D0675992

VISIONS *of* AMERICA

VISIONS of AMERICA

VOLUME 2

SINCE 1865

A HISTORY OF THE UNITED STATES

Jennifer D. Keene
Chapman University

Saul Cornell
Fordham University

Edward T. O'Donnell
College of the Holy Cross

Prentice Hall

Boston Columbus Indianapolis New York San Francisco
Upper Saddle River Amsterdam Cape Town Dubai London Madrid
Milan Munich Paris Montreal Toronto Delhi Mexico City
Sao Paulo Sydney Hong Kong Seoul Singapore Taipei Tokyo

Design concept development
by DK Education

Editorial Director: Leah Jewell
Publisher: Priscilla McGeehon
Senior Development Editor: Roberta Meyer
Development Editor: Philip Herbst
Editorial Assistant: Amanda Dykstra
Director of Marketing: Brandy Dawson
Senior Managing Editor: Ann Marie McCarthy
Project Manager: Debra Wechsler
Senior Operations Supervisor: Mary Ann Gloriande
Operations Specialist: Maura Zaldivar
Map Editor: Jeannine Ciliotta
Manager of Design Development: John Christiana
Art Director: Laura Gardner
AV Project Manager: Mirella Signoretto
Manager, Visual Research: Beth Brenzel
Photo Researchers: Barbara S. Salz; Jody Potter
Manager, Rights and Permissions: Zina Arabia
Image Permission Coordinator: Debbie Latronica
Manager, Cover Visual Research & Permissions: Karen Sanatar
Cover Art: Flappers: © Underwood & Underwood/CORBIS All Rights Reserved; Immigrant family: Courtesy of the Library of Congress; Working girl: Lewis Wickes Hines/Courtesy of the Library of Congress; Bomb over Nagasaki: National Archives and Records Administration; Obama family: © Ralf-Finn Hestoft/Ralf-Finn Hestoft/Corbis
Cover Designer: Laura Gardner
Media Director: Brian Hyland
Lead Media Project Manager: Sarah Kinney
Supplements Editor: Emsal Hasan
Full-Service Project Management: Pre-Press PMG
Composition: Pre-Press PMG
Printer/Binder: Webcrafters, Inc.
Cover Printer: Lehigh-Phoenix Color/Hagerstown

This book was set in 10.5/12.5 Minion.

Credits and acknowledgments borrowed from other sources and reproduced, with permission, in this textbook appear on appropriate page within text (or beginning on page C-1).

Copyright © 2010 Pearson Education, Inc., publishing as Prentice Hall, 1 Lake St., Upper Saddle River, NJ 07458.
All rights reserved. Manufactured in the United States of America. This publication is protected by Copyright, and permission should be obtained from the publisher prior to any prohibited reproduction, storage in a retrieval system, or transmission in any form or by any means, electronic, mechanical, photocopying, recording, or likewise. To obtain permission(s) to use material from this work, please submit a written request to Pearson Education, Inc., Permissions Department, 1 Lake St., Upper Saddle River, NJ 07458

Library of Congress Cataloging-in-Publication Data

Keene, Jennifer D.
Visions of America / Jennifer D. Keene, Saul Cornell, Edward T. O'Donnell, — 1st ed.
p. cm.
Includes bibliographical references and index.
ISBN-13: 978-0-321-06687-9
ISBN-10: 0-321-06687-1
1. United States—History—Textbooks. I. Cornell, Saul. II. O'Donnell, Edward T. III. Title.
E178.1.K24 2009
973—dc22 2009017107

10 9 8 7 6 5 4 3 2 1

Prentice Hall
is an imprint of

PEARSON

www.pearsonhighered.com

ISBN 13: 978-0-321-05310-7
ISBN 10: 0-321-05310-9

Dedication

To our parents, who imbued us with a love of history; our spouses, who have learned to share this passion; and our children, present and future students of American history.

Brief Contents

CHAPTER

14 Now That We Are Free: Reconstruction and the New South, 1863–1890 **404**

15 Conflict and Conquest: The Transformation of the West, 1860–1900 **438**

16 Wonder and Woe: The Rise of Industrial America, 1865–1900 **468**

17 Becoming a Modern Society: America in the Gilded Age, 1877–1900 **498**

18 Creating a Democratic Paradise: The Progressive Era **530**

19 Imperial America: The United States in the World, 1890–1914 **560**

20 The Great War: World War I, 1914–1918 **592**

21 A Turbulent Decade: The Twenties **624**

22 A New Deal for America: The Great Depression, 1929–1940 **654**

23 World War II: Fighting the Good War, 1939–1945 **684**

24 A Divided World: The Early Cold World, 1945–1963 **718**

25 In a Land of Plenty: Contentment and Discord, 1945–1960 **750**

26 A Nation Divided: The Vietnam War, 1945–1975 **778**

27 A Decade of Discord: The Challenge of the Sixties **810**

28 Righting a Nation Adrift: America in the 1970s and 1980s **842**

29 Building a New World Order: The United States, 1989–2009 **874**

Contents

Maps **xvii**
Charts, Graphs, and Tables **xviii**
Images as History **xix**
Competing Visions **xix**
Choices and Consequences **xxi**
Preface **xxiii**
About the Authors **xxvi**
Features **xxvii**
Supplements for Instructors and Students **xxix**
Acknowledgments **xxxi**

CHAPTER 14 Now That We Are Free: Reconstruction and the New South, 1863–1890 **404**

Preparing for Reconstruction 406
- Emancipation Test Cases **406**
- Lincoln's Ten Percent Plan **408**
- Radical Republicans Offer a Different Vision **408**

The Fruits of Freedom 409
- Freedom of Movement **409**
- Forty Acres and a Mule **409**
- Uplift through Education **410**
- The Black Church **411**

The Struggle to Define Reconstruction 412
- The Conservative Vision of Freedom: Presidential Reconstruction **412**

Competing Visions
DEMANDING RIGHTS, PROTECTING PRIVILEGE **414**
- Congressional Reconstruction and the Fourteenth Amendment **415**
- Radical Republicans Take Control **417**

Implementing Reconstruction 418
- The Republican Party in the South **418**
- Creating Reconstruction Governments in the South **419**
- The Election of 1868 **420**
- The Fifteenth Amendment **421**
- The Rise of White Resistance **421**

Reconstruction Abandoned 423
- Corruption and Scandal **423**
- The North Retreats **423**
- The Election of 1872 **424**
- Hard Times **424**

Images as History
POLITICAL CARTOONS REFLECT THE SHIFT IN PUBLIC OPINION **425**
- The Return of Terrorism **426**
- The End of Reconstruction **426**

The New South 428
- Redeemer Rule **428**
- The Lost Cause **428**
- The New South Economy **429**
- The Rise of Sharecropping **431**
- Jim Crow **432**

Choices and Consequences
SANCTIONING SEPARATION **434**

Conclusion **435**

CHAPTER REVIEW **436**

CHAPTER 15 Conflict and Conquest: The Transformation of the West, 1860–1900 **438**

Natives and Newcomers 440
- Congress Promotes Westward Settlement **440**
- The Diversity of the Native American West **442**
- Native American Tribes of the Great Plains **443**
- The Great Westward Migration **444**

The Economic Transformation of the West 447
- The Railroad Fuels Western Development **447**
- Hard Times for Farmers **448**
- The Cattle Kingdom **449**
- Fortunes Beneath the Ground: The Mining Booms **450**
- The Environmental Legacy **451**

Competing Visions
PRESERVATION VERSUS EXPLOITATION **452**

Native Americans Under Siege 453
- Mounting Problems for Native Americans **453**
- Wars on the Plains **455**
- War and Conflict in the Far West **456**
- In Pursuit of a Solution **457**

Choices and Consequences
FORCED ASSIMILATION VERSUS CULTURAL PRESERVATION **459**

Resistance and Romanticism 461
- Resistance and Persistence 461
- Creating Mythical Heroes and Images 462
- The West in Art and Literature 462

Images as History
ANNIE OAKLEY 463

- Historians Reinterpret the American West 464

Conclusion 465

CHAPTER REVIEW 466

CHAPTER 16 Wonder and Woe: The Rise of Industrial America, 1865–1900 468

The Emergence of Big Business 470
- Sources of the Industrial Revolution 470
- The Railroads 472
- Modern Business Practices 472
- Rising Concern over Corporate Power 473
- Andrew Carnegie: Making Steel and Transforming the Corporation 474
- Rockefeller and the Rise of the Trust 476

Creating a Mass Market 478
- The Art of Selling 478
- Shopping as an Experience: The Department Store 478
- Bringing the Market to the Frontier 479

Images as History
ADVERTISING AND THE ART OF CULTIVATING ANXIETY AND DESIRE 480
- Selling to the World 482

The World of Work Transformed 483
- The Impact of New Technology 483
- Hard Times for Industrial Workers 483
- Exploitation, Intimidation, and Conflict 484

Competing Visions
THE LEGITIMACY OF UNIONS 487
- New Roles and Opportunities for Women 488

Conflicting Visions of Industrial Capitalism 489
- Capitalism Championed 489
- Capitalism Criticized 491
- Power in Numbers: Organized Labor 492
- The Great Upheaval of 1886 493

Choices and Consequences
TO STRIKE OR NOT TO STRIKE? 494

Conclusion 495

CHAPTER REVIEW 496

CHAPTER 17 Becoming a Modern Society: America in the Gilded Age, 1877–1900 498

The Rise of the City 500
- To the Cities 500
- The Emergence of Ethnic Enclaves 501
- The Troubled City 502
- "Boss Rule": The Political Machine 503

Competing Visions
HOW BEST TO HELP THE POOR? 505

A Search for Solutions 506
- The Nativist Impulse 506
- A Different View: Urban Reforms 507
- Capturing a New View of Poverty 508

Images as History
SEEING THE POOR 509
- Living among the Poor: Settlement Houses 510
- The White City 510

New Habits, Roles, and Lifestyles 512
- The New Urban Landscape 512
- New Roles and Expectations for Woman 513
- New Forms of Leisure and Popular Culture 515
- Lifestyles of the Rich and Famous 517

The Challenge from Below 518
- Out of Touch Politics 519
- The People's Party 520
- Industrial Conflict and Depression 522

Choices and Consequences
THE PULLMAN STRIKE 525
- The Election of 1896 and Political Realignment 526

Conclusion 527

CHAPTER REVIEW 528

CHAPTER 18 Creating a Democratic Paradise: The Progressive Era 530

The Progressive Impulse 532
- The Angst of the Middle Class **532**
- The Progressive Vision **533**

Reining in Big Business 535
- Roosevelt's Trust-Busting **535**
- Taft and Wilson: Competing Progressive Visions **537**
- Preservation versus Conservation **539**

Competing Views on Transforming the Workplace 541
- Capitalist Visions of Industrial Harmony **541**
- Working-Class Labor Activism **543**
- The Progressives' Limited Progress **543**

Choices and Consequences
REGULATING WORKERS' HOURS **545**

Protecting Women and Children 546
- Women at Work **546**
- Stamping Out Vice **546**
- Restoring Childhood **548**

Images as History
EXPOSING THE EVILS OF CHILD LABOR **550**

Reforming the Government 552
- Containing Socialism **552**
- Ending Government Corruption **552**
- Accepting Separate but Equal **554**

Competing Visions
SEEKING RACIAL UPLIFT **556**

Conclusion **557**

CHAPTER REVIEW **558**

CHAPTER 19 Imperial America: The United States in the World, 1890–1914 560

Becoming a World Power 562
- European Imperialism **562**
- The Impulse for Expansion **563**

The Spanish-American War 565
- The Growing Conflict with Spain **565**

Images as History
ATROCITY STORIES AND PUBLIC OPINION **566**
- The Decision to Intervene in Cuba **567**
- Fighting the War against Spain **568**

Creating an American Empire 573
- The Debate over Colonies **573**

Competing Visions
THE WHITE MAN'S BURDEN **576**
- The Philippine-American War **577**

America and East Asia 579
- The Open Door in China **579**
- Relations with Japan **581**
- Angel Island **581**

Choices and Consequences
THE LEGAL CONSTRUCTION OF "WHITENESS" **583**

In America's Backyard 584
- The Panama Canal **584**
- The Roosevelt Corollary **587**

Conclusion **589**

CHAPTER REVIEW **590**

CHAPTER 20 The Great War: World War I, 1914–1918 592

The Decision for War 594
- The War in Europe **594**
- The Perils of Neutrality **596**
- America Enters the War **600**
- Conflicting Views among the Allies on the War's Purpose **601**

The War at Home 602
- Gearing Up for War **602**
- Black Migration **603**
- Female Suffrage **604**
- Rallying the Public **605**
- German Spies and Civil Liberties **606**

Images as History
PROPAGANDA POSTERS **607**

Fighting the War 609
- Raising an Army **609**
- "You're in the Army Now" **609**

Choices and Consequences
ALVIN YORK, DECIDING TO SERVE **610**
- On the Western Front **611**

World War I 613
- Flu Epidemic 614
- The Final Campaigns 614

Peace 615
- The Paris Peace Conference 615
- The Treaty Fight at Home 617

Competing Visions
JOINING THE LEAGUE OF NATIONS 619

Conclusion 621

CHAPTER REVIEW 622

CHAPTER 21 A Turbulent Decade: The Twenties 624

Cars and Planes: The Promise of the Twenties 626
- The Car Culture 626
- On the Road 627
- Welfare Capitalism and Consumer Culture 628
- The Age of Flight: Charles A. Lindbergh 630

Cultural Unrest 632
- The Lost Generation 632
- Prohibition 632
- The First Red Scare and Immigration Restrictions 634
- Fundamentalism 636

Racial Violence and Civil Rights 638
- Lynching, Racial Rioting, and the Ku Klux Klan 638
- Marcus Garvey 640
- The Harlem Renaissance 640

Competing Visions
DEBATING GARVEYISM 641

The New Woman 644
- Life for Women in the Twenties 644

Images as History
ADVERTISING THE NEW WOMAN 645
- Margaret Sanger and the Fight for Birth Control 646

Ensuring Peace: Diplomacy in the Twenties 647
- Disarmament 647
- Wartime Debts 648

Choices and Consequences
PREVENTING WAR IN EUROPE 649

Conclusion 651

CHAPTER REVIEW 652

CHAPTER 22 A New Deal for America: The Great Depression, 1929–1940 654

The Early Days of the Depression 656
- Herbert Hoover 656
- Economic Weaknesses in a Time of Prosperity 656
- The Stock Market Crash of 1929 657
- Hoover's Response to the Depression 659

Choices and Consequences
EVICTING THE BONUS MARCHERS 661

A New President and a New Deal 662
- FDR: The Politician 662
- Managing Appearances 664
- The Temper of the Poor: Passivity and Anger 664

Recovering from the Depression 666
- Revamping Banking and Financial Institutions 666
- Father Charles Coughlin 666
- Helping Industry and People 667
- Putting People to Work 668

A New Deal for Farmers 670
- Handling the Farm Crisis 670
- Hitting the Road 671
- Repatriating Mexican Immigrants 672

Images as History
"MIGRANT MOTHER," AN AMERICAN ICON 673

Reforms to Ensure Social Justice 674
- The Challenge from Huey Long: "Share Our Wealth" 674
- Social Security 674

Competing Visions
SHARING THE WEALTH 675
- Supporting Unions 676
- The Resurgence of Labor 678
- A New Deal for African Americans 679
- The Supreme Court Weighs In 680

Conclusion 681

CHAPTER REVIEW 682

CHAPTER 23 World War II: Fighting the Good War, 1939–1945 684

The Approaching War 686
- Fascism and Appeasement 686
- The Arsenal of Democracy 688
- War with Japan 690

On the Home Front 693
- Images of the Enemy 693
- Internment Camps 694
- Prosperity, Scarcity, and Opportunities for Women 695

Competing Visions
CIVIL LIBERTIES AND NATIONAL SECURITY CLASH 696
- Racial Discord 699

On the Front Lines 702
- Defeat, Then Victory 702
- The Final Push in Europe 705

Images as History
COMBAT PHOTOGRAPHY 706
- America's Response to the Holocaust 708

The Holocaust 709

Ending the Pacific War 711
- Edging Closer to Japan 711
- Dropping the Atomic Bomb 711
- The Final Surrender 712

Choices and Consequences
HOW TO USE THE ATOMIC BOMB 713

Conclusion 715

CHAPTER REVIEW 716

CHAPTER 24 A Divided World: The Early Cold War, 1945–1963 718

Origins of the Cold War 720
- Differing Goals in the Postwar World 720
- The American Vision Takes Shape: Kennan's Long Telegram 721
- The Truman Doctrine and the Marshall Plan 722
- The Berlin Airlift and NATO 725

Fighting Communism: Cold and Hot War 729
- Communism Rising: 1949 729
- The Korean War 730
- Nuclear Fallout and Fear 734

Images as History
SURVIVING AN ATOMIC BOMB BLAST 735
- Fallout Shelters 736

Spies in Our Midst 737
- The Second Red Scare 737
- HUAC against Hollywood 739
- McCarthyism 739

Competing Visions
NAMING NAMES IN HOLLYWOOD 740

Averting Nuclear War 742
- Sputnik 742
- The Berlin Wall 743
- Bay of Pigs and the Cuban Missile Crisis 745

Choices and Consequences
THE CUBAN MISSILE CRISIS 746

Conclusion 747

CHAPTER REVIEW 748

CHAPTER 25 In a Land of Plenty: Contentment and Discord, 1945–1960 750

Securing the New Deal Legacy 752
- The Labor Movement Curtailed 752
- Presidential Agendas: Truman and Eisenhower 753

A Middle-Class America 756
- Postwar Prosperity 756
- The Move to the Suburbs 758

Competing Visions
SUBURBS—AMERICAN DREAM OR NIGHTMARE? 759

Popular Culture in the Fifties 760
- The Television Age Arrives 760
- Teen Culture and Rock-and-Roll 761
- The Beats 763

Freedom Now: The Civil Rights Movement 765
- Separate and *Unequal*: Challenging Segregated Schools 765
- Emmett Till 766

Images as History
INSPIRING A NEW GENERATION TO ACT 767
- Montgomery Bus Boycott, 1955 768

Choices and Consequences
ROSA PARKS MAKES HISTORY 769
- The Little Rock Nine, 1957 770
- The Sit-ins 772

Conclusion 775
CHAPTER REVIEW 776

CHAPTER 26 A Nation Divided: The Vietnam War, 1945–1975 778

The Long Road to War 780
- The Escalating Importance of Vietnam 780
- Taking over from the French 782
- Debates within the Kennedy Administration 784
- The Kennedy Assassination 785
- The Gulf of Tonkin 786

Choices and Consequences
MAKING VIETNAM AMERICA'S WAR 788

Fighting in Vietnam 789
- The Bombing Campaign 789
- On the Ground 790
- The Tet Offensive 792

Images as History
THE ROLE OF THE PRESS IN VIETNAM 794

Controversy on the Home Front 796
- The Antiwar Movement 796
- My Lai 798

Competing Visions
WHO WAS RESPONSIBLE FOR THE MY LAI MASSACRE? 800

The Long Road to Peace 801
- Seeking Peace with Honor 801

Vietnam:
THE WAR BY THE NUMBERS 802
- Cambodia: Invasion and Outrage 803
- Withdrawal 805

Conclusion 807
CHAPTER REVIEW 808

CHAPTER 27 A Decade of Discord: The Challenge of the Sixties 810

The Liberal Moment 812
- Kennedy and the New Frontier 812
- A Liberal Court 813
- The 1964 Election 814

Choices and Consequences
IS SCHOOL PRAYER CONSTITUTIONAL? 815
- The Great Society 817

Nonviolence Triumphant: The Civil Rights Movement, 1960–1965 819
- Kennedy and the Freedom Riders 819
- Birmingham, 1963 821

Images as History
BIRMINGHAM, 1963 822
- March on Washington 824
- Freedom Summer 825
- Selma and the Voting Rights Act of 1965 826

The Fractured Left 828
- The New Left and the Counterculture 828
- Malcolm X: An Alternative to Nonviolence 830
- Watts and Chicago 831
- Black Power and the Black Panthers 832
- The Women's Liberation Movement 832

Competing Visions
DEFINING "BLACK POWER" 833

The End of an Era 835
- The Faltering Civil Rights Movement 835
- The Great Society Unravels 835
- The Demise of the Counterculture 837
- Keeping Protest Alive: Mexican Americans and Native Americans 837

Conclusion 839
CHAPTER REVIEW 840

CHAPTER 28 Righting a Nation Adrift: America in the 1970s and 1980s 842

Downturn and Scandal 844
- An Ailing Economy **844**
- Frustration at Home **847**
- The Watergate Scandal **848**

Images as History
WATERGATE THROUGH POLITICAL CARTOONS **850**

A Crisis of Presidential Leadership 851
- A Weakened Presidency **851**
- The Leadership Crisis Continues: Carter in the White House **852**
- New Paths in Foreign Affairs **855**

Choices and Consequences
ENDING THE IRANIAN HOSTAGE CRISIS **857**

The Rights Revolution 858
- The Equal Rights Amendment and Abortion Controversies **858**

Competing Visions
DEFINING THE IDEAL WOMAN **860**
- Gay Rights **862**
- Environmentalism **864**

The Rise of the Right 865
- The New Conservative Coalition **865**
- Setting a New Course: Reagan at Home **866**
- Foreign Policy Triumphs and Scandals **868**
- The Reagan Revolution **871**

Conclusion **871**

CHAPTER REVIEW **872**

CHAPTER 29 Building a New World Order: The United States, 1989–2009 874

"A Moment Rich with Promise" 876
- The Election of 1988 **876**
- Popular Revolts against Communism **877**

Images as History
THE FALL OF THE BERLIN WALL **878**
- Domestic Policy in the Bush Administration **880**
- Panama and the Persian Gulf War **881**

Contested Visions of Government 884
- Clinton's New Democrats **884**
- The Disputed Election of 2000 **866**
- Compassionate Conservatism **867**

Transforming Daily Life 888
- The Computer Age **888**
- The Changing Face of Families **889**
- A Wave of Immigration **890**

Competing Visions
THE ECONOMIC COST OF IMMIGRATION **891**
- Climate Change **892**

New Threats in the Post-Cold War World 894
- Ethnic Cleansing and Terrorism **894**
- 9/11 **896**
- The Iraq War **898**

Choices and Consequences
LAUNCHING A PREEMPTIVE WAR **899**
- The Election of 2008 **901**

Conclusion **903**

CHAPTER REVIEW **904**

Appendix **A–1**
Glossary **G–1**
Credits **C–1**
Index **I–1**
Maps **M–1**

Maps

14.18 The Readmission of Southern States and Return of White Rule **427**

14.22 Moving from Slavery to Freedom: The Barrow Plantation, Oglethorpe County, Georgia, 1860 and 1861 **432**

15.3 The Major Tribes of the Trans-Mississippi West **442**

15.7 The Spread of the Railroad **447**

15.18 The Loss of Native American Lands **460**

18.4 1912 Presidential Election Results **538**

18.10 Prohibition, 1904 and 1917 **547**

19.1 Map of the World, 1898 **562–563**

19.2 The Spanish-American War, 1898 **568–569**

19.10 Foreign Activity in China, 1901 **580**

19.15 American Involvement in Latin America, 1898–1939 **588**

20.1 World War I in Europe, 1914–1918 **595**

20.12 American Expeditionary Forces, 1918 **612**

20.13 Europe and the Middle East after the War **617**

21.15 American Loans to Europe, 1914–1925 **650**

23.1 The World at War **686**

23.14 War in the Pacific **702**

23.15 The European Theater **703**

German-run Concentration Camps in World War II **709**

24.2 The Cold War in Europe **723**

24.5 A Divided Berlin **726**

24.8 The Korean War **731**

26.10 Map of Vietnam **793**

26.12 The Presidential Election of 1968 **798**

27.5 Civil Rights Milestones, 1961–1965 **819**

28.1 Middle East and Persian Gulf, 1947–1986 **845**

28.15 American Intervention in Latin America, 1980–2000 **869**

29.4 America and the Middle East, 1980–2003 **881**

29.8 Presidential Election, 2000 **887**

29.11 Global Carbon Dioxide Emissions **893**

Charts, Graphs, and Tables

14.13 The Election of 1868 **421**

14.15 The Election of 1872 **424**

14.17 The Election of 1876 **427**

16.1 The Industrial Revolution by the Numbers **470**

16.6 Horizontal Integration versus Vertical Integration **475**

16.14 Rising Numbers of Women in the Paid Workforce **488**

17.1 Immigration to the United States, 1880–1920 **500**

17.14 Deadlocked Presidential Politics in the Gilded Age **518**

18.1 Occupational Distribution, 1900 **532**

20.2 Timeline, 1914 **595**

20.3 U.S. Exports to Europe, 1914–1917 **597**

World War I Casualties **613**

America at War: Battlefield Deaths, Deaths by Disease, and Wounded **613**

21.3 Employment Chart of the Central Tube Company, Pittsburgh, 1925 **629**

21.7 Immigration Act of 1924 **635**

21.16 The Global Flow of Reparation Payments **651**

22.2 Economic Trends in the Depression **660**

22.3 Key New Deal Legislation **662**

22.9 Soaring Unemployment **667**

23.2 Origins of World War II **687**

Jews in the Holocaust **709**

America and the Holocaust **709**

23.20 The Human Cost of Global War **714**

24.15 Nuclear Arms Race, 1950s **743**

The Human and Financial Cost of the Vietnam War, 1964–1973 **802**

Changing American Troop Levels **802**

Destruction in Vietnam, 1965–1972 **802**

Antiwar demonstrations in Washington, D.C., 1965–1975 **802**

Public Opinion and the Vietnam War, 1965–1973 **802**

27.2 Major Decisions of the Warren Court **814**

27.4 Key Great Society Legislative Achievements **818**

28.2 Inflation and Unemployment, 1960–1990 **846**

28.7 Women and Work, 1950–1990 **858**

29.9 Changes in American Family Structure, 1972–1988 **889**

Images as History

CHAPTER

14 Political Cartoons Reflect the Shift in Public Opinion **425**

15 Annie Oakley **463**

16 Advertising and the Art of Cultivating Anxiety and Desire **480**

17 Seeing the Poor **509**

18 Exposing the Evils of Child Labor **550**

19 Atrocity Stories and Public Opinion **566**

20 Propaganda Posters **607**

21 Advertising the New Woman **645**

22 "Migrant Mother," An American Icon **673**

23 Combat Photography **706**

24 Surviving an Atomic Bomb Blast **735**

25 Inspiring a New Generation to Act **767**

26 The Power of the Press in Vietnam **794**

27 Birmingham, 1963 **822**

28 Watergate through Political Cartoons **850**

29 The Fall of the Berlin Wall **878**

Competing Visions

CHAPTER

14 Demanding Rights, Protecting Privilege **414**

15 Preservation versus Exploitation **452**

16 The Legitimacy of Unions **487**

17 How Best to Help the Poor? **505**

18 Seeking Racial Uplift **556**

19 The White Man's Burden **576**

20 Joining the League of Nations **619**

21 Debating Garveyism **641**

22 Sharing the Wealth **675**

23 Civil Liberties and National Security Clash **696**

24 Naming Names in Hollywood **740**

25 Suburbs—American Dream or Nightmare **759**

26 Who Was Responsible for the My Lai Massacre **800**

27 Defining "Black Power" **833**

28 Defining the Ideal Woman **860**

29 The Economic Costs of Immigration **891**

Choices and Consequences

CHAPTER

14 Sanctioning Separation **434**

15 Forced Assimilation versus Cultural Preservation **459**

16 To Strike or Not to Strike? **494**

17 The Pullman Strike **525**

18 Regulating Workers' Hours **545**

19 The Legal Construction of "Whiteness" **583**

20 Alvin York, Deciding to Serve **610**

21 Preventing War in Europe **649**

22 Evicting the Bonus Marchers **661**

23 How to Use the Atomic Bomb **713**

24 The Cuban Missile Crisis **748**

25 Rosa Parks Makes History **769**

26 Making Vietnam America's War **788**

27 Is School Prayer Constitutional? **815**

28 Ending the Iranian Hostage Crisis **857**

29 Launching a Preemptive War **899**

Preface

Jennifer D. Keene, Saul Cornell, and Edward T. O'Donnell discuss their goals in writing *Visions of America*.

Why did you write this book? What separates it from the many fine survey texts that are available?

We conceived of *Visions of America* while teaching in the kinds of classrooms familiar to most of the instructors and students who will use this book. Many of our students are the first in their family to attend college, some are international students, most are required to take the U.S. History survey, and some are passionate students of history.

Despite their differences most share the same vision of history, but it is a distorted vision. Students often see history as a series of events that unfolded as if preordained. The colonists defeated the British, the Civil War held the Union together and abolished slavery, America defeated Nazi Germany and then prevailed in the Cold War. Yet as historians we know that history is never inevitable, that vehement disagreements have shaped the past and continue to influence the present, that events are driven by choices, and that outcomes are unknowable to those who make those choices. We wrote *Visions of America* to make those perceptions just as obvious to our readers.

How did you do that? How does Visions *change students' perceptions about history?*

The title captures our unique approach. *Visions of America* explores the competing political, social, and cultural visions *for* America that have generated conflicts in virtually every period of U.S. history. We focused on competing visions so that students can learn to appreciate the dynamic debates that shaped our nation. Every element of the text reinforces the competing visions theme, from the narrative and images to the highlighted quotes and features. The Competing Visions feature presents excerpts from key primary source documents to exemplify conflicting visions for America.

- In **Chapter 5** (page 143) students will read the opposing positions Washington and Jefferson held toward Shays's Rebellion in their own words. Excerpts from their writings convey how these two patriots interpreted the meaning of the rebellion in radically different ways.
- In **Chapter 16** (page 487) Competing Visions examines two clashing views on the legitimacy of labor unions, one a searing 1877 anti-union editorial from *Scribner's Monthly* and the other a stout defense of unions found in an 1884 labor newspaper.
- In **Chapter 19** (page 576) Competing Visions pairs Rudyard Kipling's poem, "The White Man's Burden," with a poetic parody by an anti-imperialist activist, "The Real 'White Man's Burden,'" to present the internal debate over whether the United States should create a formal colonial empire.

How did you convey that history is the product of individual choices?

Choices confronting political leaders and ordinary people are a consistent theme of the narrative, but they are graphically depicted in Choices and Consequences. In each chapter, this innovative feature diagrams the choices leaders and ordinary people grappled with at key moments in America's history. By helping students to visualize complex and sometimes agonizing choices, Choices and Consequences underscores the point that historical events are the products of human agency.

- In **Chapter 10** (page 300) students consider the choices faced by Mary Cragin, a woman who joined the Oneida perfectionist community. Did free love in nineteenth-century America represent a step toward female emancipation or was it merely another way for men to dominate woman?
- In **Chapter 14** (page 434) students see the choices that the U.S. Supreme Court confronted in *Plessy v. Ferguson*. We examine the majority decision and its consequences for establishing the policy of "separate but equal" in public facilities and schools across the South. Finally we consider the continuing controversies surrounding the strategies African Americans adopted while living under Jim Crow segregation.
- In **Chapter 25** (page 769) we examine the choices Rosa Parks faced in 1955 when asked to vacate her bus seat for a white man, her decision to stay put, the consequences of that decision, and the continuing controversies surrounding how Americans mythologized this critical moment in our history.

How does Visions of America *use images differently from other textbooks?*

Images have powerfully influenced the national debate, but history textbooks typically use them as mere illustrations. Our approach is different. We selected the nearly seven hundred paintings, photographs, line drawings, woodcuts, advertisements, engravings, film stills, political cartoons, and other images in the text. Each one is discussed and treated as historical evidence. The innovative design by DK Publishing integrates images across the pages in a way that shows detail and invites scrutiny.

- In **Chapter 4** we discuss the impact of republicanism on the family in the Revolutionary era. Accompanying the narrative on page 124, contrasting portraits of families, painted before and after the Revolution, reveal the growing ideal of companionate marriage. In the bottom portrait the husband, wife, and child are not only physically closer, but their expressions suggest greater emotional connection and intimacy, a change facilitated by republican ideology. The visuals reinforce the text, allowing students to see history as well as read about it.

- In **Chapter 17** political cartoons highlight the growing concern over the rise of political machines. On page 504 we discuss Thomas Nast's cartoon, "In Counting There Is Strength." Students discover that Nast created the image to depict William "Boss" Tweed, head of New York's Tammany Hall machine, as both corrupt and arrogant. The reference to counting suggests that Tweed's power derived from his ability to conduct fraudulent vote counts on election day.

"THAT'S WHAT'S THE MATTER."
Boss Tweed. "As long as I count the Votes, what are you going to do about it? say?"

- By reading the story behind the iconic photographic of a Vietnamese Buddhist monk setting himself on fire in **Chapter 26** (page 785), students learn to see the Vietnam War as both a civil war and part of the global Cold War. The intentional ways that activists used the Western media to publicize their cause, and the ways that one photograph can alter history, also become apparent.

How does Visions *encourage students to analyze historical images effectively?*

Beyond the analysis of images in the narrative, in each chapter, Images as History focuses on one or two images in depth. This feature encourages students to "read" images as texts with multiple meanings that speak to both the past and the present. These features include:

- A PORTRAIT OF COLONIAL ASPIRATIONS (Chapter 3, page 69). The portrait of Henry Darnall III reveals the aspirations of the colonial elite and their role in the growing Anglicization of colonial life. In the painting, next to Darnall is one of the earliest depictions of an African slave in American art, a sign of the growing importance of slavery to colonial society.

- SEEING THE POOR (Chapter 17, page 509). We dissect Jacob Riis's photograph of a poor Italian immigrant mother and child, encouraging students to appreciate how Riis's image both reflected and shaped contemporary views of immigrants in the late nineteenth century.
- ADVERTISING THE NEW WOMAN (Chapter 21, page 645). The ways that advertising both shaped and reflected public perceptions of the ideal woman become apparent when analysing the image of the "Fisher Girl" in a 1920s automobile advertisement.

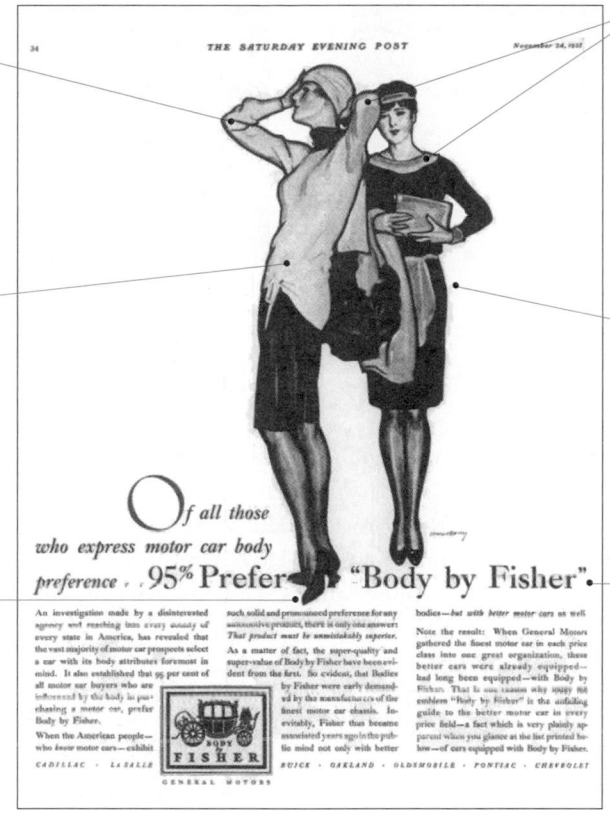

The slim Fisher girl appeared liberated from the confines of the home and the physical incapacity caused by too much weight. She seemed to be a modern woman on the move.

These tall, elongated figurines depicted an ideal female body that was slim and youthful with legs that formed a straight line from toe to thigh, pointed toes, and a giraffe-like neck. These proportions suggested the women were nearly 9 feet tall!

This female silhouette more closely resembled the body of an adolescent girl than a mature woman, encouraging a female preoccupation with dieting and self-denial that continues today.

The presence of the maid behind the Fisher girl indicates that she is rich as well as thin—an enviable combination to many women.

Most ads of the time displayed men with both feet firmly on the ground. This woman's off-balance pose with one knee bent suggested tentativeness and instability, putting limits on her independence and strength.

Her sleek body, like that of the car being advertised, served mostly as a commodity or decorative object suitable for a modern man.

"Body by Fisher"

Many students feel overwhelmed by the amount of information in history textbooks. How does Visions *help students focus on what is most important?*

Visions of America promotes active learning on every page. Each chapter opens with a large, striking image and an **enlarged quotation** designed to encapsulate the major issues of the period and spark curiosity. Throughout, lively **display quotes** from leaders and ordinary people draw students into the text. Questions running along the bottom of each page serve as **learning objectives**, prompting students to review and reflect on what they have just read. Each chapter ends with a **conclusion**, followed by a colorful **visual chronology** linking images and key events. **Review questions** help students synthesize the material in the chapter, and a list of **key terms** serves as a quick review of essential concepts.

Associating an image with a term, name, or concept can help to cement it in students' memory. *Visions of America* encourages this by providing images in abundance alongside the text to serve as mnemonic cues. For example the controversy over Andrew Jackson's Bank War produced a number of evocative cartoons. Typically most textbooks reproduce a single pro-Jackson or one anti-Jackson cartoon. *Visions of America* presents both views of the Bank War side by side so students can compare and contrast them.

Why will students read this book?

History professors and textbooks need to be good storytellers. *Visions of America's* lively writing style—active, engaging, and full of anecdotes—brings history to life. We live in an intensely visual culture, and students are always fascinated to discover the "truth" about the images they have long associated with key periods in American history, or to learn about new ones. Students will enjoy reading a text that shows them history is a living narrative open to interpretation and the product of decisions people made in the past.

Five or ten years from now, what will students remember from reading Visions of America? *How will they apply the skills they have gained?*

Students may not recall the exact terms of the Versailles Treaty or the Reconstruction Acts, but they will remember that people making individual choices are the driving force of history. When participating in the political or cultural debates of their own era, they will recall that competing visions have been a staple of the nation's historical development. The critical-thinking skills they honed while reading this book will serve them well throughout their lives. Years from now, they will know how to analyze and consume images intelligently. Most important, students will remember the moment when they realized that history was not just an endless list of names and dates but the fascinating tale of human experience.

About the Authors

Jennifer D. Keene

Jennifer D. Keene is a Professor of History and chair of the History Department at Chapman University in Orange, California. Dr. Keene has published three books on the American involvement in the First World War: *Doughboys, the Great War and the Remaking of America* (2001); *The United States and the First World War* (2000); and *World War I* (2006). She has received numerous fellowships for her research, including a Mellon Fellowship, a National Research Council Postdoctoral Award, and Fulbright Senior Scholar Awards to Australia and France. Her articles have appeared in the *Annales de Démographie Historique, Peace & Change, Intelligence and National Security,* and *Military Psychology*. Dr. Keene served as an associate editor for the *Encyclopedia of War and American Society* (2005) which won the Society of Military History's prize for best reference book. She works closely with the Gilder-Lehrman Institute, offering Teaching American History workshops for secondary school teachers throughout the country.

Saul Cornell

Saul Cornell is the Paul and Diane Guenther Chair in American History at Fordham University in New York. Professor Cornell has also taught at the Ohio State University, the College of William and Mary, and Leiden University in the Netherlands. He is the author of *A Well Regulated Militia: The Founding Fathers and the Origins of Gun Control* (Langum Prize in Legal History) and *The Other Founders: Anti-Federalism and the Dissenting Tradition in America, 1788–1828* (Society of the Cincinnati Book Prize), both of which were nominated for the Pulitzer Prize. His articles have appeared in the *Journal of American History*, the *William and Mary Quarterly, American Studies, Law and History Review*, and dozens of leading law reviews. He is also a frequent participant in Teaching American History workshops and has lectured widely on digital history both domestically and abroad.

Edward T. O'Donnell

Edward T. O'Donnell is an Associate Professor of History at the College of the Holy Cross in Worcester, Massachusetts. He taught previously at Hunter College, City University of New York. He is the author of many scholarly articles for journals such as *The Journal of Urban History, The Journal of the Gilded Age and Progressive Era*, and *The Public Historian*, as well as several books, including *Ship Ablaze: The Tragedy of the Steamboat General Slocum* (Random House, 2003) and the forthcoming *Talisman of a Lost Hope: Henry George and Gilded Age America* (Columbia University Press). Professor O'Donnell is also very active in the field of public history, curating several exhibits and consulting for others at institutions such as the Lower East Side Tenement Museum. Since 2002, he has worked with more than twenty Teaching American History grant programs across the country, offering lectures and workshops for middle and high school teachers.

Features

Dynamic **chapter openings** combine a vivid image with a narrative introduction, highlighting the major themes of the chapter. A pithy **quote** sounds a voice from the past, and a **visual outline** previews the chapter's major topics.

CHAPTER 14

Now That We Are Free

Reconstruction and the New South, 1863–1890

Preparing for Reconstruction p. 408

The Fruits of Freedom p. 409

The Struggle to Define Reconstruction p. 412

Implementing Reconstruction p. 418

Reconstruction Abandoned p. 422

The New South p. 426

"Never before had I a word of impudence from any of our black folk, but they are not ours any longer."

SUSAN BRADFORD, observing the defiant attitude among former slaves on her Florida plantation, 1865

The Civil War ended in April 1865, concluding the bloodiest and most divisive conflict in American history. The period that followed came to be known as Reconstruction for several reasons. Most obviously, the name called to mind the need to rebuild the war-torn South. It also referred to the effort to reestablish the Union torn apart by secession. Finally, it indicated the need to remake Southern society in the wake of slavery's destruction.

The complexities and challenges of this last goal are evident in Winslow Homer's 1876 painting, *A Visit from the Old Mistress*, which depicts ex-slaves being visited by their former owner. The elegant clothing worn by the "Old Mistress" suggests she has money, but clearly the relationship between the women has changed significantly in the wake of emancipation. To begin with, the mistress has come to visit the former slaves in their home, suggesting a diminishing of her status and power relative to them. The scene also lacks any sense of the affection that plantation owners always assured themselves existed between slaves and masters. Indeed, the three African American women eye the mistress warily. One of them even chooses to remain seated in what surely would have been considered a show of contempt. The old order was gone, but what would replace it remained unclear in the aftermath of the war.

Americans entered the Reconstruction period facing the profound questions raised by war and emancipation. Was it possible for whites and former slaves to live together in peace and mutual respect? What rights were the freedmen entitled to and who would guarantee these rights? The different answers articulated by freedmen and white Southerners revealed sharply divergent visions of the future and led to a bitter struggle to define the meaning of freedom. "Strike," observed ex-slave Frederick Douglass, "the work does not end with the abolition of slavery, but only begins."

How does this image reveal the uncertainty of race relations in the postwar South?

405

Historical **images** are imaginatively displayed. Authors explore each image as it documents events or expresses and shapes public opinion.

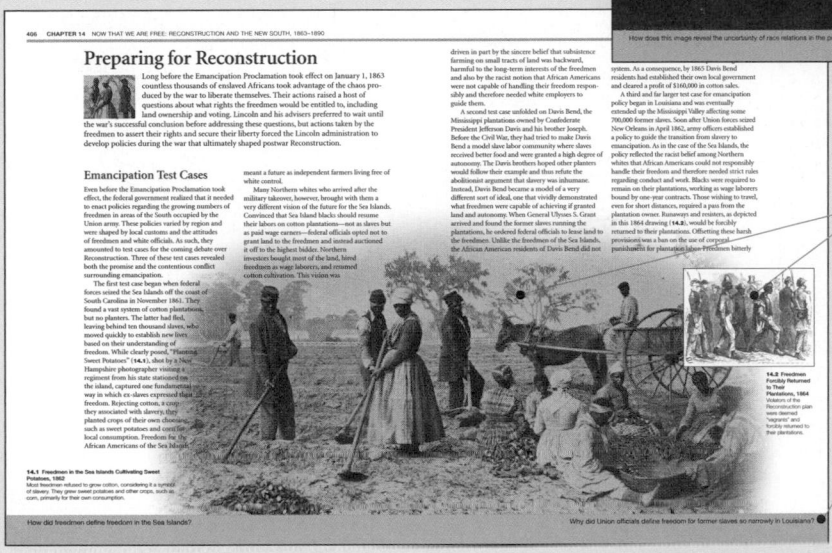

406 CHAPTER 14 NOW THAT WE ARE FREE: RECONSTRUCTION AND THE NEW SOUTH, 1863–1890

Preparing for Reconstruction

Long before the Emancipation Proclamation took effect on January 1, 1863 countless thousands of enslaved Africans took advantage of the chaos produced by the war to liberate themselves. Their actions raised a host of questions about what rights the freedmen would be entitled to, including land ownership and voting. Lincoln and his advisers preferred to wait until the war's successful conclusion before addressing these questions, but actions taken by the freedmen to assert their rights and secure their liberty forced the Lincoln administration to develop policies during the war that ultimately shaped postwar Reconstruction.

Emancipation Test Cases

Even before the Emancipation Proclamation took effect, the federal government realized that it needed to enact policies regarding the growing numbers of freedmen in areas of the South occupied by the Union army. These policies varied by region and were shaped by local customs and the attitudes of freedmen and white officials. As such, they amounted to test cases for the coming debate over Reconstruction. Three of these test cases revealed both the promise and the contentious conflict surrounding emancipation.

The first test case began when federal forces seized the Sea Islands off the coast of South Carolina in November 1861. They found a vast system of cotton plantations, but no planters. The latter had fled, leaving behind ten thousand slaves, who moved quickly to establish new lives based on their understanding of freedom. While clearly posed, "Planting Sweet Potatoes" (**14.1**), shot by a New Hampshire photographer visiting a regiment from his state stationed on the island, captured one fundamental way in which ex-slaves expressed their freedom. Rejecting cotton, a crop they associated with slavery, they planted crops of their own choosing, such as sweet potatoes and corn for local consumption. Freedom for the African Americans of the Sea Islands meant a future as independent farmers living free of white control.

Many Northern whites who arrived after the military takeover, however, brought with them a very different vision of the future for the Sea Islands. Convinced that Sea Island blacks should resume their labors on cotton plantations—not as slaves but as paid wage earners—federal officials opted not to grant land to the freedmen and instead auctioned it off to the highest bidder. Northern investors bought most of the land, hired freedmen as wage laborers, and resumed cotton cultivation. This vision was driven in part by the sincere belief that subsistence farming on small tracts of land was backward, harmful to the long-term interests of the freedmen and also by the racist notion that African Americans were not capable of handling their freedom responsibly and therefore needed white employers to guide them.

A second test case unfolded on Davis Bend, the Mississippi plantations owned by Confederate President Jefferson Davis and his brother Joseph. Before the Civil War, they had tried to make Davis Bend a model slave labor community where slaves received better food and were granted a high degree of autonomy. The Davis brothers hoped other planters would follow their example and thus refute the abolitionist argument that slavery was inhumane. Instead, Davis Bend became a model of a very different sort of ideal, one that vividly demonstrated what freedmen were capable of achieving if granted land and autonomy. When General Ulysses S. Grant arrived and found the former slaves running the plantations, he ordered federal officials to lease land to the freedmen. Unlike the freedmen of the Sea Islands, the African American residents of Davis Bend did not system. As a consequence, by 1865 Davis Bend residents had established their own local government and cleared a profit of $100,000 in cotton sales.

A third and far larger test case for emancipation policy began in Louisiana and was eventually extended up the Mississippi Valley affecting some 700,000 former slaves. Soon after Union forces seized New Orleans in April 1862, army officers established a policy to guide the transition from slavery to emancipation. As in the case of the Sea Islands, the policy reflected the racist belief among Northern whites that African Americans could not responsibly handle their freedom and therefore needed strict rules regarding conduct and work. Blacks were required to remain on their plantations, working as wage laborers bound by one-year contracts. Those wishing to travel, even for short distances, required a pass from the plantation owner. Runaways and resisters, as depicted in this 1864 drawing (**14.2**), would be forcibly returned to their plantations. Offsetting these harsh provisions was a ban on the use of corporal punishment for plantation labor. Freedmen bitterly

14.1 Freedmen in the Sea Islands Cultivating Sweet Potatoes, 1862
Most freedmen refused to grow cotton, considering it a symbol of slavery. They grew sweet potatoes and other crops, such as corn, primarily for their own consumption.

14.2 Freedmen Forcibly Returned to Their Plantations, 1864
Violators of the Reconstruction plan were deemed "vagrants" and forcibly returned to their plantations.

How did freedmen define freedom in the Sea Islands?

Why did Union officials define freedom for former slaves so narrowly in Louisiana?

At the bottom of every page, a **learning objective** in the form of a question focuses students on the key message of the page.

414 CHAPTER 14 NOW THAT WE ARE FREE: RECONSTRUCTION AND THE NEW SOUTH, 1863–1890

Competing Visions

DEMANDING RIGHTS, PROTECTING PRIVILEGE

In the aftermath of the Civil War, one question dominated the minds of Americans North and South: now that slavery was abolished, what would be the status of the freedmen? While newspaper editors, clergymen, and members of Congress debated the issue, white and black Southerners set out to answer the question themselves. As you read the following documents, one from a convention of freedmen and the other from the state legislature of Mississippi, consider the starkly contrasted visions for the future of Southern society. Why do the freedmen feel compelled to say they bear no ill will toward their "former oppressors." Why do Mississippi legislators define vagrancy in such vague terms?

"Address to the Loyal Citizens and Congress of the United States of America," Proceedings of the Convention of the Colored People of Virginia, Held in the City of Alexandria, August 2, 3, 4, 5, 1865.

We, the delegates of the colored people of the State of Virginia ... solemnly declaring that we desire to live upon the most friendly and agreeable terms with all men; we feel no ill-will or prejudice toward our former oppressors; are willing and desire to forgive and forget the past, and so shape our future conduct as shall promote our happiness and the interest of the community in which we live ...

We must, on the other hand, be allowed to aver and assert that we believe that we have among the white people of this State many who are our most inveterate enemies; who hate us as a class, who feel no sympathy with or for us; who despise us simply because we are black, and more especially, because we have been made free by the power of the United States Government ...

We claim, then, as citizens of this State, the laws of the Commonwealth [of Virginia] shall give to all men equal protection; that each and every man may appeal to the law for his equal rights without regard to the color of his skin; and we believe this can only be done by extending the franchise, which we believe to be our inalienable right as freemen, and which the Declaration of Independence guarantees to all free citizens of this Government and which is the privilege of this nation. We claim the right of suffrage:

1st. Because we can see no other safeguard for our protection.

2nd. Because we are citizens of the country and natives of this State.

3rd. Because we are as well qualified to vote who shall be our rulers as many who do vote for that purpose who have no interest in us, and do not know our wants.

Mississippi legislators in December 1865 enacted the first "Black Codes" to limit the freedoms of African Americans. Defining vagrancy in such vague terms allowed white Southerners to arrest freedmen at will and to curtail their freedom of movement. These measures were quickly copied in the remaining ex-Confederate states.

Section 1. All rogues and vagabonds, idle and dissipated persons, ... persons who neglect their calling or employment, misspend what they earn, or do not provide for the support of themselves or their families, or dependents shall be deemed and considered vagrants, ... and upon conviction thereof shall be fined not exceeding one hundred dollars, with all accruing costs, and be imprisoned ... not exceeding ten days. ...

Section 5. ... In case of any freedman, free negro or mulatto shall fail for five days after the imposition of any or forfeiture upon him or her for violation of any of the provisions of this act to pay the same, that it shall be, and is hereby, made the duty of the sheriff of the proper county to hire out said freedman, free negro or mulatto, to any person who will, for the shortest period of service, pay said fine and forfeiture and all costs ...

Colored Men's Convention 1865.

What is significant about the freedmen's use of the term citizen?

In each chapter, excerpts from personal letters, diary entries, speeches, editorials, and other written documents highlight the **Competing Visions** that have shaped every period of American history.

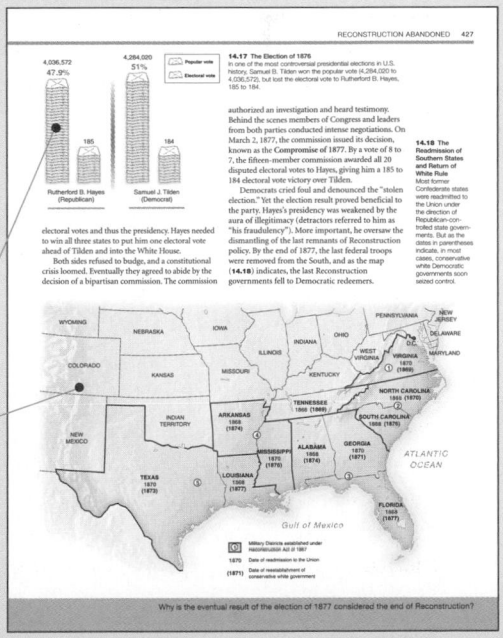

RECONSTRUCTION ABANDONED 427

14.17 The Election of 1876
In one of the most controversial presidential elections in U.S. history, Samuel B. Tilden won the popular vote (4,284,020 to 4,036,572), but lost the electoral vote to Rutherford B. Hayes, 185 to 184.

electoral votes and thus the presidency. Hayes needed to win all three states to put him one electoral vote ahead of Tilden and into the White House.

Both sides refused to budge, and a constitutional crisis loomed. Eventually they agreed to abide by the decision of a bipartisan commission. The commission authorized an investigation and heard testimony. Behind the scenes members of Congress and leaders from both parties conducted intense negotiations. On March 2, 1877, the commission issued its decision, known as the **Compromise of 1877**. By a vote of 8 to 7, the fifteen-member commission awarded all 20 disputed electoral votes to Hayes, giving him a 185 to 184 electoral vote victory over Tilden.

Democrats cried foul and denounced the "stolen election." Yet the election result proved beneficial to the party. Hayes's presidency was weakened by the aura of illegitimacy (detractors referred to him as "his fraudulency"). More important, he oversaw the dismantling of the last remnants of Reconstruction policy. By the end of 1877, the last federal troops were removed from the South, and as the map (**14.18**) indicates, the last Reconstruction governments fell to Democratic redeemers.

14.18 The Readmission of Southern States and Return of White Rule
Most former Confederate states were readmitted to the Union under the direction of Republican-controlled state governments. But as the dates in parentheses indicate, in most cases, conservative white Democratic governments soon seized control.

Why is the eventual result of the election of 1877 considered the end of Reconstruction?

Visually engaging **maps** and **graphics** make data accessible and provide geographical context. Specially designed charts clarify the results of presidential elections.

434 CHAPTER 14 NOW THAT WE ARE FREE: RECONSTRUCTION AND THE NEW SOUTH, 1863–1890

Choices and Consequences

SANCTIONING SEPARATION

In 1890 Louisiana passed a law requiring separate cars for black and white passengers on all railroads in the state. Determined to challenge the law, an African American carpenter named Homer A. Plessy bought a first-class ticket on the East Louisiana Railroad and sat in the whites-only first-class car. As expected he was arrested. Plessy argued before a local judge named John H. Ferguson that the law violated the Thirteenth Amendment's prohibition of slavery and the Fourteenth Amendment's equal protection clause. Ferguson ruled in favor of the railroad, stating that separation did not violate Plessy's rights, a decision subsequently upheld by the state's Supreme Court. When Plessy appealed to the U.S. Supreme Court, the justices considered three major options:

Choices

1. Refuse to hear the case and thus not render a judgment on the constitutionality of segregation, letting stand the Louisiana State Supreme Court decision.
2. Rule in favor of Plessy and declare Louisiana's segregation law unconstitutional.
3. Reject Plessy's appeal and uphold Louisiana's segregation law as constitutional.

Decision

On May 18, 1896, the U.S. Supreme Court by a vote of 7 to 1 chose the third option and rejected Plessy's claim that the law violated his constitutional rights. The Thirteenth and Fourteenth Amendments, argued the majority, were never intended to establish full social equality of the races. Furthermore legal separation of the races, a doctrine subsequently known as "separate but equal," was constitutional so long as states provided equal facilities. The lone dissenting justice, John Marshall Harlan, blasted the majority opinion, declaring the law a racist violation of the nation's "color-blind" Constitution.

Consequences

In sharply limiting the Fourteenth Amendment's equal protection provisions, the court allowed Southern state governments to establish separate schools, hospitals, parks, theaters, restaurants, and public transportation across the South. The decision also opened the way for segregation laws aimed at Mexicans in the Southwest and Asians in California. In practice "separate but equal" proved only half accurate as segregated facilities were indeed separate, but never equal in terms of funding, staffing, and supplies.

Continuing Controversies

How should African Americans respond to the imposition of Jim Crow laws?

Black leaders in the 1890s were divided over the best strategy to oppose segregation. Booker T. Washington, the nation's most prominent African American leader, argued that efforts to overturn segregation were doomed to failure due to black Americans' lack of political and economic power. Instead he recommended blacks focus their energy and resources on self-improvement, especially in education, a strategy that would one day empower them to challenge segregation. Founding member of the National Association for the Advancement of Colored People (NAACP), W. E. B. Dubois, rejected this policy and instead insisted that African Americans keep up a sustained legal and political effort to end segregation. Ultimately it was Dubois's vision and NAACP attorneys that ended legalized segregation. In the 1954 *Brown v. Board of Education of Topeka* decision the Supreme Court overturned *Plessy* and rejected entirely the concept of "separate but equal."

JIM CROW LAW.

UPHELD BY THE UNITED STATES SUPREME COURT.

Statute Within the Competency of the Louisiana Legislature and Railroads—East Parish Separate Cars for Whites and Blacks.

Washington, May 18—The Supreme Court today in an opinion rend by Justice Brown, sustained the constitutionality of the law in Louisiana requiring the railroads of that State to provide separate cars for white and colored passengers. There was no issue

How did the U.S. Supreme Court play a role in the imposition of segregation?

Choices and Consequences drives home the point that history is shaped by the choices we make as a nation. Each one focuses on a significant choice that confronted ordinary citizens, political leaders, or judges. The major choices are followed by the decision, an analysis of its consequences, and the controversies that often continued for years.

RECONSTRUCTION ABANDONED 425

Images as History

POLITICAL CARTOONS REFLECT THE SHIFT IN PUBLIC OPINION

One of the nation's most skilled and popular political cartoonists in the Reconstruction era was Thomas Nast. An immigrant from Germany, he landed a job in 1861 at *Harper's Weekly*, the nation's leading journal of politics and society. Nast's artistic talent, combined with *Harper's* vast circulation, soon turned him into one of the most influential illustrators of his day. As a staunch Republican and Unionist, his drawings during the Civil War were as intensely patriotic and pro-Lincoln as they were anti-Confederate.

After the war, Nast's widely distributed cartoons continued to shape Northern opinion concerning Reconstruction and the issue of freedmen's rights. Cartoons like *And Not This Man?* (August 5, 1865) proclaimed the dignity and humanity of the freedmen and their moral right to full citizenship and suffrage. In others, like *This is a White Man's Government* (September 5, 1868), he stressed the violent intent of white Southerners to reclaim power and the absolute necessity of federal authority in carrying out the goals of Reconstruction.

Nevertheless, Nast's cartoons eventually reflected the growing disillusionment of Northern Republicans regarding Reconstruction. While he rejected the Liberal Republican call for ending Reconstruction, Nast nonetheless expressed the fear that African Americans were incapable of responsible government. Note the contrast between his earlier depictions of freedmen and that in *Colored Rule in a Reconstructed (?) State*.

"Columbia," an early symbol of America and democracy, advocates black suffrage. The globe is actually a nineteenth-century ballot box.

By showing African Americans in Union army uniforms, Nast sought to earned Americans that blacks had earned the right to full citizenship through their service and sacrifice (note the missing leg in the war.

And Not This Man?

A freedman wearing a Union army uniform is crushed beneath an Irish immigrant (left), a white supremacist ex-Confederate (center), and a Northern capitalist (right). Nast saw these three groups as members of an opportunistic alliance.

A ballot box, representing the freedman's claim on citizenship and voting rights, has been kicked aside.

This is a White Man's Government

Reflecting Nast's disillusionment, "Columbia" chastises African American political leadership in the South. Nast changed his depiction of blacks from noble individuals worthy of citizenship to racist caricatures.

In 1874, frustrated with what he saw as inept and selfish African American political leadership in the South, Nast changed his depiction of blacks from noble individuals worthy of citizenship to racist caricatures.

Colored Rule in a Reconstructed (?) State

What makes political cartoons so popular and effective?

Images as History unpacks the meaning and purpose of images—including cartoons, posters, magazine illustrations, posters, fine art, and photographs. Tightly connected to the narrative, each IAH feature analyzes the way images are used to express opinions, shape perceptions, and influence policy.

RECONSTRUCTION ABANDONED 423

Reconstruction Abandoned

By the end of Grant's first term in office, supporters of Reconstruction and freedmen's rights could look with some satisfaction at the many extraordinary changes that had taken place in the South. Yet ominous signs soon appeared that suggested Reconstruction was in trouble. Despite the crackdown on the Klan, white Southerners increasingly demonstrated their commitment to seizing power and imposing a new form of servitude on African Americans. Northerners, by contrast, seemed less and less willing to support a vigorous Reconstruction policy. Slowly, between 1872 and 1877, the extraordinary experiment in multiracial democracy and progressive government in the South was dismantled in favor of oligarchy and white supremacy.

Corruption and Scandal

A major factor in the pullback from Reconstruction was a series of corruption scandals that plagued the Grant administration. Grant himself was honest, but also politically naive and given to a hands-off style of leadership that gave officials in his administration an unusual degree of independence. Many of them took advantage of Grant's implicit trust to enrich themselves in a variety of illegal schemes.

For example, in 1869 Jay Gould and Jim Fisk, two Wall Street titans, conspired with Grant's brother-in-law in a scheme to corner the gold market. The plan eventually collapsed on September 24, 1869, a day dubbed "Black Friday, but not before hundreds of innocent investors were ruined and countless workers thrown out of work in the ensuing national economic turmoil. Fisk and Gould were pilloried in the press, but emerged unscathed. When the Credit Mobilier scandal became public, it was revealed that Grant's vice president and several high-ranking members of Congress had taken large bribes from the company involved in the completion of the government-subsidized Union Pacific Railroad. Other scandals found that three of Grant's cabinet members used their office for illegal financial gain. In the so-called "Whiskey Ring" scandal, for example, Treasury secretary Orville E. Babcock made a small fortune by illegally allowing whiskey distillers to avoid paying excise taxes. Secretary of War William W. Belknap likewise accepted bribes from companies engaged in corrupt activities on Indian reservations.

The North Retreats

Corruption scandals undermined the authority of Grant's administration. Grant soon found that to secure reelection and keep the Republican Party in power he would have to minimize political controversies. With so much negative publicity stirred up by corruption scandals, Grant's administration took steps to minimize political controversies. To secure his reelection and keep the Republican Party in power, Grant adopted a more conservative approach to Reconstruction, by now a frequent source of rancor in Washington.

In the summer of 1872, for example, Grant lobbied Congress for and then signed into law the Amnesty Act, granting a general pardon to all but a few hundred former Confederate leaders. Now eligible to vote and hold office, these planters, ex-army officers, and ex-Confederate officials wasted little time in reasserting their authority.

> "It seems to me that we are drifting, drifting back under the leadership of the slaveholders. Our former masters are fast taking the reins of government."
>
> GEORGE M. ARNOLD, African American Republican

The retreat from Reconstruction in the 1870s was also hastened by growing dissention within the Republican Party. Many Republicans, including former Radicals, began to question the wisdom of maintaining a strong federal role in the affairs of Southern states. Some Republicans now believed the fundamental goals of Reconstruction—citizenship, civil rights, and suffrage for the freedmen—had been accomplished. There was, they believed, a constitutional and moral limit to what the federal government could do on behalf of the freedmen. Now was the time, they argued, for the freedmen to elevate themselves economically, socially, and politically using their new rights.

What impact did the scandals of the Grant administration have on Reconstruction?

Spread throughout each chapter, **contemporary voices** comment on the major issues of the day.

436 CHAPTER 14 NOW THAT WE ARE FREE: RECONSTRUCTION AND THE NEW SOUTH, 1863–1890 CHAPTER REVIEW 437

CHAPTER REVIEW

1863–1866

The Ten Percent Plan Lincoln proposes moderate terms for readmission of Southern states

Thirteenth Amendment (ratified 1865) Abolishes slavery in every state

Fourteenth Amendment (ratified 1868) Defines citizenship to include African Americans and guarantees equal protection before the law

1867–1868

The Reconstruction Acts South placed under military rule and freedmen guaranteed voting rights

Progressive state governments take power in South Freedmen wield their newly won right to vote and hold office

Republicans impeach Johnson Reflects the divisive politics of Reconstruction

1869–1871

Fifteenth Amendment (ratified 1870) Establishes the right to vote for all male citizens regardless of "race, color, or previous condition of servitude"

Enforcement Acts passed Empowers Grant administration to weaken Ku Klux Klan and like groups

North Carolina elects first Redeemer government Signals a return to white supremacy in the South; other Southern states soon follow

1872–1873

Amnesty Act Pardons and restores full political rights to most ex-Confederates

Panic of 1873 Begins four years of severe economic depression that weakens Northern support for Reconstruction

1874–1875

The Mississippi Plan Violence by white terrorist groups keeps thousands of blacks from voting. Restores the Democratic Party to power

Second Civil Rights Act passed Guarantees equal access to public facilities and affirms the right of blacks to serve on juries

1876–1877

Compromise of 1877 Republican Rutherford B. Hayes becomes president; Republicans promise to remove federal troops from the South. End of Reconstruction

1883–1889

Civil Rights Act of 1875 declared unconstitutional Clears the way for adoption of Jim Crow policies across the South

Tennessee enacts first poll tax Sharply reduces black voting; adopted by other Southern states. Followed by literacy test and grandfather clause

Review Questions

1. How did white prejudice toward African Americans shape early Reconstruction policy in the Sea Islands and Louisiana?
2. Why did African Americans consider acquiring land so important? How did they justify their claims to plantation lands?
3. How did violence come to play a role in the course of Reconstruction? What measures did Congress and the Grant administration take to curb it?
4. How did some feminists react to the Fifteenth Amendment? What impact did this decision have on the women's rights movement?
5. Who were the "carpetbaggers"? Where did this term originate and what does it tell us about Southern attitudes during Reconstruction?
6. What key factors led to the end of Reconstruction?
7. What was the Lost Cause? What purposes did it serve in the post-Reconstruction South?
8. Who were the "Bourbons" and what was their vision for the New South?

Key Terms

Ten Percent Plan Pardoned all Southerners (except high-ranking military officers and Confederate officials) who took an oath pledging loyalty to the Union and support for emancipation. As soon as ten percent of a state's voters took this oath, they could call a convention, establish a new state government, and apply for congressional recognition. **408**

Wade-Davis Bill A Reconstruction program designed to punish Confederate leaders and permanently destroy the South's slave society. **410**

Freedmen's Bureau Relief agency for the war-ravaged South created by Congress in March 1865. It provided emergency services, built schools, and managed confiscated lands. **410**

Black Codes Laws designed by the ex-Confederate states to sharply limit the civil and economic rights of freedmen and create an exploitable workforce. **413**

Fourteenth Amendment Drafted by Congress in June 1866, it defined citizenship to include African Americans, guaranteed equal protection before the law, and established the federal government as the guarantee of individual civil rights. **416**

carpetbagger White Southerners' derogatory term for Northerners who came south after the war to settle, work, or sell the ex-slaves. It falsely suggested they were penniless adventurers who came south merely to get rich. **418**

scalawag White Southerners' derogatory term for fellow whites considered traitors to their region and race for joining the Republican Party and cooperating with Reconstruction policy. **418**

Fifteenth Amendment Constitutional amendment passed by Congress in 1869 providing an explicit constitutional guarantee for black suffrage. **421**

Ku Klux Klan The best-known of the many secret white terrorist organizations that first arose in the South in 1866; they targeted freedmen and symbols of black self-improvement and independence and played a key role in reestablishing white supremacy by the late 1870s. **422**

Panic of 1873 A financial panic on Wall Street that touched off a national economic recession causing financial houses, banks, and businesses to fail. Hundreds of thousands of workers lost their jobs. **424**

Mississippi Plan Campaign of violence and intimidation waged by armed groups of whites closely allied with the Democratic Party that drove Republicans from power in the Mississippi state elections of 1874. Copied by other Southern states. **426**

Redeemers Name for white Southern political leaders who successfully returned their states to white Democratic rule in the mid-1870s. The name was intended to depict these leaders as saviors of Southern society from rule by freedmen, scalawags, and carpetbaggers. **426**

Civil Rights Act of 1875 Passed by Congress in 1875, it required state governments to provide equal access to public facilities such as schools and to allow African Americans to serve on juries. In 1883 the U.S. Supreme Court ruled it unconstitutional. **426**

Compromise of 1877 Resolution of the disputed presidential election of 1876 that handed victory to Republican Rutherford B. Hayes over Democrat Samuel J. Tilden. Democrats agreed to the deal in exchange for patronage and the continued removal of federal troops from the South. **427**

New South Optimistic phrase white Southerners used to describe the post-Reconstruction South, reflecting the South's development of a new system of race relations based on segregation and white supremacy and politically a renewed economic state. Accompanied by a renewed region. **428**

A **Chapter Review** provides a **visual summary** of key events, thought-provoking **review questions**, and **key terms** with definitions and page references.

Supplements for Instructors and Students

FOR QUALIFIED COLLEGE ADOPTERS

Name of Supplement	Print or Online?	Instructor or Student Supplement?	Description
Instructor's Manual 0-205-72875-8	Both	Instructor	Chapter overview, lecture supplements, discussion questions, suggested assignments, and research resources for each chapter, including both general and text-specific content.
American Stories: Biographies in United States History, Third Edition Volume 1: 0-13-182654-9 Volume 2: 0-13-182653-0	Both	Student	This two-volume collection of sixty-two biographies provides insight into the lives and contributions to American history of key figures as well as ordinary citizens. Introductions, pre-reading questions, and suggested resources help students connect the relevance of these individuals to historical events.
MyHistoryLab 0-205-75326-4	Online	Both	Along with a complete e-book version of *Visions of America,* MyHistoryLab provides several hundred primary source documents, study support, test review materials, maps and activities, many of which are assignable and feed into a gradebook. The History Bookshelf includes nearly 100 of the most commonly assigned book-length sources. A Closer Look guides users through the process of analyzing visual images. The History Toolkit offers guided tutorials and helpful links. Icons in the e-book link directly to relevant materials. Visit www.myhistorylab.com.
CourseSmart 0-205-72698-4	Online	Both	CourseSmart Textbooks Online give students an inexpensive alternative to purchasing the print textbook by subscribing to the same content online and saving up to 50% off the suggested list price of the print text. Features include search, online note-taking, a print option, and bookmarking. Visit www.coursesmart.com
Instructor's Resource Center	Online	Instructor	A password-protected Web site where instructors can download Pearson supplements. Please contact your local Pearson representative for an access code or visit www.pearsonhighered.com/educator.
MyTest 0-205-75334-5	Online	Instructor	The MyTest test bank contains over 1,700 multiple choice, short answer, and essay questions to test both general knowledge and features and content specific to *Visions of America*. Questions can be edited, and tests can be printed in several different formats. Visit www.pearsonmytest.com.
PowerPoint Presentation 0-205-74815-5	Online	Instructor	The PowerPoint slides to accompany *Visions of America* include an outline of each chapter and full-color images, maps, and figures from the text.
Comprehensive American History Transparency Set 0-673-97211-9	Online	Instructor	A vast collection of American history transparency masters. Available exclusively on the Instructor's Resource Center.
Discovering American History Through Maps and Views by Gerald Danzer 0-673-53766-8	Online	Instructor	A set of 140 full-color digital transparency masters includes cartographic and pictorial maps, views, photos; urban plans and building diagrams; and works of art. Available exclusively on the Instructor's Resource Center.
Digital Transparancy Masters	Online	Instructor	Text-specific transparency masters include all the maps that appear in *Visions of America.*

Name of Supplement	Print or Online?	Instructor or Student Supplement?	Description
Longman American History Atlas 0-321-00486-8	Print	Both	A full-color historical atlas includes approximately 100 maps covering the scope of American history from pre-Columbian Native Americans to the 1990s. Produced by a renowned cartographic firm and a team of respected historians.
Study Card for American History 0-321-29232-4	Print	Student	This timeline of major events in American social, political, and cultural history distills course information to the basics, helping students quickly master the fundamentals and prepare for exams.
Mapping America: A Guide to Historical Geography by Ken Weatherbie Volume 1: 0-321-47559-3 Volume 2: 0-321-47560-7	Print	Student	This two-volume workbook presents the basic geography of the United States, its lands and river systems, and helps students place the history of the United States into spatial perspective. The goal of this workbook is to reinforce, through practice, how to read visual materials as historical documents.
America Through the Eyes of Its People, Third Edition Volume 1: 0-321-39575-1 Volume 2: 0-321-39576-X	Print	Student	This two-volume comprehensive anthology of primary sources expertly balances social and political history and includes up-to-date narrative material.
A Short Guide to Writing About History, Seventh Edition by Richard Marius and Melvin E. Page 0-205-67370-8	Print	Student	Teaches students how to think and write like historians, to incorporate their own ideas into their papers and to tell a story about history. Covering brief essays and the documented resource paper, the text outlines the writing and researching processes, explores modes of historical writing (including argument), and offers guidelines for improving style and documenting sources.
Penguin Valuepacks	Print	Student	A variety of Penguin-Putnam texts are available at discounted prices when bundled with *Visions of America.* Complete list of available titles at http://www.pearsonhighered.com/penguin/
Library of American Biography Series	Print	Student	Pearson's renowned series of biographies spotlights figures who had a significant impact on American history. View the complete list at http://www.pearsonhighered.com/historyvaluepacks/biographies_history.html
Retrieving the American Past	Print	Student	This on-demand database offers eighty-six modules on topics such as "Women on the Frontier," "The Salem Witchcraft Scare," "The Age of Industrial Violence," and "Native American Societies, 1870–1995." Approximately thirty-five pages in length, each module includes an introduction, several primary documents and secondary sources, follow-up questions, and recommendations for further reading. Instructor-originated material can be incorporated. Contact your local Pearson representative for more information or visit http://www.pearsoncustom.com/

Acknowledgments

DEVELOPMENT STORY

More than three hundred and fifty reviewers, focus group participants, and class-testers participated in developing *Visions of America.* Each of them evaluated both the extensive visual program and the narrative text. They commented on the selection of images and on their integration into the narrative. They suggested refinements to the page design to maximize visual appeal and pedagogical effectiveness. And, through many drafts, they appraised our success in executing our twofold goal—to approach American history as the product of competing visions and to enhance that approach through an analysis of our nation's visual legacy. Always too, they focused on the value of our approach in the classroom. This book would not have been possible without their efforts, nor those of the many students who participated in focus groups and class tests.

Manuscript Reviewers

Alabama

Carl Boening, Shelton State Community College
Antoinnette Hudson, Jacksonville State University
Lawrence Kohl, University of Alabama
Lisa Lindquist Dorr, University of Alabama
Andre Millard, University of Alabama - Birmingham
Rebecca Reeves, Wallace State Community College
England Robert, Northwest-Shoals Community College
George Terrell Jr., Gadsden State Community College
John Turner, University of South Alabama
Deryl Umphrey, Calhoun Community College

Arkansas

Ken Bridges, South Arkansas Community College
James Moses, Arkansas Technical University
Charlotte Power, Black River Technical College
Carey Roberts, Arkansas Technical University
Amy Rumsey, Arkansas State University

Arizona

James Austin, Chandler-Gilbert Community College
Azusa Ono, Arizona State University
Debbie Roberts, Yavapai College
David Rudakewich, Coconino Community College

California

Guy Aronoff, California State University—Channel Islands
Josh Ashenmiller, Fullerton College
Don Bandy, Taft College
Rosemary Bell, Skyline College
Dominic Cerri, Sacramento City College
Daniel Christensen, Biola University
Tracy Davis, Victor Valley College
Philip DiMare, California State University, Sacramento
Michael Flores, Cypress College
Keith R. V. Heningburg, Sacramento City College
Jennifer Hernandez, Cuyamaca Collage
Jay Hester, Sierra College
George Jarrett, Cerritos College
Daehwan Lee, Pasadena City College
Daniel Lewis, California State Polytechnic University-Pomona
Peter Mancall, University of Southern California
Louis McDermott, Solano Community College
Aime McNamara, Cabrillo College
Jonathan Nielson, Cosumnes River College
Emily Rader, El Camino College
John Sbardellati, University of California—Santa Barbara
Bryan Seiling, Cypress College

Colorado

John Baranski, Fort Lewis College
Joanne Maypole, Metropolitan State College of Denver
Cheryl Waite, Community College of Aurora

Connecticut

Edward Donato, Sacred Heart University

Delaware

Bradley Skelcher, Delaware State University

Florida

Anthony Atwood, Florida International University
Will Benedicks, Tallahassee Community College
Tomas Bennett, Florida Hospital College of Health Sciences
Daniel Finn, Seminole Community College
David Gregory, Tallahassee Community College
Brian Harding, Lake-Sumter Community College
Kelly Minor, University of Florida
John Shaffett, The Baptist College of Florida
E. Timothy Smith, Barry University

Georgia

Don Butts, Gordon State College
Michael Hall, Armstrong Atlantic State University
Shane Hamilton, University of Georgia
Heather Lucas, Georgia Perimeter College-Dunwoody Campus
Elsa Nystrom, Kennesaw State University
George S. Pabis, Georgia Perimeter College
Jim Piecuch, Kennesaw State University
Colleen Vasconcellos, University of West Georgia

Hawaii

Allison Gough, Hawaii Pacific University

Idaho

Christian Esh, Northwest Nazarene University

Illinois

Steven DePasquale, Kankakee Community College
Melissa Dierkes, Moraine Valley Community College
Richard Filipink, Western Illinois University
Kent Gatyas, Morton College
George Gerdow, Northeastern Illinois University
Jennifer Guiliano, University of Illinois at Urbana-Champaign
Robert Harmon, Elgin Community College
Virginia Jelatis, Western Illinois University
Mark Leff, University of Illinois
Stephen Lowe, Olivet Nazarene University
Jim McIntyre, Moraine Valley Community College
Jay Nelson, DePaul University
Jay Pearce, Blackhawk Community College
Wendy Sarti, Oakton Community College
Anne Valk, Southern Illinois University—Edwardsville
Ben Whisenhunt, College of DuPage

Indiana

Eric Hall, Purdue University
Anne Kearney, Jefferson Community and Technical College
Jason Lantzer, Indiana University—Bloomington
Jonathan Nashel, Indiana University—South Bend
Dave O'Grady, University of Southern Indiana
David Vanderstel, Indiana University—Purdue University Indianapolis

Iowa

Dick Broadie, University of Northern Iowa
Kevin Gannon, Grand View University
Johanna Schoen, University of Iowa

Acknowledgments (continued from pp. xxxi)

Kansas
Andrew Lindsay, Pittsburg State University
James B. M. Schick, Pittsburg State University

Kentucky
John Bowes, Eastern Kentucky University
John Burch, Campbellsville University
Jeff Dennis, Morehead State University
Jennifer Geouge, Somerset Community College—Laurel Campus
Carol Siler, Eastern Kentucky University
Patia Tabar, Northern Kentucky University
Fiona Halloran, Eastern Kentucky University

Maine
Patricia Bixel, Maine Maritime Academy
Karen Kimball, University of Maine—Machias
David Raymond, Northern Maine Community College

Maryland
Wayne Ackerson, Salisbury University
Angela Leonard, Loyola College
David Peavler, Towson University
Alonzo Smith, Montgomery College

Massachusetts
Vincent Cannato, University of Massachusetts Boston
Gary Donato, Massachusetts Bay Community College
Charlotte Haller, Worcester State College
Kevin Kenny, Boston College
Betty Mitchell, University of Massachusetts—Dartmouth
Gail Mohanty, University of Massachusetts—Dartmouth
Elaine Pascale, Suffolk University
Cynthia Lyerly, Boston College

Michigan
Gordon Andrews, Lake Michigan College
Kevin Brown, Lansing Community College
Kimn Carlton-Smith, Ferris State University
Todd Estes, Oakland University
Roy Finkenbine, University of Detroit Mercy
Amy French, Delta Community College
Steven Garvey, Muskegon Community College
Jeff Janowick, Lansing Community College
Malcolm Magee, Michigan State University
Ed Martini, Western Michigan University
Joshua Schier, Western Michigan University
Harold Siegel, Hillsdale College
Dave Stewart, Hillsdale College
Catherine Tobin, Central Michigan University

Minnesota
Kevin Byrne, Gustavus Adolphus College
Kathleen Gorman, Minnesota State University—Mankato
Paul Harris, Minnesota State University, Moorhead
John Hendrickson, Minnesota State University, Mankato
Linda Janke, Anoka Ramsey Community College
Judy Kutulas, St. Olaf College
Scott Laderman, University of Minnesota—Duluth
David Rayson, Normandale Community College
Gregory Schmidt, Winona State University
Terry Shoptaugh, Minnesota State University, Moorhead

Mississippi
John Arnold, Itawamba Community College
Eric Bobo, Hinds Community College
Michael Namorato, University of Mississippi

Missouri
Diana Ahmad, University of Missouri—Rolla
Kay Blalock, St. Louis Community College—Meramec
Brad Lookingbill, Columbia College
John McManus, University of Missouri—Rolla
Kay Murnan, Ozarks Technical Community College
Kim Schreck, University of Missouri—St. Louis
K. Dirk Voss, Saint Louis Community College
James Whitt, Ozarks Technical Community College
Tim Wood, Southwest Baptist University

Montana
David Bibb, University of Great Falls
Debora Bibb, University of Great Falls

North Carolina
Monika Fleming, Edgecombe Community College
Michael Kennedy, High Point University

North Dakota
Jon Brudvig, University of Mary
Joseph Jastrzembski, Minot State University
Jim Norris, North Dakota State University

Nebraska
Amy Forss, Metropolitan Community College
Heather Fryer, Creighton University

Nevada
Susan Imswiler, Truckee Meadows Community College
Cyd McMullen, Great Basin College
Jerry Parker, Truckee Meadows Community College
John Reid, Truckee Meadows Community College

New Hampshire
Andrew Moore, Saint Anselm College

New Jersey
Barbara Calluori, Montclair State University
Bill Carr, Kean University
Walter Dabrowski, Mercer County Community College
Janet Golden, Rutgers University—Camden
David Wolcott, Educational Testing Service

New Mexico
Nancy Shockley, New Mexico State University

New York
Heather Barry, St. Joseph's College
Thomas Beal, State University of New York—Oneonta
Will Corprew, Broome Community College
Andrea DeKoter, State University of New York at Cortland
Tom Dublin, The State University of New York at Binghamton
Megan Elias, City University of New York—Queensborough Community College
Andrew Feffer, Union College
David Gerber, State University of New York at Buffalo
Gary Ostrower, Alfred University
William Price, North Country Community College
Daniel Prosterman, Syracuse University
Margaret Wingate, Broome Community College
Jason Young, The State University of New York at Buffalo

Ohio
Rebecca Barrett, The Ohio State University
Diane Britton, University of Toledo
Daniel Cobb, Miami University
William Coil, The Ohio State University
Hasan Jeffries, The Ohio State University
Gregory Kupsky, The Ohio State University
Mark Mengerink, Bowling Green State University
Caryn Neumann, Miami University Middletown
Paul O'Hara, Xavier University
Judith Spraul-Schmidt, University of Cincinnati Raymond Walters College
Jim Streckfuss, Miami University
Shirley Wajda, Kent State University
Jonathan Winkler, Wright State University

Oklahoma
Jeff Carlisle, Oklahoma City Community College
Frank Gilbert, Southeastern Oklahoma State University
Paul B. Hatley, Rogers State University
Stacy Reaves, Tulsa Community College
Paddy Swiney, Tulsa Community College

Oregon
Cathy Croghan Alzner, Portland Community College
John Shaw, Portland Community College—Sylvania

Pennsylvania
Jacqueline Akins, Community College of Philadelphia
Allan Austin, College Misericordia
Andy Bacha, Harrisburg Area Community College
Brian Black, Pennsylvania State University—Altoona
Michael P. Gabriel, Kutztown University
Jolyon Girard, Cabrini College
John Hepp, Wilkes University

Ben Houston, Carnegie Mellon
Jeffrey Hyson, Saint Joseph's University
John Lawlor, Jr., Reading Area Community College
Robert Malick, Harrisburg Area Community College
Rodney Ross, Harrisburg Area Community College
John Rossi, Pennsylvania State University—Erie
David Snyder, Delaware Valley College
Flo Waldron, Franklin & Marshall College

Rhode Island

Robert McCarthy, Providence College
H. Glenn Reed, Salve Regina University
Miriam Reumann, University of Rhode Island

South Carolina

Paul Christopher Anderson, Clemson University
John Barrington, Furman University
Abel Bartley, Clemson University
Bart Hayward, University of South Carolina—Sumter
Megan Shockley, Clemson University
Diane Vecchio, Furman University

South Dakota

Kurt Kemper, University of South Dakota

Tennessee

Mary Ann Bodayla, Southwest Tennessee Community College
Aram Goudsouzian, University of Memphis
Joseph Hawes, University of Memphis
Clint Madlock, Southwest Tennessee Community College
Patrick Reagan, Tennessee Technical University
Bryan Reed, Cleveland State Community College
Donald Trotter, Johnson Bible College

Texas

Javier R. Aguirre, Palo Alto College
Erika Bsumek, University of Texas at Austin
David Carlson, University of Texas-Pan American
Mike Downs, Tarrant County College Southeast Campus
Carolyn Eastman, University of Texas at Austin
Glen Findley, Odessa College
Heard Floore, Tarrant County College
Dan Greene, Baylor University
Eric Gruver, Texas A&M University-Commerce
Aimee Harris-Johnson, El Paso Community College
Andrew Hollinger, Tarrant County College
Charles Hope, Tarrant County College
Melissa Hovsepian, University of Houston-Downtown
Kenneth Howell, Prairie View A&M University
Ivy Kirkpatrick, Tyler Junior College
Don Knox, Wayland Baptist University
Carolyn Lacy, Texas A&M University—Kingsville
Andrew Lannen, Stephen F. Austin State University
Melissa LaPrelle, Collin County Community College—Spring Creek Campus
Norman Love, El Paso Community College
Alexis McCrossen, Southern Methodist University
James Mills, University of Texas at Brownsville
Daniel Murphree, University of Texas—Tyler
Eric Owens, Lamar State College-Orange
Alisa Petrovich, Brazosport College
Ashley Pettiet, Texas Technical University
Penne Restad, University of Texas
Kim Richardson, Texas Technical University
Joan Supplee, Baylor University
David Wilcox, Houston Community College
Larry Wilson, San Jacinto College Central
Chad Wooley, Eastfield College
Jane Flaherty, Texas A&M University
Katherine Pierce, Sam Houston State University

Utah

Anne Butler, Utah State University
Linda Wright, Tarrant County College—Northeast

Virginia

David Head, John Tyler Community College
Carolyn Lawes, Old Dominion University
Amy Minton, Marymount University
David Snead, Liberty University
Michael Trochim, Ferrum College
Jerrold Roy, Hampton University
Paul Gaffney, Landmark College
John Peterson, College of St. Joseph

Washington

David Brumbach, Tacoma Community College
Jaime Cardenas Jr., Seattle Central Community College
Victoria Dehlbom, Washington State University
Dan Herman, Central Washington University
Kevin Leonard, Western Washington University
Maureen Nutting, North Seattle Community College
Jason Ripper, Everett Community College

Wisconsin

John Grider, University of Wisconsin—La Crosse
Jason Hostutler, Marquette University
Abigail Markwyn, Carroll College
Kate Mollan, University of Wisconsin—Milwaukee
John C. Savagian, Alverno College
Connie Sexauer, University of Wisconsin, Marathon County
Robert Zeidel, University of Wisconsin—Stout

Wyoming

William Howard Moore, University of Wyoming

Focus Group Participants

Jaime Aguila, Arizona State University
Michael Barnhart, State University of New York—Stony Brook
John Belohlavek, University of South Florida—Tampa
George Benton, New Jersey City University
Patricia Biggs, Arizona State University
Bob Bionaz, Chicago State University
Howard Bodner, Houston Community College
Charlotte Brooks, City University of New York—Baruch College
Sharon Burnham, John Tyler Community College
Michael Camilleri, Montgomery College
Nancy Carnevale, Montclair State University
Edward Carroll, Heartland Community College
MaryLou Carroll, Columbia College
Chad David Cover, Farmingham State College
Robert Cray, Montclair State University
Carson Cunningham, DePaul University
Amy Darty, University of Central Florida-Orlando
Paul Doutrich, York College of Pennsylvania
Joanna Dyl, University of South Florida-Tampa
Mario Fenyo, Bowie State
Thomas Foster, DePaul University
Kevin Gannon, Grand View University
Matthew Garrett, Arizona State University
Steve Garvy, Muskegon Community College
George Gerdow, Northeastern Illinois University
Timothy Hack, Salem Community College
Matthew Harris, Colorado State University—Pueblo
Ann Heiss, Kent State University
Mary Kelly, Franklin Pierce University
Lionel Kimble, Chicago State University
Cranston Knight, Malcolm X CC
Paul Lafleche, Worcester State College
Tracy Lai, Seattle Central Community College
Deb Lamb, Olympic College
Bryan Lamkin, Azusa Pacific University
Kurt Leichtle, University of Wisconsin River Falls
Charles Levine, Mesa Community College
Emily Lewis, Arizona State University
Douglas Ley, Franklin Pierce University
Parandeh Lia, Mt. San Antonio College
Quinto J. Lotti, Alexandria Technical College
Alan Lucibello, Seton Hall University
Jason Martinek, New Jersey City University
Lindsey McNellis, University of Central Florida-Orlando
Paul Morgan, University of South Florida-Tampa
Karen O'Brien, Ramapo College
Lisa Ossian, Des Moines Area Community College
John Petty, Montgomery College
Jenny Piasecki, Ivy Tech Community College—North Central
Jeffrey Pilz, Northern Iowa Area Community College
Dave Price, Santa Fe College
Robert Riedl, Montgomery College
Mark Roehrs, Lincoln Land Community College

Acknowledgments (continued from pp. xxxiii)

Courtney Shah, Lower Columbia College
David Tegeder, Santa Fe College
Curtis R. Thomas, Richland College
Kathryn Tomasek, Wheaton College
Amy Tyson, DePaul University
Michael Whelan, Montclair State University
David White, McHenry County College
Kimberly Williams, Hillsborough Community College
Julie Winch, University of Massachusetts-Boston
James Wolfinger, DePaul University
Margarita Youngo, Pima Community College

Class Testers

Lee Annis, Montgomery College
Richard Byrne, Kirkwood Community College
Gary Donato, Lasell College
David Driscoll, University of Massachusetts—Lowell
David Dzurec, University of Scranton
David Hostetter, Shepherd University
Kenneth Howell, Blinn College
James Mills, University of Texas at Brownsville
Dave O'Grady, University of Southern Indiana
Elaine Pascale, Suffolk University
Charles Piehl, Minnesota State University, Mankato
Stacy Reaves, Tulsa Community College
Wendy Sarti, Oakton Community College
Jean Stuntz, West Texas A&M University
James Taw, Valdosta State University
Gray Whaley, Southern Illinois University—Carbondale

Student Reviewers

Anita Asher
Kip Bailey
Robin Baweja
Andy Bendel
Suzanne Bordelon
Jordan Bravo
Luz Calderon
Alexandra Carlier
Elham Chiali
Heidi Chohe
David Corcoran
Jacquelyn Coyle
James Creighton
Vikki Crosby
Leslie Crowl
Arik Dadez
Mercy Dicuangco
Linda Duy
Carlin Eddington
Xiomara Escobar
Rafaella Ferreira
Megan Flynn
Daniel Follosco
Janell Forgey
Yolanda Gallo
Michael Gay
Scott Geairn
David Glenn
Hector Gonzalez
Josue Gonzlaez
Harry Goodfellow
Patricia Graham
Teresa Hernandez
Tiffany Hines
Kassy Hodge
Katie Holt
Jordan Hunt
Michelle Jackson
David Johnsen
Margaret Jones
Michelle Jones
Dan Kelly
Cari Kessler
Travis Larrabee
Kamille Lau
Natalia Leal
Brian Lehtola
Jaqqi LeVasseur
Jorge Lopez
Robin Mackin
Karen Martinez
Katherine McGill
Matt Mills
Tess Nunn
Olanrewaju Olagunju
Jacob Pierce
Gina Pippin
Jessica Porter
Brendan Price
Victor Rubio
Fadi Saliba
Sofia Samrad
Meggan Schulze
Laura Sheen
Justin Simpson
Micah Spero
De'Amber Stephens
Danielle Strother
Shirley Tafoya
Chad Taska
Sarah Taylor
Otabek Tillaev
Shayra Tolliver
Gregory Trent
Chelsea Uriona
Samantha Vander Kooy
Rachel Vargas
Jenny Walters
Brittany Weathers
Sakeena White
Meghan Witmer
Rick Wolf
Bogdan Zavorotny

We offer sincere thanks for unwavering support from Michael Boezi, former Executive Editor, and Priscilla McGeehon, Publisher, through the many years it took to make our vision a reality. Roberta Meyer, Senior Development Editor, and Phil Herbst, Development Editor, also played a key part in crafting this book, as did DK Publishing who provided us with our innovative design. Other members of the Pearson team who contributed greatly to this project are: Debra Wechsler, Project Manager; Leah Jewell, Editorial Director; Ann Marie McCarthy, Senior Managing Editor; Rochelle Diogenes, Editor-in-Chief, Development; Sonya Nikolaidis, Development Assistant; Maura Zaldivar, Operations Specialist; Sue Westmoreland, Executive Marketing Manager; Ashley Fallon, Marketing Assistant; Brandy Dawson, Director of Marketing; Laura Gardner, Art Director; Mirella Signoretto, Art Editor; Maureen Prado Roberts, Market Development Coordinator; Emsal Hasan, Associate Supplements Editor; Sarah Kinney, Media Editor; Jennie Burger, Market Research Analyst; Kevin Currie, Project Manager; Patrick Barb, Editorial Assistant; David Kear, Development Editor, and Amanda Dykstra, Editorial Assistant. Pre-Press PMG executed DK's design with flair, and our thanks to Melissa Sacco, Project Editor; Amy Musto, Design Director; Brian Molloy, Designer; Maggie Sears, Copyeditor; Barbara DeVries, Proofreader; Margery Niblock, Indexer. Our image program was tremendously enhanced by the skills of Barbara S. Salz, Photo Researcher; Jeannine Ciliotta, Map Coordinator; and Peter Bull Art Studio, Cartographer. Thanks to Jay O'Callaghan who brought us together, and Betty Slack who kept us going in the initial, bumpy phases.

VISIONS *of* AMERICA

CHAPTER 14

Now That We Are Free

Reconstruction and the New South, 1863–1890

Preparing for Reconstruction p. 406

The Fruits of Freedom p. 409

> "Never before had I a word of impudence from any of our black folk, but they are not ours any longer."
>
> SUSAN BRADFORD, observing the defiant attitude among former slaves on her Florida plantation, 1865

The Civil War ended in April 1865, concluding the bloodiest and most divisive conflict in American history. The period that followed came to be known as Reconstruction for several reasons. Most obviously, the name called to mind the need to rebuild the war-torn South. It also referred to the effort to reestablish the Union torn apart by secession. Finally, it indicated the need to remake Southern society in the wake of slavery's destruction.

The complexities and challenges of this last goal are evident in Winslow Homer's 1876 painting, *A Visit from the Old Mistress,* which depicts ex-slaves being visited by their former owner. The elegant clothing worn by the "Old Mistress" suggests she has money, but clearly the relationship between the women has changed significantly in the wake of emancipation. To begin with, the mistress has come to visit the former slaves in their home, suggesting a diminishing of her status and power relative to them. The scene also lacks any sense of the affection that plantation owners always assured themselves existed between slaves and masters. Indeed, the three African American women eye the mistress warily. One of them even chooses to remain seated in what surely would have been considered a show of contempt. The old order was gone, but what would replace it remained unclear in the aftermath of the war.

Americans entered the Reconstruction period facing the profound questions raised by war and emancipation. Was it possible for whites and former slaves to live together in peace and mutual respect? What rights were the freedmen entitled to and who would guarantee these rights? The different answers articulated by freedmen and white Southerners revealed sharply divergent visions of the future and led to a bitter struggle to define the meaning of freedom. "Verily," observed ex-slave Frederick Douglass, "the work does not end with the abolition of slavery, but only begins."

How does this image reveal the uncertainty of race relations in the postwar South?

The Struggle to Define Reconstruction p. 412

Implementing Reconstruction p. 418

Reconstruction Abandoned p. 423

The New South p. 428

Preparing for Reconstruction

Long before the Emancipation Proclamation took effect on January 1, 1863 countless thousands of enslaved Africans took advantage of the chaos produced by the war to liberate themselves. Their actions raised a host of questions about what rights the freedmen would be entitled to, including land ownership and voting. Lincoln and his advisers preferred to wait until the war's successful conclusion before addressing these questions, but actions taken by the freedmen to assert their rights and secure their liberty forced the Lincoln administration to develop policies during the war that ultimately shaped postwar Reconstruction.

Emancipation Test Cases

Even before the Emancipation Proclamation took effect, the federal government realized that it needed to enact policies regarding the growing numbers of freedmen in areas of the South occupied by the Union army. These policies varied by region and were shaped by local customs and the attitudes of freedmen and white officials. As such, they amounted to test cases for the coming debate over Reconstruction. Three of these test cases revealed both the promise and the contentious conflict surrounding emancipation.

The first test case began when federal forces seized the Sea Islands off the coast of South Carolina in November 1861. They found a vast system of cotton plantations, but no planters. The latter had fled, leaving behind ten thousand slaves, who moved quickly to establish new lives based on their understanding of freedom. While clearly posed, "Planting Sweet Potatoes" (**14.1**), shot by a New Hampshire photographer visiting a regiment from his state stationed on the island, captured one fundamental way in which ex-slaves expressed their freedom. Rejecting cotton, a crop they associated with slavery, they planted crops of their own choosing, such as sweet potatoes and corn for local consumption. Freedom for the African Americans of the Sea Islands meant a future as independent farmers living free of white control.

Many Northern whites who arrived after the military takeover, however, brought with them a very different vision of the future for the Sea Islands. Convinced that Sea Island blacks should resume their labors on cotton plantations—not as slaves but as paid wage earners—federal officials opted not to grant land to the freedmen and instead auctioned it off to the highest bidder. Northern investors bought most of the land, hired freedmen as wage laborers, and resumed cotton cultivation. This vision was

14.1 Freedmen in the Sea Islands Cultivating Sweet Potatoes, 1862
Most freedmen refused to grow cotton, considering it a symbol of slavery. They grew sweet potatoes and other crops, such as corn, primarily for their own consumption. [*Source*: Collection of The New-York Historical Society, [37628]]

How did freedmen define freedom in the Sea Islands?

driven in part by the sincere belief that subsistence farming on small tracts of land was backward, harmful to the long-term interests of the freedmen and also by the racist notion that African Americans were not capable of handling their freedom responsibly and therefore needed white employers to guide them.

A second test case unfolded on Davis Bend, the Mississippi plantations owned by Confederate President Jefferson Davis and his brother Joseph. Before the Civil War, they had tried to make Davis Bend a model slave labor community where slaves received better food and were granted a high degree of autonomy. The Davis brothers hoped other planters would follow their example and thus refute the abolitionist argument that slavery was inhumane. Instead, Davis Bend became a model of a very different sort of ideal, one that vividly demonstrated what freedmen were capable of achieving if granted land and autonomy. When General Ulysses S. Grant arrived and found the former slaves running the plantations, he ordered federal officials to lease land to the freedmen. Unlike the freedmen of the Sea Islands, the African American residents of Davis Bend did not have to contend with Northerners seeking to reassert white control over the land and impose a wage labor system. As a consequence, by 1865 Davis Bend residents had established their own local government and cleared a profit of $160,000 in cotton sales.

A third and far larger test case for emancipation policy began in Louisiana and was eventually extended up the Mississippi Valley affecting some 700,000 former slaves. Soon after Union forces seized New Orleans in April 1862, army officers established a policy to guide the transition from slavery to emancipation. As in the case of the Sea Islands, the policy reflected the racist belief among Northern whites that African Americans could not responsibly handle their freedom and therefore needed strict rules regarding conduct and work. Blacks were required to remain on their plantations, working as wage laborers bound by one-year contracts. Those wishing to travel, even for short distances, required a pass from the plantation owner. Runaways and resisters, as depicted in this 1864 drawing (**14.2**), would be forcibly returned to their plantations. Offsetting these harsh provisions was a ban on the use of corporal punishment for plantation labor. Freedmen bitterly

14.2 Freedmen Forcibly Returned to Their Plantations, 1864
Violators of the Reconstruction plan were deemed "vagrants" and forcibly returned to their plantations.

Why did Union officials define freedom for former slaves so narrowly in Louisiana?

opposed the new system, arguing that it placed them in a nearly powerless position under the authority of their former masters. In New Orleans, home to the South's largest free black population before the war, African Americans began to demand equal rights for all freedmen, including the right to vote and hold office. Although their efforts failed, they sparked a national debate over freedmen's rights that would come to dominate Reconstruction.

The experiences in the Sea Islands, Davis Bend, Louisiana, and elsewhere during the war created a host of conflicting visions regarding the rights of freedmen, land redistribution, and the authority of ex-slave owners. Yet the emancipation experience also revealed the optimism of the freedmen and their commitment to defend their newly won freedom and make the most of it.

Lincoln's Ten Percent Plan

Even as the Civil War raged, President Lincoln had begun to formulate an official Reconstruction policy. A moderate on the big issues before the war, Lincoln proposed a moderate Reconstruction policy. As he suggested so eloquently in his second inaugural address, he intended to deal with the defeated South "with malice toward none" and "charity for all" to "achieve and cherish a just and lasting peace among ourselves. . . ." He believed that extending lenient terms to the South would convince Confederates to surrender sooner and speed the healing process necessary for the good of the Union. Vengeance, he held, would only delay Reconstruction. It might even inspire defeated Confederate soldiers to form renegade bands of insurgents to wage a war of terrorism for years to come.

> "A more studied outrage on the legislative authority of the people has never been perpetuated."
>
> Wade-Davis Manifesto denouncing Lincoln's veto of the Wade-Davis Bill

In December of 1863 Lincoln issued his Proclamation of Amnesty and Reconstruction, also known as the **Ten Percent Plan.** Intended to establish Southern state governments, the plan pardoned all Southerners (except high-ranking military officers and Confederate officials) who took an oath pledging loyalty to the Union and support for emancipation. As soon as ten percent of a state's voters took this oath, they could call a convention, establish a new state government, and apply for congressional recognition.

Radical Republicans Offer a Different Vision

The lenient character of Lincoln's plan enraged many Radical Republicans. In July of 1864 Radical Republican leaders Senator Benjamin Wade of Ohio and Congressman Henry W. Davis of Maryland cosponsored the **Wade-Davis Bill,** a Reconstruction program designed to punish Confederate leaders and permanently destroy the South's slave society. Southerners could reestablish new state governments only after a majority of a state's voters signed an "ironclad" oath declaring they never aided the Confederate army or government. Southerners who did serve as high-ranking army officers or government officials would be stripped of their citizenship, including the right to vote and hold office. The former Confederate states would be readmitted only after a lengthy period of punishment and a clear demonstration of their commitment to the Union, emancipation, and freedmen's rights.

Lincoln quietly pocket vetoed the bill. Undaunted, Wade, Davis, and other Radicals mounted a movement to replace Lincoln as the Republican Party presidential nominee. Although the effort failed, it exposed the deeply divided opinions regarding Reconstruction policy.

Lincoln and his fellow Republicans did manage to find common ground on two issues. In late January 1865, at the urging of Lincoln's administration, Congress passed the Thirteenth Amendment, abolishing slavery. The measure ended any ambiguity that had surrounded the Emancipation Proclamation, abolishing slavery everywhere in the United States and offering no compensation to former slaveholders. Twenty-seven states, including eight former Confederate states, would ratify the amendment by year's end.

In March Congress established the Bureau of Refugees, Freedmen, and Abandoned Lands. Known simply as the **Freedmen's Bureau,** it was to serve as an all-purpose relief agency in the war-ravaged South, providing emergency services, building schools, and managing confiscated lands. It represented the first attempt by the federal government to provide social welfare services and quickly became the bedrock institution for implementing Reconstruction policy.

What advantages did Lincoln see in proposing a moderate Reconstruction policy?

The Fruits of Freedom

Many Southerners were stunned by the response of their slaves to freedom. Clinging to self-serving paternalistic notions of the plantation as one big family under the benign authority of the master and planter, they were taken aback when their slaves refused to obey their orders or exhibited anger or disrespect toward them. Susan Bradford, a young woman living on a Florida plantation, wrote in her diary that she was "hurt and dazed" when one of her former slaves refused to prepare a dinner for her mother. "Tell her if she want any dinner," sneered the free woman, "she kin cook it herself." "I believed that these people were content, happy, and attached to their masters," wrote one South Carolina planter in 1865, unable to comprehend why slaves abandoned their masters "in [their] moment of need." It would be the first of many such shocking experiences for whites, who never imagined that slavery might one day be abolished.

INFORMATION WANTED

OF A MAN BY THE NAME OF ELIAS LOWERY McDERMIT, who used to belong to Thomas Lyons, of Knoxville, East Tennessee. He was sold to a man by the name of Sherman about ten years ago, and I learned some six years ago that he was on a steamboat running between Memphis and New Orleans, and more recently I heard that he was somewhere on the Cumberland river, in the Federal army. Any information concerning him will be thankfully received. Address Colored Tennessean, Nashville, Tenn. From his sister who is now living in Knoxville, East Tennessee.
je24-1m] MARTHA McDERMIT.

SAML. DOVE wishes to know of the whereabouts of his mother, Areno, his sisters Maria, Neziah, and Peggy, and his brother Edmond, who were owned by Geo. Dove, of Rockingham county, Shenandoah Valley, Va. Sold in Richmond, after which Saml. and Edmond were taken to Nashville, Tenn., by Joe Mick; Areno was left at the Eagle Tavern, Richmond
Respectfully yours,
SAML. DOVE.
Utica, New York, Aug. 5, 1865–3m

U. S. CHRISTIAN COMMISSION,
NASHVILLE, TENN., July 19, 1865.

14.3 Freedmen Searching for Loved Ones Sold Away during Slavery
These classified advertisements in the August 12, 1865 *Colored Tennessean* were just two of thousands published in mainly black-owned newspapers during Reconstruction. They vividly highlight the efforts of freedmen to overcome one of slavery's harshest legacies. [*Source*: Chicago History Museum]

Freedom of Movement

Even before the guns of the Civil War went silent, African Americans had begun to explore the meaning of their freedom and formulate their own vision of a reconstructed postwar South, both of which included unrestricted mobility. Under slavery, movement was sharply limited, and few slaves ventured very far from their plantations. In the chaos of war and later with official emancipation, African Americans hit the road. Many did so to get away from the plantations that were home to their former masters and countless bitter memories. Others simply reveled in the idea of free and unfettered movement. They wandered for the pleasure of it with no particular destination in mind. As these advertisements (**14.3**) from the *Colored Tennessean,* Tennessee's only African American–owned newspaper, indicate, many freedmen also journeyed in search of loved ones sold away years before.

African American mobility led to a sharp rise in the black population of Southern cities. In contrast to rural life, black settlements in cities offered more and varied job opportunities, albeit nearly always menial, difficult, and low paid. Urban life also provided freedmen access to strong black institutions such as churches, charities, and newspapers.

Southern whites reacted to black mobility with a mixture of alarm and disdain. Just as former slaves equated freedom with mobility, their former masters saw in it a shocking reminder that the old order was gone. Not surprisingly, one of the first expressions of white Southern resistance to black freedom was the passage of vagrancy laws intended to restrict African American mobility.

Forty Acres and a Mule

In addition to exercising their right to move about freely, many freedmen also tried to become landowners. If travel was a symbolic expression of their new freedom, land was freedom in concrete form. Land, the freedmen believed, would give freedom meaning by providing an independent living, free of planter control.

The idea that freedmen would receive land in addition to their freedom originated during the war. As Southerners abandoned their plantations before the advance of the Union army, ex-slaves often took control, partitioned land, and planted crops. Freedmen defended these extralegal actions as simple justice, citing the generations of unpaid labor that they and their ancestors had performed on Southern farms and plantations. "The property which they [former slaveholders] hold," asserted a freedmen's convention, "was nearly all earned by the sweat of our brows."

In early 1865 General William T. Sherman issued Field Order No. 15, supplanting these acts of unofficial confiscation. Having laid waste to the Confederate southeast, Sherman announced that 400,000 acres of abandoned land stretching from northern Florida to the South Carolina Sea Islands would be distributed to freedman in 40-acre plots. Weeks later Congress established the Freedmen's Bureau, authorizing it to rent 40-acre plots of confiscated and abandoned land, along with a mule, to freedmen. By June some forty thousand freedmen were living on Sherman lands while thousands more

Why did freedmen believe they were owed land?

> "Give us our own land and we take care of ourselves; but without land, the old masters can hire or starve us, as they please."
>
> A South Carolina freedman speaking to a Northern journalist, 1865

began renting plots under control of the Freedmen's Bureau. African Americans and Radical Republicans hoped to see this program of land redistribution, popularly known as "forty acres and a mule," enacted across the South. Before long, however, their optimism would give way to bitter disappointment.

Regardless of whether they owned or worked their land or worked as farm laborers for wages, African Americans used their freedom to change the way they worked. They often refused to work in gangs under overseers because it reminded them of slavery. Instead they preferred working independently, under the direction of elder family members. Many African American women left work in the field in order to work in their homes and care for children.

Uplift through Education

Along with land, freedmen sought education as a necessary guarantee of their freedom. Laws and customs preventing the education of slaves had left most freedmen illiterate. But with the ability to read and write they could conduct their own legal and business affairs, acquire better-paying jobs, read newspapers, and participate more fully in politics.

General O. O. Howard, the first head of the Freedmen's Bureau, shared the freedmen's belief that education should be an essential goal of Reconstruction. Working with a number of charitable societies and African American leaders, the Freedmen's Bureau helped build three thousand schools across the South that by 1870 served 150,000 students of all ages. By 1875 literacy among freedmen jumped from 10 percent to 30 percent.

Initially, most of the teachers in these schools were educated single white women from the North, like the Cooke sisters (**14.4**). Often sponsored by Northern charitable societies, these teachers saw themselves as missionaries dedicated to the uplift of the freedmen. The journal that published this image in 1866, *Frank Leslie's Illustrated Weekly,* shared this vision. Note how the artist depicted the children in spotless attire with all of them focused on their studies.

That the vision of these teachers and their sponsors went beyond merely teaching ex-slaves to read is shown in this image (**14.5**) of a brief biography of African American poet Phillis Wheatley. Published in 1866 by a Boston Christian organization, it demonstrates their effort to instill in freedmen a pride in African American achievement, believing it would aid them in their quest for education and independence.

Still, educating freedmen was no easy job. Southern whites often put up fierce resistance to African American education, especially in more remote areas. One report in 1865 provided a vivid description of the many hardships teachers faced. "Compelled to live on the coarsest diet . . . subjected

14.4 *The Misses Cooke's School Room, Freedman's Bureau,* **1866**
The Cooke sisters moved from the North to Richmond, Virginia to run one of hundreds of Freedmen's Bureau schools established across the South.

THIRD READER. 75

LESSON XXXIX.

bought	pleas-ant	daugh-ter	ap-pear-ance
chalk	char-coal	learn-ing	ea-ger-ness
health	six-teen	al-though	in-ter-est-ing

PHILLIS WHEATLEY.

PHILLIS WHEATLEY, whose likeness is on this page, was brought to this country from Africa in the year 1761. She was then between seven and eight years old. She was bought by Mrs. John Wheatley, a Boston lady, who chose her from a crowd of robust negroes, although she looked feeble and slender, because of her modest appearance and pleasant face.

14.5 Education and Inspiration
Some Northern charitable societies, like the Boston Tract Society, published and distributed books to both teach reading and inspire African Americans.

Why did education become such a priority for African Americans?

to the jeers and hatred of her neighbors . . . swamped in mud—the school shed a drip, and her quarters little better; raided occasionally by rebels, her school broken up and herself insulted, banished, or run off."

The Freedmen's Bureau and Northern aid societies also established more than a dozen black colleges, including Howard in Washington, D.C., and Hampton in Virginia. One of the most immediate goals of these new colleges was to train black teachers. By 1870 African American teachers outnumbered white teachers in freedmen's schools. Many freedmen teachers assumed roles as community leaders and many eventually ran for political office. At least seventy former teachers won seats in Southern state legislatures during Reconstruction.

The Black Church

An even greater source of community leadership came from the vast network of black churches established during Reconstruction. Black churches had existed in the South before the Civil War, but most were part of larger white congregations and subject to strict white control. Southern whites usually insisted that white ministers lead black congregations and made certain that preaching never challenged the system of slavery and white domination.

When the war ended, countless African American congregations of Methodists, Baptists, Presbyterians, and other sects separated from white ones. They resented their inferior status in white-controlled churches and longed to practice a more emotional, expressive worship style disdained by whites. Most important, they wanted black clergymen who could address their spiritual and social needs.

Often churches assumed a central place in the lives of freedmen. Religious services provided spiritual and psychological support for blacks' daily struggles. Churches also ran schools and provided charitable services to the community. As this illustration (**14.6**) of a freedmen community at Trent River, North Carolina, demonstrates, African Americans built a church in the center that doubled as a schoolhouse and meeting place. Churches also offered African Americans a degree of self-government. Members of the congregation were elected to serve as trustees and on committees overseeing many aspects of parish life and budget management. African American women, in particular, filled numerous roles in planning and managing activities, raising money, and running programs such as temperance societies. Like their white counterparts, African American churches also sponsored countless initiatives, such as burial societies, fraternal organizations, drama clubs, and youth groups.

With the church taking so prominent a place in African American life, black ministers, like black teachers, assumed major leadership roles. White hostility convinced most ministers to concentrate on building up their communities from within. Still, many ministers entered politics in an effort to advance the cause of black equality, including more than one hundred ministers elected to Southern state legislatures during Reconstruction. Reverend Richard H. Cain, for example, went to Charleston, South Carolina, in 1865, where he assisted in the reorganization of a black church. Two years later he served as a delegate to the state constitutional convention, followed by terms in the state senate and U.S. House of Representatives.

African Americans' response to emancipation showed that they possessed a clear understanding of freedom. Not simply an end to slavery, freedom meant freedmen's right to free movement and travel, to labor for themselves under conditions of their own choosing, on land granted to them by the government. It meant self-improvement through education and self-help organizations. It meant establishing their own institutions and building their own communities. It also meant full civil and social equality with whites, including the right to vote and hold office.

14.6 ***The Black Church Anchors Freedmen Communities***
African Americans organized thousands of churches across the South to address both their spiritual and their social needs. In the freedmen settlement of Trent River, North Carolina, a simple structure served as a church, school, and meetinghouse (from *Harper's Weekly,* June 9, 1866).

How did the black church become such a vital institution in freedmen communities?

The Struggle to Define Reconstruction

As freedmen in the South worked to define, protect, and extend their freedoms, political leaders in Washington, D.C., debated the best course of action to take in reconstructing the South. The debate revealed sharply divergent visions of the postwar South's social, political, and economic order. Radical Republicans wanted to replace the old slavocracy with a multiracial democracy protected by federal authority. Conservatives sought to limit Reconstruction to granting ex-slaves freedom and opposed proposals to distribute land and to grant full equality to ex-slaves. Moderates held the balance of power in deciding most of these questions, but they lacked a clear vision of the postwar South and made their decisions such as black voting in response to events as they unfolded.

The Conservative Vision of Freedom: Presidential Reconstruction

Andrew Johnson, who assumed the presidency following Lincoln's assassination, was a complicated man. Although he once owned slaves, like many other poor whites from the back country of eastern Tennessee, he grew up deeply suspicious of the planter aristocracy. As a politician, he gained a wide following among poor farmers for his populist criticism of planter power. He opposed secession and was the only senator from a seceding state who did not withdraw from the Senate in early 1861. Lincoln appointed Johnson governor of Tennessee after the state came under Union occupation. In 1864 Republicans sought to appeal to Southern unionism and picked Johnson as Lincoln's vice presidential running mate.

> "We have turned loose ... four million slaves without a hut to shelter them or a cent in their pockets. ... This Congress is bound to provide for them until they can take care of themselves."
>
> Congressman THADDEUS STEVENS, December 18, 1865

Shortly after assuming the office of president after Lincoln's assassination in April 1865, Johnson indicated that he intended to deal harshly with the South. He spoke of punishing ex-Confederate leaders for their "treason" and indicated an apparent desire to assist the freedmen. Radical Republicans, who shared these views, were thrilled.

Their joy was soon replaced first by despair and then anger. First, despite his harsh antiplanter rhetoric, Johnson held racist views about African Americans and abhorred the notion of black equality. Committed to maintaining white supremacy in the South, Johnson outlined in May 1865 a lenient policy toward the South designed to rapidly reestablish Southern state governments and restore the Union. It offered "amnesty and pardon," including the return of all property, to Southerners who took an oath of allegiance to the Constitution and Union. Former Confederate leaders and wealthy planters possessing more than $20,000 in personal wealth, however, would have to apply to him personally for a pardon.

Second, Johnson recognized the reconstructed government of North Carolina and set out the terms for readmitting the remaining ten ex-Confederate states. Johnson would appoint a governor for each state who in turn would call a constitutional convention of elected delegates (chosen by those granted amnesty or pardons). If the convention ratified the Thirteenth Amendment, renounced secession, repudiated all Confederate debts, and held elections for state office and Congress, Johnson would recognize the state as a fully reconstructed member of the Union.

With Congress out of session, Johnson's plan faced little formal opposition. By the fall of 1865, he had granted pardons to all but a small number of planters and high-ranking ex-Confederates. With

What was Andrew Johnson's primary motivation in devising his lenient Reconstruction policy?

these pardons Southerners had restored to them virtually all their lands, including the vast tracts of land that had been set aside in 40-acre plots for freedmen. In December, with all eleven former Confederate states having established new governments under his terms, Johnson announced the Union was restored and Reconstruction was over.

Johnson's actions outraged Northern Republicans, including moderates. In this political cartoon (**14.7**), the artist shows Johnson accepting bags of cash from former Confederates (depicted as the devil) in exchange for a pardon, while a "Pardoned Reconstruction Rebel" in the lower left kills "Union men and freedmen." Three developments in the supposedly "reconstructed" South also stoked Republican discontent. First, many of the state constitutional conventions had failed explicitly to accept the Thirteenth Amendment some even demanded compensation for the financial losses incurred by emancipation. Second, and even more galling, in the state elections in November 1865 Southern voters elected dozens of ex-Confederate officials and army officers. Among them was Alexander Stephens, former vice president of the Confederacy, chosen to represent Georgia in the Senate. Third, new Southern state governments, beginning in late 1865 with Mississippi and South Carolina, passed laws known as **Black Codes** to limit the civil and economic rights of freedmen and create an exploitable workforce. Observing these developments in the eight months since Confederate general Robert E. Lee surendered, many Northerners wondered if the Civil War had been fought in vain. Had hundreds of thousands died to defeat the Confederacy only to see their leaders quickly resume power? Had slavery been abolished only to be replaced with a similar system of unfree labor?

One of the Mississippi Black Codes of 1865 established the vague charge of "vagrancy"—having

14.7 Johnson's Leniency Angers the North
Johnson's pledge to punish the South ("Treason must be made odious") is ridiculed in this 1866 political cartoon. His sweeping pardons of ex-Confederate leaders and planters and easy terms for readmission of Southern states provoked anger in the North.

What events in the South in 1865 angered Northern Republicans?

Competing Visions

DEMANDING RIGHTS, PROTECTING PRIVILEGE

DEC 2009

In the aftermath of the Civil War, one question dominated the minds of Americans North and South: now that slavery was abolished, what would be the status of the freedmen? While newspaper editors, clergymen, and members of Congress debated the issue, white and black Southerners set out to answer the question themselves. As you read the following documents, one from a convention of freedmen and the other from the state legislature of Mississippi, consider the starkly contrasted visions for the future of Southern society. Why do the freedmen feel compelled to say they bear no ill will toward their "former oppressors." Why do Mississippi legislators define vagrancy in such vague terms?

"Address to the Loyal Citizens and Congress of the United States of America," Proceedings of the Convention of the Colored People of Virginia, Held in the City of Alexandria, August 2, 3, 4, 5, 1865.

We, the delegates of the colored people of the State of Virginia ... solemnly declaring that we desire to live upon the most friendly and agreeable terms with all men; we feel no ill-will or prejudice toward our former oppressors; are willing and desire to forgive and forget the past, and so shape our future conduct as shall promote our happiness and the interest of the community in which we live ...

We must, on the other hand, be allowed to aver and assert that we believe that we have among the white people of this State many who are our most inveterate enemies; who hate us as a class, who feel no sympathy with or for us; who despise us simply because we are black, and more especially, because we have been made free by the power of the United States Government ...

We claim, then, as citizens of this State, the laws of the Commonwealth [of Virginia] shall give to all men equal protection; that each and every man may appeal to the law for his equal rights without regard to the color of his skin; and we believe this can only be done by extending the franchise, which we believe to be our inalienable right as freemen, and which the Declaration of Independence guarantees to all free citizens of this Government and which is the privilege of this nation. We claim the right of suffrage:

1st. Because we can see no other safeguard for our protection.

2nd. Because we are citizens of the country and natives of this State.

3rd. Because we are as well qualified to vote who shall be our rulers as many who do vote for that purpose who have no interest in us, and do not know our wants.

Mississippi legislators in December 1865 enacted the first "Black Codes" to limit the freedoms of African Americans. Defining vagrancy in such vague terms allowed white Southerners to arrest freedmen at will and to curtail their freedom of movement. These measures were quickly copied in the remaining ex-Confederate states.

Section 1. All rogues and vagabonds, idle and dissipated persons, ... persons who neglect their calling or employment, misspend what they earn, or do not provide for the support of themselves or their families, or dependents shall be deemed and considered vagrants, ... and upon conviction thereof shall be fined not exceeding one hundred dollars, with all accruing costs, and be imprisoned ... not exceeding ten days. ...

Section 5. ...In case of any freedman, free negro or mulatto shall fail for five days after the imposition of any or forfeiture upon him or her for violation of any of the provisions of this act to pay the same, that it shall be, and is hereby, made the duty of the sheriff of the proper county to hire out said freedman, free negro or mulatto, to any person who will, for the shortest period of service, pay said fine and forfeiture and all costs ...

Colored Men's Convention 1869.

What is significant about the freedmen's use of the term citizen?

no regular home or employment—as a pretext for controlling freedmen. (See *Competing Visions: Demanding Rights, Protecting Privilege.*) Any freedman who hit the road seeking new opportunities could be arrested as a vagrant and fined. If a freedman could not pay his fine, he could be hired out for a period of time to a local plantation owner willing to pay his fine. As this drawing (**14.8**) dramatically shows, in some cases the contracts for such labor were auctioned off to local planters. The artist's intent was to conjure in the minds of Northerners a grim scene reminiscent of a slave auction, suggesting that one of the war's chief accomplishments, emancipation, was being undermined. Some Black Codes required that the children of "vagrant" freedmen be forced to accept apprenticeships that bound them to an employer until age twenty-one. Other stipulations encouraged blacks to sign long-term work contracts as proof of employment. This left them at the mercy of their employers, who were not required to pay them for any work performed if they quit before the contract expired. Other codes included laws restricting freedmen to renting land only in rural areas (to keep them on plantations), prohibiting ministers from preaching without a license, outlawing interracial marriages, and barring blacks from serving on juries.

Congressional Reconstruction and the Fourteenth Amendment

Republicans in Congress, both moderate and Radical, vowed to block Johnson's rapid and lenient Reconstruction program for both idealistic and practical reasons. Excepting emancipation, none of the Republicans' goals for changing Southern society had been accomplished, and the former slavocracy appeared poised to resume power—a result that would lead to the rebirth of the Democratic Party. A slower process of Reconstruction would allow time for the Republican Party to take root in the South, especially if African Americans were granted the right to vote, as many Radicals like Thaddeus Stephens demanded.

The confrontation began in January 1866 when Congress reconvened. Congressional Republicans, led by Sumner and Stephens, refused to admit the senators and representatives from the former Confederate states declared reconstructed by Johnson. Next they established the Joint Committee on

14.8 ***The Black Codes in Action*** Unable to pay his fine for "vagrancy" as defined in the Black Codes of Florida, a freedman is auctioned off. The high bidder won the right to a freedman's labor for months or years.

How did Black Codes calling for freedmen to sign labor contracts curtail their freedom?

14.9 *Race Riot in Memphis*
White mobs, unrestrained by local police, terrorized the freedmen community in Memphis, Tennessee on May 1–2, 1866, killing forty-six blacks. News of the atrocities, conveyed in images such as this one, stoked Northern public opinion against Johnson's lenient Reconstruction policies.

Reconstruction to investigate conditions in the South. It found widespread evidence of chaos, resistance to Northern authority, and abuse of freedmen's rights.

To counteract Southern resistance and the oppression of freedmen, Congress passed two bills. The first authorized the Freedmen's Bureau to continue operation for two more years. The second, the Civil Rights Bill, went much further. It declared African Americans and all persons born in the United States (except Native Americans) national citizens. It also defined the rights of all citizens regardless of race—for example, the right to sue and to make contracts. Taking direct aim at the Black Codes, the law prohibited state governments from depriving any citizen of these "fundamental rights." Johnson, infuriated at Congress's rejection of his Reconstruction program and determined to thwart efforts to establish racial equality, vetoed both bills.

Although Congress eventually overrode the vetoes and the bills became law, by June 1866 Republicans decided bolder action was necessary. Johnson remained opposed to freedmen's rights, and violence against the freedmen was on the rise in the South. The worst incident, depicted in the image (**14.9**), was a brutal race riot in Memphis, Tennessee, on May 1–2 that left forty-six blacks, most of them Union army veterans, and two whites dead. This drawing appeared in *Harper's Weekly,* a widely read publication that favored freedmen's rights, and was intended to arouse anger in the North over Southern intransigence and support for congressional action. The recently passed Civil Rights Bill was an unprecedented piece of legislation, but its supporters knew that it could easily be overturned by a later Congress. An amendment, on the other hand, became a permanent part of the Constitution.

On June 13, 1866, moderate and Radical Republicans passed the **Fourteenth Amendment** to the Constitution. The Fourteenth Amendment represented a radical redefining of the role of the federal government as the guarantor of individual civil rights. A complex amendment, it contained five

Why did Republicans deem the Fourteenth Amendment necessary so soon after passing the Civil Rights Act?

main provisions. First, it declared all persons born or naturalized in the United States as citizens, a definition that necessarily included all freedmen. Second, all citizens were entitled to "equal protection of the laws" of the states where they lived. Third, states that denied adult male citizens, including African Americans, the right to vote would be penalized by having their representation in Congress reduced. Fourth, all high-ranking former Confederates were prohibited from holding public office, unless pardoned by act of Congress. Fifth, it repudiated the Confederate debt (thus punishing those who lent money to the Confederacy) and denied all claims for compensation by ex–slave owners.

Johnson greeted the unprecedented amendment with an unprecedented response: he went on the campaign trail to urge its defeat. Hoping to make the midterm state and congressional elections in November 1866 a referendum on the amendment, Johnson and his allies played on white racism, conjuring up images of racial equality and racial intermarriage designed to alarm Northern whites. Republicans responded in kind, portraying Johnson and the Democrats as traitors who waged war on the Union. Republicans won a sweeping victory in November. Northern voters, while still leery of racial equality, clearly rejected Johnson's lenient form of Reconstruction because it required too little of Southerners and allowed for the restoration of planter rule.

Radical Republicans Take Control

Emboldened by their legislative and electoral success, congressional Republicans moved to take complete control of Reconstruction policy. In March 1867 Congress passed the first of four Reconstruction Acts. It divided the South (except Tennessee) into five military districts, each governed by a military commander empowered with wide authority to keep order and protect individuals, especially freedmen. As soon as order was established, the ex-Confederate states could begin a new, stricter readmission process. The act called for elections to select delegates to state constitutional conventions—elections that permitted African American men to vote, but barred Southerners who served in the Confederate government and army. The new state constitutions drawn up by these conventions had to allow universal male suffrage, regardless of race. As soon as a state's voters approved the new constitution, the state could hold elections to fill government offices. Finally, if Congress approved the state's constitution and the state legislature ratified the Fourteenth Amendment, the state would be readmitted to the Union.

Fully two years after the end of the Civil War, the federal government had finally adopted a clear Reconstruction plan. The delay was understandable, given Lincoln's assassination and the lack of any precedent. Yet delay granted Southerners time in which to recover from the war and mount an effective resistance to federal intervention.

> "The President has no power to control or influence anybody and legislation will be carried on entirely regardless of his opinion or wishes."
>
> Republican Senator JAMES W. GRIMES, Iowa, January 1867

Passage of the Reconstruction Acts further exacerbated the conflict between President Johnson and congressional Republicans. Johnson promptly vetoed the acts, and Congress passed them again over his veto. Some of the more radical Republicans had grown so embittered by the president's actions and words, they attempted to remove him from office. When Johnson dismissed Secretary of War Stanton in August 1867, Republicans charged him with violating the Tenure of Office Act, a constitutionally questionable measure they had passed back in March. It required the president to seek congressional approval before removing a cabinet official. The House voted to impeach the president, charging him with eleven offenses. The trial began in March 1868 and after two months of heated debate and accusation, the Senate failed—by one vote—to convict Johnson and remove him from office.

Johnson was saved by moderate Republicans who feared that a bad precedent would be set if they supported a largely politically motivated campaign to remove a president from office. They also knew that Johnson had less than a year left in office. Finally, many moderate Republicans had begun to lose confidence in the Radicals' Reconstruction program. Had Johnson been removed from office, the power of the Radical Republicans would have been greatly increased as one of their own, Benjamin Wade, would have succeeded him as president.

Why did moderate Republicans decide not to remove Johnson from office?

Implementing Reconstruction

As Congress engaged in its impeachment struggle with President Johnson in 1867–1868, the Reconstruction Acts took effect. A coalition of African Americans, poor up-country whites, and economically ambitious merchants (many originally from the North) and white planters came together to form the Republican Party in the South. They seized the opportunity presented by the congressional Reconstruction program and dominated the process of electing state governments and gaining readmission to the Union. The task would not be easy, especially as their different goals came into conflict with each other and with those of a majority of white Southerners who would clearly oppose—politically, economically, and violently—any attempt to establish what they called "Negro rule" in the former Confederacy.

The Republican Party in the South

The process of remaking state governments under the Reconstruction Act fell to the Republican Party, an organization comprising three distinct and in some cases antagonistic groups. Northerners who settled in the South after the war constituted one faction. White Southerners derided them as **carpetbaggers,** a term suggesting they were penniless adventurers who came south with all their possessions in a cheap suitcase, or carpetbag, intent on enriching themselves at the expense of Southerners still reeling from the war. In reality most were middle class, often former Union soldiers or merchants, ministers, artisans, and professionals who viewed the South as a region of opportunity and planned to settle permanently. Others came as idealistic relief workers, sent by Northern charitable and religious societies, intent upon aiding ex-slaves in their transition to freedom.

14.10 The Hated Scalawag Scalawags became despised figures in the popular Southern mind. Here a scalawag is depicted as an opportunist seeking political power by manipulating the black vote.

The Republican Party in the South also contained a significant number of white Southerners known derisively as **scalawags.** Most white Southerners considered them traitors to their region and race, men eager to enrich themselves and to garner political power by manipulating black voters (**14.10**). Most scalawags came from the less developed backcountry regions of the South, especially eastern Tennessee and Kentucky, northern Alabama and Georgia, and western North Carolina. They shared the view of carpetbaggers that the Republican Party offered them the best hope for economic betterment. They did not, as a rule, however, share some carpetbaggers' views on freedmen uplift and racial equality.

Former slaves made up the largest, most significant segment of the South's Republican Party. Empowered with the vote by the Civil Rights Act of 1866 and Reconstruction Act of 1867, they moved swiftly to make their political voice heard. In the fall of 1867, as Southern states held elections to select delegates to constitutional conventions, African Americans turned out in huge numbers to exercise their right to vote for the first time. For supporters

What motivated Northerners to move south after the Civil War?

> "But be sure to vote for no Southern men that was a rebel or secessionist; for, if you do, you are pulling them hemp to hang yourself with."
>
> R. I. CROMWELL, advising his fellow freedmen, *New Orleans Tribune*, April 25, 1867

of black suffrage, this extraordinary moment—persons only recently considered property now exercising the right to vote—was captured in this drawing (**14.11**). Published in *Harper's Weekly,* the hopeful, dignified scene depicts three African American voters who symbolically represent a spectrum of blacks that includes common laborers, educated blacks who were free before the war, and Union army veterans. Most of the African American political leaders that soon emerged came from the second group. They tended to come from the North and possessed more wealth and education than the average freedman.

The three factions of the Republican Party—carpetbaggers, scalawags, and freedmen—formed an uneasy alliance as they came together to reestablish Southern state governments. Nonetheless, their combined votes in the fall 1867 elections for delegates to state constitutional conventions led to a sweeping Republican victory. White Republicans won most of the seats, but 265 were won by freedmen. In South Carolina and Louisiana, freedmen constituted a majority of the delegates elected. The number was far below the proportion of African Americans in the South, but it was a striking accomplishment considering that only recently they had been considered property and incapable of citizenship.

14.11 Casting Their First Votes
For supporters of racial equality like the Northern publication *Harper's Weekly,* whose cover featured this drawing, the large turnout of black voters in the fall of 1867 elections was exhilarating.

Creating Reconstruction Governments in the South

In ex-Confederate states delegates drafted new state constitutions according to the guidelines established by the Reconstruction Acts. In a few states, notably Virginia and Texas, conservatives managed to delay the process for more than a year. Nonetheless, by the end of 1868 seven Southern states had ratified new state constitutions, created new state governments, and gained readmission to the Union.

In the coming years these Republican governments achieved remarkable results. To begin with they represented a revolutionary advance in the status of the freedmen. Held as slaves and denied citizenship only a few years before, African Americans now enjoyed the right to vote and to hold office. Between 1869 and 1901 twenty-two African Americans would serve in the U.S. Congress (twenty representatives and two senators). More than six hundred won seats in state legislatures and to other state and local offices.

What impact did African American voting have on the political situation in the South in 1867–1868?

While embittered white Southerners decried what they termed "Negro rule," statistics plainly show that white Republicans held a far greater share of offices than blacks. No African American was elected as governor, and no state legislature ever had a majority of black members (the lower house of the South Carolina legislature briefly had a black majority). What white Southerners really objected to was Republican rule and what it stood for: African American equality and empowerment.

Republican-controlled Southern state governments also achieved several significant reforms. In contrast to the tightfisted governments of the antebellum era, They funded public works projects, established hospitals and orphanages, and built thousands of schools (or took over those created by the Freedmen's Bureau). They also established more equitable tax codes and passed laws to help indebted farmers keep their land. Opponents of Republican rule denounced these initiatives (and the higher taxes needed to fund them) as wasteful and poorly managed. Fundamentally, they objected to their social and racial implications, since many of the projects were designed to aid the poor and freedmen.

But the charges of corruption, mismanagement, and debt lodged by the opponents of Reconstruction governments were not entirely groundless. The rapid expansion of government services and expenditures caused many states to run up huge budget deficits and created opportunities for graft and bribery. Many Reconstruction legislators took advantage.

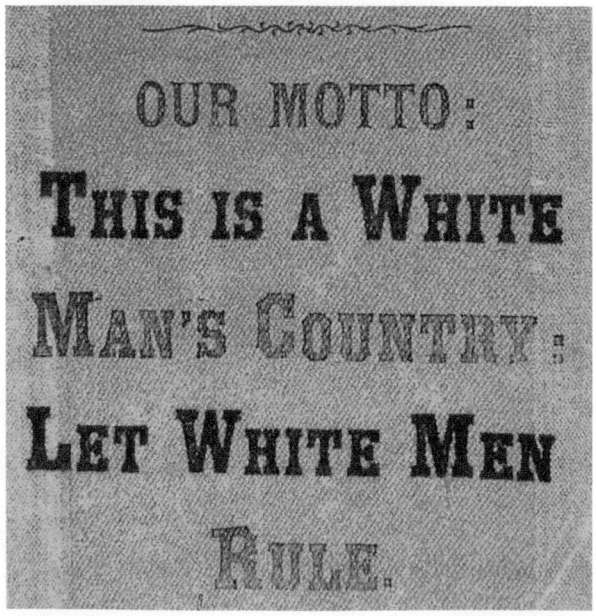

14.12 Campaign of Fear Campaigning against General Ulysses Grant, Democratic presidential candidate Horatio Seymour attempted to exploit Northern racism and anxiety about racial equality with banners such as this one.

Democratic opponents railed against these abuses as alleged evidence that blacks were incapable of holding public office and that their Northern carpetbagger allies were interested only in plunder. In reality the corruption found in Southern state governments paled in comparison to that found in the North. New York's Tammany Hall political machine, for example, under William "Boss" Tweed, stole anywhere between $20 million and $200 million from 1869 to 1871. Moreover, the amount of spending by Southern state governments on social programs looked large only in comparison to the paltry expenditures on education, health care, and public works before the war. Nonetheless, charges of corruption and excess spending, coupled with increased taxes, diminished popular support for the Southern Republican governments and created unfavorable public opinion in the North.

> "We cannot vote without all sorts of threats and intimidations. Freedmen are shot with impunity."
>
> Report of a Republican official, 1868

The Election of 1868

By the summer of 1868, there was little doubt whom the Republican Party would nominate for president. General Ulysses S. Grant enjoyed widespread popularity across the North and among Southern Republicans for defeating Robert E. Lee and ending the Civil War. Grant conveyed a tone of moderation in a time of partisan and sectional acrimony. His plea, "let us have peace," from his acceptance of the Republican nomination, became his campaign slogan.

Democrats, still weak in the aftermath of the war and the disenfranchisement of many ex-Confederates, faced an uphill battle against the popular General Grant. As their racist campaign banner makes clear (**14.12**), their nominee, Governor Horatio Seymour of New York, ran an aggressive campaign designed to arouse fears that the Republican Party and black suffrage threatened

Why did Southerners charge that Reconstruction governments were corrupt?

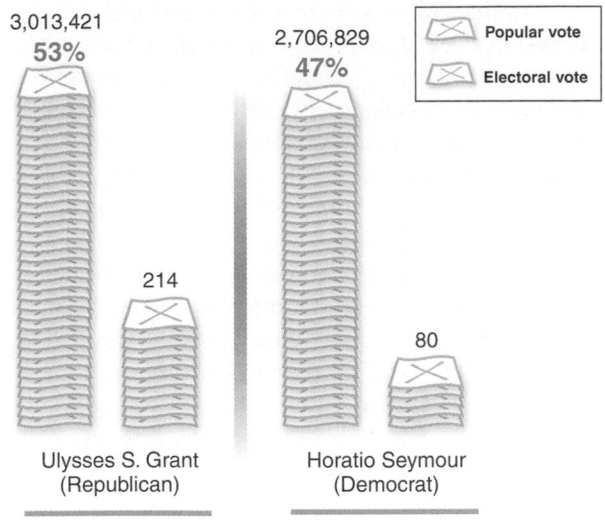

14.13 The Election of 1868
Votes from nearly 500,000 recently enfranchised African Americans proved crucial to Grant's victory in the election. (Several ex-Confederate states not yet reconstructed did not participate.)

the rights of white Americans. Republicans, the campaign claimed, must be defeated to prevent them from spreading the disastrous experiment in black political empowerment into the North.

Projecting an image of moderation, suggesting an even-handed approach to Reconstruction and fiscal responsibility, Grant won the election, garnering 214 electoral votes to Seymour's 80. The popular vote, however, was much closer: 53 percent for Grant, 47 percent for Seymour (**14.13**). This outcome reflected three things. First, it indicated the wide appeal of Seymour's blatantly racist message to conservative whites in both the North and the South. Second, it showed how vital the freedmen vote was to the future of the Republican Party. Grant received 500,000 African American votes, but won by only 300,000 votes. Third, the election outcome revealed the effectiveness of violence as a weapon in electoral politics. The reign of terror unleashed by groups of violent whites in the months before the election, especially in Georgia and Louisiana, kept thousands of black voters away from the polls.

The Fifteenth Amendment

In the wake of the 1868 election, congressional Republicans decided that black suffrage required an explicit constitutional guarantee. Black male suffrage was implied in the Fourteenth Amendment's phrase, "all male citizens," but with Southern resistance on the rise, many Republicans in Congress argued that an additional amendment was necessary to guarantee unequivocally the right of African Americans to vote.

Numerous women's rights activists agreed, but many also argued that the time had come to establish universal suffrage—the vote for all adult citizens regardless of race or gender. Bitterly disappointed over the reference to only "male citizens" in the Fourteenth Amendment, many feminists, such as Elizabeth Cady Stanton and Susan B. Anthony, demanded that any subsequent amendment guarantee universal suffrage.

Their demand was met by strong opposition from former abolitionists and Radical Republicans, including some fellow feminists like Lucy Stone and Frances Harper, who argued that gaining the right to vote for African American men was a higher priority. Extending the vote to women, they argued, would lead to the amendment's rejection because the nation was not ready for such radical change. The cause of women's suffrage could be taken up immediately after black suffrage was secured. Stanton and Anthony rejected this reasoning. Most Republicans in Congress, however, agreed with Frederick Douglass's assertion that this was the "Negro's Hour" and consequently they drafted the **Fifteenth Amendment** to read succinctly: "The right of citizens of the United States shall not be denied or abridged by the United States or by any state on account of race, color, or previous condition of servitude."

Passed by Congress in late 1869 and ratified in 1870, the Fifteenth Amendment presented a striking contradiction. It established a revolutionary experiment in multiracial democracy, something no other slave society, such as those in the Caribbean or Latin America, did so soon and so completely after emancipation. Yet its spare wording left wide open the possibility that states could devise clever ways to deny blacks the right to vote that did not directly invoke "race, color, or previous condition of servitude."

The Rise of White Resistance

The secret white terrorist organizations that first arose in 1866 and that wrought havoc in parts of the South during the 1868 election grew still bolder and more violent by 1870–1871, especially during

Why did some women's rights activists oppose ratification of the Fifteenth Amendment?

election season. Known by various names, including the White Brotherhood, Knights of the White Camelia, and especially the **Ku Klux Klan**, they functioned in much the same manner. As illustrated in a popular Northern newspaper (**14.14**), Klansmen often operated at night, wearing hoods, robes, and other regalia designed to both hide their identities and overawe the freedmen. Blacks (and occasionally carpetbaggers and scalawags) targeted for "punishment" were beaten and frequently killed. Some had their crops or homes burned or their mules killed. Klansmen also targeted symbols of black self-improvement and independence, such as black churches, businesses, and schools.

Klan terrorism served a number of purposes. For the poor whites who made up the bulk of Klansmen, the violent suppression of African Americans provided them with the psychological reassurance that they were not at the bottom of the social order. For white elites who approved of and often assisted the violence, it prevented a political alliance between poor whites and blacks and maintained a large, exploitable workforce for Southern plantations and industry by keeping African Americans powerless and poor. Klan violence also discouraged African American voting and thus threatened the Republican Party in the South.

In response to surging violence in the South, Republicans in Congress, with strong support from the Grant administration, passed several Enforcement Acts in 1870 outlawing "armed combinations" that deprived anyone of their civil or political rights. Grant's attorney general, Amos T. Ackerman, vigorously enforced these laws across the South, arresting and prosecuting thousands and leaving the Klan and similar organizations decimated by 1872.While it demonstrated that federal authority could effectively protect the rights of freedmen, it also revealed the vulnerability of freedmen should the federal commitment to Reconstruction ever wane.

14.14 *Another Victim of the Klan* Terrorist violence by white vigilante groups soared in the early 1870s. In this scene from Moore County, North Carolina, a freedman pleads for his life, surrounded by Klansmen in full regalia.

What was the purpose behind anti-black violence waged by groups like the Klan?

Reconstruction Abandoned

By the end of Grant's first term in office, supporters of Reconstruction and freedmen's rights could look with some satisfaction at the many extraordinary changes that had taken place in the South. Yet ominous signs soon appeared that suggested Reconstruction was in trouble. Despite the crackdown on the Klan, white Southerners increasingly demonstrated their commitment to seizing power and imposing a new form of servitude on African Americans. Northerners, by contrast, seemed less and less willing to support a vigorous Reconstruction policy. Slowly, between 1872 and 1877, the extraordinary experiment in multiracial democracy and progressive government in the South was dismantled in favor of oligarchy and white supremacy.

Corruption and Scandal

A major factor in the pullback from Reconstruction was a series of corruption scandals that plagued the Grant administration. Grant himself was honest, but also politically naive and given to a hands-off style of leadership that gave officials in his administration an unusual degree of independence. Many of them took advantage of Grant's implicit trust to enrich themselves in a variety of illegal schemes.

For example, in 1869 Jay Gould and Jim Fisk, two Wall Street titans, conspired with Grant's brother-in-law in a scheme to corner the gold market. The plan eventually collapsed on September 24, 1869, a day dubbed "Black Friday, but not before hundreds of innocent investors were ruined and countless workers thrown out of work in the ensuing national economic turmoil. Fisk and Gould were pilloried in the press, but emerged unscathed. When the Credit Mobilier scandal became public, it was revealed that Grant's vice president and several high-ranking members of Congress had taken large bribes from the company involved in the completion of the government-subsidized Union Pacific Railroad. Other scandals found that three of Grant's cabinet members used their office for illegal financial gain. In the so-called "Whiskey Ring" scandal, for example, Treasury secretary Orville E. Babcock made a small fortune by illegally allowing whiskey distillers to avoid paying excise taxes. Secretary of War William W. Belknap likewise accepted bribes from companies engaged in corrupt activities on Indian reservations.

The North Retreats

Corruption scandals undermined the authority of Grant's administration. Grant soon found that to secure reelection and keep the Republican Party in power he would have to minimize political controversies. With so much negative publicity stirred up by corruption scandals, Grant's administration took steps to minimize political controversies. To secure his reelection and keep the Republican Party in power, Grant adopted a more conservative approach to Reconstruction, by now a frequent source of rancor in Washington.

In the summer of 1872, for example, Grant lobbied Congress for and then signed into law the Amnesty Act, granting a general pardon to all but a few hundred former Confederate leaders. Now eligible to vote and hold office, these planters, ex-army officers, and ex-Confederate officials wasted little time in reasserting their authority.

> "It seems to me that we are drifting, drifting back under the leadership of the slaveholders. Our former masters are fast taking the reins of government."
>
> GEORGE M. ARNOLD, African American Republican

The retreat from Reconstruction in the 1870s was also hastened by growing dissention within the Republican Party. Many Republicans, including former Radicals, began to question the wisdom of maintaining a strong federal role in the affairs of Southern states. Some Republicans now believed the fundamental goals of Reconstruction—citizenship, civil rights, and suffrage for the freedmen—had been accomplished. There was, they believed, a constitutional and moral limit to what the federal government could do on behalf of the freedmen. Now was the time, they argued, for the freedmen to elevate themselves economically, socially, and politically using their new rights.

What impact did the scandals of the Grant administration have on Reconstruction?

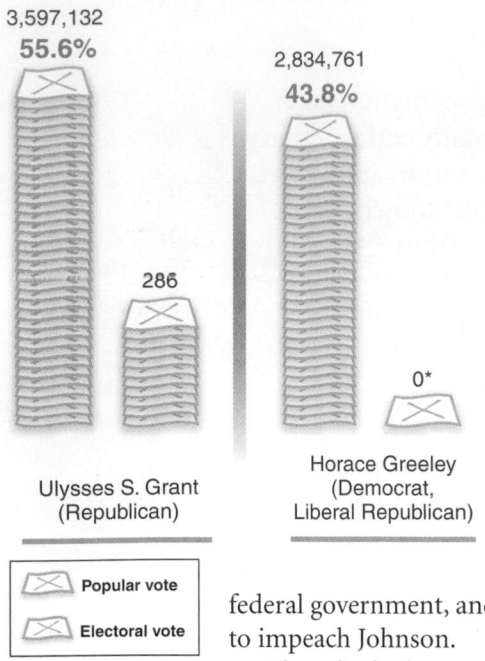

14.15 The Election of 1872 Opposed by a weak candidate, Democrat Horace Greeley, Ulysses Grant easily won reelection. Scandals and economic turmoil soon undermined his popularity and power.

Others, for less optimistic reasons, argued for an end to Reconstruction. Many Republicans, even some of the strongest advocates of abolition before the war and freedmen's rights in the first years that followed, had soured on Reconstruction. These Liberal Republicans, as they came to be called, were tired of the political strife produced by debates over freedmen's rights, concerned about the growing power of the federal government, and disgusted with the effort to impeach Johnson.

They also had grown disgusted by the corruption and mismanagement of Southern Reconstruction governments. They accepted the argument of Southerners that freedmen and their white allies were incapable of honest and effective government. No one embodied this dramatic change of heart more than Horace Greeley, the progressive editor of the *New York Tribune*. Once the outspoken champion of abolition and freedmen's rights, he was by the early 1870s an advocate of returning the South to white rule. Blacks, he wrote in 1870, were a "worthless race," unwilling to help themselves when given the option of accepting charity. Southern Reconstruction governments, as a consequence, were based on "ignorance and degradation." A similar transformation from a progressive to a reactionary view of Reconstruction was revealed in the political cartoons of Thomas Nast (see *Images as History: Political Cartoons Reflect the Shift in Public Opinion*).

The Election of 1872

The dissatisfaction of Liberal Republicans reached full bloom in the summer of 1872. Disturbed by the prospect of Grant being renominated for a second term, they broke from the Republican Party. Liberal Republicans held their own convention in Cincinnati and nominated Greeley as their candidate for president. A divided Democratic Party subsequently endorsed Greeley as well.

The election of 1872 proved disastrous for Greeley and his backers. The public viewed Greeley as an eccentric who during his long career in public life had supported many fringe causes such as vegetarianism, spiritualism, and utopianism. Even his appearance—small eyes set in a round face covered in a tangle of wispy chin whiskers—diminished him in the eyes of the public, especially in contrast to the handsome, noble bearing of Grant. Greeley's call for an end to Reconstruction and reconciliation between North and South also repelled many Northern voters who remained leery of Southerners and the Democratic Party.

In Grant's sweeping victory over Greeley in the November election (**14.15**), Republicans had good reason to cheer. The Democrats' and Liberal Republicans' call for ending Reconstruction and returning the South to white rule had been rejected. Moreover, the Grant administration's crackdown on the Klan had allowed African Americans unprecedented freedom to vote. Still, Northerners and Republicans in Congress were not prepared to support federal intervention in the South indefinitely. As new pressing issues emerged after 1872, support for Reconstruction rapidly eroded.

Hard Times

After a period of readjustment following the Civil War and conversion to peacetime production, the American economy boomed. Hundreds of thousands of new businesses were established. These included a growing number of massive factories that employed hundreds, in some cases thousands, of workers. Aiding this economic growth was the dramatic expansion of the railroad and telegraph systems and increased availability of capital through banks and stock sales.

The booming economy encouraged businesses to expand and investors to take bigger risks. When these trends reached a critical point in the fall of 1873, a panic on Wall Street ensued. Some of the nation's most prominent financial houses and banks went bankrupt. As credit became scarce businesses began to fail. Hundreds of thousands of workers lost their jobs. By early 1874 the nation's economy had plunged into a deep depression that lasted until 1877.

The **Panic of 1873** had a direct impact on Reconstruction. As hard times set in, and hundreds of thousands of workers lost their jobs, the fate of the freedmen became less of a concern to Northerners. Economic issues like currency reform and the tariff took precedence over civil rights and white vigilante violence against freedmen. The public, declared one Republican, is tired of hearing about Southern violence against the freedmen. "Hard times and heavy

Why did Liberal Republicans lose faith in Reconstruction by the early 1870s?

Images as History

POLITICAL CARTOONS REFLECT THE SHIFT IN PUBLIC OPINION

One of the nation's most skilled and popular political cartoonists in the Reconstruction era was Thomas Nast. An immigrant from Germany, he landed a job in 1861 at *Harper's Weekly,* the nation's leading journal of politics and society. Nast's artistic talent, combined with *Harper's* vast circulation, soon turned him into one of the most influential illustrators of his day. As a staunch Republican and Unionist, his drawings during the Civil War were as intensely patriotic and pro-Lincoln as they were anti-Confederate.

After the war, Nast's widely distributed cartoons continued to shape Northern opinion concerning Reconstruction and the issue of freedmen's rights. Cartoons like *And Not This Man?* (August 5, 1865) proclaimed the dignity and humanity of the freedmen and their moral right to full citizenship and suffrage. In others, like *This is a White Man's Government* (September 5, 1868), he stressed the violent intent of white Southerners to reclaim power and the absolute necessity of federal authority in carrying out the goals of Reconstruction.

Nevertheless, Nast's cartoons eventually reflected the growing disillusionment of Northern Republicans regarding Reconstruction. While he rejected the Liberal Republican call for ending Reconstruction, Nast nonetheless expressed the fear that African Americans were incapable of responsible government. Note the contrast between his earlier depictions of freedmen and that in *Colored Rule in a Reconstructed (?) State.*

"Columbia," an early symbol of America and democracy, advocates black suffrage. The globe is actually a nineteenth-century ballot box.

By showing African Americans in Union army uniforms, Nast sought to remind Americans that blacks had earned the right to full citizenship through their service and sacrifice (note the missing leg) in the war.

And Not This Man?

A freedman wearing a Union army uniform is crushed beneath an Irish immigrant (left), a white supremacist ex-Confederate (center), and a Northern capitalist (right). Nast saw these three groups as members of an opportunistic alliance.

A ballot box, representing the freedman's claim on citizenship and voting rights, has been kicked aside.

This is a White Man's Government

Reflecting Nast's disillusionment, "Columbia" chastises African American political leaders.

In 1874, frustrated with what he saw as inept and selfish African American political leadership in the South, Nash changed his depiction of blacks from noble individuals worthy of citizenship to racist caricatures.

Colored Rule in a Reconstructed (?) State

What makes political cartoons so popular and effective?

taxes make them wish the 'everlasting nigger' were in hell or Africa." The public expressed its discontent in the congressional elections of 1874 by voting in a Democratic majority for the first time since the war.

The Return of Terrorism

Reconstruction was also undone by a resumption of violence waged by white terrorist groups like the Klan. As the Grant administration bowed to political pressure to reduce federal intervention in Southern affairs, advocates of white supremacy seized the opportunity. In one notorious incident in 1873 a large band of heavily armed whites overran Colfax, Mississippi and slaughtered over one hundred African Americans.

As was the case in the late 1860s, white vigilante violence had two goals: to strip away the freedmen's hard-won economic, social, and legal rights and to prevent them from voting and holding office. This effort reached full development in Mississippi in 1875 when armed groups of whites closely allied with the Democratic Party waged a campaign of terror that came to be known as the **Mississippi Plan**. Through threats, beatings, and killings, they delivered an unambiguous message: blacks and their white allies who dared vote Republican risked their lives. But when Mississippi governor Adelbert Ames asked the Grant administration to send troops to keep the peace and protect the polls, his request was rejected.

Not surprisingly, more than sixty thousand Mississippi voters—nearly all black and Republican—stayed away from the polls on election day. Democrats swept to victory and took control of the state legislature for the first time since the Civil War.

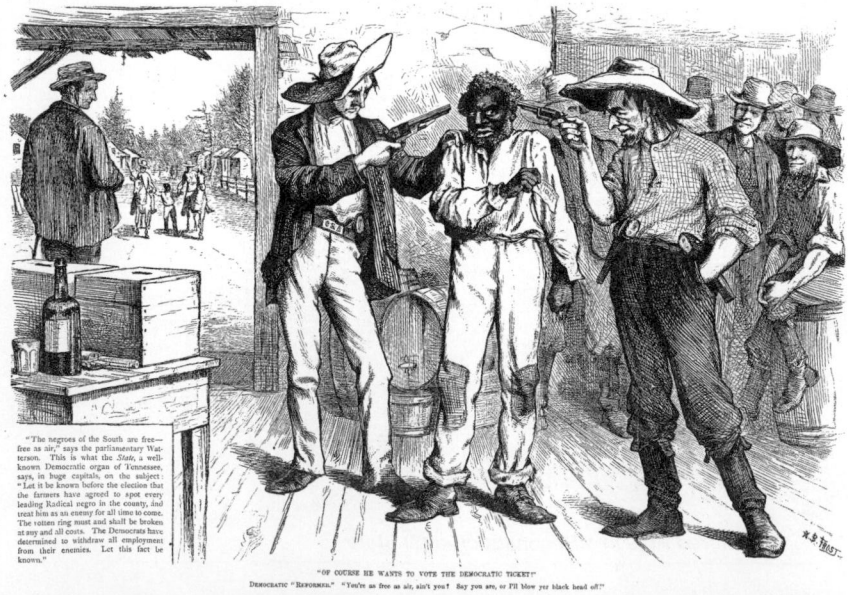

14.16 The Mississippi Plan in Action
In many parts of the South, violence kept most freedmen away from the polls. Here a freedman is threatened with death unless he votes for the Democratic Party.

Immediately they threatened Governor Ames with impeachment and forced him to resign.The success of the Mississippi Plan in intimidating black voters and demolishing the base of the Republican Party is indicated in this 1876 image, *Of Course He Wants to Vote the Democratic Ticket* (**14.16**). The artist vividly depicted the ruthless character of the white supremacy movement and the vulnerability of freedmen left without federal protection.

Other Southern states soon employed their own version of the Mississippi Plan. One by one the remaining Reconstruction governments fell to a new class of political leaders known as **Redeemers**. As the name suggests they cast themselves in almost biblical terms as saviors of Southern society. By 1876 only South Carolina, Louisiana, and Florida remained under Republican control—largely because of the presence of federal troops. The removal of these troops in 1877 opened the way for a complete "redemption" of the former Confederacy and the restoration of white supremacy.

Defenders of Reconstruction and the rights of freedmen in Congress were appalled at the rising tide of Redeemer oppression. In response they managed one final measure designed to bolster the rights of freedmen, the **Civil Rights Act of 1875**. Among its several points it required that state governments provide equal access in public facilities such as schools and allow African Americans to serve on juries. The act became law in 1875, but was largely ignored. In 1883 the U.S. Supreme Court ruled it unconstitutional.

The End of Reconstruction

The final blow to Reconstruction occurred as the result of the presidential election of 1876.With the Democratic Party reinvigorated by gaining a majority in the House in 1874 and control of most Southern state governments by 1876, a close election was expected. The Democrats nominated Samuel J. Tilden, governor of New York and a well-known reformer. Republicans nominated Ohio governor and Civil War veteran Rutherford B. Hayes. The issues centered on political corruption, the failed economy, and of course, Reconstruction.

On election day, Tilden received nearly a quarter million more popular votes than Hayes (**14.17**). But the electoral vote—the tally that actually determines the victor—was unclear. Voting irregularities in South Carolina, Louisiana, and Florida left both sides claiming victory—and the twenty electoral votes at stake. Tilden needed to be declared the winner in only one of the three disputed states to win a majority of

What was the political impact of the resurgence of white vigilante violence?

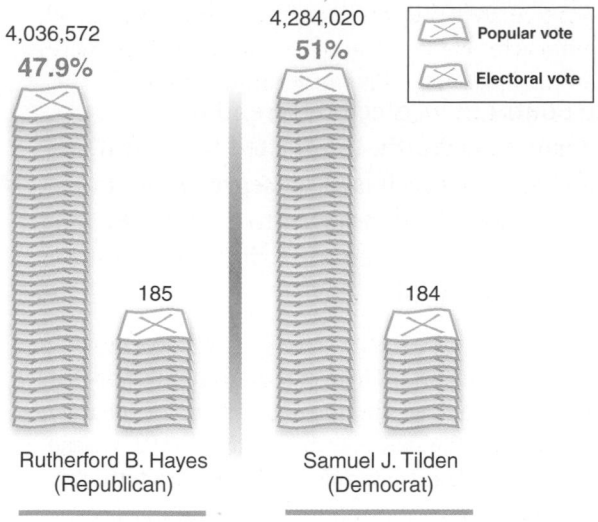

14.17 The Election of 1876
In one of the most controversial presidential elections in U.S. history, Samuel B. Tilden won the popular vote (4,284,020 to 4,036,572), but lost the electoral vote to Rutherford B. Hayes, 185 to 184.

electoral votes and thus the presidency. Hayes needed to win all three states to put him one electoral vote ahead of Tilden and into the White House.

Both sides refused to budge, and a constitutional crisis loomed. Eventually they agreed to abide by the decision of a bipartisan commission. The commission authorized an investigation and heard testimony. Behind the scenes members of Congress and leaders from both parties conducted intense negotiations. On March 2, 1877, the commission issued its decision, known as the **Compromise of 1877**. By a vote of 8 to 7, the fifteen-member commission awarded all 20 disputed electoral votes to Hayes, giving him a 185 to 184 electoral vote victory over Tilden.

Democrats cried foul and denounced the "stolen election." Yet the election result proved beneficial to the party. Hayes's presidency was weakened by the aura of illegitimacy (detractors referred to him as "his fraudulency"). More important, he oversaw the dismantling of the last remnants of Reconstruction policy. By the end of 1877, the last federal troops were removed from the South, and as the map (**14.18**) indicates, the last Reconstruction governments fell to Democratic redeemers.

14.18 The Readmission of Southern States and Return of White Rule
Most former Confederate states were readmitted to the Union under the direction of Republican-controlled state governments. But as the dates in parentheses indicate, in most cases, conservative white Democratic governments soon seized control.

Why is the eventual result of the election of 1877 considered the end of Reconstruction?

The New South

The optimism with which white Southerners greeted the end of Reconstruction gave rise to the term **New South.** It reflected the South's development of a new system of race relations based on segregation and white supremacy. Even more so, the New South pointed to a profound economic transformation that swept across the region, bringing with it a boom in manufacturing, railroad construction, and urbanization.

Redeemer Rule

The Redeemer governments that took control of Southern states by 1877 represented the arrival of a new ruling oligarchy. Before the war a small and powerful class of planters dominated Southern politics. Now in the aftermath of Reconstruction, a new elite took control. Although some were planters and former planters, most were men who drew their wealth and power from a new Southern economy based on industry, finance, commerce, and railroad construction.

As men of business their politics reflected the dominant economic theory of the era, laissez-faire (from the French "let do," meaning let things alone). It argued that the best form of government was small, frugal, and pro-business. Accordingly, Redeemer governments slashed taxes and spending on social programs and public education created during Reconstruction.

> "What I want here is Negroes who can make cotton and they don't need education to help them make cotton."
>
> A Southern planter

Redeemer politics also championed a return to white supremacy. The return of one-party (Democratic) rule in many Southern states resulted in a steady decline in office holding by African Americans and Republicans. Intimidation and violence likewise led to a marked decrease in black voting across the South. Despite these setbacks, however, African Americans in many Southern states managed to vote and hold office in appreciable numbers into the 1880s and 1890s.

Redeemers dominated state politics, but their rule did not go unchallenged. In several Southern states anger among poor farmers coalesced into full-fledged political challenges to oligarchic rule. The insurgents denounced the new elite as "Bourbons" (the name of the French royal family), a derogatory term that implied aristocratic ambitions. In Virginia, for example, a coalition of Republicans and disaffected Democrats called Readjusters turned out the Redeemer government in 1879. All of these challenges to Redeemer rule, however, ultimately failed.

The Lost Cause

Southerners after 1877 embraced not only Redeemer rule, but also an image of the prewar South as an ideal society and the Confederate bid for independence a valiant Lost Cause. Southerners clung to this image because it provided them with a psychologically soothing explanation for why they lost the war. According to the Lost Cause idea, as expressed in poems, plays, songs, speeches, sermons, and books, Confederate society was more virtuous than the North and its soldiers more brave, but the South lost because the Yankees possessed overwhelming advantages in population, industry, arms, and ruthlessness. Defeat, while bitter and painful, was also a glorious martyrdom for a people and a way of life.

The Lost Cause carried with it an obligation to keep alive the memory of Confederate glory. Southerners built elegant battlefield cemeteries to inter the war dead and monuments to celebrate Confederate victories. White Southern women, many widowed by the war, played a major role in these efforts, founding organizations such as the Ladies Memorial Association (1867) and the United Daughters of the Confederacy (1894). Southerners also erected thousands of statues honoring Southern legends like Generals Robert E. Lee, Stonewall Jackson, and Nathan Bedford Forrest. The photograph (**14.19**) vividly demonstrates how enthusiasm for the Lost Cause only grew the further the Civil War receded into history. Lee had discouraged efforts to

Who made up the political leadership of the New South?

raise monuments to the Confederate cause, but soon after he died in 1870 they sprang up all across the South, including this monumental rendering unveiled in Richmond in 1890. Thousands turned out for the dedication of the heroic statue by French sculptor Antonin Mercie and to hear Colonel Archer Anderson laud Lee for his "courage, will, energy . . . fortitude, hopefulness, joy in battle . . . [and] unconquerable soul." Nothing that day, certainly not the speeches or Lee's triumphant pose, recalled the fact that Lee had lost the war.

But the Lost Cause legend served a second purpose beyond helping Southerners cope with their defeat in the war. It celebrated a nostalgic vision of the prewar South that supported their arguments for a resumption of white rule and African American subservience. Through literature, art, and music, Southerners (and some Northerners) fashioned romantic depictions of the "Old South" as a harmonious paradise where benevolent masters treated loyal, contented slaves with kindness, where chivalrous Southern gentlemen protected delicate, charming Southern women, and where everyone revered tradition, family, and the Bible. Yet even as they glorified slavery, the proponents of the Lost Cause downplayed the importance of slavery as a cause of secession. The real issue, they insisted, was "states' rights" and attempts by Northerners to run roughshod over them in the 1850s.

The Lost Cause thus presented Southerners as victims of misguided and unjustified Yankee aggression who, in the wake of devastating war and humiliating Reconstruction, ought to be left alone to run their own affairs. The overt racism and self-serving depictions of slavery in Lost Cause rhetoric and imagery served to justify a resumption of white rule and the return of African Americans to the status of powerless, exploitable laborers.

14.19 Celebrating the Lost Cause As the commemorative ribbon indicates, this monument to Robert E. Lee was erected in the former Confederate capital of Richmond, Virginia in 1890. It was one of thousands of monuments to the Confederacy erected across the South. [*Source*: (ribbon) Lee Monument Unveiling Ribbon Accession #TBMR 277-1 (2). The Museum of the Confederacy]

The New South Economy

Even as Southerners revered the Lost Cause and Old South, their new leadership steered the region's economy into an industrial future. In the 1870s and 1880s, they joined with Northern entrepreneurs who settled in the South during Reconstruction to develop a modern, market-oriented, and diversified economy. This effort entailed not simply the establishment of banks, textile mills, and railroads, but also the celebration and spreading of capitalist values, such as hard work, risk taking, thrift, and the profit motive.

The leading figure in this movement to establish a New South economy was Henry Grady, editor

How was the Lost Cause a useful myth for Southerners?

14.20 Logging Near Laurel, Mississippi
Logging became a major industry in the New South, but like mining and cotton cultivation, it was a low-skill industry that produced a raw material rather than a finished product.

Another significant aspect of the New South economy was the lumber and furniture industry. As this photograph (**14.20**) of a logging operation near Laurel, Mississippi, in the 1890s indicates, New South entrepreneurs took advantage of the region's tremendous forest reserves and new technologies, such as rotary saws and dry kilns, and an expanded railroad system (shown here), and soon made the South the leading producer of lumber. In Mississippi alone the number of lumber mills jumped from 295 in 1880 to 608 in 1899. The furniture industry likewise boomed in the New South, especially in places like High Point, North Carolina, where a single factory opened in 1889, followed by thirty more over the next decade.

The lower South, especially the city of Birmingham, Alabama, developed into a major iron and steel producer. Birmingham had only a few hundred residents when founded in 1871, but its position at the junction of two major railroads and nearby deposits of coal, iron, and limestone soon attracted iron and steel factories and the nickname, "Pittsburgh of the South." By 1890 the South produced 20 percent of U.S. iron and steel.

of the *Atlanta Constitution*. Beginning in the mid-1870s, he wrote editorials and delivered speeches proclaiming industrialization as the solution to the South's devastated postwar economy. His message appealed to many Southerners, especially those who had never been part of the planter elite. It inspired them to start businesses, invest, and support pro-business policies. Grady also attracted the attention of many Northerners, convincing them to invest in New South enterprises.

> "The growth of the iron interests of the South during the last few years has been the marvel of the age, attracting the attention of the entire business world."
>
> New South booster,
> M. B. HILLYARD, 1887

The vast expansion of manufacturing represented the most stunning change in the New South. Drawn by low taxes, cheap labor, ample water power, proximity to cotton supplies, and the absence of unions, textile manufacturers moved their operations from New England to the South, especially the Carolinas. By 1900 the South surpassed New England in output to become the nation's leading producer of textiles. A similar transformation occurred in the tobacco industry, as the South went from merely producing raw tobacco to become the nation's leading producer of finished tobacco products like cigarettes.

As in the North the expansion of industry in the South relied upon the existence of a large pool of cheap labor. But unlike the North, where millions of immigrants and their children made up much of the workforce, the South relied on a rising population of poor white farming families pushed off the land by indebtedness, falling crop prices, and crop failure. In the rare instances where African Americans secured industrial employment, it was usually in the most menial, dangerous, and poorly paid jobs.

What weaknesses limited the success of the New South economy?

The low wages paid Southern workers reveals the limited success of the New South economy in overcoming the region's poverty and social problems. Despite decades of impressive growth in industry, mining, and railroads, the South in 1900 lagged far behind the North in virtually every category of economic and social progress. The majority of Southern industry, for example, was small-scale and focused on low-skill labor. Per capita incomes in the South remained stagnant from 1880 to 1900.

Other indications of backwardness and underdevelopment abounded. The cuts in funding for public education imposed by Redeemer governments reduced per pupil spending to half the average in the North. Rates for illiteracy and infant mortality far exceeded the national average.

14.21 Poverty and Independence
Sharecropping condemned most African Americans to a life of poverty, but it also helped to free them of immediate white control. No longer confined to slave cabins, they also worked on their own, free of white oversight and coercion.

The Rise of Sharecropping

Most revealing about the limitations of the New South economy was the preponderance, even by 1900, of Southern laborers still in agriculture. Only 6 percent of the Southern workforce in 1900 was employed in manufacturing. The region's economy remained fundamentally tied to the production of cash crops, particularly tobacco, sugar, rice, and of course, cotton.

The condition of Southern farmers, both white and black, deteriorated sharply in the last quarter of the nineteenth century. While cotton production soared the price plummeted, from eighteen cents per pound in the early 1870s to five cents per pound in 1894. Shrinking profits forced many Southern farmers to forfeit title to their land and became tenant farmers. Some rented land for a set fee and then were free to grow whatever crops they desired. But most tenant farmers resorted to the sharecropping system, whereby they received the right to farm a plot of land in exchange for rent paid in the form of a share (generally one-third to one-half) of the harvest. By 1900 more than 70 percent of the South's farmers (white and black) earned their living in this manner.

Sharecropping granted African Americans some important measure of independence. White landlords generally left their tenants alone, allowing them to control their own time and to set their own work routines. The people shown in this photograph (**14.21**) are poor and live in a ramshackle house, but like most sharecroppers they work as families free of direct white supervision. Given their slavery experience of gang labor under the brutal control of overseers, freedmen cherished this independence. And yet, as a closer look at this image shows, there is a well-dressed white man in the background—probably the landlord who arranged for the photograph to be taken. Sharecroppers were not slaves, but as this photograph makes clear, they lived under the control of their white landlords.

How did sharecropping provide a limited measure of independence to freedmen?

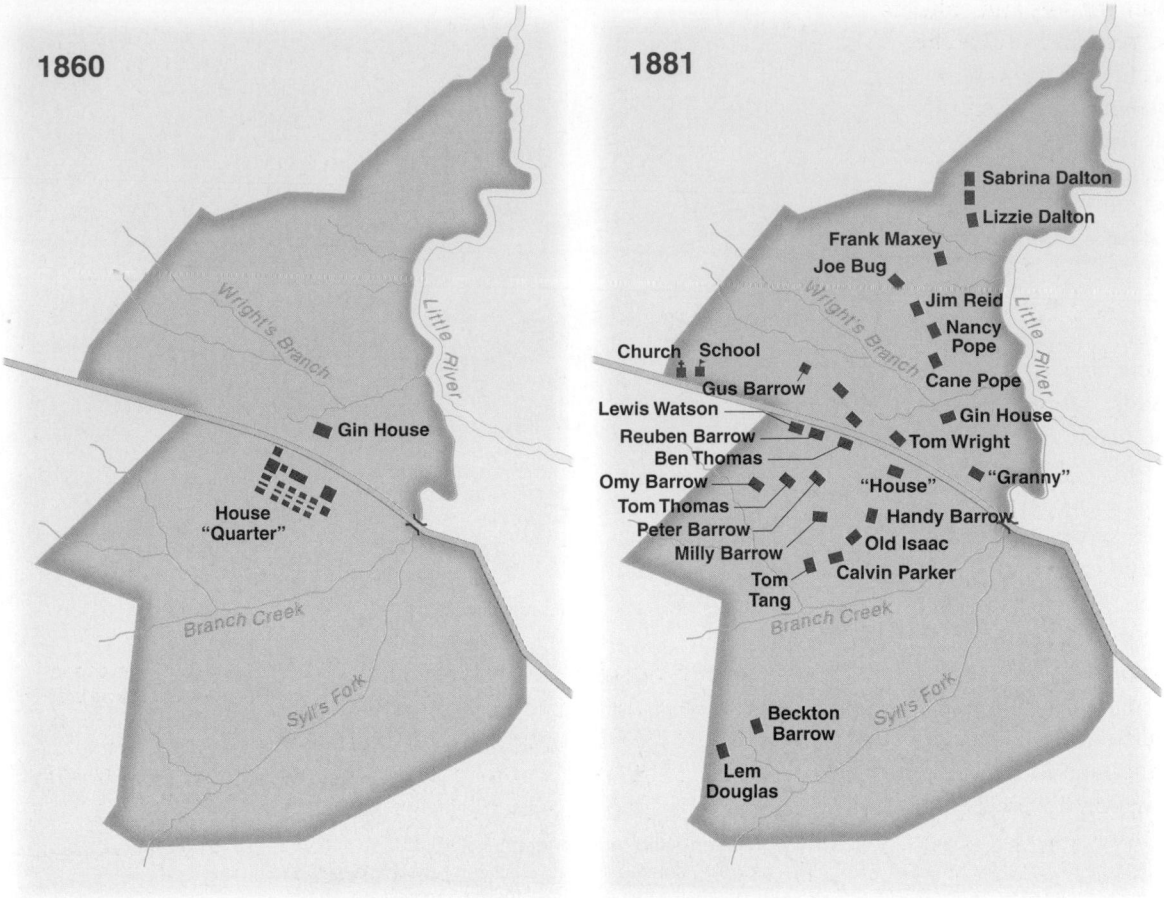

14.22 Moving from Slavery to Freedom: The Barrow Plantation, Oglethorpe County, Georgia, 1860 and 1881 Under slavery the Barrows confined their slaves' housing to a narrow section of the plantation. Sixteen years after emancipation, African Americans on the plantation, living beyond the immediate oversight of the Barrows, established a church and school.

The transformation from the tightly controlled plantation system to the relative independence of sharecropping can be seen in this map (**14.22**) of a Georgia plantation. The 1860 map shows the Barrow Family Plantation before the abolition of slavery. Notice the layout of the slave quarters—in tight rows clustered within sight and earshot of the master. Seeking maximum control over their enslaved laborers, the Barrows kept them close at hand.

Twenty-one years later, many of the Barrow's former slaves and their descendents still lived on the plantation. But as the 1881 map indicates (see 14.22), the relationship between the Barrows and their workers had changed considerably, reflecting a sharp conflict in visions regarding the social order in the postwar South. Initially the Barrows had tried, like so many other former slave owners, to limit the freedom of their former slaves, hiring them as wage workers bound by annual labor contracts and trying to coerce them into accepting gang labor under an overseer. The freedmen, however, refused these demands and eventually negotiated to work as tenant farmers. By 1881 most ex-slaves lived in separate households scattered on the former plantation. They worked as sharecroppers on 25- to 30-acre farms, doing the work as families on their own terms rather than as gang laborers. At harvest they paid a portion of their annual crop as rent. The 1881 map also indicates the presence of two key institutions of African American freedom—a church and a school. Within the narrow limits allowed by hostile whites, freedmen enjoyed privileges they had been deprived of under slavery.

Nonetheless, tenancy exploited the freedmen. Landlords demanded they grow cash crops like tobacco, wheat, and especially cotton. Because they often needed to buy seed, tools, and animals on credit (usually on unfavorable terms) from their landlords or local suppliers, most tenants found themselves in a condition of ever-mounting debt which prevented them from moving to better land or to a landlord offering better terms. It also exposed freedmen to economic reprisals should they try to vote or stand up for their rights.

Jim Crow

While life in the New South for the great majority of African Americans meant poverty and exploitation as sharecroppers, some managed to achieve a remarkable degree of economic success. Despite racism, poverty, and an often hostile white business community they bought property and started small businesses. Some of these endeavors blossomed into large, prosperous enterprises. North Carolina Mutual and Provident Insurance Company, for example, was founded by two African American men in Durham in 1898. By 1907 the company boasted more than 100,000 policy holders. Other African Americans took

What role did the black middle class play in the Jim Crow South?

advantage of the many black schools and colleges established during Reconstruction to enter the professions as teachers, professors, lawyers, doctors, nurses, and ministers. Overwhelmingly, these members of a black middle class worked in segregated settings providing services to their fellow African Americans.

These educated and relatively affluent African Americans provided leadership and direction for their communities, building social networks of churches, fraternal societies, and self-help organizations. The directors of the aforementioned North Carolina Mutual and Provident Insurance Company, for example, used their financial resources to support schools and establish a hospital, bank, and library to serve the black community of Durham. As *Heroes of the Colored Race* (**14.23**) suggests, middle-class blacks also cultivated pride in the accomplishments of African Americans after emancipation. This lithograph was published in 1881 for commercial sale to African Americans. Note its emphasis on the role of African Americans in the Civil War and later as members of Congress, as well as the significance of education.

But in the late 1870s and early 1880s, Southern political leaders began to create a social and legal system of segregation that came to be called Jim Crow (named for a derogatory black character in a popular minstrel show). It reflected their awareness that as long as some African Americans possessed civil, economic, and political rights, especially the right to vote, the idea of white supremacy was called into question. Redeemer politicians also came to recognize the political benefits of stoking racial animosity. It maintained their privileged status as a ruling elite by deflecting the frustration and anger of poor Southern whites away from them and onto African Americans. The ultimate purpose of Jim Crow was to foment racial divisions by segregating African Americans from as many aspects of everyday life as possible. Initial efforts focused on barring African Americans from hotels, restaurants, and railroad cars. Blacks denounced these violations of their constitutional rights and challenged them in court.

But an extremely conservative Supreme Court issued several decisions that sharply restricted the authority of the Fourteenth Amendment and its guarantee of equal protection. In *Hall v. DeCuir* (1878), for example, the Court ruled that a Louisiana law prohibiting racial discrimination on steamboats was unconstitutional because the vessel was engaged in interstate commerce (running routes between Louisiana and Mississippi), a realm of business that only Congress possessed the power to regulate. Five years later, in the Civil Rights Cases, the Court declared the 1875 Civil Rights Act unconstitutional, asserting that the Fourteenth Amendment did not empower Congress to outlaw racial discrimination by private individuals and organizations. The ruling cleared the way for private individuals such as hotel owners and institutions such as men's clubs to bar African Americans, but left standing the right of Congress to prohibit discrimination by state government institutions. As explained in *Choices and Consequences: Sanctioning Separation* (page 434), this matter came before the Court in an 1896 case, ***Plessy v. Ferguson.***

14.23 ***Heroes of the Colored Race*** African Americans kept alive their hopes for a better future by cultivating an appreciation for their history.

Hand in hand with the spread of segregation came an effort to eradicate the remaining vestiges of black political power by circumventing the Fifteenth Amendment. Violence and intimidation in the 1870s had reduced black voting and office holding significantly, but not completely. In Mississippi, for example, black voter turnout averaged 39 percent in the 1880s. But a rising fear among Redeemer politicians over the voting power of both blacks and disgruntled poor whites led them to commence a program of disenfranchisement.

Given the sparse and direct language of the Fifteenth Amendment, the proponents of disenfranchisement needed to devise laws that deprived African Americans of the right to vote without making specific mention of "race, color, or previous condition of servitude." In 1889 Tennessee became the first of many Southern states to enact a poll tax,

How did Southerners manage to undermine the Fifteenth Amendment?

Choices and Consequences

SANCTIONING SEPARATION

In 1890 Louisiana passed a law requiring separate cars for black and white passengers on all railroads in the state. Determined to challenge the law, an African American carpenter named Homer A. Plessy bought a first-class ticket on the East Louisiana Railroad and sat in the whites-only first-class car. As expected he was arrested. Plessy argued before a local judge named John H. Ferguson that the law violated the Thirteenth Amendment's prohibition of slavery and the Fourteenth Amendment's equal protection clause. Ferguson ruled in favor of the railroad, stating that separation did not violate Plessy's rights, a decision subsequently upheld by the state's Supreme Court. When Plessy appealed to the U.S. Supreme Court, the justices considered three major options:

Choices

1. Refuse to hear the case and thus not render a judgment on the constitutionality of segregation, letting stand the Louisiana State Supreme Court decision.
2. Rule in favor of Plessy and declare Louisiana's segregation law unconstitutional.
3. Reject Plessy's appeal and uphold Louisiana's segregation law as constitutional.

Decision

On May 18, 1896, the U.S. Supreme Court by a vote of 7 to 1 chose the third option and rejected Plessy's claim that the law violated his constitutional rights. The Thirteenth and Fourteenth Amendments, argued the majority, were never intended to establish full social equality of the races. Furthermore legal separation of the races, a doctrine subsequently known as "separate but equal," was constitutional so long as states provided equal facilities. The lone dissenting justice, John Marshall Harlan, blasted the majority opinion, declaring the law a racist violation of the nation's "color-blind" Constitution.

Consequences

In sharply limiting the Fourteenth Amendment's equal protection provisions, the court allowed Southern state governments to establish separate schools, hospitals, parks, theaters, restaurants, and public transportation across the South. The decision also opened the way for segregation laws aimed at Mexicans in the Southwest and Asians in California. In practice "separate but equal" proved only half accurate as segregated facilities were indeed separate, but never equal in terms of funding, staffing, and supplies.

Continuing Controversies

How should African Americans respond to the imposition of Jim Crow laws?

Black leaders in the 1890s were divided over the best strategy to oppose segregation. Booker T. Washington, the nation's most prominent African American leader, argued that efforts to overturn segregation were doomed to failure due to black Americans' lack of political and economic power. Instead he recommended blacks focus their energy and resources on self-improvement, especially in education, a strategy that would one day empower them to challenge segregation. Founding member of the National Association for the Advancement of Colored People (NAACP), W. E. B. Dubois, rejected this policy and instead insisted that African Americans keep up a sustained legal and political effort to end segregation. Ultimately it was Dubois's vision and NAACP attorneys that ended legalized segregation. In the 1954 *Brown v. Board of Education of Topeka* decision the Supreme Court overturned *Plessy* and rejected entirely the concept of "separate but equal."

JIM CROW LAW.

UPHELD BY THE UNITED STATES SUPREME COURT.

Statute Within the Competency of the Louisiana Legislature and Railroads—Must Furnish Separate Cars for Whites and Blacks.

Washington, May 18.—The Supreme Court today in an opinion read by Justice Brown, sustained the constitutionality of the law in Louisiana requiring the railroads of that State to provide separate cars for white and colored passengers. There was no inter-

How did the U.S. Supreme Court play a role in the imposition of segregation?

an annual tax imposed on all adult citizens in the state. Those who failed to pay it could not vote. As the image (**14.24**) of a Florida poll tax receipt for 1900 shows, the tax of one dollar was low enough so that most white voters like Henry R. Nicks could pay it, but high enough to disenfranchise thousands of impoverished African Americans. Most states also required that all unpaid poll taxes from previous years be paid off before a citizen could vote, meaning that a black man who had fallen behind in his taxes for five years would need to pay five dollars before entering a polling place.

In 1890 Mississippi enacted a poll tax and an additional measure to facilitate disenfranchisement: the literacy test. It allowed state and local officials to bar from voting anyone who failed a literacy test. The test usually required a potential voter to read a complicated section of the state constitution and explain its meaning—a provision aimed at excluding African Americans given their low levels of education.

In the mid-1890s Southern states added a third disenfranchisement policy, the so-called grandfather clause. It guaranteed the vote to anyone, even if they could not pass a literacy test, if their grandfather had been eligible to vote before 1867. Since no African Americans could vote before 1867, it left them as the only ones subject to literacy tests.

Adding to the effectiveness of the segregation and disenfranchisement movements was a stepped-up campaign of violence against African Americans. Vigilante groups across the South composed largely of poor whites, but often aided by local law officers and prominent citizens, launched an unprecedented wave of beatings, humiliations, and murders intended to intimidate blacks and "put them in their place." Often an unsubstantiated accusation of rape or murder was enough to bring out a community's lynch mob, but many killings were prompted by minor incidents of alleged disrespect such as arguing with a white man. Lynchings in the 1890s soared to an average of 187 per year, or roughly one killing every two days.

By the end of the 1890s, the cumulative effect of these disenfranchisement policies reduced overall black voting in the South by 62 percent. In some states black voting was effectively eliminated. In Louisiana, for example, the number of black voters dropped from 130,334 in 1896 to 1,342 in 1904—a reduction of 99 percent. Disenfranchisement also impacted thousands of poor whites, reducing the total white vote by 27 percent by 1900. White supremacy had triumphed.

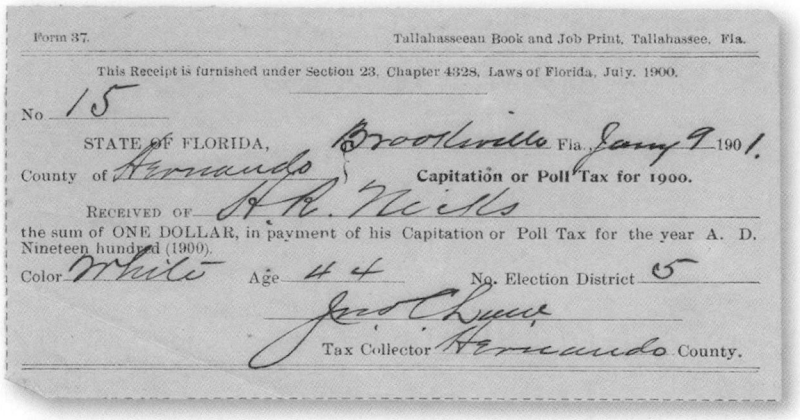
Form 37. Tallahasseean Book and Job Print, Tallahassee, Fla.

This Receipt is furnished under Section 23, Chapter 4328, Laws of Florida, July, 1900.

No. 15

STATE OF FLORIDA, Brooksville Fla., Jany 9 1901.

County of Hernando

Capitation or Poll Tax for 1900.

RECEIVED OF H. R. Nicks

the sum of ONE DOLLAR, in payment of his Capitation or Poll Tax for the year A. D. Nineteen hundred (1900).

Color White Age 44 No. Election District 5

Jno. C. Lowe

Tax Collector Hernando County.

14.24 Disenfranchisement through the Poll Tax
Because H. R. Nicks, a white man living in Hernando County, Florida, in 1900, was able to pay his poll tax of one dollar, he was eligible to vote. Mired in poverty, many African Americans could not afford the fee and lost their right to vote.

Conclusion

Reconstruction was a period of extraordinary contrasts. For the nearly four million former slaves and their supporters, it began as an era full of promise. Despite opposition, often violent, from white Southerners, by 1870 the Fourteenth and Fifteenth Amendments were ratified, declaring African Americans as citizens entitled to full civil rights, including voting, and equal protection before the law. Hundreds of thousands of freedmen joined thousands of Southern whites attracted by the progressive ideology of the Republican Party to build a reconstructed society based on democracy and equal opportunity, and social and civil equality for all. By the late-1870s, however, white Southerners who rejected this vision regained control of their state governments and began to slowly dismantle Reconstruction and impose a new form of white supremacy. Simultaneously, they guided the South toward a dramatic economic transformation. But the boom in industry, railroad construction, and urban growth that characterized the "New South" benefited mainly a small elite, leaving the South mired in poverty, illiteracy, and inequality.

How did the poll tax and literacy test allow Southerners to circumvent the Fifteenth Amendment?

CHAPTER REVIEW

1863–1866

The Ten Percent Plan
Lincoln proposes moderate terms for readmission of Southern states

Thirteenth Amendment (ratified 1865)
Abolishes slavery in every state

Fourteenth Amendment (ratified 1868)
Defines citizenship to include African Americans and guarantees equal protection before the law

1867–1868

The Reconstruction Acts
South placed under military rule and freedmen guaranteed voting rights

Progressive state governments take power in South
Freedmen wield their newly won right to vote and hold office

Republicans impeach Johnson
Reflects the divisive politics of Reconstruction

1869–1871

Fifteenth Amendment (ratified 1870)
Establishes the right to vote for all male citizens regardless of "race, color, or previous condition of servitude"

Enforcement Acts passed
Empowers Grant administration to weaken Ku Klux Klan and like groups

North Carolina elects first Redeemer government
Signals a return to white supremacy in the South; other Southern states soon follow

Review Questions

1. How did white prejudice toward African Americans shape early Reconstruction policy in the Sea Islands and Louisiana?
2. Why did African Americans consider acquiring land so important? How did they justify their claims to plantation lands?
3. How did violence come to play a role in the course of Reconstruction? What measures did Congress and the Grant administration take to curb it?
4. How did some feminists react to the Fifteenth Amendment? What impact did this decision have on the women's rights movement?
5. Who were the "carpetbaggers"? Where did this term originate and what does it tell us about Southern attitudes during Reconstruction?
6. What key factors led to the end of Reconstruction?
7. What was the Lost Cause? What purposes did it serve in the post-Reconstruction South?
8. Who were the "Bourbons" and what was their vision for the New South?

1872–1873

Amnesty Act
Pardons and restores full political rights to most ex-Confederates

Panic of 1873
Begins four years of severe economic depression that weakens Northern support for Reconstruction

1874–1875

The Mississippi Plan
Violence by white terrorist groups keeps thousands of blacks from voting. Restores the Democratic Party to power

Second Civil Rights Act passed
Guarantees equal access to public facilities and affirms the right of blacks to serve on juries

1876–1877

Compromise of 1877
Republican Rutherford B. Hayes becomes president; Republicans promise to remove federal troops from the South. End of Reconstruction

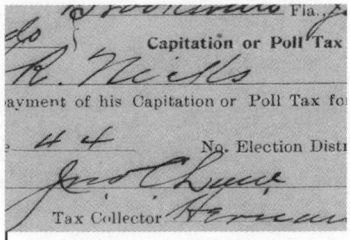

1883–1889

Civil Rights Act of 1875 declared unconstitutional
Clears the way for adoption of Jim Crow policies across the South

Tennessee enacts first poll tax
Sharply reduces black voting; adopted by other Southern states. Followed by literacy test and grandfather clause

Key Terms

Ten Percent Plan Pardoned all Southerners (except high-ranking military officers and Confederate officials) who took an oath pledging loyalty to the Union and support for emancipation. As soon as ten percent of a state's voters took this oath, they could call a convention, establish a new state government, and apply for congressional recognition. **408**

Wade-Davis Bill A Reconstruction program designed to punish Confederate leaders and permanently destroy the South's slave society. **408**

Freedmen's Bureau Relief agency for the war-ravaged South created by Congress in March 1865. It provided emergency services, built schools, and managed confiscated lands. **408**

Black Codes Laws designed by the ex-Confederate states to sharply limit the civil and economic rights of freedmen and create an exploitable workforce. **413**

Fourteenth Amendment Drafted by Congress in June 1866, it defined citizenship to include African Americans, guaranteed equal protection before the law, and established the federal government as the guarantor of individual civil rights. **416**

carpetbagger White Southerners' derogatory term for Northerners who came south after the war to settle, work, or aid the ex-slaves. It falsely suggested they were penniless adventurers who came south merely to get rich. **418**

scalawag White Southerners' derogatory term for fellow whites considered traitors to their region and race for joining the Republican Party and cooperating with Reconstruction policy. **418**

Fifteenth Amendment Constitutional amendment passed by Congress in 1869 providing an explicit constitutional guarantee for black suffrage. **421**

Ku Klux Klan The best-known of the many secret white terrorist organizations that first arose in the South in 1866; they targeted freedmen and symbols of black self-improvement and independence and played a key role in reestablishing white supremacy by the late 1870s. **422**

Panic of 1873 A financial panic on Wall Street that touched off a national economic recession causing financial houses, banks, and businesses to fail. Hundreds of thousands of workers lost their jobs. **424**

Mississippi Plan Campaign of violence and intimidation waged by armed groups of whites closely allied with the Democratic Party that drove Republicans from power in the Mississippi state elections of 1874. Copied by other Southern states. **426**

Redeemers Name for white Southern political leaders who successfully returned their states to white Democratic rule in the mid-1870s. The name was intended to depict these leaders as saviors of Southern society from rule by freedmen, scalawags, and carpetbaggers. **426**

Civil Rights Act of 1875 Passed by Congress in 1875, it required state governments to provide equal access in public facilities such as schools and to allow African Americans to serve on juries. In 1883 the U.S. Supreme Court ruled it unconstitutional. **426**

Compromise of 1877 Resolution of the disputed presidential election of 1876 that handed victory to Republican Rutherford B. Hayes over Democrat Samuel J. Tilden. Democrats agreed to the deal in exchange for patronage and the continued removal of federal troops from the South. **427**

New South Optimistic phrase white Southerners used to describe the post-Reconstruction South, reflecting the South's development of a new system of race relations based on segregation and white supremacy and pointing to a profound economic transformation that swept across the region. **428**

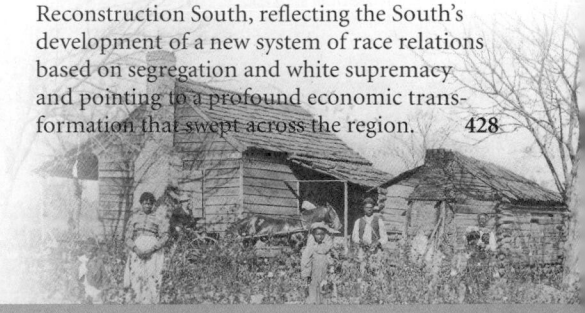

CHAPTER 15

Conflict and Conquest

The Transformation of the West, 1860–1900

> **"The destiny of the American people is to subdue the continent—to rush over this vast field to the Pacific Ocean ... to change darkness into light and confirm the destiny of the human race ... Divine task! Immortal mission!"**
>
> WILLIAM GILPIN, *The Central Gold Region,* 1859

Most Americans envisioned the conquest and transformation of the West as a tale of triumph. In John Gast's 1872 painting, *American Progress,* the beautiful goddess Liberty glides westward, stringing telegraph wire and holding a book, symbols, along with the distant railroad, of the civilization and new technology that would soon tame the wilderness. Beneath her, Gast depicts farmers and pioneers intent on taking advantage of the West's bountiful resources. Turned into a popular lithograph, it was advertised as worthy of hanging in both "the miner's humble cabin" and the "stately marble mansion of the capitalist." Publishers put the image on the cover of a popular guide to the West, *The New Overland Tourist and Pacific Coast Guide.*

Before 1840 most Americans viewed the lands west of the Mississippi as a great, untamed and dangerous wilderness of rugged terrain, extreme temperatures, wild animals, and hostile Native Americans. But beginning in the 1840s, an ever-growing number of farmers, miners, ranchers, entrepreneurs, and adventurers moved west, aided after 1869 by the completion of the transcontinental railroad and soaring demand for western products and resources.

Gast's celebratory scene reveals, doubtless unintentionally, the bitter conflict that accompanied the transformation of the West. On the painting's left border, a cluster of Native Americans flee before the advancing whites. Above them a herd of buffalo likewise make their escape. Gast's matter-of-fact portrayal of the seizure of Indian land and the near extinction of the buffalo reflected the nation's enthusiasm for "progress" and the inability—or unwillingness—to confront the human and environmental costs associated with it.

By 1900 the West had been radically transformed. Great networks of railroads and telegraph lines crisscrossed the landscape, as did untold miles of fencing that marked the boundaries of millions of farms and ranches. The western landscape also featured cities like San Francisco and Denver that rivaled their eastern counterparts. Perhaps even more remarkable than the appearance of these new aspects of western life was the disappearance of others. By 1900 the American government had confined hundreds of independent Native American tribes that had once lived in virtually every corner of the West to a series of reservations. Gone, too, were the millions of buffalo from the plains and, in areas of intensive mining, large mountain sections of once pristine landscape. The conquest of the West between 1865 and 1900 included many stories of success, achievement, and undeniable progress, but it was far more complex, violent, and tragic than Gast's dreamy vision suggests.

How did the notion of "progress" shape Americans' vision of western settlement?

Natives and Newcomers p. 440

The Economic Transformation of the West p. 447

Native Americans Under Siege p. 453

Resistance and Romanticism p. 461

Natives and Newcomers

Inspired by visions of unlimited opportunity and acts of Congress like the Homestead Act, westward migration increased dramatically after the Civil War. Contrary to the popular notions of a vacant landscape, much of the West was home to hundreds of thousands of Native Americans. Their wide variety of languages, lifestyles, and religious practices made for a rich cultural landscape, but also conflict with the rising numbers of newcomers.

Congress Promotes Westward Settlement

In 1862 Congress passed three major bills designed to facilitate settlement of the **trans-Mississippi West**, the vast region of the United States west of the Mississippi River. The Morrill Land Grant College Act of 1862 created a system whereby funds raised by the sale of public land went toward establishing colleges specializing in agricultural, mechanical, and technological education. Far more significant, however, was the **Homestead Act**. It provided 160 acres of free land to any settler willing to live on it and improve it for five years. Those who took advantage of the program included immigrants, landless farmers from the East, single women, and ex-slaves. Farmers with less patience and more capital could buy the land for a rock-bottom price of $1.25 per acre after living on it for only six months. By making available more than 600 million acres of public land to be settled and farmed, the Homestead Act touched off the largest migration of people ever within the United States.

The actual results of the Homestead Act varied widely by region. On the Great Plains and the lands farther west—regions with a harsh climate, poor soil, inconsistent supplies of water, and limited access to transportation—farmers who participated in the Homestead Act often went bankrupt. By contrast, it worked well in the northern and central portions of the Midwest, where the soil and the climate were favorable to farming.

One of the fortunate beneficiaries was Daniel Freeman, the first person to take advantage of the Homestead Act when it took effect January 1, 1863. Born in Ohio in 1826, Freeman grew up in upstate New York and Illinois. He became a doctor and served in the Union army during the Civil War. While stationed at Fort Leavenworth, Kansas, he picked out a section of land in nearby Nebraska he intended to claim as a homestead. Shortly after midnight on January 1, 1863, he woke up the land office clerk and filed his claim—the first of 417 filed that day. Freeman established a successful farm, and as this image of his certificate indicates (**15.1**), he earned clear title to the land in 1868. In addition to prospering as a farmer, Freeman practiced medicine and served terms as county coroner and county sheriff. He lived on his land until his death in 1908.

Others prospered from the Homestead Act in ways not intended by Congress. Many "homesteaders" were actually speculators who claimed their 160 acres with the intention of selling them for a quick profit in a few years. Larger enterprises like railroads and real estate companies accumulated vast holdings of land

HOMESTEAD.

Land Office at Brownville, Neb
January 20th 1868.

CERTIFICATE, No. 1 } { APPLICATION, No. 1

It is hereby certified, That pursuant to the provisions of the act of Congress, approved May 20, 1862, entitled "An act to secure homesteads to actual settlers on the public domain," Daniel Freeman has made payment in full for the W½ of NW¼ and SW¼ of SE¼ of Section Twenty-six (26) in Township Four (4) N of Range five (5) E containing 160 acres.

Now, therefore, be it known, That on presentation of this Certificate to the COMMISSIONER OF THE GENERAL LAND OFFICE, the said Daniel Freeman shall be entitled to a Patent for the Tract of Land above described.

Henry M. Atkinson Register.

15.1 Claiming a Piece of the American West
On January 1, 1863, Daniel Freeman became the first American to file a claim under the Homestead Act. Five years later he received this title, which gave him full ownership of 160 acres of Nebraska farmland. Freeman, shown here more than thirty years after he received a homestead, prospered as a farmer and doctor and served stints as county coroner and county sheriff.

What factors led to the uneven results of the Homestead Act?

by buying out farmers who failed or paying people to file homestead claims and then buying the land from them. The Homestead Act did indeed attract farmers to the West, but by 1900 only 52 percent of original homestead claimants had acquired legal title to the land.

The third major piece of legislation passed by Congress in 1862 to promote western development, the Pacific Railway Act, created two corporations to build the **transcontinental railroad**, a line spanning the continent. The Union Pacific was to build west from Omaha, Nebraska, across the Plains and the Rockies to meet the Central Pacific which was to build from California through the Sierra Nevada Mountains. To help the railroad corporations raise sufficient capital to pay for the road, Congress granted them 10 square miles of land (in a checkerboard pattern with the federal government retaining ownership of the remaining sections) for every mile of track completed. The law also granted the railroads cheap loans and cash subsidies for each mile of track laid.

It took six years of low paid, hard and dangerous (scores were killed) work by huge gangs of workers, especially Irish and Chinese, to complete the project. On May 10, 1869, a grand ceremony marking the union of the two lines took place at Promontory Point, Utah. At the appointed moment, Leland Stanford, president of the Central Pacific, drove a symbolic golden spike into place, joining two rails, one placed by a team of Chinese workers and another by an Irish crew. Telegraph wires attached to the sledge hammer and spike sent a signal out across the nation, announcing to all the long-anticipated news: the continent had been spanned. Keenly aware of the historic nature of the event, railroad officials staged this iconic photograph (**15.2**) showing the workers and locomotives of the Union Pacific and Central Pacific. It soon appeared in numerous publications across the country, often as a lithograph. Conspicuously absent from the photograph, however, are any of the thousands of Chinese workers who labored on the Central Pacific.

15.2 The Continent Spanned Conscious of the historic significance of the event, workers and officials of the Union Pacific and Central Pacific railroads pose for a photograph while celebrating the completion of the transcontinental railroad in 1869.

Why was the federal government so eager to assist the companies that built the transcontinental railroad?

15.3 The Major Tribes of the Trans-Mississippi West
More than 360,000 Native Americans, constituting some five hundred tribes, lived west of the Mississippi River.

The Diversity of the Native American West

As this map of the trans-Mississippi West (**15.3**) shows, white settlers heading west encountered Native Americans belonging to hundreds of different tribes that comprised some 360,000 persons. That number was significantly lower from what it had been a century earlier, reflecting the impact of earlier European contact, starting with the Spanish, French, and Russians, that brought conflict and devastating disease. Most Indians had lived there as far back as anyone could remember, while some had come from the East only decades earlier during the many forced removals (see Chapter 8).

Before the arrival of Europeans, dozens of Native American tribes in what is now California lived in villages as small bands of hunters and gatherers. These include the Hupa, Karok, Northern Paiute, Pomo, Wintun, and Yuki peoples. Their way of life was first disrupted in the late eighteenth century when the Spanish established a line of Christian missions on the Pacific coast running north from San Diego. While thousands of Indians lived independently beyond the reach of the missions, many were subdued by the Spanish and transformed into an exploited class of laborers. Many of them were also converted to Christianity and gradually absorbed into Spanish colonial society. Even greater change followed the discovery of gold in northern California shortly after the U.S. government seized the territory in the Mexican War. Waves of white fortune seekers soon arrived and began violently driving the Native Americans off their lands. This violence, along with

What was the impact of European contact with Indians in the trans-Mississippi West before 1850?

the starvation and disease that followed, killed upwards of ten thousand Indians (see Chapter 12).

The region of present-day Arizona, New Mexico, and west Texas likewise fell under Spanish colonial rule in the seventeenth and eighteenth centuries. But because this region was dry and remote, it attracted few Europeans. Native inhabitants, therefore, successfully retained core elements of their culture despite Spanish rule and the presence of Catholic missionaries. Indeed, missionaries managed to gain converts only by conforming their message of Christianity to fit local customs and traditions.

One major group, the Pueblo, descended from the ancient Anasazi people, included the Hopi, Zuni, and Rio Grande Pueblo tribes. They lived in settled farm communities in western New Mexico and eastern Arizona, growing corn and cotton and herding sheep. Neighboring Mexican ranchers, who prized these tribes' rich artistic traditions of decorative pottery and woven cloth, sought these native goods in trade for manufactured goods such as hoes and tools.

Eastern New Mexico and western Texas harbored more tribes, including the Jicarilla Apache and Navajo. Like the Pueblo, they lived in relative isolation from Spanish missions and thus successfully retained much of their traditional religion, language, and culture. Before the sixteenth century they had lived much like the Pueblos, but their adoption of the use of horses, brought to America by the Spanish in the seventeenth century, gradually transformed them into a more migratory people. They hunted, farmed, and tended large flocks of sheep, following them on their seasonal migrations. Sheep provided food, but also wool, which Indian women wove into cloth. The Navajo developed a tradition of silversmithing that produced beautiful jewelry.

The Pacific Northwest, comprising present-day Washington, Oregon, and northern California, was home to thriving native societies. Tribes such as the Chinook, Salish, Yurok, and Shasta lived in settled villages in large houses made from wooden planks. They divided their time between growing vegetables, hunting in the lush forests for bear, deer, and moose, and fishing along rivers and the ocean shore. Highly skilled in woodworking, the men produced excellent canoes for fishing and elaborate totem poles. Women wove intricate baskets that were both beautiful and practical. Many of these tribes enjoyed a rich material life that was offset by their custom of *potlatch*—a ceremony during which rich tribe members gave away many of their possessions as an act of benevolence and a demonstration of superior status.

Native American Tribes of the Great Plains

While Native American tribes could be found in virtually every corner of the West, by far the largest group—constituting nearly two-thirds of all Native Americans in the West—lived on the **Great Plains.** This vast open territory stretched east to west from present-day Missouri to the Rocky Mountains, and north to south from North Dakota to Texas. In the northern half (the Dakotas, Idaho, Minnesota, and Montana) lived tribes such as the Flathead, Blackfeet, Crow, Arapaho, Northern Cheyenne, and Sioux. Tribes in the southern Great Plains (present-day Nebraska, Kansas, Oklahoma, Texas, and New Mexico) included those relocated from the East during the so-called Trail of Tears ordeal (Cherokee, Choctaw, Creek, Chickasaw, and Seminole), as well as Pawnees, Comanches, Kiowas, Southern Arapahos, and Cheyenne (see Chapter 8).

The Plains tribes varied culturally, but many shared a similar tribal structure. Most tribes consisted of bands of about three hundred to five hundred related men and women, each governed by a council and widespread community involvement in the decisions the councils made. The Comanches, for example, divided their population of seven thousand (ca. 1870) into thirteen bands.

Religious beliefs and practices varied among the Plains tribes, but most shared important fundamental elements, beginning with the worship of one primary god whom the Sioux called *Wakan Tanka* (the Great Spirit). Plains Indians also believed in spirits found in everything in creation, from the earth itself, to plants, animals, stars, the moon, and sun, and they considered certain places, such as burial grounds, sacred. A shaman deemed *wakan,* or blessed, led religious ceremonies, healed the sick, and even decided where to hunt.

Many Plains tribes lived in settled villages near rivers where they tended fields of corn, beans, and squash; fished; and hunted a variety of local game, including bear, deer, and buffalo. Trade with white settlers, explorers, and trappers since the eighteenth century had allowed them to procure guns, kettles, and tools. These sedentary tribes included the Wichitas of northern Texas and Oklahoma, Pawnees of western Kansas, the Dakota Sioux of Minnesota, the Mandans of North Dakota, the Omahas of Nebraska, the Osages of western Missouri and Arkansas, and the Arikawas of South Dakota.

Although essential aspects of this Plains lifestyle had changed very little over the centuries, some of

What is significant about the diversity of Native American life in the trans-Mississippi West?

the largest tribes took to using horses (introduced by the Spanish by the eighteenth century) and adopted a migratory lifestyle. These included the Crow, Blackfeet, Cheyenne, Arapaho, Comanche, and Lakota Sioux. The horse allowed the Plains tribes to follow the seasonal migrations of the buffalo, whose population stood at 30 million in 1800. This scene, *Buffalo Chase over Prairie Bluffs,* (**15.4**), painted in 1844 by George Catlin who traveled extensively among Indian tribes in the West from the 1830s to the 1850s, reveals both the drama of the buffalo hunt and the extraordinary horsemanship skills developed by Plains Indians. It also reveals the centrality of the buffalo in Plains Indian culture, for the hunters are shown with clothing, jewelry, spear tips, and bridles made from buffalo parts. Other uses for the buffalo included flesh for food; skin for teepees and blankets; horns and hooves for glue; bones and tendons for weapons; hair for rope; teeth for ornaments; and dung for fuel.

The military advantages of the horse and the material wealth provided by the buffalo led these migratory tribes to become the dominant powers on the Plains, allowing them to oppress weaker sedentary tribes by exacting tribute. But reliance on the huge migratory beasts also meant that tribes, such as the Lakota Sioux in the north and Comanche in the central Plains, traversed enormous tracts of land during the course of their annual migrations, a practice that increasingly brought them into conflict with whites eager to acquire land. It also increased conflict between rival tribes, such as the Lakota Sioux and Crow, as white settlement forced tribes into closer contact.

While not all Native Americans were warlike, the culture of most Plains Indians relished battle. Warriors competed to develop reputations for bravery and skill, both during the hunt and in war. Warfare between tribes to determine control over land and access to game usually took the form of small skirmishes where the goal was not so much to kill their opponents as to steal their horses (a measure of a tribe's wealth and power) and drive them from the field. Individual warriors earned fame and respect by "counting coup," or making contact with an enemy with one's hand or weapon. Respect was also earned through acts of charity. Sitting Bull of the Lakota Sioux, for example, rose to prominence and eventually chief of his tribe both through his success as a warrior and due to his many exhibitions of generosity.

> "I was a famous hunter. . . . I gave the [buffalo] calves that I killed to the poor that had no horses. I was considered a good man."
>
> SITTING BULL

15.4 Plains Indians Hunting the Buffalo This 1844 painting by George Catlin shows Native American hunters pursuing the buffalo, which they relied upon as a major source of food, clothing, tools, and fuel. [*Source*: George Catlin (1796–1872) "Buffalo Chase Over Prairie Bluffs". 1832–33. Smithsonian American Art Museum, Washington, DC/Art Resource, NY]

How did the introduction of horses change the lifestyle of some Plains Indians?

The Great Westward Migration

In the late 1840s, after the Mexican War and the discovery of gold in California, a steady flow of migrant settlers into the trans-Mississippi West commenced. By the mid-1850s, thousands annually traversed the 2,000-mile Oregon Trail that stretched from Missouri to Oregon. What attracted them was a torrent of pamphlets, books, articles, and photographs produced by publicists and boosters, many employed by railroads and land companies, celebrating the virtues of the West as a region of wealth and opportunity.

Several groups led this migration westward. One was the recently freed slaves who hoped to secure new lives as independent farmers, free of the poverty and violence in the South. One of these ex-slaves, Henry Adams, who became a land promoter after emancipation, helped more than twenty thousand "**Exodusters**" on the "Exodus of 1879" from the South to farms in Kansas. This image from *Harper's Weekly* (**15.5**) captures the hopeful quality of this move-

15.5 Seeking a Better Life in the West
In response to poverty and mounting violence in the South, more than twenty thousand African Americans known as "Exodusters" migrated to Kansas in 1879–1880 to acquire homesteads and start new lives as independent farmers.

ment. Note the contrast the artist draws between the "old style" of African American migration (a desperate escaped slave hiding from a passing steamboat) and "the new" (well-dressed ex-slaves arriving at their destination by steamboat). The name Exodusters reflected the belief that, like the Israelites in the Bible's Book of Exodus, they were heading for a "promised land." The inclusion of a black veteran of the Union army symbolizes the fulfillment of the promise of emancipation won during the war. Unfortunately for many Exodusters, they settled on poor land and lacked the capital necessary to establish successful farms. As a result only about one-third stayed and the rest moved on or returned to the South.

Native-born whites constituted a second, much larger segment of the westward migration. Many were eastern and midwestern farmers who sought larger plots of land, either through purchase or by the Homestead Act, and opportunities for upward mobility. Others came to work in railroad construction or mining. Still other whites were the large numbers of soldiers in the U.S. Army who had been stationed in the West and elected to stay and settle after their terms of service expired.

One distinct subgroup of native-born whites who relocated to the West were the **Mormons**. Joseph Smith had founded this religious sect in upstate New York in 1830. But persecution, frequently violent—Smith was killed by a mob in Illinois in 1844—prompted the Mormons to head west in 1846 in search of an isolated homeland that could ensure their security and survival. They eventually chose a valley in Utah near the Great Salt Lake, territory then under Mexican rule. After the United States acquired it following the Mexican-American War, Congress created the Utah territory in 1850 (see Chapter 12), and by 1865 some twenty thousand Mormons lived in the region under a form of theocratic local rule. As more non-Mormons moved into Utah, tensions rose, since many other settlers resisted Mormon religious authority and condemned the sect's practice of polygamy (a practice they officially banned in 1896).

Joining Exodusters, Mormons, and native-born Americans in the great migration into the trans-Mississippi West were hundreds of thousands, eventually millions, of immigrants to America. Drawing them were the same desires for free, or at least inexpensive, farmland or opportunities to work in mines, on railroads, or in the rapidly expanding economies of western towns and cities. Over time large concentrations of particular ethnic groups

> "[I]f you strike off into the broad, free West, and make yourself a farm from Uncle Sam's generous domain, you will crowd nobody, starve nobody, and ... neither you nor your children need evermore beg for Something to Do."
>
> HORACE GREELEY, Editor, *New York Tribune*, 1867

What motivated the many groups that participated in the great migration into the West?

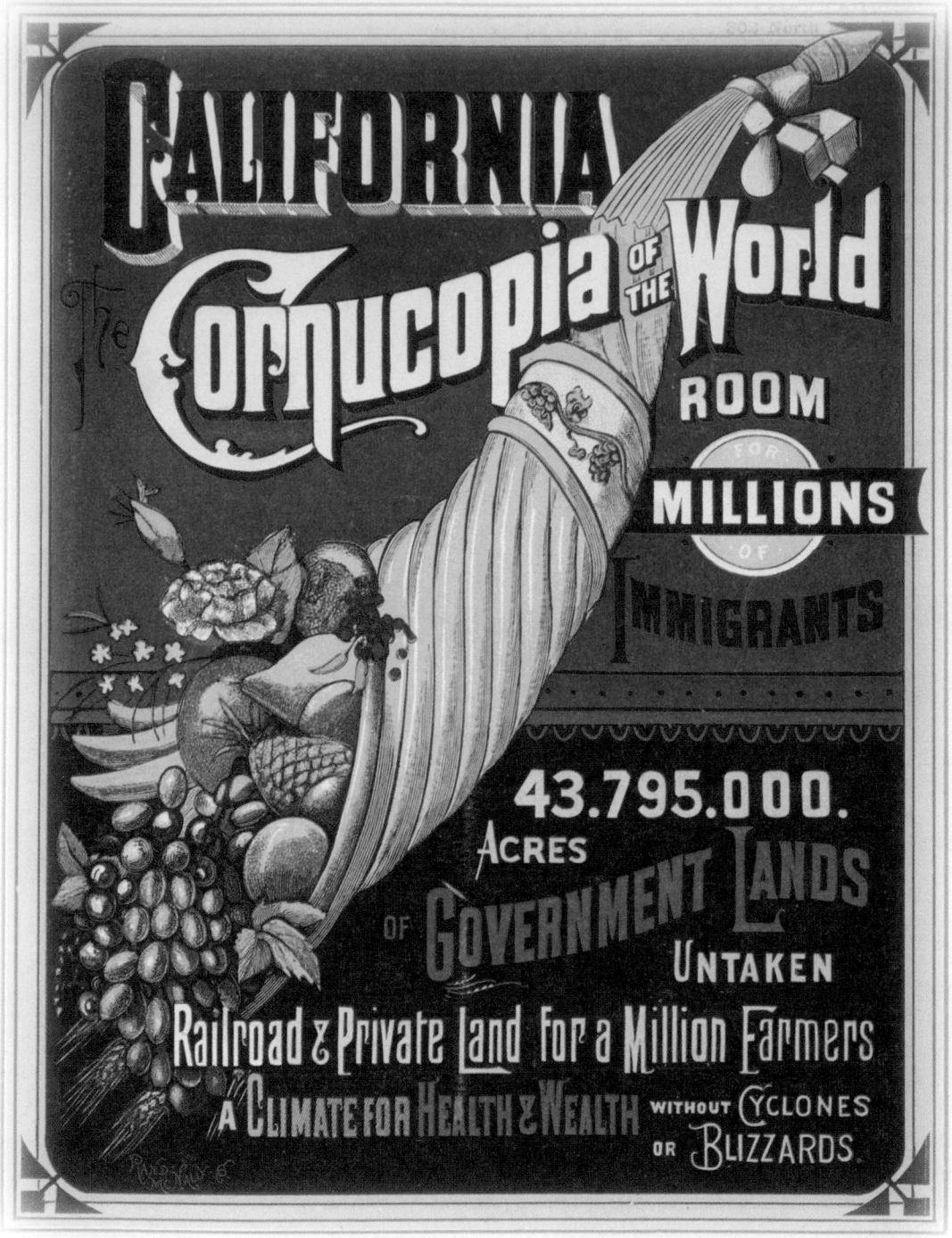

15.6 The Railroads Promote Westward Settlement
Railroads placed promotional posters such as this one from 1883 in eastern cities to entice settlers to head west to settle on land owned by the railroads, much of it acquired in land grants from the federal government.

emerged. In Minnesota, for example, 30 percent of its population in 1880 was foreign-born, including more than 66,000 Germans, over 62,000 Norwegians, and just over 39,000 Swedes. Drawn by jobs in the copper mines, thousands of Irish immigrants settled in Butte, Montana. By, 1900 it was the most Irish city in America.

As in the East, increased ethnic and racial diversity and economic competition in the West led to tension and conflict that occasionally exploded into raw violence. Frequently victims of the violence were Chinese immigrants. By 1880 California was home to 75,132 Chinese while 30,000 more lived elsewhere in the West. But anti-Chinese racism surged in the 1870s and 1880s as white laborers accused the Chinese of taking jobs and lowering wages. One attack in 1885 at Rock Springs, Wyoming, left twenty-eight Chinese miners dead. Two years later white laborers massacred at least thirty-four Chinese miners in Hells Canyon, Oregon.

Railroads and land companies played a key role in promoting immigration to the West, sending agents and advertisements to Europe to encourage migration, sometimes by entire villages, directly to the West. Railroads brought more than two million immigrants to the trans-Mississippi West between 1870 and 1900. "California, Cornucopia of the World" (1883) was one of countless posters that railroads placed in eastern seaports to attract the attention of newly arrived immigrants (**15.6**). The competition between western states for settlers is indicated in the phrase "without Cyclones or Blizzards," a clear attempt to make California more appealing than the Plains states like Kansas. Also significant is the claim of "Room for Millions of Immigrants," since only one year earlier Congress, with heavy lobbying from California, passed the Chinese Exclusion Act that barred Chinese immigration to the United States.

Why did railroads promote the migration of immigrants to the West?

The Economic Transformation of the West

While many Americans were inspired to migrate westward by notions of manifest destiny, the primary motivation was economic—a search for land and work. As a result, economic development was the chief driving force behind the profound transformations of the West after 1865. By 1900 four major industries—the railroad, farming, ranching, and mining—had fundamentally reshaped the region. These industries employed millions of workers and supplied some of the essential needs of consumers and industry in the East and internationally. Such progress, however, did not come without a cost as it was accompanied by labor exploitation, lasting environmental damage, and conflict with Indians.

The Railroad Fuels Western Development

Between 1860 and 1900 the country witnessed astonishing growth in agricultural output. The number of farms in the United States grew from two million to six million, with most of the growth taking place in the West. Agricultural output for the nation increased from $1.6 billion in 1860 to $4.3 billion in 1900.

Several factors account for this national boom in agriculture. New technologies such as the steel plow and mechanical reaper dramatically increased the acreage a typical farmer could till. The establishment of many agriculture schools, most funded by state and federal government, led to significant advances in technical knowledge of fertilization, irrigation, crop rotation, and seed selection, and the proper care of livestock.

One of the biggest factors underlying much of this booming growth in agriculture was the spread of the railroad. As the map (**15.7**) shows, the transcontinental railroad was only the beginning of a vast transportation network that spread across the West. In addition to several subsequent major east-west railroad lines, such as the Atlantic and Pacific Railroad and the Northern Pacific Railroad, companies built scores of feeder railroads, smaller lines providing access to a major one. This growing network opened up more and more western lands for farming, allowed farmers in once remote areas to sell their grain in the national market. The railroad also benefited many nonfarmers, beginning with the thousands who built the lines and who later gained employment as firemen, engineers, switchmen, mechanics, dispatchers, and clerks. It also opened up western lands for mining and ranching.

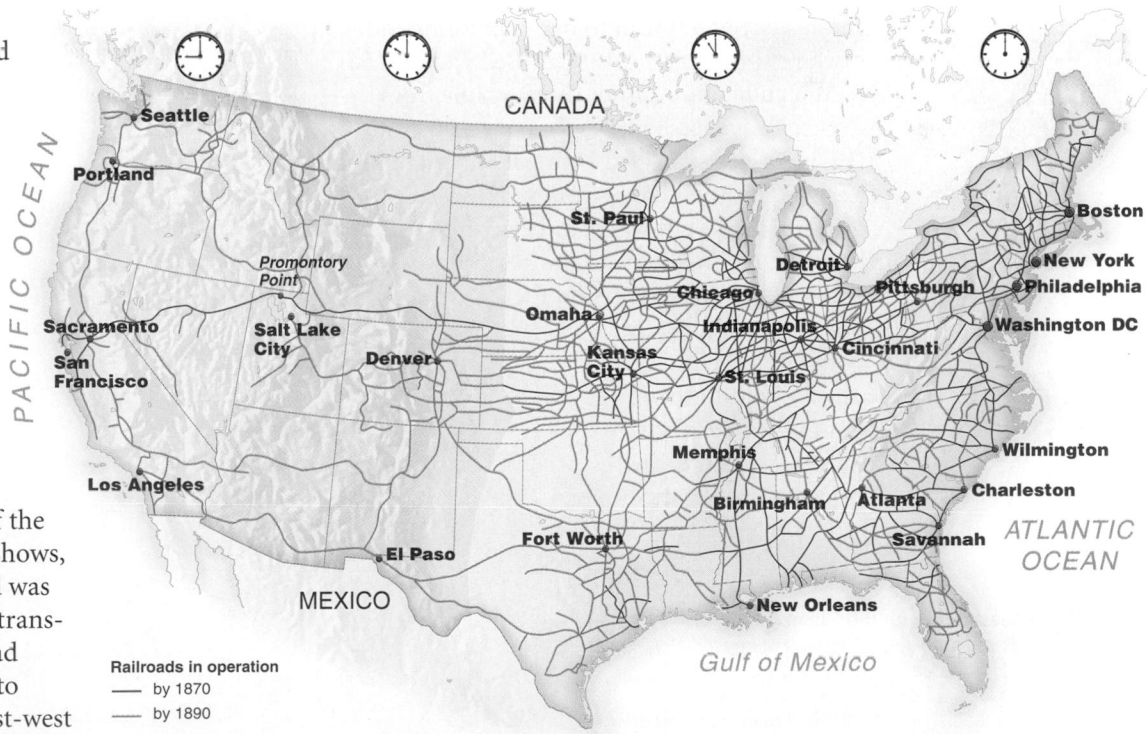

15.7 The Spread of the Railroad Government loans and land grants helped spread a railroad network across the nation, facilitating economic development and settlement in the West.

How did the railroad shape western economic development?

Railroads also transformed the West by promoting urban growth. Many western cities like San Francisco, California; Portland, Oregon; and Denver, Colorado, had arisen as significant centers of trade before the arrival of the railroad. Once connected to the national rail network, however, they boomed into major metropolises. Their economies diversified as demand for construction, food, transportation, and retail opened up new opportunities for entrepreneurs. By 1890 the West was more urbanized than any region in the United States except the Northeast. Denver's population, for example, rose from 5,000 in 1870 to 100,000 in 1890. The population of Omaha, Nebraska, soared in similar manner, from less than 2,000 in 1860 to 140,452 by 1890. Like their eastern counterparts, western cities struggled with all manner of urban problems, including crime, disorder, corruption, poor public health, inadequate water, and ethnic tensions.

Hard Times for Farmers

While the overall trend in this period was one of expansion and profit, the reality for many farmers was struggle, frustration, and failure. To begin with, farmers faced unpredictable weather patterns. Farmers on the Plains, for example, enjoyed unusually high levels of rainfall between 1878 and 1886, leading them to think this was the norm and encouraging still more farmers to acquire homesteads. But a return to dry conditions and occasional drought after 1886 caused widespread hardship and failure. Other threats came from insects such as grasshoppers that attacked crops.

Farmers also struggled with wild fluctuations in prices paid for their crops from year to year. A plentiful harvest of wheat or corn often meant a glutted market and low prices. In the 1880s wheat farmers on the Plains saw prices fall due to competition with less expensive wheat grown in South America and Australia. Sudden drops in prices pushed many farmers into foreclosure because most carried high levels of debt to finance the purchase of land and equipment such as harvesters, plows, and windmills.

These conditions favored larger farms, revealing a significant flaw in the original Homestead Act: in the more arid regions of the West the 160-acre allotment was not large enough for profitable farming. By the 1880s so-called bonanza farms of 1,000 acres or more became increasingly common in the Dakotas and California. These large enterprises had more capital and thus could better afford expensive equipment needed for plowing, sowing, and harvesting.

On top of all these challenges were the problems of the loneliness and drudgery of life on the Plains. As this photograph (**15.8**) of the four Chrisman sisters standing by their sod house in Custer County, Nebraska, illustrates, life on a western farm was often a Spartan existence. Sod houses and dugouts cut into hills lacked even the most basic amenities like running water and glass windows. Apart from occasional trips to town, church, court sessions, and harvest fairs, opportunities for social interaction were rare since farmers usually situated their homesteads far apart. The Chrisman sisters developed a strategy that diminished their isolation and allowed them to fulfill the Homestead Act's requirement that they live on their land in order to receive full title to it. Beginning with Lizzie's homestead claim in 1887 and Lutie's in 1888, the two younger sisters took turns living on the homesteads, keeping their sisters company, helping on the farm, and waiting until they were old enough to file their own claims. Hattie eventually did, but all the homestead plots were gone by the time Jennie Ruth came of age.

15.8 Homesteading on the Plains
Western farmers received 160 acres of free land through the Homestead Act, but success required years of hard work and sacrifices such as living in crude sod houses. This one, in Nebraska, was owned by one of the four Chrisman sisters shown here.

What challenges did western farmers face?

In 1867, a former clerk in the Department of Agriculture named Oliver H. Kelley founded the Patrons of Husbandry, or **Grange**. This social and educational society was dedicated to alleviating some of the problems faced by farmers by promoting fellowship, fraternity, and education. Grangers, as they were called, shared ideas about farming through a newsletter and attended lectures offered by traveling experts. Local chapters opened all across the nation, and by the early 1870s the organization had several hundred thousand loyal members.

The Grange was transformed into a powerful political movement during the severe economic depression triggered by the Panic of 1873. Hundreds of thousands of farmers faced ruin as prices plummeted, while their creditors demanded payment for loans, and railroads charged high prices to transport their produce to market. In their desperation they created Granger Parties, which in 1874 won control of the legislatures of Illinois, Wisconsin, Iowa, and Minnesota and enjoyed significant influence in several more. They enacted a series of "Granger Laws," some of the earliest regulations of banks and corporations, especially railroads. Granger-dominated state legislatures passed laws setting maximum rates for transporting or storing grain and banning abusive practices such as offering preferred customers special rates. Grangers tried, as this 1873 cartoon (**15.9**) indicates, to convince Americans not involved in farming to recognize the threat posed to them by uncontrolled railroad power. As a "Consolidation Train," a name suggesting monopoly, pulls cars labeled "extortion," "bribery," "usurpation," and "oppression," a Granger warns unsuspecting citizens of their impending doom.

Railroad magnates denounced these limitations on their power and profit as unconstitutional and sued. The Supreme Court, however, in two key cases in 1876 (*Munn v. Illinois* and *Peik v. Chicago and North Western Railroad*) ruled that state legislatures did possess the legal authority under the Constitution to regulate commerce, including especially commerce between states.

Despite this stunning legal victory, the Granger movement faded when the depression lifted and farm product prices rose in the late-1870s, ending the crisis that had produced it. In addition the Democratic and Republican parties added pro-farmer planks to their party platforms that made the Granger parties seem less necessary.

15.9 Warning of the Perils of Monopoly The Grangers saw themselves as reformers trying to warn the American public about the growing danger of powerful railroads to the survival of democracy and individual liberties.

The Cattle Kingdom

Another key emerging sector of the western economy was cattle ranching. When the United States annexed Texas in 1845, millions of longhorn cattle (introduced to Central America in the sixteenth century by the Spanish) roamed the range, raised mainly for their skins and tallow. But as Americans developed a taste for beef in the 1860s, ranchers came to envision the great profits to be made if they could get their cattle to northern markets. A longhorn that cost $4 in Texas could be sold for $40 on the northern market.

Beginning in 1866 and lasting two decades, Texas ranchers began the first of the annual **Long Drives** of more than 1,000 miles to bring the cattle to market. Ranchers Charles Goodnight and Oliver Loving drove several thousand cattle from Texas to Colorado, prompting many imitators, who moved some 260,000 Texas longhorns onto the Great Plains within a year. In 1867 another cattle entrepreneur, Joseph McCoy, established a stockyard, hotel, bank, and office in a small Kansas town along the Kansas-Pacific Railroad. Advertising heavily, he quickly turned Abilene, Kansas for a time into the premier cattle drive destination. By the early 1870s more than 600,000 longhorns arrived per year to be sold and then transported by rail to Chicago and other destinations for slaughtering.

Over time the need for the drives diminished as rail lines were extended from Kansas into Texas and entrepreneurs established large cattle ranches close to railroads in states north of Texas, such as Kansas, Nebraska, Wyoming, and Colorado.

What aspects of the railroads did western farmers resent?

The period of the great cattle drives lasted only twenty years, but it firmly established the cowboy as an enduring icon of the Old West. Nineteenth-century dime novels, paintings, books, and plays (and in the twentieth century, films) traditionally depicted cowboys as paragons of manliness, independence, and courage who spent most of their days battling fierce Indians and driving cattle (see 15.20) and nights in raucous saloons playing poker and engaging in brawls and occasional gun fights. But the life of a cowboy was far more difficult and complicated. Cattle drives exposed them to harsh weather that included searing heat, flash floods, and deadly blizzards. Cowboys' wages averaged only about a dollar a day—or less if the price of beef fell—and they survived on a relentless diet of meat, beans, and coffee. They worked from dawn until dusk and then served a shift guarding the cattle at night against rustlers and hostile Indians.

Moreover, American cowboys were a far more diverse lot than the popular images depicting them as exclusively white men would indicate. Approximately one-third of cowboys in the American West were nonwhite, the largest group being Mexican *vaqueros.* Indeed, much of the equipment, clothing, techniques, and culture of the American cowboy derived from Mexican and Spanish traditions. This borrowing is evident in the many items associated with cowboys that bear names derived from Spanish. For example, the word *cowboy* itself is a direct translation of the Spanish term *vaquero,* while other terms such as lariat (*la reata*), chaps (*chaparejos*), and wrangler (*catallerango*) are anglicized versions of Spanish words.

Native Americans worked as cowboys, as did African Americans who accounted for one in seven cowboys. The eight cowboys shown in this 1880s photograph (**15.10**) worked on the ranch of Thomas Jones (shown standing) in Texas. One of the most famous was Bose Ikard. Born a slave in Mississippi in 1847, he was later taken to Texas where he became a skilled cowboy. Freed by the Civil War, he played a key role in the first Long Drive led by Goodnight and Loving.

Ranching held out the prospect of great profits, but ranchers faced considerable challenges. In the early 1870s the invention of barbed wire effectively ended open-range ranching and the long drives as farmers enclosed their land to protect crops from cattle hooves. Cattle ranchers also clashed with other livestock enterprises, such as sheep herders, over access to water and grazing lands. These conflicts frequently led to violence and on several occasions to widespread hostilities known as "range wars." Ranchers, like farmers, also were vulnerable to extremes of weather, losing cattle in times of scorching heat and drought, as well as freezing cold and snow. Similarly, they suffered from rapid expansion of the ranching industry in the mid-1880s and consequent flooding of the market with cattle that caused a collapse of beef prices, sending many ranchers into bankruptcy.

Fortunes Beneath the Ground: The Mining Booms

While many western adventurers found fortune and failure in railroads, farms, and ranches, still others tried their luck underground in the many mining districts that emerged in the West. The second great western mining boom, after California in 1849 (see Chapter 12), began in 1859 with the discovery of vast silver deposits in Nevada. The Comstock Lode, as the Nevada site was eventually called, yielded an astonishing $300 million to $400 million in silver in the next twenty years.

As was the case in most mining booms, the initial discoverers and nearly all the small-timers who followed garnered only modest profits. The real fortunes came in the succeeding years as heavily

15.10 African American Cowboys Despite the popular image of cowboys as white men, many were African American and Hispanic.

How did the reality of cowboy life differ from that presented in popular culture?

capitalized and incorporated enterprises established mining operations to extract the ore. Among the titans who accrued stupendous fortunes were four Irishmen—John Mackay, Jim Fair, James Flood, and William O'Brien—known collectively as the "Silver Kings." They bought a controlling interest in the Consolidated Virginia Mine, an operation that many declared "spent" and virtually worthless. Yet in 1873 their miners hit the greatest silver vein of them all, the Big Bonanza that eventually yielded more than $100 million. Most fortune seekers, however, earned modest livings as wage earners working in the mines, while others flocked to the resulting boomtown, Virginia City, to work in construction, dry goods stores, and saloons. Thousands of women in Virginia City found work in hotels, laundries, and restaurants. Unfortunately, low wages and a lack of a family network to fall back upon led many women to become prostitutes.

Other mining booms for gold and silver, but also the discovery of such valuable metals as copper, lead, and zinc, followed in Colorado, Montana, Idaho, Wyoming, and the Dakotas. In every case the resulting boom followed the predictable path: the early mining claims gave way to larger, more sophisticated operations. The new corporations had the capital and knowledge to invest in the technology needed to dig deep shafts, extract the ore from rocks, process it on site, and ship it by rail to market. Like eastern industrialists such as Andrew Carnegie and John D. Rockefeller, these corporations often integrated their resources with the means and methods of production to maximize profits (see Chapter 16). The industrial revolution was not merely an eastern phenomenon.

The Environmental Legacy

Economic development in the trans-Mississippi West led to countless success stories of enterprising and risk-taking individuals who established farms, ranches, mines, and small businesses, or who simply found lucrative employment in the region's many urban centers. But such development in many cases carried with it a significant price in terms of the natural environment.

Mining, for example, came in many forms, but in nearly every case it left behind a badly scarred landscape. Open-pit mining of the Mahoning iron ore mine in Minnesota's Mesabi Range eliminated vast tracts of forest and created massive gouges in the land (**15.11**). These changes shattered the local ecosystem and choked surrounding waterways with muddy runoff water. Hydraulic mining, or the use of high-pressure water streams to wash away soil and gravel, created similar problems. Ore processing often used highly toxic chemicals to separate ore from rock or other materials that the miners simply dumped into rivers or open fields, where they eventually seeped into the water table and throughout the ecosystem.

15.11 The Price of Unchecked Economic Development Western states bowed to the powerful and profitable mining industry, leaving its practices unregulated. As a result, methods such as open-pit mining led to serious environmental damage.

The arrival of ever-growing numbers of humans in the West altered the delicately balanced western ecosystems. On the Great Plains, for example, hunting and other human activity led to the eradication or near eradication of elk, bear, wolf, and buffalo populations. Conversely, settlers introduced foreign animals and plants that, lacking natural predators, spread rapidly and disrupted the balance of the ecosystem. For example, cheatgrass, accidentally introduced to the West from Asia in the 1890s, quickly spread over millions of acres, wiping out or diminishing other flora and greatly increasing the incidence of wildfires.

Farming in some arid areas of the West, through the use of deep-cutting steel plows that loosened hard-packed dry soil, contributed to significant topsoil erosion over time. Vast herds of livestock had a similar effect as their grazing eliminated the grass whose roots held the soil in place. Likewise the practices of the timber industry led to deforestation, the loss of habitat for many animal and plant species, and without trees to shield the soil from heavy rainfall, erosion.

As *Competing Visions: Preservation versus Exploitation* (page 452) reveals, some Americans decried this environmental damage, but the great majority of Americans viewed the West through the lens of Manifest Destiny, seeing it as a place of limitless resources provided by God for the enjoyment and enrichment of human beings.

How was the environment of the West altered by human settlement and economic development?

Competing Visions

PRESERVATION VERSUS EXPLOITATION

Much of the economic damage and disruption that resulted from the development of farms, ranches, mines, and other businesses in the West followed from a prevailing attitude among Americans that all of nature was at their service. Lansford W. Hastings, a famous Western explorer, vividly expresses that view in the passage below. Less popular, but nonetheless significant, is the protest over environmental degradation set forth by George Perkins Marsh, a diplomat-turned-environmentalist. How does Hastings invoke the language of Manifest Destiny to justify his vision of the settlement of the West? How does he view the natural resources of the West? How does Marsh challenge the ideas that nature possesses limitless resources and that economic development is glorious progress?

Lansford W. Hastings, *The Emigrant's Guide to Oregon and California* (1846)

This infant country … is destined, in a very few years, to exceed by far, that of any other country of the same extent and population, in any portion of the known world. … [T]here is no country … possessing a soil so fertile and productive, with such varied and inexhaustible resources, and a climate of such mildness, uniformity and salubrity; nor is there a country, in my opinion, now known, which is so eminently calculated, by nature herself, in all respects, to promote the unbounded happiness and prosperity, of civilized and enlightened man. …

In view of their increasing population, accumulating wealth, and growing prosperity, I can not but believe, that the time is not distant, when those wild forests, trackless plains, untrodden valleys, and the unbounded ocean, will present one grand scene, of continuous improvements, universal enterprise, and unparalleled commerce: when those vast forests, shall have disappeared, before the hardy pioneer; those extensive plains, shall abound with innumerable herds, of domestic animals; those fertile valleys, shall groan under the immense weight of their abundant products: when those numerous rivers shall team [*sic*] with countless steam-boats, steam-ships, ships, barques and brigs; when the entire country, will be everywhere intersected, with turnpike roads, rail-roads and canals; and when, all the vastly numerous, and rich resources, of that now, almost unknown region, will be fully and advantageously developed. … [W]e are also led to contemplate the time, as fast approaching, when the supreme darkness of ignorance, superstition, and despotism, which now, so entirely pervade many portions of those remote regions, will have fled forever, before the march of civilization … [These accomplishments] shall forever stand forth, as enduring monuments, to the increasing wisdom of man, and the infinite kindness and protection, of an all-wise, and overruling Providence.

George Perkins Marsh, *Man and Nature,* 1864

Man has too long forgotten that the earth was given to him for usufruct [use without damage] alone, not for consumption, still less for profligate waste. … But man is everywhere a disturbing agent. Wherever he plants his foot, the harmonies of nature are turned to discords. … Indigenous vegetable and animal species are extirpated, and supplanted by others of foreign origin … The terrible destructiveness of man is remarkably exemplified in the chase of large mammalia and birds for single products … The wild cattle of South America are slaughtered by millions for their hides and horns; the buffalo of North America for his skin or his tongue … What a vast amount of human nutriment, of bone, and of other animal products valuable in the arts, is thus recklessly squandered! …

… The ravages committed by man subvert the relations and destroy the balance which nature had established between her organic and her inorganic creations … When the forest is gone, the great reservoir of moisture stored up in its vegetable mould is evaporated, and returns only in deluges of rain to wash away the parched dust into which that mould has been converted. The well-wooded and humid hills are turned to ridges of dry rock, which encumbers the low grounds and chokes the watercourses with its debris, and … becomes an assemblage of bald mountains, of barren, turfless hills, and of swampy and malarious plains.

Albert Bierstadt, *Among the Sierra Nevada Mountains, California,* 1868 [*Source:* See Credits section]

Why did few people heed the warnings of writers like Marsh?

Native Americans Under Siege

Westward expansion benefited many Americans, but it proved a devastating fate for Native Americans. They faced a relentless tide of white settlers who possessed both superior weaponry and a belief that they had a higher claim to western land. White settlers also enjoyed the support of the federal government and army. The result for Native Americans in the last third of the nineteenth century was broken treaties, devastating wars, relocation to reservations, and a policy of forced assimilation.

Mounting Problems for Native Americans

In 1851, as it became clear that the traditional government policy of simply forcing tribes into the West was no longer viable because of increased white migration into the region, Congress passed the Indian Appropriations Act. It set aside vast tracts of the Oklahoma Territory as reservations for dozens of Native American tribes. That same year the U.S. government, the Sioux, and several other Plains tribes signed the first Treaty of Fort Laramie. In exchange for declaring nearly all of the central and northern Great Plains off limits, the tribes agreed to allow white settlers to pass unmolested along the Oregon Trail as they moved westward. But the lasting peace that government officials and tribal leaders hoped the treaty would secure did not materialize. Tension and violence between white settlers and Native American tribes only increased in the coming years.

Native Americans faced a series of problems that ultimately doomed their efforts to resist Euro-American incursion onto their lands. Chief among these were the racist attitudes of white Americans that characterized Indians as backward, pagan, violent savages. who lacked a rightful claim to the lands they occupied. Many Americans believed their own culture was vastly superior and considered Native Americans obstacles to national progress that must be removed. "The Red Men are a doomed race," claimed one writer in 1877, for "the savage is giving place to a higher and more civilized race." These notions originated in the colonial period, but greater contact and conflict between whites and Indians after 1850 led to a proliferation of largely negative depictions of Native Americans in newspapers, magazines, songs, plays, and works of art like *The Rescue,* by sculptor Horatio Greenough (**15.12**). Comissioned by the federal government and placed at the entrance to the U.S. Capitol in 1853, the scene drew upon the many sensationalized stories and paintings of white settlers, especially women, being kidnapped, raped, and murdered by Native Americans. But Greenough departed from the traditional depictions and introduced a towering, dominant white settler. Notice the contrasts in the men's size, demeanor, and clothing. "I have endeavoured," Greenough explained, "to convey the idea of the triumph of the whites over the savage tribes." By 1874, the scene had merged with the life of the famous pioneer and icon of frontier masculinity, Daniel Boone (**15.13**). Both images proclaim Indian savagery and justify white domination, a message that eventually resulted in the sculpture's removal from public view in 1958.

15.12 Promoting an Image of Indian Savagery
This 1853 sculpture by Horatio Greenough promoted the idea among white Americans that Native Americans were violent savages.

15.13 Seeing Savagery
Greenough's image became so widely known that a dime novel artist easily adapted it to a Daniel Boone story.

What did the government hope to accomplish by signing treaties with Native American tribes?

White hostility to Native Americans shaped government policy, especially when it came to signing and honoring treaties. Invariably, it seemed, federal officials negotiated treaties with tribes that promised to permanently fix the boundaries of their hunting grounds and places of habitation, only to find soon thereafter that whites, hungry for land, had begun settling there. Rather than enforce the terms of the treaty and force the removal of white settlers, the government inevitably revised the treaty to further shrink designated Native American lands.

This combination of white settlers' desire for land and disregard for Native Americans' rights, and the efforts of Native Americans to resist white encroachment, led to repeated outbreaks of violence. one of the most egregious incidents was the **Sand Creek Massacre**. Angered by sporadic attacks on settlers by some Native American tribes in Colorado, a military outfit under Colonel John M. Chivington raided on November 29, 1864 a peaceful encampment of eight hundred Cheyenne at Sand Creek. With most of the Cheyenne men off hunting, Chivington's force slaughtered more than two hundred Indians, mostly defenseless women and children, mutilated their bodies, and returned to Denver with their scalps.

Native Americans also confronted epidemics of diseases such as smallpox and measles—diseases that Native Americans possessed little or no resistance to. While the worst devastation had taken place in previous centuries during initial European contact (see Chapter 1), epidemics of smallpox continued to erupt, killing thousands. For example, a smallpox outbreak in the Pacific Northwest in 1862 killed some twelve thousand Indians. The widespread abuse of alcohol, a commodity obtained through trade with whites, further compromised Native American health.

Additionally, long-standing animosities among tribes prevented Native Americans from developing a united front against the U.S. Army. White officials took advantage of these divisions to obtain help from one tribe, in the form of guides and even soldiers, against another. Disunity *within* tribes also contributed to this problem, as individual bands guarded their autonomy and resisted the idea of centralized authority. For example, in 1863 leaders of the Nez Perce tribe split over whether to sign a treaty that would confine them to a reservation. There were exceptions, of course, and some tribes managed to overcome this problem, at least temporarily.

The Plains tribes' dependence upon the buffalo left them particularly vulnerable in the 1870s. Railroad companies, disdainful of the large herds that occasionally disrupted the passage of trains, hired gunmen to kill buffalo. Entrepreneurs presently made buffalo robes fashionable in the East, thereby encouraging hunters to kill still more buffalo. The U.S. Army soon recognized the strategic value of wiping out the great herds as a means of undermining the independence of the Plains tribes and forcing them to stay on reservation lands. The scale of extermination was staggering. In this photograph (**15.14**), workers at the Michigan Carbon Works prepare thousands of skulls for processing into fertilizer, glue, and other products. The buffalo

15.14 Evidence of Extermination
This mountain of buffalo skulls gathered by a fertilizer company attests to the scale of wanton killing of buffalo in the 1870s and 1880s.

How did negative stereotypes of Native Americans influence government policy?

population, estimated at thirty million in 1800, plunged to only a few thousand by the early 1880s creating a major crisis for the Plains Indians who depended on them.

The technological disparity between white settlers and Indians gave the former an enormous advantage. Euro-American settlers and army soldiers alike were heavily armed with modern rifles. The army also possessed early machine guns (called Gatling guns) and heavy artillery. While many Native American tribes had long ago acquired firearms, they never produced guns and ammunition and they remained dependent on whites for them. The U.S. Army also benefited from the telegraph, which allowed them to communicate over great distances about troop movements and Native American military activity, and to request supplies and reinforcements as needed.

> "Women and children were killed and scalped, children shot at their mothers' breasts, and all the bodies mutilated in the most horrible manner. ... Colonel J. M. Chivington all the time inciting his troops to their diabolical outrages."
>
> MAJOR EDWARD WYNKOOP, testimony before congressional committee investigating the Sand Creek Massacre

Wars on the Plains

Despite its lack of commitment to honoring them, the federal government nonetheless signed many treaties in the late 1860s hoping to bring peace to the West and allow continued settlement by whites. Treaties were drawn up and signed with the Apache, Cheyenne, and Arapaho in 1865, the Kiowa, Comanche, and Apache in 1867 (the Medicine Lodge Treaty), and the Sioux (the second Fort Laramie Treaty) in 1868. The latter treaty ended Red Cloud's War (1866–1868), a conflict that erupted when the army announced plans to build forts along the Bozeman Trail in the Wyoming and Montana territories to protect white migrants drawn by the discovery of gold in Montana. It guaranteed to the Sioux ownership of the Black Hills and land and hunting rights in South Dakota, Wyoming, and Montana. It also explicitly barred white people from these lands. "From this day forward all war between the parties to this agreement shall for ever cease," declared the treaty in words that would soon prove false. "The government of the United States desires peace, and its honor is hereby pledged to keep it."

Despite these measures, continued violation of treaties by white settlers who ventured onto Indian lands and bands of Indians who refused to accept confinement on reservation lands led to increased bloodshed. The Red River War broke out in 1874 on the southern plains in present-day Texas, Oklahoma, and Kansas when bands of Kiowa, Comanche, southern Cheyenne, and southern Arapaho Indians, angered over the federal government's failure to uphold its obligation to provide adequate supplies and keep whites off the reservation land (the army actually organized buffalo hunting parties that devastated local herds), left the reservation and launched raids against white settlements. Led by Lieutenant General Philip Sheridan, the army crushed the rebellion by the spring of 1875, thereby ending any future Native American resistance on the southern plains.

By then the primary scenes of conflict had shifted to the northern plains. The discovery of gold in the Black Hills of South Dakota in 1874 touched off a flood of white fortune seekers into the region that was indisputably (as stipulated in the 1868 Fort Laramie Treaty) territory granted exclusively to Native American tribes. Rather than keep white trespassers out, however, the federal government demanded the Sioux vacate their Red River hunting grounds and return to their reservations. When the tribes refused to comply, the army launched an offensive.

In the late spring of 1876 the Seventh Cavalry, led by a young and vainglorious lieutenant colonel named George Armstrong Custer, closed in on a large band of Cheyenne, Sioux, and Arapaho warriors,

How did the dependence of the Plains Indians on the buffalo weaken their ability to resist the loss of their lands?

including the well-known Crazy Horse and Sitting Bull, near the Little Bighorn River in Montana. Eager to earn fame and believing there were only a few hundred Indian warriors when in fact the number was closer to four thousand, Custer attacked before the rest of the army (and other officers who might overshadow him) arrived. The **Battle of Little Bighorn** quickly disintegrated into one of the most devastating defeats ever suffered by the U.S. military as Custer and 257 of his men were killed.

Although the Battle of Little Bighorn was an overwhelming triumph for the Sioux, Cheyenne, and Arapaho, it quickly proved a hollow victory. As this cartoon (**15.15**) published in the *New York Graphic* a few weeks after the battle vividly demonstrates, the eastern media ignored Custer's blundering and instead depicted him and his men as valiant victims and demanded vengeance. Notice the artist's blunt depiction of Indians as savage, semianimal beings in stark contrast to the two white soldiers, one a heroic victim and the other a coolheaded executioner. The caption, "The Right Way to Dispose of Sitting Bull and His Braves—What the Country Expects of General Sheridan," was a not-so-subtle assertion of the popular belief that the government was showing too much leniency toward Native Americans who resisted white expansion into the West. Responding to this pressure, the U.S. government expanded military action in the Black Hills, forcing the Sioux and other defiant tribes onto reservations.

15.15 The Negative Fallout from Little Bighorn
After the Sioux, Cheyenne, and Arapaho Indians defeated Custer and the Seventh Cavalry in the Battle of Little Bighorn, negative press coverage hardened white attitudes toward Native Americans. This image appeared in the *New York Graphic* (August 15, 1876).

War and Conflict in the Far West

Farther west, native tribes encountered similar problems. During the final third of the nineteenth century, the states and territories west of the Rockies also were growing. The mining and railroad industries, the economic centerpieces of that region, required a great deal of land—land long occupied by Native Americans. Just as they were on the Great Plains, the tribes on the West Coast and in the intermountain West

How did the victory over Custer and his men ultimately prove very costly to the Plains Indians?

faced an encroaching white population that considered the land theirs for the taking.

In 1876, following the massacre of Custer and the Seventh Cavalry, army and government officials increased pressure on tribes to move to reservations. One such group targeted was a portion of the Nez Perce tribe that lived on the northwestern plateau of Idaho, Oregon, and Washington. In 1863 most of the Nez Perce tribe had agreed to move onto a reservation, but about a quarter had refused. Led by Chief Joseph, about 750 Nez Perce (500 of them women, children, and elderly non-combatants) fled the region to escape the army. Over the ensuing four months, they engaged in an epic flight of 1,500 miles, hoping to cross into Canada. Despite their small numbers and dwindling supplies, they defeated the army in several battles and came within 40 miles of the Canadian border before they were forced to surrender to the army and to life on a reservation.

> "Hear me, my chiefs! I am tired. My heart is sick and sad. From where the sun now stands, I will fight no more forever."
>
> CHIEF JOSEPH, shortly after his surrender in 1877

Similar scenes of final military resistance played out in the Southwest. An Apache warrior named Geronimo had emerged in the 1860s and 1870s as a fearless opponent to encroaching Euro-American and Mexican settlers. Eventually captured by federal authorities in 1874, Geronimo and some four thousand Apaches were sent to a reservation at San Carlos, Arizona. The grim life on the reservation led him to escape and resume his campaign of resistance. In the face of mounting pressure from the army, he surrendered again in 1884. In 1885 and again in 1886, Geronimo escaped with a small band of warriors and their families and eluded capture for months. These escapades added to his already legendary status, but he eventually surrendered for good in 1886, ending the last significant Native American resistance.

Resistance to exploitation and abuse also erupted in the Southwest among Hispanos (descendants of Spanish colonists) and Mexicans in the 1880s and 1890s. Euro-American settlers who arrived in New Mexico in the mid-nineteenth century eventually gave rise to a powerful ruling class of politicians, landowners, and ranchers. Many allied themselves with powerful gangs that provided protection and intimidated (and sometimes killed) their rivals. Poor Hispano and Mexican farmers often bore the brunt of these ruling Euro-Americans' ruthless tactics and hunger for land. When officials began to sell off to speculators and ranchers what had long been used as common grazing lands, the poor farmers resisted. The most famous of these resistors were *Las Gorras Blancas*, or The White Caps, a secret militant vigilante group of Mexican men who in the late 1880s and early 1890s wore white masks and cut fences on lands taken over by speculators. They also destroyed railroad bridges, buildings, and crops.

In Pursuit of a Solution

While most Americans expressed little concern over the fate of Native Americans in the West, a notable few did raise their voices in protest. One of the first was Helen Hunt Jackson. Inspired by an 1879 lecture by Susette La Flesche and her uncle, Chief Standing Bear, relating the plight of the Ponca tribe to an audience in Connecticut, she began speaking and lobbying on behalf of Native Americans. In 1881 she published *A Century of Dishonor*, a book that chronicled in searing detail the misguided and murderous treatment of Native Americans by the U.S. government. The book prompted Congress to appoint a commission to study Indian affairs and seek a new and more humane policy.

Another influential reformer garnered a wide audience as an authentic spokesperson for the Native Americans. Sarah Winnemucca, the granddaughter of a Northern Paiute chief, had received some education from white families in Nevada and California and worked as a translator for the army. In the late 1870s she began lecturing in the East demanding more humane treatment of the Paiutes and other tribes that brought her to the attention of eastern and western reformers. Winnemucca tried to gain credibility among whites by presenting herself as an "Indian Princess," an image firmly

Why were Native Americans so resistant to the government's demand that they settle on reservations?

established in American popular culture by the mid-nineteenth century, notably in the story of Pocahontas (see Chapter 2). In her posed portrait (**15.16**), hardly anything in her costume, especially the crown and bag embroidered with a cupid and bow and arrow, resembles traditional Paiute clothing and jewelry. Nonetheless, in an era when the political and social opinions of women, especially Native American women, were largely ignored, Winnemucca's strategy succeeded for a time in bringing extensive and respectful press coverage of her speeches and eventually her book, *Life Among the Paiutes: Their Wrongs and Claims* (1883). "In the history of the Indians," wrote one reporter in 1885, "she and Pocahontas will be the principal female characters."

Both Jackson and Winnemucca promoted education for Native Americans, but with very different goals in mind. Jackson represented the reformers who believed it the duty of the government to elevate Native Americans from "savagery" by educating and assimilating them into white Euro-American society. In particular they advocated the establishment of boarding schools for Indian children and the eventual dissolution of reservations (see *Choices and Consequences: Forced Assimilation versus Cultural Preservation*). In contrast Winnemucca believed in formal education, but not at the expense of eliminating Native American culture. She believed it was possible for Indian children to become educated and productive Americans, while retaining the core of their culture and traditions.

Jackson's ideas prevailed among reform-minded legislators in Congress, especially Senator Henry L. Dawes. He had long taken a sincere interest in the plight of Native Americans during nearly three decades in Congress. In 1887 he wrote and Congress passed the **Dawes Severalty Act**, a measure designed to break up the reservations and assimilate Native Americans into the dominant white Christian American culture. Specifically, the plan offered Native American heads of households allotments of 160 acres of reservation land (with smaller amounts going to those unmarried or under age eighteen) to encourage them to become independent family farmers. Remaining reservation lands would be sold off and the profits set aside for tools and education. Native Americans who accepted these terms then could apply for U.S. citizenship. To prevent speculators from defrauding Indians, land allotments would be held in trust for twenty-five years before full ownership was conferred.

The Dawes Severalty Act was born of high ideals and good intentions, but it nonetheless proved devastating to the Native Americans it was intended to help. The program was rife with flaws, beginning with the allotment of land that, in many cases, was of poor quality, making successful farming difficult if not impossible. It also included restrictions on hunting, further limiting options for participants. Despite safeguards, white speculators and scammers found ways to con Native Americans out of

> "For shame! For shame! You dare to cry out Liberty, when you hold us in places against our will, driving us from place to place as if we were beasts."
>
> SARAH WINNEMUCCA, *Life Among the Paiutes: Their Wrongs and Claims* (1883)

15.16 Speaking Out for Native American Rights Sarah Winnemucca, a member of the Paiute tribe in California, drew attention to the injustices being suffered by Native Americans through a speaking tour of the eastern United States and the publication of a book.

What led reformers like Dawes to believe the break up of reservations would be beneficial to Native Americans?

Choices and Consequences

FORCED ASSIMILATION VERSUS CULTURAL PRESERVATION

The Dawes Severalty Act of 1887 stipulated that revenue generated from the sale of reservation lands be applied to the education of Native American children. As with the land allotment plan, the principal motivation of people like Dawes and reformer Helen Hunt Jackson was to assimilate Indians into American society, which they believed would be facilitated by providing vocational training to enhance their job prospects. But the act did not specify what kind of education ought to be provided, and so Congress and the Bureau of Indian Affairs faced a choice.

Choices

1. Establish reservation-based schools offering a traditional public school curriculum, while allowing Native Americans to maintain their culture, including their language.
2. Establish reservation-based schools offering a traditional public school curriculum, while requiring a higher degree of assimilation (especially learning English).
3. Establish off-reservation boarding schools committed to eliminating all vestiges of Native American culture.

Decision

The federal government chose to promote the establishment of off-reservation boarding schools. The model was the Carlisle Indian School in Carlisle, Pennsylvania. Established in 1879, it operated on the simple, but brutal principle of "kill the Indian, save the man." As the "before and after" photographs indicate, Native American children sent to boarding schools were required to cut their hair, wear American clothing, take an American name, and speak only English. Some schools made conversion to Christianity a top priority.

Consequences

Removal from families and fellow Native Americans on their reservations caused many children to suffer psychological trauma. Many also suffered from physical abuse, malnutrition, and poor health care. About one in seven ran away, and an unusually high number committed suicide. Still, by 1902 twenty-five federally funded boarding schools, and many more private ones, operated in fifteen states with an enrollment of six thousand students.

Continuing Controversies

What was the long-term impact of the boarding schools?
Along with the trauma inflicted on generations of children, it hastened the demise of Native American culture, including the disappearance or near disappearance of many languages. Several Native American groups have filed lawsuits against the U.S. government and the churches that ran the schools and demanded formal apologies.

Before-and-after photos of Chiricahua Apache children at the Carlisle Boarding School, circa 1890.

What assumptions about Native American culture influenced the boarding school program?

> "The Indians must conform to "the white man's ways," peaceably if they will, forcibly if they must. They must adjust themselves to their environment, and conform their mode of living substantially to our civilization. ... They can not escape it, and must either conform to it or be crushed by it."
>
> THOMAS J. MORGAN, Commissioner of Indian Affairs, 1889

15.17 Selling off Reservation Lands
This advertisement issued by the federal government in 1911 vividly illustrates the Dawes Severalty Act in action as it exuberantly proclaims a sale of 350,000 acres of Indian land.

their allotted land long before the twenty-five-year term. The act also allowed, as indicated by the poster (**15.17**), for the government to sell land deemed "surplus" to white settlers. This poster touts the high quality of the estimated 350,000 acres being offered for sale in 1910. As the map (**15.18**) shows, by the time the Dawes Act was replaced in 1934, two-thirds of Native American reservation land had been lost.

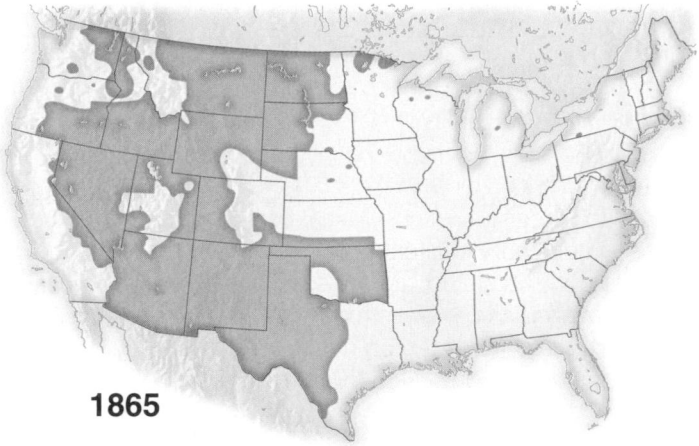

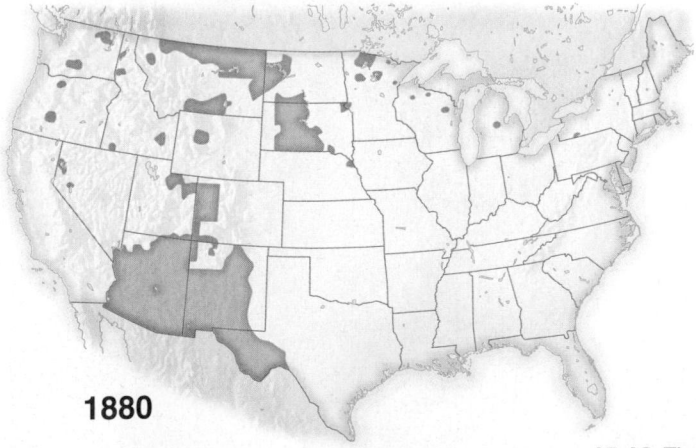

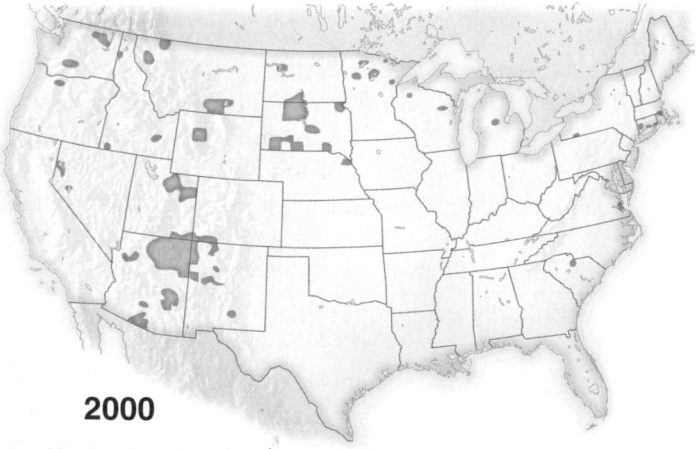

Land transferred from Indians to whites

Land held by or returned to Indians

15.18 The Loss of Native American Lands
Native American land possessions shrank steadily in the nineteenth and twentieth centuries through a combination of treaties, sales, and forced expulsion by white settlers and soldiers. In 1887 the Dawes Severalty Act accelerated this trend by encouraging the breakup of reservations.

How did the Dawes Act play a key role in the loss of Native American land?

Resistance and Romanticism

The surrender of Geronimo in 1886 symbolized the end of any significant armed resistance by Native Americans to the Euro-American settlement of the trans-Mississippi West. Nonetheless, a revival movement called the Ghost Dance, soon arose to offer one final attempt to reverse the fortunes of Native Americans. When that effort ended in brutal suppression at the hands of the army at a place called Wounded Knee, Native Americans turned to more subtle and enduring efforts to preserve their tribes, families, and culture.

At the same time, white Americans continued to fashion a pleasing image of the West as a place of adventure, heroism, individualism, and opportunity. This image found its way into art, literature, music, and innumerable aspects of popular culture in the twentieth century. Yet in recent decades, historians and activists have offered a corrective to this romantic image that takes into account the experiences of Native Americans, Mexicans, and women, as well as the impact on the environment.

Persecution and Persistence

The last major form of resistance to the Euro-American conquest of the West emerged in the late 1880s. The Ghost Dance movement originated in the 1870s, but did not become widely popular until a Northern Paiute shaman named Wovoka began preaching a message of Native American revival based on a vision he had experienced during a total eclipse of the sun in 1889. In this vision, which he related to his followers, he saw a great flood that scoured the land clean of all white settlers, leaving behind Indians who had remained true to traditional teachings and a renewed herd of buffalo. Wovoka told his followers to perform the Ghost Dance, a ritual ceremony where participants donned special shirts and danced in a circle until gradually brought to an ecstatic state that they believed drew to them the spirits of ancestors who would protect them from the white man's bullets.

The hopeful message of the Ghost Dance spread rapidly among Native Americans from the Rocky Mountains to the Great Plains, alarming federal officials who feared it contained the seeds of rebellion. They were especially concerned about its popularity among the Sioux and tried to curb it. After they moved a large group of Sioux Ghost Dancers to Wounded Knee Creek in present-day South Dakota, the army attempted to disarm them on December 29, 1890. When one of the Indians accidentally fired his gun, the soldiers attacked. The clash quickly turned into a massacre, and although estimates vary widely, between two hundred and three hundred Sioux were slaughtered. This photograph (**15.19**), titled "The Medicine Man Taken at Wounded Knee, S.D.," conveyed some of the brutality of the event. The date of January 1, 1891, on the photograph indicates that bodies were left unattended for days before being interred in a mass grave. Note the rifle placed on the body by a soldier or the photographer to present an image of a hostile Indian. It was not the bloodiest clash between Native Americans and the U.S. Army, but the **Wounded Knee Massacre** came to symbolize the brutality associated with the conquest of the West.

The end of armed conflict did not mean an end to resistance for Native Americans. In the coming decades, as they struggled with the loss of tribal lands, the cultural erosion caused by the boarding schools,

15.19 Massacre at Wounded Knee In an incident that came to symbolize American brutality toward Native Americans, U.S. soldiers killed between two hundred and three hundred Sioux at Wounded Knee, South Dakota, after a tense standoff over the Ghost Dance movement. [*Source*: © Nebraska State Historical Society Photograph Collections]

What made Wovoka's message so appealing to Indians and so frightening to military officials?

and high levels of poverty and alcoholism, Native Americans found ways to preserve their culture, including many languages, artistic forms, and religious beliefs. They did so by maintaining traditions within families and establishing informal methods of passing on traditions from one generation to the next. As a result, when a Native American rights movement emerged in the 1960s and 1970s, it included a commitment to reaffirming and strengthening traditional Native American cultures.

Creating Mythical Heroes and Images

The story of the American West has long been the object of romanticism and myth. The image of the West as a place of high adventure, heroism, rugged individualism, and endless opportunity developed with the very first enthusiastic reports of Western explorers such as Lewis and Clarke (see Chapter 7). But this image really flourished after 1850 as greater numbers of people headed west and sent back to loved ones in the East countless letters describing the marvels and perils of the frontier. Increasingly journalists sent back dispatches from the West describing wide-open lands, roaring rivers, majestic mountains, and the heroic struggles of pioneers against weather and hostile Indians. Eventually writers turned to fiction, especially a new genre known as the "dime novel."

The first Western dime novels appeared in the 1860s, and their subjects soon became pop heroes. Two early heroes were "Deadwood Dick," a cowboy dressed in black, and his girlfriend "Calamity Jane," who could handle not only her rifle and six-shooter, but also anything else that came her way. Another wildly popular Western character was Buffalo Bill. Based on the legendary exploits of a real Western scout, William "Buffalo Bill" Cody, stories about him first appeared in a newspaper and then in dime novel form as "Buffalo Bill, King of the Border Men." When it sold well its author, Ned Buntline, wrote a steady stream of Buffalo Bill stories. So, too, did other authors who flaunted copyright laws (eventually fifty thousand dime novels were published from the 1850s to the 1920s).

Cody grew famous but he earned no royalties from the novels. Seeking a way to capitalize on his fame, he created in 1883 "**Buffalo Bill's Wild West**," a circus-like production that purported to show audiences the thrilling and harrowing life on the frontier, replete with huge reenactments of cattle drives and clashes between Indians and cowboys, as well as exhibitions of marksmanship, cattle roping, and riding. The show proved hugely popular and it grew more elaborate every year, eventually topping out at 400 horses and 650 cowboys, Indians, musicians, and support staff. Over time Cody added big-name stars like the famous sharpshooter Annie Oakley and even the Sioux chief Sitting Bull.

Most Americans, indeed, much of the Western world, viewed the West, through Buffalo Bill's performances, as a place of heroism, optimism, gallantry, and success (see *Images as History: Annie Oakley*).

The West in Art and Literature

Western imagery and ideas also shaped American art and literature. Mark Twain, whose real name was Samuel Langhorne Clemens, emerged in the late nineteenth century as one of the first authentically American novelists generally unaffected by European mores. Twain headed west in the early 1860s when his older brother Orion became secretary of the Nevada territory. He had hoped his brother could provide him with a government job, but he also wanted to find his share of the gold and silver associated with the Comstock Lode. Accordingly, he headed west. The result was his classic book *Roughing It* (1872), which fit in with the evolving Western tradition of the yarn or tall tale, and the beginnings of a literary career informed by his experiences with the wild life of Virginia City. His subsequent major works, *The Adventures of Tom Sawyer* (1876) and *The Adventures of Huckleberry Finn* (1885), while not especially "Western" in that they were set along the Mississippi River, both contained Western themes of adventure, individualism, and a desire to escape the constraints of modern society for a purer, more authentic world. In keeping with this theme, when Huck Finn sets out at the end of the book to start life anew, he heads for the West.

Just as Twain's stories crackled with the realism of life on the Mississippi and in the West, Western art found its realist in Frederic Remington. Remington's background prepared him perfectly: after attending Yale's art school, he visited Montana, worked as a sheep herder and bar owner in Kansas, and started following the army, sketching battle scenes. Drawing upon earlier Western artists like George Catlin (see 15.4), he painted, drew, and sculpted vivid scenes of Western life. Most were vignettes of the lives of unknown cowboys, Native Americans, and soldiers.

Why did the West become such a popular topic in entertainment and literature?

Images as History

ANNIE OAKLEY

Two years after William Cody launched his Wild West show, he hired a woman who went on to become one of his most celebrated performers. Annie Oakley was a gifted sharpshooter, born and raised not in the West, but in Ohio. Taught to shoot at a young age, she killed game to earn money for her struggling family. At age sixteen she beat a professional in a sharpshooting match. She soon married the man and joined him on stage. In 1885 they joined Buffalo Bill's Wild West.

For sixteen seasons Oakley stunned and thrilled audiences with her marksmanship. She shot cigarettes from her husband's mouth and coins from his fingers. She blasted an endless succession of glass balls thrown in the air. She hit a target behind her by holding a mirror in one hand and shooting over her shoulder with the other. No one could match the "peerless lady wing shot."

But as this photograph and virtually every one she posed for shows, an essential part of Oakley's appeal lay in her image as an ideal frontier woman who combined Victorian femininity and rugged, almost masculine, strength.

Oakley's adoring public was not put off by her entry into the traditionally male world of guns and horses because she presented a pleasing and reassuring feminine persona. In so doing Annie Oakley, the woman from Ohio, played a key role in shaping the evolving mythical image Americans held of the Old West.

Oakley's dual image as both feminine and tough is captured in her facial expression. In all of her studio portraits, she presents herself as beautiful and composed, but unsmiling, to emphasize her grit and fearlessness.

While Oakley radiated a beguiling feminine charm (she entered the show ring skipping and blowing kisses to the audience), this hand-on-hip pose was very masculine and expressive of manly self-assuredness that audiences associated with cowboys.

Conforming to Victorian mores about proper behavior for women, Oakley always wore a dress and rode side saddle.

Her many medals were intended to lend her authenticity, as if to say that although she was a performer, her skills as a shooter were real.

Oakley's outfit was modeled on the cowboy's, but with exceptions to emphasize her femininity. Unlike the oblong cowboy hat, hers had a broad round brim. She set it on the back of her head to reveal her face and ladylike curls.

She always appeared with a gun, a central icon of how Americans in the late nineteenth century understood the West. It was a symbol they associated almost entirely with men.

Annie Oakley poses for one of her many studio portraits depicting an idealized image of a frontier woman.

What traits did Annie Oakley portray to present an ideal woman of the West?

One exception was Lt. Col. George A. Custer, whom Remington helped make into a hero after the Battle of Little Bighorn. Charles Russell, a cowboy-turned-artist, also emerged as leader of Western art, producing works that often depicted more sensational and imaginative scenes than Remington. Both men played a central role in creating the iconic image of the American cowboy. Russell's 1897 painting (**15.20**) is typical of most depictions, showing skilled and fearless cowboys roping a bull.

Historians Reinterpret the American West

Another key influence on the way Americans came to develop a particular image of the West was the work of historian Frederick Jackson Turner. In 1893 he published an essay, "The Significance of the Frontier in American History," that took as its starting point the recent announcement by the Census Bureau based on data compiled from the recent 1890 census that the American frontier was "closed," that is, for all practical purposes the United States was essentially "settled" from coast to coast. In the essay he set forth what historians long have called the Turner Thesis or the **Frontier Thesis.** According to Turner, the frontier had played a vital role in shaping the American character and consequently American institutions. The frontier's importance began with the first settlers during the colonial period along the eastern seaboard and continued in every succeeding generation as it pushed farther and farther west. This seemingly endless supply of land created widespread opportunity for upward mobility. The tough demands of the frontier, Turner argued, forced Americans to develop a spirit of rugged individualism and innovation. Frontier life also fostered values such as equality and democracy because success was determined not by one's background but rather by one's ability to work hard, sacrifice, and command the respect of others.

15.20 The Making of an American Icon
Artists such as Charles Russell, who painted this scene, *The Herd Quitters,* in 1897, played a central role in promoting the cowboy as a symbol of the West as a place of heroism, daring, and manly individualism.
[*Source*: Montana Historical Society, Helena]

Turner's thesis proved enormously influential. Several generations of Western historians based their writing and research on his ideas about the frontier. His influence also spread well beyond Western history—indeed, well beyond the study of history itself. Some American politicians and policy makers reacted to the apparent closing of the frontier in the 1890s by embracing imperialism to acquire new lands and markets that might make up for the absence of new places to conquer within the United States.

During the second half of the twentieth century, a new generation of historians reexamined Turner's thesis. In 1987 Patricia Nelson Limerick published *The Legacy of Conquest: The Unbroken Past of the American West.* Just as Turner's article was a product of the optimism and anxiety of late-nineteenth-century American society, Limerick's book offered an interpretation that reflected the fact that she was a woman raised in the 1960s, a time of social ferment, when historians began to focus more on racial, ethnic, and gender issues. Consequently she brought a far more critical eye to her study of the West than Turner.

That awareness was clear in one of the words in Limerick's title: *conquest.* Turner had seen white Euro-American settlers as triumphing over such "obstacles" as a stubborn landscape and "a fierce race of savages." Limerick and other writers, known as "new Western historians," presented a far more complicated story. While not dismissing Turner entirely they emphasized, for example, that Native Americans had inhabited the West for thousands of years before the arrival of Europeans and thus had a legitimate claim to the land. Viewed from this perspective, the story of westward migration was one of violence, exploitation, and conquest. Limerick and other historians also stressed the diversity of the West, seeing it as a meeting place of a wide array of Native American tribes, Euro-Americans, European and Asian immigrants, African Americans, Mexicans, and Hispanos that contributed to and shaped a Western culture that was not simply "white." Finally, the more critical approach of new Western historians has taken into account the environmental impact of westward economic development.

This new way of seeing the history of the West in recent years has had an impact beyond the history books. Hollywood films on Western themes began to change as well. In the classic Western epics of the

How have new Western historians changed the way many Americans understand the history of the West?

15.21 Reinterpreting the History of the West After more than 125 years of only commemorating Custer and his men, in 2003 the site of the Battle of Little Bighorn added an Indian Memorial to honor the Native Americans who fell in the battle. [*Source*: Colleen Cutschall, "Spirit Warriors". Bronze sculpture, 34 ft. × 14 ft. in an arc. Little Bighorn Battlefield National Monument, Montana. Brandon University, Canada]

1940s and 1950s, cowboys were heroes, fighting Indians who terrorized innocent white settlers. Beginning in the 1990s filmmakers began to present a more complicated view of the story of westward settlement, lawlessness, and white-Indian conflict. *Dances with Wolves* (1990), for example, presented Native Americans in very sympathetic terms. *Unforgiven* (1992) presented the West as a place of violence, lawlessness, failure, desperation, and corruption, where the line between good and evil is not at all clear. Many more such films followed.

This reassessment of the West's history has also brought significant changes in the way museums and public memorials present key chapters in American history. Nowhere is this more apparent than at the site of the 1876 Battle of Little Bighorn. For more than a century following the battle, the site was maintained as a memorial that depicted Custer and his men as heroic martyrs who died in the cause of Western settlement. The site was named for Custer (Custer Battlefield National Cemetery) and featured a memorial to the Seventh Cavalry and some Indian scouts on Last Stand Hill. Native Americans, who, of course, won the battle, were simply ignored. But the influence of new Western history and Native American activism led to the renaming in 1991 of the site Little Bighorn Battlefield National Monument and in 2003 the unveiling of the Native American memorial shown here (**15.21**). Located only 100 yards from the Seventh Cavalry monument, it features three bronze outline sculptures representing Sioux, Cheyenne, and Arapaho warriors who participated in the battle. Its official theme is "Peace through Unity," but it also represents a growing awareness that for far too long Americans relied upon an incomplete and overly simplistic understanding of the history of the American West.

Conclusion

The second half of the nineteenth century brought extraordinary changes to the United States as a whole, but especially in the trans-Mississippi West. In 1850 the primary occupants of the region were Native Americans. Most had lived there for thousands of years and developed an extraordinary diversity of lifestyles, traditions, and religious practices. White settlers, spurred on by manifest destiny, enthusiastic reports of open land, and measures such as the Homestead Act, soon began pouring into the region. They established milions of farms, founded countless towns and cities, and developed thriving railroad, ranching, and mining industries. But this rapid settlement and economic development came with a cost, most especially for Native Americans who were eventually forced onto reservations. Despite subsequent federal policies that emphasized forced assimilation and the breakup of reservations, Native Americans worked to retain essential elements of their culture in the twentieth century. Even as the final phases of western settlement and Native American defeat were playing out, Americans began to develop a mythical image of the West that, despite corrective efforts by activists and historians in recent years, remain alive and well in the American imagination.

Why are Native Americans so committed to reshaping the interpretation of historic sites like Little Bighorn?

CHAPTER REVIEW

1862–1866

Homestead and Pacific Railway Acts passed
The first distributes millions of free land to settlers; the second starts construction of the transcontinental railroad

George Perkins Marsh publishes *Man and Nature*
A widely read book that warns of environmental damage due to unrestricted exploitation of western resources

Sand Creek Massacre
Soldiers in Colorado massacre two hundred Indians

First "Long Drive" of cattle from Texas to the Great Plains
Leads to the rapid expansion of the ranching industry in the West

1867–1874

The Grange movement founded by Oliver Kelley
Becomes a powerful pro-farmer political movement by 1874 in western states

Second Fort Laramie Treaty signed
Guarantees the Sioux ownership of the Black Hills and additional land and hunting rights in South Dakota, Wyoming, and Montana

Gold discovered in Black Hills
Leads to escalating conflict as white miners move onto land reserved to Native Americans in the Second Fort Laramie Treaty

1876–1877

The Battle of Little Bighorn
Defeat of Lt. Col. Custer and Seventh Cavalry hardens white attitudes toward Native Americans

The flight of the Nez Perce fails
Symbolizes both Native American resistance to reservation policy and its ultimate failure

Review Questions

1. How was the development of the American West linked to the economy of the eastern United States?
2. What was the significance of railroad building to the West as a region and to its peoples?
3. What challenges did American farmers face in their attempts to establish successful farms in the West?
4. What significant industries, other than agriculture, developed in the West?
5. What were the critical factors that led to the conquest of Native American tribes and their forced relocation to reservations?
6. Why did U.S. government officials embrace a policy of forced assimilation for Native Americans in the late nineteenth century? How did they implement it?
7. Why did Americans develop and embrace a romanticized vision of the American West in the late nineteenth century? How close was this image to reality?
8. In what ways did the New Western History differ from traditional accounts of the settlement of the West?

1879–1881

Exoduster movement begins
To avoid violence in the South, thousands of ex-slaves migrate to Kansas, Nebraska, and Colorado to take up homestead farming

Helen Hunt Jackson publishes *A Century of Dishonor*
Brings national attention to the brutal and dishonest treatment of Native Americans

1883–1886

William Cody launches "Buffalo Bill's Wild West"
This hugely popular traveling show romanticizes the story of westward settlement

Apache resistance leader Geronimo surrenders
Ends the last major Native American military opposition to the U.S. military

1887

Dawes Severalty Act passed
Begins breakup of reservations and promotes boarding schools to encourage farming and assimilation

1890–1893

Wounded Knee massacre
Soldiers open fire on a gathering of Sioux, killing as many as three hundred

Frederick Jackson Turner publishes his frontier thesis
Bemoans the closing of the frontier, arguing that it had exerted a major influence on American values, ideals, and institutions

Key Terms

trans-Mississippi West The region of the United States west of the Mississippi River. **440**

Homestead Act Passed in 1862, it provided 160 acres of free land to any settler willing to live on it and improve it for five years; promoted massive westward migration. **440**

transcontinental railroad A line spanning the continental United States. Congress helped the Union Pacific and Central Pacific railroads build it by providing land grants, cash incentives, and loans.. **441**

Great Plains Vast open territory stretching east to west from present-day Missouri to the Rocky Mountains, and north to south from North Dakota to Texas. **443**

Exodusters More than twenty thousand ex-slaves who in 1879 left violence and poverty in the South to take up farming in Kansas. **444**

Mormons A religious sect founded in upstate New York in 1830. Driven by persecution they headed west in 1846 and settled in a valley in Utah near the Great Salt Lake. **445**

Grange Originally founded in the fall of 1867 by Oliver H. Kelley as a social and educational society for farmers, it became a major political force in the Midwest in the mid-1870s. **449**

Long Drive The annual cattle drives of more than 1,000 miles from Texas to the Great Plains that started in 1866 and established the ranching industry in the West. **449**

Sand Creek Massacre A massacre of some two hundred Cheyenne Indians on November 29, 1864, in Colorado by a military outfit known as the Colorado Volunteers under Colonel John M. Chivington. **454**

Battle of Little Bighorn Lt. Col. George A. Custer and the Seventh Cavalry are wiped out by a force of Cheyenne, Sioux, and Arapaho warriors on June 25, 1876; hardens white attitudes toward Native Americans. **456**

Dawes Severalty Act 1887 law that started the breakup of reservations by offering Native Americans allotments of 160 acres of reservation land to encourage them to become independent farmers. **458**

Wounded Knee Massacre U.S. soldiers open fire on a group of Sioux Indians on December 29, 1890, killing between two hundred and three hundred. **461**

"Buffalo Bill's Wild West" A circuslike production begun in 1883 that helped create a romantic and mythological view of the West in the American imagination. **462**

Frontier Thesis Historian Frederick Jackson Turner's 1893 theory that extolled the positive role the frontier had played in shaping the American character and consequently American institutions. **464**

CHAPTER 16

Wonder and Woe

The Rise of Industrial America, 1865–1900

> **"This association of poverty with progress is the great enigma of our times.... It is the riddle which the Sphinx of Fate puts to our civilization, and which not to answer is to be destroyed."**
>
> HENRY GEORGE, *Progress and Poverty*, 1879

This scene of industrial discontent, *The Strike* (1886) by artist Robert Koehler, was inspired by the great railroad strike of 1877. Set in an unidentified industrial town, it captures a moment of confrontation as workers pour out of a factory to gather outside the office of their employer. Unlike most scenes of labor unrest painted or drawn in the late nineteenth century, Koehler presented these workers as sympathetic characters, painting each as an individual rather than as nondescript members of a mob. Many wear square hats popular among various skilled trades, suggesting that these are more established workers. They appear as hardworking and hard-pressed men voicing their anger to the employer, perhaps over a wage cut or a round of layoffs, through the spokesman at the bottom of the stairs.

Yet the painting is fraught with tension and an atmosphere suggestive of impending violence. Notice, for example, the worker in the foreground stooping to pick up a rock. Maybe he is doing this merely as a dramatic show of anger, but perhaps he fully intends to throw it. Note also the scene to his left where a woman tries to calm down another angry worker. Again, it is not clear that she will succeed. And what about the employer? He appears to be listening patiently to the workers' representative, but whether he will accede to their demands is unclear (his stiff, emotionless bearing suggests he will not).

The uncertainty in the painting over both what is about to happen and which side—workers or employer—is in the right illuminates a central theme in American society as it experienced rapid industrialization in the late nineteenth century. The last third of the nineteenth century saw the United States thoroughly transformed by the Industrial Revolution, from a predominantly agricultural nation that ranked well behind England, Germany, and France to the world's most formidable industrial power by 1900.

While many Americans celebrated the Industrial Revolution for the unprecedented material wealth and progress it brought to American society, others grew disturbed by some of the grim consequences of industrialization, especially the immense power accrued by big businesses and capitalists and the growing number of workers living in squalid slums. The result of these conflicting visions was an intense debate—much of it vividly captured in Koehler's painting—over the proper role of government in regulating the economy, the rights of workers to form unions and strike for better wages and working conditions, and the impact of growing disparities of wealth on America's republican traditions.

What aspects of industrialization worried Americans in the late nineteenth century?

The Emergence of Big Business p. 470

Creating a Mass Market p. 478

The World of Work Transformed p. 483

Conflicting Visions of Industrial Capitalism p. 489

The Emergence of Big Business

America's huge supplies of key raw materials, its rapidly growing urban workforce, and its tradition of imposing few restraints on business enabled the explosion of industrialization after the Civil War. The railroads quickly emerged as the first big business, followed by steel and petroleum. All three industries pioneered in establishing modern business practices, but they also drew increasing criticism as Americans worried about their extraordinary power.

Sources of the Industrial Revolution

Compared to most of Western Europe, the United States was a relative latecomer to the Industrial Revolution, which made its rise to industrial supremacy by 1900 even more astonishing. Every statistical comparison between 1860 and 1900, from factory production to railroad mileage, told the same story of phenomenal growth that saw the Gross National Product rise 171 percent (**16.1**).

Several crucial factors combined to allow the United States to surpass all other industrialized countries by 1900. First, the nation possessed enormous quantities of two essential ingredients for rapid industrialization: raw materials and cheap labor. Vast deposits of bituminous coal in Pennsylvania and Kentucky, for example, provided a seemingly inexhaustible supply of inexpensive fuel to fire steam locomotives and factory machinery. Other plentiful resources included iron, lead, copper, silver, and gold, as well as wood, cotton, and oil. Cheap labor came from two sources. Record levels of immigration (see Chapter 17) in the late-nineteenth century pushed the number of foreign-born to one in five American workers (two in five in manufacturing and mining) by 1910. Likewise millions of American-born workers moved from rural settings to manufacturing centers in search of new opportunities. Women and children, both immigrant and native-born, also entered the workforce in growing numbers.

The incessant development and widespread

16.1 The Industrial Revolution by the Numbers
During the second half of the nineteenth century, every area of the economy produced enormous increases in output and value. Huge population increases helped to drive industrial and farm output.

	1860	1900	% Increase
Population	31,450,000	76,212,000	142.3
Farms	2,044,000	5,737,000	180.7
Value of Farms	$6.64 billion	$16.60 billion	150.0
Factories	140,500	510,000	263.0
Value Factory Production	$1.9 billion	$13 billion	584.0
Industrial Workers	1.3 million	5.1 million	292.3
Patents Issued	4,589	95,573	1982.7
Coal	20 million tons	270 million tons	1250
Lumber	10 billion board ft.	40 billion board ft.	300
Cotton	3.8 million bales	10.1 million bales	165.8
Oil	500,000 barrels	45,824,000 barrels	9064.8
Railroads	30,000 track miles	193,000 track miles	543.3
Steel	13,000 tons	10,382,000 tons	79,761.5
Gross National Product	$7 billion	$19 billion	171.4

What role did human migration play in fostering American industrialization?

adoption of new technology, a reflection of what many called the inventive spirit of the age, also furthered industrialization in the United States. Inventors flooded the U.S. Patent Office with applications, raising the number from an average of 1,000 per year in the 1850s to 20,000 per year in the 1890s.

Some notable inventors, such as George Eastman (Kodak camera), William S. Burroughs (adding machine), Isaac Singer (sewing machine), Alexander Graham Bell (telephone), and Thomas Edison (incandescent light bulb, phonograph, motion picture camera, mimeograph machine, and more) went on to become business giants. Less well known were the many women, immigrant, and African American inventors who filed thousands of patents in this period. For example, Jan Matzeliger, an immigrant of African and Dutch heritage from South America, invented a machine that simplified the most difficult and time-consuming step in the making of shoes (**16.2**). While much of shoemaking had become mechanized by the 1880s, the difficult "lasting" process—attaching the upper portion of a shoe to the sole—could only be done by hand. Matzeliger's lasting machine (patented in 1883) was a remarkably complex device, yet was easy for unskilled workers to operate, allowing manufacturers to greatly boost production while slashing costs.

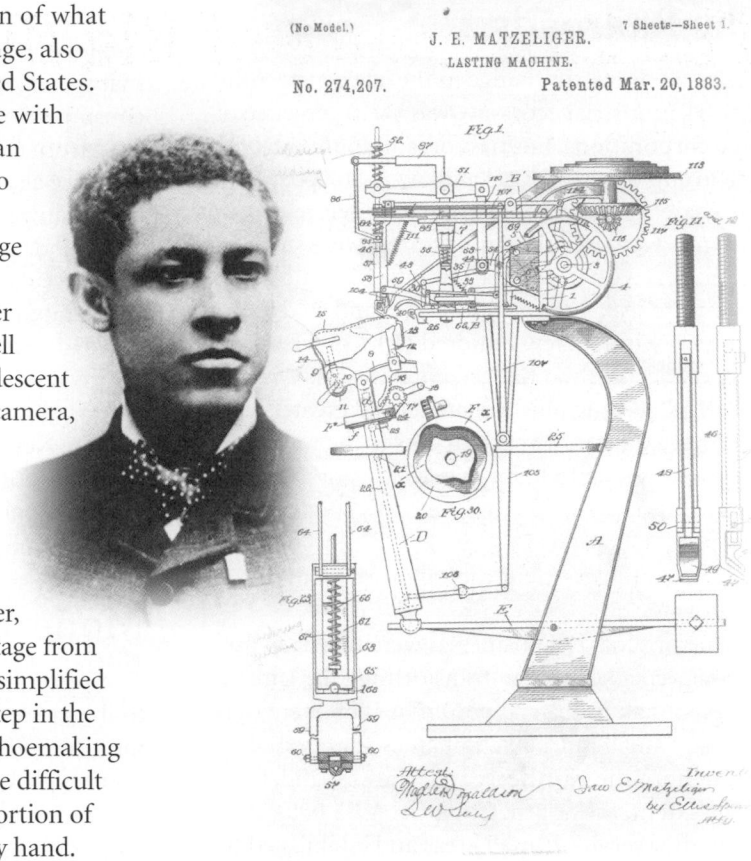

16.2 The Matzeliger Lasting Machine
Jan Matzeliger's complex sewing machine wiped out jobs for skilled shoe "lasters," who had hand-stitched shoe tops to soles, but allowed for a huge increase in mechanized shoe production.

Government policy likewise played a key role in furthering American industrialization. The federal government and the states extended substantial support to railroad projects that totaled almost 180 million acres in land grants and $500 million in loans and tax breaks (see Chapters 13 and 15). Public officials, in an argument later used to justify government support for the Interstate highway system and the Internet, defended this largess by arguing that railroads generated economic growth that benefited everyone from travelers to farmers to manufacturers. High federal tariffs that raised the price of imported goods, thereby helping domestic manufacturers, represented another government policy that promoted industrialization.

Yet the government also promoted industrialization by inaction. Public officials, business leaders, and conservatives subscribed to the philosophy of **laissez-faire** (French for "let do" or leave alone), which argued that the government should impose no restraints on business, including workers' demands for laws to regulate the hours of work, safety conditions, and wages. Government officials also ignored reformers' demands for statutes curbing cutthroat business practices and the establishment of an income tax. As Thomas Nast's political cartoon vividly shows (**16.3**), business and government leaders argued government interference harmed the American economy, depicted here as a woman weighed down by government-imposed burdens such as income taxes, laws (regulations), and "ideal" money (money not backed by gold). The closed shop and idle ship in the background and the vulture circling overhead all suggested these policies would kill the economy. Widespread support for laissez-faire among lawmakers left capitalists to operate in a market free of the restraints of government regulation.

16.3 Defending Laissez-Faire
This 1878 cartoon warns that government interference with the economy threatens the well-being of the nation.

How did government officials defend the practice of making huge land grants to the railroads?

The Railroads

The most dramatic change in the late nineteenth-century industrial economy was the emergence of large **corporations**, business organizations established by a group of individuals and owned by people who buy shares of stock in the company. Before the Civil War, most American manufacturers were small-scale operations with fewer than twenty-five employees. They were usually privately owned and sold their products within a few hundred miles of where they were made. All this changed after 1865, as entrepreneurs, seeking bigger markets and greater profits that they could now reach thanks to the railroad and telegraph, began to form massive corporations that boasted thousands of employees in a single factory complex, operations in several states, and millions of dollars of investment capital raised from the sales of stock.

The original big businesses were railroads, and they played a key role in transforming the United States into an industrial power. In 1865 there were scores of small railroad companies scattered throughout the Northeast and Midwest and, to a lesser extent, the South. Comprising 35,000 miles of track, they serviced small areas and established their own standards for things such as track gauge (the distance between the rails). Nearly all suffered from financial instability and poor management. But by 1900, this haphazard system had developed into a massive, consolidated, and integrated national railroad network of 193,000 miles dominated by just seven large corporations.

Railroads grew at such a ferocious pace because they could be built almost anywhere, creating a transportation network no longer confined to meandering rivers and expensive, slow-to-construct canals that often froze in winter. The railroad also offered another great advantage: speed. People, mail, and goods traveling by stagecoach might, on a good day, cover 50 miles. A steam locomotive pulling many times more people, mail, and goods could cover the same distance in less than two hours. And after the completion of the first of several transcontinental lines in 1869 (see map 15.7) the railroad offered service from coast to coast.

The railroad meant more quick and cheap transportation, both boosts for the national economy. Wherever railroads were built new areas of settlement opened. Farmers settled on nearby land, often sold to them by the railroad company, confident that they could get their agricultural produce to market. Shopkeepers, artisans, laborers, and railroad employees (one million by 1900) settled in towns that sprang up along the tracks. In turn they became consumers of finished goods brought by the railroad from eastern manufacturers. The railroad industry also contributed to the national economy by consuming large quantities of iron, steel, coal, and wood.

Fierce competition among railroads initially led to the rapid expansion of lines. By the 1870s, many railroads tried to diminish competition by buying out rival railroads, leading to the creation of giant corporations such as the Pennsylvania Railroad and the New York Central Railroad. Both owned thousands of miles of track in many states, employed tens of thousands of workers, and handled millions of dollars in investment capital and revenue.

Modern Business Practices

The success of the large railroad corporations led to the modernization of business practices in two important ways. First, railroad corporations allowed other types of businesses to see the advantages of incorporating and issuing stock. Stock sales allowed corporations to raise capital to expand the business (for example, to buy new and more efficient equipment, or to buy a rival company). If the company earned a profit, stockholders benefited from an increase in the value of the stock (which they could sell for a profit) and sometimes by earning dividends. Stockholders played no direct role in running a company; a professional management team performed that function. But stockholders also enjoyed "limited liability": If the company failed they were not liable for any of its debts or obligations, but they stood to lose only their shares. By the 1870s increasing numbers of companies involved in manufacturing, mining, communications, and finance had incorporated.

Second, the sudden emergence of huge railroad corporations operating in many states, employing thousands of workers, and handling millions of dollars encouraged the development of modern, sophisticated management practices. Chief among these practices was standardization. For example, in 1883, the nation's major railroads established the four time zones that are still in use today. This decision helped to combat the problem of irregular "local time" (for example, when local time in New York City was 12:00 p.m., it was 11:55 a.m. in Philadelphia and 11:47 in Washington, D.C.) that

How did railroad grants both reflect and promote national economic growth?

> "Railroad time, it appears, is to be the time of the future. And so, people will now have to marry and die by railroad time. Ministers will preach by railroad time, and banks will be required to open and close by the same time. The sun is no longer the boss of the job."
>
> *Indianapolis Sentinel,* 1883

often led to costly accidents between trains sharing a single track or crossing at a junction.

Similarly, the development of standardized equipment like couplers, signals, and brakes allowed for easier operation and maintenance of a railroad's growing fleet of rolling stock. In 1886 the railroads also established a standard gauge for track of 4 feet 8.5 inches, thereby eliminating costly delays caused by the need to transfer cargo from one train to another wherever tracks of two different gauges met. As this drawing (**16.4**) indicates, many Americans viewed standard gauge as bringing both economic and political benefits to the nation, since it promised to create both a more efficient railroad system and greater unity between the less developed South (see Chapter 14) with the rapidly industrializing North. The banner "The Last Spike in Our Commercial Union" likens the event to the 1869 completion of the transcontinental railroad.

To oversee these vast commercial operations—the largest in the world—executives of the major railroads, such as Jay Gould, Tom Scott, and Collis B. Huntington, developed complex hierarchies of superintendents, managers, and clerks and new systems of accounting, advertising information management, and pricing. Other big businesses, such as steel, oil, manufacturing, and retailing, soon copied these organizational practices, making them the norm in most large corporations.

Rising Concern over Corporate Power

Americans greeted the astonishing spread of the railroad with mixed feelings. Many agreed with poet Walt Whitman, who celebrated the railroad as "the modern emblem of motion and power—the pulse of the continent." They delighted in the benefits of inexpensive and speedy travel and increased access to finished goods in new mail order catalogs.

16.4 Celebrating the Standard Gauge, 1886
In this imagined scene Northerners and Southerners celebrate the adoption of a standard rail gauge as a measure destined to bind the country together economically.

What advantages did standardization bring to business?

16.5 Demonizing the Monopoly Americans grew increasingly worried about the rising power of railroads, the largest of which were often criticized as monopolies that strangled their competition.

Yet many Americans worried about the larger implications of the railroad. The cartoon depicting the Southern Pacific Railroad as a ravenous octopus (**16.5**) expressed their concern. The railroads and the fabulously wealthy men who ran them (shown in the eyes of the octopus) wielded immense power. The artist labeled the octopus a **monopoly**, a popular term to describe the control of an industry or market by one corporation. Was such unchecked power vested in the hands of so few people, worried the critics, compatible with the nation's republican principles? Many feared it was not—especially when it became clear that railroad executives routinely used their wealth to bribe state legislatures, members of Congress, and cabinet officials. Additional revelations of stock manipulation, price gouging of farmers and manufacturers, exploitation of workers, and shoddy construction and unsafe operation added to the railroad's tarnished image and fueled concerted efforts to curb its power. Although few critics raised the issue at the time, later generations decried the railroad for its role in hastening the defeat of the Plains Indians and the near extermination of buffalo upon which they depended (see Chapter 15).

Growing anxiety and anger over the abusive practices of many large railroads eventually compelled reformers to seek tighter regulation of the industry. Given the immense power and wealth of the railroad and a general reluctance among politicians to regulate business, reform faced many setbacks. Farmers, bitterly opposing the high rates charged by railroads to transport and store agricultural commodities, led the first significant effort to curb laissez-faire business practices. Known as the Grange (see Chapter 15) it led a successful political movement in the 1870s to pass numerous laws regulating prices and outlawing unfair business practices.

Andrew Carnegie: Making Steel and Transforming the Corporation

Of all the new things produced by the explosion of industrial output after 1865, none was more important than steel. Many times stronger than iron, steel became the essential ingredient in the transformation of America into an industrial society, allowing for the construction of the railroad and telegraph networks and tall buildings called "skyscrapers." Steel also allowed for the construction of huge factories, filled with powerful manufacturing machinery—made from steel, of course. Steel likewise accelerated the commercialization of American agriculture as the material that made possible sharp, durable, and deep-cutting plows and mechanical reapers. It also altered modern warfare, enabling the development of more accurate, powerful, and thus more deadly weapons. Steel, in short, was as influential and revolutionary a substance in the late nineteenth century as silicon (used to make computer chips) was to become in the late twentieth.

Steel was important in still another way, for it brought to prominence the single most influential big business man of the era, Andrew Carnegie.

Why did many Americans come to see railroads as potential threats to democracy?

Carnegie's success was all the more remarkable because of his humble origins. Born in Scotland in 1836, he immigrated to America with his family at the age of twelve. Settling in Pittsburgh they struggled to earn a living. Young Carnegie dropped out of school and took a job in a textile factory where he earned just $1.20 per week. Bright and ambitious, Carnegie took night classes in accounting, taught himself telegraphy, and went to work for Western Union. In 1853 Pennsylvania Railroad regional supervisor and future company president, Thomas A. Scott, hired the seventeen-year-old to serve as his personal telegrapher and eventually private secretary. In this capacity, Carnegie learned every detail of modern business practices that the railroad was developing. With his higher salary, he invested in railroads, factories, and, increasingly, the iron and steel industries.

In 1870 while running a very successful company that built steel bridges, Carnegie decided to move entirely in steel production. He built his own steel works and, drawing upon his knowledge of railroad management, he followed obsessively one fundamental business principle: reducing production costs to the lowest possible level.

To achieve this goal, Carnegie hired the brightest executives, accountants, managers, scientists, and engineers. He also invested heavily in the latest technology. He was the first to invest in the breakthrough Bessemer-Kelly process, a method of making exceptionally strong steel quickly and at low cost (in part due to reducing the need for skilled metalworkers).

Carnegie's focus on cost control led him to pioneer what is in the business practice known as **vertical integration**, the organization of a business by which one company controls all the main phases of production, from acquiring raw materials to retailing the finished product. Other industrial magnates who came to dominate their industries opted for a **horizontal integration**, a model where they bought out many companies producing the same product to eliminate competition and achieve greater efficiency (**16.6**). To provide a steady supply of cheap coal, iron, and other essential raw materials that steel production depended on, Carnegie bought mines, smelting operations, railroads, and ships.

Finally, Carnegie pursued cutthroat practices to battle rival steel producers. To drive smaller rivals out of business, Carnegie slashed his prices to levels that bankrupted his competitors, allowing him to buy them out and gain a greater share of the market.

VERTICAL INTEGRATION Seeking to bring under one company the many different products and processes that go into the making of paper, Company A has acquired forests, logging companies, railroads, and chemical companies, as well as paper manufacturing plants. The advantages in this system are lower prices for and greater control over supplies of essential materials (such as wood pulp from trees).

Paper Company A Acquires

Forests
(to supply pulp needed for paper)

Logging Company
(to harvest the trees)

Railroad
(to bring lumber and chemicals to the paper factory and to ship the finished product to market)

Chemical Company
(to manufacture chemicals like bleach needed to make paper)

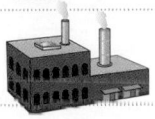

Paper Factory
(to manufacture the paper from pulp)

HORIZONTAL INTEGRATION Seeking to gain the largest share of the market for paper products, Company B has acquired five more paper manufacturing companies. The advantage of this system is that Company B can generate more revenue from the added production and sales of paper products. It can also lower costs by eliminating redundant operations like advertising, marketing, and accounting in the acquired companies in favor of single operations covering these functions. Because of its increased size, the company can also lower costs by striking deals with suppliers (wood pulp, chemicals, etc.) eager for its business.

Paper Company B Acquires

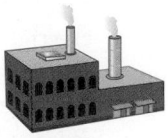

Paper Company

Paper Company

Paper Company

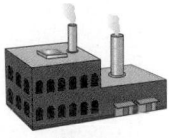

Paper Company

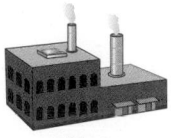

Paper Company

16.6 Horizontal Integration versus Vertical Integration
Industrialists pursued two strategies when seeking to expand the size of their corporation. With vertical integration they sought to minimize costs and increase control of production by acquiring different kinds of companies involved in the chain of production. Through horizontal integration they attempted to reduce competition by acquiring their competitors.

What policies contributed to Andrew Carnegie's success in business?

Like many other industrialists, he also signed secret deals with railroads, securing lower transportation rates for his steel than that charged by his competitors. Most of these tactics were legal at that time, but many critics considered them abusive.

The result of Carnegie's business policies was astonishing, bringing annual profits to $40 million by 1900. By then Carnegie Steel was the largest corporation in the world, with more than twenty thousand employees and related operations in many countries. Carnegie's success was part of the much larger story of the "age of steel." By 1900 the U.S. steel industry employed 272,000 workers who that year produced 10.4 million tons of steel—an output more than twice that of its nearest rivals, Germany and Great Britain.

Rockefeller and the Rise of the Trust

Carnegie was the most famous industrialist in the late nineteenth century, but countless others similarly led the way in developing key parts of the American economy. These included entrepreneurs like Philip Armour and Gustavus Swift (meat-packing), James B. Duke (tobacco products), George Eastman (Kodak camera) and Cyrus McCormick (farm equipment). Like Carnegie these industry leaders and thousands more succeeded by combining vision and ruthlessness, leading the public to both laud them as "captains of industry" who offered an ever-growing number of new products and services and denounce them as "**robber barons**," greedy capitalists who grew rich by devious business practices, exploitation of workers, and political manipulation.

The industrialist most frequently denounced as a robber baron was John D. Rockefeller. In many ways his rise to dominance in the oil industry resembled that of Andrew Carnegie. Through relentless cost-cutting, acquisition of new technology, hiring top-notch managers and scientists, and making secret deals with railroads to undermine his competition Rockefeller's Standard Oil company controlled more than 80 percent of the nation's oil-refining capacity by 1879. Unlike Carnegie, Rockefeller initially expanded his interests via horizontal integration (**16.6**), focusing almost exclusively on buying or building oil refineries. Later he followed Carnegie's vertical integration model as well, purchasing oil fields, railroad cars and warehouses, pipelines, and barrel factories.

Rockefeller's chief contribution to the rise of big business was the invention of two new forms of corporation management: the trust and the holding company. Like many industrial magnates, Rockefeller upheld the ideal of competition, but privately he believed competition between rival companies merely created waste and instability in the market. When so-called pools—secret deals between ostensibly rival companies to set production limits to keep prices high and award each participant a certain share of the market—inevitably failed, Rockefeller devised the trust.

Unlike pools, which lacked any legal basis and thus carried no penalty for cheating, **trusts** were legally binding arrangements that brought many companies in the same industry under the direction of a single board of "trustees." To join a trust, a company turned over to a board a majority of its stock in exchange for trust certificates, which guaranteed it a share of the profits. Rockefeller's Standard Oil Trust, for example, consisted of forty companies under the direction of a nine-member board of trustees selected by Rockefeller himself. As profits soared, dozens of trusts in other industries, such as sugar, lead, cotton, and oil, were formed, although not all successfully.

> "Honest labor never rusts: up with labor down with trusts."
>
> Banner in 1889 Boston Labor Day Parade

The rapid emergence of giant trusts, as with the rise of large railroads, alarmed many Americans. Fueling this rising concern was the unwillingness of Congress and the Supreme Court to curb the power of big business. In 1886 the very conservative Supreme Court declared that state railroad commissions did not have the authority to impose regulations on railroads because only Congress had the right to regulate interstate commerce (*Wabash, St. Louis & Pacific Railway Co. v. Illinois*, 1886). In a separate case (*Santa Clara County v. Southern Pacific Railroad*, 1886), the court also declared that corporations were "de facto persons" and thus subject to all the protections under the Fourteenth Amendment. No state or local government, therefore, could impose limits on corporations "without due process of law"—in other words, approval by conservative federal courts.

Why did big business find trusts so useful and attractive?

The next year in 1887 Congress attempted to curb the power of the railroads by establishing the Interstate Commerce Commission and making pools and rebates (special discounts by railroads to favored customers) illegal. But the ICC proved weak and ineffective, especially in the face of a conservative Supreme Court. Of the sixteen cases when railroads challenged a ruling by the ICC between 1887 and 1905, the Supreme Court sided with the railroads fifteen times.

Big business also benefited from enormous political influence in Congress. In this damning 1889 cartoon, *The Bosses of the Senate* (**16.7**), from the popular magazine *Puck*, the bloated trusts are clearly in charge. Congress was all too willing to do the bidding of corporate interests. Note that the doorway marked "People's Entrance" is boarded shut while a much larger "Entrance for Monopolists" is wide open. Note too the bitter conclusion that big business has subverted American democracy: "This is a Senate of the monopolists, by the monopolists, and for the monopolists."

The fate of the **Sherman Anti-Trust Act** of 1890 seemed to verify this conclusion. It was originally proposed as a law that empowered the Justice Department to prosecute any illegal contract, combination, or conspiracy among corporations that was designed to eliminate competition or in any way restrain free trade. In other words the act made trusts illegal. But months of lobbying by corporate interests influenced Congress to word the final version of the act so vaguely that it was essentially unenforceable. As a result, the Justice Department prosecuted only eighteen antitrust cases between 1890 and 1904.

Rockefeller's other major corporate management innovation—the **holding company**—replaced the trust in the 1890s as the preferred big business model. The holding company was a huge corporation that bought and ran other corporations by purchasing their stock. Rockefeller's idea caught on immediately because it offered protection from the Sherman Act and allowed for the creation of enormous corporations, many of which exercised near monopoly control of the market. Corporate mergers occurred at an astonishing pace in the 1890s, so that by 1900 a mere 1 percent of corporations controlled 33 percent of the nation's manufacturing output, a figure that rose to 44 percent by 1910. The same was true of the railroads. In 1900 seven colossal railroads controlled two-thirds of the nation's track mileage. Big business, despite the best effort of reformers, was here to stay.

16.7 The Political Power of the Trusts Reformers criticized trusts for their power to bribe and bully Congress to pass favorable legislation. Here, a meek-looking Congress sits under the domineering gaze of the bloated trusts.

Why did efforts to curb the power of trusts fail?

Creating a Mass Market

Railroads, oil refineries, textile factories, and steel mills were the most vivid symbols of the industrial era, but production was only one part of the story. Equally important was consumption—getting the public to purchase the growing array of the national economy's new products. The development of advertising would play a crucial role in creating a consumer culture, as would the department store and mail order catalogs.

The Art of Selling

To promote consumption, businesses developed sophisticated advertising techniques and marketing strategies. Many hired psychologists and other experts to develop advertising campaigns that appealed to both consumers' fears and their desires. Ads for toothpaste and deodorant, for example, stoked the public's fears of bad breath and body odor, while those for pianos and fine clothing played to desires to appear sophisticated and wealthy. Advertisers also cultivated brand loyalty through catchy slogans and impressive claims. The makers of Ivory Soap, for example, touted their product's healthful qualities with the impressive, but ridiculously exaggerated, claim that it was "99 44/100% Pure." Recognizing the value of celebrity, some manufacturers hired famous entertainers and athletes to endorse their products and allow the use of their pictures in ads. The underlying idea of advertising—spending a portion of a business's profits to generate more profit—soon became a standard business principle. Spending on advertising jumped accordingly, from $50 million in 1867 to more than $500 million by 1900.

As advertising caught on among manufacturers and retailers, competition led to increasingly complex and sophisticated advertisements. Gone were the days from before the Civil War when advertisers relied exclusively on a few bold headlines in a newspaper or magazine and some accompanying text touting a product's quality and price. With so many advertisements jamming the pages of these media, and adorning roadside signs, sides of buildings, and grocery store windows, a product's advertisement had to be eye-catching, convincing, and memorable. Advertisers began experimenting with new styles and sizes of type, developed catchy slogans, and enlisted celebrities and "experts" like doctors to vouch for their product. Once developments in print technology made it possible and affordable, they focused increasingly on images to sell their products. (See *Images as History: Advertising and the Art of Cultivating Anxiety and Desire,* page 480.)

Shopping as an Experience: The Department Store

With the emergence of advertising came the development of the department store. Irish immigrant Alexander Turney Stewart established the first in New York City in 1846. Stewart and the entrepreneurs who copied his idea built giant stores that offered a huge selection of goods, usually organized into different "departments." Customers also found a small army of clerks ready to assist them and fixed prices that eliminated uncomfortable negotiations. Retailers also offered attractive policies such as the money back guarantee and free delivery.

By the 1870s customers, increasingly called "shoppers," flocked to department stores not only for the selection, price, and convenience but also for the experience. Retailers had discovered that it was not enough to offer the finest products at good prices. Shopping had to be a pleasurable experience, so merchants built palatial, richly decorated "emporiums," an impressive Latin term meaning a

> "You can now buy your pins, your outing shirts, your wines, your prayer books, your Indian clubs, your pianolas, your false teeth, your automobiles, ... [and] your spectacles ... in the same place."
>
> *The Wall Street Journal,* 1903

Why did advertising become so important to business success?

store that displayed a large variety of merchandise. One of the first merchants to do so was John Wanamaker, who took over a Philadelphia railroad depot and in 1876 opened a massive and opulently decorated store he called the Grand Depot.

In the coming decades rival stores sought to outdo each other in size and splendor, and customers came to look forward to store openings. On September 12, 1896, for example, 150,000 New Yorkers paraded through the new Siegel Cooper store on opening day. This new "shopping resort," as the *New York Times* called it, employed eight thousand clerks and cashiers and one thousand drivers and packers. The store offered not only a huge selection of merchandise but also conveniences such as telegraph and long-distance telephone services, offices for foreign currency exchange and stock trading, and a dentist office. As this photograph (**16.8**) of the central lobby shows, the store also wowed shoppers with its lavish interior. Note the marble columns and high, decorative ceilings, as well as the statue at right of "The Republic," a copy of the one recently designed by the renowned American sculptor Daniel Chester French for the 1893 World's Fair in Chicago. It rested in a large fountain where streams of water illuminated by colorful lights flowed over it.

The success of the department store led some retail entrepreneurs to expand their operations to large regions or even the whole country. The most noted figure in this field was Frank W. Woolworth, whose "five and dime" stores specialized in low prices rather than opulence. He opened his first store in Utica, New York, in 1879. By 1900 he owned fifty-nine stores, a number that eventually topped six hundred nationwide by 1911. Like their big business counterpart in manufacturing, Woolworth and other national retailers found that with size came certain advantages. Because they bought huge quantities of goods, Woolworth received big price discounts from wholesalers and manufacturers that in turn allowed him to sell his merchandise at low prices.

Bringing the Market to the Frontier

Some entrepreneurs realized that in spite of advertising and the growth of department stores, a massive retail market remained untapped: rural America. Living on farms or in small towns far from cities, these potential customers had money and desire but lacked access to consumer goods. In 1872 Montgomery Ward set out to change that. If rural

16.8 Shopping as an Experience
Large retailers in cities built lavishly appointed shopping palaces to attract customers. The Siegel-Cooper store in New York City opened with great fanfare in 1896.

How did retailers justify spending so much money to build lavish stores?

Images as History

ADVERTISING AND THE ART OF CULTIVATING ANXIETY AND DESIRE

At first advertisers used images simply to display their product, both to show potential buyers what it looked like and to convince them of its quality. But by the 1880s advertisers began to take literally the old maxim, "a picture is worth a thousand words." They began using images to link certain powerful ideas, sentiments, values, and aspirations with the product. Often advertisers used images without ever showing the product itself. This 1887 advertisement for the Williams' Shaving Stick, a four-inch cylinder stick of shaving soap, that appeared in *Century Magazine* provides a vivid example of this new approach. There was a growing trend among American men in the late 1880s toward a clean-shaven look (or at the very least to confining facial hair to a mustache), a

Nude imagery was considered scandalous and unacceptable in late nineteenth century society. The use of a widely respected religious image, however, allowed the advertisers to grab readers' attention while not offending the public.

By asserting that "Shaggy, unkempt beards were common among the fallen, barbarous nations," the ad suggests that America's rising status in the world depends on its men taking up the razor (and Williams' Shaving Stick, of course).

This full-page advertisement omits an image of the product being sold. Instead it devotes half the page to a religious image and the rest to cleverly crafted words.

The Williams' Shaving Stick
This full-page ad ran in the November 1887 issue of *Century Magazine*.

Instead of using the image of an anonymous man sporting a whisker-free face and a smile of contentment, the advertisers opted for Michelangelo's *Adam at the Time of Creation*, an image most of their target audience—educated middle- and upper-class men who read *Century Magazine*—would recognize and respect.

Note the religious and moral imperative in this phrase: If God created Adam without a beard, the advertisement implies, then God must want all men to be clean-shaven!

How did advertisers cultivate anxiety to generate sales of their products?

trend that benefited manufacturers like J. B. Williams Co. To lure existing shavers to the Williams' Shaving Stick and to convince more men to shed their beards, the company used religious imagery and text to generate anxiety among men over their appearance. What other associations and messages do advertisers often try to convey through images?

This 1885 advertisement poster for the New Home Sewing Machine, designed to hang in a public space such as a train station or store, represents a different use of visual imagery in advertising. Unlike the Williams' Shaving Stick advertisement's effort to instill anxiety, it appeals to the consumer's desire for a more refined and wholesome life.

So central is this machine to creating a "new home" of middle-class tranquility that this woman has included it in the scene she is painting, suggesting that it is part of the family.

Liberated from the dismal, time-consuming task of sewing by the "Light-Running New Home Sewing Machine," this middle-class housewife is free to pursue more refined activities such as painting.

The quality of the sewing machine is taken for granted, for it sits in the background.

The happy child in the picture suggests that women who buy the machine will have more time to devote to the well-being and proper rearing of their children.

Even though this intricate and expensive-looking dress would most likely have been made by a professional and sold in a store, the ad implies that it is easily made with the New Home Sewing Machine.

The New Home Sewing Machine
The New Home Sewing Machine Company created this poster in 1885 to promote their product as beneficial to the American family.

America could not get to a department store, he would bring it to them—in the form of a single broadsheet offering two dozen items for sale by "mail order."

Ward's idea proved so successful he steadily expanded his list of offerings. By 1884 Ward presided over a thriving enterprise based on a catalog of 240 pages featuring some 10,000 items. By this time a rival mail order company run by Richard W. Sears and Alvah C. Roebuck had begun operation. Eager to reach this new market, established department stores like Macy's in New York, Jordan Marsh in Boston, and Marshall Field in Chicago followed the trend and brought out their own mail order catalogs.

The reach of corporate retailing beyond urban centers and into rural America (where most Americans lived until 1920) marked the emergence of a mass market. Whereas Americans had long shared a common language and republican political culture, they now developed a shared consumer culture. Exposed to the same advertising images and appeals, millions of Americans in different parts of the country began to adopt the same fashions, develop the same habits (cigarette smoking, for example), and purchase the same newfangled contraptions, including more than one million bicycles a year in the 1890s.

Selling to the World

As the nation's industrial production soared to unprecedented heights, manufacturers began to look for new markets for their goods. The United States had long been an exporter of agricultural products like cotton and wheat, but the leading trend after the Civil War was the export of manufactured goods. The total value of exports rose between 1870 and 1900 from $450 million to $1.5 billion, with the percentage of manufactured goods rising from 15 to 32 percent.

In addition to selling produce and goods overseas, American business interests also began to invest heavily in business ventures in foreign countries. By 1897 Americans had invested $635 million in mines, plantations, oil wells, and increasingly, manufacturing plants ($94 million). By the 1890s the Singer Sewing Machine Co. was an international corporation (**16.9**). With a factory in Kilbowie, Scotland, as well as in the United States, Singer sold its machines throughout the world. Note how the advertisement's text, "The Singer Seam unites Two Continents," and angelic female figures suggest that the company is pursuing humanitarian as well as capitalist goals. Farm equipment giant, International Harvester, likewise opened factories in Canada and Norrkoping, Sweden.

The globalization of the American economy brought many benefits to workers, consumers, and investors. But it also contributed to the growing sentiment in the 1890s that the United States needed to become an imperial power to protect overseas investments and ensure that markets in Asia, Africa, and Latin America remained open.

16.9 The Globalization of American Industry Like many large American corporations, the Singer Sewing Machine Co. became an international corporation by the 1890s, selling its machines throughout the world.

How did advertising promote the development of a national consumer culture?

The World of Work Transformed

The huge industrial enterprises built by Carnegie, Rockefeller, and others ultimately depended not on their individual genius but on the collective labors of American workers. As the number and size of factories grew in the late nineteenth century, the size of the industrial workforce expanded rapidly, from 1.3 million workers in 1860 to 5.1 million in 1900. Many of them faced hardships: long hours, low pay, dangerous conditions, and frequent downturns in the economy. Workers responded by forming unions, staging strikes, and protesting the surging power of business as a threat to democracy.

The Impact of New Technology

The constant introduction of new technology that marked the Industrial Revolution resulted in much more than increased manufacturing output. Even more important was its impact on the status of industrial workers. New machines produced more goods in less time and usually required only low-skilled labor to operate. Machinery transformed shoemaking, for example, from a skilled trade in the 1820s to a low-skill factory occupation by the 1860s. The same was true in the garment and textile industries. Because they could easily replace low-skilled labor, employers could pay them low wages and demand long hours. They could also simply fire or replace workers who complained or failed to keep up the pace with other unskilled workers.

This trend occurred unevenly across industrial America. For example in building trades like carpentry and bricklaying, new technology did little to undermine the position of skilled craftsmen. In other settings new technology created new opportunities for some workers. Some found well-paid skilled work as mechanics, while others became foremen and floor managers who oversaw the work of unskilled operatives. These more fortunate workers often enjoyed far higher wages, shorter hours, and better treatment compared to the unskilled.

Nonetheless for many workers new industrial technology eliminated their skilled jobs in favor of unskilled ones. Just as shoemaking changed from a skilled trade in the 1820s to a low-skill factory occupation by the 1860s, so did the garment and textile industries. In these settings, employers enjoyed increasing power over their employees for the simple reason that unskilled workers were easily replaced.

Hard Times for Industrial Workers

New technology was but one of many difficulties confronting industrial workers in the age of industrialization. Most workers complained about long hours and low wages. Although averages for both varied by industry and region, workers often toiled twelve hours each day, six days a week, for wages that barely covered weekly basic living expenses. By some estimates the average wage earner in the late nineteenth century made $400–500 per year, when living decently required a minimum of $600–800. Working-class families made up the difference by sending their children to work, taking in boarders, and bringing in "home finishing" work, performed by women, such as sewing buttons on new shirts.

Compounding the precarious economic position of wage earners was the "boom and bust" character of the industrial economy. Severe depressions (1873–1877 and 1893–1897) and recessions interrupted periods of prosperity and economic growth. Each **depression**, or "bust" as it was called, involved a contraction of economic growth, widespread business failure, and high rates of unemployment lasting several years. The severe depression of the 1870s, for example, resulted in the loss of more than a million jobs and nearly fifty thousand businesses. Those who did keep their jobs often found their wages slashed and hours increased by employers desperate to remain solvent or ruthless enough to take advantage of rising job competition between the employed and the unemployed. The monotony of industrial work likewise added to the difficulties wage earners faced. Many did work that forced them to perform the same task repeatedly, such as pulling a lever on a metal stamping machine. Workers felt, in the words of one machinist in 1883, that they were

How did new technology weaken the independence of skilled workers?

becoming "part of the machinery," a state of affairs they found "very demoralizing."

The industrial workplace was also extremely dangerous. Every year between 1880 and 1900, 35,000 workers (on average) were killed on the job and another 500,000 injured. This carnage resulted in part from the monotony of factory work, which led mind-numbed workers to make mistakes or fall asleep. But most injuries stemmed from the factory owners' negligence. With no laws compelling them to make their workplaces less lethal, few industrialists were willing to incur the expense of installing safety devices or procedures. Not until the early twentieth century did most states begin enacting laws requiring compensation be paid to injured workers or the families of killed workers.

Another disturbing trend in this era was the sharp rise in child labor. Before the Industrial Revolution children of farmers and artisans performed all sorts of work that contributed to the family economy—but always under the supervision of a parent or relative. Children working in industry, however, left their homes to work in factories and mines under the supervision of a manager rather than a parent. Between 1880 and 1900 the number of children younger than sixteen years of age working for wages—usually a fraction of those paid adults—skyrocketed from 180,000 to 1.7 million. Children as young as seven toiled long hours in dangerous conditions in mines and factories, working at jobs that exposed them to dangerous and unhealthful conditions. The boy in this photograph (**16.10**) lost his arm while operating a power saw in a box factory. Many states passed laws prohibiting child labor, but they rarely enforced them.

16.10 The Price of Child Labor Because they could pay children less than one-half the wages of an adult, employers hired increasing numbers of child laborers in the late nineteenth century, depriving them of education and often exposing them to industrial hazards.

Exploitation, Intimidation, and Conflict

Central to the transformation in the lives of workers ushered in by industrialization was the increasing power exercised by employers in the workplace. Since profit was their paramount goal, employers imposed strict discipline on their industrial workers. The clock came to dominate the workplace, as employers demanded workers begin and end their day (with a few short scheduled breaks) at precise times. Workers who arrived late or took unauthorized breaks were fined or fired. Some factories forbade workers to talk to one another—or worse, to whistle.

> "I make about three dollars a week, and my sister—she is only six years old—she does not make as much, sometimes a dollar a week, sometimes more."
>
> An eight-year-old child laborer, New York, 1871

Enforcing these new rules was an increasingly important figure in the industrial workplace: the manager or foreman. In sharp contrast to the early nineteenth-century preindustrial economy, few workers now ever saw, let alone spoke to, their employer. Instead, they dealt with managers or foremen hired to run a factory as efficiently and profitably as possible. This meant pushing workers to meet production goals and firing those who were unable to keep up or who caused trouble. Many foremen came from working-class backgrounds and treated workers fairly, but others could be abusive, especially those overseeing workers of a different ethnic background. Female workers were particularly vulnerable to abuse. In this drawing from 1888, the foreman in a garment factory shakes his fist at a weary female worker, urging her to work faster (**16.11**). In the larger inset, the overworked woman sprawls on a bed in a dingy tenement. That this image ran under the sensational title *The Female Slaves of New York* in a popular newspaper that often expressed hostility toward workers indicates the notoriety the foreman had achieved in the garment industry by the late nineteenth century.

Workers also found it difficult to organize labor unions. The first major effort to build a national labor movement after the Civil War began in 1866 when William Sylvis, a charismatic iron molder, founded the National Labor Union (NLU). A federation of independent craft unions, the NLU sought to unite skilled workers nationwide to secure demands such as a federal law establishing the eight-hour day and a federal department of labor. Its membership topped 300,000 (nearly all native-born white men in skilled trades) by 1869. But Sylvis's

What factors made industrial workplaces so dangerous?

16.11 Exploiting Female Workers
Shop floor foremen and managers became increasingly important as the size of workplaces grew. As demands for greater productivity grew, female workers were especially vulnerable to abusive foremen. The threat of overwork to the health of women is emphasized in the two insets. One depicts workers carrying heavy bundles of work home while another shows an exhausted laborer collapsed on her bed.

sudden death that year weakened the NLU, and the depression of the 1870s wiped it out completely.

Most employers saw unions as threats to their profits and freedom to run their businesses as they wanted. Many hired spies to expose labor organizers so they could fire them and put them on **blacklists**, lists of workers that employers in a particular town or industry refused to hire because they were considered trouble-makers. During strikes, employers routinely resorted to replacement workers. In this effort they usually enjoyed the cooperation of local officials, who ordered policemen to drive away or arrest pickets gathered outside a workplace. If a labor dispute went to court, an employer could more often than not count on a favorable ruling by a judge or jury. On top of all this, workers faced one over-riding problem—few unions had the financial resources to support striking workers for more than a few weeks. Strikers, one worker attested, "have had nothing to combat capital with except their empty stomachs, while the capitalists have had unlimited financial resources and have been able to starve the workingmen into submission."

Not surprisingly, rising worker frustration and anger led to an increasing number of strikes and violence. Between 1881 and 1905 American workers staged 36,757 strikes that involved more than six million workers. One particularly bitter incident took place in Pennsylvania. In response to the abusive labor policies of coal mine bosses in the 1860s, miners had formed a union called the Workingmen's Benevolent Association (WBA). Many of its members were Irish immigrants some of whom, drawing on the tradition of secret societies that resisted oppressive landlords in Ireland, formed a clandestine labor organization known as the Molly Maguires that carried out acts of intimidation, vandalism, violence, and occasionally, murder against foremen and managers. In 1874 mining interests set out to destroy the WBA by convincing the public that it was one and the same as the Molly Maguires. Within a year this campaign resulted in more than fifty arrests and numerous convictions—many on questionable testimony and with little or no evidence. In all, twenty alleged Molly Maguires were hanged for murder, including ten on a single day, June 21, 1877. Note how in this drawing (**16.12**) public officials created a powerful public spectacle designed to emphasize the men's guilt and, aware that a majority of the region's miners were Catholic, to emphasize their sinfulness.

16.12 The Pageantry of Execution
On June 21, 1877, "Black Thursday," Pennsylvania officials staged carefully planned executions of ten convicted miners known as Molly Maguires.

Why were employers so hostile to labor unions?

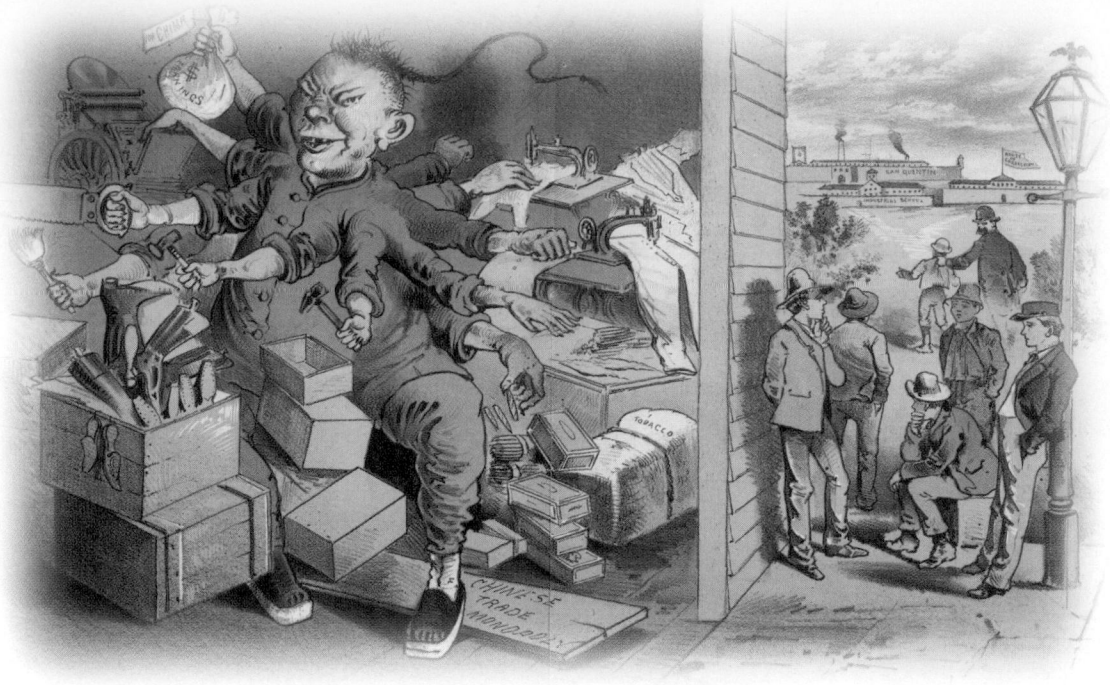

16.13 Hard Times Fuel Anti-Chinese Racism
During the depression of 1873–1878, workers blamed high levels of unemployment on Chinese immigrants, whom they accused of working long shifts for low wages.

Three weeks later, on July 14, 1877, the largest strike in the world in the nineteenth century erupted. The "Great Uprising" of railroad workers began in Martinsburg, West Virginia, and quickly spread to Baltimore, Philadelphia, Pittsburgh, St. Louis, Chicago, and other cities. The strike involved thousands of workers, and violence emanated from both sides. In Pittsburgh, for example, soldiers opened fire on striking workers and their families, killing twenty and wounding twenty-nine. Enraged by the killings, strikers and their supporters attacked the troops and the Pennsylvania Railroad stockyards, resulting in the destruction of all the terminal's buildings and other property.

The mainstream press expressed some criticism of the railroads for slashing workers' wages, but most dismissed labor activism as illegal, ill-informed, and un-American. (See *Competing Visions: The Legitimacy of Unions.*)

While workers in this period faced hostility from employers, politicians, and journalists, they also had to contend with animosity within the ranks of labor that often hindered their ability to organize. Deep hostility often existed between skilled and unskilled workers, who frequently viewed each other as having little in common. Workers were also riven by disputes arising from different ideologies, including several varieties of **socialism**, a theory that rejected capitalism and advocated common ownership of private property and greater social and economic equality. They also argued the persistent question of whether workers' interests were best served by pressuring the major political parties or by forming an independent labor party.

Perhaps the most significant divisions among workers centered on race and ethnicity. A rising tide of immigration in the late nineteenth century brought greater ethnic, racial, and religious diversity to an already diverse workforce, making more difficult the task of uniting them in common cause. For example, when hard times hit during the depression of the 1870s, anti-Chinese sentiment among American workers soared, ultimately leading to the **Chinese Exclusion Act**, a law enacted in 1882 barring Chinese immigration to the United States. As the cartoon (**16.13**) from *The Wasp* demonstrates, Chinese workers were blamed for taking jobs from Americans. The artist depicts a twelve-armed Chinese worker, drawn in racist caricature, laboring maniacally at a dozen tasks while young American-born workers stand idly near a factory. One of the workers is being hauled away by a policeman, implying that unemployment has led him to a life of crime.

African American workers also faced racist hostility from white workers, especially as they began moving to Northern cities in increasing numbers in the 1890s. Much of this hostility stemmed from the widely held racist beliefs of the day that told white workers they were superior to blacks. But it also emanated from the fear that African Americans would take jobs from white workers—a fear exacerbated when employers occasionally used black workers as strikebreakers.

Why were industrial workers so divided?

Competing Visions

THE LEGITIMACY OF UNIONS

While conflict between workers and their employers often centered on wages and hours, it also occurred over the legitimacy of labor unions. Many Americans denounced unions as illegal, foolish, and un-American. The editor of *Scribner's Monthly*, writing in the aftermath of the 1877 Great Uprising of railroad workers, reflects this view as does the accompanying image from *Puck*. Workers and their advocates like John Swinton, editor of a pro-labor newspaper in New York, offered a very different vision of labor unions as vital organizations that protected workers from the most extreme forms of exploitation. Why did employers find unions so objectionable, even dangerous? What benefits did workers see in unions?

Scribner's Monthly (October 1877)

And now that it is over, it is a good time to ask once more what good has come from this strike, and what good has come of any strike. The laws of nature which, after all, govern the laws of trade ... can never be overcome or circumvented by a strike. Labor will always command its value—no more, no less. ... Strikes are always mistakes; they are often crimes.

The day of the inauguration of trades unions and labor organizations in this country was a day the blackest and fullest of menace to the popular prosperity and peace that ever dawned upon the nation. They have been an unmitigated curse to employers and employed alike. The nature and purpose of these organizations are simply outrageous. They have been despotic toward their own members, oppressive toward the class in whose interest they pretend to have been established, impertinent and intermeddling. They have assumed the right to control property and business in which they had no more right than if they lived in the moon. There should be in the good sense of the great mass of laborers a reaction against this wretched crime, and this stupendous foolishness.

John Swinton's Paper (January 27, 1884)

There are many who cannot understand why Trades Unions exist here. They have heard them described as alien to the American craftsman, causing strikes, and raising ill-feeling generally between... employer and employe[e].

In the present state of industry, Trade Unions are a necessity, recognized as such by the great majority of intelligent workmen, ... and securing for their members a partial degree of protection without which they would sink into depths as yet unfathomed.

There is a hue and cry against the Unions as agencies that provoke strikes. In nine cases out of ten, strikes are made necessary by circumstances over which the Unions have no control whatever; sometimes they are a protest against unendurable reductions in wages ... sometimes by unjust conduct on the part of bosses or corporations. No Union to-day orders a strike that can be avoided by reasonable means; no Union orders a strike without full consideration of the subject and after a fair vote. ...

But we are told that no strike ever brings any advantage to the strikers ... This is a mistake that cannot be made by any one who has observed the results of strikes either in the United States or in any other country. ...

But strikes often fail,—yes, it is true. Capital often triumphs in the conflict with labor,—true again. Yet capital would be even harsher and more exacting than it is, if it were not for the protest of the strike, and the warning that it gives. The wages which, in many industries, are but little above the living point, would be put down and kept down to the starvation point, if the men accepted with submissive spirit every reduction of wages, and all the severe terms that capital tries to enforce.

This Puck magazine cartoon from the mid-1880s portrayed labor union officials as tyrants who hurt the interests of workers

Why do labor activists argue that unions are defensive in nature?

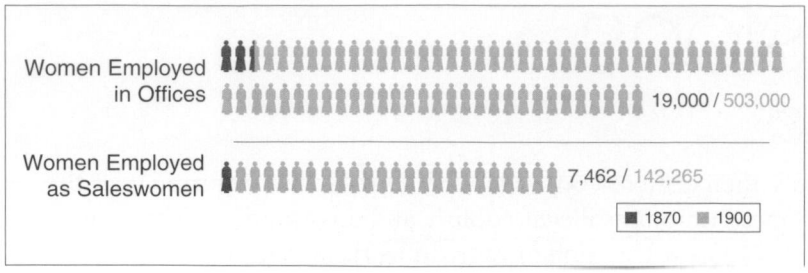

16.14 Rising Numbers of Women in the Paid Workforce Economic necessity and a desire for greater independence brought millions of women into jobs outside the home.

New Roles and Opportunities for Women

Economic necessity brought millions of women into the paid workforce. Whereas just 13 percent of women worked outside the home in 1870, 20 percent did so by 1900. Nearly all these women were single and younger than twenty-five years of age. Domestic service (cooking, cleaning, and childcare in the homes of middle- and upper-class families) remained the leading occupation for wage-earning women in this period, but increasing numbers also took on factory work, especially in the garment and textile industries. Like their male counterparts, these women factory workers labored at repetitive tasks for long hours and in unsafe conditions—but for only half (or less) the wages of men. Employers justified this disparity by claiming women worked merely for extra money whereas men worked to support whole families and therefore deserved higher pay. In fact, many working-class families depended for their survival on the earnings of their sixteen- to twenty-five-year-old daughters. Factory owners simply paid them less because women were powerless to prevent it.

While increasing numbers of women took jobs in factories, the Industrial Revolution also produced a vast array of other kinds of jobs that women came to fill. The emergence of modern corporations requiring armies of secretaries, clerks, and stenographers, combined with the invention of the telephone, adding machine, and typewriter, created new opportunities for educated, native-born, white women (**16.14**). Teaching, social work, and, as indicated in the graduation photograph of the Philadelphia School for Nurses (**16.15**), nursing emerged in the late nineteenth century as an almost exclusively female professions. These fields, even though they represented new opportunities for women, were deemed appropriate because they drew on what was widely believed to be women's "natural" role as nurturers. The pageantry evident in this photograph, especially the bright white and highly professional uniforms, the elegant setting of the Philadelphia Academy of Music, and the presence of Red Cross founder Clara Barton (seated at center), indicates the high reputation the profession had achieved by the turn of the century.

Regardless of the level of work, social custom dictated that women leave the paid workforce soon after they married (only 5 percent of married women worked outside the home in 1900). Of necessity, working-class women continued to earn money to support their families. Only now they did so from within the home by taking in boarders, laundry, and "piece work," which paid by the piece rather than by the hour.

Far larger numbers of African American women, more out of economic necessity than custom, remained in the paid workforce even after marriage. In urban areas in both the North and South, many worked as domestic servants in white middle- and upper-class homes, providing cooking, cleaning, laundry, and childcare services. These jobs required long hours and paid low wages, but racist hiring policies in industry and other sectors of the economy left African American women with few options.

16.15 Women Find Opportunities in Nursing These graduates of the Philadelphia School for Nurses, with Red Cross founder Clara Barton at center, were among the thousands of young women in the late nineteenth century who flocked to the nursing profession.

What factors explain the surge in the numbers of women entering the paid workforce?

Conflicting Visions of Industrial Capitalism

As the Industrial Revolution unfolded in the late nineteenth century, Americans of all classes, occupations, and regions felt its impact. For many it was an age of wonder, marked by a steady succession of new inventions, ideas, and possibilities. Yet one did not have to look far for signs of anxiety, fear, and discontent. Numerous critics in the last decades of the nineteenth century offered a different vision of society, emphasizing the growing poverty, gaps between the rich and poor, and inequality.

Capitalism Championed

The late nineteenth century witnessed an enthusiastic celebration of industrial capitalism and the many benefits it brought to American life. Proponents noted that every year American industry produced more consumer goods, ranging from inexpensive clothing in a dizzying array of colors and styles to exciting new products like phonographs and bicycles. It also generated new forms of transportation that allowed people, including the poor, to travel to new and different places. The introduction of industrial technology to farming led to stupendous annual harvests, falling food prices, and a more varied diet for the average American, who saw life expectancy rise from a mere 38.3 years for white men in 1850 to 50 years by 1910. Industrial technology such as the telegraph, telephone, and steam-powered printing press allowed for the unprecedented spread of information and literacy (aided by an expanded public school system). And in spite of unrest, depressions, and strikes, real wages for the average worker rose 50 percent between 1860 and 1900 (74 percent for skilled workers and 31 percent for unskilled). To these optimists industrial capitalism meant progress.

Of the enthusiastic champions of the new industrial order, none was more fervent and influential than Andrew Carnegie. He offset his hard-driving corporate style with a carefully constructed public image designed to set him apart from many of his fellow industrialists who angered the public with arrogant pronouncements. William K. Vanderbilt, for example, once brushed aside the suggestion that his business practices violated the law by saying, "Law! What do I care about the law? Hain't I got the power?"

In countless speeches and in articles in prominent magazines, the nation's most famous industrialist defended the status quo and emphasized its virtues. He argued that men of industry like him were not, as critics charged, greedy, abusive monopolists. Rather they were visionaries who built key industries that brought immeasurable benefits to Americans, including thousands of jobs for workers and countless products that improved the quality of life. Granted, Carnegie explained in what he came to call the "Gospel of Wealth," he and other entrepreneurs had grown fabulously rich, but this was a necessary and beneficial result of a free economy. Without the hope of future riches, business leaders would not have the incentive to seek new opportunities, take risks, and develop new products.

> "I can hire one half of the working class to kill the other half."
>
> Financier and railroad magnate
> JAY GOULD

Carnegie and other champions of big business also emphasized that industrial fortunes could be—and increasingly were—used to fund philanthropic projects such as schools and libraries. Carnegie was already the nation's most ostentatious philanthropist in 1901, the year he sold his steel empire to financier J. P. Morgan for $400 million. He donated millions to various causes, but most famously to his program of funding public libraries. For a man who was both conservative and optimistic, libraries appeared the perfect form of charity because they provided the

How did business leaders like Carnegie defend industrial capitalism?

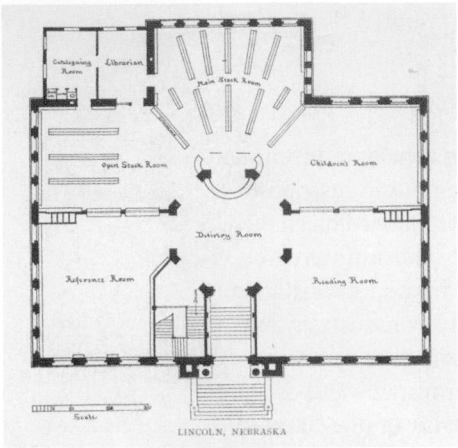

16.16 The Carnegie Library and Floor Plan in Lincoln, Nebraska
As a symbol of the virtue of industrial capitalism and the spirit of individual uplift, steel magnate Andrew Carnegie funded nearly 1,700 public libraries in America. The exterior designs reflected the popularity of classical styles circa 1900. The design of the interiors emphasized the industrial values of order and efficiency.

ambitious, hard-working, and intelligent not with a handout, but rather an opportunity to better themselves. This Carnegie library (**16.16**), built in Lincoln, Nebraska, in 1901, typified the more than 2,500 (1,689 in the United States) libraries funded by Carnegie between 1886 and 1929. Communities awarded a library were allowed pick their own architectural style. Most, like Lincoln, opted for some variation on the widely popular neoclassical style. But Carnegie and his staff that oversaw the program insisted that library interiors follow a general design that stressed efficiency and order—similar to the values reflected in the design of his steel factories. Note how the floor plan allowed for a single centrally located librarian (seated at the curved desk in the center) to monitor all the neatly organized spaces devoted to reading, children, reference, and stacks.

When Carnegie and other defenders of industrial capitalism were asked about the growing problem of poverty amid such progress, they pointed to what they claimed was the greatest virtue of a capitalist economy: the idea of the self-made man. As Carnegie's own life story seemed to attest, anyone, regardless of birthplace, family, education, or poverty, could rise up the ladder of success. Success was by no means guaranteed, noted Carnegie. But for those who possessed self-discipline, intelligence, frugality, and diligence and who avoided liquor, and debt, the future was bright.

Aiding Andrew Carnegie and other optimists in spreading this ideal of the self-made man was Horatio Alger. A former minister, Alger wrote more than one hundred young-adult books, beginning with *Ragged Dick* in 1868, all with similar plotlines, featuring a young boy, often a bootblack or a delivery boy, who lived a life of poverty and irresponsibility on the mean streets of a big city. Through the intervention of a "respectable" man, the boy eventually discovers that he need only end his prodigal ways and pursue education and opportunity to enjoy the good life. Alger sold millions of books and his success inspired imitators who churned out similar books and magazines, including the popular *Fame and Fortune* magazine (**16.17**). As this cover shows, each weekly installment offered dramatic "stories of boys who make money" by exhibiting honesty, diligence, and courage.

Not all conservative defenders of industrial capitalism shared Alger's rosy vision of a society where anyone willing to work hard, save money, and avoid liquor could find success. They subscribed to a theory known as **social Darwinism**, a corruption of British naturalist Charles Darwin's theory of natural selection (later termed "evolution"). Popularized by British philosopher and sociologist Herbert Spencer, he took Darwin's central idea that in evolution, plants and animals that are able to adapt to changing conditions survive while others become extinct,

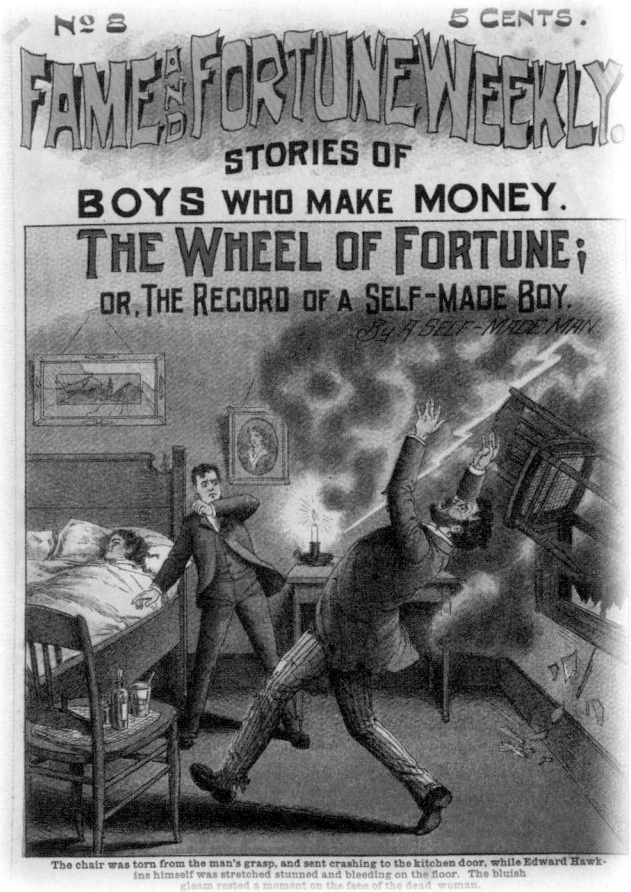

16.17 The Promise of Success
Taking their cue from the success of Horatio Alger's success in writing scores of young adult novels, many imitators published similar books and magazines preaching that reward and respectability could be had if only one worked hard, told the truth, and helped the less fortunate.

Why was the self-made man idea so popular in the age of industry?

tailoring it to fit his idea of modern industrial society as "survival of the fittest." The wealthy and powerful in society were the "fittest," people endowed with innate characteristics of intelligence, strength, and the adaptability that enabled them to succeed in the competitive world of business. And the poor? They were the "unfit," men and women consigned by nature to failure, misery, and early death. To impose government regulation on corporations, proponents argued, was both immoral and impractical, an affront to the laws of nature and God. Equally important, social Darwinism argued against any initiatives public or private to alleviate the plight of the poor, which would lead to the survival and growth of the unfit population with devastating consequences for society.

> "What a blessing to let the unreformed drunkard and his children die, and not increase them above all others. . . . How wise to let those of weak digestion from gluttony die, and the temperate live. What benevolence to let the lawless perish, and the prudent survive."
>
> *The Christian Advocate* (N.Y.), 1879

Capitalism Criticized

Despite these confident assertions on the morality and virtue of laissez-faire industrial capitalism, a host of critics decried the widening chasm between the rich and poor. While some four thousand had become "millionaires" by the early 1890s, millions of Americans lived in poverty, or perilously close to it. A tour of any city provided ample evidence of what some called the "haves and the have nots," people who dwelled in "sunshine and shadow." This cover drawing for Mathew Hale Smith's popular book of the same name from 1869 contrasts the two extremes found in New York City: merchant A. T. Stewart's Fifth Avenue mansion, and a brewery-turned-mission in the notorious Five Points district downtown (**16.18**).

In the former neighborhood were the homes of the Stewarts as well as the Vanderbilts, Astors, Morgans, and Carnegies. They attended opera at the opulent Metropolitan Opera House, entertained each other at lavish balls and dinners, and summered in their fifty-room "cottages" in coastal retreats like Newport, Rhode Island. A few miles downtown in Five Points and the surrounding Lower East Side district, nearly one million people lived in tiny, airless tenement apartments with no running water or toilets. Their neighborhoods had no parks, and their streets were filled with filth due to irregular street cleaning in poor neighborhoods.

A growing number of reformers, ministers, and social critics began to question whether American democracy, with its ideals of equal rights and individual freedom, could endure under such conditions of inequality and enslaving poverty. A self-taught political economist named Henry George, troubled by the growing social inequality and rising class conflict in the mid-1870s, wrote an influential book, *Progress and Poverty*. As the title suggested, George addressed one of the central questions of the age: Must increased poverty accompany industrial and technological progress? If so, he warned, American democracy was doomed. George claimed that the monopolization of resources, especially of land, by powerful elites was to blame for the looming social crisis. Few people understood or supported George's unorthodox solution (a "single tax" on land values), but his vivid diagnosis of the rising clash between labor and capital and his vision of a more equitable social order gained him an enormous following in the 1880s and turned *Progress and Poverty* into a bestseller. In 1886 the United Labor Party nominated George to run for mayor of New York City. He lost the contest but polled 68,000 votes—in an era when labor candidates typically only received a few hundred.

Edward Bellamy achieved a similar level of fame as a critic of laissez-faire capitalism with his

16.18 The Growing Gap between the Haves and Have-Nots The cover of Matthew Hale Smith's book about New York City, *Sunshine and Shadow*, captured the fascination and the fear with which Americans regarded growing poverty amid rising levels of wealth.

Why was the theory of social Darwinism so attractive to the wealthy and successful?

novel *Looking Backward, 2000–1887*. Published in 1887, it told the story of Julian West who, like Rip Van Winkle in another era, falls asleep in 1887 and awakens in the year 2000. To his astonishment he finds American society transformed into a socialist utopia. The class conflict, poverty, and economic inequality of the late nineteenth century are gone. The government controlled the economy, eliminating destructive competition and providing a comfortable living for all citizens. Bellamy's book became a bestseller and his largely middle-class followers established nearly five hundred clubs to spread its message.

Power in Numbers: Organized Labor

Less famous, but in many ways far more influential than critics like George and Bellamy, were the protests of those most buffeted by the Industrial Revolution: workers. Through the pages of labor newspapers and in speeches at worker rallies—and in actions such as strikes—American workers articulated a sharp critique of the new industrial order. A small percentage were socialists, but most supported the broad ideals of a free market economy. Their protest stemmed from the growing conviction that greedy monopolists, in league with unscrupulous politicians, had seized control of the economy and bent it toward their own advantage. As a result, argued workers, they received a shrinking portion of the wealth they created, while working longer hours in increasingly inhumane conditions. Try as they might, these workers claimed, the upward mobility celebrated by Andrew Carnegie and Horatio Alger was less and less attainable.

Unsettled and angered by their declining power in the face of big business, American workers renewed their efforts to organize labor unions. In 1869 a small group of Philadelphia garment cutters met to form The Noble and Holy Order of the **Knights of Labor** (KOL), a labor organization that in the 1880s accepted workers of all trades and backgrounds to become the world's largest industrial union. It called for many of the same reforms as the NLU, but added a long list of radical, even utopian, goals. For example it advocated the replacement of the existing competitive industrial system with an economy based on cooperation. In addition unlike the NLU's emphasis on craft workers, the KOL was an industrial union open to all workers, including unskilled wage earners, immigrants, and eventually women and African Americans. Leaders of the KOL believed that fundamental change in the industrial order was impossible unless this broad spectrum of workers joined forces.

To ensure success in the face of employer hostility, the organization adopted a policy of strict secrecy that necessitated holding meetings in clandestine locations. This requirement, however, combined with the severe economic depression of 1873–1877, hindered its growth. By 1879 it counted just ten thousand members, most in Pennsylvania. Two key developments that year soon propelled the KOL into the national spotlight as the world's largest industrial union. First the national economy recovered from the depression of the mid-1870s, providing wage earners with a measure of economic security that allowed them to form and join local unions in huge numbers. Second, a young machinist named Terence Powderly became the KOL's leader, or Grandmaster Workman. Powderly was a superb organizer and gifted orator who in 1882 abolished the KOL's secrecy rule, a decision that made it possible to recruit thousands of new members and fend off accusations from employers, politicians, and religious leaders that the KOL was a sinister and conspiratorial organization.

Membership soared from 10,000 in 1879 to 42,000 in 1882 (on its way to an eventual peak of more than 700,000 in late 1886). What drew many workers to the organization was the KOL's sharp critique of laissez-faire capitalism and emphasis on economic justice and democracy. Its constitution decried, "the recent alarming development and aggression of aggregated wealth" by industrialists, bankers, and stock speculators, warning that it would soon lead "to the pauperization and hopeless degradation of the toiling masses."

These sentiments and spirit of protest inspired workers in New York City, many of them KOL members, to establish the Labor Day holiday in

16.19 Establishing Labor Day
In 1882 workers in New York City held the first Labor Day celebration. It soon became a national holiday.

Why did so many workers find the Knights of Labor so appealing?

September 1882. The organizers took great care to present workers as orderly and dignified, marching in almost military fashion (**16.19**). Yet they also held aloft signs voicing their grievances ("Abolish Contract Labor" and "8 Hours to Constitute A Day's Work") and announcing their intent to reclaim their influence in the political system ("Vote for the Labor Ticket"). Others proclaimed the importance of workers ("Labor Creates All Wealth" and "Labor Pays All Taxes") and in an age of growing economic inequality, reminded the spectators of key American principles ("All Men Are Created Equal"). The annual Labor Day holiday quickly gained popularity. By 1886 it was a national event, and in 1894 President Grover Cleveland signed into law a measure establishing Labor Day as a holiday for all federal workers.

Another significant aspect of the KOL's vision, albeit one that was not embraced in every part of the country, especially the South, was its inclusion of African American workers as members. Many in the KOL's leadership argued that the union must include all workers, including blacks, because employers would inevitably use them against organized labor to break strikes and lower wages. This same argument for inclusion led the KOL to allow women members. As a result, in an era when labor unions were almost exclusively the domain of white men, the KOL garnered a membership by 1886 that was 10 percent women and 10 percent African American.

Many workers also joined the KOL because of its emphasis on practical goals. Its constitution called for the eight-hour workday, equal pay for men and women, the establishment of state bureaus of labor, and the prohibition of child and convict labor. The KOL also gained enormous support among workers for their successful leadership in strikes. But the decision to strike was difficult and carried great risks. (See *Choices and Consequences: To Strike or Not to Strike?*, page 494).

Most strikes in this period were small and local like the one at Mundell, but on several occasions the Knights of Labor enjoyed success on a grand scale. In 1885 railroad workers affiliated with the KOL won a strike against the Wabash Railroad, owned by financier Jay Gould, a man widely despised and feared by workers. Elsewhere the KOL popularized the boycott, the organized effort to discourage customers from patronizing a business engaged in anti-labor activity, as a very effective labor tactic less costly and risky than a strike.

As the Knights of Labor grew larger in membership and influence in the mid-1880s, it alarmed employers, politicians, and conservatives, who feared its radical rhetoric of class conflict and demands for economic reform. They denounced Powderly and other KOL leaders as radical socialists bent on promoting violence and class warfare. Although neither accusation was true, they made many Americans, including many wage earners, leery of the KOL union and organized labor in general.

The Great Upheaval of 1886

Fear of the KOL in particular and the labor movement in general peaked in 1886. On May 1, 340,000 workers across the country staged a one-day work stoppage to bring attention to their demand for the eight-hour day. Three days later a far more serious incident occurred that would negatively affect the labor movement for years to come. Outraged by the killing of a striking worker outside the McCormick Reaper Works in Chicago, the city's radical labor leaders called for a mass meeting in Haymarket Square on May 4. When three hundred Chicago policemen moved in to violently disperse the crowd, a bomb exploded amid their ranks. The enraged police attacked the crowd with guns and batons. In less than twenty minutes, seven policemen lay dead (most, an investigation would show, from shots fired by fellow police officers) along with four workers. The press quickly dubbed the incident the **Haymarket Incident**, and especially when accompanied by images such as this one (**16.20**), stoked vehement opposition to organized labor. Note the placement of the dead policemen in a sort of martyrs' pantheon above a riot scene depicting "murderous rioters" being gunned down.

16.20 The Haymarket Incident, 1886
The Haymarket incident sparked a nationwide backlash against organized labor. Newspapers ran images like this one, in which martyred policemen hover over a scene where, "murderous rioters" are gunned down.

What role did the press play in promoting a negative impression of labor unions?

Choices and Consequences

TO STRIKE OR NOT TO STRIKE?

Most strikes in the late nineteenth century failed, but the surge in labor activism and the emergence of the Knights of Labor in the 1880s boosted confidence among workers that strikes could succeed. In the summer of 1881, the hundreds of male shoemakers in the Knights Local Assembly 64 successfully opposed a wage reduction by the Mundell Company in Philadelphia. Management then imposed a rate cut on its female shoemakers. One of the workers, Mary Stirling, urged the workers, men and women, to strike until the company rescinded the wage cut. The workers at the Mundell Company considered essentially three major options:

Choices

1. Fearing for their jobs male and female workers refuse to strike.
2. Seeking to protect their recent victory, the men remain on the job while the women walk out.
3. Recognizing their mutual interests in opposing wage cuts for all workers, the male and female workers agree to strike together.

The Mundell Shoe Company was one of the nation's leading manufacturers of footwear in the late nineteenth century

Decision

Inspired by the Knights of Labor motto, "an injury to one is an injury to all," the seven hundred men and women of the Mundell factory decided on option 3, walking out at Mary Stirling's urging. The strike lasted several weeks, during which time the female workers formed their own KOL local assembly—even though the union did not yet allow for female members. Strikers organized pickets, rallies, and fundraisers to help pay for food and rent.

Consequences

The Mundell Company, facing lost profits and pressure to settle from other factory owners who feared worker unrest, rescinded the wage cut. The victory boosted the confidence of the workers and the reputation of the Knights of Labor locally. Within three years the shoe industry alone had eleven local assemblies that managed to win many struggles with employers over wages, firings, and work rules. Even more important, later in 1881 Mary Stirling attended the national convention of the KOL and convinced the organization to admit women. By 1887, 10 percent of the KOL's 700,000 members would be women.

Continuing Controversies

How should organized labor deal with the rising number of women in the workforce?

The admission of women into the KOL did not end the longstanding opposition of many American workers to the rights of women to work and to join unions. They continued to argue that keeping women out of the workforce would open up jobs for men and raise overall wages. When the KOL fell apart in the 1890s, so did the status of women in the labor movement. The American Federation of Labor, the organization that succeeded the KOL, admitted few female members until well into the twentieth century.

What made strikes so risky for workers?

The next day, as hysterical headlines across the nation proclaimed that revolution was at hand, Chicago police arrested eight men, all self-proclaimed anarchists, and charged them with murder. After a hasty trial in which even the prosecution conceded that no one had seen the men throw a bomb, all were convicted. Seven were sentenced to death and one to life imprisonment. Four were subsequently hanged, a fifth committed suicide in his cell. In 1893 Illinois elected a pro-labor governor who pardoned the remaining three, declaring they had not received a fair trial. Haymarket created a climate of fear and provided justification for public officials across the nation to crack down on the labor movement. Throughout the spring and summer of 1886, hundreds of labor activists were arrested—one hundred alone in New York City. In response workers in cities and towns across the nation formed labor parties and ran candidates for offices ranging from city councilor to governor. Most candidates lacked the money or experience to win, but there were some notable surprises. For example Chicago's United Labor Party polled 25,000 votes (of 92,000 cast) and elected a state senator and seven state assemblymen. In Milwaukee, the People's Party elected a mayor, a state senator, six state assemblymen, and one congressman. In one of the most widely watched contests, Henry George, the reformer and author of *Progress and Poverty,* finished a close second in the mayor's race in New York City—out polling Republican Theodore Roosevelt, who finished a distant third.

Several divisive developments, however, soon overwhelmed the unity and hope expressed by workers at the polls in November 1886. First the tumult of 1886 brought to the fore the dissatisfaction of many skilled workers within the KOL. Deeming the organization too strike prone and too influenced by socialists and radicals (who after Haymarket brought organized labor unwanted criticism), twenty-five unions of skilled workers convened in Columbus, Ohio, in December 1886 and founded the American Federation of Labor (AFL). At the same time the more radical activists within the KOL grew dissatisfied with the leadership of Powderly, decrying his growing opposition to strikes and political action. Further weakening the labor movement was a continued atmosphere of anti-labor hysteria in the press and legal repression following Haymarket. Membership dwindled rapidly, falling from its high of 700,000 in 1886 to only 100,000 by 1890.

National leadership of the labor movement after 1886 fell to the newly formed AFL. Comprised exclusively of unions of skilled workers and led by cigar-maker Samuel Gompers, the AFL shunned the KOL's idealistic vision of cooperation. Instead it accepted capitalism and the wage system and focused on what it termed "pure and simple" goals: higher wages, shorter hours, and job security.

The AFL also rejected the idea of organizing unskilled workers, arguing that they were too weak and unreliable. They similarly excluded (with a few exceptions) women, African Americans, and recent immigrants. The AFL would grow to 1.6 million members by 1904. However its narrowed vision and conservative approach to the labor question would leave the growing numbers of less skilled industrial workers without a national voice until the 1930s.

Conclusion

The United States industrialized at a rapid pace after 1865, becoming the world's most formidable industrial power by 1900. For many Americans, especially those who prospered as a result of this transformation, industrial capitalism ushered in an era of progress. But others, especially workers struggling in dangerous factories for long hours and meager wages, industrialization raised troubling questions about economic justice, social equality, and democracy. Thousands joined labor unions and participated in an unprecedented number of strikes. Many middle- and upper-class Americans also worried about the growing gap between the rich and poor and expressed anxiety over the future prospects of America's republican traditions. As a result, this period of industrialization touched off a debate over the proper role of government in regulating the economy and protecting the rights and well-being of its most vulnerable citizens—a debate that would continue into the twenty-first century.

What led to the rapid demise of the Knights of Labor?

CHAPTER REVIEW

1866–1868

William Sylvis founds the National Labor Union
First significant effort to organize workers nationally

Horatio Alger publishes *Ragged Dick*
First of one hundred "rags to respectability" novels popularizing the ideal of the self-made man

1873–1876

The Panic of 1873
Begins four years of severe economic depression

Wanamaker opens Grand Depot in Philadelphia
Sets standard for lavish department stores in an era of increasing consumerism

1877–1878

The "Great Uprising" railroad strike
Massive strike spreads to several cities. Clashes between workers and police and soldiers leave dozens killed and millions of dollars in damage

Terence Powderly elected Grandmaster Workman of the Knights of Labor
Transforms KOL into a powerful industrial union with 700,000 members by 1886

Review Questions

1. What advantages did the United States possess in terms of resources, culture, technology, and public policy that facilitated industrialization after 1865?
2. Why were the Supreme Court and Congress so slow to take steps to curb the power of big business?
3. How was advertising transformed after 1865? What impact did it have on the Industrial Revolution?
4. Why did American workers have such a difficult time uniting to oppose abusive and exploitative employers?
5. In what ways did industrialization create new opportunities for women? How and why were these opportunities limited?
6. What events, ideas, and policies explain the sudden rise of the Knights of Labor in the 1880s? Why did it collapse almost as suddenly?
7. What was social Darwinism, and why did many business leaders and wealthy Americans embrace it?
8. What was the "self-made man" ideal, and why was it so popular in the late nineteenth century? On what basis did some Americans begin to challenge its validity?

1879–1882

Henry George publishes *Progress and Poverty*
The bestseller gives voice to the growing anxiety over growing social inequality

John D. Rockefeller creates the first trust
Becomes a key feature of modern business organization and target of social critics

1882–1883

Workers in New York City establish Labor Day
Reflects strengthening of labor movement and protest against growing inequality and exploitation

Railroads establish Standard Time zones. In 1886 they establish a standard track gauge
Reflects power of railroads and the trend of standardization in business

1884–1886

Knights of Labor wins strike against Wabash Railroad
Gains publicity and credibility for the KOL, leading to a surge in membership

Police and workers clash in Haymarket
Leads to nationwide crackdown on labor union activism

The American Federation of Labor founded
Workers in skilled trades separate from Knights of Labor

1889–1890

Andrew Carnegie publishes "The Gospel of Wealth"
Popularizes the belief that opportunity and upward mobility are available to all in an industrial society

Sherman Anti-Trust Act passed
Reflects popular mood that big business must be restrained; weak and ineffective

Key Terms

laissez-faire (French for "let do" or leave alone) A philosophy that argued that the government should impose no restraints on business. **471**

corporation Businesses owned by people who buy shares of stock in the company. **472**

monopoly The control of an industry or market by one corporation. **474**

vertical integration Business organization where one company controls the main phases of production of a good, from acquiring raw materials to retailing the finished product. **475**

horizontal integration Business organization where one company buys many other companies producing the same product to eliminate competition and achieve greater efficiency. **475**

robber barons A pejorative name for big business leaders that suggested they grew rich by devious business practices, exploitation of workers, and political manipulation. **476**

trust A legally binding deal bringing many companies in the same industry under the direction of a board of "trustees." **476**

Sherman Anti-Trust Act Authorized the Justice Department to prosecute any illegal contract, combination, or conspiracy among corporations that eliminated competition or restrained free trade. **477**

holding company A huge corporation that bought and ran other corporations by purchasing their stock. **477**

depression A contraction of economic growth, widespread business failure, and high rates of unemployment lasting several years. **483**

blacklist A list of workers that employers in a particular town or industry refused to hire because they were considered troublemakers. **485**

socialism A theory that rejected capitalism and advocated common ownership of property and social and economic equality. **486**

Chinese Exclusion Act An 1882 law barring Chinese immigration to the United States for ten years. Renewed several times. It remained in effect until 1943. **486**

social Darwinism The belief that the principles of evolution, which Darwin had observed in nature, also applied to society. Advocates argued that individuals or groups achieve advantage over others as the result of biological superiority, an idea expressed as "survival of the fittest." **490**

Knights of Labor A labor organization founded in 1869 that in the 1880s accepted workers of all trades and backgrounds and became the world's largest industrial union. **492**

Haymarket Incident A violent incident touched off when a bomb exploded amid a group of policemen as they broke up a peaceful labor rally in Chicago's Haymarket Square on May 4, 1886. **493**

CHAPTER 17

Becoming a Modern Society

America in the Gilded Age, 1877–1900

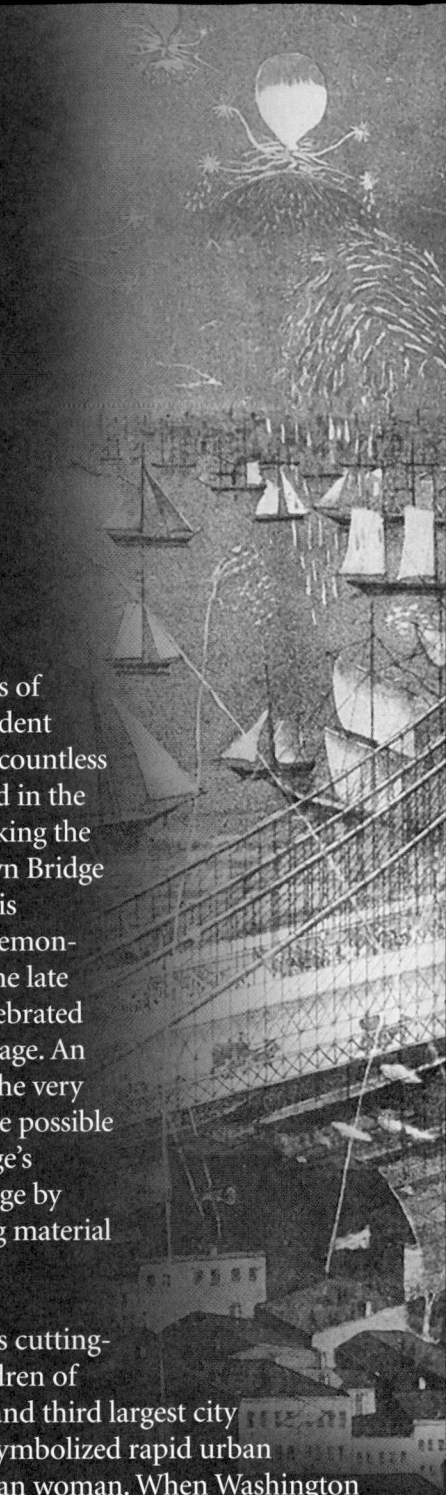

> "The day seems brought distinctly nearer when the nation, equipped with the latest implements furnished by science, shall master and use as never before its rich domain."
>
> REV. RICHARD STORRS, speech at the opening of the Brooklyn Bridge

Hundreds of thousands of people, including President Chester A. Arthur and countless dignitaries, participated in the joyful ceremonies marking the opening of the Brooklyn Bridge on May 23, 1883. As this painting of the event demonstrates, Americans in the late nineteenth century celebrated the onset of the urban age. An astonishing sight and the very embodiment of the modern age, it was the world's largest suspension bridge, a style made possible by the one product that in many ways defined the industrial revolution—steel. The bridge's designer, German immigrant John Roebling, emphasized this transition to the modern age by using a stark contrast: he constructed the bridge's twin towers out of the ancient building material (stone) and formed them into gothic archways, a style reminiscent of the great medieval cathedrals of Europe.

The Brooklyn Bridge embodied the new urban and industrial era in ways beyond its cutting-edge technology and symbolic design. Workers who were either immigrants or the children of immigrants constructed the bridge. By connecting the nation's largest city (New York) and third largest city (Brooklyn), a prelude to their consolidation into one city in 1898, the new bridge also symbolized rapid urban growth. Finally the bridge hinted at the emergence of a new, more independent American woman. When Washington Roebling (who succeeded his father as chief engineer) fell gravely ill in 1872, his wife, Emily Warren Roebling, spent the next eleven years as the project's onsite manager.

The enthusiasm that attended the bridge's opening masked the grave problems that attended rampant urban growth. Indeed the era's name, the **Gilded Age**, reflected this notion that the amazing achievements of the period were like a thin gold layer that covered many unresolved social problems. The sections of New York and Brooklyn connected by the bridge, for example, were vast working-class immigrant districts beset by high rates of poverty, crime, and disease. Equally unseen in the immediate glow of the fireworks was the rising discontent among American workers over exploitation at the hands of employers and alienation from an unresponsive political system. Indeed dozens of men had died during the bridge's construction, and on several occasions workers went on strike. These sentiments and those of hard-pressed American farmers in the heartland would explode in the 1890s, leading to the emergence of the People's Party. The party eventually faded away, but not before establishing a reform agenda that would shape the Progressive Era (1900–1920).

How did the term Gilded Age reflect both the optimism and anxiety of the late nineteenth century?

The Rise of the City
p. 500

A Search for Solutions
p. 506

New Habits, Roles, and Lifestyles p. 512

The Challenge from Below p. 518

The Rise of the City

The United States experienced explosive urban growth in the second half of the nineteenth century. Industrialization and mass immigration transformed both older cities, such as New York and Philadelphia, and newer ones, such as Denver and Chicago, into major metropolises. Their growth was often chaotic and attended by significant increases in crime, poverty, and disease epidemics. City political machines emerged in this period and grew powerful, providing relief to the vulnerable and promoting urban growth, but in the process earning a reputation for corruption.

To the Cities

The urban population of the United States grew at an astonishing rate between 1860 and 1900. In 1860 one in five Americans lived in urban areas. Forty years later the figure had doubled to two in five. In that same period the number of cities with populations greater than 100,000 jumped from nine to thirty-eight. Among these were New York (3.4 million), Chicago (2.7 million), and Philadelphia (1.3 million). Joining these cities in 1900 were seventy-eight more with 50,000 or more inhabitants.

A significant portion of this new urban population came from rural areas within the United States. As agriculture became more mechanized (see Chapter 15), thereby lowering demand for farm labor, increasing numbers of men migrated to urban areas. Similarly the rise of American manufacturing eliminated the need for rural women to make clothes and other household goods, leading many to seek economic opportunity in cities. These men and women found a wide array of job opportunities in the city, ranging from low-paid work as factory operatives, laborers, and domestic servants to more desirable positions as skilled artisans and clerks. They also faced a significant challenge in adjusting to an utterly new lifestyle.

Another rural-to-urban internal migration involved African Americans leaving the Jim Crow South. Seeking to escape the poverty, racism, and violence of the South (see Chapter 14), a growing stream of African Americans began moving to northern cities. Drawn by word of better jobs and greater freedoms, some 300,000 migrated to northern cities between 1890 and 1910. Chicago's African American population jumped from 15,000 in 1890 to 110,000 in 1920. This trend marked the beginning of what became known as the Great Migration, the relocation of some 7 million African Americans from the South to the North between 1890 and 1970.

By far, however, the greatest source of urban population growth was mass immigration from Europe, with significant numbers also from Latin America, the Caribbean, and Asia. Before 1880 the majority of immigrants to the United States came from England, Ireland, Germany, and Scandinavia. But after 1880 the sources of immigration shifted to nations in southern and eastern Europe such as Russia, Italy, Greece, and Austria-Hungary (**17.1**).

17.1 Immigration to the United States, 1880–1920 Before 1880 the majority of immigrants to the United States came from northern and western Europe, but after 1880 most were from southern and eastern Europe.

Source: U.S. Bureau of the Census.

	1880-1889	%	1890-1899	%	1900-1909	%	1910-1919	%
Austria-Hungary	314,787	6.0	534,059	14.5	2,001,376	24.4	1,154,727	18.2
German Empire	1,445,181	27.5	579,072	15.7	328,722	4.0	174,227	2.7
Greece	1,807	.1	12,732	.3	145,402	1.8	198,108	3.1
Ireland	764,061	12.8	405,710	11.0	344,940	4.2	166,445	2.6
Italy	276,660	5.1	603,761	16.3	1,930,475	23.5	1,229,916	19.4
Russia	182,698	3.5	450,101	12.7	1,501,301	18.3	1,106,998	17.4
Scandinavia	761,783	12.7	390,729	10.5	488,208	5.9	238,275	3.8
United Kingdom	810,900	15.5	328,579	8.9	469,578	5.7	371,878	5.8
Totals	5,248,568		3,694,295		8,202,388		6,347,380	

Why did so many people flock to American cities?

All told the United States accepted fourteen million newcomers between 1860 and 1900, followed by another fourteen million between 1900 and 1920.

As with all immigrants before and since, some of these newcomers chose immigration to escape problems ranging from poverty, warfare, political and religious persecution, and natural disasters. But most were drawn by the promise of economic opportunity and upward mobility in America. Some migrated to rural areas and became farmers, but the great majority headed for America's cities and the ever-expanding number of jobs in industry, construction, service, and entrepreneurship found there.

Cities already characterized by ethnic, racial, and religious diversity brought by earlier arrivals of Irish, German, and other immigrants, as well as African Americans, now saw their diversity reach unprecedented levels. By 1910 immigrants or the American-born children of immigrants comprised an astonishing 78.6 percent of New York's population of 4.8 million residents. Chicago (77.5 percent), Milwaukee (78.6 percent), San Francisco (68.3 percent) and most medium to large cities boasted similarly astounding numbers of immigrants and American-born children of immigrants. Overall the foreign-born comprised 14.8 percent of the national population in 1910.

The Emergence of Ethnic Enclaves

These new immigrants spurring the growth of cities, like the Irish and Germans before them, soon formed concentrated **ethnic enclaves** in the cities. Often they moved into neighborhoods previously dominated by immigrants who had arrived before the Civil War. As a result in New York, for example, the Lower East Side enclaves of Little Ireland, Little Germany, and Little Africa became by the 1890s Little Italy, Chinatown, and the Jewish East Side. This process of ethnic succession is captured in a World War I memorial plaque affixed to the façade of the Church of the Transfiguration on New York's Lower East Side (**17.2**). A community of native-born Americans built the church in 1801 as the English Lutheran First Church of Zion, but they sold it in the 1840s to Irish Catholics who renamed it Church of the Transfiguration. In the 1890s a massive influx of Italians and outflow of Irish to other parts of the city turned the neighborhood into Little Italy and Transfiguration into a mostly Italian Catholic church. (Mother Cabrini, later canonized a saint, worked in the church caring for Italian immigrants.) The plaque provides a snapshot of the transformation from Little Ireland to Little Italy. Of the twenty names of parishioners who died in World War I, seventeen are Italian and only three—Donahue, Durkin, and Kane—are Irish. Today the neighborhood is part of Chinatown and most of the parishioners are Chinese.

Immigrant groups formed ethnic enclaves in part because they faced hostility and discrimination from Americans and other immigrant groups. But the primary cause was their recognition that grouping together created important advantages that enhanced their chances of success in America. Italian immigrants living in Chicago's Little Italy, for example, enjoyed the comfort and practical benefits of residing among people who spoke their language. There they could find help getting a job from an immigrant aid association, fellowship in an Italian fraternal society, or solace in an Italian Catholic church. They also found things that reminded them of home: Italian food, books, newspapers, churches, theaters, and opera houses.

A closer look at these enclaves revealed that they usually comprised smaller units composed of people from a particular region or village of their home country. New York's Jewish East Side, for example, included large concentrations of Jews from Hungary, Romania, Galicia, Russia, and Levantine.

17.2 Evidence of Ethnic Succession
This 1919 plaque lists seventeen Italian and three Irish names, indicating that the neighborhood once known as Little Ireland had become Little Italy.

Why did immigrants form ethnic enclaves in cities?

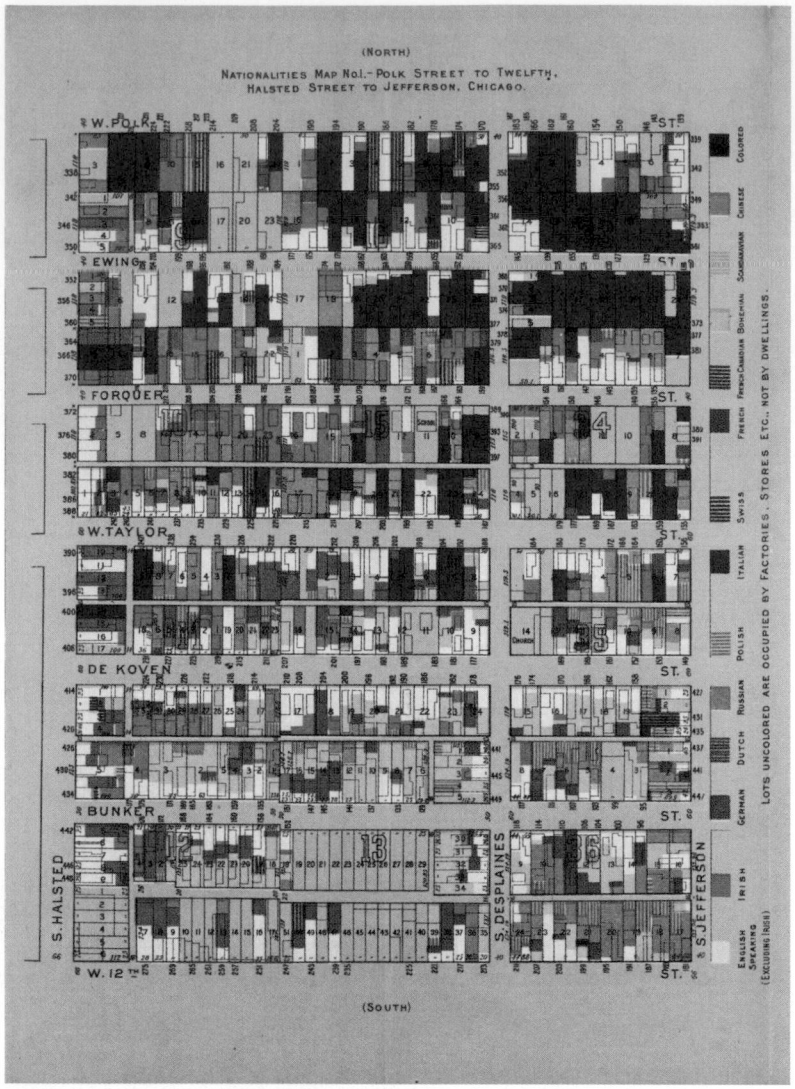

17.3 Mapping the Diversity of Ethnic Chicago
This 1895 map of the twelve-block area surrounding Hull House demonstrates the diversity of the immigrant neighborhood.

Italians living in Boston's North End clustered on certain streets depending on whether they came from Sicily, Campania, Abruzzi, or Liguria. Yet as this 1895 map (**17.3**) of the neighborhood surrounding Chicago's famous Hull House, which provided that city's immigrants with social and educational services, vividly demonstrates, immigrants—even those in ethnic enclaves—shared their neighborhoods with people of diverse origins. This twelve-block section of the city included immigrants from Ireland, Germany, Italy, Russia, Poland, Switzerland, France, Canada, Bohemia, Scandinavia, China, and the Netherlands, not to mention African Americans.

The Troubled City

Many Americans in the late nineteenth century saw cities as exciting places filled with opportunity, cultural diversity, entertainment, and new technology such as electric lighting and skyscrapers. Yet many more viewed cities as places of crowding, turmoil, filth, and despair. Both images were accurate, but the latter generated the most commentary and concern. One of the most striking features of modern urban life was the emergence of densely-packed "slums." In one ward on New York's Lower East Side in 1890, population density reached 334,000 people per square mile, numbers never seen before in history. Most of the people living in these densely packed districts were immigrants who labored for low wages as day laborers and factory operatives. Few men earned enough money to support their families and so they relied on their wives and children to produce additional income (see Chapter 16).

Squalid housing exacerbated the poverty of urban workers. **Tenements**, or multiple family dwellings of four to six stories housing dozens of families, became the most common form of housing for poor city dwellers by the 1860s. Most tenement apartments consisted of just two or three dimly lit and poorly ventilated rooms.

Tenement districts in every city suffered from high rates of disease and death, much of it caused when drinking water became contaminated by disease-causing bacteria due to primitive systems for removing sewage waste. Another source of disease were horses. In 1900 New York's 120,000 horses dropped six million pounds of manure on the city's streets every day! In most cities, as shown in this photograph (**17.4**), street cleaning was inadequate in working-class neighborhoods. Note that in this filthy working-class street in New York, vendors sell all manner of goods on the sidewalks, including food. These conditions contributed to frequent epidemics. In Chicago in 1891, for example, 2,000 people died from typhoid fever and 4,300 from bronchitis and pneumonia. Annually in the same city in the early 1890s some 10,000 to 12,000 children under the age of five died.

Despite the dreadful condition of many tenements, the surging population of American cities kept the demand for housing high, causing rents to rise continually. In New York an 1883 survey of bricklayers, among the city's best-paid wageworkers, determined that they paid 28 percent of their annual income to their landlords. Another survey a few years later revealed that cloakmakers devoted 38 percent of their income to rent. As a result evictions for falling behind in rent occurred frequently. New York averaged more than 16,000 evictions per year in the early 1880s and more than 23,000 by 1892.

What problems made life in tenement districts so difficult?

> "Thousands of small houses and cottages arranged for one family are now packed with a family in each room."
>
> Chicago Board of Health report

Late-nineteenth-century cities also suffered from high rates of crime, especially in the tenement districts. Some crime was driven by poverty or despair. Women, for example, usually turned to prostitution as a last resort means of survival. Immigration also played a role as it resulted in a disproportionately high population of young single men (typically an age cohort with higher than average crime rates). The overall growth, diversity, and mobility of urban populations also contributed to the rising crime rate because these populations fostered a greater sense of anonymity and undermined the ability and will of communities to keep a watchful eye on potential criminal activity.

"Boss Rule": The Political Machine

Another unsettling feature of urban life, in addition to poverty, crime, and disorder, was the emergence of **political machines.** Most often associated with the Democratic Party, these organizations became powerful in nearly every large American city by mobilizing large blocs of working-class and immigrant voters while developing favorable relationships with real estate and business interests. Some machines controlled small sections of big cities. Martin Lomasney, for example, was "boss" of Boston's Eighth Ward in the West End. Others, such as New York's Tammany Hall came to rule the entire metropolis by the 1860s. By the late nineteenth and early twentieth centuries, several machines extended their power to the state level.

Several trends coincided to account for the rise of political machines in American cities. First the spread of universal white male suffrage in the 1820s (see Chapter 8) meant that political success depended less on a candidate's family name or wealth and more on his ability to whip up popular

17.4 Mired in Muck Late-nineteenth-century American cities, especially in working-class neighborhoods, suffered from inadequate street cleaning, leading to public health problems.

What factors contributed to high rates of crime in cities?

enthusiasm for candidates and get out the vote on election day. Rapid urban growth also produced unprecedented opportunities for politicians and their machines to reward supporters with construction contracts and jobs such as police officers and building inspectors. Machines also garnered support from immigrants by denouncing nativism and stymieing anti-immigrant legislation such as proposals to deny public jobs to the foreign born. Finally, the growing numbers of the poor provided a needy constituency for which the machines supplied not only jobs but also a whole range of services and favors including cash handouts, payments for funerals, legal assistance, and seasonal giveaways of turkeys at Thanksgiving and bags of coal in winter. Recipients of machine largesse were expected to vote for its candidates in the coming election.

> "Tammany Hall bears the same relation to the penitentiary as the Sunday-school to the church."
>
> A reformer, 1876

The emergence of political machines horrified many wealthy and native-born Americans. They found rule by the foreign-born threatening and the rough and corrupt style of bosses offensive. One aspect of machine politics, however, aroused especially bitter criticism: the no-questions-asked charity. (see *Competing Visions: How Best to Help the Poor?*).

Political machines acquired and retained power not only by providing services to their constituents but also, as suggested by this political cartoon of boss William Tweed, the notoriously corrupt head of Tammany Hall, by engaging in voter intimidation and election fraud (**17.5**). This image shows that the ballot "box" in many cities was actually a transparent glass ball that allowed the political machine's "shoulder hitters" to intimidate voters by letting them know they were watching to see how they voted. The motto "In Counting There Is Strength" refers to the tactic of political machines to use their influence with the police department and local boards of elections to manipulate the vote count to ensure a victory for their party. Equally important was the enormous amount of money machines garnered by selling patronage jobs, demanding kickbacks from city contractors, and collecting protection fees from a vast economy of vice the machine-controlled police allowed to flourish. Reformers railed against the machine, but consistently failed to defeat it.

17.5 Winning By Any Means
Political machines often resorted to voter intimidation and election fraud. As the motto "In Counting There Is Strength" suggests, vote counts were manipulated to ensure victory.

How did political machines gain the support of working-class and immigrant voters?

Competing Visions

HOW BEST TO HELP THE POOR?

The following documents by George Washington Plunkitt, a member of New York's Tammany Hall machine, and Josephine Shaw Lowell, founder of the Charity Organization Society, offer sharply contrasting views on how best to help the urban poor. How do they differ in their understanding of the causes of poverty? How do these views shape their approach to helping the poor?

In *Plunkitt of Tammany Hall* (1905), George Washington Plunkitt explains the many kinds of aid he dispensed to his mostly poor, working-class constituents in the course of a typical day.

2 a.m.: Aroused from sleep by the ringing of his doorbell; ... found a bartender, who asked him to go to the police station and bail out a saloon-keeper who had been arrested. ... Furnished bail and returned to bed at three o'clock.

6 a.m.: Awakened by fire engines passing his house. Hastened to the scene of the fire.... Met several of his election district captains who are always under orders to look out for fires, which are considered great vote-getters. Found several tenants who had been burned out, took them to a hotel, supplied them with clothes, fed them, and arranged temporary quarters for them...

8:30 a.m.: Went to police court to look after his constituents. Found six "drunks." Secured discharge of four by a timely word with the judge, and paid the fines of two.

9 a.m.: Appeared in the Municipal District Court. Paid the rent of a poor family about to be dispossessed [evicted] and gave them a dollar for food.

11 p.m.: At home again.... Spent nearly three hours fixing things for four men [looking for jobs], and succeeded in each case.

3 a.m.: Attended the funeral [procession] of an Italian as far as the ferry. Hurried back to make his appearance at the funeral of a Hebrew constituent...

7 p.m.: Went to district headquarters and presided over a meeting of election district captains...

8 p.m.: Went to a church fair. Took chances on everything, bought ice cream for the young girls and the children. Kissed the little ones, flattered their mothers and took their fathers out for something down at the corner [at a saloon].

9 p.m.: At the clubhouse again. Spent $10 on tickets for a church excursion and promised a subscription for a new church bell.... Listened to the complaints of a dozen pushcart peddlers who said they were persecuted by the police and assured them he would go to Police Headquarters in the morning and see about it.

10:30 P.M.: Attended a Hebrew wedding reception and dance.

12 P.M. [*sic*]: In bed.

In "The Bitter Cry of the Poor in New York," (1885), Josephine Shaw Lowell explains her belief that excessive charity harms the poor.

[I]t appears that there have been, during the past three years, in New York, 220,976 *persons* who have asked for *outside* charity in one form or another.... What, then, is the secret of this ... disgraceful showing? ...

One ..., is that instead of having been encouraged and helped to be honest, upright, independent, noble, they have been tempted to lie, to cheat, to cringe, to beg; and by whom has this cruel wrong been done? By the churches, by the benevolent people of this city. It is the work of those who think and say that they want to help the poor, but ... [t]hey forget the horrible temptations they are presenting to their fellow creatures. They give, without consideration, one dollar, two dollars, five dollars, never stopping to think how many hours' *work* it takes to *earn* such sums. Imagine how utterly discouraged and disgusted must be the woman who brings home her dollar earned by a hard day's work over the washtub, when her neighbor shows her an order for a dollar's worth of groceries obtained by a trip to ... the office of some relief society. She naturally will cease to struggle so hard to earn her pittance, and will take her neighbor's advice and seek the next dollar she wants where her neighbor has found it so easy to get one.... It is like a contagion.... [H]ere is a neighbor who tells them they can get their rent, can get city coal, can get grocery orders, by going to the right sources of supply. Who could resist the temptation? And so they give up their work, and set forth on their degrading journey.... [T]hey learn to be idle, to be beggars.

Out on the Sidewalk
Eviction was an ever-present fear for many poor and working-class city dwellers.

Why did many Americans worry that the poor were receiving too much charity?

A Search for Solutions

The dark side of urbanization in the late nineteenth century prompted a wide range of competing views and responses. Some Americans concluded that the problem of urban poverty and all the troubling crime, disease, disorder, and corruption that accompanied it was the urban poor, in particular, the foreign-born. Their solution was heightened nativism and a demand for immigration restriction. Other Americans, however, worked to develop government agencies to address the emerging challenges of urban life. Still others established private institutions like settlement houses that reflected a new attitude toward the immigrant poor.

The Nativist Impulse

The rise of the modern American city was accompanied by a revival of nativism, or anti-immigrant views and sentiments. Suspicion of and hatred for the foreign-born had flared up during the Know-Nothing movement (see Chapter 12) in the 1850s, which targeted Irish and German immigrants. In the Gilded Age nativism took aim primarily at the so-called new immigrants, or those coming from southern and eastern Europe. As this 1899 image (**17.6**) illustrates, opponents of immigration in this period decried the newcomers as bearers of a wide range of unwanted habits and ideas. The immigrant, show here in racist caricature of eastern Europeans, carries according to his labels poverty, anarchy, superstition, intemperance, and Sabbath desecration (working or recreating on a Sunday). Note further Uncle Sam's disdainful reaction, but also the sarcastic inscriptions on the gateway—"admittance free," "walk in!" and "welcome"—meant to convey nativists' anger over what they considered lax immigration laws. As slums grew larger and strikes (often involving large numbers of foreign-born workers) became more violent, nativists like Josiah Strong called all the more loudly for the sharp restriction of immigration.

> The city has become a serious menace to our civilization.... It has a peculiar attraction for the immigrant.... Here is heaped the social dynamite; here roughs, gamblers, thieves, robbers, lawless and desperate men of all sorts, congregate; men who are ready on any pretext to raise riots for the purpose of destruction and plunder.
>
> — JOSIAH STRONG, *Our Country: Its Possible Future and Its Present Crisis* (1885)

In 1882 Congress responded to pressure by American workers and passed the Chinese Exclusion Act (see Chapter 16), a law that barred Chinese immigration to the United States. Five years later in 1887 a group of nativists who were especially fixated on the dangers posed by the rising immigration of Catholics formed the American Protective Association (APA) to lobby for immigration restriction. The organization grew to 500,000 members by the end of 1893. Its main base of strength lay in middle-class Protestants in the Midwest, but chapters also sprang up in most cities in the east.

Rising concerns over immigration led Congress to enact legislation in 1890 making oversight of immigration a federal responsibility and establishing immigration depots in most major port cities to screen all immigrant arrivals to weed out and deport those with incurable diseases, radical beliefs, criminal backgrounds, or so little money and skills they seemed likely only to add to the ranks of the urban poor. The largest and most famous of these facilities, Ellis Island, opened in 1892.

Many nativists, considering this new system too lenient, called for additional restrictions on immigration. In 1894 three Harvard graduates founded the Immigration Restriction League, an organization dedicated to lobbying for a literacy test for all would-be immigrants (requiring they demonstrate the ability to read and write in any language). Presidents Cleveland, Taft, and Wilson vetoed the immigrant literacy test bill, but Congress overrode the veto and it became law in 1917.

What fears about immigrants fueled nativist sentiment?

A Different View: Urban Reforms

While some Americans believed urban poverty, crime, disease, and overcrowding could be eliminated simply by restricting immigration, others developed a wide range of innovative policies and institutions to solve, or at least minimize, these problems. To meet the problem of rising crime, most cities followed the lead of New York when in 1845 it replaced the traditional night watch of a few untrained and unarmed men and established a paid professional police department. Similarly large cities disbanded their volunteer fire companies and invested in new technology, such as steam pumpers, and adopted tougher building codes.

More dangerous to a city than fire—at least to its inhabitants—were the frequent outbreaks of cholera, diphtheria, typhoid fever, and other maladies. Drawing on increasing knowledge about germ theory, cities established boards of health and took steps to improve water quality, waste removal, and street cleaning.

The latter half of the nineteenth century also witnessed a movement to build urban parks to provide the beauty and serenity of nature and to offer wholesome and healthy recreation space (as opposed to alleys and saloons) for all. New York City's Central Park, built in the 1850s and 1860s, proved so successful that nearly every large city commenced its own park projects. Because most of the grand parks were located far from the slums, however, reformers in the 1890s pushed urban governments to condemn whole blocks of tenements and build parks within working-class neighborhoods.

Urban reformers also expanded public education. Compulsory education laws (usually requiring schooling until age fourteen) and a massive building campaign saw the number of public school enrollments surge from 6.9 million to 17.8 million between 1870 and 1910. Millions more students attended parochial schools established by the Catholic church. This effort reflected the traditional belief that education made for a productive and informed citizenry. But as the photograph (**17.7**) of children reciting the Pledge of Allegiance illustrates, advocates saw expanded urban public schooling as a means of Americanizing the immigrant masses, teaching them English and respect for democracy and the law. The pledge was first published in a youth magazine in the fall of 1892 as part of an effort to promote patriotism and civic pride among school children on the eve of the four hundredth anniversary of Christopher Columbus's arrival in the New World. Educators quickly adopted the pledge, making its recitation a daily ritual in schools across the country. This earlier style, which required people to end the pledge by extending their arms out straight, was done away with in the 1930s because of its similarity to salutes used in fascist Germany and Italy.

17.6 Fear of Foreigners on the Rise
Decrying the so-called "new immigrants" from southern and eastern Europe as bearers of a wide range of unwanted habits and ideas, nativism surged in the Gilded Age.

What steps did urban reformers take to improve the safety and liveability of cities?

17.7 Promoting Loyalty and Patriotism
Advocates of public education viewed it as a means of Americanizing the urban immigrant masses. Soon after its introduction in 1892, educators quickly made the Pledge of Allegiance a daily ritual in schools.

Capturing a New View of Poverty

Reformers in the Gilded Age also developed a new way of thinking about poverty and its causes. Most Americans at this time held to the traditional view that poverty was caused by personal or moral failures such as laziness or drunkenness. The poor, as Horatio Alger and others argued so persuasively in popular literature (see Chapter 16), needed only to abandon their dissolute ways and seize the opportunities for success that abounded in American life.

But toward the end of the nineteenth century, reformers began to challenge this view of poverty by arguing that factors beyond the control of the poor caused a significant portion of poverty. A key figure in this new outlook was photojournalist Jacob A. Riis, who emigrated from Denmark to New York in 1870. After spending his first years in America struggling in poverty, he gained a foothold in journalism. By the mid-1880s he had earned a reputation as a reporter covering the city's crime beat. But Riis was deeply troubled by the poverty and suffering he saw and decided to publicize the problem in the hopes of gaining public support for reform measures. In 1887 he started taking photographs of slum life to spark public awareness, and by 1888–1889 he began showing his photographs while giving lectures before reform societies and church groups. Spurred by the positive reaction to these talks, especially to the photographs (see *Images as History: Seeing the Poor*), he wrote the book *How the Other Half Lives: Studies among the*

Why was the Pledge of Allegiance adopted in the 1890s?

Images as History

SEEING THE POOR

Riis presented a shocking exposé account of the dreadful conditions in which the poor lived. But unlike most Americans writing about urban poverty in that era, who attributed these problems to the moral failures of the poor, Riis argued that the poor were *victims* of unhealthy and unregulated tenements for which they were forced to pay most of their earnings. Adding to the book's impact were his photographs and drawings made from photographs. His carefully composed photograph, "An Italian Rag-Picker in Jersey Street," shows the viewer her desperate situation.

Riis convinced many of his readers that the growing numbers of impoverished slum dwellers were trapped in circumstances beyond their control largely due to unhealthy and expensive tenement housing. He called for improved tenements that would free the poor from their debilitating circumstances and allow them the chance to succeed. As a result of *How the Other Half Lives* and several more books, not to mention many magazine articles and speeches, Riis's work led many cities to launch investigations and eventually pass tougher laws regarding room size, windows, running water, and toilets.

Filippo Lippi, *Madonna and Child* (1445) [*Source:* Filippo Lippi, "Madonna and Child," 1440/1445. Tempera on panel, .797 × .511 (31 3/8 × 20 1/8); framed: 1.172 × .854 × .095 (46 1/8 x 33 5/8 × 3 3/4). Samuel H. Kress Collection, Photograph © 2001 Board of Trustees, National Gallery of Art, Washington. 1939.1.290.(401)/PA]

The ladder suggests her "apartment" is little more than a dingy, windowless basement room with only one piece of furniture (the chair on which she sits).

Riis presents her not as filthy or drunk; despite the dreadful circumstances, she and her baby are dressed in clean clothes.

Riis often included babies and innocent-looking children in his photographs to prompt the viewer to wonder—and worry—about their fate if action is not taken to alleviate the plight of the poor.

The man's hat on the wall prompts the viewer to wonder if this desperate woman has a husband, or if she's been abandoned.

Although poor this woman is a hard worker. A rag-picker collected discarded rags and other fabric (see sacks), laundered them on a stovetop tub, and then sold them to paper manufacturers for pennies per pound.

The mother's heavenward gaze was intended to spur sympathy in the minds of middle- and upper-class viewers by conjuring up the familiar religious imagery of the Madonna and Child.

Jacob A. Riis, "Italian Mother and Her Baby in Jersey Street" (1889) [*Source:* Jacob A. Riis "Italian Mother and Her Baby in Jersey Street", in the home of an Italian rag-picker, Jersey Street, circa 1890. Museum of the City of New York, The Jacob A. Riis Collection (#157)]

How did Jacob Riis's portrayal of the poor differ from traditional notions of poverty?

Tenements of New York, which he published in 1890. Books providing shocking accounts of prostitution, drunkenness, and violence in America's slums had appeared as early as the 1840s. Riis's book was different and it caused a sensation.

Living among the Poor: Settlement Houses

Riis was not alone in promoting a more progressive and sympathetic view of poverty and remedies to it. In the early 1880s middle-class and college-educated women began establishing in immigrant neighborhoods **settlement houses**, or institutions dedicated to helping the urban poor by providing a wide range of social and educational services. Jane Addams and Ellen Gates Starr founded the most famous and influential settlement house, Hull House, in Chicago in 1889. Born to wealthy Illinois families, they had met in college and toured Europe together in 1888, where they were inspired by a visit to Toynbee Hall, a settlement house in London's poor East End. There they saw highly educated and wealthy young men from Oxford enter the East End to offer direct assistance to the poor. They vowed to establish a similar institution in Chicago upon their return.

With financial backing from wealthy reformers, Addams and Starr rented an old mansion on Chicago's Near West Side. The neighborhood was overwhelmingly foreign born, with immigrants from dozens of countries and regions. Most lived in poverty in dreary, run-down tenements. The neighborhood also suffered from poor sanitation and high rates of crime. Unlike socially conscious elite women of earlier generations who simply raised money for the poor or lobbied the state legislature for laws against child labor, Addams, Starr, and the many women workers they subsequently attracted to Hull House consciously chose to live among the poor to get to know them and understand their needs—even learn from them.

The staff at Hull House first offered educational classes in literature and art. When these proved popular they began to offer classes on more practical subjects, such as cooking, sewing, hygiene, civics, the English language, and vocational training. They also opened their doors to fledgling labor unions, recognizing the vital role unions could play in elevating the earnings of workers, especially the foreign born.

Within a decade Hull House was a flourishing institution offering a wide array of services to the poor of Chicago. Addams and other Hull House workers like Florence Kelley also became activists to prod city authorities to improve tenement laws, increase street cleaning and garbage removal, and expand public education. They also lobbied state officials for laws against child labor and for improved factory safety. Hull House was not the first settlement in America, but it soon became its most famous, inspiring hundreds of successful imitators, including Denison House in Boston (1889) and Henry Street Settlement in New York (1893).

The White City

The optimistic vision of modern urban life articulated by reformers like Jane Addams and Jacob Riis found vivid expression in the **City Beautiful Movement**. Taking form in the late 1880s, it brought together architects, landscape architects, and urban planners who believed the many problems afflicting American cities could be ameliorated, even eliminated, through the comprehensive planning and grand redesign of urban space. City Beautiful proponents like Daniel Burnham and Frederick Law Olmsted argued for the creation of large parks and public squares linked by grand boulevards. Equally important was their emphasis on classical architectural styles for both public and private buildings.

Burnham, Olmsted, and others first demonstrated these ideas at the 1893 Chicago World's Exposition, an extraordinary event planned as a grand celebration of the four hundredth anniversary of Christopher Columbus's arrival in the New World in 1492 and of Chicago's recovery from its devastating fire in 1871. Like the many world's fairs that preceded it, the Chicago Exposition was a celebration

What services did settlement houses provide the urban poor?

of technology, culture, and commerce. It contained thousands of exhibits on science, machinery, art, history, ethnic heritage, music, and theater. But its greatest significance was its impact on architecture, design, and urban planning. Given nearly 700 acres of waterfront property along Lake Michigan, Burnham and the extraordinary team he assembled, including landscape architect Frederick Law Olmsted and architect Louis Sullivan, eventually developed a master plan that called for beautifully landscaped grounds featuring waterways and reflecting pools.

Around the waterways, (**17.8**), Burnham placed fourteen main buildings designed in the Beaux-Arts architectural style, which emphasized logic, harmony, and uniformity. The Court of Honor buildings, shown in the image, lined the Grand Basin that formed the centerpiece of the exposition grounds. Covered in bright white stucco that gave them a shimmering whiteness, the buildings of the White City astonished the estimated 27 million visitors who entered through the main gates.

Yet as this image indicates, Burnham and his team sought not simply to wow the public with grand architecture. They wanted to make a statement on the potential glory of the modern city. All cities could be—should be—as impressive as the White City. All that was needed was strong civic leadership and enlightened urban planning. This grand vision never fully caught on, but many of the City Beautiful ideals and concepts exhibited in the White City influenced a generation of urban planners and architects committed to making American cities more beautiful, healthy, and efficient.

17.8 The White City
Designed by some of the nation's leading architects and landscape architects, the White City consisted of fourteen main buildings designed in the Beaux-Arts style, set in beautifully landscaped grounds featuring waterways and reflecting pools.

How did the White City reflect an optimistic vision of the future of urban life?

New Habits, Roles, and Lifestyles

The development of vast working-class districts was but one aspect of a broad trend that reshaped urban life in the late nineteenth century. Urban and subsequent suburban growth also led to the development of middle-class and elite residential neighborhoods, as well as urban central business districts dedicated almost exclusively to commerce. Middle-class neighborhoods increasingly reflected the new values of the urban middle class, including a growing interest in leisure activities. The growth of leisure time allowed women to take on increasingly significant roles in public life through memberships in socially and politically active clubs.

The New Urban Landscape

The evolution of mass transit systems like horsecars, steam railroads, and trolleys, led to explosive urban growth and the formation of specialized districts dedicated to specific functions. Most cities, for example, developed **central business districts** where almost no residents lived. Instead the high-value real estate in downtowns from Baltimore to Chicago to San Francisco was dedicated to commerce: banks, department stores (see Chapter 16), and the offices of corporations, accountants, lawyers, and other professions. Each day mass transit systems carried thousands of shoppers and workers to central business districts from sections of cities now dedicated almost exclusively to residential use, or from residential neighborhoods just beyond the city limits.

Soaring real estate values and new technology led to another distinct feature in central business districts: skyscrapers. Before the Civil War few buildings exceeded six stories, but the invention of the elevator and new building materials like cast iron led to ten- and twelve-story buildings by the early 1880s. The big breakthrough in tall building construction came in 1885 with the completion of the Home Insurance Building in Chicago (**17.9**). It was remarkable not for its height (ten stories), but for its internal steel skeleton that allowed for thin walls and large windows. The first true skyscraper led to a boom in tall building construction in downtowns across the country. By 1900 lower Manhattan alone featured twelve buildings of 300 feet or more in height.

Equally significant, although less dramatic, than the upward reach of city skylines was the outward sprawl of urban areas due to mass transit. **Suburbs**, or residential communities established just beyond a city's boundary but connected to the urban center by mass transit, attracted middle-class families that could afford to buy a house and pay the cost of commuting to the city for work. Middle-class families found suburbs attractive for their serenity, cleanliness, and greenery—aspects that stood in sharp contrast to the crime, disease, violence, and

17.9 Reaching for the Sky
The completion of the Home Insurance Building in Chicago in 1885 marked the arrival of the skyscraper. Designed with an internal steel skeleton, it rose ten stories high and led to a boom in tall building construction in downtowns across the country.

How did new modes of transportation promote the development of specialized urban and suburban districts?

noise of the inner city. Given the prevalence of racist and nativist attitudes in Gilded Age American society, suburbs also attracted people unwilling to live with newly arrived immigrants and African Americans.

The creation of middle-class communities of like-minded people of similar ethnic and religious backgrounds fostered the development of new middle-class values, tastes, and social patterns. Middle-class families had fewer children and higher incomes than their working-class counterparts.

> "Since water hems in the business center on three sides and the nexus of railroads on the south, Chicago must grow upward."
>
> Real estate columnist, *Chicago Tribune*, 1888

Greater wealth and fewer mouths to feed allowed them to purchase an ever-increasing array of consumer products, most often by women who rode trolleys or commuter lines to the central business district. Many of these products were everyday items that came with increasingly recognizable names like Ivory Soap and Coca-Cola. Others were more substantial, such as small pianos that could be purchased on credit. The great popularity of pianos in the late nineteenth century reflected not merely the rising wealth of middle-class families, but also the significant amount of leisure time they enjoyed and their desire to develop refined tastes.

New Roles and Expectations for Women

Lower birth rates and a growing trend of hiring servants to perform duties like cooking, cleaning, and laundry left middle-class women with more free time. The dominant notions about gender roles, however, emphasized the need for women to remain in the home, focusing on creating a moral and nurturing environment for their husbands and children. According to this view the outside world of business and politics was the male sphere, full of corruption, dishonesty, immorality, and violence that threatened virtuous womanhood.

Yet two trends in the late nineteenth century led directly to new, more public roles for middle-class women. The first was a significant rise in education, especially at the college level. By 1900 women constituted nearly 20 percent of college graduates, up from just 13 percent in 1890. Education allowed women, if only temporarily, to leave the domestic sphere to interact with other young women and encounter emerging ideas of women's rights. Not surprisingly nearly every leader in the women's rights movement in the late nineteenth century had received at least some college education.

A second significant trend that reshaped the outlook, expectations, and public influence of American women in the period was their increased involvement in a growing number of clubs dedicated to charity and social reform. The General Federation of Women's Clubs, established in 1890, counted 160,000 members in more than five hundred clubs by 1900. The largest and best known organization was the Women's Christian Temperance Union (WCTU). Activism in clubs gave women the opportunity to exert political influence, build leadership skills, and learn from networks of activist, reform-minded women.

By the 1890s many of these activist women joined the **women's suffrage** movement, or the effort to obtain voting rights for women. The movement had split into rival factions in 1869 in the debate over the Fourteenth Amendment (see Chapter 14), but in 1890 they reunited to form the National American Woman Suffrage Association (NAWSA). It helped win suffrage in Colorado in 1893 and Idaho in 1896 (Utah and Wyoming had previously approved it), but voting rights for all women would not occur until ratification of the Nineteenth Amendment in 1920 (see Chapter 18).

Racism led white women to exclude black women from their clubs and the suffrage movement. Nonetheless African American women established their own clubs to pursue goals such as temperance and women's suffrage. Most of these clubs affiliated with the National Association of Colored Women, an umbrella group. Some black women pursued goals of particular concern to African Americans. Ida B. Wells launched a national campaign against lynching in the 1890s

What trends contributed to a growing public activism among women?

that drew many African American women and men into public activism for reform, especially civil rights.

By the 1890s Americans had begun to use the term "**New Woman**" to describe middle-class women who pursued higher education, engaged in political activism, delayed marriage, and bore fewer children. The New Woman had a distinct look, donning the clothing, hair style, and air of the so-called Gibson Girl. A creation of illustrator Charles Dana Gibson in 1890s popular magazines, the Gibson Girl was tall and beautiful, with a tightly cinched waist that accentuated her bosom and hair piled high on her head.

Offsetting these traditionally feminine characteristics, however, was an outgoing, even mischievous spirit that reflected the greater independence and activism of younger American women. Symbolic of this attitude was the degree to which young women took part in the great national enthusiasm for bicycling in the 1890s. Note the striking contrast between these two images. The first from 1886 (**17.10**) shows a traditional Victorian-era wife in formal attire being carried as a passenger by her husband. The second image, an 1896 advertisement poster for the Stearns Bicycle Company (**17.11**), shows a self-confident and carefree woman drawn in the Gibson Girl style breezing along on her own bicycle. Many conservative Americans condemned the bicycling craze as unnatural and immoral because it allowed young women and men the freedom to pedal off unchaperoned, away from the watchful eyes of parents and other guardians of respectability.

17.11 The New Woman
Many Americans saw a connection between the growing independence, activism, and outgoing spirit of young women and their participation in the great national enthusiasm for bicycling in the 1890s.

17.10 The Traditional Woman
Reflecting Victorian values, this conservatively dressed woman in 1886 enjoys a bicycle ride only as the passenger of her husband.

What was new about the "New Woman"?

"Bicycling has done more to emancipate women than anything else in the world. I stand and rejoice every time I see a woman ride by on a wheel. It gives women a feeling of freedom and self-reliance."

SUSAN B. ANTHONY, 1896

New Forms of Leisure and Popular Culture

As industrial life created sharp distinctions between time spent at work and time doing everything else, Americans in the Gilded Age developed the concept of leisure time. This trend was at the heart of the labor movement's persistent demand for the eight-hour day as both a call for shorter hours of toil and an insistence on the right to leisure time. Many city dwellers spent their leisure time in informal activities in their neighborhood such as walking about, playing games in streets and local parks, and socializing with their neighbors. For many working-class men, the local saloon was the preferred place of leisure.

Increasingly popular, however, were more formal leisure opportunities such as amusement parks and organized spectator sports. Amateur, semiprofessional, and professional baseball teams, for example, drew large crowds. Entrepreneurs soon came to see baseball as a business, despite its popular reputation as the "national pastime." They built large baseball stadiums near one or more streetcar lines and sold patrons not merely tickets but also food, beer, trinkets, and scorecards. By the 1880s baseball stars like Mike "King" Kelly and Adrian "Cap" Anson had emerged as high-paid celebrities. Corporations, especially true of the booming tobacco industry, quickly realized the value of celebrity endorsements for their products and in the 1880s created the original baseball cards like the one shown here (**17.12**). To legitimize tobacco use companies such as Old Judge portrayed players like Kelly as ideal men—the perfect blend of athletic masculinity and refined, almost gentlemen-like bearing. In an era when the press rarely reported on the bad behavior of athletes or politicians, few Americans could have known that the real Mike Kelly was a violent alcoholic who would drink himself to death in 1894 at the age of thirty-seven.

Other spectator sports likewise enjoyed great popularity in the late nineteenth century. Professional boxing, horseracing, track and field competitions, and bicycle races drew large crowds to venues such as Madison Square Garden in New York City, the Chicago Coliseum, and the Boston Arena. By the 1890s college football games in Boston, New York, Philadelphia, and Chicago often drew more than fifty thousand fans. Baseball, football, and other urban spectator sports proved consistent money-makers for promoters, but they also attracted criticism from ministers and some public officials who decried the violence, alcohol consumption, and gambling associated with them and the increased tendency to play them on Sundays.

Competing for the attention of the American with increased leisure time on his or her hands was a burgeoning theatrical entertainment industry. By the late nineteenth century, the typical city resident could choose from a vast array of entertainment forms on stage. In ethnic neighborhoods, for example, Old World productions like Italian melodramas based loosely on operas and Yiddish comedies drawn from eastern European traditions flourished.

Elsewhere in the city in more mainstream venues, people flocked to musical comedies, a distinctly

17.12 Selling Celebrity The booming tobacco industry created the original baseball cards to capitalize on the value of sports celebrity endorsements for their products.

How did commercial interests shape the new forms of leisure in the Gilded Age?

American innovation pioneered by the duo of Edward Harrigan and Tony Hart. They were succeeded by others such as George M. Cohan and Irving Berlin, whose popular songs like "Give My Regards to Broadway" and "Alexander's Ragtime Band" became enduring hits.

Also popular was vaudeville, a kind of variety show featuring acts from jugglers, musicians, acrobats, and family routines, to singers, wild animal acts, ribald comedians, and scantily clad women and aimed at a working-class audience. With its low admission fees and democratic approach, vaudeville was geared for the masses. A typical vaudeville production featured a series of acts by entertainers—anything. At its peak circa 1900, vaudeville shows drew two million patrons a day. Many of the great American stage and film performers from the early twentieth century, such as James Cagney, Mae West, and Al Jolson, began their careers in vaudeville.

Wealthier and better-educated city residents rejected vaudeville and the more raucous forms of musical comedy as undignified and coarse. Instead they went to opera houses to hear European classics and to what they considered legitimate theater to see productions of Shakespeare and the classics.

While these varied forms of entertainment were developed and popularized in America's large cities, they quickly spread via published sheet music and touring companies to communities of every size across the nation. The result was the beginning of a national popular culture, one that would flourish more fully with the arrival of movies, radio, and television in the twentieth century.

17.13 Imagining an American Aristocracy Wealthy Americans in the Gilded Age competed to throw the most expensive and decadent ball, wedding, or party. At Mrs. William K. Vanderbilt's 1883 ball, New York's elite arrived in costumes depicting figures of European royalty. [*Source:* Collection of The New-York Historical Society, Box1.f 10. Negative no. 80433d]

How did varied forms of leisure reflect class differences?

Lifestyles of the Rich and Famous

Another feature of urban life that became a defining feature of the Gilded Age (so much so that it informed the era's name) was the advent of lavish displays of wealth by the rich. Dubbed "**conspicuous consumption**" by sociologist Thorstein Veblen in 1899, this trend involved most prominently the construction of opulent mansions in elite urban districts such as New York's Fifth Avenue, Chicago's Lake Shore Drive, and San Francisco's Nob Hill, as well as in exclusive summer retreats like Newport, Rhode Island. Wealthy families like the Vanderbilts and Astors competed to see who could throw the most extravagant ball, weddings, and parties.

One of the most famous was a ball hosted by Alva Vanderbilt, wife of tycoon William K. Vanderbilt, on March 26, 1883, to celebrate the opening of their new $3 million mansion on upper Fifth Avenue. The elite of New York arrived in costume (**17.13**).Many dressed as Marie Antoinette, Queen Elizabeth, and Louis XV. This choice of an ostentatious theme of royalty reflected the widely shared belief among the nation's wealthy elite that they constituted an American aristocracy—a notion that ran counter to the longstanding American tradition of fear and loathing for such undemocratic pretensions (see Chapters 4 and 5). Some labor activists and social critics castigated the ball and high society's rejection of republican simplicity, but Mrs. Vanderbilt's guests paid no heed. They reveled past dawn in a party that cost $250,000—that in an age when an average worker could expect to earn less than $700 per year. By the mid-1880s most newspapers featured "Society" columns that devoted extensive coverage to the lives of the wealthy.

> "There is many a palace in Europe that would hide its diminished roof beside the sheer luxury of Fifth Avenue homes."
>
> EDGAR SALTUS

While Americans followed the exploits of the rich with a certain level of wonder, the public would accept only so much extravagance before expressing revulsion. That finally occurred in February 1897, when the Bradley Martin family hosted a $400,000 party in which eight hundred society guests arrived in costumes depicting European royalty. One society reporter described "a gorgeous, superb, and wonderful spectacle." But in 1897, when the nation was suffering from a severe economic depression, public criticism of the ball poured in from all quarters, including public officials, clergymen, and workers. The Bradley Martins fled to Europe and settled permanently in England, ending the days of diamond-necklace party favors.

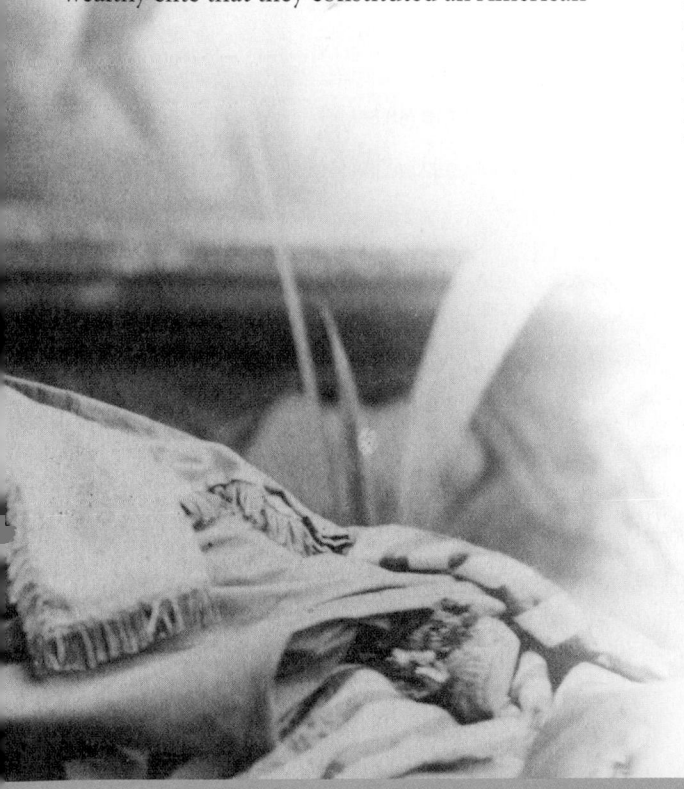

> "[Y]ou rich people put next to nothing in the collection plate, and yet you'll spend thousands of dollars on Mrs. Bradley Martin's ball."
>
> Sermon of a minister outraged over the Bradley Martin Ball

How did the great displays of wealth in the Gilded Age represent a break with America's republican traditions?

The Challenge from Below

The revulsion expressed over the Bradley Martin Ball in 1897 reflected the rising discontent of the era. Many farmers and industrial workers felt increasingly exploited by powerful corporations. When they turned to elected officials to address these problems, they found them unresponsive. Most politicians remained committed to a laissez-faire philosophy, which argued against government intervention in the economy. As a result the period was marked by some of the most bitter and violent strikes in American history and the rise of a third party comprised mainly of farmers, workers, and reformers—the **People's Party**—to challenge the two major parties, the Republicans and Democrats.

> "The popular mind is agitated with problems that may disturb social order, and among them all none is more threatening than ... the concentration of capital into vast combinations. ... Congress alone can deal with them and if we are unwilling or unable there will soon be a trust for every product and a master to fix the price for every necessity of life."
>
> Senator JOHN SHERMAN of Ohio, introducing his anti-trust bill, 1888

17.14 Deadlocked Presidential Politics in the Gilded Age With an electorate evenly divided between the two parties, Gilded Age politics were often marked by stalemate and inaction on key social and economic issues.

Year	Candidate	Party	Popular Vote	Electoral Vote
1876	**Rutherford B. Hayes***	Republican	4,036,298 (48%)	185
	Samuel J. Tilden	Democrat	4,300,590 (51%)	184
1880	**James Garfield**	Republican	4,454,416 (48.5%)	214
	Winfield S. Hancock	Democrat	4,444,952 (48.1%)	155
1884	**Grover Cleveland**	Democrat	4,874,986 (48.5%)	219
	James G. Blaine	Republican	4,851,334 (48.2%)	182
1888	**Benjamin Harrison***	Republican	5,439,853 (47.9%)	233
	Grover Cleveland	Democrat	5,540,309 (48.6%)	168
1892	**Grover Cleveland**	Democrat	5,556,918 (46%)	277
	Benjamin Harrison	Republican	5,176,108 (43%)	145
	James B. Weaver	People's	1,041,028 (9%)	22

Winner in bold

* = winner despite losing popular vote

Why were election results in the Gilded Age so close?

Out of Touch Politics

Popular enthusiasm for politics reached extraordinary heights in the Gilded Age. Indeed American voters turned out in astonishing numbers, averaging 72 percent between 1876 and 1896 (as compared with between 50 and 60 percent in recent decades). Despite such intense interest and participation in politics, politicians made little progress in resolving the major issues that dominated national politics in this period. This political stalemate stemmed from several factors. First, as indicated in (**17.14**), the electorate was evenly divided between the two parties, resulting in remarkably close elections. For example, the five presidential elections between 1876 and 1892 were decided by razor-thin margins. Indeed the contests in 1876 and 1888 saw the candidate with the highest popular vote total lose because his opponent tallied more electoral votes. No incumbent president won reelection, and only twice (each time for just two years) did one party control both houses of Congress and the presidency.

Political inaction in the Gilded Age also reflected the conservatism of most politicians who clung to longstanding political traditions that celebrated small, nonintrusive government, especially at the federal level. For many leaders government regulation of business appeared socialistic and potentially harmful to both the economy and republican principles. Political paralysis stemmed from the power of corporate interests to stymie legislation they deemed harmful to their financial interests. They did so through huge donations to political parties and outright bribery. To cite but one example, big business interests succeeded in maintaining a very high tariff, which protected their manufactures from foreign competition.The record for 1890, the year Congress took up the big issues of tariff, currency reform, and corporate regulation, provides a particularly vivid example of this ineffective political system. Support for corporate regulation reflected rising concern from many corners of American society. Industrial workers saw themselves as victims of corporate power that demanded long hours of dangerous toil for low wages. Many other Americans, as suggested by this 1889 Thomas Nast cartoon, *The Rising of the Usurpers and the Sinking of the Liberties of the People* (**17.15**), viewed trusts as a threat to the principles of democracy and equality. By monopolizing the necessities of life, trusts literally threatened to smother American liberty. The Sherman Anti-Trust Act of 1890 promised to empower the federal government to crack down on business practices that diminished competition (see Chapter 16), but opposition among pro-business legislators weakened the law to such a point that it did little in the coming years to slow the growth of big business. Indeed the 1890s saw record numbers of mergers and big business used the Sherman act to weaken labor unions by arguing that strikes amounted to restraint of trade.

Similarly, Congress also took up the contentious issue of currency reform to determine what constituted the proper basis for American currency. Advocates of "hard money," a group that included most Republicans, businessmen and the wealthy, argued for basing currency on actual gold and silver in the U.S. Treasury. They opposed the issuance of paper money, popularly known as "greenbacks," arguing that it contributed to inflation and lowered interest rates. "Soft money" proponents like farmers, workers, and Democrats, however, argued that the supply of currency in the Gilded Age was insufficient to meet the needs of an expanding commercial economy. They advocated the issuance of greenbacks and expanded coinage of silver. More money in circulation would lead to inflation, but debtors, especially farmers, welcomed inflation because it promised to raise the prices of their goods and diminish the burden of their debts. In 1890 they supported the Sherman Silver Purchase Act of 1890. It required the U.S. Treasury to purchase

17.15 Liberty Suffocated by Big Business This 1889 Thomas Nast cartoon captured the concerns of many, that trusts threatened American principles of democracy, equality, and liberty by monopolizing the necessities of life.

Why did Congress in this period fail to address major social issues?

4.5 million ounces of silver every month and issue notes (paper money) redeemable in either silver or gold.

Republicans opposed the bill but wanted to enact a higher tariff. Democrats opposed a higher tariff, arguing that it amounted to a huge subsidy paid by American consumers to business, so both sides compromised and the bills became law. Neither bill, however, had the desired effect. The higher tariff caused a surge in consumer prices, producing a widespread discontent. The silver program caused the price of silver to fall and so most of the people holding the notes redeemed them for gold, a trend that caused a severe depletion of the nation's gold reserves, which in turn contributed to the Panic of 1893 and subsequent four years of severe economic depression.

The one notable exception to the politics of stalemate was the passage of a civil service law to make certain government jobs open only to people who demonstrated their competency on a civil service exam rather than people who merely possessed strong political connections. Neither political party favored the law since it threatened to undermine their ability to reward friends and campaign contributors. It took the assassination of President James A. Garfield in 1881 by a frustrated and apparently deranged office seeker to gain passage of the Pendleton Act in 1883, a law that placed 10 percent of federal jobs under civil service.

The People's Party

Anger and resentment against the mainstream political system over its corruption and failure to act on critical issues like corporate regulation and currency and tariff reform gradually produced a popular reaction. In the late 1870s **farmers' alliances,** successors to the Granger movement (see Chapter 15), formed to alleviate the plight of farmers beset by rising costs and falling prices for their products. The Southern Farmers' Alliance (established in 1877) and Northern Farmers' Alliance (1880) grew steadily in the 1880s to a combined membership of more than 5 million. Excluded by the segregationist doctrines of the post-Reconstruction South (see Chapter 14), black farmers formed the Colored Farmers' Alliance in 1886 and soon drew a membership of more than 1.25 million.

The alliances argued that the economic woes of the American farmer were due to exploitive bankers who charged farmers exorbitant interest rates for farm mortgages, railroads that charged them extortionate rates to transport farm produce to market, and commodity brokers on Wall Street who bought their crops at rock bottom prices and then turned around and resold them at many times the original price paid. To combat this injustice the alliances promoted the establishment of cooperatives that combined the buying and selling power of farmers to gain them better prices for their produce and lower rates for loans and crop insurance. They also promoted education on agricultural topics.

In 1889 the Northern Farmers' Alliance and Southern Farmers' Alliance united to form the National Alliance. One year later, convinced that they only way to combat the power of the monopolies and trusts was to transform the National Alliance into a political movement to put pro-farmer candidates into office, delegates gathered in Ocala, Florida, and drew up a manifesto listing their grievances and proposed reforms. That fall National Alliance–backed candidates won complete or partial control of twelve state legislatures and elected six governors. They also sent fifty representatives and three senators to the U.S. Congress. Because most were Democrats, Republicans lost control of the House. These positive electoral results convinced many National Alliance activists like Ignatius Donnelly of Minnesota and Tom Watson of Georgia that they needed to form a third party and run a slate of candidates in the upcoming 1892 presidential contest.

A National Alliance convention held in St. Louis in early 1892 led to the formal creation of the People's Party (its followers would be known as "Populists") and the adoption of a preamble to the party's platform that set forth the plight of the American farmer and worker in forceful prose:

> [W]e meet in the midst of a nation brought to the verge of moral, political, and material ruin.... The fruits of the toil of millions are boldly stolen to build up colossal fortunes for a few ...

By now the strength of the People's Party movement had begun to alarm the leaders of the mainstream political parties. Worried about its potential to win enough votes in the upcoming 1892 election to determine the winner by taking votes from the major parties, they launched a campaign to discredit the Populists. In this political cartoon (**17.16**), which appeared on the cover of *Judge*, a pro-Republican magazine, the artist tries to

What grievances led to the rise of farmers' alliances?

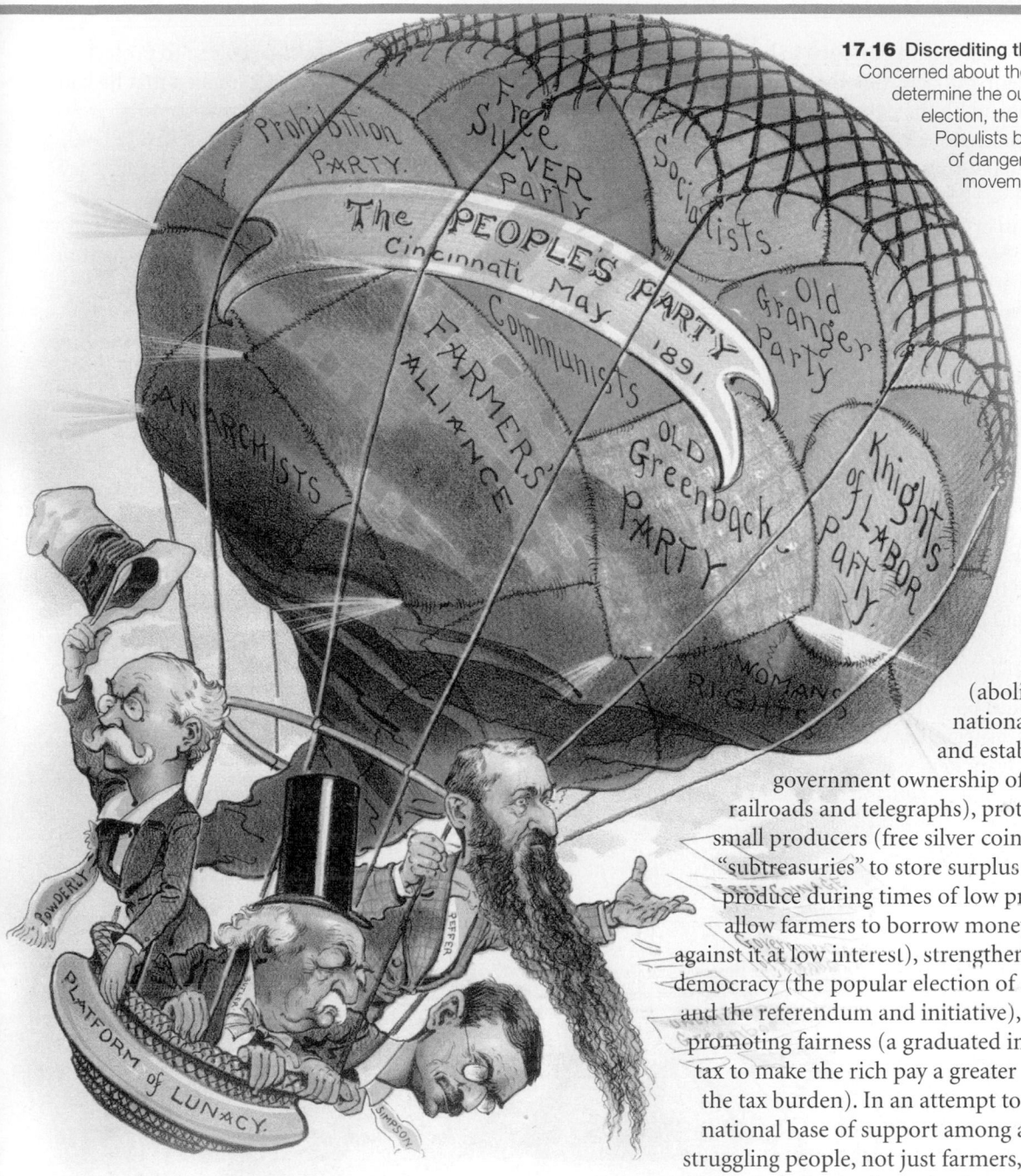

17.16 Discrediting the Populists
Concerned about the potential of the People's Party to determine the outcome of the 1892 presidential election, the major parties tried to discredit the Populists by ridiculing them as a "patchwork" of dangerous political and ideological movements like socialism and prohibition.

discredit the Populists by ridiculing them as a "patchwork" of strange and dangerous political and ideological movements like socialism and prohibition. The balloon's basket, labeled "Platform of Lunacy," carried the party leaders, depicted as eccentric fools.

Populists gathered for a national convention in July 1892 in Omaha and nominated Union Army veteran James B. Weaver for president and Confederate veteran General James G. Field of Virginia for vice president. The convention adopted a platform aimed at eliminating monopolies (abolition of national banks and establishing government ownership of railroads and telegraphs), protecting small producers (free silver coinage and "subtreasuries" to store surplus farm produce during times of low prices and allow farmers to borrow money against it at low interest), strengthening democracy (the popular election of senators and the referendum and initiative), and promoting fairness (a graduated income tax to make the rich pay a greater share of the tax burden). In an attempt to create a national base of support among all struggling people, not just farmers, the platform also included several planks that expressed sympathy with industrial workers.

In the end, the People's Party was no match for the established parties. Democrat Grover Cleveland won the election with 46 percent of the vote to Republican incumbent, Benjamin Harrison's 43 percent. Yet the Populists polled more than one million votes (9 percent) and Weaver won Kansas, Colorado, Idaho, and Nevada. Results on the local and state levels were even more impressive, as Populists elected fifteen hundred candidates to state legislatures, three governors, and five senators and ten representatives to Congress.

How did the People's Party platform reflect the concerns of farmers and industrial workers?

People's Party leaders hoped to build on this achievement, but defeating the major parties in 1896 would depend on the party's ability to overcome several challenges. Election results showed that it had performed poorly among midwestern farmers and industrial workers who opted to stay with either the Republican or Democratic parties. Finally, a successful campaign by conservatives to equate support for the People's Party with attacking white supremacy severely weakened the party in the South.

Industrial Conflict and Depression

Several events soon transpired that highlighted the unchecked power of big business and the severe consequences of a laissez-faire economy. Many People's Party activists hoped the anger and suffering produced by the Homestead strike and Panic of 1893 would prompt workers and farmers to reject the mainstream political parties and join the Populists. Workers at the Homestead Steel Works, a mammoth plant near Pittsburgh and owned by Andrew Carnegie, for years enjoyed a strong union (the Amalgamated Association of Iron and Steel Workers), high wages, and decent living conditions. But in 1892 Carnegie decided to rid the company of the union to allow him to cut costs by introducing the labor-saving machinery and reducing wages. To protect the public persona of a benevolent capitalist that he had worked for years to develop (see Chapter 16), Carnegie left the country for a vacation in Scotland, leaving his hard-nosed business partner, Henry Clay Frick, behind to take care of the dirty work.

On June 29 Frick announced a lockout and closed the mills. After a week the standoff turned violent when workers exchanged gunfire with a group of heavily armed professional strikebreakers of the Pinkerton Detective Agency, whom Frick had brought by boat to the Homestead complex. The clash claimed the lives of six strikers and five Pinkertons. The national press gave extensive coverage to the strike, and its tone in many instances was surprisingly pro-worker, probably due in part to the negative reputation of the Pinkertons. Carnegie, despite his attempt to separate himself from the conflict, drew some of the harshest criticisms. Carnegie's critics challenged his reputation as the great philanthropist who handed out libraries to communities in the United States and Europe by depicting him as a two-faced hypocrite who funded his philanthropic largesse by grinding down his workers with wage cuts (**17.17**).

But the tide of public opinion soon shifted against the strikers, for on July 23 anarchist Alexander Berkman burst into Frick's office and shot him several times. Remarkably Frick survived the assassination attempt. Even though Berkman had no

17.17 Carnegie's Reputation Takes a Hit
The Homestead strike tarnished Carnegie's image as a benevolent capitalist and friend of labor. This cartoon from the July 9 issue of the Utica, New York, *Globe* accuses him of being a two-faced hypocrite who funded his philanthropy by cutting his workers' salaries.

Why did Carnegie's actions in the Homestead strike prompt critics to accuse him of hypocrisy?

17.18 Coxey's Army Emphasizes Its Patriotism Aware that critics denounced them as violent radicals, Coxey and his "army" of protesters emphasized their patriotism and moderation by marching with American flags.

connection to Homestead workers, his actions brought widespread condemnation down upon the strikers. In September state officials arrested thirty-three members of the union's leadership and charged them with treason against the state. Two months later, on November 20, 1892, with nearly all the jobs at Homestead filled by replacement workers, the union formally ended the strike.

Six months later, on May 5, 1893, a financial crisis rocked the nation, leading to the most severe economic depression in American history to that time. Within a year the Panic of 1893 led to the failure of thousands of farms and businesses, including seventy-four railroads, and six hundred banks closed, throwing millions out of work and pushing the unemployment rate to 20 percent. The depression produced two vivid images of the widespread suffering endured by millions of Americans and the seeming indifference of public officials to do much about it. The first came from an Ohio Populist named Jacob Coxey who advocated that the government abandon its commitment to laissez-faire and create public works projects such as road building to alleviate mass unemployment and stimulate the economy (programs that the federal government adopted in the Great Depression of the 1930s). To draw attention to this idea, he organized one hundred unemployed men in Massillon, Ohio, to march to Washington, D.C. (the first such march on the capital). Setting out on March 25, 1894, they were joined by various groups along the route. As this photograph (**17.18**) and nearly every other one taken of the march shows, Coxey and his followers sought to portray an image of patriotism, earnestness, and moderation. Dressing as decently as their poverty permitted and marching with dozens of American flags, Coxey and his men rejected the accusations of their critics that they were violent radicals determined to attack the government. Rather, they asserted, theirs was a campaign to save the republic from the clutches of trusts and laissez-faire policies.

Coxey's Army, as it came to be known, numbered about five hundred by the time it reached Washington on April 30, 1894. Denied entry into the Capitol, Coxey delivered an impassioned address on the building's steps.

> We stand here to-day in behalf of millions of toilers whose petitions have been buried in committee rooms, whose prayers have been unresponded to, and whose opportunities for honest, remunerative, productive labor have been taken from them by unjust legislation, which protects idlers, speculators, and gamblers.

Coxey and several other activists were arrested for "disturbing the peace," but eventually they were convicted only for walking on the lawn of the

What did Coxey and his followers want from the federal government?

Capitol grounds. Other groups of unemployed workers staged similar protest marches, but all met with frustration and inaction.

A second image of government indifference in the face of widespread suffering arose in Chicago. The World's Columbian Exposition had opened on May 1, 1893, just four days before the panic on Wall Street. The fair's emphasis on American progress and prosperity, symbolized by the opulence and beauty of its huge complex of white neoclassical buildings, soon stood in stark contrast to the growing despair of the city's tenement districts a few blocks away. When the fair closed in October, thousands of homeless people moved into the vacant buildings that had only recently housed elaborate displays of prosperity. That winter of 1893–1894, as many as sixty thousand Chicagoans per day received a free meal from soup kitchens and missions.

> "We are born in a Pullman house, fed from the Pullman shop, taught in the Pullman school, catechized in the Pullman church, and when we die we shall be buried in the Pullman cemetery and go to the Pullman Hell."
>
> Pullman worker

Some of the hardest hit workers during the depression were employees of the Pullman Palace Car Company, located just outside Chicago. Founded by George Pullman in 1867, the company flourished as a manufacturer of luxury railroad cars. Pullman was an idealist who believed that workers and employers could work together in harmony for mutual benefit. Acting on this idea he established the town of Pullman in 1880, a **company town** built and owned by the Pullman corporation for its employees, who rented homes and patronized stores owned by the company. As this 1881 depiction of the town demonstrates (**17.19**) Pullman, like Carnegie, prided himself on being a model capitalist who earned a vast fortune but still managed to provide a decent living for his workers. This sensibility informs this drawing of Pullman's vision of the future town (since it was still under construction in 1881) as a model community of neat houses, schools, churches, stores, open spaces, and, of course, the factories that made it all possible.

So long as Pullman remained profitable, its employees considered themselves fortunate. But the depression in 1893 hit the railroad industry especially hard, and Pullman laid off hundreds of workers and announced to the rest a wage cut of 30 percent. On top of this devastating news, workers learned that Pullman would not reduce their rents, which were deducted automatically from their paychecks. Some workers soon began receiving checks for less than one dollar per week to cover the cost of food, heat, and clothing.

On May 11, 1894, Pullman's hard-pressed workers went out on strike. After a six-week standoff during which Pullman refused to negotiate, Eugene Debs, the leader of the American Railway Union (ARU) announced all of the union's 125,000 members across the country, as an act of solidarity with the Pullman workers, would refuse to handle Pullman cars. Within days of the start of the boycott, the **Pullman strike** caused the nation's railroad system to slow to a crawl.

The heads of more than two dozen railroads moved to support Pullman and break the ARU by hiring thousands of strikebreakers, pressuring the governor of Illinois, Richard Altgeld, to send in the state militia. When he refused out of sympathy for the strikers and a desire to avoid violence, the railroads turned to Washington, D.C., for help, asking President Grover Cleveland to send in federal troops (see *Choices and Consequences: The Pullman Strike*).

17.19 Capitalism and Community George Pullman's vision of himself as an enlightened and benevolent capitalist was captured in these plans for Pullman, a company town of neat houses, schools, churches, stores, open spaces, and factories.

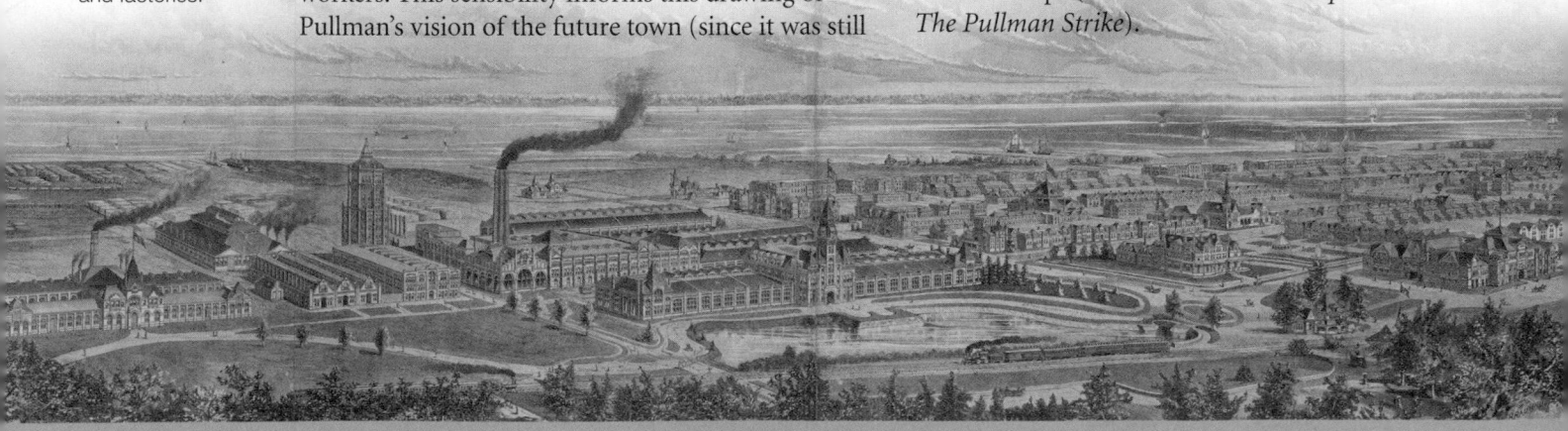

What actions by Pullman prompted his workers to strike?

Choices and Consequences

THE PULLMAN STRIKE

Grover Cleveland was not the first president to face the choice of whether to send federal troops to quell a labor dispute. President Andrew Jackson dispatched troops in 1834 to end a strike by canal workers. President Rutherford B. Hayes had sent troops to crush the great railroad strike of 1877. Despite these precedents, however, Cleveland was aware that many considered the use of the army against American citizens a violation of the key republican principles of sharply limited federal power. Cleveland also worried that the public would condemn such use of federal power if violence ensued as it did in 1877. He spent several days in late June and early July of 1894, consulting with advisors and mulling over his options.

Choices

1. Take no action, allowing the state of Illinois and its pro-labor governor to handle the matter.
2. Intervene as a neutral and insist that both sides negotiate an equitable settlement.
3. Send in the U.S. Army to break the strike and allow the railroads to use strikebreakers to operate the trains.

Decision

Despite some misgivings Cleveland was a pro-business conservative. He authorized his attorney general, Richard Olney, a man with extensive ties to the railroad industry, to obtain a court injunction declaring the ARU boycott of Pullman cars a "conspiracy in restraint of trade" that unlawfully blocked the U.S. mail. When the ARU defied the injunction, Cleveland ordered the army in to end the boycott and get the trains moving again. Eugene Debs and several other ARU leaders were arrested and the boycott ended by mid-July.

Federal troops sent by President Cleveland to break the Pullman strike escort the first meat train out of the Chicago stockyards.

Consequences

Cleveland's decision touched off extensive violence as workers destroyed railroad property and soldiers responded with rifle fire that left thirteen workers dead and scores wounded. The boycott collapsed in mid-July and with it the ARU. The Pullman strike ended in early August in complete defeat for the workers. Public opinion, however, turned against Pullman for his obstinate refusal to negotiate with his workers. A government investigation later criticized Pullman and argued that labor unions and government regulation were needed to curb the power of corporations. Yet in 1895 the Supreme Court (*In re Debs*) upheld the use of injunctions to end strikes.

Continuing Controversies

When is the use of federal troops in a strike compatible with republican principles?

Subsequent presidents, including President Woodrow Wilson, ordered military intervention during labor disputes. In 1916 the National Security Act included a provision empowering the president to federalize a state's national guard to quell a disturbance like a natural disaster, riot, or strike. The two most notable uses of this law, however, came in 1957 (Little Rock, Arkansas) and 1963 (Tuscaloosa, Alabama) to enforce federal desegregation orders.

How did President Cleveland justify using federal power to break the Pullman strike?

The Election of 1896 and Political Realignment

The turmoil caused by the economic depression and Pullman strike greatly affected the outcome of the 1894 off-year elections. Dissatisfaction with President Cleveland's administration hurt the Democrats, who lost their brief hold on both houses of Congress. The shift in power meant more stalemate for the next two years, with a Republican Congress opposed by a Democratic President.

The election of 1896 proved one of the most significant in the nation's history as it led to a major realignment in political affiliations among the American people. Republicans that year nominated former congressman and governor of Ohio William McKinley for president and affirmed their conservative commitment to the gold standard and a high tariff.

The Democrats nominated a young and dynamic congressman from Nebraska, William Jennings Bryan. Just thirty-six years old, Bryan had earned a reputation for stirring oratory against the high tariff and in support of free silver. The latter issue came to hold great symbolic importance in the middle of the depression years. Silver was the metal of the common man, argued its supporters, while gold was the metal of elites. In speeches, pamphlets, songs, and images, People's Party activists had convinced millions of Americans that free coinage of silver would both end the depression and curb the power of monopolies and trusts. Recognizing the popularity of this policy, delegates at the Democratic Party convention made free silver a key plank in the party platform.

Bryan then delivered one of the most famous speeches in American history in which he argued that average Americans were being held down by a "cross of gold," forced upon them by Wall Street and big business. Capturing this theme this campaign poster (**17.20**) included the text of the famous speech (framed by silver coins) and ribbons bearing two of its most memorable lines: "You shall not press down upon the brow of Labor this Crown of

17.20 For Silver and the People The Democratic Party emphasized Bryan's commitment to workers and farmers through his advocacy of free silver and his promise to protect Americans from being crushed by a "Cross of Gold."

Why did silver hold such political significance in the late nineteenth century?

Thorns" and "You shall not crucify mankind upon a Cross of Gold." A youthful Bryan flanked by his wife and children tops the poster, while images of a worker and farmer flank the speech text.

That left the People's Party facing a huge dilemma. Most of its activists had expected the Democrats to follow the Republicans and support the gold standard, leaving the silver issue to the Populists. Now the People's Party had to decide whether to nominate their own candidate and divide the rising support for the silver issue with the Democrats, or, as was common practice among small parties in the nineteenth century, to nominate Bryan as their candidate, a move that would diminish their standing as an independent party concerned with other issues beyond silver. In July the People's Party chose the latter option and nominated Bryan. But their ticket differed from the Democrats in choice of vice president, Populist leader Tom Watson of Georgia.

Despite longstanding tradition in American politics that argued that it was unseemly for presidential candidates to campaign, Bryan embarked on one of the remarkable campaigns in American history, traveling more than 18,000 miles through twenty-seven states and delivering more than six hundred stump speeches to audiences totaling three million people.

Bryan's campaign generated a lot of commentary and excitement, but not enough votes on election day. McKinley won with 51 percent of the vote to Bryan's 47 percent (17.15). The most significant outcome of the contest was a new and enduring political alignment. The Republican Party became strongest in the Midwest and Northeast and dominated national political power for the next three decades. Republicans would portray themselves as the party of economic prosperity (the economy recovered under McKinley) and international power. The Democrats became the party of the South and West. They would retain the Populist belief that government needed to do more to secure the well-being of the average citizen and to limit the power of big business. Given its base in the South, however, the Democratic Party also upheld a states' rights philosophy that protected white supremacy.

The People's Party disintegrated after 1896, but many of their core ideas, such as the graduated income tax and the direct election of senators, remained popular and eventually gained adoption during the next two decades, a period known as the Progressive Era.

Conclusion

The period 1877–1900 came to be known as the Gilded Age because in part it was a golden era of tremendous economic growth and dazzling innovations, such as skyscrapers and electricity, and exciting new developments in popular culture and leisure. Yet many Americans perceived these trends as superficial—just as a gilded piece of jewelry has only a thin layer of gold on its surface. Beneath the wealth and excitement that marked the rise of modern America, they argued, lay the harsh realities of urban squalor, political corruption, and worker and farmer exploitation. These problems explain the many strikes that rocked the era, as well as the emergence of the People's Party and efforts to alleviate poverty, improve public health, and curb corruption, efforts that would later form the basis of the Progressive Era.

How did the election of 1896 lead to a major political realignment?

CHAPTER REVIEW

1871

Boss Tweed's corruption ring exposed
Showed the rising influence of political machines in cities and efforts to limit their power

1874–1877

Women's Christian Temperance Union established
An early indication of growing women's activism in the Gilded Age

The Southern Farmers' Alliance established in Texas
Reflects growing discontent of American farmers that eventually leads to the formation of the People's Party

1882–1883

Charity Organization Society founded
Founded by wealthy reformers who feared that too much charity was actually harming the poor

The Vanderbilt Ball
A lavish exhibition of "conspicuous consumption" attended by the richest families in America

The Pendleton Act becomes law
Intended to diminish nepotism and corruption, it required Civil Service exams for 10 percent of federal jobs

Review Questions

1. What factors led to the dramatic growth of cities in the late nineteenth century?
2. In what ways did ethnic enclaves benefit immigrants?
3. Who supported political machines and why? Why did reformers dislike political machines so much?
4. How was the nativist movement of the late nineteenth century similar to that of the Know-Nothings in the 1850s?
5. How did the approach to poverty by reformers like Jacob Riis and Jane Addams differ from traditional approaches?
6. How did the roles and expectations for middle-class women change in the Gilded Age? What social and economic developments made this possible?
7. How did people in the Gilded Age use their leisure time? How did their choices reflect class differences?
8. What were the primary grievances of people who supported the People's Party? How did they propose to resolve them?
9. What did the outcomes of the Homestead and Pullman strikes reveal about the power of big business and the attitude of the government toward workers?
10. What was the long-term impact of the 1896 election on American politics?

1887–1889

American Protective Association founded
Signals a rise in anti-immigrant sentiment

Hull House founded in Chicago
Settlement house movement provides a wide range of social services to poor and immigrants city dwellers

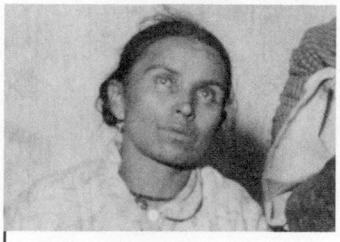

1890

Women's suffrage activists form NAWSA
Brings together two separate women's organization to concentrate on securing the vote for women

Jacob Riis publishes *How the Other Half Lives*
A shocking exposé of urban poverty that builds support for reform measures

Sherman Anti-Trust Act passed
Reflects growing concern over corporate power, but fails to curb it

1892–1893

People's Party established
A coalition of farmers, workers, and reformers committed to curbing the power of big business

The Homestead strike
A bitter and highly publicized defeat for workers

Columbian Exposition opens in Chicago
Celebrates American progress and promotes cleaner, healthier, and more beautiful cities

1894–1896

Coxey's Army marches on Washington, D.C.
Economic depression prompts many to demand relief by the federal government

The Pullman strike
President Cleveland breaks the strike by sending in federal troops

Election of 1896
Republican William McKinley defeats Democrat William Jennings Bryan

Key Terms

Gilded Age The name for the period 1877–1900 that suggested the amazing achievements of the period were like a thin gold layer that covered many unresolved social problems. **498**

ethnic enclaves Urban neighborhoods dominated by one particular immigrant group, often leading to names such as Little Germany and Little Italy. **501**

tenements Multiple family dwellings of four to six stories housing dozens of families that became the most common form of housing for poor city dwellers by the 1860s. **502**

political machines Powerful urban political organizations that mobilized large blocs of working-class and immigrant voters and often engaged in corrupt and illegal activity. **503**

settlement houses Institutions established in cities beginning in the 1880s and dedicated to helping the poor by providing a wide range of social and educational services. **510**

City Beautiful Movement A movement begun in the 1880s that advocated comprehensive planning and grand redesign of urban space to eliminate pollution and overcrowding. **510**

central business districts Sections of cities devoted exclusively to commercial enterprises such as banks, department stores, and the offices of corporations, accountants, lawyers, and other professions. **512**

suburbs Middle- and upper-class residential communities established just beyond a city's boundary but connected to the urban center by mass transit. **512**

women's suffrage The effort to obtain voting rights for women that eventually gained passage of the Nineteenth Amendment (1920). **513**

New Woman A phrase used to describe young women in the 1890s and early 1900s that reflected their rising levels of education, economic independence, and political and social activism. **514**

conspicuous consumption A term used to describe lavish displays of wealth by the rich, including construction of opulent mansions and hosting lavish balls. **517**

People's Party A third party effort launched in 1890 by a coalition of farmer organizations, reformers, and labor unions and dedicated to curbing corporate power and increasing the voice of the masses in politics. **518**

farmers' alliances Organizations in the 1870s and 1880s dedicated to helping farmers struggling with rising costs and falling crop prices by advocating farmer cooperatives and laws to regulate banks and railroads **520**

Coxey's Army A protest march from Ohio to Washington, D.C., in 1894 organized by Jacob Coxey to publicize demands for the federal government to alleviate the suffering brought on by the Panic of 1893. **523**

company town A town built and owned by a corporation and rented to its employees, reflecting both the corporation's desire to help their workers and to control them. **524**

Pullman strike A bitter strike that began on May 11, 1894, at the Pullman Palace Car Company and soon spread nationwide, paralyzing the railroad system. President Cleveland sent in federal troops and broke the strike. **524**

CHAPTER 18

Creating a Democratic Paradise

The Progressive Era, 1895–1915

The Progressive Impulse
p. 532

Reining in Big Business
p. 535

> "We have reached the point in our history when we realize that the nation has tremendous social, economic, and industrial problems."
>
> THEODORE ROOSEVELT, 1912

Female employees of the Triangle Shirtwaist Factory, many recently arrived from Italy and eastern Europe, worked on sewing machines six days a week, twelve hours a day, making blouses. On March 25, 1911, a fire engulfed the top floors of the building that housed the factory in New York City's Lower East Side. As bundles fell to the street, onlookers below assumed that workers were throwing their best cloth out the window to save it. They soon realized their mistake. Female workers were jumping by twos and threes to escape the flames. In the end, 146 women and men perished.

The memories of this horrific scene never left eighteen-year-old Victor Gatto, who stood on the corner and watched as women plunged directly onto the pavement. In 1944 Gatto, a self-taught artist, painted *Triangle Fire: March 25, 1911*. His painting depicted unprepared firefighters atop ladders too short to reach the victims above and indifferent police officers carrying a shroud-covered corpse to join a neat row of bodies that lined the street.

By the time Gatto provided this visual indictment of the government's inability to protect workers, Americans' expectations of their government had radically changed. This new vision took hold during the Progressive Era, partially in response to events like the Triangle Shirtwaist Factory Fire. In Gatto's painting the immense stone buildings tower above the lifeless workers, the artist's way of representing the complete domination of big business over labor at the beginning of the twentieth century. On the day of the fire, employers had locked the workshop doors from the outside to prevent the women from stealing materials or leaving early. With the doors bolted and flimsy fire escapes collapsing under the weight of fleeing workers, the windows offered the only means of escape for the rest.

To many Progressive Era reformers, the Triangle Shirtwaist Factory Fire illustrated the tragic consequences of capitalist exploitation and the government's lack of interest in the plight of workers. Middle-class activists championed an array of reforms that envisioned using local, state, and federal governments to protect Americans from the greed and indifference of big business. Their agenda aroused considerable criticism but Progressives, aided by three reform-minded presidents, found enough common ground to construct cross-class alliances that sought to end exploitive business practices and class conflict. Progressive-led coalitions also tackled pressing political and social issues. From the mid-1890s to mid-1900s, Progressives transformed the role of government in American society and laid the foundation for the liberal reform movements of the twentieth century.

What interpretation did this painting offer of the 1911 Triangle Shirtwaist Factory Fire?

Competing Views on Transforming the Workplace p. 541

Protecting Women and Children p. 546

Reforming the Government p. 552

The Progressive Impulse

The tide of reforms that swept across America at the turn of the twentieth century had its roots in a range of middle-class concerns. Middle-class dismay over the dismal living and laboring conditions for most working-class people turned to alarm as strikes and the appeal of socialism increased. The Progressives had unprecedented success building alliances that transcended class and political party affiliation, winning the support of three consecutive presidents. Their vision of an activist government that used regulation to safeguard the public challenged the prevailing laissez-faire notion that the government should not interfere with market forces, dramatically reshaping the nation within a decade.

The Angst of the Middle Class

At the dawn of the twentieth century, middle-class Americans looked around the nation and did not like what they saw. The upper 2 percent of the population controlled the nation's banks and industry. Even worse during the Gilded Age (Chapter 17) they openly flaunted their prodigious wealth by leading pleasure-filled lives replete with mansions, yachts, and private art collections. The upper class embraced an ethos of individualism that made each man responsible for his and his family's wealth or poverty. "Failures which a man makes in his life are due almost always to some defect in his personality, some weakness of body, mind, or character, will, or temperament," proclaimed John D. Rockefeller, the billionaire titan of Standard Oil. In the nineteenth century many middle-class Americans had uncritically echoed these same sentiments. Increasingly, however, these words rang hollow as the middle class watched the rich discard the tenets of self-discipline, frugality, and charity that had previously prevented individualism from turning into outright selfishness.

Big business came of age at the turn of the century as huge conglomerates began to dominate the economy. Smaller businesses, many run by middle-class proprietors, found it increasingly difficult to compete with these immense corporations. From 1897 to 1904 a wave of business mergers reduced 1,800 firms to just 157 in key economic sectors. Leading captains of industry vertically integrated businesses to control the production and distribution of their products from start to finish (see Chapter 16). Industrialists also integrated horizontally to eliminate competition from companies manufacturing similar items. Through such measures Rockefeller created the Standard Oil Trust and eventually produced and distributed 90 percent of refined oil in the United States, giving him the sole power to set prices for consumers and making him the richest man in the country.

American factories employed a large wage-earning working-class population that had little chance of improving their circumstances, no matter how hard they worked. More than half (**18.1**) of the nation's population toiled at manual labor in mines, factories, docks, and farms owned by others. Low wages, seasonal layoffs, sickness, and workplace accidents created a life filled with insecurity for most workers. "Father, does everyone in America live like this?" asked an eleven-year-old Russian Jewish immigrant, "Go to work early, come home late, eat and go to sleep? And the next day again work, eat, and sleep?" For the majority of the nation, the answer was a painful "yes."

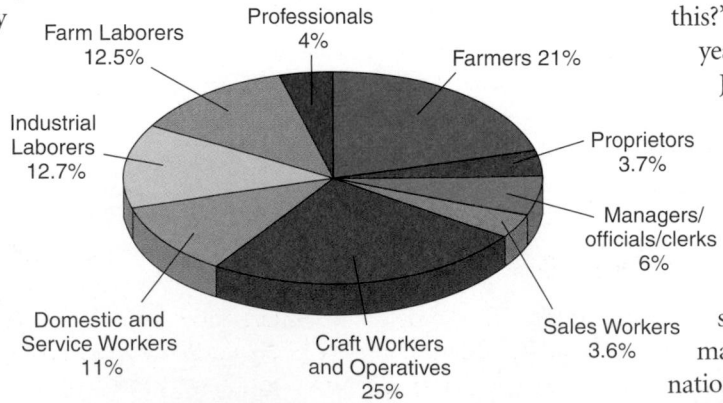

18.1 Occupational Distribution, 1900
America was a primarily working-class society during the Progressive Era.

What economic challenges did the nation face at the end of the nineteenth century?

Large corporate bureaucracies also employed a growing number of middle-class clerks whose ranks grew from 4 percent of the working population in 1900 to 8 percent by 1920. Most earned enough to maintain an acceptable middle-class lifestyle, but the middle class worried that the growing divide between the "haves" and "have-nots" put them in a precarious position. Press reports focusing on the dire living and working circumstances of the working class aroused middle-class sympathies, but fear motivated them to act as well.

The popularity of radical political ideologies, unions, saloons and dancing halls within working-class neighborhoods—each in its own way offering the promise of a better, easier life—alarmed the middle class. The classless paradise without private property championed by working-class radical leaders horrified most middle-class professionals who owned their own homes and businesses. This 1912 image of state militia confronting a parade of striking textile workers in Lawrence, Massachusetts, underscored the reality that strikes often turned violent (**18.2**). This photo's suggestion of an imminent clash between the state militia troops enforcing martial law and defiant workers offered visual evidence to middle-class Progressives that class tensions were tearing the nation apart. While sympathetic to labor unions' demands, middle-class Progressives valued law and order as well. They wanted to find a way to end both industrialist exploitation and the steady stream of strikes that disrupted their daily lives.

18.2 Troops and Striking Workers Face Off, Lawrence, Massachusetts 1912 When the governor proclaimed martial law to prevent mass union rallies, protesting workers took to the streets carrying large American flags. Middle-class Progressives hoped their reforms would end strike-related violence, like the mayhem about to unfurl in this scene.

Progressives aspired to change other aspects of working-class culture as well. They deplored what they saw as the twin evils of drink and prostitution rampant in working-class neighborhoods. In the Progressive imagination the relentless pursuit of pleasure by both the upper class and the working class signaled the overall moral decay of American society.

The Progressive Vision

Glaring problems on both sides of the class divide—an idle and exploitive upper class on one side and an increasingly radicalized and impoverished working class on the other—threatened the middle-class vision of what they felt life in America should offer. *Progressivism*, a broad term used to describe a shared philosophical approach rather than a formal organized movement, provided an answer to this threat.

Unlike Populists (see Chapter 17) or Socialists, Progressives did not form their own political party to advance their agenda. The one exception was Theodore Roosevelt's failed attempt to regain the presidency by organizing the short-lived Progressive (Bull Moose) Party in 1912. Instead Progressives built cross-class political coalitions that transcended party lines. Lacking the wealth that the upper class possessed, or the sheer numbers that gave the working class tremendous economic clout, the middle class needed the support of other classes for their reforms to succeed.

Women played a particularly visible and active role in Progressive causes. Female settlement house workers and women's civic club members, usually white, middle class, and college educated, embraced the notion of "municipal housekeeping," the Progressive conviction that women could not

How did a mix of sympathy and fear spur middle-class interest in reform?

adequately protect their children without help from the government. Female trade unionists agreed, but they also wanted to empower female workers by organizing unions to improve wages and working conditions. Tragedies like the Triangle Shirtwaist Factory fire brought these diverse female factions together, even winning support from appalled upper-class women. In the wake of the fire, this cross-class female coalition focused on bolstering city safety regulations, but only the labor activists emphasized the need for unions to end employer exploitation.

One particularly effective cross-class female alliance lobbied for legislation to ensure that mothers had clean, disease-free milk for their children. These women succeeded in their quest for local laws that prevented distributors from using chalk to make dirty milk appear white. They successfully rallied for mandatory pasteurization to kill germs, and for milk to be transported in refrigerated containers. Female-led reform campaigns also injected new energy into the suffrage movement.

"Children need pure milk and good food, good schools and playgrounds, sanitary homes and safe streets."

A female trade-union activist on why women needed the vote

Many middle-class female Progressive reformers and working-class labor organizers became convinced that without the right to vote, women lacked an essential tool they needed to keep themselves and their families safe. The National Woman Suffrage Association (NWSA) achieved some notable successes between 1910 and 1917, winning the right to vote in Washington, California, Arizona, Kansas, Oregon, and New York. Defeats in other states, however, convinced the NWSA to seek a constitutional amendment guaranteeing all women the right to vote, a campaign that succeeded in 1920 (see Chapter 20).

In a general sense the Progressives wanted to turn America into a middle-class paradise where economic security, education, health, and civility flourished. The tradition of Christian charity also helped shape the Progressive agenda. In the 1880s Protestant ministers like Josiah Strong began preaching the **Social Gospel**, the religious belief that Christians had a responsibility to create an ethically sound and morally upright society. The settlement house movement (see Chapter 17), begun in the spirit of Christian charity, became the incubator for strategies Progressives developed to attain these goals. As they confronted the problems of the poor at Hull House, a settlement house in a Chicago immigrant neighborhood, Jane Addams and Florence Kelley articulated the middle-class values that would form the cornerstone of the Progressive ethos.

Foremost among these was an emphasis on how the environment, as well as individual traits, shaped the lives of the poor. Progressives argued that poor living and working environments created many of the social problems troubling the nation. Exhibiting a typical Progressive faith in the scientific method, Addams and Kelley compiled a statistical portrait of disease, over-crowding, and crime in their Chicago neighborhood that helped Hull House devise solutions to these problems.

Improving sanitation and garbage collection, creating playgrounds for children, eliminating saloons, limiting the hours spent at work, reducing workplace accidents—these were all ways to improve the environment in working-class neighborhoods so that individuals could flourish. Personal responsibility also remained a bedrock principle for Addams and Kelley. While offering more respect for immigrant cultures than many past reformers, Addams and Kelley still believed strongly in teaching immigrants the importance of thrift, temperance, and self-discipline—lifestyle changes that some immigrants resisted.

Finally, Progressives embraced a new vision of governmental power, one that Americans from many different walks of life challenged. Their notion that governmental regulation should protect workers and curtail the excesses of big business put them at odds with industrialists and unions. Industrialists embraced the laissez-faire ethos that they had the right to control their businesses as they saw fit without government interference. Unions also viewed potential government intervention with unease, mindful that during labor conflicts the government usually sided with industrialists. Labor leaders preferred using collective action, including strikes, to win concessions from industrialists. To socialists, who wanted to nationalize all major industries, the Progressive emphasis on regulation was too timid. Essentially the Progressives sought the middle ground between these competing views. They wanted to establish a balance that avoided the excesses of unfettered laissez-faire economics, unending class conflict, or complete government control of the economy. Their aim was notable—the creation of a socially just, capitalist America.

How did the Progressive vision take shape?

Reining in Big Business

When three consecutive presidents—Theodore (Teddy) Roosevelt, William Taft, and Woodrow Wilson—embraced components of the evolving Progressive reform agenda, Progressivism entered the mainstream with a vengeance. What to do about big business aroused considerable debate within Progressive circles. Progressives held competing visions of whether to regulate, dismantle, or accept the trusts, making it hard to rally public opinion around one clear solution. Presidents Roosevelt, Taft, and Wilson devised differing regulatory and antitrust strategies to reform business practices, and openly disagreed on how to tackle the problem. Curtailing big business's access to the nation's environmental riches also provoked debate. Did business have the right to fully exploit the country's forests and water, or should these resources be preserved?

Roosevelt's Trust-busting

Roosevelt enthusiastically supported turning the government into a "steward of the public welfare." While serving as New York City police commissioner from 1895 to 1897, Roosevelt had become friendly with pioneering photojournalist Jacob Riis (Chapter 17). "The midnight trips that Riis and I took" to the tenements, Roosevelt later acknowledged, showed him "what overcrowding means, some hot summer night." Roosevelt's subsequent feats during the 1898 Spanish-American War made him a national war hero, catapulting him into winning the New York governorship. In 1900 President William McKinley selected Roosevelt as his running mate for his successful reelection bid.

On September 5, 1901, anarchist Leon Czolgosz shot President McKinley with a pistol wrapped in a handkerchief while the president was shaking hands at the Pan-American Exposition in Buffalo, New York. When McKinley died eight days later, the forty-two-year-old Roosevelt became the youngest president in American history. A robust man who appeared forever in perpetual motion dictating letters, lecturing visitors, playing tennis, or having pillow fights with his younger children in the White House, Roosevelt captured the public's affection. When Teddy Roosevelt saved a bear cub during a 1902 hunting expedition, a toymaker felt inspired to name a new children's toy after him, and so the teddy bear was born.

Like many Progressives Roosevelt believed that the country stood at a crossroads—either reform or face the end of democracy. He established his credentials as a Progressive reformer, and won public approval, by mediating the 1902 coal strike and filing suit against the Northern Securities and Standard Oil Trusts.

On May 12, 1902, 140,000 northeastern Pennsylvanian miners walked off their jobs. They demanded an eight-hour day, a 20 percent wage increase, and recognition of their United Mine Workers union. The mine owners refused to negotiate. "'The public be damned,' appears to be their motto," decried one Illinois newspaper as coal shortages forced factories to close and the poor began cooking food with oil-soaked asbestos.

President Roosevelt viewed the miners' predicament sympathetically. "I strongly favor labor unions," he declared. "If I were a wage worker in a big city I should certainly join one." Fearing widespread suffering and possible urban riots, Roosevelt threatened to use troops to take over the mine unless the owners agreed to let a government commission fashion an agreement. For the first time a president had stood up publicly against big business, winning him accolades in union circles. The resulting resolution reduced miners' hours from ten to nine and awarded them a 10 percent pay hike without forcing the owners to recognize the union. "I wish the capitalists would see," the president privately remarked, that the government-ordered compromise "is really in the interest of property, for it will save it from the danger of revolution."

Roosevelt also joined the Progressive campaign to remove the stranglehold that some trusts had on parts of the economy. In 1902 journalist Ida Tarbell began publishing a multipart series, "The History of the Standard Oil Company," in *McClure's Magazine*, a popular and influential middle-class news periodical. In her scathing critique Tarbell detailed the illicit deals that John D. Rockefeller had made with

Why did Roosevelt's personality and behavior captivate the public?

railroad companies to build his oil trust. Secret rebate agreements meant that Rockefeller paid considerably less than his competitors to ship oil. Many could not even get the railroads, which feared incurring Rockefeller's wrath, to transport their oil. Tarbell had firsthand experience with Rockefeller's cut-throat practices: They had bankrupted her father's oil business. She was convinced that Rockefeller's tactics would drive other small producers out of business, leaving a handful of industrialists in control of the entire economy.

The titans of industry offered a competing vision. There was nothing wonderful about economic competition, Rockefeller contended. Destructive price-cutting drove down wages, overproduction created regular depressions, and duplication of services wasted valuable resources. Rockefeller defended his railroad agreements as beneficial to all concerned. Standard Oil got lower rates while the railroads received guaranteed freight. Preventing too much oil from flooding the market stabilized prices and kept men in all oil-related industries profitably employed. The richest man in America also disputed claims that trusts made economic advancement impossible for average Americans, noting that he needed intelligent and skilled men to run his subsidiaries.

President Roosevelt agreed with much of Rockefeller's assessment. "The corporation has come to stay," he conceded, acknowledging that the entire nation benefited from the economies of scale that "good" trusts offered. Nonetheless, Roosevelt maintained, the government needed to break up "bad" trusts when consolidation threatened the public interest. The president soon singled out the Northern Securities Trust for dissolution, earning a reputation for **trust-busting** by taking steps to break up the monopoly.

In 1901 the financier J. P. Morgan had joined with two other powerful trust-builders, James J. Hill and E. H. Harriman, to form the Northern Securities Trust. The new transportation conglomerate meant "that you can ride from England to China on regular lines of steamships and railroads without once passing from the protecting hollow of Mr. Morgan's hand," announced journalist Ray Stannard Baker. With his eye on the 1904 presidential election, Roosevelt filed an antitrust suit charging the Northern Securities Trust with violating the 1890 Sherman Anti-Trust Act. A shocked Morgan rushed to the White House to broker a deal with the president. "If we have done anything wrong, send your man to my man and they can fix it up," suggested Morgan, an offer for a backroom deal that Roosevelt refused. In 1904 the Supreme Court upheld a Justice Department order to dissolve the Northern Securities Trust into independent railroad companies, earning Roosevelt public acclaim. One newspaper called him "the most popular man that has come into public life within recent times," after Roosevelt easily defeated the lackluster Democrat Alton B. Parker to win reelection in 1904. Roosevelt carried the Electoral College 336 to 140, the largest margin of victory in a presidential contest to date.

Standard Oil was next. In 1906 the Justice Department filed suit again, claiming that the trust had violated the Sherman Anti-Trust Act. This political cartoon (**18.3**). depicts Standard Oil as a frenzied octopus that has consumed the entire oil industry. Tentacles grasp overweight steel and copper businessmen in suits on one side and steamboats on the other, symbolizing how Standard Oil's control of the supply and price of oil strangled transportation and manufacturing industries. In the caricature state legislatures and Congress have succumbed to the monster's strength, and a leg now reaches for the White House.

When the Supreme Court finally ordered Standard Oil to dissolve in 1911, the justices avoided a blanket ruling that all trusts were illegal. The Court instead invoked a "rule of reason," stating that only unreasonable restraints of interstate trade violated the law. The Court's ruling aptly described ex-president Roosevelt's own trust-busting philosophy. Roosevelt launched highly visible assaults on the Northern Securities and Standard Oil Trusts. He did nothing, however, when Morgan bought Carnegie's steel empire in 1901 to create U.S. Steel, a trust that employed nearly one million workers.

Roosevelt balanced trust-busting with regulation to ensure that big business behaved responsibly. He strengthened the Interstate Commerce Commission (ICC), created in 1887 to address Populist Party criticism of high railroad freight rates and rebates

What competing visions did Roosevelt, the Supreme Court and leading industrialists offer on the trust issue?

18.3 Standard Oil's Tentacles In this political cartoon Standard Oil is an octopus, consuming everything in its path.

(see Chapter 17). By 1900 a series of sympathetic Supreme Court cases had essentially stripped the ICC of any real authority. During his second administration Roosevelt reinstated the power of the ICC to regulate railroad monopolies, convincing a reluctant Congress to pass the 1906 Hepburn Act. Four years later the Mann-Elkins Act further bolstered the rate-setting powers of the ICC and put the telegraph and telephone communication industries under its purview as well.

Taft and Wilson: Competing Progressive Visions

Having promised not to run again for president in 1908, Roosevelt helped his secretary of war, William Howard Taft, secure the Republican nomination. Roosevelt believed that Taft would continue his efforts to create a stronger, regulatory federal government. The Democrats countered by nominating the fiery William Jennings Bryan for a third time (see Chapter 17), trying to siphon Progressive votes away from a tepid Taft. Roosevelt's tireless campaigning for his chosen successor undercut Bryan's claim that he was the only real Progressive in the race. The Republican campaign slogan, "Vote for Taft now, you can vote for Bryan anytime," reminded voters of Bryan's two previous attempts to win the presidency and portrayed him as a perennial loser. Taft won easily, handing Bryan his worst electoral defeat.

Once Taft became president important philosophical differences between Roosevelt and Taft emerged. Like Roosevelt Taft had to work with a divided Republican party that controlled Congress. Roosevelt had sided with the Progressive faction, while

How did exposés and caricatures in the popular media shape public views of Standard Oil?

Taft gravitated to the conservatives. Unlike Roosevelt Taft viewed the president as an executor of law and protector of existing social institutions, not someone who spearheaded new reforms. A stickler for the law, Taft proved less willing than Roosevelt to make any distinction between good and bad trusts, filing more antitrust cases over four years than Roosevelt had in eight. Taft's decision to file charges against U.S. Steel enraged Roosevelt, who saw it as a personal attack on his earlier choice to leave this "good" trust alone.

Unhappy with his successor Roosevelt decided to run for president again in 1912. When Roosevelt's bid for the 1912 Republican nomination failed (the party nominated the incumbent Taft), Republican Progressives bolted and formed the short-lived Progressive (Bull Moose) Party, which nominated Roosevelt as their presidential candidate. The split in Republican ranks offered the Democrats an opportunity to capture the presidency for the first time since 1892. They nominated New Jersey Governor Woodrow Wilson, a Virginia-born politician with Progressive ideals. In contrast to the divided Republican Party, Wilson's candidacy kept the Southern base happy and prevented Progressively inclined Northern Democrats from joining the Progressive Party.

Taft, Roosevelt, and Wilson supported different degrees of federal activism, competing views that gave voters a clear choice in the election of 1912.

18.4 1912 **Presidential Election Results** Strong third-party challenges from the Progressive Party and Socialists split the national vote four ways, but Democrat Wilson prevailed to win the presidency in 1912.

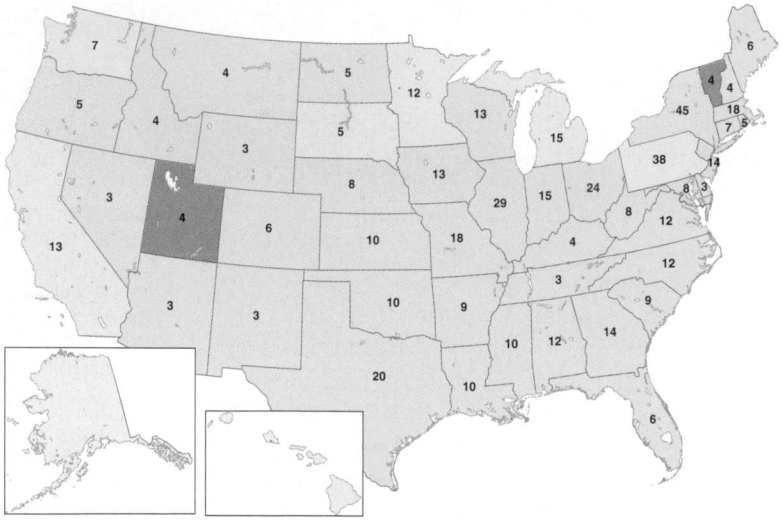

4 Electoral vote by state	Electoral Vote (%)	Popular Vote (%)
Woodrow Wilson *(Democrat)*	435 (82)	6,296,547 (41.9)
Theodore Roosevelt *(Progressive)*	88 (8)	4,118,571 (27.4)
William H Taft *(Republican)*	8 (0)	3,486,720 (23.2)
Eugene Debs *(Socialist)*	0 (0)	900,672 (6.0)

Taft was willing to zealously enforce existing Progressive reforms but had no intention of initiating any new ones. Roosevelt embraced a governing philosophy that he called "New Nationalism," a vision that emphasized increased federal regulation and widespread political reform. In contrast to Roosevelt, who wanted to regulate but not destroy big business, Wilson's "New Freedom" promised to restore a competitive marketplace where small businessmen and farmers thrived.

The 1912 slate also included Socialist Party candidate Eugene V. Debs, a railway trade union leader who had become a socialist after being jailed during the Pullman Strike of 1894. Formed in 1905 the Socialists had won numerous local elections and grown to over 100,000 dues-paying members. Roosevelt, Taft, and Wilson believed that with regulations in place (although each favored different amounts), capitalism would operate more fairly. Debs offered a competing view. He proposed transferring ownership of existing railroad, oil, and steel trusts to the government to ensure fair prices and wages. Government-run monopolies would be the first step toward ending the free-market system altogether.

The vast majority of voters agreed that the time had come to reform how the economy operated, but they overwhelmingly chose Progressivism over Socialism. Wilson won the presidency in 1912 (**18.4**) by a landslide in the Electoral College, while receiving only 41.9 percent of the popular vote. Roosevelt came in second with 27.4 percent of the popular vote, followed by Taft's 23.2 percent. Over 900,000 Americans, 6 percent of the electorate, voted for Debs. Nearly 70 percent of the country voted for Wilson or Roosevelt, an overwhelming public endorsement of Progressive principles and reforms.

Once he entered the White House President Woodrow Wilson went beyond trust-busting to weaken monopolies. He accepted the Democratic orthodoxy of cutting the tariff so foreign businesses could market lower-priced goods in the United States, thereby creating a more competitive marketplace where smaller businesses could thrive. By 1913 most industrialists had dropped their longstanding opposition to lowering the tariff. The heads of Singer Sewing Machines, Eastman Kodak, and U.S. Steel believed that other nations would reciprocate, allowing American captains of industry to conquer foreign markets as well. Wilson offset the lost tariff revenue (which the government needed to fund its operations) with the first federal income taxes, now constitutional thanks to the newly ratified **Sixteenth Amendment** (1913). Only people making more than

What clear philosophical differences separated the four candidates in the 1912 presidential election?

$4,000 a year paid federal income taxes (less than 1 percent of the population) at a time when most workers felt lucky to make $1,000 a year.

Wilson also tried to help small businesses by improving the flow of credit. Most small and big businessmen agreed with Wilson that the time had come to reform the country's chaotic banking system. They vividly remembered the Panic of 1907 when financial giant J. P. Morgan had used his own funds to shore up the national banking system. The nation's seven thousand banks operated with complete independence, issuing all forms of currency, some backed by gold and silver, others backed by government bonds. No centralized authority existed to expand or contract the currency supply as the economy demanded, or to move money throughout the country to stave off panics.

Conflicting visions soon arose over whether private financiers or the government should control the nation's financial institutions. Southern and Western populists wanted a federally run banking system that would destroy the Wall Street "money trust." Eastern bankers likened any government oversight to socialism. After much debate Congress passed the **Federal Reserve Act** (1913), creating a federally run Federal Reserve to serve as a "banker's bank" that held a portion of bank funds in reserve to help member banks in time of crisis. The Federal Reserve also set rates for business loans and issued a new national paper currency.

Wilson beefed up federal regulation of trusts as well. In 1914 the **Clayton Anti-Trust Act** prohibited interlocking directories, the practice of setting up shadow companies that appeared to compete but were actually run by the same board of directors. The law exempted trade unions from prosecution under the 1890 Sherman Anti-Trust Act, eliminating a tactic that businessmen had successfully used to undercut the labor movement. The **Federal Trade Commission** (1914) had the power to order companies to cease unfair trading practices, although its decisions were subject to court review.

Preservation versus Conservation

Roosevelt, Taft, and Wilson prescribed differing amounts of regulation and federal activism to rein in the trusts. Business's access to the nation's forests, water, and minerals provoked another set of competing visions within Progressive circles. In 1867 John Muir suffered a blinding eye injury while working as a mechanic. After his eyes healed Muir walked 1,000 miles from Indianapolis, Indiana, to the Gulf of Mexico to rejuvenate his spirit. Like Muir Roosevelt had turned to the revitalizing power of nature while recovering from personal tragedy when he retreated to his North Dakota ranch in 1884 after both his mother and twenty-two-year-old first wife died on the same day in their New York City home. In 1903 President Roosevelt went camping with Muir in Yosemite, an area of the California Sierra Nevada filled with spectacular waterfalls, massive rock formations, and Giant Sequoia trees nearly 200 feet high and three thousand years old. A photo of the pair on Glacier Point (**18.5**) before Yosemite Falls, the largest waterfall in North America, commemorated the trip. The two men dominate the frame, suggesting the power they had to decide the fate of such national treasures. This moment of unity was fleeting. Despite their mutual love of unspoiled forests, Muir and Roosevelt became formidable opponents who embraced different environmental visions.

Muir was a **preservationist** who championed preserving nature in its unspoiled state as a refuge for a "tired, nerve-shaken, over-civilized people." He accused businessmen of ravaging forests, polluting water, and destroying meadows with little regard for the long-term social costs of ruining the environment. Muir's condemnation resonated well with members of the middle class, who wanted to periodically escape the stress of urban life with holidays in the pristine wilderness. His influential writings led to the establishment of Yosemite as a national park in 1890 and the creation of the Sierra Club, an environmental group dedicated to preserving wilderness, in 1892.

18.5 John Muir and President Roosevelt in Yosemite, 1903 Despite their camaraderie during a shared camping trip, Muir and Roosevelt embraced competing environmental visions.

How did Wilson's economic vision and policies differ from the ones pursued by the Roosevelt and Taft administrations?

18.6 "The Vanishing Race," 1904
This blurry image of Navajo men riding away captured the prevailing sentiment that Indian cultures were on the verge of disappearing.

Muir's antibusiness message fit well with the Progressive determination to put the social good ahead of individual self-interest. Roosevelt agreed that a few unscrupulous entrepreneurs should not unfairly consume what belonged to the entire nation. To this end Roosevelt created five national parks, eighteen national monuments, and bird reserves that placed millions of acres off limit to development. The president parted company with Muir, however, by choosing to regulate, not ban, public access to other federally controlled lands, waterways, and mineral deposits. Roosevelt embraced a **conservationist** vision that tried to balance two goals: meeting present economic needs and conserving natural resources for future generations. When the U.S. Forestry Service director Gifford Pinchot allowed timber companies to harvest trees in designated areas, the new regulations enraged both preservationists, who wanted all economic development to cease, and Western businessmen, who demanded unfettered access to federally controlled forests.

Taft was sympathetic to Western complaints that Roosevelt had overstepped his authority. When Taft fired Pinchot, Roosevelt and his Progressive followers took it as a sign that Taft had abandoned conservation, deepening the split between the two former colleagues.

Environmentalists expressed great admiration for Native Americans' ecologically friendly farming and hunting practices, fueling mainstream curiosity about Indian cultures at the turn of the century. In 1900 photographer Edward Curtis began a thirty-year multivolume ethnographic project entitled *The North American Indian*, which recorded images of eighty different Indian civilizations. Many Indians willingly participated in Curtis's photography project, proud of the beautiful portraits he took of them in their best festive dress. Curtis wanted to capture the variety and richness of Native American cultures before they completely disappeared. Considering himself a friend to the Indian, Curtis believed (like most of his generation) that to survive Native Americans needed to assimilate into mainstream American society. The road ahead would not be easy for Native Americans, he felt. An intentionally blurred focus created a wistful aura to one of his most famous images, "The Vanishing Race" (**18.6**), which showed a line of Navajos riding off as one looks regretfully back. "The thought which this picture is meant to convey is that the Indians as a race, already shorn in their tribal strength and stripped of their primitive dress, are passing into the darkness of an unknown future," Curtis wrote.

Neither preservationists nor conservationists had any interest in reversing official policies of forced assimilation that divided collective reservation lands into individual farms, banned native languages, and sent Indian children to boarding schools (see Chapter 15). Preservationists inadvertently hastened the demise of some Indian cultures by enticing Americans to visit national forests. Tourism undercut Indians' access to traditional hunting grounds so that their economic survival increasingly depended on selling crafts to tourists and charging them to see performances of native dances.

Compare Progressive-Era debates over the environment with attitudes about disappearing Indian cultures.

Competing Views on Transforming the Workplace

In 1900 the United States earned the questionable distinction of being one of the most strike-torn nations in the world. To end class conflict and introduce more social harmony, Progressives wanted to transform the workplace into an environment where workers labored a reasonable number of hours in safe conditions for decent wages. Industry and labor each presented a competing view that challenged the Progressive vision as they sought the upper hand in their decades-long class struggle.

Capitalist Visions of Industrial Harmony

Industrialists differed on how to rid the workplace of labor conflicts that interfered with the smooth operation of their businesses. The National Civic Federation brought together moderate industrialists and labor union leaders dedicated to seeking industrial peace through compromise. Ohio senator Mark Hanna, who made his fortune in coal, argued that industrialists should turn labor into "the ally of the capitalist, rather than a foe." In return for a few minimal concessions, factory owners could demand that union leaders discipline their membership and keep workers on the job, thus ending the constant strife that permeated the industrial sector.

Hanna's voice was a decided minority. Most industrialists refused to compromise any of their authority. Staunchly antiunion they employed a host of methods to undercut unions. If forced to accept a union, they insisted upon an "open shop" that let workers choose whether to join a union, then used intimidation to stop workers from enrolling. Industrialists fired identified union members, hired private security forces to spy on workers, and created lists of fired workers, known as blacklists. Once listed a worker could not find another job. During strikes factory owners expelled families from company-owned housing and hired substitute workers (called scabs) to replace striking workers. To protect union members from these discriminatory industrialist policies and build strength, labor organizers fought to establish a "closed shop," which required all workers in the same company to join the union.

Other industrialists embraced benevolence as a way to dissuade workers from organizing. **Welfare capitalism**, the notion of using benefits to gain workers' loyalty, aimed to improve worker morale and weaken interest in unions. Some large firms instituted free medical care, pensions, kindergartens, and even baseball leagues, but these services typically evaporated at the first sign of economic downturn. Unions did not want to leave it up to the employer to decide whether to offer benefits. They preferred using collective bargaining to negotiate a contractual agreement between workers and their employers that established such benefits as a permanent right.

The drive for efficiency, a goal that many Progressives shared, was another way that industrialists undercut workers' collective power. Henry Ford's innovations in automobile manufacturing demonstrated how industrialists could boost profits by reducing manufacturing costs. The son of a prosperous Irish immigrant farmer in Dearborn, Michigan, Ford built his first car in 1896 in a shed behind his Detroit home. Forming the Ford Motor Company, Ford introduced the Model T in 1908, a moment when 515 separate companies were manufacturing automobiles. Ford standardized parts, constantly improved machinery, and used conveyor belts on his assembly line—innovations that let him produce more cars for less money. Ford passed these savings onto consumers, lowering the price of his "car for the great multitudes" from $825 in 1908 to $345 in 1916. By then Ford had captured half the market for new cars.

In 1914 Ford created headlines by offering workers a five-dollar daily wage for eight hours of work. Ford paid twice the standard wage rate because he recognized that the common practice of paying workers subsistence wages limited the markets for many consumer goods. Ford wanted his workers to be able to afford his automobiles. Working eight instead of ten hours a day, Ford reasoned, reduced fatigue-induced mistakes and worker turnover, giving the company a loyal and

What different ways did industrialists try to end labor conflict?

> "The men do their work and go home—a factory is not a drawing room."
>
> HENRY T. FORD on his rule prohibiting workers from talking to each other as they assembled automobiles

experienced workforce. The moving conveyor belt in Ford's assembly lines (**18.7**) meant that workers no longer had to lift or move the chassis as they assembled a car. Ford admitted that he "could not do the same thing day in and out," but he condescendingly believed that the average worker "wants a job in which he does not have to think." To keep workers focused and productive, Ford prohibited sitting, talking, singing, or whistling in his factories. Fearful of losing their jobs, workers only dared to criticize Ford's iron control over the production process in private.

Ford's five dollar/eight hour day came with strings attached. Ford instituted many reforms that Progressives sought because they made business sense, but he staunchly resisted government regulation and attempts to organize a union, retaining the right to make his own factory rules. Ford also firmly subscribed to industrialists' long-standing belief that they had the right, and the duty, to interfere in the private lives of their employees. For Ford this meant offering benefits only to employees who met certain moral criteria. Married men, for instance, had to live with their families. Thirty investigators working for Ford's Sociological Department visited workers' homes and sometimes imposed other requirements, such as mandatory English classes for immigrants. Gambling, excessive drinking, or having sexual relations with a prostitute were all grounds for dismissal. A Ford Motor Company investigator had to verify that a worker was morally upright (and not trying to organize a union) before he and his family could move into a spacious two-story home built by the company.

Progressives valued efficiency and expertise, and Frederick Winslow Taylor took the drive for

18.7 The Assembly Line
Ford's innovative mass production techniques included a well-lit and ventilated environment that relieved workers of backbreaking tasks. The assembly line also deadened the mind, as constant routine movements eliminated the need for any decision making. [From the Collection of the Henry Ford, THF23871]

How much did Ford's innovations and paternalism benefit workers?

efficiency further than Ford by popularizing **scientific management**, the effort to use scientific knowledge for maximizing output and profit. Taylor used stopwatches to evaluate how long each part of the manufacturing process should take. He then outlined the steps laborers should replicate to lay bricks without any wasted energy, and determined the perfect shovel size and the exact amount of rest workers needed to lift the maximum amount of pig iron each day. After establishing the optimal time and method for a specific task, Taylor argued, industrialists could then fine or fire unproductive workers who failed to maintain an acceptable pace. Taylor admitted that his system, dubbed "taylorism," intentionally eliminated workers' independence and creativity. Each man, he asserted, must "grow accustomed to receiving and obeying directions covering details, large and small, which in the past have been left to his individual judgment."

Working-Class Labor Activism

The working class had long fashioned their own solutions to surviving difficult living and working conditions. Fraternal associations assisted those who lost their jobs or needed to bury a loved one, while urban political machines (see Chapter 17) secured voters' loyalty by helping families endure personal tragedies such as fires or illness. Meanwhile unions tried to negotiate better wages and shop floor rules for dues-paying members, but organizing the working class so it could speak with one voice proved impossible. Ethnic and racial prejudices kept the working class fragmented. Italian strikebreakers, for instance, had few qualms about walking across a picket line manned by Slavic strikers. The craft-based American Federation of Labor (AFL), led by Samuel Gompers, only organized skilled, mostly white workers, refusing to let unskilled laborers, women, or blacks into their unions. Only a handful of industrial unions like the United Mine Workers and International Longshoreman's Union adopted a big umbrella approach that organized all workers in one industry into the same union.

Middle-class Progressives supported many union goals but deplored their methods. Strikes continually disrupted normal life by shutting down railroad lines, street cars, and coal mines. Government regulation, they maintained, would improve workers' lives and ensure that the economy functioned smoothly. Nevertheless many unions remained skeptical about relying on the government to solve their conflicts. The AFL preferred using its collective economic power to force industrialists to negotiate. Its members had unhappy memories of what happened when state or federal officials intervened in labor conflicts, as during the 1894 Pullman Strike (see Chapter 17).

The Roosevelt administration occasionally chose to aid labor, but Progressive Era court decisions nearly always favored industrialists. In 1908 the Supreme Court stopped workers from launching sympathy strikes or boycotts to support fellow workers, labeling them "restraints of trade" barred under the 1890 Sherman Anti-Trust Act, a law originally intended to curtail the creation of business monopolies. Another 1908 decision allowed employers to fire workers who joined unions. Reducing government interference in labor conflicts therefore remained the AFL's primary goal.

Radical trade unionists rejected the AFL vision of working within the free market system. The **Industrial Workers of the World** (IWW), formed in 1905, envisioned "one big union" that welcomed all workers regardless of sex, race, ethnicity, or skill, which would one day take over all means of production in the United States. "It is the historic mission of the working class to do away with capitalism," declared the founders of the IWW, whose members were nicknamed "Wobblies." The founding group included seventy-five-year-old Mother Mary Jones, a tireless white-haired organizer for the United Mine Workers, and William D. "Big Bill" Haywood, an organizer for the Western Federation of Miners. Their drive to abolish private property and formal government struck many Progressives as anarchy. Government harassment of the IWW limited its formal membership to around ten thousand.

The Progressives' Limited Progress

Employers had traditionally held employees responsible for workplace accidents, maintaining that workers knowingly accepted all job-associated risks. Personal carelessness caused most mishaps, they argued. Progressive organizations undertook detailed sociological studies to refute these self-serving generalizations. Lewis Hine's photographic investigation into the lives of injured Pittsburgh workers suggested that few were responsible for

What conflicting visions divided working-class union activists?

18.8 An Injured Pittsburgh Worker Portraits of maimed workers helped generate a groundswell of support for state workers' compensation laws.

their accidents. This young man (**18.8**) had his leg crushed when he fell under a coal car in a Pittsburgh coal mine. The company paid the hospital expenses for his amputation, but nothing else. In the image a nicely dressed passerby avoids making eye contact with the injured boy who stands idle on the street, suggesting that the well-off preferred to ignore the plight of disabled workers. The boy's tidy appearance reveals an effort to maintain some personal dignity while relying on private charity to survive. Studies like Hine's convinced many states to establish worker compensation programs that provided employer-funded disability payments and medical care to injured workers. As a result employers began paying more attention to workplace safety.

The drive to limit hours for male workers was less successful. Employers had traditionally maintained that as property owners they had the sole power to decide the terms of employment. In the 1874 Slaughterhouse cases, the Supreme Court had ruled that a state could not deny individuals control over their own labor. Industrialists claimed that this decision granted individual workers the constitutionally protected right to negotiate wages, hours, and workplace rules. According to this line of reasoning, state laws or unions that tried to impose restrictions on individual workers violated their right to control their own labor.

The Supreme Court, however, proved willing to abridge this right to protect public health and safety. In 1898 the Court upheld an eight-hour day for Utah miners, deciding that guarding the health of workers engaged in a dangerous occupation served the public interest. Progressives failed in their efforts to extend these protections to the entire workforce. In ***Lochner v. New York*** (1905), the Court ruled that unless long work hours directly jeopardized workers' health, the government could not abridge an employee's freedom to negotiate his own work schedule with his employer. This decision is explored more fully in *Choices and Consequences: Regulating Workers' Hours.*

Miserable and unsafe working conditions also persisted. The Colorado mining town of Ludlow sat along the Purgatory River, a telling name that suitably described what working in a mine was like. In Ludlow, the Rockefeller-owned mining company paid miners $2 a day in company-issued currency (called scrip) redeemable only in the company-run store. The mining company required that workers live in company-owned housing, and claimed no responsibility for accidents that killed two hundred miners between 1904 and 1914.

In 1913 twelve thousand miners, mostly Italian, Greek, and Serbian immigrants, went on strike to protest these conditions and demand company recognition of their United Mine Workers union. When the company expelled the strikers and their families from their homes, the workers erected a series of tent cities in the nearby hills. After armed company detectives failed to dislodge the miners, the Colorado governor sent in state troops, whose wages Rockefeller agreed to pay. The **Ludlow Massacre** ensued on April 20, 1914 when troops set fire to one striking miners' camp, and thirteen women and children suffocated to death in a shallow underground shelter where they had sought refuge.

Throughout the nation outraged laborers temporarily put their ideological divisions aside to stage protest marches in every major city. The United Mine Workers issued "a call to arms," and hundreds of neighboring miners flooded into Ludlow to defend their comrades against the state militia. Faced with the prospect of all-out class war, the Colorado governor requested federal troops and President Wilson immediately complied. Federal intervention left the union in tatters and Rockefeller free to run his mining town as he saw fit. Incidents like these convinced many unions that the Progressive proposal to rely solely on the government to solve their problems was not the answer. Throughout the twentieth century union folklore and songs used the memory of Ludlow to inspire workers to organize.

How effective were the different strategies that Progressive and unions employed to reform the workplace?

Choices and Consequences

REGULATING WORKERS' HOURS

Most city residents, especially tenement-dwellers who did not have ovens, bought their bread from bakeries. Bakers worked long hours in hot and poorly ventilated kitchens, sleeping and washing where they baked bread. In 1895 New York passed a law that set sanitary standards and limited bakers to ten hours of work per day, sixty hours per week. Joseph Lochner, a bakery owner in Utica, challenged the law after New York fined him $50 for making an employee exceed these limits. The Supreme Court faced several choices when it heard the case in 1905.

Choices

1. A state could use its police powers to protect workers' health and safety.
2. A state could not limit an individual's right to buy or sell labor in nonhazardous occupations such as baking.
3. States had the right to enact any laws not expressly forbidden in the Constitution to promote the general well-being of society.

Decision

The Court ruled 5 to 4 that the Fourteenth Amendment, which declared that "no state shall ... deprive any person of life, liberty, or property without due process of the law," prevented states from using their police powers to regulate work that did not imperil the health or safety of the public.

Consequences

The decision curtailed Progressives' attempt to use regulation to transform the workplace. During the subsequent thirty-two-year "Lochner" era, the Court struck down maximum hour, minimum wage, and child labor laws if no clear risk to the public existed. Dismayed Progressives noted that many state laws restricted an individual's ability to buy or sell labor, such as mandatory school laws or Sunday closures, to promote the general welfare. They also accused the Court of ignoring the disproportionate power that employers wielded over workers to set the terms of employment.

Lochner bakery

Continuing Controversies

Should the government limit work hours or set a minimum wage?
Lochner remained the law of the land until 1937, when the Supreme Court ruled that it was "reasonable" for Washington State hotel owners to pay female hotel maids the state-mandated minimum wage because the state had a right to protect its residents. Defining an acceptable standard for work and pay has been controversial ever since. Is a reasonable day's work six, eight, ten, or twelve hours? Does it matter if the work involves strenuous physical labor or sedentary work? Is it better for unions to negotiate the terms of employment or for the government to step in? How does regulating hours of work or setting a minimum wage hurt or benefit the general public? These are questions that Americans have debated for the last seventy years.

What competing views existed concerning a state's right to regulate the workplace?

Protecting Women and Children

Progressives never convinced unions to give up strikes, but together they demanded laws protecting women and children. Relying on mountains of sociological data and heart-rending photographs, female activists helped secure protective legislation that reduced the hours women worked and kept children in school longer. Working-class men offered more resistance when female reformers tried to make temperance the law of the land.

Women at Work

In 1908 Curt Muller, a laundry owner in Portland, Oregon, challenged a recent state law granting a ten-hour workday for female laundry workers. In making his case before the Supreme Court, Muller followed the same line of reasoning used in the *Lochner* case, arguing that the law deprived his workers of their right to control their own labor. He disputed the reformers' claim that scrubbing all day in a hot, wet workplace posed a serious risk to laundry workers' health. In its unanimous affirmative 1908 ***Muller v. Oregon*** ruling, the Supreme Court upheld maximum hour laws for female workers, accepting lawyer Louis Brandeis's argument that protecting women's reproductive health served the public good. "As healthy mothers are essential to vigorous offspring, the physical well-being of woman becomes an object of public interest and care in order to preserve the strength and vigor of the race," the Supreme Court declared.

Reactions to the ruling among women were mixed. Middle-class Progressive reformers and female trade unionists celebrated the ruling as a victory for female workers, unperturbed by the Court's emphasis on the biological inferiority of women to men. Feminists who believed in total equality were disappointed with the ruling, creating a fissure in the women's movement that widened into an open split within the next few years. The male-dominated AFL embraced the decision, believing it reduced employers' incentive to hire women instead of men. As if to prove this point, Muller responded by firing his female workers and hiring Chinese men to take their place.

Cross-class alliances between middle-class and working-class women flourished around other efforts to help working women. In 1898 the National Consumers' League (NCL) formed to coordinate local consumer boycotts of department stores that mistreated their female clerks. The NCL made the long hours and low pay endured by female working-class clerks the responsibility of every middle-class female shopper. The group soon expanded their boycotts to include stores that sold clothing made in sweatshops or with child labor. Compiling "blacklists" of stores to boycott was illegal, so the NCL instead worked with female garments' unions to create "white lists" of shops with equitable labor policies, places where socially conscientious women could shop without remorse.

18.9 Carry A. Nation Portrait and Hatchet Pin
Carry A. Nation cultivated her notoriety as a Bible-toting, ax-wielding saloon smasher by selling portraits and pins to her admirers. [*Source* (pin): Kansas State Historical Society]

Stamping Out Vice

Local and state reformers also took aim at alcohol, believing that prohibition would improve women's lives by reducing domestic violence and bolstering family income. The Woman's Christian Temperance Union (WCTU; see Chapter 17) viewed the saloon as a haven for gambling, prostitution, corrupt city political machines, and excessive alcohol consumption. The WCTU crusade took a surprising turn on June 6, 1900, when a deeply religious

Why did the campaign for maximum work hour laws succeed for women, but fail for men?

sixty-four-year-old woman named Carry A. Nation strode into a southwestern Kansas bar with a bag of bricks and smashed the liquor bottles, glassware, and mirrors, then calmly left. Nation's tactics were extreme, but many Progressives shared her sense of urgency. Drinking was on the rise in America. From 1885 to 1900 beer consumption nearly doubled from 590 million to 1.2 billion gallons. Hundreds of inspired "Home Defenders" throughout the nation organized similar attacks on neighborhood bars, hoping to convince their communities to go dry. As her fame grew Nation raised funds by selling miniature hatchet pins, her new weapon of choice (**18.9**), along with photos of herself holding her bible and hatchet. She spent time in jails from New York to Los Angeles publicizing the temperance cause before collapsing on a stage in 1911 and dying shortly thereafter.

Working-class men resolutely defended their freedom to drink, and many upper-class men were reluctant to give up a pleasure-based lifestyle that included ready access to alcohol. Attacking on multiple fronts the nonpartisan Anti-Saloon League, founded in 1893, and the WCTU established an effective coalition that included Progressives, rural Americans, and industrialists. Prohibitionists linked ridding the nation of alcohol to the broader Progressive desire to eliminate the corrupting influences of big-city political machines. Saloons, temperance advocates maintained, served as the headquarters where dishonest city politicians paid immigrants for votes and dispersed favors to supporters. Temperance advocates drew rural folk into the movement by addressing their concerns about the growing cultural influence of urban pleasures and the beer-drinking immigrants who lived in the cities. Molding their message to appeal to industrialists, temperance advocates blamed saloons for contributing to the nation's labor troubles by giving unions a place to meet and recruit.

> "You refused me the vote and I had to use a rock."
>
> CARRY A. NATION explains her saloon-smashing ways

Working through churches in the South and the West, the Anti-Saloon League and WCTU urged supporters to focus on making their state or county "dry" by banning the sale of alcohol. The "Prohibition 1904 and 1917" map (**18.10**) traces the rapid success of this strategy as the number of dry states grew from three to twenty-three. Many Western women had already secured the right to vote, and they flocked to approve prohibition in large numbers.

18.10 Prohibition, 1904 and 1917
Only three states were dry in 1904, but by 1917 over half of the people in the country lived in either a state or county that had gone dry—momentum that led to nationwide prohibition in 1919.

What diverse concerns about alcohol helped the temperance movement gain momentum?

Restoring Childhood

Middle-class Americans believed that childhood should be devoted to education and play, not work. This advertisement (**18.11**) from an 1898 Sears and Roebuck catalog portrayed the type of idyllic childhood that many middle-class families tried to give their children. In the ad an immaculately dressed young girl rides joyfully in the sunshine on a new bicycle, a portrait of health and happiness. The reality for working-class children offered a stark contrast. Census records revealed nearly 1.75 million children ages ten through fifteen worked in factories full time, a figure that did not include children employed in home sweatshops or on family farms.

To Progressives child labor epitomized the greed of employers who eagerly sent children into mining crevices where adults could not fit, used children to harvest crops in the Midwest, or dispatched an army of small boys to hawk newspapers in Northern cities. Organized labor joined this crusade, certain that child labor drove down adult wages. Industrialists offered a competing vision, arguing that jobs provided valuable training for working-class children who

18.11 "Models of 1898"
The middle class believed that children should engage in healthy and creative play, not work in dangerous and dreary factories.

What does this advertisement reveal about middle-class ideals of childhood?

needed to learn the importance of punctuality and hard work to become successful adult workers.

Many working-class families shared employers' beliefs that their children should work. In Chicago Hull House cofounder Jane Addams discovered that most immigrants, having worked themselves as children, found nothing wrong with putting their own children to work. "A South Italian peasant who has picked olives and packed oranges from his toddling babyhood, cannot see at once the difference between the outdoor healthy work which he has performed in the varying seasons, and the long hours of monotonous factory life which his child encounters when he goes to work in Chicago," she noted, adopting the Progressive tendency to gloss over the drudgery of farm work.

Most working-class families depended on their children's meager wages to survive. Child labor provided one-tenth of family income in the early twentieth century. Recently arrived immigrant men, especially unskilled, non-English speakers, realized with dismay that their English-speaking children were more apt to be hired than they were. Children in these families became the breadwinners, while their fathers stayed at home. This reversal of normal family relations often created tensions within working-class households. "I left Europe and I was a man, and here I am a what?" lamented one Russian Jewish immigrant. Idle men, frustrated over their inability to provide for their families, sometimes turned to drink, depleting the family's income even further.

The drive to end child labor gained momentum when the National Child Labor Committee formed in 1904 to lobby for state and federal laws prohibiting child labor. The group hired photographer Lewis Hine to help them build a scientific, legal, and moral case against child labor. In one photo-story, Hine paired images of children who worked in two textile mills owned by the same company. The company's mill in Huntsville, Alabama, hired children as young as eight years old, Hine noted, while Massachusetts law prohibited the Lowell factory from employing children under the age of fourteen. The National Child Labor Committee presented such regional discrepancies as evidence that the nation needed a federal child labor law. *Images as History: Exposing Child Labor*, page 550, explores Hine's images more fully.

The pervasiveness of child labor in the South particularly troubled him. In 1900 nearly 25 percent of the workers in textile factories and cotton mills were white children ages ten to sixteen. Some reformers viewed child farm work as a healthier alternative to long days in a factory. Hine disagreed. "The sunshine in the cotton fields has blinded our eyes to the monotony, overwork and the hopelessness of their lives," he wrote.

In 1916 President Wilson signed a law banning the interstate sale of products made by child labor that protected only about 150,000 industrial child laborers out of nearly 1.75 million. Two years later the Supreme Court sided with a father who argued that the law deprived him of his parental right to control his sons' labor and declared the law unconstitutional. Progressives responded by trying to amend the Constitution. In 1924 Congress approved an amendment giving the federal government the power to regulate child labor, but Southern opposition to any curtailment of states' rights prevented its ratification. A nationwide ban on child labor did not come until the 1930s, when the Court upheld a New Deal federal child labor law.

Ultimately child labor declined as states began to mandate school attendance. Embracing the notion that all children had the right to an education, local women's groups pushed hard to ensure that their neighborhood schools received appropriate funding, provided free books, offered kindergarten, paid teachers adequately, and were equipped with satisfactory fire escapes. Throughout the Progressive Era school enrollments, the number of days in a school year, and money spent per pupil all rose.

Several other Progressive endeavors also aimed to improve the lives of working-class children. The allure of pleasure and hunger at home sometimes became too strong for children, who resorted to stealing to meet their needs. "Most of these premature law breakers are in search of Americanized clothing and others are only looking for playthings," Jane Addams maintained. Some, she pointed out, were simply "eager to take home food or fuel which will relieve the distress and need they so constantly hear discussed." Reformers spearheaded the creation of a juvenile criminal system that focused on rehabilitating young offenders.

To keep young children safely off the streets when their parents went to work, Progressive activists established urban playgrounds with adult supervisors. To divert female teenagers from tempting dance halls and male adolescents from saloons or brothels, Progressives created a wide array of local boys and girls clubs that included organized sports teams and art classes. Not every child appreciated becoming the object of reform. "I can't go to the playgrounds now," complained one eleven-year-old boy. "They get on me nerves with so many men and women around telling you what to do."

What obstacles did reformers face while trying to eliminate child labor?

Images as History

EXPOSING THE EVILS OF CHILD LABOR

Trained as a sociologist, photographer Lewis Hine took nearly five thousand photographs as a staff photographer for the National Child Labor Committee from 1908 to 1918. Hine visited factories, canneries, textile mills, farms, and mines snapping photos and recording the life stories of each child, evidence the National Child Labor Committee used to argue that full-time work damaged children's health, deprived them of an education, and ruined their childhood. Hine often posed as a factory inspector or salesman to gain access to factories or mines. When a factory owner guessed his real purpose and refused to let him in, Hine took pictures of child laborers arriving at daybreak or leaving covered in grime. He carefully recorded the children's names, ages, and stories to counter industrialists' accusations that he staged his photos.

His notes for this image of a young girl tending machines in a South Carolina cotton mill read, "Sadie Pfeifer, 48 inches high, has worked half a year. One of the many small children at work in Lancaster Cotton Mills." Are Hine's photographs best understood as historical evidence or propaganda, or both?

Sadie Pfeifer was a spinner in a South Carolina cotton mill, charged with repairing breaks or snags as the machines spun the cotton into yarn or thread.

The electric lights indicate her long hours, beginning before daybreak and extending after dark.

The closed windows helped the factory maintain the hot and humid conditions that prevented thread from breaking.

The long row of machines underscores how much work she had to manage on her own, dangerous work that could cost her a finger.

The photograph does not convey the deafening noise that left some workers partially deaf.

The adult supervisor in the background represented Sadie's future and underscored her subservient position in the mill.

Lewis Hine, "Sadie Pfeifer, Lancaster Cotton Mills, South Carolina"

How did the composition of this photograph reinforce Hine's message about child labor?

Wise beyond their years, these tough-looking newsboys emulate their elders by learning to enjoy pipes and cigarettes. Newsboys also gambled, swore, and began visiting houses of prostitution at a shockingly young ages.

Camaraderie among newsboys helped make a difficult and lonely job more enjoyable.

This photo of hardened newsboys warned that without a proper education, these boys contributed to the moral breakdown of society.

Lewis Hine, "Newsies Smoking on a Monday Morning, St. Louis, Missouri, 1910"

By innocently buying a daily paper from one of the hundreds of newsboys who hawked newspapers on city corners from dawn to dusk, the middle class helped perpetuate an insidious form of child labor.

The National Child Labor Committee distributed Hine's "Making Human Junk" poster nationwide to send the message that child labor ruined individual lives and hurt the entire society.

The poster showed a group of healthy children entering a harsh and dangerous factory environment where they were powerless to control their own fates.

Appealing to middle-class self-interest, this poster suggested that sickly child workers contaminated the materials used to make clothing for the middle class.

Hine directly refuted industrialists' claims that work benefited children. "The object of employing children is not to train them, but to get high profits from their work," he wrote.

Long days in the mill turned children into broken pieces of industrial "junk" that factory owners discarded, burdening society with their care.

Lewis Hine, "Making Human Junk"

Did these images offer similar or different reasons to oppose child labor?

Reforming the Government

Progressives recognized that passing laws governing the workplace or protecting women and children was not enough. Ensuring their enforcement through the establishment of regulatory agencies required reforming how local, state, and federal governments functioned. Only then could the government become a positive force in workers' lives. Socialists agreed that the government should act, but ultimately wanted to give state and national governments control of all major industries.

Containing Socialism

Progressives discovered an unexpected ally in their drive to turn the government into a guardian that actively protected the public. Both Progressives and socialists championed the creation of city-run utilities to provide streetcar service, gas, water, and electricity. Progressives viewed such arrangements as an efficient way to deliver reliable, fairly priced public services to city residents, prevent disruptive strikes, and improve conditions for utility workers. Socialists believed that municipal-run utilities would become the opening wedge that led to eventual public ownership of railroads, mines, and banks.

In 1904 the novelist and socialist Upton Sinclair lived with workers in Chicago for nearly two months, learning firsthand about their work in the meatpacking industry. This experience became the basis for Sinclair's novel, *The Jungle*, which told the story of a Lithuanian immigrant family who came to America full of hope only to discover crushing poverty and horrific working conditions. The novelist wanted his exposé to convince Americans that socialism offered the only way to end the rampant capitalist exploitation that ground down the working class. Instead readers focused on his vivid descriptions of rotten meat, workers' fingers, and rat excrement all being tossed into the hopper to produce the sausage that Americans enjoyed each morning for breakfast. When a federal investigation confirmed Sinclair's account, the public demanded federal regulation to ensure that the nation's meat supply was safe. Faced with plummeting meat sales, packinghouse owners understood that government certification of their meat as disease-free could help them regain consumer confidence. The **Meat Inspection Act** (1906) gave federal inspectors the authority to condemn meat unfit for consumption and established federal sanitary standards for meatpacking plants.

> "I aimed at the public's heart, and by accident I hit it in the stomach."
>
> UPTON SINCLAIR laments America's reaction to his novel, *The Jungle*

Reformers also wanted manufacturers of patent medicines to list their ingredients. Lydia E. Pinkham's Vegetable Compound, a widely popular patent medicine, circulated advertising cards (**18.12**) with images of rosy-cheeked children to create the impression that the company used the purest ingredients in its syrup. The flipside of this card touted the medicine as "a positive cure for all those painful complaints and weaknesses so common to our best female population," including headaches, depression, ovarian troubles, and menopause. In 1906 the **Pure Food and Drug Act** levied fines for mislabeling food or medicine. To their dismay many female temperance advocates who had avidly consumed Lydia E. Pinkham's Vegetable Compound discovered that the serum contained 15 percent alcohol.

Ultimately the Progressive vision of government oversight prevailed over the socialist view of complete government control. Most cities balked at direct ownership of public utilities, preferring to create regulatory boards that set rules for the private companies that continued to run streetcars or gas lines. The subsequent improvement in city services reduced the appeal of socialism in many working-class neighborhoods.

Ending Government Corruption

Progressives knew that meaningful regulation required eliminating corruption within all levels of government. For an enticing bribe, city officials often

What importance did the socialist movement have during the Progressive Era?

18.12 Marketing Lydia E. Pinkham's Vegetable Compound
Ads for the patent medicine promised to cure practically every ailment and restore youthful vigor.

proved willing to look the other way when businesses broke the law. Political parties sometimes stole elections as well, creating fictitious lists of voters that let individuals use multiple aliases to vote as often as they liked.

Progressives disagreed over how to eliminate corruption. One answer was to get rid of politicians and instead rely on nonpartisan commissions of experts or city-managers to run city services. Over four hundred municipalities turned to commission-style governance, an approach that reflected the broad faith placed in expertise during the Progressive Era. Other Progressives replaced the ward system that let each neighborhood select its own councilman with city councils elected at large. Voters expected their ward representative to "bring home the bacon," patronage that Progressives felt encouraged parochialism and corruption. Impoverished working-class residents offered a competing vision. Their ward representatives provided needed job opportunities or relief. In the absence of a comprehensive social welfare system, the patronage-based ward system gave many working-class urban residents a way to survive hard times.

On the state level Progressives tried to reduce the power of corrupt political parties. Many states eliminated the previous practice of handing voters different colored ballots marked "Republican" or "Democrat" to stuff into the ballot boxes as party officials looked on. The secret ballot removed the threat of payback or shunning if one broke with the neighborhood party boss. Instead of letting party leaders chose candidates, some states introduced direct primaries that allowed party members to pick the candidates. A reform measure called the "**initiative**" provided a way, usually by gathering signatures on petitions, for the electorate to introduce legislation before state legislatures. The **referendum** put legislative proposals on the ballot, letting the voting public decide whether a measure became law. Finally the **recall** used special elections to remove unpopular or corrupt officials from office before their term expired. Wisconsin, one of the most Progressive states in the nation, adopted all these measures under the leadership of Governor Robert Lafollette.

In 1906 journalist David Graham Phillips detailed the close ties between big business and federal senators in a series of magazine articles entitled "The Treason of the Senate." Phillips viewed this alliance as threatening to "the American people as any invading army could be." Roosevelt charged Phillips with overexaggerating the extent of corruption and urged the "men with the muckrakes" to avoid stirring up needless controversy. Roosevelt's rebuke gave investigative journalists a new nickname, "**muckrakers**." Subsequent corruption scandals solidified public support for the **Seventeenth Amendment** (1913), which allowed voters, rather than state legislatures, to elect federal senators.

What reforms did Progressives introduce to improve the democratic process?

18.13 Hampton Institute Students Building a Staircase, 1900
Black educators distributed images of tidy black students working industriously to counter stereotypes that portrayed blacks as lazy or dangerous.

Accepting Separate but Equal

The Progressive campaign to remake the government into a champion of the common man did not include challenging the legal edifice constructed in the wake of the Supreme Court's 1896 "separate but equal" ruling in *Plessy v. Ferguson* (see Chapter 14). At the turn of the century, Southern states rushed to pass laws that formally segregated every public facility from railroad waiting rooms to water fountains. Use of poll taxes and literacy tests to disenfranchise blacks also exploded. When Southern-born Woodrow Wilson took office in 1913, he let the heads of federal agencies segregate their offices.

Few white Progressives spoke out against the onslaught of discriminatory laws. They convinced themselves that segregation would quell racial conflict, essentially choosing social peace over racial justice. "Good fences make good neighbors," asserted Southern Progressive leader Edgar Gardner Murphy. Jane Addams was a notable exception. She disagreed that segregation benefited the black middle class by giving black doctors and businessmen a ready clientele. Most other Northern Progressives remained content to let the South handle the "race problem" as it saw fit.

African American leaders cultivated their own reform impulse during the Progressive Era. Unlike white Progressives black leaders had little faith that government would solve their social problems. The most prominent African American leader of the Progressive Era, Booker T. Washington, instead embraced self-help as the best way to end poverty among African Americans. Born a Virginia slave in 1859, after the Civil War Washington moved with his family to West Virginia where he worked in a coal mine. As a child Washington developed an almost fanatical desire to get an education, arriving penniless

How does this photograph convey the Hampton Institute's educational philosophy?

at the doorstep of Virginia's Hampton Institute, a vocationally oriented high school founded in 1868 to educate freed slaves and Indians. He passed his entrance exam—sweeping a floor—with flying colors. Hampton taught practical skills such as brick-making, blacksmithing, and shoemaking along with more traditional academic subjects like reading and math. This staged photograph (**18.13**) of a Hampton Institute carpentering class, taken twenty years after Washington attended, encapsulated the school's educational philosophy. The photo underscored that these perfectly groomed, hard-working, and well-trained students had the skills they needed to advance step-by-step up the ladder (in this case staircase) of success.

Washington followed the Hampton model when he established his own school in 1881, the Tuskegee Institute in Tuskegee, Alabama. A captivating orator Washington popularized the notion that blacks should focus on economic advancement first, politics and civil rights later. Washington's apparent willingness to accept social segregation, as long as blacks and whites worked together toward their common economic goals, won him a large white following. Roosevelt even invited him to dine in the White House, the first African American to ever receive this honor—an invitation that provoked howls of protest throughout the South. Washington's private behavior, however, was often at odds with his public persona. Publicly he reassured whites that most blacks had little interest in demanding equality as long as they could prosper economically. Privately Washington helped fund court challenges to *Plessy v. Ferguson* and sent his own children to Northern white colleges.

Washington believed that American race relations would gradually improve. Methodist minister Henry McNeal Turner offered a competing vision, telling blacks to leave the country and immigrate to Africa. Black journalist Ida B. Wells-Barnett also disagreed with Washington. Rather than striving to prove their economic worth to whites, Wells-Barnett urged African Americans to use boycotts to win equal treatment from white-owned railroads. She also advocated armed resistance to lynch mobs. "A Winchester rifle should have a place of honour in every black home, and it should be used for that protection which the law refuses to give," she declared. Wells-Barnett began lobbying for a federal anti-lynching law after a white mob in Memphis, Tennessee, lynched three friends of hers who had opened a grocery store that drew customers away from white businesses. With her life threatened Wells-Barnett moved to Chicago where she worked with Jane Addams to prevent the segregation of city public schools and continued her anti-lynching campaign.

The most powerful challenge to Washington's vision came from the Northern-born sociologist W. E. B. Du Bois, the first African American to attend Harvard University. Du Bois argued that individuals should receive the education that best suited them, regardless of their race. He emphasized that the African American community needed educated professionals and teachers, the so-called "Talented Tenth." Economic progress was not possible without the right to vote, Du Bois contended, pointing out that discriminatory laws made it difficult for black sharecroppers or craftsmen to get ahead. *Competing Visions: Seeking Racial Uplift* (page 556) offers more detail on the debate between Washington and Du Bois. In 1909 Du Bois joined with Wells-Barnett and Addams to establish the National Association for the Advancement of Colored People. The interracial civil rights organization demanded an immediate end to all forms of racial discrimination, beginning a decades-long struggle for racial justice that would eventually overturn Jim Crow laws in the 1950s and 1960s.

> "No white American ever thinks that any other race is wholly civilized until he wears the white man's clothes, eats the white man's food, speaks the white man's language, and professes the white man's religion."
>
> BOOKER T. WASHINGTON, explaining why black students needed to learn middle-class habits of dress and decorum

What alternatives did critics of Booker T. Washington offer to improve life for African Americans?

Competing Visions

SEEKING RACIAL UPLIFT

In 1895 Booker T. Washington delivered his most famous speech, "The Atlanta Exposition Address," to an audience of Northern and Southern whites and blacks. The speech proposed a compromise that accepted social segregation in return for white support of blacks' economic advancement. In 1903 W. E. B. Du Bois accused Washington of sending blacks down a path that ensured their permanent enslavement to white America. How does Washington take into account the racially hostile climate that prevailed in the South during the Progressive Era? Is Du Bois's criticism of Washington accurate?

In this passage from his 1895 "Atlanta Exposition Address," Washington outlines his plan for racial progress and peaceful race relations.

Our greatest danger is that in the great leap from slavery to freedom we may overlook the fact that the masses of us are to live by the productions of our hands, and fail to keep in mind that we shall prosper in proportion as we learn to dignify and glorify common labour and put brains and skill into the common occupations of life. . . . No race can prosper till it learns that there is as much dignity in tilling a field as in writing a poem. It is at the bottom of life we must begin, and not at the top.

In all things that are purely social we can be as separate as the fingers, yet one as the hand in all things essential to mutual progress. . . . Nearly sixteen millions of hands will aid you in pulling the load upward, or they will pull against you the load downward. We shall constitute one-third and more of the ignorance and crime of the South, or one-third its intelligence and progress.

The wisest among my race understand that the agitation of questions of social equality is the extremest folly, and that progress in the enjoyment of all the privileges that will come to us must be the result of severe and constant struggle rather than of artificial forcing. No race that has anything to contribute to the markets of the world is long in any degree ostracized. It is important and right that all privileges of the law be ours, but it is vastly more important that we be prepared for the exercises of these privileges. The opportunity to earn a dollar in a factory just now is worth infinitely more than the opportunity to spend a dollar in an opera-house.

Charles Keck, *Booker T. Washington Lifting the Veil of Ignorance*

In this excerpt from his book, *The Souls of Black Folk* (1903), Du Bois explains why Washington's ideas would not work.

Mr. Washington distinctly asks that black people give up, at least for the present, three things,—

First, political power,

Second, insistence on civil rights

Third, higher education of Negro youth,

—and concentrate all their energies on industrial education, the accumulation of wealth, and the conciliation of the South.

Is it possible, and probable, that nine millions of men can make effective progress in economic lines if they are deprived of political rights, made a servile caste, and allowed only the most meager chance for developing their exceptional men? If history and reason give any distinct answer to these questions, it is an emphatic *No*. And Mr. Washington thus faces the triple paradox of his career.

1. He is striving nobly to make Negro artisans business men and property-owners; but it is utterly impossible, under modern competitive methods, for workingmen and property-owners to defend their rights and exist without the right of suffrage.
2. He insists on thrift and self-respect, but at the same time counsels a silent submission to civic inferiority such as is bound to sap the manhood of any race in the long run.
3. He advocates common-school and industrial training, and depreciates institutions of higher learning; but neither the Negro common [elementary] schools, nor Tuskegee itself, could remain open a day were it not for teachers trained in Negro colleges, or trained by their graduates.

His doctrine has tended to make the whites, North and South, shift the burden of the Negro problem to the Negro's shoulders and stand aside as critical and rather pessimistic spectators; when in fact the burden belongs to the nation.

Was Washington a sell-out, as Du Bois implies, or a master strategist?

"This country will not be a permanently good place for any of us to live in unless we make it a reasonably good place for all of us to live in."

THEODORE ROOSEVELT summarizes the Progressive ideal, 1912

Conclusion

The origins of twentieth century liberal reform movements such as the Civil Rights Movement and the New Deal lay in the Progressive Era. During this time, reformers first articulated the liberal vision that the government needed to play an active role in securing social, political, and economic justice. Progressives were reformers, not revolutionaries. They embraced capitalism and democracy, believing that a reformed economy and government could serve the interests of all, not just the wealthy few. The Progressives proved remarkably adept at creating coalitions that overcame class divisions and political party affiliations to advance reform causes that ranged from abolishing child labor to protecting the environment. From the mid-1890s to the mid-1910s, most Americans came to accept that it was the government's responsibility to regulate the economy, control destructive capitalistic practices, and stabilize the nation's financial system.

Using governmental power to protect workers and the environment proved more contentious. Americans debated how to balance individual freedom with social responsibility; private property with governmental action. Within a short period Progressive initiatives substantially reshaped industrial relations. States adopted varying degrees of protective legislation for female and child laborers and workers injured on the job. Federal regulators curtailed industrial access to federal forests, managed collective water resources, and became the caretakers for new nationally designated wilderness areas.

Progressives wanted to imbue Americans with a new sense of collective responsibility for their fellow citizens. Middle-class reformers worked particularly hard to create cross-class alliances to rein in exploitive capitalism and prevent workers from embracing socialism. Fissures nonetheless remained. The slew of social problems that Progressives addressed did not include the racial segregation and disenfranchisement recently sanctioned by the Supreme Court. Reformers also failed to question the prevailing "Vanishing Race" notion that Indian cultures would soon disappear.

Using regulation to transform the workplace and control big business required reforming the government as well. At the local and state level, Progressives employed a myriad of approaches to try to break the corrupt ties between businessmen and politicians and make the government more directly accountable to the voting public. Ultimately Progressives transformed the ways that American democracy and capitalism functioned. Not every Progressive reform succeeded, but the failures provided a blueprint for the next wave of social reform during the 1930s New Deal.

The link between democracy and capitalism that Progressive reformers cultivated at home influenced American foreign policy as well. The desire to achieve lasting social peace, shared prosperity, and true democracy—the heart of the Progressive reform impulse—shaped the path that the nation pursued as it stepped out in the world. The activist federal government that the Progressives had helped create set an ambitious international agenda for America at the turn of the century.

CHAPTER REVIEW

1901–1903

McKinley assassinated, Roosevelt becomes president
Progressivism gains presidential advocate

Ida Tarbell published "The History of the Standard Oil Company"
Exposé of oil trust stokes interest in trust-busting

Roosevelt and Muir camp together in Yosemite
They later champion competing preservationist and conservationist visions.

1905

Lochner v. New York
Stymies Progressive effort to mandate set working hours and wages

Socialist Party of America and IWW formed
Unlike Progressives, Socialists and IWW emphasize working-class solidarity over reform

1906

Pure Food and Drug Act and Meat Inspection Act passed
Establishes new regulatory role for the federal government

Roosevelt files suit against Standard Oil
"Trust-busting" president distinguishes between good and bad trusts

Review Questions

1. What factors led to the emergence of Progressivism?
2. What social problems did middle-class Progressives identify at the beginning of the twentieth century? How did their solutions differ from the ones embraced by the Socialists and laissez-faire industrialists?
3. What principles unified Progressives? How did they disagree?
4. Why did the Progressive notion of an activist, regulatory government create controversy on both the right and the left?
5. Evaluate the Progressive strategy for reform, giving examples of successful cross-class or bipartisan alliances they constructed.
6. How did visual images and investigative journalism transform Americans' views of poverty and corruption?
7. What role did government, including presidents, the Supreme Court, and state and local governments, play during the Progressive Era?
8. In what ways did the Progressive reform agenda succeed? How did it fail?

1908–1909

Lewis Hine begins photographing child laborers
Nationwide campaign to ban child labor fails

Muller v. Oregon
Upholds maximum work hour laws for women

National Association for the Advancement of Colored People formed (NAACP)
Seeks immediate end to segregation

1911–1912

Triangle Shirtwaist Factory Fire
Shocking tragedy confirms need to reform workplace

Supreme Court announces "rule of reason" in breaking up trusts
Makes distinction between good and bad trusts

Republican Party splits into progressive and conservative factions
Democrat Woodrow Wilson elected president

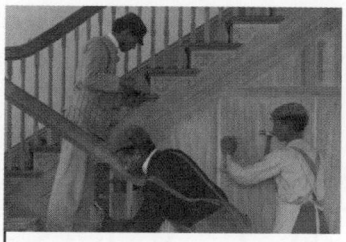

1913

Wilson allows federal agencies to racially segregate their offices
Reflects lingering impact of *Plessy v. Ferguson*

Federal Reserve Act
Creates a federally controlled currency and banking reserve system

Sixteenth Amendment ratified
Congress authorizes first federal income taxes

Seventeenth Amendment ratified
Popular election of senators intended to diminish big business's influence in politics

1914

Ford announces eight hour/five dollar workday
Secures competitive advantage through benefits and assembly lines

Ludlow Massacre
Reveals potency of class conflict during Progressive Era

Key Terms

Social Gospel Thebelief that Christians had a responsibility to create an ethically sound and morally upright society. **534**

trust-busting Governmental action to dissolve monopolies. **536**

Sixteenth Amendment (1913) The constitutional amendment authorizing federal income taxes. **538**

Federal Reserve Act (1913) The act creating a federally run Federal Reserve to serve as a "banker's bank" that held a portion of bank funds in reserve to help member banks in time of crisis, set rates for business loans, and issued a new national paper currency. **539**

Clayton Anti-Trust Act (1914) The act prohibited interlocking company directories—the practice of setting up shadow companies that appeared to compete but were actually run by the same board of directors—and exempted trade unions from prosecution under the 1890 Sherman Anti-Trust Act. **539**

Federal Trade Commission (1914) A federal agency with the power to order companies to cease unfair trading practices whose decisions were subject to court review. **539**

preservationist An environmentalist who championed preserving nature in its unspoiled state. **539**

conservationist An environmentalist who wanted to meet present economic needs and conserve natural resources for future generations. **540**

welfare capitalism The notion of using benefits to gain workers' loyalty, improve worker morale, and weaken interest in unions. **541**

scientific management The effort to use scientific knowledge to secure maximum output and profit. **543**

Industrial Workers of the World (IWW) This group envisioned "one big union" that welcomed all workers regardless of sex, race, ethnicity, or skill, which would one day take over all means of production in the United States. **543**

Lochner v. New York (1905) A Supreme Court ruling that unless long work hours directly jeopardized workers' health, the government could not abridge an employee's freedom to negotiate his own work schedule with his employer. **544**

Ludlow Massacre (1914) Colorado state troops set a striking miners' camp ablaze, killing thirteen women and children, an act that outraged laborers throughout the nation. **544**

Muller v. Oregon (1908) The Supreme Court upheld maximum hour laws for female workers because protecting women's reproductive health served the public good. **546**

Meat Inspection Act (1906) Law gave federal inspectors the authority to condemn meat unfit for consumption and established federal sanitary standards for meatpacking plants. **552**

Pure Food and Drug Act (1906) Law levied federal fines for mislabeling food or medicine. **552**

initiative Provided a way, usually by gathering signatures on petitions, for the electorate to introduce legislation before state legislatures. **553**

referendum Put legislative proposals on the ballot, letting the voting public decide whether a measure became law. **553**

recall Used special elections to remove unpopular officials from office before their term expired. **553**

muckrakers Progressive Era term for investigative journalists who wrote exposés on government and business corruption. **553**

Seventeenth Amendment (1913) A constitutional amendment that allowed voters, rather than state legislatures, elect federal senators. **553**

CHAPTER 19

Imperial America

The United States in the World, 1890–1914

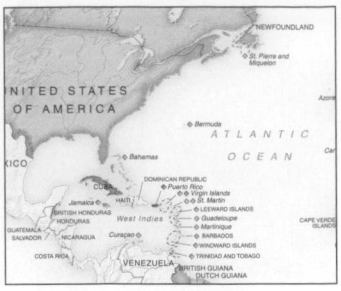

Becoming a World Power p. 562

> **"Remember the *Maine* and to hell with Spain!"**
>
> Newspaper slogan urging war with Spain in the wake of the *Maine* explosion

On February 15, 1898, a naval officer awoke President William McKinley in the middle of the night with the stunning news that the American battleship the *Maine* had exploded in Havana, Cuba, killing 266 of the 354 crew members. The explosion turned the battleship into a hunk of molten steel. This illustration depicted the blast propelling bodies and debris sky-high in Havana Harbor. Americans also read moving firsthand accounts in the press, including one from survivor James R. Young. "I was feeling a bit glum," Young recalled, "and in fact was so quiet that Lieutenant J. Hood came up and asked laughingly if I was asleep. I said, 'No, I am on watch.' Scarcely had I spoken when there came a dull, sullen roar. Would to God that I could blot out the sounds and the scenes that followed."

The United States and Spain had long been at odds over the question of independence for Cuba, then a Spanish colony. McKinley had sent the *Maine* to Havana to stop Spanish-instigated attacks on American-held property in Cuba. Many Americans suspected that Spanish saboteurs had blown up the ship to protest the U.S. incursion into Spanish territorial waters. The shocking images and accounts of the *Maine* explosion fueled public anger against Spain for its supposed attack on the U.S. Navy, creating a moment of crisis between the two nations. An official investigation confirmed these widely held views, blaming the *Maine* explosion on a Spanish mine in the harbor. The exact cause of the blast, however, remained a mystery. Some experts now cite a spontaneous combustion from the coal stored alongside ammunition as the most likely culprit, a misfortune shared by thirteen similar American naval vessels between 1895 and 1898. Others suggest that Cuban revolutionaries may have planted the explosives, expecting the United States to blame Spain and declare war.

The *Maine* explosion ignited a short, four-month war between the United States and Spain in 1898. This "splendid little war," as one official called it, ended with an overwhelming American victory. The overseas possessions that the United States gained from Spain, including Puerto Rico and the Philippines, gave the nation a new formal colonial empire. The United States simultaneously constructed an informal economic empire throughout the Caribbean and East Asia at the turn of the century. As the United States established itself as a budding world power, Americans offered conflicting visions of how the United States should behave outside its borders.

How has the meaning of this image changed since 1898?

The Spanish-American War p. 565

Creating an American Empire p. 573

America and East Asia p. 579

In America's Backyard p. 584

Becoming a World Power

Throughout the nineteenth century the Atlantic and Pacific oceans provided Americans with a sense of security and detachment from world affairs. By the 1880s, however, advancements in transportation and communication suddenly made the world seem smaller and more dangerous to Americans. Fear alone, though, did not explain Americans' growing interest in venturing overseas. Americans looked outside their borders to find markets for U.S. goods and the raw materials needed to fuel a growing industrial economy. International recognition as a world power and spreading American values also appealed to the country's growing sense of national greatness.

European Imperialism

In the seventeenth and eighteenth centuries, Britain, France, and Spain had based their world prominence on far-flung colonial empires, places that they populated with settlers and soldiers to exploit economic resources and protect ocean trade routes. In the eighteenth and nineteenth centuries, these settler communities launched a slew of successful revolutions that liberated colonies in North and South America from European rule. With the "old" colonial empires now defunct, European nations and Japan sought places to build new ones. As Britain, France, Belgium, Germany, Italy, Portugal, Spain, Russia, the Netherlands, and Japan discovered vulnerable areas around the globe to colonize, they developed a new style of empire building. **Imperialism**, the late nineteenth-century term for colonizing foreign nations and lands, relied primarily on business, political, and military structures rather than settlers to rule colonized peoples and exploit their resources. Europe's drive to create colonial empires in Africa and Asia in the late nineteenth century provided a model to either emulate or reject as the United States embarked on its campaign to become a world power.

Besides exploiting colonies for economic gain, Europeans also drew satisfaction from fulfilling a self-imposed "civilizing" mission to spread Western culture and values to nonwhite and non-Christian populations throughout Africa and Asia. The drawbacks to empires, however, included the need to defend widely dispersed territories and suppress popular uprisings against colonial rule. Americans,

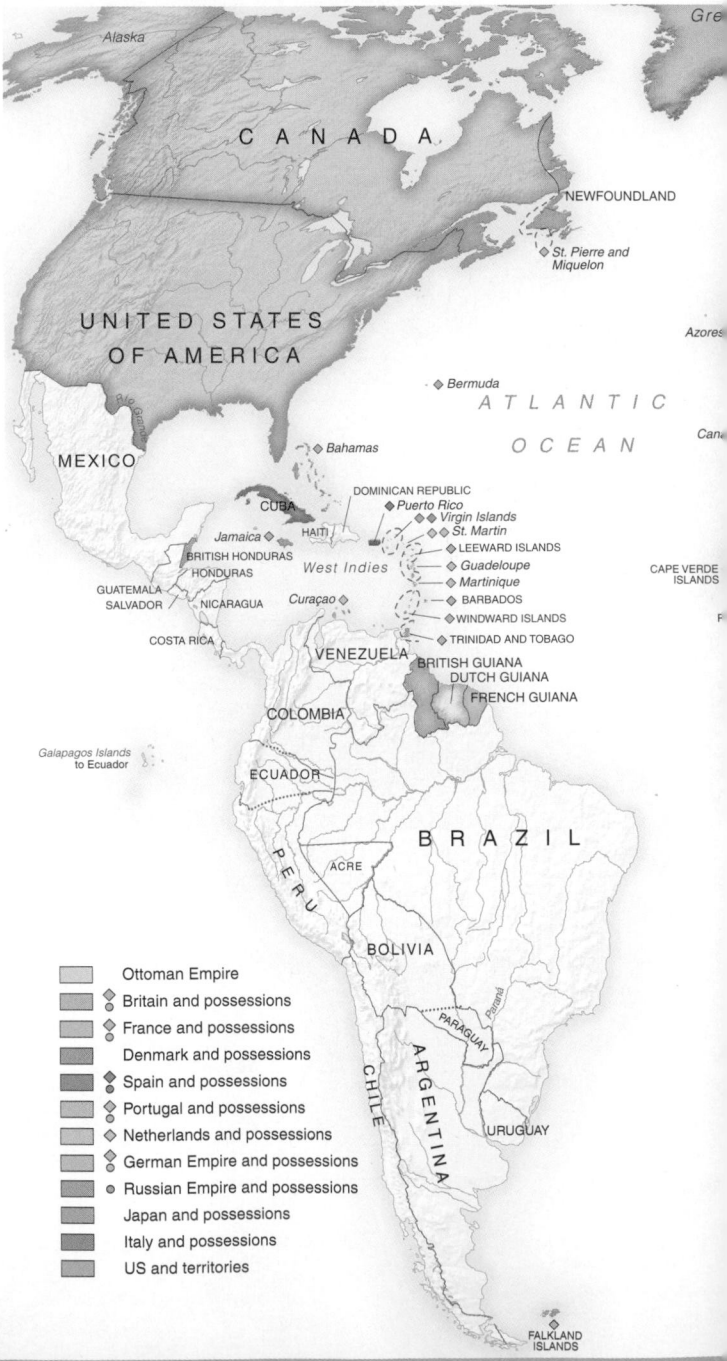

How did European imperialism affect the U.S. effort to create a formal empire?

therefore, developed conflicting visions from the lessons that they drew from the European experience. Some saw it as an inspiration; others, a cautionary tale.

As the map (**19.1**) indicates, the world situation in 1898 affected where the United States could hope to expand its influence. By the time the United States began exploring opportunities for expansion beyond the North American continent, Britain, France, Germany, and the Netherlands had already established colonial empires throughout Africa, East Asia, and South Asia. Great Britain exerted the greatest reach, making it the world's preeminent imperial power. This left the Western Hemisphere and China as possibilities for U.S. colonial expansion.

The Impulse for Expansion

Throughout American history territorial expansion played an important role in defining national identity and providing economic opportunity to Americans. In the early nineteenth century, manifest destiny, or the belief that Americans had a divine right to land in North America, fueled expansion across the continental United States. Imbued with a sense of cultural and racial superiority over the

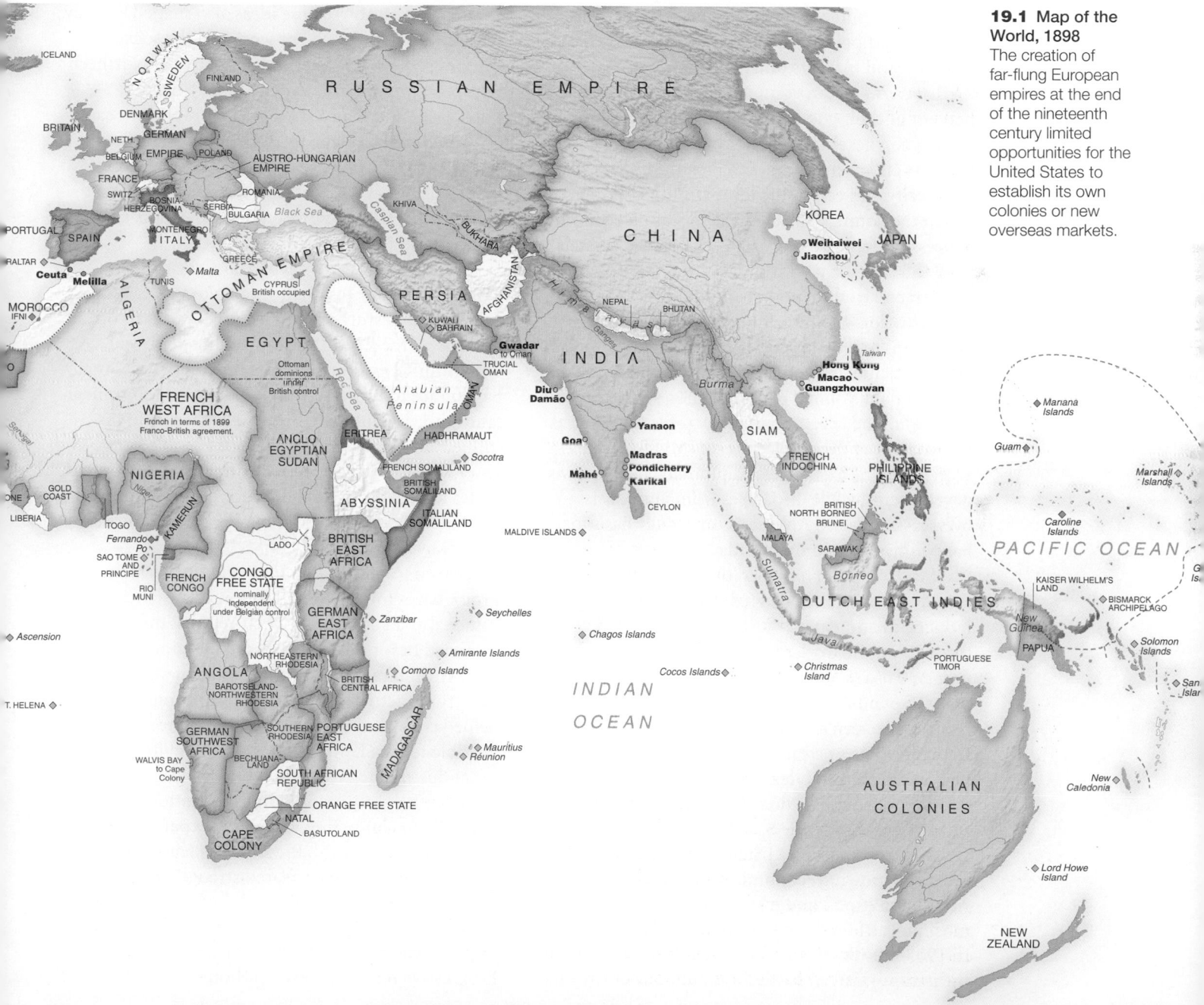

19.1 Map of the World, 1898
The creation of far-flung European empires at the end of the nineteenth century limited opportunities for the United States to establish its own colonies or new overseas markets.

Which characteristics defined a nation as a world power in the late nineteenth century?

indigenous peoples who inhabited these lands, Americans felt justified in taking away land from Indians. In their view, Native Americans had failed to make the land commercially productive. The government relocated many Indian tribes onto reservations, where officials and missionaries embraced the goal of "civilizing" Indians by teaching them Western capitalist and Christian values (see Chapter 15). The same belief in manifest destiny, quest for economic opportunity, and ideas of racial superiority that had fueled American expansion across North America throughout the nineteenth century spurred interest in expanding American influence and trade overseas.

Many prominent businessmen, commercial farmers, and politicians urged the country to seek territory and markets outside the United States. In the 1890s American companies and farmers sold 90 percent of their goods to other Americans. The time had come, these critics argued, to develop global markets and even colonies to ensure continued prosperity and economic opportunity at home. When the country suffered a devastating economic depression from 1893 to 1897, these calls crystallized into a resolve within some quarters to build a commercial and colonial empire overseas.

Technological innovations also encouraged Americans to look beyond their borders. The laying of transatlantic telegraph cables increased both the speed and the volume of information sent throughout the world. The telegraph in many respects served as the Internet of the nineteenth century. Telegrams accelerated the exchange of diplomatic notes between governments, while dispatches from journalists overseas connected Americans on a daily basis to happenings around the world.

If the telegraph hastened the flow of information, the advent of steam-powered ships dramatically reduced the time needed to move people and goods throughout the world. In his seminal 1890 work, *The Influence of Sea Power on History, 1660–1783*, U.S. Navy Captain Alfred T. Mahan traced a direct correlation between a powerful navy and world power. In the new age of steam-powered battleships, the navy's outdated wooden sailing ships, described by one congressman as "floating washtubs," were ill-suited for advancing U.S. interests in the world. From 1890 onward the United States built battleships to match its growing economic power and its expansionist ambitions, and it soon boasted the second most powerful navy in the world after Great Britain. In 1907 President Theodore "Teddy" Roosevelt sent the nation's sixteen battleships and four destroyers on a global tour to show off America's world-class steam-powered navy, a trip that took two years to complete.

Americans' growing pride in their nation's economic might and technological prowess encouraged the United States to seek international recognition as a world power. So did the ideological vision encapsulated by social Darwinism, an ideology that applied nineteenth-century naturalist Charles Darwin's theory of biological evolution to human society through the notion of "survival of the fittest." At home Americans often used social Darwinism to justify the dominance of the wealthy and powerful, considered "the fit," over the poor and weak, or "the unfit." These ideas also shaped the way that Americans viewed the world. In the social Darwinist view, the "racial superiority" of Northern European populations explained why Britain, France, and Germany were world powers that easily colonized nonwhite peoples throughout the world. To take its rightful place alongside, or even above, these world powers, the United States needed to demonstrate its fitness by entering the global competition underway for colonies.

In making a case for expansion, the congregational minister Josiah Strong linked older ideas of manifest destiny with this newer emphasis on survival of the fittest. "It seems to me that God, with infinite wisdom and skill, is training the Anglo-Saxon race to prevail" in the competition to control lands throughout the world, Strong wrote in his influential book, *Our Country: Its Possible Future and Its Present Crisis* (1885). In Strong's view the United States risked losing its chance for global eminence if it failed to join the scramble for colonies already underway worldwide.

Driven to perfect democracy at home, many Progressives found the call to spread American values abroad appealing. Their reform impulse extended beyond U.S. borders to imagine a world freed from tyranny and injustice. In many respects the strong, activist government that Progressives helped construct at the turn of the century made it possible for the United States to extend its imperial reach during the Progressive Era. Progressives never spoke with one voice on domestic matters, and they also offered competing visions on expanding U.S. influence in the world. Progressives who opposed the nation's overseas forays feared strengthening big business at the expense of exploited foreign peoples and American workers. They also believed that imperial ventures drew attention away from Progressive reform projects at home.

How did European imperialism affect the U.S. effort to create a formal empire?

The Spanish-American War

The first significant opportunity to expand U.S. influence overseas came when Cuba rose in revolt against Spanish rule. Extensive press coverage of Spanish atrocities and U.S. economic interests in Cuba prompted the nation to take note of this colonial struggle for independence. After a mysterious explosion sank the *Maine* battleship and killed hundreds of American sailors, many Americans accused Spain of deliberately attacking the ship. Fearing that Congress might declare war on its own, a reluctant President William McKinley finally agreed to an armed intervention. The war with Spain was short, but the outcome was dramatic. The peace treaty with Spain granted the United States island possessions in the Caribbean and Pacific that became the territorial foundation for the new U.S. colonial empire.

The Growing Conflict with Spain

In the early nineteenth century, when Spain's other Western Hemisphere colonies successfully fought for independence, Cuba remained loyal to Spain. By 1868, however, oppressive Spanish rule provoked a rebellion in Cuba that ended ten years later with Spain's pledge to grant the island increased autonomy. Failure to fulfill this promise, economic hardships inflicted by the 1890s depression, and continued agitation by exiled Cuban rebels living in the United States fanned the flames of rebellion once again in 1895. By the time the second revolt began, the United States and Cuba had established strong commercial ties. Cuba sent over 90 percent of its exports to the United States, and American investment totaled nearly $50 million in Cuban sugar, cattle, mining, and tobacco industries.

Spain paid a heavy price to maintain this last symbol of its imperial past. Of the 278,000 Spanish troops sent to Cuba to suppress the revolt, nearly 50,000 had died of yellow fever or malaria by 1898, and an equal number lay too sick to fight. A much smaller force of 20,000–30,000 Cuban rebels drew on their knowledge of the terrain and support from civilians to fight an effective guerrilla war that ravaged tobacco and sugar plantations to deprive the Spanish government of revenue. Rebels purposefully steered clear of American-owned plantations to avoid antagonizing the United States.

Cuban exiles in the United States drew appealing analogies between their struggle for independence and the American Revolution, highlighting the similar desire of Cuban and American colonists to free themselves from an exploitive ruler and establish democratic self-rule. If any uncertainty existed among the American public over which side they supported, Spanish General Valeriano Weyler's infamous reconcentration policy ended those doubts. Through **reconcentration** Spanish soldiers tried to crush the Cuban rebellion by herding Cuban peasants off their farms into heavily fortified cities and then systematically destroying the crops that fed the rebel armies. This policy created a humanitarian crisis in Cuba as famine and disease ravaged the civilian population, killing nearly 100,000. Outraged Americans denounced reconcentration as uncivilized and illegal warfare.

The **yellow press**, tabloid journalists and newspapers that reported sensationalist stories with a strong emotional component, fueled public anger against the Spanish. This unique name for nineteenth-century tabloid journalism derived from competing "Yellow Kid" comic strips in leading New York newspapers that portrayed the antics of a precocious boy living in the city's tenements. Yellow journalism emerged in the 1880s when Joseph Pulitzer began using melodramatic, partly fictionalized stories to bolster sales of his newspaper, the *New York World*. After William Randolph Hearst took over the *New York Journal* in 1895, the two newspapers waged daily battles over who could print the most lurid tales.

In the Cuban crisis both papers saw a chance to report the kinds of scandal-driven stories guaranteed to sell newspapers. Exiled Cuban rebels living in the United States provided a steady supply of atrocity stories (some fabricated, some true) to the yellow press, and the vivid illustrations accompanying these accounts helped the public visualize Spanish brutality.

Why did Americans take an interest in the Cuban rebellion against Spain?

Images as History

ATROCITY STORIES AND PUBLIC OPINION

Ever since the yellow press helped raise American ire against Spain in the years leading up to the Spanish-American War, Americans have pondered the power of the press in the United States. How much power do atrocity stories and pictures have to shape public opinion? Can the press convince the public to fight a war?

On February 12, 1897, the *New York Journal* published a story by Richard Harding Davis about a young Cuban woman whom Spanish authorities had expelled for carrying secret messages between Cuban rebels. Davis reported that "Spanish officers" followed Clemencia Arango and her companions onto an American ship. The Spanish officers "demanded that a cabin should be furnished to them to which the girls might be taken, and they were then undressed and searched" for messages to exiled Cuban rebels living in the United States. Frederic Remington's illustration "Spaniards Search Women on American Steamers" accompanied Davis's story.

Hearst next took up the cause of Evangelina Cisneros. Sentenced to twenty years in prison for trying to lure a Spanish officer into a rebel death trap, Cisneros was awaiting deportation to an African penal colony. According to the *New York Journal*, her only crime was calling for help from nearby Cuban rebels to stop a Spanish officer, "a beast in uniform," from raping her. On October 10, 1897 the paper stunningly announced that a *New York Journal* reporter had helped Cisneros break out of jail and sail to the United States. The yellow press presented Clemencia and Evangelina as symbols for the virtuous and victimized Cuban people, fueling public sympathy for the Cuban rebellion.

Frederic Remington (who was in the United States when this incident occurred) drew a beautiful naked white woman standing defiantly before the three overly curious and swarthy-looking Spanish officers who had undressed her. In fact, female prison matrons performed the search.

"There are things more dreadful than even war and one of them is dishonor," the *New York Journal* editorialized about the Clemencia Arango incident.

This 1897 illustration of dark-skinned men viewing and touching the body of a white woman resonated powerfully with many white Americans because it aroused their racial prejudices.

"Spaniards Search Women on American Steamers."
***New York Journal*, February 12, 1897.**

Press coverage of Cisneros's escapades generated so much interest that huge crowds gathered to hear of her adventures when she appeared in New York and Washington, D.C., where President McKinley received her in the White House.

The headline criticized diplomatic inaction and suggested that only heroic, manly military-style action could save Cuban rebels.

New York Journal accounts exaggerated Cisneros's light-skinned beauty, noble birth, and prison sufferings.

Nearly fifteen thousand women, including President William McKinley's wife, signed the newspaper's petition to Spain's Queen María Cristina demanding Cisneros's release.

NEW YORK JOURNAL AND ADVERTISER.

EVANGELINA CISNEROS RESCUED BY THE JOURNAL.

An American Newspaper Accomplishes at a Single Stroke What the Red Tape of Diplomacy Failed Utterly to Bring About in Many Months.

MISS CISNEROS BEFORE AND AFTER THIRTEEN MONTHS' INCARCERATION.

THE PETITION TO THE QUEEN.

"Evangelina Cisneros Rescued by the Journal."
***New York Journal*, October 10, 1897.**

Why did popular media accounts depict the Cubans as light-skinned and the Spanish as dark-skinned?

The importance of illustrations to the yellow press became clear in a fabled exchange between Hearst and the artist Frederic Remington. Remington, already famous for his portraits of the American West, went to Cuba to draw illustrations for the *New York Journal.* Tiring of the rebellion's slow pace, Remington told Hearst he was leaving Cuba. Hearst supposedly replied, "Please remain. You furnish the pictures, and I'll furnish the war." This exchange passed quickly into American folklore as proof of Hearst's determination to use shocking images, real or staged, to provoke a war with Spain. No evidence exists, however, that Hearst ever wrote or sent this reply. *Images as History: Atrocity Stories and Public Opinion* examines how yellow press illustrations shaped American public opinion.

The Decision to Intervene in Cuba

With the yellow press clamoring for military action, President William McKinley turned to diplomacy to end the impasse over Cuba peacefully and repeatedly asked Spain to grant Cuba more autonomy. In 1897 the Spanish government ended reconcentration by recalling Weyler and allowing Cuban peasants placed in reconcentration compounds to return to their homes. Spain also announced a plan for limited Cuban self-government, inviting protests from all sides. Cuban rebels urged Americans to help them attain complete independence. Meanwhile Cubans still loyal to Spain reacted angrily to the limited autonomy plan and rioted in the streets of Havana. An alarmed McKinley decided to send the *Maine* battleship to Havana to deter loyalists from organizing attacks on Americans or their property. Acting within the boundaries of acceptable international practice, McKinley expected the battleship's presence (with the implied threat of bombardments) to restore calm to Havana. Events in February, 1898, however, conspired against McKinley's effort to resolve the crisis peacefully. First Hearst's *Journal* published a private letter written by the Spanish ambassador, which described McKinley as "weak and a bidder for the admiration of the crowd." Although tame compared with the vicious statements American newspapers routinely made about the president, the published letter outraged the public.

> **"Worst Insult to the United States in Its History."**
>
> Yellow press headline regarding Spanish ambassador's disparaging comments about McKinley

Next the *Maine* exploded in Havana Harbor. After a month of press speculation about the cause of the explosion, an official naval investigation erroneously blamed a Spanish harbor mine for the disaster, rather than the real culprit: faulty ship design that caused an internal explosion, or perhaps sabotage by Cuban rebels who wanted the United States to declare war on Spain. In the weeks immediately following the sinking of the *Maine*, McKinley tried unsuccessfully to convince Spain to grant Cuba independence and to calm calls for war from Congress. "I have been through one war," McKinley told a friend, referring to his military service in the Civil War. "I have seen the dead piled up, and I do not want to see another." For many other Americans, however, memories of brutal Civil War battles had faded. They enthusiastically viewed war as a manly adventure that would instill discipline and vigor in American men. The assistant secretary of the navy, Theodore Roosevelt, championed this competing view, writing to a friend in 1897, "I should welcome almost any war, for I think this country needs one."

With the Democrats championing war, Republicans feared that McKinley's resistance to fighting might hurt the party at the polls. Some senators even suggested that Congress declare war whether McKinley agreed or not. The pressure on McKinley increased when Senator Redfield Proctor, several days before the navy released its findings on the *Maine* attack, gave the Senate a grim accounting of the appalling effects of Spain's reconcentration policy on the Cuban people. "I went to Cuba with a strong conviction that the situation had been overdrawn," Proctor noted, then went on to detail the starvation, squalor, and sickness he had seen. This sober address from a conservative Republican and stalwart friend of McKinley's convinced many wavering congressmen and Americans that the country had a humanitarian duty to save Cuba.

To head off a war, Spain made one last offer to grant Cuba increased autonomy, rejecting McKinley's call for total independence. "Mr. President, I can no longer hold back the Senate," Vice President Garrett Hobart told McKinley. "They will act without you if you do not act at once." Accepting that he had failed to negotiate an acceptable settlement to the crisis, McKinley asked Congress to

Why was McKinley unable to avoid war with Spain?

authorize an armed intervention to end the civil war in Cuba without declaring war on Spain. Congress complied. On April 24, 1898, however, Spain declared war on the United States. The next day Congress responded with its own declaration of war, dating it retroactively to April 21, 1898. The United States was now officially at war with Spain.

To underscore the nation's altruistic motives in declaring war, Colorado Senator Henry M. Teller added an amendment to the war resolutions that specifically disavowed any intention of annexing Cuba. The **Teller Amendment (1898)** promised "to leave the government and control of the [Cuban] Island to its people" at the end of the Spanish-American War. Congress made no such promise to other colonized peoples under Spanish control in the Caribbean and Pacific.

Fighting the War against Spain

America's victory in the Spanish-American War, which lasted from April to August 1898, paved the way for U.S. territorial expansion in the Caribbean and Pacific. One week after the war began, American Commodore George Dewey sailed into Manila Harbor, in the Spanish colony of the Philippines, (**19.2**) and destroyed the Spanish Pacific fleet. Why, Americans wondered, did the navy fight the first battle to liberate Cuba halfway around the world in the Philippines, an archipelago of seven thousand islands in the Pacific Ocean? By eliminating the Spanish Pacific fleet, Dewey prevented it from sailing to Cuba. Losing its Pacific fleet also put added pressure on Spain to sue for peace. Dewey's stunning victory at Manila catapulted the Philippines into the spotlight, and Americans learned that

> "I could not have told where those darned islands were within two thousand miles."
>
> President McKINLEY on the location of the Philippines before the Spanish-American War

the Filipinos were in the midst of their own rebellion against Spain. At first the Filipino rebels, who controlled the interior, welcomed the Americans as liberators. "I have studied the Constitution of the United States, and I find in it no authority for colonies and I have no fear," rebel leader Emilio Aguinaldo told one American general. Time would prove Aguinaldo wrong.

Besides securing the Philippines the McKinley administration also used the war against Spain as a pretext for settling the festering question of annexing Hawaii that had divided Americans for nearly a decade. Americans had a long history of

19.2 The Spanish-American War, 1898
The U.S. Navy first attacked the Spanish in the Philippines, and then blockaded Cuba as U.S. forces invaded.

Why did the United States first attack Spain in the Philippines?

involvement in Hawaiian affairs. By the 1880s American-owned sugar plantations dominated the Hawaiian economy, American missionaries had waged a successful campaign to eradicate native religions, and the U.S. Navy had established a permanent naval station at Pearl Harbor on the island of Oahu. Responding to popular discontent over the erosion of native Hawaiians' economic standing and cultural traditions, when Queen Liliuokalani assumed the throne in 1891 she promised to curtail U.S. dominance over Hawaiian politics and agriculture. Within two years, however, American businessmen and missionaries working on the islands (representing 5 percent of the islands' population) overthrew Queen Liliuokalani. U.S. Marines sent to protect American property ensured the revolution's success. Thousands of Hawaiians took to the streets to protest the coup, to no avail.

The new Hawaiian government requested annexation by the United States, a request that President McKinley endorsed to foster U.S. commercial interests in the Pacific. In 1897, however, the Hawaiian Patriotic League successfully blocked a formal U.S. takeover by presenting the Senate with a 556-page anti-annexation petition signed by over half of the native-born Hawaiian population. Faced with Hawaiians' overwhelming opposition to annexation, the Senate voted the measure down. A year later, however, with the Spanish-American War underway, the Senate reversed course. Supporters of annexation successfully argued that U.S. ships headed to the Philippines needed guaranteed access to the naval way-station in Pearl Harbor. Deciding to put its own strategic and economic needs ahead of Hawaiians' desire to remain independent, the United States assumed sovereignty over Hawaii on July 7, 1898, when McKinley signed a congressional joint resolution authorizing annexation. The president appointed a territorial governor to head the Hawaiian government, and in 1900 Congress granted Hawaiians the right to elect the territorial legislature.

Meanwhile military planners focused on defeating the Spanish in Cuba. The accompanying map, "Spanish-American War, 1898" (19.2) illustrates how the navy immediately blockaded Cuba, trapping the Spanish Atlantic Fleet in Santiago. America's traditionally small peacetime army, however, was woefully unprepared to train and equip the thousands of volunteers enlisting

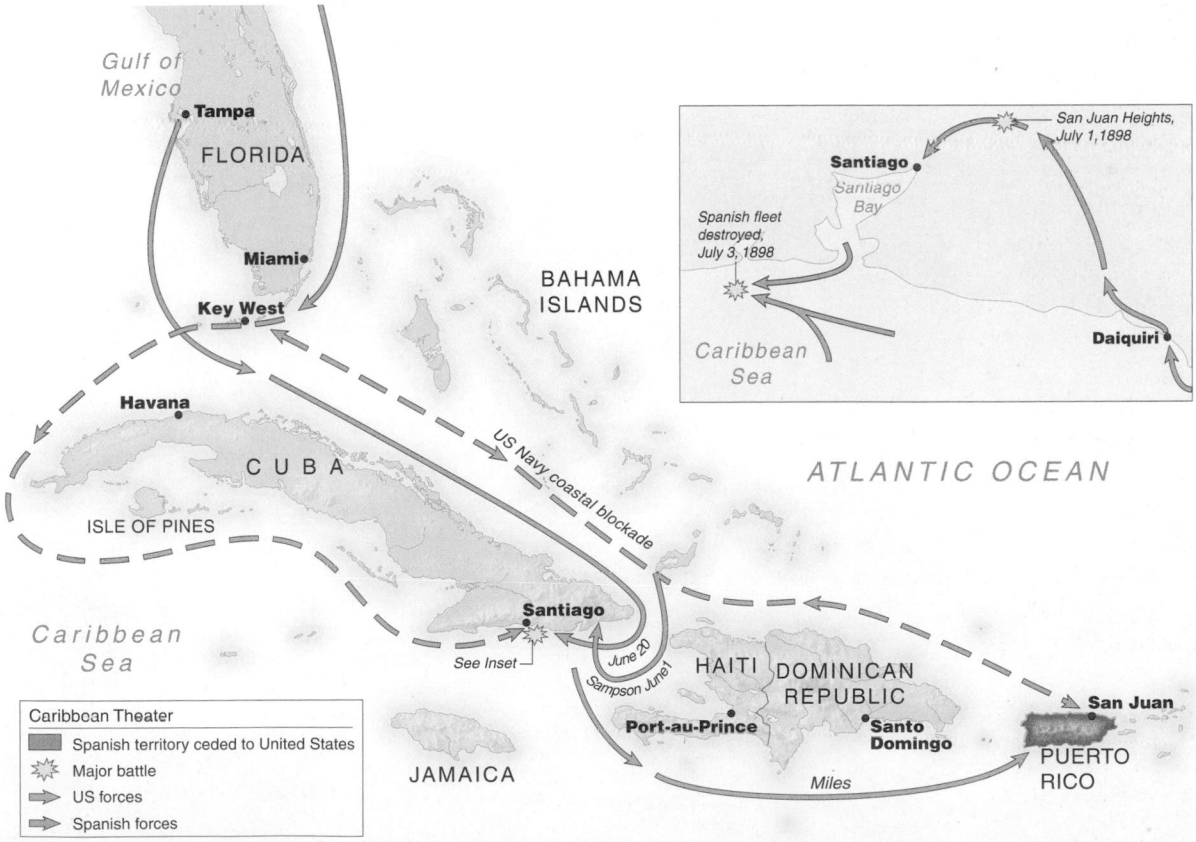

Why did Hawaii lose its independence in a war to liberate Cuba?

throughout the country. Theodore Roosevelt resigned as assistant secretary of the navy and formed the First U.S. Volunteer Calvary by recruiting Americans from wildly diverse backgrounds. Many of the recruits had personal connections to Colonel Roosevelt, a result of his eclectic lifestyle that included attending Harvard, hunting expeditions in the West, and a stint as police commissioner in New York City. Dubbed the **Rough Riders**, this collection of cowboys, Ivy League athletes, city police officers, and Pawnee scouts was one of the few volunteer units that fought in the war. Although American forces swelled from 28,000 to 275,000, the vast majority never left the United States.

On June 22, seventeen thousand U.S. troops landed in Cuba to join Cuban rebels on a slow march through heavy jungle to the port city of Santiago, which contained the bulk of the Spanish navy and army. Hidden Spanish sharpshooters harassed U.S. soldiers as they made their way to the San Juan Heights, the outlying hills that encircled Santiago. On July 1, the Americans, under the command of General William Shafter, attacked 750 Spanish soldiers along the San Juan Heights.

"I have seen many illustrations and pictures of this charge on the San Juan hills, but none of them seem to show it just as I remember it," recalled journalist Richard Harding Davis, who watched the charge from the sidelines. Like most illustrations of the battle seen in newspapers at the time, this painting (**19.3**) shows waves of eager American soldiers advancing with the flag flying, suggesting "an invincible overpowering weight of numbers," Davis noted. Yet, he continued, "I think the thing which impressed one the most, when our men started from cover, was that they were so few. It almost seemed as if someone had made an awful and terrible mistake. One's instinct was to call to them to come back." Roosevelt led the Rough Riders to the top of the San Juan Heights, a feat that garnered Roosevelt and the unit much acclaim. They stood alongside African American troops from the Ninth and Tenth Calvary who had actually reached the top first, a fact that Roosevelt and the mainstream media failed to mention when celebrating the victory.

The battle provided another opportunity for the yellow press to whip up war fervor on the home front. Responding to (false) rumors that Spanish soldiers had mutilated the corpses of American servicemen killed during the clash, a *Judge* magazine cover (**19.4**) pictured a Spaniard drenched in the

19.3 Charge up the San Juan Heights, 1898 This painting depicted the charge up the San Juan Heights as glorious and heroic, with the flag flying and no casualties. Illustrations like this contributed to the image of the Spanish-American War as a "splendid little war."

How accurate were the legends that surrounded the charge up the San Juan Heights?

blood of American soldiers who lay at his feet. In one hand the ape-like figure holds the bloody knife responsible for the recent atrocity. His other hand rests on the gravestone of U.S. sailors whom he allegedly killed by exploding the *Maine*. A brute that trampled on the American flag, the image reinforced earlier yellow press portrayals of Spain as a beast that the United States needed to subdue. The caricature also fed into racist notions of white supremacy—just like African Americans at home, and soon the Filipinos abroad, the dark-skinned Spanish posed a threat to the civilized world. In future conflicts American wartime propaganda used strikingly similar images to arouse passionate hatred of the nation's German and Japanese enemies.

Legendary accounts attributed the American success in charging up the San Juan Heights to heroic frontal charges; in fact, the Americans' three Gatling machine guns made the decisive difference. Believing his exhausted troops could go no farther after reaching the top, General Shafter decided to lay siege to Santiago instead of attacking the city directly. While American troops encircled the city atop the surrounding hills, U.S. naval ships blocked the port, thus trapping the bulk of the Spanish navy and army in Santiago. When the Spanish fleet made a dash to leave the harbor on July 3, American ships sank or beached every Spanish vessel. On July 17, Spanish troops surrendered the city and Cuba to the Americans. After defeating the Spanish in Cuba, U.S. forces landed in Puerto Rico, also a Caribbean Spanish colony, where they encountered only token opposition. American troops fought one more battle to take Manila on August 13, having not yet received word that the war between the United States and Spain had ended the day before.

19.4 ***The Spanish Brute*, 1898**
This wartime caricature portrayed the Spanish as bloodthirsty beasts who murdered and mutilated American servicemen.

The war concluded on a sour note, however, as the high costs of fighting in the tropics without adequate preparations became clear. With a limited understanding of how malaria, yellow fever, and typhoid spread among humans, U.S. Army physicians could not stop these tropical diseases from ravaging the soldier population that occupied Cuba during the summer of 1898. Victory celebrations among U.S. troops soon gave way to panic when hundreds of soldiers fell ill and healthy young men became hollow-eyed, walking skeletons. It was "a heartbreaking sight" to see her husband, a yellow fever victim whose weight had dropped from 165 pounds to 89 pounds, Grace Paulding recalled. He needed a year's nursing before he could work again.

Despairing over the lack of qualified hospital attendants, the Surgeon General turned in desperation to the female nurses offering their services to the military. Eventually, 1,500 professional and Red Cross female nurses worked side by side with army doctors at home and overseas. Overall the Americans counted 385 officers and soldiers killed in combat (excluding those killed on the *Maine*), and nearly 2,000 deaths from disease.

The peace treaty, signed on December 10, 1898, ended the Spanish-American War and set the terms of the U.S. victory. In the **Treaty of Paris**, Spain relinquished its claim to Cuba, and the United States received Puerto Rico, some smaller Caribbean

Were Americans right to characterize the Spanish-American War as "the splendid little war"?

islands, and the Pacific island group of Guam. In return for $20 million, Spain turned the Philippines over to the United States. How this territorial transfer would affect the political future of the Philippines remained in doubt. Did the United States intend to grant the Philippines independence or keep the territory as a colony? Americans soon offered competing visions on how to resolve this question.

Despite the idealistic guarantees given in the Teller Amendment, Cuba became an independent nation in name only. The United States linked the withdrawal of American occupation troops to several concessions from Cuba. The **Platt Amendment (1901)** required Cuba to give the United States the right to maintain a naval base at Guantánamo Bay and to intervene militarily in Cuba to protect "life, property, and individual liberty." Besides granting the United States a privileged trading relationship with Cuba, the Cuban government also needed permission from the United States before entering into treaties with other nations. The former Spanish colony essentially became a U.S. protectorate, a relationship in which a superior power assumes authority over a weaker country or territory to protect it from invasion and to share in managing its affairs. The United States took advantage of these rights and occupied Cuba numerous times until Congress repealed the Platt Amendment in 1934. The United States continued to maintain a naval base at Guantánamo Bay, using it to jail and interrogate foreign prisoners captured during the wars in Afghanistan and Iraq that began in 2001 and 2003, respectively.

In his successful 1900 reelection bid against Democrat William Jennings Bryan, McKinley made a strong connection between events at home and abroad. One campaign poster (**19.5**) featured portraits of the president and his war hero running mate, Theodore Roosevelt. The individual vignettes reminded Americans of the devastating 1890s depression and Cuban suffering under Spanish rule. It then noted that domestic prosperity returned and social justice prevailed overseas once the United States stepped out into the world. The claim that American intervention improved life for both U.S. and world citizens became a powerful argument in favor of constructing an American empire. Bryan focused his campaign on the evils of imperialism, but McKinley carried the election with a "full dinner pail" slogan that emphasized restored prosperity.

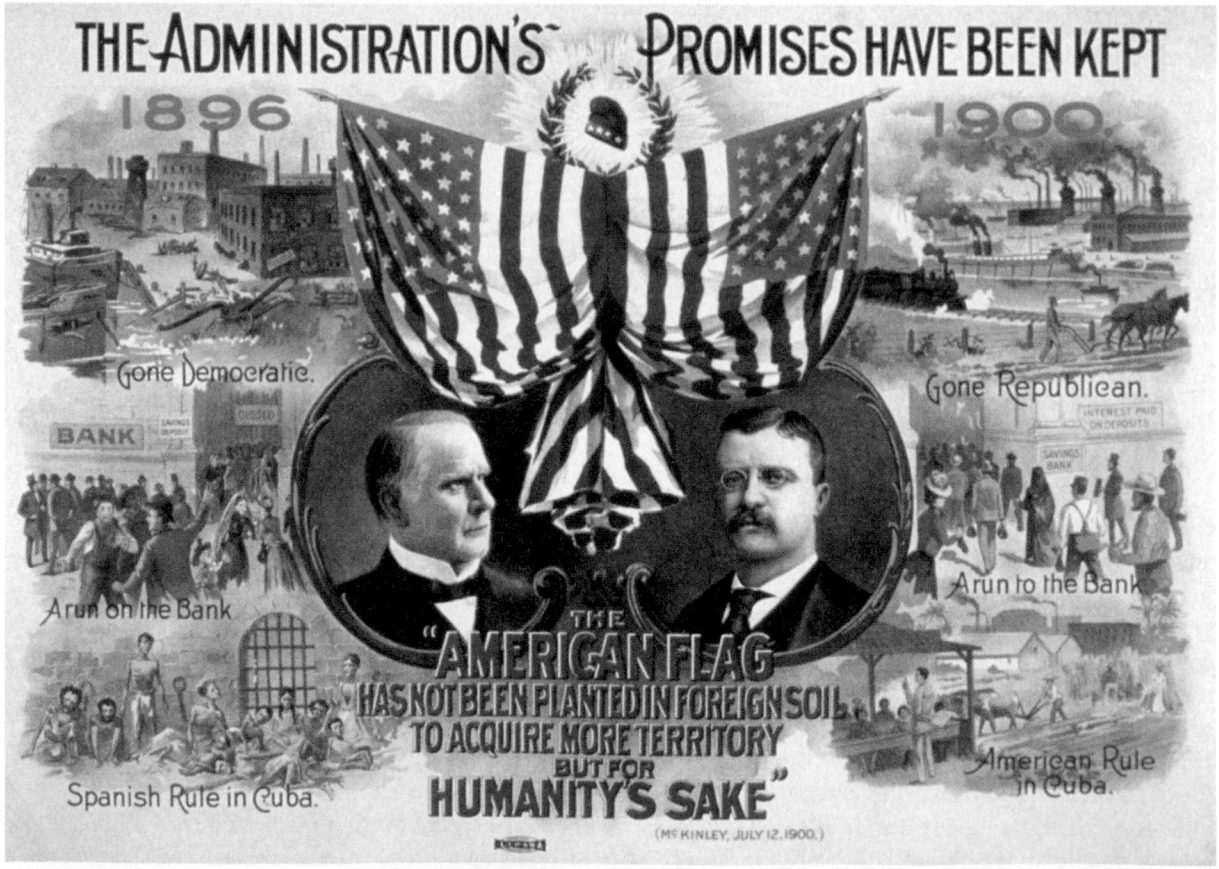

19.5 McKinley Campaign Poster, 1900
This poster helped voters visualize how expanding the nation's global influence created trading opportunities that made the whole country more prosperous. Emphasizing the American humanitarian mission abroad resonated with Progressive reformers and religious groups dedicated to spreading American values and institutions.

What steps did the United States take to construct a formal and informal empire after its victory over Spain?

Creating an American Empire

The Senate's razor-thin ratification of the Treaty of Paris, with just two votes to spare, ignited a strident internal debate over whether the United States should annex or free the Philippines. In the wake of ratification, both imperialists and anti-imperialists offered competing economic, political, and racial arguments about the wisdom of colonizing the Philippines. Unwilling to simply leave their fate in the hands of American politicians, Filipinos revolted against U.S. forces. The rebellion soon evolved into a vicious all-out war with high casualties on both sides.

The Debate over Colonies

In a risky strategic move that divided Democrats, party leader William Jennings Bryan had urged anti-imperialist Democratic senators to support ratification of the Treaty of Paris so that the United States could grant the Philippines independence once Spain relinquished control. But after the Senate had ratified the treaty, the majority of Republicans fought to keep the Philippines as a colony. Maps in the popular press helped Americans visualize the strategic and commercial importance of the nation's new island possessions. The "Map of the China Seas ... Under the National Flags, 1898" (**19.6**), published in *Harper's Weekly*, portrayed key parts of the imperialist argument for building an American empire in East Asia. By showing the proximity of the Philippine islands to European colonial possessions in East Asia, the map reinforced President McKinley's claim that another European power would certainly colonize the islands if the United States withdrew. The map also illustrated the imperialist slogan, "trade follows the flag." The closeness of the Philippines to China, for example, underscored the usefulness of the colony for developing a strong trading relationship between the United States and China.

A competing economic argument came from the Anti-Imperialist League, an organization that attracted a broad cross-section of politicians, Progressive reformers, writers, industrialists, and labor activists who opposed overseas colonial expansion. How would markets for American industrialized goods suddenly materialize in undeveloped Asian countries, the league asked. Anti-imperialists had a point, as the notion of a vast, untapped China market proved to be a seductive myth. Europe, not China, remained the most important overseas market for American goods throughout the twentieth century. Instead of economic gains anti-imperialists foresaw decades of costly expenses to maintain colonial outposts.

Debate also centered on the ability of the Filipinos to govern themselves. On the imperialist side,

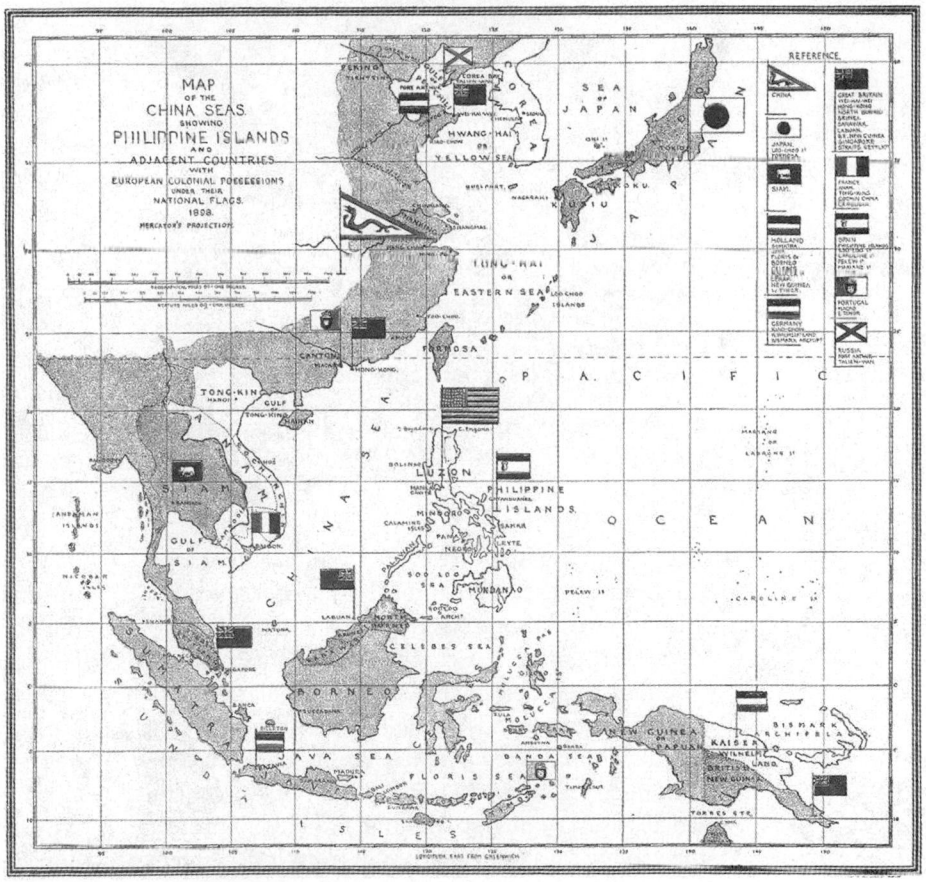

19.6 "Map of the China Seas ... Under the National Flags, 1898"
This *Harper's Weekly* map depicted the United States taking its rightful place alongside other world powers with colonial empires in East Asia.

What competing economic arguments did imperialists and anti-imperialists offer about colonies?

19.7 ***Give the Child Over to the Nurse, Uncle, and It Will Stop Crying***
Uncle Sam protects a Filipino child from ignorance and crime, portrayed as a savage black nurse, by feeding him education and civilization. This 1899 pro-expansionist political cartoon accused anti-imperialists like Hoar of failing to realize that the racially inferior Filipinos were too immature to rule themselves, no matter how much the Filipinos protested.

President McKinley adopted a strong paternalistic stance, arguing that "We could not leave them to themselves—they were unfit for self-government, and they would soon have anarchy and misrule worse then Spain's was." Caricatures helped imperialists publicize their case, incorporating popularly accepted notions of Americans' racial and moral superiority to so-called uncivilized peoples. This political cartoon contained strong racial undertones (**19.7**), depicting Uncle Sam as a nurturing white father who protects the wailing savage Filipino child from Independence (pictured as a depraved mammy-like figure) and from anti-imperialists like Senator George Hoar, a Republican from Massachusetts. The majority of Filipinos had converted to Catholicism under Spanish rule, a religion that most Americans distrusted. Besides spreading Anglo-Saxon cultural and political values, McKinley called upon Americans to take control of Filipinos' spiritual lives by turning them into Protestants.

Anti-imperialists viewed the question of governing the Filipinos differently. They claimed that subjugating the Philippines to imperial rule violated the principles of representative government outlined in the Constitution. Their slogan, "the Constitution follows the flag," conveyed their belief that Congress could not withhold constitutional rights, including the right to self-government, from colonial subjects.

In the 1900–1904 Insular Cases, the Supreme Court affirmed Congress's authority to govern the Philippines, Hawaii, and Puerto Rico as colonies. The court upheld the acquisition of colonies as constitutional and ruled that colonial populations did not become American citizens until the United States incorporated the colonies as territories. The justices offered a more mixed response on the question of extending constitutional rights to colonial subjects. In these cases the court denied colonial subjects some constitutional protections, such as procedural rights that guaranteed a fair trial, but held that Congress could not abridge the "natural rights" of free speech and religion. Recognition of these limited rights did not appease anti-imperialists, however. "Yes, as near as I can make out the Constitution follows the flag—but doesn't quite catch up with it," quipped Secretary of War Elihu Root. In 1900 Congress granted inhabitants of Hawaii and Alaska American citizenship, making them eligible for full protection under the Bill of Rights. Puerto Ricans had to wait until 1917. Filipinos never held American citizenship.

Finally some anti-imperialists envisioned that the burden of colonies would detract from solving racial problems at home. In the political cartoon *Civilization Begins at Home* (**19.8**), a woman symbolizing justice tries to draw McKinley's attention away from the map of the Philippines to the problems of racial injustice just outside his window. Other anti-imperialists, however, had racist reasons for opposing colonies. "Why do we as a people want

How did white Americans' racial views influence the debate over colonizing the Philippines?

"[T]here was nothing left for us to do but to take them all, and to educate the Filipinos, and uplift and civilize and Christianize them."

President McKINLEY explaining the imperialist vision for annexing the Philippines as a colony

to incorporate into our citizenship ten millions more of different or of differing race?" asked Senator Ben Tillman (D-SC) on the floor of the Senate.

In 1899 the British poet Rudyard Kipling entered the American debate over colonizing the Philippines when the popular magazine *McClure's* published his poem, "The White Man's Burden—The United States and the Philippine Islands." Kipling pictured Americans embracing "**the white man's burden**," the Anglo-Saxon quest to better the lives of so-called racially inferior peoples by spreading Western economic, cultural, and spiritual values and institutions. To Kipling, the term *white man* referred to more than skin color. It served as a symbol for people who embraced Anglo-Saxon moral standards and values. Theodore Roosevelt described the poem as "rather poor poetry, but good sense from the expansionist standpoint" when he sent it to Massachusetts's Republican senator Henry Cabot Lodge, who shared Roosevelt's views on expanding U.S. global influence. Black newspapers offered a competing vision, publishing an array of poems and editorials that detailed "the black man's burden" of living in a country that accepted Jim Crow practices in the South. The poem is reprinted, along with the satirical response from an anti-imperialist activist, in *Competing Visions: The White Man's Burden* (page 576).

19.8 ***Civilization Begins at Home***
In this 1898 illustration, a woman holding the scales of justice tries to draw President William McKinley's attention away from the Philippine-American War to the grisly lynchings of blacks at home.

How did imperialists define the nation's civilizing mission?

Competing Visions

THE WHITE MAN'S BURDEN

For American imperialists, Rudyard Kipling's 1899 poem "The White Man's Burden" offered a strong justification for annexing the Philippines. The poem's title became synonymous with the imperialist civilizing mission. Some disagreed, suggesting that Kipling portrayed colonies as burdens rather than assets. Others saw the poem as rife with irony. Social reformer and poet Ernest Crosby, president of the Anti-Imperialist League of New York, offered a competing vision of "the white man's burden" in his 1899 poem "The Real 'White Man's Burden.'" What views do these poems offer on the benefits and drawbacks of colonization?

Rudyard Kipling, "The White Man's Burden"

Take up the White Man's burden—
Send forth the best ye breed—
Go bind your sons to exile
To serve your captives' need;
To wait in heavy harness,
On fluttered folk and wild—
Your new-caught, sullen peoples,
Half-devil and half-child.

Take up the White Man's burden—
In patience to abide,
To veil the threat of terror
And check the show of pride;
By open speech and simple,
An hundred times made plain
To seek another's profit,
And work another's gain.

Take up the White Man's burden—
The savage wars of peace—
Fill full the mouth of Famine
And bid the sickness cease;
And when your goal is nearest
The end for others sought,
Watch sloth and heathen Folly
Bring all your hopes to nought.

Take up the White Man's burden—
No tawdry rule of kings,
But toil of serf and sweeper—
The tale of common things.
The ports ye shall not enter,
The roads ye shall not tread,
Go mark them with your living,
And mark them with your dead.

Take up the White Man's burden—
And reap his old reward:
The blame of those ye better,
The hate of those ye guard—
The cry of hosts ye humour
(Ah, slowly!) toward the light: —
"Why brought he us from bondage,
Our loved Egyptian night?"

Take up the White Man's burden—
Ye dare not stoop to less—
Nor call too loud on Freedom
To cloke your weariness;
By all ye cry or whisper,
By all ye leave or do,
The silent, sullen peoples
Shall weigh your gods and you.

Take up the White Man's burden—
Have done with childish days—
The lightly proferred laurel,
The easy, ungrudged praise.
Comes now, to search your manhood
Through all the thankless years
Cold, edged with dear-bought wisdom,
The judgment of your peers!

Ernest Crosby, "The Real 'White Man's Burden'"

With apologies to Rudyard Kipling

Take up the White Man's burden.
Send forth your sturdy kin,
And load them down with Bibles
And cannon-balls and gin.
Throw in a few diseases
To spread the tropic climes,
For there the healthy niggers
Are quite behind the times.

And don't forget the factories.
On those benighted shores
They have no cheerful iron mills,
Nor eke department stores.
They never work twelve hours a day
And live in strange content,
Altho they never have to pay
A single sou of rent.

Take up the White Man's burden,
And teach the Philippines
What interest and taxes are
And what a mortgage means.
Give them electrocution chairs,
And prisons, too, galore,
And if they seem inclined to kick,
Then spill their heathen gore.

They need our labor question, too,
And politics and fraud—
We've made a pretty mess at home,
Let's make a mess abroad.
And let us ever humbly pray
The Lord of Hosts may deign
To stir our feeble memories
Lest we forget—the *Maine*.

Take up the White's Man's burden.
To you who thus succeed
In civilizing savage hordes,
They owe a debt, indeed;
Concessions, pensions, salaries,
And privilege and right—
With outstretched hands you raised
to bless
Grab everything in sight.

Take up the White Man's burden
And if you write in verse,
Flatter your nation's vices
And strive to make them worse.
Then learn that if with pious words
You ornament each phrase,
In a world of canting hypocrites
This kind of business pays.

Is Kipling's poem best understood as imperialist propaganda or a satire of the civilizing mission?

The Philippine-American War

On January 20, 1899, the rebel Filipino leader Emilio Aguinaldo declared the Philippines independent of the United States. He formed a provisional government that concentrated power in the hands of elites from the main island of Luzon to rule the ethnically and religiously diverse societies that inhabited the archipelago. Fighting began a few weeks later on February 4, 1899, when U.S. and Filipino patrols clashed in the darkness, igniting a full-scale battle on the outskirts of Manila. The U.S. government called the conflict the Philippine Insurrection, using *insurrection*, a term used to describe an illegitimate revolt against an established government, to underscore that the Philippines was a U.S. colony, not an independent nation capable of waging war. The conflict nonetheless soon assumed the scope of a full-fledged war. In the Philippine-American War, fought from 1899 to 1902, the United States eventually defeated Filipino rebel forces. The cost of the two-and-a-half-year war in human lives differentiated it immediately from the quick American victory in Cuba. Between 1899 and 1902, 70,000 U.S. soldiers (nearly 70 percent of the army) fought a grueling war against the insurrectionists, and 4,234 lost their lives. Estimates place the number of Filipino soldiers and civilians killed as high as 220,000.

The rebels used conventional warfare tactics at first, but eventually turned to ambushes, sniping, and sabotage to drive out U.S. occupying forces. American soldiers called the Filipino way of war "amigo warfare" (amigo being the Spanish word for friend) because the guerilla fighters posed as friendly peasants during the day, then fought for the rebel army at night. The logistical difficulties of supplying troops with food and adequate medical care as they marched through the jungle in search of insurgents contributed to American soldiers' miseries. To uproot the guerilla forces, the U.S. Army adopted a mix of persuasive and coercive tactics. In many villages the army built roads, improved sanitation, vaccinated civilians, and created schools. Tens of thousands of Filipinos aided the U.S. Army during the rebellion by providing information and supplies, a sign of their gratefulness for American-engineered improvements in their daily life and their own religious, class, or ethnic disagreements with the Aguinaldo-led independence movement. Rebel soldiers, however, dealt harshly with civilians who refused to supply them with food or told the Americans where to find insurgent hideouts.

Benevolent policies won over only half of the archipelago, however. In provinces where these reforms failed to curtail guerilla attacks, U.S. troops lashed out with increasing brutality. "With an enemy like this to fight, it is not surprising that the boys should soon adopt 'no quarter' as a motto, and fill the blacks [Filipinos] full of lead before finding out whether or not they are friends or enemies," a soldier from Utah wrote home. American soldiers burned villages and crops to deprive rebels of shelter and food, tactics that created a starving civilian refugee population and encouraged resentful peasant men to join Aguinaldo's rebel force. Exposés in the American press and Senate investigations revealed the inventive tortures the army used to extract information from captured Filipino rebels, fueling the ongoing debate over whether the United States was civilizing or conquering the Philippines. In the "water cure," for example, interrogators shoved a bamboo shoot down a victim's throat to keep his mouth open while they poured water into his throat and nose until his stomach swelled and he could not breathe, and then pushed on the stomach to expel the water. The victim had a few minutes to release the desired information before his interrogators repeated the entire process.

> "Every tree seemed to shoot at us!"
>
> An American soldier confronting Filipino rebel guerilla tactics

Justifying annexation of the Philippines as part of the "white man's burden" posed a particularly thorny dilemma for the six thousand African American soldiers fighting in their own segregated regiments to subdue the Filipino rebels. White soldiers constantly referred to Filipinos as "niggers," the same derogatory term they used when speaking about their African American comrades. Knowing that many African American civilians opposed the war as "an unholy war of conquest," a term coined by activist minister Henry M. Turner, black soldiers nevertheless hoped that their honorable military record would help create more opportunities for African Americans at home and in the military. Filipino rebels posted signs on trees that chastised African Americans for fighting "against people who are struggling for recognition and freedom, [while] your people in America are being lynched and disfranchised by the same who are trying to compel

What tactics did the U.S. Army adopt to fight the Filipino rebels?

us to believe that their government will deal justly and fairly by us." Yet these Filipino appeals to lay down their arms had little effect on most African American troops, who focused instead on avenging the lives of comrades killed by Filipino rebels. One exception was Corporal David Fagan, a black soldier who had fought in Cuba and defected to the Filipino army shortly after arriving in the Philippines. He was one of five black soldiers who deserted to the other side. Fagan's reputation grew to mythic proportions as he eluded capture and successfully organized guerilla raids on his former comrades-in-arms.

Rebel leader Emilio Aguinaldo was not so fortunate. In March 1901 a captured messenger revealed the location of Aguinaldo's hideaway 50 miles into the jungle. To capture Aguinaldo General Frederick Funston assembled a group of Macabebe scouts, a Philippine ethnic group that had traditionally rendered military service to Spain and now joined the U.S. fight against the rebels. Posing as reinforcement rebel troops, the Macabebe soldiers entered Aguinaldo's camp accompanied by five American soldiers pretending to be prisoners. The group arrived as a birthday celebration for Aguinaldo was under-way, and when the infiltrators reached for their weapons, Aguinaldo's guards assumed they were preparing to fire an honor salute. Instead the Macabebe scouts began shooting, the signal for the rest of Funston's men, who were waiting on the perimeter, to invade the camp. Aguinaldo's guards fled in panic, leaving the rebel leader in the hands of the Americans.

A chastened Aguinaldo called on his followers to lay down their arms and accept U.S. rule. One by one Aguinaldo's generals surrendered, and the war ground to a halt. Theodore Roosevelt, who became president after McKinley's 1901 assassination (see Chapter 18), declared the war over on July 4, 1902. American troops nonetheless remained in the Philippines for another eleven years to subdue separate revolts by Muslim Moro tribal leaders in remote islands of the Philippines.

In 1900 William Howard Taft became the first civilian Governor General of the Philippines. When the war ended he expanded humanitarian efforts to build roads and schools, and improve sanitation. Taft also convinced Congress to purchase church-held land from the Vatican, which the colonial administration then helped peasants purchase with low-cost mortgages. To put the debate over annexing the Philippines to rest, the government sponsored exhibits at the 1904 St. Louis World's Fair that championed the imperialist vision of colonization. In the Philippine Reservation display, visitors walked through six reconstructed Filipino villages and watched partially clothed members of remote Filipino tribes demonstrate native practices that included feasts of dog and headhunting. By inviting tribes with the most exotic customs to participate, organizers intended to juxtapose the primitiveness of Filipino culture with the civilizing influence of U.S. rule. Photographs such as this (**19.9**) captured the U.S. effort to provide illiterate, nearly naked Filipinos with a Western education. The curious American visitors in the gallery observing a white female instructor teaching her pupils appear unconcerned about putting these people on display as a tourist attraction. Instead Americans who talked with Filipinos at the exhibit quickly "disabused themselves of any impression that the natives could take care of themselves," one newspaper reported. Other displays at the World's Fair championed America's scientific, economic, and cultural achievements. Collectively these exhibits suggested that as a leading nation in the civilized world the United States had the duty and right to become a colonial power.

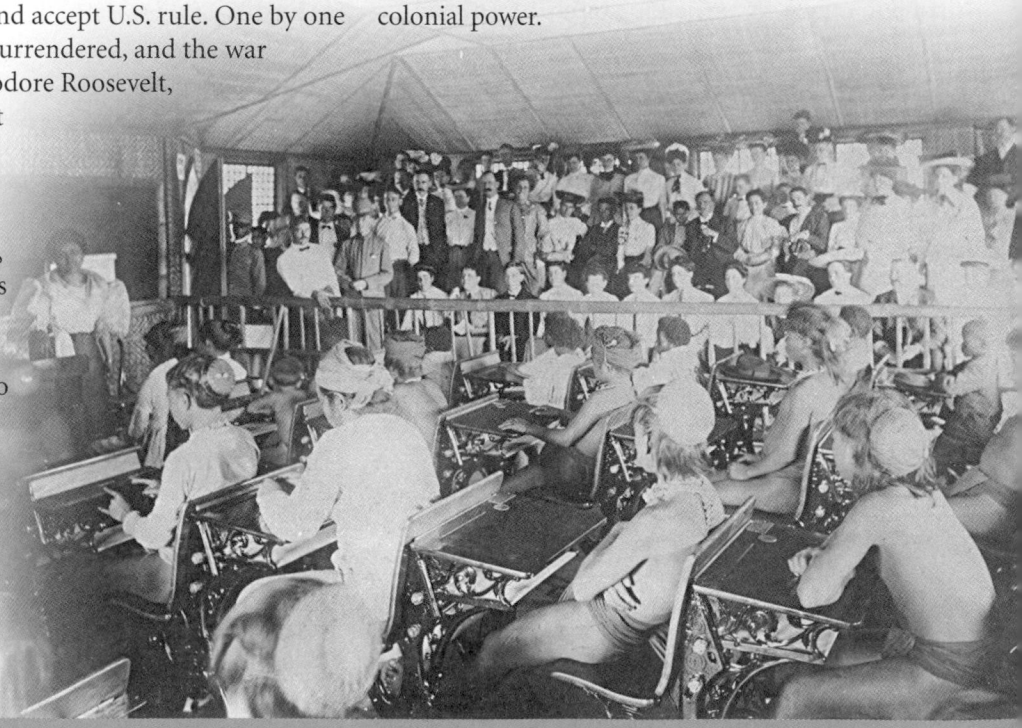

19.9 American Rule in the Philippines
The 1904 St. Louis World's Fair included exhibits on American efforts to school native tribes in the Philippines, turning these exotically dressed people into tourist attractions.

How did imperialists try to quell debate over colonizing the Philippines?

America and East Asia

The United States fought a war of conquest in the Philippines to secure an independent trade route to East Asia only to discover that the coveted China market was in danger of disappearing. To prevent the world's leading powers from carving China up into formal colonies at the turn of the century, the United States turned to diplomacy, scoring an impressive victory when it convinced these nations to keep Chinese trade open to all. Americans also viewed their nation's role in negotiating an end to the Russo-Japanese War in 1905 as an additional sign of America's growing world stature. Not all international conflicts in this period originated outside the United States, however. In 1907 President Roosevelt used diplomacy to smooth over the crisis that arose in Japanese-American relations when California initiated a campaign to segregate and ban Japanese immigrants.

The Open Door in China

Throughout the nineteenth century China granted most-favored trading status (commercial privileges) to every world power that asked. This strategy prevented any one foreign nation from gaining too much power over the Chinese economy and helped China remain independent in an age when Europe and Japan colonized many Asian lands. Any nation contemplating a campaign to colonize China risked provoking the wrath of angry competitors eager to protect their own access to Chinese trade.

In the 1880s and 1890s, American Protestant missionaries began venturing forth into the interior of China, away from the ports where foreign businessmen concentrated their commercial activity. In their letters to American churches, missionaries exaggerated Chinese interest in Western agricultural crops such as wheat and cotton. By whetting public curiosity about a vast Chinese market, missionaries hoped to bolster domestic support for their religious work in China. The debate over colonizing the Philippines also heightened the allure of an untapped Chinese market for U.S. goods.

> "There are 400,000,000 active stomachs in China, and each cries for food three times a day."
>
> A New York newspaper extolling the opportunities to export American crops

American access to these potential customers, however, appeared in danger of evaporating at the turn of the century. The world's leading nations descended on China to each claim a **sphere of influence**, the term used to describe the exclusive political and trading rights that a foreign nation enjoyed within another nation's territory. American missionaries continued their religious activities in these new spheres of influence, areas that American businessmen also coveted as future markets for U.S. goods. At this point the involved nations only demanded a monopoly over trade in a specific region, but the U.S. government feared that an outright division of China into formal colonies would soon follow. "All Europe is seizing on China and if we do not establish ourselves in the East that vast trade, from which we must draw our future prosperity" would close to the United States forever, Senator Henry Cabot Lodge warned.

Already stretched to the limit in the Caribbean and Philippines, and facing strong anti-imperialist sentiments at home, McKinley never considered sending troops to China to seize a port or territory. Instead Secretary of State John Hay circulated a carefully worded set of notes that laid the foundation for the **Open Door Policy**, a U.S.-sponsored nonbinding international agreement that kept the Chinese market open to all foreign nations. The first set of Open Door Notes asked France, Italy, Japan, and Russia to allow other nations to trade freely within their respective spheres of influence, refrain from imposing arbitrary duties on foreign goods, and allow Chinese officials to collect customs fees (thereby recognizing China's continued political control). By January 1900 Hay reported that all nations with a sphere of influence in China had

Why did Americans develop a strong interest in China at the turn of the century?

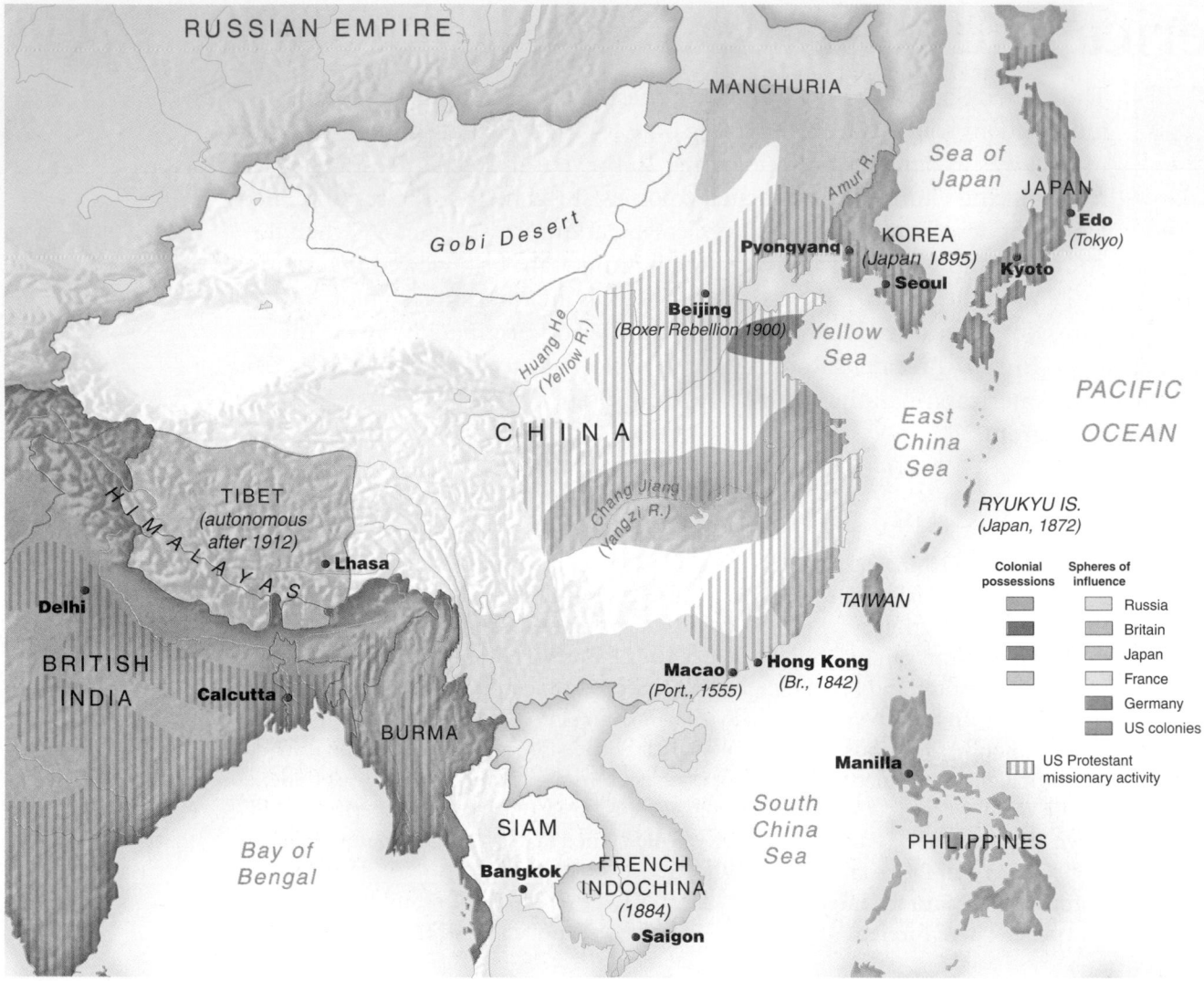

19.10 Foreign Activity in China, 1901 American missionaries and businessmen established a presence in China that the U.S. government tried to protect by negotiating with nations that had spheres of influence there.

agreed to abide by these terms. For the time being the allure of trading opportunities in the spheres of others outweighed the desire for full-fledged colonies in China. China was the only nation Hay neglected to consult in his diplomatic negotiations.

Angry over the humiliating foreign domination of China, a group of Chinese militants vowed to restore Chinese sovereignty over its land and economy. In 1900 a secret society called the Righteous and Harmonious Fists initiated a terrorist campaign to drive the "foreign devils" out of China, a crusade that some members of the Chinese imperial government secretly funded. Westerners called this group the Boxers because of the clenched fist the rebels adopted as their emblem and the militants' martial arts training. When thousands of Boxers began roaming the countryside and attacking foreigners at will, an international force of ground troops and battleships assembled to crush the insurgency. Tensions escalated dramatically when the Boxers took foreign diplomats and businessmen hostage in Beijing.

Throughout the crisis Secretary Hay worked frantically to prevent the involved nations from using the Boxer Rebellion as an excuse to colonize China. In a second round of Open Door Notes, Hay asked the same nations that had accepted the first Open Door Notes to respect the "territorial and administrative integrity" of China. To avoid any negative responses, Hay did not ask for a formal reply to his request. To further protect American missionary and economic interests in China (pictured on **19.10**), McKinley sent 2,500 U.S. soldiers to join the multinational force in freeing the foreign hostages and ending the Boxer Rebellion. As punishment for the imperial government's support of the Boxers, the international coalition demanded $333 million in indemnities from China. The United States used its share to provide scholarships for Chinese students studying at American universities.

What does this map reveal about relations between China and the world's leading powers, including the United States?

Relations with Japan

Despite the Open Door Policy, the competition for rights to control railroads, mines, and ports in China continued, and within a few years Japan and Russia fought to control the resource-rich Manchurian province of China. The Russo-Japanese War of 1904–1905 threatened to topple the careful balance of power that the United States was trying to maintain in China. Concerned that too overwhelming a Japanese victory "may possibly mean a struggle between them and us in the future," President Roosevelt offered to negotiate a peace settlement. In August 1905 a financially exhausted Japan and a militarily defeated Russia came to the peace table in Portsmouth, New Hampshire. Many Americans delighted at the sight of their president mediating a conflict between two world powers. In 1906 Roosevelt received the Nobel Peace Prize for his role in ending the Russo-Japanese War.

No sooner had Roosevelt negotiated a settlement between Japan and Russia than he faced the possibility of losing the Japanese friendship he had worked so hard to protect. In 1905 California legislators, newspapers, and labor leaders joined hands to mount a strident campaign to halt Japanese immigration. Japanese and Korean exclusion leagues urged Congress to follow the precedent established with the 1882 Chinese Exclusion Act and prohibit all Asians from entering the nation. These groups denounced Asians as a degenerative element who threatened American culture and unfairly competed for jobs that rightfully belonged to native-born white workers.

California legislators lumped all Asians together when they spoke about defending the nation from the "Yellow Peril," but Roosevelt understood the vast difference between a weak, humiliated China and a powerful, proud Japan. "If we show that we regard the Japanese as an inferior and alien race, and try to treat them as we have treated the Chinese; and if at the same time we fail to keep our navy at the highest point of efficiency and size—then we shall invite disaster," Roosevelt wrote privately. In 1906 the San Francisco Board of Education decided to send Japanese, Chinese, and Korean children to one set of segregated schools. With Japan bristling at the insult of Americans lumping Japanese together with other Asian peoples whom they viewed as inferior to themselves, Roosevelt intervened to control the damage to U.S.-Japanese relations. California agreed to revoke the segregation order in return for an end to Japanese immigration, but Hawaiian sugar planters protested that they needed Japanese workers. As a compromise Roosevelt issued an executive order that allowed Japanese workers into Hawaii. The president then negotiated a reduction in Japanese immigration to the mainland through a series of diplomatic notes between Japan and the United States. In the **Gentleman's Agreement** (1907–1908), the Japanese government agreed to deny passports to Japanese workers intending to immigrate to the United States. This informal agreement helped Japan escape the indignity of joining China as the only other nation legally banned from sending immigrant workers to the United States.

Angel Island

In the Gentleman's Agreement Japan reserved the right to issue passports to professionals and to the relatives of Japanese migrants or citizens already living in the United States. Until the United States closed this loophole in 1921, Japan gave passports to Japanese wives so they could join their husbands in the United States. Americans called these women "picture brides" because couples often exchanged photos of each other through the matchmaker who arranged long-distance marriages for Japanese men residing in the United States. The three hundred to five hundred Japanese "picture brides" who immigrated annually to the United States met their new husbands for the first time when they arrived.

The United States also experienced a surge in Chinese immigration during this period. The 1906 earthquake in San Francisco destroyed the city's birth records and without any way to prove otherwise, hundreds of Chinese men successfully claimed that they were American-born. As citizens they asserted their right to bring their families to the United States. Many brought in "paper sons," boys whose families paid a fee to Chinese men already in the United States to fraudulently claim to be their fathers.

In 1910 U.S. authorities opened up an immigration processing station on **Angel Island** in the San Francisco Bay to verify the identities of Japanese and Chinese immigrants claiming the right to enter the United States. Chinese "paper sons" endured long periods of detention on Angel Island while authorities investigated their background. Before leaving China "paper sons" memorized details about their "father," including descriptions of relatives, houses, and key events in a family's history. Once they arrived at Angel Island, inspectors quizzed sons and fathers separately and refused entry to those whose answers failed to match. Chinese men detained on Angel Island sometimes passed the time

How did domestic racial prejudices affect diplomatic relations with Japan?

by etching poetry onto the barrack walls, including one anonymous poet who expressed his angst by writing, "who was to know two streams of tears would flow upon arriving here?"

In 1919 California politicians reignited their campaign against the Japanese, successfully passing laws that made it illegal for Japanese immigrants to own property. Naturalization laws allowed just people of white or African ancestry to become citizens, preventing Japanese immigrants from seeking U.S. citizenship to circumvent these restrictions. In *Takao Ozawa v. United States* (1922), the Supreme Court held that Japanese immigrants were indeed ineligible for citizenship because they were not white. *Choices and Consequences: The Legal Construction of "Whiteness"* explores this decision.

The fact that Japanese picture brides bore children who were U.S. citizens, and therefore eligible to own property, did not escape the notice of those campaigning for a ban on Japanese property ownership. Senator James D. Phelan (D-CA) led the campaign to stop admitting picture brides to the United States, ominously predicting that a booming birthrate in the Japanese immigrant community would lead to Japanese dominance of California agriculture. To garner publicity for their anti-Japanese crusade, a congressional delegation traveled to Angel Island in 1920. The legislators invited news photographers to take photos (**19.11**) as they sternly examined the passports of bewildered, frightened young women, dressed in their best clothes to meet their new husbands. Fearful that rising anti-Japanese prejudice might lead to a Japanese exclusion law, Japan agreed to stop issuing passports to picture brides in 1921. Congress banned all immigration from Asia in 1924 (see Chapter 21).

19.11 Japanese Picture Brides, 1920
To rally public support for their drive to cut off the flow of Japanese women coming to the United States, a delegation of congressmen posed for the cameras as they examined the passports of these shy, pretty Japanese picture brides, whose ethnicity made them unwelcome.

What insights does this photo offer into issues of ethnicity and gender in the early twentieth century?

Choices and Consequences

THE LEGAL CONSTRUCTION OF "WHITENESS"

Takao Ozawa was a Japanese immigrant who lived in California and Hawaii for twenty-eight years before he applied to become a citizen of the United States. Aware that naturalization laws allowed only Caucasians and people of African ancestry to become citizens, Ozawa argued that he was white. He emphasized his complete assimilation into American society and the lightness of his skin. When the Supreme Court heard his case in 1922, the justices faced several options about how to define "whiteness."

Choices

1. Differing physical features divided the human species into white, black, and yellow races.
2. Skin color established racial identity.
3. Whiteness was a socially constructed notion with no scientific basis.
4. Assimilating into American culture made one "white."

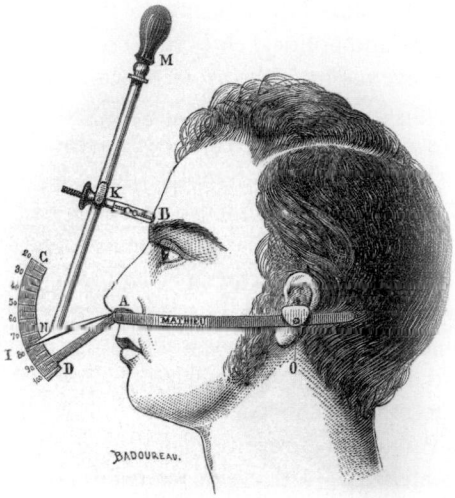

Measurement of the Head and Face, 1883

Decision

The Court rejected Ozawa's contention that skin pigmentation signified whiteness and his claim of complete assimilation. In a unanimous decision the justices ruled that "the words 'white person' are synonymous with the words 'a person of Caucasian race.'" This decision accepted contemporary anthropologists' assertions that measurements of facial features provided scientific evidence to classify the Japanese as members of the "Mongolian race."

Consequences

Within three months the court unanimously reversed its reasoning, deciding instead that whiteness was a socially, not scientifically, constructed category. When Indian immigrant Bhagat Singh Thind applied for citizenship, he argued that anthropologists categorized Asian Indians as Caucasians. In rejecting Thind's claim of whiteness, the Supreme Court now ruled that "the words 'free white persons' are words of common speech, to be interpreted in accordance with the understanding of the common man." Deciding who was legally white now depended on the whims of the larger culture, not the claims of scientists.

Continuing Controversies

What determines racial identity?

Well into the twentieth century, many Americans continued to believe that biologically based racial differences existed, even within the Caucasian race. In the 1920s the United States severely curtailed immigration from eastern and southern Europe, viewing northern Europeans as racially superior (see Chapter 21). The fear that light-skinned blacks were "passing" as whites caused many Southern states to bar individuals with any African ancestry, the so-called "one-drop" of blood rule, from using "whites-only" facilities. The view of racial identity as a social construct also drew adherents. Radical black civil rights leaders tried to cultivate a racial identity based on African Americans' cultural distinctiveness, while others sought a color-blind society that did away with racial identities completely.

What differing ways have Americans defined racial identity?

In America's Backyard

Establishing a U.S. presence and maintaining favorable relations in East Asia became key aims of American foreign policy at the turn of the century. Americans also, however, explored opportunities to expand closer to home. The government focused in particular on constructing an isthmian canal through Central America to facilitate U.S. trade with China and better protect the nation's coastlines. Earlier transportation breakthroughs such as the Erie Canal, National Road, and transcontinental railroad quickened the movement of people and goods and helped the United States expand across the continent. The Panama Canal secured U.S. dominance of the Caribbean, and the government resolved to keep other foreign powers out of the region.

The Panama Canal

At the end of the nineteenth century, American canal advocates emphasized increased trade and better defense as reasons for building the **Panama Canal**, a manmade waterway through Panama completed in 1914 to link the Pacific and Atlantic oceans. The canal project received a boost when one of its strongest advocates, Theodore Roosevelt, assumed the presidency. Roosevelt took up the canal project immediately. "No single great material work which remains to be undertaken on this continent is of such consequence to the American people," Roosevelt told Congress the first time he addressed the legislators.

Roosevelt intended to take up where Ferdinand de Lesseps, the French mastermind who built the 1869 Suez Canal in Egypt that linked the Mediterranean and Red seas, had left off. In the 1880s de Lesseps had begun building a canal through Panama (then part of Colombia). Battling mudslides and earthquakes de Lesseps eventually abandoned the project and sold his concession from the Colombian government to the New Panama Canal Company, a French company headed by Philippe Bunau-Varilla, a longtime engineer on the project.

In 1902 the United States offered the New Panama Canal Company $40 million for its concession and assets, a sum that Bunau-Varilla eagerly accepted. Colombia, however, rejected Roosevelt's offer of $10 million to secure the rights to maintain a U.S.-controlled canal in Panama indefinitely. The Colombian government knew that the New Panama Canal Company's concession expired in 1904, and by stalling Colombia expected to pocket the $40 million earmarked for the company. "Those contemptible little creatures in Bogotá [the capital of Colombia] ought to understand how much they are jeopardizing things and imperiling their own future," Roosevelt wrote in frustration to his secretary of state John Hay.

In 1903 Panama revolted against Colombia. The timing was not coincidental. Fearing it would lose everything, the New Panama Canal Company encouraged and financed the rebellion by Panamanian business and political elites who did not want to share revenue from the projected canal with the rest of Colombia. Bunau-Varilla not only set the date for the revolution but also provided its leader, Manuel Guerrero Amador, with money, defense plans, a declaration of independence, and even a flag. Roosevelt never gave Bunau-Varilla any direct promises of U.S. support but, the president later recalled, it was Bunau-Varilla's "business to find out what he thought our Government would do . . . in fact, he would have been a very dull man had he been unable to make such a guess."

Once the Panamanian revolt began, Roosevelt acted immediately to ensure events turned in favor of the United States. The difficult mountain terrain separating the rest of Colombia from Panama forced Colombian troops to come by sea. When they arrived U.S. naval ships patrolling both coasts prevented them from landing in Panama. Roosevelt claimed that an 1846 agreement with Colombia gave the United States the authority to control transit across Panama. The nineteenth-century pact, however, envisioned using U.S. forces to protect, not destroy, Colombian sovereignty in Panama. In the 1920s Congress apologetically sent Colombia $25 million for Roosevelt's transgression.

With America's help the revolution in Panama succeeded. The United States immediately received its reward from Bunau-Varilla, the newly appointed

How did U.S. intervention in Panama compare with its colonization of the Philippines?

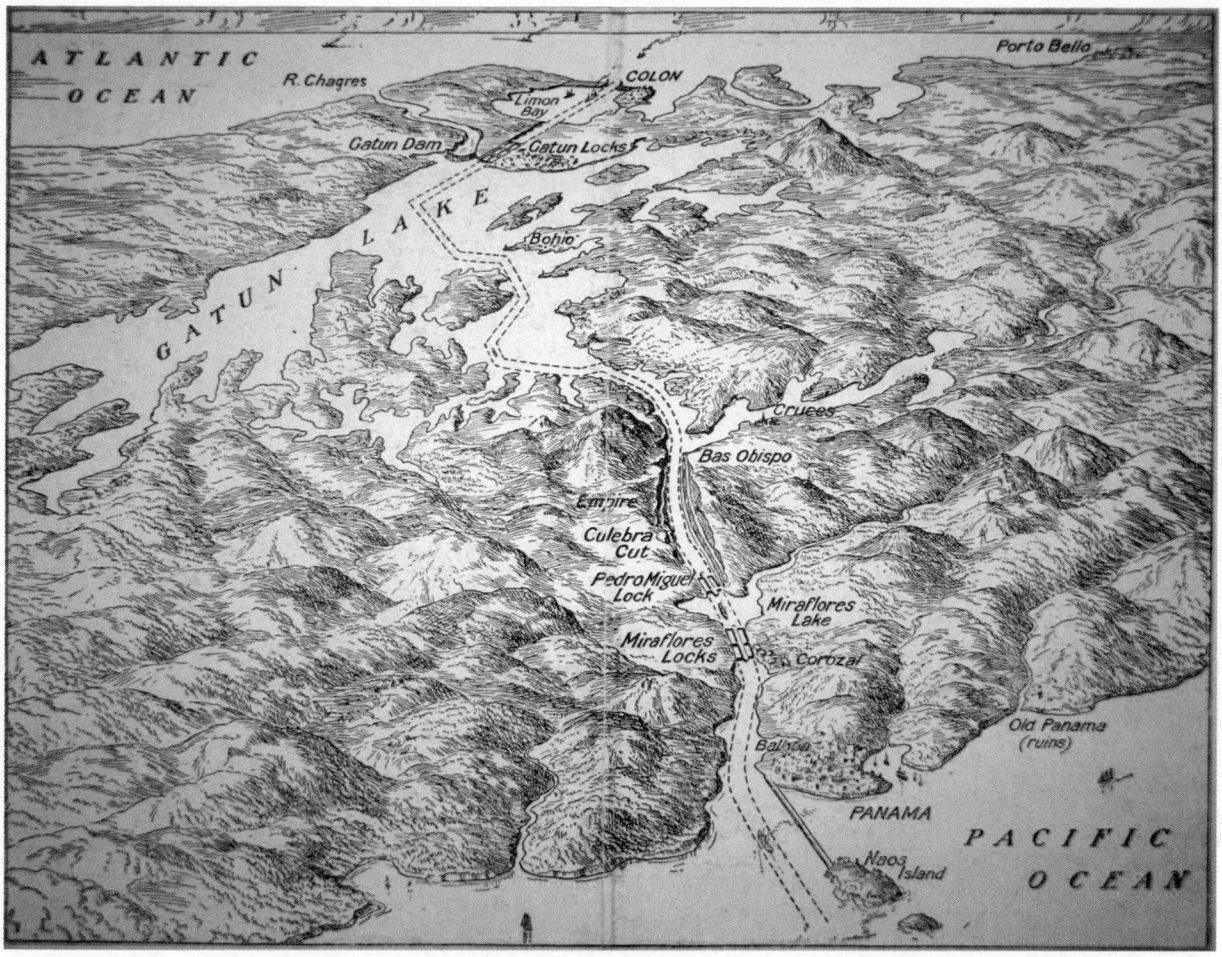

19.12 Building the Panama Canal
The Americans used a system of locks and dams to construct the waterway through a mountainous terrain subject to flooding and mudslides.
[*Source:* Map of the Panama Canal from the Atlantic to the Pacific Ocean, 1913 (litho), American School, (20th century) / Private Collection / Peter Newark American Pictures / The Bridgeman Art Library International]

minister to the United States for the Republic of Panama. The Hay–Bunau-Varilla Treaty (1903) gave the United States perpetual control over a strip of land 10 miles wide that included the Panama Canal for $10 million and an annual rent of $250,000. These terms remained in effect until December 31, 1999, when the United States turned control of the canal over to Panama.

When American engineers took over building the Panama Canal in 1904, they confronted a host of geological challenges. At several points the Chagres River crisscrossed the route selected for the canal. Tropical rains regularly poured down the mountains into the Chagres, which, if not diverted, would dump floodwaters and huge silt deposits into the planned canal. By damming the Chagres River, U.S. engineers created the artificial Gatun Lake that ships reached through a stairway of locks on either side. This approach used water rather than shovels to create a large portion of the waterway. The accompanying map (**19.12**) shows the 164 square miles of rain forest that construction crews flooded to create Gatun Lake. The five thousand American engineers, skilled workers, and foremen at the construction site relied on thousands of foreign workers, mostly blacks from the British West Indies, to dig the rest of the canal.

President Theodore Roosevelt shared the public's fascination with the feat of building the canal, and visited the site in 1906. His two-week trip made Roosevelt the first American president to leave the country while in office. Not content merely to watch the huge steam shovels through the window of the train bringing him to the Culebra Cut, the project's largest excavation site, Roosevelt tramped through the mud to reach one and climbed into the driver's seat. As photographers snapped away Roosevelt

> "It is an epic feat, and one of immense significance."
>
> President ROOSEVELT, after visiting the Panama Canal construction site

How did U.S. engineers overcome the geological obstacles to building the Panama Canal?

"You had to pray every day for God to carry you safe, and bring you back."

A black worker on felling giant trees and surviving mudslides while building the Panama Canal

learned that the Bucyrus steam shovel picked up 8 tons of dirt in a single scoop, required a crew of ten, and dug five times more than older machines.

This photo of Roosevelt sitting at the controls of a Bucyrus steam shovel (**19.13**) captured the adventurous spirit of an era dedicated to overseas economic expansion, technological innovation, and world prominence. "The real builder of the Panama Canal was Theodore Roosevelt," wrote Major George W. Goethals, chief engineer on the project.

Americans usually saw photos of their formally dressed presidents standing on podiums, sitting at desks, or posing with visiting dignitaries. In this photograph Roosevelt appears as the larger-than-life personality he was, literally building the canal he played such a large part in securing for the United States.

Americans solved more than the engineering riddle of constructing the canal. They also conquered the disease-carrying mosquito. Guided by the recent discovery that mosquitoes transmitted malaria and yellow fever among humans, Dr. William C. Gorgas undertook a relentless fumigation campaign that

19.13 Theodore Roosevelt Visits the Canal Zone
Instead of observing construction of the Panama Canal from a safe distance, Roosevelt climbed into the seat of a steam shovel to work its controls.

What does this photograph convey about Roosevelt and the feat of building the Panama Canal?

saved thousands of lives. Nonetheless poor sanitary conditions in the black workers' laboring camps (which Roosevelt criticized during his visit) and the dangers posed by mudslides and working with dynamite still exacted a toll. Nearly 4,500 foreign black workers and 500 white Americans died during the American phase of construction.

The Roosevelt Corollary

The completed Panama Canal stood as a symbol for U.S. technological achievement, naval power, and economic strength. The canal also increased the importance of the Caribbean to U.S. national security. "America's interests in this hemisphere are greater than those of any European power," Roosevelt stated, therefore the United States intended to "police and protect" the canal alone. Roosevelt had reason to worry about European naval incursions into the region. Anxious about overdue debts, Britain and Germany blockaded Venezuela in 1902 and two years later several European nations threatened to intervene with force in the Dominican Republic for the same reason. To head off a European invasion, the Dominican Republic asked Roosevelt to accept the nation as a protectorate. Roosevelt privately remarked he had "about the same desire to annex it as a gorged boa constrictor might have to swallow a porcupine wrong-end-to." He nonetheless agreed to help the Dominican Republic, but only after deciding to use the incident to establish a new principle in U.S. foreign policy.

To prevent European military incursions into the Western Hemisphere, Roosevelt announced a corollary to the 1823 Monroe Doctrine (see Chapter 7), which had declared the Western Hemisphere off-limits to further European colonization. The **Roosevelt Corollary** of 1904 stated that when confronted with "flagrant cases" of wrongdoing by Latin American nations, such as not paying their debts to Western nations, the United States intended to act as an "international police power" in the region. In this political cartoon (**19.14**), a gigantic Roosevelt, dressed as a Rough Rider, holds a big stick as he pulls U.S. ships labeled "sheriff" and "debt collector" around the Caribbean. Americans dubbed the Roosevelt Corollary the "big stick" policy in reference to a West African proverb that Roosevelt favored: "Speak softly and carry a big stick, and you will go far." The corollary exempted Argentina, Brazil, and Chile because Roosevelt considered them civilized nations capable of meeting their international commitments and running their own domestic affairs. Satisfied that the United States would help Europe recoup its loans to Central and South American nations, European nations reacted positively to the Roosevelt Corollary.

19.14 *Theodore Roosevelt's Big Stick*
In this cartoon illustrating the impact of the Roosevelt Corollary, the president pulls a line of naval vessels around the Caribbean to keep nearby nations in line and prevent the creation of European empires too close to U.S. shores.

Roosevelt's successor in the White House, William Howard Taft, further expanded U.S. influence over Latin America. Not content to simply ensure that Caribbean nations paid their debts, Taft initiated a policy of Dollar Diplomacy that encouraged U.S. investment in Latin America to ensure U.S. economic dominance over the region.

How did the Roosevelt Corollary bolster U.S. stature as a world power?

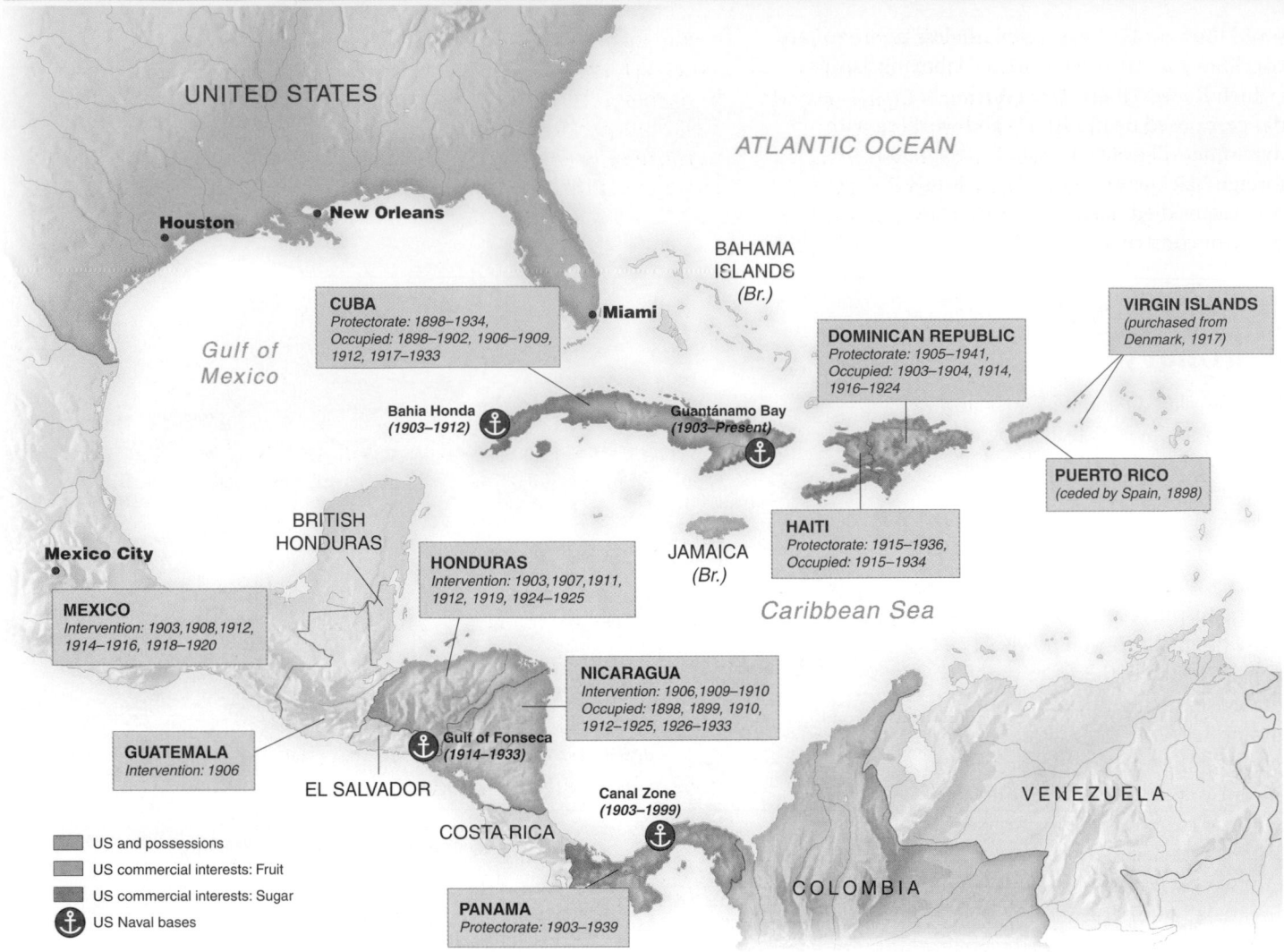

19.15 American Involvement in Latin America, 1898–1939
The United States intervened continually in the domestic affairs of its southern neighbors to protect the area as a U.S. sphere of influence.

Hoping to substitute "dollars for bullets," Taft shared Roosevelt's desire to turn the Caribbean into an American lake. When Democrat Woodrow Wilson became president in 1912, he followed in Roosevelt and Taft's footsteps by acting aggressively to protect U.S. business interests and curtail European access to the Western Hemisphere. The map, "American Involvement in Latin America, 1898–1939," (**19.15**) lists the many U.S. military incursions that occurred in areas where American businessmen had invested heavily in fruit and sugar industries. During this period U.S. troops invaded Mexico, Guatemala, Honduras, Nicaragua, Haiti, the Dominican Republic, and Cuba for a variety of strategic, commercial, and humanitarian reasons. American occupying armies often stayed for years, and in 1915 Haiti joined Cuba, the Dominican Republic, and Panama as a U.S. protectorate. Exerting influence over the domestic affairs of its Caribbean neighbors, through military invasions and protectorships, became a mainstay of twentieth-century U.S. foreign policy.

America's emerging role as a mediator in international disputes also included sending delegates abroad to resolve conflicts among European nations, including an agreement that partitioned Morocco in North Africa between Spain and France in 1906. Many congressional leaders feared that this diplomatic intervention represented a dangerous precedent. They made clear their refusal to support any departure from the traditional U.S. policy of

What steps did Taft and Wilson take to protect the Caribbean as a U.S. sphere of influence?

neutrality in the precarious game of European geopolitics. Their concerns proved well founded. On August 15, 1914, the Panama Canal officially opened. Newspapers buried this news about America's crowning achievement of the imperial age in their back pages, instead devoting their headlines to the eleven-day-old war sweeping through Europe. The beginning of World War I ushered in a new era in world history, one of global warfare made possible by the powerful empires constructed in the late nineteenth century. Now actively engaged in the world, the United States would find it difficult to stay out of this spreading conflict.

Conclusion

From 1890 to 1914 U.S. imperialists identified key commercial, strategic, and moral reasons for the United States to play an active role on the world stage. Americans increasingly saw expansion overseas, through war or trade, as the answer to its domestic and foreign concerns. Opportunity for expansion came first in Cuba. Shocked by stories of Spain's reconcentration program and worried about U.S. business interests in Cuba, Americans agreed to help Cuba liberate itself from Spain when the *Maine* exploded in Havana Harbor. After its victory in Cuba, the United States established a protectorate there, acquired Puerto Rico and Guam, and purchased the Philippine islands. These territorial possessions in the Caribbean and Pacific formed the basis of the U.S. empire for the next forty years.

Americans offered conflicting visions over the virtues of creating a U.S. colonial empire. Imperialists asserted that acquiring colonies would enhance the prestige of the United States, provide valuable economic resources, and help establish a trade route to China. Advocates also viewed imperialism as a mission to improve the lives of native peoples. Anti-imperialists voiced concern over subjugating people against their will and the costs of maintaining an empire. As Americans argued, Filipino rebels took up arms against the American occupying force. The costly Philippine-American War cooled American enthusiasm for using military conquest to acquire more colonies.

Establishing a strong trading relationship with East Asia also required diplomacy. The implementation of the Open Door Policy guaranteed American businessmen unfettered access to China by preventing other foreign nations from colonizing China. To maintain the balance of power in East Asia, President Roosevelt took a leading role in negotiating the peace treaty that ended the Russo-Japanese War. Roosevelt also forged the Gentleman's Agreement, which limited Japanese immigration to the United States.

In return for helping Panama win independence from Colombia, the United States received permission to build and control a canal across Panama. The construction feat evoked pride in the nation's industrial achievements. The Roosevelt Corollary announced the U.S. intention to police the Western Hemisphere to ensure that the region remained an American sphere of influence. By building the Panama Canal, establishing protectorates in Central America, acquiring territory in the Pacific, and authoring the Open Door Policy in China, the United States emerged as a world power at the turn of the century. With the American economy increasingly dependent on overseas markets, the United States would find it difficult to ignore the threat that World War I posed to its trade, and eventually to its borders.

CHAPTER REVIEW

1893

Four-year depression begins
Intensifies interest in finding foreign markets for American goods

1898

The *Maine* explodes in Havana Harbor
Major cause of Spanish-American War

Spanish-American War
United States defeats Spain in four months

Treaty of Paris signed
Ends war with Spain; United States gains Caribbean and Pacific islands

1899

Philippine-American War begins
Ignites debate within United States over keeping Philippines as a colony

Rudyard Kipling publishes "The White Man's Burden"
Imperialists believe it articulates the civilizing mission; others see it as a parody

Review Questions

1. What concerns and fears encouraged the United States to look outside its borders in the 1890s?
2. How did Americans' longstanding interest in Cuba become a full-blown crisis in 1898? What image did Americans have of Spanish rule in Cuba and the American war against Spain?
3. How did the United States benefit from its victory against Spain?
4. What conflicting visions did imperialists and anti-imperialists hold toward colonizing the Philippines? How did each reconcile their ideas with traditional American values and ideals?
5. How did American views about race and racial identity shape the nation's development as a world power?
6. What different tactics did the United States use to protect its economic and strategic interests in East Asia versus those used in the Caribbean at the turn of the century?
7. How did the United States overcome political, engineering, and medical challenges to build the Panama Canal?

1900–1901

Open Door Notes
Protects American access to China market

Platt Amendment
Cuba becomes a protectorate of the United States

1904

Roosevelt Corollary
Establishes United States as international police presence in the Caribbean

St. Louis World's Fair
Exhibits highlight industrial progress and "civilizing" mission in colonies

1907–1908

Gentleman's Agreement
Limits Japanese immigration

1914

Panama Canal opens
Symbol of U.S. technological, military, and economic might

World War I begins
Global war engulfs Europe and its empires

Key Terms

imperialism The late nineteenth-century term for colonizing foreign nations and lands, relying primarily on business, political, and military structures rather than settlers to rule colonized peoples and exploit their resources. **562**

reconcentration Spanish policy that herded Cuban peasants off their farms into heavily fortified cities followed by systematic destruction of the crops that fed the rebel armies. **565**

yellow press Tabloid journalists and newspapers that reported sensationalist stories with a strong emotional component. **565**

Teller Amendment Congressional promise "to leave the government and control of the [Cuban] Island to its people" at the end of the Spanish-American War. **568**

Rough Riders A volunteer unit of cowboys, Ivy League athletes, city police officers, and Pawnee scouts led by Theodore Roosevelt that gained fame by charging up the San Juan Heights during the Spanish-American War. **570**

Treaty of Paris Agreement that ended the Spanish-American War with Spain relinquishing its claim to Cuba and the United States receiving Puerto Rico, some smaller Caribbean islands, and the Pacific island group of Guam. In return for $20 million, Spain turned the Philippines over to the United States. **571**

Platt Amendment Law linking U.S. withdrawal from Cuba to Cuban government granting the United States the right to maintain a naval base at Guantánamo Bay, to intervene militarily in Cuban domestic affairs, and to establish a privileged trading relationship with Cuba. The Cuban government also needed permission from the United States before entering into treaties with other nations. **572**

"the white man's burden" The Anglo-Saxon quest to better the lives of so-called racially inferior peoples by spreading Western economic, cultural, and spiritual values and institutions. **575**

sphere of influence The term used to describe the exclusive political and trading rights that a foreign nation enjoyed within another nation's territory. **579**

Open Door Policy A U.S.-sponsored nonbinding international agreement that kept the Chinese market open to all foreign nations. **579**

Gentleman's Agreement (1907–1908) Japanese agreement to deny passports to Japanese workers intending to immigrate to the United States. **581**

Angel Island Immigration processing station in the San Francisco Bay for Asian immigrants. **581**

Panama Canal A manmade waterway through Panama completed in 1914 to link the Pacific and Atlantic oceans. **584**

Roosevelt Corollary (1904) Corollary to the 1823 Monroe Doctrine that announced the U.S. intention to act as an "international police power" in Latin America. **587**

CHAPTER 20

The Great War

World War I, 1914–1918

> "The world must be made safe for democracy."
>
> President WOODROW WILSON, 1917 War Address

On May 7, 1915, Ernest Cowper was chatting with a friend aboard the *Lusitania*, a British passenger ship traveling from New York to the British Isles, as it passed the lush, green coast of Ireland. Looking into the water, Cowper suddenly felt a stab of terror when he spotted a German torpedo just seconds before it hit the ship. Peering through the periscope the German submarine captain watched hundreds of people jumping into the water in a desperate attempt to reach empty lifeboats. The ship sank within eighteen minutes, killing 1,198 passengers, including 128 Americans. Cowper was one of the lucky survivors, a Toronto newsman whose vivid recollections soon appeared in American newspapers.

The sinking of the *Lusitania* was a defining moment for the United States during World War I, often also called the Great War. The nation had remained neutral when the war began nine months earlier in August 1914, refusing to chose sides among the European powers involved, led by Great Britain and France on one side and Germany and Austria-Hungary on the other. When, however, the war spread to the high seas and American business initiated a lucrative arms trade with Great Britain, Americans increasingly found themselves in the line of fire.

American newspapers highlighted the tragic deaths of innocent women and children on the *Lusitania*, stirring outrage against Germany. One U.S. news report described the corpse of a mother embracing her three-month old baby, noting that "her face wears a half smile. Her baby's head rests against her breast. No one has tried to separate them." This description inspired the first American war-era propaganda poster, pictured here. The image, by artist Fred Spear, showed a mother and her baby sinking into the depths of the sea accompanied by one word—"Enlist."

Not all Americans, however, blamed Germany for the attack. German Americans pointed out that the *Lusitania* was secretly transporting munitions from New York to Britain. Rural Americans castigated Northeast business interests for trading primarily with Britain, fearful that favoring Britain and its allies would draw America into the war. President Woodrow Wilson offered a competing vision of the *Lusitania's* importance. Through increasingly strident diplomacy Wilson decided to defend the rights of neutrals to travel wherever they liked. This stance put the United States on a collision course with Germany that resulted in America entering the war two years later. Once America entered the war, President Wilson gave the country a larger purpose than defeating Germany. Introducing a new, and controversial, vision of American world leadership, Wilson promised to achieve a lasting peace by spreading democracy throughout the world.

To mobilize the nation's economic and manpower resources to fight the grim trench warfare underway along the Western Front, the government unfurled a far-reaching propaganda campaign, offered unprecedented support to labor unions, and raised a mass army through conscription. Americans suffered severe casualties in a short time, and their war effort helped the Allies defeat Germany by November 1918. The nation expected a peace treaty that embodied Wilson's promise to make this conflict "the war to end all wars." Americans held conflicting visions, however, over how to achieve this goal.

What meaning does this poster attach to the sinking of the *Lusitania*?

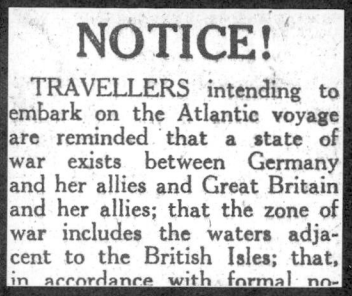

NOTICE!

TRAVELLERS intending to embark on the Atlantic voyage are reminded that a state of war exists between Germany and her allies and Great Britain and her allies; that the zone of war includes the waters adjacent to the British Isles; that, in accordance with formal no-

The Decision for War
p. 594

The War at Home p. 602

Fighting the War p. 609

Peace p. 615

The Decision for War

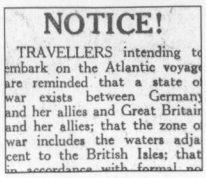
NOTICE!

TRAVELLERS intending to embark on the Atlantic voyage are reminded that a state of war exists between Germany and her allies and Great Britain and her allies; that the zone of war includes the waters adjacent to the British Isles; that in accordance with formal no

In the summer of 1914, Europe ignited as war swept across the continent (**20.1**). Instead of the easy victory that many Europeans expected, the war turned into a prolonged global struggle that took the lives of millions of men. World War I pitted the **Allies**, initially composed of Britain, France, Belgium, and Russia, and eventually totaling eighteen nations including Italy and the United States, against the **Central Powers** of Germany and Austria-Hungary, expanding by 1915 to include the Ottoman Empire and Bulgaria.

Europeans rushed into battle without taking the time to pause and consider what a general war would mean. Americans, however, followed a completely different road to war, openly debating whether this was their war to fight. It took two and a half years for the United States to enter the war. By then few illusions remained about the horror of modern warfare. Unlike Europeans in 1914 Americans knew they were committing to total war—and that winning would require the complete economic and psychological mobilization of the home front.

The War in Europe

On June 28, 1914, a nineteen-year-old Bosnian Serb named Gavrilo Princip arrived in Sarajevo, the capital of Bosnia, as part of a terrorist band that intended to assassinate the heir to the Austro-Hungarian throne, who was also visiting the city. Princip belonged to the Black Hand, a Slavic nationalist group based in the neighboring independent country of Serbia that longed to free Bosnia, then part of the Austro-Hungarian Empire. The group's first attempt to assassinate Archduke Franz Ferdinand failed when the bomb that one of Princip's coconspirators threw at the archduke's motorcade bounced off the side of the car carrying him, injuring two Austrian officers instead. Eluding the police Princip disappeared into the crowd. Later in the day the archduke made a fateful decision to visit his injured staff members. On the way to the hospital, the driver made a wrong turn down a narrow street and began slowing down to put the car in reverse. Standing at the end of the street was Princip, who could barely believe his good fortune as he saw the archduke and his pregnant wife coming toward him. Seizing the opportunity he stepped forward, pulled a pistol from his pocket, and fired, killing them both.

World War I began with these two deaths and ended four years later with more than nine million more. In responding to the assassination, Austria-Hungary, Russia, and Germany all tried to leverage the crisis to fulfill longstanding territorial ambitions, events summarized on the timeline, "Countdown to War, 1914" (**20.2**). Austria-Hungary and Russia vied for control of the Balkans, which offered ready access to the Mediterranean Sea and the Middle East. Germany hoped to become the dominant power in Europe and had recently challenged the world dominance of France and Britain by building a strong navy, acquiring colonies, and winning the Franco-Prussian War in 1871.

> "Mr. Mayor, it is perfectly outrageous! We have come to Sarajevo on a visit and have had a bomb thrown at us."
>
> ARCHDUKE FRANZ FERDINAND after surviving the Black Hand's first assassination attempt

Austria-Hungary held Serbia responsible for the assassination and demanded that the Serbian government make amends. In response Serbia chose appeasement over confrontation. Serbia accepted all of Austria-Hungary's demands except the one insisting that Austro-Hungarian judges participate in the trials of any Black Hand terrorists captured in Serbia. Without actually reading the Serbian response, German Kaiser Wilhelm II encouraged Austria-Hungary to quickly invade and annex Serbia. The next day, when the Kaiser read the Serbian statement, he jotted in the margins: "a great moral victory for Vienna; but with it every reason

What role did nationalism and imperialism play in bringing about World War I?

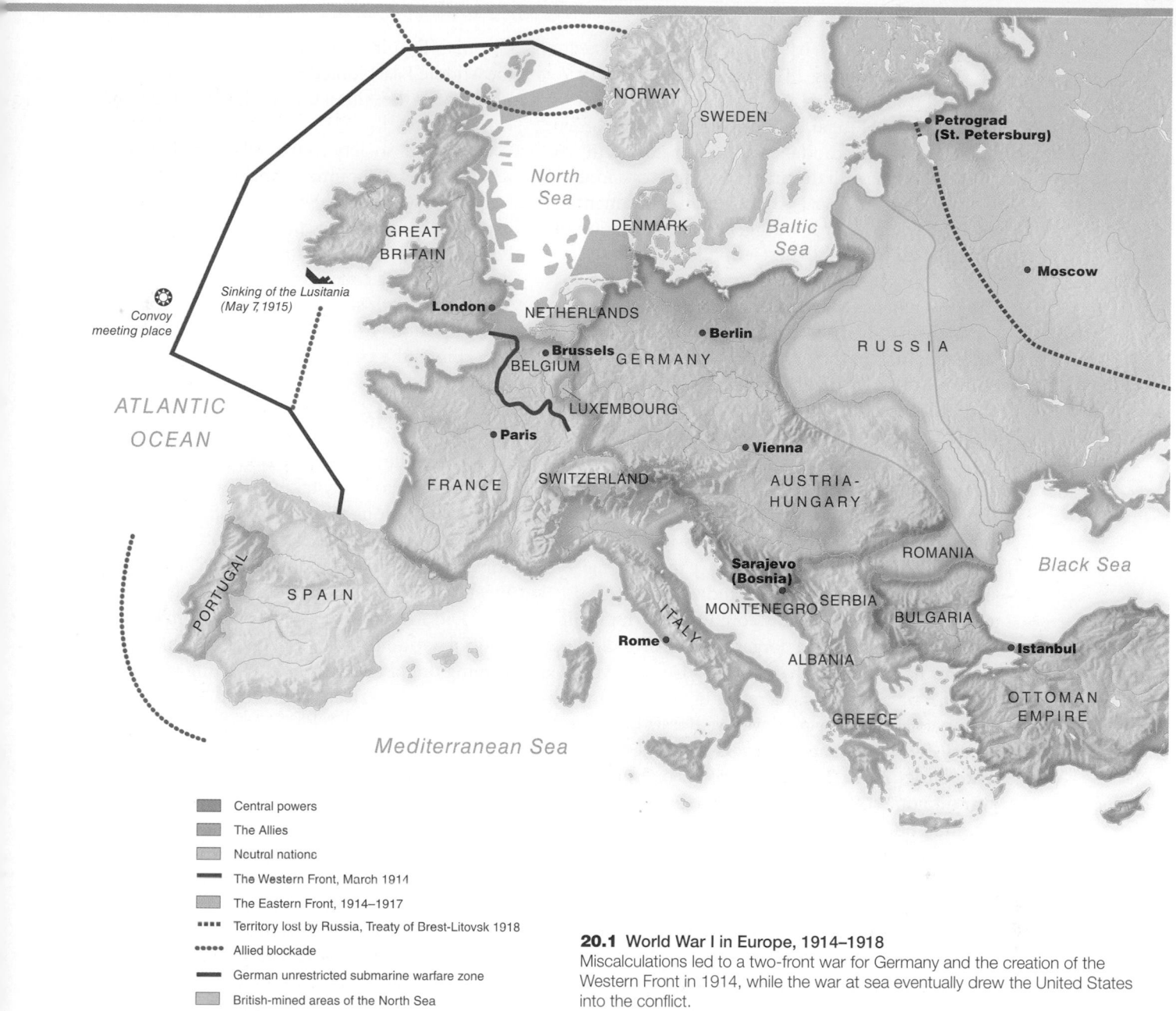

20.1 World War I in Europe, 1914–1918
Miscalculations led to a two-front war for Germany and the creation of the Western Front in 1914, while the war at sea eventually drew the United States into the conflict.

Countdown to War, 1914

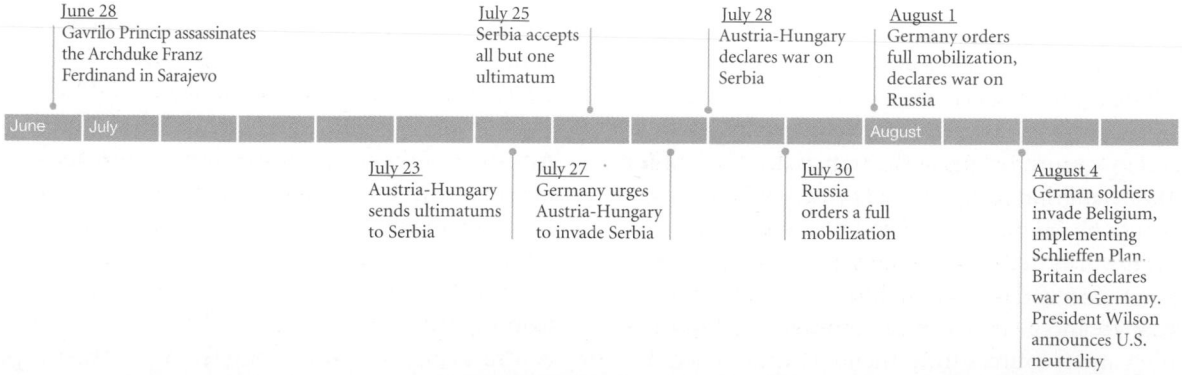

20.2 Timeline, 1914
Choices made after the assassination of the Archduke Franz Ferdinand led to World War I.

Why did the assassination of Archduke Franz Ferdinand spark a general European war that soon spread to the world?

for war is removed." His comments came too late. An hour later, on July 28, 1914, Austria-Hungary declared war on Serbia.

As Austro-Hungarian naval artillery bombarded Belgrade, Serbia's capital city, Russia resolved to stand by Serbia and defend its own interests in the Balkans. Russian Tsar Nicolas II made a momentous decision when he ordered a general mobilization of his army on July 30, 1914. Germany viewed the Russian mobilization as a direct threat. Ever since the 1894 alliance between Russia and France, Germany had worried about fighting a two-front war sometime in the future. In 1905 the German chief of staff Alfred von Schlieffen developed a plan that called for Germany, in the event of war, to attack and quickly defeat France while the cumbersome Russian army mobilized. **The Schlieffen Plan** avoided the well-defended border between France and Germany and instead sent German troops on a northward arch. Passing quickly through Belgium German troops would enter France through the undefended northern border and encircle Paris within six weeks. Germany could then turn its full forces against the much larger Russian army.

For the Schlieffen Plan to work, Germany needed to strike first. With Russia refusing to halt its mobilization, Germany declared war on Russia on August 1, 1914, and put a modified version of the Schlieffen Plan into motion. Two days later Germany declared war on France. When German troops crossed into Belgium on August 4, Britain declared war on Germany, fulfilling its 1839 pledge to guarantee Belgium independence.

The Schlieffen Plan quickly unraveled. German troops encountered unexpected resistance from the Belgian army and had difficulty resupplying a mass army on the move, giving the French and British time to mobilize. In the east Russia attacked with its partly mobilized army sooner than Germany expected, prompting German Chief of Staff Helmuth von Moltke to divert some troops from France to defend Berlin. At the Marne River, 35 miles northeast of Paris, the French and British successfully stopped the German drive toward Paris. Instead of defeating France quickly, Germany's attack ignited a general European war. As each army dug defensive trenches in France and Belgium, the trench deadlock of the **Western Front** took shape. For nearly four years men would live and die in the complex system of earthworks that ran for 550 miles from the North Sea to Switzerland. To bolster their forces Britain, France, and Germany began immediately enlisting men and resources from their colonies. When the Ottoman Empire (which ruled Turkey and most of the Middle East) joined the Central Powers and Italy joined the Allies, the conflict became a true world war.

American society contained many first- and second-generation immigrants from both the Central Powers and the Allied nations who disagreed over which nation had started the war. In 1914 President Woodrow Wilson believed that all belligerents shared collective responsibility for the war. Wanting to both stay out of the war and prevent bitter divisions from ripping America apart, Wilson proclaimed the United States neutral.

The Perils of Neutrality

As war engulfed Europe Wilson advised Americans to avoid "passionately taking sides" and to "remain impartial in thought, as well as action." Neutrality, however, turned out to be a difficult concept for Americans to define and maintain. Did neutrality mean trading with both sides selectively, or with no one? Did Americans have the right as members of a neutral nation to travel wherever they liked without coming under attack? The conflicting visions that emerged as Americans confronted these questions created a strident debate as the war wore on.

The dilemma was how to remain neutral without inflicting serious damage on the American economy. Since the 1890s American foreign policy had focused on protecting American business interests abroad (see Chapter 19). Cutting off trade completely with Europe would have had severe consequences for American citizens. At first Wilson tried to limit America's financial involvement in the war by banning private American bank loans to the belligerent nations. Secretary of State William Jennings Bryan believed the loan ban would "hasten a conclusion to the war" by making it impossible for the countries at war to buy the arms that they needed to continue fighting. Wilson, however, lifted the ban in 1915. The Allies were running short of cash, and Wilson feared a widespread U.S. recession if these nations stopped buying American goods.

Trading with or loaning money to both sides was another possible way to stay neutral. In theory American manufacturers and banks were free to do business with both Britain and Germany. In practice, however, the chart of U.S. Exports to Europe, 1914–1917 (**20.3**) reveals that they chose primarily to help the Allies. By 1917 American banks were loaning Britain an average of $10 million a day. In contrast American trade with Germany had dropped

What miscalculations stymied German expectations of a short war?

U.S. Trade with Nations at War

	1914	1915	1916	1916 Figure as a Percentage of 1914 Figure
Britain	$594,271,863	$911,794,954	$1,526,685,102	257%
France	$159,818,924	$369,397,170	$628,851,988	393%
Italy*	$74,235,012	$184,819,688	$269,246,105	364%
Germany	$344,794,276	$28,863,354	$288,899	0.08%

*Italy joined the Allies in April 1915.

20.3 U.S. Exports to Europe, 1914–1917
The nation's robust trade with Britain, France, and Italy—allied nations fighting Germany—provoked debate among Americans holding conflicting visions of neutrality.

to less than 1 percent of what it had been in 1914. Even if American manufacturers and banks had wanted to help Germany, trade became nearly impossible when Britain used its navy to blockade waterways leading to Germany and cut the international cable between the United States and Germany. The country's financial elite, however, had no desire to trade with both sides. Many upper-class Americans revered British culture and had warm feelings towards the French. Widespread publicity of German atrocities against Belgian civilians also fanned anti-German sentiment. Newspapers published vivid accounts of German soldiers burning homes, ransacking museums, and executing random Belgian civilians in retaliation for guerilla attacks against the German army. The press embellished these stories with fabricated tales of German soldiers cutting off women's breasts and children's hands.

Some Americans remained skeptical of such reports, seeing them as little more than British propaganda. America's disproportionate aid to the Allies alarmed the sizable German American and Irish American communities (the latter hated British rule of Ireland). People in the Midwest and South accused Eastern banks of violating the principle of neutrality, thereby pulling the nation slowly into a war most Americans did not want to fight. These critics embraced a strict vision of neutrality and wanted the government to announce an arms embargo that would prevent American companies from trading with nations at war.

When the war spread to the high seas, these conflicting visions provoked heated debate over America's role in the war. Facing a trench stalemate on the Western Front, Britain used its superior navy to establish a blockade around the Central Powers that included mining the North Sea. The blockade immediately affected American trade. American ships could not sail through the North Sea to Germany without first allowing the British to search their cargo for contraband, merchandise such as guns or ammunition that Britain wanted to stop from entering Germany. In mounting its blockade Britain soon violated international law by adding cotton and food to the contraband list. The 1915 political cartoon, *Britannia Must be More Careful How She Waves the Rules* (**20.4**), inverted the traditional motto associated with British naval dominance, "Britannia Rules the Waves," to criticize the blockade's effect on neutral countries, especially the United States. The cartoon depicts American shipping as a crying child that Uncle Sam is trying to comfort. Other neutral countries affected by the blockade (Norway and Sweden) bawl inconsolably, while John Bull, the symbol of Great Britain, tells Uncle Sam that "I'm trying to hit him," pointing to the German Kaiser, who raises a menacing sword at his foe. In March 1915 Wilson formally protested British blockading

20.4 *Britannia Must Be More Careful How She Waves the Rules*
This 1915 political cartoon criticizes Britain for mining the North Sea and preventing American ships from trading with Germany.

What competing visions did Americans offer on the question of trading with warring Europeans nations?

"The American people do not want to go to war to vindicate the right of a few people to travel or work on armed vessels."

Missouri Senator WILLIAM J. STONE to President Wilson, 1916

"I cannot consent to any abridgement of the rights of American citizens in any respect. The honor and self-respect of the nation is involved."

WILSON'S reply

practices. The British eventually agreed to buy enough American cotton to offset the loss of the German market.

The president proved less accommodating when Germany declared all the waters around Britain a war zone and threatened to attack any ship that entered the area. To combat the British blockade Germany turned to a new weapon, its **U-boat**, or submarine, to launch surprise torpedo attacks against Allied merchant and naval ships. International law recognized a naval blockade as a legal weapon of war, but required that the attacking ship give the merchant vessel's crew time to evacuate, and if necessary, take them aboard before sinking the ship and cargo. These pre-war customs rendered the U-boat useless, removing the element of surprise that made it such an effective weapon. Once spotted, armed merchant vessels did not hesitate to attack fragile U-boats.

20.5 German Warning to Travelers in the War Zone
When Wilson criticized Germany for sinking the *Lusitania*, German Americans pointed out that the German government had published warnings like this ahead of time urging Americans to stay off ships headed to the war zone.

NOTICE!

TRAVELLERS intending to embark on the Atlantic voyage are reminded that a state of war exists between Germany and her allies and Great Britain and her allies; that the zone of war includes the waters adjacent to the British Isles; that, in accordance with formal notice given by the Imperial German Government, vessels flying the flag of Great Britain, or of any of her allies, are liable to destruction in those waters and that travellers sailing in the war zone on ships of Great Britain or her allies do so at their own risk.

IMPERIAL GERMAN EMBASSY
WASHINGTON, D. C., APRIL 22, 1915.

On May 7, 1915, a German U-boat sunk the *Lusitania*, a British passenger ship sailing off the coast of Ireland. Calls for war swept through the press. "Germany must surely have gone mad," surmised one Richmond newspaper. Wilson sent a series of notes demanding that Germany pay reparations and accept the right of Americans to travel on any ship they wished. The Germans defended the sinking, pointing out that they had published warnings to passengers in American newspapers (**20.5**) and that the *Lusitania* was carrying munitions as part of its cargo.

The *Lusitania* sinking was an ideological turning point for the United States. In reaction to the crisis, Wilson redefined the meaning of neutrality, thus putting the United States on an eventual collision course with Germany. The president moved away from his initial definition of neutrality as remaining "impartial in thought, as well as action." The president now embraced neutrality as a concept that first and foremost gave neutral nations the irrevocable right to trade and travel wherever they liked. Secretary of State Bryan urged Wilson to ban Americans from traveling on ships headed to the U-boat–patrolled waters around Great Britain. Wilson refused. Convinced that the president's preoccupation with the rights of neutrals would lead to war, Bryan resigned in protest.

As the United States and Germany argued over the *Lusitania*, a German U-boat sunk another British passenger ship, the *Arabic*, in August 1915, leaving two Americans among the dead. Worried about further provoking the United States, Germany stepped back. On September 1, 1915, Germany issued the *Arabic* Pledge, promising not to sink passenger ships without warning. Germany renounced surprise attacks on merchant ships in May 1916 following another controversial sinking. For the moment Germany's pledges averted war with the United States.

The debate deepened when prominent pro-Ally political, business, and financial leaders formed the National Security League and began lobbying for universal military training to give all men of fighting age instruction in drilling and marksmanship. In response Progressive reformers formed the American Union Against Militarism to denounce any preparations for war. The appeal of the pacifist

Why was the sinking of the *Lusitania* a turning point in the neutrality debate?

vision made the 1916 song "I Didn't Raise My Son to be a Soldier" a hit. Taking stock of the controversy swirling around the preparedness versus peace debate, Congress authorized only a modest, but still controversial, increase in the size of the peacetime army.

Recognizing the potency of antiwar sentiment, Wilson ran for reelection in 1916 on the slogan "He Kept Us Out of War." The banners covering a Wilson reelection campaign truck (**20.6**) revealed the strong connections that Wilson drew between domestic and foreign issues. Wilson reminded voters of his Progressive reform agenda, which included a Federal Reserve System that "broke the money trust" and passage of an eight-hour day for railroad workers (see Chapter 18). The slogan "Peace with Honor" referred to Wilson's success in securing pledges from Germany that respected America's right to trade with the Allies. This overseas commerce created the prosperity that Democrats boasted about on the same sign. During the campaign Wilson noted that twice he had sent his trusted advisor Colonel Edward House to Europe to negotiate a peace settlement, lamenting that House had returned home empty-handed each time. At the same time he campaigned on the slogan of preparedness to underscore his commitment to defending the country if necessary.

20.6 Wilson Campaign Slogans
In a tight race for reelection in 1916, Woodrow Wilson emphasized his progressive legislative agenda and championed his success at keeping the nation out of the war without sacrificing national honor or economic prosperity. [*Source* (buttons): Cornell University, Carl A. Kroch Library, Division of Rare and Manuscript Collections]

In contrast to the Wilson campaign, the Republican challenger Supreme Court Justice Charles Evan Hughes never developed an effective slogan or theme. The Hughes campaign believed that Woodrow Wilson had won the presidency in 1912 because progressive Republicans had supported Theodore Roosevelt's run as a third-party Progressive Party candidate over the incumbent Republican president William Howard Taft (see Chapter 18). With the conservative and progressive factions of the Republican Party now reunited, Hughes tried to avoid controversy with vague calls "for law and liberty" and "undiluted Americanism." On election night, with returns from California still uncounted, Wilson went to bed certain that he had lost the election. He awoke to discover that he had won reelection by only 23 electoral votes, 277–254.

After the election Wilson tried once again to negotiate a settlement. On January 22, 1917, he outlined a plan for "peace without victory" based on "American principles, American policies." Democracy, freedom of the seas, no entangling alliances, and equality of rights among nations were, Wilson asserted, "the principles and policies of forward-looking men and women everywhere, of every modern nation, of every enlightened community." Wilson's desire to export democracy overseas while simultaneously protecting American access to foreign markets promised to greatly expand America's imperial reach. No longer limiting American intervention to its Pacific colonies or nearby Latin American countries (see Chapter 19), Wilson proposed remaking Europe in the image of America.

Wilson's words had little effect on European leaders. Unbeknownst to the president Germany had already decided to resume unrestricted submarine warfare. Having staked everything on Germany's

How did Wilson link domestic and foreign issues during the 1916 presidential campaign?

willingness to let Americans travel unmolested in the war zone, Wilson's neutrality policy collapsed.

America Enters the War

Germany expected the Allies to capitulate quickly once German submarines cut off the lifeline between the United States and Britain. Even if the resumption of unrestricted submarine warfare brought the United States into the war, Germany knew that it would take at least a year for the American government to raise, train, and equip an overseas force. By then Germany would have won the war.

To further hamper the deployment of American troops to France, the German government tried to distract the U.S. government by provoking a border conflict between the United States and Mexico. Throughout 1914–1917, German spies had spent nearly $12 million to support rebel factions in Mexico hostile to the United States who resented the U.S. government's active involvement in Mexican domestic politics. In 1916 Francisco "Pancho" Villa raided American border towns, hoping to draw U.S. troops into Mexico and destabilize the new U.S.-backed constitutional government headed by Venustiano Carranza. Much as Villa anticipated, Wilson sent a twelve thousand–troop punitive expedition under the command of Brigadier General John J. Pershing into Mexico in 1916 to arrest Villa. Carranza angrily denounced the American expedition as an invasion of Mexico. Tensions between the two countries escalated dramatically after a deadly clash in Carrizal on June 21, 1916. Wilson began planning for war with Mexico, but just in time learned that American troops had attacked first at Carrizal. After months of talks between U.S. and Mexican negotiators, American troops left Mexico in January 1917.

That same month the German foreign minister Arthur Zimmermann sent the **Zimmermann Telegram** to Mexico stating that in the event of war with the United States, Germany would help Mexico recover Texas, New Mexico, and Arizona (territory lost in the nineteenth century) if Mexico started a borderland war with the United States. Zimmermann also asked Mexico to mediate between Germany and Japan (which had joined the Allied side in 1914), hoping to entice Japan into attacking America's Pacific colonial possessions. Carranza had no interest in fighting the United States after the American withdrawal from Mexico, and Germany had no men or munitions to offer. Carranza, however, never had a chance to respond. In one of the war's greatest intelligence coups, British intelligence agents intercepted and deciphered the secretly coded telegram. When the State Department released the Zimmermann Telegram to the press six weeks later, many Americans viewed it as evidence that Germany had hostile intentions against the United States. Antiwar activists denounced the telegram as a forgery, but Zimmermann confessed to sending the note. With war between Germany and the United States growing more likely, Zimmermann wanted the United States to believe the threat was real so they would keep troops at home to protect the border.

Despite the public outcry over the Zimmermann Telegram, Wilson still hesitated. The president broke off diplomatic ties with Germany, but still no declaration of war came. German submarines began sinking over half a million tons of Allied shipping per month, and the Allies warned Wilson that without these supplies they were doomed. Finally, on April 2, 1917, Wilson went before Congress to ask for a declaration of war, laying out war goals that went far beyond simply defeating Germany. "We are glad, now that we see the facts," Wilson proclaimed ". . . to fight thus for the ultimate peace of the world and for the liberation of its peoples . . . for the rights of nations great and small and the privilege of men everywhere to chose their way of life and of obedience."

> "It is a fearful thing to lead this great peaceful people into war."
>
> President WILSON, 1917 war address before Congress

Congress declared war with a vote of 90 to 6 in the Senate and 373 to 50 in the House, but a vocal minority opposed going to war. Republican Senator George W. Norris from Nebraska expressed the "rich man's war, poor man's fight" sentiment that ran deep in rural America. Only four days into her term as the first female member of Congress, Jeannette Rankin (R-Montana) caste her maiden vote against the war. She lost her reelection in 1919, but returned to Congress in 1940. Sticking to her pacifist principles, she was the only legislator who voted against entering World War II after the Japanese attacked Pearl Harbor. Critics expressed their opposition freely during the debate over declaring war, but once the nation was officially fighting Germany, most Americans rallied behind the flag.

Why did the United States finally decide to fight Germany?

Conflicting Views among the Allies on the War's Purpose

Wilson claimed that the United States "had no selfish ends to serve" by going to war. Skeptical voices from revolutionary Russia soon prompted Wilson to defend this claim. On November 7, 1917, seven months after the United States entered the war, the Bolshevik revolutionary Vladimir Lenin seized power in Russia with promises of peace, land, and bread. Lenin's Communist government immediately published secret Allied treaties, revealing that Tzarist Russia, Britain, and France had agreed to enlarge their empires at the expense of Germany, Austria-Hungary, and the Ottoman Empire if they won the war. This disclosure exposed evident competing visions on the Allied side: Wilson's vague promises that the war was about democracy and the now-revealed territorial ambitions of the Allies.

Trying to bridge this gap, Wilson outlined a broad statement of Allied war goals in his **Fourteen Points** speech to Congress on January 8, 1918. In the Fourteen Points Wilson envisioned a world dominated by democracy, free trade, disarmament, self-determination, resolved territorial disputes in Europe, and a league of nations to mediate future international crises. He explicitly linked the spread of democracy with the expansion of capitalism, a position that gained new urgency as Russian Communists began confiscating private property and promising to redistribute wealth throughout the population. Whether spreading democracy meant increasing political rights and free trade or reallocating wealth became a cornerstone of the ideological debate between the United States and the newly formed Soviet Union throughout the twentieth century.

> "God gave us his Ten Commandments and we broke them. Wilson gave us his 14 points—well, we shall see."
>
> French Prime Minister GEORGE CLEMENCEAU, 1918

Free trade and freedom of the seas offered more than an antidote to communism, however. These principles also advanced American economic interests at the expense of major imperialist powers like Britain and France. The Fourteen Points speech revealed some contradictions in Wilsonian idealism. Like other world leaders Wilson advanced principles that protected the interests of his own country. Yet Wilson also demanded some sacrifices from Americans to make this "the war to end all wars." Once they joined the general association of nations that Wilson proposed, Americans faced modifying their traditional desire to act unilaterally in the Western Hemisphere.

Wilson's Fourteen Points further declared that all peoples should enjoy **self-determination**, or a voice in selecting their own government. Using this principle Wilson proposed redrawing the map of Eastern and Central Europe along ethnic lines and even proposed extending this right to colonial populations. Robert Lansing, who replaced Bryan as secretary of state, remained dubious. The principle of self-determination "is simply loaded with dynamite," Lansing noted. "It will raise hopes which can never be realized."

Shortly after Wilson issued his Fourteen Points, another model emerged for how the war might end when Lenin negotiated a separate peace with Germany. The Treaty of Brest-Litovsk officially ended the war between Russia and Germany on March 3, 1918. This treaty reflected Germany's complete victory over Russia and exposed the full imperialist thrust of German war goals. The treaty made Ukraine, parts of Poland, Finland, Lithuania, Estonia, and Latvia satellite states of Germany. Map 20.1 illustrates Russia's territorial losses in 1918. With these gains Germany intended to eliminate Russia as a future rival and expand its empire into resource-rich eastern lands.

The Brest-Litovsk treaty gave the Allies an idea of the terms that a victorious Germany might impose on them. This knowledge hardened the British and French resolve to achieve total victory and inflict equally punitive terms of their own. The treaty even convinced Wilson that maintaining peace in Europe would require weakening Germany militarily and economically.

With Russia out of the war, Germany finally had the opportunity to fight the one-front war it had sought in 1914. Now holding a clear manpower advantage, Germany prepared to strike along the Western Front. As the American government raced to mobilize the nation's men and industry for total war, many in Europe feared that the United States had entered the war too late to save the Allied side.

How did the Fourteen Points lay the foundation for future domestic and international debates?

The War at Home

America could not mobilize, supply, and feed an army without granting new powers to the federal government. The federal government used a mix of incentives, threats, and patriotic appeals to negotiate the preexisting class, gender, and racial conflicts that threatened to make wartime cooperation difficult. Official propaganda urged unity, but Americans retained conflicting visions about regulating big business, unionizing, female suffrage, and racial equality.

Gearing Up for War

Wilson's democratic rhetoric convinced many Progressive reformers that they could count on the president to use his wartime powers to rein in big business (see Chapter 18). The president, however, feared that the war would make corporations more powerful than ever. "We shall be dependent upon the steel, oil, and financial magnates," Wilson privately worried. "They will run the nation." Wilson's concerns were well-founded. Increased wages and federal protections for unions improved the lives of many workers, but the resurgent power of big business prevented Progressives from making these wartime reforms permanent.

In the winter of 1917, gridlock paralyzed the railroad system. Blizzard conditions, fuel shortages, and poor coordination among private railway companies prevented trains from delivering tons of war-related freight. Labor unrest also created havoc as skilled railway workers left in droves for better-paying factory jobs and railway unions prepared to strike. To sort out this mess, the federal government took over management of the railroads for the duration of the war. The Railroad Administration met union demands for high wages, standardized equipment, and coordinated the use of tracks. To improve the flow of needed materials, the newly created War Industries Board (WIB) ranked industries so that those most critical to the war effort received raw materials ahead of nonessential wartime businesses. Steel, for example, went first to manufacturers producing guns and ships, while factories making civilian cars, freezers, and corsets (they needed steel for the inner stays) had to wait. The government paid railroad companies handsomely for wartime use of their trains and track to mute their objections to government management of the railroads. When private companies regained control of railroad lines in 1920, the nation's railroad network lay in shambles, a victim of heavy wartime traffic and the government's failure to properly maintain the lines.

Food Administration director Herbert Hoover chose a different path to ensure that the country produced enough to feed civilians at home, soldiers, and refugees overseas. Congress had given the president near dictatorial powers to regulate the food and fuel industries in the 1917 Lever Food and Fuel Act. Hoover, however, opted to use high prices and patriotic appeals to control the nation's food supply rather than rationing. To stimulate production Hoover had the American and Allied governments pay high prices for agricultural goods. To curb civilian demand Hoover organized a massive propaganda campaign around the slogan "food will win the war." Citizens signed pledge cards vowing to observe wheatless Mondays, meatless Tuesdays, and porkless Saturdays. Urging Americans to conserve wheat for shipment overseas, the Food Administration plastered the country with posters that tried to popularize cornmeal, which did not transport well, as a tasty and acceptable substitute for wheat flour. The agency offered housewives cornmeal recipes and cooking classes, and even tried to enlist the

20.7 "Little Americans Do Your Bit!" This propaganda poster showing a three-year-old saluting a bowl of corn-based porridge underscored the total mobilization of American society.

What varying strategies did the government use to mobilize economic resources?

cooperation of finicky toddlers (**20.7**) by urging them to eat cornmeal instead of oatmeal.

Americans responded well to Hoover's patriotic appeals to conserve food, but whether the government could quell labor unrest for the duration of the war remained questionable. Wilson quieted industrial class conflict by throwing money at the problem. The steel, copper, petroleum, and meatpacking industries enjoyed a healthy increase in profits once they began selling their products to the government. Wilson also offered industrialists, still bristling over Progressive-era laws that curtailed monopolies and regulated working conditions (see Chapter 18), an olive branch by giving them a role in setting the government's wartime price, wage, and production codes.

Labor benefited during the war as well. The government built high wages and union protection into its wartime contracts in exchange for a no-strike pledge from labor. The National War Labor Board (made up of representatives from government, business, and labor) required industries that accepted government contracts to honor the eight-hour day and forty-hour week. These companies also had to pay a living wage, maintain high safety standards, and recognize a union's right to recruit members at work. Not all labor groups benefited equally from the sudden government attention. Official support for collective bargaining helped the more moderate unions that formed the American Federation of Labor. Radical labor groups that continued to oppose the war suffered when the government arrested their leaders and members for sedition.

Even the gains for moderate labor unions proved fleeting, however. Workers received higher wages, but after adjusting for the considerable wartime inflation, real wages only increased 4 percent. When the war ended and the government canceled its contracts, workers lost federal protection for organizing unions. Without the government stopping them, many manufacturers quickly returned to their old union-busting ways (see Chapter 21).

Black Migration

Immigrants had long provided American industry with a source of inexpensive labor. The war disrupted the flow of immigrants to the United States at the exact moment that the demand for industrial goods exploded. In 1914, 1.2 million immigrants entered the country. In 1917 only 110,618 arrived. Labor recruiting agents soon turned to white and black Southerners to fill the void. During the war over half a million African Americans migrated from Southern farms and cities to the North, lured by offers of high-paying industrial jobs. The African American painter Jacob Lawrence celebrated this mass exodus in a series of paintings he completed in the 1940s. His first painting showed brightly dressed streams of families preparing to board trains through doors marked "Chicago," "New York," and "St. Louis" (**20.8**). Many migrants exalted at their newfound freedom in the North. "I can quit any time I want," noted one migrant, without forfeiting a year's pay as in the sharecropping system. Another man realized that in Chicago he was no longer afraid "to rub up against a white person" accidentally on the street or sit down next to one on a streetcar. In the South he had constantly feared the consequences of an unintended breach of Southern racial etiquette. Migrants also discovered, however, that despite the absence of overt segregation or intimidation, racial prejudice existed in the North as well.

20.8 The First Wave of the Great Migration (1916–1919)
"Around the time of WWI, many African-Americans from the South left home and traveled to cities in the North in search of a better life," wrote artist Jacob Lawrence to explain this 1940 painting.

How did workers and unions fare during the war?

The migration of Southern blacks northward also unveiled regional and class tensions within the black community. Working through organizations like the Urban League and the Young Men's Christian Association, paternalistic Northern middle-class blacks tried to help Southern migrants adjust to the rhythms of industrial jobs and urban life. Besides wanting to genuinely assist recent arrivals, middle-class blacks worried that migrants' rural customs might harm the reputation of the entire Northern black community. A list of dos and don'ts published by the *Chicago Defender*, a newspaper serving the African American community, entreated migrants to watch their language, mind their manners, respect the law, keep their houses clean, and send their children to school.

The Urban League had reason to fear that racial rioting might accompany the arrival of black workers from the South. The explosive combination of economic competition, housing shortages, and latent racial hostility triggered a series of racial riots in Northern cities during the war. The most deadly one occurred in East St. Louis, Illinois, in July 1917. In East St. Louis companies intentionally recruited immigrants and Southern blacks to undermine union activism. Company owners knew that racial and ethnic prejudices would prevent native-born whites from allowing these new workers to join their unions, which in turn undermined the union's ability to mount a strike. Viewing black migrants as potential strikebreakers, white workers initiated a series of minor attacks on black workers that escalated into a full-fledged racial riot on July 2, 1917. The anti-lynching crusader Ida B. Wells-Barnett interviewed over fifty black eyewitnesses for a report that she submitted to Congress, including one witness who recalled seeing black men exit homes with their hands raised. As they pled for their lives, mobs stoned them to death. Overall the riot left nine whites and thirty-nine blacks dead and hundreds wounded on both sides. The subsequent congressional investigation held white employers, labor leaders, and politicians responsible, but six thousand African Americans left the city anyway.

Female Suffrage

The war inadvertently provided an opportunity for women to gain suffrage and for the temperance reform movement (see Chapter 21), where women held leading roles, to build momentum. Mobilizing the home front meant securing the active cooperation of women. Over the course of the war, savvy female leaders successfully parlayed their newly recognized economic clout into a demand for political power.

Women did the shopping and cooking in most homes, so the Food Administration needed their full support for its food conservation efforts to succeed. "Will you have a part in Victory?" queried one propaganda poster above the image of a young woman in a stars and stripes gown scattering seeds in a "victory garden" to provide vegetables for her family. Over eight million women volunteered for Red Cross work, producing surgical dressings, sweaters, socks, and mittens for soldiers and refugees. With workers in short supply, companies increasingly recruited women to fill positions in factories, and the government hired many as clerks. In desperate need of laborers, companies in Bridgeport, Connecticut, even hired airplanes to scatter leaflets throughout residential neighborhoods that urged housewives to apply for jobs in munitions factories. Overall, however, few homemakers entered the workforce. Instead, the eight million women already at work shifted positions, taking advantage of new, albeit temporary, opportunities to work at better paying and higher skilled jobs.

Suffragists wanted the nation to thank women for their war work by giving them the right to vote. The vision of an engaged female citizenry working actively to defend the nation reduced the appeal of longstanding arguments against votes for women. In the past the close ties between female suffragists and the temperance movement had led some urban and midwestern male residents to resist enfranchising women because so many women supported prohibition. The South feared that female suffrage meant extending the right to vote to black women. Other opponents argued that the male head of the household adequately represented his family's interests in the public domain, holding fast to a vision of women as primarily domestic, not public, figures.

In the 1910s the middle- and upper-class women leading the suffragist movement had divided into radical and conservative factions (see Chapter 18) and each offered a competing vision of how to obtain the vote for women. For months members of the militant National Woman's Party stood outside the White House with banners asking "how long must women wait for liberty?" Once the United States entered the war, militant suffragists turned Wilson's democratic rhetoric against him. They erected a sign (**20.9**) intended to embarrass Wilson as he greeted a Russian delegation from the parliamentary government that ruled Russia for a short time in 1917 before Lenin seized power. Wilson hoped to

What class and regional tensions did the war reveal in the African American community?

convince the delegates to keep Russia in the war so democracy could triumph over autocracy in Europe. The suffragists instead focused on the recent introduction of female suffrage in Russia, urging the envoys to "help us make this nation really free" by convincing Wilson to support female suffrage.

Daily scuffles broke out between outraged war supporters and the picketing suffragists, whom the press vilified as unpatriotic. After the police arrested the suffragists, the women initiated a hunger strike to protest their poor treatment in prison. After news accounts of prison guards forcing feeding tubes down the throats of suffragists leaked out, Wilson pardoned them. Unbowed the female militants returned to the White House gates, where they burned Wilson in effigy.

The more moderate National American Woman Suffrage Association (NAWSA) followed a different tack. The NAWSA presented the vote, not as a question of equality or democracy, but as a way to reinforce the traditional desire of women to protect their families (see Chapter 18). The NAWSA also seized upon wartime prejudices against German Americans, whose loyalty many Americans increasingly questioned. "It is a risk, a danger to a country like ours to send 1,000,000 men out of the country who are loyal and not replace those men by the loyal votes of the women they have left at home," NAWSA president Carrie Chapman Catt proclaimed. All these arguments eventually swayed Wilson. In September 1918 he became the first president to endorse national female suffrage, convinced that the female pacifist nature could help secure his postwar goals for a lasting peace. Congress sent the **Nineteenth Amendment**, a constitutional amendment that granted women the right to vote, to the states on June 4, 1919, seven months after the war ended. Final ratification came on August 26, 1920.

20.9 Suffragists Picket the White House
The radical wing of the suffragist movement criticized Wilson, who claimed that an Allied victory would spread democracy, for refusing to support female suffrage.

Rallying the Public

To control the flow of information and shape public opinion about the war, Wilson formed the **Committee on Public Information** (CPI). Headed by George Creel, a Progressive muckraking journalist, the CPI disseminated propaganda posters, pamphlets, and films. The CPI translated its pamphlets into multiple languages to reach the nation's huge immigrant population. The agency also recruited so-called Four-Minute Men to speak before audiences in movie halls, markets, fairs, and churches. The CPI limited each speech to four minutes to fill the time that it took to change the reels for silent films in movie theatres. Creel estimated that 75,000 Four-Minute Men gave nearly seven million impassioned speeches during the war on topics such as German submarine warfare and German espionage. Hollywood helped the official propaganda effort by making movies like *To Hell With the Kaiser*, a film that depicted the German leader as a depraved lunatic who receives a much-deserved punch in the mouth from the American soldier who captures him.

What competing arguments and strategies did moderate and radical female suffragists develop?

The government also used war bond campaigns to win over hearts and minds. Rather than angering the public with higher taxes to pay for the war, the government financed two-thirds of the war's costs with **war bonds**, short-term loans that individual citizens made to the government. Secretary of the Treasury William G. McAdoo believed that Americans who bought a fifty-dollar liberty bond, a five-dollar war savings certificate, or a twenty-five cent thrift stamp felt personally connected to the war. "Any great war must necessarily be a popular movement," McAdoo noted. Financing the war through war bonds, however, made the war more expensive because eventually the government had to pay interest to each bondholder.

With the government reaching out to immigrants from Russia, Poland, and Italy through war bond campaigns and military recruitment, the war gave many immigrants a chance to feel American for the first time. Recent arrivals often lived in ethnic neighborhoods and worked alongside their compatriots, circumstances that had made assimilation difficult. Rather than having to choose between their homelands and their new country, these immigrants could openly support both during the war. "By Helping the American Red Cross You are Helping Italy," read an ad in one Italian American newspaper.

> "When the nation is at war many things that might be said in time of peace ... will not be endured so long as men fight."
>
> Supreme Court Justice OLIVER WENDELL HOLMES Jr., upholding the constitutionality of the Espionage Act

Immigrants from the Allied nations thrived during the war, but for German-Americans the war years were bleak. Wartime propaganda accentuated Americans' sense of duty, concern for troops in the field, and fears of a German invasion. *Images as History: Propaganda Posters* discusses the impact of this anti-German imagery more fully. Propaganda posters whipped up patriotic fervor and hate for the enemy to justify the war and motivate young Americans to fight. To their dismay, Progressive reformers soon realized that the same publicity techniques they had perfected to expose corrupt business practices and spur interest in reform during the Progressive Era (see Chapter18) could also incite war hysteria. Wartime propaganda ultimately served its purpose. Americans spent nearly $21.4 billion on war bonds purchases.

German Spies and Civil Liberties

Throughout the period of U.S. neutrality, German spies and saboteurs in the United States tried to disrupt the munitions trade between the United States and Britain. Spies planted tiny egg-shaped bombs on ships carrying munitions and detonated dynamite in several munitions factories. The most spectacular prewar strike by German saboteurs occurred at a munitions depot in Black Tom, New Jersey, on the Hudson River. Citizens as far away as Philadelphia, Pennsylvania, heard the huge explosions on the morning of July 30, 1916. Shrapnel left holes in the Statue of Liberty, and shock waves shattered thousands of windows in lower Manhattan. Anxious to keep the country neutral, the government labeled each incident an accident despite clear evidence of sabotage. The government could not explain away the actions of Eric Muenter, a German American professor who planted a bomb that exploded in an empty U.S. Senate reception room on July 2, 1915. Muenter then broke into the house of financier J. P. Morgan, whose bank acted as the purchasing agent for the British government, where he shot and wounded Morgan.

Once the country entered the war, government propaganda urged the public to stay alert for "spies and lies" and report "the man who spreads pessimistic stories, divulges—or seeks—confidential military information, cries for peace, or belittles our efforts to win the war." The 1917 **Espionage Act** made it a crime to obstruct military recruitment, to encourage mutiny, or to aid the enemy by spreading lies. These prohibitions had a chilling effect on speech. The **Sedition Act**, passed in 1918, went even further by prohibiting anyone from uttering, writing, or publishing "any abusive or disloyal language" concerning the flag, constitution, government, or armed forces. Civil liberties and antiwar advocates challenged both laws in court, but the Supreme Court upheld the Espionage Act and Sedition Act as constitutional.

What effect did revelations of German spying and wartime propaganda have on the public?

Images as History

PROPAGANDA POSTERS

In his war address Wilson told the American people that "we have no quarrel with the German people." But Wilson also privately predicted that "a nation couldn't put its strength into a war and keep its head level; it had never been done." The government soon plastered the nation with propaganda posters that relied on negative images of Germany and Germans to rally the public to support the war. Teaching Americans to despise anything German had negative consequences on the home front, where German Americans went from being one of the most respected immigrant groups to one of the most hated. Wartime propaganda also questioned the patriotism and masculinity of men who refused to serve. What made these wartime posters effective propaganda?

This 1917 army recruiting poster depicts the Germans as savage beasts who raped, pillaged, and killed.

In 1939 Adolf Hitler rallied German opinion against the former Allied nations by reprinting this poster with the caption: "When they assaulted us 25 years ago, they wrote on their rotten slanderous poster: 'Destroy this mad beast'—they meant the German people!"

Europe lays in ruins behind the gorilla-like German soldier who carries his limp female victim, a ravaged Lady Liberty, as he makes his way to American soil.

The gorilla carries the club of culture, alerting Americans to reject the contaminating influences of Germany's culture. Nearly half of the states banned or restricted the teaching of German, and Americans renamed the hamburger a "liberty sandwich."

The image of Germany threatening the American coastline reminded viewers that German U-boats patrolled the Atlantic coast looking for troop and merchant ships to sink.

"Destroy this Mad Brute"

The poster shows a fearful man hiding shamefully in the dark with his back turned against the bright, vibrant scene of virile men marching proudly under a large flag.

This man's wistful look implies that he will regret his decision to stand apart from his countrymen.

This loner is a man of privilege, reflecting concerns about the emasculating effect of urban life on middle- and upper-class American men.

Several cities held "slacker raids" where policemen stormed into movie theaters and arrested those who could not produce a draft registration card.

"On Which Side of the Window Are You?"

How did visual depictions of the Germans compare to media images of the Spanish during the Spanish-American War?

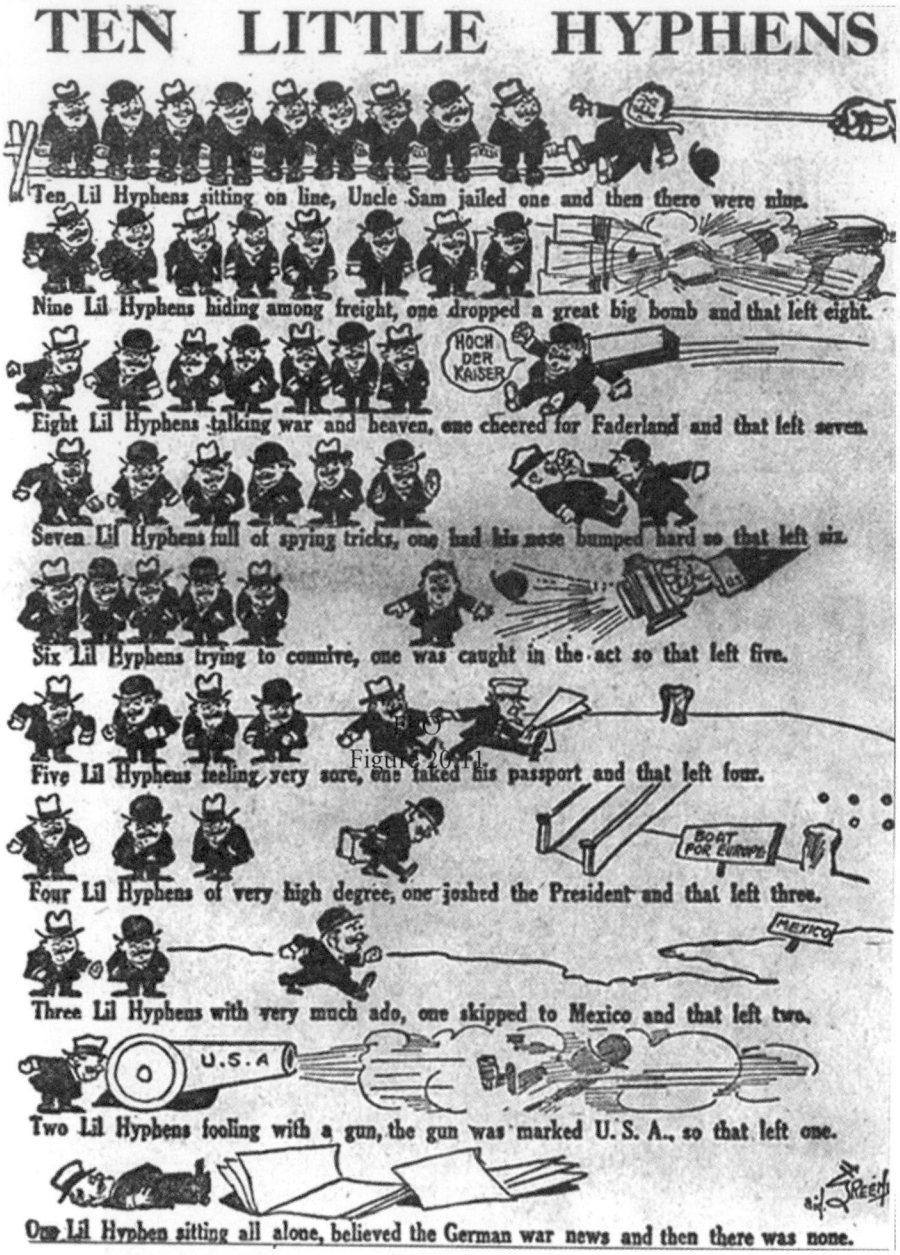

20.10 *Ten Little Hyphens*
Capturing the public's fears of German espionage, this caricature implied that "hyphenated Americans" retained dangerous loyalties to their homelands. This song identified blowing up a munitions factory and criticizing the president as equal threats to national security.

Some Americans decided to take matters into their own hands, attacking German Americans and their businesses. In the war's most infamous incident of vigilante justice, a mob murdered German American Robert Prager in Collinsville, Illinois. When the first attempt to hang Prager failed, the assailants granted his request to write a letter, expecting him to detail a plot to dynamite a mine. Instead Prager wrote a letter to his mother and father who still lived in Dresden, Germany. "Dear parents," he wrote in German, "I must on this fourth day of April, 1918, die. Please pray for me, my dear parents." The murder went unpunished. To protect themselves from similar assaults, many German American families changed their names, stopped teaching German to their children, and purchased multiple war bonds.

The caricature *Ten Little Hyphens* (**20.10**) captured the growing sense that dual loyalty meant disloyalty. The lyrics in the ditty refer to real incidents of German espionage in the United States, including German agents who blew up munitions, assumed false identities by faking passports, or fled to Mexico. The caricature also referenced the demand from some patriots that "German-Americans," so-called "hyphenated Americans," drop their allegiance to their native lands and become 100 percent American. "We can have no fifty-fifty allegiance in this country," proclaimed Theodore Roosevelt.

This caricature underscored another dilemma facing the nation: how to protect itself from terrorist attacks without denying residents the right to free speech. The lyrics reveal that during the war, officials considered words as dangerous as acts of sabotage, punishing German Americans who "cheered for Faderland," or their fatherland.

Besides routing out suspected spies the Espionage and Sedition acts also helped the federal government suppress pacifists who refused to give up opposition to the war and radical political groups like the Socialist Party and Industrial Workers of the World that had long opposed capitalism. "The master class has always declared the wars; the subject class has always fought the battles," declared Eugene Debs, the leader of the Socialist Party. During the debate over declaring war, before passage of the Espionage Act, members of Congress had uttered similar denunciations of the rich and powerful. But as punishment for uttering these words in 1918, a federal judge sentenced Debs to ten years in prison. Debs became a hero in some quarters for his steady opposition to the war. In 1920, two years after the war ended, Debs made his fifth and final bid for the presidency from his jail cell and received one million votes. President Warren Harding pardoned Debs in 1921.

How does this song capture the tension between preventing espionage and protecting civil liberties?

Fighting the War

Germany had good reason to assume that it would take time for the United States to pose a threat on the Western Front. The country confronted significant challenges raising and training an army quickly. In 1917 the American armed forces numbered just over 300,000. Over the next nineteen months, however, the military grew to over four million and managed to arrive overseas just in time to prevent a German victory.

Raising an Army

When the nation entered the war, the government faced the choice of raising its armed forces with volunteers, instituting conscription immediately, or waiting until enlistments began to flag before turning to a draft. In previous wars the government had selected the third option. Wilson, however, chose to implement conscription immediately. Wilson knew that the United States needed to supply the Allies with troops, munitions, and food. The draft gave the government the power to decide who stayed at home to work in essential wartime industries and who went into the army. Letting individuals decide might deprive industry of its best workers or leave the military understrength once the initial enthusiasm for enlisting subsided. To combat the impression that conscription forced reluctant men to fight, the government renamed the draft "selective service." Selective service, the government repeatedly told the American public, placed men where they could best serve the war effort.

To offer the public a visible demonstration of male patriotism, all men registered publicly for selective service on the same day. On June 5, 1917, ship horns, church bells, and factory whistles rang out and crowds gathered to cheer for men filling out their draft registration cards. Three million men, or 11 percent of the draft-eligible population, refused either to register or to serve. Some went to jail; others managed to elude authorities by changing jobs often. The Selective Service Act allowed **conscientious objectors** from recognized pacifist sects to apply for noncombatant duty. Those who opposed fighting for philosophical or political reasons had no legal way to stay out of fighting units. The most famous conscientious objector of the war was Sergeant Alvin C. York who, like 80 percent of drafted conscientious objectors, eventually agreed to fight. *Choices and Consequences: Alvin York, Deciding to Serve* (page 610) explores York's decision to serve in the army. Conscripts ultimately accounted for 72 percent of the four million men in the wartime army. Overall, 20 percent of the draft-eligible male population (ages 18–45) served in the wartime military, 15 percent of the adult male population overall.

"You're in the Army Now"

In makeshift training camps across the country, soldiers trained (sometimes with wooden rifles) and spoke eagerly of getting to France before the "big show" ended. The army reflected the diversity of the American population. Approximately 18 percent of the entire force, or one in five, were foreign-born. Nearly twelve thousand Native Americans served, composing only a small fraction of the total military force, but representing nearly 25 percent of the Native American male population. Sixteen thousand women went overseas as nurses, telephone operators, or welfare workers working in army canteens.

African Americans made up 13 percent of the military, though they were only 10 percent of the country's population. The wartime army remained strictly segregated. Black soldiers received few chances to demonstrate bravery or leadership since 89 percent served as labor troops under mostly white officers. Although they received little recognition from white authorities, these troops performed important logistical services by constructing the roads and bridges required to keep a modern army in the field. In France many black troops discovered a more racially tolerant environment where white French had no qualms socializing with African American soldiers. "You now know that the mean contemptible spirit of race prejudice that curses this land is not the spirit of other lands," noted the African American minister Francis J. Grimké to a group of returning black soldiers. The fear that black servicemen intended to bring the fight for democracy home provoked numerous postwar riots and lynchings that often targeted black veterans in uniform. Determined to fight back against white supremacists, black veterans helped forge a more

Why did the government choose to draft the wartime army?

Choices and Consequences

ALVIN YORK, DECIDING TO SERVE

Alvin York grew up poor in the Tennessee Appalachian Mountains, where he became an expert marksman hunting wild turkeys in the forests. He spent his youth carousing, gambling, and drinking. As an adult he underwent a religious conversion and joined the Church of Christ in Christian Union, a pacifist Christian sect. Drafted six months before his thirtieth birthday, York faced an agonizing decision on whether or not to fight. "I believed in my Bible," he said. "And it distinctly said. 'THOU SHALT NOT KILL.'" But, York acknowledged, "I wanted to be a good Christian and a good American too."

Choices

1. Request noncombatant duty as a conscientious objector.
2. Refuse to serve in any form of military duty.
3. Agree to serve and fight.

Decision

Like many men claiming conscientious objector status, York faced intense pressure to fight once he entered a training camp. After several conversations about the Bible with his commanding officers, York eventually decided that the biblical injunction "Blessed are the peacemakers" overrode the Sixth Commandment prohibiting killing because the war promised to be "the war to end all wars." York agreed to fight.

Consequences

York became the most celebrated American hero of the war for his feats on the battlefield in France. On October 8, 1918, York was credited with killing 24 German soldiers, silencing 35 machine guns, and capturing 132 enemy soldiers during the Meuse-Argonne campaign. Surviving combat without a scratch reaffirmed York's faith in God, but on his deathbed he still wondered whether God would punish him for killing men in battle.

Continuing Controversies

What is the ultimate meaning of York's experience? Some historians note that York's transformation from pacifist to warrior demonstrated that Wilsonian ideals inspired many American soldiers to fight in World War I. With Americans divided in 1941 (before the Japanese attacked the American naval base in Pearl Harbor, Hawaii) over the merits of entering World War II, the Hollywood film *Sergeant York* sent the message that fighting to defend the country was a citizen's Christian and patriotic duty. Others note that York personified the poorly educated and underprivileged conscript who did the bulk of the fighting along the Western Front. Some believe that the army exaggerated York's feats to boost morale. Rather than a cause for celebration, his experience reveals the difficulty of becoming a conscientious objector during the war—an experience repeated in future conflicts, especially the Vietnam War.

Sergeant Alvin C. York, with his mother in front of his home in Tennessee

What factors constrained or influenced York's choice to serve?

militant postwar civil rights movement (see Chapter 21).

To help the army turn this polyglot force into a functioning military force, civilian psychologists administered intelligence tests to soldiers in the training camps. Quickly assessing a recruit's intelligence could help the army immediately identify whether a man was officer material or better suited for unloading boxes of supplies off ships in France. To their surprise 25 percent of the soldier population had to take the test designed for illiterates. The majority of native-born white soldiers had completed only 7 years of school, while foreign-born men averaged 4.7 years and Southern black men 2.6 years of schooling.

Psychologists claimed their intelligence tests measured native intelligence, but the test questions suggest they primarily assessed level of education, economic background, and familiarity with mainstream American culture (**20.11**). Tabulated exam results claimed that the white American soldiers had a mental age of 13, while the average mental age was 11.01 for Italians, 11.34 for Russians, 10.74 for Poles, and 10.41 for American-born blacks. Some critics argued that the tests only showed that immigrants and blacks needed more comprehensive schooling. Social Darwinists, who used Charles Darwin's ideas of survival of the fittest to establish a racial hierarchy of superior and inferior human races, believed these figures validated existing ideas of white northern European superiority. After the war public schools began administering intelligence tests to determine the aptitude of their pupils, a trend that continues today.

On the Western Front

The United States entered the war at a critical moment. The peace with Russia gave Germany a clear manpower advantage on the battlefield. As U-boats began sinking Allied shipping indiscriminately, the Germans transferred over one million men from the Eastern Front with Russia to the Western Front in France. In March 1918 the Germans accomplished what many had thought impossible: They broke through the trench stalemate

222 MEMOIRS NATIONAL ACADEMY OF SCIENCES. [Vol. XV.

TEST 3

This is a test of common sense. Below are sixteen questions. Three answers are given to each question. You are to look at the answers carefully; then make a cross in the square before the best answer to each question, as in the sample:

SAMPLE — Why do we use stoves? Because
☐ they look well
☒ they keep us warm
☐ they are black

Here the second answer is the best one and is marked with a cross. Begin with No. 1 and keep on until time is called.

1 Cats are useful animals, because
☒ they catch mice
☐ they are gentle
☐ they are afraid of dogs

2 Why are pencils more commonly carried than fountain pens? Because
☐ they are brightly colored
☒ they are cheaper
☐ they are not so heavy

3 Why is leather used for shoes? Because
☐ it is produced in all countries
☒ it wears well
☐ it is an animal product

4 Why judge a man by what he does rather than by what he says? Because
☒ what a man does shows what he really is
☐ it is wrong to tell a lie
☐ a deaf man cannot hear what is said

5 If you were asked what you thought of a person whom you didn't know, what should you say?
☐ I will go and get acquainted
☐ I think he is all right
☒ I don't know him and can't say

6 Streets are sprinkled in summer
☐ to make the air cooler
☐ to keep automobiles from skidding
☒ to keep down dust

7 Why is wheat better for food than corn? Because
☒ it is more nutritious
☐ it is more expensive
☐ it can be ground finer

8 If a man made a million dollars, he ought to
☐ pay off the national debt
☒ contribute to various worthy charities
☐ give it all to some poor man

☞ Go to No. 9 above

9 Why do many persons prefer automobiles to street cars? Because
☐ an auto is made of higher grade materials
☒ an automobile is more convenient
☐ street cars are not as safe

10 The feathers on a bird's wings help him to fly because they
☒ make a wide, light surface
☐ keep the air off his body
☐ keep the wings from cooling off too fast

11 All traffic going one way keeps to the same side of the street because
☐ most people are right handed
☐ the traffic policeman insists on it
☒ it avoids confusion and collisions

12 Why do inventors patent their inventions? Because
☒ it gives them control of their inventions.
☐ it creates a greater demand
☐ it is the custom to get patents

13 Freezing water bursts pipes because
☐ cold makes the pipes weaker
☒ water expands when it freezes
☐ the ice stops the flow of water

14 Why are high mountains covered with snow? Because
☐ they are near the clouds
☐ the sun seldom shines on them
☒ the air is cold there

15 If the earth were nearer the sun
☐ the stars would disappear
☐ our months would be longer
☒ the earth would be warmer

16 Why is it colder nearer the poles than near the equator? Because
☐ the poles are always farther from the sun
☒ the sunshine falls obliquely at the poles
☐ there is more ice at the poles

Fig. 20.—Group Examination Alpha, Form 5, Test 3, Practical Judgment.

20.11 Intelligence Tests for Soldiers
These questions come from an intelligence test on logic given to literate soldiers in training camps. The pictorial exam for illiterates and non-English speakers required that soldiers draw in the missing item.

Take these intelligence tests yourself. Who would fare well on these tests and why?

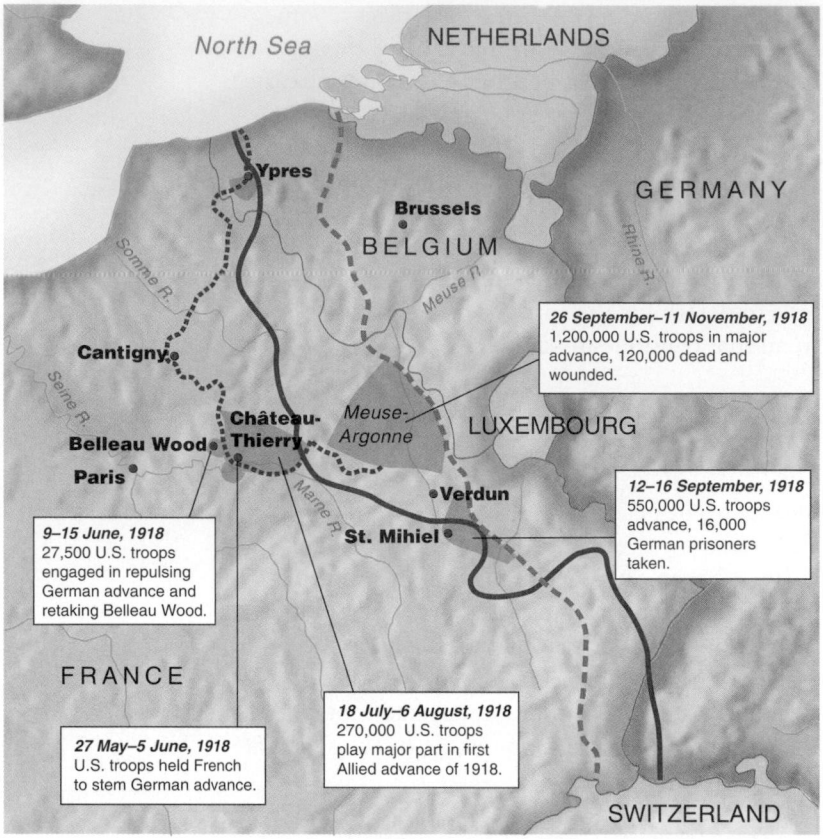

Western Front, March 1918
German offensive, spring 1918
Armistice line, Novemder 11, 1918
U.S. military activity

20.12 American Expeditionary Forces, 1918
U.S. troops fought hard for six months along the Western Front, winning key victories at Chateau-Thierry, St. Mihiel, and during the Meuse-Argonne campaign.

> "I hope that you have not arrived too late."
>
> The American ambassador to General JOHN J. PERSHING upon his arrival in France

and began marching once again toward Paris. The map (**20.12**) reveals how much French territory the Germans captured during their spectacularly successful spring offensives against the British and French armies.

As in 1914, however, the pace of the offensive exhausted German troops, who quickly outran their supply lines. The arriving **American Expeditionary Forces**, the American soldiers who fought overseas under the command of General John J. Pershing, played a critical role in stopping the German drive toward Paris in battles at Cantigny, Belleau Wood, and Chateau-Thierry. In July American soldiers fought with the French in a successful six-week counteroffensive that pushed the German army back to where it had begun the spring offensives. These campaigns initiated American soldiers to the reality of fighting along the Western Front. Men collapsed from the strain of continuous artillery bombardments and the sight of bodies blown to bits. Soldiers diagnosed with shell shock suffered from panic attacks, and some could not sleep or speak. Private Duncan Kemerer arrived at a military hospital in such poor condition that the sound of a spoon dropping sent him frantically searching for cover under his bed.

American soldiers soon settled into the predictable routine of trench warfare. The three-dimensional trench shown in the *World War I* special feature portrays the different components of a working trench. A strip of land known as No-Man's Land separated the Allied and German trench systems. The actual distance between the two lines averaged 250 yards. Scores of barbed wire covered this barren strip of land, which was filled with huge craters formed by artillery shells.

The U.S. Army rotated soldiers, putting them in the trenches for twenty-one days, with a week to recuperate in the rear before their next rotation. Each day just before sunrise, the men assembled and went on alert. If dawn passed with no enemy attack, then the men spent the day trying to stay out of sight from enemy snipers and airplanes that strafed troops with machine gun fire. By feasting on corpses rats grew to gigantic proportions and multiplied by the thousands. Adding to the misery of trench life was the constant rain in northern France, which created a thick, gooey mud. At night, No-Man's Land came alive as small patrols scrambled out of the trenches to repair damaged wire or raid enemy lines for prisoners who might reveal valuable military information.

German artillery bombed the Allied lines, day and night. "To be shelled is the worst thing in the world," noted one American soldier. "It is impossible to adequately imagine it." Troops developed an array of superstitions to try to make sense of who lived and who died in the trenches. "They claim that a man's shell has his name on it, if it's for him," joked Sergeant Harry Weisburg. "But it is the part of a wise man to keep his nose out of the way of another man's shell." By 1918 one of every four shells fired on the Western Front contained poison gas. Troops especially feared odorless, colorless mustard gas, which caused painful burns on any exposed skin and was deadly if inhaled. Slow-moving tanks also made their first appearance on the battlefield, but the war ended before either side could exploit their full potential as an offensive weapon.

What was it like to fight in the trenches along the Western Front?

World War I

The trenches along the Western Front were intricate defense systems that both protected soldiers and added to their misery in the front lines. As a straight line, the trenches ran for 460 miles from the North Sea to Switzerland. The network of trenches, however, encompassed nearly 35,000 miles, disfiguring the Belgian and French countryside. France suffered the heaviest casualties of the Allied nations: On the whole, the number of Frenchmen who died each day (900) was twice as high as the number of British (457) and more than four times higher than the number of Americans (195). But in the last six months of the war, the American death rate jumped to 820 a day as U.S. troops experienced their share of brutal fighting. Overall fewer American soldiers perished, but the cost to the United States was still high. More Americans died on the battlefield in World War I than in Korea or Vietnam, both much longer wars.

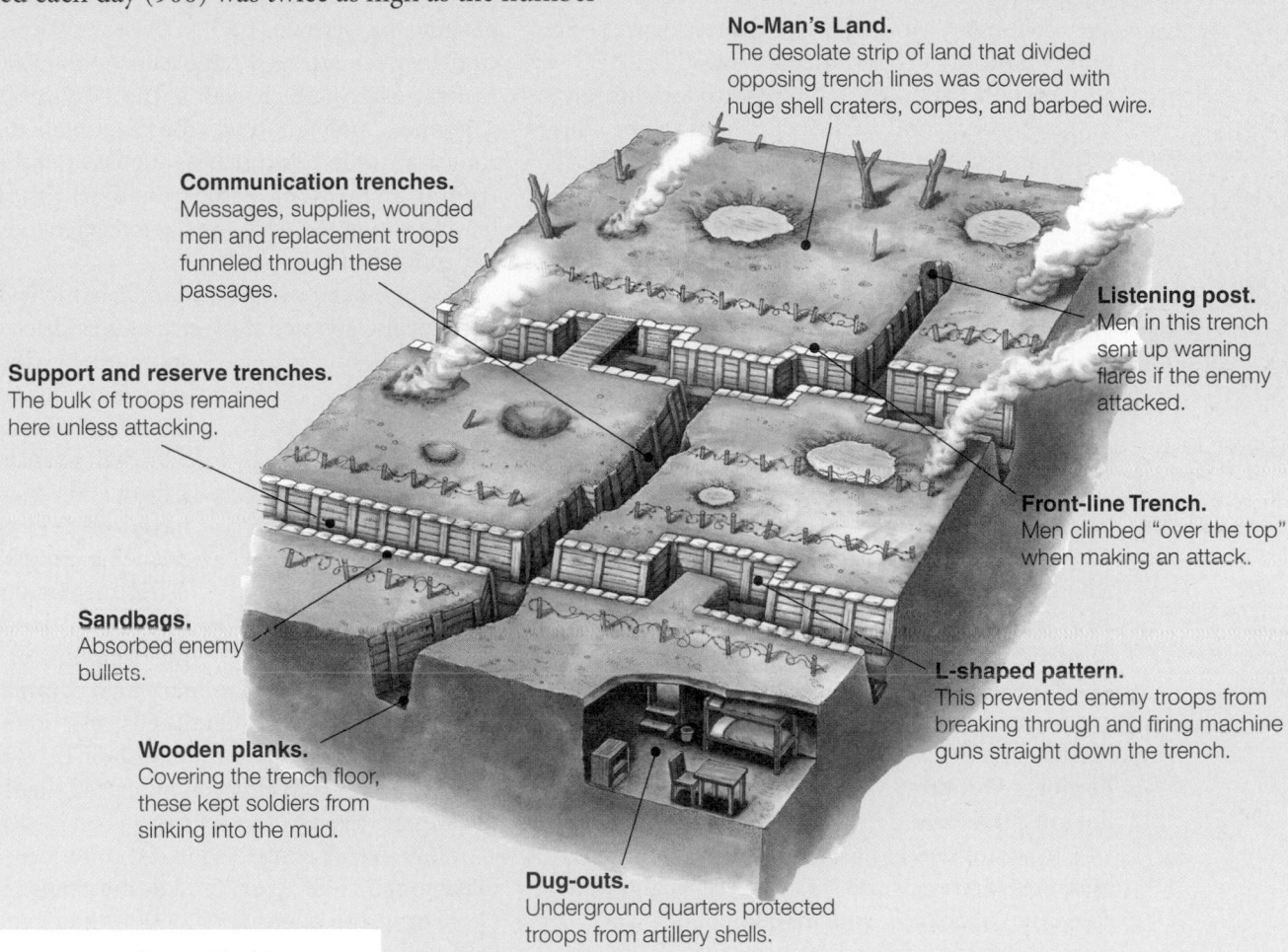

	Deaths	Wounded
France	1.3 million	3.0 million
Britain	950,000	2.1 million
Germany	1.8 million	4.2 million
Russia	1.7 million	4.9 million
United States	116,000	204,000
Austria-Hungary	1.2 million	3.6 million

World War I Casualties

Conflict	Total Serving	Battle Deaths	Other Deaths	Wounded
Civil War (1861–1865)				
Union	2,213,363	140,414	224,097	281,881
Confederate	600,000–1,500,000	74,524	59,297	—
World War I (1917–1918)	4,734,991	53,402	63,114	204,002
World War II (1941–1945)	16,112,566	291,557	113,842	670,846
Korean War (1950-1953)	5,720,000	33,741	2,833	103,284
Vietnam War (1964–1973)	8,744,000	47,355	10,796	153,303

America at War: Battlefield deaths, deaths by disease, and wounded

What differing perspectives do these charts and trench diagram offer on the U.S. battlefield experience?

Flu Epidemic

In 1918, in the midst of mounting battlefield casualties, the world suddenly encountered a new vicious killer. Without warning a particularly lethal strain of influenza traversed the globe. The virus became known as **Spanish Influenza** because the Spanish press first reported its outbreak. Biologists speculate that the influenza germ began as a mutated version of avian (bird) flu in the American Midwest in March 1918. American soldiers carried the germ to France, and the virus spread rapidly from Europe to Africa, Asia, and Central America. Nearly twenty-five million Americans fell ill, a quarter of the entire population, and 675,000 died.

Anecdotes of people who went to work healthy in the morning, only to die before dinnertime, illustrated how suddenly the lethal virus could strike. Influenza was usually the most severe for children and the elderly, segments of the population with weak immune systems. This flu virus attacked young adults especially hard—making it particularly unique and terrifying.

Public officials closed movie houses, schools, churches, and office buildings in an effort to contain the epidemic. Nearly one million American soldiers also fell ill, further hampering an overseas military campaign that already faced considerable challenges fighting with an inexperienced force. General John Pershing, Assistant Secretary of the Navy Franklin D. Roosevelt, and President Woodrow Wilson all suffered from the flu, but survived.

> "I had a little bird/Its name was Enza/I opened up the window/And in-flu-enza."
>
> A children's rope-skipping rhyme inspired by the 1918 influenza epidemic

Physicians devised some useless precautionary measures to prevent transmission. Throughout the epidemic Americans wore masks in public (the microscopic virus passed easily through the fabric), boiled their dishes, and sprayed public areas with disinfectants. In mid-1919, as suddenly as it had come, the virus disappeared, having run out of susceptible human beings to infect.

The Spanish Influenza pandemic had a catastrophic effect worldwide. From 1918 to 1919, the disease killed thirty million people. Nine million men died in battle from 1914–1918. The bloodiest war to date thus coincided with the deadliest influenza epidemic yet recorded.

The Final Campaigns

In September 1918 the American army attacked at St. Mihiel (20.12). The battle successfully reduced a bulge in the lines (called a "salient"), thereby weakening German defenses. Two weeks later, the Allies began a massive coordinated assault along the entire Western Front. The Americans hit the Germans hard in the Meuse-Argonne region of France, while the British and French struck farther north and west. Advancing in heavily wooded and hilly terrain against dense German fortifications, the American effort stalled. Regrouping, the Americans began pushing the Germans back in October. Battle casualty rates averaged 2,550 a day, with 6,000 Americans dying each week of the 47-day Meuse-Argonne campaign. "It was most assuredly the Americans who bore the heaviest brunt of the fighting on the whole battle front during the last few months of the war," the German General Erich Ludendorff later recalled.

Besides making headway on the battlefield, Allied convoys also stymied the German unrestricted submarine warfare campaign. Instead of letting individual ships take their chances at sea, British and American naval vessels began escorting groups of Allied merchant vessels across the Atlantic. At the beginning of November, the German military high command requested an armistice. On the eleventh hour of the eleventh day of the eleventh month of 1918, the Armistice went into effect and guns fell silent along the Western Front.

What overall contribution did American troops make to the final victory? At key moments in the German spring offensives in 1918, American soldiers helped stop the Germans from taking Paris. American divisions provided key strength for the French-led counteroffensives over the summer, and in the Meuse-Argonne campaign American soldiers leveled a devastating blow to the German army that helped make British and French advances to the north possible. Also important, the prospect of fighting a million more fresh American recruits in 1919 convinced Germany to seek a negotiated peace.

Did the Allies win the war, or did Germany lose it?

Peace

The Armistice ended active fighting, but the details of the peace settlement took months to negotiate. Twenty-seven nations and four British dominions sent delegates to the Paris Peace Conference. Germany expected to join the negotiations, but instead the terms of peace were determined in secret by the Big Four: Wilson, Clemenceau, the British Prime Minister Lloyd George, and the Italian Premier Vittorio Orlando. The **Versailles Peace Treaty** required Germany to pay reparations and disarm. Germany signed the treaty under protest on June 28, 1919, the same date of Archduke Franz Ferdinand's assassination five years earlier. In the end the flawed and controversial Versailles Peace Treaty laid the groundwork for future conflict in Europe and raised questions at home about the future role America wanted to play in the world.

The Paris Peace Conference

Woodrow Wilson enjoyed worldwide popularity on Armistice Day. Throughout the United States and Europe, Wilson's idealistic pronouncements had raised hopes that the war's slaughter might pave the way for a lasting peace. Wilson broke with tradition and decided to travel overseas to negotiate the peace treaty himself, rather than sending representatives to hash out the details. As Wilson toured Paris, London, Rome, and Milan, papers greeted him as "The Savior of Humanity." British and French leaders, however, knew that four years of suffering had created a deep-seated desire for revenge against Germany within their nations. The war had hardened Wilson's view of Germany as well, and he agreed to weaken postwar Germany by eliminating its navy and colonies. He disagreed, however, with the French insistence on eviscerating the German economy and military permanently.

Certain that America had played a vital role in winning the war, Wilson felt confident asserting his equal right, along with Britain and France, to shape the terms of peace. British and French leaders, however, publicly downplayed America's contribution to defeating Germany, hoping to limit Wilson's say in the peace treaty. At the request of Allied leaders, the British and French press began printing increasingly disparaging reports about the American army's inexperience and leadership. Resentful over the Allies' apparent ingratitude for their wartime sacrifices, Americans' postwar disillusionment only grew as the treaty-making process got underway.

Wilson's domestic political problems weakened his negotiating position. In November the Republicans won control of Congress despite Wilson's plea to voters to return a Democratic majority as a vote of confidence for his peace proposals. The reasons for the Republican victory were complex, a result of unease with conditions at home as well as concern about Wilson's ideals. The Democrats' loss energized opponents of the **League of Nations**, a Wilson-supported collective security organization where member nations agreed to mediate future international disputes to prevent wars and work together to improve global human conditions.

Domestic opponents of the League of Nations worried that by joining the international organization America would lose control over its own foreign policy and invite international meddling in the Western Hemisphere. They also doubted that the League could successfully maintain world peace. League critics divided into two camps, each offering conflicting visions of America's role in the postwar world. Isolationists, led by Republican Senator William E. Borah from Idaho, preferred adopting an official policy of neutrality. The isolationists believed that if the United States kept out of all foreign disagreements, the country could avoid going to war in the future. By contrast the faction headed by Massachusetts Senator Henry Cabot Lodge, the Republican majority leader and chairman of Senate Foreign Affairs Committee, favored a return to the former balance of power system in Europe. Lodge wanted the United States to help rebuild, and perhaps join, a strong alliance among democratic European nations that could contain Germany indefinitely.

Eager to shore up support for the League of Nations at home, Wilson briefly sailed home to

What opposition did Wilson face overseas and at home to his peace plan?

confer with Republican leaders who were still upset that Wilson had not invited any leading Republicans to join his Paris negotiating team. The possibility of compromise appeared slim. Lodge had an intense personal dislike for Wilson, whom he regarded as sanctimonious. Wilson returned the distain, viewing Lodge as narrow-minded. Discussion soon stalled. On the day before Wilson left to return to Paris, Lodge handed the president a pledge signed by thirty-nine senators who vowed to reject the League covenant in its present form.

Hoping to appease his Republican critics, Wilson managed to incorporate key Republican demands in the final League covenant. The League of Nations now agreed to respect the Monroe Doctrine, the 1823 American pronouncement that the Western Hemisphere was off-limits to other world powers, and to allow nations to withdraw from the League. Wilson also tried outmaneuvering his domestic critics. He opted against creating two international agreements, a peace treaty and a covenant creating the League of Nations, that would each require a separate Senate ratification. Instead Wilson decided to incorporate the League covenant into the peace treaty. The Senate, Wilson gambled, would never refuse to ratify the peace treaty, even one that contained a controversial League of Nations.

> "With his mouth open and his eyes shut, I predict that he will make a Senator when he grows up."
>
> WILSON'S joke about his infant grandson touched upon his political troubles with Republican Senators

Allied leaders pressured Wilson to compromise as well. To get them to accept the League of Nations, Wilson gave up his idea of peace without victory. When Supreme Commander of Allied Armies Ferdinand Foch read the harsh demands of the Versailles Peace Treaty, he accurately predicted, "this isn't a peace, it's a twenty year truce." The treaty required that Germany pay reparations to French and Belgian civilians for the coal mines, factories, and fields its troops had destroyed during "the war imposed upon them by the aggression of Germany." This war guilt clause held Germany alone responsible for starting World War I. The treaty also forced Germany to disarm. The Reparations Committee set Germany's initial bill at $33 billion in gold, although commissions in the 1920s significantly reduced the amount owed. The United States accepted no reparation payments, and in the 1920s even loaned Germany money to help it pay this debt. The war guilt clause and the reparations bill created tremendous resentment in Germany. In the 1930s the German chancellor Adolf Hitler cultivated this anger to fuel a resurgent national fervor dedicated to restoring German economic and military strength.

The Versailles Treaty settled old territorial disputes in Europe, but the dismemberment of the Russian, German, and Austro-Hungarian empires created new sources of tensions. The redrawn map of eastern Europe reflected Wilson's principle of self-determination, fulfilling the ambitions of ethnic groups in Czechoslovakia, Poland, Yugoslavia, Croatia, Latvia, Lithuania, and Estonia to create their own nations (**20.13**). To limit Germany's postwar strength, the Allied side disregarded the desires of German-speaking peoples in Poland, Czechoslovakia, and Austria to unite with Germany. These three weak independent states remained vulnerable to future German and Soviet expansionist schemes. Twenty years later, Hitler justified his invasions of Austria (1938), Czechoslovakia (1938), and his joint invasion of Poland with Soviet leader Josef Stalin (1939) as a drive to reunite the German-speaking world separated by the terms of the Versailles Treaty (see Chapter 23).

Other nations also left the conference feeling slighted. Italy resented the Allies for denying it Austrian territory, a humiliation that the fascist leader Benito Mussolini vowed to avenge when he seized power in 1922. Japan protested the failure to incorporate into the League Covenant a statement protecting the rights of nonwhite nations, helping breed Japanese resentment against the West. In the Middle East, Africa, and Asia, the peace treaty transferred colonial possessions from the losers (the Ottoman and German empires) to the victors under a mandate system. In theory the mandate system named a Western nation as a League of Nation trustee for territories in need of political instruction before they assumed the responsibilities of self-government. In reality the mandate system simply cloaked old-style imperialism in the new rhetoric of

What complaints did critics make about the Versailles Peace Treaty?

20.13 Europe and the Middle East after the War. The victorious Allies dismantled the German, Austro-Hungarian, and Ottoman empires to create independent nations in Central Europe and colonies for themselves in the Middle East.

self-determination. By redrawing the map of the Middle East to expand their global influence, Britain and France set in motion political, religious, and cultural conflicts in the region that created tremendous strife throughout the century. Denying Arab nationalist demands for independence, France took control of newly created Lebanon and Syria. Britain ruled Transjordan (present-day Jordan) and brought together three distinct ethnic groups—the Kurds, Sunnis, and Shiites—who had previously lived in autonomous regions to form the country of Iraq. When the British took over Palestine, they kept wartime promises to open up part of the territory to Jewish immigration, angering Arab residents in the process. Competing claims to this territory continue to this day.

The Treaty Fight at Home

Wilson saw the flaws in the final treaty, but he hoped that over time the League of Nations could modify the treaty's worst excesses. To counter the initial burst of public enthusiasm for joining the League of Nations, Republicans challenged Wilson's idealistic pronouncements promising world peace. "Are you ready to put your soldiers and your sailors at the

What significance did the re-drawn maps of Europe and the Middle East have?

disposition of other nations?" Senator Lodge asked the American people. The political cartoon *Looking a Gift Horse in the Mouth* (**20.14**) captured the public's mounting concern about the League. While Wilson tries to assure Uncle Sam that the League is better than nothing, the Senate carefully examines the mule. Wary of going against public opinion too strongly, Lodge did not urge outright rejection of the Versailles Treaty. He instead proposed adding fourteen American reservations. The most important one required explicit congressional approval before American troops went overseas. Wilson refused to accept modifications. Instead Wilson tried to create a groundswell of public support for the League that would force the Republicans to accept the treaty as written.

To reignite public enthusiasm for the League of Nations, the president traveled 10,000 miles in three weeks and made forty speeches to hundreds of thousands of people. The political cartoon *Ratification Rapids* (**20.15**) offered a sympathetic portrayal of Wilson, shown here using all his strength to steer the treaty and League Covenant to safety. In the cartoon a young woman clutches both documents to her breast, symbolizing both the besieged nation and innocent victims of war. In his speeches Wilson dismissed Republican concerns about sending American troops throughout the world as impractical. "If you want to put out a fire in Utah, you don't send to Oklahoma for the fire engine. If you want to put out a fire in the Balkans, if you want to stamp out the smoldering flames in some part of Central Europe, you don't send to the United States for troops," Wilson told an audience in Salt Lake City. *Competing Visions: Joining the League of Nations* further explores the debate between Wilson and Lodge.

20.14 *Looking a Gift Horse in the Mouth*
This political cartoon expresses skepticism about the League of Nations. By taking a closer look, the Senate realizes that the League (represented here as a broken-down mule) is not strong enough to handle the hard work of keeping the peace.

20.15 *Ratification Rapids*
This sympathetic portrait of Woodrow Wilson trying to steer the Versailles Treaty through the ratification process illustrates how contentious the treaty debate became.

What competing views do these political cartoons offer on the question of ratifying the Versailles Treaty?

Competing Visions

JOINING THE LEAGUE OF NATIONS

In 1919 President Woodrow Wilson and Senator Henry Cabot Lodge debated the wisdom and value of joining the League of Nations. Consider the exact wording of Article X, and then the differing interpretations of it offered by Lodge and Wilson. What changes in American foreign policy does each foresee arising from the League? Are there any points of agreement between the two about the future world role of the United States?

Article X of the League Covenant ignited tremendous controversy over whether the United States should join the League of Nations.

The Members of the League undertake to respect and preserve as against external aggression the territorial integrity and existing political independence of all the members of the League. In case of any such aggression or in case of any threat or danger of such aggression the Council shall advise upon the means by which this obligation shall be fulfilled.

Republican senator Henry Cabot Lodge contended that the League Covenant stripped Congress of its power to declare war in this August 12, 1919, congressional address.

We should never permit the United States to be involved in the internal conflict in another country, except by the will of her people expressed through the Congress which represents them.

With regard to wars of external aggression on a member of the league, the case is perfectly clear. There can be no genuine dispute whatever about the meaning of the first clause of article 10. In the first place, it differs from every other obligation in being individual and placed upon each nation without the intervention of the league. Each nation for itself promises to respect and preserve as against external aggression the boundaries and the political independence of every member of the league. ... It is, I repeat, an individual obligation. It requires no action on the part of the league, except that in the second sentence the authorities of the league are to have the power to advise as to the means to be employed in order to fulfill the purpose of the first sentence. ...

We may set aside all this empty talk about isolation. Nobody expects to isolate the United States or to make it a hermit Nation, which is a sheer absurdity. But there is a wide difference between taking a suitable part and bearing a due responsibility in world affairs and plunging the United States into every controversy and conflict on the face of the globe.

Wilson defended the League in a speech on September 25, 1919, in Pueblo, Colorado, that recalled the sacrifices of soldiers during the war, bringing many in the audience to tears.

But you will say, "what is the second sentence of article 10? That is what gives very disturbing thoughts." The second sentence is that the Council of the League shall advise what steps, if any, are necessary to carry out the guaranty of the first sentence, namely, that the members will respect and preserve the territorial integrity and political independence of the other members. I do not know of any other meaning for the word "advise" except "advise." The Council advises, and it can not advise without the vote of the United States [as a member of the Council]. ... Whether we use it wisely or unwisely, we can use the vote of the United States to make impossible drawing the United States into any enterprise that she does not care to be drawn into...

My friends, on last Decoration Day I went to a beautiful hillside near Paris, where was located the cemetery of Suresnes, a cemetery given over to the burial of the American dead. ... I wish some men in public life who are now opposing the settlement for which these men died could visit such a spot as that. I wish that the thought that comes out of those graves could penetrate their consciousness. I wish that they could feel the moral obligation that rests upon us not to go back on those boys, but to see the thing through, to see it through to the end and make good their redemption of the world. For nothing less depends upon this decision, nothing less than the liberation and salvation of the world.

Who has the more compelling argument regarding the League of Nations, Wilson or Lodge?

Pushing himself to the limit to defend the League of Nations, an exhausted Wilson paid the price. On September 25, 1919, hours after he reminded a Pueblo, Colorado, audience that American soldiers had died to protect "the liberty of the world," the president fell ill. His personal physician rushed a twitching and nauseated Wilson back to Washington, D.C., where two days later he suffered a stroke. His life in the balance and permanently paralyzed on his left side, Wilson spent the rest of his presidency hidden in the White House. Wilson, the British Prime Minister Lloyd George remarked, was "as much a victim of the war as any soldier who died in the trenches."

The White House kept the president's illness a secret, issuing a vague statement that he was recovering from exhaustion. For weeks, however, Wilson only spent three hours a day out of bed and saw no one except his physician, Dr. Cary Grayson, and his family. His wife carefully controlled all correspondence reaching the president and helped compose his replies. Critics later accused her of serving as a shadow president during Wilson's convalescence, but Edith Wilson steadfastly maintained that Wilson made every decision himself. Wilson rejected all private suggestions that he resign, and still refused to accept any reservations to the Versailles Treaty.

With Wilson absent from the public stage, opposition to the League of Nations spread. Wilson's refusal to compromise doomed the treaty to defeat. The Senate rejected both the original treaty and one with Lodge's reservations attached. The Senate therefore never ratified the Versailles Treaty. It took two more years for the war to end officially for the United States. In October, 1921, the Senate finally ratified separate peace treaties with Germany, Austria, and Hungary.

Nations that ratified the Versailles Peace Treaty also agreed to join the League, with the exception of Germany, which was not allowed to join until 1926. The League remained headquartered in Geneva, Switzerland, from 1920 until 1946, when the United Nations took its place. Wilson won the Nobel Peace Prize for his efforts to establish the League of Nations, but without American membership the League became little more than a place to air grievances.

Wilson never regained his health, and he died in 1924. The war altered countless other lives as well. Most American families of fallen soldiers opted to have their remains returned from France at government expense. John Steuart Curry's painting, *The Return of Private Davis from the Argonne* (**20.16**) captured the mixture of commemorative ritual and private mourning that accompanied the reburial of his friend in a small Kansas town. The flag-draped

20.16 ***The Return of Private Davis from the Argonne***
John Steuart Curry's 1940 painting of gathered mourners burying a fallen soldier reflected Americans' ambiguity over how to remember World War I. The artist juxtaposed the intense personal grief of the soldier's family and community with a vast void behind them. [Property of the Westervelt Company and displayed in The Westervelt-Warner Museum of American Art in Tuscaloosa, AL]

Why did Americans feel disillusioned at the end of World War I?

coffin, wreaths, and honor guard offer official assurances that Davis died in service to his nation and humanity, but the emptiness of the landscape behind the mourners suggests that nothing constructive resulted from his death. Like Curry, the nation remained undecided over whether to remember the war as a great victory or tragedy.

Conclusion

Conflicting visions over America's role in the world shaped both the American road to war and the outcome of World War I. From 1914 to the spring of 1917, the nation debated whether neutrality required ending trade with Europe, trading equally with all sides, or instead gave Americans the right to trade and travel wherever they liked. When Wilson embraced the last definition of neutrality in 1915, he managed to keep the country out of the war only by convincing Germany to curtail submarine attacks on passenger and merchant ships. When Germany resumed unrestricted submarine warfare in 1917 and sent Mexico the Zimmermann Telegram, Wilson decided that German aggression now threatened the nation's economic and territorial interests and asked Congress to declare war.

The war left a lasting imprint on the nation. Leading a divided nation into war, the Wilson administration quickly rallied pubic support through a massive propaganda drive, a complete mobilization of the industrial and agricultural economies, conscription, espionage and sedition laws, and war bond campaigns. All these efforts greatly extended the reach of the federal government into the private lives of American citizens. The home front experience during World War I set the precedent for how the United States would marshal its resources to combat the Great Depression and fight a much longer World War II.

After the war women had the vote and African Americans continued their migration northward. The wartime coalition had included a place for labor, but the government abandoned its support of unions when the war ended. Progressive faith in expertise and efficiency infused some parts of the war effort, such as relying on experts to manage governmental wartime agencies and embracing conscription as the most efficient way to mobilize the armed forces. However, the Progressive drive to regulate big business languished as the war strengthened industrialists' influence within governmental circles, and the Progressive Era came to an end.

World War I shaped the twentieth century. Fledgling democratic nations replaced the former German, Russian, and Austro-Hungarian empires, redrawing the map of Central Europe. The war laid the foundation for World War II, and gave the world an ideal of self-determination that helped encourage colonized peoples to seek independence. The creation of the Soviet Union in 1922 would also have severe consequences for future generations.

Americans went to war to stop German aggression and make the world safe for democracy. The country remained divided, however, over what role America should have in the postwar world. The domestic debate over the League of Nations revealed strong conflicting visions—isolationism, balance of power, collective security—over how to maintain peace. Although the nation never joined the League of Nations, Wilson's democratic ideals inspired American foreign policy for decades to come. The United States continued to mold its own distinct imperial tradition—eschewing the addition of formal colonies, but continuing to extend its economic and ideological reach throughout the world.

CHAPTER REVIEW

1914

Archduke Franz Ferdinand assassinated in Sarajevo, Bosnia
Triggers breakdown of European balance of power system

Germany invades Belgium and France
World War I begins; Wilson declares United States neutral

1915

Britain mines the North Sea; German U-boats patrol British waters
Incites domestic debate over how to stay neutral

German U-boat sinks *Lusitania*
Wilson asserts rights of neutrals to travel unmolested

1916

Villa raids American bordertowns
U.S. troops sent to Mexico; war narrowly avoided

Germany renounces unrestricted submarine warfare
Wilson wins reelection, promising "peace with honor"

Review Questions

1. Was any one nation primarily responsible for starting World War I or did Europe share collective responsibility?
2. Why was neutrality so difficult to define and maintain for the United States?
3. How did the government rally public support for the war? Consider the various types of approaches taken in presidential speeches, in propaganda posters, and by wartime governmental agencies. What were the positive versus negative consequences of these various approaches?
4. How well did the government balance the need to uncover German espionage with protecting civil liberties during the war?
5. How did women and African Americans fare during the war? Which changes were temporary? Which were more permanent?
6. What challenges did soldiers face in the trenches? How was fighting this war different from previous American wars such as the Civil War or Spanish-American War?
7. Evaluate the key flaws of the Versailles Treaty. What concerns did Americans raise about the League of Nations? In what ways did the treaty create the groundwork for future world problems?

1917

Germany resumes unrestricted submarine warfare; Zimmermann Telegram sent to Mexico
Congress declares war against Germany

Race riot in East St. Louis, Illinois
Racial animosities intensify as Southern blacks migrate north

Bolsheviks seize power in Russia
Communist victory sets the stage for future conflicts

1918

Wilson gives Fourteen Points Speech
Establishes democracy, free trade, and collective security as key postwar goals

Congress passes Sedition Act
Dilutes civil liberties and freedom of speech

Peak of influenza pandemic
Deadly flu virus kills 675,000 Americans; 30 million worldwide

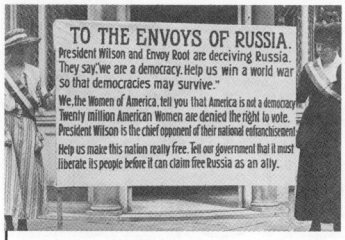

1918

Wilson supports female suffrage
Ends picketing outside White House by suffragists

Armistice between Allies and Germany
Germany capitulates before Allies cross into Germany

1919

Germany signs the Versailles Treaty
Punitive terms create resentments Hitler will later exploit to rise to power

Senate rejects the Versailles Treaty
Ends strident debate on the merits of joining the League of Nations

Key Terms

Allies (World War I) Initially composed of Britain, France, Belgium, and Russia, and would eventually total eighteen nations, including Italy and the United States. **594**

Central Powers Initially Germany and Austria-Hungary, expanded by 1915 to include the Ottoman Empire and Bulgaria. **594**

The Schlieffen Plan A military plan that called for Germany to attack and quickly defeat France while the cumbersome Russian army mobilized. **596**

Western Front Complex system of trenches and earthworks that ran for 550 miles from the North Sea to Switzerland that pitted Germany against Belgium, France, Britain, and the United States. **596**

U-boat German submarine, a new weapon that launched surprise torpedo attacks against Allied merchant and naval ships. **598**

Lusitania British passenger ship sunk by a German U-boat on May 7, 1915, an attack that killed 1,198 passengers, including 128 Americans. **598**

Zimmermann Telegram German foreign minister Arthur Zimmermann offered to help Mexico recover Texas, New Mexico, and Arizona if Mexico would start a borderland war with the United States and ask Japan to join them. **600**

Fourteen Points Speech by Woodrow Wilson to Congress on January 8, 1918, that outlined a postwar world dominated by democracy, free trade, disarmament, self-determination, the settlement of territorial disputes in Europe, and a league of nations to mediate future international crises. **601**

self-determination Giving people a voice in selecting their own government. **601**

Nineteenth Amendment Constitutional amendment that granted women the right to vote; it was ratified August 26, 1920. **605**

Committee on Public Information Government agency that controlled the flow of information and shaped public opinion about the war with posters, Four-Minute Men, pamphlets, and films. **605**

war bonds Short-term loans that individual citizens made to the government that financed two-thirds of the war's costs. **606**

Espionage Act (1917) Legislation that made it a crime to obstruct military recruitment, to encourage mutiny, or to aid the enemy by spreading lies. **606**

Sedition Act (1918) Legislation that went even further than the Espionage Act by prohibiting anyone from uttering, writing, or publishing "any abusive or disloyal language" concerning the flag, constitution, government, or armed forces. **606**

conscientious objectors Those who opposed participating in military service because of religious, philosophical, or political belief. **609**

American Expeditionary Forces Two million American soldiers who fought overseas under the command of General John J. Pershing. **612**

Spanish Influenza A lethal flu virus that killed millions worldwide. **614**

Versailles Peace Treaty The controversial treaty that required Germany to pay reparations and disarm. **615**

League of Nations An international collective security organization composed of member nations where member nations agreed to mediate future international disputes to prevent wars and work together to improve global human conditions. **615**

CHAPTER 21

A Turbulent Decade

The Twenties

Cars and Planes: The Promise of the Twenties p. 626

Cultural Unrest p. 632

> "Was every decent standard being overthrown?"
>
> Journalist FREDERICK LEWIS ALLEN, commenting on youthful rebellion in the twenties

On a cold December afternoon in 1926, two young women posed for the camera as they danced on the ledge of a Chicago hotel. With their short skirts, bobbed hair, and heel-kicking dance steps, they displayed a carefree lifestyle that defied the stricter morals embraced by their mothers' generation. The pair embodied the high spirits of a generation ready to put the tragedy of World War I behind them and move forward into the modern era. Novelists and journalists referred to these women as flappers, a decades-old slang term for young girls. Now it was used to describe independent young women who smoked, drank, danced to jazz, and flaunted their sexual liberation by wearing revealing clothes. Rebellious postwar writers made flappers a cultural icon. Their youthful exuberance and daring behavior excited some Americans and created a sense of moral outrage in others.

The flapper controversy was one of many cultural conflicts that turned political in the turbulent twenties. Flappers and the equally controversial birth control movement championed the right of women to take control of their bodies. Other Americans preferred using the government to control behavior. Prohibition of the manufacture and sale of alcoholic liquors became the law of the land, promising to rid the nation of poverty, crime, and disease. To prevent the communist-inspired Russian Revolution from spreading to the United States, the government arrested suspected political radicals and drastically reduced the flow of European immigration. Meanwhile religious Fundamentalists argued that the country was morally adrift and launched a well-publicized crusade against teaching evolution in public schools. African Americans, too, played an important role in changing America's cultural landscape, creating new artistic centers and political movements that challenged the methods of established civil rights leaders.

Putting the Progressive-era faith in trust-busting aside, the government allowed large industrial conglomerates to dominate key industrial sectors, such as steel and automobiles. Still staunchly antiunion, some factory owners nonetheless became more responsive to workers' grievances to reduce labor strife. Mass production, accompanied by mass consumption, spurred the decade's economic prosperity. Cars, suburbs, and asphalt highways soon dotted the American horizon, changing the living habits of millions.

Domestic cultural conflict dominated political discourse in the twenties, yet a distinct foreign policy also took shape during the decade. Despite its refusal to join the League of Nations, the country remained active in world affairs. By exerting rising international influence through diplomacy and foreign aid, Republican presidential administrations offered an alternative way to maintain world peace.

How much of the old order would America jettison or protect as it entered the postwar age? Throughout the twenties Americans held competing visions of what modernity had to offer.

What qualities define the women in the photo as flappers?

Racial Violence and Civil Rights p. 638

The New Woman p. 644

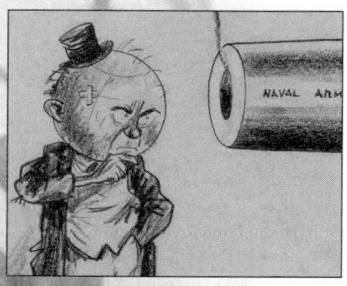

Ensuring Peace: Diplomacy in the Twenties p. 647

Cars and Planes: The Promise of the Twenties

During the twenties America became a car culture. Car registration jumped from 9.2 million in 1920 to 26.5 million ten years later. By 1927 the United States contained 80 percent of the world's cars. Conflicting ideas soon emerged, however, over how much car-based commerce should transform the American landscape and whether all Americans could be trusted with the new freedom their cars bestowed.

The push to produce cars and other consumer goods more efficiently caused industrialists to change how they treated their workforce. Competing visions of industrial work culture between industrialists and workers emerged alongside ongoing clashes over wages and hours. Did America's increased reliance on machines render individual skill or initiative irrelevant? When aviator Charles A. Lindbergh made his historic solo flight across the Atlantic Ocean, he became an instant hero to a society needing reassurance that people and machines could coexist harmoniously.

The Car Culture

At the turn of the century, cities were smelly, dirty places. In New York City alone, horses dumped 2.5 million tons of manure and 60,000 gallons of urine on city streets yearly. The car seemed to offer a clean, flexible solution to city transportation problems. Paving the streets with asphalt would remove the dust that often forced dwellers to keep their windows shut. No one foresaw that a fleet of privately owned cars would soon clog city streets, or that their exhaust would become a serious public health hazard.

Although initial expectations focused on the improvements that cars would make in cities, farmers also benefited significantly from the new technology. Tractors made plowing easier, while trucks transported produce more quickly to market. Whole families piled into cars on Saturday morning to head into town, ending the isolation that had previously characterized farm life.

A car represented a significant purchase for a family. Cars cost between 20 and 45 percent of a non-farm family's annual income, and between 50 and 100 percent of a farm household's yearly earnings. Credit plans required that purchasers pay one-third in cash as a down payment and spread the remaining payments over one year. Most plans also came with hefty interest rates averaging around 16 percent.

Besides enriching automobile manufacturers the explosion in car ownership meant boom times for numerous other industries. To satisfy the unquenchable thirst for gasoline, the petroleum industry underwent a major expansion with new oil wells appearing daily in Texas and California. The building trades saw their business take off when millions took advantage of the mobility that cars afforded and moved to the suburbs. An acute need soon developed for tunnels and bridges to link cities by car to ever-dispersed commuter suburbs. In 1927 the Holland Tunnel, the nation's first underwater motor vehicle tunnel, opened between New York City and New Jersey. On its first day of operation, nearly fifty thousand people paid fifty cents to drive through the tunnel that ran under the Hudson River.

21.1 Cottage Gas Station
Many businessmen built gas stations that looked like country cottages to assure passing motorists that their establishments were safe and clean.

How did cars transform urban and rural lifestyles?

On the Road

Many Americans took vacations away from home for the first time, and to satisfy their wanderlust, the public demanded good roads through rural areas. The government responded with a massive road-building and paving program. Following the precedents set in the nineteenth century when the federal government had funded canal construction and given railroad companies huge land grants to build railroads (see Chapter 15), the federal government now helped states build a new national highway system.

Car travelers also needed food, lodging, and gas. To entice tourists to stop at their establishments, rural businessmen erected eye-catching signs and buildings. A revolution in commercial roadside architecture was soon underway. Small clusters of cottages where tourists could spend the night on long road trips, forerunners of today's motels, appeared in remote areas. The miniature house (**21.1**) emerged as the most popular type of commercial roadside building in the twenties, a way to assure passersby that the restaurant, store, or gas station was a safe and respectable establishment.

Other retailers used surreal images to entice motorists to stop. An array of giant milk bottles, toads, and hot dogs soon lined the highways of America. The Teapot Dome Service Station (**21.2**), built in 1922 along a highway in Zillah, Washington, humorously reminded patrons of the Teapot Dome political scandal that rocked the Harding White House in the early twenties. The Republicans had selected Warren Harding, an unassuming senator from Ohio, as their 1920 presidential candidate because his easygoing nature and call for "a return to normalcy" presented the electorate with a welcome respite from the sternness of Democrat Woodrow Wilson's wartime leadership. Winning 60 percent of the popular vote, Harding easily defeated Democrat James Cox, who suffered when he stood by Wilson and his failed League of Nations crusade (see Chapter 20). Harding's two years in office (he died of a heart attack in 1923, making his vice president Calvin Coolidge president) were, however, tarnished by scandal. The largest scandal involved Secretary of the Interior Albert B. Fall, who went to jail for accepting bribes from two wealthy businessmen to lease government-controlled oil reserves in Teapot Dome, Wyoming. The enterprising owner of this service station gave his customers a laugh at the president's expense by selling oil and gasoline in a teapot-shaped gas station.

21.2 Teapot Dome Gas Station, Zillah, Washington Roadside architecture in the twenties often included whimsical structures designed to entice passing motorists to stop. This gas station shaped like a teapot made a joke of the Teapot Dome scandal.

What messages did the architecture of roadside gas stations convey?

Throughout the twenties Americans embraced conflicting visions of the architectural merits of such buildings. Some celebrated them as a vernacular form of pop art, while others dismissed them as eyesores. The controversy surrounding America's nascent car culture extended beyond competing aesthetic ideals of roadside architecture. Some traditionalists also lamented Americans' changing recreational habits. Ministers complained that instead of spending Sundays in church, many families chose instead to take all day drives. Cars let teenagers take their courting out of the family parlor and into the backseat of the family automobile, to the dismay of parents everywhere. "The best way to keep children home is to make the home atmosphere pleasant—and let air out of the tires," quipped author Dorothy Parker. Automobiles also made it harder for town officials to regulate red-light districts, causing one judge to declare that "the automobile has become a house of prostitution on wheels."

Welfare Capitalism and Consumer Culture

During World War I the government had mandated that industrialists with wartime contracts pay high wages, provide clean and safe working conditions, and allow unions to organize within their factories (see Chapter 20). In return for this official protection, the government demanded a no-strike pledge from unions. When the war ended in 1918, the government abruptly canceled its orders and withdrew from managing worker-industrial relations. The government's hands-off attitude emboldened many industrialists to reinstate low wages, long hours, and blacklists for union members. To protect their wartime gains, unions orchestrated the greatest wave of strikes in American history in 1919. Although they rallied millions of workers to the picket lines, outmatched unions lost this battle.

Industrialists accused unions of following in the footsteps of the recent Russian Revolution and trying to spread communism in the United States. These accusations won industrialists the support of local governments, who once again forcefully broke up many picket lines. Defeated steel, coal, and garment unions, however, did not give up organizing and continued to attract members. In the early 1920s union ranks grew to five million, the largest to date. When faced with the dismal vision of unending labor strife, Progressives had crafted government regulation to rein in business and improve working conditions (see Chapter 18). In the 1920s industrialists used the guarantee of government noninterference to pursue a different vision.

Throughout the decade the Harding and Coolidge administrations left industrialists free to fashion their own solutions to such labor troubles, adopting an openly pro-business stance. *The Wall Street Journal* exulted that "never before, here or anywhere else, has a government been so completely fused with business," referring to Commerce Department workshops that helped businesses eliminate wasteful practices, a Justice Department that largely stopped enforcing anti-trust laws, and a high protective tariff that made imported goods more expensive than American industrial products.

Progressive-era innovations aimed at improving industrial efficiency, however, remained popular. Scientific management and welfare capitalism gained even more adherents in the twenties. Mirroring how army psychologists had used intelligence tests to rank the aptitudes of different racial and ethnic groups in World War I (see Chapter 20), the Central Tube Company in Pittsburgh devised a chart (**21.3**) assessing the abilities of various nationalities to perform skilled and unskilled jobs. The new profession of psychology accepted pseudoscientific social Darwinian ideas that "race" determined aptitude, and the factory owner used this "scientific" information to organize and run his business more efficiently. Unsurprisingly, given this racial climate, white Americans topped the list as good at all types of tasks. Jews were considered bad at every job and American blacks were listed as only suited for unskilled jobs. There were some surprises on the chart, however. While social Darwinists usually viewed northern Europeans as superior to southern and eastern Europeans, in the factory's ethnic hierarchy Italians and Poles actually outscored Germans and French as desirable skilled workers.

Some innovative industrialists tried to put aside the prevailing idea that the interests of capitalists and workers inevitably clashed. Rather than driving their workers relentlessly to secure a profit, advocates of welfare capitalism suggested that industrialists offer a wide range of benefits such as medical insurance, pensions, and stock ownership plans to create a loyal workforce.

As the vogue for welfare capitalism spread, many industrialists began to change their management practices. To develop a stable, well-trained workforce, industrialists introduced fringe benefits (including paid vacations and sick pay), created industrial committees where workers could air grievances,

How did ethnic profiling and welfare capitalism promise to help industrialists run their factories more efficiently?

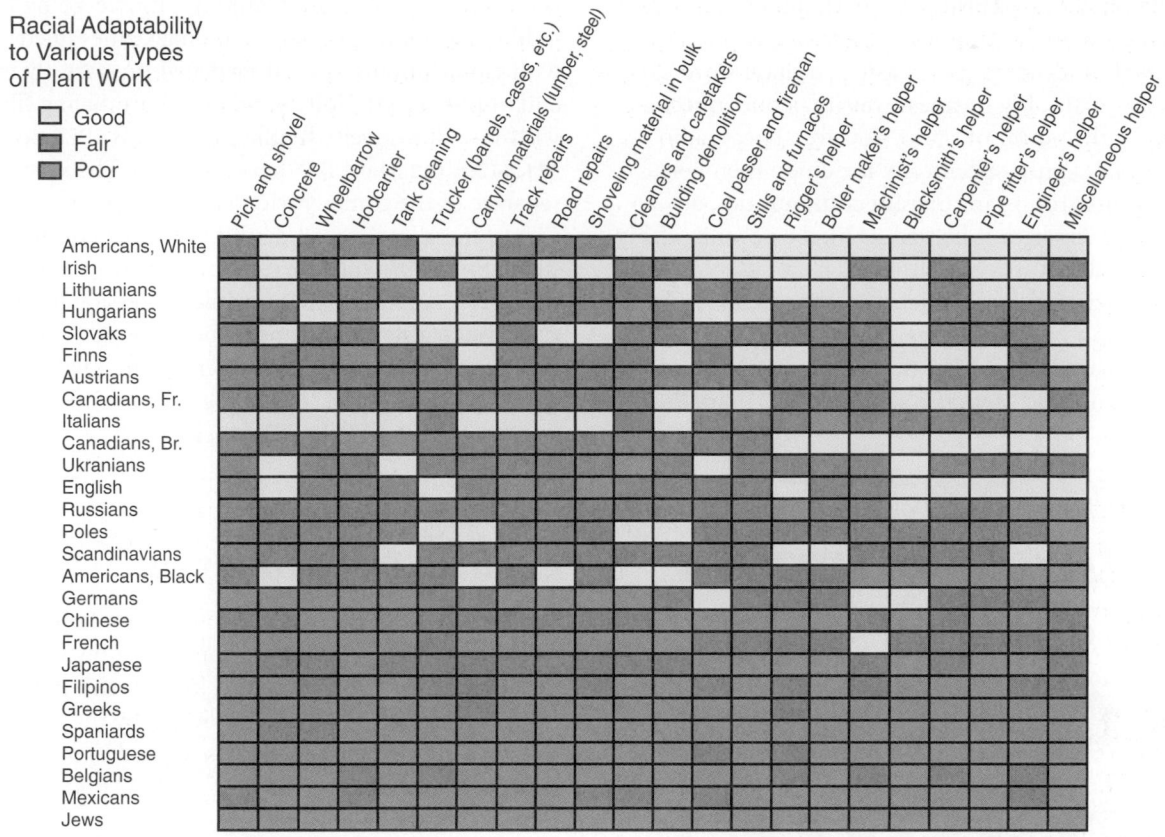

21.3 Employment Chart of the Central Tube Company, Pittsburgh, 1925 Social Darwinian ideas about the innate abilities of different racial and ethnic groups determined where individuals could work in this factory.

and offered bonuses for workers who exceeded production quotas. A worker usually needed at least twenty-five years with one company to qualify for a pension, so this policy alone could potentially keep workers from leaving to pursue other job opportunities. Industrialists also experimented with offering employees stock options, hoping to dilute class antagonism by making each worker an investor who would share in the company's profits.

Despite workers' enthusiasm for welfare capitalism, the reality rarely matched the rhetoric. Seasonal lay-offs continued, wage rates fluctuated constantly, and long hours in unhealthy factories persisted. As one worker complained, "we had to wait five years for one week's vacation. And I've seen men work four and one-half years and then get laid off." Industrialists' promises ended up simply whetting workers' appetites for stable well-paid jobs with benefits. During the Great Depression in the 1930s (see Chapter 22), the labor movement would demand that the government fulfill the hopes that industrialists had raised in the twenties.

Increased industrial productivity and efficiency created an unprecedented abundance of affordable goods in the twenties. Blue-collar workers toiling in dead-end jobs in factories staffed with salaried white-collar employees performing unsatisfying clerical tasks produced these items. Frustrated at work, many working- and middle-class Americans used their growing leisure time and access to material goods to create more fulfilling lives. A modern consumer culture arose that deemphasized traditional Victorian values of thrift and restraint. Americans instead increasingly relied on credit to buy cars, radios, and household appliances.

Radio played a key role in forging a national mass culture. Over 60 percent of American homes acquired radios in the twenties, which until 1924 required headphones. Americans from all walks of life now simultaneously gathered around their radios to learn election results. Baseball fans throughout the nation listened to the play-by-play of the World Series, radio broadcasts that made New York Yankee player Babe Ruth a national sports hero. Farmers closely followed weather reports, and bankers digested the day's financial news. "There is radio music in the air, every night, everywhere," one newspaper observed. Big companies like Walgreen Drugs and Palmolive Soap started sponsoring nationally syndicated radio shows to boost sales of their products. These weekly comedies and dramas, filled with plugs for the sponsor's merchandise,

What job could you have gotten in this factory?

cultivated shared tastes in entertainment and brand-name products. Americans increasingly bought the same brand-name toothpaste at a chain store like Woolworths. Big business was not alone in recognizing the power of radio, however. Local radio shows designed specifically for union members, religious groups, immigrant communities, or African Americans helped strengthen bonds within these subcultures as well.

Movie stars and athletes enjoyed nationwide adulation in the twenties. Silent-film actors like the comedian Charlie Chaplin, the sex symbol Rudolph Valentino, and "America's Sweetheart" Mary Pickford became household names among a movie-going public that avidly purchased fan magazines filled with glossy photos of their favorite film stars. By the end of the decade Hollywood began producing films with sound, a novelty highlighted in this 1929 poster (**21.4**) for the Marx Brothers' first film. The verbal repartee of the comedy trio delighted audiences. As silent films disappeared, so did the careers of many silent-film stars whose artistic talents lay in physical, not vocal, expression. Meanwhile professional sports gave rise to a slew of national sports heroes, such as the boxer Jack Dempsey. In an era dominated by cultural heroes, none rose to greater prominence than the pilot Charles A. Lindbergh.

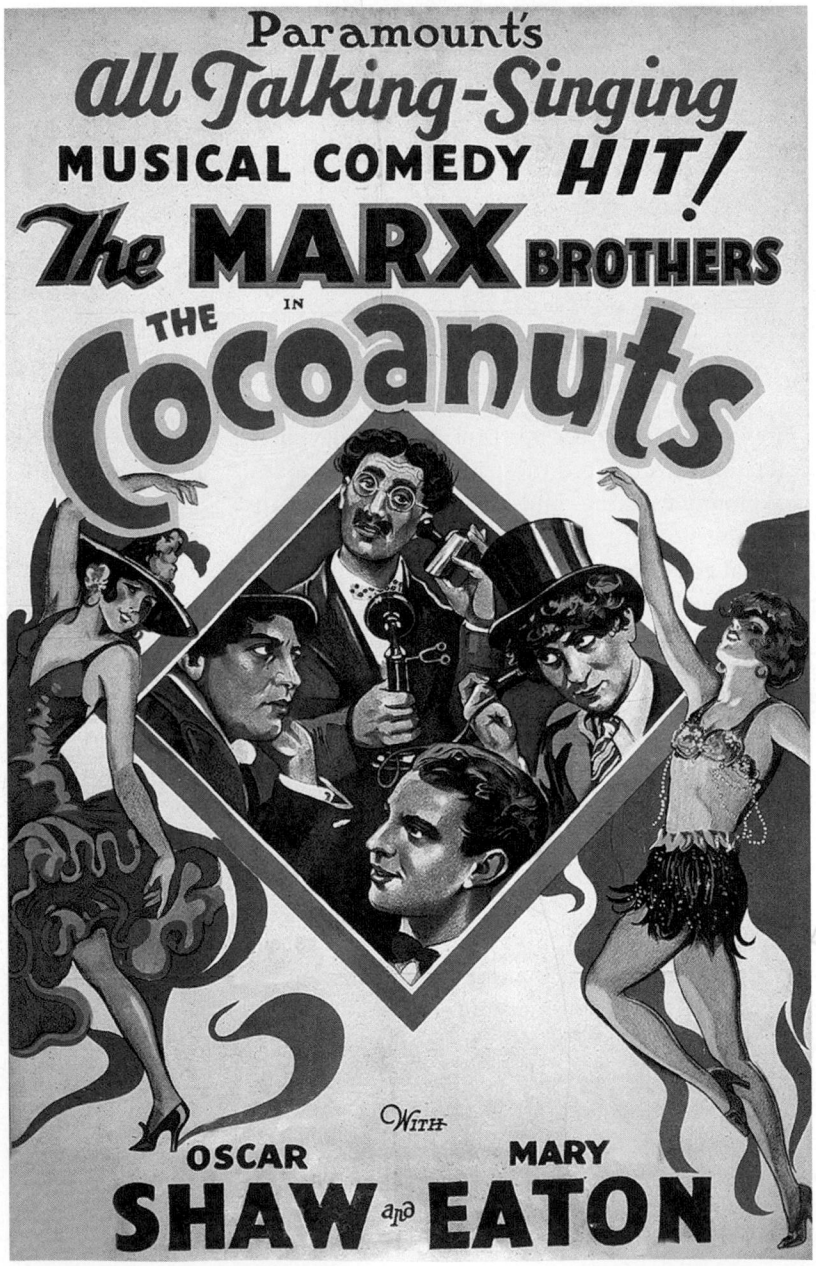

21.4 The End of Silent Films
By the end of the decade Hollywood began advertising "all talking-singing" movies like "Cocoanuts."

The Age of Flight: Charles A. Lindbergh

The feats of pilot Charles A. Lindbergh ushered the nation into the age of flight. Commentators called the sky the new frontier, a label loaded with potent historical significance for Americans. By the late twenties, a time when machines seemed to matter more than people, the image of the lone pilot against the vast blue sky recalled the pioneer spirit of the nineteenth century.

Lindbergh piloted his plane, the *Spirit of St. Louis,* on the first-ever nonstop solo flight from New York to Paris on May 21, 1927. Flying without the radio or radar that help modern pilots navigate, Lindbergh relied on a few navigational instruments and looking out the window to locate his position on a paper map as he flew. Sitting in a wicker chair with sandwiches and water under it, Lindbergh had a rubber raft on board in case he was forced to land in the cold Atlantic and a flashlight to examine his wings for ice.

Lindbergh's flight lasted 33.5 hours, enough time to make him the hero of the decade. This photomontage (a composite photo made by pasting together separately taken images) of the *Spirit of St. Louis* (**21.5**) passing by the Eiffel Tower combined the signature symbol of Paris with the image of Lindbergh's iconic plane. "Had we searched all America we could not have found a better type than young Lindbergh to represent the spirit and high purpose of our people," the jubilant American ambassador to France wired President Coolidge amid the celebrations that followed Lindbergh's landing in Paris. Lindbergh's triumph assured Americans that individual initiative still mattered and that technological advancement benefited humankind at a time when the recent industrialized

How did a mass popular culture emerge in the twenties?

> "The *Spirit of St. Louis* is a wonderful plane. It's like a living creature, gliding along smoothly, happily, as though a successful flight means as much to it as to me."
>
> CHARLES LINDBERGH, evoking the perfect symmetry between man and machine

slaughter on the Western Front (see Chapter 20) suggested otherwise. The vision of planes serving a peaceful purpose by transporting mail and tourists replaced wartime images of aerial dogfights. Lindbergh toured the nation tirelessly to promote commercial air travel, and also flew flood relief missions in China with his wife, the author Anne Morrow Lindbergh, in 1931 to demonstrate the humanitarian good that planes made possible.

In exalting Lindbergh's achievement Americans channeled their own conflicting visions of the modern age. Some praised Lindbergh for exhibiting the same adventurous spirit that had propelled American pioneers across the West in the nineteenth century, values that seemed increasingly at risk in a machine-dominated age. "Charles Lindbergh is the heir of all that we like to think is best in America," opined *Outlook* magazine. Others, including Lindbergh, rejected the idea that his flight epitomized a return to the past. Lindberg asserted that his flight illustrated the nation's industrial march forward, "the culmination," he said, ". . . of all that was practicable and best in American aviation." Although differing on whether the flight represented the revival of traditional values or the modern ethos of industrial might, Americans agreed that his flight renewed faith in the benefits of technology.

Lindbergh suffered, however, in the public spotlight. The 1933 kidnapping and murder of his firstborn son became the most reported tabloid story of the day. Later in the decade Lindbergh tarnished his image by expressing admiration for Nazi Germany and joining with those who initially argued against American intervention in World War II. After Japan's bombing of Pearl Harbor in 1941, Lindbergh changed his position. He went on to fly combat missions against the Japanese, and his reputation recovered when he took a strong anti-communist stand during the Cold War in the 1950s.

21.5 Photo Montage of the *Spirit of St. Louis* Flying Near the Eiffel Tower
In this imagined scene an unnamed photographer celebrated the moment that pilot Charles Lindbergh arrived in Paris by pasting an image of his famous plane flying past Paris's most recognized monument.

Why did Americans celebrate Lindbergh's solo flight to Paris?

Cultural Unrest

Celebrating Lindberg's achievement was a unique moment of national unity in a decade dominated by cultural turbulence and strife. During the 1920s Americans initiated a series of societal-wide debates that reflected competing visions over what values the nation should embrace as it entered the modern age. Cultural conflict turned political in the twenties as Americans debated the need for legislation to protect the nation's morals, ethnic purity, and capitalist economy.

The Lost Generation

"I've kissed dozens of men. I suppose I'll kiss dozens more," declared the flapper heroine of F. Scott Fitzgerald's novel *This Side of Paradise* (1920), announcing a new attitude of living for the moment that defined the era's youth culture. With his wife Zelda by his side, Fitzgerald put this philosophy into practice, moving from party to party in his fast-paced life as an expatriate in Europe. The Paris-based American writer Gertrude Stein coined the term "the Lost Generation" to describe white intellectuals and artists like Fitzgerald who rebelled against Victorian values in the twenties and lived primarily overseas.

Lost Generation writers used Austrian psychologist Sigmund Freud's theories to justify their revolt against "repressive" codes of conduct. Freud believed that subconscious sexual impulses drove human behavior and that repressed desires sometimes found expression in dreams. Fitzgerald was one of a host of writers including Ernest Hemingway, e. e. cummings, and John Dos Passos who championed sexual liberation as one way to escape the sterile and deadly confines of modern life. Men and women "spend their lives going in and out of doors and factories ... they live their lives and find themselves at last facing death and the end of life without having lived at all," asserts a character in Sherwood Anderson's *Many Marriages* (1923) who, in the throes of a passionate extramarital affair, is preparing to end his marriage and leave his job.

The hedonistic lifestyles depicted in many Lost Generation novels, while rarely bestowing lasting happiness on the protagonists, still rankled more traditionally minded Americans. Agreeing that modern culture was flawed, these Americans wanted to bolster, rather than reject, traditional values. These clashing cultural visions had strong political overtones. Alcohol remained central to the Lost Generation ethos of pleasure-seeking, an indulgence that became illegal in the twenties thanks to temperance reformers who felt that drinking threatened the moral fabric of American society.

Prohibition

Temperance, one of the nation's longest lasting reform movements (see Chapters 17 and 18), took on a new life during World War I. Wartime temperance propaganda claimed that "German brewers in this country have rendered thousands of men inefficient." Organized "wet" opposition to the dry campaign materialized slowly, partly because critics of the temperance movement could not easily counter its emphasis on health, thrift, and morals. Some wets focused on personal freedom. Senator James Wadsworth contended that it seemed unfair to tell exhausted workers at the end of the day "you shall not have a glass of beer." Other critics felt uneasy about increasing the power of the federal government so it could enforce prohibition. Once the debate centered on a possible constitutional amendment prohibiting alcohol, they argued that such an amendment would violate states' rights. The middle-class Anti-Saloon League's highly structured propaganda and lobbying campaign, however, easily overpowered this disjointed wet response on the local, state, and national level.

Evangelical preacher Billy Sunday converted many churchgoers to the temperance cause, delivering impassioned sermons on the evils of alcohol. Sunday, a former professional baseball player turned preacher, littered his sermons with slang, winning a large following among the rural poor and urban working class who flocked to his revival meetings throughout the Midwest. The political elite also embraced the preacher. Sunday often dined at the White House and considered the oil tycoon John D. Rockefeller a friend. In his most famous temperance speech, Sunday urged his listeners in 1908 to "get on the water wagon; get on for the sake of your wife and babies, and hit the booze a blow."

What critique did the Lost Generation offer of American society?

On December 18, 1917, Congress approved the **Eighteenth Amendment**, which banned the sale, manufacture, and transportation of intoxicating liquors. By January 16, 1919, the required thirty-six states had ratified the amendment. By the time every state had voted, only Rhode Island and Connecticut had rejected it. When prohibition went into effect in 1920, Congress clarified what constituted an intoxicating beverage in the **Volstead Act (1919)**, a law that defined any beverage with more than 0.5 percent alcohol as intoxicating liquor and established criminal penalties for manufacturing, transporting, or possessing alcohol.

Congress never appropriated enough money for wide-scale enforcement, hampering Justice Department efforts to curb illegal drinking. The police raided working-class neighborhoods to shut down illegal distilleries, but the well-to-do drank their bathtub gin or homebrewed beer without interference. Many reform goals of the temperance movement remained unmet. Belying the expectation that prohibition would create a more virtuous, law-abiding society, prohibition gave birth to a much more insidious form of crime. Organized crime syndicates ran profitable bootlegging operations that financed beer breweries and liquor distilleries, bribed cops, and stocked the shelves of illegal bars throughout major metropolitan areas. Trafficking in forbidden alcohol, the publicity-crazed gangster Al Capone became a powerful figure in the Chicago underworld, a position he maintained with unprecedented violence. In the 1929 St. Valentine's Day Massacre, Capone's men, posing as cops, pretended to arrest rival gang members and then lined them up against a wall and used submachine guns to mow them down. Tabloid papers vividly recounted every detail of Capone's "new technique of wholesale murder" to a shocked American public. Suffering from syphilis that he contracted from a prostitute in one of his own brothels, Capone became increasingly unstable and violent before he went to prison for tax evasion in 1931.

Secret bars called speakeasies proliferated. To demonstrate Americans' widespread disrespect for prohibition, federal agent Izzy Einstein timed how long it took him to find alcohol in most major cities. It took him 21 minutes in Chicago, and only 31 seconds in New Orleans when he asked a taxi driver where he could get a drink and the man replied, "right here," as he pulled out a bottle. Einstein personally shut down over four thousand speakeasies nationwide, prompting bartenders to post his picture with the caption "watch for this man."

Illicit drinking became fashionable among the young urban elite, whose escapades Lost Generation writers helped glamorize. This image of a well-dressed woman barhopping with her male companions (**21.6**) revealed new social acceptance for public drinking by respectable middle- and upper-class women. Americans had previously viewed saloons as male establishments that only women of low moral character, like prostitutes, dared to enter.

21.6 Well-Dressed Trio Entering a Speakeasy
Frequenting speakeasies, which patrons entered by giving a secret password to the doorman, became fashionable for women during prohibition. Gone was the stigma that had stopped respectable women from drinking in public.

The competing visions of whether illegal drinking was harmless fun or a vice that destroyed families kept the political debate over prohibition alive throughout the 1920s. "Drys" credited prohibition for the prosperous economy. By putting alcohol aside, they claimed, workers had become more productive, could afford to buy cars and furniture, and had more savings. Critics of prohibition argued that the amendment generated disrespect for the law as it became socially acceptable for Americans to commit a crime by purchasing alcohol. States' rights advocates increasingly resented the arrival of federal officials trying to track down local bootleggers. Picking up the Anti-Saloon League's longstanding emphasis on protecting women and children, the wet lobby emphasized the dangers of teenagers drinking contaminated "moon-shine" (a slang term for illicitly manufactured alcohol) in speakeasies run by the mob. Better to have them drink safely in public cafes, the wets argued.

The beginning of the Great Depression in 1929, which thrust the nation into an unprecedented financial crisis, undermined the dry claim that prohibition brought prosperity. Wets made headway with the argument that enforcing the law drained the federal treasury. When Democrat Franklin D. Roosevelt entered the White House in 1933, he immediately asked Congress to repeal prohibition. With lightening speed the states ratified the **Twenty-First Amendment** (1933), which repealed the

Why did Americans eventually conclude that national prohibition was a failed experiment?

Eighteenth Amendment. The temperance vision remained regionally popular, however, especially in Southern and Midwestern rural areas that continued to enforce local prohibition statutes. A few states also passed minimum-age drinking laws in the 1930s to curtail alcohol consumption, but most states did not enact such laws until the 1980s.

The First Red Scare and Immigration Restrictions

The vision of America as the land of opportunity for peoples worldwide came under severe attack in the 1920s. Debates over immigration were not new (see Chapter 17), but for the first time the nativist vision prevailed. In the early twenties the United States underwent a historic shift, changing from a nation that admitted over 1 million immigrants a year in the decade leading up to World War I to one that grudgingly allowed fewer than 200,000 to enter the country annually.

World War I was the catalyst that turned longstanding nativist attacks against immigrants (see Chapter 17) into a mandate for dramatic change. Alarm over German Americans' continued ties to Germany linked concerns about assimilation to the more potent political question of national security. After the war Congress passed the 1921 Emergency Immigration Act. This law temporarily allowed a total of 350,000 European immigrants to enter the country each year and set limits on how many immigrants could come from each European nation. Three years later Congress made these quotas permanent. The **Immigration Act of 1924** allowed unrestricted immigration from the Western Hemisphere, curtailed all Asian immigration, and used quotas to control how many immigrants emigrated from individual European nations. The law authorized a total of 165,000 immigrants from Europe, a figure that Congress reduced to 150,000 in 1929 at the start of the Great Depression.

Assumptions about the racial superiority of northern European races strongly influenced the new national quotas portrayed on the "Immigration Act of 1924" chart (**21.7**). In this new quota system, Germany received the highest quota. If Americans no longer feared German immigrants, then why did the country feel compelled to adopt immigration restrictions? The answer: The Communist-inspired Russian Revolution, a critical wartime event that some Americans envisioned politically radical immigrants from Russia and Eastern Europe recreating in the United States. To meet this threat the Justice Department arrested and deported alien anarchists and Communists suspected of trying to destroy American democracy and capitalism during the **First Red Scare (1919–1920)**.

Like Communists, anarchists believed that capitalist exploitation of the working class created widespread social suffering. While Communists wanted to create a workers' government that controlled property, anarchists viewed all governments as corrupt. The anarchist movement's most famous spokesperson was Emma Goldman, an eloquent speaker who had emigrated from Russia as a young girl. Anarchism, she wrote, "stands for the liberation of the human mind from the dominion of religion; the liberation of the human body from the dominion of property; liberation from the shackles and restraint of government." Some radical anarchists felt justified using violence to advance their cause (one had assassinated President William McKinley in 1901, see Chapter 18). Goldman, however, disavowed armed conflict and instead tried to popularize the anarchist philosophy through lectures and the magazine that she founded, *Mother Earth*.

In 1919 post office clerk Charles Kaplan helped avert disaster after reading a newspaper account of two anarchist mail-bomb attacks, one against the mayor of Seattle and another against a senator from Georgia, as he rode the subway home. Kaplan realized that the description of the booby-trapped packages matched that of sixteen parcels he had recently set aside for insufficient postage, including one addressed to oil tycoon John D. Rockefeller. Kaplan's discovery triggered a nationwide investigation that netted eighteen more mail bombs.

As anxiety over national security mounted, terrorists exploded dynamite outside the home of Attorney General A. Mitchell Palmer, the man heading the Justice Department's hunt for Bolshevik and anarchist terrorists. Palmer warned that "on a certain day which we have been advised of," radicals were planning "to rise up and destroy the Government at one fell swoop." To head off this revolutionary uprising, Palmer raided the homes and offices of suspected radicals and deported a few hundred immigrants with ties to radical organizations, including Emma Goldman.

While the government focused on the need to ensure public safety, radicals asserted their right to freedom of speech and peaceful assembly. Without concrete evidence of their participation in any criminal activity, they argued, the government was prosecuting them merely for their beliefs. Coming

Why did the nation enact strict immigration restrictions in the twenties?

Northwest Europe and Scandinavia		Eastern and Southern Europe		Other Countries	
Country	**Quota**	**Country**	**Quota**	**Country**	**Quota**
Germany	51,227	Poland	5,982	Africa (other than Egypt)	1,100
Great Britain and Northern Ireland	34,007	Italy	3,845	Armenia	124
Irish Free State (Ireland)	28,567	Czechoslovakia	3,073	Australia	121
Sweden	9,561	Russia	2,248	Palestine	100
Norway	6,453	Yugoslavia	671	Syria	100
France	3,954	Romania	603	Turkey	100
Denmark	2,789	Portugal	503	Egypt	100
Switzerland	2,081	Hungary	473	New Zealand & Pacific Islands	100
Netherlands	1,648	Lithuania	344	All others	1,900
Austria	785	Latvia	142		
Belgium	512	Spain	131		
Finland	471	Estonia	124		
Free City of Danzig	228	Albania	100		
Iceland	100	Bulgaria	100		
Luxembourg	100	Greece	100		
Total (Number)	142,483	**Total (Number)**	18,439	**Total (Number)**	3,745
Total (%)	86.5	**Total (%)**	11.2	**Total (%)**	2.3

21.7 Immigration Act of 1924
The United States enacted a quota system in the 1920s that allotted most slots for immigrants from northern Europe.

on the heels of wartime arrests under the Espionage and Sedition acts, the government's harassment of radical activists during 1919–1920 made it practically impossible for radical groups to organize, distribute literature, or give public speeches championing their political ideals.

Radicals tried to fight back by taking up the cause of anarchists Nicola Sacco and Bartolomeo Vanzetti, two Italian immigrants arrested in Massachusetts for the robbery and murder of a payroll guard in 1920. Poor Italian immigrants and left-leaning union members made numerous small donations to the Sacco-Vanzetti Defense Committee, which sponsored picnics and wrestling matches to raise funds for their defense. Many intellectuals also supported the pair, including Roger Baldwin, who had recently founded the American Civil Liberties Union (ACLU), an organization dedicated to protecting constitutional liberties. Foreign-born, openly radical, in possession of guns and anarchist pamphlets when arrested: The portrait that prosecutors painted of Sacco and Vanzetti epitomized the terrorist threat many Americans feared. Sacco and Vanzetti's radical and liberal supporters embraced a competing vision, blaming growing xenophobia for the pair's conviction and 1927 electrocution. Recent findings suggest that Sacco and Vanzetti were indeed dedicated anarchists with close connections to those who planned the spate of 1919 bombings, but no conclusive evidence ties them to the 1920 murder.

The First Red Scare ended quickly. As the anarchist attacks ceased, the press began to poke fun at Palmer's "hallucinations" of a mass uprising and accused him of exaggerating the "revolutionary menace" as part of a failed campaign to win the Democratic Party presidential nomination in 1920. Although the arrests and deportations stopped, the First Red Scare gave credence to the anti-immigration argument that the country needed protection from foreigners who might import dangerous radical political theories.

Other arguments also helped tip the balance in favor of immigration restriction. Urban elites and rural folk worried about protecting the "racial purity" of American stock, while unions and African Americans feared economic competition from immigrant laborers. By the early twenties industrialists had dropped their complaint that immigration restrictions would deprive business of a traditionally inexpensive labor source. Many now believed that machines would increasingly replace unskilled immigrant workers in factories, and felt confident that there were enough African American or Mexican workers readily available to alleviate any labor shortage. With the consensus in the nation moving toward immigration restrictions, immigrant

What competing visions over radicalism emerged during the Sacco-Vanzetti trial?

associations focused their lobbying efforts on ensuring that their nationality received the highest quota possible.

Official quotas, however, do not reveal the exact numbers of immigrants who entered the country. If denied entry under the quota system, which remained intact from 1924 through 1965, determined immigrants found loopholes to exploit. The 1924 law contained two key provisions that have remained staples of American immigration legislation since the 1920s: the principle of family reunification, which let resident immigrants bring in members of their immediate families, and the desirability of certain skills. The law, for example, established exemptions for trades facing worker shortages in the United States, such as domestic service. Other savvy European immigrants simply entered the country illegally, often by way of Mexico or Canada, two nations that still enjoyed unrestricted immigration to the United States.

Fundamentalism

The cultural debates surrounding prohibition and immigration restrictions assumed a decidedly political edge in the 1920s. Christian Fundamentalists added to the decade's cultural turbulence when they initiated a campaign to stop the teaching of biologist Charles Darwin's views on evolution. Religious conservatives felt that Darwin's theories contradicted the Bible's depiction of God creating the world and humankind in seven days. They instead subscribed to the tenets of **fundamentalism**, an evangelical Christian theology that viewed the Bible as an authentic recounting of historical events and the absolute moral word of God. By critiquing Darwin Fundamentalists offered a conservative alternative to **modernism**, a liberal Christian theology embraced in many urban areas that emphasized the ongoing revelation of divine truth. Offering competing religious visions Fundamentalists accepted the Bible as errorless, while Modernists reinterpreted the Bible when confronted with new scientific knowledge (such as fossil evidence of evolution).

Believing that "monkey men mean monkey morals," the World Christian Fundamentals Association lobbied for state laws that prohibited teaching evolutionary ideas in public schools. In 1925 Tennessee passed a law making it a punishable crime to teach "any theory that denies the story of the Divine Creation as taught in the Bible, and to teach instead that man has descended from a lower order of animals." Passed mostly to make sweeping school reforms more palatable to Fundamentalist voters, the state made no effort to enforce the law and even adopted a biology textbook that included an extended discussion of Darwin's ideas.

The ACLU viewed the law as a violation of the First Amendment's guarantee of free speech. Hoping to test the law's constitutionality, the ACLU offered to help any teacher in Tennessee who wanted to challenge the law in court. A group of civic boosters in Dayton, Tennessee, responded to the offer. A trial highlighting the clash between science and religion was bound to attract huge crowds, they reasoned, and by hosting this national extravaganza Dayton expected to draw an influx of visitors with cash to spend. The boosters approached twenty-four-year-old John Scopes, a science teacher and part-time football coach, who agreed to step forward so officials in Dayton could arrest him. The infamous Scopes trial was underway.

Interest in Scopes, the ACLU, and Dayton faded once William Jennings Bryan agreed to prosecute the case and the attorney Clarence Darrow arrived to defend Scopes. Bryan was the former leader of the Democratic Party who had unsuccessfully run for president three times and resigned as secretary of state when President Woodrow Wilson abandoned complete neutrality during World War I. The devout Bryan blamed Germany's embrace of evolutionary notions like "survival of the fittest" for causing the brutal global war. Darrow was an acknowledged agnostic, famous for defending both radical labor leaders, such as the socialist Eugene Debs, and wealthy murderers.

Hundreds of journalists descended on the town to observe the courtroom confrontation between Bryan and Darrow. Their dispatches helped build publicity for the "monkey trial," a reference to evolutionists' claim that humans had descended from apes. Urban-based reporters billed the case as a conclusive struggle between modern America and the ignorant rural masses (few of whom shared in the general prosperity of the 1920s) whose alleged backward thinking threatened to impede the country's progress. In his widely read reports, nationally syndicated columnist H. L. Mencken regularly referred to Fundamentalists as hillbillies and yokels. Fundamentalists fought back. The carnival-like atmosphere outside the courtroom soon included Fundamentalist revival meetings and performances by trained chimpanzees that mocked evolutionists. Vendors did a brisk business selling monkey dolls, like the one held by Lena Ruffner

Why did Fundamentalists object to teaching evolution in public schools?

Dueling newspaper headlines during the Scopes Trial: "'They Call Us Bigots When We Refuse to Throw Away Our Bibles,' Bryan says."

"We say 'Keep Your Bible,' but keep it where it belongs, in the world of your conscience."

(**21.8**), who announced her support of Bryan by pinning a sign "they can't make a monkey out of me" to her dress.

Both Bryan and Darrow argued that they were protecting American democratic institutions. Bryan maintained that the Tennessee legislature had the right to pass any law that the majority wanted; Darrow contended the state had violated the constitution by establishing Christianity as an official religion and limiting freedom of expression. The mainstream press viewed the trial as a showdown between science and religion, with science winning a decisive victory. In their account, the climatic moment came when Darrow called Bryan to the witness stand and trapped him into confessing he did not accept the entire Bible as the literal truth. "We have the purpose of preventing bigots and ignoramuses from controlling the education of the United States," Darrow declared in court, expressing Modernists' view of fundamentalism. The national press labeled Bryan a broken man when he passed away in his sleep five days after Scopes was found guilty and fined. The courtroom, however, had burst into applause when during his cross-examination Bryan had thundered, "I am simply trying to protect the word of God against the greatest atheist or agnostic in the United States." Southern folk songs popularized this competing heroic image of Bryan among his supporters, viewing him as someone who "fought for what was righteous and the battle it was won / Then the Lord called him to heaven for his work on earth was done."

After Scopes's conviction the ACLU appealed to the Tennessee Supreme Court, which upheld the law's constitutionality and then overturned the verdict because the judge rather than the jury had imposed the fine. Scopes's acquittal meant that the ACLU had to find a new case to take before the U.S. Supreme Court. After the ridicule heaped on Dayton, however, no town or teacher was willing to help the ACLU try again. The Tennessee state legislature did not repeal the law until 1967. A year later the U.S. Supreme Court declared anti-evolution laws unconstitutional.

Although soon forgotten by mainstream America, throughout the twentieth century Fundamentalists created a thriving minority subculture of churches, schools, universities, publishing houses, radio ministries, and missionary societies. Fundamentalists rejoined the cultural and political mainstream in the 1970s and are generating headlines once again with their challenges to teaching evolution in public schools. In one striking break from the past, Fundamentalists now use Darrow's line of reasoning to argue that keeping the biblical theory of creation out of high school biology classes violates the constitutional guarantee to freedom of expression.

21.8 Young Woman Holds Monkey Doll during the Scopes Trial A supporter of prosecutor William Jennings Bryan wears a sign ridiculing the theory of evolution and displays the monkey doll she bought from a vender outside the courthouse.

What cultural and religious tensions were exposed during the Scopes Trial?

Racial Violence and Civil Rights

Advocates of prohibition, immigration restrictions, and fundamentalism had varying degrees of success reshaping American society after the war. Throughout the twenties African Americans were also active, employing new strategies to advance their vision of racial equality. Continued lynchings and a resurgent Ku Klux Klan in the South and Midwest exposed the willingness of many whites to use violence to maintain their competing vision of white supremacy. A new generation of black political activists emerged, determined to fight back when whites attacked. Jamaican immigrant Marcus Garvey won both praise and criticism within the African American community by calling for black economic self-sufficiency at home and the creation of a homeland in Africa. The **Harlem Renaissance**, an outpouring of African American artistic expression in the 1920s and 1930s also stirred debate within the African American community over the best way to improve the lives of African Americans.

Lynching, Racial Rioting, and the Ku Klux Klan

Lynch mobs tortured and killed nearly five thousand victims between 1880 and 1930, roughly two per week. The souvenir postcard (**21.9**) depicting the lynching of Thomas Shipp and Abram Smith is a disturbing relic from this grisly past. Professional photographers often attended lynchings and sold hundreds of picture postcards to perpetrators and witnesses, who put them in family scrapbooks or sent them to friends and relatives. Besides buying souvenir postcards whites sometimes took other relics from the victim, including hair, clothing, fingers, and ears. Both the existence of this postcard and the scene it depicts raise chilling questions about the ritual of lynching. Rather than viewing their murder as a shameful act or believing that they needed to conceal their identities to avoid prosecution, these participants smile openly for the camera. Local and state police rarely arrested anyone for committing a lynching, preferring instead to claim that the victims died "at the hands of persons unknown."

Trumped-up accusations that the victim had raped or murdered a white person usually fueled a lynching frenzy. Local police had arrested Shipp and Abram for robbery, murder, and rape. The purpose of lynching, however, went beyond simply administering extralegal justice. Lynching also created a climate of terror that helped whites maintain social control over all blacks, not just the ones killed. James Weldon Johnson, a well-regarded poet who served as director of the National Association for the Advancement of

21.9 Souvenir Postcard, Thomas Shipp and Abram Smith Lynching, Marion, Indiana
After witnessing the lynching of two black men, smiling men and women had their pictures taken as a memento. The two girls to the left clutch pieces of the victims' hair.

What does this souvenir postcard reveal about the ritual of lynching?

Colored People (NAACP) in the twenties, coined the term "The Red Summer of 1919" to describe the wave of vicious assaults against black communities that left at least forty-three African Americans dead. Some whites also used organized violence to prevent blacks from competing with whites economically. Mobs intentionally attacked thriving black business centers and middle-class homes in Tulsa, Oklahoma, in 1921, and in Rosewood, Florida, in 1923. A headline in a local Tulsa newspaper even helped mobilize whites by issuing the call "To Lynch A Negro Tonight."

In both the Tulsa and Rosewood race riots, African Americans fought back against their attackers, but enraged white crowds still burned both communities to the ground. Officials in Tulsa declared martial law and imprisoned one-half of the city's black population in internment camps. After gaining their freedom a few weeks later, one thousand families spent the winter in tents before beginning the huge task of rebuilding their community. In 1994 the Florida state government awarded survivors of the Rosewood race riot $150,000 each in monetary reparations. For the first time African Americans received compensation for past racial injustices, raising the question of whether victims of other racially motivated attacks deserved financial settlements.

With the states unwilling to prosecute the members of lynch mobs, the NAACP lobbied to make lynching a federal crime. Hoping to shock the rest of the nation into supporting an anti-lynching law, the NAACP used graphic images of lynchings in their pamphlets, parades, and posters. Southern congressmen, however, successfully blocked the passage of a federal anti-lynching bill by claiming that it violated the constitutional right of states to police themselves.

The lynching documented by this souvenir postcard reveals another key aspect of racial violence in the twenties. Although most lynchings took place in the South, the attack pictured here actually occurred in Marion, Indiana. Indiana was home to the largest chapter of the Ku Klux Klan in the 1920s, enrolling nearly one-half of the state's white male population even though only 3 percent of the state's population was black. The federal government had suppressed the original Ku Klux Klan during Reconstruction (see Chapter 15). The Klan revived in the 1910s, and in its second incarnation became a national organization that drew members from all parts of the country with membership fluctuating between three and six million throughout the twenties.

21.10 Ku Klux Klan in Washington, D.C., 1925
Klan members unfurl a giant American flag on the steps of the Capitol, equating patriotism with their call for white supremacy.

The new Klan organized their call for white Protestant supremacy under the banner of 100 percent Americanism, and their list of enemies included any group that threatened the traditional order. Anxieties aroused by blacks' wartime migration to Northern and Midwestern industrial centers, the Red Scare, women's suffrage, mass immigration, prohibition, and postwar strikes caused many conservative whites to listen sympathetically to Klan outbursts against blacks, Jews, Catholics, immigrants, radicals, feminists, and bootleggers. The 1925 Klan march in Washington, D.C. (**21.10**), exposed the group's national appeal. City officials required the forty thousand assembled Klan members to march from the White House to the Capitol without their masks. Like lynch mobs these Klan members were unafraid to reveal their identities as they proudly unfurled an American flag that championed the Klan's "patriotic" slogan of "native, white, Protestant supremacy." The march represented the high tide of Klan power in the twenties. As fears of social upheaval diminished, Klan membership rolls also decreased.

Why did membership in the Ku Klux Klan surge in the twenties?

Marcus Garvey

The African American community had long debated how to end racial attacks and segregation. In the 1890s Booker T. Washington squared off against W. E. B. Du Bois over whether blacks should focus first on improving their economic position or demanding political rights (see Chapter 18). Washington died in 1915 and in the 1920s Jamaican immigrant Marcus Garvey took up Washington's idea of empowering blacks economically. Garvey founded the **Universal Negro Improvement Association (UNIA)** to encourage economic self-sufficiency by creating black-owned businesses. The UNIA organized the Black Star Line, a short-lived capitalist venture that sold $5 stock certificates to finance the world's only black-owned and staffed fleet of steamships. Garvey's working-class followers, native-born African Americans and recently arrived immigrants from the West Indies, purchased stock enthusiastically. Poor management, however, forced the Black Star Line to dissolve in 1922.

Despite their shared message of economic empowerment, the black nationalist Garvey was much more militant than Washington. There was nothing shameful in being black, Garvey told his audiences, criticizing African Americans who used skin lighteners and hair straighteners to make themselves appear more white. God, Garvey said, "made no mistake when he made us black with kinky hair. We have outgrown slavery, but our minds are still enslaved to the thinking of the Master Race. Now take these kinks out of your mind, instead of out of your hair." Like Washington, Garvey rejected the political goal of dismantling Jim Crow that dominated other civil rights organizations. But unlike Washington, who wanted to improve life for blacks within the United States, Garvey spoke often of acquiring enough economic power to establish an independent African nation that could reunite the world's dispersed black peoples.

21.11 Marcus Garvey
The leader of the UNIA often appeared in full military dress to project an image of strength and racial pride. He challenged prevailing racial stereotypes of black subservience by adopting regalia usually worn by kings.

Pageantry was a hallmark of the UNIA. The group's meetings often included a uniformed male African Legion dressed in blue and female Black Cross Nurses in white. To give these gatherings an official air, participants waved flags that were "black for our race, red for our blood, and green for our hope," Garvey said. Black middle-class detractors ridiculed Garvey's tendency to appear, as pictured here (**21.11**), wearing a plumed hat and military regalia. These critics called him "a clown" in a "gaudy uniform" who led "big parades of ignorant people down the street selling pie in the sky." Garvey, however, believed that seeing a black man dressed as an aristocrat inspired confidence among his followers and challenged the stereotype of black subservience perpetuated by white America. The Justice Department took notice of Garvey's theatrics. Worried that his movement was sowing the seeds of a violent black rebellion, government spies monitored his activities.

Competing Visions: Debating Garveyism explores Marcus Garvey's vision for black America and the criticism he received from W. E. B. Du Bois, a leader in the NAACP who supported immediate integration. Some of Garvey's other black critics organized a "Garvey Must Go" campaign and helped the government convict him of fraudulent use of the mails in 1923. He served four years in prison and upon his release immigration authorities deported him. Without Garvey the UNIA collapsed. Garveyism, however, offered African Americans an important alternative to the integrationist vision of the NAACP and introduced separatist ideas that Black Power advocates would resurrect in the 1960s (see Chapter 27).

The Harlem Renaissance

Garvey based the UNIA in Harlem, a thriving African American neighborhood in New York City that became the hub of black politics and culture in the 1920s during the **Harlem Renaissance**. African

Why did Garvey elicit such strong emotions among both followers and critics?

Competing Visions

DEBATING GARVEYISM

Many of the traditional civil rights elite despised Marcus Garvey, whom they accused of swindling the poor of their hard-earned money and stirring up racial animosity within the United States. Garvey in turn accused light-skinned African American leaders of racial prejudice, arguing that they could not accept the dark-skinned Garvey as their equal. In the following excerpts Garvey lays out his reasons for urging black Americans to go "Back to Africa," while W. E. B. Du Bois, one of the light-skinned elites Garvey attacked, criticizes Garvey's vision. How does Garvey propose to stop "crimes against the race"? What portrait does Du Bois offer of Garvey?

In "The True Solution of the Negro Problem" (1922) Marcus Garvey argued that creating a homeland in Africa could solve the problem of racial violence in the United States.

We cannot allow a continuation of these crimes [lynching and disenfranchisement] against our race. As four hundred million men, women and children, worthy of the existence given us by the Divine Creator, we are determined to solve our own problem, by redeeming our Motherland Africa from the hands of alien exploiters and found there a government, a nation of our own, strong enough to lend protection to the members of our race scattered all over the world, and to compel the respect of the nations and races of the earth.

Do they lynch Englishmen, Frenchmen, Germans or Japanese? No. And Why? Because these people are represented by great governments, mighty nations and empires ... ever ready to shed the last drop of blood and spend the last penny in the national treasury to protect the honor and integrity of a citizen outraged anywhere. Until the Negro reaches this point of national independence, all he does as a race will count for naught, because the prejudice that will stand out against him even with his ballot in his hand, with his industrial progress to show, will be of such an overwhelming nature as to perpetuate mob violence and mob rule. ...

If the Negro were to live in this Western Hemisphere for another five hundred years he would still be outnumbered by other races who are prejudiced against him. He cannot resort to the government for protection for government will be in the hands of the majority of the people who are prejudiced against him, hence for the Negro to depend on the ballot and his industrial progress alone, will be hopeless as it does not help him when he is lynched, burned, jim-crowed and segregated. The future of the Negro therefore, outside of Africa, spells ruin and disaster.

Button won by Marcus Garvey supporters

In this 1923 biographical sketch, "Marcus Garvey," W. E. B. Du Bois views Garvey as misguided and inept.

Garvey soon developed in America a definite and in many respects original and alluring program. He proposed to establish the "Black Star Line" of steamships under Negro ownership and with Negro money, to trade between the United States, the West Indies, and Africa. He proposed to establish a factories corporation which was going to build factories and manufacture goods both for local consumption of Negroes and for export. ... When Mr. Garvey brought his cohorts to Madison Square Garden, and when, ducking his dark head at the audience, he yelled, "We are going to Africa to tell England, France and Belgium to get out of there," America sat up, listened, laughed, and said here at least is something new. ... Thus the Black Star Line arose and disappeared, and with it went some $800,000 of the savings of West Indians and a few American Negroes. ...

His African program was made impossible by his own pigheadedness. He proposed to make a start in Liberia with industrial enterprises. From this center he would penetrate all Africa and gradually subdue it. Instead of keeping this plan hidden and working cautiously and intelligently toward it, he yelled and shouted and telegraphed it all over the world. Without consulting the Liberians, he apparently was ready to assume partial charge of their state. ... [H]is talk about conquest and "driving Europe out," aroused European governments. ...

The present generation of Negroes has survived two grave temptations, the greater one, fathered by Booker T. Washington, which said, "Let politics alone, keep in your place, work hard, and do not complain," and which meant perpetual color caste for colored folk by their own cooperation and consent ... and the lesser, fathered by Marcus Garvey, which said, "Give up! Surrender! The struggle is useless; back to Africa and fight the white world."

How did Garvey and Du Bois link the U.S. Civil Rights Movement to international politics?

Claude McKay

"If We Must Die"

(1919)

If we must die, let it not be like hogs
Hunted and penned in an inglorious spot,
While round us bark the mad and hungry dogs,
Making their mock at our accursed lot.
If we must die, O let us nobly die,
So that our precious blood may not be shed
In vain; then even the monsters we defy
Shall be constrained to honor us though dead!
O kinsmen we must meet the common foe!
Though far outnumbered let us show us brave,
And for their thousand blows deal one deathblow!
What though before us lies the open grave?
Like men we'll face the murderous, cowardly pack,
Pressed to the wall, dying, but fighting back!

Countee Cullen

"Incident"

(1924)

Once riding in old Baltimore,
Heart-filled, head-filled with glee,
I saw a Baltimorean
Keep looking straight at me.
Now I was eight and very small,
And he was no whit bigger,
And so I smiled, but he poked out
His tongue, and called me, "Nigger."
I saw the whole of Baltimore
From May until December;
Of all the things that happened there
That's all that I remember.

American artists, photographers, musicians, and writers openly celebrated the distinctiveness of black culture. Many writers published their works in black magazines such as *The Crisis* and *The Messenger*. White literary figures like Carl Van Vechten also became patrons of the Harlem Renaissance, helping black writers publish their works with commercial presses that exposed white America to black artistic endeavors for the first time. The African American philosopher Alain Locke captured the creative impulse of the Harlem Renaissance in 1925 when he published *The New Negro*, an anthology of essays and poems by emerging literary voices. According to Locke the **New Negro** embodied a spirit of black racial pride and militancy that set a younger generation of African American artists and civil rights leaders apart from their predecessors, who had emphasized assimilating into white culture.

Harlem Renaissance writers took up themes previously absent from serious works of literature. Poet Langston Hughes discussed black Americans' aspirations; Jean Toomer's novel *Cane* explored the rhythms of working-class life in the countryside and city; Zora Neale Huston exposed the power of female sexuality in her novel *Their Eyes Were Watching God*; poet Countee Cullen confronted the psychological impact of racism; and Claude McKay celebrated manly violence in his poems and novels. The poems displayed here show how McKay, Cullen, and Hughes protested racial discrimination through their poetry.

The Harlem Renaissance also included the jazz music innovations of trumpeter Louis Armstrong, pianist and arranger Fletcher Henderson, and pianist and composer Ferdinand "Jelly Roll" Morton. Jazz was an original American musical style that melded African American and European musical traditions. White and black patrons flocked to Harlem jazz clubs to listen to black bands at venues like the Cotton Club and the Savoy, while white musicians nationwide formed jazz bands of their own. Thanks to new commercial radio stations and the growing phonographic record industry, jazz became so popular that Americans began calling the twenties **"The Jazz Age."** Jazz music, the white conductor Leopold Stokowski rejoiced, was "an expression of the times, of the breathless, energetic, superactive times in which we are living."

James Weldon Johnson's poem "The Prodigal Son" highlighted the dangers awaiting new arrivals unschooled in big-city ways, who flocked to Harlem's jazz clubs. In the two-dimensional drawing by African

In these poems how do responses to racism vary?

American artist Aaron Douglas that accompanied the poem (**21.12**), female dancers surround a young man and gyrate to the music provided by a hovering jazz trombone. The fragments of a dollar, playing card, and gin label evoke the temptations confronting this young man. Johnson's poem echoed the rhythms of sermons that folk preachers delivered to their Southern congregations who might be planning to go to Harlem, warning that these "sweet-sinning women stripped him of his money / And they stripped him of his clothes / And they left him broke and ragged / In the streets of Babylon."

As Johnson's poem suggested African Americans expressed conflicting views about jazz. Many artists celebrated the music's originality and exuberance. Like Southern preachers, however, the urban black middle class viewed jazz as "the devil's music," believing that its syncopated rhythms aroused sexual impulses and encouraged lewd behavior. Jazz clubs often served illegal alcohol purchased from organized crime rings, linking jazz music to the immoral lifestyle that many black middle-class prohibition advocates wanted to eradicate. The middle class preferred religious spirituals, a distinctive African American musical tradition that they felt projected a more respectable image of black culture to mainstream America.

Langston Hughes

"I, Too, Sing America"

(1925)

I, too, sing America.

I am the darker brother.
They send me to eat in the kitchen
When company comes,
But I laugh,
And eat well,
And grow strong.
Tomorrow,
I'll be at the table
When company comes.
Nobody'll dare
Say to me,
"Eat in the kitchen,"
Then.

Besides,
They'll see how beautiful I am
And be ashamed—

I, too, am America.

The literature of the Harlem Renaissance drew fire as well. Du Bois criticized novelist Claude McKay for depicting black working-class culture as a collection of pimps, petty criminals, drunks, and whores in his novel *Home to Harlem*. Du Bois lambasted McKay for reinforcing the negative stereotypes that white America held of African American culture, thereby undermining the possibility of using art to challenge the racial status quo. Defending New Negro aesthetics and the principle of artistic freedom, Langston Hughes countered, "We younger Negro artists who create now intend to express our dark-skinned selves without fear or shame. If white people are pleased we are glad. If they are not, it doesn't matter. We know we are beautiful."

21.12 *Prodigal Son,* 1927
Aaron Douglas's innovative angular style evoked the fast pace of modern life in an illustration that both portrayed and epitomized the artistic innovations of the Harlem Renaissance.

What competing views arose over the purpose of art during the Harlem Renaissance?

The New Woman

Women began the decade with a significant political victory when the Nineteenth Amendment gave them to right to vote in 1920. Female reformers expected newly enfranchised women to care deeply about issues affecting their gender, but the much-anticipated "women's vote" never materialized. Throughout the twenties Americans offered competing visions of women's proper place in American society. Former suffragists envisioned modern women playing an active role in politics. Popular culture, however, consistently defined the "new woman" as someone who kept herself thin, pretty, and lively for her husband.

Women in the Twenties

When women got the right to vote nationwide, an aging generation of feminists tried immediately to organize the female vote behind causes that particularly affected women. Black women had actively supported suffrage as a step toward politically empowering the African American community. Throughout the South, however, authorities used poll taxes, literacy tests, and intimidation to stop black women from registering to vote. The League of Women Voters, created by the National American Women Suffrage Association in 1920, drew up a list of issues that it expected to resonate among female voters including child labor, protective legislation for female workers, and cleaning up city politics. This list did not include demanding that the Nineteenth Amendment be enforced for black and white women alike.

Responding to studies that revealed high rates of infant mortality and women dying in childbirth, the League of Women Voters successfully lobbied Congress for the nation's first major social welfare measure to help impoverished women and children. The Sheppard-Towner Act (1921) offered eight years of matching funds to states for classes that taught poor mothers about nutrition, hygiene, and prenatal care. It also provided visiting nurses for low-income pregnant women and new mothers.

By 1929, however, it became clear that women did not vote as a bloc. Therefore despite evidence of the law's success, Congress did not renew the program. Rather than rallying to gender-specific causes, the best predictor of how a woman would vote was how her husband voted.

Feminists also failed in their effort to amend the constitution by adding an **Equal Rights Amendment** (ERA), a proposed constitutional amendment which stated that "equality of rights under the law shall not be denied or abridged by the United States or by any State on account of sex." The radical National Women's Party, chaired by Alice Paul, argued that such an amendment would eradicate in one fell swoop all the legal barriers that a dizzying array of archaic state legislation created for women. These laws, advocate Elsie Hill noted, denied a woman "control of her children equal to the father's; they deny her, if married, the right to control her earnings; they punish her for offenses for which men go unpunished," such as adultery. The moderate Progressive reformers who dominated the League of Women Voters, like future first lady Eleanor Roosevelt, worried that the Equal Rights Amendment might endanger the protective legislation for women that they had so carefully crafted in recent years, such as the maximum hour laws designed to shield mothers from overwork (see Chapter 18). They opposed the amendment, arguing that it was better to remove troubling laws individually, like the ones that prevented women from serving on juries or inheriting property.

Over the course of the decade, younger women displayed little interest in the social movements championed by their elders. Instead many women in their twenties and thirties focused on their economic prospects. Women made up 23.6 percent of the workforce by 1920, although they remained restricted to professions considered appropriate for their gender. During the decade clerical work as secretaries and telephone operators became primarily female occupations. Rapid expansion of corporate bureaucracies created a new need for office workers, a demand that the growing numbers of white female high school graduates filled. Women earned less than men, but companies were certain that married women made most of the purchasing decisions in American households. Product advertising in the 1920s, therefore, carefully targeted female consumers. *Images as History: Advertising the New Woman* explores how advertisements in the popular media also helped define the feminine ideal in the twenties.

What different strategies did women develop to improve their lives in the twenties?

Images as History

ADVERTISING THE NEW WOMAN

Popular advertising characterized the "new woman" as an efficient homemaker, devoted mother, high fashion sophisticate, and engaging spouse with the time and energy for a dizzying circle of friends and club activities. Manufacturing discontent about a woman's lifestyle and insecurity about her looks was another advertising strategy designed to get women to purchase products.

Advertisements that featured attractive women to entice potential customers, as in the Fisher car ad pictured here, reflected changing ideas about the ideal female body type. In the nineteenth century upper-class women proudly displayed their corpulence as evidence of their wealth and health. In the twenties, the popular media depicted the vigorous, alert modern woman as thin. But according to a 1928 study, only 17 percent of American women were both slender and over 5 feet 3 inches tall. How does this Fisher car ad both celebrate the new freedoms that women enjoyed in the twenties and perpetuate traditional stereotypes about women?

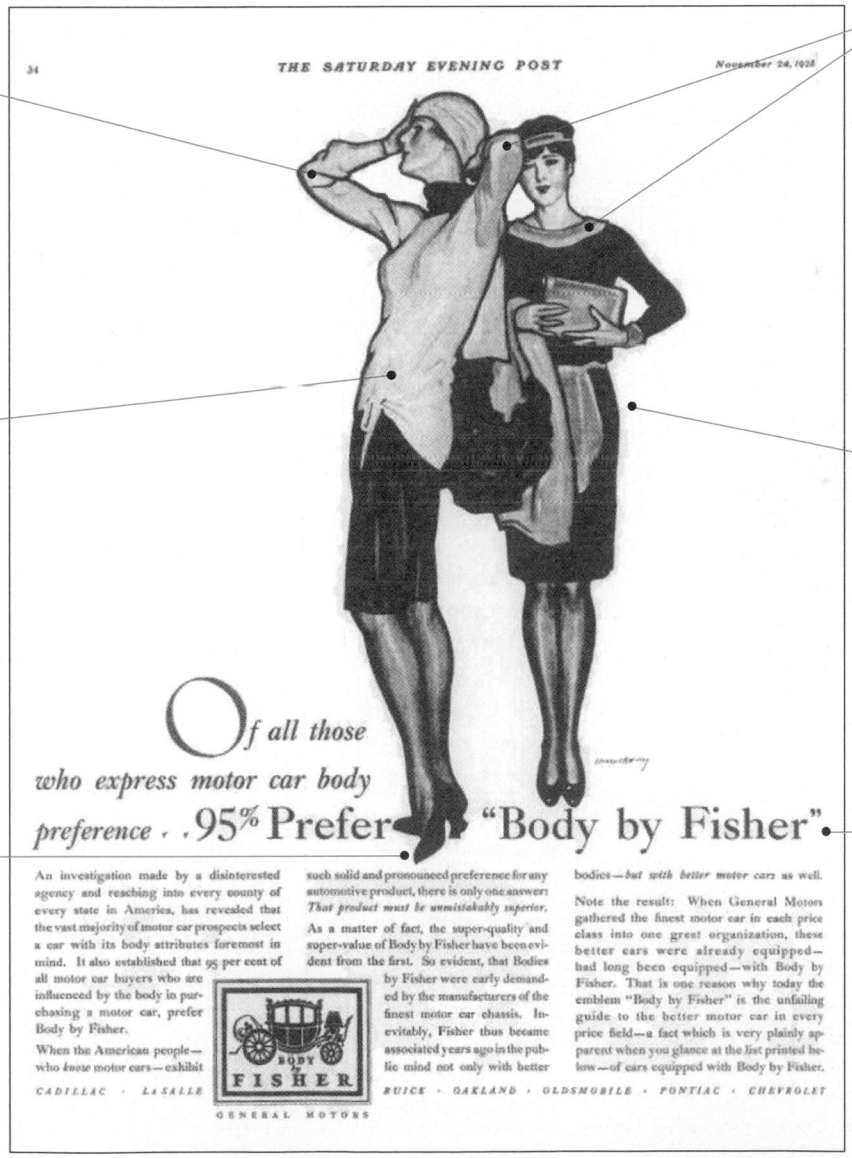

The slim Fisher girl appeared liberated from the confines of the home and the physical incapacity caused by too much weight. She seemed to be a modern woman on the move.

These tall, elongated figurines depicted an ideal female body that was slim and youthful with legs that formed a straight line from toe to thigh, pointed toes, and a giraffe-like neck. These proportions suggested the women were nearly 9 feet tall!

This female silhouette more closely resembled the body of an adolescent girl than a mature woman, encouraging a female preoccupation with dieting and self-denial that continues today.

The presence of the maid behind the Fisher girl indicates that she is rich as well as thin—an enviable combination to many women.

Most ads of the time displayed men with both feet firmly on the ground. This woman's off-balance pose with one knee bent suggested tentativeness and instability, putting limits on her independence and strength.

Her sleek body, like that of the car being advertised, served mostly as a commodity or decorative object suitable for a modern man.

"Body by Fisher"

How did the popular media define "the new woman"?

Margaret Sanger and the Fight for Birth Control

Advertisers promised that modern electrical appliances would give women more time to spend with their children, and women's popular magazines offered a plethora of articles on how to use this additional time to raise children properly. Birth control advocate and trained nurse Margaret Sanger viewed the mother's plight somewhat differently. Too many children, Sanger argued, ruined women's health and relegated them to the ranks of the poor. In her view providing women with information on safe and reliable contraception was more important than dispensing advice on how to raise children.

> "No woman can call herself free who does not own and control her own body."
>
> Birth control advocate MARGARET SANGER

In 1916 Sanger opened the nation's first birth control clinic in Brooklyn, New York, where she passed out flyers to advertise the benefits of contraception over illegal and dangerous back-alley abortions. For nine days Sanger dispensed information on diaphragms, condoms, douches, and withdrawal to women who waited in long lines to enter the clinic. The police then shut the clinic down and arrested Sanger for distributing information about birth control. Since 1873 the Comstock Act had prohibited sending information about contraception, abortion, or pornography through the mails, and by 1878 every state except New Mexico banned all means of circulating material about contraception. Sanger served thirty days in jail, one of many unsuccessful attempts to silence her. In 1929, after she spoke on birth control before the Harvard Liberal Club in Boston, the outraged mayor threatened to revoke the license of any hall that allowed her to speak again. In response Sanger appeared with her mouth bandaged before an audience in Boston's Ford Hall Forum (**21.13**). Her silent protest won headlines across the nation, helping Sanger publicize her cause even more widely.

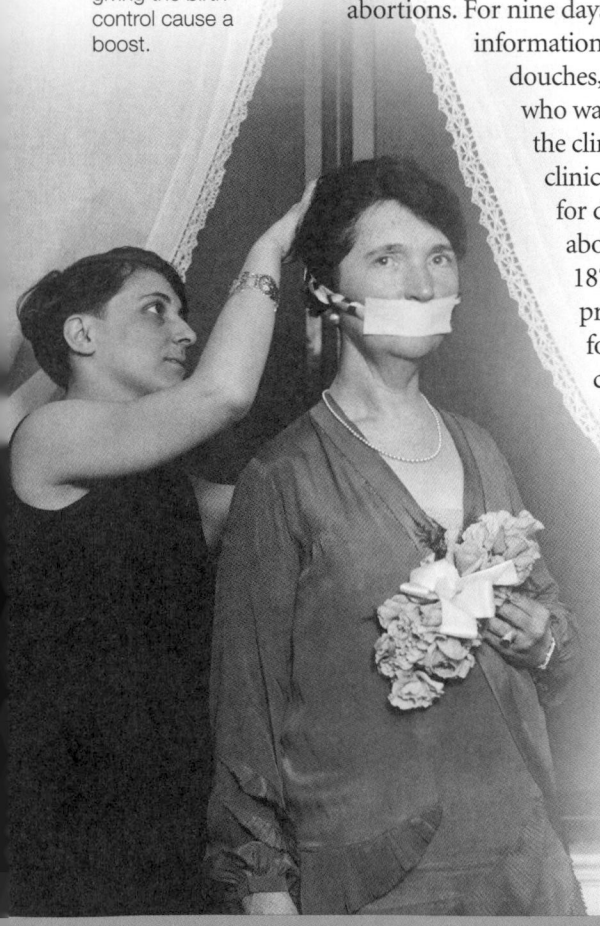

21.13 Margaret Sanger Protests When officials in Boston refused to let Margaret Sanger speak publicly about birth control, she appeared before a crowd with her mouth bandaged to protest their censorship. Her ploy garnered headlines across the nation, giving the birth control cause a boost.

By openly discussing birth control, Sanger made public the private contraception practices of middle-class couples. Poor mothers, she said, pleaded for her to share "the secret the rich have." Studies suggested that at least twice in their lifetimes, women living in poverty pulled their shawls over their heads to visit the five-dollar abortionist down the street. Sanger often told the story of Sadie Sachs (whose authenticity was never verified), a woman whom Sanger, as a young nurse, met when she accompanied a physician into the tenements to care for Sadie after she fell ill from a botched self-induced abortion. When Sadie begged the middle-class doctor to give her the information she needed to avoid another pregnancy, he replied, "Tell Jake to sleep on the roof." The next time Sanger saw Sadie, she lay in a coma dying from another abortion. Sanger used the story to personalize the extent of the abortion problem (nearly one million abortions that resulted in fifty thousand female deaths each year) and to dispel the misguided belief that no "decent" woman needed information about contraception.

Rather than counseling women to avoid sex, Sanger asserted that women had as much right as men to enjoy sexual intercourse without fearing for their lives. Contraception would not make women more promiscuous, she predicted. Once freed from the constant strain of childbearing, women would become more interesting spouses by developing their intellectual, political, and cultural interests much as popular advertising encouraged them to do.

Through her arrests, clinics, and public lectures, Sanger gradually helped change attitudes toward birth control. Although laws censoring information about birth control remained part of the legal code until the 1970s, enforcement became rarer and rarer. By the late 1920s thirty birth control clinics operated nationwide. **Eugenicists**, who wanted to improve the human race by controlling its hereditary qualities, also developed a strong interest in birth control. For Eugenicists contraception could prevent those they viewed as "unfit" from reproducing. Under their influence many states authorized compulsory sterilization of the institutionalized mentally handicapped, criminals, and epileptics until the 1960s.

What arguments did Sanger make to support her campaign for legal contraception?

Ensuring Peace: Diplomacy in the Twenties

Leaders in the birth control movement developed close ties with women's right groups in other countries, just one example of the global presence that Americans maintained throughout the twenties. Although the nation focused mostly on domestic concerns, international issues sometimes dominated the headlines. In 1920 the Senate refused to ratify the Versailles Treaty, which officially ended the war with Germany, or to join the League of Nations, which President Woodrow Wilson had championed to protect world peace. Rejection of Wilson's vision of collective security through the league did not signal a withdrawal from world affairs. American presidents Warren Harding and Calvin Coolidge tried instead to use disarmament and dollars to prevent armed conflict.

Disarmament

The high point of the disarmament movement came when Republican President Warren Harding convened the **Washington Conference (1921–1922)** in Washington, D.C., to negotiate a set of agreements that would limit naval arms. The conference also reaffirmed America's Open Door Policy (see Chapter 19) that kept Chinese trade open to all and secured pledges of cooperation among the world's leading military powers, including Britain, Japan, Italy and France.

Through the Washington Conference, Harding reshaped the political vision of his Democratic predecessor, Woodrow Wilson. Harding rejected Wilson's idea of using an open-ended commitment to the League of Nations to ensure world peace. He agreed with other Republicans who felt membership in this world body would unduly restrict America's ability to set its own foreign policy. Harding instead sought to prevent another war by convincing all major powers to disarm and to agree to mediation when disputes arose. Harding knew that Congress's penny-pinching mood meant certain rejection of any administration proposal to maintain a large military or embark on a major shipbuilding campaign. What better way to balance this domestic reality with the need to protect American shores from heavily armed naval competitors than by negotiating multinational disarmament treaties?

The White House and press referred to the meetings in Washington as a "peace conference" to cultivate the image that the negotiations would correct Wilson's blundering in Paris during the Versailles Treaty proceedings (see Chapter 20). The opening ceremonies underscored the symbolic comparisons that the Harding administration wanted to draw between the two international conferences. Delegates first attended the solemn burial in Arlington National Cemetery of an unidentified American soldier who had fallen on the battlefields of France. The Tomb of the Unknown Soldier was a memorial to all deceased soldiers who went missing or unidentified during the war. Next, Secretary of State Charles Evans Hughes opened the conference with a detailed public statement of his objectives, putting into practice the open diplomacy that Wilson had called for in the Fourteen Points and then quickly abandoned for closed door sessions in Paris.

Japan's 1905 victory in the Russo-Japanese War had signaled its emergence as the premier military power in East Asia. To contain Japan and Britain, which still controlled the world's greatest navy, Hughes proposed scrapping thirty American, twenty-three British, and seventeen Japanese battleships. One thrilled observer noted that Hughes had single-handedly sunk more British battleships "than all the admirals of the world had destroyed in a cycle of centuries." The Japanese, who unlike the British and Americans had only one ocean to patrol, accepted a naval tonnage ratio of 5:5:3 between the United States, Great Britain, and Japan. This meant that for every 5 tons of naval shipping that America and Great Britain maintained, Japan retained 3. Besides arms limitation, negotiations focused on settling potentially explosive issues in the Pacific. There American objectives included curtailing Japanese expansion in East Asia and preserving the Open Door in China. The American delegation met these goals, but at some cost. Japan accepted a smaller navy in

How did Harding's foreign policy vision differ from Wilson's?

21.14 ***Looking into the Black Hole of Ruin***
This 1927 political cartoon forecasts disaster if the world powers failed to reach a second naval disarmament agreement. In the cartoon the world is in disarray after a naval gun showers it with gun powder.

return for a pledge that the others would refrain from improving their naval bases or fortifications in the western Pacific. American naval experts warned that this concession would leave American Pacific possessions vulnerable to a future Japanese attack. Hughes, who doubted that Congress would approve funds to improve naval defenses, accepted the deal. The resulting Five Power Treaty (which included smaller tonnage limits for France and Italy) set a ten-year moratorium on battleship construction and limited the number of guns that ships could carry. The treaty, however, made no mention of limits for submarines, light cruisers, aircraft, or land forces.

The Washington Conference also negotiated an accompanying Four Power Treaty, in which France, the United States, Britain, and Japan agreed to respect one another's Pacific possessions and to consult if any dispute arose. The Nine Power Treaty was the conference's final achievement. In this agreement the above five nations and Portugal, the Netherlands, Belgium, and China all agreed to respect the Open Door in China, a policy advocated by the United States since the turn of the century (see Chapter 19).

The resulting agreements essentially protected the United States, Britain, and Japan from an aggressive naval attack on their borders. They left Britain in control of the European seas, gave the United States charge of the Americas, and recognized Japanese predominance in East Asia. For the time being, avoiding an arms race and maintaining the status quo served the interests of the world's major powers.

Calvin Coolidge, Harding's successor in the White House, continued the Republican effort to find alternative ways to maintain world peace. Leading powers met again in Geneva in 1927 to broker another disarmament pact. This 1927 political cartoon (**21.14**) offered support for the proceedings by showing a disheveled world covered with gunpowder from a recently fired naval gun. This time, however, the leading powers failed to reach an agreement. Coolidge's secretary of state Frank Kellogg had more success negotiating the **Kellogg-Briand Pact (1928)**, whose signatories renounced aggressive war as an instrument of national policy and agreed to resolve their disagreements through peaceful means. *Choices and Consequences: Preventing War in Europe* examines why President Coolidge chose to support a multinational treaty that outlawed war.

Wartime Debts

World War I revealed the importance of European trade to American prosperity, but in the twenties the politically sensitive question of securing repayment from Allied nations for American wartime loans threatened to undermine Europe's economic recovery. From 1914 to 1925 the United States had loaned the Allies nearly $10 billion to finance wartime purchases of American goods and to help rebuild war-torn Europe (**21.15**). In the 1920s the Allied governments urged the United States to cancel the loans. How, they asked, could America insist on repayment when the Allies had sacrificed a whole generation of men to the joint cause of defeating Germany? Americans had supplied money while the Allies gave their blood, they argued. The United States, the Allies claimed, could easily afford to cancel the loans as the country had profited enormously from the war.

Americans remained vehemently opposed to canceling the debt. "They hired the money, didn't they," retorted President Calvin Coolidge in the mid-twenties, expressing a common American view that Europe had a moral obligation to repay its debts. Coolidge did, however, agree to lower the interest rate on the loans, which reduced the total amount due by 43 percent. Further complicating the debate, the high American tariff enacted in 1922 made it difficult for Allied nations to sell manufactured goods in the United States, revenue that they needed to repay their war loans. Using a high tariff to protect American industries from foreign competition had tremendous domestic appeal and the United States refused to lower it.

The Allies consequently relied on reparation payments from Germany (authorized in the Versailles Treaty) to repay their U.S. war loans. This punitive aspect of the Versailles Treaty troubled many Americans, who viewed the $33 billion reparation bill imposed on Germany as excessive. The United States denied any connection between war loans and reparation payments, seeing the first

What benefits and drawbacks did the Washington Conference agreements offer the United States?

Choices and Consequences:

PREVENTING WAR IN EUROPE

In 1928 France invited the United States to sign a treaty renouncing war between the two nations, hoping to coax the American government into playing a more active peacekeeping role in Europe. President Coolidge faced several choices about how to respond. Americans had conflicting visions of the best way to avoid another war, and vocal supporters backed each option.

Choices

1. Adopt a non-interventionist policy that kept the United States out of European affairs.
2. Sign a nonaggression pact with France as the first step toward creating a formal defensive alliance that rebuilt the pre-WWI balance of power system in Europe.
3. Reject bilateral agreements and instead join the League of Nations.
4. Negotiate a multinational nonaggression pact.

Decision

Coolidge rejected any suggestion that the United States join the League of Nations but knew that the idea of outlawing war had strong appeal at home. Consequently he agreed to let Secretary of State Frank Kellogg meet with French Foreign Minister Aristide Briand to fashion a multinational nonaggression pact. By opening the treaty up to other nations, Coolidge avoided the impression that the United States was allying itself with France. The resulting Kellogg-Briand Pact was eventually signed by sixty three nations, including Germany and Japan.

Consequences

The Kellogg-Briand Pact proved popular with Americans because its vagueness allowed it to be all things to all people. Non-interventionists saw the pact as insulating the country from ever fighting another war overseas. They liked that the United States resolved to stay peaceful yet made no binding commitments to defend other nations. Internationalists, who wanted the United States to play a more active role in maintaining world peace, saw the treaty as the first step toward creating an American presence in international arbitration bodies like the World Court and the League of Nations.

"A Christmas Carol: Peace on Earth, Good Will Towards Man"

Continuing Controversies

What value did the Kellogg-Briand Pact have?
Critics called the treaty a "letter to Santa Claus" and dismissed it as "not worth a postage stamp," pointing out that the world's major powers signed the agreement but continued to arm their nations for war. The Kellogg-Briand agreement still allowed for wars of "self-defense," a slippery term that nations could easily manipulate. As if to prove the point, when the Senate enthusiastically ratified the treaty with only one dissenting vote, it added a reservation stating that preserving the Monroe Doctrine constituted self-defense. Others acknowledge that the treaty did not prevent World War II but point out that it gave the victorious nations a legal way to punish Nazi officials who were convicted of violating the Kellogg-Briand Pact in postwar war crimes trials.

21.15 American Loans to Europe, 1914–1925
The United States demanded that Europe repay loans given to help nations defeat Germany and rebuild after World War I.

as an honest debt and the latter as blood money. The Allies, however, refused to reduce the reparation bill as long as the United States insisted on collecting Allied war loans.

In 1923 skyrocketing inflation caused Germany to miss a reparation payment, and in retaliation France and Belgium occupied the Ruhr Valley, a German industrial center. This crisis threatened to undermine American economic interests abroad by thrusting Europe into recession. Having ruled out lowering the tariff or canceling Allied war loans as ways to foster Europe's economic recovery from the war, the United States resolved to help Germany make its reparation payments. Twice in the decade international committees of experts convened to discuss reparations. In 1924 Secretary of State Hughes sent Chicago banker General Charles G. Dawes and General Electric Company head Owen D. Young to Europe. The resulting **Dawes Plan** (1924) loaned Germany $200 million in gold to pay a reduced reparation bill and gave Germany more time to meet its debt. Certain that a German recovery was imminent, American bankers eagerly provided half the funds for the Dawes Plan, and made private loans and investments that helped Germany even more. Dawes went on to become vice president during Coolidge's successful reelection bid in 1924 and won the Nobel Peace Prize in 1925. In 1929 the Young Plan further reduced Germany's final bill to $8 billion and restructured the payment schedule once again.

American money kept the whole system afloat. Between 1923 and 1930 American banks loaned $2.6 billion to Germany; Germany made $2 billion in reparation payments; and the Allies repaid $2.6 billion of their American war loans (one-fifth of the amount owed). The "Global Flow of Reparation

How did lingering financial issues from World War I shape relations between the United States and Europe?

Payments" (**21.16**) details the journey that American money took around the world through Germany, France, and Great Britain until it landed back in American coffers. When the stock market crashed in 1929, American bankers drastically reduced their overseas loans. The withdrawal of American funds caused the whole arrangement to collapse. First Germany, then the Allied governments defaulted on their payments. In 1931 President Herbert Hoover successfully called for a one-year moratorium on all international debts. With the connection between reparation payments and war loans now formally acknowledged by the United States, the Allied governments canceled most of Germany's remaining reparation payments. By 1934 all governments except Finland defaulted on their wartime American loans. Finland was the only nation that finally repaid its entire debt of $8 million to the United States by 1969.

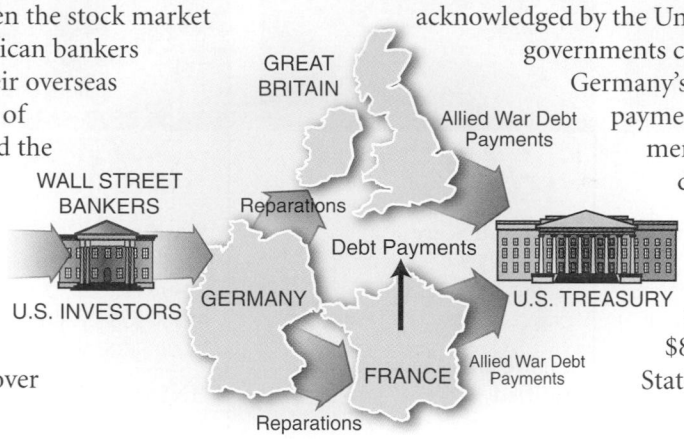

21.16 The Global Flow of Reparation Payments
American capital kept the reparation system created by the Versailles Treaty afloat in the twenties.

Conclusion

The 1920s proved a pivotal decade for the United States, a period when Americans both embraced and resisted modernity. The health of the automobile industry became essential to the country's economy, and cars refashioned daily life, inner cities, and the rural landscape. Welfare capitalism offered the promise of better industrial working conditions. Lindbergh's solo flight across the Atlantic captured the public's imagination and provided evidence of American technological prowess. Meanwhile multinational agreements that limited armaments and outlawed war promised to keep the world peaceful without entangling America in defensive alliances or the League of Nations.

In the twenties Americans embraced conflicting visions over what values should dominate the nation in the modern era. The Fundamentalist-Modernist cultural divide fueled the controversy that surrounded the Scopes Trial over teaching evolution in public schools. Temperance advocates viewed alcohol as a scourge that increased vice and corrupted politics. They led the nation into a thirteen-year experiment with prohibition that ended when the increase in organized crime and widespread flouting of the law convinced Americans that prohibition was unenforceable and misguided.

The birth control movement and Lost Generation writers challenged traditionally accepted notions of female sexuality in the twenties, but a consumer culture focused on improving appearance urged the "new woman" to continue thinking of her husband and children first. Fearing that unchecked immigration would infect American culture with foreign ideologies, especially communist ideals, the nation supported drastic immigration restrictions. Meanwhile the desire to protect a racial status quo based on white, Protestant supremacy fueled a resurgence of lynchings and the Ku Klux Klan. Embodying a new militant spirit, the New Negro clashed with traditional civil rights leaders over whether the solution to breaking down the barrier of racial discrimination lay in demonstrating artistic merit, economic self-help, or leaving the United States altogether.

Blinded by prosperity in the industrial sector, few Americans focused on farmers' difficulties or the growing concentration of wealth at the top in the twenties. All this changed quickly when the stock market crashed in 1929. Suddenly the plight of the common people became the nation's top concern.

Why did the United States intervene to settle European financial crises in the 1920s?

CHAPTER REVIEW

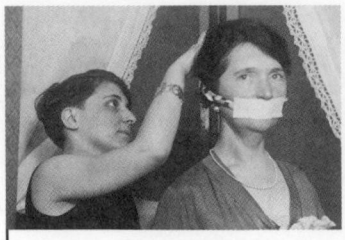

1916

Margaret Sanger opens first birth control clinic
Sanger champions birth control to improve female health and eliminate poverty

1919

First Red Scare
Anti-communist campaign destroys radical political organizations

Eighteenth Amendment ratified
Initiates era of national Prohibition

1921–1922

Washington Conference held
Disarmament becomes a major goal of American foreign policy

UNIA Black Star Line founded
Short-lived black-run steamship operation line embodies Marcus Garvey's ideal of economic self-help

Teapot Dome Scandal
Corruption weakens Harding's presidency

Review Questions

1. What features and controversies characterized America's transformation into a car culture in the 1920s? How did lifestyles and labor relations also change during the decade?
2. What symbolic significance did Americans attach to Charles Lindberg's solo flight across the Atlantic?
3. Compare the various manifestations of cultural conflict in the twenties. What similar impulses motivated Americans to enact prohibition, immigration restrictions, and laws prohibiting the teaching of Darwin's theory of evolution? What differing impact did these various reforms have on American society?
4. Why were the Harlem Renaissance and Marcus Garvey controversial?
5. Were the 1920s a time of political, economic, and social liberation for women? What traditional concerns or ideas remained intact?
6. How did the United States fashion a new role for the nation in world affairs in the twenties? What ideals informed American foreign policy in this era?

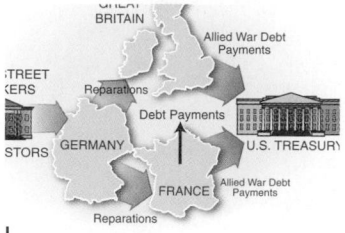

1924

Immigration Act of 1924
Severely reduces immigration and establishes nationality-based quota-system

Dawes Plan
United States uses financial aid to stabilize postwar European economies

1925

Scopes Trial
Highlights cultural conflict between religion and science

Ku Klux Klan marches in Washington, D.C.
White-instigated racial violence surges as the Klan becomes national organization

Publication of *The New Negro*
Harlem Renaissance gives rise to African American artistic outpouring

1927

Charles A. Lindbergh flies nonstop from New York to Paris
Reassures Americans that man and machine can coexist harmoniously

1928

Kellogg-Briand Pact
America uses world influence to secure global pledges of peace

Key Terms

Spirit of St. Louis The plane that Charles Lindbergh piloted on the first-ever nonstop solo flight from New York to Paris on May 21, 1927. **630**

Eighteenth Amendment (1919) Constitutional amendment that banned the sale, manufacture, and transportation of intoxicating liquors. **633**

Volstead Act (1919) Law that established criminal penalties for manufacturing, transporting, or possessing alcohol. **633**

Twenty-First Amendment (1933) Constitutional amendment that repealed the Eighteenth Amendment. **633**

Immigration Act of 1924 Law that allowed unrestricted immigration from the Western Hemisphere, curtailed all Asian immigration, and used quotas to control how many immigrants emigrated from individual European nations. **634**

First Red Scare (1919–1920) Period when the Justice Department arrested and deported alien anarchists and Communists suspected of trying to destroy American democracy and capitalism. **634**

fundamentalism An evangelical Christian theology that viewed the Bible as an authentic recounting of historical events and the absolute moral word of God. **636**

modernism A liberal Christian theology embraced in many urban areas that emphasized the ongoing revelation of divine truth. **636**

Harlem Renaissance An outpouring of African American artistic expression in the 1920s and 1930s. **638**

Universal Negro Improvement Association (UNIA) Organization founded by Marcus Garvey to spread his message of racial pride, economic self-sufficiency, and returning to Africa. **640**

New Negro Spirit of black racial pride and militancy that set a younger generation of African American artists and civil rights leaders apart from their predecessors. **642**

The Jazz Age Nickname for the twenties that reflected the popularity of jazz music. **642**

Equal Rights Amendment (ERA) A proposed constitutional amendment, which stated that "equality of rights under the law shall not be denied or abridged by the United States or by any State on account of sex." **644**

Eugenicists Those who wanted to improve the human race by controlling its hereditary qualities. **646**

Washington Conference (1921–1922) Meeting of world powers that resulted in agreements that limited naval arms, reaffirmed America's Open Door policy that kept Chinese trade open to all, and secured pledges of co-operation among the world's leading military powers. **647**

Kellogg-Briand Pact (1928) Treaty that renounced aggressive war as an instrument of national policy. **648**

Dawes Plan (1924) International agreement that loaned Germany $200 million in gold to pay a reduced reparation bill and gave Germany more time to meet its debt. **650**

CHAPTER 22

A New Deal for America

The Great Depression, 1929–1940

The Early Days of the Depression p. 656

A New President and a New Deal p. 662

> "I pledge you, I pledge myself, to a new deal for the American people,"
>
> FRANKLIN D. ROOSEVELT, 1932

When Franklin D. Roosevelt accepted the Democratic nomination for president in 1932, he promised to remember "the forgotten man at the bottom of the economic pyramid." FDR won the election and took office in the throes of the Great Depression, the most devastating and longest economic crisis in American history. Four years later the photographer Walker Evans traveled to Alabama to document the hardships of three struggling sharecropping families. While there he photographed Floyd Burroughs, who spent his days toiling in the cotton fields alongside his wife and children. For seven years, through the worst of the Depression crisis, Burroughs had struggled to provide the minimal basics for his family without any government help.

To gain public support for new government programs designed to help sharecroppers, the Farm Security Administration had commissioned this and photos like it to show Americans the faces of poverty-stricken farmers. Evans's portrait of the "forgotten man" aroused more than sympathy, however.

Americans had different visions of how the government should respond to the crisis, and throughout the decade political debate centered on whether and how much the government should intervene. Presidents Herbert Hoover and Franklin D. Roosevelt both championed initiative, freedom, and opportunity. They disagreed, however, over what government action preserved or destroyed these values. In the early thirties President Herbert Hoover, who preferred minimal government intervention in the economy, took a few historic steps by lending money to banks and businesses and helping farmers. More attuned to the mood of the public, Roosevelt initiated a broad array of public works programs and social reforms to satisfy the demand for direct government intervention in the economy.

Taken together, policy initiatives by Hoover and Roosevelt paved the way for a complete transformation of the role that the federal government played in American society. The New Deal did not end the Depression; that honor belonged to World War II. It was, however, one of the most important periods of legislative activity in American history.

Farmers, migrants, and industrial workers did not just passively wait for help during these hard times. They demanded a "new deal" from the federal government that alleviated the sufferings of common people. Organized labor and charismatic populist politicians on the left helped create a groundswell of support for active government intervention in the economy. The decade, therefore, was not just the story of unrelenting hardship. The era also had moments of triumph for ordinary Americans, like Burroughs, who found their political voice.

What emotions does Walker Evans's portrait of the "forgotten man" arouse?

Recovering from the Depression p. 666

A New Deal for Farmers p. 670

Reforms to Ensure Social Justice p. 674

The Early Days of the Depression

In 1928 the future looked rosy to most Americans, and even President Herbert Hoover believed that permanent prosperity was at hand. Americans venerated Hoover as the "Great Humanitarian" when he began his term. He left four years later amid bitter denunciations that he cared more for banks than for people, earning him the new nickname of the "Great Scrooge." The causes of the Depression were complex, giving rise to competing visions over what action, if any, the government should take and how far it should go to engineer an economic recovery. Hoover went further than any other president to date in offering federal assistance to businesses and farmers, but his awkward manner along with his refusal to approve direct governmental relief made him appear uncaring to most Americans by 1932.

Herbert Hoover

Herbert Hoover's personal story was a classic rags-to-riches tale that reaffirmed faith in the American Dream. Orphaned at nine years old, he later recalled that "my boyhood ambition was to be able to earn my own living, without the help of anybody, anywhere." This personal ethos shaped his lifelong political views.

Starting as a mine laborer working for $2.50 a day, by the age of forty Hoover was a respected engineer with millions in the bank. During World War I Hoover became the country's most famous humanitarian when he served as food administrator and organized relief missions to help feed a starving postwar Europe. Hoover's organizational talents and dedication to good works inspired such awe that the first time his name ever appeared on a ballot in 1928, he won, becoming president of the United States. Hoover was a poor public speaker, lacked charisma, and closely guarded his private life. But when he became president, he enjoyed immense popularity. After all, Hoover was a success in business, he had fed starving people, and he believed that people would do the right thing once the government showed them the way.

> "Just making money isn't enough."
>
> HERBERT HOOVER, explaining his decision to leave a lucrative engineering career for public service

Like most Americans, Hoover believed that able-bodied individuals should make their own way in the world. He maintained that if the government stepped in too often to manage the economy, individuals and businesses lost their initiative. For Hoover individualism meant more than individuals selfishly pursuing their own well-being. He felt that Americans and American business also had a responsibility to serve the community; like Progressive reformers he believed that self-interest often caused great harm to others (see Chapter 18). Hoover, however, did not share the Progressive desire to use government regulation to solve economic problems. Hoover envisioned a more cooperative, voluntary approach. Instead of passing more laws, Hoover wanted the government to organize meetings so industrialists, labor, and farmers could craft their own agreements to address issues such as overproduction, price wars, low wages, and strikes. The beginning of the Depression gave the country a chance to see if Hoover's voluntary and cooperative approach to economic problems could stem the crisis.

Economic Weaknesses in a Time of Prosperity

The economic downturn in 1929 took the country by surprise. However, a hard look at the twenties reveals that problems in the nation's economy existed even during the boom years, both in large-scale industries and on family-run farms.

Some industries, especially textiles and mining, suffered throughout the decade from overproduction and falling demand. By the end of the twenties, even

What qualities made Hoover a popular president when he was first elected?

automobile, construction, and appliance industries found it difficult to turn a profit. Cooling demand for automobiles soon rippled outward to industries such as steel and rubber. Some of the reasons for the slump lay in the unequal distribution of income in American society. From 1923 to 1929 corporate profits rose 62 percent, while workers' hourly wages increased by only 8 percent. With economic growth now linked to consumer spending, the limited purchasing power of working-class Americans contributed to the growing financial crisis.

High tariffs (taxes levied against imported products) kept the prices of foreign-made goods high, protecting American companies from overseas competition. Foreign countries responded by levying high tariffs against American goods, reducing overseas markets for U.S. companies. When demand for American-made goods declined at home, American companies were slow to lower prices. By the time they did, demand had fallen so dramatically that massive layoffs were inevitable. As the chances for making money in manufacturing lessened, investors stopped buying industrial stocks. This loss of capital further dampened manufacturers' efforts to recover their earlier momentum. Together, these problems revealed an ailing industrial sector.

More evident problems existed in the farming sector. Farmers' boom times had come during World War I, when high demand, generous prices, and easy access to credit induced many to expand their crop production. When the war ended and demand fell, farmers were left with debts, large farms, and falling crop prices. The long-term trend toward mechanized farming also contributed to the country's looming agricultural crisis. With tractors, farmers could plow and harvest more land on a daily basis. The ability to grow more crops, more easily, paradoxically hurt farmers because overproduction drove prices down even further.

Even before the Depression officially began, Hoover had devised a plan to help farmers escape the vicious cycle of overproduction and low prices that kept them from sharing in the prosperity of the twenties. The Agricultural Marketing Act (1929) created a Farm Board with the power to buy and store crops to reduce the harvest-time market glut, which lowered crop prices. In keeping with his ethos of self-help, Hoover expected farmers to do their part to keep agricultural prices high by growing less. These measures, however, were too little, too late. Unsure about what his neighbors would do, no farmer wanted to be the only one to reduce his crop and then suffer both low prices *and* a small harvest. The nation's farmers continued to plant crops in record numbers.

> "In the 93 years of my life, depressions have come and gone. Prosperity has always returned and will again."
>
> Oil Magnate J. D. ROCKEFELLER, doubting the need for government action

The Stock Market Crash of 1929

These underlying problems all laid the foundation for an economic downturn, but by themselves did not predict a worldwide depression. Any chances for a mild recession disappeared in the **stock market crash of 1929**, a ten-day period beginning on October 20, 1929, when the value of stocks plummeted as panicked investors sold off their stock in droves. This moment is usually considered the official start of the Depression.

Before the crash the stock market promised investors easy profits. When investors buy stock they own pieces of the company and receive dividends (their share of the profits). Normally the price of a share fluctuates in relation to the expected profitability of the company. By the late 1920s, however, speculators had taken over the stock market. Speculators did not care about holding on to their share purchases to earn dividends. Instead, they sold their shares as soon as the share price rose.

The epidemic of speculation created three key financial problems:

1. The influx of money into the stock market inflated share prices to such an extent that a stock's price soon bore little relation to the actual worth of a company.
2. Many speculators bought on margin, the name given to the short-term loans used to purchase stock, and planned to cover these loans by quickly reselling their shares at a higher price. When stock prices began to fall, too many investors could not pay these debts.

Why did farmers fail to prosper in the 1920s?

3. Many investors were speculating with other people's money, funds from ordinary Americans' savings accounts that banks used to finance speculative stock market purchases. That explains why, although only 10 percent of Americans actually owned stock, the life savings of millions disappeared in October 1929.

On Monday, October 20, 1929, the downward spiral began. Stock prices plummeted three days later on Black Thursday when a record 12.9 million shares changed hands. On Black Tuesday the following week, October 29, 1929, 16 million shares were traded and losses totaled $14 billion. That evening James Rosenberg, a Wall Street bankruptcy lawyer who was also a trained artist, etched an expressionist portrait of the chaotic scenes he had witnessed. Rosenberg's *Day of Wrath 1929* (**22.1**) captured the panic that swept Wall Street as

22.1 ***Oct. 29 Dies Irae (Days of Wrath) 1929***
James Rosenberg used apocalyptic biblical imagery of God's wrath as the world comes to an end to convey the panic that swept Wall Street after the stock market crashed. The photo shows investors racing to the New York Stock Exchange. [*Source* (left): James N. Rosenberg, American, (b. 1874). Oct 29 Dies Irae, 1929, Lithograph. Philadelphia Museum of Art, Lola Downin Peck Fund]

What factors led to the stock market crash in 1929?

investors raced to the New York Stock Exchange. In the lithograph the nation's financial institutions teeter on the verge of collapse, frightened crowds gather in the streets, and dark clouds hover over a sky filled with stockbrokers jumping to their deaths. Throughout the crisis rumors circulated about ruined investors committing suicide from the city's skyscrapers and ambulance sirens wailed continually as crews responded to false alarms.

Hoover's Response to the Depression

When the stock market crashed, no one knew that this was the beginning of a ten-year ordeal. The **Great Depression** lasted from 1929 to 1939, the most devastating and longest economic crisis in American history. In the 1920s the federal government played a relatively minor role in the economy, and conservative businessmen urged Hoover to keep it that way. Do nothing, the laissez-faire capitalists told the president, setting in motion a political debate over government intervention that would dominate the Depression era.

Rejecting the laissez-faire suggestion, Hoover envisioned the government fostering a spirit of teamwork that encouraged Americans to work together as the nation weathered the economic downturn. In keeping with his ideas of service-minded individualism, he brought the leaders of banking, industry, and labor to the White House and urged them to do their bit to keep the economy afloat. Responding to Hoover's plea, industry agreed not to lay off workers or cut wages, and labor leaders accepted a shorter workday to create more jobs. Hoover asked state governments to accelerate their road and public building projects to add jobs in their communities.

Hoover also stepped up hiring for long-planned federal construction projects including the Hoover Dam and asked Congress to extend the already existing tariff on manufactured goods to agricultural imports. Congress complied in 1930, raising tariffs to their highest level ever. When other nations retaliated with their own high tariffs, American companies and farmers lost overseas markets. As a result the world and the United States plunged deeper into economic depression.

In orchestrating this unprecedented federal response to an economic depression, Hoover stayed within limits acceptable to most conservatives. Most fiscal conservatives wanted government-built roads and a high protective tariff and preferred non-governmental solutions to economic problems. When it came to helping needy citizens directly, Hoover went no further than asking local governments and charities to assume their traditional role of distributing food and clothing to the poor. This stance surprised Hoover's Progressive supporters, given the president's previous triumph organizing a massive international relief effort to feed hungry Europeans after World War I. It was not a question of helping people, Hoover asserted. "It is solely a question of the best method by which hunger and cold shall be prevented," he explained. To Hoover the American tradition of self-help made relief the responsibility of local governments and charities.

How did Hoover respond to the initial economic crisis?

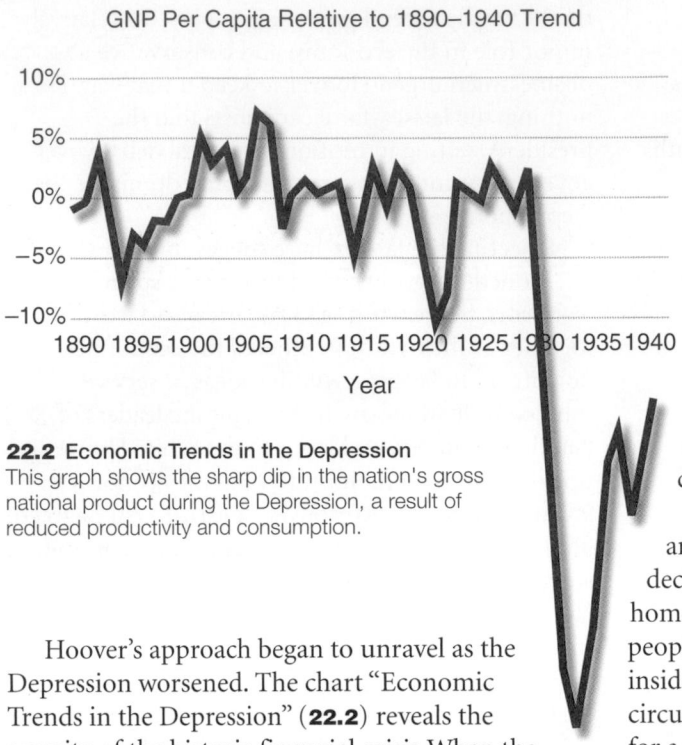

22.2 Economic Trends in the Depression
This graph shows the sharp dip in the nation's gross national product during the Depression, a result of reduced productivity and consumption.

Hoover's approach began to unravel as the Depression worsened. The chart "Economic Trends in the Depression" (**22.2**) reveals the severity of the historic financial crisis.When the crisis entered its second year, U.S. Steel announced a 10 percent wage cut. Other companies followed suit, and within ten days American business had slashed millions of workers' wages and begun massive layoffs. The nation's deepening financial woes convinced Hoover to lend federal money to businesses and states. This decision was a dramatic break from past practice. In previous financial panics and depressions, private bankers had put up the money needed for recovery and presidents had cut federal spending to ensure a balanced budget. In 1932, by proposing a direct economic role for the government in ending the Depression, Herbert Hoover—the man who wanted to decrease Americans' reliance on the government to solve their problems—went further than any previous peacetime president in similar circumstances.

By providing money to banks, insurance companies, farm mortgage associations, and railroads through the Reconstruction Finance Corporation (RFC) Act of 1932, Hoover helped institutions that were vital to the prosperity of any community. In its first year the government loaned more than $1.5 billion to these businesses, but little relief trickled down to workers. When critics pressured the president to provide direct help to those without work or food, Hoover responded with the Emergency Relief Act (1932), which lent money to the states for public works programs. Although his farm program, the RFC, and state loans failed to bring about recovery, Hoover had unknowingly set a precedent for direct governmental management of the economy that Franklin D. Roosevelt would continue and expand.

With the unemployment rate hovering around 20 percent in 1932, Hoover's popularity declined steadily. Shantytowns constructed by the homeless became known as "Hoovervilles" and people waved "Hooverflags" (empty pockets turned inside out) during their street protests. A well-circulated joke began with Hoover asking an aide for a nickel to call a friend from a public telephone. "Here," said the man, tossing him a dime, "call them both."

In the 1932 presidential campaign, Hoover faced off against Franklin D. Roosevelt (commonly referred to as FDR), a fifth cousin of Theodore Roosevelt. In sharp contrast to how he would govern, Franklin D. Roosevelt ran a fairly conservative campaign and let Hoover's missteps win him the election. One of those mistakes was the violent eviction of a group of war veterans from the nation's capital. Throughout the summer of 1932 the **Bonus March**, a two-month-long demonstration by forty thousand impoverished World War I veterans in Washington, D.C., transfixed the nation. The Bonus March ended violently when the army expelled the protesters, further damaging Hoover's popularity at a key moment during the 1932 presidential campaign. *Choices and Consequences: Evicting the Bonus Marchers* explores how Hoover lost control of the decision to evict the Bonus Marchers from the city and paid the consequences.

"We didn't admit it at the time, but practically the whole New Deal was extrapolated from programs that Hoover started."

REXFORD TUGWELL, key advisor to FDR

What innovative solutions did Hoover propose as the economic crisis continued?

Choices and Consequences

EVICTING THE BONUS MARCHERS

In 1924 World War I veterans had received a federal bond certificate (worth an average of $1,500) set to mature in 1945. In May, 1932, veterans arrived en masse in the nation's capital to demand immediate payment of this bonus. They set up a huge "Hooverville" of makeshift shacks and tents and staged continuous demonstrations on the Capitol steps. Hoover faced several choices about how to deal with the demonstration, depending on what interpretation of the protest he embraced.

Choices

1. Accept the veterans' argument that the government should pay the bonus immediately to alleviate their Depression-caused suffering.
2. Accept his advisers' view that the Bonus March was a communist-inspired plot to incite revolution and use force to thwart it.
3. Reject their claim but treat the veterans as essentially harmless, if misguided, citizens in desperate financial straits.

Decision

While many in the general public and press viewed the Bonus Marchers as down-on-their-luck citizens, Hoover grew convinced that they were a dangerous, radical force. After a skirmish between veterans and the local police in August, Hoover opted to send in troops with instructions to restore order.

Consequences

Once the troops were deployed, Chief of Staff General Douglas MacArthur exceeded Hoover's orders and decided to drive the veterans out of the city using tear gas and bayonets. Hoover never publicly revealed MacArthur's insubordination. When Democratic presidential candidate Franklin D. Roosevelt heard of the violent eviction, he reportedly told an adviser, "Well, Felix, this will elect me."

Continuing Controversies

Was the government right to use force to evict the Bonus Marchers?

To justify the eviction the White House mounted a furious public relations campaign that included false accusations of discovering dynamite in the main veterans' encampment. Some upper-class Americans applauded the government's actions, hoping to dampen any revolutionary impulse brewing among the poor. Many working-class and middle-class Americans saw their own destroyed lives in the smoldering ruins of the veterans' shantytown and turned against Hoover for refusing to aid men who had served the nation loyally.

The ruins of a Bonus Army encampment

Why was Hoover's choice to evict the bonus marchers significant?

A New President and a New Deal

FDR became president in 1933 during the lowest moment of the Depression with 25 percent of the workforce unemployed. Half of those with home mortgages had defaulted on their loans, and the entire banking system appeared ready to collapse. Empathy for the common people encouraged FDR to act, but so did fear that a social revolution might result if Washington did nothing for them. "I pledge you, I pledge myself, to a new deal for the American people," FDR had proclaimed during his campaign. FDR entered office dedicated to protecting America as a capitalist society, and his vision of government activism came under severe scrutiny from both sides of the political spectrum.

FDR: The Politician

"Only a foolish optimist can deny the dark realities of the moment," noted FDR upon taking office in 1933. If FDR had a mandate for anything, it was bold action. He met that expectation with the **New Deal**, an avalanche of legislation from 1933 to 1938 intended to promote economic recovery, reform American capitalism, and offer security to ordinary Americans. The chart "Key New Deal Legislation" (**22.3**) shows the most significant laws passed under Roosevelt's watch.

22.3 Key New Deal Legislation

1933	**Reconstruction Finance Corporation** continued Businesses and banks receive federal loans
1933	**National Industrial Recovery Act** Allows business to set price, wage, production codes
1933	**Agricultural Adjustment Act** Paid farmers to plant less to raise crop prices establishing key precedents in government farm policy
1933	**Civilian Conservation Corps** Employed young men in reforestation and construction
1933	**Public Works Administration** Construction projects provide work relief to poor
1933	**Glass-Steagall Act of 1933** Insures bank deposits; separates commercial and investment banking
1933	**Tennessee Valley Authority** Brings electricity to rural areas, stops devastating floods
1935	**Social Security Act** Guaranteed eligible workers a pension, unemployment insurance, aid to disabled and widows with dependent children
1935	**Wagner Act** Offers government protection to unions
1935	**Works Progress Administration** Extensive public works program employed 8 million ranging fromartists to construction workers
1938	**Fair Labor Standards Act** Established federal minimum wage and maximum hours per week

Having campaigned as a fiscal conservative who would balance the budget, FDR did not have a blueprint for ending the Depression when he came into office. He did, however, have a fairly well-shaped social philosophy. "He had a profound feeling for the underdog, ...a very keen awareness that political democracy could not exist side by side with economic plutocracy," according to one of his key advisers. "We are going to make a country," the president told a Cabinet member, "in which no one is left out." FDR sought advice for specific programs and regulations from the Brain Trust, a group of leading academics who served as presidential advisers in the early years of the New Deal. The Brain Trust wanted to revive the Progressive-era practice of using government regulation to solve economic problems and protect the common good (see Chapter 18). Brain Trust members Raymond Moley, Rexford Tugwell, and Adolf Berle diagnosed underconsumption as the main cause of the Depression, blaming the unequal distribution of income, the farm crisis, the rigidity of prices, and low wages as the key culprits. This cartoon (**22.4**) depicts the conservative complaint that the Brain Trust hurt the country with New Deal programs intended to correct these economic problems. Posing as doctors, these professors have anesthetized the country with propaganda. Now the patient lies on an operating table oblivious to the knives and drills about to destroy his body. Besides attacking the New Deal as a set of unwise experiments, the cartoon touches on conservatives' concern that too much government involvement in the economy (like too

How did the competing social philosophies of Hoover and FDR differ?

22.4 Conservatives Attack the New Deal
This 1934 cartoon mocks the Brain Trust for experimenting with the nation's well-being, implying that New Deal policy initiatives did more harm than good.

many pointless operations) would result in more harm than good.

In formulating his policies FDR leaned on another critical adviser: his wife. Eleanor Roosevelt served as the president's "eyes and ears" by traveling around the country and reporting to him what she observed. In her first year Eleanor Roosevelt traveled 30,000 miles visiting Americans where they worked and lived. In 1935 the Washington *Star* felt it newsworthy to print the headline "Mrs. Roosevelt Spends the Night at the White House."

Over time Eleanor Roosevelt became more outspoken in advancing causes dear to her heart concerning racial injustice and poverty. She invited prominent African Americans to the White House to talk directly to the president on civil rights matters. Eleanor Roosevelt's visible participation in political affairs set her apart from former First Ladies, who had mostly served as official hostesses at White House functions. Her activism opened up political opportunities for other women. There were many firsts for women in the thirties: first ambassador, first judge on the Court of Appeals, and first cabinet secretary, Secretary of Labor Frances Perkins.

Americans differed in their reactions to Eleanor Roosevelt's left-leaning political activities. Conservative detractors advised her to "stay at home and make a home for your husband." Her civil rights

"If it fails, admit it frankly and try another. But above all, try something."

FDR's approach to shaping the New Deal

activism particularly upset southern Democrats in Congress. She had equally ardent supporters, and consistently won a two-thirds approval rating in Gallup polls—often bettering her husband. Thousands of Americans wrote to her each week, to ask for financial help, or to praise her work.

Like his wife, FDR connected well with the public. Throughout his presidency FDR used weekly radio addresses that he called "fireside chats" to speak directly to the nation. After the president's death in 1945, people stopped Eleanor on the street to tell her how much "they missed the way the President used to talk to them," she recalled. "They'd say, 'He used to talk to me about my government.'" FDR was often photographed smiling and smoking from an elegant-looking cigarette holder (**22.5**), and the public found his visible cheerfulness refreshing.

FDR infused hope into a time of trouble and confusion. Yet little in his background suggested that he would understand the plight of common people. The only son of doting, wealthy parents who imbued him with tremendous self-confidence, the athletic, charming, and brilliant FDR attended Harvard and passed the New York State bar exam after just one year at Columbia Law School. In 1929 he became governor of New York. A personal tragedy in FDR's life, however, convinced the public that he understood what it meant to overcome adversity. In 1921 at the age of thirty-nine, FDR contracted polio. It left him partially paralyzed for the rest of his life, and in pain much of the time. His disability "made it possible for the common people to trust him to understand what it is to be handicapped by poverty and ignorance, as well as by physical misfortune," Secretary of Labor Frances Perkins noted.

22.5 FDR's Trademark Cigarette Holder and Smile
Most Americans found FDR's cheerfulness reassuring, and he inspired confidence in America's security and future prosperity.

What role did Eleanor Roosevelt play during her husband's administrations?

Managing Appearances

Although FDR benefited from people knowing that he had overcome a misfortune, he also believed that visual images of his handicap would convey the impression that he was weak and physically unfit for his responsibilities. FDR made a personal and political decision to conceal his paralysis. To hide his heavy leg braces, he wore extra long pants and had the visible portion painted black to blend with his shoes. He learned to stand upright by holding onto a cane with one hand and the arm of an aide, usually his son, with the other (**22.6**). He would then use his hips to swing his legs forward in a semiarch to give the illusion of walking. All of this required tremendous physical exertion. James Roosevelt later noted that he often had bruises on his arms from the force of his father's grip. Father and son disguised their physical effort by smiling and joking as they "walked" together before audiences.

Away from the crowds, aides carried FDR up stairs or from the car to a wheelchair. In public he often used his automobile as a prop to hide his disability, and by holding a bar installed in the backseat of an open touring car, he could pull himself up to address crowds. At one stadium rally a ramp was constructed so that the president's car could be driven onto the stage in the center of the field. FDR gave his speech without leaving the car.

The press obeyed White House rules that prohibited taking photos of the president in a wheelchair or being carried. As a result there are only two known photographs of FDR in a wheelchair. This self-censorship even extended to political cartoons, which never once depicted the president as incapacitated. Instead, these caricatures usually portrayed an energetic FDR running or jumping like this 1936 caricature from the *Kansas City Star* (**22.7**), in which a running FDR replicates Benjamin Franklin's kite-flying experiment to bring electricity to the rural poor.

22.7 FDR Running
Political cartoons never showed the president's physical disabilities. [Reproduced with permission of *The Kansas City Star* © Copyright 2007 *The Kansas City Star*. All rights reserved. Format differs from original publication. Not an endorsement.]

22.6 FDR Walking
Shunning his wheelchair, candidate FDR holds onto his son's arm as the two greet supporters during his first presidential campaign in 1932.

The Temper of the Poor: Passivity and Anger

Hoover kept his distance from common people and paid the price. FDR was a more astute politician. But what was the temper of the people he needed to help? Two competing images of the poor soon emerged. One emphasized their helplessness and suffering; the other saw them as teetering on the brink of revolt.

> "There is something about the first anniversary of your layoff which makes you feel more hopeless."
>
> A worker during the Great Depression

How and why did FDR manage his political image?

Countless government investigators detailed the plight of hardworking family men suddenly without jobs. "I find them all in the same shape—fear, fear driving them into a state of semi-collapse; cracking nerves; and an overpowering terror of the future," reported one social worker. Many Americans chose to suffer silently, making their own decisions about how to cope, sometimes blaming themselves rather than the Depression for their troubles. This portrait by Dorothea Lange (**22.8**) conveys this "quiet desperation" of the poor. In Lange's image an unemployed man grasps his empty tin cup and leans over the rail as if he is kneeling at a church altar praying for salvation. The man's plight is moving, but his passivity is also vaguely reassuring to those who feared angry demonstrations or social revolution.

As the Bonus March revealed, however, not all Americans were waiting patiently for conditions to improve. Federal investigator Lorena Hickok feared that a social revolution was brewing. "I still feel that vast numbers of unemployed in Pennsylvania are 'right on the edge,' so to speak—that it wouldn't take much to make Communists out of them," she concluded. The Communist Party hoped that she was right. Unlike Roosevelt and his conservative critics, Communists had no interest in saving capitalism. They instead hoped that the crisis would provoke a social revolt that ended all forms of private property. The 1930s are sometimes referred to as the "heyday of American Communism," as the party grew from seven thousand members in 1930 to a hundred thousand in 1939. Across the country Communists organized unemployed councils that blocked evictions from city apartments, mounted hunger marches, and reconnected gas and electricity lines for workers who had fallen delinquent in their bills.

Grocery store robberies were also common, although newspapers rarely reported these events. When the manager of a grocery store in Detroit denied a group of men credit, they ransacked his store. Witnessing the food riot, the novelist John Dos Passos wondered why the manager did not call the police. "If more people heard about affairs like this, there would be more trouble," the manager replied.

While the urban poor stole food, farmers organized public demonstrations to demand higher prices for their crops. Across the Midwest farmers disrupted food shipments by blocking highways with logs and pouring milk onto roads. When banks seized land, cattle, or farm machinery from farmers who defaulted on their loans, the police stood guard to ensure that public sales of the seized property went smoothly. At some farm auctions farmers devised an effective strategy to help their neighbors by offering only a penny for the property on sale. Nooses hung on barn doors at penny auctions warned prospective buyers that bidding on a farm family's possessions would not be a wise thing to do. "If anyone in the farmyard might be so ignorant of what was going on as to put in a serious bid, a suitably burly man would be likely to step up and put a hand on his shoulder with the words, 'That bid's a little high, ain't it?'" one farmer recalled.

22.8 "Breadline," San Francisco, 1933
The man's empty cup symbolized his pervasive hunger. His unthreatening pose created sympathy for his plight, while the militant poor provoked fears of social revolution.

What competing responses did the poor offer to the ongoing Depression?

Recovering from the Depression

"First of all," FDR stated in his inaugural address, "let me assert my firm belief that the only thing we have to fear is fear itself." These courageous words inspired confidence in the country's new leader at a time when financial institutions were on the brink of collapse. Jump-starting the economy involved restoring confidence in the banking system, putting people to work and keeping businesses afloat. Following Hoover's lead, FDR established a cooperative relationship between the government and business and provided federal money for banks and businesses. But FDR differed from Hoover in a major way: he was willing to provide jobs through extensive public works programs and to fund temporary direct relief to average citizens.

Revamping Banking and Financial Institutions

By the time FDR took office, Americans had lost nearly $2.5 billion in nine thousand bank failures. The new president declared an immediate bank holiday on March 6, 1933, that closed the nation's banks for a week. An obedient Congress quickly passed emergency banking legislation that allowed only banks with the Federal Reserve's stamp of approval to reopen. "I can assure you that it is safer to keep your money in a reopened bank than under the mattress," FDR told the public in his first fireside address. When the "holiday" ended, millions of Americans demonstrated their faith in the president by depositing more money than they withdrew in the weeks that followed. "Capitalism," a FDR adviser said later, "was saved in [those] eight days."

"It was the Government's job to straighten out this situation," FDR told radio listeners. His administration soon proposed more reform measures intended to inspire public confidence in the nation's banks. The Glass-Steagall Act of 1933 created the Federal Deposit Insurance Corporation (FDIC), insuring the accounts of small depositors in member banks. The FDIC still exists. The same legislation protected the deposits of ordinary Americans by separating investment and commercial banking so bank officials could no longer make speculative loans or stock purchases with depositors' money. This provision was repealed in 1999.

Finally, the New Deal tackled the problems caused by an unregulated stock market that had contributed to the crash of 1929. A series of laws established the Securities and Exchange Commission (SEC) and reformed the practices of buying and selling stock. The SEC required companies to disclose financial details to potential investors so they could make an informed stock purchase. The SEC also regulated the practice of buying stocks on margin.

Reforms in home mortgage lending practices probably had a more immediate impact on the lives of ordinary Americans than stock market reform. In 1933 forty percent of homeowners were on the brink of losing their homes to bank foreclosures. In response FDR created a program that refinanced one out of every ten home mortgages and spread the payments out over twenty years instead of the usual five. Designed to encourage Americans to purchase homes (and thereby give the construction industry a boost), the Federal Housing Authority (FHA), founded in 1934, offered insurance to private lenders who financed home mortgages for new homes. FHA backing allowed creditors to reduce the amount of the down payment required, lower interest rates, and lengthen the life of the loan. These government-supported initiatives helped form the modern mortgage lending practices that enabled the percentage of Americans who owned their own homes to increase by one-third over the next forty years.

Father Charles Coughlin

Many businessmen and bankers supported these reforms because they renewed public faith in the basic structures of capitalism. With internal battles dividing members, the Communist Party never mounted an effective challenge to the New Deal. Instead, the most influential dissenter on the left who challenged New Deal banking reforms was Father Charles Coughlin.

A popular "radio priest" from Detroit who spoke with an Irish brogue, Father Coughlin gave sermons

How did FDR reform the nation's banking and financial institutions?

on a weekly radio program that drew audiences of thirty to forty million. In 1934 Coughlin received more mail than anyone in the United States, including Roosevelt, most of it from adoring fans making donations to advance Coughlin's cause. Coughlin singled out financiers and international bankers as the culprits who caused the Depression. The popularity of Father Coughlin's relentless attacks on the elite helped push FDR increasingly to the left over the course of his first administration.

Following the lead of the Populists of the nineteenth century (see Chapter 17), Coughlin focused on how existing currency and banking arrangements helped bankers but hurt the common people. With currency in short supply, average citizens had to work harder to pay off their debts. Putting more money into circulation made sense in the midst of a depression, but bankers held firm to their old orthodoxy that all sound economies were based on the gold standard. Coughlin proposed a revaluation of the price of gold and the monetization of silver to allow the government to put more dollars into circulation. He also wanted to nationalize the banks to take money lending out of the hands of private bankers.

Coughlin initially supported the New Deal in sermons like "The New Deal Is Christ's Deal" and praised the president when he took the country off the gold standard in 1933. The president welcomed Coughlin's support at first but eventually grew tired of the priest's impromptu visits to the White House. As their relationship soured Coughlin began criticizing the administration for doing too little to rein in powerful banking and capitalist interests. Many of his followers begged him to reconsider his break with FDR, then withdrew from the short-lived third party that he headed. By 1938 Coughlin's star was in decline. His broadcasts became increasingly strident, filled for the first time with anti-Semitic diatribes against an imagined international Jewish banking conspiracy. He stayed on the air until 1942, when his bishop ordered him to cease all political activities.

Helping Industry and People

Besides shoring up banks, FDR also immediately sought ways to get people back to work. As the graph (**22.9**) reveals, FDR faced the most severe jobs crisis in American history. At first FDR followed in his predecessor's footsteps. The Reconstruction Finance Corporation, begun under Hoover's watch, continued to make loans and began buying bank stocks to help banks acquire the liquid capital needed to stay open. The National Recovery Administration (NRA), established by the 1933 National Industrial Recovery Act, was the cornerstone of FDR's efforts to devise a Hoover-like cooperative solution to the crisis. Temporarily suspending antitrust laws, the NRA established industrial boards for each sector of the economy that brought competitors together to set prices, production quotas, and wages. Architects of the NRA believed these industrial codes would stop manufacturers from cutting wages to subsidize lower prices, a practice that reduced the purchasing power of workers, contributing to overproduction and underconsumption.

When prices rose without any corresponding increase in wages, however, many Americans became unhappy with the NRA. Even the larger corporations that benefited from the price codes remained leery of the NRA, fearful that the agency might force them to negotiate with labor unions. To everyone's relief the Supreme Court declared the NRA unconstitutional in 1935, ruling that it delegated too much power

Unemployed Persons as a Percentage of the Civilian Labor Force

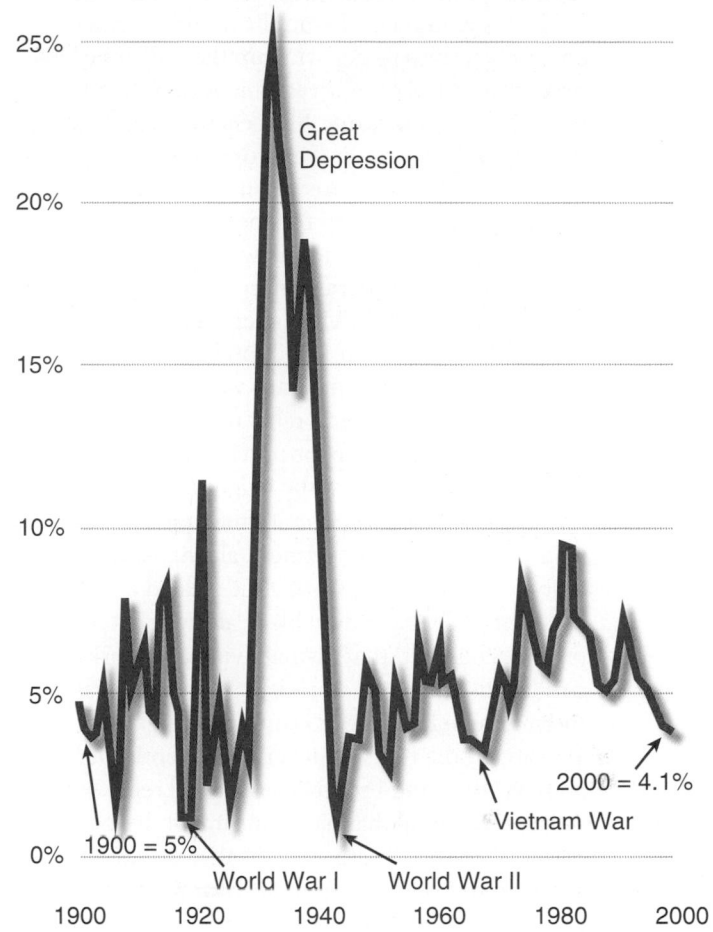

22.9 Soaring Unemployment This graph reveals the historically high unemployment rate during the Great Depression.

Why did New Deal banking reforms and relief programs generate criticism?

from the legislative to the executive branch and regulated more than interstate commerce.

FDR's reading of the public mood quickly encouraged him to depart from the policies of his predecessor and offer direct financial relief to individuals out of work. FDR encouraged Americans to write to him, and in their correspondence destitute Americans bared painful details of their poverty and often asked for specific items, such as a coat or shoes. Attuned to the widespread misery, FDR created the Federal Emergency Relief Administration (FERA), a federal agency that distributed more than $1 billion in three years.

Although many Americans were grateful for this help, applying for federal relief or a "dole" was a humiliating experience for previously self-sufficient working people. Even at the height of the Depression, accepting relief carried the stigma of personal failure. Conservatives felt that laziness, alcoholism, lack of ambition, and a poor work ethic created a class of indigent poor that would likely always exist. Progressives believed that dismal living and working conditions deadened workers' spirits, encouraging them to turn to drink or crime. Although they envisioned the roots of poverty differently, both conservatives and Progressives viewed relief with suspicion, fearful that handouts might discourage workers from trying to support themselves in the future. One could feel sympathy for the poor, therefore, and still worry about the negative consequences of distributing charity or relief.

Like many of his contemporaries, FDR disliked using federal monies to fund direct relief. FDR always preferred federal programs that employed the poor over those that simply handed out food or money. In 1935 he decided to stop providing direct cash grants to the needy. "To dole out relief in this way is to administer a narcotic, a subtle destroyer of the human spirit," FDR told Congress. From this point on the states handled relief while the federal government tackled the problem of putting "employable" persons to work.

Putting People to Work

To the dismay of conservatives and gratitude of the unemployed, the New Deal created a variety of programs, each administered by a different agency, which provided 15 million jobs over the course of the Depression. The Civil Works Administration (CWA), Civilian Conservation Corps (CCC), and Public Works Administration (PWA) were all founded in 1933. During its four-month existence, the CWA provided jobs that helped more than 4 million workers survive the winter of 1933–1934 and stemmed growing unrest among the unemployed. The CCC (which lasted until World War II) focused on giving economically disadvantaged young men a chance to gain work experience. It undertook major reforestation projects, constructed campgrounds, restored historic battlefields, and stocked rivers and lakes with fish. The PWA, run by Harold Ickes, funded public works projects, especially roads and buildings, to help revive the construction industry.

After deciding in 1935 to fund only work relief programs, Roosevelt created the Works Progress Administration. The WPA, managed by Harry Hopkins, was a major public works program that employed more than 8 million workers from 1935 to 1943, one-fifth of the workforce. Over the course of its existence, the WPA constructed 200,000 buildings and bridges along with 600,000 miles of roads. The agency also funded the arts, subsidizing painters and writers. Thanks to massive New Deal government spending on work-relief, and the subsequent strengthening of consumer spending power, the economy began gradually recovering in the mid-thirties.

"I gave the best part of my life to the American country, and I spent every cent I made here. They owe it to me to take care of me."

A worker, happily accepting a WPA job

"I wouldn't plow nobody's mule from sunrise to sunset for 50 cents per day when I could get $1.30 for pretending to work on a DITCH."

A Georgia farmer, criticizing the WPA work ethic

Who was helped by the wide range of New Deal work relief programs?

22.10 *Turning a Corner*
Like most Depression-era post office murals, this one celebrated workers as the backbone of the nation. "My interest," artist Joe Jones noted, "was in portraying man at work—his job before him—and how he goes about it with his tools—man creating."

Even permanent government agencies put Americans to work during the Depression. The Treasury Department, for instance, hired artists to decorate post offices throughout the nation. Edward Bruce, who directed the Treasury Department program, wanted to "enrich the lives of all our people" by making "beauty part of their daily lives" when they visited the post office. Post office murals celebrated Americans and their communities. In rural areas these murals projected images of prosperous farmers running family farms. Joe Jones painted *Turning a Corner* (**22.10**) for the Anthony, Kansas, post office, a mural that showed a farmer using a tractor to harvest a beautiful field of golden wheat before an approaching storm damaged his crops. The mural made no reference to the drought or dust storms that ravaged farms during the thirties, nor criticized farmers for overproducing and causing crop prices to fall. Instead, the artist celebrated the farmer for growing the food that fed the nation and romanticized his relationship with the land.

Americans had different visions of work relief, disagreeing over whether it was ruining or saving the country. For critics of work relief, the sight of WPA construction crews workers standing around talking instead of working led to jokes that WPA stood for "We Piddle Around." Farmers looking for day laborers also complained bitterly that federal work relief often paid more than working in the fields. Many WPA employees, however, saw government-provided jobs as a right that they had earned.

In a 1935 *Fortune* magazine survey, nearly 90 percent of lower-middle-class and working-class respondents answered yes when asked "Do you believe that the government should see to it that every man who wants to work has a job?" Roosevelt agreed to a point. FDR consistently tried to terminate these programs at the slightest sign of recovery in an effort to balance the federal budget, remaining true to his conservative fiscal values. The government reduced funds to the WPA when unemployment dropped in 1937 to 7.7 million from a high of 12.8 million in 1933. However, the sharp reduction in government spending, combined with new taxes and higher interest rates, all caused the fledgling recovery to grind to a halt. During the 1937 recession automobile production declined by 50 percent, steel by 70 percent, rubber by 40 percent, and the unemployment rate rose to 9.5 million (17 percent of the working population). With no federal funds for new relief projects available, New Jersey responded by issuing licenses to beg on the streets. The next year FDR restored public works funding.

What competing visions arose over New Deal work relief programs?

A New Deal for Farmers

New Deal public works programs dotted the American landscape with new roads, murals, and dams, a lasting legacy of Depression-era recovery efforts. Reforms in the agricultural sector also outlived the immediate crisis, part of FDR's commitment to save American capitalism and create "greater security for the average man than he has ever known before in the history of America." Americans from all walks of life, however, questioned the government's desire to help displaced farm workers.

Handling the Farm Crisis

Assisting farmers protected an American way of life with strong mythic connections to the nation's beginnings as a land of opportunity. Farmers received more direct aid than any other group during the Depression. The Agricultural Adjustment Act (AAA) of 1933 tried to ensure that farmers earned an adequate income by paying them to take land out of cultivation, which the administration hoped would cause crop prices to rise. When reducing acreage failed to sufficiently lower output, FDR approved a series of laws that established marketing quotas for each commodity. If farmers tried to sell more than their allotted quota, they were hit with a heavy fine.

The administration departed temporarily from this approach when the Supreme Court ruled the AAA unconstitutional in 1936. The Court decided that the tax on food-processing plants used to finance the acreage-reduction program was an illegal sales tax because the plants passed the cost of the program on to consumers. Congress passed a second AAA in 1938, but in the midthirties the problems facing farmers in some parts of the country had changed.

In the **Dust Bowl** drought and soil erosion caused massive dust storms across southern and plains states throughout the thirties. During one storm in May 1934, experts estimated that the winds transported 350 million tons of soil from the West to the East. Dust fell like snow on Chicago, the sun was obscured in Washington, D.C., and ships 300 miles out to sea reported dirt settling on their decks. This photo (**22.11**) captures an approaching dust storm carrying deadly amounts of dirt. Each storm left piles of dead cattle and wildlife in its wake as

22.11 "Approaching Dust Storm" Ominous clouds of dirt descend on a small town in Colorado during one of the dust storms that plagued the plains states and the southwest in the thirties. The storms killed livestock and kept people inside for days.

How did FDR tackle the problems of rural America?

residents barricaded themselves inside their houses with damp towels over their mouths to avoid suffocation or wore Red Cross-provided gas masks. But even these precautions did not completely prevent deaths from occurring when a duster hit.

To encourage better farming practices, the government began paying farmers in the Dust Bowl to plant soil-improving crops like legumes instead of traditional cash crops such as wheat, cotton, and tobacco that exhausted the soil. In one innovative program the government planted 220 million trees in a 100-mile-wide swath from Childress, Texas, to the Canadian border. These trees stopped western dust from traveling east by cooling the air and reducing the wind velocity of dust storms.

Bringing electricity to rural areas was another way the New Deal improved the quality of life for the rural poor. Most of the urban population had electricity to ease the daily tasks of pumping water and washing clothes, advantages available to only one in ten rural families in 1930. Begun in 1933, the Tennessee Valley Authority (TVA) was a government-owned utility company that provided thousands of jobs as it built a series of dams that generated power, provided flood relief, and created recreational lakes throughout the seven states (Tennessee, Alabama, Mississippi, Kentucky, Virginia, North Carolina, and Georgia) serviced by the Tennessee River. These areas soon enjoyed good fishing, cheap electricity, and relief from debilitating floods.

Government-sponsored low-interest loans enabled rural cooperatives to string electrical lines and manufacture power. "The women went around turning the switches on and off," noted an observer after one home received its hookup. "The light and wonder in their eyes was brighter than that from the lamps." By 1941 almost half of all American farms had access to electricity, a figure that rose to 90 percent by 1950.

Native Americans were another rural population aided by New Deal policies. Commissioner for Indian Affairs John Collier pressed successfully for passage of the 1934 Indian Reorganization Act that ended the land allotment policies sanctioned under the 1887 Dawes Act (see Chapter 15) and returned a degree of self-government to Indian reservations. The stage was set for a gradual rebirth of Native American cultures in the twentieth century.

Overall, New Deal subsidies succeeded in improving farm owners' lives. Farm income doubled from $2 billion in 1929 to $4.6 billion in 1939. Although farmers still made only 37.5 percent of what nonfarm workers made, farming had become a much more profitable business. These agricultural policies created some unexpected problems, however, by helping landowners at the expense of tenant farmers and farm laborers whose services were no longer needed once the government began paying farm owners to take land out of cultivation. The Farm Security Administration helped a small number of tenants purchase land, offering sharecroppers a way to break out of the traditional cycle of debt that bound them to landowners. But millions of tenant farmers and farm laborers, white and black, had to find their own way out of the crisis.

Hitting the Road

Nearly 2.5 million farmers hit the road in search of work in the thirties. Besides families traveling together in cars, nearly 250,000 teenagers, usually young men, "rode the rails" by hopping into empty railroad freight cars. Constantly on the move, these wandering youths found companionship in "hobo jungles" (homeless encampments) as they looked for jobs, lived off handouts, and sometimes stole to get by. Nearly 400,000 Americans left farming areas in the middle of the country and headed to California. Old trucks piled high with personal belongings flooded western highways, demonstrating how completely the United States had become a car culture. The United States was "the only Nation in the history of the world that ever went to the poor house in an automobile," quipped the cowboy humorist Will Rogers.

California state officials tried to discourage migrants. A billboard on Route 66, the main highway that migrants took west, near Tulsa, Oklahoma, proclaimed: "NO JOBS in California, If YOU are looking for work—KEEP OUT, 6 men for Every Job, No State Relief Available for Non-Residents." The signs did little to discourage families from heading to California.

The majority of new California arrivals settled into the nomadic life of the migrant worker, traveling an average of 516 miles during the six-month harvest season. Despite their dependence on migrant workers to pick the crops, native Californians did not welcome "Okies," the pejorative term for Dust Bowl refugees, with open arms. "Okies" were now subject to the same kinds of discrimination that migrant workers of Mexican, Chinese, Japanese, and Filipino descent had suffered for

How did displaced farmers act to improve their own lives?

22.12 Migrants Hit the Road Rickety trucks piled high with possessions and children filled western highways as families fled the Dust Bowl in search of employment elsewhere.

years in California. Migrant workers often lived in makeshift roadside camps near disease-ridden water ditches. When the government tried to create camps that offered migrants better and cleaner facilities, some Californians objected. Growers worried that concentrating migrant workers in government-run camps would make it easier for them to organize unions and strikes. Other Californians believed that improving living conditions would draw even more displaced farmers to their state.

In 1935 California-based photographer Dorothea Lange began taking photographs for the Resettlement Administration to document the extent of migrant workers' suffering and arouse the public's sympathy. This photo (**22.12**) shows a father from Arkansas changing the tire on his truck as he and his seven children followed the crops in Oklahoma and Texas. "We'll be in California yet," he proclaimed. Lange was renowned for her ability to take photographs that revealed her subjects' true feelings. Left lame by polio, Lange believed that her own disability made strangers trust her. Her photographs, discussed more fully in *Images as History: Migrant Mother, an American Icon*, had a distinct political purpose: to cement public support for migrant worker aid programs.

Repatriating Mexican Immigrants

Reducing competition from immigrants seeking work was another way that the government tried to help native-born farm workers. In 1929 the government effectively ended legal immigration from Mexico for the duration of the Depression to protect jobs for American citizens. Foreshadowing today's debate over the benefits and drawbacks of immigration, California officials argued that alien workers held jobs that should rightfully go to native-born Americans. Large-farm owners disagreed, predicting that they would face a serious labor shortage if they lost their traditional workforce since few Americans wanted these jobs.

Anti-immigration forces prevailed. Faced with the offer of a free trip back to their original homes (financed by the United States and Mexico) or the option of staying in a country where employment options had dwindled, thousands of Mexican workers accepted repatriation. Local and federal officials arrested and then deported others who had entered the country illegally. With the advent of the New Deal, immigrants' interest in voluntary repatriation dwindled. New Deal agency regulations made legal aliens eligible for food relief, although most public works programs gave jobs only to citizens. The deportation of undocumented workers continued. Overall approximately 415,000 Mexicans left the United States during the 1930s, both voluntarily and involuntarily.

"Social change is a difficult thing in our society unless you have sentiment."

President FRANKLIN D. ROOSEVELT

What happened to Mexican immigrants during the Depression?

Images as History

"MIGRANT MOTHER," AN AMERICAN ICON

In March 1936 the photographer Dorothea Lange entered a makeshift migrants' camp and saw a thirty-two-year-old woman sitting with four of her seven children and all the family's possessions. Taking six quick pictures, she jotted down a few notes about the family: "Destitute in pea pickers' camp, Nipomo, California, because of the failure of the early pea crop. These people had just sold their tires in order to buy food. Of the 2500 people in this camp most of them were destitute."

Lange's final portrait, "**Migrant Mother**," was a masterpiece. The viewer has the sense of intruding on an intensely personal moment, but Lange made no apologies for invading this woman's privacy. "She asked me no questions," the photographer later recalled. Instead, she "seemed to know that my pictures might help her, and so she helped me." When these photographs appeared in the *San Francisco News* in 1936, relief authorities immediately sent food to the entire camp of starving pea pickers. In later years Florence Thompson, the subject of "Migrant Mother," tried to suppress the diffusion of this photograph because she felt that it stigmatized her as poor. As she lay dying of cancer in 1983, however, her children successfully used the image to raise funds for their mother's medical expenses.

This initial photograph did not send the clear message that Lange wanted. In subsequent photos she focused on the despair of the mother and her small children rather than their general poverty.

The father was nowhere in sight, conveying either the comforting possibility that he was out looking for work or the discomforting suggestion that he had abandoned the family.

"Migrant Mother series, no. 2"

The presence of an older daughter raised potentially troublesome questions about when the woman began having children, why she continued to have so many, or why the teenager was not working to help the family.

In her next shots, Lange carefully framed out the open luggage and trash to erase any suggestion that the family lacked discipline.

"Migrant Mother series, no. 6"

Because they wanted their photographs to arouse public sympathy, government photographers always depicted the migrants as heroic victims. They were never shown smiling, angry, or in any way responsible for their misery.

The mother clearly wants to love and care for the children who lean on her, but her anxiety severs her from them emotionally and leaves her alone with her thoughts.

Lange's composition suggests "a sort of anti-Madonna and Child," wrote one critic.

What was the purpose and impact of Dorothea Lange's migrant farmer photographs?

Reforms to Ensure Social Justice

In 1935 the New Deal moved beyond measures intended to help the nation recover from the Depression to policies designed to correct basic inequities in American society and provide security to ordinary Americans. Reforms protected unions, guaranteed many elderly a government pension, established a minimum wage for factory workers, and abolished child labor. The momentum for these New Deal reforms came from the growing strength of left-leaning politicians, unions, and senior citizens who were unafraid to press the popular president to adopt their vision of a more just society.

The Challenge from Huey Long: "Share Our Wealth"

Roosevelt's move to the left toward the end of his first administration was partially a response to the combined popularity of Father Coughlin (see page 000) and Senator Huey Long. Before he became a senator, Huey Long was an adored, although corrupt, governor of Louisiana who provided free school textbooks, built much needed roads and hospitals, and curbed the power of the state's oil industry. "They do not merely vote for him," a reporter wrote of Louisianans in 1935, "they worship the ground he walks on."

Long supported the New Deal at first, but his dissatisfaction with the pace of change and his own political ambitions caused a break with FDR. As an alternative to the New Deal, Long proposed a **share our wealth** plan to redistribute money from the rich to the poor. Long wanted to limit every person to $1 million in income and $8 million in capital investments each year. The government would confiscate all other personal income and corporate profits and redistribute $2,000 annually to every American family. Besides offering Americans a guaranteed income, Long also championed old-age pensions, expanded veterans' benefits, a shorter working day, and government support for education. He created a Share Our Wealth Society and claimed a membership of 5 million, promising to make "every man a King."

Long argued that under his plan the rich would still enjoy a life of luxury, and even published a budget for a family of four on $1 million a year to show that they could easily afford $10,000 of jewelry each season and a new $100 suit a day. Yet even the great fortunes amassed by the richest Americans were too small to support the kind of program Long proposed. Despite the flaws in his plan, Long successfully tapped into public anger at the rich, whom many blamed for causing the Depression, and long-standing resentments about the concentration of wealth in the hands of a few. Long never had a chance to challenge FDR as a third-party candidate, however, because a disgruntled man who detested Long assassinated him on the steps of the Louisiana state capital in the fall of 1935. "I wonder why he shot me," Long asked before he died, a question the assassin, killed on the spot by Long's bodyguards, could never answer. *Competing Visions: Sharing the Wealth* explores the Depression-era debate over redistributing income.

Social Security

Alongside the larger-than-life personas of Huey Long and Father Coughlin stood Dr. Francis Townsend, an unassuming sixty-six-year-old physician who organized a campaign for old-age pensions in 1933 after seeing three old women outside his house in Long Beach, California, rummaging through the trash. The combined activism of these three men helped push FDR to the left in 1935. The outpouring of support each enjoyed convinced FDR that the time was right to create a comprehensive social-welfare system that protected the aged, the unemployed, and those unable to care for themselves.

Townsend's call for government pensions for the elderly struck a nerve, setting in motion a powerful

> "It is hard to be old and not have anything."
>
> A woman from North Dakota, writing to Roosevelt

How did critics from the left shape the social justice programs of FDR's second administration?

Competing Visions

SHARING THE WEALTH

Should money be redistributed from the haves to the have-nots? During the Depression, many Americans answered a resounding "yes." Below are two views, reflecting different visions of how income redistribution might affect the future of American capitalism and democracy. What justification or objection does each give for redistributing wealth throughout the population?

In this 1935 radio address, Senator Huey Long outlines his proposal to redistribute wealth from the rich to the poor.

We find not only the people going further into debt, but that the United States is going further into debt.... And with it all, there stalks a slimy specter of want, hunger, destitution, and pestilence, all because of the fact that in the land of too much and of too much to wear, our president has failed in his promise to have these necessities of life distributed into the hands of the people who have need of them....

But we have been about our work to correct this situation. That is why the Share Our Wealth societies are forming in every nook and corner of America ...

Here is what we stand for in a nutshell:

Number one, we propose that every family in America should ... have a home and the comforts of a home up to a value of not less than around $5,000 or a little more than that.

Number two, we propose that no family shall own more than three hundred times the average family wealth, which means that no family shall possess more than a wealth of approximately $5 million—none to own less than $5,000, none to own more than $5 million.

Number three,... We propose that no family will have an earning of less than around $2,000 to $2,500 and that none will have more than three hundred times the average less the ordinary income taxes, which means that a million dollars would be the limit on the highest income.

We also propose to give the old-age pensions to the old people, not by taxing them or their children, but by levying the taxes upon the excess fortunes to whittle them down, and on the excess incomes and excess inheritances, so that the people who reach the age of sixty can be retired from the active labor of life ... We also propose the care for the veterans, including the cash payment of the soldiers' bonus. We likewise propose that there should be an education for every youth in this land and that no youth would be dependent upon the financial means of his parents in order to have a college education.

In the following letter to Eleanor Roosevelt, a woman from Columbus, Indiana, protests that government-distributed relief robbed hardworking honest men to help "good-for-nothing loafers."

Dec. 14, 1937

Mrs. Roosevelt: ... We have always had a shiftless, never-do-well class of people whose one and only aim in life is to live without work. I have been rubbing elbows with this class for nearly sixty years and have tried to help some of the most promising and have seen others try to help them, but it can't be done. We cannot help those who will not try to help themselves and if they do try a square deal is all they need and by the way that is all this country needs or ever has needed: a square deal for all and then, let each one paddle their own canoe, or sink .... As for the old people on beggars' allowances: the taxpayers have provided homes for all the old people who never liked to work, where they will be neither cold nor hungry: much better homes than most of them have ever tried to provide for themselves. They have lived many years through the most prosperous times of our country and had an opportunity to prepare for old age, but they spent their lives in idleness or worse and now they expect those who have worked like slaves, to provide a living for them and all their worthless descendants.... There is many a little child doing without butter on its bread, so that some old sot can have his booze and tobacco: some old sot who spent his working years loafing around pool rooms and saloons, boasting that the world owed him a living..... During the worst of the depression many of the farmers had to deny their families butter, eggs, meat, etc. and sell it to pay their taxes and then had to stand by and see the dead-beats [who qualified for relief] carry it home to their families by the arm load, and they knew their tax money was helping pay for it.... Is it any wonder the taxpayers are discouraged by all this penalizing of thrift and industry to reward shiftlessness, or that the whole country is on the brink of chaos?

What competing images of the poor do Long and this Indiana woman offer?

22.13 Three Steps to Security
This 1936 poster deliberately emphasized the monthly check workers would receive during retirement, not the payroll deductions that would reduce their take-home pay to help finance immediate pensions for the elderly.

grassroots movement. For many working-class Americans their final years had always been a steady decline into poverty. Unable to work due to age, illness, or the unwillingness of employers to hire them, most relied on family members or charities to survive. The plight of the aged assumed crisis proportions when Depression-era bank failures swept away the savings of many older Americans. Townsend clubs, formed to promote government pensions for the elderly, barraged Congress with petitions signed by 10 million supporters, sending a clear message to the president and legislators in Washington, D.C.

Roosevelt responded. In drafting the bill that provided pensions for the elderly, he attached some controversial measures. Unwilling to take the political risk of voting against extremely popular pensions for the elderly, many conservative congressmen ended up grudgingly voting for a law that also provided unemployment benefits, assistance to the disabled, and aid for dependent children.

FDR wanted to help the "**deserving poor,**" needy Americans legitimately entitled to public support, a category open to differing interpretations. What made someone deserving of aid in the new social security system? This poster (**22.13**) urging Americans to apply for their old-age benefits clearly noted that only industrial workers working for a salary or wage were eligible for the new pension program. The system did not cover agricultural and domestic workers until 1950, a concession to southern and agricultural business interests who claimed they could not afford the mandatory employers' contribution to their employees' Social Security accounts (employers paid half). The Social Security Act of 1935 also set the following criteria for its other categories of aid: being laid off (not fired for cause) from an industrial job and being physically disabled or a widow (not an unwed mother) with children to raise.

The Social Security pension system operated along the same lines as private insurance by collecting premiums from individual subscribers in the form of payroll taxes. The public embraced Social Security as a system that simply returned these earlier deposits to retirees. Retired workers, however, began receiving checks in 1940, clearly too soon for these recipients to have paid enough to cover the costs of their pension benefits. Ida May Fuller, a retired legal secretary, received the nation's first Social Security check for $22.54 after paying a total of $24.75 in payroll taxes. She lived until the age of one hundred, collecting more than $22,000 in Social Security checks before she died in 1975.

Supporting Unions

Political pressures from the left and empathy for the poor had encouraged Roosevelt to create the Social Security system. These same forces influenced the president as he faced a different set of choices concerning the standoff between business and labor. His desire to curtail political challenges from the left and solidify his voter base by building a new coalition that included unions encouraged Roosevelt to choose the side of labor in this simmering industrial dispute. Business leaders' open hostility to

Who was considered part of the "deserving poor" in the new Social Security system?

New Deal relief and public works programs also prompted FDR to ally himself with labor in 1935. When FDR proposed a heavy tax on the rich (again inspired by Long), the business elite denounced the wealthy president as "a traitor to his class."

FDR openly mocked his opponents when running for reelection in 1936. "I should like to have it said of my first Administration that in it the forces of selfishness and of lust for power met their match. I should like to have it said of my second Administration that in it these forces met their master," declared Roosevelt in his last campaign speech before defeating the Republican candidate, Kansas governor Alf Landon. The general public's antipathy to the rich was captured perfectly in this photo (**22.14**) by Dorothea Lange of a gas station in Kern County, California, which displayed a sign declaring "This is your country, don't let the big men take it away from you" next to the free air pump.

Roosevelt's actions matched his antibusiness rhetoric. Throughout the great strikes of the nineteenth century, the federal government had usually sided openly with industrialists to break workers' movements. Thanks to important legislation passed during the New Deal, the federal government suddenly became labor's friend.

The National Industrial Recovery Act (1933), the same law that created the NRA, provided the first hint of things to come by declaring that workers had the right to organize and bargain collectively. Labor officials often referred to this section of the law, 7a, as the "Magna Carta" of organized labor because it recognized a right that many industrialists still refused to acknowledge. When the Supreme Court declared the National Industrial Recovery Act unconstitutional, FDR took a historic step by signing the Wagner Act (1935), a law sponsored by Senator Robert Wagner (D-NY) to increase the purchasing power of workers by giving them the power to negotiate for higher wages. The Wagner Act created the National Labor Relations Board (NLRB) to supervise unions' elections for their collective bargaining agents. The law prevented employers from firing or blacklisting workers who joined a union, or infiltrating unions with spies. With this government protection, the union movement exploded. Between 1933 and 1941, union membership rose from 2.9 million to 8.7 million workers.

In 1938 FDR went even further with the Fair Labor Standards Act, which established a national minimum hourly wage (set initially at twenty-five cents, rising gradually to forty cents), set maximum hours for the workweek (forty-four hours), and outlawed labor by children under sixteen (with some exemptions, such as newspaper carriers). Aimed at industrial workers, the act excluded agricultural and domestic workers. FDR again demonstrated political savvy in maneuvering the bill through Congress. FDR attached the controversial wage and hours measures to a bill prohibiting child labor, knowing that few congressmen would vote against such as a popular measure.

22.14 This Is Your Country
This sign reflected the general resentment toward the rich that encouraged Roosevelt to attack business and support unions in 1935.

How did government support of unions change during the 1930s?

The Resurgence of Labor

Government regulation gave crucial support to unions, but the task of building a successful labor movement lay with workers. Overcoming workers' fears that they would lose their jobs if they joined a union posed a significant hurdle for all organizers. When the United Auto Workers (UAW) took on Henry Ford, a strident opponent of unions, organizers passed out handbills assuring workers that "the Wagner Bill is behind you! Now get behind yourselves!" Ford had offered the best terms of employment with his five-dollar-a-day wages and eight-hour workdays in the 1910s and revolutionized American industry with his introduction of the assembly line (see Chapter 18). By the thirties, however, workers in unionized auto plants had much higher wages and guaranteed benefits.

Ford ruled his plants with an iron fist, and when five labor organizers tried to pass out handbills to workers entering the Ford motor plant in Dearborn, Michigan, in 1937, forty members of the company's private security force attacked them. As seen in this photo (**22.15**), the Ford guards unleashed a flurry of punches and kicks, throwing each man face first onto the pavement before tossing him down a set of stairs. One man's back was broken, and another recounted how two men held his legs apart while the security guards kicked him repeatedly in the groin.

A few news photographers managed to smuggle out photographs of the attacks, thwarting the attempt by Ford's security force to confiscate their film. The shocking images caused a public outcry. The NLRB ordered Ford to stop interfering with union organizing, but securing industry-wide recognition of the UAW required more dramatic action at Ford Motor Company and elsewhere. Ford's antiunion intimidation had worked in the past, but by the midthirties, many workers were ready to fight back. In 1934 alone 1.5 million workers participated in eighteen hundred strikes.

Support from the government helped the labor movement grow but so did a new vision of who could join a union. The **American Federation of Labor (AFL)** was a craft-based organization that accepted only skilled workers, like carpenters or cigar makers, who practiced a trade. Excluding unskilled workers from the labor movement made little sense once assembly-line mass production began to dominate the manufacturing process. John L. Lewis, head of the United Mine Workers, argued that unions needed to find room for unskilled workers, no matter their race or ethnicity, to become truly powerful. When the AFL

22.15 Ford Security Guards Attack Labor Organizers
Ford's guards pull a labor organizer's jacket over his head to immobilize his arms as they pummel him. Signaling new support for the labor movement, the federal government intervened after these photos were published.

Why were the CIO's innovative organizing and strike tactics effective?

expelled Lewis for trying to organize these groups, he formed the **Congress of Industrial Organizations (CIO)**, a new type of labor organization that organized workers within an entire industry rather than by their trade orientation.

The AFL and CIO offered competing visions of how to construct a successful union. The CIO organized all workers in the automobile industry into one union, rejecting the AFL idea of creating separate unions for auto mechanics, welders, and so on. The CIO warned workers not to fall for their employers' old tricks. "The man working beside you, be he Negro, Jew or Pollock [Polish] is a working man like yourself ... You work together—FIGHT TOGETHER," one CIO labor organizer told steelworkers. "We were making a *religion* of racial unity," noted another CIO official. In sharp contrast to its enlightened racial views, the CIO made no effort to recruit women. The CIO instead joined with the AFL in urging women to voluntarily leave their jobs so men could have them. Within two years of its founding, the CIO boasted 3.7 million members as compared to the 3.4 million workers who belonged to the AFL.

Besides recruiting unskilled and minority workers into its ranks, the CIO reversed the labor movement's indifference to electoral politics. Now that the government was actively supporting unions, keeping sympathetic officials in public office became a major CIO goal. "Every worker owes it to himself, his family, his union and his country to go to the polls himself, and to see that his fellow workers go too, to cast their votes in organized fashion for the labor-endorsed candidates," a CIO newsletter told meat packinghouse workers in 1938. Recruiting members became easier when the CIO devised new methods of collective action that bore results. Automobile workers seized the spotlight when they pioneered a new and effective tactic: the sit-down strike. During a **sit-down strike** workers occupied a factory to paralyze production lines and prevent strikebreakers or management from entering the building. Because sit-down strikes caused the employer, as well as his striking employees, to lose money, this tactic brought employers to the negotiating table more quickly than traditional picket lines. Nearly 400,000 workers participated in sit-down strikes in 1937 alone, causing *Time* magazine to comment that "sitting down has replaced baseball as the national pastime."

When the UAW took over the main General Motors plant in Flint, Michigan, in 1937, the governor of Michigan and FDR (who had just received 84 percent of the votes cast by organized labor and 81 percent from low-income voters in the 1936 presidential election) refused to authorize the use of troops to retake the plant. By standing with the strikers, FDR solidified his support among the working class. Within six weeks General Motors capitulated and recognized the union. Ford held out until 1941, when he finally recognized the UAW. Having lost the battle on the ground, the automobile companies fought back through the courts. In 1939 the Supreme Court ruled that sit-down strikes were illegal seizures of property.

The union movement's successes in the automobile, steel, and textile industries markedly improved the daily lives of workers, but even with these gains, workers had few material comforts in comparison to laborers today. By 1941 factory workers earned an average of $1,449 a year, enough for a married father with two children to buy two dresses for his wife every year, shoes for his children every other year, and a coat for himself every six years while living in a five-room apartment and driving a used car.

A New Deal for African Americans

FDR's turn to the left also included a new willingness to advance the cause of civil rights. As late as 1932 the majority of black northern voters (few African Americans could vote in the South) remained loyal to the Republican Party and Herbert Hoover. Four years later Gallup polls estimated that 76 percent of northern blacks had voted for FDR. What had FDR done to deserve this newfound loyalty among black voters? At first glance it seemed very little.

During his first administration, the power that southern Democrats held in Congress prevented FDR from proposing any civil rights legislation or guaranteeing equal treatment by New Deal agencies. He knew Congress would never approve such measures, and he needed southern legislators' support to pass New Deal legislation. Still, New Deal programs offered African Americans more federal and state aid than they had ever received before. Southern blacks usually received smaller relief payments than whites, but before 1933 most state agencies had given them nothing. In the 1936 presidential election, Democratic campaigners emphasized the benefits that the New Deal had brought to the African American community, proclaiming on billboards: "Do not bite the hand

Why did many African Americans switch their allegiances from the Republican to the Democratic Party in the 1930s?

22.16 "There's No Way Like the American Way" The photo captured the irony of trumpeting America as the land of opportunity for whites, while needy black citizens stood in line at a soup kitchen in 1937.

that feeds you." An African American preacher offered the same message to his congregation, telling them, "Let Jesus lead you and Roosevelt feed you." Eleanor Roosevelt's well-known interest in civil rights also helped draw many black voters to FDR.

When black voters abandoned the Republican Party for the Democratic Party, they joined the **New Deal coalition**, a political partnership formed in the midthirties among liberals, trade unionists, Catholics, and northern blacks that redrew the nation's political map. The strength of the New Deal coalition increased the president's freedom to pursue his legislative agenda. In the newly elected 75th Congress, the president did not need a single southern or Republican vote to pass New Deal legislation.

As the black vote gained new importance to the Democratic Party, the administration became more responsive to African American demands. During FDR's second term public works projects hired more black workers. FDR also appointed the first black federal judge and convened an unofficial Black Cabinet to investigate civil rights abuses and advise him on racial matters. Nonetheless, racial discrimination continued to plague the lives of African Americans in the thirties. In Margaret Bourke-White's 1937 photo (**22.16**), black residents wait for emergency relief during the Louisville, Kentucky flood, while above them, a billboard poster shows a carefree well-dressed white family driving a car. The image symbolically showcased the racial divide that remained intact throughout the decade.

The Supreme Court Weighs In

FDR's popularity made it difficult for opponents to organize a sustained campaign against him. In 1936 he won reelection with 61 percent of the popular vote, carrying every state except Maine and Vermont in the Electoral College. Clearly the majority of Americans supported the New Deal. The same could not be said of the Supreme Court. Of the nine justices, four consistently opposed New Deal legislation and two remained unpredictable. By 1937 the Court had declared two major pieces of early New Deal legislation, the NRA and AAA, unconstitutional. With lawsuits against the Wagner Act and Social Security Act on the Court's docket, Roosevelt decided to act.

Suggesting that advanced age (rather than conservative ideology) was hampering the work of the Supreme Court, FDR proposed increasing the number of justices to a maximum of fifteen by adding one new justice for every one over seventy who had served more than ten years on the Court. With the conservative bloc all over seventy, Roosevelt's plan would either increase the size of the court or force the older justices to retire. Either way FDR would have a chance to appoint judges who were sympathetic to the New Deal.

The campaign to expand the size of the Court soon exposed the limits of FDR's power. Dubbed the "Court-packing scheme" by detractors, the clash consumed a whole session of Congress and ended

What role did the Supreme Court play during the New Deal?

with a resounding defeat for FDR. FDR always maintained that though he lost the battle, he won the larger war with the Court. As Congress debated his proposal to add more justices, the Supreme Court surprised everyone by upholding the constitutionality of the Wagner Act and the Social Security Act. Over the next few years, deaths and retirements gave FDR the chance to appoint seven justices.

The fallout from the Court struggle had some negative repercussions for the president, however. Although the Court began upholding New Deal legislation, the battle alienated progressive Republicans who had previously supported the president and pushed conservative Democrats into an alliance with like-minded Republicans. In 1938 Republicans narrowed the Democratic majority in Congress. The bipartisan conservative coalition was now strong enough to thwart any new reform initiatives and to begin cutting expenditures for New Deal recovery programs. The New Deal thus ground to a halt in 1938, after five years of public policy initiatives, experiments, and reforms.

What did the New Deal accomplish over those five years? It alleviated much human suffering, fashioned an institutional apparatus that strengthened the capitalist market structure, and provided economic security to ordinary Americans where none had existed before. New Deal reforms bolstered financial institutions, protected the housing market, kept farmers afloat, improved industrial wages, and created old-age pensions. This legacy outlived the Depression crisis, shaping the lives of countless Americans for decades to come. FDR's legislative program reached workers, farmers, African Americans, and migrant workers, forging a new, permanent relationship between the federal government and common people. Despite the New Deal's accomplishments, the nation's financial crisis continued. It took unprecedented government spending during World War II to end the Depression.

Conclusion

The New Deal was one of the most important periods of legislative activity in American history. Before 1932 a stroll down Main Street or a visit to a private home would have uncovered little evidence of the federal government. The situation by the end of the decade could not have been more different. By 1940 the American landscape was dotted with the highways, campgrounds, tunnels, and bridges constructed by government-sponsored work relief projects. The federal government subsidized farmers, guaranteed pensions, regulated the stock market, insured the life savings of small bank depositors, gave industrial workers unemployment insurance, protected unions, and for the first time, set a federal minimum wage. The federal government was now an active presence in the lives of millions, provoking a debate that continues into the twenty-first century over the proper role of the government in the economy and who is deserving of help.

Clashes that pitted unions against industry, Mexican immigrants against government officials, and migrant farmers against native Californians roiled the nation during the Depression. The decade was more than unrelenting hardship or confrontation, however. The era also had moments of triumph for ordinary Americans. African Americans were now valued members of the New Deal coalition. Industrial unions attracted many new members and won benefits with their new tactic of sit-down strikes.

By the late thirties international affairs began to intrude on the mostly insular vision that Americans had maintained throughout the decade. The outbreak of war in Europe helped the American economy recover, but forced the country to confront the question of whether to join another overseas war. Eventually, Japan's attack on Pearl Harbor in 1941 made this decision for the United States. For the next four years Americans would focus on winning World War II.

Why did the New Deal end in 1938?

CHAPTER REVIEW

1929

Stock Market Crashes
Signals beginning of Depression

1932

Reconstruction Finance Corporation established
Hoover's effort to help businesses and banks with federal loans

Bonus March
Public outrage over army's eviction of protesting veterans from Washington, D.C.

1933

FDR inaugurated president
Restores faith and confidence in government and capitalism

Review Questions

1. What were the causes of the Great Depression?
2. What groups of people did the New Deal help? What new role did the New Deal establish for the federal government in their lives?
3. How did the government publicize the plight of farmers and Dust Bowl refugees in the thirties? Why did these images become an enduring symbol of Depression-era suffering?
4. What factors account for labor protests in the thirties, a time when one might expect workers simply to be grateful for any job on any terms?
5. What conflicting visions prompted the right and left to criticize the New Deal?
6. What was the short-term versus long-term significance of the New Deal?

1933–1938

New Deal created
Slew of federal agencies, laws, and reforms restructure American capitalism and provide economic security to citizens

1935

Share Our Wealth Movement
Senator Huey Long's proposal to redistribute wealth pushes FDR to the left

CIO founded
Organizes workers by industry rather than by trade

1936

Dust Bowl crisis worsens
Drought, soil erosion result in major ecological disaster

FDR wins reelection
New Deal coalition formed

CIO begins sit-down strikes
Wins union recognition, but later ruled unconstitutional

1937

FDR tries to reform Supreme Court
Proposal failure exposes limits of FDR's power

Social Security payroll taxes begin
Establishes funding mechanism for federal pensions

Key Terms

stock market crash of 1929 A ten-day period beginning on October 20, 1929, when the value of stocks plummeted as panicked investors sold off their stock in droves. This moment is usually considered the official start of the Depression. **657**

Great Depression The most devastating and longest economic crisis in American history that lasted from 1929 to 1939. **659**

Bonus March A two-month-long demonstration by forty thousand impoverished World War I veterans in Washington, D.C., that ended violently when the army expelled the protesters. **660**

New Deal An avalanche of legislation from 1933 to 1938 intended to promote economic recovery, reform American capitalism, and offer security to ordinary Americans. **662**

Dust Bowl Drought and soil erosion caused massive dust storms across southern and plains states throughout the thirties. **670**

"Migrant Mother" Dorothea Lange's 1936 photograph of a destitute woman, which became an iconic portrait of Depression-era suffering. **673**

share our wealth Louisiana Senator Huey Long's plan to redistribute money from the rich to the poor. **674**

deserving poor Needy Americans who were legitimately entitled to public support, a category open to differing interpretations. **676**

American Federation of Labor (AFL) A craft-based organization that accepted only skilled workers, like carpenters or cigar makers, who practiced a trade. **678**

Congress of Industrial Organizations (CIO) A brand-new type of labor organization that organized workers within an entire industry rather than by their trade orientation. **679**

sit-down strike Workers occupy a factory to paralyze production lines and prevent strikebreakers or management from entering the building. **679**

New Deal coalition A political partnership formed in the mid-thirties among liberals, trade unionists, Catholics, and northern blacks that redrew the nation's political map. **680**

CHAPTER 23

World War II

Fighting the Good War, 1939–1945

> "Yesterday, December 7, 1941—a date which will live in infamy—the United States of America was suddenly and deliberately attacked by naval and air forces of the Empire of Japan."
>
> President FRANKLIN D. ROOSEVELT

In early December 1941 a Japanese naval convoy secretly traveled toward Hawaii, stopping within 250 miles of the Hawaiian island of Oahu. At 6:00 a.m. on December 7, Admiral Chuichji Nagumo launched two consecutive attacking waves of bombers, torpedo planes, and dive-bombers. As Japanese pilots approached Pearl Harbor, a naval station on Oahu, they saw a line of American battleships parked in a neat row. Moments later those battleships were on fire.

Before Pearl Harbor debate raged over how to respond to the growing threat of war in the Pacific and Germany's conquest of Europe. Non-interventionists and interventionists offered competing visions of how to protect America's vital interests in a world torn apart by war. Now Americans needed no other explanation than this photo of a battleship engulfed in flames to understand why they were at war. Questions instead arose over why the United States had given the Japanese such an inviting target. Hoping to pressure Japan into withdrawing from China, President Franklin D. Roosevelt had sent the U.S. Pacific Fleet to Hawaii. There, he believed, the battleships were far enough away from Japan to escape attack but close enough to convince Japan to end its expansionist drive into East Asia. Roosevelt erred on both counts. Instead, Japan resolved to drive the Western powers out of East Asia.

In their attack on Pearl Harbor, the Japanese sank or damaged eighteen American ships and killed 2,405 Americans. Congress declared war on Japan the day after the attack. On December 11 Germany and Italy declared war on the United States, and Romania, Bulgaria, and Hungary quickly followed suit. The United States now faced the challenge of fighting resolute and capable enemies in Europe and the Pacific against whom victory was not certain.

The attack on Pearl Harbor silenced all political debate about whether America needed to fight, but were all the war-generated changes in American society positive ones? World War II thrust the United States into a new position of global leadership. Mobilizing the nation's resources to fight also created vast economic and social changes at home. The United States eventually prevailed against its enemies, but the cost of victory was high on the battlefield and on the home front.

How did the attack on Pearl Harbor compare to the sinking of the *Maine* in 1898?

The Approaching War p. 686

On the Home Front p. 693

On the Front Lines p. 702

Ending the Pacific War p. 711

The Approaching War

From 1939 to 1945 war engulfed nearly the entire globe, as shown on the map (**23.1**). Huge areas fell under German and Japanese control, naval battles occurred on vast stretches of sea, and colonies provided key materials needed by warring nations. Until 1941, however, the United States remained on the sidelines as Germany attacked continuously in Europe, and Japan launched steady invasions throughout East Asia. As long as the fighting remained far from their shores, Americans disagreed over whether these wars were theirs to fight. Still coping with the social and financial problems created by the Great Depression, **non-interventionists** urged the nation to put "America First" and stay out of overseas conflicts. By the late thirties, however, **interventionists** increasingly challenged this view, arguing that only direct engagement could prevent the world conflagration from reaching American shores.

Fascism and Appeasement

In the midst of the Depression, the United States had to formulate responses to Adolf Hitler's rise to power in Germany in 1933, Italy's invasion of Ethiopia in 1935, and the Spanish Civil War in 1936–1939.

Appointed chancellor in 1933, Hitler immediately began turning Germany into a **fascist state** under Nazi control, a dictatorial form of government that glorified the state over the individual. Widespread economic suffering, lingering resentments against the harsh terms of the Versailles Treaty (see Chapter 20), and virulent anti-Semitism created fertile ground for Nazism to flourish. Stripped of their German citizenship, Jews could not practice medicine or law, attend public school after the age of fourteen, or enter public parks and libraries. Promising to restore Germany's economic and military prowess and protect the presumed "racial superiority" of the German people, Hitler rearmed the country and sought allies.

In formulating their response to the rise of fascism in Europe, non-interventionists in Congress sought to avoid repeating the mistakes of the past that had led to involvement in the bloodbath of

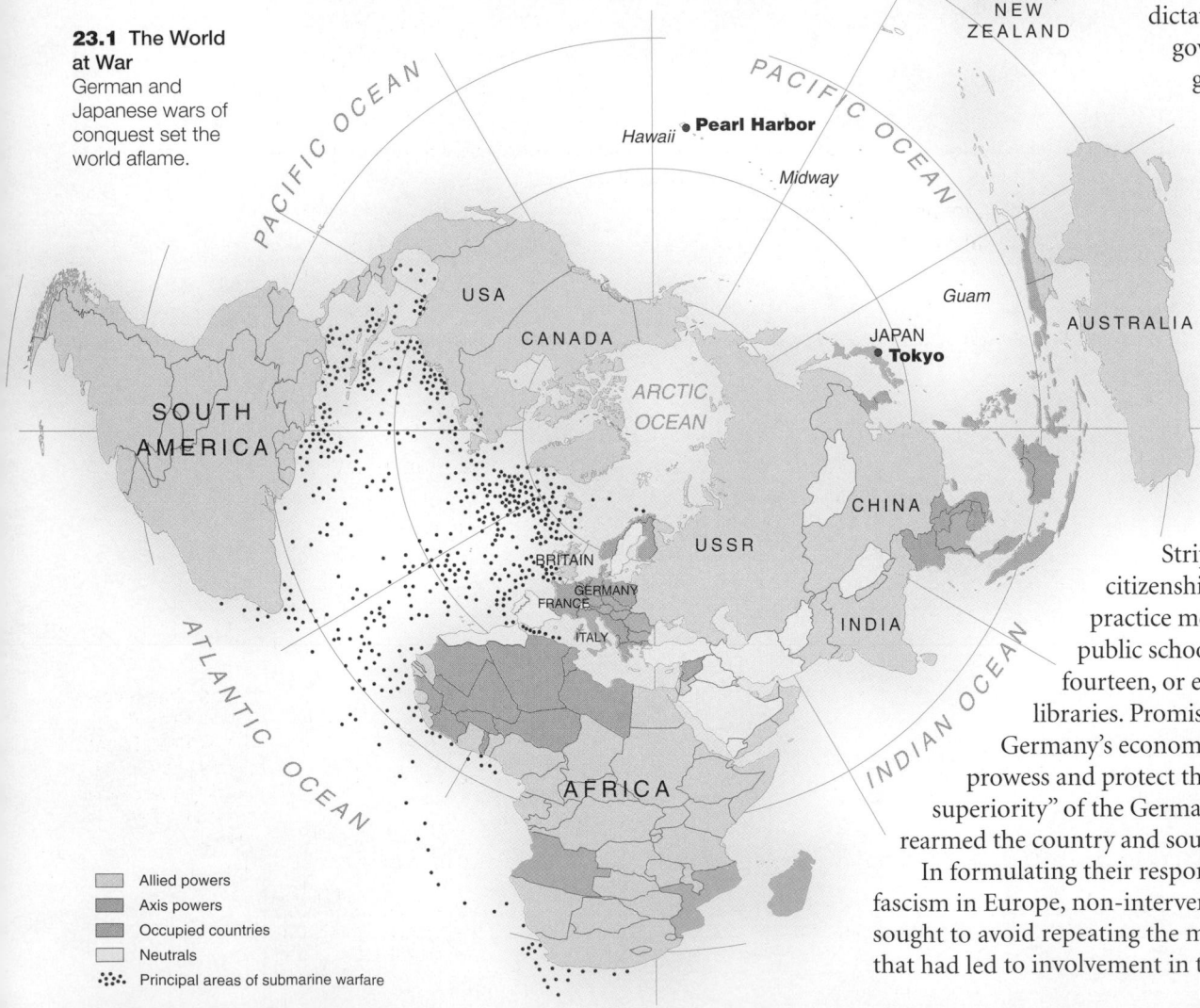

23.1 The World at War
German and Japanese wars of conquest set the world aflame.

What does this map convey about the scope of World War II?

World War I. Senator Gerald P. Nye, a Republican from North Dakota, chaired a series of Senate investigations in the midthirties into the role that American arms manufacturers had played in the nation's decision to enter World War I. Although the investigations unearthed little hard evidence of a conspiracy, they did buoy the consensus that the United States had entered that war to continue profitable arms sales and to guarantee that the Allies, the powers who had fought Germany, repaid their war loans to private banks. When these European countries defaulted on their loans during the Depression, public sentiment hardened against helping foreign nations.

To ensure that trading with belligerent nations did not drag the country into another war, Congress passed the **Neutrality Acts**, a series of laws from 1935 to 1939 that restricted arms sales, loans, and transport of goods with nations at war (see U.S. Countdown to War timeline, **23.2**). These popular laws encapsulated the widespread non-interventionist vision of avoiding involvement in an overseas conflicts that did not directly threaten U.S. territory. Depending on the official policy pursued, the Atlantic and Pacific Oceans could serve as buffers protecting the nation or as pathways to war. Trying to ensure the former, the 1935 Neutrality Act prohibited the sales of arms and ammunition to nations at war. In 1936 Congress barred all loans to warring nations. The 1937 Neutrality Act allowed belligerent nations to purchase non-war-related goods if they paid cash for them and transported them on their own ships, a policy known as "**cash and carry.**"

FDR momentarily challenged the non-interventionist vision with his 1937 Quarantine Speech which urged peace-loving countries to isolate aggressor nations and actively seek peace. Outraged non-interventionists accused FDR of trying to turn the United States into the world's policeman. "It's a terrible thing to look over your shoulder when you are trying to lead – and find no one there," the president remarked to an aide before he publicly reaffirmed his support for the Neutrality Acts. The zenith of non-interventionist sentiment was reached in 1938 when Congress considered a constitutional amendment that required public approval through a national referendum for any declaration of war, except in the event of an enemy invasion. The amendment was debated, but never approved by Congress.

The United States was not alone in its desire to remain at peace. Eager to avoid war with Germany, Britain and France recalled how a relatively minor incident (the assassination of Archduke Franz Ferdinand) had become the catalyst for war in 1914 (see Chapter 20). Instead of mobilizing their armies when Germany violated the terms of the Versailles Treaty by rearming and threatening its neighbors, France and Britain turned first to negotiation. In 1938 Germany annexed Austria and then demanded the Sudetenland, a German-speaking province made part of Czechoslovakia against its will when the Allies dissolved the Austro-Hungarian Empire at the end of the World War I. By the thirties many Europeans felt that the Versailles Peace Treaty had punished Germany too severely, creating the widespread impression that Hitler's actions and demands were reasonable. Taking Hitler at his word that he was interested only in reuniting German-speaking peoples into one nation, Britain and France agreed at the **Munich Conference** in 1938 to let Germany occupy the Sudetenland.

Instead of dampening Hitler's ambitions, the Munich Conference convinced the dictator that the Western democracies were too weak to oppose him militarily. Arguing that Germany needed "living space" in the East for its people, Hitler initiated his master plan to displace what he demeaningly called the "inferior" Slavic "races," the peoples living in Eastern Europe, and to exterminate the European Jews. Intent on avoiding the mistakes of World War I, when Germany had fought a two-front war, Hitler resolved to fight one war at a time. To accomplish

U.S. Countdown to War, 1931 – 1941

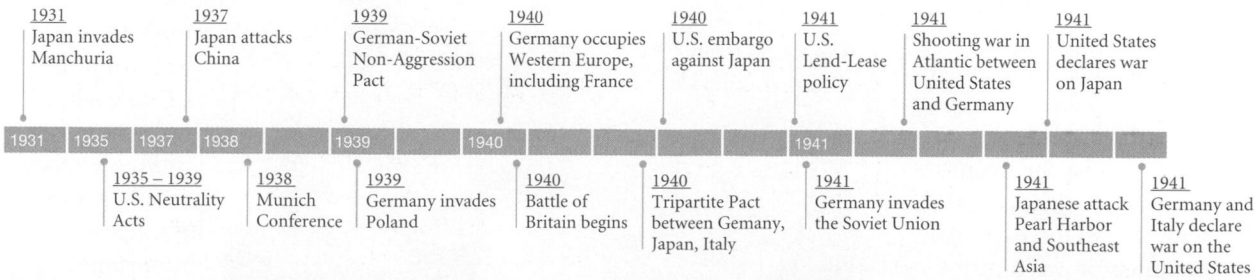

23.2 Origins of World War II
The United States remained neutral until the Japanese attacked Pearl Harbor.

What different lessons did America and other world powers draw from World War I?

this, in the late summer of 1939 Hitler signed a non-aggression pact with Josef Stalin, the dictator of the Soviet Union (USSR). In this agreement Germany and the Soviet Union agreed to jointly partition a defeated Poland and other parts of Eastern Europe, and the USSR offered Hitler supplies for his pending attack on France and Britain. The non-aggression pact ensured that Germany's eastern border remained peaceful when it attacked western and southeastern Europe. Only days after signing the pact, Hitler invaded Poland, bringing a declaration of war from Britain and France and the official beginning of World War II.

In the spring of 1940, Hitler began his massive assault on Western Europe by invading Norway and Denmark. He then marched through Luxembourg, Holland, and Belgium to invade France. Unlike in 1914, when Germany's broad attack against French lines ended in a trench stalemate, in May 1940 Germany's Blitzkrieg (lightning war) punched holes in the French defense system and then sent tanks, infantry, artillery, and aircraft through these openings to disrupt communications and threaten the French army from the rear. When German troops entered Paris, Hitler underscored his triumph by visiting Paris's Eiffel Tower. In this photograph (**23.3**) Hitler is posing before the landmark monument, transforming a banal tourist excursion into an act that, by symbolizing his control of Western Europe, carried sinister and tragic overtones. With France under Nazi domination, Italy formally entered the war on the side of Germany. Through a combination of alliances and force, the **Axis**, those nations fighting on the German side, quickly took control of the rest of Eastern Europe and the Balkans.

As German troops were rolling toward Paris, the British army had escaped capture at the French port town of Dunkirk. For a full year Britain fought Germany alone, surviving a massive bombing campaign known as the Battle of Britain. That changed in June 1941, however, when Hitler invaded the Soviet Union. Frustrated in his efforts to subdue Britain, and without the means to launch an invasion across the English Channel, Hitler decided that with British forces off the continent it was time to conquer Russia. Up until this point Hitler had successfully fought a series of isolated wars, but he made his first major strategic error when he invaded the Soviet Union. Instead of advancing quickly to Moscow, German troops found themselves bogged down in a massive battle along a far-flung Eastern Front.

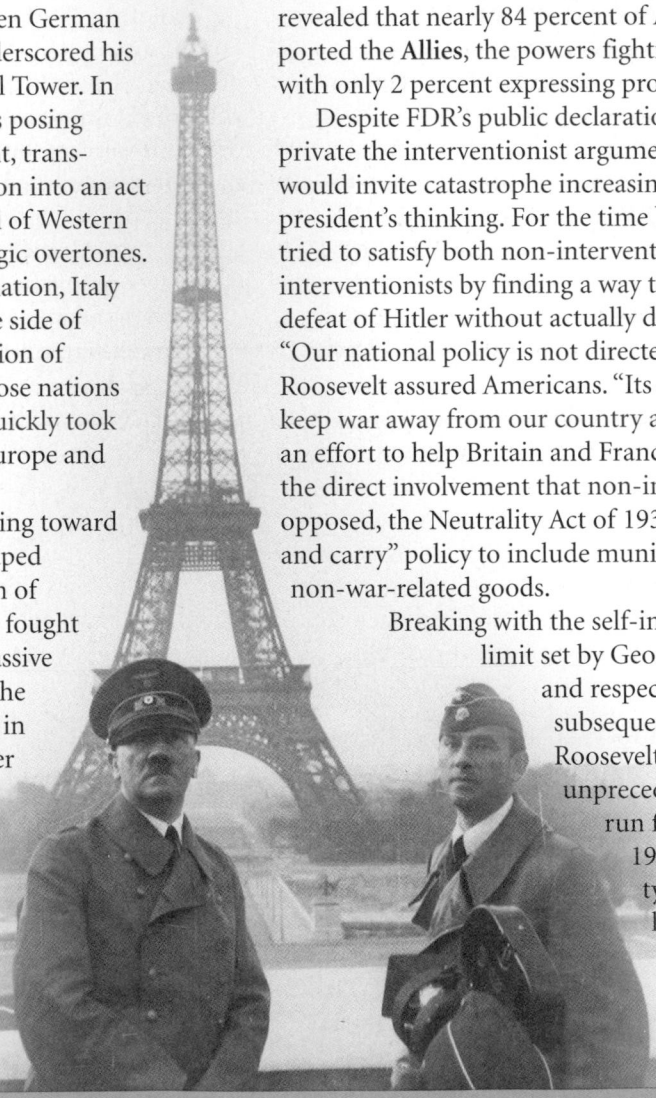

23.3 Hitler in Paris Adolf Hitler's quick subjugation of Western Europe brought him to Paris by June 1940. Hitler posed in front of the city's most recognizable monument, the Eiffel Tower, to underscore France's defeat and his power over Western Europe.

The Arsenal of Democracy

As these events developed in Europe, both President Franklin D. Roosevelt and the majority of the American people opposed going to war. Publicly embracing non-interventionists measures during his first two terms, Roosevelt adopted an officially neutral stance as the war spread. Unlike Wilson in World War I, however, Roosevelt did not ask Americans to remain impartial in thought. Immigration restrictions had limited the number of first-generation immigrants from Europe, and Roosevelt had few concerns that well-assimilated Americans of German ancestry might retain strong loyalties to Germany. Indeed public opinion polls in 1939 revealed that nearly 84 percent of Americans supported the **Allies**, the powers fighting Germany, with only 2 percent expressing pro-German views.

Despite FDR's public declaration of neutrality, in private the interventionist argument that inaction would invite catastrophe increasingly influenced the president's thinking. For the time being Roosevelt tried to satisfy both non-interventionists and interventionists by finding a way to ensure the defeat of Hitler without actually declaring war. "Our national policy is not directed toward war," Roosevelt assured Americans. "Its sole purpose is to keep war away from our country and our people." In an effort to help Britain and France without risking the direct involvement that non-interventionists opposed, the Neutrality Act of 1939 revised the "cash and carry" policy to include munitions as well as non-war-related goods.

Breaking with the self-imposed two-term limit set by George Washington and respected by every other subsequent president, Roosevelt made the unprecedented decision to run for a third term in 1940. Roosevelt, who typically kept even his closest advisers guessing before he reached an important

How did Hitler accomplish his rapid conquest of Eastern and Western Europe?

decision, surprised everyone, even his wife, with his announcement. FDR never explained his decision to anyone, but the shock of France falling to Nazi control undoubtedly influenced his decision to run again. Roosevelt's candidacy and his selection of a liberal New Dealer, Henry Wallace, as his vice president caused some grumbling among conservative Democrats, who nonetheless rallied around Roosevelt in the general election. The Republican challenger Wendell Willkie and Roosevelt each argued that the nation should offer all the help it could to the Allies short of entering the war. Willkie tried to paint Roosevelt as bent on direct intervention, but this charge and Willkie's anti-New Deal rhetoric resonated poorly with voters. Roosevelt easily won a third term as president.

FDR saw his task as satisfying "the wish of 70% of Americans to keep out of the war" and "the wish of 70% of Americans to do everything to break Hitler, even if it means war." To accommodate the public's conflicting emotions, Roosevelt proposed turning the nation into a "great arsenal of democracy." By telephone and telegraph British Prime Minister Winston Churchill pressed FDR continually for aid. Stressing America's vulnerability, Churchill warned that "overwhelming sea power would be in Hitler's hands" if Germany defeated Britain. FDR responded as Churchill hoped. Besides selling Britain arms, FDR agreed to trade fifty old American destroyers for ninety-nine-year leases on seven British air and naval bases in the Western Hemisphere. Britain needed these ships to transport weapons overseas. He also supported the introduction of a peacetime draft and invited a leading interventionist, Republican Henry Stimson, to join his cabinet as secretary of war.

Interventionists countered the non-interventionists' slogan of "America First" with Churchill's argument that a Nazi-controlled Europe directly threatened America's well-being. As part of the heated exchange between non-interventionists and interventionists, Dr. Seuss (the alias used by Theodore Geisel, who was to gain fame in the 1950s as the author-illustrator of *The Cat in the Hat* and many other children's books) drew editorial cartoons for *PM,* a short-lived left-wing New York magazine, that denounced non-intervention as folly. Dr. Seuss depicted non-interventionists as ostriches with their heads in the ground, anti-Semites, and appeasers. This Seuss cartoon (**23.4**) shows a non-interventionists wearing an "America First" hat in a bathtub that is jumping with predatory sea creatures adorned with swastikas, the symbol of the Nazi Party. His eyes closed tight, the man ignores the lurking danger, saying with a satisfied smile, "The old Family bath tub is plenty safe for me." This cartoon challenged the non-interventionists' belief that the Atlantic Ocean would protect the United States from a Nazi attack. As he moved closer to the interventionist position, FDR voiced similar concerns about the vulnerability of the American coastline.

By 1941 Britain had run out of cash, and neutrality laws still prohibited the United States from loaning the British the money they needed to buy munitions. FDR circumvented these restrictions with a policy called **Lend-Lease** that loaned rather than sold arms to Britain. The United States would "say to England, we will give the guns and ships that you need, provided that when the war is over you will return to us in kind the guns and ships that we have loaned you," Roosevelt told Secretary of the Treasury Henry Morgenthau. Lend-Lease, FDR explained to the nation, was simply one neighbor helping another to put out a fire. No one would say, FDR noted, "Neighbor, my garden hose cost me $15; you have to pay me $15 for it . . . I don't want $15—I want my garden hose back after the fire is over." As the

23.4 Dr. Seuss Lampoons Non-Interventionists Dr. Seuss lampooned non-interventionists for closing their eyes to the threat that Hitler's navy (depicted here as swastika-marked monsters) posed to American shores.

Did the competing visions of non-interventionists and interventionists influence FDR's rhetoric and actions?

> "Some of our people like to believe that wars in Europe and in Asia are of no concern to us. But it is a matter of most vital concern to us that European and Asiatic war-makers should not gain control of the oceans which lead to this hemisphere."
>
> President FRANKLIN D. ROOSEVELT, radio "fireside chat," December 29, 1940

Lend-Lease bill worked its way through Congress, however, non-interventionists successfully attached an amendment that prohibited the U.S. Navy from escorting British convoys carrying American goods across the Atlantic. Fittingly, given the analogy that FDR used to explain Lend-Lease, one of the first shipments to Britain contained boxes of fire hoses.

When Hitler attacked the USSR in 1941, the United States extended Lend-Lease aid to the Soviets as well. FDR had formally recognized the Soviet Union in 1933, hoping to find another overseas market for American goods. Trade with the Soviets remained minimal during the Depression, but exploded during the war. By 1945 the United States had provided $50 billion of materiel to the Allies under this program. No one, however, expected Britain and the Soviet Union to return "loaned" ammunition or arms to the United States. Instead, the law left it up to the president to decide what form repayment would take. After the war President Harry Truman accepted favorable postwar trade relations as repayment from Britain and demanded $2.6 billion from the Soviet Union for nonmilitary lend-lease goods. Russia did not pay its debt until after the fall of communism in 1991.

Securing American guns and ammunition solved only half the problem for Britain. Because of the number of German submarines patrolling the Atlantic, Secretary of War Henry Stimson warned, sending arms to Britain was like pouring water into a leaky bathtub. When the American destroyer *Greer* gave chase and exchanged fire with a German submarine, FDR used the incident to invoke his authority as commander in chief by ordering U.S. naval ships to escort all ships headed to Britain and "shoot on sight" any German submarine or ship. Although it remained unclear whether the Germans knew that the *Greer* was an American ship, FDR denounced the skirmish as a deliberate attack in American waters. "We have sought no shooting war with Hitler. We do not seek it now," FDR declared in September 1941. "But when you see a rattlesnake poised to strike, you do not wait until he has struck before you crush him. These Nazi submarines and raiders are the rattlesnakes of the Atlantic." Three months before Japan's attack on Pearl Harbor, the United States was fighting an undeclared naval war with Germany.

War with Japan

The catalyst for America's formal entry into the war did not come in the Atlantic, however, but on the other side of the globe when Japanese pilots attacked **Pearl Harbor**, a naval base in Hawaii, on December 7, 1941. The attackers discovered a neat line of battleships, reproduced in this miniature version of Pearl Harbor (**23.5**) that Japanese filmmakers constructed for a wartime propaganda film that reminded Japanese audiences of their nation's great victory against the United States.

The Japanese attack on Pearl Harbor was the culmination of two decades of tension and growing mistrust between the two nations. Japan's desire to establish itself as the major power in the Pacific alarmed the United States, which maintained an array of island possessions and a strong naval presence in the Pacific to support its trading relationship with China. Access to Chinese markets had been a cornerstone of American foreign policy since the Spanish-American War. From the Japanese perspective, claiming East Asia as Japan's proper sphere of influence was no different from the United States declaring the Western Hemisphere off-limits to foreign powers through the 1823 Monroe Doctrine and 1904 Roosevelt Corollary. Japan aimed to build the Greater East Asia Co-Prosperity Sphere, creating satellite states throughout Asia that would free Japan from dependence on Western-controlled resources like oil. In the twenties the United States and Japan successfully mediated their differences, with Japan agreeing to reduce the size of its navy and renouncing war as an instrument of foreign policy (see Chapter 21). The Japanese army's 1931 invasion of Chinese-held Manchuria (land long disputed by China, Russia, and Japan), however, signaled the

Were there significant differences between FDR's version of neutrality and Wilson's in World War I?

beginning of a direct confrontation between Japan and the United States. Claiming that Manchuria rightfully belonged to Japan, the Japanese army assumed control of all raw materials and industry to support Japan's military endeavors.

In July 1937 Japan attacked China. The Japanese unleashed a brutal war of conquest; during the infamous Rape of Nanking, a Chinese city, over 350,000 Chinese perished, including 20,000 women, who were raped, tortured, and then executed. "Soldiers impaled babies on bayonets and tossed them still alive into pots of boiling water," a Japanese soldier later admitted. More than 6 million Chinese died at the hands of Japanese soldiers over the next eight years.

Growing American sympathy for Chinese victims and concern over protecting American economic interests in Asia coincided with rising tensions in Europe. By 1940 aiding Britain had become President Roosevelt's foreign policy priority. Containing Japan with a series of escalating economic sanctions and warnings, FDR reasoned, was the best way to defuse the situation in the Pacific so the nation could focus on problems in the Atlantic and Europe. Hoping that a show of force would convince Japan to abandon its imperialist ambitions, the United States embarked on a naval building program and stationed the Pacific Fleet in Pearl Harbor, on the Hawaiian island of Oahu, 2,500 miles from California (see 23.1). Roosevelt also sent aid to China and in July 1940 imposed a limited embargo on scrap iron and high-octane aviation fuel to Japan.

Japan was not deterred. Instead of withdrawing from China, Japan seized parts of French Indochina, a French colony in Southeast Asia, the site of present-day Vietnam. In response, on September 26, 1940, the United States announced a total embargo on scrap metal shipments to Japan. The following day Tokyo signed the Tripartite Pact with Germany and Italy, an agreement dedicated to "the establishment of a new order" in East Asia and Europe. Aimed at offering mutual aid in the event that the United States attacked, the pact did not envision any strategic coordination between the European and Asian theaters of war. Japan and Germany shared mutual enemies during the war, but little else.

When Japan increased its incursions into French Indochina in the summer of 1941, the American government froze Japanese assets in the United States and stopped oil shipments (which accounted for four-fifths of Japan's oil supply). Diplomatic

23.5 Japanese Model of Pearl Harbor
This mock-up of Pearl Harbor, constructed for a Japanese wartime film of the attack, showed American battleships lined up in a row, making them easy targets for aerial bombs.

How did the United States respond to increasing Japanese aggression?

> "The United States was in the war, up to the neck and in to the death. . . . Being saturated and satiated with emotion and sensation, I went to bed and slept the sleep of the saved and thankful."
>
> British Prime Minister WINSTON CHURCHILL, upon learning of the 1941 Japanese attack on Pearl Harbor

exchanges continued until the eve of the attack on Pearl Harbor, even though Japan decided in September to launch an expansionist war into resource-rich Southeast Asia to push the United States and Britain out of the region.

The Japanese calculation that the United States would withdraw from East Asia after a devastating attack on Pearl Harbor proved as faulty as the American belief that sanctions were the best way to prevent a war with Japan. The Japanese assault on Pearl Harbor ended all debate over entering the war. Having agonized over how far to pull the country toward war, Roosevelt reportedly told an aide that the attack took the matter "entirely out of his hands, because the Japanese had made the decision for him."

Despite catching the Americans by surprise, the Japanese victory at Pearl Harbor was far from complete. Although the attack prevented the United States from interfering with Japan's subsequent invasion of Southeast Asia, Japan failed to destroy America's Pacific Fleet. Fearing a counterattack Nagumo, on the day of the attack, called off a third air strike on storage tanks containing millions of gallons of fuel oil and repair facilities. Most American sailors in Hawaii survived the attack, and the navy eventually repaired six of the eight damaged battleships. In another stroke of luck, the Pacific Fleet's two aircraft carriers were at sea and escaped the attack. The navy also had eleven battleships and two aircraft carriers stationed elsewhere to defend the nation from further attack. Nonetheless the short-term damage was severe. Over the next twenty-four hours, Japan attacked American territory and countries throughout Southeast Asia. While the attack on Pearl Harbor horrified Americans, it brought hope to the British. Churchill knew immediately that the United States would soon be in the war against Germany.

After Pearl Harbor some die-hard non-interventionists immediately questioned whether the Japanese attack could have been prevented. Charges of dereliction of duty against the commanders of Pearl Harbor and suspicions that Roosevelt had allowed the attack to take place in order to enter the war against Hitler (through the back door) surfaced. By early December, American commanders expected a Japanese attack against American Pacific possessions. Most intelligence data, however, indicated that the Japanese would invade the Philippines and mainland Southeast Asia, as they subsequently did. American officials simply overlooked the few bits of information indicating that Hawaii was both a possible and a probable first target. The extent to which the Japanese took the Americans by surprise is reflected in this telegram (**23.6**),which alerted all ships in Pearl Harbor to take the air sirens seriously. American radar had picked up the waves of aircraft approaching the naval base, but officials assumed these were American planes arriving from the mainland. The telegram, therefore, was not sent until the bombs had already started falling.

23.6 Pearl Harbor Under Attack
Caught off guard, the navy rallied their defenses against the Japanese attack on Pearl Harbor with this telegram.

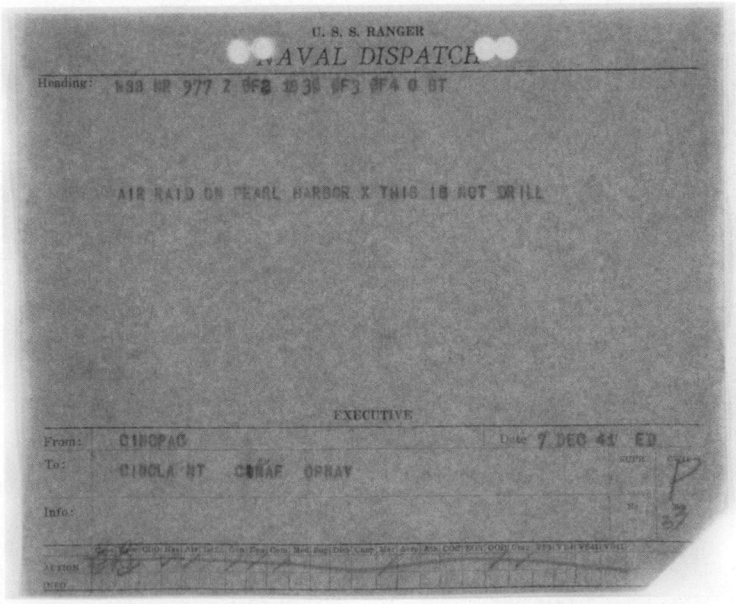
U. S. S. RANGER
NAVAL DISPATCH
Heading:
AIR RAID ON PEARL HARBOR X THIS IS NOT DRILL
EXECUTIVE
From: CINCPAC
Date: 7 DEC 41
To: CINCLANT CINCAF OPNAV
Info:

How significant was the attack on Pearl Harbor in the short and long run?

On the Home Front

The U.S. government made the formal declaration of war, but winning it required the active participation of the American people. Americans remember World War II as the "good war" not only because it ended the Depression but also because it united the nation against its enemies. While unified in the desire to prevail on the battlefield, Americans embraced conflicting visions that kept ethnic, gender, race, and class divisions intact. Motivating the country to fight the Japanese was easy after the attack on Pearl Harbor, but cultivating hatred of the enemy had direct consequences for Japanese immigrants and Japanese Americans. The wartime economic boom ended years of financial struggle and hardship, but prosperity brought its own share of strains. Cities with major defense industries found themselves inundated with migrants from rural areas and struggled to contain rising racial and ethnic tensions between white inhabitants and black and Hispanic communities.

Images of the Enemy

Americans had long exhibited disdain for Asian immigrants and Americans of Asian descent. Before the war localities and the federal government had passed a series of discriminatory laws that targeted Asian immigrants generally and their American-born children. These laws segregated swimming pools and dance halls, denied Asians the right to own land, prohibited intermarriage with whites, and prevented Asian immigrants from becoming citizens. The attack on Pearl Harbor provoked more virulent expressions of hatred for the Japanese, leading to even greater discrimination.

In the opening days of the war, *Life* and *Time* magazines offered the nation a crash course in "how to tell a Chinese from a Jap." Understanding the difference was crucial, *Life* magazine asserted, to protect the Chinese Americans, "whose homeland is our staunch ally," from unwarranted attacks. As the Chinese embassy prepared to hand out identification buttons for Chinese immigrants and Chinese Americans to wear, *Life* and *Time* instructed the nation in distinguishing pseudoscientific, stereotypical "racial" characteristics. *Life* magazine used photos (**23.7**) to compare the facial features and expressions of a Chinese civil servant with those of General Hideki Tojo, the minister of war who ruled Japan during the war. The magazine called on readers to note Tojo's heavy beard and cheekbones and humorless expression, all supposedly key traits of Japanese physiognomy. *Time* and *Life* were not alone in feeling a sudden need to distinguish members of the "yellow race." Congress lifted the ban on Chinese naturalization and granted China an annual quota of 105 immigrants a year. This act symbolically differentiated the Chinese from the Japanese (banned as immigrants in 1924 and prohibited from becoming naturalized citizens, see Chapters 19 and 21), but protected the nation from any substantial increase in Chinese immigration.

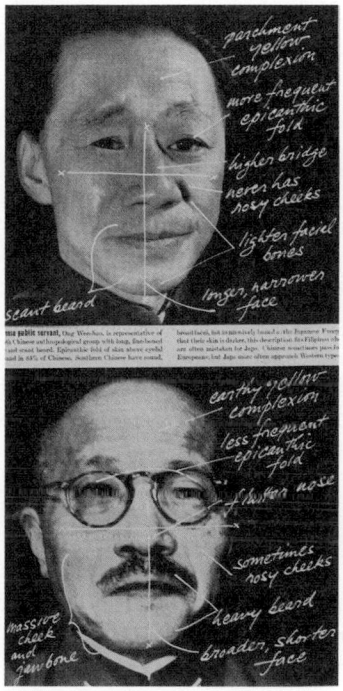

23.7 "How to Tell Japs from the Chinese" Lamenting the American tendency to lump all Asians together, *Life* magazine analyzed the facial features of Chinese and Japanese men to instruct readers in the difference between the two groups—one an ally, the other the enemy.

Renewed outrage against Japan greeted news of ongoing atrocities in the Pacific war, such as the April 1942 Bataan Death March. When American and Filipino soldiers finally surrendered their position on the Bataan Peninsula in the Philippines, their Japanese captors forced the sick, starving troops to walk almost 90 miles through the intense heat and jungle to a prisoner of war camp. Out of 76,000 men who began the trek, 22,000 succumbed to illness, starvation, and severe beatings from Japanese soldiers.

Still these horrors were not enough to explain Americans' deep-seated hatred for the Japanese. "In Europe we felt that our enemies, horrible and deadly as they were, were still people," Ernie Pyle wrote in one of his newspaper columns toward the end of the war. "But out here I soon gathered that the Japanese were looked upon as something subhuman and

What distinctions did Americans now make between the Japanese and Chinese?

repulsive; the way some people feel about cockroaches or mice." As Pyle noted, general views toward the Germans were decidedly different. Remembering the vigilante attacks against German Americans in World War I (see Chapter 20), government propaganda took great care to focus on Hitler and Nazism as the enemy, not the German people.

Internment Camps

In the immediate wake of the attack on Pearl Harbor, Americans were eager for explanations. Rumors circulated that Japanese American farmers on Hawaii had plowed arrows in their fields to show Japanese pilots the way to military installations. Yet no evidence of internal spying ever surfaced, and suggestions that the government round up and quarantine these Hawaiian residents went nowhere. Composing one-third of Hawaii's population, people of Japanese descent were too important to the local economy to deport, and there were no ships available to transport replacement workers to the islands.

The 110,000 Japanese and Japanese Americans who lived in California, Oregon, and Washington, where they were not so vital to the economy, met a different fate. The day after the attack on Pearl Harbor, air raid sirens wailed in San Francisco. Then, when a Japanese submarine torpedoed an American ship off the California coast, Americans feared that the West Coast would soon be under attack. Frenzied officials instituted blackouts; Coast Guard units patrolled the seas. Throughout the war West Coast defense factories camouflaged their plants, as illustrated in these "Plant Camouflage, Before and After" photos (**23.8**). This aircraft factory in Burbank, California, stretched a tarp over its facilities to make it look like a suburban housing development from the air. The camouflagers hoped that an attacking Japanese pilot would pass over the site in search of a more recognizable military target.

Within this atmosphere of heightened anxiety, Japanese immigrants and Japanese Americans on the West Coast found themselves targeted as potential enemy agents. Increasingly the larger public and the government embraced a vision that viewed their presence near vital ports and military bases as a threat to national security. On February 19, 1942, President Roosevelt signed Executive Order 9066, giving the military the ability to declare certain areas off-limits to any or all persons. Lieutenant General John L. DeWitt, head of the Western Defense Command, immediately declared the entire West Coast a military zone closed to "all persons of Japanese ancestry, both alien and non-alien." The order called for the evacuation of anyone of Japanese descent; even orphanages had to comply by relocating Japanese American babies.

In mid-March 1942 Roosevelt created the War Relocation Authority to oversee the forced removal of 38,000 Japanese immigrants and 72,000 Japanese American citizens to **internment camps** where they were held under armed guard in isolated areas. Posted "Instructions to All Persons of Japanese Ancestry" (**23.9**) informed Japanese inhabitants that they had only a few days to sell their belongings and settle their affairs. "It is difficult to describe the feeling of despair and humiliation experienced by all of us," one internee later said, "as we watched the Caucasians coming to look over our possessions and offering such nominal amounts knowing we had no recourse but to accept whatever they were offering." Evacuees were allowed to take only what they could carry. With numbers pinned on their coats, they

23.8 Plant Camouflage, Before and After
This aircraft factory in Burbank, California, camouflaged its facility with a painted tarp and cardboard houses to create the facade of a suburban housing development, in the hopes of deceiving Japanese pilots on the lookout for military targets.

What do these photos reveal about American fears of a Japanese attack?

rode trains to recently abandoned stables or stockyards to await transport to one of ten internment camps scattered in remote areas throughout the interior West.

Offering a conflicting vision that emphasized their loyalty to the United States, the overwhelming majority of Japanese and Japanese Americans complied quietly with the evacuation order. A few, however, found ways to register their protest against this wholesale violation of their civil rights. For propaganda purposes the Office of War Information hired photographer Dorothea Lange to document that the government was treating evacuees humanely as it contained this suspect population. Sympathetic to the plight of Japanese Americans, Lange managed to capture this scene (**23.10**) of a Japanese American veteran reporting to a Santa Anita assembly center in his old military uniform, a silent demonstration of his long-standing loyalty to the country.

In January 1943 the army decided to recruit Nisei men, the American-born children of Japanese immigrants. While their parents remained in the camps, these men joined with Japanese Americans from Hawaii to form the 442nd Regimental Combat Team, a unit that became the most decorated American unit in the nation's history. These men opted to prove their loyalty by fighting for their country. Other Japanese Americans sought redress in the courts, but the Supreme Court upheld the government's evacuation policy in 1944. *Competing Visions: Civil Liberties and National Security Clash* (page 696) examines this controversy in more detail.

As the tide of the war began to turn in America's favor, the military justification for interning people of Japanese descent weakened. In 1945 the government let inmates return to their West Coast homes. Three years later the federal government offered some restitution to those who had lost homes or businesses. It took until 1988, however, for Congress to offer an apology and reparation payment of $20,000 to each of the 60,000 surviving internees.

Prosperity, Scarcity and Opportunities for Women

Japanese Americans were among the few to suffer financially from the war. For most Americans jobs were plentiful and wages high. Over the course of the war the nation's gross national product rose 60 percent, and 17 million new jobs were created. To mobilize the economy the government quickly established a slew of agencies to allocate scarce resources, help business convert their factories to a wartime footing, and enlist the public's full support for the war. After the difficult years of the Depression, the war-fueled economic boom came as a welcome relief. "People are crazy with money," one store owner exclaimed. "They don't care what they buy. They purchase things . . . just for the fun of spending." Madison Avenue advertising firms assured the public that consumerism was essential to the American way of life. "Will you ever own another car?" asked one ad. "Another radio? Another gleaming new refrigerator? Those who live under dictators merely dream of such possessions."

Concerns over unemployment gave way to worries about inflation as the additional money flowing into the economy sent prices soaring. The government tried to curb inflation by instituting price and wage controls. Because the nation's

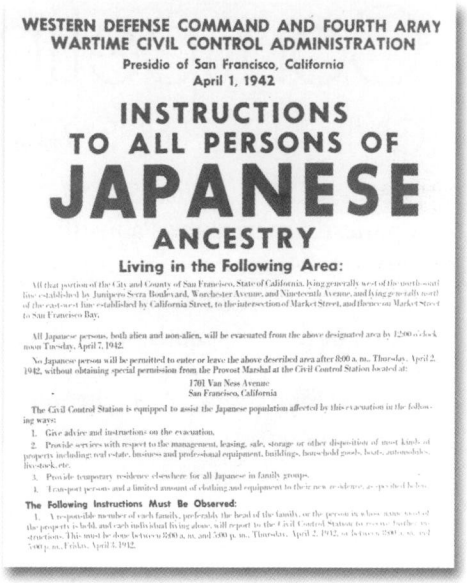

WESTERN DEFENSE COMMAND AND FOURTH ARMY
WARTIME CIVIL CONTROL ADMINISTRATION
Presidio of San Francisco, California
April 1, 1942

INSTRUCTIONS TO ALL PERSONS OF JAPANESE ANCESTRY

Living in the Following Area:

All that portion of the City and County of San Francisco, State of California, lying generally west of the north-and-south line established by Junipero Serra Boulevard, Winchester Avenue, and Nineteenth Avenue, and lying generally north of the east-and-west line established by California Street, to the intersection of Market Street, and thence on Market Street to San Francisco Bay.

All Japanese persons, both alien and non-alien, will be evacuated from the above designated area by 12:00 o'clock noon Tuesday, April 7, 1942.

No Japanese person will be permitted to enter or leave the above described area after 8:00 a. m., Thursday, April 2, 1942, without obtaining special permission from the Provost Marshal at the Civil Control Station located at:

1701 Van Ness Avenue
San Francisco, California

The Civil Control Station is equipped to assist the Japanese population affected by this evacuation in the following ways:

1. Give advice and instructions on the evacuation.
2. Provide services with respect to the management, leasing, sale, storage or other disposition of most kinds of property including: real estate, business and professional equipment, buildings, household goods, boats, automobiles, livestock, etc.
3. Provide temporary residence elsewhere for all Japanese in family groups.
4. Transport persons and a limited amount of clothing and equipment to their new residence, as described below.

The Following Instructions Must Be Observed:

1. A responsible member of each family, preferably the head of the family, or the person in whose name most of the property is held, and each individual living alone, will report to the Civil Control Station to receive further instructions. This must be done between 8:00 a. m. and 5:00 p. m., Thursday, April 2, 1942, or between 8:00 a. m. and 5:00 p. m., Friday, April 3, 1942.

23.9 "Instructions to All Persons of Japanese Ancestry" This poster illustrates the hasty pace of the evacuation of Japanese Americans. They had just seven days to leave their homes.

23.10 A Japanese American Protests Internment Government officials censored this photograph of a Japanese American veteran who reported to the evacuation center in his old uniform. He gave his name to a Japanese-American staff member who decided instead to cooperate openly with authorities.

What competing responses did Japanese Americans have to internment?

Competing Visions

CIVIL LIBERTIES AND NATIONAL SECURITY CLASH

In *Korematsu v. United States* (1944), the Supreme Court upheld the constitutionality of relocating and interning Japanese Americans as a justifiable military measure. Three Supreme Court justices dissented from the majority opinion, concluding that internment violated the constitutional rights of Japanese American citizens. Which side made the stronger argument? How has America resolved a similar dilemma over national security versus civil rights in the aftermath of the 9/11 attacks (see Chapter 29)?

Justice Hugo Black wrote the majority opinion that upheld the constitutionality of interning Japanese Americans.

Exclusion of those of Japanese origin was deemed necessary because of the presence of an unascertained number of disloyal members of the group, most of whom we have no doubt were loyal to this country. ... We are not unmindful of the hardships imposed by it upon a large group of American citizens. ... But hardships are part of war, and war is an aggregation of hardships. All citizens alike, both in and out of uniform, feel the impact of war in greater or lesser measure. Citizenship has its responsibilities as well as its privileges, and in time of war the burden is always heavier. Compulsory exclusion of large groups of citizens from their homes, except under circumstances of direct emergency and peril, is inconsistent with our basic governmental institutions. But when under conditions of modern warfare our shores are threatened by hostile forces, the power to protect must be commensurate with the threatened danger. ...

Regardless of the true nature of the assembly and relocation centers—and we deem it unjustifiable to call them concentration camps with all the ugly connotations that term implies.... Korematsu was not excluded from the Military Area because of hostility to him or his race. He was excluded because we are at war with the Japanese Empire, because the properly constituted military authorities feared an invasion of our West Coast and felt constrained to take proper security measures, because they decided that the military urgency of the situation demanded that all citizens of Japanese ancestry be segregated from the West Coast temporarily, and finally, because Congress, reposing its confidence in this time of war in our military leaders—as inevitably it must—determined that they should have the power to do just this. There was evidence of disloyalty on the part of some, the military authorities considered that the need for action was great, and time was short. We cannot—by availing ourselves of the calm perspective of hindsight—now say that at that time these actions were unjustified.

Justice Frank Murphy disagreed with the majority opinion, arguing that internment was racially motivated.

This exclusion of "all persons of Japanese ancestry, both alien and non-alien," from the Pacific Coast area on a plea of military necessity in the absence of martial law ought not to be approved. Such exclusion goes over "the very brink of constitutional power" and falls into the ugly abyss of racism ... it is essential that there be definite limits to military discretion, especially where martial law has not been declared. Individuals must not be left impoverished of their constitutional rights on plea of military necessity that has neither substance nor support. ...

No one denies, of course, that there were some disloyal persons of Japanese descent on the Pacific Coast who did all in their power to aid their ancestral land. Similar disloyal activities have been engaged in by many persons of German, Italian and even more pioneer stock in our country. But to infer that examples of individual disloyalty prove group disloyalty and justify discriminatory action against the entire group is to deny that under our system of law individual guilt is the sole basis for deprivation of rights. ... To give constitutional sanction to that inference in this case, however well-intentioned may have been the military command on the Pacific Coast, is to adopt one of the cruelest of the rationales used by our enemies to destroy the dignity of the individual and to encourage and open the door to discriminatory actions against other minority groups in the passions of tomorrow. ...

I dissent, therefore, from this legalization of racism. Racial discrimination in any form and in any degree has no justifiable part whatever in our democratic way of life.

Japanese American girl saying the Pledge of Allegiance

Did a legitimate military reason exist to place Japanese Americans in internment camps?

resources were now being poured into producing military equipment and supplying the troops, consumers faced shortages of all kinds. To deal with the scarcity of resources, the government rationed many goods, including gas and sugar, by distributing coupon books that allotted families a set amount of each item. In an effort to save wool, cotton, and nylon, the War Production Board (WPB) dictated fashion trends by forbidding tailors to make cuffs, vests, or double-breasted jackets for men. The WPB's demand that bathing suit manufacturers use 10 percent less material meant that skintight one-piece bathing suits soon took the place of billowing bathing costumes on America's beaches. Hemlines on ladies' skirts also rose to save fabric.

The government spent as never before, expanding the federal budget from $9 billion in 1939 to $100 billion by 1945. As in World War I, the nation used conscription to fill the ranks and enlisted the help of big business to provide the masses of guns, tanks, ships, and bullets that a modern army needed. Numbers help convey the immensity of the American war effort. The military grew from 227,000 to 16 million, of whom 10 million were conscripted. American industry produced 77,000 ships, 300,000 airplanes, 2.5 million trucks, and 20 million small arms for the American and Allied armed forces. Nearly 15 million civilians relocated during the war to take advantage of opportunities in cities with booming wartime industries such as Los Angeles, New Orleans, Seattle, Detroit, and Philadelphia. The sudden growth of many cities forced hundreds of thousands of recent migrants to live in "the backs of stores, in public buildings, warehouses, and garages," the Bureau of Labor reported.

To combat the growing labor shortage, the War Manpower Commission, a wartime agency charged with keeping American workers on the job, tried to lure "Mrs. Stay-at Home" into the wartime workforce. Whether swayed by wartime propaganda or attracted instead by new employment opportunities and higher wages, droves of married women entered the workplace. Nearly 19 million women held jobs during the war, for the moment a record high. Many of these women would have worked anyway. Only 3 million new female workers entered the wartime workforce. Not all Americans supported this change in the domestic life of the nation, however. Male workers resented competing with women for desirable positions. Many mothers also expressed mixed feelings about leaving their children in day care.

Over 350,000 women served in the armed forces, including 150,000 in the Women's Army Corps (WAC). The majority of women in uniform served as nurses and clerks, fulfilling vital communication and record-keeping services. Many men and the media found these clerical roles easy to deride. The press nicknamed the WACs the "Petticoat Army" and their quarters "Fort Lipstick." The recruiting slogan for the WACs—"Release a man for combat"—publicly underscored the different risks faced by women and men in the military.

> "Instead of cutting the lines of a dress, this woman cuts the pattern of aircraft parts."
>
> 1943 newsreel, *Glamour Girls of '43.*

Female soldiers also performed more traditionally "male" tasks, serving as gunnery instructors, mechanics, and truck drivers, and 1,000 women even flew combat aircraft from domestic manufacturers to overseas bases. General Douglas MacArthur called female troops "my best soldiers." At least one congressman, however, offered a competing vision, wondering "what has become of the manhood of America?" now that women had a formal place in the armed forces.

Once victory seemed ensured in 1944, government-sponsored propaganda reversed course, embracing a vision that emphasized women's domestic responsibilities instead of their public duties. Toward the end of the war, the *Saturday Evening Post* carried this "Mothers at Work" ad (**23.11**) that urged women to consider the toll that working outside the home had on their children. The ad also emphasized this woman's imminent postwar need for new appliances. As expected the overall percentage of women working returned to 28 percent (from a wartime high of 36 percent) in 1947 as women quit their

23.11 "Mothers at Work"
As the war drew to a close, official posters and private advertisements encouraged women to revert to their traditional roles as homemakers.

What competing visions of working women emerged over the course of the war?

jobs to raise families or employers fired them to free up positions for returning veterans. Similarly, only a few thousand women remained in uniform as the military cut slots reserved for female troops. Their position within the armed forces rebounded a bit, however, when an act of Congress in 1948 gave women a permanent, though segregated, place in the army, navy, and air force. The debate over whether to limit female soldiers to support tasks or use them in active operations was only just beginning.

Even children pitched in to help the war effort. To encourage children's active participation, the government released photographs of small girls and boys doing their bit (**23.12**). This young boy takes care of the family shopping while his parents work in war-related jobs, handing the family's ration card to the merchant. At home this little girl carefully saves tin and foil in separate jars for the local scrap drive, all scarce materials needed by the military. Classrooms across the nation collected pennies and nickels for war bonds, which the federal government sold to Americans to help finance the war. The remoteness of the war often made it seem like a great adventure to children, who enthusiastically scoured their neighborhoods for aluminum, rubber, and tin foil, sometimes banging pots and pans outside homes until residents came forth with a donation. War games gained popularity on the nation's playgrounds, and some children joined the Junior Commandos, a group that let young uniformed recruits, only a few years away from qualifying to fight in the army, train on a rugged obstacle course.

With the wartime economy booming, many Americans concluded that wars, by nature, were good for the economy. However, a set of unique factors made World War II particularly beneficial for the American economy.

- The war effort withdrew 16 million servicemen and women from the workforce just as millions of new positions were created, absorbing all surplus labor and creating a labor shortage.
- Massive government spending on the war, not the war per se, ended the Depression. If the government had been willing to spend $323 billion (the total cost of the war) on New Deal programs, then the economy would likely have rebounded earlier.
- The wartime boom years came at the expense of future generations. Direct taxation paid for less than half of the war's cost. It took until 1970 for the government to finish paying off its war debts.

During the war, prosperity and unity of purpose failed to guarantee tranquility in labor relations on the home front. Competing visions on the meaning of wartime sacrifice emerged immediately. The chairman of the National War Labor Board dramatized the difficulty of asking unions for wage

23.12 Children and War
Children helped in the war effort by collecting metal for neighborhood scrap drives and by shopping with a ration card while their parents worked.

Why was World War II unique in comparison to other American wars?

concessions by noting, "If you say to the boys, 'Why don't you make a sacrifice for your country?' they are going to say, 'That is fine. I am making a sacrifice for my country, but I am not going to make it to increase the profits of General Motors.'" Workers were right to suspect that big business profited tremendously from the war. Government contracts with generous profit margins, federal loans for factory conversion or expansion, and tax write-offs went overwhelmingly to the nation's one hundred largest companies. Even companies that at first glance appeared peripheral to the war effort prospered. Both Coca-Cola and Wrigley's Gum, for instance, managed to get their products declared essential war commodities, thus gaining access to carefully rationed sugar and shipping space. By following American servicemen around the globe, Coca-Cola cultivated a worldwide taste for its beverage. Wrigley's Gum convinced the War Department that gum reduced stress in war workers and combat troops. The company provided a free stick for every soldier's combat rations.

> "If you are going to ... go to war ... in a capitalist country, you have to let business make money out of the process or business won't work."
>
> Secretary of War HENRY L. STIMSON

During the war, labor's clout, like that of big companies, also expanded. Union rolls swelled from 8.7 to 14.7 million thanks in part to supportive War Labor Board policies. Industrialists tried to use the wartime rhetoric of sacrifice to rein in these growing unions. In one published advertisement, for example, the Jenkins Valve firm linked work slowdowns (used to pressure a company to agree to labor's demands) to the unnecessary deaths of American sailors. The ad showed a small child staring at a sailor's cap that had washed up along the shore; above ran the caption "Is a Plant Slow Down Worth It?" Unions did not completely abandon strikes, but overall the war ushered in a less militant era of collective bargaining.

Racial Discord

The war provided many opportunities for racial minorities to assert their claims for equal rights in all aspects of American social and political life. These groups offered a strikingly different view of the war's ultimate purpose. Unlike the majority of white Americans who confined their thoughts to the struggle against fascism abroad, many civil rights leaders championed a competing vision that sought to eradicate discrimination at home. Using the war to promote a **double-victory campaign** against both fascism overseas and racial prejudice at home, these activists promoted a vision of an egalitarian and color-blind society.

At first the wartime boom threatened to leave African Americans behind because many essential wartime industries refused to hire blacks. In 1941, the African American labor leader A. Philip Randolph threatened to assemble 10,000 blacks in front of the Lincoln Memorial in Washington, D.C., to "demand the right to work and fight for our country." Nationally known for successfully organizing a union for black railroad porters, Randolph realized that FDR's lock on the black vote gave him little reason to offer more than sympathy in private meetings with black leaders about rampant racial discrimination. To pressure FDR to act on blacks' behalf, a step certain to anger the president's white Southern supporters, Randolph resolved to publicly protest employment discrimination.

Randolph's idea for a march on Washington immediately attracted the support of civil rights groups and the ire of the White House. When FDR tried to convince Randolph to call off the march, Randolph stood firm, telling the president, "We feel as you have wisely said: 'No people will lose their freedom fighting for it.'" Seeking to avoid an embarrassing demonstration that highlighted racial problems at home, FDR agreed to issue an executive order that forbade discrimination in the defense industry and government if Randolph canceled the march. Roosevelt's order also established the Fair Employment Practices Committee to handle complaints of discrimination. For the first time since Reconstruction, the period following the Civil War, the federal government was intervening directly to protect the civil rights of African Americans. Randolph's aborted demonstration later inspired the 1963 march on Washington, where black civil rights leader Martin Luther King Jr. delivered his "I Have a Dream" speech standing before the Lincoln Memorial (see Chapter 27).

Why did big business prosper during the war?

Interest in direct action grew throughout the war. The Fellowship of Reconciliation's Committee on Racial Justice initiated a wave of sit-ins where groups of blacks and whites entered segregated restaurants together and refused to leave when denied service. In Washington, D.C., Howard University students successfully picketed segregated restaurants with signs that read "We Die Together. Let's Eat Together" and "Are You for Hitler's Way or the American Way? Make Up Your Mind."

Nearly 1 million blacks served in the armed forces during the war, including Brigadier General Benjamin O. Davis, the first African American general in the U.S. Army. The War Department finally agreed to train African American pilots, and the Tuskegee Airmen (who received their stateside training at Alabama's Tuskegee Institute) amassed an admirable war record in Europe. The military remained segregated, however, and the overwhelming majority of black soldiers served in noncombatant units where they cleared beaches in France of mines, manned supply lines transporting food and ammunition to front-line troops, and built roads and railroads for the advancing army.

Within the United States black servicemen continued to receive daily reminders of their second-class status. When a group of black soldiers entered a whites-only restaurant in Salina, Kansas, the owner stopped them. We "just stood there inside the door, staring at what we had come to see—the German prisoners of war who were having lunch at the counter. . . . This was really happening. It was no jive talk. The people of Salina would serve these enemy soldiers and turn away black American G.I.'s," one soldier recalled. The proper epitaph to mark each black soldier's grave in the Pacific, African Americans sarcastically told one another, would be "here lies a black man killed fighting a yellow man for the protection of a white man."

The double-victory campaign laid the groundwork for the postwar civil rights movement by pioneering new strategies that would later prove extraordinarily successful. The accelerated migration northward also created new bases of political power that would aid the civil rights movement in the 1950s and 1960s. Throughout the war hundreds of thousands of African American civilians hit the road in search of job opportunities in midwestern and western cities. In 1943 Los Angeles welcomed 10,000 black migrants a month, most from Texas and Louisiana. Overcrowding and changing demographics created explosive racial situations in many urban areas. The most serious wartime race riot took place in 1943 in Detroit, Michigan. Home to the nation's largest automobile manufacturers, Detroit became the leading producer of military goods when these companies began manufacturing jeeps and tanks for the military. Plentiful jobs drew thousands of migrants to the city, including African Americans, who had trouble finding adequate lodging in the strictly (albeit unofficially) segregated city housing market. White workers, resentful at working next to black workers, staged work slowdowns in the city's wartime defense plants. To protest racial discrimination some black residents initiated a "bumping campaign," purposefully nudging whites off sidewalks. The anticipated confrontation finally came on a warm spring afternoon when several groups of black and white teenagers tussled at a crowded amusement park located on Belle Isle. As the violence escalated, a mob of 5,000 whites formed to attack blacks as they crossed the bridge back to the mainland. Racial rampaging soon engulfed the entire city. Hundreds of African Americans were injured and twenty-five were killed before state and federal troops restored order. Nine whites also died in the rioting.

Horace Pippin, a self-taught African American painter who rocketed to fame in the late thirties, took note of the racial discord on the home front in his 1943 painting *Mr. Prejudice* (**23.13**). Pippin's composition expressed doubt that the double-V campaign would succeed. In the painting a racist white worker, backed by a Klansman, hammers a chisel down the center of a V, the symbol of victory. A fellow worker stands to his left, holding a noose—a reference to lynching. The Statue of Liberty, portrayed as an African American woman, is toppling down as the dream of racial unity unravels. The fractured V threatens to crack into two, permanently dividing the friendly white soldiers reaching out to their black comrades in arms—a doctor, sailor, aviator, and soldier who are all serving loyally during the war.

African Americans were not the only targets of racial violence, however. The same summer that racial violence rocked Detroit, white sailors and soldiers on leave in Los Angeles began a ten-day rampage against Mexican American **zoot-suiters**, youths who wore baggy pants, long oversize coats, and broad-brimmed hats. The zoot-suit was a fashion trend established by African American men in the thirties. By the war years white Americans viewed zoot-suiters at best as juvenile delinquents

How did African Americans challenge racial discrimination during the war?

who refused to dress and act properly, and at worst as marauding criminal gangs bent on robbery and rape. Some *pachucos*, as zoot-suiters called themselves, engaged in criminal activity, but most limited their adolescent rebellion to wearing different clothes from adults.

The explosive growth in the Mexican American community, coupled with a general intolerance for any nonconformity in time of war, set the stage for the conflict in Los Angeles. Street fights between sailors and Mexican American men escalated into full-scale rioting when organized groups of servicemen began attacking boys as young as twelve and Mexican American businesses. Local white civilians joined in the rioting, and when a mob came upon a zoot-suiter, they often beat and stripped him and sometimes even burned his clothes. The casualties included more than a hundred seriously injured Mexican Americans, and at least a hundred more who refused hospital care. Newspapers in Los Angeles egged on the white crowds by praising their efforts to rid the city of the "hoodlums" and "gangsters." Federal investigators cited racial prejudice as the cause of the riots, but Los Angeles nonetheless passed an ordinance that prohibited wearing zoot-suits on city streets. The image of Mexican Americans as disaffected youths belied the reality that 500,000 Latinos served alongside whites in the armed forces during the war, playing a large role in the doomed defense of the Philippines and heavily represented among Medal of Honor winners.

23.13 Horace Pippin, *Mr. Prejudice* (1943)
The fractured V in Pippin's painting suggested that the African American vision of using the war to secure democracy at home and abroad was in jeopardy. [*Source:* Horace Pippin (1888–1946), "Mr. Prejudice," 1943. Oil on canvas, 18 × 14 inches. Philadelphia Museum of Art, Gift of Dr. and Mrs. Matthew T. Moore. Photo by Graydon Wood. 1984-108-1]

Perceived as natural-born warriors, Native Americans encountered less hostility within the armed forces than blacks or Latino Americans. More than 25,000 Native Americans served, including the famed Navajo code talkers who transmitted secret messages between units in their native language, baffling the Japanese, who never deciphered it. Military service offered many young Native Americans their first decent wages and a chance to leave the reservation. Government officials expected military service to hasten the process of assimilation, since Native American soldiers lived among whites. Yet sending men into combat also gave some tribes a reason to resurrect rituals surrounding battle, such as requiring returning soldiers to spend time in a sweat hut to cleanse themselves of the evils associated with war. Serving in the military, therefore, became a catalyst that both expanded veterans' knowledge of the wider world and reinforced their own cultural traditions, helping them to see themselves and mainstream society in a different light.

How did the wartime experiences of African Americans compare to those of Latino Americans?

On the Front Lines

No bombs fell on American cities and no occupying armies marched through the streets, but with 16 million men in the armed forces, nearly everyone knew someone who might not make it home. The United States essentially fought two separate wars in World War II, one against Germany and its allies in Europe; the other against Japan in the Pacific. The initial news from the battlefront was not good, as the American armed forces encountered one setback after another. America had determined foes in Japan and Germany, and defeating them required time and patience. Important first victories finally came, but the closer the Allies got to Japan and to Germany, the harder their enemies fought. Initially leery of exposing Americans to blood and gore, over time magazines and newspapers began to publish photographs that registered the rising toll of death at the front. The public welcomed photographs of enemy destruction as evidence that the nation was nearing victory, but reacted strongly to any sign of suffering by American soldiers. Nothing prepared the public, however, for the shocking details that emerged from liberated Nazi concentration camps in 1945.

23.14 War in the Pacific
Allied victories at Guadalcanal, the Coral Sea, and Midway halted the Japanese expansionist drive, preparing the way for the Allied island-hopping campaign in 1944–1945.

Defeat, Then Victory

Until mid-1942 the American military reeled from one defeat to another in the Pacific. The attack on Pearl Harbor prevented the United States from interfering with Japan's sweeping conquest of Southeast Asia and the western Pacific island chains, as shown in this map (**23.14**). American and Filipino soldiers fought courageously in the Philippines; but lacking supplies these troops finally surrendered in the spring of 1942.

To solidify its control of East Asia, Japan planned to attack Australia through Port Moresby, on the island of New Guinea, and then fight a decisive battle with the American navy in the western Pacific that would force the United States to sue for a negotiated peace. The Americans thwarted these plans in the Battle of Coral Sea (May 3–8, 1942) and the Battle of Midway (June 4–6, 1942). In the former a duel of naval aircraft ended with Japan calling off its planned invasion of Australia. In

What does this map reveal about the military challenges facing the United States in the Pacific?

the latter American dive-bomber squadrons surprised a convoy of Japanese aircraft carriers in the midst of refueling their planes. Japan's heavy losses at Midway prevented Japan from launching any major naval offensives for the rest of the war. Midway was a crucial turning point that put Japan permanently on the defensive.

America adopted a "Europe First" strategy, but the war in the European theater began equally poorly for the Allies. Initially the United States wanted to get needed supplies across the Atlantic and open up a second front against Germany in Western Europe. Meeting the first goal required winning the Battle of the Atlantic. For eighteen months the Allied cause looked grim as German submarines controlled the seas and sank an average of one hundred ships a month. The extensive submarine activity on Map 23.1 illustrates the ferocity of the struggle to control the Atlantic. Finally, in the summer of 1943, the tide began to turn in the Allies' favor. Better air surveillance, improved radar, the discovery that the Germans had broken the convoy-routing code, and breaking the German submarine code all contributed to Allied success in the Atlantic.

The issue of opening a second front in Europe remained. Roosevelt was reluctant to commit large numbers of American land forces until he could field an army that was better equipped and supplied than those of its adversaries. But he recognized that committing American ground troops to the war in Europe would build morale at home; it would also prevent the Russians from seeking a separate peace with Germany.

Soviet leader Joseph Stalin urged Britain and the United States to invade Nazi-occupied France in 1943. Churchill and FDR refused. Britain worried about repeating the trench stalemate of World War I, while the Americans doubted that their inexperienced army could prevail against the first-rate German troops stationed in France. As an alternative FDR and Churchill decided to attack through "the soft underbelly of Europe" by first establishing supply and air bases in North Africa and then attacking Italy. Despite some American blunders on the battlefield, by the summer of 1943 the Allies had gained control of North Africa and invaded Sicily, as shown in the map "The European Theater" (**23.15**).

Italy's surrender on September 8, 1943, meant little, however. German forces invaded the Italian peninsula, saving Mussolini's regime and keeping Allied troops bogged down in a bloody campaign that lasted until the spring of 1945. When Mussolini tried to escape in 1945 with the retreating Germans, Italian resistance fighters captured him and his mistress, shot them, and strung them upside down in a

23.15 The European Theater The Soviet army fought alone in Europe until the United States invaded Italy in 1943 and joined with Great Britain to launch the D-Day invasions in 1944.

Why did the United States attack the Axis powers first in Italy, rather than France?

public square in Milan where resistance fighters had been executed.

In 1943 the Allies launched the first major incendiary attack of the war. The bombing raids on Hamburg, a major industrial German city, ignited a firestorm in the hot, dry conditions that killed 45,000 and wounded nearly 40,000. Germany's aerial attacks during the Battle of Britain in 1940–1941 had hardened British views about bombing civilians in Germany, while the Americans preferred trying to hit actual military and industrial installations. Dresden, home to key railroad lines, was the site of another devastating incendiary bombing raid in February 1945, which killed approximately 35,000 Germans. Although many American bombs failed to hit their precisely designated industrial or military targets, in fighting Germany, the United States never formally adopted terror bombing, the strategy of dropping high concentrations of bombs on civilian populations to create panic and misery.

In late November 1943 FDR and Churchill met with Stalin for the first time in Tehran, the capital of Iran, to discuss Allied strategy for the coming year. During the conference FDR privately described Stalin as "altogether quite impressive," and the president purposefully stayed in the Soviet Embassy to build a good rapport with the Soviet leader. Churchill remained more leery of Soviet intentions to expand its influence into Eastern Europe after the war. The Soviet's victory at Stalingrad (January–February 1943), a pivotal battle that put the Allies on the path to victory, buoyed optimism that the tide had turned in Russia's favor on the Eastern Front. Within a few months, the Soviets would also prevail in Leningrad, ending a 900-day German siege of the city that lasted from September 1941–January 1944. Churchill wanted to join the fight in the East by launching an Anglo-American invasion of the Balkans through the Adriatic Sea. FDR doubted that Americans would support a sustained campaign in Eastern Europe when the nation's traditional interest lay in defending Britain and France. In addition the president was reluctant to send American troops into a region that the USSR clearly intended to dominate after the war. The president was wary of antagonizing the Soviet Union when he still hoped to convince Stalin to declare war against Japan once the European war ended. Instead, the United States persuaded Britain to join the United States in an invasion of France in 1944.

The campaign in the Pacific followed a similar strategy of attacking Japan in the "soft underbelly" of its empire in the South Pacific. The Allies opened this campaign with successful, but difficult attacks on Guadalcanal in the Solomon Islands and on New Guinea. In early 1943 Japan accepted its defeat in the South Pacific by withdrawing its fleet and aircraft to a new defensive line that extended through Southeast Asia, the Philippines, and the Mariana Islands.

To keep up the pressure on Japan, the Allies decided to launch a two-pronged attack on Japanese forces in the Central and South Pacific. From the Central Pacific the Americans hoped to establish a naval blockade that cut Japan off from supplies in the south. The United States quickly took the Gilbert and Marshall Islands. During the subsequent invasion of the island of Saipan in the Marianas, the Americans destroyed so many Japanese naval aircraft in the Battle of the Philippine Sea (June 19–20, 1944) that the battle became known as "the Great Marianas Turkey Shoot." The final capture of the Mariana Islands in August 1944 put the United States, armed with massive and heavily-loaded B-29s that could travel up to 2,000 miles, within striking distance of Japan.

"I shall return," General Douglas MacArthur had proclaimed when FDR ordered him to head to Australia and leave his embattled troops on the Philippines in 1942. On October 20, 1944, he fulfilled this promise by wading ashore in the Leyte Gulf four hours after the first American force

23.16 General MacArthur's Return to the Philippines MacArthur used the press to publicize his return to the Philippines in 1944. Military photographers captured his purposeful stride ashore, and that evening MacArthur proclaimed in a radio address, "People of the Philippines: I have returned ... Rally to me."

How did the tide gradually turn in favor of the Allies in Europe and the Pacific?

23.17 "A Wartime Souvenir"
In 1944, *Life* magazine chose this photo as its picture of the week. The young woman's fiancé sent her a Japanese skull with an inscription that read: "This is a good Jap—a dead one picked up on the New Guinea beach." Collecting enemy body parts as war trophies was common among American troops fighting in Japan, but not in the European theater.

landed in a carefully choreographed act that MacArthur insisted on filming several times to get just right. To build morale and enhance his reputation as a fearless leader, MacArthur presented himself as part of the invasion force, a general who was willing to get his boots wet and resolutely press forward, as seen in this photo (**23.16**). The Battle of Leyte Gulf (October 23–25, 1944), the largest naval battle in history, ended with an American victory. It took until July 1945, however, to completely liberate the Philippines from isolated infantry garrisons.

With the war advancing well in the Pacific, Americans began to feel optimistic about achieving a swift victory. These hopes faded, however, when Japan switched from fighting a strategic war to waging a war of attrition. Mounting losses, Japan's leaders reasoned, would force the United States to the negotiating table. With conventional weapons like ships, guns, and planes in short supply, Japan introduced a set of suicidal battlefield tactics on land and sea in the fall of 1944 that dramatically intensified the struggle. In the western Caroline Islands, Japanese soldiers resolved to fight to the last man. Forcing the Americans to rout out every enemy soldier from an interlocking system of caves and bunkers prolonged the battle and raised American casualties. During the Battle of Leyte Gulf, the first kamikaze pilots plowed their planes into the decks of six American ships, setting off a cascade of explosions from the ships' gasoline and ordnance that damaged five and sank one.

A month later seaman James Fahey was on a ship under attack. He and the sailors battled for hours, shooting down a steady stream of incoming aircraft. "The explosions were terrific as the suicide planes exploded in the water . . . the water looked like it was on fire," Fahey wrote in his diary. Parts of the destroyed planes fell onto his ship, and during a lull in the action, the sailors went sifting through the debris for souvenirs. "The deck near my mount was covered with blood, guts, brains, tongues, scalps, hearts, arms etc. from the Jap pilots," Fahey recalled. Fahey watched men select body parts to preserve in alcohol and send home to relatives. Soldiers involved in the Pacific island–hopping campaigns exhibited a similar macabre interest in collecting Japanese soldiers' body parts. In May 1944 *Life* magazine published "A Wartime Souvenir," showing an attractive young woman writing a thank-you note to her fiancé for sending her a souvenir Japanese skull (**23.17**). "The armed forces disapprove strongly of this sort of thing," *Life* noted. Yet the image of this woman calmly contemplating her war trophy elicited no controversy. Instead, many Americans exorcised their own desire for revenge against Japan through such images. The press had to handle photographs of American war dead more carefully (see *Images as History: Combat Photography*, page 706).

The Final Push in Europe

On June 6, 1944, the Allies launched the D-Day invasion, their long-anticipated invasion of Normandy, a region of northern France, under the command of General Dwight D. Eisenhower. "The eyes of the world are upon you," the popular leader told his troops. Eisenhower, raised in a poor Jehovah Witness Kansas family, became a national hero for his successful planning and execution of the D-Day invasions and subsequent offensives through France and Germany. His achievements and sunny personality would make him an appealing postwar presidential candidate in 1952 (see Chapter 24).

What do media images of the Japanese suggest about American wartime culture?

Images as History

COMBAT PHOTOGRAPHY

War photography brings the realities of combat into the homes of ordinary citizens. How do pictures of combat force viewers to think about the overall meaning and worthiness of the conflict?

For the first year and a half of American involvement, when there was little good news to report, the military believed that photographs of dead American soldiers would weaken morale on the home front. In 1943 Allied victories in the South Pacific and North Africa raised spirits at home—perhaps a bit too much in the eyes of some officials. Aware of the long road ahead and the need for continued sacrifice on the home front, the War Department now approved the dissemination of bloody battlefield photographs.

In September 1943 *Life* magazine published a photograph of three American soldiers lying partially buried in the sand in New Guinea. In the accompanying editorial *Life* anticipated the public's shock at seeing the first photograph of American war dead. "Why print this picture, anyway, of three American boys dead upon an alien shore? Is it to hurt people? To be morbid?" *Life* editors wrote. "Those are not the answers. The reason is that words are never enough."

Magazine editors chose their images from an ever-increasing supply of casualty pictures. Two-thirds of the 291,557 American troops killed in battle during the war died in 1944–1945. Photographer Joe Rosenthal's "Old Glory Goes Up on Mt. Suribachi, Iwo Jima," a candid shot of five marines and one navy corpsman raising a flag on the Pacific Island of Iwo Jima on February 23, 1945, remains the most famous image from World War II. Rosenthal's Pulitzer Prize–winning photograph would inspire a Marine Corps statue, erected in Washington, D.C., in 1954.

Military censors forbade publication of photographs containing identifiable war dead or badly mutilated corpses, worried that such pictures might depress morale on the home front.

"Publication of photos showing some of our boys killed in action had a sobering effect on people and brought the realities of war closer to home," a satisfied War Department official noted.

"Here Lie Three Americans"

The image of six men working together to push the flag upright conveyed the teamwork necessary to defeat Japan, and that the uphill struggle to victory was not quite completed.

Critics later accused Rosenthal of staging this photo, a charge that he denied.

Three of the marines in Rosenthal's photograph died in the ensuing battle. The others returned home and toured the country in an overwhelmingly successful war bond campaign.

"Old Glory Goes Up on Mount Suribachi, Iwo Jima"

How did the political and military situation influence the way Americans viewed these photographs?

Although stormy weather made traversing the English Channel treacherous, and the Americans faced fierce resistance on Omaha Beach, the D-Day invasion was an overwhelming success. The heavy buildup for the attack, involving 175,000 troops, 6,000 aircraft, and 6,000 naval vessels, made complete surprise impossible. But the Allies had dramatically increased the invasion's chances of success by deceiving the Germans into expecting the attack to come farther north. Diversionary bombing, false agent reports, and misleading radio communications convinced the Germans to station the majority of their first-rate infantry divisions farther north. Hitler continued to hold these units in reserve even after the D-Day invasion began, certain that the Normandy landings were just a diversion. The German delay in responding gave the Allies the time they needed to establish a beachhead that stretched for 55 miles by the end of the first day.

Life photographer Robert Capa hit the beaches with the troops, living up to his famous statement, "If your pictures aren't good enough, you aren't close enough." Anxious to see Capa's photographs, a rushing darkroom technician used too much heat to dry the film and inadvertently melted nearly all his images. The excessive heat blurred the remaining few, creating a surreal aura to this instantly iconic image (**23.18**) of an American soldier struggling through the turbulent surf to reach the shore. Capa put down his camera long enough to pull this soldier to safety after a bullet struck him in the right shoulder.

It was still a long way from Normandy to Berlin, however. After two more months of hard fighting, the Allies finally began to push forward. On August 15, 1944, the Americans launched a second invasion through the south of France. Within a month these troops had joined with the Normandy invasion forces to establish a continuous Allied front from the English Channel to the German frontier. Hitler had no intention of going down without a fight. In December 1944 the Germans launched a massive counteroffensive. The Battle of the Bulge, so named for the Germans' pocket of penetration into Allied lines, was the largest battle fought by the American Army in Europe. Fighting in the snow and bitter cold, the Allies suffered 77,000 casualties before finally halting the German counterattack a month later.

> "Two kinds of people are staying on this beach, the dead and those who are going to die."
>
> Colonel GEORGE TAYLOR, urging his dazed troops forward on Omaha Beach during the D-Day invasions

When Roosevelt, Churchill, and Stalin met in February 1945 at Yalta, a town in the Ukraine, to discuss their next step, Roosevelt was fresh off an unprecedented fourth-term victory in the 1944 presidential election. The Republican candidate Thomas Dewey, a popular New York State governor, had attacked Roosevelt as a "tired old man" no longer up to the challenge of running the war. Roosevelt solidified support within the Democratic Party by replacing the controversial liberal Henry Wallace with Harry S Truman, a straight-talking moderate senator from Missouri, as his vice-presidential candidate. The selection of an acceptable vice-presidential candidate was important to Democratic Party bosses who feared that the ill Roosevelt might not live to complete a fourth term in office. Suffering from advancing heart disease and the strain of war, Roosevelt nevertheless managed to display renewed energy during the campaign, convincing Americans not to "change horses in mid-stream." He won 432 to 99 votes in the Electoral College, receiving 54 percent of the popular vote.

23.18 D-Day Invasion, 1944 Robert Capa's grainy photograph conveyed the chaos and danger American soldiers faced when they hit the beaches in Normandy, France.

Why did the Allies prevail on D-Day?

At the Yalta Conference the larger question of how to defeat Germany was behind the Allies. The issues now on the table included governing postwar Germany, ensuring victory over Japan, and maintaining peace in the postwar world. At the conference FDR secured a Soviet promise to enter the war against Japan three months after Germany capitulated. In return Stalin wanted the United States and Britain to grant the Soviet Union territorial concessions in Japan and China. For the moment FDR acceded to Soviet control of Eastern Europe, but secured a pledge from Stalin to hold free elections in a liberated Poland.

The decision at the Yalta Conference to name the United States, Britain, France, China, and the USSR as permanent members of the proposed United Nations Security Council, each with the power to veto any resolution, cleared the way to officially create a United Nations (UN) to replace the now-defunct League of Nations. Delegates from fifty nations met in San Francisco between April 25 and June 26, 1945, to found the UN, an international organization that offered nations a place to discuss their differences and collectively promote economic development and peace throughout the world. To ensure that the United States joined the UN, its creators made participation in UN peacekeeping missions voluntary. In addition the Security Council veto gave the United States (and other major powers) a way to control UN activities. Unlike after World War I, when the United States failed to join the League of Nations, the United States was one of the first countries to join. The UN subsequently built its headquarters in New York City.

Now unstoppable in Europe, the Allies crossed the Rhine River into Germany in March. On April 30, 1945, Hitler committed suicide in a bunker 55 feet under the ground in Berlin. After dictating his will and marrying his longtime companion Eva Braun, Hitler bit into a cyanide capsule and shot himself in the head. Two days later Russian soldiers entered Berlin, where they destroyed the bunker and took Hitler's burned remains so an autopsy could confirm he was dead. Germany surrendered unconditionally on May 7, 1945.

America's Response to the Holocaust

In the spring of 1945, Allied troops began liberating the concentration camps holding Jews, Poles, prisoners of war, and a host of other groups that the German state considered enemies or racially inferior. News of the Final Solution, Hitler's plan to systematically murder the Jews and other "lesser" peoples, first reached the West in August 1942. Along with ten other nations, the United States condemned "in the strongest possible terms this bestial policy of cold-blooded extermination." During the war mainstream American newspapers, fearful of reporting falsified atrocity stories amid a glut of war news, had published little about the **Holocaust**, the term used to describe this Nazi-engineered extermination. The United States did little initially to aid European Jews. In January 1944, however, the Secretary of the Treasury, Henry Morgenthau, who was Jewish, protested to FDR that anti-Semitism within the State Department had thwarted a plan to ransom 70,000 Rumanian Jews with private funds, leaving the United States open to charges that it was acquiescing to the "murder of the Jews." FDR immediately issued an executive order establishing the War Refugee Board (WRB). Over the next year the WRB saved approximately 200,000 lives by convincing Rumania and Hungary to stop deportations and helping Jews and other victims of Nazi persecution escape or survive in hiding. *The Holocaust* special feature depicts both the response of the United States to the Holocaust and the scope of German atrocities.

Pressed by some Jewish groups to undertake a dramatic rescue of Europe's Jews by bombing either the concentration camps or the railroads leading to them, Roosevelt demurred. He argued that any diversion of military resources from the ultimate goal of winning the war would only prolong the Jews' suffering. In February 1944 the War Department decided not to send armed forces to rescue "victims of enemy oppression unless such rescues are the direct result of military operations conducted with the objective of defeating the armed forces of the enemy." Bombing Auschwitz, the main Nazi extermination camp in Poland, became a real possibility only in the summer of 1944. In August Allied planes dropped more than 1,000 bombs on synthetic-oil plants less than 5 miles from Auschwitz.

Whether the Allies should have also targeted the gas chambers has provoked heated debate since the war. Advocates of bombing the camps argue that destroying the railroad lines leading to Auschwitz or its gas chambers would have slowed down the killing as liberating Allied troops approached the camps, perhaps saving as many as 100,000 Jews. These would have included Anne Frank, a thirteen-year-old German refugee who was sent to Auschwitz after her

What significant decisions were reached at the 1945 Yalta Conference?

The Holocaust

The United States reacted slowly to Hitler's persecution of Jews in the Depression-plagued thirties. Strict immigration quotas and anti-Semitism limited visas for Jewish refugees fleeing Nazi persecution. After Kristallnacht, a 1938 German rampage against Jewish businesses and homes, FDR granted more Jews asylum, but acceded to public concern over increasing immigration dramatically. In 1939 the United States turned back the *St. Louis*, a ship carrying Jewish refugees who did not have visas to enter the country. Of all nations, the United States, despite its strict immigration quotas, accepted the largest number of Jewish refugees fleeing Nazi persecution. Once at war FDR refused to bomb the concentration camps from the air, worried that any diversion from attacking the German military would lengthen the war. Instead, American ground troops liberated major concentration camps in Western Europe, including Buchenwald, Dachau, and Mauthausen. The Germans killed over 6 million Jews, 3 million Soviet prisoners of war, 2 million non-Jewish Poles, nearly 200,000 disabled individuals, 10,000 Jehovah Witnesses, and an undetermined number of homosexuals.

> "I have gotten rid of the Jews."
> ADOLF HITLER, 1944

German-run Concentration Camps in World War II

Jews in the Holocaust

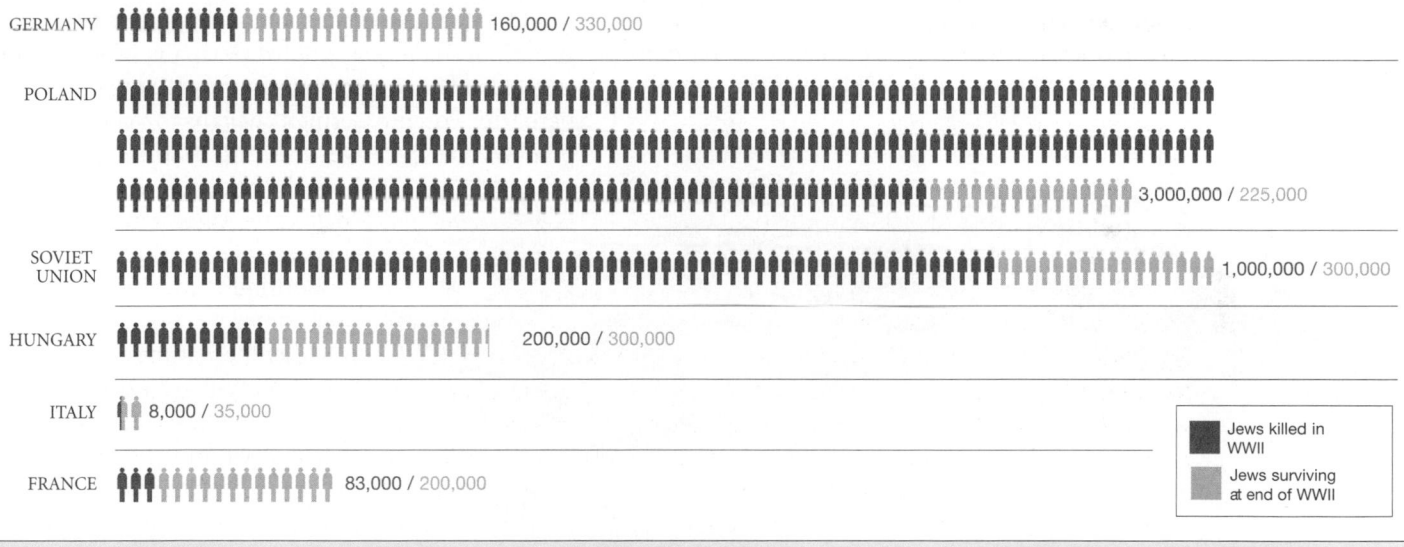

America and the Holocaust

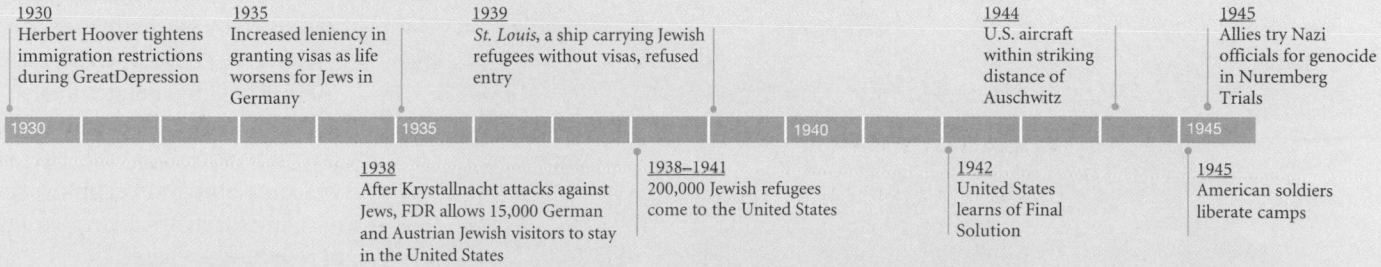

What insights does this data offer on the scope of the Holocaust and the American response?

> "The wrongs which we seek to condemn and punish have been so calculated, so malignant, and so devastating, that civilization cannot tolerate their being ignored, because it cannot survive their being repeated."
>
> American prosecutor, Supreme Court Justice ROBERT JACKSON, in opening the Nuremberg War Crimes Trials

family's capture in Amsterdam and whose journal of her experience in hiding, *The Diary of Anne Frank*, became a postwar literary classic. Detractors note the determination of the Nazis to use any means possible to slaughter the Jews, including mass executions by firing squads and forced marches, until the very end of the war.

As the camps were liberated, reporters tried through words and pictures to convey how 6 million Jews had met their deaths. Even though Americans had grown accustomed to seeing photos of war dead, nothing prepared them for images from the concentration camps. American commanders invited the press into the camps to head off any possible denials over the scope of the Holocaust. Photographs of concentration camps were, one reporter wrote, "so horrible that no newspaper normally would use them, but they were less horrible than the reality."

Soldiers set themselves up as witnesses (a term used to describe both survivors and liberators) who could personally vouch for the extent of the horrors by posing in photographs before piles of corpses, next to the ovens used to cremate bodies, or in showers that dispersed cyanide gas instead of water to asphyxiate victims. "You can photograph results of suffering but never suffering itself," observed one British politician.

By documenting the act of discovering Nazi atrocities, witness photographs helped Americans share the horror that soldiers felt. The American military also posted photographs of concentration camp atrocities in German towns and villages for civilians to see, but many American commanders went further. In the photo shown here (**23.19**), American soldiers assembled German civilians before a truckload of corpses to listen to a lecture on the barbarity. Forcing German civilians to view the carnage with their own eyes, and in some cases bury the bodies, was part of a deliberate Allied campaign to make all Germans accept responsibility for their nation's war crimes.

After the war the Allies jointly tried twenty-two Nazi leaders in the Nuremberg War Crimes Trials. In these trials individual Germans were charged with starting the war, authorizing the killing of prisoners of war, and orchestrating the wartime genocide against victims who mostly came from nations occupied by Germany (see the "Jews in Holocaust" chart, page 709). The United States independently tried thousands of other German officials as well. These trials were not enough to calm the fears of many survivors. Many left Europe to resettle elsewhere.

23.19 German Civilians Viewing Corpses in a Concentration Camp
Photographs from liberated concentration camps, like this one from Buchenwald, Germany, shocked the world. American military commanders forced German civilians, who professed ignorance about the Final Solution, to view and bury the dead.

How did images instruct Americans about the meaning of the Holocaust and their role as liberators?

Ending the Pacific War

Germany was now under Allied control, but in the Pacific the war raged on. There the fighting took a desperate turn in 1945, and each victory cost the United States dearly. Despite a mounting death toll, American troops edged closer to Japan and officials began planning an invasion of the mainland. News of a successful atomic bomb test detonation in the New Mexico desert dramatically altered existing political and military calculations on how to achieve victory. Employing this new, terrible weapon eventually generated conflicting views within the United States over the ethics of atomic warfare.

Edging Closer to Japan

Japan's use of "cave and bunker" tactics on land and kamikazes at sea dramatically raised the cost of capturing Iwo Jima (February 19–March 26, 1945) and Okinawa (April 1–June 21, 1945), the last two islands that remained before the United States could launch an invasion of the Japanese homeland. Battles on Iwo Jima and Okinawa produced some of the toughest fighting of the war.

The Americans coveted the 7-mile pork–chop–shaped island of Iwo Jima for its airstrips, both to stop Japanese fighter planes from harassing B-29s headed to Japan and to provide emergency landing fields for crippled B-29s returning from mainland bombing raids. In their conquest of Iwo Jima, the Americans took only 216 prisoners out of 21,000 enemy troops, the rest perishing in the fighting. As the marines shot flamethrowers into caves to extract hiding enemy soldiers, "the scene became wild and terrible," one correspondent recalled. "More Japs rushed screaming from the caves. They tumbled over the rocks, their clothes and bodies burning fiercely." The capture of Okinawa, needed as a staging area for the actual invasion of Japan, was equally bloody. Weeks of kamikaze attacks alone took the lives of 5,000 sailors, while ground troops squared off against an entrenched enemy determined to fight to the last man.

As on Iwo Jima vast numbers of Japanese soldiers (70,000) perished. In this battle, however, an equal number of Japanese civilians either took their own lives (they had been told of mass rape and torture if taken prisoner) or were killed by Japanese soldiers if they tried to surrender. The Americans suffered 75,000 casualties in capturing Okinawa. With the actual invasion of the Japanese homeland up next, the Americans feared facing, in the words of Harry Truman, "an Okinawa from one end of Japan to the other."

Meanwhile American pilots brought the war home to the Japanese people from newly established air bases in the Marianas. When the bombing campaign began in earnest in the Pacific theater in 1945, the United States quickly abandoned efforts to differentiate between civilian and military targets as it had in Germany. "There are no civilians in Japan," declared one air force official. "We are making War and making it in the all-out fashion which saves American lives, shortens the agony which War is, and seeks to bring about an enduring peace." The United States targeted sixty-seven Japanese cities for incendiary bombing in 1945, resulting in the destruction of 187 square miles and approximately 300,000 deaths. During one night-time raid the entire city of Toyama burned to the ground. The most destructive air attack of the war came on March 9–10, 1945, when incendiary bombs dropped on Tokyo ignited fires that American bombers kept going by spreading gasoline and chemicals over the city. This attack destroyed 16 square miles and killed nearly 90,000 Japanese—more than would perish from the atomic bomb blast over Hiroshima five months later.

Dropping the Atomic Bomb

Franklin D. Roosevelt died at the age of 65 of a cerebral hemorrhage on April 12, 1945, while at his cottage in Warm Springs, Georgia. Throngs of mourners lined railroad tracks and city streets as the casket holding FDR's remains traveled first to Washington, D.C., for funeral services in the White House and then to his final resting spot at his home in Hyde Park, New York. Throughout the grieving nation many Americans could barely remember a time when FDR had not been president.

FDR's firm grip on power had kept his vice president Harry Truman in the dark about the four-year, $20 billion **Manhattan Project**, the code-named secret government research program established to

What new tactics raised the death toll in the Pacific war?

produce the atomic bomb. Thrust overnight into the presidency, Truman faced a host of critical strategic decisions in Europe and the Pacific, none more important than what to do with the newly developed atomic bomb. In mid-July 1945 the United States exploded its first atomic bomb in the New Mexico desert. *Choices and Consequences: How to Use the Atomic Bomb* traces Truman's options and the consequences of his decision to use the bomb against Japan.

> "The crux of the matter is whether total war in its present form is justifiable, even when it serves a just purpose."
>
> German Jesuit Priest in Nagasaki, when the atomic bomb was dropped

On August 6, 1945, a B-29 bomber christened the *Enola Gay* dropped an atomic bomb on the Japanese city of Hiroshima. As pilot Captain Paul Tibbets turned the *Enola Gay* away from Hiroshima, Sergeant George Caron snapped several photographs, giving Americans their first look at the telltale mushroom cloud formation that came to signify nuclear annihilation.Three days later, acting on a standing order to use the atomic bomb "as made ready," an American plane dropped a second atomic bomb on Nagasaki.

Saved from firebomb attacks because of their minimal military value, Hiroshima and Nagasaki presented virgin ground for a clear demonstration of the bomb's force. The United States wanted to make a profound impression on the Japanese. Secretary of War Stimson believed "the atomic bomb was more than a weapon of terrible destruction; it was a psychological weapon." The firebombed ruins of cities like Tokyo, therefore, presented a much less appealing target for demonstrating the full power of a nuclear bomb.

American soldiers scheduled to take part in the planned invasion gave little thought to civilian victims on the ground. "When we learned to our astonishment that we would not be obliged in a few months to rush up the beaches near Tokyo assault-firing while being machine-gunned, mortared, and shelled, for all the practiced phlegm of our tough facades we broke down and cried with relief and joy. We were going to live. We were going to grow to adulthood after all," recalled literary critic Paul Fussell in a 1988 essay, "Thank God for the Atom Bomb."

The Final Surrender

Truman and his advisers recognized that American possession of the atomic bomb was certain to reshape postwar relations between the United States and the Soviet Union. In the minds of several key presidential advisers, America's nuclear monopoly increased the chances of limiting Soviet influence over Eastern Europe and ending the Pacific war without any Soviet help. Soviet spies in the Manhattan Project had already alerted Moscow of the bomb's existence when Truman finally told Stalin in July 1945 at the Potsdam Conference, held near Berlin, that the United States had developed a potent new weapon. When the first bomb destroyed Hiroshima, the Soviets quickly invaded Manchuria on August 8 to seize their planned territorial objectives before the war ended.

By August 10 the combination of two atomic bomb blasts and the Soviet entry into the war caused Japanese Emperor Hirohito to take the unprecedented step of imposing his own views on official policy. Traditionally the emperor simply approved decisions taken by his cabinet. With the peace and militarist factions within his government still strongly divided over whether to make one last stand against the Allies, Hirohito pleaded for peace. After several key military leaders accepted the emperor's wishes, Japan sued for peace with the condition that the Imperial Institution remain. Truman agreed, thereby modifying the original goal of unconditional surrender. Could a Japanese surrender have come sooner if the United States had guaranteed the emperor's office earlier? Before August 6 Truman likened keeping Hirohito to allowing Hitler to remain in power, and he believed that the American people would never accept these terms for peace. In mid-August, however, Truman concluded that letting Hirohito tell the Japanese people to lay down their arms would facilitate the occupation of Japan. Hirohito paved the way for a peaceful surrender when he addressed the Japanese people on the radio for the first time ever, calling on them to accept his decision. The formal surrender took place on September 2 aboard the battleship *Missouri* in Tokyo

How did the war against Japan finally end?

Choices and Consequences

HOW TO USE THE ATOMIC BOMB

President Harry Truman considered the bomb a legitimate weapon to use alongside the more conventional tactics of terror bombing, an economic blockade, and a planned invasion of Japan. He did, however, face some choices over how to exploit this new weapon to meet his goals of securing an unconditional surrender from Japan, saving American lives, and establishing American postwar supremacy over the Soviet Union.

Choices

1. Demonstrate the bomb's destructive power in a trial demonstration on an uninhabited area to convince Japan to surrender.
2. Drop one atomic bomb and give Japan time to react.
3. Drop the two atomic bombs in American possession.
4. Inform the Soviet Union of the bomb's existence before dropping it.

Decision

Truman chose to drop both atomic bombs on virgin sites to magnify the psychological shock of one bomb causing so much destruction. Senior advisers rejected a test demonstration of the bomb as impractical. Truman vaguely informed Stalin of "a new weapon of unusual destructive force," unaware that spies in the Manhattan Project had already alerted Stalin of the bomb's existence.

Consequences

On August 6, 1945 "Little Boy," the atomic bomb dropped on Hiroshima, destroyed three-fourths of the city and killed 80,000 people instantly. "Fat Man" destroyed two-fifths of Nagasaki and killed 35,000 people on August 9. The Emperor announced Japan's surrender on August 14. Truman's attempted secrecy increased Soviet distrust of the United States and unleashed a nuclear arms race between the two nations.

Continuing Controversies

Should the United States have dropped the bomb?
Supporters of Truman's decision claim that dropping the bomb ended the war. It saved 1 million American lives by making an invasion of Japan unnecessary and convinced the Japanese government to end the war. Not all supporters, however, agree that the second bomb on Nagasaki was militarily necessary. Critics counter that the bomb was not needed to end the war. Traditional bombing, the blockade, and Soviet invasion of Manchuria would have ended the war without the planned invasion, critics claim. Because the United States accepted a modified surrender that allowed Japan to retain the Emperor, abandoning the demand for unconditional surrender earlier may have convinced Japan to surrender sooner. Finally, some detractors accuse Truman of using the bomb mainly to curtail Soviet territorial ambitions in postwar Europe and Asia.

Bomb over Nagasaki

Why does so much controversy surround the dropping the atomic bomb and not conventional weapons?

Bay, attended by delegates from Japan and the Allied nations. The deadliest war in human history, whose death toll is charted in "The Human Cost of Global War" (**23.20**), had finally ended.

When news of the Japanese surrender hit the United States, Americans swarmed into the streets to celebrate the good news. "Every female was grabbed and kissed by men in uniform," recalled one woman who joined the crowd in Times Square, New York City. The celebrants included a sailor whose impromptu kiss with a passing nurse was captured in *Life* photographer Alfred Eisenstaedt's candid "Kiss in Times Square" photograph, known as "the smack seen round the world"(**23.21**). Eisenstaedt never revealed the identity of the kissing couple, preferring to let their shielded faces symbolize the exuberance of young men and women who had survived the war. In the ensuing years three nurses and eleven sailors stepped forward to claim that they were the individuals in the photograph.

Hirohito escaped facing trial as a war criminal, but the Allies intended to punish other Japanese leaders for their part in the war. In the few weeks between the Japanese surrender and the Allied occupation of Japan, more than 1,000 officials and officers committed suicide and others destroyed thousands of documents concerning Japanese mistreatment of prisoners of war and massacres of civilians in occupied countries. Nonetheless the Allies convicted thousands of Japanese in a series of war crimes trials throughout East Asia, including twenty-eight major Japanese leaders in Tokyo.

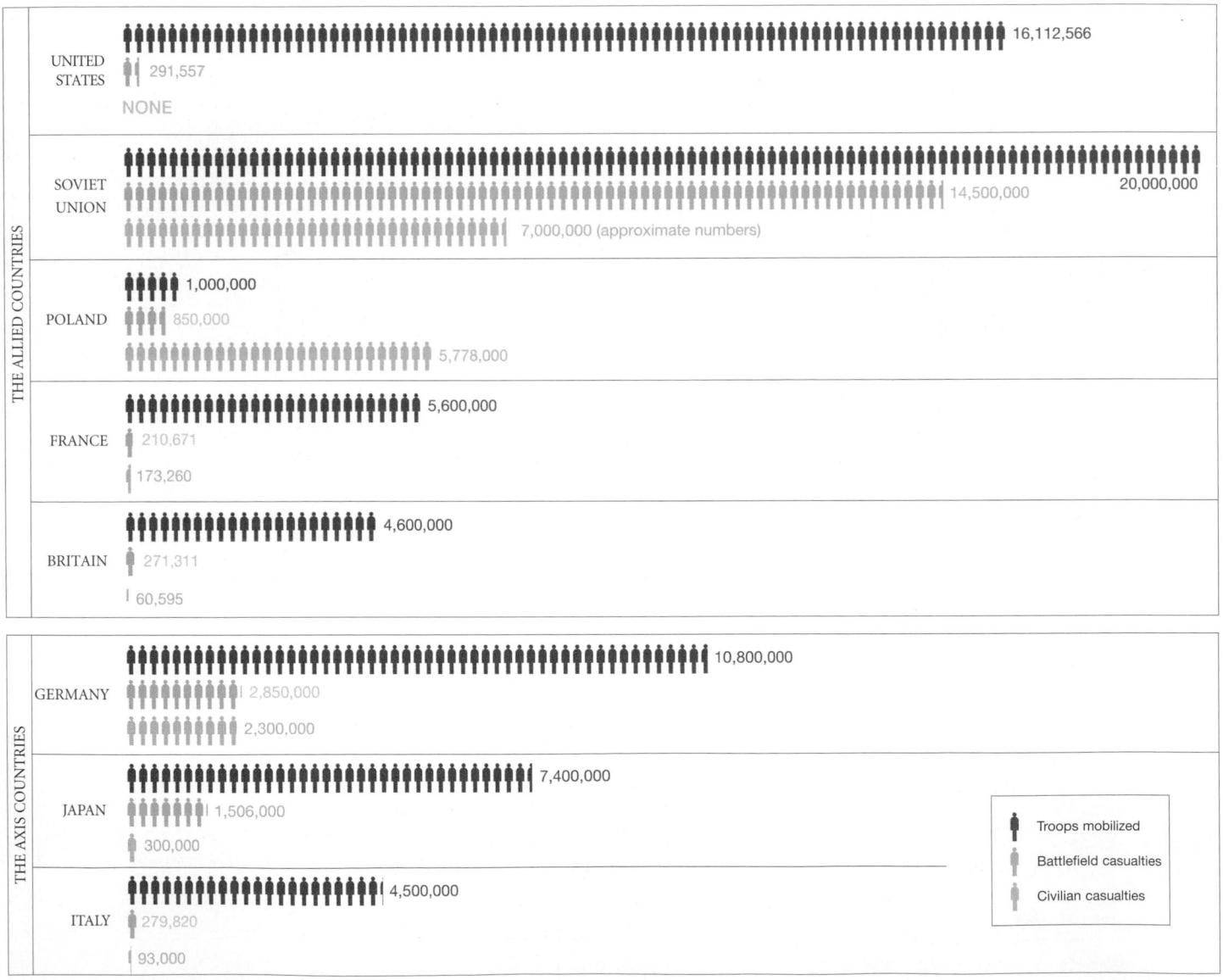

23.20 The Human Cost of Global War Worldwide wartime casualties, those killed and wounded, numbered in the millions.

How might this distribution of wartime casualties shape the postwar world?

23.21 Kiss in Times Square
Jubilation greeted the news that Japan had surrendered. Two strangers shared a passionate kiss in Times Square, conveying the life-affirming energy that filled the air.

Conclusion

Combat, genocide, and terror bombing took millions of lives during World War II. Americans could rightly see themselves as having both suffered and caused the war's deadly violence. After two years of debating conflicting visions of how best to help Britain defeat Germany in Europe, the impetus for war came from the other side of the globe when Japan attacked Pearl Harbor. Fighting on multiple fronts, against enemies that took modern warfare to a new level of brutality, the United States eventually found itself willing to adopt an ends-justifies-the-means approach to winning the war.

At home the U.S. government placed Japanese Americans in internment camps, mounted a massive propaganda campaign to rally support for the war, and took control of the economy by rationing scarce commodities. Americans became accustomed to seeing photographs of death and destruction, but nothing prepared the public for the shock of the Holocaust. The cruelty unleashed during the war and the deadly power of the atom bomb changed the position of the United States in the world, giving the nation new moral and strategic reasons to stay engaged in world affairs after its victory against Germany and Japan.

During the war millions of rural Americans moved to cities, married women entered the workplace in record numbers, and civil rights activists scored significant victories. As men came home from war and Americans rushed to spend their wartime savings, the expected period of peace failed to materialize. Instead, the United States became immediately embroiled in a Cold War with the Soviet Union. For the second time in the same decade, Americans confronted the challenges of exercising world leadership. This time, however, Americans faced the threat of nuclear annihilation.

CHAPTER REVIEW

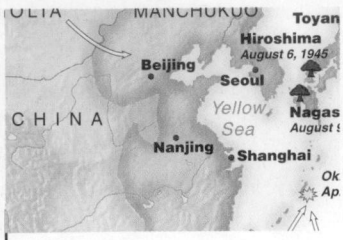

1937

Japan attacks China
Initiates Japan's expansionist drive in East Asia

1939

Germany invades Poland
Beginning of World War II

Neutrality Acts completed
Restrictions on arms sales reflected strong non-interventionist sentiments

1940

France falls to Germany
Completes Hitler's conquest of continental Europe

Economic sanctions against Japan
FDR attempts to halt Japanese aggression

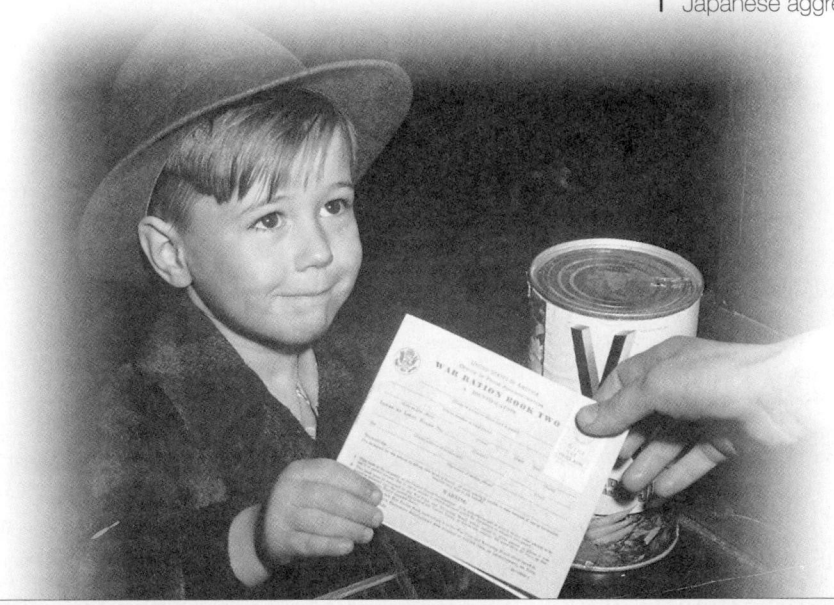

Review Questions

1. What conflicting visions did Americans offer in response to the expansionist drives of Germany and Japan? How did they influence the American path to war?
2. How did visual images influence Americans' views of the war and their enemies?
3. How did the war affect racial, labor, and gender relations on the home front? What conflicting visions emerged?
4. What distinct strategic challenges and battlefield conditions did the United States face in the Pacific and European theaters? How did the United States prevail against Japan and Germany?
5. Why did the United States drop the atomic bomb?

1941

Lend-Lease begins
Interventionist vision prevails as America offers economic aid to Allied side

U.S. ships exchange gunfire with German U-boats
Beginning of unofficial shooting war with Germany in the Atlantic Ocean

Japanese attack Pearl Harbor
United States officially enters World War II

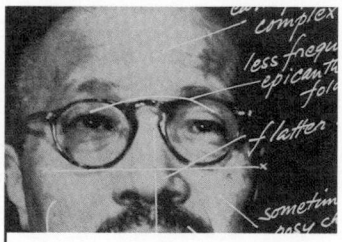

1942

FDR issues Executive Order 9066
Creation of Japanese American internment camps

Battle of Midway
Puts Japan on defensive in Pacific naval war

U.S. government learns of Final Solution
Limited exposure of Hitler's plan to exterminate the Jews

1944

D-Day landings
Beginning of Anglo-American march to Berlin

Supreme Court upholds constitutionality of internment camps
Rules that national security outweighs civil rights

1945

American troops enter concentration camps
Published images confirm German atrocities

FDR dies
Harry Truman assumes presidency

Germany surrenders
End of European war

United States drops atomic bomb on Hiroshima and Nagasaki
Ends war in Pacific, initiates nuclear arms race

Key Terms

non-interventionists Those urging the nation to stay out of overseas conflicts. **686**

interventionists Those advocating direct engagement in overseas conflicts. **686**

fascist state A type of dictatorial regime that arose in Germany, Italy, and Spain that glorified the state over the individual. **686**

Neutrality Acts A series of laws from 1935 to 1939 that restricted arms sales, loans, and transport of goods with nations at war. **687**

"cash and carry" A policy that required belligerent nations to pay cash for goods and transport them on their own ships. **687**

Munich Conference (1938) Hoping to avoid war, Britain and France agreed to let Germany occupy the Sudetenland, a German-speaking part of Czechoslovakia. **687**

Axis Name for nations fighting the Allies, including Germany, Italy and Japan. **688**

Allies (World War II) Name for powers fighting Germany, eventually including the United States, Britain, France, and the Soviet Union. **688**

Lend-Lease A 1941 policy that circumvented "cash and carry" by loaning rather than selling arms to the Allies. **689**

Pearl Harbor A U.S. naval base in Hawaii that the Japanese attacked on December 7, 1941. **690**

internment camps Camps in the United States that held people of Japanese descent under armed guard in isolated areas. **694**

double-victory campaign Civil rights call for victory against both fascism overseas and racial prejudice at home. **699**

zoot-suiters Name given to Mexican American youths who wore oversize suits. **700**

Holocaust German-engineered wartime extermination of Jews and other peoples that Germans considered inferior. **708**

Manhattan Project Secret U.S. wartime project to develop an atomic bomb. **711**

CHAPTER 24

A Divided World

The Early Cold War, 1945–1963

Origins of the Cold War p. 720

> "Communism is on the march on a worldwide scale, which only America can stop."
>
> Senator ARTHUR VANDENBERG, April 26, 1946

As World War II ended, Soviet and American troops, converging from different directions, met and shook hands on a bridge spanning the Elbe River in Germany. Each side was pleasantly surprised by this first encounter with their wartime ally. "They looked like ordinary people. We had imagined something different," recalled one Soviet soldier of American troops. "I guess we didn't know what to expect from the Russians," an American soldier said after the meeting. "If you put an American uniform on them, they could have been American!" Within two years the lost promise of this friendly encounter was obvious to all. A 1947 U.S. propaganda film replayed footage of this historic meeting and struck a lightning bolt across the frozen image of Soviet and American soldiers shaking hands. "Here two worlds actually met," the narrator thundered, "but this coalition was to be torn asunder" by Soviet postwar incursions in Eastern Europe that the United States viewed as part of a Soviet plan for global conquest.

In the decade after the Allies' victory against Hitler, relations between the United States and the Soviet Union soured dramatically. As the contours of the Cold War between the United States and the Soviet Union took shape, two competing ideological visions, an escalating nuclear arms race, and confrontations in Europe and Asia, including a war in Korea, heightened fears that another world war was in the making.

From 1946 to 1965 most Americans viewed the world as sharply divided into free and totalitarian societies. American leaders proclaimed that the United States was engaged in an epic struggle with the Soviet Union over the future of humankind. Protecting the world from the menace of Soviet-led communism became a key American foreign policy goal in this era. Americans fought the Cold War at home as well, where citizens expressed differing views on whether government tactics in rooting out Soviet spies undermined American democracy or saved it. On the other side of the ideological divide, Soviet leaders developed an abiding distrust of Western motives as they sought to counter the American nuclear advantage with territorial and technological gains. As each nation struggled to extend its world influence, Americans once again confronted the crucial question of defining their nation's role in the world.

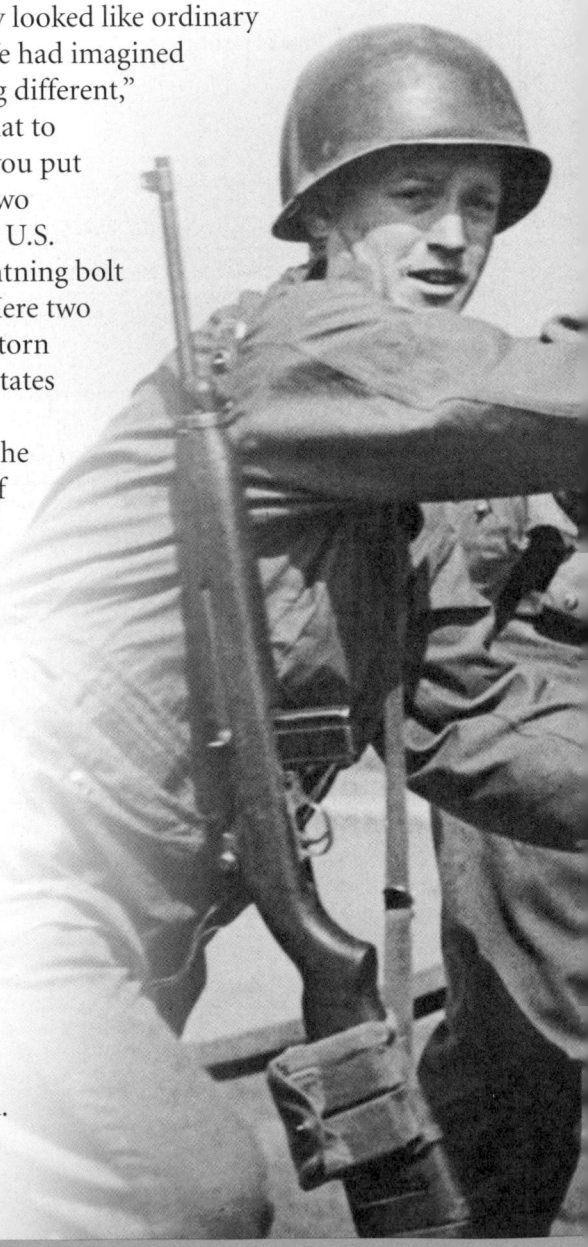

What was the significance of this brief 1945 encounter between U.S. and Soviet soldiers?

Fighting Communism: Cold and Hot War p. 729

Spies in Our Midst p. 737

Averting Nuclear War p. 742

Origins of the Cold War

The United States and the Soviet Union worked effectively together in World War II to defeat Adolf Hitler, but each nation had dramatically different visions of the postwar world. The United States remained dedicated to free markets and democracy, while the Soviet Union embraced a Marxist vision that eschewed private property ownership and celebrated concentrated state authority. Each nation also drew different lessons from the recent war. For the Soviet leader Josef Stalin, Hitler's invasion of the Soviet Union underscored the need to secure his nation's borders by controlling vast amounts of territory in Eastern Europe. The United States feared that Stalin was another Hitler-like dictator, intent on controlling all of Europe. American political leaders believed that maintaining peace in Europe hinged on spreading capitalism and democracy. These differing, often conflicting, visions triggered an immediate postwar clash between the former allies.

Differing Goals in the Postwar World

The origins of the Cold War hark back to World War II. The victory against Hitler came at a huge cost for the Soviet Union. An estimated twenty-five million Soviet soldiers and civilians died, almost ninety times the 291,551 Americans who perished in combat. Germany had attacked the Soviet Union twice in the last thirty years, a fact that contributed to Stalin's obsession with protecting his nation from future attack. Stalin also suspected that the Americans and British had delayed opening up a second front in Europe (see Chapter 23)

24.1 Soviet Soldier Raises Flag over Reichstag, 1945
The Soviet triumph over Germany in World War II came at a high cost for both nations. Stalin sought future security for his nation by keeping war-destroyed Germany weak and installing friendly regimes throughout Eastern Europe.

What important symbolism does this photograph contain regarding the Soviet victory over Germany?

"I have never been talked to like that in my life,"
Soviet foreign minister VYACHESLAV MOLOTOV to Truman

"Carry out your agreements and you won't get talked to like that."
TRUMAN'S retort, angered over the Soviet's refusal to hold Democratic elections in postwar Poland

to further weaken the Soviet Union, causing him to distrust of the United States. This photo (**24.1**) of a soldier waving the Soviet flag from the roof of the Reichstag, the German parliament building, above the ruins of Berlin, illustrated Germany's complete defeat at the end of World War II. It also represented a past that the Soviet Union had no intention of repeating. To protect his nation's borders, Stalin installed friendly Communist governments throughout Eastern Europe to create a buffer zone between Germany and the Soviet Union. He also tried to keep Germany as weak as possible by carting off German heavy machinery to the Soviet Union, disarming the Germany military, and requiring large reparation payments.

In the postwar era Stalin fully expected to retain his firm grip on power within the Soviet Union. Standing only 5 feet tall with a thin mustache, yellowed teeth, and a pockmarked face, Stalin was not physically imposing. In this case, however, images were deceiving. "An unforewarned visitor would never have guessed what depths of calculation, ambition, love of power, jealously, cruelty and sly vindictiveness lurked behind this unpretentious façade," one American diplomat noted. Stalin had been responsible for the deaths of nearly ten million Soviet citizens before World War II, a result of failed agricultural policies that created widespread famine and relentless executions of all suspected political opponents. The Soviet dictator was willing to sacrifice the lives of countless others to achieve his new territorial objectives.

The postwar goals on the American side reflected lingering dismay over the nation's failure to prevent the rise of expansionist regimes in Japan and Germany during the 1930s. Before his death in April 1945, President Franklin D. Roosevelt had argued that American leadership in the newly formed United Nations (UN) could promote a peaceful future by deterring and punishing any aggression before it spun out of control. Roosevelt also stressed the importance of preventing another global depression like the one that had helped bring Hitler to power and had fueled non-interventionist sentiment in the United States.

By themselves these differing ideas on how to maintain peace in Europe did not necessarily guarantee a future clash between the United States and the Soviet Union. During the war the United States and Britain had accepted that the Soviet Union would exert considerable postwar political influence over Eastern Europe. FDR and British Prime Minister Winston Churchill, however, had tried to rein in the Soviet dictator by making him promise to hold free elections in the region. Stalin had offered some backing for Western postwar schemes as well, agreeing to support the United Nations and to a joint occupation of a defeated Germany. When Harry Truman assumed the presidency after Roosevelt's death, even the first signs of Soviet intransigence on fulfilling its wartime agreements failed to produce a permanent rift. To put pressure on Stalin to hold free elections in Soviet-occupied Poland, Truman abruptly canceled Lend-Lease payments, thereby denying much needed aid to the war-torn Soviet Union. When the Soviet foreign minister Vyacheslav Molotov called on the new president in the White House, Truman went even further, personally berating Molotov for Stalin's failure to schedule the promised elections. The long-term impact of this heated exchange was minimal, however. Truman quickly sent an emissary to Moscow to patch things up with Stalin. As a gesture of goodwill, he also reversed his initial decision to suspend Lend-Lease shipments to the Soviet Union.

The American Vision Takes Shape: Kennan's Long Telegram

Over time, however, these initial skirmishes between the United States and the Soviet Union developed into the **Cold War**. This intense ideological conflict between the United States and the Soviet Union and

How did differing memories of the recent past shape U.S. and Soviet goals in postwar Europe?

their allies led to several hot wars around the globe, although the Americans and Soviets never fought each other directly. In the opening phases of the Cold War, each side focused on defining the exact threat that the other posed. At the heart of this clash lay both conflicting visions of the future and a mutual distrust that only deepened whenever the balance of power threatened to shift dramatically in favor of one nation or the other. To Stalin the American monopoly on nuclear weapons placed the Soviet Union at a distinct strategic disadvantage that he intended to remedy as quickly as possible. For the United States Stalin's attempt in 1946 to use military force to extend his reach into the Middle East and Mediterranean raised concerns that the Soviet leader sought world domination.

Tensions mounted further in 1946 when Stalin gave a belligerent speech predicting the inevitable triumph of communism over capitalism. U.S. State Department officials were now concerned enough to ask the American embassy in Moscow for more information about Stalin's intentions. The response was the "**long telegram**," an influential five-thousand-word missive in which diplomat George F. Kennan outlined why America needed to develop an aggressive foreign policy aimed at containing Soviet expansionist impulses. Kennan concluded that Stalin needed an outside enemy to keep himself in power because an external threat kept the Soviet public from focusing on his ruthless dictatorship. Stalin, Kennan also explained, believed that conflicts between capitalist societies would lead to their demise, thus allowing communism to triumph when capitalist societies collapsed. Given this Soviet mindset, negotiations to resolve differences between the two nations would be fruitless, Kennan advised. Kennan suggested strengthening Western-style capitalist and democratic structures to foil communist efforts to woo impoverished peoples. He predicted that Stalin would moderate his ambitions only if he encountered strong and steady resistance from the West each time he tried to expand beyond the Western-accepted Soviet sphere of influence in Eastern Europe. "It is clear that the main element of any United States policy toward the Soviet Union must be that of a long-term, patient but firm and vigilant *containment* of Russian expansive tendencies," Kennan wrote in a version of the telegram that he published in 1947 under the pseudonym Mr. X in *Foreign Affairs* magazine. With this one statement Kennan articulated the philosophical foundation for **containment**, the label affixed to multiple American foreign policy initiatives meant to prevent the Soviet Union from increasing its influence around the globe. Kennan had economic and political policies in mind when he penned these words, but hard-liners in the Truman administration seized on his analysis to craft a new vision of U.S. military engagement in the world.

A month after Kennan sent his long telegram, the former British prime minister Winston Churchill visited Westminster College in Fulton, Missouri, where he used Kennan's words to underscore that a military, not just ideological, standoff lay ahead. In his speech Churchill declared that there was nothing the Soviets "admire so much as strength, and there is nothing for which they have less respect than for military weakness." Stalin accused Churchill of trying to provoke a war with his comment that an "**iron curtain**," Churchill's characterization of the military and ideological barrier erected by the Soviet Union, separated Western and Eastern Europe into free and unfree halves. Many American newspapers agreed, denouncing Churchill's speech as too belligerent.

The Truman Doctrine and the Marshall Plan

Turning the principles of containment into concrete action that had public approval took another year. By the end of 1947, the Truman Doctrine and the Marshall Plan established containment as the new course of American foreign policy, a direction strengthened even further in 1949 with the creation of a post-World War II military alliance between the United States and Western European powers through the **North Atlantic Treaty Organization**(NATO). These initiatives evolved in response to a series of crises in Europe, portrayed in **24.2**.

In 1947 Truman briefly returned to FDR's notion of working through the UN to resolve international disputes. That year the UN successfully pressured Stalin into removing Soviet troops from northern Iran. At the same time Truman stationed the American Sixth Fleet in the Mediterranean to prevent the Soviets from seizing Turkish-controlled shipping lanes through the Dardanelles. Stalin accepted the setback in oil-rich Iran without fanfare, but he continued to demand unrestricted naval access through the Dardanelles passage, the only way for Soviet military and commercial vessels to travel

What analysis did Kennan's Long Telegram offer of Stalin's beliefs and behavior?

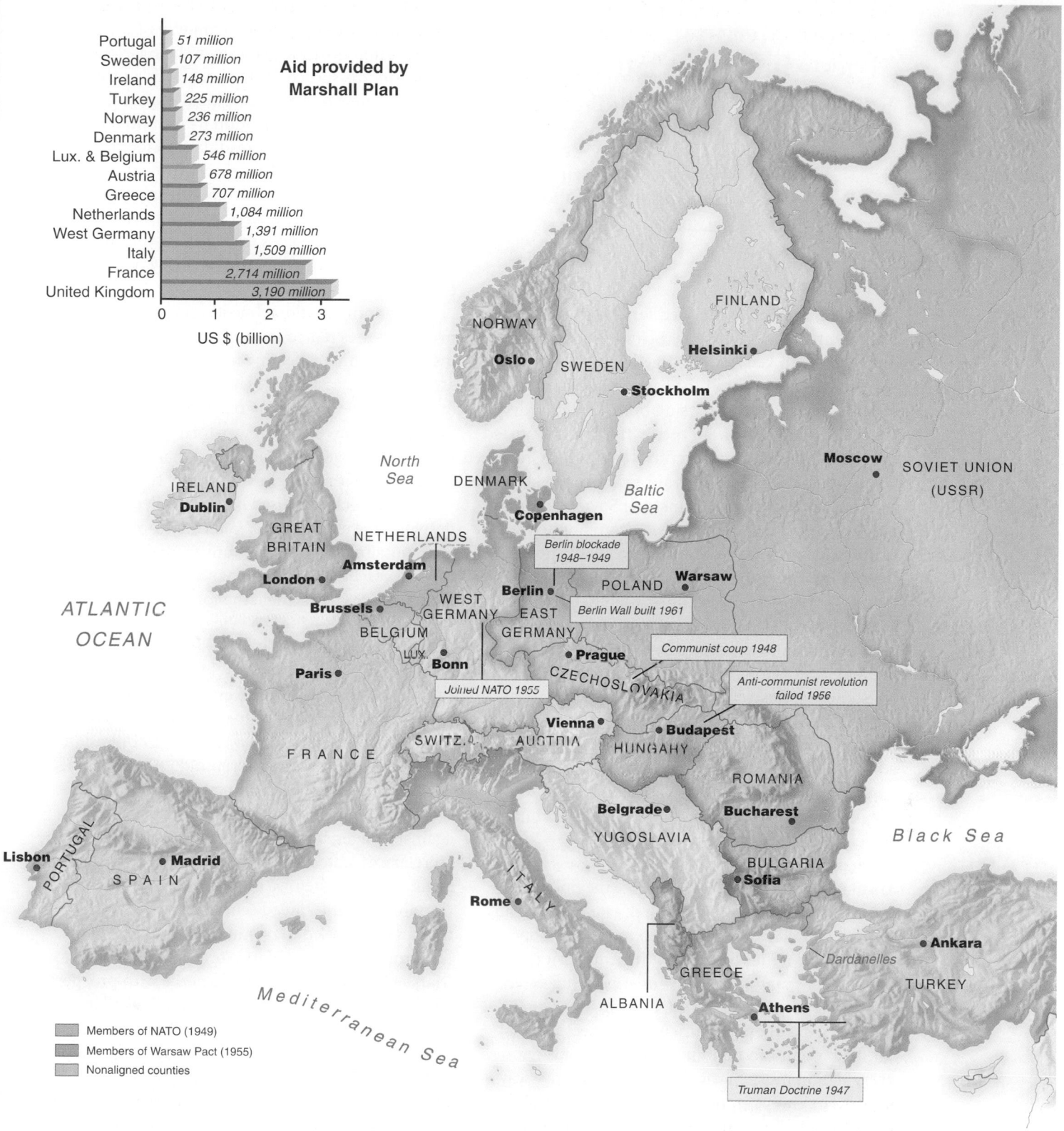

24.2 The Cold War in Europe
Europe divided into two competing alliance systems after World War II. The United States used the NATO alliance and Marshall Plan aid to strengthen ties with Western Europe.

What new role did the United States play in Western Europe after World War II?

> "From Stettin in the Baltic to Trieste in the Adriatic, an iron curtain has descended across the continent."
>
> Former British Prime Minister WINSTON CHURCHILL in Fulton, Missouri, March 1946

from the Black Sea to the Mediterranean. In 1947 Stalin sent troops to the Turkish-Soviet border to force Turkey to keep the passage open.

The sense of crisis in the eastern Mediterranean soon deepened, encompassing both Turkey and Greece. Throughout 1946 the British had supported the Greek monarchy in its efforts to subdue Greek Communist rebels and sent aid to Turkey to help the country stand firm against the Soviet Union. In 1947 as part of a general decision to renounce its world-wide imperial role, a financially strapped Britain informed the United States that it could no longer give economic or military aid to Greece and Turkey. Fearing that the British withdrawal meant certain Communist success in Greece and Turkey, Truman asked Congress to grant American assistance to these countries. Secretary of State Dean Acheson outlined the threat to America in a meeting with congressional leaders. "Like apples in a barrel infected by one rotten one," Acheson explained, "the corruption of Greece" would "carry the infection" of communism to Western Europe, Africa, and the Middle East.

In preparing his speech before Congress in 1947, Truman pondered how to convince the public that events in far-off Greece and Turkey necessitated an unprecedented peacetime interference in European affairs. "Scare [the] hell out of the American people," Republican senator Arthur Vandenberg suggested. Truman followed this advice. Dividing the world into "us" and "them," Truman told Americans that "at the present moment in world history nearly every nation must choose between alternative ways of life. The choice is too often not a free one." The Western side of the divide championed democracy and freedom. On the other were Communist states where "terror and oppression, a controlled press and radio, fixed elections, and the suppression of personal freedom" were parts of daily life. Drawing a line in the sand to stop the spread of communism was the nation's responsibility to the world and the only way to protect the American way of life at home. While asking specifically to help Greece and Turkey, in this speech Truman set forth a more expansive view of America's global responsibilities, asking the country to abandon its traditional non-interventionist stance. Instead the president proposed the **Truman Doctrine**, a foreign policy initiative that gave the United States an active role in stopping the global spread of communism by supporting "free peoples who are resisting attempted subjugation by armed minorities or by outside pressures."

The administration almost immediately used the principles articulated in the Truman Doctrine to justify extending a helping hand to Western Europe as well. In the eastern Mediterranean the United States wanted to prevent Communist armies from taking over the region. In war-torn Western Europe, the American government feared that hungry, exhausted citizens might voluntarily turn to communism, which promised bread for all, out of despair. Free elections in Western Europe offered the grim possibility that Communists might be voted into power. Embracing Kennan's vision, Secretary of State George C. Marshall, the former army chief of staff who had designed the victorious American strategy in World War II, suggested offering massive amounts of financial aid to help European capitalistic economies recover. **The Marshall Plan (1948–1952)** aimed to restore Europeans' faith in capitalism by sending $13 billion ($119 billion in today's dollars) overseas to rebuild Europe's ruined roads, bridges, factories, and farms. "Our policy is directed not against any country or doctrine but against hunger, poverty, desperation, and chaos," the secretary of state claimed, avoiding the dualistic "us" against "them" rhetoric of the Truman Doctrine. Certain that widespread economic suffering in the thirties had caused desperate people to embrace fascism, which then led to World War II, the Marshall Plan explicitly linked peace with prosperity. All European nations (including the Soviet Union) were invited to submit proposals for aid. Stalin briefly entertained the idea of applying for American funds to rebuild his devastated nation, but as Marshall and Truman expected, he quickly abandoned this idea. Instead the Soviets publicly denounced the plan as an American plot to colonize Europe and refused to allow Eastern European nations to participate. Besides cash, the Marshall Plan offered European nations technical and management advice that helped spread American farming

How did the Truman Administration convince the public to accept a new direction in U.S. foreign policy?

24.3 American View of the Marshall Plan
The Marshall Plan is portrayed as a lifeline offered by the United States to help a desperate Western Europe pull itself out of war-inflicted misery and away from the powerful influence of the Soviet Union, seen in the distance.

techniques, labor policies, and manufacturing practices.

The recovery of Western European markets under the Marshall Plan furthered the ideological divide between the United States and the Soviet Union. These conflicting political cartoons (**24.3** and **24.4**) reflected the American view that free markets fostered independence and the contrasting Soviet critique of capitalism as an exploitive, class-based system that enriched some at the expense of others. In his illustration (24.3) the American cartoonist Daniel R. Fitzpatrick viewed the Marshall Plan as a lifeline to Western Europe pulling people out of war-inflicted misery and away from the looming Soviet menace in the distance (represented in the cartoon by the distant towers of the Tsar's former palace in Leningrad, a readily recognizable symbol of the Soviet Union to Americans). Americans took pride in the wave of Western European prosperity that resulted from the Marshall Plan, making it one of the great economic success stories of the Cold War. In sharp contrast the Soviet magazine *Krokodil* showed European leaders groveling at the feet of their American lord, depicted in the cartoon (24.4) as a paunchy Uncle Sam relaxing with his feet on their backs. This cartoon implied that the Marshall Plan, rather than fostering recovery, enslaved Western Europe to the United States, which grew richer by the day. There was some truth to the Soviet claim that the Marshall Plan, which ran from 1948 to 1952, strengthened the American economy. Western European nations spent most of their funds in the United States on raw materials, food, machines, and fuel, creating a taste for American goods that continued even after the Marshall Plan ended.

The Berlin Airlift and NATO

The American policy of containment quickly evolved into more than a vision of financial assistance for struggling governments and economies overseas. By 1949 containment also meant a firm military commitment from the United States to come to the defense of Western European nations that allied themselves with America. Almost overnight the United States shed its traditional reluctance to intervene militarily in European affairs as Americans became convinced that they were the only ones who could stop Stalin from controlling Europe.

In 1948 Stalin supported a coup by Czech Communists that overthrew the only democratic government in Eastern Europe. The quick demise of democracy in Czechoslovakia caused the West to fear that an emboldened Stalin might

24.4 Soviet View of the Marshall Plan
In this Soviet cartoon, European leaders grovel at the feet of their American capitalist master, who has used the Marshall Plan to conquer Europe.

What conflicting views of the Marshall Plan are presented in these two cartoons?

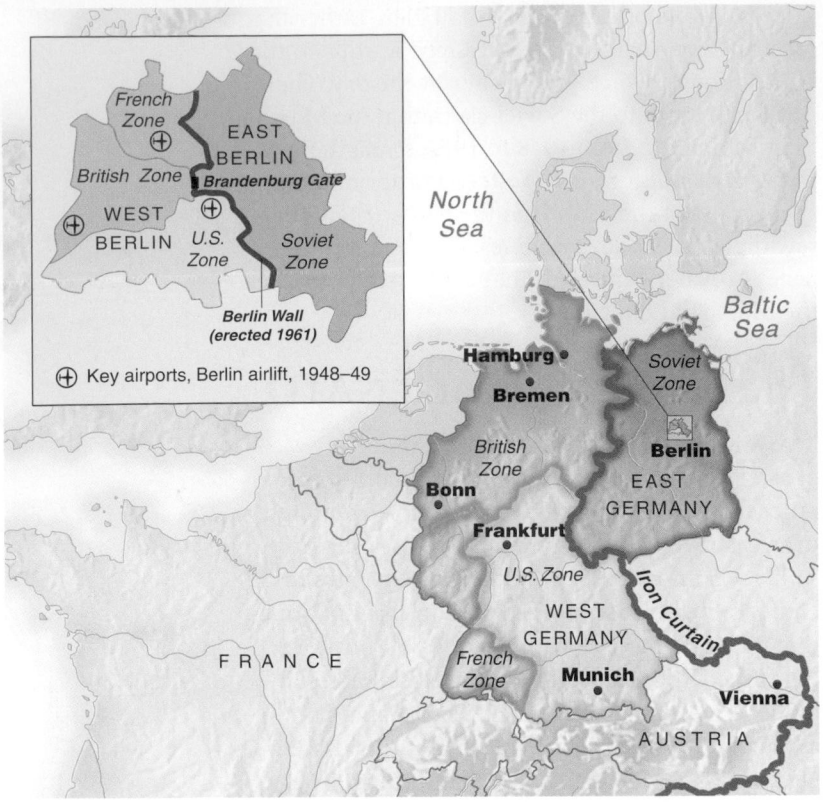

24.5 A Divided Berlin
Key showdowns during the Cold War took place in Berlin, including the Berlin airlift in 1948–1949 and the construction of the Berlin Wall in 1961.

have Germany, with its wrecked economy and nonexistent military, in mind as the next target for a Soviet-inspired communist revolution. With the country still divided into four occupied zones, the German economy was in shambles. Keeping Germany weak to punish it for World War II, initially a shared American and Soviet objective, increasingly made little strategic sense as the Soviet menace grew. By 1948 the United States saw strengthening Germany as a way to halt the Soviet expansionist drive across Europe. With this goal in mind, the United States, Britain, and France began discussing the possibility of consolidating their separately occupied sections of Germany to form a new democratic German government and offering it Marshall Plan funds to bolster the economy. The Soviet Union firmly opposed any plan for rebuilding Germany and protested that its former allies were violating the 1945 Yalta agreement that all four nations had to agree before any restructuring of Germany could occur.

As the West and the Soviet Union argued over how to deal with Germany, the stakes rose precipitously. Trying to pressure the United States, Britain, and France to abandon either their plan to reunify Germany or their stake in Berlin, Stalin ordered his army to stop all road, railroad, and canal traffic between the Western and Soviet zones of Germany. Berlin lay in the heart of the Soviet-occupied sector, but at the end of World War II the Allies had agreed to divide the German capital into four zones of occupation, portrayed on the map (**24.5**). To supply and reach their respective zones in Berlin, the Americans, British, and French needed to travel on roads, rail lines, and waterways that ran through the Soviet sector of Germany. Stalin now barred them from using these transportation facilities, setting in motion the first direct military confrontation of the Cold War between the United States and the Soviet Union.

The United States faced a set of difficult choices. One option was to try to breach the blockade by sending an armed convoy down the autobahn (the German name for freeway) with permission to fire back if attacked by Soviet forces. In the midst of a difficult reelection campaign, Truman doubted Americans' willingness to fight the Soviet Union to help a recent enemy. The other option was to try to circumvent the blockade by supplying the Western-occupied sectors of Berlin from the air. The chances of an airlift working appeared slim since each plane could carry only 3 tons of supplies and the West normally sent an average of 12,000 tons of supplies a day to sustain a combined population of 2.3 million in their three zones. Faced with two unappealing choices, Truman gambled on the airlift and won.

> "The situation was dark and full of danger."
>
> State Department official GEORGE F. KENNAN on the Soviet blockade of Berlin in 1948

In the **Berlin airlift (1948–1949)**, American and British planes resupplied West Berlin for nearly a year to stymie the Soviet blockade of the city. It was a brilliant success, both a spectacular logistical feat and a propaganda coup for the United States worldwide. In sharp contrast to dour Soviet soldiers turning away convoys carrying needed food and medicine, the world saw photographs of German

Which international disputes led to the 1948–1949 Soviet blockade of Berlin?

children cheering the arrival of American and British planes. This photo (**24.6**) underscored how much the world had changed in a mere three years. The children stood on the rubble from a building destroyed by Allied bombers during the war. Instead of fleeing for their lives as American planes approached, they now welcomed the Americans as saviors for a city where strict rationing meant most children received only gruel (hot milk and flour) for their noontime meal. One American pilot was so touched by the sight of children scanning the skies for food planes that he attached miniature parachutes to candy bars and gum to drop to them when he flew by. "The spectacle of the British and Americans trying to feed the 2,000,000 Germans in Berlin, while the Soviet Union was trying to starve them, has been an object lesson to the German people far beyond anything that words could convey," Churchill noted.

Images like these convinced Americans that their help was both welcome and needed overseas. They also boosted Truman in the 1948 presidential campaign as he squared off against the Republican challenger, Thomas Dewey, who led in the polls, and two other third party candidates. Faced with public dissatisfaction over rampant inflation at home and a badly divided Democratic Party, these photos bolstered Truman's image as a resolute leader.

Truman could not correct all his political problems with photographs, however. The 1948 presidential campaign presented voters with sharply competing visions of what direction the country should take. Angry over Truman's proposal that the federal government investigate racial discrimination in voting and employment, many conservative Southern Democrats supported Strom Thurmond, the governor of South Carolina, in his presidential bid as a segregationist candidate for the States' Rights Party. Meanwhile liberal factions of the Democratic Party, upset with Truman's tepid reform agenda (see Chapter 25), formed the Progressive Party and nominated Henry A. Wallace who championed national health insurance. The former vice president's downplaying of the Soviet threat brought charges that Wallace had communist sympathies. Dewey, who had run against FDR in 1944, was a moderate Republican who, like Truman, supported civil rights and containing communism. Many believed that the president's unpopularity and the three-way split within the Democratic Party assured Dewey's election. Determined to "give them hell," Truman traveled nearly 32,000 miles during the campaign, appealing to the New Deal coalition of farmers, Northern blacks, Catholics, unions, and

24.6 The Berlin Airlift, 1948–1949 Photographs of waving German children welcoming American food planes convinced Americans that their help was both needed and welcomed overseas.

What political impact did this photo have?

24.7 Truman's Triumph
On election night in November 1948, Truman celebrated his reelection by holding the *Chicago Daily Tribune,* with its mistaken headline, from his campaign train.

liberals that had secured FDR's victory in 1936. Dewey's unwillingness to attack the president's foreign policies during this time of international crisis also helped Truman. In the summer of 1948, Truman issued an executive order desegregating the military to prevent the defection of black voters to Wallace, who called for an immediate end to Jim Crow. Thanks to votes from African Americans and labor, Truman won a second term, with 303 electoral votes and 49.5 percent of the popular vote, defeating Dewey who received 189 electoral votes and 45.1 percent of the popular vote, Thurmond (39 electoral votes; 2.4 percent of the popular vote), and Wallace (no electoral votes; 2.4 percent of the popular vote). This victory came as a surprise to many, including the *Chicago Daily Tribune,* which tried to get a jump on the competition by declaring Dewey the victor on election night before all the votes were counted. In a photo (**24.7**) that became an instant classic, a jubilant Truman held the paper and its erroneous headline "Dewey Defeats Truman" above his head the next morning when his victory was confirmed.

Besides helping Truman win reelection, the sight of wave after wave of planes arriving twenty-four hours a day in Berlin also demonstrated America's strength and resolve to the Soviet Union. After nearly a year, Stalin finally admitted defeat and revoked the blockade on May 12, 1949. The capitalist enclave in the heart of the Soviet sector of Germany had survived. By that time the Americans, British, and French had merged their zones within Berlin and the rest of Germany to create the Federal Republic of Germany, or West Germany. In response the Soviets organized a Communist-led German government in their sector, the German Democratic Republic, or East Germany. Germany was now formally divided into two separate nations.

In the wake of the Soviet-backed coup in Czechoslovakia and the blockade of Berlin, the United States refined its policy of containment even further. These events had shattered any chance of creating consensus within the Truman administration around Kennan's vision that economic aid through the Marshall Plan was enough to safeguard democracy and prosperity in Western Europe. If peace were to prevail, it would be an armed peace. Western European nations took the first step by allying themselves in the Brussels Pact in 1948. This alliance blossomed into the American-led NATO alliance in April 1949. The Soviet Union responded with their own alliance, the Warsaw Pact, among Eastern European nations. The map of the Cold War in Europe portrays the two alliance systems that formally divided Europe into capitalist and communist camps (see 24.2).

By joining NATO the United States created its first formal military alliance since the Revolutionary War. There would be no repeat of World War I or World War II, when the United States had waited over two years each time before declaring war. As a member of NATO, the United States was obligated to come immediately to Western Europe's defense in the event of a Soviet attack. Besides putting American bases and soldiers permanently in Europe, NATO extended the protection of America's atomic shield to its NATO partners.

Like the Marshall Plan NATO was designed to do many things at once. Besides creating a permanent role for the United States overseas and containing communism, NATO also helped keep peace among European nations that had clashed repeatedly in the last hundred years. A popular saying claimed that NATO kept "the Soviets out, the Americans in, and the Germans down" by ensuring that West Germany remained friends with Western democracies even after the nation regained its economic vigor.

Why was NATO an important development in the Cold War?

Fighting Communism: Cold and Hot War

As the Cold War took shape, the United States did not gain any noticeable advantage from its atomic monopoly in dealing with Stalin. Losing it, nonetheless, caused great angst in the United States. In 1949 the Soviet Union successfully tested its own atomic bomb, challenging Americans' view of their own nation as the world's dominant military power. Suddenly the chances of an international crisis escalating into nuclear war appeared greater. As Americans digested this news, the epicenter of the Cold War shifted to Asia. By 1950 a Communist government controlled China, and the Korean War had begun. In the **Korean War (1950–1953)**, the United States fought Communist North Koreans and Chinese to a stalemate, frustrating Americans.

Communism Rising: 1949

The United States did not have long to celebrate its achievements during the Berlin airlift. Three months after Stalin admitted defeat in Berlin, an American spy plane detected a large amount of radioactive fallout in the desert of Kazakhstan, a Soviet republic. This unusual finding could mean only one thing: the Soviet Union had successfully tested its own atomic bomb. This news shattered the American certainty that it would retain a nuclear monopoly for at least ten years. Waiting impatiently for a formal announcement from the Kremlin, Truman finally broke the news to the world in September 1949. The Soviet Union confirmed the American report, but gave no other information about Stalin's plans for his nuclear-building program.

Fearful that Stalin might use nuclear weapons to expand beyond the iron curtain, the Truman administration broadened the scope of America's containment strategy beyond NATO and the Marshall Plan. Truman decided to station American troops in Western Europe permanently to both deter and, if necessary, respond to a nuclear attack. At the same time the United States began stockpiling atomic bombs to gain a numerical advantage over the Soviet Union. Finally Truman authorized the development of a "superbomb," a thermonuclear hydrogen bomb that was a thousand times more powerful than the uranium-enriched atomic bomb dropped on Hiroshima and the plutonium one that destroyed Nagasaki.

Americans were still recovering from the shock of the Soviet bomb when they received more bad news. The twenty-five-year-old Chinese Civil War had finally ended with the Communist Mao Zedong victorious over the Nationalist leader Jiang Jieshi (Chiang Kai-shek), who fled with his government to Taiwan, an island off the southeast coast of mainland China. Mao was an avid swimmer who refused even as an old man to be deterred by the human waste floating in China's polluted rivers. A master of staying afloat in water and in politics, Mao adopted Stalin and Soviet-style policies as his model, inflicting similarly painful waves of famine and political oppression on the Chinese people that killed more than twenty million. Fearful that the United States intended to attack China and restore Jiang to power, Mao immediately reached out to Stalin. "There should be some division of labor between us," Stalin suggested, with the Soviet Union furthering the communist cause in Europe and Mao doing the same in Asia. Accepting Stalin's offer Mao spent two months in Moscow devising a joint strategy that resulted in the 1950 Sino-Soviet Treaty, which pledged mutual assistance in the event of an enemy attack. This alliance created a second front in the Cold War that forced the United States to divide its attention between Europe and Asia.

> "There is only one thing worse than one nation having the atomic bomb—that's two nations having it."
>
> American physical chemist
> HAROLD ULREY, September 1949

In light of these new threats on the world stage, Truman ordered a full review of American foreign

How did the USSR acquiring nuclear weapons and the rise of communist China change the contours of the Cold War?

policy. The State Department responded with a document known as National Security Council Memorandum 68, or NSC-68. Not mincing words NSC-68 declared that "the issues that face us are momentous, involving the fulfillment or destruction not only of this Republic but of civilization itself." Secretary of State Acheson later admitted that NSC-68's cataclysmic vision of a Soviet enemy "animated by a new fanatic faith" and bent on worldwide domination was meant to convince the president to use all means "short of war" to halt the apparent Soviet drive for world conquest. NSC-68 crystallized the piecemeal developments of the last four years into one clear vision: The United States must build up "the political, economic, and military strength of the free world to frustrate the Kremlin design of a world dominated by its will." This message was transmitted to the public not only through political speeches but also through films and novels. Perhaps no writer better encapsulated the public's fears of worldwide communist domination than George Orwell in his classic novel *1984,* which hit bookstores in 1949. In the novel Orwell envisioned a future where totalitarianism has triumphed and the people's loyalty to a Stalin-like dictator "Big Brother," who watches over everyone and censors their behavior, is ensured by a cycle of endless wars and torture. As the main character Winston Smith undergoes another round of torture, his tormentor tells him, "Imagine a boot stamping on a human face—forever." This image neatly encapsulated the American public's view of communism in the Cold War.

The Korean War

At the end of World War II, the United States and the Soviet Union had agreed to divide the former Japanese colony of Korea, a peninsula along the Asian Pacific Coast, into two zones of occupation. The country was split along the 38th parallel, with the USSR occupying the north and the United States in the south. In 1945 partitioning the country seemed like a good way to both deprive Japan of Korean resources and prevent the Soviet Union from completely taking over the peninsula. When the Soviet Union organized a Communist government under Kim Il-sung in North Korea and the United States selected Syngman Rhee to head a capitalist government in the south, the previously unified nation appeared permanently divided.

By 1949, however, the United States had begun to reevaluate its military commitment in South Korea. The military occupation was expensive to maintain, and Pentagon officials increasingly doubted the strategic importance of the peninsula. The State Department agreed, believing that economic aid and political reforms could strengthen South Korea enough to discourage a North Korean attack. In January 1950 Secretary of State Acheson openly questioned the importance of South Korea to the overall defense of American interests in East Asia. In a speech before the National Press Club, Acheson outlined a defensive perimeter in the Pacific that the United States would defend against Communist incursions that included Japan, Okinawa, Formosa, and the Philippines, but not South Korea. Accordingly Truman began withdrawing American soldiers from South Korea. To deter North Korea from attacking, the United States left a stockpile of conventional weapons and promised continued financial aid.

Yet when North Korea launched a surprise invasion of South Korea in June 1950, Truman dramatically reversed course. Within days Truman decided to send American ground troops to help roll back the offensive. The speed and success of the North Korean attack alarmed Truman. Within two days North Korean troops had entered Seoul, the capital of South Korea (**24.8**), and by the end of one week North Korea had pushed the bulk of the South Korean army into the toe of the Korean peninsula around Pusan. Viewing this overpowering offensive as confirmation of the vision encapsulated in NSC-68, Truman immediately suspected that the USSR was behind the attack. Truman was partly right. Kim Il-sung had secured reluctant support from Stalin and Mao Zedong for the invasion by promising an easy victory. In the event that the United States intervened in Korea, Stalin saw advantages to diverting American attention away from Europe.

Other global and domestic events by June 1950 left many Americans feeling that the West was losing the Cold War. Worldwide these events included China falling to communism and the explosion of a Soviet atomic bomb. At home sensational spy trials fueled continued doubts about Truman's leadership. In this political climate doing nothing was hardly an option for Truman.

Truman's intimate understanding of World War I (he had served as an artillery captain in France) and World War II encouraged him to break with the precedent set by these recent conflicts. In each of these wars, Americans had debated the merits of fighting for more than two years before declaring war. "I remembered how each time the democracies

Why did the United States decide to fight in Korea?

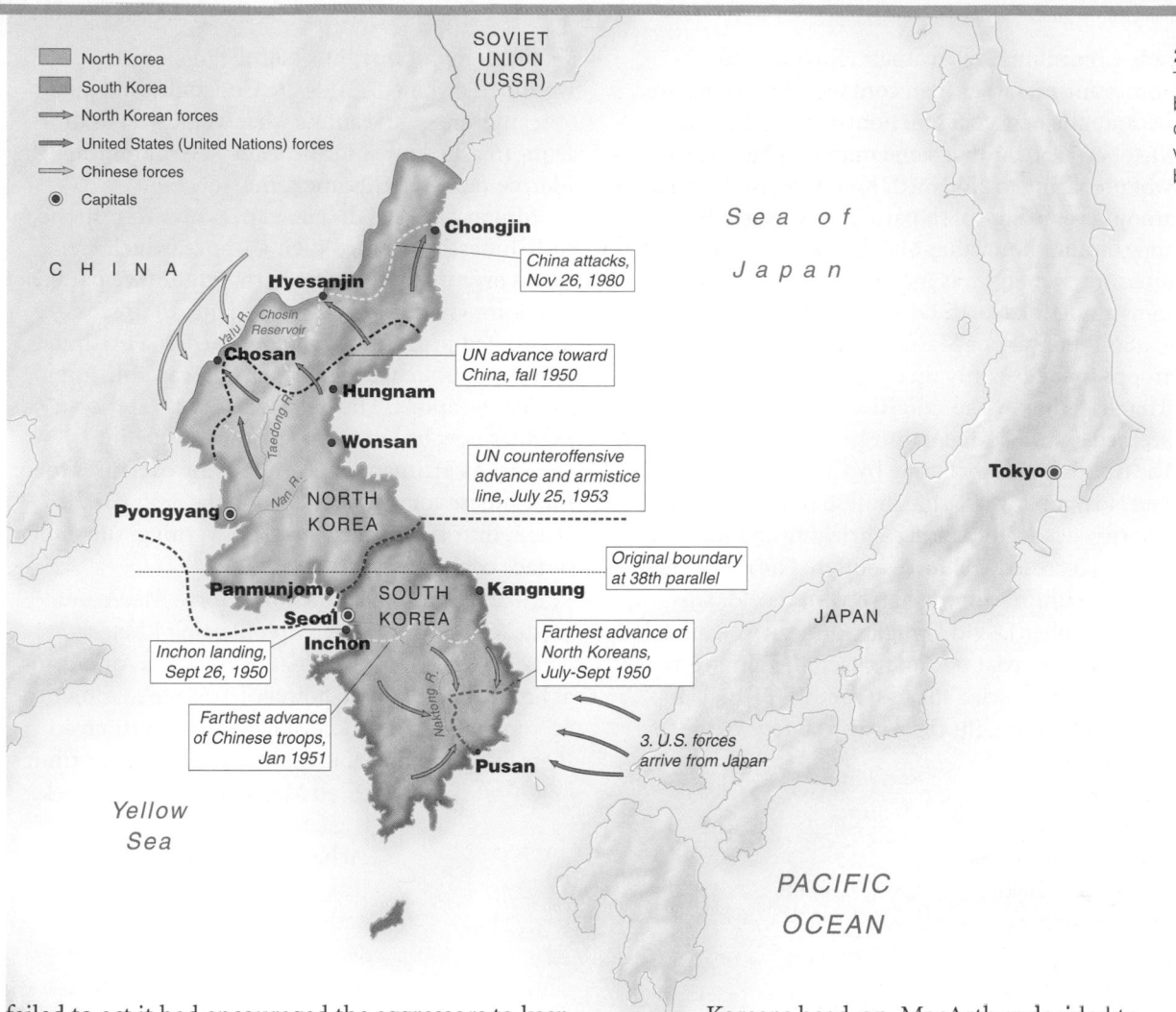

24.8 The Korean War The advantage on the battlefield changed quickly during the war's first year before becoming a stalemate.

failed to act it had encouraged the aggressors to keep going ahead," Truman noted. Determined to respond quickly this time, Truman committed American troops to combat within a matter of days. Although Truman consulted Congress, he never asked for a declaration of war against North Korea. Truman instead decided to work through the UN, which authorized the use of force to restore the original 38th-parallel boundary between North and South Korea. Sixteen nations sent troops to Korea to serve in the UN police force, but the United States provided the bulk of troops and commanded military operations. When polled three-quarters of Americans approved of Truman's decision to send military aid to South Korea. Americans, for the time being anyway, subscribed to Truman's vision that "the future of civilization depends on what we do."

The situation on the battlefield, however, was grim, with South Korean soldiers holding on precariously around Pusan. To reverse the situation General Douglas MacArthur, the Supreme United Nations commander, devised a dramatic and risky strategy. Rather than simply confronting the North Koreans head-on, MacArthur decided to stage an amphibious landing at Inchon, a port city near Seoul. This attack on the North Koreans' rear would cut their supply lines and force them to fight on two fronts. The tides at Inchon, however, were the second highest in the world, varying twenty-nine feet between high and low tides. Within a matter of minutes, the quickly receding tide could mire a boat in mud. Inchon, MacArthur reasoned, was the right place to attack precisely because it was so uninviting and would take the enemy by surprise. As he predicted the North Koreans had stationed only 2,000 troops there, and the UN force of 70,000 encountered little resistance in taking the city. The success of this operation turned MacArthur, already famous for his feats in World War II, into a national hero. Following the Inchon invasion UN forces quickly drove North Korean troops out of South Korea.

In the wake of this victory, Truman pondered giving the war a new purpose. Instead of simply restoring the status quo of a divided Korea, Truman now decided to try to reunify Korea under an

What accounted for America's initial successes on the battlefield?

anti-Communist government. Rolling back communism, rather than containing communism, became the new goal sanctioned by the UN in October 1950. At that same moment, however, China was preparing to aid North Korea. When American troops crossed the 38th parallel into North Korea, they did not know that Mao had already resolved to enter the war and was massing Chinese troops and guns along the North Korean-Chinese border.

Still unaware of Mao's intentions, American troops moved swiftly up the peninsula to celebrate Thanksgiving by the Yalu River. Imminent victory seemed assured: MacArthur promised Truman that the troops would be home by Christmas. Then in late November waves of Chinese troops began pouring across the border, shrieking and blowing bugles. Terrified UN forces suffered heavy casualties as they withdrew in the harsh winter cold. *Life* photographer David Douglas Duncan, warming his camera in his coat pocket to keep the film from breaking, chronicled the bitter retreat of 10,000 Marines who fought their way to safety. Nearly every soldier suffered frostbite; half the men were wounded or killed. "If I were God and could give you anything you wanted, what would you ask for?" Duncan asked one Marine. After several minutes the Marine replied, "Give me tomorrow."

Military leaders disagreed over how to respond as the Chinese continued their advance, which UN forces eventually contained around the 38th parallel. The Joint Chiefs of Staff urged Truman to seek a negotiated peace, advice he followed. MacArthur, however, publicly endorsed all-out war utilizing nuclear weapons. The president and theater commander now began to pursue two competing visions. As Truman made diplomatic overtures to the Chinese for a ceasefire along the 38th parallel, MacArthur issued the Chinese a warning: surrender or face complete destruction.

"There is no substitute for victory," MacArthur wrote to Congressman Joseph Martin of Massachusetts, echoing the feelings of countless Americans at home. This was not, however, Truman's vision of how to end the war successfully; when Martin read these words on the House floor, he sealed MacArthur's fate. Truman fired MacArthur the next week, triggering, as Secretary of State Acheson had predicted, "the biggest fight of your administration."

MacArthur came home, not in disgrace, but to great acclaim. Many Americans shared MacArthur's frustrations with the stalemate on the battlefield. Six years after defeating two great military powers in World War II, the United States found itself unable to reunify Korea under an anti-Communist government. Responding to MacArthur's vision of total victory, huge crowds greeted the general when his ship docked in San Francisco, and he reveled in a ticker-tape parade held in his honor in New York City. Congress debated impeaching Truman but then opted instead to hold hearings into MacArthur's removal. During the hearings MacArthur's critics interrogated the general about the possibility

24.9 "The Price of Victory: A Soldier Grieves for His Lost Buddy" An American soldier comforts a comrade distraught over the death of a friend during the Korean War in the fall of 1950.

How did the entry of the Chinese into the Korean War affect political and military debates within the United States?

that using nuclear weapons in Korea might lead to a global nuclear war. MacArthur's response, "that doesn't happen to be my responsibility," caused the general's popularity to plummet. The cooling enthusiasm for MacArthur's vision of all-out war did little to bolster public confidence in Truman, however. In public opinion polls only 24 percent of Americans approved of how Truman was handling the presidency, reflecting public disappointment over the situation in Korea, continued anger at Truman over "losing China," and several well-publicized Soviet spy scandals that together revived the image of Truman as an ineffectual leader. Truman's aggressive support for civil rights and his domestic reform agenda (see Chapter 25), too much for conservatives and too little for liberals, also contributed to his poor rating.

Korea was the last American war that the public viewed primarily through photographs. Only 34 percent of American homes were equipped with television sets in 1952, rising to 86 percent by 1960. In 1950 *Newsweek* published the photograph "The Price of Victory: A Soldier Grieves for His Lost Buddy" (**24.9**). One reader's suggestion that this image should serve as the iconic photo of the Korean War, just as "Old Glory Goes Up on Mt. Suribachi, Iwo Jima" had served to represent World War II, revealed a significant shift in the public's attitudes over the last five years (see *Images as History: Combat Photography,* Chapter 23, page 706). The World War II image of five marines and one navy corpsman raising the flag suggested teamwork, victory, and the triumph of democracy. In sharp contrast "The Price of Victory" looked at the personal cost of war—the sorrow and compassion that drew men together on the battlefield—even as the photograph reaffirmed the willingness of soldiers to die for their country. Photographers and the public were beginning to probe the impact of fighting on the ground soldier, stoking the ambivalence that the country increasingly felt about the war.

With MacArthur out of the picture, General Matthew Ridgway took over command of UN operations in 1951 and armistice negotiations began. Talks were still underway two years later when a new president, Dwight D. Eisenhower, took office. Eisenhower's sunny demeanor offered a sharp contrast to Truman's more combative and coarser personality. Whereas Truman cussed, told off-color jokes, and picked fights with reporters, Eisenhower was gregarious and friendly to all. Some Democrats had tried to draft Eisenhower as a presidential candidate in 1948. Four years later the Republican "We Like Ike" campaign finally convinced Eisenhower to seek office. The young women adorned here (**24.10**), with "Ike" dresses and umbrellas, illustrate Republicans' enthusiasm for Eisenhower on the eve of the nominating convention where delegates enthusiastically selected him as their presidential candidate.

24.10
"We Like Ike"
The enthusiasm for his candidacy displayed by Republicans in 1952 convinced Eisenhower to run for president.

Admired by Americans for his command of the D-Day invasion in World War II, Eisenhower's military experience convinced Americans that he would be a capable leader in a time of war. The negotiations remained deadlocked, however, until Eisenhower threatened to reconsider the question of employing nuclear weapons. Finally the two sides agreed to a permanent ceasefire in July 1953.

The war was costly on all sides. More than 600,000 Chinese soldiers and nearly two million North and South Koreans perished. For the first time in its history, the United States could not claim outright victory over its opponent despite nearly 33,000 men killed in combat and 103,000 men wounded. "What the hell is there to celebrate?" remarked one soldier when news of the armistice reached the front. The silence at home offered a marked contrast to the jubilant demonstrations that had filled the streets

How did the Korean War compare to World War II?

eight years earlier when Japan surrendered. China embraced a competing vision of the stalemate, reveling in their ability to hold their own against the United States.

The Korean War had major geopolitical consequences by turning the Cold War into a global conflict. The war tied South Korea and Japan, economically resurgent thanks to American aid, even more closely to the United States, and these two nations became staunch allies in creating a defensive perimeter against communism in East Asia. Holding the line against communism in Korea increased America's interest in other regional civil wars, including one underway in Vietnam. The war poisoned relations with China, and the two nations did not reestablish diplomatic relations until 1979. Pledged to defend South Korea, the United States to this day maintains a large military presence along what continues to be the most heavily armed border in the world.

24.11 Godzilla
A 1954 Japanese horror film used the ravages of a nuclear-spawned dinosaur named Godzilla to criticize American use and testing of its nuclear arsenal. This political message was edited out of the version shown in the United States.

Nuclear Fallout and Fear

While soldiers fought and died on the battlefield, Americans at home waged their own defensive war against nuclear weapons. The government sponsored atmospheric and underwater tests of nuclear bombs in the 1940s and 1950s both in the United States and on the Bikini Atoll in the Marshall Islands in the Pacific. Even when the United States had a secure monopoly on nuclear weapons, many Americans expressed concern about **nuclear fallout**, the deadly pollution that descends through the air after a nuclear bomb explosion.

Over the course of the decade, popular science fiction writers and filmmakers tapped into this preoccupation with nuclear fallout. In the Japanese film classic *Godzilla,* for example, a nuclear explosion awakes a fire-breathing monster who, as the film's promotional poster (**24.11**) illustrated, terrorizes Tokyo. Like the atomic bomb that ravaged Hiroshima and Nagasaki, Godzilla is an unstoppable nuclear force that obliterates everything in his path. Americans, however, saw only a carefully edited version of the film, with all critical commentary on America's ongoing nuclear testing program in the Pacific carefully excised. In a similar vein two popular Marvel comic book characters, the Incredible Hulk and Spiderman, were spawned by contact with radioactive material. In the *Incredible Hulk*, a scientist exposed to gamma rays is transformed into a green, 300-pound giant, while a bite from an irradiated spider turns nerdish lab assistant Peter Parker into Spiderman.

Teaching Americans how to live with the constant threat of nuclear war meant convincing citizens to remain vigilant and calm. To combat both indifference and panic, governmental propaganda underscored the seriousness of the threat, while also reassuring the public that they could survive an atomic bomb blast if they took precautionary measures such as building fortified fallout shelters or remembering to "duck and cover." *Images as History: Surviving an Atomic Bomb Blast* explores how government-generated images presented competing visions that both reassured and frightened Americans about the likely effect of a nuclear bomb attack.

What insights does popular culture offer into Americans' concerns about nuclear weapons?

Images as History

SURVIVING AN ATOMIC BOMB BLAST

Controlling how people react to advice or propaganda can be difficult to predict. What was the government's purpose in disseminating images of a possible nuclear attack? What were the possible unintended effects that these images could have on the Americans viewing them?

By 1950 schoolchildren throughout the nation had learned to jump out of their seats and under their desks with their hands clasped firmly over their heads when their teachers shouted "Drop!" during civil defense drills. In government-produced civil defense films and comic books distributed to schools, a cartoon character named Bert the Turtle instructed children to "duck and cover" during a nuclear attack. Advocates of the "duck and cover" approach argued that flying debris and shattered windows had killed many victims in Hiroshima and Nagasaki; therefore, teaching children to "duck and cover" was practical advice.

To ensure that Americans remained vigilant in preparing for a nuclear attack, the government also released "before" and "after" photographs from a test explosion in the Nevada desert on March 17, 1953. *Time* magazine estimated that nearly three-quarters of the nation saw these pictures.

The stick of dynamite dangling from a stick symbolized a nuclear attack, exactly the kind of danger children needed to learn to recognize.

A catchy jingle accompanied this lesson in civil defense: "There was a turtle by the name of Bert, and Bert the Turtle was very alert / When danger threatened him he never got hurt / He knew just what to do / He'd Duck and Cover / Duck and Cover."

The intact shell implies that one could safely survive a nuclear attack by hiding under something.

Authorities advised children—who did not carry their shelters on their backs like Bert—to seek protection behind walls and trees or under tables if an atomic bomb hit.

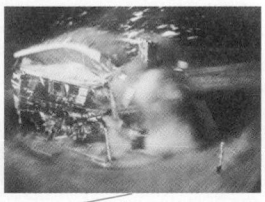

The "before" blast images portrayed a normal middle-class suburban home and yard.

The "after" blast photographs showed these suburban houses engulfed in flames and blown to bits within two seconds of being hit with a nuclear bomb.

This image directly contradicted the vision that one could survive a nuclear attack by seeking shelter under a bed as "Bert the Turtle" advised.

Did these images offer competing or complimentary visions of the nuclear threat?

Fallout Shelters

With the successful test explosion of the hydrogen bomb in 1954, the Eisenhower administration embraced mass evacuation from city centers as the best civil defense against nuclear attack. The president's decision to construct an interstate highway system changed official policy "from 'Duck and Cover' to 'Run Like Hell,'" the *Bulletin of the Atomic Scientists* concluded. Multilane highways served peacetime needs by linking cities to suburbs and military needs by making the evacuation of civilians and the mobilization of the military easier if the United States was attacked. Practice evacuation runs were not encouraging, however. "Operation Kids," for example, an effort to move 37,300 schoolchildren in Mobile, Alabama, out of the city without warning resulted in heavy traffic jams.

Eisenhower also urged Americans to build private family shelters at their own expense. The government distributed pamphlets with suggested floor plans, and advised women to store enough food and medical supplies to sustain their families if a nuclear attack contaminated water supplies or destroyed grocery stores. "Grandma's pantry was ready" whenever guests unexpectedly arrived; "is your 'pantry' ready in event of emergency?" one government pamphlet asked.

Given their high cost (even a barebones shelter cost $1,000, about one-fifth an average family's annual income) only a small number of Americans could afford to construct their own fallout shelters. At a moment of crisis in 1961 when the United States and the Soviet Union clashed once again over the fate of Berlin, Eisenhower's successor, John F. Kennedy, dedicated some public funds to preparing mass underground shelters in schools and public buildings. Signs with three yellow triangles superimposed on a black circle (**24.12**) that pointed toward underground public fallout shelters now became ubiquitous in schools and government buildings throughout the country.

In 1956 the government began constructing secret centers scattered throughout the nation to house officials in the event of a nuclear attack. The government did not make these preparations public, avoiding uncomfortable questions about what would happen to the rest of the country. These secret plans sought to ensure the continued functioning of Congress by transporting legislators and some staff members (without their families) to an underground shelter in White Sulphur Springs, West Virginia. As part of its preparations, the Treasury Department put an eight-month supply of one-dollar bills and a two-year supply of five-, ten-, and twenty-dollar bills in bombproof shelters. The military scattered mini-Pentagons throughout the country, including underground facilities for the president and his cabinet near Gettysburg, Pennsylvania. Plans to whisk the government to safety during a nuclear attack remained in place until 1995.

24.12 Fallout Shelter Sign
In the early 1960s, fallout shelter signs posted in neighborhoods, schools, and public buildings were daily reminders of the nuclear threat that hung over the nation.

What defensive measures did the public and government take against a possible nuclear attack?

Spies in Our Midst

Recently released documents from the Soviet Union suggest that as many as three hundred Americans spied for the USSR during the 1930s and 1940s. Does this reality justify the attack on civil liberties that occurred during the anti-communist crusade that swept across the country during the 1940s and 1950s? During the Cold War many Americans believed that this anti-communist campaign made the country safer and freer; a minority voiced the competing vision that the government was using spy investigations to limit the scope of legitimate political discourse by eliminating the radical left. The government's crusade against communism in the First Red Scare (1919) after World War I lasted only a few short months. The widespread effort to root out Communist spies after World War II lasted for nearly a decade.

The Second Red Scare

To a country reeling from the loss of China to communism and the detonation of a Soviet bomb, the suggestion that the government was rife with Communist spies offered a simple explanation for these complex events. The House Un-American Activities Committee (HUAC), which had investigated fascist activities in the United States during World War II, now probed the communist threat. Other World War II–era measures also took on new life during the **Second Red Scare**, including the Smith Act (1940), which outlawed advocating the forceful destruction of the government. Acting on a precedent set by Franklin D. Roosevelt in World War II, Truman created a federal employee loyalty program in 1947 that gave the Federal Bureau of Investigation (FBI), the police arm of the Justice Department, the right to investigate the backgrounds of federal workers. In 1950 Congress tightened restrictions on radical political activity even further by passing the McCarran Act, which stopped Communists from entering the country and required Communist or Communist-front organizations to register with the attorney general.

Most of the individuals investigated by HUAC and the FBI had once belonged to the Communist Party, which had attracted many new members during the labor unrest of the 1930s (see Chapter 22). Whether past or even present membership in the Communist Party made one a traitor was another question. When David Wellman was a young boy, his family was under constant police surveillance. Two unmarked cars sat outside their Detroit home and followed him and his sister to school, ball games, and the store. "Trying to turn fear into fun, we made shaking them a game," he later recalled. Wellman maintained that his father, a wounded World War II veteran and leader in the Michigan Communist Party, and his mother, a communist active in trade unions, were not traitors but people who believed that revolution was an American ideal.

The constant surveillance took a toll on the family. "It felt as if the government penetrated the deepest recesses of our lives every minute of the day," Wellman recalled. Paranoia caused the family to censor speech within the home and on the telephone, certain that the police were always listening. As an adult Wellman got access to his family's police file and was stunned to learn that the actual reports contained almost no information about his parents' political activism. The police had discovered very little through this constant surveillance, succeeding mostly in terrorizing the family, which, Wellman suspected, was their true intent all along.

> "They were trying to put the fear of police power in the minds of the people they spied on. To a large degree, it worked."
>
> DAVID WELLMAN, whose family was under police surveillance during the Second Red Scare

The two biggest spy cases of the era involved Alger Hiss and Ethel and Julius Rosenberg. In 1948 Whittaker Chambers, a *Time* magazine editor and former member of the Communist Party, accused Alger Hiss, a high-ranking official during the

What insights does Wellman's story offer into the Second Red Scare?

Roosevelt administration, of being a communist. Hiss denied the charge before HUAC, announcing under oath that "I am not and never have been a member of any Communist-front organization." Chambers responded by charging that Hiss spied for the Soviet Union in the 1930s and as proof produced several rolls of microfilm that Chambers had hidden in a hollow pumpkin in his garden. The "pumpkin patch" microfilm contained copies of secret State Department papers from 1938 regarding the Soviet Union, Nazi Germany, and the Spanish Civil War that had been typed on Hiss's typewriter. The "pumpkin patch" papers corroborated Chambers's account, and recently declassified intelligence documents have confirmed that Hiss worked as a Soviet spy through at least 1945. Because the statute of limitations on espionage had expired, a federal court convicted Hiss of perjury for lying to HUAC about his communist ties. Hiss served four years in jail. Congressman Richard Nixon, a member of HUAC, believed that the "Hiss case, for the first time, forcibly demonstrated to the American people that domestic communism was a real and present danger to the security of the nation." Nixon's leading role in the Hiss investigation catapulted him into the national spotlight. His prominence increased even further when he ran successfully for vice president on the Republican ticket with Eisenhower in 1952.

24.13 The Rosenbergs Spy Case, 1953
Protesters urge the government to execute convicted spies Julius and Ethel Rosenberg, reflecting the fury many Americans felt toward anyone believed to have betrayed the United States.

In 1953 another spy case involving Ethel and Julius Rosenberg, the Jewish parents of two young boys, captivated the nation. The federal government charged Julius with passing atomic bomb secrets to the Soviet Union during World War II, information he had supposedly gathered from his brother-in-law, a Soviet spy working for the Manhattan Project who later testified against the couple. Although Julius's wife Ethel was never personally implicated in the spy ring, the government charged her with knowing of her husband's involvement. Arrested to spur her husband into confessing, both went on trial for espionage. They each maintained their innocence even when convicted and sentenced to death by electric chair.

As the execution date neared, demonstrators from the right and the left took to the streets, offering the public two competing visions of the Rosenbergs and the government's anti-communist investigations. Men carrying signs that read "Burn All Reds" and "No Mercy for Spies" picketed before the White House (**24.13**). Supporters who believed that the Rosenbergs were being persecuted for their radical beliefs organized marches for clemency. Radio and television reporters witnessing the execution shared intimate details with a nation riveted on the couple's final moments, including Ethel's botched electrocution on June 19, 1953, when it took three tries to kill her. Their two young sons, aged ten and six, endured intense media scrutiny as well. Relatives put them in an orphanage, and New Jersey revoked their right to attend public school. Two of their parents' supporters eventually adopted the boys and changed their names. As adults they were active in leftist causes and until recently steadfastly maintained their parents' innocence. For decades the right and the left embraced two competing visions of the Rosenbergs case. The right viewed the couple as traitors whose cooperation with the Soviet Union demonstrated the clear internal threat that the nation faced from Soviet spies. The left, believing the Rosenbergs innocent, felt that mainstream politicians exaggerated the Communist menace to gain public support for eradicating all left-leaning political groups from American society. In some respects both portraits were accurate. Newly released Soviet documents reveal that Julius did indeed pass valuable atomic data to the Soviet Union, but it appears that Ethel knew nothing of her husband's espionage activities, making her, along with countless others in the 1950s, a victim of overzealous investigators who equated leftist politics with treason.

What competing visions arose over the Hiss and Rosenbergs spy cases?

HUAC against Hollywood

The effort to expose the evildoings of communists went far beyond punishing government officials who spied for the Soviet Union. In 1947 HUAC began an investigation into alleged communist activities in Hollywood. Over the next few years, hundreds of screenwriters, producers, directors, and actors were called to testify in Washington, D.C. Initial hearings focused on the supposedly subversive plotlines and imagery of selected motion pictures, such as *Mission to Moscow,* a World War II–era film that presented the Soviet Union as paradise on earth. Jack Warner, the head of Warner Studies, had produced *Mission to Moscow* after the Roosevelt administration requested a film that would improve the public's impression of the nation's wartime ally. This episode in producing left-wing political propaganda was the exception rather than the rule in Hollywood. Most studio heads subscribed to Sam Goldwyn's view that "if you want to send a message, use Western Union." The iron grip of the Hollywood studio system allowed directors little independence to include political content in their films that was not approved by the studio bosses. As a result HUAC could find little evidence of "subversive" content in Hollywood films. Rather than abandoning its investigation of Hollywood, however, HUAC shifted focus to the political affiliations and beliefs of the individuals involved in making movies.

After ten screenwriters, dubbed the "Hollywood Ten," were convicted of contempt of Congress for refusing to cooperate and sentenced to a year in prison, studio executives announced the creation of a **Hollywood blacklist**, a list of individuals with suspected past or present communist ties whom film studios refused to hire. The FBI had already infiltrated the Communist Party and provided HUAC with the names of all those in Hollywood with present or past communist affiliations. HUAC nonetheless pressured subpoenaed witnesses to publicly name names, not to gain information, but to test witnesses' loyalty. Many cooperated with HUAC to salvage their film careers. The vast majority who refused to testify or to name names never worked in films again. Others, like future president Ronald Reagan, then the president of the Screen Actors Guild, joined the anti-communist crusade by privately providing the FBI with the names of individuals in Hollywood with potential communist connections. Reagan testified before HUAC as a liberal Democrat (his shift to the right came a few years later), where he denied that communists "have ever at any time been able to use the motion-picture screen as a sounding board for their philosophy."

Director Elia Kazan and playwright Arthur Miller used their artistic work to explain the different choices they made when asked to testify by HUAC. Kazan's film *On the Waterfront* (1954) starred Marlon Brando as an ex-prizefighter turned longshoreman who overcomes his aversion to "ratting on your friends" and testifies against his corrupt union bosses. Kazan, who had been a member of the Communist Party in the 1930s, intended for the film to justify his own decision in 1952 to provide HUAC with the names of eight former Communist Party colleagues (see *Competing Visions: Naming Names in Hollywood,* page 740). *On the Waterfront* won Academy Awards for Best Picture, Best Director, and Best Actor. Conversely Miller refused to testify when called before HUAC in 1956 and criticized the hysteria created by the Second Red Scare in his play *The Crucible,* which likened the HUAC investigations to the 1692 Salem witch trials in colonial Massachusetts.

> "We will not knowingly employ a Communist nor a member of any party or groups which advocates the overthrow of the Government of the United States by force or by illegal or unconstitutional methods."
>
> Studio executives' statement announcing the creation of a Hollywood blacklist, 1947

McCarthyism

The government's anti-communist crusade during the Second Red Scare also became known as **McCarthyism**, named for the media-savvy Republican senator Joseph McCarthy from Wisconsin, who, along with HUAC, spearheaded numerous governmental investigations into communist activities, many of them spurious. Anti-communist spy investigations predated McCarthy, but his flair for the dramatic made the senator an instant media sensation. McCarthy burst onto the scene after waving around a piece of paper during a speech before the Women's Republican Club in Wheeling, West Virginia, on

What was the purpose and impact of HUAC's Hollywood investigations?

Competing Visions

NAMING NAMES IN HOLLYWOOD

The following opinions, one from former first lady Eleanor Roosevelt who wrote a syndicated magazine column, "My Day," and the other from film director Elia Kazan, offer opposing views on aiding the HUAC investigations. Consider how Roosevelt and Kazan defined the threat to American democracy in this period. What risks were involved in following the different suggestions each made? Could their two views be reconciled in any way?

In a 1947 "My Day" column, Eleanor Roosevelt expressed concerns that HUAC was creating a police state atmosphere that would squash artistic creativity and freedom of expression.

I have waited a while before saying anything about the Un-American Activities Committee's current investigation of the Hollywood film industry. I would not be very much surprised if some writers or actors or stagehands, or what not, were found to have Communist leanings, but I was surprised to find that, at the start of the inquiry, some of the big producers were so chicken-hearted about speaking up for the freedom of their industry.

One thing is sure—none of the arts flourishes on censorship and repression. And by this time it should be evident that the American public is capable of doing its own censoring.... The film industry is a great industry with infinite possibilities for good and bad. Its primary purpose is to entertain people. On the side, it can do many other things. It can popularize certain ideals, it can make education palatable. However, in the long run, the judge who decides whether what it does is good or bad is the man or woman who attends the movies. In a democratic country I do not think the public will tolerate a removal of its right to decide what it thinks of the ideas and performances of those who make the movie industry work.... What is going on in the Un-American Activities Committee worries me primarily because little people have become frightened and we find ourselves living in the atmosphere of a police state, where people close doors before they state what they think or look over their shoulders apprehensively before they express an opinion.... If you curtail what the other fellow says and does, you curtail what you yourself may say and do. In our country we must trust the people to hear and see both the good and the bad and to choose the good. The Un-American Activities Committee seems to me to be better for a police state than for the USA.

Many people in Hollywood never forgave Elia Kazan for cooperating with HUAC. In his 1988 autobiography Kazan refused to apologize for his actions. Instead he asserted his right to protect his career and the need to defend the country.

I believed it was the duty of the government to investigate the Communist movement in our country. I couldn't behave as if my old "comrades" didn't exist and didn't have an active political program. There was no way I could go along with their crap that the CP [Communist Party] was nothing but another political party, like the Republicans and the Democrats. I knew very well what it was, a thoroughly organized, worldwide conspiracy. This conviction separated me from many of my old friends ...

Did I really want to change the social system I was living under? Apparently that was what I'd stood for at one time. But what s**t. Everything I had of value I'd gained under that system ...

Why had I taken so long to even consider telling the country—that's what it amounted to—everything I knew? Was it because of the moral injunction against "informing," which was respected only depending on which side you were on? ... If the situation were reversed, wouldn't the "comrades" protect themselves without hesitation and by any means? Including naming me.... I began to measure the weight and the worth of what I was giving up, my career in films, which I was surrendering for a cause I didn't believe in. It seemed insane. What was I if not a filmmaker? ... If you expect an apology now because I would later name names to the House Committee, you've misjudged my character.... The people who owe you an explanation (no apology expected) are those who, year after year, held the Soviets blameless for all their crimes.

Hearings before the House Committee on Un-American Activities during the Second Red Scare

What different perspectives do Roosevelt and Kazan offer on protecting the right to freedom of expression?

February 9, 1950, thundering that he had a list of 205 known communists who worked in the State Department. (The paper turned out to be just a prop.) When pressed for the names of the individuals on his list, McCarthy stalled and announced that he would only show their names to Truman, which he never did. In each subsequent speech the number cited by McCarthy dropped until he finally settled on fifty-seven.

> "When a great democracy is destroyed, it will not be from enemies from without, but rather because of enemies from within."
>
> Senator JOSEPH R. MCCARTHY, Wheeling, West Virginia, 1950.

As a Republican attacking a Democratic administration, McCarthy's accusations had a distinctly partisan ring. Taking advantage of the media spotlight, McCarthy issued new charges against an assortment of State Department officials, ruining the careers of numerous individuals who could not mount an effective defense against his bullying. Reveling in the press attention that every new allegation brought, McCarthy sought increasingly bigger targets, even attacking Secretary of Defense George C. Marshall, who had authored the Marshall Plan while secretary of state, for having joined "a conspiracy so immense and an infamy so black as to dwarf any previous such venture in the history of man."

A year after the Rosenbergs were executed, the personal career of Joseph McCarthy as an anti-communist crusader ended when the senator began investigating the army for subversion. National television broadcast the hearings, and Americans watched aghast for thirty-six days as McCarthy intimidated witnesses, ignored facts, and made ludicrous charges. The climactic moment in the hearing came when the army's attorney Joseph Welch rebuked McCarthy, telling him, "You have done enough. Have you no sense of decency, sir, at long last?" Public approval ratings for McCarthy plummeted from 50 percent to 35 percent in Gallup polls.

The public unraveling of support for McCarthy mirrored growing concerns among his fellow Republicans in Congress. By 1954 Eisenhower and former HUAC member Richard Nixon were in the White House. Attacking a Republican-controlled administration yielded fewer political benefits, and some Republicans privately urged Eisenhower to rein in McCarthy. Leary of having his own anti-communist credentials challenged, Eisenhower refused to confront McCarthy directly. Instead the president tried to take the high road. "I will not get down in the gutter with that guy," Eisenhower vowed, reasoning that if he gave McCarthy enough rope, he would eventually hang himself. This hands-off approach allowed McCarthy to run wild until 1954, when, as Eisenhower predicted, he went too far. Eventually it was the mainstream press, not the president, who denounced McCarthy. In the wake of the Army-McCarthy hearings, the esteemed television journalist Edward R. Murrow exposed McCarthy's slander and lies in a television documentary. McCarthy, Murrow pointedly told his audience, "didn't create this situation of fear; he merely exploited it." However when the Senate censured McCarthy on December 2, 1954, for violating Senate rules, the legislators chose to depict McCarthy as solely responsible for the excesses of anticommunism. McCarthy left the Senate in disgrace, and died from liver failure caused by alcoholism four years later at the age of forty-nine.

> "No one man can terrorize a whole nation unless we are all his accomplices."
>
> Journalist EDWARD R. MURROW during a 1954 television exposé on McCarthy

As Murrow suggested the end of McCarthy's career as a red-baiter did not stop the government's anti-communist crusade. Republicans and Democrats alike took their cue from McCarthy and freely attacked any suspected radical working in local or state governments, public schools, or universities. The Smith Act remained in place, as did loyalty oaths, Hollywood blacklists, and police surveillance of suspected radicals. By the 1950s using the charge of communism to discredit political opponents or liberal activists (such as Martin Luther King Jr.) was commonplace in American politics.

Is the term McCarthyism a useful or misleading way to characterize the Second Red Scare?

Averting Nuclear War

The worldwide ideological, political, and military struggle between the United States and the Soviet Union fueled Americans' abiding fear of communism, both at home and throughout the world. The vision of fighting a nuclear war continued to haunt Americans even after the ceasefire in Korea. Technological advances in long-range ballistic missiles and satellites provoked a new moment of crisis in the Cold War standoff between the United States and the Soviet Union. A missile fitted with a nuclear warhead could now travel through space to reach the United States within half an hour from the Soviet Union. A series of armed uprisings in Eastern Europe, renewed Soviet demands that the West abandon Berlin, and the Cuban Missile Crisis combined to create a climactic moment when the world teetered on the edge of all-out nuclear war.

Sputnik

On October 4, 1957, the Soviet Union successfully sent the world's first satellite, nicknamed Sputnik ("fellow traveler"), into outer space. The size of a basketball and weighing just 183 pounds, Sputnik (**24.14**) nonetheless became a symbol of Soviet technological superiority, a satellite that could orbit the earth in ninety-eight minutes. Today satellites serve a host of peaceful functions, transmitting television images and telephone calls throughout the globe. In 1957, however, Americans focused primarily on the new strategic advantage that satellite technology gave the Soviets. The Soviets could easily fit a missile that sent Sputnik into orbit with a nuclear warhead and launch it at the United States. Fearing that the United States was in danger of losing the "space race," the government created the National Aeronautics and Space Administration (NASA) to launch America's own investigation of space, and the Defense Department scrambled to develop American satellite technology.

Predicting how the Soviet Union's volatile new leader might use this technological breakthrough kept Americans on edge. In the power struggle that followed Stalin's death from a brain hemorrhage in March 1953, Nikita Khrushchev emerged as the new Soviet premier. A poorly educated peasant who rose through the ranks to become a Stalin protégé, Khrushchev reveled in rhetorical excess. He proclaimed that the USSR was producing missiles "like sausages," and enjoyed keeping his American visitors off-balance. During a visit by Minneapolis senator Hubert Humphrey to Moscow, Khrushchev stopped his threatening tirade long enough to ask Humphrey where he was from. "That's so I don't forget to order them to spare the city when the rockets fly," he said good naturedly.

Eager to catch up with the Soviet Union in missile technology and cut the defense budget (conventional military forces cost more than building nuclear weapons), Eisenhower oversaw a tremendous increase in American nuclear weaponry, which grew from eight hundred to nearly eight thousand warheads between 1953 and 1960. This nuclear arms build-up was part of a strategic vision called the "New Look." In 1954 Eisenhower's tough-talking secretary of state John Foster Dulles announced that the United States would focus on developing "massive retaliatory power" to deter Soviet aggression. The National Security Council agreed with Dulles that the country would go bankrupt trying to develop adequate defenses against Soviet nuclear weapons and policing the world with ground troops. Dulles maintained that building a strong arsenal of intercontinental missiles armed with nuclear warheads would allow the United States to "retaliate, instantly, by means and at places of our choosing" when the Soviets stepped out of line. Eisenhower particularly liked the New Look because it offered a way to counter the Soviet manpower advantage while maintaining a small peacetime army at home. The appeal of "massive retaliation" was simple—it provided "more bang for the buck," some commentators noted.

Getting accurate data on the Soviet arsenal became critical once the United States embraced the doctrine of massive retaliation. The year before the Soviets launched Sputnik, the Americans began

24.14 Sputnik, 1957
For Americans this small satellite symbolized Soviet technological superiority over the United States, fueling the ongoing arms race between the two nations.

What caused the nuclear arms race to escalate in the late 1950s?

using a new spy plane, the U-2, to take photographs of Soviet military installations. Soviet radar could detect the U-2, but the plane flew at altitudes out of range for Soviet fighter pilots or antiaircraft missiles. For four years the United States used U-2 missions to collect intelligence about the number of Soviet long-range missiles before turning to spy satellites. The photographs were reassuring. At the end of 1959, the United States learned, the Soviet Union had only six intercontinental ballistic missile (ICBM) sites, which were places to launch a missile carrying a nuclear warhead. Because it took twenty hours to fuel each missile, which could travel through space to reach targets 5,000 to 6,000 miles away in half an hour, the United States would have ample time to respond if the Soviet Union launched a first strike with six missiles. Despite Khrushchev's claims that the Soviets possessed a huge nuclear arsenal, in fact American stockpiles of nuclear warheads and ICBMs far exceeded those of the Soviet Union.

Having made much of the claim that the Soviet Union possessed more ICBMs than the United States in his successful 1960 presidential campaign against Richard Nixon, newly elected Democratic president John F. Kennedy waited a few months before revealing the truth. Calling Khrushchev's bluff Kennedy announced to the world that the United States had a "second strike capability which is at least as extensive as what the Soviets can deliver by striking first. Therefore, we are confident that the Soviets will not provoke a major nuclear conflict." The gap only kept growing in America's favor. Continuing the policy of massive retaliation, Kennedy oversaw an increase in the American ICBM stockpile from 63 to 424 from 1961 to 1963.

The attention given to the missile gap during the 1960 presidential campaign revealed the constant pressure that Americans felt to retain the upper hand in the ever-evolving nuclear arms race. The chart (**24.15**) lists the key developments in early Cold War nuclear weaponry, illustrating the intense competition between the United States and Soviet Union to develop nuclear weapons, including nuclear-powered submarines that could stay submerged for two months and fire nuclear-fitted missiles.

INNOVATION	USA	USSR
Nuclear-powered submarine	1954	1958
First Trial of ICBM	1958	1957
ICBM operational	1960	1959
Submarine-launched ICBM operational	1960	1957

24.15 Nuclear Arms Race, 1950s The United States and Soviet Union tried to best each other by developing more sophisticated nuclear weapons.

The Berlin Wall

Americans weighed Kennedy's reassuring words about the missile gap against recent events that once again demonstrated the heavy hand of Soviet authority in Eastern Europe. In 1956 Khrushchev publicly denounced Stalin's crimes against the Soviet people. Khrushchev's speech, taken as a cue that the new Soviet regime would be more open and tolerant, set off rebellions in Poland and Hungary. Soviet troops immediately rolled into Hungary to crush the rebellion, revealing that Khrushchev intended to retain Soviet control over Eastern Europe.

Khrushchev also moved to consolidate Soviet power over Berlin, twice issuing ultimatums to the West to vacate its territory in the divided city. The stark differences between life in East and West Berlin had become a public embarrassment to the Soviet Union. Lavishly rebuilt by West Germany and the Marshall Plan, West Berlin teemed with new housing, industry, and commerce. Moving freely between the more prosperous western half and the areas under Communist control, many Berliners voted with their feet. Nearly a million East Germans defected in 1956, traveling easily from West Berlin into West Germany to start new lives.

Khrushchev viewed the forty-four-year-old Kennedy as an inept, inexperienced leader whom he could easily intimidate. A botched U.S. invasion of Cuba in 1961 (discussed more fully later) only reaffirmed Khrushchev's low opinion of Kennedy. Believing that Kennedy would crumble under pressure, Khrushchev demanded that the West leave Berlin when the two met for the first time in Vienna. To Khrushchev's surprise the president stood firm. Kennedy left the summit "shaken and angry," one reporter claimed. He never met with Khrushchev again. Instead he returned home and requested funds for additional nuclear and conventional forces. The public fully supported their president. More

How did the new Soviet premier Khrushchev compare to Stalin?

24.16 Brandenburg Gate, 1961
For Americans the desolate scene before the Brandenburg Gate, the traditional entry point into the city of Berlin, symbolized the heavy hand of Soviet oppression as the Berlin Wall went up.

than 82 percent favored maintaining American, French, and British forces in Berlin, even if it meant war with the Soviet Union.

With Kennedy unwilling to abandon the city, Khrushchev resisted the temptation to erect another blockade. Instead of revoking permission for the West to use roads through East Germany to supply the city, as Stalin had in 1948, he made the controversial decision to build a wall between East and West Berlin. In the twilight hours of August 13, 1961, construction of a barbed wire fence began. East German tanks and troops rolled up to the monumental Brandenburg Gate, the traditional entry point into the city of Berlin, to prevent a popular protest from breaking out in front of this symbol of German nationhood. East German workers quickly laid a thin line of barbed wire in front of the Brandenburg Gate, turning the popular square into a desolate no-man's land (**24.16**). As tensions mounted the British strung a second line of barbed wire on the western side as a safety measure to prevent irate West Berliners from instigating a shooting war between the two sides. The sign initially placed at the site, "Attention—You Are Now Leaving West Berlin," was hardly necessary now.

> "Freedom has many difficulties and democracy is not perfect, but we have never had to put a wall up to keep our people in, to prevent them from leaving us."
>
> President JOHN F. KENNEDY, in a speech before the Berlin Wall, 1963

Photos put a human face on the suffering. In one (**24.17**) two young girls, standing on the western side, chat with their grandparents over the makeshift fence that now divided them. East Germany eventually replaced the barbed wire with 12-foot-high concrete walls that ran for nearly 30 miles, and was dotted with guard towers, spotlights, guard dogs, and minefields. West Germans flocked to the construction site, curious and in shock. Some East Germans made desperate last-minute escapes, jumping from the windows of buildings that straddled the boundary into nets held by West German firefighters. East German soldiers first bricked up the windows, then demolished the buildings to create 100 yards of empty space between the wall and any other structure. The "dead zone" on the eastern side made it impossible for people to approach the wall. Guards along the wall had strict orders to shoot anyone who tried to cross it. Nearly a thousand people died trying to escape to West Berlin during the wall's twenty-eight-year existence.

The wall succeeded in stopping the flow of people from East to West Berlin without provoking a major confrontation with the United States. As the wall went up in 1961, Kennedy remarked to his aides that "a wall is a hell of a lot better than a war." The Soviet success came at a cost, however. For over two decades the Berlin Wall served as the most visible symbol to the world of Soviet oppression. When Kennedy finally visited the wall in June 1963, he expressed

24.17 Berlin Wall
Two sisters living in West Berlin chat with their grandparents across the barbed wire that divided East and West Berlin. Before East Germany replaced the barbed wire with a concrete wall, many East Germans escaped to the West by jumping over the flimsy barricade.

What meaning did photographs of the Berlin Wall have for Americans?

solidarity with the people on both sides of the divided city by announcing, "Ich bin ein Berliner" (which Kennedy thought meant "I am a Berliner," not realizing that *ein Berliner* was the name for a popular German doughnut). Over the years the wall on the western side became covered in graffiti and required continual repair from saboteurs' efforts to destroy parts of it.

Bay of Pigs and the Cuban Missile Crisis

Americans viewed Communist activities in Germany with dismay, but the prospect of a Communist Cuba alarmed the government more: Cuba lay just 90 miles south of Florida. In 1959 Fidel Castro had emerged as the victor in the Cuban Revolution, overthrowing the dictator Fulgencio Bastista y Zaldívar. Castro moved quickly to consolidate his power. He declared himself a communist, confiscated a billion dollars in American property, and accepted aid from the Soviet Union. In response an alarmed Eisenhower broke off diplomatic relations and imposed economic sanctions, including an embargo that banned the export of American goods to the island. The Central Intelligence Agency (CIA) urged more forceful action and began planning the covert **Bay of Pigs operation**, a failed amphibious invasion by Cuban exiles in 1961 to overthrow the Cuban dictator Fidel Castro.

Eisenhower left office before the scheduled invasion, but Kennedy quickly gave his blessing to the plan. Problems arose immediately. Two days before the ground attack, American planes (painted to look like stolen Cuban aircraft) bombed Cuban air defenses. On April 17, 1961, fourteen hundred exiles landed and were all immediately killed or captured. Kennedy's unconvincing public statement that the United States was not involved in this "struggle of Cuban patriots against a Cuban dictator" hurt his credibility at home and overseas.

The Bays of Pigs fiasco hardened the resolve of Kennedy, Khrushchev, and Castro to gain the upper hand in this new Cold War hotspot. The CIA devised various schemes for overthrowing Castro that involved sabotage and terrorism. In November 1961 CIA agents and Cuban exiles formed attack squads that covertly traveled in speedboats from Florida to Cuba, where they burned sugar plantations and blew up factories and oil depots. The CIA also plotted to assassinate Castro by trying to poison his ice cream and cigars and enlisting Mafia crime bosses to kill him. Castro complained to Khrushchev about America's murderous intentions, and in return received an influx of Soviet economic and military aid. Protecting communism in Cuba now became a major goal for the Soviet Union.

On October 22, 1962, President Kennedy appeared on national television to deliver the stunning news that the Soviet Union was building missile launching pads in Cuba for short- and intermediate-range nuclear missiles. The United States maintained bases in Italy, Britain, and Turkey that housed nuclear missiles aimed at the Soviet Union. Putting Soviet missiles in Cuba, a mere 90 miles from the American coast, would teach Americans "just what it feels like to have enemy missiles pointing at you," Khrushchev told his advisors. The **Cuban Missile Crisis**, a showdown in 1962 between the United States and the Soviet Union over Khrushchev's decision to place Soviet missiles in Communist Cuba aimed at America, was underway.

Instead of accepting the Soviet view that missiles in Cuba simply leveled the playing field, Kennedy responded with a competing vision that the Soviet actions represented "a provocative change in the delicate status quo both countries have maintained." Short- and intermediate-range Soviet missiles in Cuba threatened to reduce the strategic advantage that America held with its larger long-range nuclear arsenal. This was unacceptable to Kennedy. Intelligence officials estimated that the missile sites would become operational in two weeks, giving Kennedy only a small window of time before the Soviets would double their ability to launch a devastating nuclear strike against the United States.

Kennedy ultimately decided to use a naval blockade to prevent Soviet ships from arming the launching sites with nuclear missiles. (Only later would Kennedy discover that missiles were already in Cuba. The president never learned that the estimate of 10,000 Soviet troops in Cuba was wrong—there were actually 42,000).

How did the United States respond when communism took hold in Cuba?

Choices and Consequences

THE CUBAN MISSILE CRISIS

Long-range Soviet missiles (4,000–5,000 miles) launched from the USSR could already reach America, but short-range (1,100 miles) and intermediate-range (2,200 miles) nuclear-armed missiles in Cuba helped close the missile gap by giving the Soviets more weapons to use against the United States. Determined to get Soviet missiles out of Cuba, Kennedy and his advisors debated how to respond on October 16, 1962.

Choices

1. Use air and ground forces to attack Cuba and destroy the missile sites.
2. Follow up an attack on Cuba with a full-scale invasion to depose Castro.
3. Negotiate with the Soviet Union and Cuba.
4. Enact a naval quarantine to prevent Soviet-supplied missiles from reaching Cuba.

Decision

Kennedy opted for the quarantine. He sent the American navy 500 miles offshore of Cuba to intercept Soviet vessels carrying missiles, and threatened a nuclear attack on the Soviet Union if missiles were launched from Cuba.

Consequences

For two tense days Soviet ships steamed toward American naval vessels. At the last minute Khrushchev called the ships back and offered to negotiate by removing the missiles if Kennedy pledged not to attack Cuba and the United States dismantled its missiles in Turkey. Kennedy privately agreed to these terms. By deciding against an air strike, Kennedy may have unknowingly averted a nuclear war. Unbeknownst to the president nuclear warheads were already in Cuba. Soviet commanders on the ground had permission to use them if the United States attacked and considered using them against the blockade.

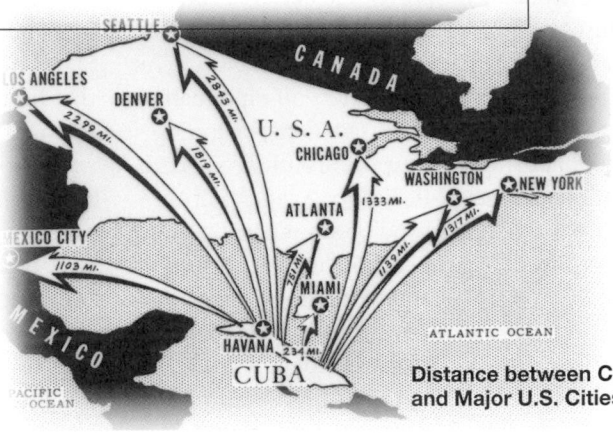

Distance between Cuba and Major U.S. Cities, 1962

Continuing Controversies

Did Kennedy react correctly during the Cuban Missile Crisis?

Supporters argue that Kennedy effectively used the threat of an American nuclear attack, traditional naval tactics, and old-fashioned diplomacy to end the crisis without resorting to war. By doing so he maintained America's strategic advantage against the Soviet Union and improved the nation's image worldwide after the Bay of Pigs fiasco.

Detractors claim that Kennedy provoked a crisis where there was none. Short- and medium-range missiles in Cuba did not alter the ability of the Soviets to attack with long-range missiles or of the United States to respond. Supporters counter that the improved accuracy of shorter-range missiles fired from Cuba posed a real threat. Critics also point out that because Kennedy made concessions privately to Khrushchev, the crisis gave rise to the myth that "brinkmanship," or threatening nuclear war, rather than diplomatic negotiations, caused the Soviets to back down. American overconfidence in the wake of the Cuban Missile Crisis would lead to missteps in America's growing military involvement in the Vietnam War and elsewhere in the next few years.

What political and military considerations influenced Kennedy during the Cuban Missile Crisis?

Choices and Consequences: The Cuban Missile Crisis, outlines the options facing Kennedy during this tense fortnight, the closest that the world ever came to fighting an all-out nuclear war. The world waited for thirteen days as Soviet ships steamed toward the American fleet guarding Cuban ports. American pilots sat in planes loaded with nuclear weapons, waiting to take off for Cuba at a moment's notice. Finally Khrushchev called Soviet ships back and offered to negotiate. The public breathed a collective sigh of relief that nuclear war had been averted, but the crisis lingered on behind closed doors for another month. As Soviet engineers continued to work on the missile sites, Kennedy and Khrushchev debated the exact terms of an agreement. In the end the American navy won the right to inspect ships carrying dismantled missiles out of Cuba. In return the United States agreed to dismantle its missiles in Turkey and pledged to respect Cuban independence by not launching another Bay of Pigs–type invasion. Over the next few years land-based missile sites lost significance as more American and Soviet submarines equipped with nuclear missiles began patrolling the world.

> "We're eyeball to eyeball, and I think the other fellow just blinked."
>
> Secretary of State DEAN RUSK, upon receiving word that Soviet ships had turned back during the Cuban Missile Crisis in 1962

Having teetered on the brink of nuclear war, both the United States and the Soviet Union opted to deescalate tensions. Kennedy and Khrushchev agreed to establish a hotline connection between Washington and Moscow so the two leaders could speak directly in the event of another crisis. In June 1963 Britain, the Soviet Union, and the United States also signed the Limited Test Ban Treaty, which banned atmospheric and underwater testing of nuclear weapons.

Conclusion

By 1950 conflicting visions within the U.S. government over how to respond to Soviet aggression gave way to an American strategy focused on containing communism. The United States sent financial aid to Western Europe, offered assistance to nations resisting Communist aggression, and stationed American soldiers permanently overseas. When the Soviet Union acquired the atomic bomb and China fell to communism, the United States responded by building a hydrogen bomb and stockpiling an enormous arsenal of nuclear weapons. The Cold War turned hot when North Korea invaded South Korea and the United States decided to intervene. After three years of fighting, a ceasefire ensured South Korean independence.

At home some Americans built bomb shelters to protect themselves from radioactive fallout, and civil defense drills taught schoolchildren to "duck and cover" during a nuclear bomb attack. Fears that Soviet spies were infiltrating the military, government, and film industry led to the Second Red Scare. After a brief lull Cold War tensions reignited when East Germany built the Berlin Wall in 1961 and the Soviets attempted to place missiles in Cuba in 1962. The Cuban Missile Crisis passed without either side launching a nuclear strike, but this was the closest the world came to nuclear annihilation during the Cold War.

Throughout the Truman, Eisenhower, and Kennedy administrations, America made critical choices about how to handle the new threat that the Soviet Union posed to the nation's economy, global influence, and national security. Eschewing diplomacy three presidents chose instead to contain communism with a mix of international aid, military alliances, and direct fighting with Communist nations presumably financed and controlled by Moscow. In the early 1960s American policymakers decided that defeating the North Vietnamese Communist regime was essential for America to win the Cold War, a strategic vision that the peace movement soon challenged.

What was the ultimate significance of the Cuban Missile crisis?

CHAPTER REVIEW

1946

Kennan's Long Telegram
Makes containing communism a key American goal

1947

Truman Doctrine
Gives United States a role in helping other nations resist communism

HUAC begins investigating Hollywood
Leads to establishment of blacklist

1948

Marshall Plan
Grants U.S. aid to rebuild war-torn Europe and prevent spread of communism

Berlin airlift
Highly visible Cold War victory for the United States

Review Questions

1. In the postwar period, the United States assumed the role of global protector against Communist aggression. What competing visions did policymakers offer on the role that the United States should play in world affairs? How did the Truman Administration justify its foreign policy decisions from 1945–1950?
2. Evaluate the impact that international crises had on domestic politics from 1945 to 1963. Consider the reverse as well: How did domestic politics affect foreign policy during the early Cold War?
3. How did images and popular culture shape Americans' ideas about the Soviet Union and the atomic bomb?
4. What factors contributed to the Second Red Scare? What differing views did Americans have about its impact on American society?
5. Compare how Truman and Kennedy each handled a Soviet-instigated crisis over Berlin. Why did Americans consider West Berlin so important? What key decisions and risks did each leader take in resolving the crisis?
6. What key contributions did Truman, Eisenhower, and Kennedy make to the strategy of containment?

1949

NATO formed
First formal American military alliance since the Revolutionary War

Soviet Union acquires atomic bomb
United States loses atomic monopoly

China falls to communism
Provokes fears that communists are winning the Cold War

1950

Joseph McCarthy gives Wheeling, West Virginia, Speech
Begins career as major figure in Second Red Scare

Korean War begins
United States enters fighting; Cold War extends into East Asia

1953

Stalin dies; Khrushchev assumes power
Ruthless dictator replaced by brash and unpredictable one

Armistice announced in Korea
Limited victory that restores initial boundary between North and South Korea

Julius and Ethel Rosenberg executed
Spy case fuels Second Red Scare

1961–1962

Bay of Pigs invasion
Failed attempt to oust Castro in Cuba embarrasses the United States

Berlin Wall built
Becomes symbol of communist oppression

Cuban Missile Crisis
Nuclear showdown between the United States and the USSR prompts fears of nuclear war

Key Terms

Cold War A full-scale ideological and military conflict between the United States and the Soviet Union and their allies that led to several hot wars around the globe, although the Americans and Soviets, fearful of a nuclear showdown, never fought each other directly **721**

"long telegram" An influential five-thousand-word missive by diplomat George F. Kennan that outlined why America needed to develop an aggressive foreign policy aimed at containing Soviet expansionist impulses. **722**

containment The label affixed to multiple American foreign policy initiatives meant to prevent the Soviet Union from expanding its influence around the globe. **722**

iron curtain Churchill's characterization of the military and ideological barrier erected by the Soviet Union that separated Western and Eastern Europe into free and unfree halves. **722**

North Atlantic Treaty Organization (NATO) A post-World War II military alliance between the United States and Western European powers. **722**

Truman Doctrine A foreign policy initiative that gave the United States an active role in stopping the global spread of communism by supporting "free peoples who are resisting attempted subjugation by armed minorities or by outside pressures." **724**

Marshall Plan (1948–1952) Aimed to restore Europeans' faith in capitalism by sending $13 billion ($119 billion in today's dollars) overseas to rebuild Europe's ruined roads, bridges, factories, and farms. **724**

Berlin airlift (1948–1949) Americans and British used planes to resupply West Berlin to stymie the Soviet blockade of the city. **726**

Korean War (1950–1953) The United States fought Communist North Koreans and Chinese to a stalemate, frustrating Americans who had to learn to accept only a partial victory. **729**

nuclear fallout The deadly pollution that descends through the air after a nuclear bomb explosion. **734**

Second Red Scare Widespread effort to root out Communist spies after World War II that lasted for nearly a decade. **737**

Hollywood blacklist A list of individuals with suspected past or present communist ties whom film studios refused to hire. **739**

McCarthyism The government's anti-communist crusade named for Senator Joseph McCarthy from Wisconsin, who, along with the House Committee on Un-American Activities (HUAC), spearheaded numerous governmental investigations into communist activities, many of them spurious. **739**

Bay of Pigs operation (1961) Failed attempt to use an amphibious invasion by Cuban exiles to overthrow the Cuban dictator Fidel Castro. **745**

Cuban Missile Crisis (1962) A showdown between the United States and the Soviet Union over Khrushchev's decision to place Soviet missiles in Communist Cuba aimed at America. **745**

CHAPTER 25

In a Land of Plenty

Contentment and Discord, 1945–1960

> **"It was the longest block I ever walked in my whole life."**
>
> ELIZABETH ECKFORD, confronting a mob as she walked from the bus stop to school in Little Rock, Arkansas

On September 3, 1955, a young black teenager, Elizabeth Eckford, walked past an angry mob after state troopers refused to let her enter the all-white Central High School in Little Rock, Arkansas. This photo captures her harrowing ordeal as a young white woman, her face contorted with rage, screamed at Eckford.

In the days that followed a sympathetic white man put an ad in the local newspaper featuring this photograph. "Study this picture and know shame," he told his neighbors. Instead for years Hazel Bryan received congratulatory letters from diehard segregationists for her verbal assault on Eckford that day. Five years later Bryan tracked down Eckford in Little Rock to apologize. Eckford went on to graduate from college, served in the army, and then started a career as a probation officer.

This photograph challenges the traditional image of the fifties as a tranquil period of material contentment and ideological consensus. Americans did enjoy unprecedented prosperity during the decade. They also, however, experienced a fair amount of domestic discord along racial, generational, and political lines. New energy surged into the Civil Rights Movement in the 1950s. Acts of extraordinary bravery by Elizabeth Eckford and others like her took on new significance in an era of favorable Supreme Court rulings that pushed the federal government to take an active role in protecting the civil rights of African Americans. Leadership from black churches and black students infused the movement with an ethos of nonviolent direct action that forced white America to see the injustice of Jim Crow, the southern legal structure that relegated African Americans to second-class citizenship.

A different type of discord permeated American home-life throughout the 1950s. In many respects families were the focus of American society from 1945 to1960. Enjoying a rising standard of living in generally prosperous times, American families grew at an unprecedented rate. Lured to fast-growing suburbs by low-cost loans and affordable housing prices, an exploding middle class filled their homes with an array of possessions previously out of reach for most Americans. The baby boom generation, those 76.4 million Americans born between 1946 and 1964, now coming into adolescence, embraced new standards in dress, music, and movies that distinguished the "teen" generation from their parents. Some teenagers rebelled against authority in more overtly political ways. High school and college students, for instance, were the ground troops in many civil rights demonstrations. Others joined the counterculture beat movement to express their rebellion against social norms through poetry, novels, and art.

From 1945 to 1960 Americans debated the divergent political paths that the country could take domestically during the Cold War era. They pondered the effects of New Deal programs, unions, suburbs, civil rights, and consumption on American society. Altogether the changing American way of life created a sense of both contentment and crisis for the nation.

What symbolism made this photograph an icon of the Civil Rights Movement?

Securing the New Deal Legacy p. 752

A Middle-Class America p. 756

Popular Culture in the Fifties p. 760

Freedom Now: The Civil Rights Movement p. 765

Securing the New Deal Legacy

Once prosperity returned after World War II, Republicans launched a campaign to undo the New Deal, arguing that these Depression-era laws and benefits programs hampered the free market and deprived industrialists of the freedom to run their companies as they saw fit. Moderate Democrats, like President Harry Truman, focused on ensuring the permanency of past reforms. When labor unions launched a series of unpopular postwar strikes, Republicans joined with conservative Southern Democrats to successfully roll back New Deal legislation that had benefited the labor movement. The victory over labor, however, did not provide enough momentum for conservatives to achieve their ultimate goal: the entire dismantlement of the New Deal.

The Labor Movement Curtailed

In 1945 the labor movement enjoyed unparalleled strength. Government support for union organizing during the New Deal and World War II, combined with a wave of successful sit-down strikes in the 1930s, had made labor a powerful force in American society. This was the high point of the labor movement in American history. Over fourteen million workers belonged to unions, nearly 35 percent of the industrial workforce. Labor flexed its muscle in 1946, when the lifting of wartime price controls sent prices skyrocketing. Nearly 4.6 million

25.1 Striking Steel Workers, 1946
Picketing steel workers carried signs with slogans meant to win sympathy from ordinary Americans, but widespread strikes caused a public backlash against labor unions.

What overall arguments do these signs make in favor of labor's demands?

workers participated in five thousand strikes nationwide in 1945–1946, demanding not just higher wages and benefits but also the right to participate in management decisions regarding investments, product lines, production methods, and plant locations. The signs held by striking steelworkers in this photo (**25.1**) outside a Bethlehem Steel Plant were intended to mobilize public support. The slogans demanded fairness to returning veterans, gave assurances that higher wages would not lead to higher prices, and proposed a living wage for workers who made such a valuable commodity. Black and white steelworkers manned this picket line together, reflecting the success of the Congress of Industrial Organizations (CIO) in mending racial divisions that had previously weakened the labor movement (see Chapter 22).

As the scale of labor unrest widened, popular support for strikes diminished. The public had little sympathy for threats to shut down the steel and car industries, which formed the core of the national economy. Strikes in the coal and meatpacking industries also caused public dismay by making it more expensive for Americans to heat their homes and eat meat. When railroad workers went on strike, Truman intervened. The railroad strike "threatens to paralyze all our industrial, agricultural, commercial, and social life," leading to potential starvation at home and abroad, the president proclaimed. Although supportive of New Deal labor legislation, Truman announced he would use the army to run the railroads and draft striking workers into the military if they did not return to work. Moments before he was scheduled to address Congress to ask for authorizing legislation, Truman received word that the strikers had returned to work.

Workers in other industries fared a bit better. Negotiated settlements in the steel and auto industries set the benchmark for wages, benefits, and shop floor practices that other companies, even nonunionized ones like the general merchandiser Sears Roebuck, adopted to maintain peaceful labor relations. Industrialists gained as well in these agreements. Longer contracts ensured a lengthy period of tranquility with no strikes, and in all settlements company owners maintained control over management decisions.

The Republicans' successful mid-term campaign slogan, "Had Enough? Vote Republican," capitalized upon voters' dismay over labor conflicts and higher prices. For the first time since 1933, the Republican Party won majorities in both the House and the Senate in the 1946 congressional elections. Republicans hoped to use this victory as a springboard for unseating Truman from the White House in 1948. The Eightieth Congress immediately passed strong anti-labor legislation over Truman's veto. Although dismayed with the strikes of 1946, Truman knew that he would need labor's vote in the upcoming presidential contest. The **Taft-Hartley Act (1947)** abolished the closed shop, a practice that required all workers who benefited from a union-negotiated contract to join the union. The law also banned so-called sympathy boycotts, strikes by workers who wanted to support another union's protest. Finally the law's requirement that all union officers sign affidavits certifying that they were not members of the Communist Party encouraged unions to purge its most radical members, often those who had pioneered new tactics, like the sit-down strike in the 1930s. The Taft-Hartley law was a serious blow to the labor movement. The merger in 1955 between the CIO and the more conservative American Federation of Labor (AFL) ushered in a more cautious era of labor organizing that mostly ignored unskilled and southern workers.

Presidential Agendas: Truman and Eisenhower

Conservative Republicans hoped that the Taft-Hartley law would spearhead a drive to dismantle the New Deal. Instead the curtailment of labor removed the most visible symbol of what was supposedly "wrong" with the New Deal just as the 1948 presidential campaign got underway. To win Truman decided that the votes of labor and northern African Americans were more important than retaining the solid South. The Democratic Party adopted the slogan "Don't let them take it away," referring to the minimum wage, unemployment insurance, and Social Security that the New Deal granted to industrial workers. Liberals in the Democratic Party successfully pushed Truman to take a stronger stand on civil rights. In July 1948, for both principled and pragmatic reasons, Truman ordered the desegregation of the armed forces, an important civil rights milestone.

Truman's embrace of civil rights caused Southern conservatives to bolt from the Democratic Party; his earlier confrontations with labor convinced social progressives to leave the party as well. Vowing to

What differing responses did postwar labor conflicts provoke?

preserve segregation conservative Southern Democrats formed the States Rights Party and nominated South Carolina governor Strom Thurmond to run against Truman and the Republican candidate, Thomas Dewey. On the political left former Vice President Henry Wallace ran on the Progressive Citizens of America ticket, representing a coalition of liberals and radicals upset about the assault on civil liberties at home and the nation's aggressive foreign policy as the Cold War took shape. Truman's campaign assault on big business as "gluttons of privilege," strong support from labor and blacks, and the success of the Berlin airlift (see Chapter 24) propelled him to a clear victory in the Electoral College (303 to 189), but he led Dewey by just 2 million in the popular vote. The concentrated segregation and states' rights vote in the South garnered Thurmond 39 electoral votes in return for the 1.2 million popular votes he received. Wallace received nearly the same number of votes as Thurmond nationwide, but won no electoral votes.

> "The time has come to walk out of the shadow of states' rights and into the sunlight of human rights."
>
> Minneapolis Mayor HUBERT HUMPHREY, urging Democrats to adopt a strong civil rights stance in the 1948 presidential election

For much of his second term, Truman focused on managing foreign affairs and fending off assaults on his administration from Senator Joseph McCarthy (see Chapter 24). Abandoning his earlier stance of merely sustaining the New Deal, Truman advanced the **Fair Deal**, proposals for national health care, public housing, education, and public works projects. The Democratic majority that controlled the Eighty-First Congress funded state school systems and urban public housing, increased the minimum wage, and continued bringing electricity and telephones into rural areas. Proposals for national health insurance stalled, but Congress did vote to build more hospitals and expanded public health facilities for the poor.

In June, 1950, North Korea invaded South Korea and political debate shifted to the Korean War (see Chapter 24). Truman, wary of undermining bipartisan support for his Cold War policies and the Korean War, did not push hard for highly controversial Fair Deal initiatives such as repealing the antiunion Taft-Hartley Act, price and wage controls, or universal health care. Only a fraction of Truman's Fair Deal proposals became law, but his program foreshadowed the more successful and extensive liberal agendas of future presidents John F. Kennedy and Lyndon B. Johnson, both Democrats.

By the end of the Truman administration, most Americans could not imagine a society without Social Security or a minimum wage, expectations that shaped the political vision of the nation's next president. In 1952 and again in 1956, the Republican candidate Dwight Eisenhower won in landslide elections, both times defeating Democrat Adlai E. Stevenson, the governor of Illinois. The virtually unknown Stevenson faced the daunting challenge of overcoming southern anger at Truman's civil rights reforms (which Stevenson supported) and America's affection for Eisenhower, a World War II hero. A gifted orator Stevenson stuck to traditional stump speeches, while Eisenhower became to the first presidential candidate to use televised political ads. He honed his folksy image in short television ads that aired during the commercial breaks of popular nighttime programs. America voted overwhelmingly for the man they knew and liked, with Eisenhower defeating Stevenson by 422 to 89 electoral votes. In 1956, running on a slogan of "peace and prosperity" that noted his success in ending the Korean War, Eisenhower polled even higher numbers, receiving 457 electoral votes to Stevenson's 73.

Republican critics like Senator Robert Taft attacked the Fair Deal as "creeping socialism" because these expensive programs required high taxes and, in Republicans' view, gave the government too much power. The 1953 editorial cartoon *Who Said 'Creeping Socialism'* (**25.2**) reflected the conservatives' fear that Eisenhower would have trouble taming New Deal and Fair Deal programs. The congressman, a symbol of runaway big government, holds a briefcase labeled "Govt. in Business, Housing, Power, Transport," and his running head start makes it impossible for Eisenhower to catch up. In fact, though, the cartoon misrepresented Eisenhower's intentions. The president liked to say that he was "conservative when it comes to money and liberal when it comes to human beings." To appeal to the moderates in each party, Eisenhower announced that he had no intention of

How did foreign affairs influence domestic politics in the postwar era?

25.2 *Who Said 'Creeping Socialism,'* 1953
During the 1952 presidential election, conservative Republicans criticized the New Deal and Fair Deal as "creeping socialism." This caricature portrays the newly elected Republican President Dwight Eisenhower struggling to catch a runaway congressman who clutches onto programs enacted during previous Democratic administrations.

dismantling popular New Deal programs. "Should any political party attempt to abolish social security and eliminate labor laws and farm programs, you would not hear of that party again in our political history," Eisenhower concluded, to the dismay of conservatives in the Republican Party. His "victory of the moderates," as some commentators termed it, underscored that New Deal reforms were here to stay. Eisenhower did curb the Fair Deal by vetoing new public housing and public works projects and never offered any new social welfare measures of his own.

Fiscally conservative, Eisenhower believed that balancing the budget and limiting government expenditures created a favorable business environment that promoted jobs and prosperity. He worked hard to foster strong ties between government and the defense industry as the Pentagon amassed a huge nuclear arsenal. In the president's view a nuclear shield protected the nation more cheaply and effectively than conventional arms or troops, which were expensive to maintain. But Eisenhower expressed misgivings about the domestic costs of a large defense budget as early as 1953: "Every gun made, every warship that is launched, every rocket fired, signifies, in the final sense, a theft from those who hunger and are not fed, those who are cold and are not clothed." Nine years later, as he prepared to vacate the White House, Eisenhower suggested that he had gone too far in promoting the convergence of military and industrial interests. In a well-remembered speech, he urged Americans to monitor vigilantly the growth of the "**military-industrial complex**," Eisenhower's term for the close ties between the defense industry and the Pentagon that might influence government policy. "We must never let the weight of this combination endanger our liberties or democratic processes," Eisenhower warned.

"I have always assumed that what was good for the United States was good for General Motors, and vice versa."

Secretary of Defense CHARLES E. WILSON, when asked about a possible conflict of interest between his government position and his former job as the head of General Motors, 1953

What significance did Eisenhower's "victory of the moderates" have?

A Middle-Class America

By any measurement the 1950s was a prosperous decade. From 1945 to 1960 per capita consumption rose 50 percent, wages grew by one-third, and unemployment averaged 4.6 percent. American productivity boomed as well. Inhabited by only 6 percent of the world population, the United States produced half of the world's manufactured goods in the 1950s. The 1950s gave the generation raised in the austerity of the Great Depression something they had never known: prosperity. For the first time many Americans enjoyed the trappings of middle-class life—a suburban home filled with modern appliances and a car in the garage—previously available only to a small segment of the population. By 1960 the nation crossed a significant historic threshold when 60 percent of Americans were classified as middle class. The United States was no longer a primarily working-class society.

Postwar Prosperity

In 1948 Vernon Presley brought his family to Memphis, Tennessee, hoping to escape the grinding poverty of Mississippi. Gladys Presley later recalled that her son, Elvis, "would hear us worrying about our debts, being out of work and sickness and he'd say, 'Don't you worry none, Baby. When I grow up, I'm going to buy you a fine house . . . and get two Cadillacs—one for you and Daddy, and one for me." Elvis Presley fulfilled this promise to his parents when he became the most famous rock-and-roll star of the era. For the rest of his life, Elvis, an extreme example of the era's conspicuous consumption, gave away cars to friends and family.

Few Americans enjoyed this level of financial success, but the kind of deprivation that Elvis experienced as a child became a relic of the past for millions in the 1950s. The typical American "has access to amenities—foods, entertainment, personal transportation, and plumbing—in which not even the rich rejoiced a century ago," economist John Kenneth Galbraith noted. Having discretionary

25.3 and 25.4 Buying on Credit
"What They Have" vs. "What They Own." The before and after photos of this *Life* magazine spread demonstrated Americans' heavy reliance on credit to accumulate the trappings of middle-class life in the fifties.

What factors caused standards of living to improve for many Americans in the 1950s?

income for things such as a television, vacations, or sending a child to college transformed the lives of American workers. "If what we lived through in the 1950s was not liberation," Jack Metzgar, the son of Pennsylvania steelworkers, noted, "then liberation never happens in real human lives."

An aggressive union movement seeking higher wages and benefits and the New Deal safety net of guaranteed pensions and unemployment insurance helped fuel this leap into the middle class for many industrial workers. Other government initiatives also helped transform the way Americans lived. In 1944 just 44 percent of Americans owned their homes. By 1960 this figure had risen to 60 percent thanks to the 1944 GI Bill of Rights that offered returning veterans low-interest loans and a tax code that provided incentives for homeowners. In addition state and federal governments constructed the roads, schools, bridges, and sewers that new suburban developments required.

During World War II production of consumer goods was scant, and many Americans had accumulated savings that they were now eager to spend. In 1950 alone Americans snatched up 6.2 million refrigerators, 14.6 million radios, and 6.2 million automobiles. This represented three-quarters of the appliances purchased worldwide. Installment plans helped millions of Americans purchase these key consumer items. Consumer debt rose from 8.3 billion in 1946 to 56.1 billion in 1960, a trend that caught *Life* magazine's attention in 1953. To illustrate the newly affluent lifestyle of middle-class Americans, *Life* photographer Loomis Dean put a couple with their two children in front of their Los Angeles suburban home alongside all their furnishings and car. The first picture (**25.3**) showed "what they have": an oven, refrigerator, two television sets, car, and furniture. The second photograph (**25.4**), "what they own," put the family in front of the foundations of a house and a pair of wheels to reflect how far along they were in their mortgage and car payments. The refrigerator, couch, stove, and one television set—all bought on credit—were missing. By purchasing so heavily with credit, this family risked losing nearly everything if a recession hit and the father lost his job.

American leaders felt that their nation's material abundance clearly demonstrated the superiority of the capitalist societies over communist ones, where basic consumer items were often in short supply. Others condemned American materialism. In his biting social commentary *The Status Seekers*, Vance Packard criticized Americans for jettisoning the frugality of the past in favor of status-seeking conspicuous consumption. Manufacturers played an active role in creating this new consumerist

Compare this family's possessions and home life to those of previous generations.

orientation. One executive conceded that it was the advertisers' job to "see to it that Americans are never satisfied." A middle-class family now considered their car or refrigerator "obsolete after two or three years even though it works well," financial columnist Sylvia Porter noted.

The Move to the Suburbs

Suburbs built in the 1920s ringed major cities and remained connected to the metropolitan core by streetcars or rail lines. In the 1950s suburbs moved farther away from cities, becoming insular communities that depended increasingly on cars to transport people. The roads Eisenhower built to help evacuate urban areas if the nation came under nuclear attack (see Chapter 24) were now filled with suburbanites running errands and commuting to work. Of the thirteen million new homes constructed between 1948 and 1958, 85 percent were built in suburban neighborhoods. By 1960 thirty-seven million Americans lived in suburbs.

When developer William Levitt erected thousands of mass-produced homes on the former potato fields of Long Island, New York, he pioneered building techniques that transformed the housing market. Applying Henry Ford's automobile assembly line–style innovations to the housing industry, Levitt built "**Levittowns**,"—planned suburban communities where developers standardized every part of the construction process. Levitt claimed that his crews could assemble a house in fifteen minutes, while it took only three minutes to complete the paperwork to purchase one. Levitt passed these savings onto homebuyers, dropping the prices of new homes from $14,000 to $8,000. When other developers copied his techniques nationwide, the low price of suburban homes, coupled with readily available government-backed financing, brought home ownership within reach of millions of Americans.

These new suburban homes typically contained living room picture windows that developers installed to make their 1,000-square-feet houses feel more spacious. When the curtains were open, these large windows also displayed a family's possessions and prosperity to the neighborhood. Suburban homes had "living kitchens" where families both prepared and ate their meals and "family rooms" to accommodate the television, toys, and games that brought the family together at the end of the day. A garage sheltered the automobile that every suburban family needed to own.

Americans offered competing visions on whether suburban living improved daily life or encouraged mindless conformity. Conflicting interpretations greeted images of idealized suburban life. "For literally nothing down" Americans could purchase a "box" in a suburban development "inhabited by people whose age, income, number of children, problems, habits, conversation, dress, possessions and perhaps even blood type are also precisely like [theirs]," wrote John Keats in *The Crack in the Picture Window* (1957). Abraham Levitt, the son of developer William Levitt, fought back against these charges. "Houses are for people, not critics . . . — and the people for whom we do it think it's pretty good." This debate is explored in *Competing Visions: Suburbs—American Dream or Nightmare?*

The move to the suburbs converged with an explosion of childbearing among couples who had put off having children during the Depression and World War II and younger couples encouraged by boom times to start their families immediately. Between 1935 and 1955 the birth rate jumped nearly 40 percent. Levittown's nickname, "Fertility Valley," underscored this link between the suburbs and the **baby boom generation**, the 76.4 million Americans born between 1946 and 1964.

The baby boom generation shaped American society for decades to come. As babies and children they helped stimulate a huge industry devoted to diapers, baby formulas, and toys. Teenagers, a term coined after World War II to describe adolescents, formed the backbone of fifties popular culture and the antiwar movement and cultural upheavals of the sixties. In the twenty-first century, as the baby boomers begin to retire, the imperative to care for a large aging population poses significant challenges for American society.

The fifties ushered in other key lifestyle changes besides suburban living and an emphasis on family life. As more Americans entered the middle class, they increasingly worked at white-collar jobs ranging from clerks to professionals to corporate executives. The effect of corporate culture on American society was as hotly debated as the impact of suburban life. In an era when McCarthyism eliminated radical discourse as a legitimate form of political expression, social critics worried that suburbs and corporations were bleaching individuality and innovation out of the national character. "When white-collar people get jobs, they sell not only their time and energy but their personalities as well," sociologist C. Wright Mills contended. Others, including *Fortune* magazine, regularly defended corporations for extending job security and prosperity to millions.

Why did suburbs boom in the 1950s?

Competing Visions

SUBURBS—AMERICAN DREAM OR NIGHTMARE?

As the suburbs grew social critics debated whether suburban life represented the epitome of the American dream or a nightmarish existence that isolated Americans from one another. To challenge historian Lewis Mumford's assertion that the suburbs were cultural wastelands, sociologist Herbert J. Gans moved his family into a Levittown to study the habits and behaviors of its residents. As you read the following excerpts from Mumford and Gans, consider how each links the suburbs to changing lifestyles. What positive and negative changes do these writers attribute to suburban life? What different futures do they envision for a suburban-based American culture?

Lewis Mumford in *The City in History* (1961) contended that suburban life bred conformity, loneliness, and alienation.

In the mass movement into suburban areas a new kind of community was produced ... a multitude of uniform, unidentifiable houses, lined up inflexibly, at uniform distances, on uniform roads, in a treeless communal waste, inhabited by people of the same class, the same income, the same age group, witnessing the same television performances, eating the same tasteless pre-fabricated foods, from the same freezers, conforming in every outward and inward respect to a common mold ...

The town housewife, who half a century ago knew her butcher, her grocer, her dairyman, her various other local tradesmen, as individual persons, with histories and biographies that impinged on her own, in a daily exchange, now has the benefit of a single weekly expedition to an impersonal supermarket, where only by accident is she likely to encounter a neighbor. ...

The cost of this detachment in space from other men is out of all proportion to its supposed benefits. The end product is an encapsulated life, spent more and more either in a motor car or within the cabin of darkness before a television set.

Levittown Street Scene

Herbert J. Gans defended suburbanites in *The Levittowners: Ways of Life and Politics in a New Suburban Community* (1967).

[Levittowners] are not apathetic conformists ripe for takeover by a totalitarian elite or corporate merchandiser; they are not conspicuous consumers and slaves to sudden whims of cultural and political fashion. ... even though Levittowners and other lower middle class Americans continue to be home-centered, they are much more "in the world" than their parents and grandparents were. Those coming out of ethnic working class backgrounds have rejected the ... ethnocentrism which made other cultures and even other neighborhoods bitter enemies. This generation trusts its neighbors, participates with them in social and civic activities, and no longer sees government as inevitably corrupt. Even working class Levittowners have begun to give up the suspicion that isolated their ancestors from all but family and childhood friends. Similarly, the descendants of rural Protestant America have given up the xenophobia that turned previous generations against the Catholic and Jewish immigrant, they have almost forgotten the intolerant Puritanism which triggered attacks against pleasure and enjoyment, and they no longer fully accept the doctrine of laissez-faire that justifies the defense of all individual rights and privileges against others' needs.

These and other changes have come about not because people are now better or more tolerant human beings, but because they are affluent. For the Levittowners, life is not a fight for survival any more; they have been able to move into a community in which income and status are equitably enough distributed so that neighbors are no longer treated as enemies, even if they are still criticized for social and cultural defiance. By any yardstick one chooses, Levittowners treat their fellow residents more ethically and more democratically than did their parents and grandparents. They also live a "fuller" and "richer" life. ... superior to what prevailed among the working and lower middle classes of past generations."

What competing visions emerged over suburban living and corporate jobs?

Popular Culture in the Fifties

The introduction of television sets into family living rooms transformed the home life of millions of Americans. So did the emergence of an autonomous youth culture, with its own slang, rock-and-roll music, and modes of dress. Were these harmless expressions of adolescent rebellion or signs of the disintegration of American culture? These stirrings of generational conflict in the 1950s exploded a decade later into full-fledged revolt.

The Television Age Arrives

The first commercial television transmission occurred in 1939 when President Franklin D. Roosevelt visited the New York World's Fair. The war slowed the introduction of televisions into the consumer market, but by the 1950s, the television age had arrived. In 1948 just 178,000 homes had televisions. Seven years later three-quarters of American households owned one.

President Dwight Eisenhower set the tone for the decade with the widely publicized image of the president and his wife, Mamie, eating dinner each night off tray-tables set up in front of a television in their private White House parlor. Whereas in the forties Americans had flocked to movie theaters for entertainment, now they stayed home. "Don't be a Living Room Captive—Step Out and See a Great Movie," film studios urged Americans. Many Americans, however, appeared to agree with President Eisenhower, who wrote in his diary, "If a citizen has to be bored to death it is cheaper and more comfortable to sit at home and look at television than it is to go outside and pay a dollar for a ticket." Throughout the nation movie theaters closed and the studios made fewer films. Only drive-in theaters in suburban towns, where customers sat in their cars next to individual speakers to watch a movie on a giant outdoor screen, thrived. Drive-in theaters appealed to young parents who could pile their children into the car for a night out and teenagers who could escape the watchful eyes of adults for a few hours.

What were Americans watching at home? Many early television shows dealt with the social conditions and cultural values of the day, paying particular attention to family and consumerism. In *The Honeymooners*, the working-class Kramdens lived in a sparsely furnished apartment and often clashed, particularly when one of the get-quick-rich schemes devised by bus driver Ralph (played by comedian Jackie Gleason) started to unravel. His wife Alice always stood her ground, even when Ralph threatened her with one of the show's trademark lines: "One of these days, Alice . . . one of these days . . . POW, right in the kisser." By the end of each episode, the couple had reconciled, with Ralph often telling his wife, "Baby, you're the greatest."

I Love Lucy began in a small Manhattan apartment, but eventually Lucy Ricardo (played by Lucille Ball) and her Cuban husband Ricky (Ball's real-life husband Desi Arnez) relocated to suburban Connecticut to raise their son. Lucy's farcical adventures to get a job, enter show business, or best her husband always ended with Lucy realizing that being a wife and mother was fulfilling enough. Situation comedies like *Father Knows Best* and *Leave it to Beaver* focused on the roles that each member of an ideal white suburban family played: Father worked hard and came home in time to resolve the minor crises of the day; mother kept a spotless home, volunteered, and supported her husband's career; and children learned to tell the truth, work hard, and obey their parents. These television shows mirrored the general preoccupation with child-rearing during the baby boom, a time when family and religion were at the center of white middle-class suburban life. Yet because plotlines never involved the working class, people of color, politics, or domestic discord, these shows offered little insight into the social realities that shaped family life for millions of Americans during the 1950s.

Television programming in the 1950s provided plenty of escapist fare. Nightly news broadcasts, however, brought glimpses of the wider world into American homes and played an increasing role in politics. Politicians quickly learned to use the new medium to their advantage. Republican vice presidential candidate Richard M. Nixon was the first politician to give a televised speech to defuse a political scandal. During the 1952 presidential election, the press revealed that Nixon had a secret fund financed by California businessmen. Hoping to stem the damage, Nixon appeared on television

What insights do 1950s television shows offer into American culture?

to refute charges that the money was for his personal use or that these businessmen were buying "secret favors" from him with their donations. Laying out the details of his personal finances, Nixon defiantly told viewers that without campaign donations only the rich could run for office. In the speech's most famous passage, Nixon mentioned one personal gift that he would not return. "A man down in Texas heard Pat [his wife] on the radio mention the fact that our two youngsters would like to have a dog" and surprised the family with the gift of a black-and-white cocker spaniel. "And our little girl Tricia, the six year old, named it 'Checkers.' And you know, the kids, like all kids, love the dog, and I just want to say this, right now, that regardless of what they say about it, we're gonna keep it," Nixon declared.

In the aftermath of the speech, Nixon posed with his family and Checkers in this photo (**25.5**). The Checkers speech saved Nixon's place on the Republican ticket alongside Eisenhower. Like Nixon, John F. Kennedy also astutely used posed photographs, like this one with his attractive young family (**25.6**). By creating such images Kennedy hoped to distract attention from his inherited wealth and Catholicism, long considered an undesirable religious affiliation for a politician.

On September 26, 1960 in the **Kennedy and Nixon debate**, the two candidates faced off in the first televised presidential election debate. Nearly 77 million Americans, or 60 percent of the adult population, watched this historic event. Nixon, still pale and underweight from a recent two-week stint in the hospital, squared off against a tan and fit Kennedy, who impressed viewers with his comfortable presence before the cameras. By contrast Nixon refused to wear make-up, looked like he needed a shave, wore a poorly fitted shirt, and was visibly sweating throughout the exchange. The majority of Americans who watched the debate felt that Kennedy had won, while most Americans who listened on the radio gave the edge to Nixon. Kennedy went on to narrowly win the election, revealing the power of images to sway political judgments.

Teen Culture and Rock-and-Roll

Teenagers came into their own in the 1950s. Their parents remained haunted by visions of Depression-era deprivation and the life-and-death struggle of World War II. By contrast in the fifties many middle-class teenagers grew up with an abundance of material possessions. Most teenagers agreed with their parents when it came to politics, sharing their concern about communist expansion throughout the world and the growing Soviet nuclear threat. Many however adopted

25.5 and 25.6 Two candidates, one family portrait Throughout their political careers, Richard M. Nixon and John F. Kennedy used portraits of their family life to connect with voters. These images fit with the era's idealized image of the perfect American family, which included a supportive wife, two children, and at least one dog.

How did politicians use television and photographs to shape their public image?

an ethos of pleasure-seeking that often put them at odds with their parents who emphasized thrift and self-discipline. Unlike their parents' generation teenagers were no longer expected to earn money to help support their families. Millions of young people experienced unprecedented leisure time, longer schooling, and were free to spend money earned from after-school jobs as they liked.

Teenagers flocked to buy record players and radios to play music marketed specifically to them. In 1958 the Coasters scored a number-one record with their song, "Yakety Yak," which depicts a teenager rebelling against household chores. In one refrain, the parent orders the teenager to "Take out the papers and the trash / Or you don't get no spendin' cash," to which the teenager replies "yakety yak," with the parent then retorting: "don't talk back."

"Teenagers are my life and triumph. I'd be nowhere without them."

ELVIS PRESLEY, whose stardom demonstrated the strength of teen culture in the 1950s

Teens' freedom to create their own social world filled with slang and fads that adults did not understand disturbed some critics. By the end of the decade, sociologist Edgar Friedenberg noted that "the 'teen-ager' seems to have replaced the Communist as the appropriate target for public controversy and foreboding." In this cultural clash traditionalists lambasted horror comic books and teen films for encouraging teenagers to revolt against their parents and social norms. But rock-and-roll music and musicians provoked the most outrage.

Rock-and-roll burst onto the national scene when Bill Haley and the Comets recorded "Rock Around the Clock" in 1955, the first rock-and-roll tune. The following year Chuck Berry thundered "Roll over, Beethoven, and tell Tchaikovsky the news!" proclaiming rock-and-roll the music of choice for this teenage generation. It took Elvis Presley, however, to make rock-and-roll (which got its name from a rhythm and blues slang term for sexual intercourse) a phenomenon. Exposed to the raw sexuality and powerful rhythms of African American rhythm and blues music as a young boy growing up in Mississippi, Presley also sang gospel and country music in church. Melding the sounds and explosive delivery of these musical traditions with catchy pop lyrics, Presley developed his own highly eroticized dancing style. "If I could find a white man who had the black sound and the black feel, I could make a billion dollars," predicted record producer Sam Phillips, the owner of Sun Records, a small recording company in Memphis, Tennessee. Philips found his man when Presley walked into Sun Records to record a song as a gift for his mother.

Americans embraced competing visions over whether the growing popularity of rock-and-roll meant the triumph of consumer tastes or the downfall of American civilization. Nicknamed "Elvis the Pelvis" for his suggestive hip thrusts while dancing, partially captured in this photograph (**25.7**), Presley became a lightening rod for critics who denounced rock-and-roll from the pulpit, in the press, and even in congressional hearings. When teenager Ron Kovic's family watched Presley on television's *Ed Sullivan Show*, his sister went "crazy in the living room jumping up and down," his mother sat "on the couch with her hands folded in her lap like she was praying" and his dad shouted from the other room that "watching Elvis Presley could lead to sin." In introducing Presley the affable TV host Sullivan assured parents that the twenty-two-year-old Presley was "a real decent, fine boy." To avoid controversy, however, Sullivan ordered camera crews to frame out Presley's legendary pelvic thrusts and gyrations, showing only his head and chest. It took the draft to tame Elvis. "Presley wriggled off to military service," one newspaper columnist wrote, "but comes marching home . . . shorn of his sideburns and behaving the way a sedate, serious-minded youngster should." The new "clean-cut" Presley kept his original fan base but had limited appeal to the teenage generation coming of age in 1960.

Ed Sullivan showcased a range of music, skits, and comedy acts designed to keep the whole family watching together during the hour-long show. Dick Clark, however, helped pioneer television programming exclusively for teenagers with his daily afternoon show *American Bandstand,* which featured Philadelphia high-school students dancing to the latest hits. The advent of pocketsize transistor radios meant that teenagers could listen to radio stations broadcasting the top forty best-selling records or independent rhythm and blues stations in the privacy of their bedrooms, away from critical adult ears.

Hollywood also catered to teenage tastes with films like *The Wild Ones* (1953), which featured Marlon Brando as part of a rebellious motorcycle gang, and *Rebel Without a Cause* (1955). In the latter

How did larger economic and technological changes make a mass teen culture possible?

25.7 Elvis Presley Nicknamed "Elvis the Pelvis," Elvis Presley's suggestive dancing enraged parents but earned the singer thousands of adoring teenage female fans.

film James Dean and Natalie Wood played teenagers from upper-middle-class suburban homes; unsure how to handle their racing hormones, the two become defiant. Dean's character tries to prove his masculinity by drag racing, while Wood's character uses promiscuity to rebel against an overprotective father. This view of the suburbs as hotbeds of intergenerational conflict and alienated youth frightened some adults but thrilled teenagers. Embracing the persona of an angry youth discontented with mainstream society, Dean (who died at the age of twenty-four in a car accident) became an icon of teenage rebellion in the fifties.

Parental norms often prevailed in the end. Teenagers in the fifties grew up quickly. Students who dated a lot in high school tended to marry within a few years of graduation. As much as they may have rebelled as adolescents, once married, they quickly started families, conforming to the lifestyle standards set by their parents.

The Beats

Teens in the fifties used their purchases—of music, clothes, cars—to define their generational identity, while their parents announced their newly acquired middle-class status by buying cars and suburban houses. **Beats** or beatniks, members of the bohemian communities of poets, novelists, and artists that flourished in New York's Greenwich Village and San Francisco's North Beach, offered an alternative vision. The Beats rejected home ownership, career, and marriage in favor of individual freedom and immediate pleasure (including drugs and casual sex).

The national spotlight briefly shined on City Lights Bookstore in San Francisco when it published the controversial poem "Howl" (1955) by then-struggling Beat poet Allen Ginsberg. "I saw the best minds of my generation destroyed by madness, starving hysterical naked, dragging themselves through the negro streets at dawn looking for an angry fix," began the opening stanza of "Howl." The poem sent readers on a journey into the underground lives of the drug addicts, musicians, artists, radicals, and homosexuals who lived on the margins of mainstream society. In the 1950s most states had so-called antisodomy laws that criminalized same-sex intercourse. Ginsberg's open celebration of gay sex in "Howl" offended anti-obscenity crusaders in San Francisco. The police arrested the owner of the City Lights Bookstore for selling the poem, but a judge

What competing visions of youth rebellion did rock-and-roll and the Beat movement embody?

25.8 Mark Rothko, *Number 10*
The Abstract Expressionist painter Mark Rothko expressed his personal feelings rather than reproducing objects or addressing politics in his paintings. Refusing to title or explain his paintings, Rothko wanted viewers to interpret his work freely. [*Source*: Mark Rothco (1903–1970), "Number 10". 1950. Oil on canvas. 7' 6 3/8" × 57 1/8". Gift of Philip Johnson. (38.1952) Location:The Museum of Modern Art, New York, NY, U.S.A. Digital Image © The Museum of Modern Art/Licensed by SCALA / Art Resource, NY. Estate of Mark Rothco © 2010 Artists Rights Society (ARS), NY]

dismissed the charge, arguing that "Howl" was a socially significant artistic work.

In his novel *On the Road* (1955), the Beat novelist Jack Kerouac celebrated the spiritual quest for a meaningful life away from the suffocating materialism and conformity of middle-class society. Guilty at times of over-romanticizing working-class life for its "authenticity" without appreciating the deadening effects of poverty, the Beats nonetheless laid the foundation for the youth protests of the sixties (see Chapter 27).

Most Americans never read "Howl" or *On the Road*. They instead formed their impressions of the Beats from watching *The Many Loves of Dobie Gillis*, a television series that showcased a beatnik best friend who urged Dobie to reject his father's single-minded drive to make money and instead enjoy life to the fullest. This televised depiction of Beat culture helped interject new words, such as "dig it," "cool," and "man" that the Beats took from African American culture, into the vocabulary of white teenagers.

> "What sphinx of cement and aluminum bashed open their skulls and ate up their brains and imagination?"
>
> Beat poet ALLEN GINSBERG, critiquing suburban life in "Howl"

Beat poets and novelists were not the only artists rebelling against received traditions in the fifties. American modern artists formulated a new mode of visual art called Abstract Expressionism that broke with the predominant painting styles of the previous generation. Before World War II leading artists included the Cubist painter Pablo Picasso who reordered the physical world in his paintings and American social realist painters who captured the lives of ordinary people during the Depression. Politics informed much artistic work in the 1930s and 1940s. In the fifties a restless generation of new artists chose instead to emphasize personal expression over politics. "The big moment came when it was decided to paint. . . . Just TO PAINT. The gesture on the canvas was a gesture of liberation, from Value—political, aesthetic, moral," wrote art critic Harold Rosenberg in 1952. American painters such as Jackson Pollock, who dripped paint on the canvas, and Mark Rothko, who painted fields of color, created signature styles that epitomized the rebellious nature of Abstract Expression (**25.8**). Young artists idolized these painters for refusing to represent reality or use their art to send a message. More tradition-bound artists denounced their work as trivial. Like James Dean in films and Elvis Presley in music, the painters Pollock and Rothko embodied the rebellious streak of fifties youth culture.

How does Rothko's painting compare to social realist paintings in the 1930s (see Chapter 22)?

Freedom Now: The Civil Rights Movement

The Civil Rights Movement entered a pivotal phase in the 1950s. Key Supreme Court rulings, new leadership, and innovative strategies emboldened thousands of black and white people to demand the end of racial segregation in the South. The National Association for the Advancement of Colored People (NAACP) successfully challenged the constitutionality of segregated public schools. Martin Luther King Jr. emerged as a major leader, alongside a generation of activist black and white college students who employed new nonviolent strategies to compel white Americans to confront the harsh realities of Jim Crow. Favorable decisions from the Supreme Court pressured the federal government to intervene on behalf of African Americans. Meanwhile television and news magazines transmitted shocking images of racial violence that made it impossible for the nation to ignore the demands of civil rights activists.

Separate and *Unequal*: Challenging Segregated Schools

"Tastes the same to me, Mom."

LEO LILLARD, after secretly sampling water from "white" and "colored" fountains as a boy in Nashville

Black and white southern children, as this photo of a street scene in a small southern town suggests (**25.9**), grew up in two separate worlds. They lived in different parts of town, went to segregated schools, drank from separate water fountains, ate in different restaurants, waited for buses in different waiting rooms, sat in separate sections of movie theatres, and often shopped in different stores. For many black children segregation meant daily humiliation and unanswered questions. "I guess if you are from a small Georgia town, as I am," one black college student recalled, "you can say that your first encounter with prejudice was the day you were born. . . . My parents never got to see their infant twins alive because the only incubator in the hospital was on the 'white' side."

After World War II ethnic and racial minorities successfully challenged the legality of segregated schools. In 1947 the Supreme Court ruled that educating children of Mexican ancestry in separate California schools was illegal because state law only authorized segregated schools for children of Asian decent. In the wake of this ruling, California repealed this discriminatory law. Ending legalized racial segregation came next.

In 1954 the Supreme Court overturned the 1896 *Plessy v. Ferguson* "separate but equal" ruling that had allowed the South to maintain segregated schools from elementary school to graduate school. In *Plessy v. Ferguson* the Court had concluded that separate facilities (schools, waiting rooms, railroad cars) for whites and blacks were constitutional as long as they offered each race similar amenities. (See *Choices and Consequences,* Chapter 14.) In practice legalized segregation usually resulted in inferior

25.9 A Southern Town
On their visit to town, these white and black children carefully avoided mixing, demonstrating how early children in the South learned to respect their region's racial customs.

In what ways did racial discrimination shape southern children's lives?

25.10 Emmett Till and his mother
"If you have to get on your knees and bow when a white person goes past, do it willingly," Emmett's mother told her northern-raised son before he left to visit relatives in Mississippi, instructions that the teenager tragically disregarded.

accommodations and schools for black citizens. The Supreme Court ruled in ***Brown v. Board of Education*** (1954) that segregated schools indeed violated the equal protection clause of the Fourteenth Amendment.

The *Brown* case concerned seven-year-old Linda Brown, whose parents wanted to send her to an all-white school closer to their home. In mounting the case NAACP lawyer Thurgood Marshall (who later became the first African American appointed to the Supreme Court) and his team based their argument on more than the law. To convince the public and the Supreme Court that segregation was wrong, they needed to dramatize the effects of segregation. "To show damage and a violation of equal protection under the Fourteenth Amendment, you had to show that being segregated actually damaged children," psychologist Kenneth Clark asserted.

To demonstrate the irreversible effects of segregation on African American children, the NAACP cited Clark's controversial research. In a series of studies, Clark asked white and black children whether they liked a white or black doll best. The majority of children picked a white doll because it was "nice" and rejected the black doll as "bad." Clark next asked the children to identify the doll that was the most like them. The black children now had to pick the doll that many of them had just rejected as "bad." In the North black children often burst into tears rather than respond. In the South, however, reactions like the one from a young boy in Arkansas, who laughed, "pointed to the brown doll, and said, 'That's a nigger. I'm a nigger,'" convinced Clark that segregation taught African American children to accept their inferiority to whites.

Not everyone agreed with Clark's methodology, so the NAACP relied heavily on his findings in preliminary court challenges and then mentioned them only briefly in their Supreme Court filing. The wording of the *Brown v. Board of Education* decision, however, revealed that the NAACP had guessed right in emphasizing the impact of segregation on the self-esteem of black children. In reaching their unanimous decision, the Court noted that "to separate [black children] from others of similar age and qualifications solely because of their race generates a feeling of inferiority as to their status in the community that may affect their hearts and minds in a way unlikely ever to be undone."

Emmett Till

In 1955 Emmett Till was just another fourteen-year-old posing for the camera with his mother. Their portrait reveals a boy with a beaming smile and a mother's pride in her growing son (**25.10**). That summer Mamie Till-Bradley sent Emmett from his home in Chicago to visit relatives in Mississippi. To prepare her northern-raised son for the racial customs of southern society, his mother warned him to think of his safety when encountering southern whites. One morning at a country store in Money, Mississippi, Emmett forgot his mother's warning. While playing with some black teens on the porch of the store, Emmett bragged that he had a white girlfriend in Chicago. "Hey, there's a [white] girl in that store there," one of the boys retorted, "I bet you won't go in there and talk to her." Responding to the dare Emmett walked into the store, bought some candy, then grabbed the arm of Carol Byrant, who ran the store with her husband, and allegedly asked, "How about a date, baby?" Till's aghast cousin ran in and pulled him out of the store.

Three days later a car pulled up to Emmett's granduncle's house in the middle of the night. Two white men burst into the house and dragged Emmett out of bed. The husband of the young woman in the store, Roy Bryant, and her brother, J. W. Milam, threw a terrified Emmett into their truck and drove away. This was the last time his relatives saw him alive. The white men drove to an abandoned shed on a nearby plantation where they beat Till severely, then drove to the Tallahatchie River and forced Emmett to strip before they shot him in the head and tossed his body into the river. With his mother's permission, *Jet* magazine and the *Chicago Defender*, stalwarts of the black press, published the grisly photos of the corpse. *Images as History: Inspiring a New Generation to Act* discusses the transforming effect that images of Emmett Till's murder had on the Civil Rights Movement.

Why did the Supreme Court rule that segregated schools were unconstitutional?

Images as History

INSPIRING A NEW GENERATION TO ACT

The photo of Emmett Till's broken body, printed in African American newspapers and magazines, became the wake-up call for a group of young people destined to play major roles in the future Civil Rights Movement. The Emmett Till case gave the nation more than a clear image of the victim. It also provided a snapshot of the killers and the vigilante justice dealt out in many small towns across the Deep South. At first, some southern officials and citizens denounced the murder. But when the northern press castigated the entire South for the crime, southerners fought back with competing claims that Emmett Till was alive and in hiding or that the NAACP had set up the murder to embarrass the South. Why are these images important for understanding the history of race relations and the Civil Rights Movement?

Deciding that "the world is going to have to look at this," Mamie Till-Bradley took her son's body back to Chicago where she insisted on an open casket funeral that thousands attended.

The black northern press provoked outrage over the killing by pairing this gruesome image of Emmett's battered corpse with the photograph of him smiling with his mother (25.10).

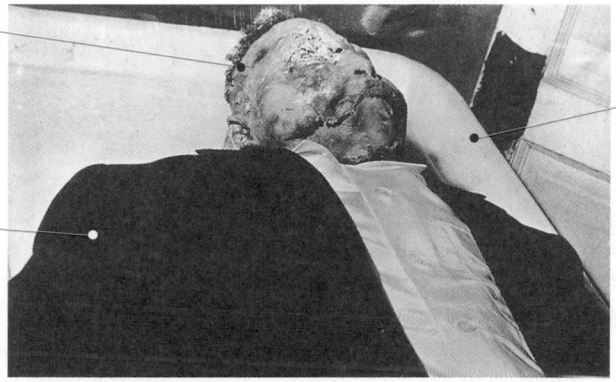

Emmett Till's corpse

After seeing these photos future civil rights activist Julian Bond "felt vulnerable for the first time in my life—Till was a year younger—and [I] recall believing that this could easily happen to me—for no reason at all."

The accused men's nonchalance in the courtroom and the show of support from the white observers sent a warning to the African American witnesses who testified against the pair, illustrating how communities like Money, Mississippi, at that time preserved the racial status quo.

Bringing their children into the courtroom bolstered the accused men's image as upstanding family men and helped teach white youth about the importance of maintaining white supremacy.

Men on trial for Emmett Till's murder, sitting with their families.

For many of his neighbors, Roy Bryant's defense of his wife protected her honor, his reputation, and fulfilled his duty to help the white community keep the color bar intact.

How do these photos compare to postcards of lynchings (see Chapter 21)?

What made Emmett Till's murder different from previous racially inspired killings of African Americans in the South was the courageous decision of his family to fight back. Ignoring the kidnappers' warnings to keep quiet (so Emmett would become yet another black boy who went mysteriously "missing"), Emmett's cousin called the sheriff and Emmett's mother the next day. The sheriff found Emmett's body and three days later arrested Roy Bryant and J. W. Milam. When Mamie Till-Bradley saw her son's tortured body, a sight that would have caused many mothers to fall apart, she instead vowed that "here's a job that I got to do now."

Emmett's granduncle, Moses Wright, had begged the white men to just whip Emmett, while his wife offered them money to leave Emmett alone. Now Moses Wright decided to seek justice by testifying against the pair when they went on trial for murder. The sixty-four-year-old Wright later recalled that as he entered the courtroom he could "feel the blood boil in hundreds of white people as they sat glaring." When the prosecutor asked him to identify Milam as one of the men who took Emmett, Wright stood up, pointed his finger, and said, "Thar he." News of Wright's testimony emboldened other black sharecroppers to step forward and testify about hearing Emmett crying for his mother as he was beaten. Fearing for their lives all of these sharecroppers left town after appearing in court.

At first it seemed they had risked everything for naught. The all-white male jury took less than an hour to proclaim the men not guilty. They would have returned the verdict sooner, the jury foreman bragged, "If we hadn't stopped to drink pop." A second jury acquitted the men on the charge of kidnapping. Two months after their murder trial, Bryant and Milam sold their story to an Alabama journalist for $4,000 and admitted killing Emmett. Double jeopardy, a legal concept that prevents authorities from retrying someone for the same crime, protected the pair from prosecution after their confession. Nonetheless the sight of ordinary black citizens standing up in court to accuse their white oppressors electrified a generation ready to strike back. Four months later, partly because of the Emmett Till case, the Montgomery Bus Boycott began.

Montgomery Bus Boycott, 1955

The *Brown v. Board of Education* decision was a milestone in the fight for racial equality, but by the mid-1950s civil rights activists were no longer content simply to fight for justice through the courts. Many resolved to use economic boycotts, picketing, and mass demonstrations to force white America to take notice of the injustice and violence experienced daily by African Americans. Courageous men and women, ordinary people who took extraordinary risks, set this new direction in civil rights protest.

On December 1, 1955, Rosa Parks, a forty-three-year-old black seamstress, boarded a bus in downtown Montgomery, Alabama, and selected a seat. She was one of forty thousand blacks who paid a dime twice a day to the white driver, then stepped down and entered the bus through the rear door. When a white man demanded her seat, Parks had to decide whether or not to comply. *Choices and Consequences: Rosa Parks Makes History* explores her decision to stay seated.

As soon as English professor Jo Anne Robinson heard of the arrest, she mimeographed 35,000 handbills urging black citizens to stage a one-day bus boycott on the day of Parks' trial. Robinson was president of the Montgomery Women's Political Council, which had been planning a one-day bus boycott for months. The Parks' arrest offered a perfect moment to act. Two of her students helped Robinson distribute the handbills to black schools, businesses, and churches. "Negroes have rights, too, for if Negroes did not ride the buses, they could not operate," the handbill read. When the day-long boycott succeeded, community leaders decided to continue it indefinitely.

The **Montgomery Bus Boycott (1955–1956)** was a year-long boycott that brought a new leader, Martin Luther King Jr., and a new strategy of nonviolent protest to the forefront of the Civil Rights Movement. The boycotters' initial demands were moderate: courteous treatment from bus drivers, first-come-first-served segregation so no one would have to give up a seat, and the hiring of some black bus drivers. The city administrators and bus company executives refused. The Montgomery Improvement Association (MIA) now prepared for a lengthy boycott. Mass meetings twice a week kept boycotters' spirits high and helped disseminate accurate information within a black community that had no radio station or newspaper. The MIA also set up an elaborate carpool system to transport black workers to their jobs and back home. Volunteers picked up passengers from one of forty-two collection points throughout the city, which became the target of terrorist bombings on several occasions. Images of black workers waiting peacefully for carpools contrasted with the burnt remains of

Which individual choices mattered in the Till case?

Choices and Consequences

ROSA PARKS MAKES HISTORY

Unlike the signs above water fountains or posted in waiting rooms, there was no clear section marked "colored" on Montgomery city buses. Instead as more white passengers boarded the bus, black passengers had to vacate their seats for them. When three other black passengers heeded the white driver's request to move on the afternoon of December 1, 1955, Rosa Parks faced a set of choices over how to respond.

Choices

1. Move to the back of the bus.
2. Refuse to give up her seat.
3. Vacate her seat but express her outrage by participating in a planned one-day bus boycott.

Decision

Rosa Parks refused to give up her seat. When the driver threatened to call the police, Parks quietly replied, "You may do that." She was arrested.

Consequences

On the day of Parks's trial (she was found guilty and fined), the Montgomery Women's Political Council organized a one-day boycott that it had been planning for months and nearly all Montgomery's black citizens stayed off the buses. That evening the city's black male clergy met and formed the Montgomery Improvement Association (MIA), which voted to continue the boycott. The group chose Martin Luther King Jr., a twenty-six-year-old Baptist minister who headed the church that Rosa Parks attended, as their president. When the Supreme Court ruled that bus segregation was unconstitutional in 1956, the year-long boycott ended.

Continuing Controversies

Who was the real Rosa Parks?
The folklore is that Parks was simply a tired seamstress who impulsively decided to stay seated. This narrative leaves out key details. Parks was also secretary of the Montgomery chapter of the NAACP and had attended the left-leaning Highlander Folk School in Tennessee where civil rights and labor leaders trained. She knew that the NAACP wanted to test the bus segregation law in the courts and had recently participated in a mass meeting protesting Emmett Till's murder. Boycott leaders played down Parks's activist past, worried that it would diminish her "everyman" appeal and that moderates might view her as a radical agitator. Some activists later suggested that this simplified tale sent the wrong message about how to initiate social change. Rosa Parks's bravery mattered, they agreed, but so did careful preparation, organization-building, and ideological dedication.

What is the enduring legacy of Rosa Parks's decision?

bombed cars provided good television footage for the national television networks that covered the boycott extensively. Television interviews with King, a twenty-six-year-old Baptist minister, turned him into a celebrity overnight and allowed him to appeal directly to moderates throughout the nation. To raise money and garner publicity for the boycott, King also toured the country giving speeches.

> "If Martin Luther King had never been born this movement would have taken place. I just happened to be there."
>
> MARTIN LUTHER KING JR., commenting on his role in the Montgomery Bus Boycott.

Instead of discouraging the protesters, white resistance convinced the MIA to broaden its demands to include the complete desegregation of the buses. The violence now threatened to spiral out of control. When King's house was bombed, a crowd of supporters arrived carrying knives and guns. "If you have weapons, take them home," King told the crowd as news cameras rolled. Publicizing the new civil rights ethos of nonviolence, King declared, "'He who lives by the sword will perish by the sword.' . . . We must meet hate with love."

Over time white opposition to the boycott began to fracture. Some whites had been openly sympathetic to the boycott from the beginning, even though their businesses and social life suffered as a result. Others had more pragmatic reasons for helping black workers reach their jobs. When the mayor chastised white women for chauffeuring their black maids to and from work, one defiant white woman wrote to the newspaper: "If the mayor wants to do my wash and wants to cook for me and clean up after my children let him come and do it."

After nearly a year the boycott was victorious. In November 1956 the Supreme Court ruled that segregated buses were unconstitutional. On December 21, 1956, Martin Luther King Jr. boarded the first integrated bus in Montgomery with the African American minister Ralph Abernathy and the white Reverend Glenn Smiley, both key leaders in the boycott. In their carefully choreographed ride, pictured here (**25.11**), all three followed the guidelines that the MIA had established for integrating buses. An MIA pamphlet advised: "For the first few days try to get on the bus with a friend in whose non-violence you have confidence. You can uphold one another by a glance or a prayer." The MIA cautioned black riders not to respond to curses or shoves. When King entered the bus, the presence of newspaper reporters and cameramen protected him from violence. "We are glad to have you here this morning," the bus driver cordially greeted King as he climbed aboard. The ride was not so smooth for other Montgomery citizens. In the weeks to come, snipers fired into buses and Abernathy's house was bombed.

Two months later King met with ministers from eleven other southern states to form the **Southern Christian Leadership Conference** (SCLC). Black churches, they decided, could help the Civil Rights Movement devise a new nonviolent strategy of direct action that challenged segregation and discrimination throughout the South. At first King saw nonviolence mostly as a way to gain sympathy and to prevent authorities from using violence against demonstrators. King employed a bodyguard throughout the boycott and had applied for a permit to allow him to carry a gun (which the police refused). "King sees the inconsistency, but not enough. He believes and yet he does not believe . . . if he can *really* be won over to a faith in nonviolence there is no end to what he can do," Smiley noted privately.

Over the next few years, King would develop that faith. King's social justice fundamentalism evolved from his reading of Jesus's biblical "Sermon on the Mount" that urged Christians to create "a beloved community" by winning over enemies with love and humility rather than seeking to punish or defeat them. King was also influenced by activists like Reverend James Lawson who had traveled to India to study the Hindu religion's version of nonviolence pioneered by the Indian activist Mahatma Gandhi in the 1930s to win independence from Britain. Lawson was in India during the Montgomery Bus Boycott but returned in time to instruct members of the SCLC and university students as they broadened their attack on Jim Crow in the early 1960s.

The Little Rock Nine, 1957

The *Brown v. Board of Education* case launched a decades-long struggle to integrate public schools. Many white southerners had grown up without ever questioning segregation. The Brown ruling now forced them to either formulate a defense and

Why was the Montgomery Bus Boycott a turning point in the Civil Rights Movement?

rationale for segregation or consider changing generations-old habits. Throughout the South diehard segregationists dug in. "The Negro race, as a race, plainly is not equal to the white race, as a race," asserted James Jackson Kilpatrick, the editor of a Richmond newspaper. Segregationists also advanced a states' right argument, arguing that the federal government had no right to dictate racial policies to the South. Sympathetic to claims that it would be difficult to change ingrained habits overnight, the Supreme Court issued only a vague directive for school systems to desegregate "with all deliberate speed" in 1955. This ruling encouraged entrenched segregationists to try to delay integration indefinitely.

In a scattering of southern cities, moderate whites proved willing to accept the piecemeal dismantlement of Jim Crow. Little Rock, Arkansas, for instance, had desegregated its parks, buses, and libraries with little controversy. After the Brown decision the school board made plans to integrate slowly by inviting nine black teenagers to attend high school alongside two thousand white students. Nicknamed the **Little Rock Nine**, the nine teenagers who integrated Central High School in Little Rock, Arkansas, in 1957 became the focus of a national crisis that required the intervention of federal troops to resolve.

Segregationists quickly organized statewide opposition to the planned integration of Central High School. Concern about states' rights and segregationists' claims that integration would lead to white and black students dancing together at school social functions won over some moderates. Two weeks before the school year started, the threats began. One night a rock shattered the living room window of Daisy Bates, secretary of the local NAACP chapter. The note tied around the rock read "stone this time. Dynamite next."

Influenced by poll numbers showing 85 percent of white Arkansans opposed school integration, Arkansas governor Orval Faubus, who faced a

25.11 First Ride on an Integrated Montgomery Bus, 1958
Martin Luther King Jr., seated on the left, rides with other activists on the first day that buses were integrated in Montgomery after a year-long bus boycott. Fearing vigilante attacks from angry whites, King urged all black bus riders to exude steely resolve and to ride in pairs.

What messages did this planned scene send to whites and blacks?

difficult reelection campaign, declared he would not "force acceptance of change to which the people are so overwhelmingly opposed." In September 1957 Faubus decided to ring Central High with state troops on the first day of school to stop the black students from entering the high school. Using state troops to defy a federal mandate fit well with the desire of moderate whites and die-hard segregationists to protect the sanctity of states' rights.

To protect the black teenagers, Daisy Bates asked parents to drop the students off at her house so they could go to school together. However Elizabeth Eckford, whose family did not have a telephone, never received the message. Instead she took a bus to the school by herself and confronted the angry mob alone. At first she felt reassured when she saw the troops, whom she assumed were there to protect her. She quickly realized her error. When she tried to squeeze past a guard, "He raised his bayonet, and then the other guards moved in." As she stood there confused, the crowd started to chant "Lynch her! Lynch her!" Television cameras, tempering the crowd's enthusiasm for a lynching, likely saved Elizabeth's life. Also a godsend Grace Lorch, a white woman, came out of the crowd to help Elizabeth flag down a city bus and escape.

Over the next few days, as the crowds in front of the high school grew, attacks against news photographers and cameramen became more common. The television footage coming out of Little Rock, reporter David Halberstam noted, "made it hard for people watching at home not to take sides" as they saw "orderly black children behaving with great dignity" being assaulted by a "vicious mob of poor whites." Outrage outside of the South over such images put pressure on President Eisenhower to act, as did the negative worldwide attention that the Little Rock incident garnered. "Our [Communist] enemies are gloating over this incident and using it everywhere to misrepresent our whole nation," Eisenhower warned the country.

Resistance to Supreme Court–mandated integration created more than a racial crisis. It also led to a showdown between the federal government and the state of Arkansas. Under pressure from the White House, Faubus withdrew state troops. It was the president's responsibility to enforce federal law, Eisenhower told the American people, announcing his decision to send federal troops to Little Rock to ensure that Arkansas obeyed the Supreme Court's ruling. With paratroopers from the 101st Airborne Division ringing the school, the Little Rock Nine walked up the front steps surrounded by armed guards.

This was the first time that the federal government had used troops to protect the civil rights of African Americans since the Reconstruction era. The troops, Melba Pattillo Beals recalled, meant a "declaration of war" in the hallways of Central High where white teenagers insulted, kicked, shoved, and ostracized the Little Rock Nine, who were each sent to different classrooms. Eight of the nine finished the year. (Minnijean Brown was expelled for dumping chili on a white student's head after he insulted her in the cafeteria line.) The following year Faubus defied the order to integrate by keeping the schools closed all year. In 1959 Central High reopened with one black student in attendance; in 1960 there were five; then eight in 1961. The small numbers of black students in Central High signified the long, slow road to complete the process of school integration.

The Sit-ins

By the end of the fifties, with the nonviolent Civil Rights Movement in full bloom, the movement's attention shifted from schools to segregated lunch counters. In 1958 James Lawson began conducting SCLC workshops for local college students in Nashville to prepare them for a sit-in campaign to desegregate the city's lunch counters. At these meetings students studied Christian pacifist principles, Gandhi's theories of nonviolence, and the nineteenth-century philosopher Henry David Thoreau's ideas on civil disobedience. During **sit-ins** protesters occupied seats at whites-only lunch counters and remained there even after they were refused service, sometimes for hours. The sit-ins employed the tactic of **civil disobedience**, breaking the law in a peaceful way to call attention to an unjust law, and replicated a tactic used successfully by the CIO in the 1930s when workers had occupied factories during strikes (see Chapter 22). Sit-ins, like sit-down strikes, disrupted business, making it impossible for white businessmen to ignore the protesters' demands. Highly visible sit-ins in downtown Nashville department stores were also guaranteed to attract press attention.

Lawson warned the students that their anger over Jim Crow was not enough to sustain them through the challenges ahead. Instead they needed to truly embrace nonviolence as the governing principle of their lives. They were fighting back, he assured his students, but in a way that broke the cycle of violence. Armed resistance was not only morally wrong, Lawson argued, but it was also futile to believe that blacks could take on the police and army with guns.

Why did Eisenhower send troops to integrate Central High School in Little Rock?

> "Do show yourself friendly on the counter at all times. Do sit straight and always face the counter. Don't strike back, or curse if attacked. Don't laugh out. Don't hold conversations. Don't block entrances. ... Remember the teachings of Jesus, Gandhi, Thoreau, and Martin Luther King, Jr."
>
> Instructions to sit-in demonstrators in Nashville, Tennessee, 1960

Students learned how to ignore the taunts and blows that whites would heap on them during a sit-in, to go limp when pulled from the seats, and to curl into a protective fetal position if attacked with blows. Lawson's Nashville workshops identified and trained students who would become major leaders in the Civil Rights Movement, including John Lewis, Diane Nash, and Jim Bevel.

Black civil rights protesters had intermittently organized sit-ins since 1942, but it was the spontaneous decision in 1960 of four freshmen from the all-black North Carolina Agricultural and Technical College to request service at a Woolworth's lunch counter in Greensboro, North Carolina, that ignited the national sit-in movement. By acting on impulse these four teenagers ignored SCLC rules, which emphasized careful preparation and planning before launching any civil rights protest. The evening television news broadcast images of their defiance throughout the nation, demonstrating that the actions of ordinary people could make a difference. In this posed photo taken of the four when they returned to the lunch counter the following day, the young men "had a certain look on their faces, sort of sullen, angry, determined. Before, the Negro in the South had always looked on the defensive, cringing," Bob Moses later recalled (**25.12**). Their courage inspired Moses to leave his job teaching math in Harlem and head south to join the movement. He would go on to spearhead the 1964 voter registration drive in Mississippi known as "Freedom Summer" (see Chapter 27).

25.12 Second Day of Woolworth's Lunch Counter Sit-In, 1960
These freshmen from the North Carolina Agricultural and Technical College ignited the southern sit-in movement when they decided to request service at a whites-only lunch counter in Greensboro. They sat unmolested day after day for a week, until the store shut down the lunch counter.

What principles lay at the heart of nonviolent direct action?

25.13 Mississippi Sit-In, 1963
Assaults on sit-in protesters grew more vicious as the demonstrations moved into the Deep South.

Over the following weeks churches and students worked together to unleash waves of sit-ins throughout the South. In Nashville Lawson's group unfurled the longest and most sustained series of sit-ins. After a month of letting roving gangs of thugs punch and kick the students, the Nashville police tried to end the sit-ins by arresting the demonstrators for "disorderly conduct." The students responded with a "jail-no bail" strategy. "Only so many can fit into a cell; if you remain here, there can be no more arrests! Imprisonment is an expense to the state; it must feed and take care of you. Bails and fines are an expense to the movement, which it can ill afford," SCLC organizer Bayard Rustin told the students. With the jails full and the sit-ins continuing, the SCLC increased the pressure with a successful boycott of the downtown stores.

The standoff came to a head when the home of a prominent black lawyer (who had represented the students in court) was bombed. Marching to city hall the students demonstrated the power of nonviolence to change minds. Confronting the mayor, Diane Nash asked: "Mayor West, do you feel it is wrong to discriminate against a person solely on the basis of their race or color?" Answering as "a man had to answer, not a politician," Mayor Ben West, a moderate on racial issues, agreed it was wrong. Three weeks later the lunch counters in Nashville were desegregated. Energized by their success the Nashville group staged "stand-ins" in the city's segregated movie theaters and "sleep-ins" in the lobbies of whites-only hotels.

Throughout the upper South photographs of the sit-ins provoked a similar awakening among moderate whites. The contrast between "the colored students, in coats, white shirts, ties" quietly requesting service at a lunch counter and the ragtag gangs of "white boys come to heckle" was hard to ignore, noted the *Richmond News Leader* when sit-ins hit the capital of Virginia. Resistance to sit-ins in the Deep South proved more formidable and vicious. In 1963 Tougaloo College student Anne Moody sat at a Woolworth's lunch counter with two white activists in Jackson, Mississippi. As this photo shows (**25.13**) a lunchtime crowd of high school students ferociously assaulted the three and poured condiments on their heads. Egging them on was the older man in the picture, who urged the mob to get the demon-

Why were sit-ins successful in the upper South?

strators off the stools and pour salt on their wounds. The crowd's heated anger convinced Moody that "many more will die before it is over with."

By the spring of 1960, Jim Lawson and SCLC organizer Ella Baker saw that students had emerged as a powerful force within the Civil Rights Movement. The two leaders urged university students to form their own civil rights organization. Students, they realized, were willing to take more risks than were many adult activists. Employing the lyrics of a movement song that urged protesters to "keep your eyes on the prize," Baker told the students that their goal needed to be "bigger than a hamburger." The students responded by forming their own civil rights organization, the **Student Nonviolent Coordinating Committee**, or **SNCC** (pronounced Snick) in 1960.

In the struggles ahead SNCC and SCLC often forged a crucial partnership between black churches and university students. Idealistic and enthusiastic college students, white and black, eagerly put themselves in the frontlines during civil rights demonstrations. Black churches provided the experienced organizers, meeting spaces, and funds necessary to organize successful protests. Often SNCC acted alone. Commenting on the importance of SNCC to the modern civil rights crusade, Diane Nash noted that "the media and history seem to record it as Martin Luther King's movement, but young people should realize that it was people just like them, their age, that formulated goals and strategies, and actually developed the movement."

The Civil Rights Movement brought together many critical features of the 1950s. While print media remained important, film footage shown on evening television news broadcasts of confrontations between racist whites and nonviolent protesters forced the rest of the nation to confront the realities of Jim Crow and racial violence in the South. Thanks to television what happened in the South no longer remained in the South. The rise of a distinctly teenage culture within the baby boom generation also helped to create a strong generational bond among those young adults who joined the movement. Finally the ideological overtones of the Cold War that pitted democratic capitalism against communism helped civil rights protesters focus attention on the inherent contradictions between America's self-proclaimed goal of spreading democracy throughout the world and visible racial discrimination at home.

Conclusion

Americans enjoyed unprecedented prosperity from 1945 to 1960. A strong labor movement, readily available credit, and generous veterans' benefits fueled a booming consumer and housing market. Growing American families headed to the suburbs, where cars and televisions played prominent roles in their daily lives. Americans debated the meaning of their newfound prosperity throughout the decade. For some this wealth offered a clear demonstration of the superiority of capitalism over communism and made people more tolerant. To others the suburbs were places where all people learned to think and act alike. Conflict also followed Americans into their homes, where parents railed against teenage tastes in music and films.

In the realm of politics, the federal government made only minor adjustments to the New Deal reforms inherited from the Roosevelt administration. The Supreme Court issued path-breaking rulings on the unconstitutionality of segregated schools and buses. In the wake of Emmett Till's murder and Rosa Parks's arrest, a new generation of civil rights activists fought back against racial injustice by employing the tactics of nonviolent direct action and civil disobedience. The publicity given to individual acts of tremendous bravery demonstrated the ability of ordinary Americans to ignite extraordinary changes in the American polity. Overall the fifties planted the seeds for the cultural conflict that traversed the nation in the sixties, a time when youth culture, civil rights, the television age, and an unpopular war in Vietnam created division and discord.

What different strengths did students and churches bring to the Civil Rights Movement?

CHAPTER REVIEW

1945–1946

Five thousand labor strikes sweep the country
Creates public backlash against unions

Baby Boom begins
Generation sets cultural trends from cradle to grave

1947–1948

Taft-Hartley Act
Puts restrictions on labor unions

First Levittown built
Mass migration to suburbs begins

Truman desegregates the armed forces
First major U.S. institution to integrate in the twentieth century

1952

Nixon's "Checkers" speech
First use of television to diffuse a political crisis

Review Questions

1. How did efforts to undo the New Deal and curtail the Fair Deal fare from 1945 to 1960?
2. How did Americans react to rising prosperity in the United States? What internal debates arose over suburbanization and teen culture?
3. Consider the role of the media in the 1950s. How did the media affect intergenerational conflicts? What role did the media play during the Civil Rights Movement? How did activists, both conservative and liberal, use the media to sway opinions?
4. What key social conditions and events triggered the modern Civil Rights Movement?
5. What means were available to African Americans to fight against Jim Crow?
6. Why was the Civil Rights Movement successful in the fifties? What role did ordinary citizens play? How important were its leaders?

1954

Brown v. Board of Education
Supreme Court orders integration of public schools

1955

Emmett Till murdered
Images of corpse spark civil rights protest

Three-quarters of American homes have televisions
Leisure habits shift as families spend more time inside the home

Montgomery Bus Boycott
Martin Luther King Jr. emerges as civil rights leader

1957

Elvis Presley appears on *The Ed Sullivan Show*
Culture clash over rock-and-roll

Little Rock Nine integrate high school in Arkansas
Showdown between federal and state governments over *Brown* ruling

1960

Sit-ins across the South
College students become a major force in the Civil Rights Movement

Sixty percent of Americans classified as middle class
American standard of living rises

Nixon-Kennedy debate
Television shapes public opinion of presidential candidates

Key Terms

Taft-Hartley Act (1947) Law that abolished the closed shop, banned so-called sympathy boycotts, and required that all union officers sign affidavits certifying that they were not members of the Communist Party. **753**

Fair Deal Truman's proposals for national health care, public housing, education, and public works projects. **754**

military-industrial complex Eisenhower's term for the close ties between the defense industry and the Pentagon that might influence government policy. **755**

Levittowns Planned suburban communities where developers standardized every part of the construction process. **758**

baby boom generation The 76.4 million Americans born between 1946 and 1964. **758**

Kennedy and Nixon debate First televised presidential election debate in 1960 watched by nearly 77 million Americans, or 60 percent of the adult population. **761**

Beats Members of the bohemian communities of poets, novelists, and artists that flourished in New York's Greenwich Village and San Francisco's North Beach and who rejected middle-class suburban values. **763**

***Brown v. Board of Education* (1954)** Supreme Court decision that segregated schools violated the equal protection clause of the Fourteenth Amendment. **766**

Montgomery Bus Boycott (1955–1956) A year-long bus boycott that brought a new leader, Martin Luther King Jr., and a new strategy of nonviolent protest to the forefront of the Civil Rights Movement. **768**

Southern Christian Leadership Conference (SCLC) Civil rights organization founded by Martin Luther King Jr. that used black churches to devise a new nonviolent strategy of direct action. **770**

Little Rock Nine Nine black teenagers who integrated Central High School in Little Rock, Arkansas, in 1957 and became the focus of a national crisis that required the intervention of federal troops to resolve. **771**

sit-ins Nonviolent demonstrations where civil rights protesters employed the tactic of civil disobedience to occupy seats at whites-only lunch counters. **772**

civil disobedience A strategy of nonviolence used by demonstrators to protest a law or a policy considered unjust. **772**

Student Nonviolent Coordinating Committee (SNCC) Student-run civil rights organization founded in 1960. **775**

CHAPTER 26

A Nation Divided

The Vietnam War, 1945–1975

> **"We will not be defeated. We will not grow tired. We will not withdraw."**
>
> President LYNDON B. JOHNSON in 1965

Vietnam was America's longest war, a conflict that over time divided the nation to an extent not seen since the Civil War. For thirty years the United States invested money and then eventually soldiers in the struggle to prevent the establishment of communism in the small Southeast Asian country of Vietnam. From 1945 to 1964 the United States fought a proxy war by funneling supplies and aid to others willing to take up arms against the Vietnamese Communists. In 1965 the conflict became an American war when President Lyndon Johnson sent U.S. ground forces to fight in Southeast Asia.

By 1967 the antiwar movement had taken to the streets to protest America's involvement in Vietnam. On October 21, 1967, antiwar protesters gathered to hold a peace rally before the Lincoln Memorial in Washington, D.C., after which thirty thousand demonstrators linked arms and marched to the Pentagon, the national headquarters for the Department of Defense. When they arrived armed guards greeted them. As the soldiers advanced toward the crowd with their guns drawn, an eighteen-year-old actor from New York with a flare for the dramatic stepped forward holding a bouquet of pink carnations and carefully placed each one into soldiers' rifles. *Washington Star* news photographer Bernie Boston captured this poetic gesture in his photograph "Flower Power," an iconic photo of the civil strife that the war triggered. Competing interpretations of this image revealed key divisions of the era. For peace advocates the photograph illustrated the stark contrast between government-sponsored violence in Vietnam and American citizens' demand for peace. Critics of the peace movement, who accused activists of destroying respect for law and order, viewed the gesture as a ploy meant to distract the soldiers moments before demonstrators stormed the steps of the Pentagon and armed guards beat them back.

The Vietnam War originated as an anticolonial struggle to win independence from France, and then evolved into a civil war between North and South Vietnam. At first the crucial debates about Vietnam took place behind closed doors in the White House. Over the course of the country's thirty-year engagement in Vietnam, despite being presented continuously with other viewpoints, five American presidents chose escalation when faced with the option of pulling back or pressing forward. Viewing the Vietnamese conflict through the prism of the global Cold War, each president feared that losing all of Vietnam to communism would set off a chain reaction of communist revolutions throughout Southeast Asia.

World War II had united the nation. Vietnam fractured it. The guerilla war under way in South Vietnam, in which Communist soldiers intermingled with the civilian population to avoid detection, made it particularly difficult for Americans to separate enemy combatants from civilians. When the American military tried using overwhelming force to flush Communist guerillas out of South Vietnamese villages, the rising civilian death toll turned many Americans against the war. The conflict ultimately tore apart both Vietnam and America before the United States finally withdrew in 1973. The war ended with a Communist victory in 1975.

How did differing views on the war influence interpretations of this photograph in 1967?

The Long Road to War
p. 780

Fighting in Vietnam
p. 789

Controversy on the Home Front p. 796

The Long Road to Peace
p. 801

The Long Road to War

From 1945 to 1965 America gradually shifted its Cold War focus from Europe to Asia. The United States first supported French efforts to recover Vietnam as a colony, and then sustained an independent anti-communist South Vietnam with financial aid. At home some American policymakers envisioned the war as part of the worldwide struggle between democracy and communism. In Vietnam, however, Americans confronted a country torn apart by a civil war that reflected long-standing religious and political divisions within the nation. No American president sought a war in Vietnam, and key presidential advisors offered competing assessments of America's chances for victory. Yet at critical moments when the intractable political and military situation called for a response, each president chose to bolster the American commitment rather than turn back.

The Escalating Importance of Vietnam

America first became involved in Vietnam during World War II, when Japan took over the French colony of Indochina (present-day Laos, Cambodia, and Vietnam). In 1945 U.S. intelligence operatives worked with Ho Chi Minh, the leader of an underground Vietnamese communist resistance movement that launched guerilla attacks against the Japanese occupiers. When the war ended Ho Chi Minh and his rebel force formed a provisional government in Hanoi and declared independence from France. Eager to reestablish its position as a world power after the humiliating occupation by Germany in World War II, France sent in troops to crush the Vietnamese independence movement.

In search of international support for Vietnamese independence, the Western-educated Ho Chi Minh turned to the United States. Ho Chi Minh had previously tried to interest the United States in the cause of Vietnamese independence by submitting a petition to the American delegation at the Paris Peace Conference in 1919 after World War I that called for democratic reforms in French-held Indochina. The American delegation ignored Ho Chi Minh's request, mindful that his proposal would anger the French, whose support President Woodrow Wilson needed to create the League of Nations (see Chapter 20). After the rebuff in Paris, Ho Chi Minh became a communist, attracted by communism's revolutionary promise to free colonized peoples. "It was patriotism, not communism, that inspired me," he later claimed. In 1941 after nearly three decades abroad working as a Soviet spy, Ho Chi Minh returned to Vietnam to help organize a communist resistance to the Japanese occupation. Despite this revolutionary background Ho Chi Minh held out hope that the United States would support Vietnamese independence when Japan withdrew in 1945. Ho Chi Minh's communist credentials, however, tainted him in the eyes of President Harry S. Truman, who remained unmoved by Ho Chi Minh's truthful assurances that the Soviet Union did not control or finance him.

In the 1940s the Americans saw Ho Chi Minh as a communist puppet doing Moscow's bidding. His Vietnamese followers, however, viewed him as a charismatic leader ignited with a patriotic desire to free his nation from French colonial control. As one disciple recalled, the fifty-five-year-old "Uncle Ho" spoke with an "ardent and idealistic nationalism" that encouraged many Vietnamese to join the **Vietminh**, the term initially used to describe all Vietnamese communists, and used after 1954 solely for North Vietnamese communists. This photograph (**26.1**) of Ho Chi Minh sitting with a group of children reinforced his reputation in Vietnam as a beloved, wise elder. The image tapped into prevailing Confucian ideals, including filial piety (respect toward living and dead relatives), loyalty, and humane treatment of others. Ho Chi Minh broadened his appeal by eschewing personal luxuries and living simply in a small cottage. By the time American troops arrived in the late 1960s, an ailing Ho Chi Minh played almost no official role in the conflict. He nonetheless remained the face of Vietnamese communism for supporters and opponents throughout the war.

Who was Ho Chi Minh to his supporters and foes?

Cold War geopolitics consistently influenced how Americans reacted to the Vietnamese Communist revolt. As the emerging Cold War with the Soviet Union in the 1940s made containing communism in Europe a national obsession, Vietnam took on new political significance for the United States. The United States needed help from a vigorous and cooperative France to defend Western Europe from Soviet incursion. To rebuild the French economy and build goodwill, the United States gave France arms and funds beginning in 1947 (see Chapter 24). The French government used some of this aid to finance the war in Vietnam. The United States also agreed to support French efforts to regain control of its Vietnamese colony.

In 1950 the strategic importance of Vietnam for the United States also changed dramatically. The fall of China to communism in 1949 and the outbreak of the Korean War in 1950 when Communist-led North Korea invaded the anti-communist South Korea created fears that all of Asia might fall to communism. The "who lost China" debate severely hurt Truman politically, and no subsequent president wanted to be the one blamed for Vietnam falling to communism. Containing communism in both Europe and Asia became cornerstones of American foreign policy from this point on, requiring the United States to maintain military bases throughout Western Europe and along a string of Pacific islands from Japan to the Philippines.

As the Cold War spread to Asia, key presidential advisors insisted on seeing the hand of the Soviet Union behind every communist victory. By the early 1950s National Security Council Memorandum 68, or NSC-68, a document that described a global communist monolith, set the tone for U.S. foreign policy (see Chapter 24). Any more territory "under the domination of the Kremlin," the National Security Council warned, would make the Soviet Union invincible in any future military conflict. The threat would deepen if the Soviets gained control of resource-rich Southeast Asia, whose rubber, rice, tin, and oil were important economically to the United States. These resources were even more for vital for Japan, now a key American ally in the struggle against communism, and the United States wanted to ensure Japanese access to these materials by preventing them from falling into unfriendly communist hands.

Hardliners in the Truman and Eisenhower administrations embraced the **domino theory**, the fear that a communist Vietnam would open the door to a complete communist takeover of Southeast Asia, with communists repeating how Japan had conquered the region in World War II. Announcing the domino theory President Dwight D. Eisenhower explained in a 1954 press conference: "You have a row of dominos set up, you knock over the first one, and what will happen to the last one is the certainty that it will go over very quickly. So you could have a beginning of a disintegration that would have the most profound influences." Key events in the 1950s gave credence to these fears. Josef Stalin's success in pressuring China and North Korea to accept an

26.1 Ho Chi Minh Poses with Children, 1954
Ho Chi Minh developed a strong bond with his followers, who revered him as a wise elder who loved his nation.

What political and strategic importance did Vietnam assume in U.S. foreign policy by the mid-1950s?

26.2 ***How About the Other Buttons?*** This 1953 illustration shows Soviet leader Josef Stalin pressing his finger on a button labeled "Korea" to end the Korean War. This cartoon suggested that Stalin had the power to stop other conflicts that he had initiated throughout the world, including the war in Indochina.

armistice to end the Korean War strengthened the American conviction that the Soviet Union had the power to start or stop communist insurgencies around the globe. This political cartoon (**26.2**) by illustrator Marcus Edwin showed Stalin pressing the stop button for Korea, and suggested that he could also stop the conflict in Indochina (Vietnam) if he wished. Indeed Stalin had encouraged the Chinese leader Mao Tse-tung to take the lead in promoting communist revolution throughout Asia. The immediate influx of Communist Chinese advisors to train Vietminh officers, plus mountains of Chinese-manufactured vehicles, arms, and ammunition, seemingly confirmed that the Vietminh were part of an international communist conspiracy masterminded in Moscow.

American policymakers failed to appreciate, however, that a shared belief in communism did not override the nationalistic ambitions of the Soviet Union, China, or Vietnam. Ho Chi Minh accepted help from the Chinese, but remembering the Chinese ancient colonization of Vietnam, he remained suspicious of their ulterior motives and had no intention of turning Vietnam over to them. "It is better to sniff French dung for a while than eat China's all our life," warned Ho Chi Minh. In an American worldview that saw every communist revolution as part of the Soviet Union's master plan, however, the specific grievances or goals of the Vietminh became irrelevant.

Taking Over from the French

To hold the line in Vietnam, the American government was willing to foot the bill but wanted the French to do the actual fighting. The United States upheld its end of the bargain. By 1954 the United States was paying for 80 percent of the war's costs, money used to both purchase arms and fund humanitarian projects including free health clinics, food for refugees, and seeds for farmers. Increasingly, however, the United States doubted, in the words of Truman's outgoing secretary of state Dean Acheson, the "French will to carry on." As Acheson anticipated, the incoming Eisenhower administration soon faced a crisis in Vietnam. In 1954 the Vietminh defeated the French at Dien Bien Phu, in the northwest corner of the country, prompting the French to seek an international agreement with the Vietminh. The resulting **Geneva Accords (1954)** called for a temporary partition of Vietnam along the seventeenth parallel, with the Vietminh in the north and the French in the south, and a general election in two years to reunify the country under one government. Refusing to sign the Geneva Accords, the Eisenhower administration instead resolved to use the two-year period to ease the French out of South Vietnam and create a new government capable of raising and training a strong military to resist communist aggression.

To head the new South Vietnamese government, the United States selected Ngo Dinh Diem, a wealthy Catholic who had served as minister of the interior in the French colonial administration before resigning when the French refused to enact reforms he proposed. A staunch nationalist Diem moved to the United States, where he became well known to American policymakers. Neither Diem nor the United States intended to let the scheduled election take place, certain that Ho Chi Minh's authoritarian government would use force and fraud to ensure victory in the north and perhaps in the south as well. Instead the United States tried to destabilize Ho Chi Minh's fledgling Communist government by creating political turmoil in North Vietnam. Central Intelligence Agency (CIA) operatives destroyed government printing presses, contaminated the oil used in bus engines, sabotaged railway tracks, and planted rumors of Chinese troops raping North Vietnamese women.

Eisenhower supported the creation of an anticommunist South Vietnam to stem the tide of communism in Southeast Asia. As an additional defense against communism, the United States

What key choices did Eisenhower make in 1954 that increased U.S. involvement in Vietnam?

formed the **Southeast Asian Treaty Organization (SEATO)** in 1954. Through SEATO the United States, Britain, France, Australia, New Zealand, Thailand, the Philippines, and Pakistan pledged to "meet common danger" in Southeast Asia together. A separate agreement identified Vietnam, Laos, and Cambodia as areas that would endanger the "peace and security" of SEATO members if any of these three nations came under attack. Unlike the North Atlantic Treaty Organization (NATO), which guaranteed the mutual defense of member nations in Europe, the SEATO treaty left each nation's exact commitment vague. Secretary of State John Foster Dulles wanted it that way, reluctant to overextend American military responsibilities around the world by guaranteeing the borders of SEATO members. Even if this loosely worded pact failed to deter communist aggression, Dulles reasoned, it would provide a justification for direct American involvement in Vietnam to protect SEATO members if the United States decided to escalate its involvement in the future. An important development in America's ever-increasing involvement in Vietnam, SEATO illustrated how completely the United States linked the civil war in Vietnam to the global crusade against communism.

With the United States poised to embark on a major campaign to create an independent South Vietnam, dissenting voices within the government urged the president to pull back. Secretary of Defense Charles E. Wilson warned that he could "see nothing but grief in store for us if we remained." The joint chiefs of staff complained it would be impossible to build a capable South Vietnamese army without a "reasonably strong, stable civil government in control." This "chicken and egg" argument over which needed to come first, a strong South Vietnamese government or a strong military, divided American policymakers for the next fifteen years.

With Diem the United States got neither. A short, stocky man who always dressed in white, Diem's stiff and privileged appearance contrasted poorly with the plain dress and manners of Ho Chi Minh. The Eisenhower administration recognized Diem's shortcomings, but Secretary of State Dulles accepted the American ambassador's conclusion "that there is no one to take his place who would serve U.S. interests better." The United States quickly realized that Diem intended to build a dictatorial regime in South Vietnam. Diem modeled his rule on Vietnamese emperors of the nineteenth century, issuing decrees and refusing to abide any criticism. "I know what is best for my people," he declared in one interview. The secret police, headed by Diem's brother-in-law, Ngo Dinh Nhu, arrested, tortured, and executed thousands of South Vietnamese accused of opposing his rule.

Most Vietminh had relocated to North Vietnam when the country split into two, but remnants of the Communist guerilla force still existed in the south. They found ample discontent with Diem among peasants, students, Buddhists, and even some South Vietnamese soldiers. Attempting to destabilize the Diem regime, the Communists unleashed a wave of assassinations targeting wealthy landlords and rural officials who worked for the repressive Diem regime. Diem fought back by trying to cut off guerilla fighters from their supply base. He moved peasants off their ancestral lands and into "strategic hamlets" protected by moats and walls and imprisoned thousands of civilians suspected of aiding the rebels. Enraged over the forced removal program, the peasants were like a "mound of straw ready to be ignited," claimed one Vietnamese Communist.

The U.S. government and press revealed none of Diem's internal difficulties to the American people. When Diem visited the United States in 1957, the American press praised him as the "tough little miracle man" who had brought stability to South Vietnam. "We can take pride in our support," *Newsweek* magazine trumpeted.

In the mid-1950s Ho Chi Minh offered southern Communists little support. He was instead preoccupied with subduing the widespread protests that greeted his forced land redistribution program in North Vietnam, a campaign that sent armed posses into the countryside to confiscate land. These "land reforms" left thousands of property owners dead, destroyed communities, and created famine. By the end of the decade, however, the North Vietnamese government began sending soldiers and supplies to southern Communists, unleashing a terror campaign meant to pave the way for a Communist takeover of South Vietnam. In 1960 the southern Communists formed the National Liberation Front (NLF) to bring the various factions in South Vietnamese society opposed to the Diem regime together into a fighting coalition. Diem derogatorily called South Vietnamese Communists **Vietcong**, slang meaning "Vietnamese Commies." The name stuck. From this point on Americans called all Communists from South Vietnam "Vietcong" and Communists from North Vietnam "Vietminh."

Why did the civil war in Vietnam reignite in the late 1950s and early 1960s?

Debates within the Kennedy Administration

John F. Kennedy assumed the presidency in 1961 having proclaimed Vietnam the "cornerstone of the free world in Southeast Asia." Kennedy also understood the negative political consequences of "losing" a nation to communism. While in the Senate Kennedy had joined the chorus hurling criticism at Truman when China succumbed to communism. In 1961 Kennedy suffered two setbacks of his own in the global war against communism with the botched Cuban Bay of Pigs invasion and his inability to stop the Soviets from constructing the Berlin Wall (see Chapter 24). His leadership during the Cuban Missile Crisis in 1962, however, eventually redeemed his reputation as a Cold War warrior. In the meantime Kennedy did not intend to let the conflict in Vietnam bring his administration down.

Faced with a worsening political and military situation in Vietnam, Kennedy received conflicting recommendations from his advisors. One group envisioned dramatically escalating the American commitment by sending in combat troops. Another wanted to seek a diplomatic resolution to the conflict. Faced with these divided opinions, Kennedy chose a middle path. Instead of infantry troops Kennedy sent more financial aid and increased the number of American military "advisors" in South Vietnam from one thousand to sixteen thousand. Officially these advisors helped train the South Vietnamese Army. In actuality many "advisors" were Green Berets, the army's special-force troops who organized South Vietnamese attacks on Vietcong supply lines, flew planes when South Vietnamese pilots were unavailable, and picked up the dead and wounded in helicopters after skirmishes. When word of these activities leaked out, Kennedy publicly denied that Americans were participating in active combat operations in Vietnam.

"Supporting the Diem regime while applying pressure for reform appears to be the only practicable alternative at this time," the joint chiefs of staff convinced Kennedy, cautioning that "any reversal of U.S. policy could have disastrous effects" throughout Southeast Asia. As South Vietnamese anger against his rule intensified, Diem privately voiced his own mounting frustration with the growing American presence in South Vietnam. "All these soldiers," he fumed, referring to the Green Berets and military advisors. "I never asked them to come here." To rid South Vietnam of Americans, Diem and his police chief brother Nhu decided to seek a negotiated settlement with North Vietnam in 1963. Upset with Diem's overture to North Vietnam, the turning point for the Kennedy administration came in June, when a Buddhist monk set himself on fire in a busy street in Saigon, the capital of South Vietnam.

The Catholic Diem had long discriminated against Buddhists. Thousands of North Vietnamese Catholics fled to the south when the Communists took over in 1954, and Diem guaranteed their loyalty by rewarding them with land and governmental positions. In May 1963 Nhu refused to let the Buddhists fly a multicolored flag honoring Buddha on his birthday. Widespread street protests ensued, which Nhu violently suppressed with soldiers who used water hoses, tear gas, and on one occasion bullets, killing a woman and eight children. On June 10, 1963, a Buddhist monk telephoned Associated Press photographer Malcolm Browne to invite him to witness "something important" the next morning. Browne arrived at the designated street crossing on June 11, 1963, and watched monks take a canister of gasoline out of the white car shown in this picture (**26.3**) and place a brown mat in the middle of the street. Moments later a Buddhist monk, Thich Quang Duc, sat down on the mat in the lotus position. After another monk poured gasoline over him, Duc struck a match. Flames instantaneously engulfed his body. "His eyes were closed, but his features were twisted in apparent pain," Browne recalled. As Browne snapped this memorable photo, a monk shouted into a microphone in Vietnamese and English: "A Buddhist priest burns himself to death. A Buddhist priest becomes a martyr." Monks (seen in the background) lined the streets to prevent any one from trying to save Duc. Immediately proclaimed a Buddhist saint, Duc's ashes were distributed to pagodas, towering Buddhist temples, throughout South Vietnam.

Duc carefully staged his suicide to gain maximum exposure for the Buddhists' political protest, using the Western press to help rally opposition to Diem within South Vietnam and the United States. The burning monk image shocked but also bewildered Americans. The American government and press had continually praised Diem as a valiant Cold War ally, but this photo suggested strong opposition to his rule at home. Students, Buddhist priests, and soldiers in South Vietnam responded to the suicide as a call to action. Street protests erupted, the military began planning a coup, and six other monks set themselves

What conflicting recommendations did Kennedy receive from his advisors about Vietnam?

26.3 Burning Monk Thich Quang Duc wanted the Western press to photograph his 1963 suicide to publicize the Buddhist protest against the corrupt Diem regime.

on fire in front of Western journalists. With a framed copy of Browne's burning monk image on his desk, Kennedy secretly agreed to support a military coup to overthrow the Diem regime.

> "I must say that during the monk episode, I had no impulse to try to go in and save him. I knew for one thing that he intended it this way."
>
> Photographer MALCOLM BROWNE, on photographing Thich Quang Duc's self-immolation in 1963

The Kennedy Assassination

The military coup supported by President Kennedy led to the murder of Diem and Nhu, but Americans had little time to reflect on these events. Three weeks later, on November 22, 1963, Lee Harvey Oswald shot and killed President Kennedy in Dallas, Texas, as Kennedy waved to onlookers from an open convertible with his wife by his side. In the midst of his presidential reelection bid, Kennedy was visiting Dallas to shore up his fading popularity among Texans angered by his support for the Civil Rights Movement (see Chapter 27). This was the first trip that Jackie Kennedy had taken with her husband since the death of their two-day-old son Patrick three months before. Kennedy decided to ride in an open-air convertible, rejecting the suggestion from his Secret Service guards that he sit within a bulletproof clear glass bubble for the ride past the gathered crowds. An amateur movie by Abraham Zapruder, a Russian immigrant and Kennedy supporter, gave the nation its most enduring images of this killing, film stills that provoked countless controversies over who killed the president. In its investigation of the assassination, the Warren Commission cited the Zapruder film as evidence that Oswald acted alone, claiming that the film footage showed bullets entering the president's body from only one

What insights does the story behind this 1963 photo offer into the Vietnam War?

direction. Counterclaims that the assassination was the result of a wider conspiracy involving other gunmen, the mafia, Cuban dictator Fidel Castro, and the CIA continue to this day.

Vice President Lyndon Baines Johnson (LBJ), who had been riding two cars behind Kennedy in the Dallas motorcade, appreciated the potent political symbolism attached to the president's grieving widow. When Kennedy died within hours of the shooting, Johnson, who was next in line to assume the presidency, insisted on taking the oath of office before Judge Sarah Hughes with Jackie Kennedy on one side and his wife on the other before the presidential airplane Air Force One left Dallas. The presence of the slain president's widow would, Johnson felt, immediately legitimatize the transfer of power in the eyes of the American people. Already on board the plane, which was carrying her husband's body back to Washington, D.C., Jackie Kennedy complied with Johnson's request, but had no chance to change her clothes. In this portrait (**26.4**) of Johnson's swearing in, photographer Cecil Stoughton carefully framed out Jackie Kennedy's skirt, which was stained with her husband's blood. Her pale and drawn expression nonetheless reflected the day's ordeal.

A wealthy Massachusetts-born Catholic, Kennedy had selected Johnson, a powerful Texan politician, as his vice presidential running mate to help broaden his appeal in the South. Johnson grew up poor and worked as a middle and high school teacher before entering national politics as an avid supporter of the New Deal in 1937. Johnson relied heavily on his superior political instincts and outgoing personality to rise to prominence. While serving in the Senate, Johnson became the most powerful majority leader in history. A larger-than-life figure, his brashness contrasted sharply with the slain president's debonair manner. His most legendary gaff came in 1965, when he lifted his shirt during a press conference to show reporters his 12-inch scar from recent gallbladder surgery. Johnson wanted to reassure the nation about his recovery, but critics lampooned the act as crude and undignified.

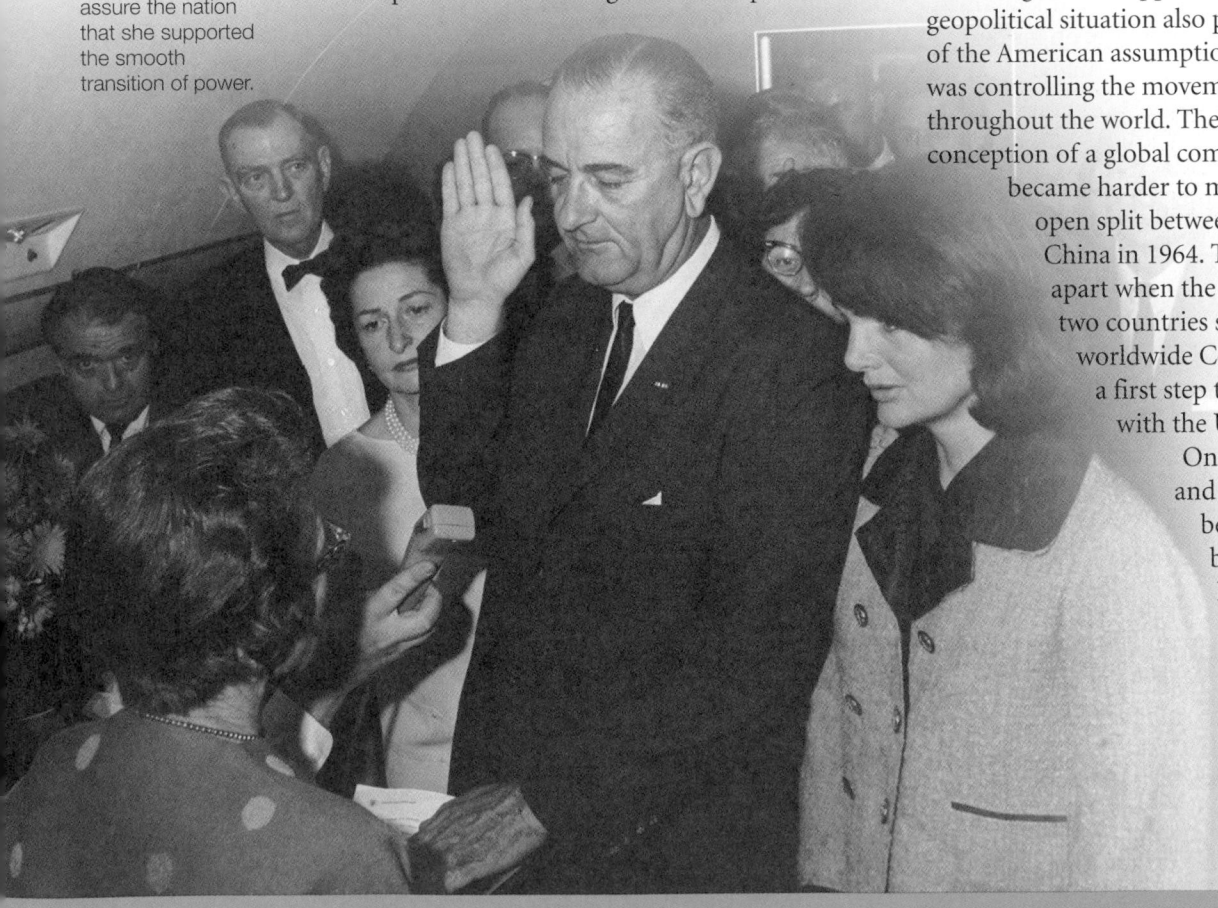

26.4 Jackie Kennedy
On November 22, 1963, the day President John F. Kennedy was assassinated in Dallas, Texas, the First Lady's personal tragedy became enveloped in political symbolism. Here she stands by as the new president, Lyndon B. Johnson, takes the oath of office to visibly assure the nation that she supported the smooth transition of power.

How did images both provoke and quell controversy surrounding the Kennedy assassination?

The Gulf of Tonkin

Lyndon Baines Johnson inherited a rapidly deteriorating situation in Vietnam in the wake of the Diem assassination. Like his predecessors he faced the choice of pulling back or escalating the American commitment, which at this point consisted of sixteen thousand military advisors and Green Beret troops and substantial financial aid to South Vietnam. After the Diem assassination, South Vietnam slipped into perpetual political instability as a succession of rulers failed to gain the support of the people. The shifting geopolitical situation also prompted a reappraisal of the American assumption that the Soviet Union was controlling the movements of communists throughout the world. The previous American conception of a global communist conspiracy became harder to maintain in the face of the open split between the Soviet Union and China in 1964. The Sino-Soviet alliance fell apart when the Soviets suggested that the two countries scale back their support of worldwide Communist insurgencies as a first step toward improving relations with the United States. Mao refused.

Once again elected officials and policymakers differed behind closed doors on the best course of action. National Security Advisor McGeorge Bundy told Johnson that "the right course is to continue to strengthen our struggle against the Communist terror (which is exactly what this is)." Senator

Richard Russell, a close confidant of the president, disagreed with those who claimed that "we'll lose everything in Southeast Asia if we lose Vietnam." For his part Johnson feared that withdrawal would mark him as a weak leader, emboldening conservative challenges to the civil rights laws and expanded social welfare programs for the poor that he wanted to enact. "I was determined to keep the war from shattering that dream," Johnson later admitted, by which time the war had indeed consumed the financial resources and political goodwill that the president needed to fully realize this dream (see Chapter 27).

> "No one ever won a battle sitting on his ass."
>
> General EARLE WHEELER, supporting the troop buildup in Vietnam

Events in the Gulf of Tonkin, the body of water off the shore of North Vietnam, soon gave Johnson an excuse to act boldly. On August 2, 1964, North Vietnamese torpedo boats attacked an American destroyer, the USS *Maddox*, in the Gulf of Tonkin. The *Maddox* easily repelled the confirmed attack. Two days later the crew of the *Maddox* and a second destroyer, the USS *Turner Joy*, both reported coming under attack from North Vietnamese torpedoes. After failing to locate any North Vietnamese boats, U.S. Navy pilot James Stockdale landed on the *Maddox* where officers met him "all with sheepish grins on their faces." Citing improperly working radar, overeager sonar operators, and no visual sightings of the torpedo boats, the ships' joint commander now doubted that a second attack had taken place. Accepting initial reports of a second attack as conclusive, Secretary of Defense Robert McNamara told Johnson that "we cannot sit still as a nation and let them attack us on the high seas and get away with it." A television reporter asked Secretary of State Dean Rusk why North Vietnam would attack an American ship. "I can't come up with a rational explanation for it," Rusk answered. Behind closed doors the president admitted to knowing better, acknowledging in a private conversation that "there have been some covert operations in that area that we have been carrying on—blowing up some bridges ... roads and so forth. So I imagine they wanted to put a stop to it."

Besides ordering reprisal bombing against North Vietnam, President Johnson used the Gulf of Tonkin incident to win congressional approval for further military action in Vietnam. In August of 1964, rallying behind the president, Congress approved the **Gulf of Tonkin Resolution** with only two dissenting votes in the Senate. The resolution gave Johnson permission "to take all necessary measures to repel any armed attack against the forces of the United States and to prevent further aggression" in Vietnam.

On March 8, 1965, the first American Marines landed at Da Nang along the northern coast of South Vietnam, where young women put leis around their necks during an official ceremony. In the years that followed, troops received a distinctly less warm welcome. As the American air force began a major bombing campaign against North Vietnam called Rolling Thunder, General Westmoreland requested a dramatic escalation in American ground forces. "You must take the fight to the enemy," General Earle Wheeler, the joint chiefs of staff chairman, agreed.

Choices and Consequences: Making Vietnam America's War (page 788) explores how Johnson reached his decision to intensify America's involvement in the war. By choosing escalation Johnson sealed his legacy as the American president who made winning the war a priority for the United States. In 1966 the political cartoonist David Levine reimagined the 1965 scene of Johnson lifting his shirt to expose his gallbladder incision. In Levine's rendition (**26.5**) the mark now assumed the shape of Vietnam, the conflict destined to scar Johnson's presidency and the nation. Johnson's willingness to expose the minute details of his health to the public contrasted sharply with the ethos of misinformation and secrecy (suggested by the Pinocchio-like nose of the caricature) he embraced as commander-in-chief.

26.5 ***Johnson's Scar***
In 1966 the political cartoonist David Levine transformed President Lyndon Johnson's scar into the shape of Vietnam, portraying the conflict as an ugly mark on Johnson's administration.

Why was the 1964 Gulf of Tonkin incident a turning point in the Vietnam War?

Choices and Consequences

MAKING VIETNAM AMERICA'S WAR

In the first part of 1965, Johnson initiated a regular bombing campaign against North Vietnam and sent 82,000 ground troops to South Vietnam. The theater commander General William Westmoreland soon requested 150,000 more. In deciding how to respond to Westmoreland's request, the president's advisors gave Johnson the following choices in the summer of 1965.

Choices

1. Avoid a war likely to become protracted with little chance for a military or political victory over the Communists and seek a negotiated settlement in Vietnam.
2. Continue at the present level of military aid to South Vietnam and push for political reforms in South Vietnam to bolster internal support for a more democratic anti-Communist government.
3. Send the requested troops, expand the bombing campaign, and work for political reforms in South Vietnam.

Decision

Johnson viewed a negotiated settlement as tantamount to losing Vietnam to communism, an outcome he viewed as a threat to both Southeast Asia and his presidency. Certain that South Vietnam would lose the war without additional U.S. aid, he publicly agreed to send fifty thousand troops immediately. He privately guaranteed Westmoreland an additional fifty thousand and promised to send more as needed. He also approved heavy bombing of Vietcong strongholds in South Vietnam and tried to institute political reforms in South Vietnam to erode support for the Vietcong.

Consequences

The United States was no longer simply aiding South Vietnam in its struggle against communism, but now took the lead in fighting the Vietcong and the North Vietnamese. By 1967 there were nearly half a million American troops in Vietnam. Over the course of the war the United States dropped more bombs there than it had in World War II.

Johnson's Dilemma. He is shown here with Defense Secretary, Robert McNamara.

Continuing Controversies

Should the United States have fought a major war in Vietnam?

Detractors claim that Johnson committed the United States to an unwinnable war by trying to use the military to solve a political problem in South Vietnam. He underestimated the will of the Vietcong and exaggerated the importance of South Vietnam to containing communism in the rest of Southeast Asia. He failed to build strong domestic support for a long war, leading to eventual unrest at home over the draft and rising casualties. Johnson's supporters argue that he honored a commitment to South Vietnam made by his predecessors. This reassured American allies worldwide that they could count on the United States. Retreat would only have invited further Communist aggression in Southeast Asia and Europe. Losing Vietnam would have weakened Johnson politically, putting his controversial domestic reform and civil rights legislative agenda in jeopardy.

Why was Johnson's decision to escalate U.S. troop levels in 1965 important?

Fighting in Vietnam

David Halberstam, reporting for the *New York Times* in 1962, summed up the military dilemma in Vietnam perfectly: "It is often impossible to separate the cruel and dedicated foe you want to kill from the simple and illiterate peasant you want to woo." America and North Vietnam embraced competing strategic visions in fighting the war. While the American military preferred fighting against uniformed soldiers on a clearly defined battlefield, the Communists embraced guerilla warfare where troops blended into the civilian population or stayed hidden in underground tunnels. The American military tried to defeat Vietnamese guerilla forces by bombing enemy bases and destroying their village refuges. These tactics created another set of competing visions about the war: the soldiers' view of an unending conflict versus the image of imminent victory that the government championed at home.

The Bombing Campaign

The American military relied heavily on bombing to defeat the Vietcong and North Vietnamese. The American bombing campaign was the largest air war in world history, with American planes dropping nearly 5 million tons of bombs in eight years. The Americans hoped to pressure North Vietnam into ending the war. The North Vietnamese instead learned to live with bombs. The sighting of American planes over the North Vietnamese capital city of Hanoi sent inhabitants scurrying into bombproof underground shelters. The government built 30,000 miles of tunnels, which moved the nation's transportation and communication infrastructure underground. The sustained bombing campaign bred anti-American feelings among the civilian population that made it easier for the North Vietnamese government to mobilize the country to "foil the war of aggression of the U.S. imperialists."

Navy Captain James Stockdale led the first American air strike against North Vietnamese oil tanks in the wake of the Gulf of Tonkin incident. A year later during another air raid, he was shot down over a small coastal village in North Vietnam where angry villagers beat him and broke his knee. Stockdale spent the next seven and a half years in a prisoner of war (POW) camp. His jailers subjected Stockdale to brutal rounds of torture when he taught fellow POWs a wall-tapping code so they could communicate with one another during their long years in solitary confinement.

American planes targeted the **Ho Chi Minh Trail** as well, a 600-mile North Vietnamese supply route that ran along the western border of Vietnam through the mountainous rain forest of neighboring Laos and Cambodia. Nearly five thousand Communist soldiers and workers completed the arduous three-month journey each month, bringing additional troops, munitions, and food to the Vietcong. North Vietnamese propaganda glorified the difficult journey with images that emphasized the toughness and determination of its people. This photo (**26.6**) shows a North Vietnamese camera crew filming male and female teenage volunteers from the north as they push bicycles, which the North Vietnamese called "steel horses," through the woods to carry rice and guns to Communist troops in the south. Continued improvements turned the dirt paths into an open road by the 1970s. Surface-to-air missiles and antiaircraft guns stationed along the way helped protect trucks from bombing.

26.6 Hardships along the Ho Chi Minh Trail
North Vietnamese propaganda relentlessly publicized the arduous journey along the Ho Chi Minh Trail to highlight how Communist ingenuity had stymied the world's greatest military power. Here, a Communist movie crew films teenage volunteers transporting bags of rice and guns strapped to their bicycle handlebars in 1970.

What messages did North Vietnamese propaganda send?

Americans also extensively bombed South Vietnamese "free fire zones," the name given to villages that supposedly contained only enemy combatants. The American air campaign included spraying defoliants, usually **Agent Orange**, that stripped trees of their leaves to expose Vietcong hideouts and killed the crops that might feed enemy troops. "Only you can prevent forests," American pilots quipped, a satirical reworking of a popular environmental slogan "only you can prevent forest fires." Defoliants ultimately destroyed half of Vietnam's forests and caused lasting health problems for both American pilots and the Vietnamese that included cancers and birth defects. Responding to negative publicity at home, the military stopped using defoliants in 1971. American pilots also dropped napalm, a jellylike gasoline that ignited on impact, to destroy South Vietnamese villages hiding enemy troops. Napalm inflicted severe burns on the human body, contributing to the misery of civilians subject to bombing attacks.

> "I wanted to be a hero."
>
> Vietnam veteran RON KOVIC, explaining why he joined the Marines

Reports of mounting civilian suffering energized the U.S. **peace movement**, a loose coalition of antiwar activists that included pacifists, students, professors, clergy, hippies (young people who rejected middle-class values and adopted a bohemian lifestyle), civil rights activists, and middle-class liberals. In making his decision to go to war, Johnston had focused on placating his hawkish critics without considering the political fallout of antagonizing the left. By 1967, however, belatedly realizing the price he was paying for waging the war, the president noted, "The major threat we have [politically] is from the doves."

On the Ground

The initial wave of American troops sent to Vietnam consisted mostly of army volunteers. Raised on tales of heroism during World War II, Phil Caputo viewed joining the Marines as a way to escape suburbia and serve their country. "I saw myself charging up some distant beachhead, like John Wayne in *Sands of Iwo Jima*," noted Caputo, recalling a popular 1949 film that romanticized the battle responsible for the iconic World War II photo of six men raising the flag over Mount Suribachi (see *Images as History*, Chapter 23). The 1966 hit song "The Ballad of the Green Berets" sold nine million singles and topped the charts for five weeks, evidence of widespread popular support for the war that lasted until 1967. The song praised each member of this specially trained force as "one of America's best" who fought courageously with conviction to free the oppressed. The song's lyrics, "one hundred men, we'll test today, but only three, win the Green Beret," promoted military service as a legitimate way for young men to demonstrate their masculine prowess—a message that encouraged many working-class men to volunteer.

The realities of combat, however, quickly shattered the idealism of men like Caputo. In 1965, *Life* photojournalist Larry Burrows spent a month with helicopter crews, documenting their heroism and the harrowing combat. In this photo (**26.7**) gunner James Farley fires on enemy troops below as the pilot lands to rescue a downed American helicopter crew. Subsequent photos captured the anguish on Farley's face when he realized that the rescued pilot had died.

The drafted men sent to Vietnam in later years had fewer illusions than the initial volunteers. Conscripts were often working-class men who did

26.7 American Gunner Rescues Downed Comrades, 1965
Life photographer Larry Burrows captured the harrowing nature of combat in a photo that shows a U.S. soldier clearing the ground of enemy fire as his helicopter lands to aid a downed American helicopter crew.

What motivated American men to volunteer to fight in Vietnam?

not qualify for draft deferments, which only college-bound and married men enjoyed. Volunteers and conscripts served one-year tours in Vietnam, and as the time to return home neared, they often became more averse to taking risks in combat. Some soldiers even used their helmets as calendars, openly marking off the days left until their tour of duty ended.

In World War II American soldiers had fought against a clearly distinguishable enemy in the Pacific island jungles. Vietcong forces, however, infiltrated the civilian population. They wore civilian clothes, stored arms in the walls of huts, and sent spies to work on American military bases. Civilians gave the Vietcong crucial support, some by choice and some out of fear that the Vietcong would torture or murder them. On search-and-destroy missions, American soldiers tried to draw the enemy out of hiding to kill them and destroy their supply base with combined ground force action and air attacks. To locate the enemy American soldiers marched in darkness through the steamy jungle and tried to stay alert while sweat poured down their faces and saw-edged grass cut into their skin. They walked gingerly, on the lookout for enemy ambushes, land mines, and leaf-covered punji stake traps (holes in the ground lined with sharpened spears that would impale a soldier who fell into one).

Search-and-destroy missions reduced villages that were suspected of aiding Vietcong to mounds of rubble. American troops blew up or contaminated wells, burned straw huts, and salted the ground so no crops would grow. Even in the middle of search-and-destroy missions, however, American soldiers remained capable of compassion. It was "the paradoxical kindness-and-cruelty that made Vietnam such a peculiar war," Marine Phil Caputo remembered. On one search-and-destroy mission, for instance, men in his unit tried to treat and comfort a baby with skin ulcers. Only a few yards away, other soldiers threatened to kill an old woman for preparing metal stakes that the Vietcong placed in fields to prevent helicopters from landing.

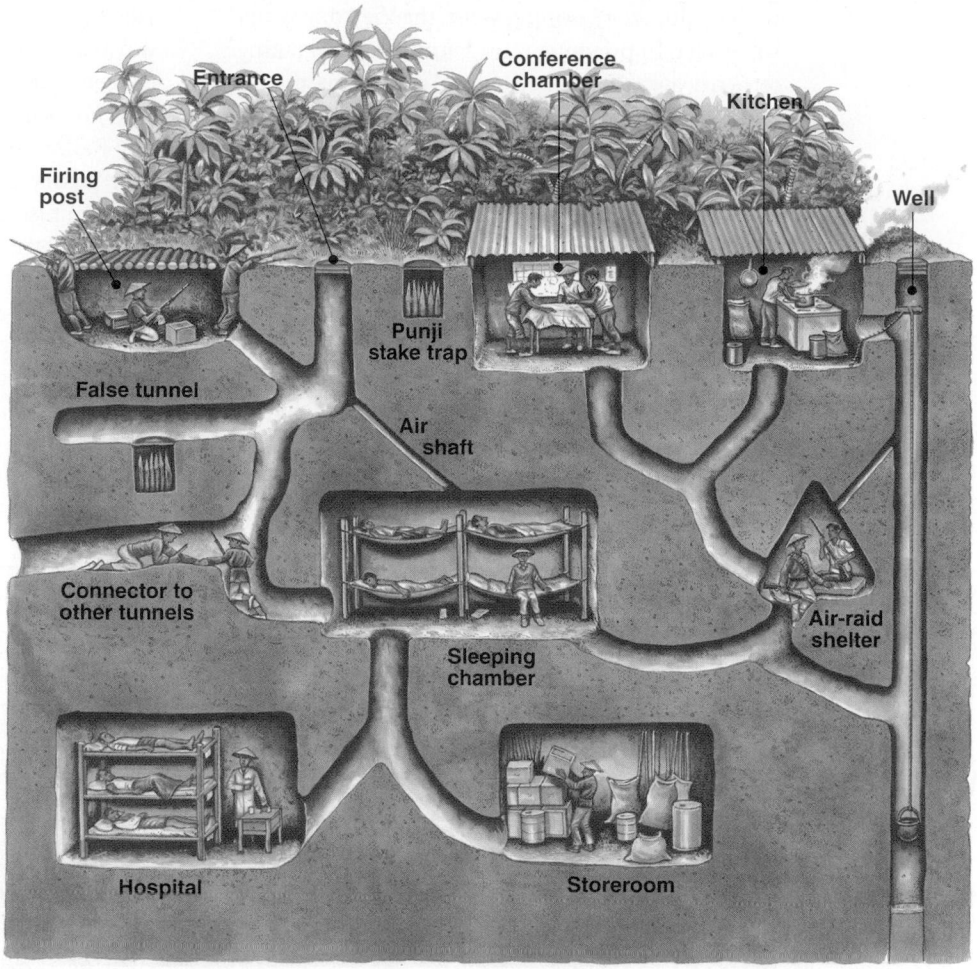

26.8 Drawing of Vietcong Hideout Intricate tunnel complexes concealed Vietcong guerilla forces beneath villages.

To combat American air superiority, the Vietcong moved many of their command posts, dormitories, and supply depots underground. This drawing (**26.8**) illustrates an example of an elaborate Vietcong tunnel complex. Village huts camouflaged some entrances. Punji stake traps, pictured on one side of the tunnel entrance, and hidden snipers, hiding in a hole on the other side, protected another. The Vietcong also laid traps for American "tunnel rats" who entered the complex in search of enemy troops. A wrong turn down the false tunnel meant overturning baskets of scorpions and poisonous snakes or falling into a punji stake trap. The twisted tunnel design stymied American attempts to fill the tunnels with water, while poisonous gas escaped through the airshafts. Heavy bombing ultimately demolished many tunnel complexes, but at the high cost of destroying homes and forests as well.

American soldiers fought a war of attrition, trying to kill as many Vietcong as possible while also destroying their resources and thus sapping their morale. When the enemy could no longer replace its fighters

What tactics did the military adopt to fight the Vietcong?

in the field, the reasoning went, the Vietcong would surrender. In previous wars, winning meant taking territory away from the enemy. In Vietnam, the United States measured victory by accumulating a high body count of enemy dead. The Communists had the same goal, hoping to create so many American casualties that the United States would abandon the war.

Compiling an accurate tally of enemy dead proved impossible, however. Soldiers encountered genuine difficulties determining how many Vietcong they had killed. The aftermath of battle often littered the jungle with assorted body parts and trails of blood rather than intact bodies to count. The military also unintentionally created incentives for soldiers to lie. "You guys want a day off, we got to be getting more kills," one commander told his men. In comparing their body counts, troops made little effort to separate friend from foe. The American soldier credo, "If it's dead and it's Vietnamese, it's VC [Vietcong]," lumped enemy soldiers with innocent civilians. Eventually the inaccuracy of body counts became common knowledge. Satirist Gary Trudeau mocked the preoccupation with body count in this Doonesbury comic strip (**26.9**). Trudeau's rendition of an American captain using the day's date as his official body count echoed an uncomfortable truth about the value of these officially circulated figures.

26.9 Doonesbury Lampoons Body Counts
Cartoonist Gary B. Trudeau underscored the meaninglessness of the official body count figure. Many Americans were becoming skeptical of the government's claim that victory was imminent.

The Tet Offensive

In 1967 Americans' support for the war began to flounder. Nearly thirteen thousand American soldiers had died so far, and each month draft boards inducted another thirty thousand into the military. Johnson's call for new taxes to meet rising war expenses further dismayed Americans. Some leading policymakers changed their minds as well. Secretary of Defense Robert McNamara underwent the greatest shift in views. McNamara went from strenuously advocating war (some critics called it "McNamara's war") to conceding that "Ho Chi Minh is a tough old S.O.B. And he won't quit no matter how much bombing we do." Rather than making his breach with the president over Vietnam public, however, McNamara quietly left the administration.

In the same year General Westmoreland assured Johnson that the war of attrition had reached a crossover point, meaning that American soldiers had killed more enemy soldiers than the Communists could replace in the field. To boost morale at home, General Westmoreland publicly assured the nation that "we have reached an important point where the end begins to come into view." Johnson was also upbeat. "The enemy is not beaten," Johnson told the nation before Christmas, "but he knows that he has met his master in the field."

A major Vietnamese offensive in 1968 exposed the hollowness of these claims. On January 30, 1968, during the Vietnamese New Year holiday known as Tet, North Vietnamese and Vietcong forces launched the **Tet Offensive**, a massive, coordinated assault against more than a hundred cities and towns in South Vietnam. The map of Vietnam (**26.10**) depicts the wide-ranging attacks. "Uncle Ho was very old and we had to liberate the south before his death," one North Vietnamese officer recalled. By demonstrating their determination to fight forever, the North Vietnamese wanted to convince Johnson that the cost of any American victory was too high. The Communists also expected their attack on previously calm cities to spark a revolution within South Vietnam.

Before the Tet Offensive the Communists had successfully lured nearly fifty thousand American troops away from the cities by laying siege to a remote Marine garrison in Khe Sanh and making smaller attacks on a few isolated towns. The weakened

What problems surfaced from using enemy body counts to measure victory?

American presence in the urban centers left them vulnerable to enemy attack. A shocked American public watched on television as nineteen Vietcong commandos entered the courtyard of the American Embassy complex in Saigon and battled guards there for six hours. It took heavy fighting and more than a month before American troops regained control of South Vietnamese towns and cities. In the end the Communists paid a heavy price for forsaking the jungles and tunnels that provided such effective cover, suffering forty thousand casualties and military defeat. Nearly twelve thousand civilians died during the battle, along with thirty-five hundred American and South Vietnamese soldiers.

Yet rather than celebrating this victory over the Communists, Americans' support for the war plunged. The daily televised images of the month's fierce fighting undercut the recent rosy predictions of imminent victory issued by the White House. At a time when 60 percent of Americans got their news from television, Vietnam became the first war in which Americans viewed the fighting in the comfort of their living rooms on a nightly basis. Televised news reports suggested that no matter who won the battle the fighting would go on. These newscasts stoked the shift in public sentiment already well under way before Tet. *Images as History: The Power of the Press in Vietnam* (page 794) considers how viewers' political leanings influenced their interpretation of photographs from the battlefront. The revered CBS-TV news anchor Walter Cronkite spoke for millions when he declared the war a stalemate. "We have been too often disappointed by the optimism of the American leaders, both in Vietnam and Washington, to have faith any longer in the silver linings they find in the darkest clouds," Cronkite told his listeners on February 27, 1968. He urged the government to seek a negotiated peace.

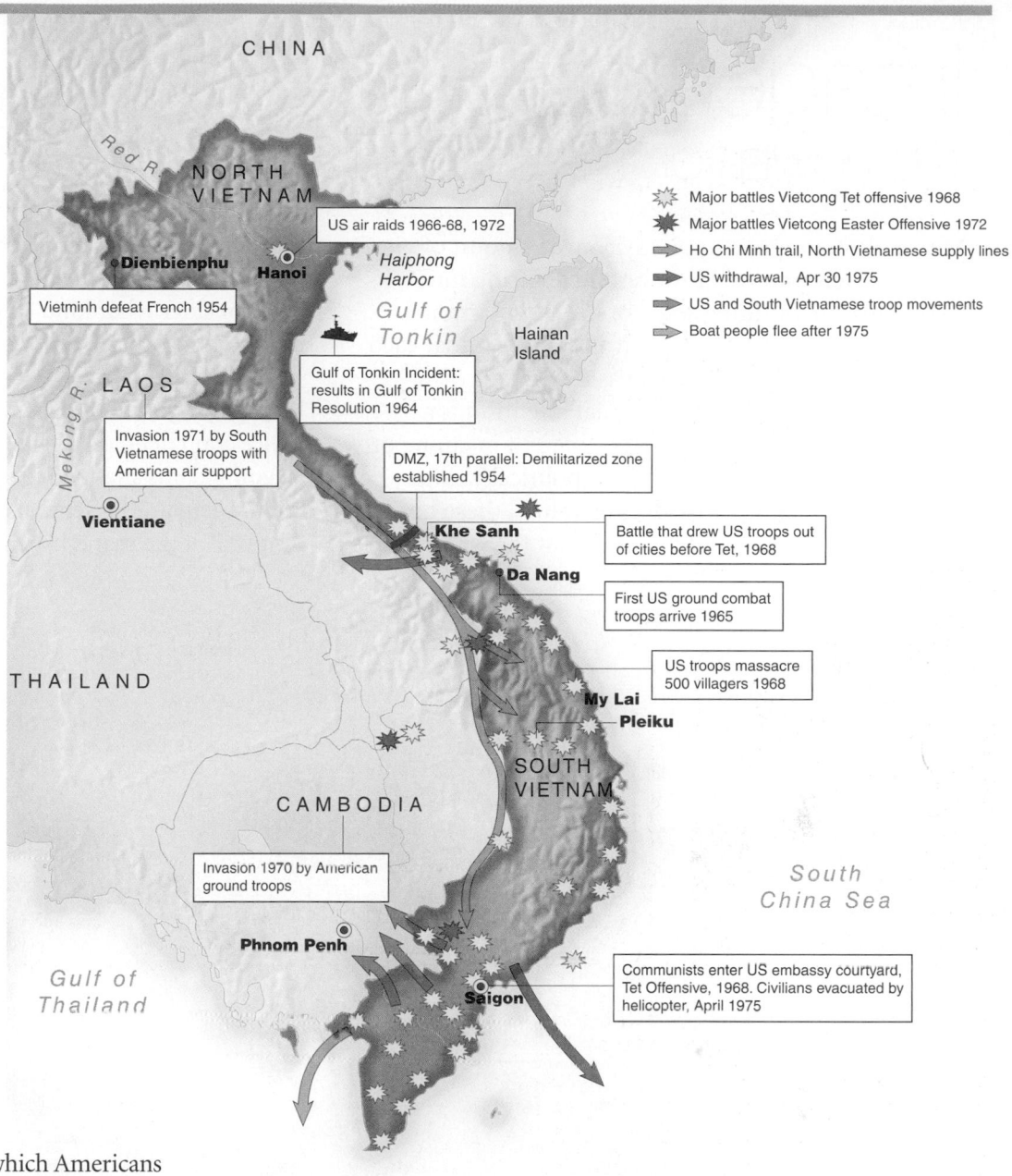

26.10 Map of Vietnam
From the French defeat at Dien Bien Phu in 1954 to the final evacuation of U.S. personnel in 1975, the United States actively tried to defeat Communist forces in Vietnam.

Cronkite's assessment mirrored reports from the president's new secretary of defense Clark Clifford. As the joint chiefs pressed the president for more troops, "I couldn't get hold of a plan to win the war" [from the military], Clifford later complained. "When I asked how many more men it would take, would 206,000 more men do the job, no one could be certain." Responding to these rising doubts, Johnson made a surprise announcement in a televised address to the nation on March 31, 1968. "I want to speak to you of peace in Vietnam," Johnson told listeners. He would not seek reelection, he said. Instead of campaigning he would halt most bombing of North Vietnam and devote the rest of his time in office to peace negotiations.

Why did the 1968 Tet Offensive have such tremendous political fallout?

Images as History

THE POWER OF THE PRESS IN VIETNAM

Media photographers typically convey a point of view through their photos. However the differing interpretations surrounding some of the most famous photographs from the Vietnam War suggest that each photo took on a life of its own as Americans disregarded the photographer's original intention for taking the photo and imposed a different meaning on the image that reflected their own political views. Rather than creating new ideas or values, these images became iconic visual statements about the war because they reinforced strongly held beliefs within the population. In examining the text and photos in this box, consider what kind of power the press had to mold public opinion about the war.

In the midst of the 1968 Tet Offensive, Associated Press photographer Eddie Adams saw South Vietnamese police apprehend a Vietcong suspect in the streets of Saigon. Adams snapped his prize-winning photo just as South Vietnamese General Nguyen Ngoc Loan aimed his pistol at the man's head and pulled the trigger.

"He killed many of my men and many of your people," Loan told Adams. The *New York Times* caption echoed Loan's justification for his act. "GUERILLA DIES: Brig. Gen. Nguyen Ngoc Loan, national police chief, executes man identified as a Vietcong terrorist in Saigon. Man wore civilian dress and had a pistol."

Instead of just retribution many Americans saw an execution. Prisoners of war have the right to a trial under international law, critics argued.

This striking image of one man's death became a symbol of the failed U.S. effort to establish the rule of law in South Vietnam, prompting fears that American soldiers were killing prisoners of war as well.

Adams regretted taking a photo that forever tarnished the reputation of Loan, whom he felt had simply acted impetuously in the heat of combat. "Pictures do not always tell the full story, and this is one case where that is true," Adams contended.

Supporters of Loan noted that the Vietcong ruthlessly executed thousands of South Vietnamese officials and police during the Tet Offensive.

Why did this image become the defining one of the Tet Offensive?

In 1966 *Life* photographer Larry Burrows went into the field with a group of marines trying to stop North Vietnamese infiltration through the demilitarized zone along the seventeenth parallel, a combat-free strip of land that separated North and South Vietnam. He snapped this image of a wounded black soldier reaching out to a white buddy sprawled on the ground. *Life* magazine published the photo twice, once right after Burrows took it and again in 1971 to eulogize Burrows when a helicopter crash in Laos took his life.

In their letters to *Life* magazine, many readers felt that Burrows's portrait illustrated how the shared burden of combat inspired men to transcend the "great racial problems" of American society. Burrows's photo gave some viewers hope that whether "purple, polka-dotted or streaked," Americans could also learn to live together as brothers at home.

In his captioning Burrows emphasized soldiers' suffering in the midst of combat, simply noting, "At a first-aid center, during Operation Prairie, a wounded GI reaches out towards a stricken comrade."

The interracial compassion captured by Burrows's photo told only one side of the story. Racial conflict permeated the armed forces in the rear and on ships, suggesting that fighting together did not magically heal the racial divide.

The wounded soldier lies in a crucifix position, establishing a symbolic link between Christ who suffered on the cross to redeem humankind and a soldier sacrificing his life to save his nation.

How does this image compare to combat photographs from World War II and the Korean War (see Chapters 23 and 24)?

Controversy on the Home Front

Advocates for peace have opposed every American war, but their dissent rarely influenced the mainstream political debate. During the Vietnam War these rebellious voices offering an alternative vision of peace moved from the fringes to the center of American political life. Building in strength as more Americans began to oppose the war, the peace movement made itself visible through mass demonstrations, propaganda posters, and press coverage of celebrities who joined. The very existence of a vocal peace movement in the midst of a war, however, also invited controversy because Americans held differing views on the legitimacy of wartime dissent. Many peace activists believed they were preserving the American tradition of freedom on speech. Public opinion polls from 1965 to 1973, however, consistently showed that the majority of Americans disliked both the war and the peace movement.

The Antiwar Movement

In announcing his 1968 decision not to run for reelection, Johnson noted that "there is division in the American house right now." In the 1960s the rise of a youth-based counterculture and a powerful civil rights movement roiled the country (see Chapter 27). The night of his announcement, however, Johnson was referring to the domestic debate over the war in Vietnam.

Although many working- and middle-class people opposed the war, overcoming existing cultural and class divisions in American society to create a unified antiwar movement proved difficult. The organized antiwar movement tended to attract mostly white, middle-class, college-educated Americans or individuals already engaged in crusades of social justice. Working-class women and African Americans, many with grade-school educations and low-paying jobs, opposed the war in large numbers, but had little interest in marching alongside middle-class college students in street demonstrations.

> "Hey, hey LBJ, how many kids did you kill today?"
>
> A popular chant during antiwar demonstrations

Uniting around one universal vision also posed difficulties for the antiwar movement. All peace activists wanted to end the war in Vietnam, but they offered different arguments for doing so. Some made a primarily moral argument. They claimed that a war involving napalm, search-and-destroy missions, and forced relocation into strategic hamlets hurt the Vietnamese more than living under Communist rule did. Others focused on the futility of fighting an unwinnable civil war. Another group accepted that the nation needed to stop Communist China from expanding its influence. They argued that working with Ho Chi Minh could accomplish this goal more effectively than fighting a war in Vietnam. These critics noted that while Ho accepted Chinese aid to fight the United States, he was leery of Chinese ambitions to control Vietnam. America had worked successfully in Europe with the independently minded communist leader Josip Broz Tito in Yugoslavia to contain Soviet ambitions in the Balkans. Why could it not do the same in Vietnam? Other activists saw a chance to open the nation's eyes to injustice at home, as well as overseas. Student leaders from the nation's top universities founded the Students for a Democratic Society (SDS) at Port Huron, Michigan, in 1962. A leader in the New Left movement, SDS combined staunch opposition to the war with a scathing critique of the inequities of capitalism (see Chapter 27).

Although peace advocates differed on their reasons for opposing the war, they agreed that the war was destroying American democracy. They noted a number of violations of American democratic values: going to war without a formal declaration of war from Congress, presidential secrets and lies, FBI surveillance of peace protesters, and unjust draft deferments for middle- and upper-class men who could afford to go to college. When civil rights leader Martin Luther King Jr. spoke out against the war in 1967, he denounced both the destruction of Vietnamese culture and the war's negative impact on African Americans. The war's

What differing visions did peace activists offer on the war?

high cost diverted funds away from antipoverty programs at home, King rightly contended. The disproportionately high numbers of African American men fighting and dying in Vietnam further illustrated ongoing racial injustice within the United States, he continued. (King's criticism was valid in 1967, but over the course of the entire war black soldiers did not incur higher casualty rates than the rest of the population.) One antiwar poster (**26.11**) captured this link between racial inequality and the war by picturing two African American soldiers as they advanced into the jungle under the headline, "The only time we're in the front is when it's time to die." The rebuke against King for these statements was swift and severe, including criticism from civil rights activists who worried that his antiwar views would discredit their cause. King died a year later from an assassin's bullet, cutting short his career as a civil rights leader and antiwar activist.

The peace movement brought the debate over the war out of the halls of government and into the streets. In 1965 University of Michigan faculty and students organized the first teach-in, a series of public lectures and debates protesting the war. Over the next eight years, scholars and students on hundreds of other college campuses held teach-ins. Some teach-ins invited counterprotests. At the conclusion of a teach-in at the University of Wisconsin, for example, six thousand students signed a petition supporting President Johnson. Like other segments of American society, college students held differing views about the war.

The draft made the war more than an abstract humanitarian or foreign policy question for millions of American men. Male college students would lose their draft deferments once they graduated, giving many personal, as well as political and moral, reasons to oppose the war. Peace activists organized ceremonies where men burned the notices from their draft boards ordering them to report for induction. When fifteen hundred peace activists gathered in New York City in 1965 to watch five men burn their draft cards, an onlooker bolted from the crowd with a fire extinguisher and doused the protesters before the cards caught fire. The shower failed to deter the activists, however, who managed to ignite their soggy draft cards while hundreds of New Yorkers stood on the other side of police barricades and chanted "Burn yourselves, not your cards!" a macabre reminder, perhaps unintentional, of the Buddhist suicides in Vietnam in 1963.

Going on the offensive Johnson tried to discredit the peace movement by claiming it was communist-run and gave solace to the enemy. Other defenders of the war openly charged the peace movement with treason. Some war supporters felt differently, however. Revulsion against the peace movement, they contended, helped bolster the resolve of Americans in the political center to stay the course.

The outcome of the 1968 presidential election suggested that the peace movement had helped the conservative cause. The presumption that Senator Robert Kennedy, brother of the slain president, would seek the Democratic Party nomination as a peace candidate had encouraged Johnson to abandon a quest for a second term. On June 4, 1968, Sirhan Sirhan, a Jordanian immigrant upset with Kennedy's pro-Israel stance, shot and killed the senator as he walked through the kitchen of a California hotel moments after finishing his victory speech for winning the state primary. At the Chicago nominating convention, the Democratic Party

26.11 Stop the War. It's Killing Us This antiwar poster highlighted the disproportionate numbers of African Americans fighting and dying on the frontlines in the late 1960s, linking that imbalance to continued racial inequity in American society.

How did domestic concerns influence the peace movement?

Dueling Bumper Stickers

"Peace Through Victory in Vietnam"

"Join the Army; travel to exotic distant lands; meet exciting, unusual people and kill them."

selected Vice President Hubert Humphrey as their presidential candidate, a man much like Johnson who supported liberal causes at home and the war in Vietnam. Instead of uniting liberal and conservative Democrats, Humphrey's candidacy badly fractured the party. Outside the convention hall radical antiwar protesters denounced his nomination and clashed violently with police. "The war is destroying our country as we are destroying Vietnam," the writer I. F. Stone lamented.

Believing that the protesters, rather than the police, had gone too far in Chicago, many working- and middle-class Americans responded positively to Republican candidate Richard Nixon's call for a return to "law and order." During the campaign Nixon suggested that he had a "secret plan" to bring about a "peace with honor" that he could not reveal to the enemy. The election became a three-man race when Alabama governor George Wallace entered as an independent candidate, attracting conservative southern whites and white northern blue-collar workers with his attacks on integration, elites in Washington, D.C., and antiwar protesters. "If any demonstrator ever lays [*sic*] down in front of my car," Wallace proclaimed, "it'll be the last car he'll ever lay [*sic*] down in front of." As election day neared Humphrey picked up some liberal support by pledging to end bombing over North Vietnam immediately. Despite losing some conservatives votes to Wallace, Nixon won the electoral college vote handily but only received 40 percent of the popular vote (**26.12**).

Rising public opposition to the war never resulted in widespread support for the peace movement. Most Americans remained staunchly anticommunist, even as their dissatisfaction with the war in Vietnam grew. Gallup Polls in 1969 revealed that by a margin of 55 percent to 31 percent, Americans labeled themselves as doves not hawks and most described the war as indefensible. Three-fifths, however, also believed that the peace movement helped the enemy and made it more difficult for the president to end the war. Americans, it seemed, wanted an end to the fighting overseas and at home.

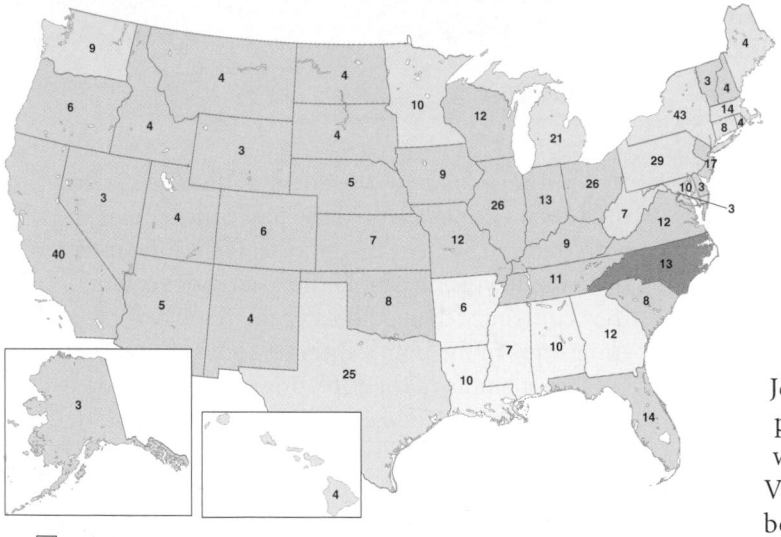

4 Electoral vote by state	Electoral Vote (%)	Popular Vote (%)
Richard M. Nixon *(Republican)*	301 (56)	31,785,480 (44)
Hubert H. Humphrey *(Democratic)*	191 (35)	31,275,166 (42)
George C. Wallace *(American Independent)*	46 (%)	9,906,473 (14)
North Carolina *(Electors split)*	12 for Nixon 1 for Wallace	

26.12 The Presidential Election of 1968 Republican Richard Nixon won easily in the electoral college, but he received only about a half million more popular votes that his Democratic Party opponent, Hubert Humphrey.

My Lai

Johnson had calmed the American public in March 1968 by announcing he would open negotiations with the North Vietnamese. Keeping his promise, he began fruitless negotiations between Hanoi and Washington. Johnson continued trying, however, to win the war before he left office. Believing that a final push against a severely weakened enemy could finish the job, American soldiers renewed their attacks on the Vietcong. The largest search-and-destroy missions of the war occurred in March and April, involv-

Why did the peace movement have trouble winning support from mainstream America?

ing more than a hundred thousand troops. During one of these in the village of **My Lai**, American soldiers massacred five hundred civilians, an atrocity that fueled the strident domestic debate over the American mission in Vietnam.

On March 16, 1968, seventy-five American soldiers in two platoons under the command of Lieutenant William Calley entered My Lai. Leading up to the mission, these troops had spent long days wading through the rice paddies and even longer nights battling snipers and insects, looking for Vietcong forces who had killed a popular sergeant the week before. By the time the men approached My Lai, they were in an ugly mood. In making their attack during the morning hours, the company's officers anticipated that their troops would confront 250 enemy troops and very few civilians, whom the Americans expected would follow the usual daily ritual of leaving the village to visit a local market. None of these predictions came to pass. Upon entering the village the men found only unarmed women, children, and elderly in the village. The Vietcong force had retreated into the western mountains before the Americans arrived.

Rather than leaving, however, the American soldiers engaged in a systematic orgy of rape, torture, and slaughter that took four hours to complete and left more than five hundred villagers dead. Army photographer Ron Haeberle snapped this image (**26.13**) of terrified women and children huddled together moments before American soldiers killed them. "Guys were about to shoot these people, I yelled, 'Hold it' and I shot my pictures. As I walked away, I heard M-16s open up, and from the corner of my eye I saw bodies falling but I did not turn to look," Haeberle recalled. Seeing the carnage from the air, pilot Hugh Thompson landed his helicopter between the soldiers and one group of eleven survivors, whom he flew to safety. Thompson reported the atrocity to his superiors to no avail. Only the perseverance of Ron Ridenhour, a sergeant who was not even at My Lai, finally brought the massacre to light. After hearing stories from men who took part, an outraged Ridenhour wrote to President Nixon, the Pentagon, and members of Congress. When the story broke in 1969 Haeberle sold his photos to *Life* magazine. An official military investigation headed by Lieutenant General William Peers followed, resulting in the court martial of Lieutenant Calley for premeditated murder.

Calley's arrest, trial, and 1971 conviction exposed Americans' conflicting views over the meaning of My Lai. Was the atrocity a unique episode or representative of American conduct in Vietnam? *Competing Visions: Who Was Responsible for the My Lai Massacre?* (page 800) explores this question in further detail. Responding to the public outcry over Calley's conviction, the secretary of the army Howard "Bo" Callaway first reduced Calley's life sentence to ten years, and then eventually pardoned Calley after he had served only five months in prison. By this time Calley had undergone a striking transformation from villain to hero in the American imagination. People on both the left and the right of the political spectrum defended Calley. The left saw him as a scapegoat for failed American policies, while the right argued that civilians were fair targets in a guerilla war.

26.13 My Lai Villagers Moments before their Execution, 1968 Americans expressed more outrage over the publication of photographs from My Lai than over the actual killings.

Why did photos of the My Lai massacre provoke conflicting responses from Americans?

Competing Visions

WHO WAS RESPONSIBLE FOR THE MY LAI MASSACRE?

Americans disagreed over who bore responsibility for the massacre at My Lai. Some commentators focused on the individuals directly involved in the killings, others on the orders given by higher-ranking officials to destroy the village. As you read the following excerpts, try to reconstruct the domestic dispute over My Lai. Is one argument stronger than the other? Who was to blame: Calley, the two platoons, the commanding officers, or the American people?

Fellow soldier Dennis Conti told army investigators that he saw Calley and Private Paul Meadlo kill civilians in the village of My Lai.

They were bringing people out [of their huts], and then we pushed them out into the rice paddy, onto the dike there … Lieutenant Calley came back, and said: "Take care of them." So we said: "Okay." And we sat there and watched them like we usually do. And he came back again, and he said: "I thought I told you to take care of them." I said: "We're taking care of them," and he said: "I mean kill them." So I looked at Meadlo and he looked at me, and I didn't want to do it, and he didn't want to do it … then [Calley] said: "Come on, we'll line them up here, we'll kill them." So I told him: "I'll watch the tree line" … Then they opened up, and started firing. Meadlo fired a while. I don't know how much he fired, a clip, I think. It might have been more. He started to cry, and he gave me his weapon.

This *New York Times* editorial suggested that higher-ranking officials than Calley bore some responsibility for ordering and observing the My Lai massacre.

Who gave the orders? Who knew what was going on? Was any attempt made to stop it? Who is responsible? … [Paul Meadlo] was one of 18 witnesses to describe a briefing the night before the assault at which Captain [Ernest L.] Medina told the men they were going into battle with a hardened Vietcong battalion; that their mission was "search and destroy" and they were to destroy everything in the hamlet—houses, crops and people … Helicopter pilots, radio men and artillery observers said the higher officers had flown over the scene for several hours and had seen bodies on the ground, had conference with the other officers and, as one pilot said, "knew what was going on" all through the day … the Geneva conventions, the Nuremburg doctrines and the Army's own rules of land warfare make plain that obedience to orders is not a blanket defense, that orders that to a "prudent" or "reasonable" man seem patently illegal need not be obeyed. The question here, then, is whether the order, if that is what it was, to kill everything was one that a prudent man should obey when he found that everything included women, children, and infants.

The *National Review* rejected suggestions that the nation bore the blame and should abandon the war in Vietnam.

"That America and Americans must stand in the larger dock of guilt and human conscience for what happened at My Lai seems inescapable." So observed *Time* [magazine], adding: "Men in American uniforms slaughtered the civilians of My Lai, and in so doing humiliated the U.S. and called in question the U.S. mission in Vietnam in a way that all the antiwar protesters could never have done." One's mind staggers: Are "America and Americans" generally guilty, the same America and Americans now preparing to bring the accused to trial? And even if it turns out that atrocities were committed, how does this call in question the U.S. mission in Vietnam? Do the innumerable atrocities committed by both sides in World War II add up to the proposition that resistance to the Nazis ought to have been abandoned? … Irrational and irresponsible comment on [My Lai] has become collective madness.

***Time* Magazine Cover, Lieutenant William Calley**

What was the ultimate historic significance of the My Lai massacre?

The Long Road to Peace

When Richard Nixon entered the White House in 1969, he told his advisors, "I'm going to stop that war. Fast." Nixon was also intent, however, on preserving America's international reputation. He had a different vision from his predecessor, he assured the public, pledging to seek "peace with honor." Nixon's promises proved empty, however. The war did not end quickly, but continued for four more years. At home Nixon benefited politically by portraying the peace movement as out of step with the values of law-abiding citizens. When Nixon extended the war into Laos and Cambodia and became embroiled in political scandal, his actions fueled the ongoing political debate over whether Americans could trust their government.

Seeking Peace with Honor

For Nixon a peace with honor meant winning the war. Nixon and his national security advisor , Henry Kissinger, pursued four different tactics to achieve this goal. First Nixon implemented **Vietnamization**, a policy that turned the bulk of the ground fighting over to the South Vietnamese Army. The gradual reduction of American forces in Vietnam took until 1971 to dramatically shrink the American presence in Vietnam. In many respects this was a return to the pre-1965 approach, when America propped up an independent South Vietnam with financial and military aid. Announcing Vietnamization in November 1969, Nixon asked for support from "the great **silent majority** of Americans," referring to the large number of Americans who supported the war quietly in the privacy of their homes. He also issued a rebuke to the peace movement. "Let us be united for peace. Let us also be united against defeat. Because let us understand: North Vietnam cannot defeat or humiliate the United States. Only Americans can do that." Polls indicated that the "silent majority" overwhelmingly supported the president's plan.

Vietnamization promised to give the country exactly what it wanted: victory with minimal loss of American lives. The United States quickly transformed the South Vietnamese Army into one of the largest and best-equipped military forces in the world. At the ongoing peace talks, a North Vietnamese negotiator wondered aloud how the United States, when it could not win with its own troops, thought it could "succeed when you let your puppet troops do the fighting." That dilemma, Kissinger admitted, "also torments me."

In implementing Vietnamization Nixon hoped to disarm the peace movement by replacing images of civilian suffering on the evening news with pictures of troops withdrawing and returning home. In March 1970 Nixon announced the incremental withdrawal of another 150,000 soldiers to "drop a bombshell on the gathering spring storm of anti-war protest." He simultaneously reformed the draft, replacing the controversial deferment system with a lottery that randomly drafted men by date of birth. Nixon hoped these policy changes would buy his administration enough time to win the war.

The controversial actions of some peace activists inadvertently helped Nixon solidify the support of Middle America. In 1972 the actress Jane Fonda accepted an invitation from the North Vietnamese government to visit Hanoi. While in the enemy capital city, she made a series of radio broadcasts urging American pilots to mutiny. A photo of Fonda joking with North Vietnamese soldiers as she sat on an antiaircraft gun used to shoot down American planes created a backlash against the peace movement that Nixon effectively exploited.

Vietnamization was more than a reaction to declining popular support for fighting in Vietnam. It was also part of Nixon's attempt to reshape the role that the United States played in global geopolitics. Nixon and Kissinger viewed the longstanding vision of a bipolar world that pitted the United States against the Soviet Union as obsolete. They embraced a competing strategic vision of multipolarity that focused on negotiating with Europe, China, Japan, and the Soviet Union to construct a new balance of power system to keep the peace. In this foreign policy reformulation, the United States would refrain from direct involvement in regional conflicts, such as Vietnam. The Nixon Doctrine, formulated in 1969 and 1970, announced that the United States expected its friends to take the lead in defending themselves.

Nixon's second tactic linked Vietnamization to the resumption of massive bombing in North Vietnam, which Johnson had halted when he

What motivated Nixon to implement Vietnamization?

Vietnam

THE WAR BY THE NUMBERS

Millions of Americans and Vietnamese fought in America's longest war to date, a conflict that exacted a high death toll and left many soldiers and civilians with lifelong wounds. The United States tried to use its air superiority to win the war, dropping more bombs in the Vietnam War than in World War II. The reliance on air power increased dramatically when the United States began pulling out troops in 1969. The numbers of draft evaders fleeing to Canada, the rising number of antiwar demonstrations, and public opinion polls illustrated the growing unpopularity of the war at home.

Total Serving in the American Military (worldwide)	8.7 million men 250,00 women
Total Serving in Vietnam	3.4 million men 6,421 women
Total Killed in Vietnam	47,415 battle deaths 10,785 other causes
Total Wounded	153,303
Total Draft Evaders	600,000 (tens of thousands fled to Canada)
Vietnamese Casualties (North and South)	2 million
Total Cost of War	$173 billion

The Human and Financial Cost of the Vietnam War, 1964–1973

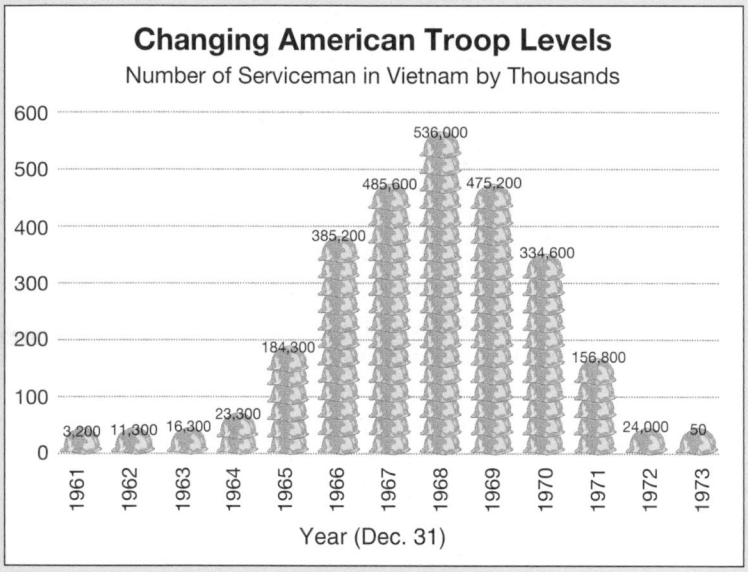

	Defoliation in South Vietnam (acres)	Crop Destruction in South Vietnam (acres)	Bombs Dropped on North Vietnam (tons)
1962	4,940	741	0
1963	24,700	247	0
1964	83,486	10,374	100
1965	155,610	65,949	63,000
1966	741,247	103,987	136,000
1967	1,486,446	221,312	226,000
1968	1,267,110	63,726	175,000
1969	1.198,444	64,961	659
1970	220,324	32,604	892
1971	0	0	1,842
1972	0	0	218,561
Total	**4,747,587**	**481,897**	**822,054**

Destruction in Vietnam, 1962–1972

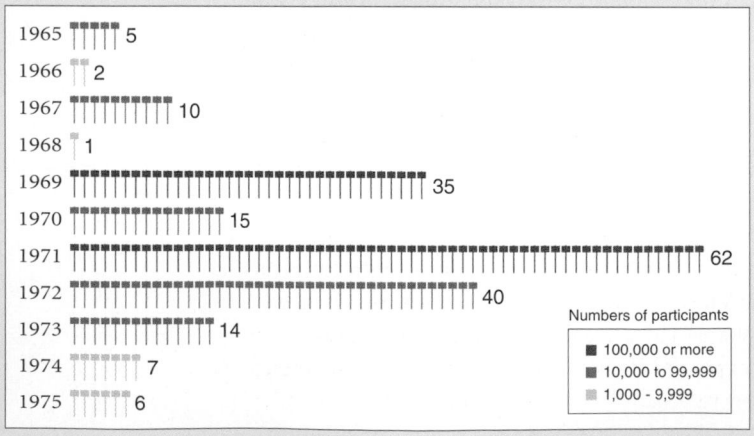

Antiwar demonstrations in Washington, D.C., 1965–1975

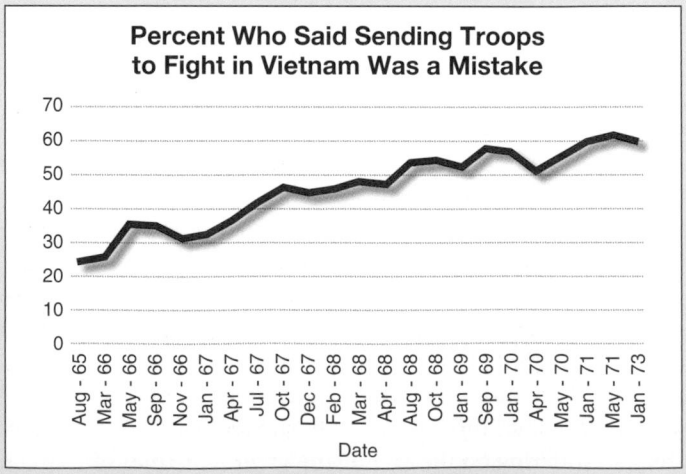

Public Opinion and the Vietnam War, 1965–1973

What does this data reveal about the various stages of America's involvement in Vietnam?

initiated peace talks in 1968. As American troops left Vietnam between 1969 and 1972, the number of bombs dropped increased spectacularly (see this shift in the "Changing American Troops Levels" and "Destruction in Vietnam, 1965–1973" charts in *Vietnam: The War by the Numbers*). America had not used enough military force to achieve victory, the president and Kissinger concluded. They intended to correct this problem. For a while the news of troop withdrawals successfully diverted attention from the intensified bombing of North Vietnam.

Alongside Vietnamization and renewed bombing of North Vietnam, Nixon and Kissinger's third tactic used diplomacy to decrease Soviet and Chinese support for North Vietnam. Recognizing the existing discord between China and the Soviet Union, Nixon pursued independent negotiations with each nation to strengthen their ties to the United States and deepen their distrust of each other. Nixon reshaped the Cold War by pursuing his vision of multipolarity through **détente**, using diplomatic, economic, and cultural contacts to improve U.S. relations with China and the Soviet Union. Fearing that the United States might form an alliance with the other, the Soviet Union and China each eagerly accepted these overtures. In return for a more congenial relationship with the United States, Nixon expected China and the Soviet Union to end their support of North Vietnam. Although both countries continued to send aid to North Vietnam, once they decided to normalize trade relations and enter into arms limitations agreement with the United States, the Soviet Union and China began pressuring Hanoi to seek a negotiated peace.

Cambodia: Invasion and Outrage

The fourth tactical component of Nixon's Vietnam policy involved the neutral country of Cambodia, which bordered Vietnam to the west. In 1969 Nixon initiated a secret bombing campaign of Cambodia. He hoped to cut off supplies filtering through the Ho Chi Minh Trail and thus pressure North Vietnam into accepting the American terms for peace that included an independent South Vietnam.

In April 1970 Nixon shattered the public consensus he had carefully created for Vietnamization by ordering an American ground force invasion of Cambodia. Before the invasion Nixon sought inspiration from repeated showings of the movie *Patton* in the White House, a film that portrayed the hard-nosed and belligerent World War II tank commander leading American forces to victory. Going public with his plans, Nixon announced in a televised speech that American troops needed to destroy Communist bases in Cambodia to help the South Vietnamese army defeat the Vietcong. The two-month-long incursion succeeded only in pushing the North Vietnamese farther into the interior of Cambodia, where they began supporting the Khmer Rouge, Communist rebels who assumed power in Cambodia in 1975 and unleashed a wave of mass murder so brutal that the country became known as "the killing fields."

Nixon's claim that he was expanding the war to end it sooner persuaded few. Protest erupted on college campuses nationwide and in Congress where the Senate symbolically terminated the Gulf of Tonkin Resolution. Many university demonstrations turned violent as protesters clashed with police and set fire to college buildings. A defiant Nixon stood his ground, assuming that the "silent majority" agreed with his assessment that the protesters were just "bums blowing up the campuses."

In Kent, Ohio, student-organized demonstrations protesting the invasion of Cambodia took a nasty turn, recalled Phil Caputo, who had left the Marines after two tours in Vietnam and was now a reporter for the *Chicago Tribune*. In a May weekend rampage, "store windows had been smashed in town, [and] radicals had burned down the ROTC building," according to Caputo. Calling the protesters "the worst sort of people we harbor in America," Ohio governor James Allen Rhodes promised to "use every weapon possible to eradicate the problem," as he sent National Guardsmen to restore order.

On Monday morning a few hundred students gathered on the campus of Kent State University for a rally, defying a campuswide ban on protests. National Guardsmen fired tear gas into the crowd to disperse the demonstrators, who responded by throwing rocks, unexploded tear gas cans, and obscenities at the troops. Suddenly, as bystanders and students on their way to class watched the mini-battle unfurl, the troops sprayed bullets into the crowd, leaving four dead and nine wounded. The National Guardsmen claimed that they had fired in self-defense when protesters began throwing concrete slabs. Two of the victims were passers-by, however, and all four were too far away from the troops to have hit them with anything more than pebbles.

How did Nixon try to win the war?

Responding to Nixon's earlier characterization of the protesters, the father of one of the dead girls told reporters, "My child was not a bum." The cover of *Life* magazine (**26.14**) showed terrified students trying to save the life of one victim, underscoring that the war's killing had come home to America. This photo, along with the others inside the magazine, inspired musician Neil Young to write the song "Ohio" to protest the shootings, the war, and the Nixon administration. "A nation driven to use the weapons of war upon its youth is a nation on the edge of chaos," concluded the presidential commission that investigated the Kent State incident.

> "Tin soldiers and Nixon coming,
> We're finally on our own.
> This summer I hear the drumming,
> Four dead in Ohio."
>
> Lyrics from Neil Young's song "Ohio," written in response to the Kent State shootings

The Kent State shootings unmasked the growing "town and gown" divide over the war and latent anger at the peace movement. "They should have shot more of them," suggested one Kent resident, still angry over the weekend riot. Many radio stations refused to play Young's "anti-Nixon" song. While protests over the shooting engulfed more than half the nation's college campuses, working-class unions staged counter-protests in support of the war. In New York City hundreds of longshoremen wearing hard hats attacked students who were protesting the Cambodian invasion. During a subsequent meeting at the White House, sympathetic labor leaders presented the president a "commander-in-chief" hard hat.

The wave of protests after the Kent State shootings nonetheless bothered Nixon. At the end of a sleepless night on May 9, 1970, the president made an impulsive decision to have his valet drive him, without his Secret Service detail, to the Lincoln Memorial at five o'clock in the morning so he could talk to the antiwar demonstrators camped out there. According to the protesters Nixon talked disjointedly about college sports and surfing and assured them that he shared their wish for peace in Vietnam.

Despite his clumsy attempt to talk directly with peace activists, Nixon remained determined to see the war through to victory. Clinging to the belief that success would vindicate his methods, Nixon expanded the theater of war once again in February 1971 by ordering an invasion of Laos. This time South Vietnamese troops fought on the ground with American air support. Once again, however, the hopes of permanently disrupting enemy supply lines along the Ho Chi Minh Trail bore meager results. Administration officials claimed that the Laos invasion illustrated the success of Vietnamization. Skeptics pointed to the sight of South Vietnamese soldiers clinging in panic to the skids of departing helicopters during their chaotic retreat back into South Vietnam.

In the summer of 1971 the *New York Times* published the Pentagon Papers, a secret Department of Defense study that criticized the way Kennedy and Johnson had handled the war, further stoking the flames of antiwar sentiment in the wake of the Calley conviction, the failed Cambodian and Laos invasions,

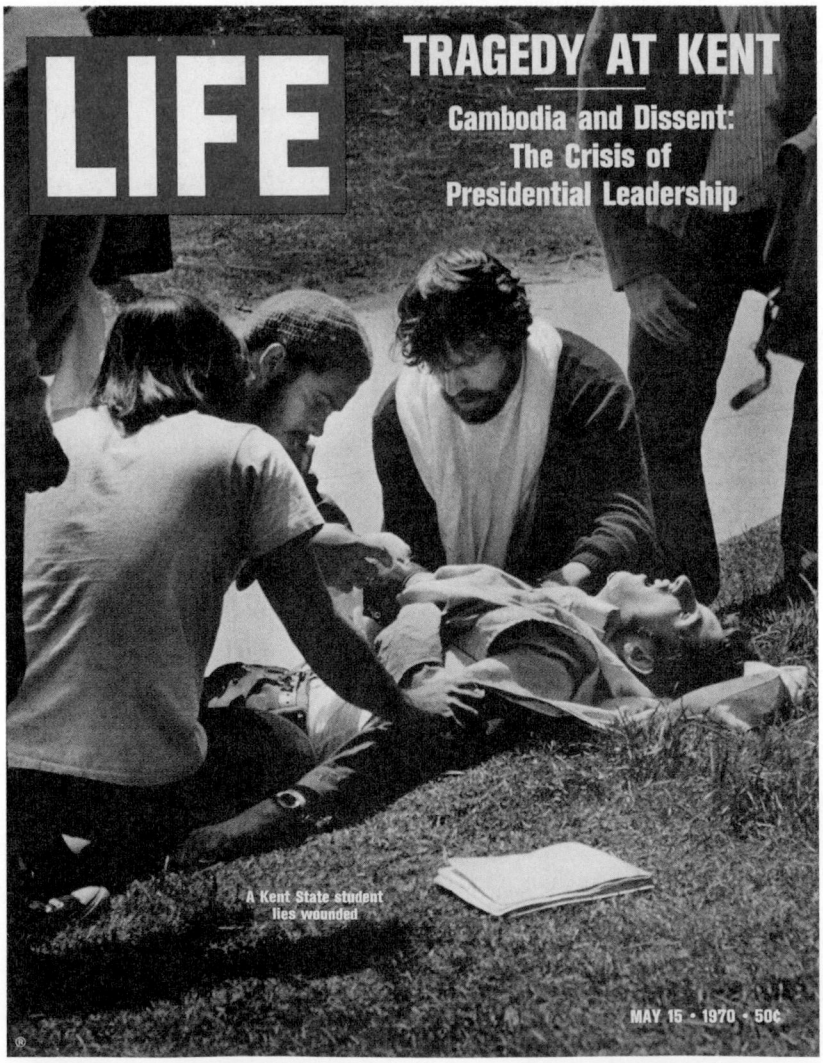

26.14 Kent State University, 1970
The images of students wounded and killed at Kent State University by National Guardsmen prompted fears in some quarters that a war undertaken to protect American democracy was instead destroying it.

What competing visions emerged in response to the Kent State killings?

and the Kent State killings. Pentagon official Daniel Ellsberg leaked the Pentagon Papers which confirmed that presidents Kennedy and Johnson had intentionally lied to the public about the extent of previous American involvement in the war. Many Americans assumed that Nixon was misleading the country as well. By now only 34 percent of Americans approved of Nixon's handling of the war.

Controversy over the war seeped into the military as well. Morale plummeted as soldiers became increasingly unwilling to put their lives on the line for a cause that the nation seemed poised to abandon. Disobedience took a deadly turn in 1970 when the military reported nearly two hundred incidents of "fragging," deadly attacks by enlisted men on officers, named for the hand grenade fragments that did most of the damage in these fraternal attacks. Escalating use of marijuana, opium, and heroin, all readily available in Vietnam, among servicemen served as another sign of disintegrating discipline.

> "How do you ask a man to be the last man to die for a mistake?"
>
> Vietnam veteran and antiwar activist
> JOHN KERRY

Withdrawal

Nixon envisioned détente creating a new world order in which the United States used trade agreements and arms limitation treaties to curtail the expansionist ambitions of its enemies. The Nixon administration made great headway with this approach in 1972, beginning with a highly publicized trip to China in February and culminating with a May summit meeting in Moscow. The carefully orchestrated pictures of the staunch anticommunist Nixon toasting China's communist leader Mao during an official banquet and lauding the achievements of Chinese civilization during a trek to the Great Wall signaled an important turning point in Sino-American relations. Improved relations with China also demolished one of the main arguments used to justify the war in Vietnam. American leaders had always linked the war in Vietnam to the larger American goal of containing communism in Southeast Asia. They considered the region, rather than the country, vital to American strategic interests overseas. Nixon now demonstrated that diplomacy could perhaps achieve the goal of containing communism in Southeast Asia more effectively. Why then, many Americans wondered, was the nation still fighting in Vietnam?

North Vietnam reacted with alarm to improving relations between its communist benefactors and the United States. When the North Vietnamese grumbled about Mao shaking hands with Nixon, Mao advised them to sign a peace treaty, regroup while the Americans withdrew, and then resume the war. North Vietnam eventually followed Mao's advice. They first tried, however, to replicate the political success of the Tet Offensive by launching a major invasion of the south. The North Vietnamese timed the so-called Easter Offensive of March 1972 to coincide with the start of the American presidential campaign. In response Nixon ordered a massive retaliation against North Vietnam that included bombing, a blockade, and the mining of a key harbor.

Unlike Tet the Easter Offensive did not greatly alter the political equation in the United States or worldwide. At home Nixon's approval ratings rose for defending South Vietnam from attack. Moving from his successful meeting in China to Moscow, the U.S.-Soviet summit proceeded as planned. When Nixon returned with the first disarmament agreement ever signed by the Soviet Union, he bolstered his image as a tough negotiator who got results. The Strategic Arms Limitation Treaty (SALT I) set limits on how many intercontinental ballistic missiles and submarine-launched missiles each side could stockpile, and restricted the number of antimissile launching pads. Once again, however, Nixon's diplomatic success undercut his argument that the United States needed an anti-Communist South Vietnam to win the Cold War.

By the summer of 1972, both the United States and North Vietnam concluded that the costs of continued fighting had become too great. Recognizing that Democratic presidential candidate Senator George McGovern of South Dakota, a peace advocate who promised to withdraw U.S. troops from Vietnam, was trailing in the polls, the North Vietnamese decided to seek the best terms possible from Nixon. Although Nixon had successfully discredited McGovern by suggesting that he would abandon American POWs in Vietnam, the president was also eager to negotiate. With his reelection assured Nixon wanted to fulfill his earlier campaign promise to end the war so he could pursue his larger goal of refashioning Cold War relations among the world's superpowers.

Despite this renewed willingness on both sides to negotiate, it still took months to seal the deal.

How did Nixon reshape the contours of the Cold War?

The final 1973 peace treaty called for American withdrawal, allowed North Vietnamese troops to remain in South Vietnam, and left the existing South Vietnamese government in place. All left the Paris negotiating table knowing that the cease-fire existed only on paper. The war would go on, only now without American advisors, soldiers, or pilots.

Despite the spiral downward in Vietnam, Nixon retained a durable base of domestic support due to the success of détente with China and the Soviet Union and his effective portrayal of the antiwar movement as out of step with mainstream America. This political base, however, eroded quickly when Nixon became embroiled in a major political scandal. The **Watergate scandal (1972)**, a botched Republican-engineered break-in of the Democratic National Committee headquarters in Washington, D.C., eventually forced Nixon to resign in 1974. On June 17, 1972, members of Nixon's campaign staff had broken into the Watergate building office to fix broken wiretaps (listening devices on telephones) that they had installed during a previous burglary in May. The combined force of steady congressional challenges to his Vietnam policies and ongoing investigations into potential criminal activity by Nixon and members of his administration (see Chapter 28), severely weakened Nixon politically as he began his second term.

In the midst of the Watergate crisis, Congress passed the War Powers Resolution to curtail presidential war-making powers. The 1973 law required congressional approval for any deployment of American troops overseas that lasted for more than sixty days. Some critics pressed for even greater restrictions, arguing that the constitutional authority to declare war lay solely with Congress whether a war lasted sixty days or sixty years. Nixon countered that the law interfered with the president's constitutional role as commander in chief of the armed forces. Ignoring Congress's desire to end American involvement in Vietnam, Nixon tried to continue funneling money and arms to South Vietnam. In response Congress sharply reduced funding for South Vietnam in 1974.

When Nixon resigned the presidency on August 9, 1974 to avoid impeachment, Vice-President Gerald Ford assumed office. (Nixon had appointed Ford as his vice president in 1973 when Spiro Agnew resigned following an unrelated corruption scandal.) The political controversy at home and Americans' widespread distrust of executive power in the wake of the failed war in Vietnam and the Watergate scandal weakened President

26.15 The Final Evacuation
Fleeing Vietnamese scramble for a spot aboard an American helicopter as the North Vietnamese Army approaches Saigon in 1975, a final portrait of the failed American mission in Vietnam.

How did the Vietnam War finally end for the United States and the Vietnamese?

Ford's ability to respond to the imminent collapse of South Vietnam. In March 1975 North Vietnam renewed its offensive. With no American help in the offing, South Vietnam quickly succumbed. Within eight weeks North Vietnamese troops neared Saigon. They walked along highways littered with boots and uniforms discarded by deserting South Vietnamese Army soldiers who hoped to blend into the civilian population and avoid execution.

Ho Chi Minh did not live to see the end of the war (he died in 1969), but the Communists renamed Saigon "Ho Chi Minh City" in his honor. Final victory in the thirty-year conflict did not end civilian suffering in Vietnam, however. Famine and prison camps caused thousands to flee in overcrowded boats for refuge camps in Thailand and Malaysia where they faced an uncertain future waiting for permanent asylum in the United States or Europe.

For America the war concluded with the image of South Vietnamese citizens climbing a ladder on the roof of the American Embassy to board one of the American helicopters that flew American citizens and 150,000 South Vietnamese to safety in the final days of the war (**26.15**). The frantic evacuation provided a disheartening end to America's longest war. How to remember such a divisive and controversial war continued to provoke debate within the United States. The 1982 Vietnam Veterans Memorial in Washington, D.C., listed all the names of American war dead on two black marble slabs that descended into the ground. "Hidden in a hole, as if in shame," complained one veteran. "It is exactly the right memorial for that war," countered another. Festering rumors that Vietnam was still holding American soldiers hostage deepened public bitterness against the nation's former foe. The United States finally normalized diplomatic relations with Vietnam in 1995, twenty years after the fall of Saigon. It was time, one veteran wrote, "to recognize the truth. The war is over."

Conclusion

The Vietnam War divided the country as no war had since the Civil War. The United States entered the conflict incrementally over the course of four administrations, with President Johnson taking the fateful step of sending ground troops to fight in Vietnam in 1965. His effort to win the war backfired. The political and military quagmire in Vietnam instead consumed thousands of lives and $173 billion. Antiwar activists focused unprecedented attention on the civilian casualties of war, provoking internal debate over the increasingly unpopular war and an equally disliked peace movement. On the ground American soldiers struggled against a determined guerilla force, often finding it difficult to separate friend from foe. President Nixon's attempt to parlay victory on the battlefield into success at the negotiating table also failed. When the United States withdrew in 1973, both South Vietnam and the United States suffered the consequences of the unsuccessful American war effort. North Vietnam quickly overran South Vietnam.

The war made Americans leery of embarking on other overseas military adventures and created a deeply felt cynicism that caused many to distrust any statement coming from the president. The breach of faith between Americans and the federal government temporarily weakened the presidency as Congress reasserted some control over foreign policy. The war, however, was only one part of the upheaval that Americans experienced during the 1960s. The Civil Rights Movement, the new youth counterculture, and President Johnson's effort to create a Great Society that eliminated crushing poverty combined to create a strong liberal vision that enthralled some Americans and repulsed others.

Why does the Vietnamese War continue to provoke controversy among Americans?

CHAPTER REVIEW

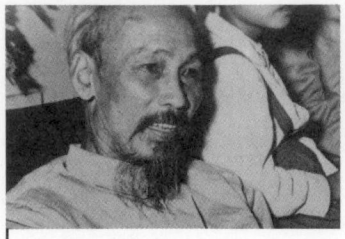

1950

Truman offers aid to French in Vietnam
United States begins financing 80 percent of France's war effort

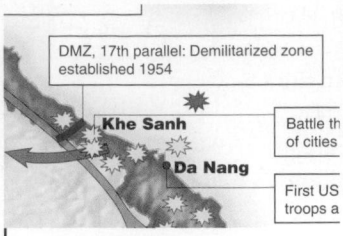

1954

Geneva Accords
Peace settlement between France and Vietminh divides Vietnam at seventeenth parallel

Eisenhower uses domino theory to explain U.S. involvement in Vietnam
Links defeating communism in Vietnam to protecting U.S. interests in Southeast Asia

1963

Buddhist monk sets himself on fire to protest corrupt Diem regime
Kennedy supports overthrow of Diem

President Kennedy assassinated
Johnson resolves to stay the course in Vietnam

Review Questions

1. Consider the nation's gradual intervention in Vietnam. How important were early decisions (1945–1954) in setting the course of U.S. involvement in the Vietnam War?
2. How did the Cold War influence presidential decision making about Vietnam from 1945 to 1975?
3. How did the political situation within Vietnam shape the war?
4. What military challenges did American troops face fighting in Vietnam?
5. How did competing images of the war create turmoil at home?
6. What do the debates surrounding the My Lai massacre and Kent State shootings reveal about Americans' competing visions about the war?

1964–1965

Gulf of Tonkin Resolution
After alleged North Vietnamese attack on U.S. destroyers, Congress gives Johnson permission for military action in Vietnam

American ground forces arrive in Vietnam
Vietnam becomes America's war

1968

Tet Offensive
Major North Vietnamese attack convinces majority of Americans that war is futile

Johnson withdraws from presidential race
Tries to win war before leaving office

My Lai Massacre
Controversy erupts over who was responsible for U.S. troops killing five hundred unarmed villagers

Nixon wins presidency
Promises peace with honor and quick withdrawal from Vietnam

1970

U.S forces invade Cambodia
National Guardsmen fire on protesters at Kent State University, killing four

1973–1975

Paris Peace Accords
Ends direct American involvement in war

North Vietnamese troops enter Saigon
North Vietnam wins the war

Key Terms

Vietminh The term initially used to describe all Vietnamese communists, and used after 1954 solely for North Vietnamese communists. **780**

domino theory The fear that a communist Vietnam would open the door to a complete communist takeover of Southeast Asia. **781**

Geneva Accords (1954) Called for a temporary partition of Vietnam along the seventeenth parallel, with the Vietminh in the north and the French in the south, and a general election in two years to reunify the country under one government. **782**

Southeast Asian Treaty Organization (SEATO) 1954 alliance among the United States, Britain, France, Australia, New Zealand, Thailand, the Philippines, and Pakistan who pledged to "meet common danger" in Southeast Asia together. **783**

Vietcong Slang term for South Vietnamese communists. **783**

Gulf of Tonkin Resolution (1964) Gave Johnson permission "to take all necessary measures to repel any armed attack against the forces of the United States and to prevent further aggression" in Vietnam. **787**

Ho Chi Minh Trail A 600-mile North Vietnamese supply route that ran along the western border of Vietnam through neighboring Laos and Cambodia. **789**

agent orange A defoliant that stripped trees of their leaves to expose Vietcong hideouts and killed crops. **790**

peace movement A loose coalition of antiwar activists that included pacifists, students, professors, clergy, hippies, civil rights activists, and middle-class liberals. **790**

Tet Offensive (1968) A massive, coordinated Communist assault against more than a hundred cities and towns in South Vietnam. **792**

My Lai A Vietnamese village where American soldiers massacred five hundred civilians in 1968. **799**

Vietnamization A Nixon administration policy that turned the bulk of the ground fighting over to the South Vietnamese Army. **801**

silent majority Nixon's term for the large number of Americans who supported the war quietly in the privacy of their homes. **801**

détente Relaxing Cold War tensions by using diplomatic, economic, and cultural contacts to improve U.S. relations with China and the Soviet Union. **803**

Watergate scandal (1972) A botched Republican-engineered break-in of the Democratic National Committee headquarters in Washington, D.C., that eventually forced Nixon to resign in 1974. **806**

CHAPTER 27

A Decade of Discord

The Challenge of The Sixties

> "We know through painful experience that freedom is never voluntarily given by the oppressor; it must be demanded by the oppressed."
>
> MARTIN LUTHER KING JR., 1963

In April 1968 civil rights leader Martin Luther King Jr. traveled to Memphis, Tennessee, to offer his support for a black garbage men's strike. Around 6:00 pm on April 5, 1968, as King leaned over a balcony railing outside his second-story room at the Lorraine Motel to chat with two friends in the courtyard below, shots rang out. A wounded King collapsed on the floor of the balcony, and colleagues frantically tried to stem the bleeding with towels while waiting for the ambulance to arrive. Within an hour hospital doctors pronounced the thirty-eight-year-old minister dead. As news of King's assassination spread, rioting erupted in black communities throughout the nation, and images of violence saturated the television airwaves. In this photo King's thirteen-year-old daughter Yolanda sits inside a car peering at mourners, reflected in the car window, while her mother Coretta Scott King sits solemnly behind her as they leave King's funeral in Atlanta, Georgia. This somber photograph, as much as the images of rioters had, captured the crushing disappointment of dashed dreams. It was a sentiment shared by many Americans in the 1960s, white and black, who failed to fully realize their goals of either reforming America or ending the cultural turmoil.

America was rife with discord during the sixties. Much debate centered on liberalism and its willingness to use the government to protect civil rights and expand economic opportunity. Throughout the decade social reformers working within the liberal tradition advanced competing visions of social justice and shared prosperity. Some visions were bold; some, truly radical. King dreamed of using nonviolence to achieve racial equality; more militant activists advocated armed self-defense. Building on the reform legacies of the Progressive Era and the New Deal, Democratic presidents John F. Kennedy and Lyndon B. Johnson launched their own wars against poverty. Their legislative agendas were too timid for young radical activists who wanted to revolutionize American capitalism. Feminists, Chicano activists, and Native American protesters all mobilized as well to demand equal rights.

These visions of reform, especially the more radical revolutionary ones, appeared like nightmares to conservative segments of the population that abhorred liberalism. Southern segregationists organized to prevent any government-mandated dismantling of Jim Crow, and white northerners increasingly resented taxpayer-supported programs for unruly minorities. The rise of a hippie counterculture that emphasized love and pleasure convinced many working- and middle-class whites that liberalism meant the end of law and order and traditional values.

If there was one point of agreement throughout the sixties, it was that the political and cultural battles that defined the decade, for good or ill, transformed the nation. By the end of the decade, frustration over unfulfilled dreams left Americans divided over whether the nation had changed too much or not enough.

What was the larger political significance of the King family's personal tragedy?

The Liberal Moment p. 812

Nonviolence Triumphant: The Civil Rights Movement, 1960–1965 p. 819

The Fractured Left p. 828

The End of an Era p. 835

The Liberal Moment

The 1960s was the heyday of American liberalism, thanks in part to the reform agendas of presidents Kennedy and Johnson and pivotal Supreme Court rulings. Kennedy and Johnson viewed themselves as heirs to the New Deal legacy, and they intended to follow in Harry Truman's footsteps, who as president had desegregated the American military and secured federal funds for urban public housing, education, and public works projects. Kennedy and Johnson each believed in the power of the federal government to positively reform American society, but each faced intense resistance from conservatives who were certain that the less the government interfered in the economy or society, the better.

Kennedy and the New Frontier

Nearly 20 percent of Americans, 70 percent of them white, lived in dire poverty during the most prosperous moment in American history. Many middle- and upper-class Americans learned this startling statistic by reading Michael Harrington's *The Other America: Poverty in the United States* (1962). Harrington documented the deteriorating schools, substandard hospitals, and dead-end jobs that created a cycle of poverty that continued unabated for generations. Just like Jacob Riis's nineteenth-century exposé, *How the Other Half Lives* (see Chapter 17), Harrington made the lives of the nation's poor "visible" to the rest of the nation. Harrington claimed that a "culture of poverty" filled with extramarital sex, illegitimate children, and broken families created "a different kind of people" who did not share the values or outlook of middle-class America. Like Riis seventy years earlier, Harrington succeeded in awakening the social consciousness of affluent liberals, including John F. Kennedy.

While campaigning in West Virginia during his 1960 presidential bid against Republican Richard Nixon, Kennedy came face to face with appalling poverty as he sat and talked with coal miners, pictured here (**27.1**), about their lives. This moment of intimate conversation, one of his speechwriters noted, was "Kennedy at his best" as he gathered details about children who never drank milk and their fathers' dangerous

27.1 Presidential Candidate John F. Kennedy Speaking with Coal Miners, 1960
Kennedy's personal touch and charisma helped him create a strong connection with voters, who educated him about the entrenched poverty endemic to many rural communities.

What social problems associated with poverty became visible in the early 1960s?

work underground. "I was better off in the war than they are in the coal mines," Kennedy, a World War II veteran, told his campaign staff after this photo was taken. "It's not right."

"Let us begin anew," John F. Kennedy told the nation in his 1961 inaugural address, setting a tone of hope that inspired young people and liberals throughout the nation. After eight years with the moderate Republican Dwight Eisenhower in the White House, Kennedy wanted to reinvigorate the liberal agenda through a legislative program called the **New Frontier**. Kennedy's proposed reforms included raising the minimum wage, reducing overcrowding in schools, and providing health care for the elderly. Kennedy also advocated cutting taxes and increasing government spending to stimulate the economy, reasoning that as incomes rose more tax revenue would flow into federal coffers to pay for these programs.

> "Ask not what your country can do for you—ask what you can do for your country."
>
> Kennedy's Inaugural Address, 1961

Kennedy also needed large sums for the ongoing space race with the Soviet Union, begun when the Soviets launched Sputnik in 1957 (see Chapter 24). The Soviets sent the first astronauts into space in 1961, prompting Kennedy to announce that the United States intended to recover its reputation as the world's technological leader by putting a man on the moon.

The youngest elected president in American history, Kennedy's charisma and idealism inspired many baby boomers who were just reaching adolescence or entering college. Thousands rushed to join the **Peace Corps**, an agency established by Kennedy that sent recent college graduates to work on humanitarian projects overseas in developing nations. "I really believed that I was going to change the world," recalled one teenager. By the end of the decade, over ten thousand Peace Corps volunteers had traveled abroad to teach, build hospitals, set up water treatment plants, and establish irrigation systems.

Kennedy succeeded in raising unemployment and Social Security benefits, as well as the minimum wage, but he had trouble implementing other parts of his liberal legislative program. Unskilled in lobbying individual legislators, just over one-third of his proposals became law. Conservative congressmen balked at using deficit spending to fund the tax cuts and programs Kennedy proposed. Southerners objected to northerners' insistence that federal education funds only go to racially integrated schools, while Protestants resisted offering public monies to private Catholic parochial schools. It was one of the "great ironies of American politics," a *New York Times* reporter noted, that "JFK, the immensely popular president, could not reach his legislative goals."

A Liberal Court

Under the leadership of Chief Justice Earl Warren from 1953–1969, the Supreme Court became an aggressive champion of individual rights, fostering the liberal agenda better than Kennedy and Democrats in Congress did. Warren believed that the Constitution gave the government the power, and the responsibility, to protect the relatively powerless against oppression by the majority. By choosing to render opinions on a wide range of social justice issues, the **Warren Court** brought about a legal revolution in the United States that permanently altered American schools, politics, the criminal justice system, and cultural norms. Northern liberals cheered these court decisions, but conservatives in both parties viewed the Warren Court as an activist court that rewrote rather than upheld the Constitution.

In 1954 the *Brown v. Board of Education* decision (see Chapter 25) paved the way for school desegregation. Throughout the fifties and sixties, the court continued to dismantle Jim Crow piece by piece, striking down segregated interstate and city buses, upholding the rights of civil rights protesters to hold sit-ins, and embracing mid-1960s federal laws that desegregated public places and guaranteed the right to vote as constitutional.

Another innovative judicial premise, the right to privacy, accompanied the Supreme Court's new support for civil rights. The Court struck down a host of state laws that outlawed possession of obscene publications, prohibited the use of contraception, and prevented interracial marriages. Individual Americans, the Court ruled, had the right to decide what to read, to use birth control, and to marry whom they wanted. Other court decisions redefined how the police arrested and interrogated suspected criminals. The police now had to inform individuals of their constitutional right to have a state-funded attorney present during questioning and their right not to answer questions that might incriminate them in a crime.

Why did many young people find Kennedy inspiring?

1954	**Brown v. Board of Education** outlawed racial segregation in public schools.
1962	**Baker v. Carr** gave federal courts right to intervene if states created voting districts of unequal size.
1962	**Engle v. Vitale** outlawed official school prayer in public schools.
1963	**Gideon v. Wainwright** gave accused felons the right to free legal counsel.
1965	**Griswold v. Connecticut** established "right to privacy," overturning state laws banning use of contraception.
1966	**Miranda v. Arizona** required that police inform suspect of right to remain silent and have a lawyer present during police questioning.
1967	**Loving v. Virginia** prohibited state laws banning interracial marriages.

27.2 Major Decisions of the Warren Court
The Supreme Court presided over a major "rights revolution" in the sixties.

The Court also championed freedom of speech, ruling against Red Scare–era laws that required Communist Party members to register with the government and striking down official school prayer. For many years children across America had begun their school days by reciting the "Pledge of Allegiance," to which Congress added the words "under God" in 1954 as a Cold War measure intended to contrast American religiosity with the godless communism embraced by the Soviet Union. Most schoolchildren then sang a patriotic song like "America," and some concluded this opening ritual with a short reading from the Bible. The Court's ruling against official school prayer in *Engle v. Vitale* (1962) is explored in *Choices and Consequences: Is School Prayer Constitutional?* The decision ignited a firestorm of controversy among conservative Protestants and Catholics. President Kennedy, however, endorsed the decision. Having encountered strong anti-Catholic bigotry during his 1960 presidential campaign, Kennedy welcomed the chance to make religion a strictly private matter as he geared up for his reelection campaign. The chart, *Major Decisions of the Warren Court* (**27.2**), summarizes key court decisions.

The 1964 Election

When Lyndon B. Johnson (LBJ) assumed office in the wake of Kennedy's assassination on November 22, 1963 (see Chapter 26), he took up the slain president's liberal agenda. "Let us continue," President Lyndon Johnson proclaimed, echoing Kennedy's earlier entreaty, "let us begin." Unlike Kennedy Johnson excelled at forging the deals needed to move legislation through Congress, and under his stewardship liberalism gained tremendous momentum. Over the next few months, Johnson adroitly used the nation's grief to great political advantage by cajoling Congress into enacting key pieces of Kennedy's legislative initiatives, including civil rights legislation, a tax cut, and federally funded public housing. Johnson also announced his own War on Poverty, creating an Office of Economic Opportunity that formed the Jobs Corps to teach inner-city youth vocational skills and created Volunteers in Service to America (VISTA), a domestic Peace Corps that sent privileged young adults to work on community projects in impoverished rural and urban areas.

Despite these legislative successes, Johnson knew that "for millions of Americans I was still illegitimate . . . a pretender to the throne," because he had not been elected president. Johnson saw the 1964 election as an opportunity to validate his presidency. His campaign, however, got off to a rocky start. LBJ expected to lose southern votes for having openly supported federal civil rights legislation. Alabama segregationist and former governor George Wallace's strong showing in a few northern Democratic primaries was unwelcome evidence that racism was strong in northern white working-class ethnic neighborhoods and some middle-class suburbs as well.

Racial controversy also rocked the Democratic Party's presidential nominating convention in Atlantic City when two separate delegations from Mississippi appeared. Disenfranchised blacks could not vote in Mississippi's official Democratic primary, so the Mississippi Freedom Democratic Party (MFDP) had held a shadow primary to elect their own convention delegates. This delegation traveled to Atlantic City and challenged the all-white Democratic Party's claim to represent the state.

How did the Warren Court advance the liberal reform agenda?

Choices and Consequences

IS SCHOOL PRAYER CONSTITUTIONAL?

In 1962 a group of parents in New York State challenged the constitutionality of the short nondenominational prayer that the state Board of Regents had adopted in 1951 for use in the public schools. The question was whether government-directed prayer violated the First Amendment clause that "Congress shall make no law respecting an establishment of religion, or prohibiting the free exercise thereof." The Fourteenth Amendment made this clause applicable to state law.

Choices

1. The prayer was constitutional because students were not required to recite it.
2. An officially composed prayer, regardless of its content, violated the First Amendment.
3. School prayer simply recognized the importance of religion in American society without establishing an official religion.

Decision

In *Engle v. Vitale* (1962) the Supreme Court ruled 6 to 1 that state-directed school prayer was unconstitutional. Justice Hugo Black wrote the majority opinion, stating that the First Amendment prohibited "official prayers for any group of American people to recite as part of a religious program carried on by government."

Consequences

The Warren Court received more mail opposing this case than any other. In 1963 the Court also banned reciting the Lord's Prayer and Bible-reading in public school, ruling that to remain truly neutral the government could not support "the tenets of one or all religions." Shared outrage over school prayer rulings helped forge a new political coalition between southern fundamentalist Protestants and northern orthodox Catholics, whose grassroots activism against liberalism contributed greatly to the conservative right's resurgence in the late 1960s. Subsequent court decisions in the 1980s and 1990s prohibited moments of silence for private prayer, minister-led prayers at high school graduation ceremonies, and student-led prayers at high school football games.

First-graders praying

Continuing Controversies

Does school prayer violate the First Amendment?
Those who answer "yes" believe that the Founding Fathers included the establishment clause in the constitution because the union of government and religion often leads to religiously based persecution of those not adhering to mainstream religious views. Freedom of religion requires a completely secular government that neither advances nor inhibits religious beliefs. Many conservatives disagree. They argue that the Court's decisions violated their First Amendment right to exercise free speech and destroyed the spiritual heritage of the nation that stretched back to the Pilgrims.

Why did so many Americans object to the Supreme Court's ruling against school prayer?

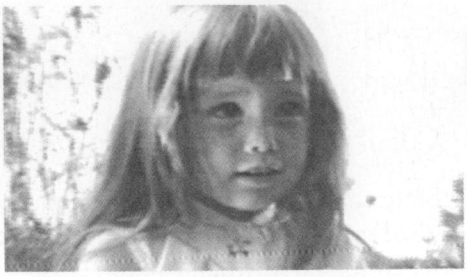
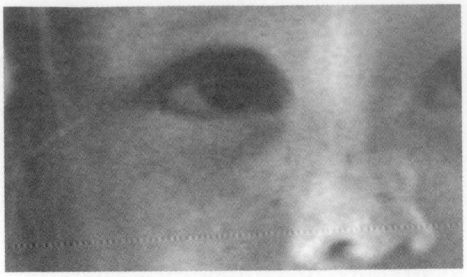

27.3 Sequence of Stills from the Daisy Girl Campaign Ad, 1964 This Democratic campaign ad implied that Republican candidate Barry Goldwater would start a nuclear war if elected. The ad script included these directions: "Ominous male voice counts down launch sequence, 10, 9, 8, 7, 6, 5, 4, 3, 2, 1. Close up of girl's face as camera progressively zooms in on her eye. Overlay an atomic explosion into the pupil of her eye."

In deciding which delegation to seat as the official delegates from Mississippi, the convention's Credentials Committee heard gripping testimony from MFDP delegate Fannie Lou Hamer. Thanks to the live television feed covering the proceedings, Americans throughout the nation heard Hamer describe being beaten, losing her job, and receiving a $9,000 water bill even though her house had no running water—all retribution for trying to register to vote. "Is this America, the land of the free and the home of the brave, where we are threatened daily because we want to live as decent human beings?" she asked before the cameras. Suddenly the networks broke away for an impromptu presidential news conference that Johnson had called to interrupt news coverage of Hamer's moving personal story. Johnson did not want the convention and his subsequent campaign to center on civil rights. To end the matter Johnson tried to broker a deal off-camera. When the MFDP rejected the offer of two delegate seats, the all-white Mississippi delegation took the floor.

In the election of 1964, the Democrat and Republican parties fielded candidates who offered starkly different visions of the role that government should play in American society. The Democrats selected Johnson, who spoke of creating a **Great Society** with social welfare reforms that would make the amenities of modern life—a decent standard of living, education, health care, clean water—available to all Americans. Like turn-of-the-century Populists and Progressives, and 1930s New Dealers, Johnson wanted to use the power of the federal government to reign in the wealthy and help economically disadvantaged Americans. Having begun his congressional career as an avid New Dealer in the 1930s, Johnson shared Franklin D. Roosevelt's desire to provide the deserving poor with a decent standard of living. Johnson, however, believed even more strongly than previous generations of liberal reformers in the ability of the government to improve the quality of life in America. Under Johnson the federal government began combating pollution, supporting the arts, and planting trees and flowers along the nation's highways—a beautification project strongly endorsed by his wife, Lady Bird Johnson. Johnson aspired to do more than put food in people's bellies; he wanted to nurture their spirits as well.

Barry Goldwater, a conservative Republican senator from Arizona, offered a radically different view of what responsibilities the government should assume. Instead of more government Goldwater proposed dismantling most of the New Deal, including Social Security, and opposed federal civil rights laws because he saw them as the first step toward creating "a police state." "My aim is not to pass laws but to repeal them," he declared. Goldwater spoke for the radical right, staunch conservatives who felt that the government's interference in the economy and society did more harm than good. Goldwater's extreme conservative views, however, alarmed some prominent moderate Republicans who openly supported Johnson.

The Democrats astutely used Goldwater's most extreme pronouncements against him in the campaign, making the liberal Johnson look almost moderate in comparison. Amplifying a remark by Goldwater that NATO commanders should have the authority to use nuclear weapons, a Democratic television campaign ad pictured a little girl counting as she picked the petals off a daisy (**27.3**). When she reached nine the camera froze on the image of her uplifted face before dissolving into the scene of a countdown to a nuclear bomb explosion. As the mushroom cloud dissipated, the screen turned dark and these words appeared: "Vote for President Johnson on November 3. The stakes are too high for you to stay home." The ad provoked its own firestorm of controversy and only aired once. It succeeded, however, in planting the image of

What competing views of government emerged during the 1964 presidential election?

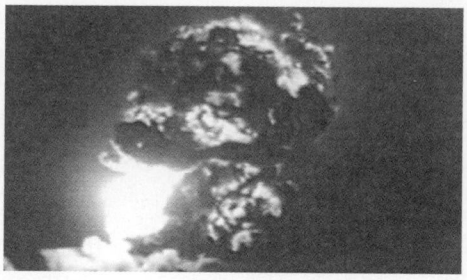

"In Your Heart You Know He's Right."

Republican billboards

"In Your Guts You Know He's Nuts."

Democratic bumper stickers

Dueling campaign slogans in the 1964 presidential election centered on Republican candidate Barry Goldwater

Goldwater as a dangerous extremist who might lead the nation into nuclear war.

Johnson won the election with over 61 percent of the popular vote, the largest percentage of any presidential candidate in American history. The Democrats also widened their control of Congress, further strengthening Johnson's hand. Johnson knew that he had to strike immediately to enact his legislative agenda. "Hurry, boys, hurry," he told his staff. "Get that legislation up to the hill and out. Eighteen months from now Landslide Lyndon will be Lame-Duck Lyndon."

The Great Society

Admiring the trees and landscaping along a national highway, reading a food label listing nutritional content in the supermarket, buying unleaded gas at a service station, and watching a documentary on the Public Broadcasting System (PBS): these are all experiences of modern life made possible by Johnson's Great Society. Reflecting liberal faith in the power of the government to do good, the Great Society hoped to remove the causes of debilitating poverty by improving the nation's educational system, providing health care to the aged and indigent, and creating a new cabinet-level position in housing and urban affairs to oversee housing and economic relief to struggling cities. Johnson's Great Society also included a new Department of Transportation to manage the federal funds pouring into highway construction and landscaping.

Johnson worked hard to create consensus for his liberal ideals. He offered conservative industrialists tax breaks in return for supporting his social welfare programs, arguing that his programs would create highly skilled workers who consumed more. "Doing something about poverty is economical in the long run," he told them. From his long years in Congress, Johnson knew how to lobby individual legislators. To secure a needed vote, Johnson brought legislators to the White House and subjected them to "The Treatment," a mixture of cajoling, horse-trading, and intimidation. One congressman recalled the 6-foot Johnson grabbing him by the lapels of his coat, pulling him close and holding his face inches away while he "talked and talked. I figured it was either getting drowned or joining." Johnson succeeded in pushing through over 65 percent of his proposals, a level of success only surpassed by Franklin D. Roosevelt's 80 percent legislative passage rate. Unable to stop the Great Society juggernaut, Republicans complained bitterly of "the three-B Congress—bullied, badgered, and brainwashed."

What made Johnson such an effective politician?

1964 **Economic Opportunity Act** – created VISTA, a domestic version of the Peace Corps, and community-based antipoverty programs that residents designed and administered.

Wilderness Act – protected public lands from development to preserve their unspoiled state.

1965 **Social Security Act** – created Medicare, government health insurance for Americans over 65, and Medicaid, government health insurance for the poor.

Department of Housing and Urban Development – established a new Cabinet-level position to administer Great Society legislation intended to clear slums and build new public housing.

Elementary and Secondary Education Act – allocated $1 billion to improve education for impoverished children.

Higher Education Act – created federal scholarships and loans for students in need.

Immigration Act – eliminated national quotas, set new guidelines privileging family unification and desirable occupational skills.

Highway Beautification Act – provided funds for landscaping along nation's highways.

Motor Vehicle Air Pollution Control Act – set first federal standards for motor vehicle emissions.

1966 **The Department of Transportation** – established a new Cabinet-level position to administer federal funds to improve highways and urban mass transit.

Fair Packaging and Labeling Act – required manufacturers to label number of servings and nutritional information on food packages.

1967 **Public Broadcasting Act** – created public television and radio stations dedicated to educational programming.

27.4 Key Great Society Legislative Achievements
The Great Society built on liberal legislation initiated during the Progressive Era and New Deal to give the federal government an expanded role in American society.

After pushing first for federal aid to schools, Johnson turned to providing health care to senior citizens and the poor. Facing strong opposition from health insurance companies and medical professionals to government-provided health care, Johnson compromised. Medicare, government-funded health insurance for the elderly, reimbursed doctors and hospitals whatever they charged senior citizens instead of establishing government rates. Johnson also agreed to let the states, not the federal government, run Medicaid, which provided health services to the poor.

In creating the Great Society, Johnson wanted to restore America's identity as the land of opportunity for immigrants. The Immigration Act of 1965 eliminated the quota system established in the 1920s that set stringent caps on immigration from southern and eastern Europe and barred all Asian immigration (see Chapter 21). In the first great wave of immigration since the 1910s, unprecedented numbers of Koreans, Chinese, Filipinos, and Vietnamese migrated to the United States over the next thirty years. Whether immigration benefited or hurt the nation once again became a topic on which Americans offered competing visions (see Chapter 29).

By detailing the destructive impact of pesticides, Rachel Carson's best-selling book *Silent Spring* (1962) helped create a politically favorable climate for the environmental regulation that Johnson proposed. *Silent Spring* vividly detailed the destructive impact of pesticides on native bird populations, provoking general alarm over the possibility of a future silent spring when no bird songs would be heard. Johnson noted that Americans had always been proud of "America the beautiful," but the reality of polluted air, disappearing forests, and filthy rivers had already tarnished this image. The air in some major cities was so bad that motorists had to use their headlights after noon. The pronouncement that Lake Erie was "dead" and the sight of oil slicks on the Cuyahoga River in Cleveland burning for eight days after a man tossed a lit cigar into the water underscored the seriousness of environmental deterioration. These ecological catastrophes helped spawn an exploding grassroots environmental movement that included Greenpeace, a radical direct-action group, and the Sierra Club, a long-standing conservation society. Responding to environmental activism and growing middle-class concerns, Congress enacted a slew of bipartisan environmental measures that required pollution controls on cars and established national standards for acceptable air and water pollution. Johnson also created federally protected wilderness areas to safeguard endangered domestic species at risk of extinction, such as the whooping crane. *The Great Society* chart (**27.4**) contains a list of Johnson's most significant pieces of legislation.

What social problems did Great Society laws and programs address?

Nonviolence Triumphant: The Civil Rights Movement, 1960–1965

Kennedy's and Johnson's strong civil rights agendas came in response to a series of carefully planned grassroots protests against segregation and disenfranchisement in Alabama and Mississippi. These highly visible demonstrations put many civil rights workers in peril, and civil rights leaders hoped to win support from white liberals and moderates nationally by showing them the face of southern segregationists' resistance. Putting increased pressure on the federal government to act, the Civil Rights Movement successfully brought an end to legalized segregation and disenfranchisement by 1965.

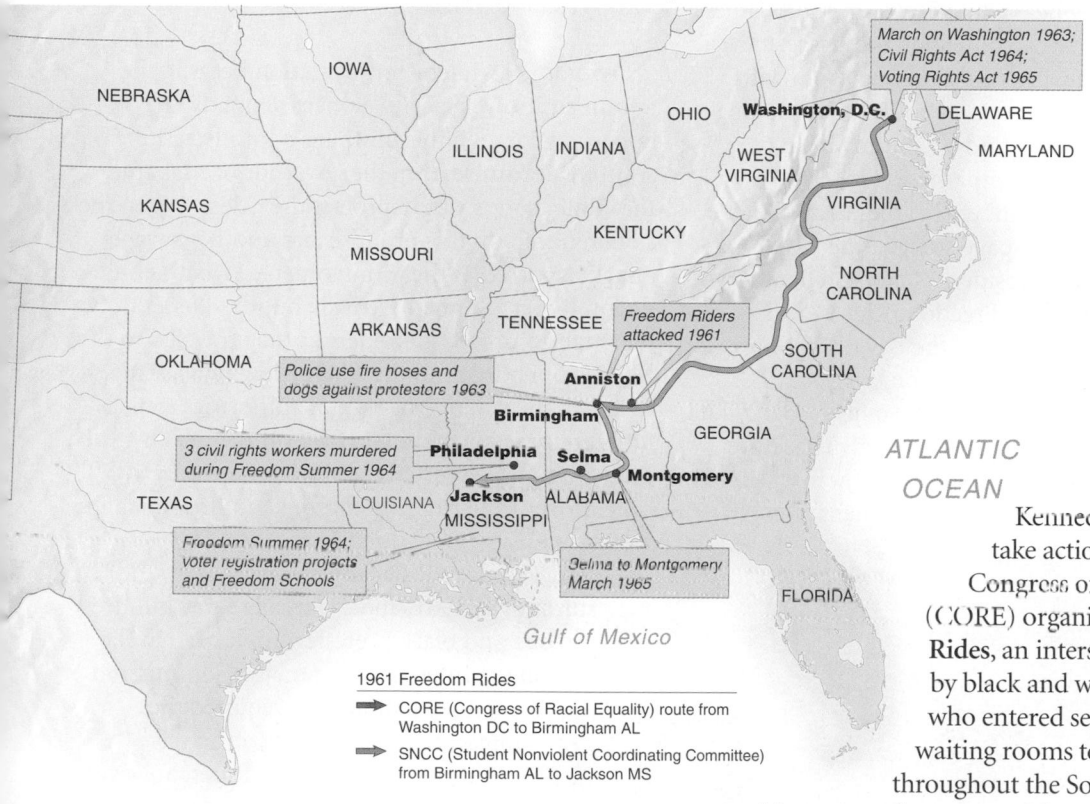

27.5 Civil Rights Milestones, 1961–1965
The Civil Rights Movement fanned out across the Deep South in the early sixties, pushing for an end to legalized segregation and disenfranchisement.

Kennedy and the Freedom Riders

Inspired by Kennedy's pronouncement during his inaugural address that "the torch has been passed to a new generation of Americans," civil rights leaders expected the new president to aggressively seek an end to Jim Crow. Kennedy, however, adopted a cautious stance, and like his predecessors, remained silent on civil rights. The movement would have to compel the new president to act.

The immediate issue centered on the enforcement of recent Supreme Court rulings that desegregated bus terminals serving interstate travelers. Faced with Kennedy's reluctance to take action, the interracial Congress of Racial Equality (CORE) organized the **Freedom Rides**, an interstate bus journey by black and white activists who entered segregated bus waiting rooms together throughout the South. "We felt we could count on the racists of the South to create a crisis so that the federal government would be compelled to enforce the law," the African American CORE leader James Farmer recalled.

The Freedom Rides began when a group of thirteen whites and blacks (including Farmer and John Lewis, a veteran of the 1960 Nashville sit-ins) boarded an interstate bus on May 4, 1961, in Washington, D.C., headed for the Deep South. Expecting the worst several riders left sealed letters for their families to open if they were killed. The map of "Civil Rights Milestones, 1961–1965" (**27.5**) traces their route. After a smooth ride through the upper South, in Atlanta the Freedom Riders decided to take two separate buses into the heart of the

What was the purpose of the Freedom Rides?

rigidly segregated Deep South. When the first bus carrying Freedom Riders entered the Anniston, Alabama, bus depot, a waiting mob pelted the bus with stones and slashed its tires. The bus driver drove away without stopping, pursued by fifty cars carrying vigilantes. When a flat tire forced the driver to stop along a deserted country road, a firebomb thrown at the bus forced the Freedom Riders into the waiting gauntlet of sticks and crowbars. State troopers arrived in time to save the lives of the traumatized Freedom Riders, two of whom sit stunned on the ground in this photo (**27.6**) of the bus burning. Meanwhile the second bus arrived in Birmingham, where a large group of Ku Klux Klansmen savagely beat white Freedom Rider James Peck, a forty-seven-year-old labor and peace activist, when he entered a white-only waiting room with a black colleague. "When you go somewhere looking for trouble, you usually find it," the governor of Alabama remarked unsympathetically.

A photo of Klan members beating Peck accompanied the front-page story in the *New York Times* that informed President Kennedy about the organized attacks on the Freedom Riders. Still dealing with the fallout from the Bay of Pigs invasion that had ended in disaster four weeks earlier and preparing for a summit with Soviet leader Nikita Khrushchev (see Chapter 25), Kennedy urged the Freedom Riders to call off the rest of their scheduled journey. Instead members of the Student Non-Violent Coordinating Committee (SNCC), the student-run civil rights group founded in 1960 during the sit-ins (see Chapter 25), rushed to Birmingham to ride alongside John Lewis, a founding member of SNCC, taking the place of riders unable or unwilling to continue.

> "We can't let them stop us with violence. If we do, the movement is dead,"
>
> SNCC leader DIANE NASH upon resuming the Freedom Rides, 1961

Avoiding a violent confrontation became the administration's priority. Robert Kennedy, the attorney general in his brother's administration, secured a promise from the governor of Alabama that state troops would protect the riders. When the state reneged on this promise and another savage attack occurred at the Montgomery, Alabama bus depot, Robert Kennedy sent six hundred federal marshals to protect the riders as they traveled to the Mississippi border. Rather than allowing vigilantes to attack the riders, Mississippi authorities took a different tack. As the riders filed off the bus in Jackson, police escorted them into waiting patrol cars. Most of the riders spent four months in jail for violating local segregation laws.

The Freedom Rides continued through the summer of 1961, and eventually three hundred white and black protesters took part. In the fall the Interstate Commerce Commission issued regulations that required the integration of all interstate travel facilities. The Freedom Rides, however, did not achieve organizers' broader goals of securing President Kennedy's enthusiastic support for the Civil Rights Movement. Despite his own integrationist views, President Kennedy remained preoccupied with protecting his white Democratic southern base and feared that open discussion of America's racial problems provided fodder for Soviet propaganda. It would take a shocking visual demonstration of racial violence in Birmingham, Alabama, to make President Kennedy a champion of civil rights.

27.6 Freedom Riders Attacked in Anniston, Alabama, 1961
Traumatized civil rights activists sit on the ground after a mob firebombed the bus the Freedom Riders were riding to protest the continued segregation of interstate bus facilities.

Who made key choices that affected the course and outcome of the Freedom Rides?

Birmingham, 1963

In 1963 the Southern Christian Leadership Conference (SCLC), Martin Luther King Jr.'s church-based civil rights organization, unfurled a carefully coordinated campaign to desegregate Birmingham, perhaps the most segregated city in the nation. SCLC's goals went beyond desegregating lunch counters or drinking fountains. "We were trying to launch a systematic, wholehearted battle against segregation that would set the pace for the nation," explained the Birmingham-based SCLC leader Fred Shuttlesworth. The city's volatile police chief Bull Connor made the city an especially dangerous place to launch such a protest. SCLC accurately predicted that they would gain the attention of the president once the world saw Connor's police force attacking nonviolent demonstrators with high-power water hoses and police dogs. Television was vital to this campaign: The images of violence pouring into living rooms would make it impossible for moderate white Americans to ignore the nation's racial problems.

In April 1963 King and the SCLC initiated their **Birmingham campaign** with economic boycotts and a limited number of sit-ins. Press coverage increased dramatically when King and Shuttlesworth led a march in defiance of a state injunction that prohibited public demonstrations. Police immediately arrested and jailed the pair. King purposefully timed his arrest to occur on Good Friday, the day that Jesus carried his cross to the site of his crucifixion, using religious symbolism to underscore the immorality of racial persecution.

As King sat in solitary confinement, the *Birmingham News* published an open letter to him from a group of white liberal southern clergymen who criticized the demonstrations as "unwise and untimely" for trying to intentionally provoke hard-core segregationists. The opinion of liberal and moderate southern whites mattered to King. The nonviolent strategy depended on swaying those who may have traditionally supported segregation but were not die-hard racists. Visitors to King smuggled out his response, written on the margins of newspapers and scraps of toilet paper during his eight-day jail stay. King's "Letter from a Birmingham Jail" did not influence the course of events in Birmingham (by the time it was published, the protests had ended), but the text was one of King's most eloquent statements on the dehumanizing aspects of racial discrimination. "For years now I have heard the word 'Wait!' It rings in the ear of every Negro with piercing familiarity. This 'Wait' has almost always meant 'Never,'" King wrote. How would whites feel about sleeping in their cars when traveling because "no motel will accept you," telling their children that they could not go to the segregated amusement parks advertised on television, and "living constantly on tiptoe stance, never quite knowing what to expect next"? These were the reasons, King explained, "why we find it difficult to wait."

Hoping to put a stop to downtown demonstrations that were keeping shoppers away and worried that the federal government might intervene, moderate white business owners initiated secret talks with SCLC leaders without Police Chief Connor's knowledge. To put increased pressure on the business owners, SCLC went ahead with a series of planned marches despite lukewarm support from Birmingham churches and adults. To fill the ranks Jim Bevel, another veteran of the Nashville sit-ins, proposed turning Birmingham into a "children's crusade" by recruiting from the city's high schools and, if necessary, middle and elementary schools. "A boy from high school has the same effect in terms of being in jail, in terms of putting pressure on the city, as his father, and yet there's no economic threat to the family, because the father is still on the job," Bevel argued convincingly.

On May 3, 1963, the second day of the protests, Carolyn McKinstry, like many others, left her high school without telling her parents that she was joining the demonstrations. When the teenagers arrived downtown, Connor was waiting with water hoses and police dogs. A shocked nation viewed television and newspaper images of firefighters directing torrents of water at McKinstry and her friends and police dogs biting protesters. (See *Images as History: Birmingham, 1963*, page 822.)

As the SCLC had hoped, northerners reacted with outrage to this blatant display of police brutality, while moderates in the South worried that Connor's heavy-handed tactics would invite more federal scrutiny of southern politics and racial customs. The Civil Rights Movement scored a major victory in Birmingham. Besides winning a commitment to desegregate lunch counters and schools as well as the promise of jobs, the protests renewed President Kennedy's interest in civil rights. Concerned about losing momentum in the Cold War, Kennedy asked the nation: "Are we to say to the world—and much more importantly to each other—that this is the land of the free, except for the Negroes . . . ?"

What various strategies made the Birmingham campaign a success?

Images as History

BIRMINGHAM, 1963

In Birmingham civil rights activists developed a strategy that included using television and news photos to their advantage. The Civil Rights Movement succeeded in getting exactly the images the activists wanted in 1963 when the Birmingham police chief Bull Connor unleashed extreme violence against protesters in the downtown area. How important was the press to the success of the Birmingham campaign? Why did the public react so strongly to these photos?

As a white child in rural Alabama, *Life* photojournalist Charles Moore had accepted segregation "as the way things were." Birmingham proved a crucial turning point in his own evolving social consciousness. "My emotional involvement in the story grew

"The water hoses hurt a lot," recalled Carolyn McKinstry, the high school sophomore girl pictured here.

Three teenage protesters clung to a doorway as water whipped their bodies, an ordeal that Moore immortalized in this iconic photograph of the Birmingham protests.

Fire Hoses, Birmingham, 1963

McKinstry remained "proud of what I had done," but afterwards she questioned "the tactics that they [SCLC] were using because I think I felt that you could actually be hurt."

Moore avoided taking photos that might send a mixed message to the public. He took no pictures of students, only partly schooled in nonviolent techniques, who threw pieces of concrete at the police—even after a slab hit him and injured some tendons.

Does knowing more about McKinstry and Moore alter this photograph's meaning?

as I saw what was happening," he noted. On the afternoon of May 3, 1963, Moore arrived in downtown Birmingham just as firefighters turned their high-pressure hoses and police dogs on teenage demonstrators. When Moore's photos appeared in *Life*, a magazine read by half of American adults in the sixties, his images, along with television coverage of the mayhem, helped transform Birmingham from a local crisis into an event that prompted national soul-searching about the state of democracy in America. Drawing inspiration from these images, civil rights activists initiated one thousand demonstrations in nearly one hundred cities throughout the South in subsequent months.

Movement leaders wanted liberal and moderate Americans to blame the police for escalating the violence in Birmingham, and Moore's pictures left little room for an alternative explanation.

The police arrested Moore when he refused to stop taking pictures. "It was scary to be a victim" of abusive police, Moore recalled, an experience that strengthened his sense of solidarity with the protesters.

Police Dogs, Birmingham, 1963

"The sight of snarling dogs, and the possibility of dogs ripping flesh, was revolting to me," Moore recalled.

Moore sided with the protesters, but the story that accompanied his photos blamed extremists on both sides for the melee. "[The pictures] are frightening because of the brutal methods being used by white policemen in Birmingham, Ala. against Negro demonstrators. They are frightening because the Negro strategy of 'nonviolent direct action' invites that very brutality—and welcomes it as a way to promote the Negroes' cause, which, under the law, is right," *Life* told readers.

How did *Life* magazine and Moore differ over the meaning of this photo?

In his address Kennedy proposed a civil rights act that would outlaw racially segregated public facilities nationwide. The white supremacist response came immediately. The next day a Klansman shot and killed Medgar Evers, the head of the National Association for the Advancement of Colored People (NAACP) in Mississippi, as Evers stood in the driveway of his Jackson home. Evers's killing was the first, but not the last, politically motivated assassination of a major political figure of the sixties.

March on Washington

Birmingham had given the civil rights cause national and international visibility, and Evers's shocking assassination reinforced Kennedy's determination to enact a sweeping civil rights bill. Southern Democratic senators were equally prepared to filibuster to prevent its passage. Intent on winning this legislative battle, King and other civil rights leaders decided to organize the **March on Washington**, a massive demonstration in the nation's capital that would demand passage of a federal civil rights act. Adopting the slogan, "Jobs and Freedom," organizers underscored the link between greater economic opportunity and civic equality. The organizing committee included African American labor leader A. Philip Randolph, founder of the Brotherhood of Sleeping Car Porters. Randolph had planned his own March on Washington in 1941, but he cancelled it when President Franklin D. Roosevelt agreed to guarantee fair protection at the workplace during World War II (see Chapter 23).

On August 28, 1963, the March on Washington for Jobs and Freedom took place as more than 200,000 marchers walked from the Washington Monument to Lincoln Memorial to listen to a three-hour program of music and speeches, forming the nation's largest political protest to date. This photo (**27.7**) of Martin Luther King Jr. talking to a reporter reveals why organizers chose to put their speakers' platform before the Lincoln Memorial. On the hundredth anniversary of Lincoln's Emancipation Proclamation, the larger-than-life statue of President Abraham Lincoln in the background offered a potent reminder of how long African Americans had waited for equal rights. "I have a dream that my four little children will one day live in a nation where they will not be judged by the color of their skin, but by the content of their character," declared King in the day's most memorable speech.

The march received the national media's full attention. It was also among the first events that television viewers throughout the world could watch live, thanks to a newly launched communications satellite. From Cairo to Amsterdam people participated in sympathy marches before American embassies and sent supportive petitions to Kennedy. By August nearly 78 percent of white Americans believed that images of racial discrimination in the United States made it harder for the nation to achieve its Cold War foreign policy goals.

Two weeks after the March on Washington, a bomb tossed into Birmingham's Sixteenth Street Baptist Church killed four little girls attending Sunday school. Carolyn McKinstry, the young woman that Charles Moore had photographed during the Birmingham protests, was in the church at the time, a friend to all four girls. The attack convinced her that she too would one day die at the hands of white supremacists. "I guess this bombing is Birmingham's answer to the march," exclaimed an enraged Anne Moody, who was working on a voter registration campaign in Mississippi. President Kennedy's assassination two months later only underscored her growing conviction that "nonviolence is through."

27.7 March on Washington, 1963 Martin Luther King Jr. speaks to a reporter while standing inside the Lincoln Memorial to underscore that one hundred years after Lincoln issued the Emancipation Proclamation blacks were still second-class citizens in the segregated South.

What symbolism and rhetoric connected the 1963 March on Washington to the past and future?

Freedom Summer

With SCLC's Birmingham campaign to desegregate public facilities successfully concluded, the spotlight turned to Mississippi. **Freedom Summer**, a multi-pronged attack on white supremacy in Mississippi during the summer of 1964, was a turning point in the Civil Rights Movement.It forced the federal government to deepen its commitment to equal rights, laid bare the rising tensions within the Civil Rights Movement, and trained a new generation of student activists who would soon spearhead new leftist and feminist movements.

In the summer of 1964, the Council of Federated Organizations (COFO) coordinated the efforts of several civil rights groups to launch Freedom Summer, including SNCC and CORE. With ambivalence SNCC recruited large numbers of northern whites to work on the voter registration projects. SNCC had reluctantly concluded that the national media, which had started to ignore blacks-only protests, would pay attention to Freedom Summer only if white students were involved. SNCC, CORE, and COFO hoped that the media spotlight would offer Freedom Summer workers some protection from racial violence, protection that the federal government was unwilling to give. This calculation proved incorrect.

> "At night, people should not sit in their rooms without drawn shades."
>
> Rule from CORE security handbook meant to protect Freedom Summer workers from sniper attacks

On the first day of Freedom Summer, three CORE workers went missing in Mississippi. Twenty-four-year-old Michael Schwerner was a white Jewish social worker from Manhattan who, one coworker recalled, "had been deeply affected by the photographs of Negroes sprawling under the dogs and fire hoses" in Birmingham. On June 21, 1964, Schwerner went with James Chaney, a twenty-one-year-old Mississippi black activist, and twenty-year-old Andrew Goodman, another white Jewish volunteer from New York, to inspect a church that the Ku Klux Klan had burned to the ground to stop CORE from opening a school there. On the return home they passed near Philadelphia, Mississippi, where local sheriff (and Klansman) Cecile Price recognized Schwerner's car and license plate from a circular the governor's office had issued concerning "outside agitators." Price arrested the trio on charges of speeding then alerted fellow Klansmen to join him for an ambush after he released the three men from jail in the middle of the night.

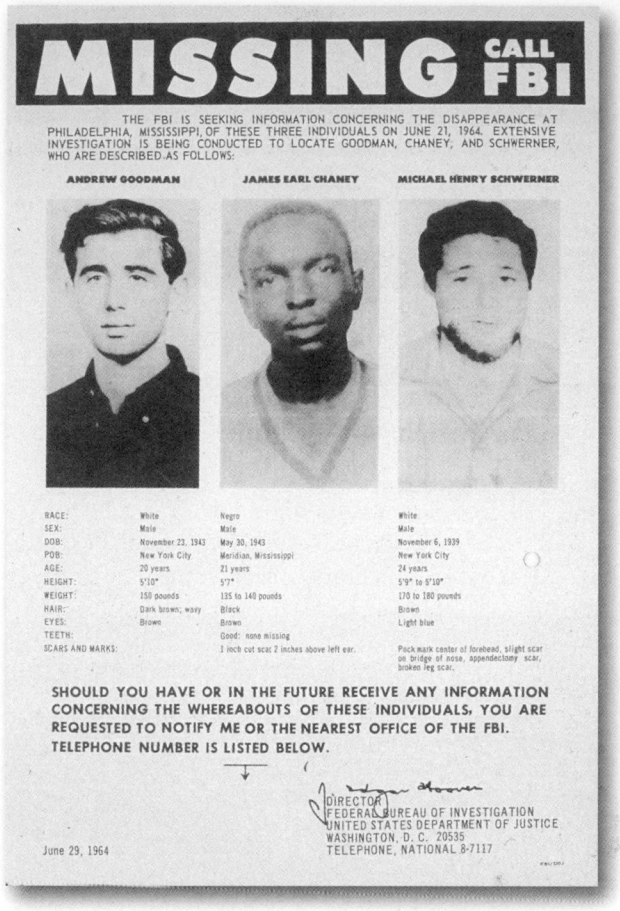

MISSING CALL FBI

THE FBI IS SEEKING INFORMATION CONCERNING THE DISAPPEARANCE AT PHILADELPHIA, MISSISSIPPI, OF THESE THREE INDIVIDUALS ON JUNE 21, 1964. EXTENSIVE INVESTIGATION IS BEING CONDUCTED TO LOCATE GOODMAN, CHANEY, AND SCHWERNER, WHO ARE DESCRIBED AS FOLLOWS:

	ANDREW GOODMAN	JAMES EARL CHANEY	MICHAEL HENRY SCHWERNER
RACE:	White	Negro	White
SEX:	Male	Male	Male
DOB:	November 23, 1943	May 30, 1943	November 6, 1939
POB:	New York City	Meridian, Mississippi	New York City
AGE:	20 years	21 years	24 years
HEIGHT:	5'10"	5'7"	5'9" to 5'10"
WEIGHT:	150 pounds	135 to 140 pounds	170 to 180 pounds
HAIR:	Dark brown; wavy	Black	Brown
EYES:	Brown	Brown	Light blue
TEETH:		Good; none missing	
SCARS AND MARKS:		1 inch cut scar 2 inches above left ear.	Pock mark center of forehead, slight scar on bridge of nose, appendectomy scar, broken leg scar.

SHOULD YOU HAVE OR IN THE FUTURE RECEIVE ANY INFORMATION CONCERNING THE WHEREABOUTS OF THESE INDIVIDUALS, YOU ARE REQUESTED TO NOTIFY ME OR THE NEAREST OFFICE OF THE FBI. TELEPHONE NUMBER IS LISTED BELOW.

DIRECTOR
FEDERAL BUREAU OF INVESTIGATION
UNITED STATES DEPARTMENT OF JUSTICE
WASHINGTON, D. C. 20535
TELEPHONE, NATIONAL 8-7117

June 29, 1964

27.8 FBI Poster of Three Slain Freedom Summer Civil Rights Workers, 1964
The murder of these three CORE workers hardened the resolve of many Freedom Summer volunteers to continue their work registering blacks to vote, but some blacks resented that the nation seemed to care only if white activists disappeared.

The trio's disappearance created national headlines, forcing the FBI to launch a massive manhunt across five states to find them. The FBI posted this circular (**27.8**) seeking information about the men's whereabouts, haunting images that conveyed more than the dangers of vigilante violence. Putting her own grief aside, Schwerner's wife Rita, herself a dedicated CORE field worker, publicly voiced her suspicion that "if Mr. Chaney, who is a native Mississippian, had been alone at the time of the disappearance, . . . this case, like so many others that have come before it, . . . would have gone completely unnoticed." As if to prove her point, sailors sent to comb through Mississippi swamps for the bodies of the three men (now assumed to be dead) discovered the corpses of three lynched black men whose previous disappearances authorities had ignored.

What interracial tensions within the Civil Rights Movement did Freedom Summer expose?

27.9 COFO Freedom School, 1964
Refusing to be intimidated when the Ku Klux Klan burned a cross in front of their Freedom School, Freedom Summer workers painted "freedom" on the blackened wood.

As the FBI investigation unfolded, Freedom Summer continued. Nearly one thousand black and white activists fanned out throughout Mississippi to register blacks in rural areas. Hoping to recruit and train a new generation of student leaders, SNCC and COFO founded summer Freedom Schools that taught high school students African American history to build pride in the long legacy of black accomplishment and gave remedial instruction in basic subjects to remedy their deficient public education. In a state with no mandatory school laws, black children often spent more time in the cotton fields than in the classroom. COFO volunteers refused to be intimidated when the Klan left a burning cross in front of a Freedom School in the Mississippi Delta (**27.9**). Writing their own counter-message of "Freedom" on the cross, Freedom Summer workers openly asserted that "COFO=Freedom Now" to underscore that it would take determined activism to meet their goals of "One Man, One Vote."

In the midst of Freedom Summer, Congress passed the **Civil Rights Act of 1964**, which banned segregation in businesses and places open to the public (such as restaurants and public schools) and prohibited discrimination in employment on the basis of race, religion, ethnicity, or sex. This landmark legislation, the most sweeping civil rights law since Reconstruction, came about because thousands of individuals risked arrest, murder, or unemployment to participate in boycotts, sit-ins, and street demonstrations in towns and cities throughout the South. Their activism went unnoticed in the national press, which focused mostly on a few dramatic moments such as the disappearance of Schwerner, Chaney, and Goodman.

A month after the Civil Rights Act's passage, after six weeks of searching, the FBI paid $30,000 to an informant who helped officers locate the three men's bodies buried in an earthen dam. All three had been shot in the head, and Chaney's shattered bones attested to the savage beating he had received. No one was ever convicted of the murders, although Price and nine others were found guilty on federal conspiracy charges in 1967 and served a few years in jail.

Like Kennedy, Johnson knew that the world was watching events unfold in Mississippi. Passage of the Civil Rights Act was front-page news overseas, and world leaders rushed to congratulate Johnson. Winning the 1964 Nobel Peace Prize, King was now an international figure who inspired social justice activists worldwide.

Passage of the 1964 Civil Rights Act was a great victory for the Civil Rights Movement, but the strain of combat-like conditions during Freedom Summer took its toll. Becoming increasingly fearful some SNCC volunteers began to arm themselves for self-defense. Many blacks resented the media attention given to white activists. Meanwhile female civil rights workers, black and white, increasingly objected to males' expectations that they would clean and cook for them. The stage was set for a fracturing within the activist community.

Selma and the Voting Rights Act of 1965

The nonviolent Civil Rights Movement registered one more significant victory before that fracturing occurred, using a stand-off in Selma, Alabama, to secure President Johnson's open support for federal

What pivotal role did college-age students play in Freedom Summer?

legislation guaranteeing blacks the right to vote. On Sunday March 7, 1965, a day soon known as "Bloody Sunday," about six hundred marchers left the small town of Selma, Alabama, and began walking across the Edmund Pettis Bridge that spanned the Alabama River. They intended to march 50 miles to Montgomery, the state capitol, to demand voting rights. At the other end of the bridge, a line of county troopers armed with clubs and tear gas waited for them. When the marchers knelt in prayer at the end of the bridge, Sheriff Jim Clark ordered the troopers to attack as white spectators cheered.

Photographers and television crews witnessed the violent attack in Selma. That evening ABC interrupted the film *Judgment at Nuremburg*, a dramatized account of the war crimes trials that convicted Nazi leaders of crimes against humanity, to show news footage of the Bloody Sunday assault. The juxtaposition between the film's portrayal of the Holocaust and events in Selma haunted many viewers. Late that evening the door opened to the chapel in Selma that served as the marchers' headquarters. "We have seen on the television screen the violence that took place today, and we're here to share it with you," announced a group of blacks and whites from New Jersey who had chartered a plane to arrive that night.

On Monday, March 15, 1965, President Johnson, who had spoken privately with King before Selma about how to win public support for voting rights legislation, announced in a televised address that he was sending a federal voting rights act to Congress. "It's not just Negroes, but really it's all of us, who must overcome the crippling legacy of bigotry and injustice," Johnson told the nation. "And we shall overcome," he concluded, quoting the anthem of the Civil Rights Movement.

> "I asked my mother and father for my birthday present to become registered voters."
>
> Eight-year-old SHEYANN WEBB, youngest member of the first Selma to Montgomery march.

A triumphant march from Selma began the following Sunday, March 21, 1965, a moment captured by James Karales's stirring photograph for *Look* magazine (**27.10**). The photograph accompanied an article on the decision of northern white ministers to join the march in Selma, reaffirming the mainstream media focus on the role of whites in the Civil Rights Movement. When the marchers arrived in Montgomery five days later, King addressed the crowd on the steps of the state capitol building, looking down at the Dexter Avenue Baptist Church where he had helped initiate the Montgomery Bus Boycott ten years earlier (see Chapter 25). "I know you are asking today, 'How long will it take?' . . . How long? Not long, because no lie can live forever," King said hopefully. Five months later Johnson signed the **Voting Rights Act of 1965**, legislation that prohibited literacy tests and poll taxes, plus authorized the use of federal registrars to register voters if states failed to respect the Fifteenth Amendment. Within a year over nine thousand blacks had registered in Dallas County, Alabama, enough to block Jim Clark's reelection as sheriff.

27.10 March from Selma to Montgomery, March 21–25, 1965
Storm clouds hovered as marchers walked along the rural highway that linked Selma to Montgomery, creating a poetic image that captured their resolve to keep moving forward, no matter what the obstacle.

How did the media, public, and government respond to events in Selma?

The Fractured Left

Conservative Republicans and Democrats never liked the antipoverty legislative initiatives of Kennedy and Johnson, while die-hard segregationists adamantly opposed the integrationist goals of nonviolent civil rights leaders like King. The most potent attacks on these progressive visions, however, came from the left where competing visions proliferated. By the mid-sixties disaffected student activists increasingly dismissed the Great Society as too cautious and protested openly against "Johnson's War" in Vietnam, while others renounced all ties to mainstream culture. Within the Civil Rights Movement, militancy replaced nonviolence as the dominant ethos. Meanwhile many white women left the Civil Rights Movement to pursue the goal of women's liberation.

The New Left and the Counterculture

The baby boom generation came of age in the sixties. By 1968 over half of the American population was under the age of twenty-five. By then a core of white middle-class college students had created the **New Left**, a small, but highly visible, coalition of left-leaning student-based organizations that attacked racial discrimination, poverty, and the war in Vietnam.

Al Haber formed Students for a Democratic Society (SDS) in 1960 at the University of Michigan, believing "that if any really radical liberal force is going to develop in America, it is going to come from the colleges and the young." In 1962 Tom Hayden, a white activist in the Civil Rights Movement, penned the group's manifesto, "The Port Huron Statement." Hayden urged his peers to act, noting "we are people of this generation, bred in at least modest comfort, housed now in universities, looking uncomfortably to the world we inherit."

Although the majority of college-age Americans did not attend university, their ranks were increasing. By 1965 nearly 6.5 million students attended colleges or universities, compared with 2.2 million in 1950. Strict rules governed student behavior. Students lived in single-sex dormitories, had to obey curfews each evening and abide by dress codes that prohibited female students from wearing pants. The University of California, Berkeley, went one step further by forbidding all political debate or discussion on campus, a rule in place since the 1930s to prevent communist student groups from recruiting.

For years students had used a small strip just outside the campus main gate to hand out political pamphlets or give speeches. In the fall of 1964, the university administration shut this down as well, provoking the Free Speech Movement, a mass student protest that accused the University of California of denying students the right to freedom of speech. Protest leader Mario Savio, who had just returned from Freedom Summer, pointed out that "the two battlefields [in Mississippi and Berkeley] may seem quite different to some observers, but this is not the case. The same rights are at stake in both places—the right to participate as citizens in a democratic society." Aided greatly by sympathetic television coverage, the Free Speech Movement succeeded after four months of demonstrations and inspired left-leaning students on other university campuses. Most college students never joined any organized protests, but in response to those who did universities eliminated codes of conduct, introduced more elective courses into curriculums, and established black and women's studies.

After 1964 local SDS chapters took the lead in organizing antiwar demonstrations on university campuses that included teach-ins and draft-card burnings (see Chapter 26). SDS at first embraced the liberal vision of using representative government to implement incremental reforms, but in the course of its antiwar protests the group became more radical. By 1968 New Left leaders expressed open admiration for Marxist-inspired communist revolutionaries like the Vietnamese leader Ho Chi Minh and Ernesto "Che" Guevara, a colleague of Cuban dictator Fidel Castro trying to foster revolution in Bolivia and the Congo. When student-led protests roiled Europe and South America in 1968, the American New Left assumed they were part of a global youth rebellion that would ultimately reshape the world.

Once the novelty of student demonstrations wore off, getting television reporters to cover their protests

What impact did the New Left have on university life?

required more outlandish theatrics, images that increasingly radicalized student leaders eagerly provided. Press scrutiny sometimes backfired, however. Nightly news reports of demonstrators hurling bricks and expletives frightened many moderates, who increasingly viewed the New Left as unpatriotic and dangerous.

The challenge to the liberal vision went beyond the New Left. An emerging counterculture, the heir to the Beat cultural ethos of the 1950s (see Chapter 25), emphasized rejecting middle-class lifestyles more than agitating for political change. **Hippies**, youthful social rebels who renounced material acquisition and used drugs to explore their inner spiritual selves, refused to dedicate their lives to acquiring the same suburban home, car, and corporate job as their parents. The hippie utopian vision embraced peace, pleasure, sexual liberation, and sharing of material resources., an ethos captured in this 1968 photograph (**27.11**) of a hippie gathering by Robert Altman (who became a renowned filmmaker).

Drugs, especially marijuana and lysergic acid diethylamide (LSD), formed an essential part of the counterculture's challenge to the established values of middle-class society. Rock music exposed many young people to these counterculture ideals. Bob Dylan, a folk troubadour whose songs had inspired civil rights protesters, transformed himself into a rock musician with poetic lyrics steeped in drug references. The Beatles underwent a similar transformation after taking America by storm. Nearly 60 percent of the nation watched the four mop-headed British musicians sing their masterful pop concoctions during the band's first televised performance on the *Ed Sullivan Show* in 1964. In just three years the group underwent a complete makeover with the release of an album, *Sgt. Pepper's Lonely Hearts Club Band,* that broadcasted the counterculture message, "I'd love to turn you on"—a reference to taking drugs and having sex. The heyday of the marriage between rock music and the counterculture was Woodstock, a free three-day drug-infused music festival held on a farm in upstate New York, in August 1969.

New Left and young civil rights activists increasingly adopted a hippie-style of dress and experimented with drugs, but unlike hippies they remained dedicated to political activism. Most black civil rights activists, rather than rejecting white middle-class materialism, were fighting for their fair share of the nation's wealth and prosperity. New Left radicals shared the hippie belief that acquisitive capitalism bred inequality and injustice, but they were committed to engaged social action, not "tuning out."

Out of the spotlight conservatively minded college students were also active, laying the foundation

27.11 Holding Together
In their quest to define an alternative lifestyle, hippies emphasized love and harmony in their gatherings—sometimes wearing clothes, sometimes not.

How did the New Left, Civil Rights Movement, and counterculture disagree?

for the future conservative resurgence within a Republican Party dominated by moderates. A group of college students formed the Young Americans for Freedom (YAF) in 1960 under the guidance of *National Review* founder William F. Buckley. Throughout the sixties the Radical Right YAF attracted more members than the New Left SDS. Strong Goldwater supporters in 1964, these conservative students championed limited economic regulation, states' rights, respect for law and order, and staunch anticommunism. For the time being, however, the New Left had center stage.

Malcolm X: An Alternative to Nonviolence

The New Left and counterculture did not speak with one voice, and by the mid-sixties fractures within the Civil Rights Movement were also apparent. The **Nation of Islam**, an African American religious sect founded in the 1930s, rejected integration as the path to salvation for the black community and instead wanted to establish a separate black nation within the United States. As with conventional Muslims followers of Nation of Islam leader Elijah Muhammad prayed to Mecca five times a day, dressed modestly, and avoided pork and alcohol. The Nation of Islam departed from traditional Islamic thought, however, by viewing whites as "blue-eyed devils" whom Allah would condemn to eternal damnation on a forthcoming day of judgment.

> "I don't see any American dream; I see an American nightmare."
>
> MALCOLM X, ridiculing King's "I Have a Dream Speech" during the 1963 March on Washington

Nation of Islam leader Malcolm X moved ideas of armed self-defense and black separatism from the fringes to the center of the civil rights debate. A magnetic speaker Malcolm X had converted to Islam while serving a six-year stint in prison. After his release he changed his name from Malcolm Little to Malcolm X, the X signifying the lost name of his African ancestors.

Even during the heyday of nonviolence in the 1950s and early 1960s, more militant voices within the black community championed a competing vision of self-defense and racial pride that extended back to Marcus Garvey (see Chapter 21). Malcolm X openly ridiculed the nonviolent strategy of the Christian-led SCLC. "If someone puts his hand on you, send him to the cemetery," proclaimed Malcolm X in 1963. His statements received an increasingly sympathetic hearing among northern blacks who could already vote and sit alongside whites at lunch counters but encountered racial prejudice that relegated them to segregated ghettos, limited their employment opportunities, and subjected them to continued harassment by the police.

Malcolm X linked the domestic black struggle for civil rights to the global anticolonial movements underway in Africa and Asia, underscoring that the American Civil Rights Movement was just one of many liberation movements underway in the world, including a campaign to end apartheid in South Africa. Malcolm X's rhetorical links with Africa resonated well among northern blacks, who were incorporated African styles of clothing, hairstyles, and music into their daily lives. Many jettisoned the old label of "Negro" in favor of "black" to reflect their growing color consciousness and racial pride.

This photo (**27.12**) of Malcolm X smiling as he takes a photograph of boxer Muhammad Ali in a Miami restaurant after he won the heavyweight championship in 1964 conveys the charisma that each man radiated, and the strong bonds they maintained to the black urban community. Ali, who called himself "the greatest," gained fame not just for his athletic feats but, like Malcolm X, also for his defiance of authority. The day after this photo was taken he announced his conversion to the Nation of Islam, changing his name from Cassius Clay to Muhammad Ali. His mentor Malcolm X applauded Ali's announcement, knowing that the magnetic boxer would help attract other converts.

By the time Malcolm X's ideas began to gain widespread currency among disaffected blacks, however, his own philosophies were starting to shift. Viewing the increasingly powerful Malcolm X as a potential rival, Nation of Islam leader Elijah Muhammad had silenced Malcolm X a few months before this photo was taken. Malcolm X's transgression was calling the assassination of President Kennedy "a case of 'the chickens coming home to roost'" because whites were finally experiencing the vigilante violence that had terrorized blacks for years. Malcolm X left the Nation of Islam soon afterwards,

Why did some northern blacks find Malcolm X's vision appealing?

and Ali severed all ties with him. Malcolm X went on to experience a change of heart about the possibility of interracial cooperation following a 1964 pilgrimage to Mecca, Islam's holiest city, in Saudi Arabia, where he saw pilgrims "of all colors" coming together to worship. His more moderate stance did little to mollify his Nation of Islam critics. On February 21, 1965, as he stood to address a gathering in Harlem, three Nation of Islam members shot him dead.

27.12 Malcolm X Snaps a Photo of Muhammad Ali, 1964.
This meeting between two mid-sixties icons of black manhood came just after Ali won the heavyweight boxing title. Both Black Muslims, Malcolm X and Muhammad Ali enjoyed keeping whites on edge with militant rhetoric that emphasized black pride and physical prowess.

Watts and Chicago

Malcolm X did not live to help heal the fractures that ultimately unraveled the Civil Rights Movement. In the mid-sixties tensions among activists led to an overt split between those who continued to advocate nonviolence and integration and those who assumed a more militant, nationalistic approach. Stalwart civil rights veterans like John Lewis and Martin Luther King, Jr. never stopped advocating their vision of nonviolent collective action. But after 1965 the vision of armed self-defense won many new adherents.

August 6, 1965, the day that President Johnson signed the Voting Rights Act of 1965, represented the high-water mark of the nonviolent Civil Rights Movement. Five days later, with activists still basking in the afterglow of this major achievement, riots erupted in Watts, a Los Angeles black ghetto rife with high unemployment, poor schools, and rampant drug use. A routine arrest of a black man for drunk driving, which residents viewed as yet another example of the police harassment that plagued them daily, sparked the uprising. Watts burned for six days before sixteen thousand national guardsmen managed to stop the violence. The Watts riot left thirty-four dead and destroyed $35 million in property, including many businesses and homes owned by blacks.

Watts changed the image of African American protest in the white imagination from a portrait of nonviolent protesters kneeling in prayer before their attackers to one of lawless mobs shouting "burn, baby, burn." The same television cameras that helped awaken the liberal and moderate white consciousness now stoked white fears about unchecked black violence. The press ignored residents' complaints about police harassment and instead portrayed Los Angeles police as heroes who toiled tirelessly to prevent black rioters from destroying their own community. Watts was the prelude to several long, hot summers of racial rioting that rocked cities throughout the nation from 1965–1968.

The Watts riot convinced leaders like King to move aggressively to end economic inequality nationwide now that battles against legalized segregation and disenfranchisement were won. The SCLC's 1966 Chicago campaign dramatically demonstrated the limits of moderate northern whites' support for racial equality. When protesters marched through all-white neighborhoods to protest racial discrimination in renting and selling homes, white crowds pelted them with bottles and rocks, which some marchers threw back. "I have never seen—even in Mississippi and Alabama—mobs as hostile and hate-filled as I've seen in Chicago," King noted with dismay. After King's death in 1968,

> "It's much easier to integrate lunch counters than it is to eradicate slums."
>
> MARTIN LUTHER KING JR.

What caused many northern whites to lose sympathy for the Civil Rights Movement?

President Johnson successfully lobbied Congress to pass the Fair Housing Act that prohibited discrimination in selling, renting, or financing housing as a memorial to the slain leader.

Black Power and the Black Panthers

27.13 Black Panther Leader Huey Newton, 1967 This staged photo showed Newton dressed in guerrilla-style clothing surrounded by symbols of African warrior culture to convey the Black Panthers' militant, nationalistic ideology.

The "black power" slogan emerged during James Meredith's 1966 "March against Fear" in Mississippi. Meredith had faced down hostile crowds in 1962 when he became the first black student to graduate from the University of Mississippi. Four years later he decided to march 220 miles by himself from Memphis, Tennessee, to Jackson, Mississippi, hoping that his courage would inspire blacks to register to vote. On the second day of his march, a sniper waiting in the bushes shot and wounded Meredith. When activists flocked to continue Meredith's march, SNCC leader Stokely Carmichael told participants "we been saying freedom for six years, and we ain't got nothing. What we gonna start saying now is black power." **Black Power**, however, soon became a slippery term that different people employed in various ways. *Competing Visions: Defining "Black Power"* explores how black leaders with completely different ideologies embraced competing definitions of Black Power.

In 1966 Black Power militants came to the forefront of traditionally nonviolent civil rights organizations like SNCC, which expelled whites from the organization to foster black community leadership. That same year Bobby Seale and Huey Newton founded the Black Panther Party for Self-Defense in Oakland, California. The **Black Panthers** were a militant civil rights group dedicated to armed self-defense, racial pride, and inner-city renewal. The paramilitary group initiated several community projects including free breakfasts for school children and health clinics, but the press only saw their rifles. The Black Panthers organized paramilitary patrols that openly carried weapons (then legal under California law) and, Newton explained, "stopped whenever we saw the police questioning a brother or a sister" to ensure that no beatings or abuse occurred.

To project an image of strength that would appeal to inner-city youth, the Black Panthers wore commando-style attire including black leather jackets, black pants, black berets, and dark sunglasses, items already fashionable among young black men. The 1967 photo (**27.13**) that became the emblem of the Black Panther Movement depicted Newton sitting in a throne-like wicker chair surrounded by a zebra rug and warrior shields, symbols of a racial identity rooted in African culture. Wearing Western military-style clothing and holding a rifle in his right hand and a spear in his left, Newton stared into the camera with the steely resolve of a modern revolutionary.

By October, 1967 Newton was under arrest, wounded by police during a shoot-out and accused of killing a white policeman who died in the melee. FBI chief J. Edgar Hoover viewed the Panthers as "the greatest threat to the internal security of the country" and used spies to plan raids on Panther offices and create rifts within the group to weaken the Panthers internally. When the courts overturned Newton's conviction in 1970, he emerged from jail to find the Black Panthers in shambles.

The Women's Liberation Movement

Another fracture within the Civil Rights Movement, this one between men and women, energized the modern women's movement. When young white

Did the tactics used by the Black Panthers to publicize their militant vision help or hurt them?

Competing Visions

DEFINING "BLACK POWER"

The powerful image of a raised, clenched black fist became the most enduring symbol of "Black Power," but it only represented one view of the slogan's meaning. In the following excerpts civil rights leaders debate the meaning and implications of Black Power. Malcolm X never used the term directly, but his separatist message laid the groundwork for Black Power nationalism later in the decade. In contrast Martin Luther King, Jr. advocated using nonviolent methods to empower the black community. Political scientist Charles Hamilton notes the various interpretations given to the "Black Power" slogan and embraces one that emphasizes pride in being black. Are there any points of agreement among these competing definitions? How does this debate compare to the one between Marcus Garvey and W. E. B. DuBois in the 1920s (see Competing Visions, Chapter 21)?

The revolutionary, nationalist rhetoric in Malcolm X's fiery 1963 "Message to the Grassroots" greatly influenced later advocates of Black Power.

There's no such thing as a nonviolent revolution. The only kind of revolution that is nonviolent is the Negro revolution. The only revolution in which the goal is loving your enemy is the Negro revolution. It's the only revolution in which the goal is a desegregated lunch counter, a desegregated theater, a desegregated park, and a desegregated public toilet; you can sit down next to white folks—on the toilet. That's no revolution. Revolution is based on land. Land is the basis of all independence. Land is the basis of freedom, justice, and equality ...

Whoever heard of a revolution where they lock arms ... singing "We Shall Overcome"? You don't do that in a revolution. You don't do any singing, you're too busy swinging.

In a "Conversation with Martin Luther King," March 25, 1968, King offered a definition of Black Power that supported his strategy of nonviolence.

We have always stood up against injustices. We have done it militantly. Now, so often the word 'militant' is misunderstood because most people think of militancy in military terms. But, to be militant merely means to be demanding and to be persistent, and in this sense I think the nonviolent movement has demonstrated great militancy. It is possible to be militantly nonviolent. ... I haven't advocated violence, because I do not see it as the answer to the problem. I do not see it as the answer from a moral point of view and I do not see it as the answer from a practical point of view. ...

Let me briefly outline the positives [of Black Power]. First, Black Power in the positive sense is a psychological call to manhood. This is desperately needed in the black community, because for all too many years black people have been ashamed of themselves. ... Secondly, Black Power is pooling black political resources in order to achieve our legitimate goals. ... Thirdly, Black Power in its positive sense is a pooling of black economic resources in order to achieve legitimate power. ... Withdrawing economic support from those who will not be just and fair in their dealings is a very potent weapon.

Writing to white America in the *New York Times Magazine* in 1968, Charles Hamilton outlined competing views of Black Power and stressed the importance of maintaining black racial identity.

Black Power has many definitions and connotations in the rhetoric of race relations today. To some people, it is synonymous with premeditated acts of violence to destroy the political and economic institutions of this country. Others equate Black Power with plans to rid the civil rights movements of whites who have been in it for years. The concept is understood by many to mean hatred of and separation from whites; it is associated with calling whites 'honkies' and with shouts of 'Burn, baby, burn!' Some understand it to be the use of pressure-group tactics in the accepted tradition of the American political process. And still others say that Black Power must be seen first of all as an attempt to instill a sense of identity and pride in black people. ...

Black Power rejects the lessons of slavery and segregation that caused black people to look upon themselves with hatred and disdain. To be 'integrated' it was necessary to deny one's heritage, one's own culture, to be ashamed of one's black skin, thick lips and kinky hair. ... The black man must change his demeaning conception of himself; he must develop a sense of pride and self-respect. Then, if integration comes, it will deal with people who are psychologically and mentally healthy, with people who have a sense of their history and of themselves as whole human beings ...

Why do all three writers emphasize the importance of racial pride and manhood?

27.14 Feminists Picket the Miss America Pageant, 1968
This satirical portrait of a woman carved up like a side of beef criticizes beauty pageants for reducing a woman's value to the quality of her body parts.

female activists began leaving the Civil Rights Movement to join the women's movement, they joined a crusade already well underway. In 1963 journalist Betty Friedan reignited the feminist movement, which had faltered since the 1920s, with her treatise the *Feminine Mystique*. Calling it "the problem that has no name," Friedan challenged the widely accepted notion that women found homemaking and child-rearing fulfilling. In 1966 she founded the **National Organization for Women** (NOW), an organization dedicated to securing equal rights for women in employment, education, and politics—areas traditionally seen as male domains. NOW also wanted to give women control over their own bodies through unfettered access to contraception and legal abortions. A relatively small organization with only five thousand members in the late sixties, NOW nonetheless convinced President Johnson to issue an executive order that required government agencies and federal contractors to create affirmative action programs to hire and promote women and minority men.

The women's movement continued to grow as younger female activists, unhappy with gender discrimination within the Civil Rights Movement and New Left, took up the cause of female liberation. The feminists who founded NOW lobbied for legislative solutions to women's problems. In contrast, more radicalized feminists, steeped in New Left ideology and nonviolent tactics, adopted a grassroots approach that used consciousness-raising—heightening awareness of social and political issues—to help women "understand the universality of our oppression." They emphasized changing attitudes rather than lobbying for legislative changes. To combat the ways that sexism pervaded normal social interactions, feminists introduced the word "Ms." into American lexicon to replace "Miss" or "Mrs.," titles that linked a woman's identity to her marital status. When activist Robin Morgan brought busloads of women to Atlantic City to protest the annual Miss America pageant in 1968, she sought maximum media coverage. Demonstrators carried the photograph (**27.14**) of an attractive, naked young woman with lines dividing her body into cuts of beef to protest how beauty pageants dehumanized women. "Welcome to the Miss America Cattle Auction," they chanted while filling a trash can with bras, high heeled shoes, mainstream fashion magazines, and copies of *Playboy*, items they believed reinforced "the Mindless Sex Object Image" of women. In deference to a local ordinance, the protesters never set the trash can on fire, but from this point onwards detractors used the dismissive term "bra-burners" to describe feminists.

Despite their different styles and messages, both moderate and radical feminists had trouble expanding their base of support beyond the white middle class. "If your husband is a factory worker or a tugboat operator, you don't want his job," noted Democratic Congresswoman Barbara Mikilski to explain why NOW's emphasis on equality in employment failed to resonate among working-class women. Similarly few black women joined the women's movement, convinced that racial oppression affected them more severely than sexual discrimination.

How did activists' competing visions and media coverage shape the women's liberation movement?

The End of an Era

As the Civil Rights Movement unraveled, the Great Society also floundered. Republicans widened their political appeal by promising to end the cultural strife that was tearing the nation apart. Although most liberal and radical causes lost energy after 1968, activists in the Chicano and Native American communities helped keep the protest tradition alive as the decade came to a close.

The Faltering Civil Rights Movement

Embittered by years of violent attacks in the South, young activists either left the movement altogether or migrated to more militant organizations. By 1967 King's weakening leadership reflected a movement adrift. When King spoke out against the Vietnam War, he strained his relationship with President Johnson, losing a valuable ally in the White House. King's call for a complete reconstructing of American capitalism to eliminate poverty also cost him the support of moderate blacks and whites. In the fall of 1967, after a summer of deadly race riots in Detroit and Newark, King proposed setting up a poor people's encampment in front of the White House. When the Poor People's Campaign stalled, King had time to make a quick trip to Memphis to offer his support for a garbage men's strike.

On April 4, 1968, a sniper's bullet tore through the knot in King's necktie and fatally wounded him as he leaned over the balcony of his Memphis motel. Within hours *Life* photographer Steve Schapiro entered King's motel room and snapped a haunting photograph of King's open suitcase containing a copy of his book *Strength to Love*, a wrinkled shirt, and the remnants of a meal (**27.15**). "The half-drunk cup of coffee gave me a moment of pause," Schapiro noted. "He had left his room planning to return." Completing this eerie scene King's portrait appeared on the motel television during a newscast reporting his death. The three-week urban rampage in one hundred cities across the nation that followed King's murder only further alienated the white community, who increasingly supported using troops to restore "law and order." Two months later a white man, James Earl Ray, confessed to the killing, a confession that he later retracted.

The Great Society Unravels

Diminishing sympathy for the Civil Rights Movement also meant less support for Great Society programs directed at the urban poor. Congress had written much of the legislation quickly, but the public had no appetite for waiting patiently while the Great Society worked through its growing pains. Critics from the left and right continued their attacks. The New Left advocated redistributing corporate profits more equitably throughout society. Meanwhile the Radical Right denounced the Great Society as a "hodgepodge" of

27.15 King's Room in the Lorraine Motel, April 4, 1968
King stepped out of this motel room to chat briefly with friends over the motel balcony and never returned. The television above King's suitcase announces his death to an empty room.

Why was King's death a serious blow to the Civil Rights Movement?

programs that humiliated the poor and encouraged dependency on government welfare. Ethnic working-class whites and left-leaning suburbanites, groups that had traditionally supported the Democratic liberal agenda, began to resent federal programs that they felt primarily helped black minorities. The shift in attitudes among the white working class had a significant political impact. In 1964 nearly 60 percent had voted for the Democratic ticket; four years later that percentage had dropped to 35 percent.

The Great Society's troubles reflected more than persistent racism, however. Johnson's unwillingness to raise taxes to pay for an exploding array of domestic programs and a costly war in Vietnam also contributed to its undoing. As the economy overheated interest rates doubled, the national debt exploded, and inflation caused prices to rise without any corresponding increase in wages. Americans reacted with dismay to this sudden decline in the standard of living after several decades of continued prosperity.

This 1967 Herblock political cartoon (**27.16**) illustrated Johnson's dilemma in trying to fund both the Vietnam War and the Great Society. In the drawing President Johnson prepares for an evening out with his mistress, a robust and expensively attired woman wearing a mink stole emblazoned with the words "Vietnam War." As they leave Johnson tries to assure the other woman in his life, a thin homemaker wearing a tattered apron labeled "U.S. Urban Needs," that "There's Money Enough to Support Both of You—Now, Doesn't That Make You Feel Better?" As this cartoon suggested the administration was neglecting its domestic programs and giving the war the bulk of its attention and funds. In 1968 Johnson agreed to raise taxes to finance the expanded war in Vietnam but southern conservative congressmen refused to vote for the measure until the president made substantial funding cuts to his domestic programs.

"There's Money Enough To Support Both Of You — Now, Doesn't That Make You Feel Better?"

27.16 Torn between Two Mistresses, 1967
This Herblock cartoon illustrated how Johnson's escalation of the war in Vietnam deprived his Great Society programs of needed funds.

The Democratic Convention in 1968 pulled together these various strands of disenchantment with liberal politics. With Vice President Hubert Humphrey on track to secure the nomination, ten thousand antiwar activists led by New Left leader Tom Hayden organized a mass protest before the television cameras outside the Chicago Convention Center to support the antiwar candidate Eugene McCarthy. Yippies, a New Left splinter group that stood for blending "pot and politics," joined the protest. Led by Abbie Hoffman and Jerry Rubin, the Yippies issued outlandish warnings that they planned to put LSD in Chicago's water supply. As Democratic Party delegates debated the administration's Vietnam policy inside the convention hall, the police launched a premeditated attack on the demonstrators outside. Televised images of long-haired, pot-smoking protesters who waved North Vietnamese flags and threw excrement had a greater impact on public opinion than news reports of police brutality. Over 70 percent of adults supported the police crackdown.

Critics of liberalism found the public suddenly much more receptive to their competing political vision. Richard Nixon won the presidency in 1968 promising to restore "law and order," a Republican catch-phrase that fueled the political shift already underway in many traditionally Democratic blue-collar and suburban neighborhoods. With grassroots conservatism on the rise, the liberal vision appealed to fewer and fewer Americans by the end of the decade.

At the end of this divisive decade, a rare moment of national celebration occurred on July 20, 1969 when astronaut Neil Armstrong became the first man to walk on the moon. Watching the event unfurl on their television sets, Americans heard Armstrong declare "that's one small step for a man, one giant leap for mankind" as he began to stride across the moon's surface. Announcing the U.S. space race victory over the Soviet Union to the world, astronaut Buzz Aldrin planted an American flag (**27.17**) near manmade

How did presidential choices and public attitudes undermine Johnson's Great Society agenda?

footprints that would permanently mark the moon's surface. This iconic photo of the United States conquering the moon bolstered many citizens' faith in the superiority of the American way of life, giving them another reason to reject the New Left and counterculture critique of American culture.

27.17 The First Moon Landing, 1969
National pride surged at the sight of an American flag planted on the moon. For many Americans, beating the Soviets to the moon challenged the radical left's view that American society was faltering.

The Demise of the Counterculture

As with the Civil Rights Movement and the Great Society, the hippie counterculture unraveled by the end of the decade. Heightened media coverage drew large crowds to the 1967 "Summer of Love" in San Francisco's Haight-Ashbury neighborhood, a hippie gathering dedicated to free food, drugs, sex, and music. In the fall hippie stalwarts organized a mock "Death of Hippie: Son of Media" funeral procession, blaming the over-hyped media image of the free-loving hippie for the drug-related violence and epidemic of rapes that now beset Haight-Ashbury. They then departed en masse, moving the foci of hippie culture to rural communes away from the media glare, where some succeeded in keeping the hippie utopian ideal alive.

> "Beautify America, Get a Haircut."
>
> A billboard in Rochester, New York, criticizes counterculture fashion

Ronald Reagan, the Republican governor of California, echoed the views of mainstream America in 1969 when he characterized a hippie as someone who "dresses like Tarzan, has hair like Jane, and smells like Cheetah," a reference to the counterculture's embrace of public nudity, long hair, and disdain for underarm deodorant. Worried that the counterculture had made addictive drugs such as heroin popular among the young, many states passed stringent anti-drug laws. At the federal level, in 1972 President Nixon announced a "war on drugs" aimed at disrupting the illicit drug trade.

The quick commercialization of the counterculture also hastened its demise as a potent alternative social vision. Modes of hippie dress, hippie slang, and hippie values (albeit in diluted form) swept into the mainstream. Granola appeared on supermarket shelves, and middle-aged men began growing their hair long. Affluent and educated adults increasingly smoked marijuana and listened to rock music. More sexually explicit movies and highly profitable rock record sales fueled rather than undermined acquisitive capitalism.

Keeping Protest Alive: Mexican Americans and Native Americans

The declining fortunes of the Civil Rights Movement and the counterculture did not mean the end of all campaigns for social justice in the late sixties. Mexican American and Native American activists drew inspiration from the African American struggle and launched their own highly visible, if short-lived, crusades to end ethnic discrimination. Ultimately, however, the same problems of factionalism and police harassment hurt these crusades as well.

How did media exposure affect the counterculture?

In the 1960s the life expectancy for Mexican American migrant workers hovered around fifty years old, while infant mortality was double the national average. The short-handed hoe represented the nearly complete exploitation of California migrant workers. "The short one" forced workers to bend all day (**27.18**) as they worked in the fields, often causing crippling back pain that sidelined workers who could not afford health care. California regulators finally banned the tool in 1975.

Rallying Mexican Americans around the slogan *Si Se Puede* ("Yes, it can be done"), César Chávez, head of the United Farm Workers union, used strikes and marches to secure better working and living conditions. Chávez also appealed directly to consumers, convincing seventeen million Americans to stop buying nonunion-picked grapes, but also provoking a backlash among some. One Safeway grocery store manager reported antiunion customers loading up "their car with grapes and nothing else," while school children in the East refused to eat the grapes provided as part of their school lunches. By 1970 the economic toll of the boycott forced growers to recognize the United Farm Workers union and raise wages.

Latino urban radicals in Texas, California, and Colorado embraced a competing vision called La Raza (The Race) that emphasized racial identity over union organizing. The Brown Berets modeled themselves after the Black Panthers and proudly called themselves "Chicanos," embracing their Mexican American heritage while demanding an end to Anglo-American discrimination. In March 1968, ten thousand high school students in East Los Angeles staged a "blowout" by walking out of their classrooms and into the streets to protest the poor education they received in their mostly Hispanic schools. By this point most white Americans had little tolerance for radical political protest and overwhelmingly supported the police for shutting the demonstrations down. Internal divisions within the Mexican American community over the wisdom of confrontational tactics like mass demonstrations and steady harassment from the police hastened the demise of the short-lived Chicano student movement.

Native American activists also drew inspiration from the integrationist vision that championed equality and the competing militant one that emphasized maintaining racial identity. After encouraging Indians to move off their reservations in the 1950s, the Bureau of Indian Affairs (BIA) began terminating the rights of some Indian tribes to federal protection. Ending their dependence on the BIA to run schools, manage their lands, and provide health care, the agency argued, would encourage Indians to assimilate into mainstream culture more quickly. Indian activists wanted the federal government to continue its financial

27.18 Hispanic Farm Workers Using Short Hoes Workers nicknamed short hoes "the devil's arm" because using them caused intense back pain. Every time César Chávez saw a head of lettuce in the supermarket, he thought of what the suffering workers had endured to grow it and was newly resolved to use strikes and boycotts to improve their working conditions.

How did the Civil Rights and labor movements influence Hispanic activists?

assistance, while at the same time allowing more self-government on Indian reservations.

On November 20, 1969, a group calling themselves "Indians of All Tribes" grabbed headlines when they occupied the abandoned federal prison on Alcatraz Island in San Francisco Bay. During their occupation of Alcatraz, Indian activists issued the sardonic **Alcatraz Proclamation** that offered to purchase the island for $24 in glass beads and red cloth, the same amount that the Dutch had paid indigenous people for Manhattan Island in 1626. The proclamation further described Alcatraz as the perfect site for an Indian reservation because it lacked running water, sanitation, schools, mineral resources, and productive soil, plus "the population has always been held as prisoner and kept dependent upon others." Eventually the cold and isolation took its toll, and the protest ended in June 1971.

In the fall of 1972 a caravan of cars and vans left the West Coast to follow "The Trail of Broken Treaties," a slogan meant to remind Americans of the "Trail of Tears," the 1838 forced removal of southeastern Indian tribes to interior lands. Stopping at individual reservations, the protesters urged tribes to fight for their legal rights. When they reached Washington, D.C., the group temporarily occupied BIA offices. Native Americans staged nearly seventy other occupations throughout the nation, including the American Indian Movement's armed takeover of the village of Wounded Knee, South Dakota, in 1973, the site of the army's massacre of three hundred Sioux in 1890. These highly visible protests prompted Nixon to increase funds for social services on Indian reservations and establish the Office of Indian Water Rights. In the early 1970s the federal government ended the policy of termination and Congress increased Indian self-rule on the reservations. Indian tribes also began suing the government for past treaty violations. At the same time, however, government harassment eviscerated radical Indian groups, part of a general crack-down on revolutionary political movements in the early seventies.

Conclusion

Whether the 1960s represented the heyday of progressive social change or a nightmare from which America needed to awake remained a point of disagreement among liberals and conservatives for decades to come. By the mid-sixties the legal edifice that had supported racial segregation and disenfranchisement through the South was gone, thanks to countless grassroots protests including the Freedom Rides, the Birmingham campaign, Freedom Summer, and the march from Selma to Montgomery. The movement effectively used mass media to create a groundswell of support for civil rights legislation, and celebrated figures like Martin Luther King Jr. along with numerous other activists lost their lives while pursuing racial justice. Nonviolent direct action lost momentum when the competing militant call for Black Power and the focus on economic inequality moved the spotlight from the South to northern ghettos. Although the movement faltered in the closing years of the sixties, it left a legacy that permanently altered the social and political fabric of the nation.

Radical and liberal politics also left a mark. Student activists transformed university life. Counterculture rejection of traditional values seeped into the mainstream, changing attitudes toward sex, drugs, and authority. Women, Hispanics, and Native Americans made the larger society aware of longstanding discrimination that limited their chances to share the American Dream. America emerged from the sixties with a new vision of itself as a multicultural society.

The Great Society laid bare a vigorous set of competing visions among radicals, liberals, and conservatives over the role of the government in American society and the value of capitalism. Dismay over Supreme Court decisions that outlawed prayer in school, Great Society programs that primarily helped minorities, and the counterculture pervaded Middle America. Unhappy with the direction of the liberal vision, many former Democrats joined a new conservative coalition whose vision appealed to more and more Americans in the 1970s.

What problems did Native Americans face in the 1960s?

CHAPTER REVIEW

1961

Peace Corps Established
Program sends U.S. aid volunteers worldwide

Freedom Rides
Convinces Kennedy administration to enforce Supreme Court ruling against segregated interstate travel

1962

Supreme Court rules school prayer unconstitutional
Furor lays the foundation for religiously-based conservative resurgence

Port Huron Statement
Motivates student activists to join SDS

1963

Birmingham
Outrage over fire hose and dog attacks on civil rights protesters prompts Kennedy to support a federal civil rights law

March on Washington
International press coverage turns the peaceful march into a triumphant movement for the nonviolent Civil Rights Movement

***Feminine Mystique* published**
Inspires creation of the modern feminist movement

Review Questions

1. Compare the goals and strategies of the Freedom Rides and the Birmingham civil rights campaign. Why was each an effective episode of nonviolent protest?
2. How did the Great Society compare to the New Deal? What continuities or differences existed? What lasting impact did the Great Society have on American society?
3. Why did black nationalist sentiment become more popular among African Americans after 1965?
4. What alternative visions did the counterculture and the New Left offer? What were the differences and similarities in their critiques of American society?
5. How important was leadership in the civil rights and black nationalism movements? How did grassroots activism make these movements successful? Which reform and protest movements in the 1960s were the most successful? Why?
6. Why did conservative ideals gain strength as the decade progressed?
7. How did the sixties transform American society?

1964

Freedom Summer
Murder of three Civil Rights workers in Mississippi prompts Congress to pass the Civil Rights Act of 1964

Great Society begins
Largest legislative liberal reform effort since the New Deal

1965–1966

March from Selma to Montgomery
Congress responds to vigilante attacks on marchers by passing the Voting Rights Act of 1965

Watts Riot
Violent rampage in Los Angeles ghetto generates white backlash against Civil Rights Movement

Black Panthers founded
Black militants reject nonviolent tactics and instead advocate Black Power

1967

"Summer of Love"
Hippie gathering in Haight-Ashbury publicizes counterculture

1968

King assassinated
Nationwide rioting signals the end of the nonviolent Civil Rights Movement

Chicago Democratic presidential convention
Police crackdown on demonstrators wins general support for reinstating law and order

Feminists picket Miss America pageant
Feminists use media coverage to challenge sexist stereotypes

Key Terms

New Frontier Kennedy's legislative program that proposed raising the minimum wage, reducing overcrowding in schools, and providing health care for the elderly. **813**

Peace Corps Government agency that President Kennedy established to send recent college graduates to work on humanitarian projects overseas in developing nations. **813**

Warren Court Supreme Court that brought about a legal revolution in the United States by permanently altering American schools, politics, the criminal justice system, and cultural norms. **813**

Great Society President Johnson's wide-ranging social welfare reforms intended to make the amenities of modern life—a decent standard of living, education, health care, and clean water—available to all Americans. **816**

Freedom Rides An interstate bus journey by black and white activists who entered segregated bus facilities together throughout the South. **819**

Birmingham campaign Civil rights effort to desegregate Birmingham, Alabama, where shocking images of police brutality prompted Kennedy to push for a federal civil rights act. **821**

March on Washington, 1963 Massive demonstration in the nation's capital that demanded passage of a federal civil rights act and more economic opportunities. **824**

Freedom Summer, 1964 Multipronged attack on white supremacy in Mississippi that included a voter registration drive and the creation of Freedom Schools. **825**

Civil Rights Act of 1964 Legislation that banned segregation in businesses and places open to the public (such as restaurants and public schools) and prohibited racial and gender discrimination in employment. **826**

Voting Rights Act of 1965 Legislation that prohibited literacy tests and poll taxes, plus authorized the use of federal registrars to register voters if states failed to respect the Fifteenth Amendment. **827**

New Left A small, but highly visible, coalition of left-leaning student-based organizations that attacked racial discrimination, poverty, and the war in Vietnam. **828**

hippies Youthful social rebels who renounced material acquisition and used drugs to explore their inner spiritual selves. **829**

Nation of Islam African American sect that rejected integration as the path to salvation for the black community and instead wanted to establish a separate black nation. **830**

Black Power A call for blacks to unite politically and economically in black-only organizations to protect their racial identity as they fought for equality. **832**

Black Panthers Militant civil rights group dedicated to armed self-defense, racial pride, and inner-city renewal. **832**

National Organization for Women (NOW) An organization dedicated to securing equal rights for women in employment, education, and politics. **834**

Alcatraz Proclamation Sardonic statement issued by Indian activists who occupied the island of Alcatraz and described it as the perfect site for an Indian reservation because it lacked running water, sanitation, schools, mineral resources, and productive soil. **839**

CHAPTER 28

Righting a Nation Adrift

America in the 1970s and 1980s

> "Government is not the solution to our problem; government is the problem,"
>
> President RONALD REAGAN, 1981

The vision of the United States as a great and powerful nation suddenly seemed less assured in the 1970s. In 1973 a dispute between the United States and oil-producing Arab nations led to an oil embargo that severely restricted oil imports. Gas stations across the nation posted signs like this one as they ran out of gas, dotting the American landscape with humiliating reminders that foreign nations had the power to wreak havoc on the U.S. economy. Gas shortages also threatened the vision of America as a prosperous car culture where it was the birthright of every citizen to work, live, and shop wherever they liked thanks to the freedom of movement that automobiles provided. To many Americans images of closed gas stations (which reappeared in 1979) were just one sign of a nation adrift. Domestic political scandals, a troubled economy, and lost international prestige made the future look dim.

Americans lost confidence in the federal government in the 1970s as the Watergate scandal and cover-up brought down President Richard Nixon and the post-World War II boom times finally ended, leaving high inflation and unemployment. Ongoing economic woes and troubles abroad hampered the efforts of presidents Gerald Ford and Jimmy Carter to restore respect for the presidency. Americans did not agree over how to move the nation back onto the path of glory. Women's and gay rights groups fought to extend the social justice campaigns of the sixties, while the environmental movement focused Americans' attention on conserving its natural heritage. A new and powerful conservative coalition, however, formed around a competing vision that focused on protecting traditional values, limiting the role of the government in the economy, and flexing the nation's power overseas. In the 1980s, after two decades of grassroots activism, the conservative ascendancy was complete.

When Ronald Reagan, an ideologically committed conservative, became president in 1981, he refused to accept the notion that America had entered an age of limits. Reagan rejected the liberal vision and diagnosed government as part of the problem, not the solution to the nation's economic woes. He also moved aggressively to restore America's image as a powerful world power. An immensely popular president, Reagan restored the nation's confidence in the economy and the presidency, despite suffering some political scandals of his own.

Why did signs like this one provoke anxiety throughout the nation?

Downturn and Scandal p. 844

A Crisis of Presidential Leadership p. 851

The Rights Revolution p. 858

The Rise of the Right p. 865

Downturn and Scandal

Americans enjoyed unprecedented prosperity in the 1950s and 1960s, and few expected the bubble to eventually burst. By the 1970s, however, periodic recessions returned, a shocking development for a nation that had grown accustomed to a steadily improving standard of living. The political repercussions were significant. Still reeling from the cultural and civil rights upheavals of the sixties, the nation's new economic problems exacerbated the growing feeling that the country was adrift. The economic downturn, partly caused by turmoil overseas, coincided with a decade-long crisis of presidential leadership that began when political scandal enveloped the Nixon White House.

An Ailing Economy

An ailing economy created the sense of a nation adrift by the 1970s. In the sixties Lyndon Johnson had tried to pay for both the Vietnam War (see Chapter 26) and the Great Society programs (see Chapter 27) without raising taxes. Heavy governmental spending created both a ballooning federal deficit and, by pumping so much cash into the economy, inflation. The end of the Vietnam War (see Chapter 26) added rising unemployment to the growing list of economic woes. Returning veterans entered a job market hit hard by the cancellation of government defense contracts that triggered massive layoffs in the industrial sector.

Americans also faced rising energy costs. The United States contained 6 percent of the world's population, but consumed nearly 40 percent of global energy resources. Due to increased U.S. reliance on Middle Eastern oil, the unending strife in the region affected the daily lives of Americans. The United States had offered Israel strong financial and moral support ever since the United Nations created a homeland for the Jewish people in 1947 by partitioning Palestine into Jewish and Palestinian areas. Israel claimed territory in Palestine as their ancestral land, a view supported by the United States, which also believed that the world owed the Jewish people some reparation for the horrors of the Holocaust. Arab nations viewed the creation of Israel completely differently. In their eyes the arrival of Jewish immigrants perpetuated the long history of hated Western colonization in the Middle East. A series of clashes between neighboring Arab nations and Israel ensued (detailed on **28.1**), and disputes over the fate of Palestinian refugees and Israeli land seizures continue to roil the region to this day.

Richard Nixon and subsequent presidents faced a thorny foreign policy dilemma in the Middle East. The U.S. government steadfastly supported Israel's right to exist, but given America's growing dependence on Middle Eastern oil exports, the United States could not afford to alienate oil-producing Arab nations. The Soviet push to form strong alliances in the Middle East also threatened to turn the oil-rich region into the new Cold War battlefield.

In 1973 Egypt and Syria (both armed with Soviet-provided weapons) attacked Israel on Yom Kippur (Judaism's holiest day) to regain territory lost to Israel in 1967. Nixon's decision to send military aid to Israel enraged the Arab world. In retaliation the **Organization of the Petroleum Exporting Countries (OPEC)**, an international consortium of oil-producing nations that regulates the price and quantity of oil exported to the world market, announced an oil embargo of the United States. By this point the United States depended on the Middle East for 12 percent of the oil consumed domestically. The embargo lasted five months, enough time to ravage the American economy (see image on page 843). OPEC finally lifted the embargo after Nixon persuaded Israel to withdraw from Egyptian and Syrian lands seized during the Yom Kippur War.

In 1974 the nation entered its worst recession since the Great Depression. In typical periods of recession and depression, high unemployment went hand in hand with declining prices and wages. The financial crisis of the mid-1970s was unique, however, because the economy suffered from both

How did domestic energy needs affect U.S. foreign policy?

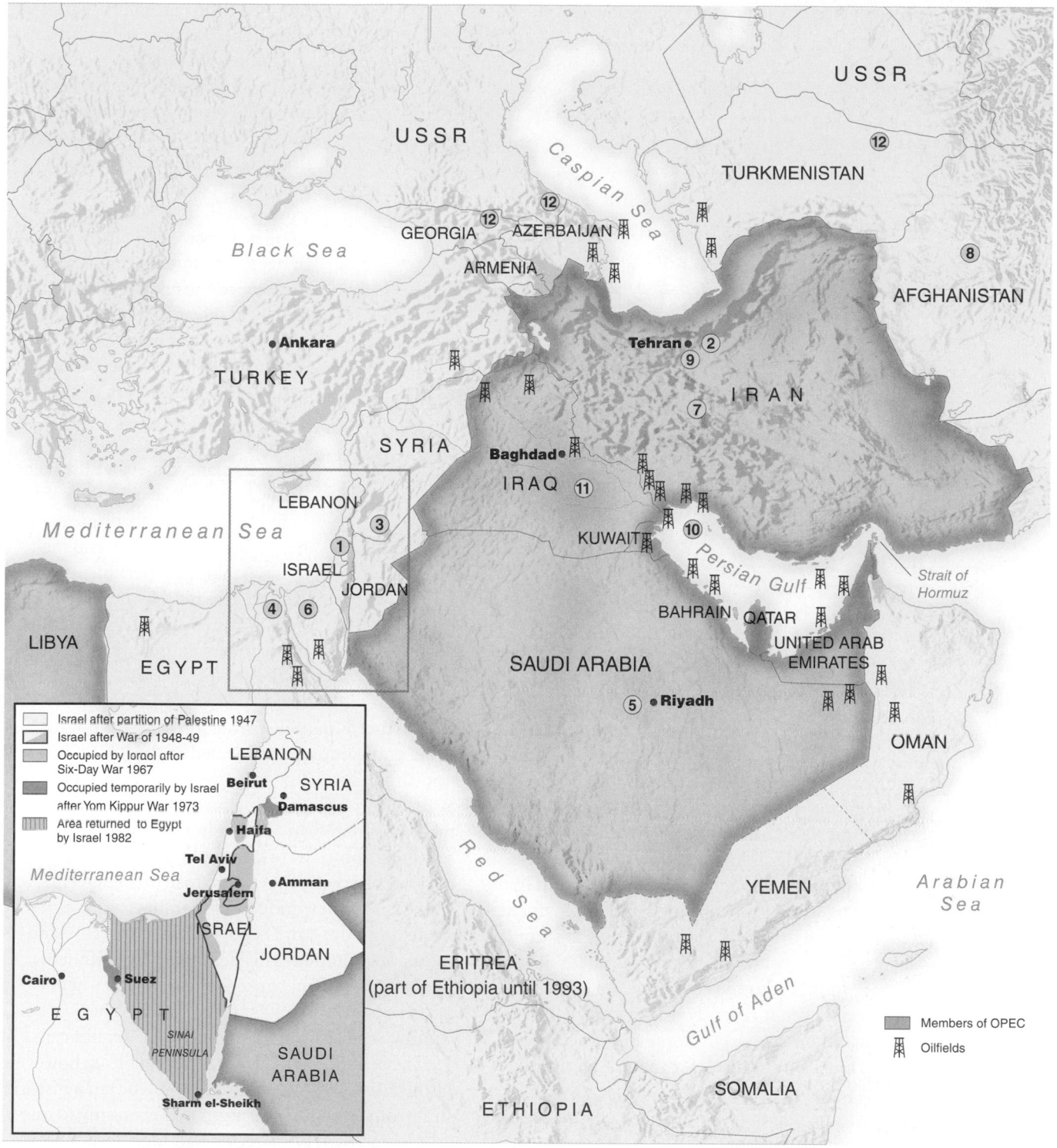

1. 1948-49: Egypt, Syria, Jordan, Lebanon attack Israel
2. 1953 Shah of Iran installed with US help
3. 1967 Six-Day War: Israel vs. Egypt, Syria, Jordan
4. 1973 Yom Kippur War: Egypt, Syria attack Israel
   1974 Israel withdraws from Suez
5. 1973 OPEC oil embargo of US
6. 1978 Camp David Accords between Egypt and Israel
7. 1979 Iranian revolution deposes Shah
8. 1979 Soviet invasion of Afghanistan
9. 1979-81 Iranian hostage crisis
10. 1980 Carter Doctrine: US will defend Persian Gulf
11. 1980-1988 Iraq-Indian War
12. Part of USSR until 1991

28.1 Middle East and Persian Gulf, 1947–1988
U.S. dependence on Middle-Eastern oil increased the importance of conflicts in this region for Americans.

Why did Israel's troubled relations with its neighbors concern the United States?

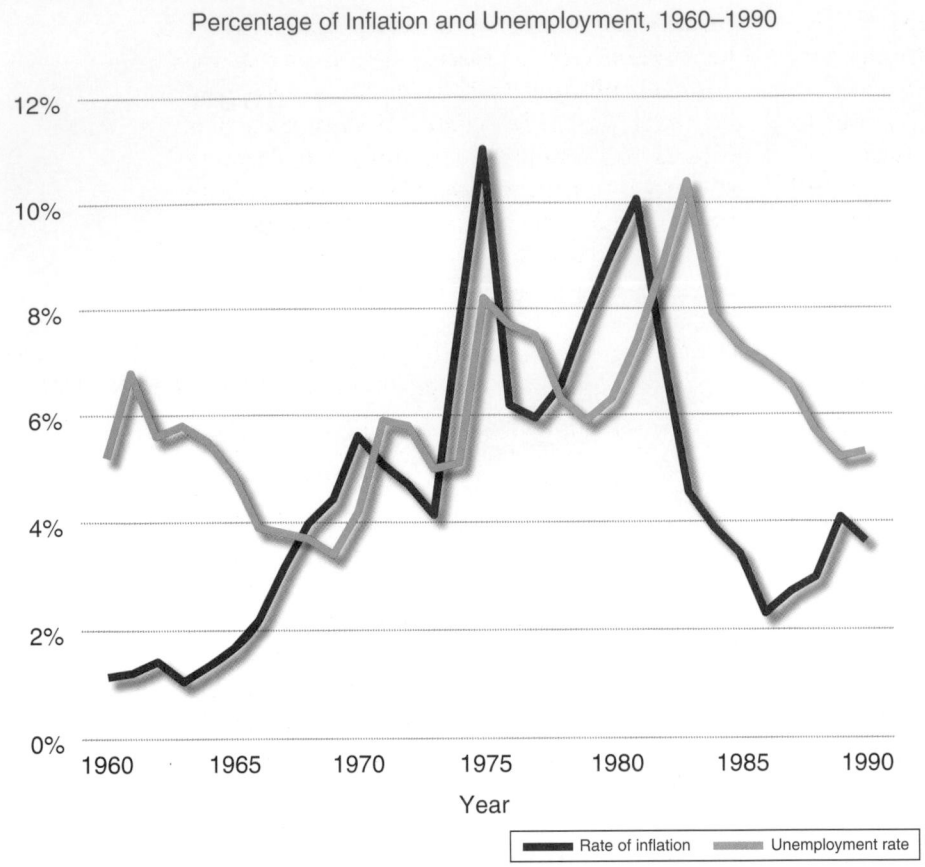

28.2 Inflation and Unemployment, 1960–1990
The combination of high unemployment and inflation created a phenomenon dubbed "stagflation" in the 1970s.

high unemployment and mounting inflation that kept prices rising, pictured on the graph *Inflation and Unemployment, 1960–1990* (**28.2**), an unusual combination dubbed "stagflation." In the 1930s pumping more federal money into the economy through the New Deal did not end the Depression, but it did ease unemployment and stabilize prices so farmers and businessmen could make a profit. In the 1970s trying to solve one problem, unemployment, often worsened inflation. Tax cuts meant to stimulate a business recovery and create more jobs, for instance, put more money into the economy and caused prices to rise even further. Trying to curtail inflation by raising interest rates put home mortgage and business loans out of reach for many Americans. Without access to credit the business recovery stalled. Meanwhile the federal deficit skyrocketed as tax revenue declined, but high spending on defense and entitlement programs like Social Security, welfare, and Medicaid continued.

The problem of rising unemployment had deep roots in the ailing auto and steel industries, long the backbone of the American economy. In 1970 the Big Three automakers, General Motors, Ford, and Chrysler, sold 89 percent of the cars marketed in the United States. Within ten years their market share dropped to 66 percent. Faced with higher gas prices, American consumers flocked to purchase smaller, more fuel-efficient cars imported from Japan. The decline in the steel industry was even more dramatic. In 1950 the U.S. steel industry produced nearly half of the world's steel. By 1980 that figure stood at 14 percent, a fall hastened by aggressive foreign competitors that reaped the rewards of investing heavily in research and innovation. New furnace technology, for instance, allowed Japanese competitors to produce a ton of steel for a third of the price it cost American factories. As American automobile and steel plants closed, a **Rust Belt** of decaying industrial cities appeared in the Midwest, places plagued with high unemployment, crumbling roads, bankrupt governments, and high welfare rolls. By the end of the decade, Americans increasingly chose to buy household appliances, textiles, and television sets manufactured abroad in places like Japan and Taiwan.

Northern manufacturing jobs also evaporated as American companies relocated to the South, where non-unionized labor costs were cheaper and newly available air-conditioning made the hot climate more hospitable. In 1960 only 18 percent of southern homes were air-conditioned; within the next twenty years, that figure rose to 73 percent. A "Sun Belt" of new industrial manufacturing centers stretching from San Diego, Phoenix, and Houston to Atlanta boomed. This demographic shift had important political consequences as well when grassroots conservativism took hold in the Sun Belt, shifting the electoral map in favor of Republicans.

The economic picture was not all bleak, however. In the 1970s the American economy began a historic shift from a manufacturing-based economy to one dominated by service-sector and high-tech jobs. No longer a leader in auto or steel manufacturing, America gained new preeminence in high-tech fields like aerospace, electronics, and eventually computers. In the 1890s Henry Ford had built his first car in his garage before going on to revolutionize the auto industry (see Chapter 21). In 1976 Steven Jobs and Stephen Wozniak, twenty-one and twenty-six years old respectively, followed in Ford's footsteps

What economic problems plagued the United States in the 1970s?

by constructing their first personal computer in a family garage. The pair founded Apple Computers a year later, envisioning a machine that would transform daily life. The first Apple logo showed the seventeenth-century mathematician Sir Isaac Newton sitting under the apple that supposedly fell and hit him on the head, inspiring him to develop his theory of universal gravitational pull that revolutionized modern scientific thought. The subsequent, permanent logo just retained the apple. In 1976 the claim that computers could transform the world as much as Newton's theories seemed ludicrous. Yet within a year the computer age got underway when Apple released the first home computer designed for the general public. The computer revolution received another boost when twenty-nine-year-old Bill Gates, the cofounder of an obscure start-up company called Microsoft, signed an agreement with International Business Machines (IBM) to provide operating software for its home computers. The 1980 deal made Gates a billionaire within two years.

Frustration at Home

Nixon initially embraced the same moderate course as President Dwight Eisenhower, with whom he had served as vice president from 1953 to 1961. Like Eisenhower, Nixon billed himself as a fiscal conservative who was willing to accept popular social welfare programs like Social Security and Medicare. As the economic outlook worsened, however, Nixon instituted wage and price controls in 1971 to curb inflation, the most drastic government intervention in the economy since World War II.

Conservative outrage over his fiscal policies had little effect on Nixon, who intended to stay in the political center. He hoped to bolster the moderate wing of the Republican party by turning the disgruntled southerners and northern white blue-collar and suburbanite Democrats who had voted for him in 1968 (see Chapter 27) into lifelong Republicans. Called "the silent majority" these voters rejected some, but not all, of the liberal vision. The silent majority disliked Great Society programs that primarily aided minorities, but they still subscribed to the New Deal orthodoxy that made the government responsible for ensuring permanent prosperity. Nixon's budget-cutting, therefore, targeted social-welfare programs for minorities and the poor, measures that partially appeased fiscal conservatives without touching New Deal programs like Social Security that former Democrats and many moderate Republicans viewed as sacrosanct. Nixon also tried unsuccessfully to reduce the jumble of laws and programs that made welfare assistance to the poor expensive to administer. His proposal to guarantee all Americans a minimum income drew criticisms from the poor who viewed the suggested amount of $1,600 ($8,500 in today's dollars) as too low and from conservatives who opposed redistributing income.

Nixon gained the loyalty of the silent majority by trying to tame the Supreme Court, which under the leadership of Chief Justice Earl Warren from 1953–1969 (see Chapter 27) had issued a series of controversial rulings on school prayer and desegregation. When Warren retired in 1969, Nixon appointed Warren Burger to replace him, believing that Burger would direct his colleagues to offer a more restrained interpretation of the Constitution than Warren had. Burger, however, had no intention of reducing the Court's commitment to school integration. The Court insisted that the North develop school busing programs to catch up with the South where, by 1971, 77 percent of black children attended school with white children.

The 1954 *Brown vs. Board of Education* decision outlawing segregated schools had set off waves of massive resistance throughout the South (see Chapter 26). In the 1970s opposition to court-mandated integration moved northward as members of the silent majority found their collective voice and took to the streets. Busing sent black and white children to schools outside their neighborhoods, generating tremendous opposition in northern, ethnic white enclaves where angry white parents objected to "big government" turning their children into "guinea pigs."

Boston became a hotbed of anti-busing fervor throughout the seventies. On April 5, 1976, two hundred white working-class Irish American teenagers assembled in downtown Boston to begin an adult-supervised anti-busing march. Joseph Rakes, one of the teenage protesters, who brought along his family's American flag, later recalled feeling "blind anger" at busing policies that were destroying his close-knit South Boston community. "They took half the guys and girls I grew up with and said, 'You're going to school on the other side of town.' Nobody understood it at 15," Rakes explained. When Ted Landsmark, an African American lawyer on his way to a meeting. crossed the protesters' path, the students pounced on him.

How did the concerns and views of the "silent majority" shape politics in the 1970s?

28.3 "The Soiling of Old Glory," 1976
The image of an anti-busing protester in Boston preparing to ram an African American lawyer with a flagpole underscored that deeply ingrained racial prejudices were more than just a southern problem.

Boston Herald news photographer Stanley Forman's Pulitzer-Prize winning photo "The Soiling of Old Glory" (**28.3**) showed Rakes poised to attack Landsmark with his flagstaff. In the photo Landsmark apparently struggles to free himself from the grip of another white man grabbing him from the rear. Contrary to the impression given by the photo, however, the man holding Landsmark was actually helping him to his feet after several white youths had thrown him to the ground and beaten him. Rakes never hit Landsmark with the flagstaff. Yet when Landsmark, a seasoned civil rights activist who had marched from Selma to Montgomery in 1965 (see Chapter 27), went to the hospital, he had doctors put a large bandage on his broken nose. Landsmark knew that the appearance of severe injuries would draw more press attention. The portrait of raw racial hatred captured in the photograph, and Landsmark's heavily bandaged face at a press conference the following day, shocked white Boston and encouraged the city's political leaders to initiate a sustained campaign to deescalate racial tensions. When the new school year began in September, *Time* magazine trumpeted the "Truce in Boston." By this time, however, the Supreme Court's stance had shifted, thanks to Nixon's more conservative appointments. After the court ruled that independent suburban school districts did not have to participate in inner-city busing programs, accelerated "white flight" to the suburbs created a core of all-black urban schools ringed by suburban white schools in Boston and in other cities nationwide.

The Watergate Scandal

By reshaping the political landscape, Nixon won a landslide victory against antiwar Democratic challenger George McGovern in 1972(see Chapter 27). Yet rather than ushering in an era of unchallenged Republican control, Nixon became embroiled in the **Watergate scandal**, an episode of presidential criminal

How does this photograph compare to the images of racially-inspired violence in the South seen in earlier chapters?

"When the president does it that means that it is not illegal."

RICHARD NIXON in 1977, defending his actions as necessary for national security

"A government of laws was on the verge of becoming a government of one man."

Attorney general ELLIOT RICHARDSON

wrong-doing that created a constitutional crisis, ended Nixon's political career, and helped the Democrats retake the White House in 1976.

On June 17, 1972, a night watchman caught five burglars breaking into the offices of the Democratic National Committee located in a Washington, D.C., building complex called Watergate. The plan, financed by Nixon's reelection campaign and approved by White House staffers, called for the burglars to fix a broken telephone wiretap installed during a previous break-in so the Nixon campaign could listen to Democratic phone calls. After Nixon vigorously disavowed any previous knowledge of the plot, the story slid off the front pages and Nixon easily won the 1972 election.

When the burglars went on trial in early 1973, however, one confessed to accepting a bribe to keep quiet about the White House's involvement in planning the break-in. In response the Justice Department and Senate launched two separate investigations. *Washington Post* reporters Carl Bernstein and Bob Woodward detailed the growing scandal in a series of articles based on information from a secret informant whom they identified only by the nickname, Deep Throat (recently revealed as William Mark Felt, the FBI's deputy director).

During one Senate committee hearing, Senator Howard Baker asked the key question: "What did the President know, and when did he know it?" Secret tapes that Nixon had made of all White House conversations promised to provide the answer. The showdown over gaining access to these tapes and what they eventually revealed transformed the Watergate burglary into a constitutional crisis over whether the president was above the law.

Two competing visions of presidential power emerged. Nixon refused to turn over the tapes to the Justice Department or Congress, claiming that the constitutionally protected right of executive privilege gave him the right to keep advice from counselors private. Investigators argued that the president had no constitutional right to withhold evidence of corruption or abuse of power. Nixon next tried to use his authority to control the investigation. When Archibald Cox, who headed the Justice Department investigation, secured a special court order for the tapes on Saturday, October 20, 1973, Nixon ordered his attorney general Elliot Richardson to fire Cox. Richardson refused and resigned, as did the deputy attorney general. The head of the Justice Department finally agreed to fire Cox. Public outrage greeted news of the "Saturday Night Massacre" and Nixon endured a steady cacophony of car horns sounding outside the White House day and night where protesters urged passing motorists to "Honk for Impeachment."

After much delay and controversy, Nixon finally turned over highly edited versions of his taped White House conversations, enraging his critics even further. Liberal political cartoonists lampooned Nixon as a tyrant and a crook (see *Images as History: Watergate through Political Cartoons*, page 850). In July 1974 the House Judiciary Committee issued several articles of impeachment against Nixon, charging him with obstruction of justice, abusing his presidential powers by ordering the CIA, FBI, and Internal Revenue Service (IRS) to harass his political enemies, and violating the Constitution by refusing to honor congressional subpoenas. In July the Supreme Court unanimously ruled that Nixon could not withhold information pertaining to his own potential criminal wrongdoing.

On August 6, 1974, Nixon finally released the remaining tapes, and the nation heard the president authorize a cover-up plan. On June 23, 1972, Nixon had instructed the CIA to tell the FBI to end its Watergate investigation to protect "national security." Two days later, on August 8, 1974, to avoid impeachment proceedings almost certain to remove him from office, Nixon became the first president in U.S. history to resign, and Vice President Gerald Ford became president. "Our long national nightmare is over," the new president assured the nation.

What competing views of presidential power emerged during the Watergate crisis?

Images as History

WATERGATE THROUGH POLITICAL CARTOONS

Political cartoons have been a mainstay of political debate in American society since the colonial era. "If the prime role of a free press is to serve as critic of government, cartooning is often the cutting edge of that criticism," stated Herb Block, who drew under the pseudonym Herblock. Political cartoonists like Herblock and Paul Conrad followed the long career of Richard Nixon from his early days as a Red-hunting congressman through his resignation as president. Their illustrations caricatured his face and shoulders, depicting a long beak-like nose, dark circles under his eyes, five o'clock shadow, and slumping shoulders.

Some conservative political cartoonists steadfastly defended Nixon, even as the Watergate scandal deepened. One caricature depicted the media as piranhas nipping at Nixon's heels as he tried to reach calmer waters, suggesting that he was the victim of a media witch hunt. When Nixon resigned, a Bert Whitman political cartoon in the *Phoenix Gazette* showed the president exiting center stage, leaving behind spotlights that illuminated his foreign policy successes such as ending the Vietnam War and improving relations with China and the Soviet Union. To these conservative commentators Nixon's record as a strong leader in the world mattered more than his transgressions at home.

The cartoon, Herblock later noted, "comments not only on his situation at the time, but on his veracity and honesty—without using any words other than his own."

Nixon struggles to pull the two ends of a severed tape together, a reference to the severely edited tapes of White House conversations that Nixon had released to Watergate investigators.

By depicting Nixon with the word "not" in his mouth, Herblock transformed Nixon's 1973 statement, "I'm not a crook" into "I am a crook" in this 1974 cartoon.

Herblock, *Nixon Hanging Between the Tapes*, *Washington Post*, 1974

Conrad satirized the president's paranoia by depicting Nixon as a despot sitting in the dark, creating pages of "enemies lists" (which eventually included thirty thousand people).

By 1973 the public knew that Nixon had instructed the FBI and IRS to harass people he considered political "enemies." The list included Paul Conrad, who drew political cartoons for the *Los Angeles Times*.

To prevent future presidents from using the FBI to spy on their domestic critics, Congress passed the Foreign Intelligence Surveillance Act (1978), which required secret judicial approval for any internal surveillance of U.S. citizens. After the terrorist attacks on September 11, 2001, Congress loosened these restrictions on monitoring Americans at home.

The cartoon title suggested that Nixon, rather than his opponents, destroyed his presidency.

His Own Worst Enemy

Paul Conrad, *His Own Worst Enemy*, *Los Angeles Times*, 1973

Are political cartoons an effective way to comment seriously on heady political issues of the day?

A Crisis of Presidential Leadership

The Watergate scandal and the lingering scars from the Vietnam War severely tested Americans' faith in the federal government. Congress moved to limit the powers of the president, and Americans remained divided over what direction to take in foreign policy post-Vietnam. The challenges were significant: dealing with renewed Soviet aggression, ensuring that support for Israel did not alienate oil-producing Arab nations, and fostering better relations with Central America.

A Weakened Presidency

When Gerald R. Ford became president, for the first time a man unelected as either president or vice president led the nation. Nixon had appointed Ford, then Republican House Minority leader, as his vice president in 1973, invoking the newly ratified Twenty-Fifth Amendment to fill the office after disgraced Vice President Spiro Agnew resigned for having accepted bribes while governor of Maryland. During his twenty-four years in Congress, Ford built a solid reputation as an honest, fiscally conservative Republican and won the respect of legislators in both parties. "I'm a Ford, not a Lincoln," he said when he became vice president, distancing himself from both the elite who bought luxurious Lincoln automobiles and the political genius of the nation's sixteenth president.

Ford's modesty compared favorably with Nixon's obsessive quest for power. Believing that the nation wanted to turn the page quickly on the Watergate scandal, Ford announced that he was giving Nixon a "full, free, and absolute pardon" for any illegal acts that he might have committed as president. A long trial and possibly imprisoning the former president would only prolong the nation's agony, he believed. The new president, however, had misread the public's mood. Ford's approval rating sank to 42 percent amid accusations that he was fulfilling the terms of a backroom deal made while Nixon was still president—a pardon in return for the presidency. Nixon went free but over seventy others were eventually convicted of Watergate-related crimes. Ford never fully recovered from this loss of public confidence in his leadership.

An emboldened Congress took steps to rein in presidential power. Nixon had accepted large donations from businessmen in return for favors and influence. In response Congress amended existing election laws in 1974 to create a Federal Election Commission (FEC) to monitor federal elections. Congress also set new limits on campaign contributions by individuals and official political organizations, and created a system of public funding for presidential elections. Opponents immediately challenged the constitutionality of these restrictions. In 1976 the Supreme Court struck down a provision that limited how much an individual could spend of his or her own money to win elected office, claiming that such restrictions (except for candidates who accepted matching federal funds) violated the First Amendment right to free speech. These efforts to curb influence-peddling through campaign donations had some unintended consequences. Political action committees (PACs), which represented private interest groups, such as labor, business, and retired people, were allowed to donate more money than individuals, giving them increased sway over the politicians they supported.

To repair public faith in the presidency, President Ford tried to shape a post-Vietnam foreign policy that restored America's image as an invincible superpower without reigniting fears that the nation was overextending its reach or behaving unethically. Damaging press exposés about how the United States was conducting the Cold War acquainted Americans with their government's willingness to support dictators in South America, the Middle East, and Africa who pledged friendship to the United States over the Soviet Union. In 1974 the *New York Times* exposed the CIA's covert involvement in the overthrow of Salvador Allende, the democratically elected Marxist president of Chile. With aid from CIA operatives, anti-Soviet and pro-American General Augusto Pinochet seized power and established a brutal sixteen-year dictatorship that tortured, imprisoned, and killed dissenters. Congressional investigations also exposed CIA plots to assassinate leftist leaders in the Congo, Cuba, and the Dominican Republic.

Hoping to regain public confidence in how the government was waging the Cold War, Ford issued

How did Congress and Ford respond to Nixon's past wrongdoing?

an executive order that prohibited any government employee from engaging or conspiring in political assassination plots. Complaints over human rights violations influenced him less. Ford refused to cut off U.S. aid to Pinochet and supported the military junta that seized power in Argentina in 1976.

President Ford also tried to build on the foreign policy successes of the Nixon administration by retaining Henry Kissinger, a powerful cabinet member in the Nixon administration, as secretary of state and national security advisor. Ford initially accepted Kissinger's view that détente, the policy of using diplomatic, economic, and cultural contacts to improve U.S. relations with China and the Soviet Union, would promote global stability by lowering the risk of nuclear war. Consequently Ford abided by the terms of the 1972 **SALT I**, the first treaty between the Soviet Union and the United States that limited the deployment of intercontinental and submarine-launched ballistic missiles.

Nixon had also signed the 1972 Anti-Ballistic Missile (ABM) Treaty, in which the United States and the Soviet Union agreed to refrain from creating national missile defense systems. This treaty embraced the long-standing logic of **mutually assured destruction** (**MAD**), the belief that the guarantee of a devastating nuclear counterattack would deter the United States and Soviet Union from ever employing their nuclear arsenals. By pledging to remain defenseless against a nuclear attack, each side hoped to dampen fears that it ever planned to launch a first strike against the other. Seeking further accommodation with the Soviet Union, Ford joined with the Soviet Union and thirty-one other nations to sign the 1975 Helsinki Accords, an agreement that accepted the current East-West balance of power on the continent.

Ford's moderate course invited pounding criticism from the left and the right, ultimately spelling the demise of détente. Conservative critics, led by California governor Ronald Reagan, lambasted Ford for "giving" away Eastern Europe to the Soviet Union. This objection resonated with liberal critics who shared conservatives' concerns about Soviet treatment of dissidents within the Soviet Union. Bipartisan objections also arose over letting the Soviets maintain a larger arsenal of long-range and submarine-launched nuclear missiles than that of the United States. Over time Ford began to share bipartisan concerns that the Soviet Union was untrustworthy. Certain that the Soviets were continuing to build long-range intercontinental ballistic missiles, Ford heeded the advice of his hawkish defense secretary Donald Rumsfeld and poured money into the American missile program.

The Leadership Crisis Continues: Carter in the White House

As the 1976 presidential contest approached, Ford faced a strong challenge in the Republican primaries from sixty-five-year-old Ronald Reagan, a former film actor who had just finished his second term as governor of California. Reagan's father had kept the family afloat during the Depression by working for the Works Project Administration, but some key adult experiences gradually transformed this son of the New Deal into a staunch conservative. During the Second Red Scare, Reagan became concerned about communism's influence in Hollywood, and he objected to paying nearly 70 percent of his film earnings in taxes. In 1962 he joined the Republican Party, enthusiastically supported Barry Goldwater in 1964, and became governor of California in 1966. In a breathtakingly close vote, Ford prevailed at the Republican presidential nominating convention, but Reagan vowed to "rise and fight again."

> "Don't Vote, It Only Encourages Them."
>
> A bumper sticker that reflected widespread voter apathy in the 1976 presidential election

Ford's Democratic opponent was former Georgia governor Jimmy Carter, a surprise choice who was virtually unknown to most Americans when he declared his candidacy. Carter's political ambitions even surprised his own mother. When Carter told her that he was running for president, she replied, "President of what?" Carter's strong Baptist faith and the image he cultivated of an uncorrupted Washington outsider who could restore honor to the White House attracted conservative Democrats who had voted for Nixon. "I will never lie to you," Carter assured voters.

Neither candidate generated much enthusiasm during the campaign. The made-up campaign

What competing visions arose over Nixon's efforts to reshape U.S.-Soviet relations?

slogans in this political cartoon (**28.4**)—"Gerald R. Ford: a perfectly adequate guy for the seventies" and "Oh . . . Why Not? Ford in '76"—captured the general apathy surrounding Ford's campaign. An equally lackluster campaigner, Carter benefited mostly from the nation's ongoing economic woes, residual anger over Watergate and Ford's misstep in pardoning Nixon. In winning the presidency Carter managed to temporarily reassemble the New Deal coalition of white southerners, urban blacks, and union members to carry the election by 297 to 240 electoral votes. Fewer than 55 percent of the electorate even bothered to vote, however, a historic low and disappointing follow-up to the 1960s, when countless civil rights activists had put their lives on the line to secure this right.

" DO YOU GET THE FEELING THIS CAMPAIGN LACKS A LITTLE SOMETHING? "

28.4 ***Do You Get the Feeling This Campaign Lacks a Little Something?*** Like Carter, Ford failed to generate much enthusiasm among the electorate in the 1976 presidential election.

On his inauguration day Carter chose to walk from his swearing in on the Capitol steps to the White House with his wife and family rather than ride in a limousine, the type of populist gesture that he frequently made as president. Ford had pardoned Nixon in an attempt to heal wounds quickly. Carter tried to remove another source of festering discord by immediately pardoning ten thousand Vietnam War draft resisters, many of whom had fled to Canada during the war, a move that enraged conservatives but earned him the gratitude of liberal Democrats. Seeking to solidify liberal Democratic support, Carter moved quickly to build on the liberal vision of Democrats John F. Kennedy and Lyndon B. Johnson by creating the Department of Education and successfully working with Congress to establish a "Superfund" to clean up the nation's most polluted areas. He also appointed the most women and minorities to federal office of any previous president.

Carter's outsider status and his tendency toward self-righteousness, however, soon hampered his presidency. A hard worker who rose early and went to bed late, he pored over every memorandum, even going so far as to personally handle requests to use the White House tennis court during his first six months in office. The fiscally conservative Carter had strong philosophical differences with many liberal Democrats who emphasized the advantages of deficit-spending over balancing the federal budget. Carter believed that too much government regulation was hampering the business recovery, while liberal Democrats felt certain that regulation was necessary to protect the public. The president eventually prevailed, convincing Congress to deregulate the trucking, communication, and airline industries.

Identifying rising oil costs as the linchpin of the nation's economic woes, Carter urged the nation to consume less oil in a 1977 television address that recalled Franklin D. Roosevelt's famous fireside chats. As a fire crackled behind him, Carter, dressed in a cardigan sweater, called the energy crisis "the moral equivalent of war," which was the title of a famous essay by nineteenth-century philosopher William James. To discourage consumption Carter proposed ending the price controls that kept oil and gas prices low and imposing higher federal taxes on gasoline. To prevent price-gouging he also wanted oil and gas companies to pay higher taxes on their profits. Carter tried to craft a vision that would appeal to both laissez-faire adherents who liked the idea of lifting price controls so the market determined the price of oil and liberals who believed in using government regulation to rein in corporate profits and protect the environment. The resulting energy law in 1978 offered a compromise between these conflicting visions. The law lifted price controls, raised the sales taxes on gas-guzzling cars, and

Why did the 1976 presidential election fail to engage the country?

offered tax incentives for using alternative energy sources such as coal and solar heating. It did not, however, include a windfall profits tax on oil and gas company profits.

The country soon felt the effects of lifting price controls without also raising taxes on oil and gas company profits. In 1979 OPEC raised prices four times in five months, and a new war between Iran and Iraq created oil shortages. Images of motorists waiting for hours in line to buy gas, last seen during the 1973 oil embargo (see the chapter opener on page 843), once again dominated the news. The crisis reached its zenith on June 13, 1979, when over half of the nation's service stations ran out of gas. Meanwhile Exxon, an American company that imported oil from overseas, announced first quarter earnings of $1.9 billion in 1980, a record profit by any American corporation.

Carter renewed his call for a windfall-profit tax on oil and gas companies, hoping to use this revenue to fund public transportation, develop alternative energy sources, and help the poor pay for heating. Trying once again to stimulate public interest in energy conservation, Carter took to the airwaves to deliver an address soon dubbed the "malaise speech." America, he lamented, was a nation enmeshed in a moral and spiritual crisis. The nation had gone from one that celebrated "hard work, strong families, close-knit communities, and our faith in God" to one that worshiped "self-indulgence and consumption." Carter's call for Americans to "seize control again of our national destiny" fell flat, arousing only resentment over his presidential sermonizing.

These two political cartoons, both drawn in 1980, encapsulated competing notions of where blame for the energy crisis lay. Bob Taylor, drawing for the *Dallas Times Herald*, focused on the nation's insatiable appetite for oil (**28.5**). He portrayed Uncle Sam as a drug addict willing to pay any price for his next fix of oil. "Hey, man . . . like I don't CARE what it's costing . . . I need it," a disheveled and stony-eyed Uncle Sam says as he prepares to inject a barrel of oil into his vein. By contrast John Milt Morris's "Profit-sharing plan!" indicted OPEC and American oil companies for price-gouging, viewing the consumer as a victim of their conspiracy to empty his pockets (**28.6**). A sign posted outside one gas station presented a third view by proclaiming "Higher prices, More Sass, Bad President, Out of Gas," putting the blame squarely on Carter's shoulders.

28.5 *Hey, man . . . like I don't CARE what it's costing me*
This political caricature blamed Americans' oil addiction for the nation's ongoing energy problems.

28.6 *Profit Sharing Plan*
Expressing more sympathy for the average consumer, this caricature accused oil-producing nations and oil companies of creating artificial shortages to gouge consumers.

What different opinions surfaced about the root of America's energy problems?

New Paths in Foreign Affairs

Carter had more success in foreign affairs than in domestic matters, although not without encountering serious opposition to his Wilsonian-inspired vision of America championing democracy worldwide. Constant meddling in the domestic affairs of neighboring nations, he noted, had earned the United States the reputation as an imperial exploiter throughout Latin America. Liberal Democrats rejoiced when Carter resolved to make human rights and the spreading of democracy the centerpieces of his foreign policy.

The president's first major achievement was consistent with his desire to forge a new path in American diplomatic relations. Making amends for past American wrongdoing (see Chapter 19), Carter negotiated a treaty that returned the Panama Canal to Panama in 2000. The United States had controlled the Canal Zone since 1903, but by the 1970s America's bigger submarines and ships did not fit through the canal, reducing the waterway's importance to national security and the economy. Three previous presidents had recognized these facts and opened negotiations, but Carter pushed harder than his predecessors to seal the deal and won Senate ratification for the agreement in 1978.

Giving up control of the Panama Canal failed to dramatically improve relations between the United States and Latin America. Overtures to normalize relations with the Communist Cuban dictator Fidel Castro went nowhere. Carter also faced a severe test in Nicaragua, where civil war pitted the anti-communist dictator Anastasio Somoza against the Cuban-supported Sandinista rebel force. When the Sandinistas prevailed Carter offered them economic aid in the vain hope that he could dissuade them from creating a Cuban-like authoritarian communist state. Turning to Asia, Carter continued along the path forged by Nixon and established diplomatic relations with the People's Republic of China in 1979. This decision angered conservatives who viewed Taiwan, where the nationalist government had established residence after the Communist takeover of the mainland in 1949, as the rightful government of China. "To the Communists and those others who are hostile to our country," Reagan fumed, "President Carter and his supporters in the Congress seem like Santa Claus. They have given the Panama Canal away, abandoned Taiwan to the Red Chinese, and they're negotiating a SALT II treaty (with the Soviets) that could very well make this nation NUMBER TWO."

> "An inordinate fear of communism has led us to embrace any dictator who joined in our fear."
>
> President JIMMY CARTER, making human rights a guiding principle in U.S. foreign policy

Ignoring these criticisms Carter signed the SALT II pact in June 1979, an agreement that capped missiles and bombers on each side. But as Reagan's comments revealed, American disaffection with détente ran deep. In the mid-late 1970s, Soviet-backed regimes took control of Angola, Somalia, Ethiopia, and Afghanistan, confirming skeptics' fears that détente had strengthened the enemy. Additional signs of Moscow's aggressive intentions came in 1977 when the Soviets began aiming new, highly accurate intermediate-range missiles (SS-20s) at Western Europe. Carter responded to this threat by securing the North Atlantic Treaty Organization's (NATO) authorization to install Pershing II missiles in Western Europe, missiles that could reach Moscow in ten minutes.

Strained Soviet-American relations took another hit when the Soviet Union invaded Afghanistan in December 1979 to prop up its faltering Marxist government. The Soviets were eager to keep a friendly regime in power along their border, but the United States feared their ambitions might stretch into the oil-rich Middle East. Calling the invasion "the most serious threat to peace since the Second World War," Carter announced the Carter Doctrine, a declaration that the United States would use armed forces to stop any outside power from making inroads into the Persian Gulf region. He withdrew the SALT II arms limitation treaty from the Senate, increased defense spending, cut off shipments of grain and technology to the Soviet Union, and announced that the United States would boycott the summer Olympics in Moscow. The Carter administration also sent aid to Muslim fundamentalist rebels battling the Soviets in Afghanistan, whose ranks included the Saudi-born Islamic militant Osama bin Laden. A wealthy recent college graduate dedicated to establishing an Islamic state in Afghanistan, bin Laden would later found al-Qaeda, an Islamic fundamentalist terrorist organization.

The Cold War had long held the attention of American presidents. The United States was just learning, however, to take conflicts in the Middle East as seriously. Carter hoped to remove one source

Did Carter's dealings with the Soviet Union continue or undo initiatives undertaken by Nixon and Ford?

of festering tension by negotiating an end to hostilities between Israel and Egypt. In 1978 Carter invited Egyptian leader Anwar El Sadat and Israeli leader Menachem Begin to Camp David, a presidential mountain retreat in Maryland 60 miles north of the White House. Thirteen days of tense negotiations ended with the **Camp David Accords**. Israel agreed to give the Sinai Peninsula back to Egypt in 1982 (see 28.1). In return Egypt became the first Arab state to recognize Israel's right to exist. The United States rewarded each side with pledges of substantial military aid, support that continues to this day. Befriending Egypt neutralized the only credible military threat to Israeli security and brought a previous Soviet ally into the American fold, strengthening the American position in the Middle East.

If the Middle East gave Carter his greatest diplomatic victory, it also provided the low point of his presidency. In 1953 the United States helped overthrow the left-leaning Iranian government and installed the reliably anticommunist Shah of Iran to ensure American access to Iranian oil. In 1979 radical Islamists overthrew the Shah, who fled the country. An Islamic cleric and revolutionary, the Ayatollah Ruhollah Khomeini, became the head of the world's first radical Islamist government. Khomeini's intense dark eyes, long snowy beard, and flowing robes made him appear dark and dangerous to Americans, who recoiled at his ferocious denunciations of the United States as "the Great Satan."

In October 1979 Carter made a fateful decision when he reluctantly agreed to let the ailing Shah of Iran, who was living in Mexico, into the United States for medical treatment. If the United States "turned our backs on the fallen Shah, it would be a signal to the world that the U.S. is a fair-weather friend," National Security Advisor Zbigniew Brzezinski told Carter. At 3:00 a.m. on November 4, 1979, the State Department received a telephone call from panicked officials in the American embassy in Teheran, the capital of Iran, reporting that a mob of Iranian university students had broken into the compound. The students proceeded to take embassy employees hostage. Khomeini had not ordered the hostage-taking, but he supported the students' demands that the United States return the Shah and his fortune to Iran to secure their release. Khomeini's government, worried that the United States might try to organize a counterrevolution and return the Shah to power, wanted him in hand.

The **Iranian hostage crisis** became the defining event in Carter's presidency as Iranian revolutionaries held fifty-two Americans captive for 444 days. The media coverage was unprecedented for a single event, and most reporters viewed the crisis as a humiliating blow to America's honor. ABC news created a late-night show, "Nightline," that gave constant updates on "America Held Hostage" and repeatedly showed film footage of Iranian crowds chanting "Death to America" and the blindfolded captives. Public frustration with Carter's inability to resolve the crisis caused his approval ratings to sink to 28 percent.

How to proceed was not clear, however, and Carter's key advisors offered him a competing set of recommendations. Secretary of State Cyrus Vance focused on saving the hostages' lives and argued that the United States needed to negotiate patiently, no matter how long it took. National Security Advisor Brzezinski worried more about protecting America's image as a global superpower. Brzezinski felt that the longer the crisis lasted, the weaker America appeared to the rest of the world, emboldening America's enemies to strike. The Soviet invasion of Afghanistan a month into the hostage crisis seemingly corroborated Brzezinski's vision. *Choices and Consequences: Ending the Iranian Hostage Crisis* explores Carter's options and the repercussions of his decision to try to rescue the hostages.

> "The release of the American hostages had become almost an obsession with me."
>
> President JIMMY CARTER comments on the Iran hostage crisis in his memoirs

Five months later Iraq invaded Iran, and Khomeini finally decided to negotiate in earnest. Iran could no longer afford its diplomatic isolation, needing to reestablish its global trading networks to fend off the invasion by Iraqi leader Saddam Hussein. After months of negotiations the United States agreed to give Iran $7.9 billion (the estimated value of the Shah's holdings in the United States) and pledged not to interfere in Iranian domestic affairs. Carter hoped to deliver the good news to the American people that the hostages were coming home before he left office on January 20, 1981. Instead, Khomeini waited until a few minutes after the new president Ronald Reagan was sworn into office to release the hostages, denying Carter any final moment of triumph.

How did Carter respond to old and new problems in the Middle East?

Choices and Consequences

ENDING THE IRANIAN HOSTAGE CRISIS

When Iranian students stormed the U.S. Embassy and took Americans hostage in 1979, President Carter faced a choice over whether to follow the advice of Secretary of State Vance, who recommended patient negotiations, or National Security Advisor Brzezinski, who favored using military force to end the crisis. For five months Carter brokered a compromise between these two positions by freezing Iranian financial assets in the United States, engaging in secret negotiations, and beefing up the American naval presence in the Arabian Sea. Mounting public frustration as Carter began his 1980 reelection bid, along with concern that American inaction had encouraged the Soviet Union to invade Afghanistan, increased the pressure on Carter for decisive action.

Choices

1. Wait for Iran to tire of its diplomatic isolation, and then negotiate the hostages' release without alienating the rest of the Arab world.
2. Make a show of strength by bombing Iranian oil refineries and military bases and by mining harbors.
3. Use Special Forces to rescue the hostages.

Decision

When an Iranian negotiator told the administration that a possible diplomatic resolution was months away, Carter decided to act. In April, 1980, while Vance was out of town, Carter authorized a rescue mission by Special Forces.

Consequences

Swirling desert sands and a collision between American aircraft doomed the rescue mission in its first stages, further humiliating the United States. Vance immediately resigned and in July the Shah died in Egypt, ending the question of returning him to Iran. When Iraq invaded Iran in September, seeking oil-rich territory, Khomeini decided to end Iran's diplomatic isolation. Winning concessions from the United States, Iran released the hostages on January 20, 1981, the day that Ronald Reagan was inaugurated president.

"All the News That's Fit to Print"

The New York Times

LATE CITY EDITION

VOL.CXXX ... No. 44,645 — NEW YORK, WEDNESDAY, JANUARY 21, 1981 — 35 CENTS

REAGAN TAKES OATH AS 40TH PRESIDENT; PROMISES AN 'ERA OF NATIONAL RENEWAL'

MINUTES LATER, 52 U.S. HOSTAGES IN IRAN FLY TO FREEDOM AFTER 444-DAY ORDEAL

'ALIVE, WELL AND FREE'

Captives Taken to Algiers and Then Germany — Final Pact Complete

Teheran Captors Call Out Insults As the 52 Leave

FREEZE SET ON HIRING

Carter Orders Steps to Restrict Government and Busy Economy

11:57 A.M.: Ronald Reagan being sworn in as 40th President by Chief Justice Warren E. Burger. Nancy Reagan holds the Bible and Senator Mark O. Hatfield witnesses the ceremony.

Anxious Families and Towns Erupt Into Long-Postponed Celebrations

More News And Pictures

Headline Announcing the Hostage Release, 1981

Continuing Controversies

How important was the hostage crisis for the United States in the long-term?

Some say it was very important. The hostages' prolonged captivity branded Carter as inept and contributed to his reelection loss. To gain revenge against Iran, the United States supported the Iraqi leader Saddam Hussein's regime during his ten-year war with Iran, once again using a repressive Middle Eastern dictator to advance American interests in the region. The hostage crisis also created a negative image of Islam in the United States that future Islamic terrorist attacks reinforced. The crisis was not so important, others counter, rejecting it as a major reason for Reagan's victory. In the 1980s the failed Soviet invasion of Afghanistan, the Camp David Accords, and using a secular Iraq to contain Iranian influence protected U.S. economic interests in the region, diminishing the long-term significance of the hostage crisis.

What larger significance did Carter's advisors attach to the Iranian hostage crisis?

The Rights Revolution

The nation's foreign policy problems revealed that that turbulence overseas did not end with the Vietnam War. Feminists and gay activists carried the 1960s' rights revolution into the 1970s and 1980s, demanding equal opportunities and legal protections against discrimination. These movements struck at the heart of gender identity in American society, arousing conservative fears that traditional values were disappearing. The environmental movement, seeking to reverse the toll of industrial pollution on the nation's natural habitats, had more success than the women's and gay rights movements uniting Americans around a common cause.

The Equal Rights Amendment and Abortion Controversies

Feminist political demands received unprecedented attention in the seventies. Hoping to eradicate gender discrimination and sexual inequality at the workplace, feminist organizations lobbied for equal pay for equal work, ending sexual harassment, affordable day care, and paid maternity leave. These bread-and-butter issues became even more pressing as the economic downturn of the 1970s forced more women into the workplace. The chart *Women and Work, 1950–1990* (**28.7**) shows the steady increase in the percentage of women who worked outside the home over the second half of the twentieth century. In 1950, 32.5 percent of white women and 41.5 percent of black women worked, rising to 58.8 percent and 59.1 percent by 1980. Between 1950 and 1970 the percentage of white married women holding jobs nearly doubled from 22.3 percent to 41.8 percent, compared with 33.7 percent and 53.5 percent of black married women over the same period.

The feminist movement, however, faced considerable challenges convincing these working women that feminism provided the answer to the problems they faced balancing work and home life or advancing in the workplace. The press, one activist noted, portrayed the feminist as "a total weirdo—bra-burner, man-hater, lesbian, sickie!" —exaggerated stereotypes that threatened the movement's growth. Many women proved reluctant to publicly identify themselves as feminists even if they privately supported the women's movement goals, fearing social stigmatization as unfeminine. Divisions within the women's movement created another major obstacle. Poor minority women often saw racial and ethnic prejudice as bigger obstacles to their economic advancement than gender discrimination, and regarded white, upper-middle-class feminists with suspicion. Feminism, in the words of one black woman, was "basically a family quarrel between White women and White men." Divisions between radicals and moderate feminists (see Chapter 27) also prevented women from speaking with one voice.

Despite negative media portrayals and problems attracting working-class women, the feminist

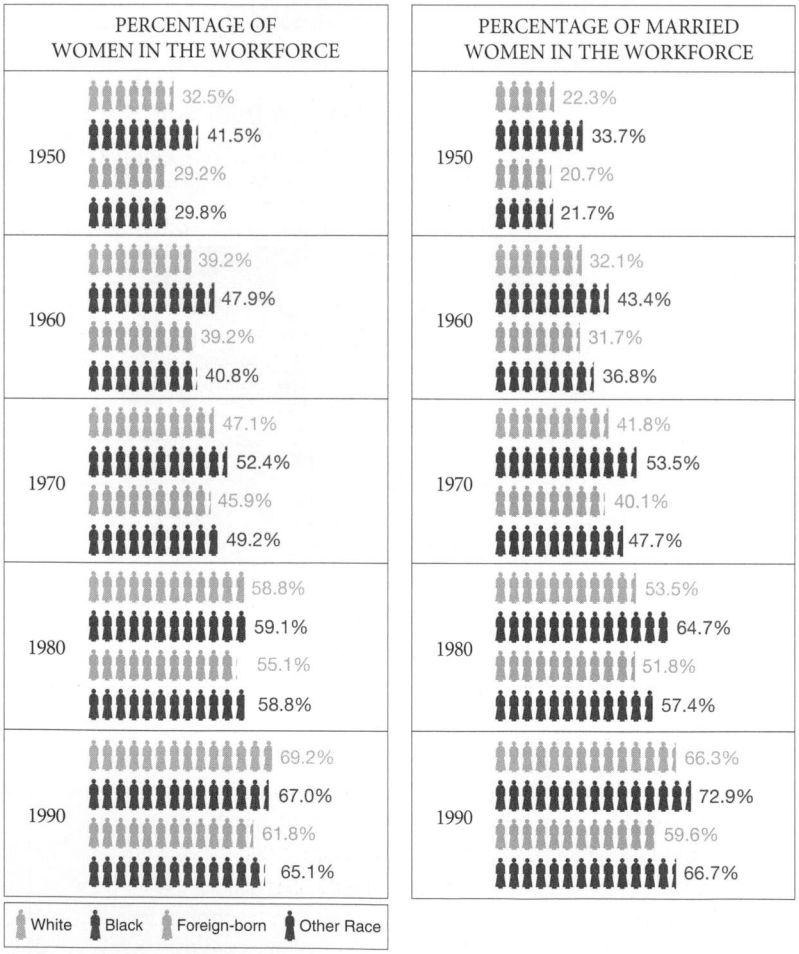

28.7 Women and Work, 1950–1990
As more women entered the workforce, combating discrimination in the workplace became a major issue for the women's movement.

What were the social, cultural, and political consequences of shifting trends in the female workforce?

movement enjoyed a wave of success in the early seventies. Cities established shelters for battered women and rape-crisis centers. Feminist campaigning led to the passage of Title IX of the 1972 Education Act, prohibiting gender discrimination in education. This law revolutionized high school and college sports by forcing administrators to create more teams and scholarships for female students. Congress also passed the **Equal Rights Amendment** (ERA) in 1972, a proposal that congressional supporters had introduced regularly since 1923 that stated, "equality of rights under the law shall not be denied or abridged by the United States or by any State on account of sex." Within three years thirty-four of the thirty-eight states needed for ratification of the ERA had approved the measure, endorsing the feminist vision that the ERA guaranteed complete equality between women and men.

This avalanche of change outraged cultural conservatives who charged that the ERA would hasten the destruction of the American family. Phyllis Schlafly, a conservative Illinois lawyer with six children, led the anti-ERA crusade. Catapulting into the national spotlight, Schlafly helped forge the coalition among Catholics, southerners, antifeminists, religious fundamentalists, and fiscal conservatives that pushed the Republican Party to the right throughout the decade. Feminists branded Schlafly a hypocrite, pointing out that she was a well-educated woman who had enjoyed a satisfying career in Republican politics before spearheading the anti-ERA campaign. "She's an extremely liberated woman," asserted Karen DeCrow, the president of the feminist National Organization for Women. *Competing Visions: Defining the Ideal Woman* (page 860) further explores the spirited debate over female gender identity in the seventies. Schlafly's anti-feminist message resonated in the southern and mountain states, areas without strong local feminist organizations to offer a competing view of how gender discrimination adversely affected women in the workplace. In the end the anti-ERA forces prevailed. The ERA remained three states short when the deadline for approving the measure came in 1982, the first of many conservative political victories to come in the 1980s.

The rancor surrounding the issue of legalized abortion, however, soon far surpassed the barbs exchanged over the Equal Rights Amendment. Between 700,000 and 800,000 women a year sought illegal abortions, and botched procedures by incompetent practitioners working in unsanitary conditions killed 2,000–3,000 patients annually.

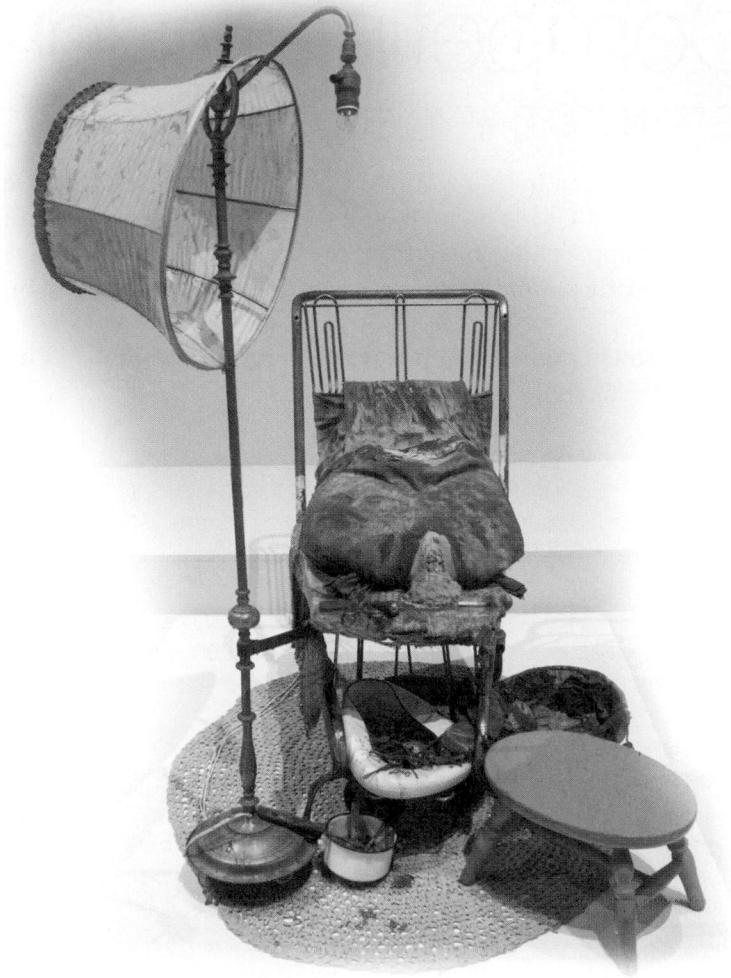

28.8 ***The Illegal Operation,*** **1962**
Edward Kienholz's sculpture of a back-alley abortionist's office evoked pain and fear to protest the inability of women to secure a safe and legal abortion in the United States.
[*Source:* Edward Kienholz, "The Illegal Operation", 1962. Sculptural installation of shopping cart, wooden stool, concrete, pots, blanket, hooked rug, medical equipment, polyester resin, pigment, etc. Dimensions: 59 x 48 x 54 in. Los Angeles County Museum of Art. Photograph © 2009 Museum Associates/LACMA]

Edward Kienholz's 1962 sculpture *The Illegal Operation* evoked the gruesomeness of visiting a back-alley abortionist (**28.8**). In the sculpture a lifeless, torn cushion (representing a woman's body) sits in a metallic chair above a white bowl filled with stained rags and crude kitchen utensils. The small stool in the foreground beckons viewers to take a seat and confront the realities of this secret butchery. The sculpture provoked little controversy when it appeared as part of a 1966 exhibition in Los Angeles. By then many Californians supported changing what the *Los Angeles Times* called "Our Archaic Abortion Law" that only allowed a woman to end a pregnancy if her life was in danger.

Bending to the popular will, then-California governor Ronald Reagan reluctantly signed a bipartisan-supported bill in 1967 that let women

What symbols does Kleinholz incorporate into his sculpture to present his view on abortion?

Competing Visions

DEFINING THE IDEAL WOMAN

What did it mean to be a woman? Cultural conservatives answered "wife and mother"; feminists disagreed. In 1972 journalist Gloria Steinem, founder of *Ms.*, a popular feminist magazine, argued that both women and men would be happier once freed from the straitjacket of culturally constructed gender roles. Conservative activist Phyllis Schlafly countered that gender identity was rooted in biology.

Gloria Steinem argued that women's liberation would benefit men as well as women.

I don't think most women want to pick up briefcases and march off to meaningless, depersonalized jobs.... We want to liberate men from those inhuman roles as well. We want to share the work and responsibility, and to have men share equal responsibility for the children. Probably the ultimate myth is that children must have fulltime mothers, and that liberated women make bad ones. The truth is that most American children seem to be suffering from too much mother and too little father.

Women now spend more time with their homes and families than in any other past or present society we know about. To get back to the sanity of the agrarian or joint family system, we need free universal day care. With that aid, as in Scandinavian countries, and with laws that permit women equal work and equal pay, man will be relieved of his role as sole breadwinner and stranger to his own children.

No more alimony. Fewer boring wives. Fewer childlike wives.... No more wives who fall apart with the first wrinkle because they've been taught that their total identity depends on their outsides. No more responsibility for another adult human being who has never been told she is responsible for her own life, and who sooner or later says some version of, "If I hadn't married you, I could have been a star." Women's Liberation really is Men's Liberation, too. ... Colleague marriages, such as young people have now, with both partners going to law-school or the Peace Corps together, ... Communes; marriages that are valid for the child-rearing years only, there are many possibilities.

The point is that Women's Liberation is not destroying the American family. It is trying to build a human compassionate alternative out of its ruins.

Gloria Steinem

Phyllis Schlafly claimed that the "Positive Woman" embraced her distinctly female role.

The first requirement for the acquisition of power by the Positive Woman is to understand the differences between men and women.... She rejoices in the creative capability within her body and the power potential of her mind and spirit. She understands that men and women are different, and that those very differences provide the key to her success as a person and fulfillment as a woman.

The women's liberationist, on the other hand, is imprisoned by her own negative view of herself and of her place in the world around her.... Women must be made equal to men in their ability *not* to become pregnant and *not* to be expected to care for babies they may bring into the world. This is why women's liberationists are compulsively involved in the drive to make abortion and childcare centers for all women, regardless of religion or income, both socially acceptable, and government-financed.... The Positive Woman looks upon her femaleness and her fertility as part of her purpose, her potential, and her power. She rejoices that she has a capability for creativity that men can never have ...

A Positive Woman cannot defeat a man in a wrestling match or boxing match, but she can motivate him, inspire him, encourage him, teach him, restrain him, reward him, and have power over him that he can never achieve over her with all his muscle.... The overriding psychological need of a woman is to love something alive. A baby fulfills this need in the lives of most women. If a baby is not available to fill that need, women search for a baby-substitute. This is the reason why women have traditionally gone into teaching and nursing careers. They are doing what comes naturally to the female psyche.

Phyllis Schlafly

Do Steinem and Schlafly offer realistic or clichéd depictions of women's lives, or a combination of both?

terminate pregnancies in cases of rape and incest and fetuses with severe physical and mental defects, a decision he later called a mistake. Texas, however, still only allowed abortions if a pregnancy jeopardized a woman's life. Feminists felt that women, not male doctors, should have the right to make medical decisions about their own bodies. In 1970 Norma McCorvey, an unmarried, poor, pregnant twenty-five-year-old, sued the state of Texas under the pseudonym Jane Roe claiming that she had the right to a legal and safe abortion based on her constitutional "right to privacy." The Supreme Court dealt the feminist movement a stunning victory when it legalized abortion in its 1973 ***Roe v. Wade*** decision. The ruling came too late for McCorvey, who gave birth to a baby girl and gave her up for adoption as the case moved through the courts.

In rendering the *Roe v. Wade* decision, the Supreme Court ruled that the "right to privacy . . . is broad enough to encompass a woman's decision whether or not to terminate her pregnancy." The Court decision prohibited states from criminalizing abortion in the first trimester, but allowed states to regulate abortion in the second trimester and prohibit it during the third trimester when a fetus became viable. The Court, however, sidestepped a key question that would provoke much future controversy. "We need not resolve the difficult question of when life begins," the Court asserted in granting women the legal right to an abortion. Critics argued that the Court had invented a right to privacy that did not exist in the Constitution. Supporters countered that court decisions over the last hundred years had firmly established this right. The debate soon seeped into national politics when the Democrats assumed the mantle of the party dedicated to maintaining a woman's right to choose an abortion and the Republicans became predominantly against the right to abortion, a position that came to be known as "pro-life."

The vocabulary embraced by each side in the abortion debate revealed competing visions of what abortion meant. Supporters of legalized abortion called themselves "pro-choice," a label encapsulating their view that abortion was a question of personal liberty. In contrast "pro-life" forces believed that human life began at conception (not when a fetus was viable outside the womb); they therefore viewed abortion as tantamount to murder. Both sides employed the language of rights, the "rights of women" (pro-choice usage) squaring off against those of "unborn children" (pro-life term). The activist women facing off in this debate had very different life experiences and conceptions of motherhood. Pro-life activists had often built their lives around children and the home, and were outraged by their suspicion that pro-choice women had abortions "as a matter of convenience." Pro-choice activists often wanted careers as well as children and refused to allow biology to dictate their life choices.

McCorvey eventually changed her mind about abortion. Twenty years after *Roe v. Wade*, she became a born-again Christian who joined the anti-abortion crusade. Her reversal illustrated the growing momentum of the pro-life movement, which used images of children, like the one affixed to the sign of this 1979 pro-life demonstrator protesting in Washington, D.C. (**28.9**), to emphasize the rights of children. In the twenty-first century, the pro-life movement took advantage of new ultrasound portraits of fetuses in the womb that showed beating hearts to underscore their argument that life began at conception. Unable to overturn the *Roe* directly, pro-life activists secured a ban on federal funding for abortions. Some states also passed laws that required parental notification when minors sought abortions.

28.9 Pro-life Protest, 1979 Pro-life demonstrators who opposed legalized abortion put the focus on the right of unborn children to have a life rather than the right of women to control their own bodies.

What different visions separated the pro-life and pro-choice camps?

Gay Rights

The rights revolution also encompassed the gay and lesbian subcultures that existed in the shadows of mainstream society until the 1960s. Unlike blacks, women, and other minority groups, gay Americans did not have a long history of organizing to defend their rights. Heterosexual Americans uniformly disparaged gays as deviant and morally reprehensible. The American Psychiatric Association categorized homosexuality as a "mental disorder," a position they did not jettison until 1973. Taking the psychological stereotyping a step further, *Time* magazine viewed homosexuality as "a pernicious sickness." "If you were gay and you accepted those societal norms, then you were at war with yourself," recalled one college student of his own private struggle to come to terms with his homosexuality. Within this social climate exposure as a homosexual or lesbian meant losing everything—job, spouse, friends, and social position.

In the sixties the black Civil Rights Movement and the hippie counterculture assault on sexual taboos inspired some gay people to "come out of the closet" and challenge the ways that American society ostracized them. The true awakening of the gay rights movement came during the **Stonewall riot** on June 28, 1969, when patrons frequenting the Stonewall Inn, a Greenwich Village male gay bar, fought back during a New York City police raid. This image of open defiance electrified the gay community, and the next morning a huge crowd gathered outside the Stonewall Inn, chanting "Gay Power," a modification of the "Black Power" slogan that black militants embraced (see Chapter 27). Energized homosexuals and lesbians founded the radical Gay Liberation Front in response to Stonewall, while hundreds of smaller gay rights groups sprouted up throughout the country. Collectively these organizations formed gay support groups on university campuses, lobbied for antidiscrimination laws, marched openly in Gay Pride parades, and followed the "sit-in" model of the Civil Rights Movement by staging "kiss-ins" in restaurants. "We should have the same right to express our affection publicly as heterosexuals have," asserted lesbian activist Barbara Gittings.

The increased visibility of the gay rights movement soon provoked a conservative response. In 1977 the deeply religious pop singer Anita Bryant, known to most Americans for her television commercials singing the praises of Florida orange juice, spearheaded a successful campaign to overturn a newly enacted gay rights law in Dade County, Florida. Her victory galvanized forces across the country on both sides of the gay rights debate.

28.10 AIDS Memorial Quilt, 1987
The panels of the AIDS Memorial Quilt portrayed the disease's victims as sons, brothers, and lovers with strong ties to their families and communities to challenge stereotypes of homosexuals as diseased pariahs.

How similar were the Gay Rights and Civil Rights Movements?

Fundamentalist churches geared up to oppose any legislation granting gays legitimacy, lobbying particularly strongly for laws that prevented homosexuals from teaching in public schools. Gay rights groups ridiculed the notion that male homosexuals, because they preferred men over women as sexual partners, were pedophiles. A new, more insidious challenge loomed ahead, however.

In 1981 the mainstream press began printing stories of a mysterious ailment sweeping through the sexually charged homosexual communities in New York and San Francisco. Acquired Immune Deficiency Syndrome (AIDS), a virus transmitted through the exchange of bodily fluids, ravaged the immune system of its victims. Acquiring AIDS was a virtual death sentence in the 1980s; the disease killed over 100,000 Americans by 1990. Because in the United States AIDS disproportionately struck homosexuals, the nation viewed the epidemic as more than a public health crisis.

The raging political debate over the status of homosexuals in American society colored the competing visions about AIDS. Extreme religious conservatives viewed AIDS as God's retribution against the "morally degenerate," ignoring evidence that AIDS could strike the heterosexual population as well. Having just recently repudiated the notion that gay people were mentally ill, homosexuals now confronted widespread fears that they were all diseased. AIDS patients told heartbreaking stories of losing their jobs, being turned away from hospital emergency rooms, and facing eviction from apartment buildings by landlords who feared contamination. The gay community lobbied vigorously for increased federal funds to find a medical cure for the disease. Still, having fought so long to escape police harassment and end legal penalties for consensual homosexual acts, many gay activists were initially leery about urging homosexual men to modify their sexual behaviors. Larry Kramer chastised gay activists who "took the position that sexual promiscuity was the one freedom we had and that we had to fight to maintain it—even if it killed us. And it did kill us, a lot of us." Kramer instead worked to popularize the "safe sex" message that eventually gained currency in the gay community.

The two images shown here illustrate the competing visions within the gay community over how to best draw media attention to the mounting AIDS death toll. In 1987 the AIDS Memorial Quilt, the brainchild of San Francisco AIDS activist Cleve Jones, began touring the country after an inaugural unfurling on the National Mall in Washington, D.C. The nation's largest-ever public art endeavor, the quilt (**28.10**) made the individual stories of AIDS visible by allowing family and friends to create a square for a loved one, homosexual or heterosexual, lost to the disease. Squares were the size of a human grave and the stories they contained varied considerably, portraying a mixture of embroidered personal remembrances and treasured possessions like jewelry.

28.11 ACT-UP Protestors Stage a Funeral Demonstration in Wall Street
Militant gay activists used civil disobedience to protest high prices and slow federal approval of life-saving anti-AIDS drugs.

Radical activists adopted a less poignant and more militant tone. Embracing the slogan "silence = death," the AIDS Coalition to Unleash Power (ACT-UP) staged its first "funeral" demonstration in 1987 to demand better medical treatment. Protesters lay prone on a busy Wall Street intersection until police carried them away (**28.11**), employing the same civil disobedience tactics used successfully by the Civil Rights Movement in the 1960s. ACT-UP also conducted phone "zaps" that barraged local, state, and federal officials with calls on AIDS-related issues, and barricaded the doors to the Food and Drug Administration to protest delays in approving AIDS-fighting drugs. A *New York Times* headline called ACT-UP, "rude, rash, effective." By 1996 a drug "cocktail" became available that dramatically reduced AIDS-related deaths. A relentless safe-sex campaign and screening of donated blood lowered the infection rate as well.

What competing strategies did gay activists develop to publicize the AIDs crisis?

Environmentalism

On April 22, 1970, communities throughout the nation celebrated their first Earth Day. New York City crowds walked through a block-long plastic bubble to breathe pure air; demonstrators in Boston protested noise pollution; and population control advocates in Bloomington, Indiana, handed out free birth control pills. Earth Day made environmentalism visible, but the wide variety of causes that activists championed revealed the competing visions within the environmental movement. For New Left and counterculture environmentalists, eating organically produced food grown without pesticides became a symbolic way of purging the poison of mainstream American values out of their lives. Politicians interested in securing environmentally friendly legislation framed pollution as a straightforward health issue. They focused, for example, on how lead poisoning damaged children's developing brains to win widespread support for laws mandating lead-free gas and paint. Traditional conservationist societies like the Sierra Club and Audubon Society concentrated their efforts on preserving pristine wild habitats from development. They strongly supported expanding the National Park Service to safeguard wildness areas and provide recreational sanctuaries for over-taxed citizens living in the industrial world.

Presidential support for environmental reforms had begun during the Kennedy and Johnson administrations (see Chapter 27), and in the 1970s Nixon and Carter also gave their blessing to increased federal environmental controls. New laws controlling toxic substances required the removal of asbestos (a cancer-causing building material) from schools. Companies had to reduce the amount of airborne toxins that their factories produced and clean up sites they had chemically contaminated. Car manufacturers installed required catalytic converters that helped reduce automobile pollution by 75 percent. Meanwhile the consumer protection movement spearheaded by activist Ralph Nader led to the creation of a federal Consumer Product Safety Commission that could ban the sale of hazardous products, from cribs to cars. While the general public applauded changes that made their lives healthier and safer, some blue-collar workers feared that new, expensive pollution controls on industry simply encouraged industrialists to move their factories overseas. "If you're hungry and out of work, eat an environmentalist," read one popular labor union bumper sticker.

28.12 Three Mile Island Nuclear Reactor Towers America rejected nuclear power after the accident at the Three Mile Island nuclear power plant. That decision, coupled with limited federal support for solar and wind-generated power, increased the nation's dependence on overseas oil.

Two well-publicized environmental scandals, however—one at Love Canal, a waterway near Niagara Falls, New York, and the other at Three Mile Island in Pennsylvania—convinced most Americans that their well-being depended on strict federal environmental regulation. After years of ignoring residents' complaints about rising levels of miscarriages and birth defects, New York State finally admitted in 1978 that the foul-smelling industrial waste dumped into Love Canal contained deadly toxins that had polluted the area's ground and air. Congress responded by creating a Superfund to clean up dangerously polluted areas, spending $400 million and twenty years to restore the Love Canal region.

In 1979 the partial meltdown of a nuclear reactor at the Three Mile Island nuclear power plant in Pennsylvania caused the panicked exodus of nearly 100,000 residents when radioactive steam poured into the air. No one was hurt, but the government-sponsored clean-up took fourteen years. Despite new, more stringent federal regulations for nuclear reactors, Americans equated the image of nuclear reactor towers with danger (**28.12**) and steadfastly refused to accept new nuclear power plants in their neighborhoods despite a strong industry-wide safety record.

Not all Americans applauded new environmental regulation. A "Sagebrush Rebellion" arose in the West among conservatives demanding that the federal government return federally controlled lands to the states. Viewing environmentalists as East Coast liberal elitists, Western miners, ranchers, and loggers chafed under new federal restrictions that limited their access to water, their ability to hunt predators, and their grazing rights on federal lands. Western votes helped Ronald Reagan win the presidential contest in 1980, and as president he listened sympathetically to their complaints concerning federal environmental policies. An avid outdoorsman who enjoyed riding horses at his California ranch, Reagan did not believe that the environment was in serious jeopardy. Emphasizing economic growth Reagan loosened recently enacted pollution controls on industry and reduced the size and budget of the Environmental Protection Agency (EPA), an agency founded under Nixon's watch and charged with enforcing federal environmental regulations.

Which environmental visions prevailed in the 1970s and 1980s?

The Rise of the Right

Successful conservative attacks on environmental regulation were just one component of a resurgent conservative coalition that emerged as the dominant force in American politics in the 1980s. Through right-leaning policy institutes, magazines, lobbying groups, and direct mail campaigns, conservatives spearheaded a powerful political movement whose vision Ronald Reagan championed when he entered the White House. A charismatic leader, Reagan's unrelenting optimism changed the national mood. The vision of a nation adrift evaporated as confidence in the economy and government rebounded.

The New Conservative Coalition

The emerging conservative coalition known as the New Right created alliances among groups with very different concerns and views of what America and American government should be, reshaping the Republican Party in the process. Conservatives differed on whether a balanced budget or cutting taxes would guarantee prosperity. They disputed whether the government should play an active role in promoting conservative values or adopt a more libertarian approach that reduced governmental activity in all spheres. In the 1970s the mix of ideas grew even more complicated when neoconservatives, defectors from the liberal ranks, joined the conservative coalition. Seeking to explain his own political journey from the left to the right, Irving Kristol defined neoconservatives as "liberals who've been mugged by reality." Neoconservatives focused mostly on foreign affairs, urging the nation to cast off its Vietnam hangover and stand proud in the world once again. Their insistence that America had the right to act unilaterally in world affairs soon prevailed over lingering noninterventionist currents in conservative thinking.

Former working-class and southern Democrats also joined the emerging conservative coalition. Angry over court-ordered integration and busing, affirmative action programs that reserved jobs or school slots for minorities, and rising crime, these newcomers accepted the conservative orthodoxy of smaller government when it came to programs that primarily benefited minorities. Ethnic northern whites in the Rust Belt resented their declining economic clout as industrial jobs evaporated, and they responded well to Republican claims that "limousine liberal" elites were out of touch with the concerns of working-class America. Finally the popularity of grassroots conservative movements among burgeoning Sun Belt populations from Florida to Arizona completed the political realignment in the 1980s.

In the late 1970s simmering resentment against increasing taxes exploded into open revolt. Big business and the well-to-do had long championed lower income and corporate taxes. Now the working class and middle class joined the tax revolt by demanding lower property taxes. Voters in California spearheaded the tax rebellion in 1978 when they approved **Proposition 13**. This ballot referendum reduced property taxes by 57 percent, lost tax revenue that caused drastic cuts in funding for public schools and universities. Voters in other states soon followed suit, and increasingly found the Republican anti-tax message appealing.

The Republican Party also benefited from the rise of the **Religious Right**, a collection of conservative Christian groups that defended traditional values and supported right-wing political causes, the most sustained grassroots movement of the late twentieth century. Ronald Reagan immediately saw the benefits of reaching out to the Religious Right, hoping to create a strong conservative coalition that, in his words, would "attract those interested in the so-called 'social issues' and those interested in economic issues."

Protestant fundamentalists had mobilized their ranks for battle in the 1920s to end the teaching of evolution in southern public schools. After the Scopes Trial (see Chapter 21), the mainstream media paid little attention to religious conservatives, but Protestant fundamentalist radio stations, publishing houses, and revival meetings thrived in the South. Fundamentalists ended their self-imposed exile from mainstream politics in the 1950s when religious conservatives voiced strong support for the nation's Cold War crusade against godless communism. The

Did any significant tensions exist within the New Right?

Supreme Court's 1962 ruling against school prayer (see Chapter 27) incensed Fundamentalists, as did Carter's attempts to revoke the tax-exempt status of religious schools that failed to integrate racially.

But politics alone does not completely explain why fundamentalism became a nationwide phenomenon in the 1970s, a time when nearly a quarter of Protestant Americans (fifty million people) described themselves as born-again Christians. In an era when sprawling suburbs and rancorous cultural debates created a sense of social fragmentation, close-knit fundamentalist churches offered members cohesive communities where people with similar values spoke the same language. The fundamentalist vision of leading a morally upright life in keeping with divine will attracted white, middle-class suburbanites along with white, rural residents, creating a strong grassroots religious movement that cut across class and regional, if not racial, lines. A series of highly effective evangelical preachers, such as Pat Robertson, Jerry Falwell, Oral Roberts, Jimmy Swaggart, Robert Sculler, and Jim and Tammy Bakker, built media empires that preached the literal truth of the Bible to millions of television viewers—further popularizing the appeal of the Fundamentalist vision.

In the late 1960s Nixon claimed to speak for the "silent majority" who objected to liberal policies in the privacy of their living rooms. In the 1980s Republican politicians showered attention on the "moral majority," a well-organized network of politically active religious conservatives. In 1979 Falwell founded the Moral Majority, which he described as a "pro-life, pro-family, pro-morality, and pro-American" organization. The cover of Falwell's 1979 book, *America Can Be Saved*, showed a drawing of the preacher in front of a huge American flag, melding patriotism with religious fervor to create a vision of faith and conservative politics providing salvation to a nation adrift (**28.13**). The Moral Majority joined with other conservative religious groups to register two million new voters in time for the presidential contest of 1980. In the past Fundamentalists had distrusted Catholicism, but now, political concerns outweighed doctrinal differences. Fundamentalists formed a new political alliance with conservative Catholics who shared their concerns about religious instruction in schools, abortion, and gay rights. Along with other members of the New Right, the Religious Right voted overwhelmingly for Reagan when he ran against Carter in the 1980 presidential election.

28.13 ***America Can Be Saved*** (1979)
The cover of Jerry Falwell's book illustrated the new connection between religious fundamentalism and political activism forged in the 1970s.

Setting a New Course: Reagan at Home

During the 1980 presidential campaign, Reagan focused voters' attention on the nation's continuing economic woes by repeatedly asking "are you better off than you were four years ago?" Reagan's cheerfulness, humor, and athleticism offered a stark contrast to Carter's more drawn and weary demeanor. Memorizing his speeches ahead of time and delivering them in a soothing baritone voice, Reagan's charisma helped him amass a devoted and almost worshipful following. Reagan's victory capped the rise of the New Right, a two-decade ascendancy that Watergate and Carter's subsequent election had temporarily interrupted. Reagan won the election by an impressive margin: 489 to 49 electoral votes. In his inaugural address Reagan entreated the nation "to believe in our capacity to perform great deeds . . . after all, why shouldn't we believe that? We are Americans." Commentators likened Ronald Reagan's victory over the unpopular Carter in the 1980 presidential election to Franklin D. Roosevelt's triumph over Herbert Hoover in 1932 (see Chapter 22). Each man created lasting political coalitions that reshaped the political landscape; each inspired the country at a moment when the nation felt besieged.

Reagan entered the presidency passionate about cutting income and corporate taxes, reducing social welfare spending, and fighting communism. He immediately sent Congress a budget that contained

Why did the Religious Right thrive in the 1980s?

dramatic cuts in spending for social programs, increased allocations for defense, and lowered taxes considerably. Embracing the theory of **supply-side economics**, pro-business officials in the Reagan administration believed that letting entrepreneurs keep more of their profits would fuel economic growth, creating more and better-paying jobs that generated enough tax revenue to offset the increases in military spending that Reagan proposed.

Liberal Democrats, however, suspected that Reagan had a more sinister reason for slashing taxes. Reagan, they charged, planned to starve the budget to force Congress to undertake even more draconian cuts in New Deal and Great Society social welfare programs that conservatives longed to abolish. Liberal Democrats derided his budget proposal as trickle-down economics, an approach discredited during the Hoover administration (see Chapter 22) when aid to the wealthy failed to create more jobs for the poor.

Democrats in Congress were determined to fight Reagan's budget proposals. Then a nearly tragic turn of events gave Reagan an unexpected advantage. On March 30, 1981, a deranged twenty-five-year-old named John Hinckley (seeking to impress teenage film actress Jodie Foster) shot Reagan, his press secretary James Brady, and two others as they were leaving a Washington hotel. After hearing a firecracker-like pop, news photographer Ron Edmonds took three quick photos (**28.14**): The first shows the president grimacing as the bullet hit him; the second shows him turning to locate the source of the noise; in the third, Secret Service agent Jerry Parr pushes Reagan into the presidential limousine. In the hospital, with a bullet lodged near his heart, Reagan maintained his trademark cheerfulness, telling his distraught wife, "Honey, I forgot to duck."

Americans rallied to his side, and when Reagan returned to work a month later, he presented his 70 percent approval ratings as evidence that the nation supported his budget proposal. It passed easily with bipartisan support from conservative Democratic legislators. The top tax rate dropped from 70 percent to 50 percent, subsequently lowered to 28 percent in 1986. Reagan's image as a resolute leader got another boost when he fired eleven thousand striking air traffic controllers in August 1981, enforcing a ban on strikes by federal employees working in critical industries. Liberal critics lamented that the president's act sent a chilling message to organized labor, whose membership rolls and willingness to strike declined throughout the decade.

> "Please tell me you're all Republicans."
>
> A wounded President RONALD REAGAN to the emergency surgical team before they operated, 1981

In 1984 Reagan easily won his reelection bid against Democratic challenger Walter Mondale. Mondale energized the Democratic Party when he selected New York congresswoman Geraldine

28.14 President Reagan Shot, 1981
The first photo shows the president flinching as a bullet hits him, but Reagan did not realize that he had been shot until his limousine started driving away.

What accounted for Reagan's popularity with the electorate?

Ferraro as his running mate, the nation's first female vice presidential candidate, but he made a key strategic error by stating that he would raise taxes to close the deficit. Mondale expected Americans to reward him for his candor about the worrisome federal debt, but the nation was in no mood to fret. Reagan scored well with a series of television campaign ads that centered on the theme "Morning Again in America." The ads featured scenes of small-town America where content citizens celebrated marriages, schoolchildren pledged allegiance to the flag, and friends laughed together. "America is prouder, stronger, better. Why would we want to return to where we were less than four short years ago?" the voiceover asked. Many Americans agreed and Reagan won every state in the Electoral College except Mondale's home state of Minnesota and the District of Columbia, with a landslide total of 525 to 13.

Reagan remained relentlessly pro-business throughout his presidency. Driven to free private industry from government regulations that, in his view, restricted its growth, Reagan convinced Congress to deregulate the savings and loan industry. Once freed from strict government oversight, these banks subsequently lost huge amounts of depositors' money in speculative investments. In 1989 President George H. W. Bush, Reagan's successor in the White House, convinced Congress to bail them out at great cost to taxpayers rather than accept wide-scale bank failures that would certainly send the economy into a deep recession.

As the budget battles and savings and loan debacle revealed, Reagan's fiscal policies remained controversial. During his time in office, the federal debt nearly tripled (from $997 billion in 1981 to $2.6 trillion in 1988) as the hoped-for tax revenue failed to materialize and the military build-up continued unabated. After a serious recession in 1981–1983, the economy began to improve as inflation lessened and business activity picked up. The return of prosperity muted the impact of liberal criticism and helped Republicans argue that people at all class levels were doing better financially under Reagan's stewardship.

Democrats and Republicans offered competing visions on the state of the economy throughout the 1980s. Democrats lamented the increased concentration of income in the hands of the top fifth of the population. "What I want to see above all is that this remains a country where someone can always get rich," Reagan stated in 1983. Chief executive officers (CEOs) of leading corporations had no reason for complaint. Their average salaries, adjusted for inflation, rose from $3 million to $12 million a year during Reagan's eight years in office while outlays for subsidized housing dropped from $30 billion to $7 billion. In 1980 the average CEO made forty times more than the average factory worker. By 1989 CEOs earned ninety-three times more. To Democrats Reagan's economic policies helped the rich get richer while the poor got poorer. Republicans countered that consumption was a better measurement of the Americans' overall financial health than income distribution. In the 1980s Americans went on a buying spree that rivaled the postwar boom of the 1950s, purchasing nearly 88 million cars, 63 million VCRs, and 62 million microwave ovens. Items previously available only to the wealthy, such as refrigerators and telephones, were found in nearly every American household by 1990. While the poorest Americans were not living as well as the richest, their material circumstances were much improved when compared with those of previous generations.

Reagan spoke eloquently about cutting taxes and slashing welfare. He was decidedly less passionate about education, housing, health care, and the environment, often letting subordinates make key decisions in these areas. His hands-off management style differed vastly from Carter's micromanaging tendencies. Reagan rarely worked more than eight hours a day, enjoyed many vacations to his California ranch, and usually took an afternoon nap. "It's true that hard work never killed anyone, but I figure why take the chance?" he joked. Reagan's detractors viewed his detachment as senility and charged that he was just a figurehead. Supporters sometimes agreed that Reagan put his trust in the wrong hands. Over one hundred members of his administration were indicted or forced to resign amid corruption charges, stemming in part from Reagan's lax oversight of his subordinates who often acted without consulting him.

Foreign Policy Triumphs and Scandals

President Reagan did more than reject the liberal economic vision; he also overturned the foreign policy initiatives set in place by his Republican predecessors. He changed the rules of the Cold War by abandoning MAD, the doctrine embraced by American and Soviet policymakers since the 1950s, as the basis for U.S. defense against the Soviet Union. Remaining defenseless against enemy nuclear weapons was an essential component of MAD.

Why did Democrats and Republicans come to different conclusions about the state of the economy in the 1980s?

The ability to shoot down incoming missiles, the doctrine asserted, might encourage the enemy, who no longer feared its own destruction, to attack.

Reagan offered a competing view. "Let me share with you a vision of the future which offers hope," Reagan declared in 1983, announcing the **Strategic Defense Initiative (SDI)**. Challenging the view that vulnerability made America more secure, Reagan proposed building a missile shield that used lasers from space satellites to destroy incoming missiles. Publicly, Reagan argued that his plan was compatible with the 1972 ABM treaty (a point that critics disputed) since he intended to share the technology with the Soviets. Privately, he expected the Soviet Union to go bankrupt trying to match the United States in building its own missiles defenses.

Despite the billions spent on research, the SDI project failed. SDI nonetheless hurt the Soviet Union. A quick succession of elderly Soviet leaders responded to Reagan's challenge much as he expected. They increased military spending, ignoring the devastating consequences for average Soviet citizens. In the 1980s the Soviet Union spent between 15 and 20 percent of its GNP on defense, compared to 6.5 percent by the United States. Pervasive shortages meant that Soviet citizens spent hours waiting in long lines outside poorly stocked supermarkets, stoking internal discontent with Communist rule.

Closer to home, Reagan looked for ways to destabilize communist and leftist regimes in the Caribbean and Central America, activities portrayed on the map, *American Intervention in Latin America, 1980–2000* (**28.15**). In Nicaragua Reagan hoped to unseat the Sandinistas, leftist rebels who had overthrown the American-supported dictator Anastasio Somoza in 1979. Sandinista aid to Marxist rebels battling the pro-American government in nearby El Salvador confirmed Reagan's fears that communism was on the march in Central America. Reagan consequently approved covert Central Intelligence Agency (CIA) assistance to the contras, counterrevolutionary forces in Nicaragua that opposed the Sandinistas.

Congress had a different view of events in Central America. Hoping to continue the move away from direct interference in other nations' domestic affairs (a process begun by Ford and Carter), Congress prohibited the CIA and Department of Defense from funding any effort to overthrow the Sandinistas. National Security Council (NSC) Director Robert McFarlane and his assistant Marine Lt. Col. Oliver North convinced Reagan that these restrictions did not prevent the NSC from soliciting millions from the Saudi Arabian government and other private donors to aid the contras. When Congress heard about these donations in 1984, they prohibited the government from using non-American funds to unseat the Sandinistas.

Hoping to score a quick victory in thwarting the regional expansion of communism, in October 1983 Reagan ordered U.S. troops to invade the tiny

28.15 American Intervention in Latin America, 1980–2000
The United States continued to maintain Latin America as a sphere of influence in the 1980s.

Which of Reagan's foreign policy initiatives broke with policies set by Nixon and Carter?

28.16 *Speak Softly and Carry a Big Stick,* 1986
Political cartoonist Herblock suggested that the Iran-Contra scandal would mar Reagan's place in history, comparing his tepid response to the scandal with the stirring phrases associated with presidents Theodore Roosevelt, Franklin D. Roosevelt, and Harry Truman.

Caribbean island of Grenada. The president ostensibly dispatched U.S. forces to rescue American medical students trapped in Grenada when a leftist government seized control. The troops' real mission was to remove a government actively seeking Cuban and Soviet military aid. By ordering troops into battle without consulting Congress ahead of time, Reagan also used his powers as commander-in-chief (some argued unconstitutionally) to restore the strength of the presidency, badly damaged since Watergate.

Reagan supporters celebrated America's swift victory in Grenada, but critics viewed the event differently. They accused Reagan of using the Grenada invasion to distract Americans from more dismal news coming out the Middle East. Two days before the Grenada invasion, a militant Islamist suicide bomber had plowed a vehicle loaded with explosives into an unsecured barracks housing U.S. peacekeeping troops in Beirut, Lebanon, killing 241 servicemen. Over the next few months, Iranian-backed Islamist terrorist groups (angry over U.S. support for Israel and Iraq, Iran's enemy) increased their assaults against the United States by taking individual Americans hostage in Lebanon. Reagan's dual desire to end the burgeoning Middle Eastern hostage crisis and halt the spread of communism in Central America led to the biggest political scandal of his administration.

In the **Iran-Contra scandal**, Reagan administration officials sold arms to Iran to secure the hostages' release and then illegally used the proceeds to support the anti-Communist contras in Nicaragua. The problems began in 1985 when Reagan asked his new NSC director John Poindexter and North to devise a covert plan to sell arms to Iran, which needed the weapons for its ongoing war with Iraq. As part of the secret agreement, the United States demanded that Iran use its influence to secure the release of hostages held in Lebanon. After the deal went through, a few hostages were freed, but the arms-for-hostages deal soon backfired. Reagan's willingness to pay bribes to free American hostages only encouraged militant Islamist groups to seize more over the next two years. Even more troubling, Poindexter and North secretly decided to divert profits from the arms sales to the contras in Nicaragua—directly violating the congressional ban on aid to the anti-Communist rebels. When an American cargo plane carrying arms to the contras crashed in 1986, their illegal action was exposed. Convicted of breaking the law, the pair won appeals based on legal technicalities and went free.

Poindexter and North claimed that Reagan knew nothing about their illegal diversion of funds to the contras. "I made a very deliberate decision not to ask the president so I could insulate him," Poindexter testified before Congress. The public accepted this explanation, viewing Reagan as a hands-off administrator who could not always control his subordinates. This Herblock cartoon (**28.16**) reinforced that image by portraying Reagan as lacking the leadership skills of presidents Theodore Roosevelt, Franklin D. Roosevelt, and Harry Truman. With his approval rating dipping to below 50 percent, Reagan hoped to restore confidence in his leadership by improving relations with the Soviet Union.

The night before the Soviet Politburo appointed him the nation's leader in 1985, fifty-four-year-old Mikhail Gorbachev admitted to his wife, "We can't go on living like this." Gorbachev was referring to both the ironclad Soviet control over the domestic economy and the Soviet government's decades-long obsession with a possible American nuclear attack. Gorbachev embraced reform to save the Soviet Union, not destroy it. Eager to reduce Soviet outlays for defense so he could pump needed funds into the long-ignored economy, Gorbachev also moved to reduce tensions with the United States.

When Reagan and Gorbachev met in Washington, D.C., in December 1987, the pair took a historic step by signing the **Intermediate-Range Nuclear Forces Treaty** that approved the destruction of all U.S. and Soviet intermediate-range missiles in Europe. Past arms treaties had focused on curtailing the growth of nuclear stockpiles. For the first time a U.S.-Soviet pact actually reduced nuclear arms. The thaw in U.S.-Soviet relations continued when Gorbachev

Why was Reagan able to weather the Iran-Contra scandal?

withdrew Soviet forces from Afghanistan in 1988 and reduced support for Communist regimes throughout the world.

The Reagan Revolution

Reagan was an overwhelmingly popular president, but supporters' claims of a "Reagan Revolution" appear exaggerated. Reagan lowered taxes for the wealthy and he established limits that permanently curtailed the growth of the welfare state. He appointed right-leaning judges to the federal judiciary and the Supreme Court, including Sandra Day O'Connor as the first female Supreme Court justice. Cultural conservatives remained loyal to Reagan even though he offered little more than lip-service to their goals of outlawing abortion, returning prayer to public schools, or ending affirmative action.

As president Reagan always won applause when he proclaimed, "government is not the solution to our problem; government is the problem." Yet when Reagan left office, the New Deal and Great Society were as vibrant and relevant as the day he entered the White House. Americans still expected the federal government to pay pensions, guarantee unemployment benefits, curb pollution, and help educate poor children. Rather than leaving a strong institutional legacy that endured, Reagan presided over a profound shift in political vision. His pro-business policies reinvigorated faith that an unfettered free market could make Americans prosperous, and his open alliance with the Religious Right brought discussion of issues that concerned cultural conservatives into the center of American political discourse. In foreign policy neoconservatives' interventionist ideas now exerted considerable influence in Republican circles. Finally, "Reagan succeeded in reviving national confidence at a time when there was a great need for inspiration. This was his great contribution as president," reporter Lou Cannon concluded.

Conclusion

Spiritual malaise gripped the country in the 1970s as a poor economy and dissatisfying foreign policy made many Americans feel that the nation was adrift. Conflicting visions arose over women's roles and abortion, the increased visibility of homosexuals, and federal environmental regulation as Americans debated whether the country was on the right path. A crisis of presidential leadership defined American politics throughout the decade. Nixon resigned during the Watergate scandal; the first nonelected vice president, Gerald Ford, assumed the presidency; and a southern born-again Democrat, Jimmy Carter, lost support when he floundered during the Iranian hostage crisis. In the 1980s Reagan's charisma and conservative principles enthralled his supporters, but vocal critics lamented his casual style and free market economic policies. The ascendancy of the Religious Right, an important component of the new conservative coalition that elected Reagan, introduced vigorous debate over cultural issues into the political arena. Followers credited Reagan with jump-starting the economy, detractors worried about an exploding federal deficit and the inequitable distribution of wealth. Both acknowledged that Reagan presided over a rightward shift in political values in the 1980s.

The country's dependency on foreign oil and escalating tensions with the Soviet Union required a new approach to foreign affairs, a challenge that Carter met by returning the Panama Canal to Panama and injecting human rights issues into foreign policy debates. Like Carter, Reagan would enjoy his greatest successes and failures in the foreign policy arena. He rewrote the rules of the Cold War and achieved a new accommodation in U.S.-Soviet relations, but wrongdoing in the Reagan White House resulted in the Iran-Contra scandal, which brought back fears in some circles that the imperial presidency of the Nixon years had returned. In a testament to Reagan's popularity, George H. W. Bush became the first vice president since Martin Van Buren (who followed the well-liked Andrew Jackson in 1837) to win election immediately after the president under whom he served completed his term.

How does Reagan's legacy compare to the one left by Franklin D. Roosevelt?

CHAPTER REVIEW

1972–1973

Congress passes ERA
Provokes heated debate over gender roles in American society

OPEC oil embargo against the United States
Dramatizes American dependence on overseas oil exports

Watergate investigations heat up
Constitutional crisis over Nixon's abuse of power

***Roe v. Wade* legalizes abortion**
Religious conservative coalition forms in opposition

1974

Nixon resigns
Gerald Ford, the first unelected vice president, becomes president

Ford pardons Nixon
Shakes public confidence in Ford's leadership

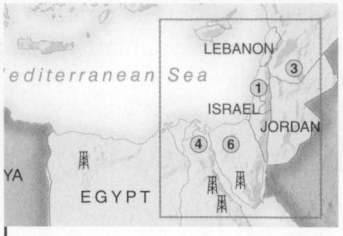

1977–1978

First home computer marketed
Computer revolution begins

Senate ratifies treaty returning Panama Canal
Redresses past U.S. wrongdoing but provokes controversy at home

Camp David Accords
Secures lasting peace between Egypt and Israel

Review Questions

1. Why was the Watergate scandal politically significant? What different portraits of Nixon emerged in political cartoons of the 1970s? How did the Watergate scandal compare to the Iran-Contra scandal during the Reagan Administration?
2. What accounted for the nation's economic problems throughout the 1970s?
3. What changes and continuities existed in American foreign policy in the post-Vietnam 1970s and 1980s? How did concerns over human rights, communism, and the domestic economy influence the direction of foreign relations during these two decades?
4. Why did presidents Ford and Carter lose public confidence? How did Ronald Reagan's political vision differ from the ones embraced by his predecessors in the White House?
5. What different constituencies united to form the New Right?
6. What competing visions animated debates over feminism, gay rights, and environmentalism?
7. What was Ronald Reagan's lasting legacy in domestic and foreign affairs?

1979

Meltdown of nuclear reactor at Three Mile Island
Americans reject nuclear energy as an alternative to oil

Iranian Hostage Crisis begins
Carter's approval ratings plummet

Soviet Union invades Afghanistan
U.S.-Soviet relations deteriorate

1980–1981

AIDS epidemic begins
Stigmatizes gay people as diseased

President Reagan shot
Upsurge in popularity helps controversial budget plan pass

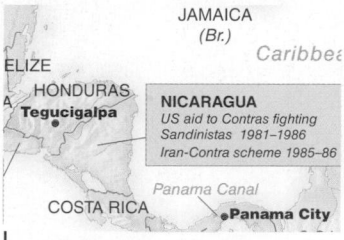

1983–1985

Reagan announces SDI
Challenges MAD doctrine

Iran-Contra scandal
Most serious presidential scandal since Watergate

1987–1988

ACT-UP stages first funeral demonstration
Puts pressure on government to fund anti-AIDS research

Intercontinental-Range Nuclear Forces Treaty signed
Spells the final phases of the Cold War

Key Terms

Organization of the Petroleum Exporting Countries (OPEC) An international consortium of oil-producing nations that regulated the price and quantity of oil exported to the world market. **844**

Rust Belt Decaying industrial cities in the Midwest, places plagued with high unemployment, crumbling roads, bankrupt governments, and high welfare rolls. **846**

Watergate scandal An episode of presidential criminal wrongdoing that created a constitutional crisis and brought an end to Nixon's political career. **848**

SALT I (1972) The first treaty between the Soviet Union and the United States that limited the deployment of intercontinental and submarine-launched ballistic missiles and the creation of missile-defense systems. **852**

mutually assured destruction The claim that the guarantee of a devastating nuclear counterattack would deter the United States and Soviet Union from ever employing their nuclear arsenals. **852**

Camp David Accords (1978) Israel agreed to give the Sinai Peninsula back to Egypt; in return Egypt became the first Arab state to recognize Israel's right to exist. **856**

Iranian hostage crisis Defining event in Carter's presidency as Iranian revolutionaries held fifty-two Americans captive for 444 days. **856**

Equal Rights Amendment (ERA) A proposed constitutional amendment, which stated that "equality of rights under the law shall not be denied or abridged by the United States or by any State on account of sex." **859**

***Roe v. Wade* (1973)** Supreme Court decision that legalized abortion. **861**

Stonewall riot A 1969 battle between patrons of a Greenwich Village male gay bar and police that became the catalyst for the gay rights movement. **862**

Proposition 13 Referendum in California that dramatically reduced property taxes, spearheading grassroots tax rebellion nationwide. **865**

Religious Right A collection of right-wing Christian groups that defended traditional values and supported conservative political causes. **865**

supply-side economics Reagan administration theory that letting entrepreneurs keep more of their profits would fuel economic growth, job creation, and more tax revenue to offset military spending. **867**

Strategic Defense Initiative (SDI) Reagan's proposal to build a missile shield that used lasers from space satellites to destroy incoming missiles. **869**

Iran-Contra scandal A law-breaking scheme that sold arms to Iran to secure the hostages' release and used the proceeds to support anti-Communists in Nicaragua. **870**

Intermediate-Range Nuclear Forces Treaty (1987) Approved the destruction of all U.S. and Soviet intermediate-range missiles in Europe. **870**

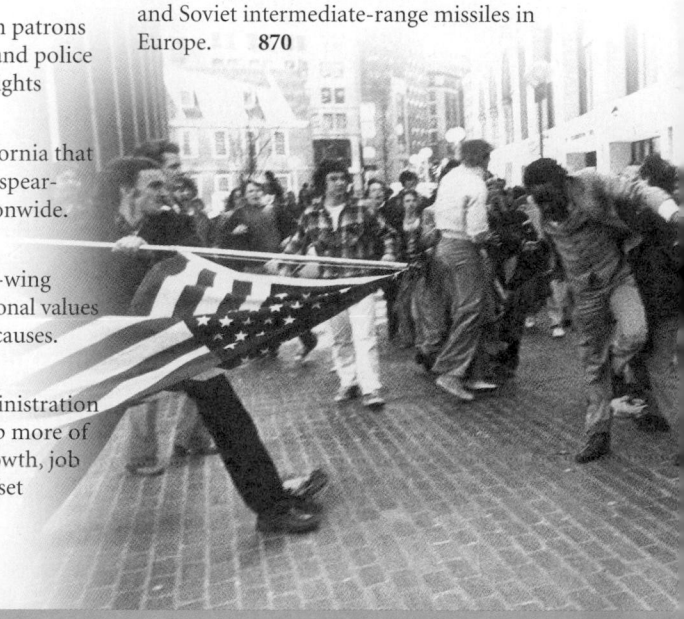

CHAPTER 29

Building a New World Order

The United States, 1989–2009

> **"None of us will ever forget this day, yet we go forward to defend freedom and all that is good and just in our world."**
>
> President GEORGE W. BUSH, speaking to the nation on the evening of September 11, 2001

On the morning of September 11, 2001, nineteen young Arab men boarded four planes on the East Coast. All belonged to the Islamic extremist organization known as al-Qaeda. Within a half an hour after take-off, they stormed the cockpits of their respective planes with box cutters and mace, killed the American pilots, and installed their own pilots (who had each received flight instruction in private American aviation schools) to fly the planes into predetermined targets.

At 8:46 a.m. the first plane plowed into the North Tower of the World Trade Center in New York City, an internationally recognized landmark that symbolized American dominance over the world economy. Seventeen minutes later a second plane hit the South Tower. The nation now understood that what had first looked like an unfortunate and tragic accident was actually a coordinated attack against the United States. A third plane crashed into the Pentagon, headquarters of the U.S. Department of Defense, in Virginia, the building most closely associated with U.S. military might in the eyes of the world. Meanwhile passengers in the fourth hijacked plane reached the cockpit and prevented the terrorists from flying the plane into the Capitol, a worldwide symbol of democratic government. This plane instead crashed into a Pennsylvania field.

The blazing World Trade Center towers quickly crumbled, with the office workers and firefighters still inside the buildings as onlookers ran for cover. The skeletal ruins and mountains of debris became the burial site for thousands. One onlooker echoed the nation's sense of disbelief: "This is America. How can it happen in America? How?"

The 9/11 attacks, as they came to be known, reshaped the ongoing debate about America's role in the world and the best way to protect American citizens. Only twenty years earlier Americans had savored their victory in the Cold War as communist governments in Eastern Europe and the Soviet Union collapsed. When the Cold War ended, Americans believed that their nation would take the lead in creating a new world order even as they disputed how best to spread democracy, protect the U.S. economy, and flex the nation's military muscle. Enjoying prosperous times for most of the 1990s, the country paid little attention to the new threat that loomed before the world's sole remaining superpower—terrorist strikes by anti-American Islamist extremists, such as al-Qaeda. Political debate instead centered on whether the liberal or conservative vision of government would prevail at home.

After 9/11 President George W. Bush moved with resolve to restore the image of America as a powerful and triumphant nation. He led the country into two wars: the first in Afghanistan; the second, far more controversial, in Iraq. In 2008, Americans provided a different sort of history-making moment by electing the first African American president of the United States. By then, the worst financial crisis since the Great Depression posed an additional challenge for the nation.

What meaning did Americans attach to photographs of 9/11?

"A Moment Rich with Promise" p. 876

Contested Visions of Government p. 884

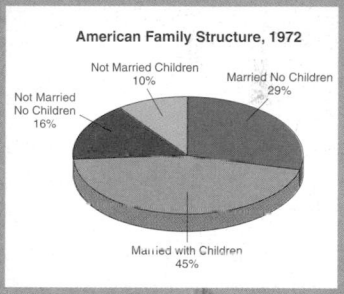

Transforming Daily Life p. 888

New Threats in the Post-Cold War World p. 894

"A Moment Rich with Promise"

On his inauguration day in 1989, George H. W. Bush announced that he had become president "at a moment rich with promise." The fall of communism throughout Eastern Europe and the Soviet Union within the next two years seemed to confirm this judgment. However, the end of the Cold War did not mean peace; the United States immediately fought two short wars in Panama and the Persian Gulf. Conflict arose at home as well, as a huge federal deficit and simmering racial tensions that occasionally exploded into violence left some feeling that America's promise lay unfulfilled.

The Election of 1988

The son of a former Connecticut senator, George H. W. Bush served as a congressman, ambassador, Central Intelligence Agency (CIA) director, and vice president before becoming the Republican candidate for president in 1988. In this sense the decorated World War II pilot and former oilman was the ultimate insider, a man familiar with the corridors of power in Washington, D.C., and the exclusive private clubs where financial deals were negotiated. A moderate Republican with a patrician style, Bush never projected the same charisma or the passion for conservative causes that had drawn voters to Ronald Reagan, the man he hoped to follow as president. Bush's campaign had to overcome these obstacles when he faced Massachusetts Democratic governor Michael Dukakis in the 1988 presidential contest.

When Dukakis proposed increased spending on health care, education, and housing, the Bush team ridiculed the Democrat as a big-spending liberal and began calling him the governor of "Taxachusetts." In his stump speeches Bush also tapped into white peoples' fears of so-called black criminality by frequently mentioning Willie Horton, an African American prisoner who had taken advantage of a weekend furlough program in Massachusetts and gone on a crime rampage that included raping a white woman. Adding to his woes Dukakis made some critical missteps, including one ill-advised photo-op during which he donned an oversized helmet and military jumpsuit to ride a tank (**29.1**). Most

29.1 A Failed Photo-Op
Seeking to appear like a commander in chief, 1988 Democratic presidential candidate Michael Dukakis was instead ridiculed for riding around in a tank in a suit and tie.

How did George H. W. Bush prevail in the 1988 presidential election?

Americans felt that the photo made Dukakis look ridiculous, not presidential. By Election Day Bush had successfully defined Dukakis as someone who would raise taxes and let criminals out of jail, and as someone who was unprepared to be commander in chief. He defeated Dukakis 426 to 111 in the Electoral College, capturing 53 percent of the popular vote.

Popular Revolts against Communism

When Bush became the 41st president of the United States in 1989, the former director of the CIA remained suspicious about Soviet Premier Mikhail Gorbachev's true motives for instituting internal reforms and reaching out to the United States (see Chapter 28). Bush administration officials worried that Gorbachev "was attempting to kill us with kindness," according to National Security Advisor Brent Scowcroft. Gorbachev was equally distrustful of Bush and his inner circle. "These people were brought up in the years of the Cold War and still do not have any foreign policy alternative," he complained to the Politburo. Caught off guard by the quick demise of communism in Eastern Europe, within a year Bush had changed his mind about Gorbachev "by 180 degrees."

In the first sign of the upheaval to come, Hungary decided to take down the barbed wire fence between Communist Hungary and democratic Austria in May 1989. The East German government watched in dismay as thousands of its citizens drove to the Hungarian-Austrian border and then walked across to defect to the West. Turning to Moscow for help, East Germany received a surprising reply: "We can't do anything about it." A similarly uncharacteristic Soviet reaction greeted news that candidates from the democratic Polish workers' union Solidarity had won control of Poland's newly created bicameral Parliament, forming the first democratic government in postwar Eastern Europe. "This is entirely a matter to be decided by Poland," a Soviet official announced.

Soviet, Hungarian, and Polish leaders lifted restrictions on speech, voting, and economic activity to save their Communist regimes, unleashing a tide of popular revolt against Communist rule that soon overwhelmed them. Perhaps nowhere did the fall of communism come faster, and more unexpectedly, than in East Germany. On November 9, 1989, a botched news conference by a harried East German official triggered the destruction of the Berlin Wall. Instead of announcing a relaxation in rules governing travel between East and West Berlin, a confused East German official mistakenly told the press that starting immediately, East Germans could freely leave "through any of the border crossings." Electrified by the news that the wall was open, thousands of people gathered at armed crossing points, places where 1,000 East Germans had been shot trying to cross over the last twenty-eight years. When confused guards opened the gates, streams of East Germans poured across and joined with West Germans to rejoice atop the Berlin Wall.

Images as History: The Fall of the Berlin Wall (page 878) examines the media images that shaped Americans' reactions to this event. Further evidence of television's power to mold history came in the following days as thousands of East Berliners entered West Berlin and headed straight for downtown department stores. Concrete walls had not prevented East Berliners from viewing American sitcoms (dubbed in German) showing the abundance of goods available in the West. Television-stoked desires for "work-saving gadgets, [well-stocked pantries], attractive surroundings and a touch of luxury," one reporter contended, played an important role in bringing the Berlin Wall down. Gorbachev's refusal to intervene with armed force was also critical. Within a year East and West Germany had reunified into one democratic nation, an American goal since the Cold War began in the late 1940s.

By the end of 1989, the Soviet Union no longer dominated Eastern Europe, losing territory that it had controlled since the end of World War II. One by one the individual states that formed the Soviet Union demanded their independence as well, secession movements that Gorbachev tried to squash with economic embargos and, occasionally, troops. Desperate to stop the hemorrhaging, a group of hard-line Communist insiders orchestrated a coup attempt in August 1990. They put Gorbachev under house arrest in his vacation home and ringed the Soviet Parliament in Moscow with troops and tanks. Hesitating, the coup leaders lost the military's support and the overthrow attempt failed. With the populace now demanding widespread economic reforms and Communist Party officials blaming Gorbachev for losing control, the freed premier resigned on August 24, 1990. Five days later the Soviet Communist Party dissolved. By December 25, 1991, the Soviet Union ceased to exist as all its member states, including Russia, became independent nations. After decades

What role did ordinary citizens play in ending communism in East Germany and the Soviet Union?

Images as History

THE FALL OF THE BERLIN WALL

Photographs of Berlin had already punctuated key moments in the Cold War for Americans, beginning with images of the 1948–1949 Berlin airlift to the wall's construction in 1961 to prevent East Berliners from defecting to West Berlin (see Chapter 24). Presidents John F. Kennedy and Ronald Reagan had made well-documented pilgrimages to the site where they publicly denounced the Berlin Wall as a towering symbol of Communist oppression. Now, from the comfort of their living rooms, TV-viewing Americans watched as East and West Berliners climbed atop the wall throughout the night on November 9, 1989 to demand the reunification of their divided city.

The fall of communism in Europe reinforced American faith in the superiority of capitalism over communism, but some commentators urged the United States to undertake economic reforms at home to ensure that capitalism operated more fairly. What competing views do this photograph and political cartoon offer Americans about the importance of the Berlin Wall falling? What counter-arguments could critics offer?

After the evening celebrations East German guards reclaimed the top of the wall and impassively watched German civilians attack the graffiti-laden western side of the wall with chisels and hammers.

President Bush told the press that he had no desire "to dance on the wall," worried that any gloating might goad Gorbachev into sealing up the wall or prompt Soviet hardliners to overthrow Gorbachev.

Both reporters and ordinary people brought cameras to document this historic moment.

The image of one man destroying the wall piece-by-piece with his hammer resonated with Americans—it symbolized the ability of common people to make history and their desire to collect pieces of the wall as souvenirs.

Attacking the Berlin Wall with a Hammer

Would the fall of Communism usher in a better world? Many Americans believed so, but cartoonist Pat Oliphant offered a competing view by implying that free market capitalism did not always benefit everyone equally.

Pat Oliphant Questions the Triumph of Capitalism over Communism

The befuddlement of the hungry, homeless man dressed in rags suggests that there is no "we" in the United States—rich and poor view events like the fall of the Berlin Wall differently.

In the 1980s, the number of homeless people living and begging on the streets grew to a level not seen in urban America since the Progressive era.

Many Americans celebrated the fall of the Berlin Wall as a triumph of the nation's democratic, capitalist vision over a competing autocratic, anti-capitalist Communist one.

What symbolic importance did the Berlin Wall have during the Cold War?

of devising strategies to contain, weaken, and defeat the Soviet Union, the United States declared victory in the Cold War. "The Soviet Union did not simply lose the Cold War; the Western democracies won," Bush announced.

The U.S. battle against communism was not over, however. On the other side of the world, the Chinese Communist regime made different choices when faced with a popular revolt. In April 1989 university student demonstrators occupied Tiananmen Square in central Beijing to protest the removal of a high-ranking Communist official who had called for economic and political reforms. A vigorous debate took place behind closed doors among Chinese Communist officials over whether to end the demonstrations with troops or adopt a Gorbachev-like approach and accommodate some of the students' demands. On the morning of June 4, tanks appeared in Tiananmen Square, signaling that discussion within the inner circle had ended. Troops shot hundreds as they cleared the area of protesters. Two days later a lone man walking down the deserted Avenue of Eternal Peace made a solitary gesture of defiance by standing steadfast in the middle of the street as a column of seventeen patrolling tanks approached. When the lead tank swerved right to avoid hitting him, the man stepped right. When it swerved left, he stepped left. Finally the tanks stopped and the man jumped onto the first one, shouting to its driver, "Why are you here? My city is in chaos because of you." Associated Press photographer Jeff Widener captured this encounter in an award-winning photo seen on newspaper front-pages around the globe (**29.2**). Americans hailed "Tank Man," as he became known, for his inspirational defense of peace and human rights. No one in China, however, except for the bystanders who whisked him away and the Chinese authorities who probably executed him, ever knew of this encounter.

As the economic relationship between the United States and China changed, China's violent suppression of democracy movements provoked competing visions over how to proceed. In 1900 America wanted to sell China goods; by 1990 American companies increasingly outsourced work on manufactured products to China, using cheap Chinese labor to satiate American consumers' demands for affordable goods. Some critics argued that by aiding the Chinese government in its quest to improve the standard of living for ordinary citizens, Americans were helping autocratic Communist leaders stay in power. Others countered that recent events in Eastern Europe demonstrated that exposing Chinese citizens to Western values and goods would sow the seeds for an eventual democratic and capitalist revolution. A third faction saw the issue differently; they worried that a prosperous and industrially strong China might eventually replace the United States as the world's strongest power.

29.2 Standing Up for Democracy in China, 1989
Two days after the Chinese military brutally suppressed a popular rebellion in Tiananmen Square, a lone man stopped army tanks in their tracks; the world cheered his courageous stand.

Why did popular uprisings against communism in Europe and China have different outcomes?

Domestic Policy in the Bush Administration

The growing trade deficit with China (the United States bought more than it sold) was only one economic issue troubling Americans during the Bush years. "Read my lips: No new taxes," Bush had proclaimed during the 1988 campaign. Once in office, however, Bush reneged on his pledge by raising income taxes. Faced with the largest deficit in American history, the result of increased defense spending during the Reagan years without any corresponding tax increases and Bush's own decision to bail out the failing savings and loan industry in 1989 (see Chapter 28), he saw no other option. Bush's decision angered many conservative Republicans, and some never forgave him. "Read My Lips: I Lied," ran one condemning *New York Post* headline.

The combination of a huge deficit and an unfriendly Democratic majority in Congress discouraged Bush from proposing any dramatic new domestic initiatives. A revolution of sorts nonetheless occurred when Bush signed the **Americans with Disabilities Act**, a 1990 civil rights law that prohibited discrimination against the disabled in employment, public accommodations, and telecommunications. The disabled gained unprecedented freedom of movement as legally required elevators, ramps, and sloped curbs became commonplace.

During the campaign Bush had courted the conservative wing of the Republican Party by promising to appoint like-minded judges. He fulfilled this pledge by nominating a conservative African American lawyer, Clarence Thomas, to the Supreme Court when Thurgood Marshall, the Court's first African American judge, retired. Controversy erupted when Anita Hill, a former colleague, accused Thomas of sexual harassment and Thomas responded by calling the televised confirmation hearings a "high-tech lynching." The Senate ultimately confirmed Thomas by a narrow majority in 1991. With workplace sexual harassment front-page news, an unprecedented number of women won congressional seats in the 1992 elections, including the first female African American senator, Carol Mosley Braun, a Democrat from Illinois.

While the Thomas hearings exposed gender discord, the 1991 Los Angeles riots brought simmering racial and ethnic tensions to the surface. In March a 78-mile car chase along Los Angeles freeways ended with white police brutally beating Rodney King, an African American, when he resisted arrest for speeding. A nearby resident captured the incident on film, but Americans differed on what the video revealed (**29.3**). Most blacks and some sympathetic whites saw a poorly trained and racist police force that unfairly harassed blacks, echoing complaints that had set off the Watts riots in 1965 (see Chapter 27).

29.3 Los Angeles Police Beat Motorist Rodney King, 1991
Many whites saw the police trying to control an unruly black man who had resisted arrest for speeding, but many blacks saw racist police brutality.

Which gender and racial issues dominated the headlines in the early 1990s?

Others, including the jury (consisting of ten whites, one Latino, and one Asian American) that eventually acquitted the officers, offered a competing vision. They saw overworked police doing their job to protect law and order in a dangerous neighborhood. The "not guilty" verdict set off four days of rioting in Los Angeles during which Latinos also took to the streets to air their frustration with failing schools and entrenched poverty. Television networks continuously aired footage of black youths assaulting a white truck driver, but paid little attention to the Asian American–owned stores that blacks and Latinos ransacked as payback for allegedly having previously refused to serve or hire young men of color.

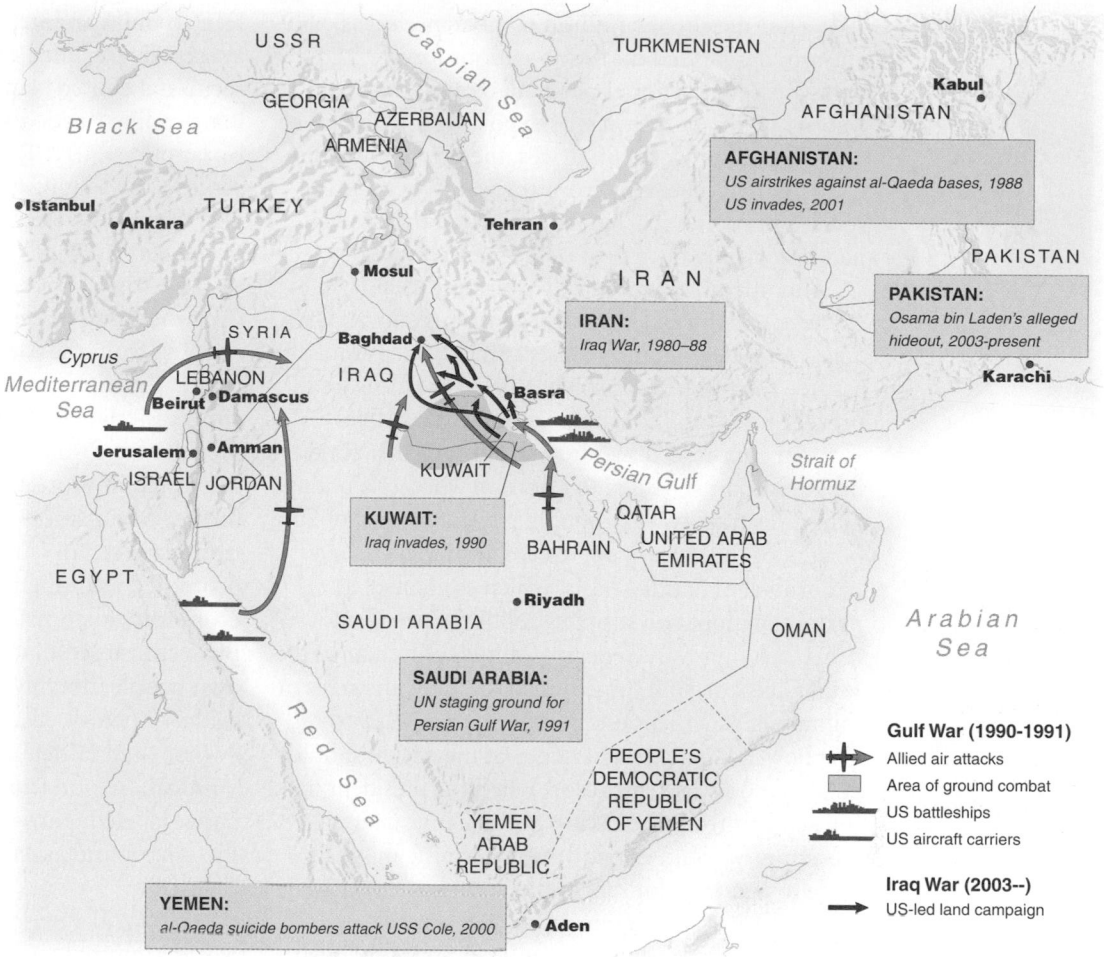

29.4 America and the Middle East, 1980–2003 The United States fought two major wars against Iraq, one in 1991 and the other beginning in 2003.

Panama and the Persian Gulf War

Bush did not propose any new initiatives to address gender, racial, or ethnic inequities; his real interest lay in foreign affairs. As he contemplated the new role that the United States should assume in a post–Cold War world, Bush moved to address a festering problem close to home. The Bush administration felt particularly uneasy about returning the Panama Canal in 1999 (see Chapter 28) to a Panamanian dictator who ruthlessly suppressed political opponents and oversaw lucrative drug-trafficking schemes. In December 1989 Bush launched Operation Just Cause, the largest American military campaign since the Vietnam War, to remove Manuel Noriega from power. The Panamanian invasion continued the nation's long tradition of maintaining Central America as a U.S. sphere of influence.

A crisis in the Middle East, however, offered Bush the opportunity to propose a new focus for U.S. foreign policy now that the Cold War was over. Bush faced the severest test of his administration when Iraqi dictator Saddam Hussein, whose nation's oil fields supplied 11 percent of global oil exports, invaded the neighboring nation of Kuwait, a small country that provided 9 percent of the world's oil, on August 2, 1990 (**29.4**). The 1979 Carter Doctrine (see Chapter 28) had already established the oil-rich Persian Gulf as a region vital to national economic and strategic interests. Throughout the 1980s Iranian-financed terrorist attacks and hostage crises in Lebanon (see Chapter 28) convinced the U.S. government that the fundamentalist Islamic government in Iran, not Iraq, posed the major threat in the Persian Gulf. During the eight-year Iran-Iraq War over a disputed waterway that separated the two nations, the United States supplied Iraq with weapons and intelligence. Oil-rich Arab nations, including Saudi Arabia and Kuwait, had also lent Iraq billions of dollars to prevent Iranian revolutionary religious fervor from spreading to their kingdoms. When the war ended inconclusively in

What problems did the United States face in the Middle East from 1980–2003?

1988 after nearly one million combatant deaths, Hussein demanded that Arab nations forgive Iraq's debt. Hussein harbored particular animosity against Kuwait, which he accused of exporting too much oil and depressing world oil prices, thereby hurting the Iraqi financial recovery from the war. When Kuwait refused his demands, Hussein declared that Kuwait had historically been part of Iraq, and invaded.

After the Iraqi army easily overran Kuwait, President Bush rushed American troops and ships to Saudi Arabia. Operation Desert Shield, the president assured the public, was solely a defensive measure to prevent Iraq from attacking Saudi Arabia. After Hussein announced that he was permanently annexing Kuwait, Bush began to question whether a purely defensive strategy was enough. Now in control of 20 percent of the world's oil, overnight Iraq became a major rival of Saudi Arabia, which contained 26 percent of global oil supplies. With the president now contemplating war, General Colin Powell, chair of the Joint Chiefs of Staff, urged Bush to follow the rules of military engagement established in the Reagan years. The **Powell Doctrine** asserted that the nation should go to war only as a last resort when the president had full support from the nation and the international community, could employ overwhelming military force to win without serious loss of American life, and had a clear exit strategy.

To amass overwhelming military strength, Bush sent Secretary of State James Baker on a diplomatic tour to build an international coalition that eventually included thirty-four nations. Bush secured a United Nations (UN) resolution authorizing military action if Hussein did not withdraw by January 15, 1991. With Saudi Arabia agreeing to serve as the staging ground for the invasion, 460,000 U.S. troops and sixty-five warships made their way to the Persian Gulf.

The Powell Doctrine called for more than overwhelming force; it also required enthusiastic support from the American people for an overseas military campaign. Bush faced stiff opposition from congressional Democrats, who argued that the president, a former Texas oilman, was primarily interested in protecting the lucrative profits of his former oil-business associates who imported oil from the Persian Gulf. Instead of war, Democrats promoted a competing vision that relied on economic sanctions to force Hussein to withdraw. Bush countered that Hussein's atrocities against his own people, notably his 1988 poison gas attacks against Kurdish villagers in northern Iraq, made him "worse than Hitler." Echoing Bush's claim, this political cartoon (**29.5**) showed Hussein holding a paper labeled "Kuwait takeover" as he looked into the mirror and asked Adolf Hitler's smiling reflection, "how'm I doing?" Bush, a decorated World War II veteran, reminded Americans that the world's failure to act when Hitler began his wars of conquest in 1939 had led to World War II. If an emboldened Hussein next attacked Saudi Arabia, he would control nearly half of the world's oil reserves. Bush also claimed that Hussein was actively trying to acquire nuclear weapons, and if he succeeded, he would be unstoppable. These arguments did not sway Democrats. With a vote split mostly along partisan lines, Congress voted to authorize war according to the terms spelled out in the UN resolution. When the UN deadline for withdrawal passed, the American-led UN coalition attacked Iraq the next day. Once the fighting started public debate ceased and Americans rallied around the flag.

29.5 "Mirror, Mirror on the Wall–How'm I doing?"
This 1990 political cartoon supported President George H. W. Bush's claim that Iraqi dictator Saddam Hussein was a modern-day Hitler.

How did the Powell Doctrine influence Bush's preparations for war against Iraq in 1991?

The Persian Gulf War unfolded in two phases. In the first phase U.S. forces bombed Iraqi installations in Kuwait and major cities in Iraq for thirty-nine days. In Kuwait the massive bombing terrified many poorly trained occupying Iraqi soldiers, and nearly one-quarter of the 400,000-man force deserted. A news team from the cable television news network CNN stayed in Baghdad, the capital of Iraq, throughout the bombing, and each night Americans watched their own nation's missiles streak across the sky and explode. The bombing inside Iraq destroyed the nation's power grid, water treatment plants, radio and television stations, and roads—hampering its military activities but also leaving civilians without power or clean water.

With Iraqi defenses in shambles from the air attacks, the war's second phase began when ground troops attacked the Iraqi forces occupying Kuwait on February 23, 1991. General Norman Schwarzkopf led coalition forces during **Operation Desert Storm**, a massive assault that soundly defeated the Iraqi army within four days, pushing it out of Kuwait. When American soldiers crossed into Iraq, Bush ordered an abrupt halt to the fighting. The total war had lasted forty-two days.

deaths) and successfully avoided widening the war beyond its original goal, Bush's approval ratings soared to 89 percent.

The UN peace agreement prohibited Hussein from rearming or acquiring nuclear weapons, restrictions enforced by UN inspectors who stayed in Iraq until 1998. The establishment of no-fly zones over Shiite and Kurdish areas prevented Hussein and his Sunni-dominated government from launching aerial attacks against these minorities within his own nation. The UN also instituted an oil embargo to prevent Hussein from acquiring funds to reconstitute his nuclear weapons program. Critics charged that the embargo led to widespread food and medicine shortages among the civilian population, and failed to prevent Iraq from rearming. Instead of caring for his people, Hussein used the nation's meager cash flow to continue his lavish lifestyle and secured funds to amass a large arsenal of conventional weapons by illegally smuggling oil through Jordan, Turkey, Syria, and Egypt. When the UN initiated a "food-for-oil" program in 1996 that allowed Hussein to export some oil legally if he used the profits for humanitarian purposes, civilian conditions improved slightly.

"By God, we've kicked the Vietnam Syndrome once and for all."

An exultant President GEORGE H. W. BUSH at the end of the Persian Gulf War, 1991

American forces, Bush declared, had met their goal of ending Hussein's occupation of Kuwait and had no intention of conquering Iraq. The United States would henceforth rely on sanctions to curb Hussein, returning to the strategy of containment that the United States had employed successfully against the Soviet Union to win the Cold War. Neoconservatives embraced a competing vision. They viewed the war as an opportunity to remove Hussein from power. Bush advisors, including Secretary of Defense Dick Cheney, however, saw no advantage to staying in Iraq. They argued that it would be difficult, if not impossible, to bring together the nation's three different ethnic groups (Sunnis, Shiites, and Kurds), each of which inhabited distinct regions, to form a democratic government. Abiding by the Powell Doctrine's emphasis on a clear exit strategy, Bush wanted to avoid a long, protracted war that could become a Vietnam-like quagmire. Having suffered relatively few casualties (148 battlefield

Victory in the Persian Gulf War, along with the end of the Cold War, led to a revaluation of American foreign policy goals. After defeating Iraq Bush took to the airwaves to announce that the United States would build a "new world order," which he defined as playing an active global peacekeeping role dedicated to spreading democracy and prosperity. Some of Bush's defense advisors encouraged the president to go even further to protect American dominance. In 1992 Cheney and his neoconservative aide Paul Wolfowitz asserted that the United States needed to respond immediately, and preemptively, to any foreign nation that challenged American military superiority or attempted to "overturn the established political and economic order." Bush never publicly embraced these neoconservative principles, but his son George W. Bush, the 43rd president of the United States, proved more receptive to these ideas.

What vision of American world leadership did neoconservatives promote?

Contested Visions of Government

The Reagan years had redefined the American political landscape, shifting the political center away from New Deal and Great Society liberal assumptions that government could be a positive force in citizens' lives. To succeed in this changed political climate, a new breed of Democratic politician was needed—socially liberal but fiscally conservative. The most successful and most controversial "New Democrat" was William "Bill" Jefferson Clinton, who defeated George H. W. Bush in the 1992 presidential election and won reelection in 1996 against Kansas Senator Bob Dole. When Republican George W. Bush won the presidency in the heavily disputed 2000 election, he moved swiftly to restore the conservative vision of low taxes and limited regulation that the political right had long championed.

Clinton's New Democrats

Clinton was relatively unknown when the 1992 presidential campaign began. While governor of Arkansas, at just forty-four years of age, Clinton had chaired the Democratic Leadership Council, a group committed to shifting the Democratic Party to the political center by accepting market-based solutions to social problems and ending deficit spending. Exuding boundless energy and a vast knowledge of government policy, Clinton's magnetic personality and compassionate nature soon won him a dedicated following. "I feel your pain," became Clinton's mantra as he bear-hugged voters on the campaign trail. Clinton, one commentator noted, cultivated the image of "the president as the guy next door," who "struggles like the rest of us with his weight, his marriage, and his golf game."

Worried about the nation's finances, third-party candidate Ross Perot, a self-made Texas billionaire, entered the race and focused his campaign almost exclusively on how the federal deficit had ballooned under Bush's watch. Winning 19 percent of the popular vote, Perot registered the best third-party showing since Theodore Roosevelt's run as the Progressive Party candidate in 1912. Clinton defeated Bush in the Electoral College, 370 to 168, but only 43 percent of the electorate voted for him.

Widely praised for his superior political skills, Clinton nonetheless stumbled badly during his first few weeks in office when he tried and failed to fulfill a campaign pledge to lift the ban against gays in the military. Proponents viewed the issue as a straightforward question of protecting civil rights; opponents countered that ignoring heterosexual soldiers' objections to serving alongside gay soldiers would undermine military discipline and hurt recruitment. Clinton pleased no one with his compromise approach. Rather than lift the ban, Clinton instituted a policy of **"Don't Ask, Don't Tell,"** which allowed closeted homosexuals and lesbians—gays who kept their sexual preferences hidden—to serve in the military.

Clinton's domestic agenda contained a number of other ambitious proposals, including a comprehensive plan to provide all Americans with health care. Clinton delegated this major policy initiative to Hillary Rodham Clinton, his wife, an attorney with extensive experience in public service. Republicans successfully attacked the plan as "socialized medicine" that would deprive Americans of the freedom to choose their healthcare providers. The plan failed to win congressional approval. Clinton achieved a more modest victory with his tax proposals. Overcoming Republican opposition, he passed an economic stimulus package that offered tax incentives for job creation and increased taxes for large corporations and wealthy Americans—reversing Reagan's decision to lower taxes on the richest citizens.

Clinton also addressed economic problems caused by the recent globalization of the American economy. As late as 1970 most U.S. businesses manufactured strictly for the American market, and few stores stocked items made overseas. By the early 1980s the United States exported and imported more goods than ever before. Exports rose from $43 billion in 1970 to $178 billion in 2000, while imports surged from $40 billion to $519 billion in 2000 (all figures adjusted for inflation). Importing more than it exported, the nation questioned whether this trade deficit hurt or helped the overall economy. American companies selling products at home now faced stiff competition from

How did Clinton's centrist vision affect his policy decisions?

foreign manufacturers, while U.S. companies shifted production to places like China and Mexico where workers earned less. Globalization, however, also lowered costs for consumers and gave them a greater selection of products.

Clinton helped accelerate the trend toward globalization when he broke with organized labor to back the 1992 **North American Free Trade Agreement (NAFTA)**, a treaty that lifted trade barriers between the United States, Mexico, and Canada. Labor unions opposed NAFTA because they feared that it would encourage U.S. factories to relocate to Mexico, resulting in fewer jobs for American workers. American businesspeople liked NAFTA because it prohibited Mexican companies from manufacturing knock-offs of American films, drugs, clothing, and accessories—essentially protecting their overseas and domestic markets by stopping the flow of counterfeit goods.

Clinton's emphasis on free trade reflected his desire to move the Democratic Party to the political center, but his Republican opponents cited his failed healthcare initiative as evidence that Clinton subscribed to the same 1960s liberal vision that had spurred the creation of the Great Society (see Chapter 27). In the 1994 midterm elections, Georgia congressman Newt Gingrich successfully mobilized the New Right (see Chapter 28) with his call to end the "corrupt liberal welfare state." The Republicans captured both the House and the Senate for the first time since 1952. Gingrich's manifesto, **"The Contract with America,"** envisioned smaller government, less regulation, term limits for members of Congress, welfare reform, and adding a balanced budget amendment to the Constitution. Little of Gingrich's ambitious agenda was enacted, partly because Clinton stole some of his thunder by undertaking his own program of welfare reform. Modifying legislation passed during the New Deal, Clinton joined with Republicans and conservative Democrats in Congress to reduce the time that families (mostly single mothers) with dependent children could receive financial assistance. Clinton also tried to appeal to fiscal conservatives by balancing the federal budget for the first time in thirty years.

Clinton used his superior political skills not only to weaken the Republican resurgence but also to survive the scandals that plagued his presidency. In 1994 a special federal prosecutor, Kenneth Starr, began investigating charges that the president had participated in a fraudulent land deal during his tenure as Arkansas attorney general. In the course of his investigation, Starr learned that President Clinton had engaged in a sexual relationship with a White House intern named Monica Lewinsky. Clinton was not the first or only president to have extramarital dalliances, but when giving testimony under oath on an unrelated matter he denied the affair. Seven months later the president publicly acknowledged that he had lied as seen in this *New York Daily News* headline reporting his televised address to the nation (**29.6**). Republicans argued that Clinton's failure to tell the truth warranted impeachment. In 1998 the Republican-controlled House of Representatives completed the first stage of impeachment by voting that the president had lied under oath and obstructed justice. The Senate now had to decide whether these infractions met the constitutional test of "high crimes and misdemeanors" needed to remove a president from office. Ten Republican senators joined with Democrats in defeating the first charge of perjury by a vote of 55 to 45. The second charge of obstructing justice resulted in a 50 to 50 tie. Neither charge obtained the requisite two-thirds vote required to remove Clinton from the White House.

Clinton survived impeachment by cultivating the same "everyman" appeal that won him the presidency. "The essence of Clinton's success has been to persuade America that this scandal is about human weakness, not crime, and that at its core is not a string of felonies but a sin familiar to all—adultery," lamented conservative commentator Patrick Buchanan. The strong economy also helped keep Clinton's approval ratings near 60 percent throughout the ordeal.

29.6 Clinton's Sex Scandal
When Clinton finally admitted to an "inappropriate relationship" with White House intern Monica Lewinsky, the lies he had previously told to cover it up led to his impeachment.

How does Clinton's sex scandal compare to the Reagan-era Iran-Contra scandal (see Chapter 28)?

The Disputed Election of 2000

The election of 2000 once again offered voters two competing notions of the role that the government should play in American society. Democrat Al Gore, then serving as vice president under Bill Clinton, ran against Republican George W. Bush, the son of former president George H. W. Bush. More liberal than Clinton, Gore was a well-known environmentalist whose pedantic manner often made him appear wooden. Bush was a born-again evangelical Christian who had cultivated a folksy persona while governor of Texas.

Reflecting the generally prosperous times, the two candidates put forward competing visions on how to spend the projected federal surplus. Calling it "the people's money," Bush proposed enormous tax cuts that he argued would fuel investment and economic growth. Rejecting the Democrat emphasis on federal government activism, Bush vowed to create an "ownership society" where people had more control over their wealth, Social Security retirement accounts, health care, and property. Gore adhered to the traditional competing Democratic vision of using government regulation and federally funded programs to promote equity, environmental responsibility, and prosperity. He charged that Bush's tax cuts would disproportionately help the wealthy and starve federal programs for the poor. Gore proposed saving the surplus to prepare for the coming explosion in Social Security payments once the baby boom generation began retiring. Green Party candidate Ralph Nader, a consumer advocate who railed against corporate greed, and the Conservative Patrick Buchanan, who ran on the Reform Party ticket, also entered the race.

In an age of machine-counted votes and instantaneous communication, Americans expected complete results on election night. However, with several states too close to call that evening, it took a few days before Gore emerged with 267 electoral votes, three short of the 270 required to win the presidency, to Bush's 246. All eyes now turned to Florida where a riveting thirty-six-day drama unfurled over recounting ballots that vote-counting machines had rejected because voters had not completely punched the perforated box next to the candidate's name. Gore's team went to state court and won a hand recount in four primarily Democratic counties. Election inspectors, like the one pictured here (**29.7**), spent hours examining "hanging chads," the name given to partially punched boxes, to determine voters' intent. Arguing that time for a recount had run out, Republican Florida officials certified that Bush had won the state.

The battle now moved to the Supreme Court, where conservative justices accepted the Republican argument that the different standards used by inspectors to include or reject ballots violated the "equal protection" clause of the Fourteenth Amendment. As the map (**29.8**) shows, although Gore won the national popular vote, by winning Florida, Bush had the 271 electoral votes that he needed to win the election. Echoing the outraged Democratic response to the Supreme Court's decision to halt the recount, Justice John Paul Stevens wrote, "Although we may never know with complete certainty the identity of the winner of this year's Presidential election, the identity of the loser is perfectly clear. It is the Nation's confidence in the judge as an impartial guardian of the rule of law." Subsequent privately funded recounts undertaken by several major news organizations all concluded that Bush had indeed won Florida.

The election results continued to rankle Democrats. Besides questioning poor ballot design and Supreme Court partisanship, Democrats charged that Florida Republicans had used a variety of shady tactics to disenfranchise some African Americans, such as incorrectly claiming they were felons who could

29.7 Hanging Chads
A Florida election worker uses a magnifying glass to try to determine which candidate this voter had selected, reflecting the closeness of the 2000 presidential election.

Why was the 2000 presidential election so controversial?

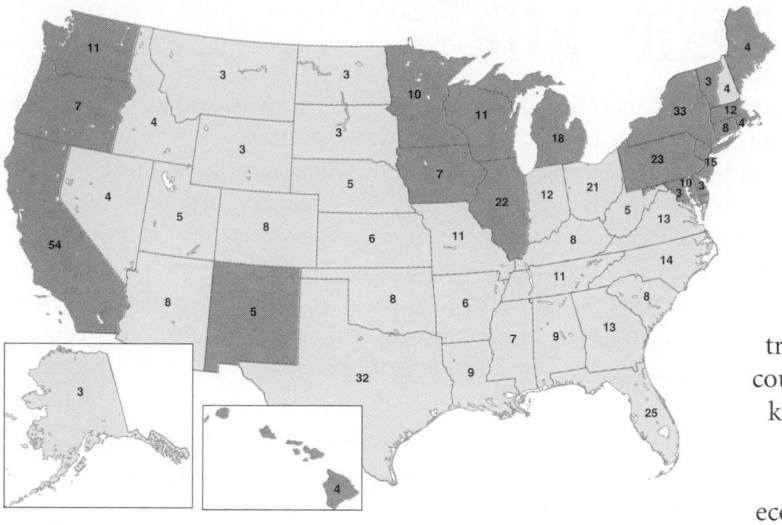

29.8 Presidential Election, 2000
A mere 537 votes in Florida decided the outcome of the 2000 presidential contest.

4 Electoral vote by state	Electoral Vote (%)	Popular Vote
George W. Bush *(Republican)*	271 (50)	50,456,062 (48)
Albert Gore, Jr. *(Democrat)*	266 (50)	50,996,582 (48)
Ralph Nader *(Green Party)*	0 (0)	2,882,955 (3)

not vote. The post-election recriminations also targeted liberals who had rejected the centrist direction of the Democratic Party and voted for Nader. The Green Party candidate received 97,488 votes in Florida—a state that Bush won by a mere 537 votes.

Compassionate Conservatism

Bush entered office proclaiming that his administration would move away from the laissez-faire, antigovernment message championed by past Congressional Republican leaders like Gingrich. He instead embraced a new vision termed "**compassionate conservatism**," a philosophical approach to governing that emphasized using private industry, charities, and religious institutions, rather than the government, to provide community services. Adherents to compassionate conservatism argued that the poor quickly became dependent on government-run social welfare programs, losing the motivation and drive to improve their circumstances themselves. As one Bush administration official put it, compassionate conservatives believed that "the government should encourage the effective provision of social services without providing the service itself." In keeping with this philosophy, the president championed faith-based initiatives that funded church-run community programs, arguing that local clergy understood their neighborhood problems better than government bureaucrats. Federal money flowed to churches offering after-school tutoring to students, transportation for the elderly, counseling for drug addicts, and soup kitchens for the homeless.

Critics saw little compassion for the poor in some of Bush's other economic initiatives. Ignoring the election's evidence that strong competing visions of governing continued to divide the nation, President Bush relied on the Republican-controlled Congress to win swift congressional approval for the tax cuts and deregulation of financial markets that he had proposed during the campaign. Faced with the beginnings of a recession as overinflated stock prices collapsed, Bush and other conservative Republicans offered a new rationale for slashing taxes by an average of 15 percent. Over 40 percent of the tax cuts went to the wealthy, the very people whose companies and investments would provide the jobs and capital needed to jump-start the economy, the president argued. When the short recession ended, Bush and his congressional supporters credited their tax cutting. Some economists suggested that the overinflated housing market was the real reason for the economic rebound. Home prices increased nearly 45 percent between 1997 and 2005 as speculators bought and sold homes quickly to take advantage of rising prices. Low-interest loans encouraged homeowners to use their houses as collateral to borrow money, which they used to purchase consumer goods. For the moment the credit-fueled rise in housing prices infused cash into the economy, but the day of reckoning was ahead.

Despite his antigovernment philosophy Bush sometimes proved willing to strengthen the federal government's power. The bipartisan 2001 "No Child Left Behind" law tried to improve public schools by linking federal funding to student performance on annual standardized exams. Bush also dramatically increased the investigative powers of the Justice Department in the wake of the terrorist attack against the United States on September 11, 2001.

How did George W. Bush reshape the conservative vision of governing?

Transforming Daily Life

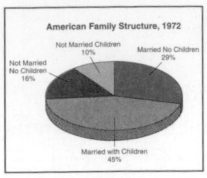

In the 1990s computers altered daily life in countless ways, quickly becoming essential to work and leisure. The Monica Lewinsky scandal broke on the Internet, revealing how the emergence of the World Wide Web transformed the way Americans communicated with one another in the 1990s. Key demographic shifts also reshaped American society. Fewer heterosexual American couples married, while the desire of gay couples to wed provoked heated debate over the meaning of marriage. A sizable population of senior citizens emerged, and new immigrant communities formed across the nation. Meanwhile environmentalists worried about human-induced climate changes and entreated Americans to stop using fossil fuels to run their cars and factories.

The Computer Age

At key moments in American history, transportation or communication breakthroughs transformed the contours of daily life. Past accomplishments such as building the intercontinental railroad and federal highway system quickened the movement of goods and people throughout the nation. Telegraphs, telephones, and televisions broke down the barrier of distance among people living in different regions. Thanks to these inventions Americans could speak directly to loved ones living elsewhere, learn instantaneously about events far from home, and laugh at the same jokes told on weekly television shows. In the 1990s computer technology, especially personal computers and the Internet, once again changed how Americans communicated, shopped, and received information.

First introduced in the 1980s (see Chapter 28), by the late 1990s millions of Americans spent hours a day at work or home typing on personal computers. The lucrative computer industry, fueled by the constant invention of ever-improving components and programs, supplanted the car and steel industry as the engine that drove prosperity. As manufacturing plants continued to close in the Midwest, areas where high-tech enterprises clustered, like Silicon Valley in northern California, boomed. Computer giants Microsoft (which produced the computer operating system Windows) and Apple became powerful corporations that employed highly educated workers and developed global markets for their products.

Going the way of the horse and buggy when cars were invented, typewriters became obsolete when people ranging from office workers to students began using computers to write letters and essays. At first computer-users printed copies of these documents and delivered them in traditional ways—such as mailing letters or handing a teacher a completed assignment. By the end of the decade, however, more and more Americans relied on the Internet to deliver business and social correspondence electronically.

The Internet evolved from a primitive computer system designed in the sixties to facilitate the exchange of computer information among geographically disparate military installations. The creation in the late 1980s of a computer network linking universities and five national supercomputer centers paved the way to providing instantaneous computer communication among civilians. At the same time engineers in Switzerland developed the **World Wide Web**, a system for organizing electronic information transmitted through the Internet. With these tools in place, Internet use exploded. In 1994 six million Americans were connected to the Internet. By 2001 the 130 million Americans who surfed the web daily in offices, libraries, schools, or at home accounted for a quarter of all global Internet traffic.

> "When I took office [in 1993], only high energy physicists had ever heard of what is called the Worldwide Web... Now even my cat has its own page.
>
> President BILL CLINTON, 1996

Computers and the Internet quickly reshaped how Americans worked and played at the dawn of the twenty-first century. Virtual business meetings now took place among geographically dispersed colleagues who looked into small cameras attached

Which technological innovations of the twentieth century had the greatest impact on daily life?

to their computers to converse with the people they saw on their screens. Office workers working in the same building sent a steady stream of e-mails to each other throughout the day, rather than telephoning or delivering a message in person. Many companies jettisoned paper records in favor of computer databases that stored personal and commercial data.

Americans differed on the benefits that children derived from this new technology. A generation of youth hooked on computer games alarmed commentators who worried that their sedentary lifestyle was fueling an epidemic of childhood obesity. Others fretted that children who played violent computer games became desensitized to real-world violence. Schools, however, quickly brought the Internet into the classroom. By simply typing a phrase into an Internet search engine, researchers of all ages gained instant access to information from libraries throughout the world. The Internet facilitated the spread of misinformation as well. Anyone could create a Web site, allowing virtual communities to form around almost any issue. A great resource for researching a medical condition, the Internet also helped terrorists publicize their causes and killings around the world.

The Internet reshaped commerce as well, becoming a virtual shopping mall and entertainment center as entrepreneurs rushed to market their wares. Shopping on the Internet, however, differed from taking a stroll down Main Street. The Internet-based company Amazon.com not only sold books more cheaply but built virtual communities in which readers posted their own reviews of books and sold used copies. The privacy and accessibility that the Internet afforded gave the pornography and gambling industries a boost, drawing millions of customers on a daily basis. To pay the credit card bills that they accumulated while shopping online, many Americans stopped sending checks through the mail and began using the Internet to pay their bills electronically. Droves of Americans stopped watching their favorite shows on TV, preferring instead to watch them on the Internet when it was convenient.

The Changing Face of Families

In 1992 George H. W. Bush's vice president Dan Quayle attacked a popular television series *Murphy Brown* for positively portraying the unmarried title character's decision to have a child. Quayle voiced the New Right's lament that marriage had lost ground to other nontraditional family arrangements. The charts "American Family Structure, 1972" and "American Family Structure, 1998" (**29.9**) show that the composition of the American family had indeed changed radically in less than a generation. By 1998, 47 percent of American families lived in non-married households, both with and without children, compared to 26 percent in 1972. Longstanding gender roles within families also changed. In the traditional model of marriage, the husband worked and the wife stayed at home. By the end of the 1990s, most married couples worked outside the home.

Changing family structure prompted sometimes acrimonious debate between the New Right who wanted to reverse these trends and liberal Democrats who championed the right of non-married partners to cohabitate and single women to have children. Many people who considered themselves liberal on a myriad of economic and social issues, however, joined with the New Right in condemning same-sex or gay marriage. The gay rights movement had made overt discrimination against homosexuals and lesbians less socially acceptable (see Chapter 28).

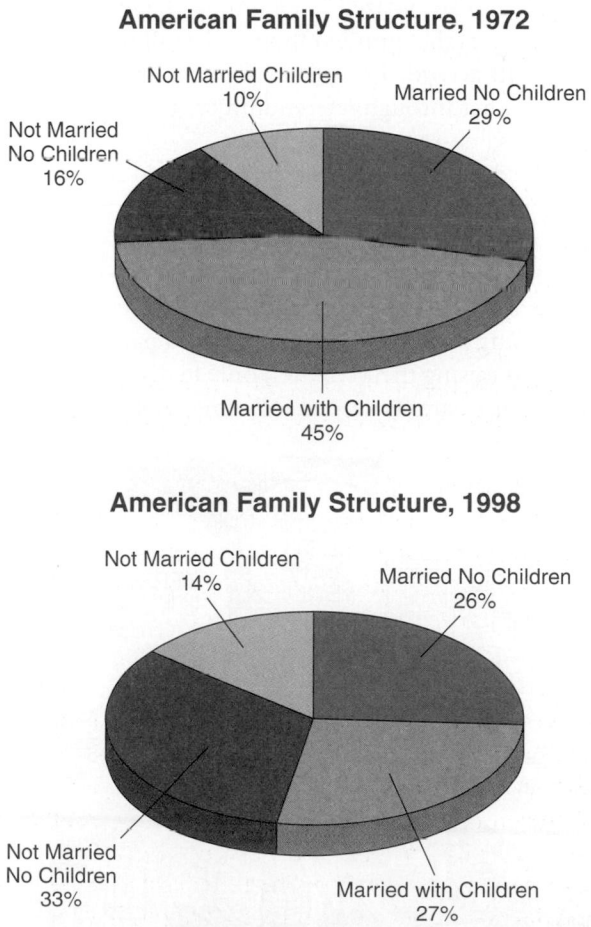

29.9 Changes in American Family Structure, 1972–1998
These graphs reveal that the percentage of married households with children dropped significantly by the end of the twentieth century.

What changes in family structure do these graphs illustrate?

"Regardless of how you feel about marriage, it's wrong to treat people differently under the law."

An ad equating bans against gay marriage with past laws prohibiting interracial marriages

"I can marry a princess."

In a competing ad a young girl suggests that schools will promote legalized gay marriage

While many Americans were willing to tolerate same-sex couples living together, people on both ends of the political spectrum drew the line at same-sex marriages. In 1996 Congress overwhelmingly passed the Defense of Marriage Act, a law that defined marriage as a legal union between a man and a woman. Under this statute states that banned same-sex marriages did not have to accept legal marriages performed in other states if a gay couple moved to their jurisdiction. Gay-rights advocates argued, with limited success, that every American had the right to marry a partner of their choosing. In 2009 only Massachusetts, Connecticut, Vermont, Maine, and Iowa allowed same-sex marriages. Seven other states authorized "civil unions" between same-sex partners that granted them either all or some of the rights accorded married couples. The remaining states, either through referendum or stature, prohibited same-sex marriage.

The debate over gay marriage received a tremendous amount of press exposure, but few reporters paid much attention to how the graying of America was altering family life. Life expectancy had increased thanks to improved medical care and decreasing poverty. Many middle-aged parents finished raising their children only to discover that their aging parents needed full-time caretaking.

29.10 Competing Views on Immigration Americans continue to debate whether immigrants are a burden or an asset.

What competing visions emerged over same-sex marriage?

As the population aged, Social Security and Medicare payments went up, but a declining birthrate meant that there were fewer native-born workers available to pay the taxes that kept this social welfare system afloat. Over the last twenty-five years, the birth rate had declined from 18.4 births for every 1,000 people in 1970 to 14.8 in 1996. Faced with a labor shortage of able-bodied workers, the nation turned, as it had in the past, to immigrants to fill available jobs.

A Wave of Immigration

The massive wave of immigration that began after Congress eliminated national quotas in 1965 initiated another important social transformation. Between 1931 and 1965 around 5 million immigrants came to the United States. These numbers skyrocketed to 4.5 million in the 1970s; 7.3 million in the 1980s; and 9.1 million in the 1990s. Hundreds of thousands more entered the country illegally. Most of these immigrants came from Asia, Africa, and Latin America—only two million Europeans settled in the United States between 1980 and 2000. Some Americans satirically referred to the exploding Hispanic immigrant population in the Southwest as the *reconquista*, or re-conquering of territory that Mexico had lost to the United States in the nineteenth century after the Mexican-American War of 1848 (see Chapter 11). Overall the United States attracted twice as many immigrants as all of the other nations in the world combined.

Competing claims about the economic benefits of immigration emerged, a debate explored more fully in *Competing Visions: The Economic Costs of Immigration*. The different meanings attached to the word "benefits" in this political cartoon by Brian Fairrington (**29.10**) encapsulated the debate over whether immigrants drained the economy by seeking a wide array of taxpayer-funded social services or contributed to overall prosperity by working for very little. The New Right also feared dire cultural

Competing Visions

THE ECONOMIC COSTS OF IMMIGRATION

To this day Americans continue to disagree about the economic costs associated with immigration. In the following passage Harvard economist George J. Borjas paints a pessimistic economic portrait. Tamar Jacoby disputes Borjas's claim that three decades of high immigration have hurt the U.S. economy. What different factors does each emphasize to make his case?

George J. Borjas suggested that immigration affected socioeconomic groups differently in his 1996 article "The New Economics of Immigration: Affluent Americans Gain: Poor Americans Lose."

New research has established a number of points. The relative skills of successive immigrant waves have declined over much of the postwar period. In 1970, for example, the latest immigrant arrivals on average had 0.4 fewer years of schooling and earned 17 percent less than natives. By 1990 the most recently arrived immigrants had 1.3 fewer years of schooling and earned 32 percent less than natives ...

The large-scale migration of less-skilled workers has done harm to the economic opportunities of less-skilled natives. Immigration may account for perhaps a third of the recent decline in the relative wages of less-educated native workers ...

The increasing welfare dependency in the immigrant population suggests that immigration may create a substantial fiscal burden on the most-affected localities and states ...

There exists a strong correlation between the skills of immigrants and the skills of their American-born children, so that the huge skill differentials observed among today's foreign-born groups will almost certainly become tomorrow's differences among American-born ethnic groups. In effect, immigration has set the stage for sizable ethnic differences in skills and socioeconomic outcomes, which are sure to be the focus of intense attention in the next century ...

Current immigration redistributes wealth from unskilled workers, whose wages are lowered by immigrants, to skilled workers and owners of companies that buy immigrants' services, and from taxpayers who bear the burden of paying for the social services used by immigrants to consumers who use the goods and services produced by immigrants. ... Immigration changes how the economic pie is sliced up. ... The harmful effects of immigration will not go away simply because some people do not wish to see them.

In his 2002 article "Too Many Immigrants," Tamar Jacoby argued that large-scale immigration benefited the United States economically.

The most commonly heard complaint about foreign workers is that they take jobs from Americans. Not only is this assertion untrue—nobody has found real evidence to support it—but cities and states with the largest immigrant populations (New York, Los Angeles, and others) boast far faster economic growth and lower unemployment than cities and states that do not attract immigrants. In many places, the presence of immigrants seems to reduce unemployment even among native-born blacks—probably because of the way immigrants stimulate economic growth. ... Even if Borjas is right that a native-born black worker may take home $300 less a year as a result of immigration, this is a fairly small amount of money in the overall scheme of things. More to the point, globalization would have much the same effect on wages, immigrants or no immigrants ...

What about the costs imposed by immigrants, especially by their use of government services? It is true that many immigrants—though far from all—are poorer than native-born Americans, and thus pay less in taxes. It is also true that one small segment of the immigrant population—refugees—tends to be heavily dependent on welfare. As a result, states with large immigrant populations often face chronic fiscal problems. ... [But] If we shift the lens to the federal level, and include the taxes that immigrants remit to the IRS, the calculation comes out very differently: immigrants pay in more than they take out. ... 28 million immigrants form but a small part of the $12-trillion U.S. economy, and most of the fiscal costs and benefits associated with them are relatively modest. Besides, fiscal calculations are only a small part of the larger economic picture. How do we measure the energy immigrants bring—the pluck and grit and willingness to improvise and innovate?

Not only are immigrants by and large harder-working than the native-born, they generally fill economic niches that would otherwise go wanting.

Are contemporary concerns about immigration similar or different from objections made earlier in the twentieth century?

consequences as the nation fragmented into permanent ethnic enclaves. "If America is to survive as 'one nation, one people' we need to call a 'time-out' on immigration, to assimilate the tens of millions who have lately arrived," exhorted conservative columnist Patrick Buchanan, who unsuccessfully ran for president in 2000. To protect the nation's cultural cohesion, these right-leaning critics organized campaigns to make English the nation's official language.

Both Democrats and Republicans worried that immigrants, who were willing to work for less, took jobs away from native-born workers. Critics especially denounced illegal immigration, arguing that people who sneaked across the border often violated other laws as well. Illegal immigrants sent their children to school and received health care in hospitals, all at taxpayer expense, they charged. Unions and their supporters complained that undocumented workers could not join labor unions, making it more difficult to organize labor to improve working conditions and wages.

Champions of immigration, mostly from the political left, pointed to the nation's past success in assimilating large numbers of immigrants and argued that immigrants took the low-paying jobs such as busboys, gardeners, and nannies that few Americans wanted. Countering claims that new immigrants failed to assimilate, advocates of immigration noted the high rate of interethnic marriages among second-generation immigrants. They also viewed complaints about multiculturalism as a racist attempt to protect the United States as a primarily white society.

Climate Change

The computer revolution and shifting demographics were not the only factors changing American daily life. Scientists worried that accelerated climate change threatened to reshape the physical space that Americans inhabited and urged the nation to take steps to reverse human-induced environmental damage. They entreated Americans to alter their consumption habits by switching from gas-guzzling cars like sport-utility vehicles (SUVs) to automobiles that burned little or no fossil fuels. Americans, 4.5 percent of the global population, drove 24 percent of the 590 million cars in the world. Ingrained driving habits, however, were hard to change.

Environmental scientists claimed that average temperatures had risen 1.8 degrees Fahrenheit over the last one hundred years, a phenomenon called **global warming**. They attributed this climate shift to the widespread burning of fossil fuels (coal and oil) that pumped carbon dioxide into the air. Carbon dioxide was one of several greenhouse gases that trapped the sun's heat in the Earth's atmosphere. While the sun's rays were essential to human life, environmentalists blamed the rapidly rising levels of greenhouse gases for global warming.

This 2007 world map (**29.11**) shows which nations emitted the greatest amount of carbon dioxide from burning fossil fuels. The United States, China, Russia, India, and Japan head the list. Developing nations in Africa with few cars or heavy industry emitted relatively little carbon dioxide. Besides emitting more total greenhouse gases than most other nations, the United States ranked tenth in the amount of greenhouse emissions per person.

Why did global warming matter? The quicker-than-normal melting of the Arctic ice cap, environmentalists warned, was causing sea levels to rise. If unchecked, rising waters would soon wash over sea-level lands throughout the world including the Mississippi Delta in the United States. Scientists also speculated that global warming affected rainfall patterns and storms, leading to an increase in devastating droughts, wildfires, and hurricanes. Not everyone in the United States accepted these dire predictions. Some Americans questioned the scientific evidence linking climate change to human activity. Fluctuations in the earth's average temperature had occurred before, they argued, disputing the claim that any permanent or catastrophic change in the atmosphere was underway.

In 1997 the United States signed the Kyoto Protocol, an international agreement that set targets for reducing greenhouse emissions in industrial nations. In 2001, however, President George W. Bush argued that the agreement was flawed because it exempted China and relied on governmental controls, not market incentives, to develop "green" technology. The United States subsequently became the only nation besides Australia to sign, but not ratify, the treaty.

For Americans to reduce the amount of fossil fuels burned in cars and factories, a significant shift in lifestyle needed to occur. Enjoying low gas prices few Americans felt compelled to invest time or money into developing "green" technology. National security concerns proved more effective in motivating the nation to re-examine its energy

What core arguments support and refute the theory of global warming?

29.11 Global Carbon Dioxide Emissions
This 2007 map depicts the proportion of carbon dioxide gases emitted from burning fossil fuels (mostly in factories and cars) by each nation. The United States and China were the worst polluters, along with Japan, Russia, and India.

policy. The United States imported 65% of its oil, with Canada providing the largest share. After 9/11 a consensus emerged that the ongoing American presence in the Middle East (which provided 11% of the oil Americans consumed) bred resentment among Arab populations that helped Islamist fundamentalist terrorist groups. Republicans and Democrats, however, disagreed over how to wean the nation off its dependence on foreign oil. The Bush administration championed bolstering oil production at home by lifting restrictions on drilling in the Arctic National Wildlife Refuge, a nationally protected wilderness area in Alaska. This proposal enraged a wide swath of environmentalists and Democrats who worried that drilling accidents could potentially contaminate this pristine wilderness. They also feared losing valuable time in the battle against global warming by continuing, rather than ending, fossil fuel consumption.

"We are entering a period of consequences."

AL GORE, who won the 2007 Nobel Peace Prize for publicizing the global warming crisis

"Global warming—at least the modern nightmare version—is a myth."

British botanist DAVID BELLAMY

What accounts for the disparity in carbon dioxide emissions on this map?

New Threats in the Post–Cold War World

Access to oil in the Middle East remained critical to the American economy throughout the 1990s and 2000s. Containing Iraqi leader Saddam Hussein presented an ongoing challenge for President Bill Clinton and President George W. Bush. Ethnic cleansing in Eastern Europe and Africa raised additional questions of much responsibility American should assume to prevent massacres worldwide. When Islamic fundamentalist terrorists attacked U.S. targets overseas and at home, competing visions also arose over how to best defend the nation from this new threat.

Ethnic Cleansing and Terrorism

In the 1990s the nation faced a new foreign policy dilemma: when to intercede on humanitarian grounds to stop massacres in parts of the world strategically unimportant to the United States. In 1992 images of a civil-war induced famine in Somalia, a country in East Africa, flooded American airwaves and newspapers. This image of a Somali woman and her starving child (**29.12**) echoed the Madonna and child compositions used by Jacob Riis during the Gilded Age (see Chapter 17) and Dorothea Lange during the Depression (see Chapter 22) to rally popular support for aiding the poor. President George H. W. Bush responded to the public outcry by sending U.S. troops to help UN peacekeepers restore order, aid that incoming president Bill Clinton continued. Public opinion shifted dramatically in 1993 when news cameras captured the image of cheering Somalis dragging the corpse of an American soldier through the streets of Mogadishu, the capital city of Somalia, after rebel Somali warlords downed a U.S. Black Hawk helicopter (**29.13**). The public now demanded

29.12 and 29.13 Competing Views of Civil Turmoil in Somalia, 1992 and 1993
Photographs like this one of a starving Somali woman and child prompted Americans to demand that the United States send troops to end the civil war responsible for the famine. A year later, angered by a photograph of Somali rebels dragging the corpse of an American soldier through the streets, Americans called for the return of U.S. troops. Both images encouraged Americans to view African nations as dysfunctional places where famine and fighting were endemic.

How did media coverage influence American views of Africa?

an immediate withdrawal, and Clinton complied. The UN withdrew its troops as well, and years of anarchy in Somalia followed. Reluctant to put American soldiers' lives in jeopardy again, Clinton proceeded cautiously in April 1994 when Hutus, the majority ethnic group in Rwanda, another East African nation, unleashed a one-hundred-day genocidal rampage that killed 800,000 Tutsis, a minority ethic group. This time Clinton came under attack for failing to intervene decisively with force.

The photo of Somalis desecrating the corpse of an American soldier had other repercussions as well. Osama bin Laden, the Saudi exile who headed **al-Qaeda**, a fundamentalist Islamic terrorist organization, concluded that terrorist attacks against the United States would work because Americans had no stomach for casualties. "One American pilot was dragged in the streets of Mogadishu [and] you left. . . . the extent of your impotence and weaknesses became very clear," he jeered in 1996. Such pronouncements caused Paul Watson, the photojournalist who took the Pulitzer-prize winning image, to conclude that the "storm of outrage" over his photo taught terrorists that they could rely on publicity in the Western media to amplify the impact of their terrorist attacks.

During his first few years in office, Clinton also had to formulate a response to "**ethnic cleansing**," the intentional mass killing of one ethnic group by another, in the Balkans, a mountainous region of southeastern Europe. When Communist Yugoslavia dissolved in 1991, ethnic and religious differences provoked a civil war among Croatia, Bosnia, and Serbia, all former parts of Yugoslavia. Clinton resisted intervening until July 1995 when Serbian forces forced 25,000 Bosnian Muslim women and children to leave the town of Srebrenica, and murdered the 7,500 Muslim men and boys who remained behind. The United States participated in North American Treaty Organization (NATO) air strikes of Serbian military positions and helped broker the 1995 Dayton Peace Accords, which settled disputed territorial boundaries and placed NATO troops (including Americans) on the ground as peacekeepers.

Preoccupied with humanitarian tragedies overseas, Americans paid less attention in the early 1990s to signs that the terrorist threat was moving closer to home. Many residents in Arab nations saw the United States and Israel as one, blaming both for taking away land that rightfully belonged to the Palestinians. A spate of overseas hostage-takings and plane hijackings in the 1970s and 1980s kept the Arab-Israeli conflict in the news. In 1993 Kuwaiti and Iraqi-born terrorists exploded a massive car bomb in the parking garage of the World Trade Center, two towering skyscrapers located in the heart of New York City's financial district that housed governmental agencies and companies involved in foreign trade. The explosion killed six people and created a six-story hole in the ground. The FBI captured the culprits easily when one tried to recover his deposit from a car rental agency for the van used in the attack. Reassured that law enforcement agencies had done their job and that the terrorists were inept, the public and government quickly forgot the incident.

But al-Qaeda, which maintained training bases in Afghanistan, resolved to try again. Determined to launch a *jihad*, or holy war against Western nonbelievers, bin Laden relied on his family's fortune and large donations from individuals in Saudi Arabia to construct a clandestine terrorist network that recruited disciples from the Middle East, Asia, and Africa.

Not all terrorist threats during this period originated overseas. On April 19, 1995, Timothy McVeigh parked a rental truck filled with explosives in front of a federal building in Oklahoma City. The blast killed 168 people, including many children in the building's day care center, and wounded 800. McVeigh and his accomplice Terry Nichols viewed the attack as payback for the federal government's recent assaults against private paramilitary groups and their rural compounds filled with large caches of weapons. Militia supporters like McVeigh rejected any legal restriction on their Second Amendment right to bear arms, citing gun laws as just one example of government tyranny. The attack stunned the country and remained the deadliest terrorist attack against American civilians until 9/11.

Meanwhile al-Qaeda made plans to attack U.S. targets overseas. Issuing a *fatwa*, or death sentence, against all Americans, bin Laden demanded that the United States remove its troops from Saudi Arabia (stationed there since the 1991 Persian Gulf War) and end its support of Israel. "It is more important for Muslims to kill Americans than other infidels," bin Laden declared. This pronouncement was more than rhetoric. In August 1998 al-Qaeda terrorists bombed the U.S. embassies in Nairobi, the capital of Kenya, and Dar es Salaam, a city in Tanzania. Clinton ordered an immediate retaliatory attack, and tomahawk cruise missiles rained down on eight al-Qaeda training camps in Afghanistan and on a pharmaceutical plant in Sudan accused of supplying bin Laden with chemical weapons.

What motivated foreign and domestic terrorists to attack Americans?

29.14 The World Trade Center Collapses
This photograph conveyed the panic that spread through lower Manhattan as rubble and smoke from the collapsing World Trade Center towers rained down on the streets.

The president's advisors presented Clinton with a set of competing views over the next step to take. Clinton's antiterrorist advisor recommended continuing the bombing until the Taliban, Afghanistan's fundamentalist Islamic government, turned bin Laden over to the United States. Pentagon officials opposed sustained bombing, worried that mounting civilian casualties would inflame anti-American sentiments throughout the Middle East. Assassinating bin Laden, others argued, would turn him into a martyr whose death fundamentalists would certainly avenge. Faced with these conflicting views, Clinton chose instead to rely on the CIA to thwart terrorist attacks against U.S. targets overseas. These covert agents uncovered several planned attacks but failed to prevent al-Qaeda from sending a small explosive-laden boat into the side of an American navel vessel, the *USS Cole*, which was anchored near the Middle Eastern country of Yemen. The October 12, 2000, assault killed seventeen sailors and injured forty more. Clinton left office still waiting for verification that al-Qaeda was behind this attack. Incoming President George W. Bush received that confirmation, but had not yet settled on a clear policy response when al-Qaeda struck again on September 11, 2001.

9/11

On the morning of September 11, 2001, in an attack that became known as **9/11**, nineteen terrorists operating from al-Qaeda cells located inside the United States hijacked four planes. The terrorists, from Saudi Arabia, Egypt, Lebanon, and the United Arab Emirates, flew two planes into the World Trade Center towers, and a third into the Pentagon. The fourth plane crashed in Shanksville, Pennsylvania, after the passengers seized control of the cockpit, thwarting the terrorist plan to fly the plane into the Capitol. On this "day of terror," Americans watched in horror as the World Trade Center towers crumbled, causing rescue workers, victims, and onlookers to run for safety as the massive structures collapsed in a heap (**29.14**). A total of 2,973 people died in the attacks.

President Bush immediately announced that "we will make no distinction between the terrorists who committed these acts and those who harbor them." He issued an ultimatum to Afghanistan's Taliban government: turn over al-Qaeda members living there, including bin Laden, or face invasion. The Taliban refused. Receiving overwhelming support from Congress, the American people, and most foreign nations, the United States attacked Afghanistan on October 7, 2001. U.S. forces first bombed al-Qaeda training camps and arms depots, and then joined with the Northern Alliance, an Afghan rebel group, to drive the Taliban from power. The two-month conflict failed, however, to capture bin Laden, who had likely escaped into the mountains of neighboring Pakistan with help from Pakistani sympathizers.

How did the nation and government respond to the 9/11 attacks?

29.15 Security versus Privacy, 2002
This cartoon suggests that invading the privacy of Americans under the guise of increasing security reduced, rather than improved, their standard of living.

Most Americans had supported the invasion, but a growing number grew uneasy about how the Bush administration was conducting the war. These critics accused Bush of condoning torture by allowing CIA agents to use water-boarding, an interrogation tactic that simulated drowning, in an effort to extract information from captured al-Qaeda suspects held prisoner at the U.S. naval base in Guantánamo Bay in Cuba. The decision to incarcerate captured prisoners indefinitely at Guantánamo Bay, denying them the right to a fair trial, also aroused controversy.

Responding to criticism that the nation's security agencies had failed to prevent the 9/11 attack, the president created the Department of Homeland Security, a new umbrella organization that housed the nation's intelligence-gathering and law enforcement agencies. He also secured congressional approval for the 2001 **Patriot Act**, a law that greatly expanded the government's investigative and police powers. Critics soon attacked the law as an unconstitutional assault on civil liberties. This 2002 Pulitzer Prize–winning political cartoon (**29.15**) by Clay Bennett exposed a familiar wartime dilemma—how to protect the nation against enemy agents operating on American soil while simultaneously safeguarding the privacy rights of Americans. In the cartoon determined federal workers remove planks from a couple's home to build a security fence, exposing their personal lives to public scrutiny. In the weeks after the 9/11 attacks, the FBI arrested hundreds of Arabs and Muslims in an effort to destroy any remaining al-Qaeda cells in the United States. Acting hastily, and often on flimsy evidence, resulting in innocent people getting caught up in the FBI dragnet and some spent substantial periods in jail before being released. Scores of Arab Americans, like Japanese Americans in World War II, hung American flags outside their businesses to counter lingering suspicions that all Muslims were terrorists. In 2007 a federal court overturned parts of the Patriot Act that made it easier for the government to secure search warrants and Internet and phone records.

Were governmental efforts to prevent internal enemy attacks after 9/11 similar to the steps during World War I and II?

The Iraq War

America's "war on terror" soon spread to Iraq. Containing Hussein's ambition to acquire weapons of mass destruction (nuclear, chemical, and biological weapons) had been an ongoing issue since the end of the 1991 Persian Gulf War. In 1998 the UN halted its weapons inspection program after Hussein refused to continue cooperating. President Clinton subsequently authorized Operation Desert Fox, a four-day bombing campaign in December 1998 against one hundred Iraqi military targets to punish Hussein and destroy any weapons he was hiding. Neoconservatives publicly urged Clinton to make removing Hussein a key goal of American foreign policy. They had the chance to advance their views more forcefully once Bush appointed key neoconservatives to defense-related positions, including Secretary of Defense Donald Rumsfeld and Deputy Secretary of Defense Paul Wolfowitz.

This core of key neoconservative defense policy advisors included Vice President Dick Cheney. Reversing his previous stand when he had urged the first President Bush to stop the Persian Gulf War without attacking Bagdad, Cheney, along with others, urged the president to attack Iraq while public concern about national security remained high. "Do we wait and hope he doesn't do what we know he is capable of, which is distributing weapons of mass destruction to anonymous terrorists, or do we take preemptive action?" asked neoconservative Richard Perle, chairman of the Defense Policy Board. These advisors championed the doctrine of **preemptive war**, the notion that the United States should remove hostile regimes with force before they could pose a serious threat.

> "Our security will require all Americans to be forward-looking and resolute, to be ready for preemptive action when necessary to defend our liberty and to defend our lives."
>
> President GEORGE W. BUSH, announcing a shift in foreign policy from containment to preemption, 2002

State Department officials, especially Secretary of State Colin Powell, disagreed. They offered a competing vision that relied on the same Cold War–era containment policies that had eventually toppled the Soviet Union. Those urging restraint worried that a hostile fundamentalist Islamic government might replace Hussein's secular regime, fueling rather than dampening the terrorist threat against the United States. "Better the devil we know than the one we don't," one high-ranking intelligence official reasoned. *Choices and Consequences: Launching a Preemptive War* examines the options before Bush as he made his decision to attack Iraq.

Having privately resolved to topple Hussein, Bush began laying the groundwork for sending American troops into Iraq. In September 2002 his administration announced a new national security strategy. The **Bush Doctrine** established the unilateral right to attack nations that harbored terrorists, to launch preemptive military strikes to prevent future attack on the United States, and to replace autocratic governments with democratically elected ones. The inclusion of preemptive war was new, but other parts of the Bush Doctrine reiterated key principles announced by Bush's father when he defined a new post–Cold War direction for American foreign policy in 1992. Neoconservative Paul Wolfowitz played a key role in both administrations, devising a foreign policy that aggressively protected America's singular status as the world's strongest military power.

In building his case for war, the president repeatedly claimed that Hussein possessed weapons of mass destruction and had links to terrorist organizations, including al-Qaeda. By the summer of 2002, this rhetoric had convinced 72 percent of the American public of the falsehood that Hussein was responsible for the 9/11 attacks. Working to win support in the international community and at home, Bush sought both a UN resolution demanding that Iraq readmit weapons inspectors and a congressional joint resolution authorizing the use of force to enforce UN mandates and remove the "continuing threat" that Hussein posed. In arguing for war the administration pointed to secret correspondence between Iraq and Niger provided by Italian intelligence agents indicating that between 1999 and 2001 Hussein had tried to buy uranium oxide, material used to build a nuclear bomb, from Niger. Some CIA agents, including the envoy sent to Niger to investigate, privately doubted that Hussein had made any direct overture to buy uranium from Niger. This charge, however, convinced wavering Democrats to support the war. When the International Atomic Energy Agency later anounced that these letters were indeed forgeries, antiwar advocates charged that Bush had deliberately misled the country while building his case for war.

What debates occurred within the Bush administration over going to war against Iraq in 2003?

Choices and Consequences

LAUNCHING A PREEMPTIVE WAR

In 2002 the Bush administration feared that Iraqi dictator Saddam Hussein had acquired, or was on the verge of acquiring, nuclear weapons and was actively developing chemical and biological weapons. President Bush worried that once Hussein acquired a sizeable arsenal, he would use it against his neighbors, including Israel, and help terrorists attack the United States. Facing a critical decision about how to proceed, his advisors gave Bush several options.

Choices

1. Launch a preemptive war to remove Hussein from power.
2. Work through the UN to impose economic sanctions and send weapons inspectors to Iraq.
3. Support Iraqi exiles' plan to organize a coup d'état that might trigger a mass uprising.

Decision

In February 2002 Bush decided to fight. He announced that Hussein harbored weapons of mass destruction and had aided al-Qaeda. He made a half-hearted effort to work with the UN to reconstitute the weapons inspection program halted in 1998, and secured support from a handful of potential allies if the United States declared war. Announcing that Hussein had refused to cooperate with UN weapons inspectors adequately, the United States attacked Iraq on March 20, 2003.

Consequences

Active combat operations lasted three weeks and successfully removed Hussein from power. No weapons of mass destruction were found. Iraq elected a democratic government that struggled to contain ethnic and religious strife. U.S. forces came under daily attack until a surge of troops in 2008 weakened rebel insurgencies.

***Looking for a coherent Iraq policy*, Jack Ohman, *The Oregonian*, 2002**

Continuing Controversies

Was the Iraq War justified?

Supporters of Bush's policies argued that removing Hussein benefited the Iraqi people and the world. Building a stable, democratic and militarily weakened Iraq was necessary to protect American interests in the strategically and economically important Persian Gulf. The 9/11 attacks demonstrated that the United States must act aggressively and preemptively overseas to prevent future strikes on its own soil.

Critics argued that Bush misled the American people by making false claims that Hussein possessed weapons of mass destruction and had ties to al-Qaeda. The war made America less secure by fanning anti-American sentiments in the Middle East that helped al-Qaeda recruit and diverted needed resources from the war in Afghanistan, where al-Qaeda was regrouping. Preemptive war set a dangerous precedent that lowered the threshold for declaring war to simply feeling threatened by another nation.

What justifications and criticisms did the doctrine of preventative war arouse?

The Iraq War followed the same pattern as the 1991 Persian Gulf War—intense bombing followed by a ground troop invasion. The bombing campaign began on March 19, 2003, and within three weeks American troops were in Baghdad. On April 10, 2003, *USA Today* was one of many newspapers and television newscasts (**29.16**) showing an Iraqi crowd enlisting the aid of U.S. Marines to pull down a huge statue of Hussein. "The toppling of Saddam Hussein's statue in Baghdad will be recorded alongside the fall of the Berlin Wall as one of the great moments of liberty," Bush subsequently proclaimed. Although the event was initially seen as emblematic of Iraqi happiness over the fall of Hussein, subsequent reports suggested that American army personnel had staged it in a square across from the hotel housing international journalists to create a positive iconic image of the war similar to the World War II image of U.S. Marines raising the flag on Iwo Jima (see Chapter 23). The controversy over the picture mirrored Americans' ongoing debate over whether the war was based on lies or was, as Bush and his supporters maintained, spreading democracy to the Middle East.

After active combat operations ceased, American troops faced a host of problems that kept them in Iraq. Widespread looting greeted the fall of Saddam Hussein, who eluded capture until December 13, 2003. He was held in prison, then put on trial and executed on December 30, 2006. Restoring law and order and creating a new democratic government proved difficult as Sunnis, Shiites, and Kurds divided along ethnic and religious lines. American soldiers caught up in the emerging civil war provided inviting targets for suicide bombers, while Iran and al-Qaeda penetrated Iraq to expand their influence in the region.

Controversy over the war continued at home, especially when scandalous photographs taken by soldiers at the American-run Abu Ghraib prison circulated in the mainstream media and on the Internet in 2004. While interrogating prisoners U.S. guards had taken photos of the prisoners forced into humiliating sexual positions and being threatened with dogs. Some photos showed smiling American soldiers standing beside beaten and bloody corpses. As with the 1968 My Lai massacre in Vietnam (see Chapter 26), Americans held strong competing visions on what they felt the photos represented. Some saw rogue soldiers acting on their own; others blamed the president for authorizing brutal

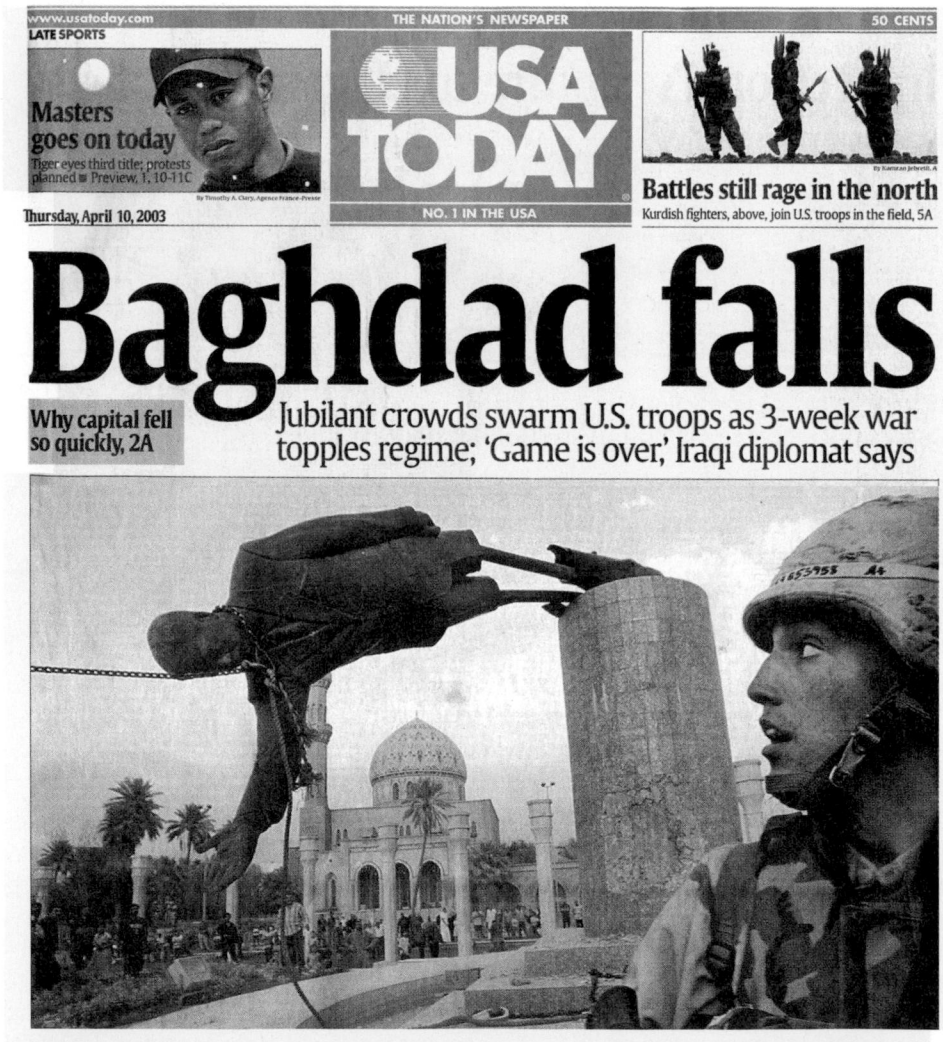
www.usatoday.com
THE NATION'S NEWSPAPER
50 CENTS
LATE SPORTS
Masters goes on today
Tiger eyes third title; protests planned ■ Preview, 1, 10-11C
By Timothy A. Clary, Agence France-Presse
USA TODAY
NO. 1 IN THE USA
Battles still rage in the north
Kurdish fighters, above, join U.S. troops in the field, 5A
Thursday, April 10, 2003
Baghdad falls
Why capital fell so quickly, 2A
Jubilant crowds swarm U.S. troops as 3-week war topples regime; 'Game is over,' Iraqi diplomat says

29.16 "Baghdad Falls," April 10, 2003
Initial news reports spoke of jubilant crowds cheering as U.S. Marines helped them pull down a statue of Saddam Hussein, but later reports suggested that the army had staged the incident.

What accomplishments and setbacks did the United States experience in the Iraq War?

interrogating techniques on suspected terrorists. Another group sidestepped the moral question and instead debated whether torture produced valuable information or simply encouraged suspects to say what interrogators wanted to hear.

When an influx of U.S. troops in 2008 reduced insurgent attacks, the public's views of the war improved. Debate nonetheless continued over how long American troops would stay in Iraq and whether the war had made the nation safer. How the new president who entered the White House in 2009 would handle these questions remained to be seen.

The Election of 2008

In 2004 Bush successfully won reelection against Democratic challenger Massachusetts senator John Kerry, a Vietnam War veteran whose record both as a decorated officer and peace activist came under Republican attack during the campaign. Despite the growing unpopularity of the war in Iraq, the fresh memories of 9/11 bolstered Bush's argument that only he could adequately protect the nation against terrorism. In a close election Bush won the popular vote by 3 percent and captured the Electoral College 286 to 252.

By 2008, however, the president's approval rates had sunk to historic lows. These lows reflected the nation's unease with its seemingly permanent presence in Iraq and recoil at the White House's initial failure to react when Hurricane Katrina devastated predominantly black New Orleans neighborhoods in 2005. In the 2008 presidential contest, Democrat and Republican candidates all repudiated the Bush administration and ran campaigns that promised change.

The election soon assumed historic dimensions when Hillary Rodham Clinton, the former First Lady and now a senator from New York, announced her candidacy. Clinton had a long record of public service dedicated to healthcare issues, but her initial support for the war in Iraq angered staunch antiwar Democrats. First-term Illinois senator Barack Obama, the forty-seven-year-old son of a white woman from Kansas and an African father, astutely campaigned on his own consistent opposition to the war. When the crowded Democratic field narrowed to Clinton and Obama, the 2008 election was guaranteed to make history. For the first time either a woman or an African American would head the national Democratic Party ticket. At the end of a bruising primary battle, Obama prevailed and became the Democratic nominee. Fervent Clinton supporters, holding fast to their dream of electing the first female president, for the moment appeared reluctant to switch allegiances to Obama.

In the general election Obama faced Republican John McCain, a former military pilot whom the Communist Vietnamese had held captive for six years during the Vietnam War. The seventy-two-year-old senator from Arizona had developed a reputation as a maverick for occasionally breaking ranks with fellow Republicans. Hoping to make some history of his own, and perhaps woo some Clinton supporters, McCain selected Alaska governor Sarah Palin as his running mate—only the second time that a woman had received this honor.

Obama pledged to end the war in Iraq quickly and roll back the Bush-era tax cuts for the wealthy, while McCain supported both. Debate over the Iraq War faded when a cascade of bank and insurance company failures sent the stock market into a tailspin. In the midst of the crisis, economists offered the following explanation for the downturn that future investigations may or may not confirm. During the last five years, as housing prices rose dramatically and Congress deregulated the banking and financial industries, banks had made numerous risky loans that let some people purchase homes they could not afford, and Wall Street brokers had invested heavily in mortgage-backed securities. When housing prices started declining in the summer of 2007, the dominos began to fall. Bank foreclosures on people who could not pay their mortgages increased, and even more ominously, the declining value of mortgage-backed securities threatened to bankrupt leading Wall Street firms, wiping out many Americans' retirement investments. Trying to stabilize the mortgage market, the government took over two leading lenders, Freddie Mac and Fannie Mae. Treasury Secretary Henry Paulson refused to intervene when Lehman Brothers, a major investment firm, went bankrupt in September 2008. This bankruptcy sent shock waves through the financial sector. Credit markets froze as banks stopped lending and investors began moving money from stocks and bonds to government-backed Treasury notes.

By mid-September the Bush administration decided that an infusion of $700 billion was needed to unfreeze the credit markets and stop the stock market's freefall. Enraged House Republicans revolted. In their view the government "bail-out" used taxpayer money to reward bad behavior. Many Democrats accepted the competing view that the government would recoup this money when the

What factors led to the economic downturn in 2008?

29.17 "Out of Many, We are One" Almost overnight Barack Obama became an American icon, and his soaring rhetoric inspired this flag-shaped montage of his supporters.

economy and value of these investments improved. Congress eventually authorized the funds, which Paulson used to infuse capital directly into banks rather than buying low-valued assets. What happened to this money emerged as a major political question in the months to come.

Obama was a captivating orator who drew thousands to his rallies. His supporters came to hear him speak of "that American spirit, that American promise, that pushes us forward even when the path is uncertain; that binds us together in spite of our differences; that makes us fix our eye not on what is seen, but what is unseen, that better place around the bend." Inspired by his trademark phrase "out of many, we are one," photographer Anne Savage superimposed Obama's image on snapshots of people who attended his campaign events, and arranged them to look like an American flag (**29.17**). As the mosaic reveals, Obama succeeded in drawing enthusiastic support from whites and blacks; young and old; Hispanic and Asian. Eventually even Hillary Clinton campaigned for him. Exuding confidence, calm, and charm, Obama amassed an inspired following who put his likeness on posters, vans, t-shirts, bridges, and boats. Some supporters even sported Obama tattoos.

With the nation facing its most severe economic crisis since the Great Depression, the focus of the 2008 presidential race changed. An intensely disciplined candidate, Obama stuck to a clear message of economic reform. The McCain campaign was more erratic, one day highlighting economics; the next portraying Obama as the heir to sixties-era radical politics. Thanks to support from swing voters (those without strong ideological convictions), momentum for Obama built steadily throughout the fall. As this *New York Times* headline announced (**29.18**), on November 4, 2008, Barack Obama became the first African American elected president of the United States by winning a decisive victory: 365 to 173 electoral votes, and 53 percent of the popular vote.

How did past civil rights activism help make Obama's election possible?

"If there is anyone out there who still doubts that America is a place where all things are possible, who still wonders if the dream of our founders is alive in our time, who still questions the power of our democracy, tonight is your answer."

BARACK OBAMA after becoming the first African American elected president, 2008

Conclusion

Americans had good reason to feel hopeful when the forty-year Cold War came to an end as Communist governments collapsed in Europe and the Soviet Union disintegrated. Rather than entering into a period of sustained peace, however, the United States almost immediately faced new challenges from an aggressive dictator in the Middle East and Islamic fundamentalist terrorist attacks that culminated in 9/11. Taking stock of these new threats, three consecutive presidents tried to set a new direction in post–Cold War foreign policy. George H. W. Bush spoke of using U.S. leadership to create a new world order where democracy and prosperity prevailed, a vision that his son expanded to include the use of preventative war to ensure that America remained the world's sole superpower. Clinton accepted that the nation had a global responsibility to prevent massacres and used missile strikes to punish rogue states. These new foreign policy forays, which included several wars, all sparked controversy at home over the role that the United States should play in the world.

Competing visions also emerged over how to manage domestic affairs. Americans disagreed over whether to place faith in an activist, regulatory government or the free market to protect prosperity and individual rights. With the political center shifting toward the right, Democratic president Bill Clinton embraced issues popular with moderates in both parties such as welfare reform and free trade agreements. Adept at surviving political scandal, Clinton's attempt to reinvigorate the liberal vision by melding fiscal conservatism with social liberalism halted when George W. Bush won a hotly contested presidential race in 2000. Bush and the Republican-controlled Congress moved quickly to cut taxes and deregulate the financial and banking sector, but his administration failed to foresee the economic meltdown that began in the summer of 2008.

Bush was widely unpopular when he left office in 2009, and high expectations to end the war in Iraq and solve the nation's growing financial crisis awaited the incoming president Barack Obama. In difficult economic times the liberal vision of government gained new currency amid demands for increased government spending and regulation. How Obama planned to shape the liberal vision to meet these new circumstances, and the competing conservative response, lay in the future.

The New York Times

NEW YORK, WEDNESDAY, NOVEMBER 5, 2008

OBAMA

RACIAL BARRIER FALLS IN DECISIVE VICTORY

Democrats in Congress Strengthen Grip

29.18 Obama Makes History
The United States turned a page on its troubled racial past when it elected Barack Obama as the nation's first African American president in 2008.

CHAPTER REVIEW

NO GAS

1989

Fall of the Berlin Wall
Symbolizes demise of communism in Eastern Europe

Chinese students occupy Tiananmen Square
Communist government violently suppresses pro-democracy movement

1991

Persian Gulf War
United States announces intention to build "a new world order"

Soviet Union ceases to exist
United States declares victory in the Cold War

Los Angeles police acquitted of wrongfully beating Rodney King
A four-day riot erupts in Los Angeles minority neighborhoods

1998

UN withdraws weapon inspectors from an uncooperative Iraq
Growing U.S. alarm over Hussein's drive to acquire nuclear weapons

Home prices begin to surge
Encourages banks and Wall Street to invest in risky mortgages

President Bill Clinton impeached
Cleared of charges, but scandal mars Clinton's second term

Review Questions

1. What factors contributed to the ending of the Cold War?
2. What competing ideas emerged over the role that America should play in the world from 1989 to 2009? How did these ideas shape key American foreign policy decisions in this period?
3. How did technological and demographic changes affect American society? What controversies emerged over immigration, gay marriage, and computers?
4. How did liberals and conservatives modify their long-standing visions of the role government should play? How successful were they in realizing their new, modified visions?
5. Compare the differences and similarities in the U.S path to war in the 1991 Persian Gulf War and the 2003 Iraq War. Why was the 2003 war more controversial at home than the 1991 one?
6. What role did the media play in shaping American attitudes about world events?
7. How did the United States reconcile its domestic values with its new imperialistic ventures in the world from 1989-2009?

2000

al-Qaeda attacks *USS Cole* near Yemen
Precursor to 9/11 attacks inside the United States

George W. Bush elected president
Controversy over disputed recount in Florida divides the nation

2001

al-Qaeda terrorists attack U.S. targets
United States begins "war on terror" overseas and at home

United States rejects Kyoto Protocol
Stalls domestic campaign to reduce greenhouse gas emissions

Congress passes the Patriot Act
Americans debate whether law protects nation or violates civil liberties

2003

Iraq War begins
Preemptive war puts U.S. troops in Iraq indefinitely

2008

Economic downturn begins
Economists predict worst financial crisis since the Great Depression

Barack Obama elected president
First African American elected president

California rejects gay marriage
Joins majority of states in banning same-sex marriages

Key Terms

American with Disabilities Act A 1990 civil rights law that prohibited discrimination against the disabled in employment, public accommodations, and telecommunications. **880**

Powell Doctrine General Colin Powell's assertion that the nation should go to war only as a last resort when the president had full support from the nation and the international community, could employ overwhelming military force to win without serious loss of American life, and had a clear exit strategy. **882**

Operation Desert Storm A massive U.S. ground assault during the Persian Gulf War that soundly defeated the Iraqi army within four days. **883**

"Don't Ask, Don't Tell" The policy instituted during the Clinton era that allowed closeted homosexuals and lesbians, gays who kept their sexual preferences hidden, to serve in the military. **884**

North American Free Trade Agreement (NAFTA) A 1992 treaty that lifted trade barriers between the United States, Mexico, and Canada. **885**

"The Contract with Americas" A 1994 Republican manifesto that envisioned reducing the size of government, less regulation, term limits for members of congress, welfare reform, and adding a balanced budget amendment to the Constitution. **885**

"compassionate conservatism" A philosophical approach to governing that emphasized using private industry, charities, and religious institutions, rather than the government, to provide community services. **887**

World Wide Web A system for organizing electronic information transmitted through the Internet. **888**

global warming The scientific theory that widespread burning of fossil fuels emitted greenhouse gases into the atmosphere that caused average global temperatures to rise. **892**

al-Qaeda A fundamentalist Islamic terrorist organization led by Saudi exile Osama bin Laden. **895**

"ethnic cleansing" The intentional mass killing of one ethnic group by another. **895**

9/11 September 11, 2001, was the day of al-Qaeda attacks on the United States; terrorists hijacked four planes and flew two into the World Trade Center towers and one into the Pentagon; one crashed on a field in Shanksville, Pennsylvania. **896**

Patriot Act A controversial 2001 law that greatly expanded the government's investigative and police powers. **897**

preemptive war The notion that the United States should remove hostile regimes with force before they could pose a serious threat. **898**

Bush Doctrine Established the unilateral right to attack nations that harbored terrorists, to launch preemptive military strikes to prevent future attack on the United States, and to replace autocratic governments with democratically elected ones. **898**

Appendix

- **The Declaration of Independence**
- **The Articles of Confederation**
- **The Constitution of the United States of America**
- **Amendments to the Constitution**
- **Presidential Elections**
- **Presidents and Vice Presidents**

For additional reference material, go to
www.pearsonamericanhistory.com
For the on-line appendix, click on Pearson American History Study Site.
The on-line appendix includes the following:

- The Declaration of Independence
- The Articles of Confederation
- The Constitution of the United States of America
- Amendments to the Constitution
- Presidential Elections
- Vice Presidents and Cabinet Members by Administration
- Supreme Court Justices
- Presidents, Congresses, and Chief Justices, 1789–2001
- Territorial Expansion of the United States (map)
- Admission of States of the Union
- U.S. Population, 1790–2000
- Ten Largest Cities by Population, 1700–1900
- Birthrate, 1820–2000 (chart)
- Death Rate, 1900–2000 (chart)
- Life Expectancy, 1900–2000 (chart)
- Urban/Rural Population, 1750–1900 (chart)
- Women in the Labor Force, 1890–1990
- United States Physical Features (map)
- United States Native Vegetation (map)
- Ancient Native American Communities (map)
- Native American Peoples, c. 1500 (map)
- Present-Day United States (map)

The Declaration of Independence

In Congress, July 4, 1776

The Unanimous Declaration of the Thirteen United States of America

When, in the course of human events, it becomes necessary for one people to dissolve the political bonds which have connected them with another, and to assume, among the powers of the earth, the separate and equal station to which the laws of nature and of nature's God entitle them, a decent respect to the opinions of mankind requires that they should declare the causes which impel them to the separation.

We hold these truths to be self-evident: That all men are created equal; that they are endowed by their Creator with certain unalienable rights; that among these are life, liberty, and the pursuit of happiness; that, to secure these rights, governments are instituted among men, deriving their just powers from the consent of the governed; that whenever any form of government becomes destructive of these ends, it is the right of the people to alter or to abolish it, and to institute new government, laying its foundation on such principles, and organizing its powers in such form, as to them shall seem most likely to effect their safety and happiness. Prudence, indeed, will dictate that governments long established should not be changed for light and transient causes; and accordingly all experience hath shown that mankind are more disposed to suffer, while evils are sufferable, than to right themselves by abolishing the forms to which they are accustomed. But when a long train of abuses and usurpations, pursuing invariably the same object, evinces a design to reduce them under absolute despotism, it is their right, it is their duty, to throw off such government, and to provide new guards for their future security. Such has been the patient sufferance of these colonies; and such is now the necessity which constrains them to alter their former systems of government. The history of the present King of Great Britain is a history of repeated injuries and usurpations, all having in direct object the establishment of an absolute tyranny over these states. To prove this, let facts be submitted to a candid world.

He has refused his assent to laws, the most wholesome and necessary for the public good.

He has forbidden his governors to pass laws of immediate and pressing importance, unless suspended in their operation till his assent should be obtained; and, when so suspended, he has utterly neglected to attend to them.

He has refused to pass other laws for the accommodation of large districts of people, unless those people would relinquish the right of representation in the legislature, a right inestimable to them, and formidable to tyrants only.

He has called together legislative bodies at places unusual, uncomfortable, and distant from the depository of their public records, for the sole purpose of fatiguing them into compliance with his measures.

He has dissolved representative houses repeatedly, for opposing, with manly firmness, his invasions on the rights of the people.

He has refused for a long time, after such dissolutions, to cause others to be elected; whereby the legislative powers, incapable of annihilation, have returned to the people at large for their exercise; the state remaining, in the mean time, exposed to all the dangers of invasions from without and convulsions within.

He has endeavored to prevent the population of these states; for that purpose obstructing the laws for naturalization of foreigners; refusing to pass others to encourage their migration hither, and raising the conditions of new appropriations of lands.

He has obstructed the administration of justice, by refusing his assent to laws for establishing judiciary powers.

He has made judges dependent on his will alone, for the tenure of their offices, and the amount and payment of their salaries.

He has erected a multitude of new offices, and sent hither swarms of officers to harass our people and eat out their substance.

He has kept among us, in times of peace, standing armies, without the consent of our legislatures.

He has affected to render the military independent of, and superior to, the civil power.

He has combined with others to subject us to a jurisdiction foreign to our constitution, and unacknowledged by our laws, giving his assent to their acts of pretended legislation:

For quartering large bodies of armed troops among us;

For protecting them, by a mock trial, from punishment for any murder which they should commit on the inhabitants of these states;

For cutting off our trade with all parts of the world;

For imposing taxes on us without our consent;

For depriving us, in many cases, of the benefits of trial by jury;

For transporting us beyond seas, to be tried for pretended offenses;

For abolishing the free system of English laws in a neighboring province, establishing therein an arbitrary government, and enlarging its boundaries, so as to render it at once an example and fit instrument for introducing the same absolute rule into these colonies.

For taking away our charters, abolishing our most valuable laws, and altering fundamentally the forms of our governments;

For suspending our own legislatures, and declaring themselves invested with power to legislate for us in all cases whatsoever.

He has abdicated government here, by declaring us out of his protection and waging war against us.

He has plundered our seas, ravaged our coasts, burned our towns, and destroyed the lives of our people.

He is at this time transporting large armies of foreign mercenaries to complete the works of death, desolation, and tyranny already begun with circumstances of cruelty and perfidy scarcely paralleled in the most barbarous ages, and totally unworthy the head of a civilized nation.

He has constrained our fellow-citizens, taken captive on the high seas, to bear arms against their country, to become the executioners of their friends and brethren, or to fall themselves by their hands.

He has excited domestic insurrection among us, and has endeavored to bring on the inhabitants of our frontiers the merciless Indian savages, whose known rule of warfare is an undistinguished destruction of all ages, sexes, and conditions.

In every stage of these oppressions we have petitioned for redress in the most humble terms; our repeated petitions have been answered only by repeated injury. A prince, whose character is thus marked by every act which may define a tyrant, is unfit to be the ruler of a free people.

Nor have we been wanting in our attentions to our British brethren. We have warned them, from time to time, of attempts by their legislature to extend an unwarrantable jurisdiction over us. We have reminded them of the circumstances of our emigration and settlement here. We have appealed to their native justice and magnanimity; and we have conjured them, by the ties of our common kindred, to disavow these usurpations, which would inevitably interrupt our connections and correspondence. They, too, have been deaf to the voice of justice and of consanguinity. We must, therefore, acquiesce in the necessity which denounces our separation, and hold them, as we hold the rest of mankind, enemies in war, in peace friends.

We, therefore, the representatives of the United States of America, in General Congress assembled, appealing to the Supreme Judge of the world for the rectitude of our intentions, do, in the name and by the authority of the good people of these colonies, solemnly publish and declare, that these United Colonies are, and of right ought to be, FREE AND INDEPENDENT STATES; that they are absolved from all allegiance to the British crown, and that all political connection between them and the state of Great Britain is, and ought to be, totally dissolved; and that, as free and independent states, they have full power to levy war, conclude peace, contract alliances, establish commerce, and do all other acts and things which independent states may of right do. And for the support of this declaration, with a firm reliance on the protection of Divine Providence, we mutually pledge to each other our lives, our fortunes, and our sacred honor.

John Hancock

Button Gwinnett
Lyman Hall
Geo. Walton
Wm. Hooper
Joseph Hewes
John Penn
Edward Rutledge
Thos. Heyward, Junr.
Thomas Lynch, Junr.
Arthur Middleton
Samuel Chase
Wm. Paca
Thos. Stone
Charles Carroll of Carrollton
George Wythe
Richard Henry Lee
Th. Jefferson
Benj. Harrison
Thos. Nelson, Jr.
Francis Lightfoot Lee
Carter Braxton
Robt. Morris
Benjamin Rush
Benja. Franklin
John Morton
Geo. Clymer
Jas. Smith
Geo. Taylor
James Wilson
Geo. Ross
Caesar Rodney
Geo. Read
Tho. M'kean
Wm. Floyd
Phil. Livingston
Frans. Lewis
Lewis Morris
Richd. Stockton
Jno. Witherspoon
Fras. Hopkinson
John Hart
Abra. Clark
Josiah Bartlett
Wm. Whipple
Saml. Adams
John Adams
Robt. Treat Paine
Elbridge Gerry
Step. Hopkins
William Ellery
Roger Sherman
Sam'el Huntington
Wm. Williams
Oliver Wolcott
Matthew Thornton

The Articles of Confederation

Between the States of New Hampshire, Massachusetts Bay, Rhode Island and Providence Plantations, Connecticut, New York, New Jersey, Pennsylvania, Delaware, Maryland, Virginia, North Carolina, South Carolina, Georgia

ARTICLE 1

The stile of this confederacy shall be "The United States of America."

ARTICLE 2

Each State retains its sovereignty, freedom and independence, and every power, jurisdiction, and right, which is not by this confederation expressly delegated to the United States, in Congress assembled.

ARTICLE 3

The said states hereby severally enter into a firm league of friendship with each other for their common defence, the security of their liberties and their mutual and general welfare; binding themselves to assist each other against all force offered to, or attacks made upon them, or any of them, on account of religion, sovereignty, trade, or any other pretence whatever.

ARTICLE 4

The better to secure and perpetuate mutual friendship and intercourse among the people of the different states in this union, the free inhabitants of each of these states, paupers, vagabonds, and fugitives from justice excepted, shall be entitled to all privileges and immunities of free citizens in the several states; and the people of each State shall have free ingress and regress to and from any other State, and shall enjoy therein all the privileges of trade and commerce, subject to the same duties, impositions, and restrictions, as the inhabitants thereof respectively; provided, that such restrictions shall not extend so far as to prevent the removal of property, imported into any State, to any other State of which the owner is an inhabitant; provided also, that no imposition, duties, or restriction, shall be laid by any State on the property of the United States, or either of them.

If any person guilty of, or charged with treason, felony, or other high misdemeanor in any State, shall flee from justice and be found in any of the United States, he shall, upon demand of the governor or executive power of the State from which he fled, be delivered up and removed to the State having jurisdiction of his offence.

Full faith and credit shall be given in each of these states to the records, acts, and judicial proceedings of the courts and magistrates of every other State.

ARTICLE 5

For the more convenient management of the general interests of the United States, delegates shall be annually appointed, in such manner as the legislature of each State shall direct, to meet in Congress, on the 1st Monday in November in every year, with a power reserved to each State to recall its delegates, or any of them, at any time within the year, and to send others in their stead for the remainder of the year.

No State shall be represented in Congress by less than two, nor by more than seven members; and no person shall be capable of being a delegate for more than three years in any term of six years; nor shall any person, being a delegate, be capable of holding any office under the United States, for which he, or any other for his benefit, receives any salary, fees, or emolument of any kind.

Each State shall maintain its own delegates in a meeting of the states, and while they act as members of the committee of the states.

In determining questions in the United States, in Congress assembled, each State shall have one vote.

Freedom of speech and debate in Congress shall not be impeached or questioned in any court or place out of Congress: and the members of Congress shall be protected in their persons from arrests and imprisonments, during the time of their going to and from, and attendance on Congress, except for treason, felony, or breach of the peace.

ARTICLE 6

No State, without the consent of the United States, in Congress assembled, shall send any embassy to, or receive any embassy from, or enter into any conference, agreement, alliance, or treaty with any king, prince, or state; nor shall any person, holding any office of profit or trust under the United States, or any of them, accept of any present, emolument, office or title, of any kind whatever, from any king, prince, or foreign state; nor shall the United States, in Congress assembled, or any of them, grant any title of nobility.

No two or more states shall enter into any treaty, confederation, or alliance, whatever, between them, without the consent of the United States, in Congress assembled, specifying accurately the purposes for which the same is to be entered into, and how long it shall continue.

No State shall lay any imposts or duties which may interfere with any stipulations in treaties entered into by the United States, in Congress assembled, with any king, prince, or state, in pursuance of any treaties already proposed by Congress to the courts of France and Spain.

No vessels of war shall be kept up in time of peace by any State, except such number only as shall be deemed necessary by the United States, in Congress assembled, for the defence of such State or its trade; nor shall any body of forces be kept up by any State, in time of peace, except such number only as, in the judgment of the United States, in Congress assembled, shall be deemed requisite to garrison the forts necessary for the defence of such State; but every State shall always keep up a well regulated and disciplined militia, sufficiently armed and accoutred, and shall provide, and constantly have ready for use, in public stores, a due number, of field pieces and tents, and a proper quantity of arms, ammunition and camp equipage.

No State shall engage in any war without the consent of the United States, in Congress assembled, unless such State be actually invaded by enemies, or shall have received certain advice of a resolution being formed by some nation of Indians to invade such State, and the danger is so imminent as not to admit of a delay till the United States, in Congress assembled, can be consulted; nor shall any State grant commissions to any ships or vessels of war, nor letters of marque or reprisal, except it be after a declaration of war by the United States, in Congress assembled, and then only against the kingdom or state, and the subjects thereof, against which war has been so declared, and under such regulations as shall be established by the United States, in Congress assembled, unless such States be infested by pirates, in which case vessels of war may be fitted out for that occasion, and kept so long as the danger shall continue, or until the United States, in Congress assembled, shall determine otherwise.

ARTICLE 7

When land forces are raised by any State for the common defence, all officers of or under the rank of colonel, shall be appointed by the legislature of each State respectively, by whom such forces shall be raised, or in such manner as such State shall direct; and all vacancies shall be filled up by the State which first made the appointment.

ARTICLE 8

All charges of war and all other expences, that shall be incurred for the common defence or general welfare, and allowed by the United States, in Congress assembled, shall be defrayed out of a common treasury, which shall be supplied by the several states, in proportion to the value of all land within each State, granted to or surveyed for any person, as such land and the buildings and improvements thereon shall be estimated according to such mode as the United States, in Congress assembled, shall, from time to time, direct and appoint.

The taxes for paying that proportion shall be laid and levied by the authority and direction of the legislatures of the several states, within the time agreed upon by the United States, in Congress assembled.

ARTICLE 9

The United States, in Congress assembled, shall have the sole and exclusive right and power of determining on peace and war, except in the cases mentioned in the 6th article; of sending and receiving ambassadors; entering into treaties and alliances, provided that no treaty of commerce shall be made, whereby the legislative power of the respective states shall be restrained from imposing such imposts and duties on foreigners as their own people are subjected to, or from prohibiting the exportation or importation of any species of goods or commodities whatsoever; of establishing rules for deciding, in all cases, what captures on land or water shall be legal, and in what manner prizes, taken by land or naval forces in the service of the United States, shall be divided or appropriated; of granting letters of marque and reprisal in times of peace; appointing courts for the trial of piracies and felonies committed on the high seas, and establishing courts for receiving and determining, finally, appeals in all cases of captures; provided, that no member of Congress shall be appointed a judge of any of the said courts.

The United States, in Congress assembled, shall also be the last resort on appeal in all disputes and differences now subsisting, or that hereafter may arise between two or more states concerning boundary, jurisdiction or any other cause whatever; which authority shall always be exercised in the manner following: whenever the legislative or executive authority, or lawful agent of any State, in controversy with another, shall present a petition to Congress, stating the matter in question, and praying for a hearing, notice thereof shall be given, by order of Congress, to the legislative or executive authority of the other State in controversy, and a day assigned for the appearance of the parties by their lawful agents, who shall then be directed to appoint, by joint consent, commissioners or judges to constitute a court for hearing and determining the matter in question; but, if they cannot agree, Congress shall name three persons out of each of the United States, and from the list of such persons each party shall alternately strike out one, in the petitioners beginning, until the number shall be reduced to thirteen; and from that number not less than seven, nor more than nine names, as Congress shall direct, shall, in the presence of Congress, be drawn out by lot; and the persons whose names shall be drawn, or any five of them, shall be commissioners or judges to hear and finally determine the controversy, so always as a major part of the judges who shall hear the cause shall agree in the determination; and if either party shall neglect to attend at the day appointed, without shewing reasons which Congress shall judge sufficient, or, being present, shall refuse to strike, the Congress shall proceed to nominate three persons out of each State, and the secretary of Congress shall strike in behalf of such party absent or refusing; and the judgment and sentence of the court to be appointed, in the manner before prescribed, shall be final and conclusive; and if any of the parties shall refuse to submit to the authority of such court, or to appear or defend their claim or cause, the court shall nevertheless proceed to pronounce sentence or judgment, which shall, in like manner, be final and decisive, the judgment or sentence and other proceedings being, in either case, transmitted to Congress, and lodged among the acts of Congress for the security of the parties concerned: provided, that every commissioner, before he sits in judgment, shall take an oath, to be administered by one of the judges of the supreme or superior court of the State where the cause shall be tried, "well and truly to hear and determine the matter in question, according to the best of his judgment, without favor, affection, or hope of reward": provided, also, that no State shall be deprived of territory for the benefit of the United States.

All controversies concerning the private right of soil, claimed under different grants of two or more states, whose jurisdictions, as they may respect such lands and the states which passed such grants, are adjusted, the said grants, or either of them, being at the same time claimed to have originated antecedent to such settlement of jurisdiction, shall, on the petition of either party to the Congress of the United States, be finally determined, as near as may be, in the same manner as is before prescribed for deciding disputes respecting territorial jurisdiction between different states.

The United States, in Congress assembled, shall also have the sole and exclusive right and power of regulating the alloy and value of coin struck by their own authority, or by that of the respective states; fixing the standard of weights and measures throughout the United States; regulating the trade and managing all affairs with the Indians not members of any of the states; provided that the legislative right of any State within its own limits be not infringed or violated; establishing and regulating post offices from one State to another throughout all the United States, and exacting such postage on the papers passing through the same as may be requisite to defray the expences of the said office; appointing all officers of the land forces in the service of the United States, excepting regimental officers; appointing all the officers of the naval forces, and commissioning all officers whatever in the service of the United States; making rules for the government and regulation of the said land and naval forces, and directing their operations.

The United States, in Congress assembled, shall have authority to appoint a committee to sit in the recess of Congress, to be denominated "a Committee of the States," and to consist of one delegate from each State, and to appoint such other committees and civil officers as may be necessary for managing the general affairs of the United States, under their direction; to appoint one of their number to preside; provided that no person be allowed to serve in the office of president more than one year in any term of three years; to ascertain the necessary sums of money to be raised for the service of the United States, and to appropriate and apply the same for defraying the public expences; to borrow money or emit bills on the credit of the United States, transmitting, every half year, to the respective states, an account of the sums of money so borrowed or emitted; to build and equip a navy; to agree upon the number of land forces, and to make requisitions from each State for its quota, in proportion to the number of white inhabitants in such State; which requisitions shall be binding; and, thereupon, the legislature of each State shall appoint the regimental officers, raise the men, and cloathe, arm, and equip them in a soldier-like manner, at the expence of the United States; and the officers and men so cloathed, armed, and equipped, shall march to the place appointed and within the time agreed on by the United States, in Congress assembled; but if the United States, in Congress assembled, shall, on consideration of circumstances, judge proper that any State should not raise men, or should raise a smaller number than its quota, and that any other State should raise a greater number of men than the quota thereof, such extra number shall be raised, officered, cloathed, armed, and equipped in the same manner as the quota of such State, unless the legislature of such State shall judge that such extra number cannot be safely spared out of the same, in which case they shall raise, officer, cloathe, arm, and equip as many of such extra number as they judge can be safely spared. And the officers and men so cloathed, armed, and equipped, shall march to the place appointed and within the time agreed on by the United States, in Congress assembled.

The United States, in Congress assembled, shall never engage in a war, nor grant letters of marque and reprisal in time of peace, nor enter into any treaties or alliances, nor coin money, nor regulate the value thereof, nor ascertain the sums and expences necessary for the defence and welfare of the United States, or any of them: nor emit bills, nor borrow money on the credit of the United States, nor appropriate money, nor agree upon the number of vessels of war to be built or purchased, or the number of land or sea forces to be raised, nor appoint a commander in chief of the army or navy, unless nine states assent to the same; nor shall a question on any other point, except for adjourning from day to day, be determined, unless by the votes of a majority of the United States, in Congress assembled.

The Congress of the United States shall have power to adjourn to any time within the year, and to any place within the United States, so that no period of adjournment be for a longer duration than the space of six months, and shall publish the journal of their proceedings monthly, except such parts thereof, relating to treaties, alliances or military operations, as, in their judgment, require secrecy; and the yeas and nays of the delegates of each State on any question shall be entered on the journal, when it is desired by any delegate; and the delegates of a State, or any of them, at his, or their request, shall be furnished with a transcript of the said journal, except such parts as are above excepted, to lay before the legislatures of the several states.

ARTICLE 10

The committee of the states, or any nine of them, shall be authorized to execute, in the recess of Congress, such of the powers of Congress as the United States, in Congress assembled, by the consent of nine states, shall, from time to time, think expedient to vest them with; provided, that no power be delegated to the said committee for the exercise of which by the articles of confederation, the voice of nine states, in the Congress of the United States assembled, is requisite.

ARTICLE 11

Canada acceding to this confederation, and joining in the measures of the United States, shall be admitted into and entitled to all the advantages of this union; but no other colony shall be admitted into the same, unless such admission be agreed to by nine states.

ARTICLE 12

All bills of credit emitted, monies borrowed and debts contracted by, or under the authority of Congress before the assembling of the United States, in pursuance of the present confederation, shall be deemed and considered as a charge against the United States, for payment and satisfaction whereof the said United States and the public faith are hereby solemnly pledged.

ARTICLE 13

Every State shall abide by the determinations of the United States, in Congress assembled, on all questions which, by this confederation, are submitted to them. And the articles of this confederation shall be inviolably observed by every State, and the union shall be perpetual; nor shall any alteration at any time hereafter be made in any of them, unless such alteration be agreed to in a Congress of the United States, and be afterwards confirmed by the legislatures of every State.

These articles shall be proposed to the legislatures of all the United States, to be considered, and if approved of by them, they are advised to authorize their delegates to ratify the same in the Congress of the United States; which being done, the same shall become conclusive.

The Constitution of the United States of America

PREAMBLE

We the People of the United States, in Order to form a more perfect Union, establish Justice, insure domestic Tranquility, provide for the common defence, promote the general Welfare, and secure the Blessings of Liberty to ourselves and our Posterity, do ordain and establish this Constitution for the United States of America.

ARTICLE 1

Section 1

All legislative Powers herein granted shall be vested in a Congress of the United States, which shall consist of a Senate and House of Representatives.

Section 2

The House of Representatives shall be composed of Members chosen every second Year by the People of the several States, and the Electors in each State shall have the Qualifications requisite for Electors of the most numerous Branch of the State Legislature.

No Person shall be a Representative who shall not have attained to the Age of twenty five Years, and been seven Years a Citizen of the United States, and who shall not, when elected, be an inhabitant of that State in which he shall be chosen.

Representatives and direct Taxes shall be apportioned among the several States which may be included within this Union, according to their respective Numbers, *which shall be determined by adding to the whole Number of free Persons, including those bound to Service for a Term of Years, and excluding Indians not taxed, three fifths of all other Persons.** The actual Enumeration shall be made within three Years after the first Meeting of the Congress of the United States, and within every subsequent Term of ten Years, in such Manner as they shall by Law direct. The Number of Representatives shall not exceed one for every thirty Thousand, but each State shall have at Least one Representative; *and until such enumeration shall be made, the State of New Hampshire shall be entitled to chuse three, Massachusetts eight, Rhode-Island and Providence Plantations one, Connecticut five, New York six, New Jersey four, Pennsylvania eight, Delaware one, Maryland six, Virginia ten, North Carolina five, South Carolina five, and Georgia three.*

When vacancies happen in the Representation from any State, the Executive Authority thereof shall issue Writs of Election to fill such Vacancies.

The House of Representatives shall chuse their Speaker and other Officers; and shall have the sole Power of Impeachment.

Section 3

The Senate of the United States shall be composed of two Senators from each State, chosen by the Legislature thereof, for six Years; and each Senator shall have one Vote.

Immediately after they shall be assembled in Consequence of the first Election, they shall be divided as equally as may be into three Classes. The Seats of the Senators of the first Class shall be vacated at the Expiration of the second Year, of the second Class at the Expiration of the fourth Year, and of the third Class at the Expiration of the sixth Year so that one third may be chosen every second Year; and if Vacancies happen by Resignation, or otherwise, during the Recess of the Legislature of any state, the Executive thereof may make temporary Appointments until the next Meeting of the Legislature, which shall then fill such Vacancies.

No Person shall be a Senator who shall not have attained to the Age of thirty Years, and been nine Years a Citizen of the United States, and who shall not, when elected, be an Inhabitant of that State for which he shall be chosen.

The Vice President of the United States shall be President of the Senate, but shall have no Vote, unless they be equally divided.

The Senate shall chuse their other Officers, and also a President *pro tempore,* in the Absence of the Vice President, or when he shall exercise the Office of President of the United States.

The Senate shall have the sole Power to try all Impeachments. When sitting for that Purpose, they shall be on Oath or Affirmation. When the President of the United States is tried the Chief Justice shall preside: And no Person shall be convicted without the Concurrence of two thirds of the Members present.

Judgment in Cases of Impeachment shall not extend further than to removal from Office, and disqualification to hold and enjoy any Office of honor, Trust or Profit under the United States: but the Party convicted shall nevertheless be liable and subject to Indictment, Trial, Judgment and Punishment, according to Law.

Section 4

The Times, Places and Manner of holding Elections for Senators and Representatives, shall be prescribed in each State by the Legislature thereof; but the Congress may at any time by Law

*Passages no longer in effect are printed in italic type.

make or alter such Regulations, except as to the Places of chusing Senators.

The Congress shall assemble at least once in every Year, *and such Meeting shall be on the first Monday in December, unless they shall by Law appoint a different Day.*

Section 5

Each House shall be the Judge of the Elections, Returns and Qualifications of its own Members, and a Majority of each shall constitute a Quorum to do Business; but a smaller Number may adjourn from day to day, and may be authorized to compel the Attendance of absent Members, in such Manner, and under such Penalties as each House may provide.

Each House may determine the Rules of its Proceedings, punish its Members for disorderly Behaviour, and, with the Concurrence of two thirds, expel a Member.

Each House shall keep a Journal of its Proceedings, and from time to time publish the same, excepting such Parts as may in their Judgment require Secrecy; and the Yeas and Nays of the Members of either House on any question shall, at the Desire of one fifth of those Present, be entered on the Journal.

Neither House, during the Session of Congress, shall, without the Consent of the other, adjourn for more than three days, nor to any other Place than that in which the two Houses shall be sitting.

Section 6

The Senators and Representatives shall receive a Compensation for their Services, to be ascertained by Law, and paid out of the Treasury of the United States. They shall in all Cases, except Treason, Felony and Breach of the Peace, be privileged from Arrest during their Attendance at the Session of their respective Houses, and in going to and returning from the same; and for any Speech or Debate in either House, they shall not be questioned in any other Place.

No Senator or Representative shall, during the Time for which he was elected, be appointed to any civil Office under the Authority of the United States, which shall have been created, or the Emoluments whereof shall have been encreased during such time, and no Person holding any Office under the United States, shall be a Member of either House during his Continuance in Office.

Section 7

All Bills for raising Revenue shall orginate in the House of Representatives; but the Senate may propose or concur with Amendments as on other Bills.

Every Bill which shall have passed the House of Representatives and the Senate, shall, before it become a Law, be presented to the President of the United States; If he approve he shall sign it, but if not he shall return it, with his Objections to the House in which it shall have originated, who shall enter the Objections at large on their Journal, and proceed to reconsider it. If after such Reconsideration two thirds of that House shall agree to pass the Bill, it shall be sent, together with the Objections, to the other House, by which it shall likewise be reconsidered, and if approved by two thirds of that House, it shall become a Law. But in all such Cases the Votes of both Houses shall be determined by yeas and Nays, and the Names of the Persons voting for and against the Bill shall be entered on the Journal of each House respectively. If any Bill shall not be returned by the President within ten Days (Sundays excepted) after it shall have been presented to him, the Same shall be a Law, in like Manner as if he had signed it, unless the Congress by their Adjournment prevent its Return, in which Case it shall not be a Law.

Every Order, Resolution, or Vote to which the Concurrence of the Senate and House of Representatives may be necessary (except on a question of Adjournment) shall be presented to the President of the United States; and before the Same shall take Effect, shall be approved by him, or being disapproved by him, shall be repassed by two thirds of the Senate and House of Representatives, according to the Rules and Limitations prescribed in the Case of a Bill.

Section 8

The Congress shall have Power To lay and collect Taxes, Duties, Imposts and Excises, to pay the Debts and provide for the common Defence and general Welfare of the United States; but all Duties, Imposts and Excises shall be uniform throughout the United States;

To borrow Money on the credit of the United States;

To regulate Commerce with foreign Nations, and among the several States, and with the Indian Tribes;

To establish an uniform Rule of Naturalization, and uniform Laws on the subject of Bankruptcies throughout the United States;

To coin Money, regulate the Value thereof, and of foreign Coin, and fix the Standard of Weights and Measures;

To provide for the Punishment of counterfeiting the Securities and current Coin of the United States;

To establish Post Offices and post Roads;

To promote the Progress of Science and useful Arts, by securing for limited Times to Authors and Inventors the exclusive Right to their respective Writings and Discoveries;

To constitute Tribunals inferior to the supreme Court;

To define and punish Piracies and Felonies committed on the high Seas, and Offences against the Law of Nations;

To declare War, grant Letters of Marque and Reprisal, and make Rules concerning Captures on Land and Water;

To raise and support Armies, but no Appropriation of Money to that Use shall be for a longer Term than two Years;

To provide and maintain a Navy;

To make Rules for the Government and Regulation of the land and naval Forces;

To provide for calling forth the Militia to execute the Laws of the Union, suppress Insurrections and repel Invasions;

To provide for organizing, arming, and disciplining, the Militia, and for governing such Part of them as may be employed in the Service of the United States, reserving to the States respectively, the Appointment of the Officers, and the Authority of training the Militia according to the discipline prescribed by Congress;

To exercise exclusive Legislation in all Cases whatsoever, over such District (not exceeding ten Miles square) as may, by Cession of particular States, and the Acceptance of Congress, become the Seat of the Government of the United States, and to exercise like Authority over all Places purchased by the Consent of the Legislature of the State in which the Same shall be, for the Erection of Forts, Magazines, Arsenals, dock-Yards, and other needful Buildings;—And

To make all Laws which shall be necessary and proper for carrying into Execution the foregoing Powers, and all other Powers vested by this Constitution in the Government of the United States, or in any Department of Officer thereof.

Section 9

The Migration or Importation of such Persons as any of the States now existing shall think proper to admit, shall not be prohibited by the Congress prior to the Year one thousand eight hundred and eight, but a Tax or duty may be imposed on such Importation, not exceeding ten dollars for each Person.

The Privilege of the Writ of Habeas Corpus shall not be suspended, unless when in Cases of Rebellion or Invasion the public Safety may require it.

No Bill of Attainder or ex post facto Law shall be passed.

No Capitation, or other direct, Tax shall be laid, unless in Proportion to the Census or Enumeration herein before directed to be taken.

No Tax or Duty shall be laid on Articles exported from any State.

No Preference shall be given by any Regulation of Commerce or Revenue to the Ports of one State over those of another: nor shall Vessels bound to, or from, one State, be obliged to enter, clear, or pay Duties in another.

No Money shall be drawn from the Treasury, but in Consequence of Appropriations made by Law; and a regular Statement and Account of the Receipts and Expenditures of all public Money shall be published from time to time.

No Title of Nobility shall be granted by the United States: And no Person holding any Office of Profit or Trust under them, shall, without the Consent of the Congress, accept of any present, Emolument, Office, or Title, of any kind whatever, from any King, Prince, or foreign State.

Section 10

No State shall enter into any Treaty, Alliance, or Confederation; grant Letters of Marque and Reprisal; coin Money; emit Bills of Credit; make any Thing but gold and silver Coin a Tender in Payment of Debts; pass any Bill of Attainder, ex post facto Law, or Law impairing the obligation of Contracts, or grant any Title of Nobility.

No State shall, without the Consent of the Congress, lay any Imposts or Duties on Imports or Exports, except what may be absolutely necessary for executing its inspection Laws: and the net Produce of all Duties and Imposts, laid by any State on Imports or Exports, shall be for the Use of the Treasury of the United States; and all such Laws shall be subject to the Revision and Controul of the Congress.

No State shall, without the Consent of Congress, lay any Duty of Tonnage, keep Troops, or Ships of War in time of Peace, enter into any Agreement or Compact with another State, or with a foreign Power, or engage in War, unless actually invaded, or in such imminent Danger as will not admit of delay.

ARTICLE II

Section 1

The executive Power shall be vested in a President of the United States of America. He shall hold his Office during the Term of four Years, and, together with the Vice President, chosen for the same Term, be elected, as follows:

Each State shall appoint, in such Manner as the Legislature thereof may direct, a Number of Electors, equal to the whole Number of Senators and Representatives to which the State may be entitled in the Congress: but no Senator or Representative, or Person holding an Office of Trust or Profit under the United States, shall be appointed an Elector.

The Electors shall meet in their respective States, and vote by Ballot for two Persons, of whom one at least shall not be an Inhabitant of the same State with themselves. And they shall make a List of all the Persons voted for, and of the Number of Votes for each; which List they shall sign and certify, and transmit sealed to the Seat of the Government of the United States, directed to the President of the Senate. The President of the Senate shall, in the Presence of the Senate and House of Representatives, open all the Certificates, and the Votes shall then be counted. The Person having the greatest Number of Votes shall be the President, if such Number be a Majority of the whole number of Electors appointed; and if there be more than one who have such Majority, and have an equal Number of Votes, then the House of Representatives shall immediately chuse by Ballot one of them for President; and if no Person have a Majority, then from the five highest on the List the said House shall in like Manner chuse the President. But in chusing the President, the Votes shall be taken by States, the Representation from each State having one Vote; A quorum for this Purpose shall consist of a Member or Members from two thirds of the States, and a Majority of all the States shall be necessary to a Choice. In every Case, after the Choice of the President, the Person having the greatest Number of Votes of the Electors shall be the Vice President. But if there should remain two or more who have equal Votes, the Senate shall chuse from them by Ballot the Vice President.

The Congress may determine the time of chusing the Electors, and the Day on which they shall give their Votes; which Day shall be the same throughout the United States.

No person except a natural born Citizen, *or a Citizen of the United States, at the time of the Adoption of this Constitution,* shall be eligible to the Office of President; neither shall any Person be eligible to that Office who shall not have attained to the Age of thirty five Years, and been fourteen Years a Resident within the United States.

In Case of the Removal of the President from Office, or of his Death, Resignation, or Inability to discharge the Powers and Duties of the said Office, the Same shall devolve on the Vice President, and the Congress may by Law provide for the Case of Removal, Death, Resignation or Inability, both of the President and Vice President, declaring what Officer shall then act as President, and such Officer shall act accordingly, until the Disability be removed, or a President shall be elected.

The President shall, at stated Times, receive for his Services, a Compensation, which shall neither be encreased nor diminished during the Period for which he shall have been elected, and he shall not receive within that period any other Emolument from the United States, or any of them.

Before he enter on the Execution of his Office, he shall take the following Oath or Affirmation:—"I do solemnly swear (or affirm) that I will faithfully execute the Office of President of the United States, and will to the best of my Ability, preserve, protect and defend the Constitution of the United States."

Section 2

The President shall be Commander in Chief of the Army and Navy of the United States, and of the Militia of the several States, when called into the actual Service of the United States; he may require the Opinion, in writing, of the principal Officer in each of the executive Departments, upon any Subject relating to the Duties of their respective Offices, and he shall have Power to grant Reprieves and Pardons for Offences against the United States, except in Cases of Impeachment.

He shall have Power, by and with the Advice and Consent of the Senate, to make Treaties, provided two thirds of the Senators present concur; and he shall nominate, and by and with the Advice and Consent of the Senate, shall appoint Ambassadors, other public Ministers and Consuls, Judges of the supreme Court, and all other Officers of the United States, whose Appointments are not herein otherwise provided for, and which shall be established by Law: but the Congress may by Law vest the Appointment of such inferior Officers, as they think proper in the President alone, in the Courts of Law, or in the Heads of Departments.

The President shall have Power to fill up all Vacancies that may happen during the Recess of the Senate, by granting Commissions which shall expire at the End of their next Session.

Section 3

He shall from time to time give to the Congress Information of the State of the Union, and recommend to their Consideration such Measures as he shall judge necessary and expedient; he may, on extraordinary Occasions, convene both Houses, or either of them, and in Case of disagreement between them, with Respect to the Time of Adjournment, he may adjourn them to such Time as he shall think proper; he shall receive Ambassadors and other public Ministers; he shall take Care that the Laws be faithfully executed, and shall Commission all the officers of the United States.

Section 4

The President, Vice President and all civil Officers of the United States, shall be removed from Office on Impeachment for, and Conviction of, Treason, Bribery or other high Crimes and Misdemeanors.

ARTICLE III

Section 1

The judicial Power of the United States, shall be vested in one supreme Court, and in such inferior Courts as the Congress may from time to time ordain and establish. The Judges, both of the supreme and inferior Courts, shall hold their offices during good Behaviour, and shall, at stated Times, receive for their Services, a Compensation, which shall not be diminished during their Continuance in Office.

Section 2

The judicial Power shall extend to all Cases, in Law and Equity, arising under this Constitution, the Laws of the United States, and Treaties made, or which shall be made, under their Authority;—to all Cases affecting Ambassadors, other public Ministers and Consuls;—to all Cases of admiralty and maritime Jurisdiction;—to Controversies to which the United States shall be a Party;—to Controversies between two or more States;—between a State and Citizens of another State;—between Citizens of different States;—between Citizens of the same State claiming Lands under Grants of different States, and between a State, or the Citizens thereof, and foreign States, Citizens or Subjects.

In all Cases affecting Ambassadors, other public Ministers and Consuls, and those in which a State shall be Party, the supreme Court shall have original Jurisdiction. In all the other Cases before mentioned, the supreme Court shall have appellate Jurisdiction, both as to Law and Fact, with such Exceptions, and under such Regulations as the Congress shall make.

The Trial of all Crimes, except in Cases of Impeachment, shall be by Jury; and such Trial shall be held in the State where the said Crimes shall have been committed, but when not committed within any State, the Trial shall be at such Place or Places as the Congress may by Law have directed.

Section 3

Treason against the United States, shall consist only in levying War against them, or in adhering to their Enemies, giving them Aid and Comfort. No person shall be convicted of Treason unless on the Testimony of two Witnesses to the same overt Act, or on Confession in open Court.

The Congress shall have Power to declare the Punishment of Treason, but no Attainder of Treason shall work Corruption of Blood, or Forfeiture except during the Life of the Person attainted.

ARTICLE IV

Section 1

Full Faith and Credit shall be given in each State to the public Acts, Records, and judicial Proceedings of every other State. And the Congress may by general Laws prescribe the Manner in which such Acts, Records and Proceedings shall be proved, and the Effect thereof.

Section 2

The Citizens of each State shall be entitled to all Privileges and Immunities of Citizens in the several States.

A Person charged in any State with Treason, Felony, or other Crime, who shall flee from Justice, and be found in another State, shall on Demand of the executive Authority of the State from which he fled, be delivered up, to be removed to the State having Jurisdiction of the Crime.

No Person held to Service or Labour in one State, under the Laws thereof, escaping into another, shall, in Consequence of any Law or Regulation therein, be discharged from such Service or Labour, but shall be delivered up on Claim of the Party to whom such Service or Labour may be due.

Section 3

New States may be admitted by the Congress into this Union; but no new State shall be formed or erected within the Jurisdiction of any other State; nor any State be formed by the Junction of two or more States, or Parts of States, without the Consent of the Legislatures of the States concerned as well as of the Congress.

The Congress shall have Power to dispose of and make all needful Rules and Regulations respecting the Territory or other Property belonging to the United States; and nothing in this Constitution shall be so construed as to Prejudice any Claims of the United States, or of any particular States.

Section 4

The United States shall guarantee to every State in this Union a Republican Form of Government, and shall protect each of them against Invasion; and on Application of the Legislature, or of the Executive (when the Legislature cannot be convened) against domestic violence.

ARTICLE V

The Congress, whenever two thirds of both Houses shall deem it necessary, shall propose Amendments to this Constitution, or, on the Application of the Legislatures of two thirds of the several States, shall call a Convention for proposing Amendments, which, in either Case, shall be valid to all Intents and Purposes, as Part of this Constitution, when ratified by the Legislatures of three fourths of the several States, or by Conventions in three fourths thereof, as the one or the other Mode of Ratification may be proposed by the Congress; Provided that *no Amendment which may be made prior to the Year One thousand eight hundred and eight shall in any Manner affect the first and fourth Clauses in the Ninth Section of the first Article;* and that no State, without its Consent, shall be deprived of its equal Suffrage in the Senate.

ARTICLE VI

All Debts contracted and Engagements entered into, before the Adoption of this Constitution, shall be as valid against the United States under this Constitution, as under the Confederation.

This Constitution, and Laws of the United States which shall be made in Pursuance thereof; and all Treaties made, or which shall be made, under the Authority of the United States, shall be the supreme Law of the Land; and the Judges in every State shall be bound thereby, any Thing in the Constitution or Laws of any State to the Contrary notwithstanding.

The Senators and Representatives before mentioned, and the Members of the several State Legislatures, and all executive and Judicial Officers, both of the United States and of the several States, shall be bound by Oath or Affirmation, to support this Constitution; but no religious Test shall ever be required as a Qualification to any Office of public Trust under the United States.

ARTICLE VII

The Ratification of the Conventions of nine States, shall be sufficient for the Establishment of this Constitution between the States so ratifying the Same.

Done in Convention by the Unanimous Consent of the States present the Seventeenth Day of September in the Year of our Lord one thousand seven hundred and Eighty seven and of the Independence of the United States of America the Twelfth* IN WITNESS whereof We have hereunto subscribed our Names,

*The Constitution was submitted on September 17, 1787, by the Constitutional Convention, was ratified by the Convention of several states at various dates up to May 29, 1790, and became effective on March 4, 1789.

George Washington
President and Deputy from Virginia

Delaware
George Read
Gunning Bedford, Jr.
John Dickinson
Richard Bassett
Jacob Broom

Maryland
James McHenry
Daniel of St. Thomas Jenifer
Daniel Carroll

Virginia
John Blair
James Madison, Jr

North Carolina
William Blount
Richard Dobbs Spraight
Hugh Williamson

South Carolina
John Rutledge
Charles Cotesworth Pinckney
Charles Pinckney
Pierce Butler

Georgia
William Few
Abraham Baldwin

New Hampshire
John Langdon
Nicholas Gilman

Massachusetts
Nathaniel Gorham
Rufus King

Connecticut
William Samuel Johnson
Roger Sherman

New York
Alexander Hamilton

New Jersey
William Livingston
David Brearley
William Paterson
Jonathan Dayton

Pennsylvania
Benjamin Franklin
Thomas Mifflin
Robert Morris
George Clymer
Thomas FitzSimons
Jared Ingersoll
James Wilson
Gouverneur Morris

Amendments to the Constitution

AMENDMENT I

Congress shall make no law respecting an establishment of religion, or prohibiting the free exercise thereof; or abridging the freedom of speech, or of the press; or the right of the people peaceably to assemble, and to petition the Government for a redress of grievances.

AMENDMENT II

A well regulated Militia being necessary to the security of a free State, the right of the people to keep and bear Arms, shall not be infringed.

AMENDMENT III

No Soldier shall, in time of peace be quartered in any house, without the consent of the Owner, nor in time of war, but in a manner to be prescribed by law.

AMENDMENT IV

The right of the people to be secure in their persons, houses, papers, and effects, against unreasonable searches and seizures, shall not be violated, and no Warrants shall issue, but upon probable cause, supported by Oath or affirmation, and particularly describing the place to be searched, and the persons or things to be seized.

AMENDMENT V

No person shall be held to answer for a capital, or otherwise infamous crime, unless on a presentment or indictment of a Grand Jury, except in cases arising in the land or naval forces, or in the Militia, when in actual service in time of War or public danger; nor shall any person be subject for the same offense to be twice put in jeopardy of life or limb; nor shall be compelled in any criminal case to be a witness against himself, nor be deprived of life, liberty, or property, without due process of law; nor shall private property be taken for public use, without just compensation.

AMENDMENT VI

In all criminal prosecutions, the accused shall enjoy the right to a speedy and public trial, by an impartial jury of the State and district wherein the crime shall have been committed, which district shall have been previously ascertained by law, and to be informed of the nature and cause of the accusation; to be confronted with the witnesses against him; to have compulsory process for obtaining witnesses in his favor, and to have the Assistance of Counsel for his defence.

AMENDMENT VII

In Suits at common law, where the value in controversy shall exceed twenty dollars, the right of trial by jury shall be preserved, and no fact tried by a jury, shall be otherwise reexamined in any Court of the United States, than according to the rules of the common law.

AMENDMENT VIII

Excessive bail shall not be required, nor excessive fines imposed, nor cruel and unusual punishments inflicted.

AMENDMENT IX

The enumeration in the Constitution, of certain rights, shall not be construed to deny or disparage others retained by the people.

AMENDMENT X *

The powers not delegated to the United States by the Constitution, nor prohibited by it to the States, are reserved to the States respectively, or to the people.

AMENDMENT XI

[ADOPTED 1798]

The Judicial power of the United States shall not be construed to extend to any suit in law or equity, commenced or prosecuted against one of the United States by Citizens of another State, or by Citizens or Subjects of any Foreign State.

AMENDMENT XII

[ADOPTED 1804]

The Electors shall meet in their respective states, and vote by ballot for President and Vice President, one of whom, at least, shall not be an inhabitant of the same state with themselves; they shall name in their ballots the person voted for as President, and in distinct ballots the person voted for as Vice President, and they shall make distinct lists of all persons voted for as President, and of all persons voted for as Vice President, and of the number of votes for each, which lists they shall sign and certify, and transmit sealed to the seat of the government of the United States, directed to the President of the Senate;—The President of the Senate shall, in the presence of the Senate and House of Representatives, open all the certificates and the votes shall then be counted;—The person having the greatest number of votes for President, shall be the President, if such number be a majority of the whole number of Electors appointed; and if no person have such majority, then from the persons having the highest numbers not exceeding three

*The first ten amendments (the Bill of Rights) were ratified and their adoption was certified on December 15, 1791.

on the list of those voted for as President, the House of Representatives shall choose immediately, by ballot, the President. But in choosing the President, the votes shall be taken by states, the representation from each state having one vote; a quorum for this purpose shall consist of a member or members from two-thirds of the states, and a majority of all the states shall be necessary to a choice. And if the House of Representatives shall not choose a President whenever the right of choice shall devolve upon them, before the fourth day of March next following, then the Vice President shall act as President, as in the case of the death or other constitutional disability of the President.—The person having the greatest number of votes as Vice President, shall be the Vice President, if such number be a majority of the whole number of Electors appointed, and if no person have a majority, then from the two highest numbers on the list, the Senate shall choose the Vice President; a quorum for the purpose shall consist of two-thirds of the whole number of Senators, and a majority of the whole number shall be necessary to a choice. But no person constitutionally ineligible to the office of President shall be eligible to that of Vice President of the United States.

AMENDMENT XIII

[ADOPTED 1865]

Section 1

Neither slavery nor involuntary servitude, except as a punishment for crime whereof the party shall have been duly convicted, shall exist within the United States, or any place subject to their jurisdiction.

Section 2

Congress shall have power to enforce this article by appropriate legislation.

AMENDMENT XIV

[ADOPTED 1868]

Section 1

All persons born or naturalized in the United States, and subject to the jurisdiction thereof, are citizens of the United States and of the State wherein they reside. No State shall make or enforce any law which shall abridge the privileges or immunities of citizens of the United States; nor shall any State deprive any person of life, liberty, or property, without due process of law; nor deny to any person within its jurisdiction the equal protection of the laws.

Section 2

Representatives shall be apportioned among the several States according to their respective numbers, counting the whole number of persons in each State, excluding Indians not taxed. But when the right to vote at any election for the choice of electors for President and Vice President of the United States, Representatives in Congress, the Executive and Judicial officers of a State, or the members of the Legislature thereof, is denied to any of the male inhabitants of such State, being twenty-one years of age, and citizens of the United States, or in any way abridged, except for participation in rebellion, or other crime, the basis of representation therein shall be reduced in the proportion which the number of such male citizens shall bear to the whole number of male citizens twenty-one years of age in such State.

Section 3

No person shall be a Senator or Representative in Congress, or elector of President and Vice President, or hold any office, civil or military, under the United States, or under any State, who, having previously taken an oath, as a member of Congress, or as an officer of the United States, or as a member of any State legislature, or as an executive or judicial officer of any State, to support the Constitution of the United States, shall have engaged in insurrection or rebellion against the same, or given aid or comfort to the enemies thereof. But Congress may by a vote of two-thirds of each House, remove such disability.

Section 4

The validity of the public debt of the United States, authorized by law, including debts incurred for payment of pensions and bounties for services in suppressing insurrection or rebellion, shall not be questioned. But neither the United States nor any State shall assume or pay any debt or obligation incurred in aid of insurrection or rebellion against the United States, or any claim for the loss or emancipation of any slave; but all such debts, obligations and claims shall be held illegal and void.

Section 5

The Congress shall have power to enforce, by appropriate legislation, the provisions of this article.

AMENDMENT XV

[ADOPTED 1870]

Section 1

The right of citizens of the United States to vote shall not be denied or abridged by the United States or by any State on account of race, color, or previous condition of servitude.

Section 2

The Congress shall have power to enforce this article by appropriate legislation.

AMENDMENT XVI

[ADOPTED 1913]

The Congress shall have power to lay and collect taxes on incomes, from whatever source derived, without apportionment among the several States, and without regard to any census or enumeration.

AMENDMENT XVII

[ADOPTED 1913]

The Senate of the United States shall be composed of two Senators from each State, elected by the people thereof, for six years; and each Senator shall have one vote. The electors in each State shall have the qualifications requisite for electors of the most numerous branch of the State legislatures.

When vacancies happen in the representation of any State in the Senate, the executive authority of such State shall issue writs of election to fill such vacancies: *Provided*, That the legislature of any State may empower the executive thereof to make temporary appointments until the people fill the vacancies by election as the legislature may direct.

This amendment shall not be so construed as to affect the election or term of any Senator chosen before it becomes valid as part of the Constitution.

AMENDMENT XVIII

[ADOPTED 1919, REPEALED 1933]

Section 1

After one year from the ratification of this article the manufacture, sale, or transportation of intoxicating liquors within, the importation thereof into, or the exportation thereof from the United States and all territory subject to the jurisdiction thereof for beverage purposes is hereby prohibited.

Section 2

The Congress and the several States shall have concurrent power to enforce this article by appropriate legislation.

Section 3

This article shall be inoperative unless it shall have been ratified as an amendment to the Constitution by the legislatures of the several States, as provided in the Constitution, within seven years from the date of the submission hereof to the States by the Congress.

AMENDMENT XIX

[ADOPTED 1920]

The right of citizens of the United States to vote shall not be denied or abridged by the United States or by any State on account of sex.

Congress shall have power to enforce this article by appropriate legislation.

AMENDMENT XX

[ADOPTED 1933]

Section 1

The terms of the President and Vice President shall end at noon on the 20th day of January, and the terms of Senators and Representatives at noon on the 3d day of January, of the years in which such terms would have ended if this article had not been ratified and the terms of their successors shall then begin.

Section 2

The Congress shall assemble at least once in every year, and such meeting shall begin at noon on the 3d day of January, unless they shall by law appoint a different day.

Section 3

If, at the time fixed for the beginning of the term of the President, the President elect shall have died, the Vice President elect shall become President. If a President shall not have been chosen before the time fixed for the beginning of his term, or if the President elect shall have failed to qualify, then the Vice President elect shall act as President until a President shall have qualified; and the Congress may by law provide for the case wherein neither a President elect nor a Vice President elect shall have qualified, declaring who shall then act as President, or the manner in which one who is to act shall be selected, and such person shall act accordingly until a President or Vice President shall have qualified.

Section 4

The Congress may by law provide for the case of the death of any of the persons from whom the House of Representatives may choose a President whenever the right of choice shall have devolved upon them, and for the case of the death of any of the persons from whom the Senate may choose a Vice President whenever the right of choice shall have devolved upon them.

Section 5

Sections 1 and 2 shall take effect on the 15th day of October following the ratification of this article.

Section 6

This article shall be inoperative unless it shall have been ratified as an amendment to the Constitution by the legislatures of three fourths of the several States within seven years from the date of its submission.

AMENDMENT XXI

[ADOPTED 1933]

Section 1

The eighteenth article of amendment to the Constitution of the United States is hereby repealed.

Section 2

The transportation or importation into any State, Territory, or possession of the United States for delivery or use therein of intoxicating liquors in violation of the laws thereof, is hereby prohibited.

Section 3

This article shall be inoperative unless it shall have been ratified as an amendment to the Constitution by conventions in the several

States, as provided in the Constitution, within seven years from the date of the submission hereof to the States by the Congress.

AMENDMENT XXII

[ADOPTED 1951]

Section 1

No person shall be elected to the office of the President more than twice, and no person who has held the office of President, or acted as President, for more than two years of a term to which some other person was elected President shall be elected to the office of the President more than once. But this Article shall not apply to any person holding the office of President when this Article was proposed by the Congress, and shall not prevent any person who may be holding the office of President, or acting as President, during the term within which this Article becomes operative from holding the office of President or acting as President during the remainder of such term.

Section 2

This article shall be inoperative unless it shall have been ratified as an amendment to the Constitution by the legislatures of three-fourths of the several States within seven years from the date of its submission to the States by the Congress.

AMENDMENT XXIII

[ADOPTED 1961]

Section 1

The District constituting the seat of Government of the United States shall appoint in such manner as the Congress shall direct:

A number of electors of President and Vice President equal to the whole number of Senators and Representatives in Congress to which the District would be entitled if it were a State, but in no event more than the least populous State; they shall be in addition to those appointed by the States, but they shall be considered, for the purposes of the election of President and Vice President, to be electors appointed by a State; and they shall meet in the District and perform such duties as provided by the twelfth article of amendment.

Section 2

The Congress shall have power to enforce this article by appropriate legislation.

AMENDMENT XXIV

[ADOPTED 1964]

Section 1

The right of citizens of the United States to vote in any primary or other election for President or Vice President, for electors for President or Vice President, or for Senator or Representative in Congress, shall not be denied or abridged by the United States or any state by reason of failure to pay any poll tax or other tax.

Section 2

The Congress shall have the power to enforce this article by appropriate legislation.

AMENDMENT XXV

[ADOPTED 1967]

Section 1

In case of the removal of the President from office or his death or resignation, the Vice President shall become President.

Section 2

Whenever there is a vacancy in the office of the Vice President, the President shall nominate a Vice President who shall take the office upon confirmation by a majority vote of both houses of Congress.

Section 3

Whenever the President transmits to the President pro tempore of the Senate and the Speaker of the House of Representatives his written declaration that he is unable to discharge the powers and duties of his office, and until he transmits to them a written declaration to the contrary, such powers and duties shall be discharged by the Vice President as Acting President.

Section 4

Whenever the Vice President and a majority of either the principal officers of the executive departments or of such other body as Congress may by law provide, transmit to the President pro tempore of the Senate and the Speaker of the House of Representatives their written declaration that the President is unable to discharge the powers and duties of his office, the Vice President shall immediately assume the powers and duties of the office as Acting President.

Thereafter, when the President transmits to the President pro tempore of the Senate and the Speaker of the House of Representatives his written declaration that no inability exists, he shall resume the powers and duties of his office unless the Vice President and a majority of either the principal officers of the executive department or of such other body as Congress may by law provide, transmit within four days to the President pro tempore of the Senate and the Speaker of the House of Representatives their written declaration that the President is unable to discharge the powers and duties of his office. Thereupon Congress shall decide the issue, assembling within 48 hours for that purpose if not in session. If the Congress, within 21 days after receipt of the latter written declaration, or, if Congress is not in session, within 21 days after Congress is required to assemble, determines by two-thirds vote of both houses that the President is unable to discharge the powers and duties of his office, the Vice President shall continue to discharge the same as Acting President; otherwise, the President shall resume the powers and duties of his office.

AMENDMENT XXVI

[ADOPTED 1971]

Section 1

The right of citizens of the United States, who are 18 years of age or older, to vote shall not be denied or abridged by the United States or any state on account of age.

Section 2

The Congress shall have the power to enforce this article by appropriate legislation.

AMENDMENT XXVII

[ADOPTED 1992]

No law, varying the compensation for the services of the Senators and Representatives shall take effect, until an election of Representatives shall have intervened.

Presidential Elections

Year	Candidates	Parties	Popular Vote	Electoral Vote	Voter Participation
1789	**George Washington**		*	**69**	
	John Adams			34	
	Others			35	
1792	**George Washington**		*	**132**	
	John Adams			77	
	George Clinton			50	
	Others			5	
1796	**John Adams**	**Federalist**	*	**71**	
	Thomas Jefferson	Democratic-Republican		68	
	Thomas Pinckney	Federalist		59	
	Aaron Burr	Dem.-Rep.		30	
	Others			48	
1800	**Thomas Jefferson**	**Dem.-Rep.**	*	**73**	
	Aaron Burr	Dem.-Rep.		73	
	John Adams	Federalist		65	
	C. C. Pinckney	Federalist		64	
	John Jay	Federalist		1	
1804	**Thomas Jefferson**	**Dem.-Rep.**	*	**162**	
	C. C. Pinckney	Federalist		14	
1808	**James Madison**	**Dem.-Rep.**	*	**122**	
	C. C. Pinckney	Federalist		47	
	George Clinton	Dem.-Rep.		6	
1812	**James Madison**	**Dem.-Rep.**	*	**128**	
	De Witt Clinton	Federalist		89	
1816	**James Monroe**	**Dem.-Rep.**	*	**183**	
	Rufus King	Federalist		34	
1820	**James Monroe**	**Dem.-Rep.**	*	**231**	
	John Quincy Adams	Dem.-Rep.		1	
1824	**John Quincy Adams**	**Dem.-Rep.**	**108,740 (31%)**	**84**	**26.9%**
	Andrew Jackson	Dem.-Rep.	153,544 (44%)	99	
	William H. Crawford	Dem.-Rep.	40,856 (12%)	41	
	Henry Clay	Dem.-Rep.	47,531 (14%)	37	
1828	**Andrew Jackson**	**Democratic**	**647,286 (56.0%)**	**178**	**57.6%**
	John Quincy Adams	National Republican	508,064 (44.0%)	83	
1832	**Andrew Jackson**	**Democratic**	**688,242 (54.2%)**	**219**	**55.4%**
	Henry Clay	National Republican	473,462 (37.4%)	49	
	John Floyd	Independent		11	
	William Wirt	Anti-Mason	101,051 (7.8%)	7	

Year	Candidates	Parties	Popular Vote	Electoral Vote	Voter Participation
1836	**Martin Van Buren**	**Democratic**	**762,198 (50.8%)**	**170**	**57.8%**
	William Henry Harrison	Whig	549,508 (36.6%)	73	
	Hugh L. White	Whig	145,342 (9.7%)	26	
	Daniel Webster	Whig	41,287 (2.7%)	14	
	W. P. Magnum	Independent		11	
1840	**William Henry Harrison**	**Whig**	**1,274,624 (53.1%)**	**234**	**80.2%**
	Martin Van Buren	Democratic	1,127,781 (46.9%)	60	
	J. G. Birney	Liberty	7069	—	
1844	**James K. Polk**	**Democratic**	**1,338,464 (49.6%)**	**170**	**78.9%**
	Henry Clay	Whig	1,300,097 (48.1%)	105	
	J. G. Birney	Liberty	62,300 (2.3%)	—	
1848	**Zachary Taylor**	**Whig**	**1,360,967 (47.4%)**	**163**	**72.7%**
	Lewis Cass	Democratic	1,222,342 (42.5%)	127	
	Martin Van Buren	Free-Soil	291,263 (10.1%)	—	
1852	**Franklin Pierce**	**Democratic**	**1,601,274 (50.8%)**	**254**	**69.6%**
	Winfield Scott	Whig	1,386,580 (43.9%)	42	
	John P. Hale	Free-Soil	155,825 (5.0%)	—	
1856	**James Buchanan**	**Democratic**	**1,832,955 (45.3%)**	**174**	**78.9%**
	John C. Frémont	Republican	1,339,932 (33.1%)	114	
	Millard Fillmore	American	871,731 (21.6%)	8	
1860	**Abraham Lincoln**	**Republican**	**1,865,593 (39.8%)**	**180**	**81.2%**
	Stephen A. Douglas	Democratic	1,382,713 (29.5%)	12	
	John C. Breckinridge	Democratic	848,356 (18.1%)	72	
	John Bell	Union	592,906 (12.6%)	39	
1864	**Abraham Lincoln**	**Republican**	**2,213,655 (55.0%)**	**212**[†]	**73.8%**
	George B. McClellan	Democratic	1,805,237 (45.0%)	21	
1868	**Ulysses S. Grant**	**Republican**	**3,013,421 (53%)**	**214**	**78.1%**
	Horatio Seymour	Democratic	2,706,829 (47%)	80	
1872	**Ulysses S. Grant**	**Republican**	**3,597,132 (55.6%)**	**286**	**71.3%**
	Horace Greeley	Dem.; Liberal Republican	2,834,761 (43.8%)	66[‡]	
1876	**Rutherford B. Hayes**[§]	**Republican**	**4,036,572 (48.0%)**	**185**	**81.8%**
	Samuel J. Tilden	Democratic	4,284,020 (51.0%)	184	
1880	**James A. Garfield**	**Republican**	**4,454,416 (48.5%)**	**214**	**79.4%**
	Winfield S. Hancock	Democratic	4,444,952 (48.1%)	155	
1884	**Grover Cleveland**	**Democratic**	**4,874,986 (48.5%)**	**219**	**77.5%**
	James G. Blaine	Republican	4,851,981 (48.2%)	182	
1888	**Benjamin Harrison**	**Republican**	**5,439,853 (47.9%)**	**233**	**79.3%**
	Grover Cleveland	Democratic	5,540,309 (48.6%)	168	
1892	**Grover Cleveland**	**Democratic**	**5,556,918 (46.1%)**	**277**	**74.7%**
	Benjamin Harrison	Republican	5,176,108 (43.0%)	145	
	James B. Weaver	People's	1,041,028 (9%)	22	

Year	Candidates	Parties	Popular Vote	Electoral Vote	Voter Participation
1896	**William McKinley**	**Republican**	**7,104,779 (51.1%)**	**271**	**79.3%**
	William Jennings Bryan	Democratic People's	6,502,925 (47.7%)	176	
1900	**William McKinley**	**Republican**	**7,207,923 (51.7%)**	**292**	**73.2%**
	William Jennings Bryan	Dem.-Populist	6,358,133 (45.5%)	155	
1904	**Theodore Roosevelt**	**Republican**	**7,623,486 (57.9%)**	**336**	**65.2%**
	Alton B. Parker	Democratic	5,077,911 (37.6%)	140	
	Eugene V. Debs	Socialist	402,400 (3.0%)	—	
1908	**William H. Taft**	**Republican**	**7,678,908 (51.6%)**	**321**	**65.4%**
	William Jennings Bryan	Democratic	6,409,104 (43.1%)	162	
	Eugene V. Debs	Socialist	402,820 (2.8%)	—	
1912	**Woodrow Wilson**	**Democratic**	**6,296,547 (41.9%)**	**435**	**58.8%**
	Theodore Roosevelt	Progressive	4,118,571 (27.4%)	88	
	William H. Taft	Republican	3,486,720 (23.2%)	8	
	Eugene V. Debs	Socialist	900,672 (6.0%)	—	
1916	**Woodrow Wilson**	**Democratic**	**9,129,606 (49.4%)**	**277**	**61.6%**
	Charles E. Hughes	Republican	8,538,221 (46.2%)	254	
	A. L. Benson	Socialist	585,113 (3.2%)	—	
1920	**Warren G. Harding**	**Republican**	**16,152,200 (60.4%)**	**404**	**49.2%**
	James M. Cox	Democratic	9,147,353 (34.2%)	127	
	Eugene V. Debs	Socialist	917,799 (3.4%)	—	
1924	**Calvin Coolidge**	**Republican**	**15,725,016 (54.0%)**	**382**	**48.9%**
	John W. Davis	Democratic	8,386,503 (28.8%)	136	
	Robert M. La Follette	Progressive	4,822,856 (16.6%)	13	
1928	**Herbert Hoover**	**Republican**	**21,391,381 (58.2%)**	**444**	**56.9%**
	Alfred E. Smith	Democratic	15,016,443 (40.9%)	87	
	Norman Thomas	Socialist	267,835 (0.7%)	—	
1932	**Franklin D. Roosevelt**	**Democratic**	**22,821,857 (57.4%)**	**472**	**56.9%**
	Herbert Hoover	Republican	15,761,841 (39.7%)	59	
	Norman Thomas	Socialist	884,781 (2.2%)	—	
1936	**Franklin D. Roosevelt**	**Democratic**	**27,751,597 (60.8%)**	**523**	**61.0%**
	Alfred M. Landon	Republican	16,679,583 (36.5%)	8	
	William Lemke	Union	882,479 (1.9%)	—	
1940	**Franklin D. Roosevelt**	**Democratic**	**27,244,160 (54.8%)**	**449**	**62.5%**
	Wendell L. Willkie	Republican	22,305,198 (44.8%)	82	
1944	**Franklin D. Roosevelt**	**Democratic**	**25,602,504 (53.5%)**	**432**	**55.9%**
	Thomas E. Dewey	Republican	22,006,285 (46.0%)	99	
1948	**Harry S Truman**	**Democratic**	**24,105,695 (49.5%)**	**304**	**53.0%**
	Thomas E. Dewey	Republican	21,969,170 (45.1%)	189	
	J. Strom Thurmond	State-Rights Democratic	1,169,021 (2.4%)	38	
	Henry A. Wallace	Progressive	1,157,326 (2.4%)	—	

Year	Candidates	Parties	Popular Vote	Electoral Vote	Voter Participation
1952	**Dwight D. Eisenhower**	**Republican**	**33,778,963 (55.1%)**	**442**	**63.3%**
	Adlai E. Stevenson	Democratic	27,314,992 (44.4%)	89	
1956	**Dwight D. Eisenhower**	**Republican**	**35,575,420 (57.6%)**	**457**	**60.6%**
	Adlai E. Stevenson	Democratic	26,033,066 (42.1%)	73	
	Other	—	—	1	
1960	**John F. Kennedy**	**Democratic**	**34,227,096 (49.9%)**	**303**	**64%**
	Richard M. Nixon	Republican	34,108,546 (49.6%)	219	
	Other	—	—	15	
1964	**Lyndon B. Johnson**	**Democratic**	**43,126,506 (61.1%)**	**486**	**61.7%**
	Barry M. Goldwater	Republican	27,176,799 (38.5%)	52	
1968	**Richard M. Nixon**	**Republican**	**31,785,480 (44%)**	**301**	**60.6%**
	Hubert H. Humphrey	Democratic	31,275,166 (42%)	191	
	George Wallace	American Indep.	9,906,473 (14%)	46	
1972	**Richard M. Nixon**	**Republican**	**46,740,323 (60.7%)**	**520**	**55.2%**
	George S. McGovern	Democratic	28,901,598 (37.5%)	17	
	Other	—	—	1	
1976	**Jimmy Carter**	**Democratic**	**40,828,587 (50.0%)**	**297**	**53.5%**
	Gerald R. Ford	Republican	39,147,613 (47.9%)	241	
	Other	—	1,575,459 (2.1%)	—	
1980	**Ronald Reagan**	**Republican**	**43,901,812 (50.7%)**	**489**	**52.6%**
	Jimmy Carter	Democratic	35,483,820 (41.0%)	49	
	John B. Anderson	Independent	5,719,437 (6.6%)	—	
	Ed Clark	Libertarian	921,188 (1.1%)	—	
1984	**Ronald Reagan**	**Republican**	**54,455,075 (59.0%)**	**525**	**53.3%**
	Walter Mondale	Democratic	37,577,185 (41.0%)	13	
1988	**George H. W. Bush**	**Republican**	**48,886,097 (53.4%)**	**426**	**50.3%**
	Michael S. Dukakis	Democratic	41,809,074 (45.6%)	111	
1992	**William J. Clinton**	**Democratic**	**44,908,254 (43%)**	**370**	**55.1%**
	George H. W. Bush	Republican	39,102,343 (37.5%)	168	
	H. Ross Perot	Independent	19,741,065 (18.9%)	—	
1996	**William J. Clinton**	**Democratic**	**45,590,703 (50%)**	**379**	**49%**
	Robert Dole	Republican	37,816,307 (41%)	159	
	Ross Perot	Reform	7,866,284	—	
2000	**George W. Bush**	**Republican**	**50,456,062 (47.88%)**	**271**	**49.3%**
	Al Gore	Democratic	50,996,582 (48.39%)	266[‖]	
	Ralph Nader	Green	82,955 (2.72%)	—	
	Other		834,774 (less than 1%)	—	
2004	**George W. Bush**	**Republican**	**60,934,251 (51.0%)**	**286**	**55.6%**
	John F. Kerry	Democratic	57,765,291 (48.0%)	252	
	Ralph Nader	Independent	405,933 (less than 1%)	—	
2008	**Barack H. Obama**	**Democratic**	**69,456,897**	**365**	**56.8%**
	John McCain	Republican	59,934,814	173	
	Ralph Nader	Independent	738,475	0	

*Electors selected by state legislatures.

†Eleven secessionist states did not participate.

‡Greeley died before the electoral college met. His electoral votes were divided among the four minor candidates.

§Contested result settled by special election.

‖One District of Columbia Gore elector abstained.

Presidents and Vice Presidents

	President	Vice President	Term
1.	**George Washington**	John Adams	1789–1793
	George Washington	John Adams	1793–1797
2.	**John Adams**	Thomas Jefferson	1797–1801
3.	**Thomas Jefferson**	Aaron Burr	1801–1805
	Thomas Jefferson	George Clinton	1805–1809
4.	**James Madison**	George Clinton (d. 1812)	1809–1813
	James Madison	Elbridge Gerry (d. 1814)	1813–1817
5.	**James Monroe**	Daniel Tompkins	1817–1821
	James Monroe	Daniel Tompkins	1821–1825
6.	**John Quincy Adams**	John C. Calhoun	1825–1829
7.	**Andrew Jackson**	John C. Calhoun	1829–1833
	Andrew Jackson	Martin Van Buren	1833–1837
8.	**Martin Van Buren**	Richard M. Johnson	1837–1841
9.	**William H. Harrison (d. 1841)**	John Tyler	1841
10.	**John Tyler**	—	1841–1845
11.	**James K. Polk**	George M. Dallas	1845–1849
12.	**Zachary Taylor (d. 1850)**	Millard Fillmore	1849–1850
13.	**Millard Fillmore**	—	1850–1853
14.	**Franklin Pierce**	William R. King (d. 1853)	1853–1857
15.	**James Buchanan**	John C. Breckinridge	1857–1861
16.	**Abraham Lincoln**	Hannibal Hamlin	1861–1865
	Abraham Lincoln (d. 1865)	Andrew Johnson	1865
17.	**Andrew Johnson**	—	1865–1869
18.	**Ulysses S. Grant**	Schuyler Colfax	1869–1873
	Ulysses S. Grant	Henry Wilson (d. 1875)	1873–1877
19.	**Rutherford B. Hayes**	William A. Wheeler	1877–1881
20.	**James A. Garfield (d. 1881)**	Chester A. Arthur	1881
21.	**Chester A. Arthur**	—	1881–1885
22.	**Grover Cleveland**	Thomas A. Hendricks (d. 1885)	1885–1889
23.	**Benjamin Harrison**	Levi P. Morton	1889–1893
24.	**Grover Cleveland**	Adlai E. Stevenson	1893–1897
25.	**William McKinley**	Garret A. Hobart (d. 1899)	1897–1901
	William McKinley (d. 1901)	Theodore Roosevelt	1901
26.	**Theodore Roosevelt**	—	1901–1905
	Theodore Roosevelt	Charles Fairbanks	1905–1909
27.	**William H. Taft**	James S. Sherman (d. 1912)	1909–1913

	President	Vice President	Term
28.	**Woodrow Wilson**	Thomas R. Marshall	1913–1917
	Woodrow Wilson	Thomas R. Marshall	1917–1921
29.	**Warren G. Harding (d. 1923)**	Calvin Coolidge	1921–1923
30.	**Calvin Coolidge**	—	1923–1925
	Calvin Coolidge	Charles G. Dawes	1925–1929
31.	**Herbert Hoover**	Charles Curtis	1929–1933
32.	**Franklin D. Roosevelt**	John N. Garner	1933–1937
	Franklin D. Roosevelt	John N. Garner	1937–1941
	Franklin D. Roosevelt	Henry A. Wallace	1941–1945
	Franklin D. Roosevelt (d. 1945)	Harry S Truman	1945
33.	**Harry S Truman**	—	1945–1949
	Harry S Truman	Alben W. Barkley	1949–1953
34.	**Dwight D. Eisenhower**	Richard M. Nixon	1953–1957
	Dwight D. Eisenhower	Richard M. Nixon	1957–1961
35.	**John F. Kennedy (d. 1963)**	Lyndon B. Johnson	1961–1963
36.	**Lyndon B. Johnson**	—	1963–1965
	Lyndon B. Johnson	Hubert H. Humphrey	1965–1969
37.	**Richard M. Nixon**	Spiro T. Agnew	1969–1973
	Richard M. Nixon (resigned 1974)	Gerald R. Ford	1973–1974
38.	**Gerald R. Ford**	Nelson A. Rockefeller	1974–1977
39.	**Jimmy Carter**	Walter F. Mondale	1977–1981
40.	**Ronald Reagan**	George H. W. Bush	1981–1985
	Ronald Reagan	George H. W. Bush	1985–1989
41.	**George H. W. Bush**	J. Danforth Quayle	1989–1993
42.	**William J. Clinton**	Albert Gore, Jr.	1993–1997
	William J. Clinton	Albert Gore, Jr.	1997–2001
43.	**George W. Bush**	Richard Cheney	2001–2005
	George W. Bush	Richard Cheney	2005–2009
44.	**Barack H. Obama**	Joseph R. Biden, Jr.	2009–

Glossary

agent orange (p. 790) A defoliant that stripped trees of their leaves to expose Vietcong hideouts and killed crops.

Alcatraz Proclamation (p. 839) Sardonic statement issued by Indian activists who occupied the island of Alcatraz and described it as the perfect site for an Indian reservation because it lacked running water, sanitation, schools, mineral resources, and productive soil.

Allies (World War I) (p. 594) Initially composed of Britain, France, Belgium, and Russia, and would eventually total eighteen nations, including Italy and the United States.

Allies (World War II) (p. 688) Name for powers fighting Germany, eventually including the United States, Britain, France, and the Soviet Union.

American Expeditionary Forces (p. 612) Two million American soldiers who fought overseas under the command of General John J. Pershing.

American Federation of Labor (AFL) (p. 678) A craft-based organization that accepted only skilled workers, like carpenters or cigar makers, who practiced a trade.

Angel Island (p. 581) Immigration processing station in the San Francisco Bay for Asian immigrants.

Axis (p. 688) Name for nations fighting the Allies, including Germany, Italy and Japan.

baby boom generation (p. 758) The 76.4 million Americans born between 1946 and 1964.

Battle of Little Bighorn (p. 456) Lt. Col. George A. Custer and the Seventh Cavalry are wiped out by a force of Cheyenne, Sioux, and Arapaho warriors on June 25, 1876; hardens white attitudes toward Native Americans.

Bay of Pigs operation (1961) (p. 745) Failed attempt to use an amphibious invasion by Cuban exiles to overthrow the Cuban dictator Fidel Castro.

Beats (p. 763) Members of the bohemian communities of poets, novelists, and artists that flourished in New York's Greenwich Village and San Francisco's North Beach and who rejected middle-class suburban values.

Berlin airlift (1948–1949) (p. 726) Americans and British used planes to resupply West Berlin to stymie the Soviet blockade of the city.

Birmingham campaign (p. 821) Civil rights effort to desegregate Birmingham, Alabama, where shocking images of police brutality prompted Kennedy to push for a federal civil rights act.

Black Codes (p. 413) Laws designed by the ex-Confederate states to sharply limit the civil and economic rights of freedmen and create an exploitable workforce.

blacklist (p. 485) A list of workers that employers in a particular town or industry refused to hire because they were considered troublemakers.

Black Panthers (p. 832) Militant civil rights group dedicated to armed self-defense, racial pride, and inner-city renewal.

Black Power (p. 833) A call for blacks to unite politically and economically in black-only organizations to protect their racial identity as they fought for equality.

Bonus March (p. 660) A two-month-long demonstration by forty thousand impoverished World War I veterans in Washington, D.C., that ended violently when the army expelled the protesters.

***Brown v. Board of Education* (1954) (p. 766)** Supreme Court decision that segregated schools violated the equal protection clause of the Fourteenth Amendment.

"Buffalo Bill's Wild West" (p. 462) A circuslike production begun in 1883 that helped create a romantic and mythological view of the West in the American imagination.

Camp David Accords (1978) (p. 856) Israel agreed to give the Sinai Peninsula back to Egypt; in return Egypt became the first Arab state to recognize Israel's right to exist.

carpetbagger (p. 418) White Southerners' derogatory term for Northerners who came south after the war to settle, work, or aid the ex-slaves. It falsely suggested they were penniless adventurers who came south merely to get rich.

"cash and carry" (p. 687) A policy that required belligerent nations to pay cash for goods and transport them on their own ships.

central business districts (p. 512) Sections of cities devoted exclusively to commercial enterprises such as banks, department stores, and the offices of corporations, accountants, lawyers, and other professions.

Central Powers (p. 594) Initially Germany and Austria-Hungary, expanded by 1915 to include the Ottoman Empire and Bulgaria.

Chinese Exclusion Act (p. 486) An 1882 law barring Chinese immigration to the United States for ten years. Renewed several times. It remained in effect until 1943.

City Beautiful Movement (p. 510) A movement begun in the 1880s that advocated comprehensive planning and grand redesign of urban space to eliminate pollution and overcrowding.

civil disobedience (p. 772) A strategy of nonviolence used by demonstrators to protest a law or a policy considered unjust.

Civil Rights Act of 1875 (p. 426) Passed by Congress in 1875, it required state governments to provide equal access in public facilities such as schools and to allow African Americans to serve on juries. In 1883 the U.S. Supreme Court ruled it unconstitutional.

Civil Rights Act of 1964 (p. 826) Legislation that banned segregation in businesses and places open to the public (such as restaurants and public schools) and prohibited racial and gender discrimination in employment.

Clayton Anti-Trust Act (1914) (p. 539) The act prohibited interlocking company directories—the practice of setting up shadow companies that appeared to compete but were actually run by the same board of directors—and exempted trade unions from prosecution under the 1890 Sherman Anti-Trust Act.

Cold War (p. 721) A full-scale ideological and military conflict between the United States and the Soviet Union and their allies that led to several hot wars around the globe, although the Americans and Soviets, fearful of a nuclear showdown, never fought each other directly

Committee on Public Information (p. 606) Government agency that controlled the flow of information and shaped public opinion about the war with posters, Four-Minute Men, pamphlets, and films.

company town (p. 524) A town built and owned by a corporation and rented to its employees, reflecting both the corporation's desire to help their workers and to control them.

Compromise of 1877 (p. 427) Resolution of the disputed presidential election of 1876 that handed victory to Republican Rutherford B. Hayes over Democrat Samuel J. Tilden. Democrats agreed to the deal in exchange for patronage and the continued removal of federal troops from the South.

Congress of Industrial Organizations (CIO) (p. 679) A brand-new type of labor organization that organized workers within an entire industry rather than by their trade orientation.

conscientious objectors (p. 609) Those who opposed participating in military service because of religious, philosophical, or political belief.

conservationist (p. 540) An environmentalist who wanted to meet present economic needs and conserve natural resources for future generations.

conspicuous consumption (p. 517) A term used to describe lavish displays of wealth by the rich, including construction of opulent mansions and hosting lavish balls.

containment (p. 722) The label affixed to multiple American foreign policy initiatives meant to prevent the Soviet Union from expanding its influence around the globe.

corporation (p. 472) Businesses owned by people who buy shares of stock in the company.

Coxey's Army (p. 523) A protest march from Ohio to Washington, D.C., in 1894 organized by Jacob Coxey to publicize demands for the federal government to alleviate the suffering brought on by the Panic of 1893.

Cuban Missile Crisis (1962) (p. 745) A showdown between the United States and the Soviet Union over Khrushchev's decision to place Soviet missiles in Communist Cuba aimed at America.

Dawes Plan (1924) (p. 650) International agreement that loaned Germany $200 million in gold to pay a reduced reparation bill and gave Germany more time to meet its debt.

Dawes Severalty Act (p. 458) 1887 law that started the breakup of reservations by offering Native Americans allotments of 160 acres of reservationland to encourage them to become independent farmers.

depression (p. 483) A contraction of economic growth, widespread business failure, and high rates of unemployment lasting several years.

deserving poor (p. 676) Needy Americans who were legitimately entitled to public support, a category open to differing interpretations.

détente (p. 803) Relaxing Cold War tensions by using diplomatic, economic, and cultural contacts to improve U.S. relations with China and the Soviet Union.

domino theory (p. 781) The fear that a communist Vietnam would open the door to a complete communist takeover of Southeast Asia.

double-victory campaign (p. 699) Civil rights call for victory against both fascism overseas and racial prejudice at home.

Dust Bowl (p. 670) Drought and soil erosion caused massive dust storms across southern and plains states throughout the thirties.

Eighteenth Amendment (1919) (p. 633) Constitutional amendment that banned the sale, manufacture, and transportation of intoxicating liquors.

Equal Rights Amendment (ERA) (p. 858) A proposed constitutional amendment, which stated that "equality of rights under the law shall not be denied or abridged by the United States or by any State on account of sex."

Espionage Act (1917) (p. 606) Legislation that made it a crime to obstruct military recruitment, to encourage mutiny, or to aid the enemy by spreading lies.

ethnic enclaves (p. 501) Urban neighborhoods dominated by one particular immigrant group, often leading to names such as Little Germany and Little Italy.

Eugenicists (p. 646) Those who wanted to improve the human race by controlling its hereditary qualities.

Exodusters (p. 444) More than twenty thousand exslaves who in 1879 left violence and poverty in the South to take up farming in Kansas.

Fair Deal (p. 754) Truman's proposals for national health care, public housing, education, and public works projects.

farmers' alliances (p. 520) Organizations in the 1870s and 1880s dedicated to helping farmers struggling with rising costs and falling crop prices by advocating farmer cooperatives and laws to regulate banks and railroads.

fascist state (p. 686) A type of dictatorial regime that arose in Germany, Italy, and Spain that glorified the state over the individual.

Federal Reserve Act (1913) (p. 539) The act creating a federally run Federal Reserve to serve as a "banker's bank" that held a portion of bank funds in reserve to help member banks in time of crisis, set rates for business loans, and issued a new national paper currency.

Federal Trade Commission (1914) (p. 539) A federal agency with the power to order companies to cease unfair trading practices whose decisions were subject to court review.

Fifteenth Amendment (p. 421) Constitutional amendment passed by Congress in 1869 providing an explicit constitutional guarantee for black suffrage.

First Red Scare (1919–1920) (p. 634) Period when the Justice Department arrested and deported alien anarchists and Communists suspected of trying to destroy American democracy and capitalism.

Fourteenth Amendment (p. 416) Drafted by Congress in June 1866, it defined citizenship to include African Americans, guaranteed equal protection before the law, and established the federal government as the guarantor of individual civil rights.

Freedmen's Bureau (p. 408) Relief agency for the war ravaged South created by Congress in March 1865. It provided emergency services, built schools, and managed confiscated lands.

Freedom Rides (p. 819) An interstate bus journey by black and white activists who entered segregated bus facilities together throughout the South.

Freedom Summer, 1964 (p. 825) Multipronged attack on white supremacy in Mississippi that included a voter registration drive and the creation of Freedom Schools.

Frontier Thesis (p. 464) Historian Frederick Jackson Turner's 1893 theory that extolled the positive role the frontier had played in shaping the American character and consequently American institutions.

fundamentalism (p. 636) An evangelical Christian theology that viewed the Bible as an authentic recounting of historical events and the absolute moral word of God.

Geneva Accords (1954) (p. 782) Called for a temporary partition of Vietnam along the seventeenth parallel, with the Vietminh in the north and the French in the south, and a general election in two years to reunify the country under one government.

Gentleman's Agreement (1907–1908) (p. 581) Japanese agreement to deny passports to Japanese workers intending to immigrate to the United States.

Gilded Age (p. 498) The name for the period 1877–1900 that suggested the amazing achievements of the period were like a thin gold layer that covered many unresolved social problems.

Grange (p. 449) Originally founded in the fall of 1867 by Oliver H. Kelley as a social and educational society for farmers, it became a major political force in the Midwest in the mid-1870s.

Great Depression (p. 659) The most devastating and longest economic crisis in American history that lasted from 1929 to 1939.

Great Plains (p. 443) Vast open territory stretching east to west from present-day Missouri to the Rocky Mountains, and north to south from North Dakota to Texas.

Great Society (p. 816) President Johnson's wideranging social welfare reforms intended to make the amenities of modern life—a decent standard of living, education, health care, and clean water—available to all Americans.

Gulf of Tonkin Resolution (1964) (p. 787) Gave Johnson permission "to take all necessary measures to repel any armed attack against the forces of the United States and to prevent further aggression" in Vietnam.

Harlem Renaissance (p. 638) An outpouring of African American artistic expression in the 1920s and 1930s.

Haymarket Incident (p. 493) A violent incident touched off when a bomb exploded amid a group of policemen as they broke up a peaceful labor rally in Chicago's Haymarket Square on May 4, 1886.

hippies (p. 829) Youthful social rebels who renounced material acquisition and used drugs to explore their inner spiritual selves.

Ho Chi Minh Trail (p. 789) A 600-mile North Vietnamese supply route that ran along the western border of Vietnam through neighboring Laos and Cambodia.

holding company (p. 477) A huge corporation that bought and ran other corporations by purchasing their stock.

Hollywood blacklist (p. 739) A list of individuals with suspected past or present communist ties whom film studios refused to hire.

Holocaust (p. 708) German-engineered wartime extermination of Jews and other peoples that Germans considered inferior.

Homestead Act (p. 440) Passed in 1862, it provided 160 acres of free land to any settler willing to live on it and improve it for five years; promoted massive westward migration.

horizontal integration (p. 475) Business organization where one company buys many other companies producing the same product to eliminate competition and achieve greater efficiency.

Immigration Act of 1924 (p. 634) Law that allowed unrestricted immigration from the Western Hemisphere, curtailed all Asian immigration, and used quotas to control how many immigrants emigrated from individual European nations.

imperialism (p. 562) The late nineteenth-century term for colonizing foreign nations and lands, relying primarily on business, political, and military structures rather than settlers to rule colonized peoples and exploit their resources.

Industrial Workers of the World (IWW) (p. 543) This group envisioned "one big union" that welcomed all workers regardless of sex, race, ethnicity, or skill, which would one day take over all means of production in the United States.

initiative (p. 552) Provided a way, usually by gathering signatures on petitions, for the electorate to introduce legislation before state legislatures.

internment camps (p. 694) Camps in the United States that held people of Japanese descent under armed guard in isolated areas.

interventionists (p. 686) Those advocating direct engagement in overseas conflicts.

Intermediate-Range Nuclear Forces Treaty (1987) (p. 870) Approved the destruction of all U.S. and Soviet intermediate-range missiles in Europe.

Iran-Contra scandal (p. 870) A law-breaking scheme that sold arms to Iran to secure the hostages' release and used the proceeds to support anti-Communists in Nicaragua.

Iranian hostage crisis (p. 856) Defining event in Carter's presidency as Iranian revolutionaries held fifty two Americans captive for 444 days.

iron curtain (p. 722) Churchill's characterization of the military and ideological barrier erected by the Soviet Union that separated Western and Eastern Europe into free and unfree halves.

The Jazz Age (p. 642) Nickname for the twenties that reflected the popularity of jazz music.

Kellogg-Briand Pact (1928) (p. 648) Treaty that renounced aggressive war as an instrument of national policy.

Kennedy and Nixon debate (p. 761) First televised presidential election debate in 1960 watched by nearly 77 million Americans, or 60 percent of the adult population.

Knights of Labor (p. 492) A labor organization founded in 1869 that in the 1880s accepted workers of all trades and backgrounds and became the world's largest industrial union.

Korean War (1950–1953) (p. 729) The United States fought Communist North Koreans and Chinese to a stalemate, frustrating Americans who had to learn to accept only a partial victory.

Ku Klux Klan (p. 422) The best-known of the many secret white terrorist organizations that first arose in the South in 1866; they targeted freedmen and symbols of black self improvement and independence and played a key role in reestablishing white supremacy by the late 1870s.

laissez-faire (p. 471) (French for "let do" or leave alone) A philosophy that argued that the government should impose no restraints on business.

League of Nations (p. 615) An international collective security organization composed of member nations where member nations agreed to mediate future international disputes to prevent wars and work together to improve global human conditions.

Lend-Lease (p. 689) A 1941 policy that circumvented "cash and carry" by loaning rather than selling arms to the Allies.

Levittowns (p. 758) Planned suburban communities where developers standardized every part of the construction process.

Little Rock Nine (p. 771) Nine black teenagers who integrated Central High School in Little Rock, Arkansas, in 1957 and became the focus of a national crisis that required the intervention of federal troops to resolve.

***Lochner v. New York* (1905) (p. 544)** A Supreme Court ruling that unless long work hours directly jeopardized workers' health, the government could not abridge an employee's freedom to negotiate his own work schedule with his employer.

Long Drive (p. 449) The annual cattle drives of more than 1,000 miles from Texas to the Great Plains that started in 1866 and established the ranching industry in the West.

"long telegram" (p. 722) An influential five-thousand-word missive by diplomat George F. Kennan that outlined why America needed to develop an aggressive foreign policy aimed at containing Soviet expansionist impulses.

Ludlow Massacre (1914) (p. 544) Colorado state troops set a striking miners' camp ablaze, killing thirteen women and children, an act that outraged laborers throughout the nation.

***Lusitania* (p. 598)** British passenger ship sunk by a German U-boat on May 7, 1915, an attack that killed 1,198 passengers, including 128 Americans.

Manhattan Project (p. 711) Secret U.S. wartime project to develop an atomic bomb.

March on Washington, 1963 (p. 824) Massive demonstration in the nation's capital that demanded passage of a federal civil rights act and more economic opportunities.

Marshall Plan (1948–1952) (p. 724) Aimed to restore Europeans' faith in capitalism by sending $13 billion ($119 billion in today's dollars) overseas to rebuild Europe's ruined roads, bridges, factories, and farms.

McCarthyism (p. 739) The government's anticommunist crusade named for Senator Joseph McCarthy from Wisconsin, who, along with the House Committee on Un-American Activities (HUAC), spearheaded numerous governmental investigations into communist activities, many of them spurious.

Meat Inspection Act (1906) (p. 552) Law gave federal inspectors the authority to condemn meat unfit for consumption and established federal sanitary standards for meatpacking plants.

"Migrant Mother" (p. 673) Dorothea Lange's 1936 photograph of a destitute woman, which became an iconic portrait of Depression-era suffering.

military-industrial complex (p. 755) Eisenhower's term for the close ties between the defense industry and the Pentagon that might influence government policy.

Mississippi Plan (p. 426) Campaign of violence and intimidation waged by armed groups of whites closely allied with the Democratic Party that drove Republicans from power in the Mississippi state elections of 1874. Copied by other Southern states.

modernism (p. 636) A liberal Christian theology embraced in many urban areas that emphasized the ongoing revelation of divine truth.

monopoly (p. 474) The control of an industry or market by one corporation.

Montgomery Bus Boycott (1955–1956) (p. 768) A year-long bus boycott that brought a new leader,Martin Luther King Jr., and a new strategy of nonviolent protest to the forefront of the Civil Rights Movement.

Mormons (p. 445) A religious sect founded in upstate New York in 1830. Driven by persecution they headed west in 1846 and settled in a valley in Utah near the Great Salt Lake.

muckrakers (p. 533) Progressive Era term for investigative journalists who wrote exposés on government and business corruption.

mutually assured destruction (p. 852) The claim that the guarantee of a devastating nuclear counterattack would deter the United States and Soviet Union from ever employing their nuclear arsenals.

***Muller v. Oregon* (1908) (p. 546)** The Supreme Court upheld maximum hour laws for female workers because protecting women's reproductive health served the public good.

Munich Conference (1938) (p. 687) Hoping to avoid war, Britain and France agreed to let Germany occupy the Sudetenland, a German-speaking part of Czechoslovakia.

My Lai (p. 799) A Vietnamese village where American soldiers massacred five hundred civilians in 1968.

National Organization for Women (NOW) (p. 834) An organization dedicated to securing equal rights for women in employment, education, and politics.

Nation of Islam (p. 830) African American sect that rejected integration as the path to salvation for the black community and instead wanted to establish a separate black nation.

Neutrality Acts (p. 687) A series of laws from 1935 to 1939 that restricted arms sales, loans, and transport of goods with nations at war.

New Deal (p. 662) An avalanche of legislation from 1933 to 1938 intended to promote economic recovery, reform American capitalism, and offer security to ordinary Americans.

New Deal coalition (p. 680) A political partnership formed in the midthirties among liberals, trade unionists, Catholics, and Northern blacks that redrew the nation's political map.

New Frontier (p. 813) Kennedy's legislative program that proposed raising the minimum wage, reducing overcrowding in schools, and providing health care for the elderly.

New Left (p. 828) A small, but highly visible, coalition of left-leaning student-based organizations that attacked racial discrimination, poverty, and the war in Vietnam.

New Negro (p. 642) Spirit of black racial pride and militancy that set a younger generation of African American artists and civil rights leaders apart from their predecessors.

New South (p. 428) Optimistic phrase white Southerners used to describe the post-Reconstruction South, reflecting the South's development of a new system of race relations based on segregation and white supremacy and pointing to a profound economic transformation that swept across the region.

New Woman (p. 514) A phrase used to describe young women in the 1890s and early 1900s that reflected their rising levels of education, economic independence, and political and social activism.

Nineteenth Amendment (p. 605) Constitutional amendment that granted women the right to vote; it was ratified August 26, 1920.

non-interventionists (p. 686) Those urging the nation to stay out of overseas conflicts.

North Atlantic Treaty Organization (NATO) (p. 722) A post-World War II military alliance between the United States and Western European powers.

nuclear fallout (p. 734) The deadly pollution that descends through the air after a nuclear bomb explosion.

Organization of the Petroleum Exporting Countries (OPEC) (p. 844) An international consortium of oil-producing nations that regulated the price and quantity of oil exported to the world market.

Panama Canal (p. 584) A manmade waterway through Panama completed in 1914 to link the Pacific and Atlantic oceans.

Panic of 1873 (p. 424) A financial panic on Wall Street that touched off a national economic recession causing financial houses, banks, and businesses to fail. Hundreds of thousands of workers lost their jobs.

Peace Corps (p. 813) Government agency that President Kennedy established to send recent college graduates to work on humanitarian projects overseas in developing nations.

peace movement (p. 790) A loose coalition of antiwar activists that included pacifists, students, professors, clergy, hippies, civil rights activists, and middle-class liberals.

Pearl Harbor (p. 690) A U.S. naval base in Hawaii that the Japanese attacked on December 7, 1941.

People's Party (p. 518) A third party effort launched in 1890 by a coalition of farmer organizations, reformers, and labor unions and dedicated to curbing corporate power and increasing the voice of the masses in politics.

Platt Amendment (p. 572) Law linking U.S. withdrawal from Cuba to Cuban government granting the United States the right to maintain a naval base at Guantánamo Bay, to intervene militarily in Cuban domestic affairs, and to establish a privileged trading relationship with Cuba. The Cuban government also needed permission from the United States before entering into treaties with other nations.

political machines (p. 503) Powerful urban political organizations that mobilized large blocs of working-class and immigrant voters and often engaged in corrupt and illegal activity.

preservationist (p. 539) An environmentalist who championed preserving nature in its unspoiled state.

Proposition 13 (p. 865) Referendum in California that dramatically reduced property taxes, spearheading grassroots tax rebellion nationwide.

Pullman strike (p. 524) A bitter strike that began on May 11, 1894, at the Pullman Palace Car Company and soon spread nationwide, paralyzing the railroad system. President Cleveland sent in federal troops and broke the strike.

Pure Food and Drug Act (1906) (p. 552) Law levied federal fines for mislabeling food or medicine.

recall (p. 553) Used special elections to remove unpopular officials from office before their term expired.

reconcentration (p. 565) Spanish policy that herded Cuban peasants off their farms into heavily fortified cities followed by systematic destruction of the crops that fed the rebel armies.

Redeemers (p. 426) Name for white Southern political leaders who successfully returned their states to white Democratic rule in the mid-1870s. The name was intended to depict these leaders as saviors of Southern society from rule by freedmen, scalawags, and carpetbaggers.

referendum (p. 553) Put legislative proposals on the ballot, letting the voting public decide whether a measure became law.

Religious Right (p. 865) A collection of right-wing Christian groups that defended traditional values and supported conservative political causes.

robber barons (p. 476) A pejorative name for big business leaders that suggested they grew rich by devious business practices, exploitation of workers, and political manipulation.

***Roe v. Wade* (1973) (p. 861)** Supreme Court decision that legalized abortion.

Roosevelt Corollary (1904) (p. 587) Corollary to the 1823 Monroe Doctrine that announced the U.S. intention to act as an "international police power" in Latin America.

Rough Riders (p. 570) A volunteer unit of cowboys, Ivy League athletes, city police officers, and Pawnee scouts led by Theodore Roosevelt that gained fame by charging up the San Juan Heights during the Spanish-American War.

Rust Belt (p. 865) Decaying industrial cities in the Midwest, places plagued with high unemployment, crumbling roads, bankrupt governments, and high welfare rolls.

SALT I (1972) (p. 852) The first treaty between the Soviet Union and the United States that limited the deployment of intercontinental and submarine-launched ballistic missiles and the creation of missile-defense systems.

Sand Creek Massacre (p. 454) A massacre of some two hundred Cheyenne Indians on November 29, 1864, in Colorado by a military outfit known as the Colorado Volunteers under Colonel John M. Chivington.

scalawag (p. 418) White Southerners' derogatory term for fellow whites considered traitors to their region and race for joining the Republican Party and cooperating with Reconstruction policy.

The Schlieffen Plan (p. 596) A military plan that called for Germany to attack and quickly defeat France while the cumbersome Russian army mobilized.

scientific management (p. 543) The effort to use scientific knowledge to secure maximum output and profit.

Second Red Scare (p. 737) Widespread effort to root out Communist spies after World War II that lasted for nearly a decade.

Sedition Act (1918) (p. 606) Legislation that went even further than the Espionage Act by prohibiting anyone from uttering, writing, or publishing "any abusive or disloyal language" concerning the flag, constitution, government, or armed forces.

self-determination (p. 601) Giving people a voice in selecting their own government.

settlement houses (p. 510) Institutions established in cities beginning in the 1880s and dedicated to helping the poor by providing a wide range of social and educational services.

Seventeenth Amendment (1913) (p. 553) A constitutional amendment that allowed voters, rather than state legislatures, to elect federal senators.

share our wealth (p. 674) Louisiana Senator Huey Long's plan to redistribute money from the rich to the poor.

Sherman Anti-Trust Act (p. 477) Authorized the Justice Department to prosecute any illegal contract, combination, or conspiracy among corporations that eliminated competition or restrained free trade.

silent majority (p. 801) Nixon's term for the large number of Americans who supported the war quietly in the privacy of their homes.

sit-down strike (p. 679) Workers occupy a factory to paralyze production lines and prevent strikebreakers or management from entering the building.

sit-ins (p. 772) Nonviolent demonstrations where civil rights protesters employed the tactic of civil disobedience to occupy seats at whites-only lunch counters.

Sixteenth Amendment (1913) (p. 538) The constitutional amendment authorizing federal income taxes.

social Darwinism (p. 490) The belief that the principles of evolution, which Darwin had observed in nature, also applied to society. Advocates argued that individuals or groups achieve advantage over others as the result of biological superiority, an idea expressed as "survival of the fittest."

Social Gospel (p. 534) The religious belief that Christians had a responsibility to create an ethically sound and morally upright society.

socialism (p. 486) A theory that rejected capitalism and advocated common ownership of property and social and economic equality.

Southeast Asian Treaty Organization (SEATO) (p. 783) 1954 alliance among the United States, Britain, France, Australia, New Zealand, Thailand, the Philippines, and Pakistan who pledged to "meet common danger" in Southeast Asia together.

Southern Christian Leadership Conference (SCLC) (p. 770) Civil rights organization founded by Martin Luther King Jr. that used black churches to devise a new nonviolent strategy of direct action.

Spanish Influenza (p. 614) A lethal flu virus that killed millions worldwide.

sphere of influence (p. 579) The term used to describe the exclusive political and trading rights that a foreign nation enjoyed within another nation's territory.

***Spirit of St. Louis* (p. 630)** The plane that Charles Lindbergh piloted on the first-ever nonstop solo flight from New York to Paris on May 21, 1927.

stock market crash of 1929 (p. 657) A ten-day period beginning on October 20, 1929, when the value of stocks plummeted as panicked investors sold off their stock in droves. This moment is usually considered the official start of the Depression.

Strategic Defense Initiative (SDI) (p. 869) Reagan's proposal to build a missile shield that used lasers from space satellites to destroy incoming missiles.

Student Nonviolent Coordinating Committee (SNCC) (p. 775) Student-run civil rights organization founded in 1960.

Stonewall riot (p. 862) A 1969 battle between patrons of a Greenwich Village male gay bar and police that became the catalyst for the gay rights movement.

suburbs (p. 512) Middle- and upper-class residential communities established just beyond a city's boundary but connected to the urban center by mass transit.

supply-side economics (p. 867) Reagan administration theory that letting entrepreneurs keep more of their profits would fuel economic growth, job creation, and more tax revenue to offset military spending.

Taft-Hartley Act (1947) (p. 753) Law that abolished the closed shop, banned so-called sympathy boycotts, and required that all union officers sign affidavits certifying that they were not members of the Communist Party.

Teller Amendment (p. 568) Congressional promise "to leave the government and control of the [Cuban] Island to its people" at the end of the Spanish-American War.

Ten Percent Plan (p. 408) Pardoned all Southerners (except high-ranking military officers and Confederate officials) who took an oath pledging loyalty to the Union and support for emancipation. As soon as ten percent of a state's voters took this oath, they could call a convention, establish a new state government, and apply for congressional recognition.

tenements (p. 502) Multiple family dwellings of four to six stories housing dozens of families that became the most common form of housing for poor city dwellers by the 1860s.

Tet Offensive (1968) (p. 792) A massive, coordinated Communist assault against more than a hundred cities and towns in South Vietnam.

"the white man's burden" (p. 575) The Anglo-Saxon quest to better the lives of so-called racially inferior peoples by spreading Western economic, cultural, and spiritual values and institutions.

transcontinental railroad (p. 441) A line spanning the continental United States. Congress helped the Union Pacific and Central Pacific railroads build it by providing land grants, cash incentives, and loans..

trans-Mississippi West (p. 440) The region of the United States west of the Mississippi River.

Treaty of Paris (1898) (p. 571) Agreement that ended the Spanish-American War with Spain relinquishing its claim to Cuba and the United States receiving Puerto Rico, some smaller Caribbean islands, and the Pacific island group of Guam. In return for $20 million, Spain turned the Philippines over to the United States.

Truman Doctrine (p. 724) A foreign policy initiative that gave the United States an active role in stopping the global spread of communism by supporting "free peoples who are resisting attempted subjugation by armed minorities or by outside pressures."

trust (p. 476) A legally binding deal bringing many companies in the same industry under the direction of a board of "trustees."

trust-busting (p. 536) Governmental action to dissolve monopolies.

Twenty-First Amendment (1933) (p. 633) Constitutional amendment that repealed the Eighteenth Amendment.

U-boat (p. 598) German submarine, a new weapon that launched surprise torpedo attacks against Allied merchant and naval ships.

Universal Negro Improvement Association (UNIA) (p. 640) Organization founded by Marcus Garvey to spread his message of racial pride, economic self-sufficiency, and returning to Africa.

Versailles Peace Treaty (p. 615) The controversial treaty that required Germany to pay reparations and disarm.

vertical integration (p. 475) Business organization where one company controls the main phases of production of a good, from acquiring raw materials to retailing the finished product.

Vietcong (p. 783) Slang term for South Vietnamese communists.

Vietminh (p. 780) The term initially used to describe all Vietnamese communists, and used after 1954 solely for North Vietnamese communists.

Vietnamization (p. 801) A Nixon administration policy that turned the bulk of the ground fighting over to the South Vietnamese Army.

Volstead Act (1919) (p. 633) Law that established criminal penalties for manufacturing, transporting, or possessing alcohol.

Voting Rights Act of 1965 (p. 826) Legislation that prohibited literacy tests and poll taxes, plus authorized the use of federal registrars to register voters if states failed to respect the Fifteenth Amendment.

Wade-Davis Bill (p. 408) A Reconstruction program designed to punish Confederate leaders and permanently destroy the South's slave society.

war bonds (p. 606) Short-term loans that individual citizens made to the government that financed two-thirds of the war's costs.

Warren Court (p. 813) Supreme Court that brought about a legal revolution in the United States by permanently altering American schools, politics, the criminal justice system, and cultural norms.

Washington Conference (1921–1922) (p. 647) Meeting of world powers that resulted in agreements that limited naval arms, reaffirmed America's Open Door policy that kept Chinese trade open to all, and secured pledges of cooperation among the world's leading military powers.

Watergate scandal (1972) (p. 806) A botched Republican-engineered break-in of the Democratic National Committee headquarters in Washington, D.C. that eventually forced Nixon to resign in 1974.

welfare capitalism (p. 541) The notion of using benefits to gain workers' loyalty, improve worker morale, and weaken interest in unions.

Western Front (p. 596) Complex system of trenches and earthworks that ran for 550 miles from the North Sea to Switzerland that pitted Germany against Belgium, France, Britain, and the United States.

women's suffrage (p. 513) The effort to obtain voting rights for women that eventually gained passage of the Nineteenth Amendment (1920).

Wounded Knee Massacre (p. 461) U.S. soldiers open fire on a group of Sioux Indians on December 29, 1890, killing between two hundred and three hundred.

yellow press (p. 565) Tabloid journalists and newspapers that reported sensationalist stories with a strong emotional component.

Zimmermann Telegram (p. 600) German foreign minister Arthur Zimmermann offered to help Mexico recover Texas, New Mexico, and Arizona if Mexico would start a borderland war with the United States and ask Japan to join them.

zoot-suiters (p. 700) Name given to Mexican American youths who wore oversize suits.

Credits

Page abbreviations are as follows: **T** *top,* **C** *center,* **B** *bottom,* **L** *left,* **R** *right.*

CHAPTER 14

405 National Museum of American Art, Smithsonian Institution/Art Resource, N.Y. **14.1** Collection of The New-York Historical Society, [37628] **14.2** The Granger Collection, New York **14.3T&B** Chicago History Museum **14.4** The Granger Collection, New York **14.5** Courtesy of the Library of Congress **14.6** The Granger Collection, New York **14.7** Picture History **414** The Granger Collection, New York **14.8** The Granger Collection, New York **14.9** The Granger Collection, New York **14.10** Used with Permission of Documenting the American South, The University of North Carolina at Chapel Hill Libraries **14.11** Corbis/Bettmann **14.12** David J. and Janice L. Frent **14.14** Frank Leslie's Illustrated Newspaper, October 7, 1871/The Granger Collection, New York **425T** Harper's, Aug. 5, 1865/Courtesy of the Library of Congress **425BL** Harper's Sept. 5, 1868/Courtesy of the Library of Congress **425BR** The Granger Collection, New York **4.16** The Granger Collection, New York **14.19L** Keene **14.19R** Lee Monument Unveiling Ribbon Accession #TBMR 277-1 (2). The Museum of the Confederacy **14.20** Lauren Rogers Museum of Art **14.21** Brown Brothers **14.23** Courtesy of the Library of Congress **434** The Granger Collection, New York **14.24** Charles Blankenship, descendant of H. R. Nicks

CHAPTER 15

439 © Christie's Images Inc. 2004 **15.1L** Courtesy of the Library of Congress **15.1R** U.S. National Archives and Records Administration **15.2** The Granger Collection, New York **15.4** George Catlin (1796–1872) "Buffalo Chase Over Prairie Bluffs". 1832–33. Smithsonian American Art Museum, Washington, DC/Art Resource, NY **15.5** The Granger Collection, New York **15.6** The Burndy Library, Dibner Institute for the History of Science and Technology, Cambridge, Massachusetts **15.8** © Nebraska State Historical Society Photograph Collections **15.9** The Granger Collection, New York. **15.10** George Ranch Historical Park **15.11** Minnesota Historical Society **452** Albert Bierstadt (1830–1902), "Among the Sierra Nevada Mountains, California", 1868. Oil on Canvas, 71 × 120" (183 × 305 cm). Smithsonian American Art Museum, Washington DC. Copyright © Smithsonian American Art Museum, Washington DC/Art Resource, NY. **15.12** Courtesy of the Library of Congress **15.13** Getty Images Inc.—Hulton Archive Photos **15.14** "Courtesy of the Burton Historical Collection, Detroit Public Library" **15.15** Collection of Sandy Bernard, Wake Forest, NC/AST Press **15.16** The Granger Collection, New York **459T&B** Bureau of Indian Affairs/U.S. Department of the Interior **15.17** Getty Images **15.19** © Nebraska State Historical Society Photograph Collections **463** Getty Images Inc.—Hulton Archive Photos **15.20** Montana Historical Society, Helena **15.21** Colleen Cutschall, "Spirit Warriors". bronze sculpture, 34 ft. × 14 ft. in an arc. Little Bighorn Battlefield Natioal Monument, Montana. Brandon University, Canada

CHAPTER 16

469 Robert Koehler (1850–1917), "The Strike" 1886. Oil on canvas. Deutsches Historisches Museum, Berlin, Germany/The Bridgeman Art Library, NY. **16.2L** AP Wide World Photos **16.2R** Lynn Historical Society **16.3** Provided courtesy HarpWeek., LLC **16.4** Manning's Books, Prints Old & Rare **16.5** Courtesy of The Bancroft Library. University of California, Berkeley. **16.7** The Granger Collection, New York **16.8** Getty Images Inc.—Hulton Archive Photos **480** Reproduced from "The Century Magazine", November, 1887 in The History and Development of Advertising by Frank Presbrey, Doubleday, Dowan & Company, Inc. 1929 **481** Courtesy of David Briggs; briggsdavi@gmail.com **16.9** National Museum of American History/Smithsonian Institution **16.10** Courtesy of George Eastman House **16.11** Special Collections & Archives **16.12** The Granger Collection, New York **16.13** Courtesy of The Bancroft Library. University of California, Berkeley. **487** Special Collections & Archives **16.15** Courtesy of the Clara Barton National Historic Site, CLBA #659 **16.16T&B** Reproduced from the original held by the Department of Special Collections of the University Libraries of Notre Dame, Photo by Cornell Engraving Company, Lincoln, Neb., Fisher & Lawrie, Architects, Omaha, Neb. **16.17** Courtesy of Center for Southwest Research, University Libraries, University of New Mexico, Seder Dime Novel Collection, MSS 312 BC, Box 3, Folder 63 **16.18** John Hay Library, Brown University **16.19** The Granger Collection, New York **16.20** Courtesy of the Library of Congress **494** Bryan Mawr College Library

CHAPTER 17

499 Collection of the New York Historical Society **17.2** Edward T. O'Donnell **17.3** Chicago Historical Museum **17.4** Culver Pictures, Inc. **17.5** The Granger Collection, New York **505** The Granger Collection, New York **17.6** Ohio State University Cartoon Research Library **17.7** Courtesy of the Library of Congress **509T** Filippo Lippi, "Madonna and Child," 1440/1445. Tempera on panel, .797 × .511 (31⅜ × 20⅛); framed: 1.172 × .854 × .095 (46⅛ × 33⅝ × 3¾). Samuel H. Kress Collection, Photograph © 2001 Board of Trustees, National Gallery of Art, Washington. 1939.1.290(401)/PA **590B** Jacob A. Riis "Italian Mother and Her Baby in Jersey Street", in the home of an Italian rag-picker, Jersey Street, circa 1890. Museum of the City of New York, The Jacob A. Riis Collection (#157) **17.8** © Bettmann/CORBIS **17.9** The Granger Collection, New York **17.10** National Archives and Records Administration **17.11** The Granger Collection, New York **17.12** Courtesy of the Library of Congress **17.13** Collection of the New-York Historical Society, Box 1.f 10. Negative no. 80433d **17.15** The Granger Collection, New York **17.16** The Granger Collection, New York **17.17** From "The River Ran Red, Homestead 1892" by David P. Demarest Jr. Editor, University of Pittsburg Press, with image credited to Marge Rybar. **17.18** The Ohio Historical Society **17.19** Chicago Historical Museum **525** Library of Congress **17.20** The Granger Collection

CHAPTER 18

531 Victor Joseph Gatto (1893–1965), "Triangle Fire: March 25, 1911". c. 1944 [depicting 1911], oil on canvas, 19 × 28", Gift of Mrs. Henry L. Moses, 54.75. The Museum of the City of New York **18.2** Brown Brothers **18.3** Courtesy of the Library of Congress **18.5** Corbis/Bettmann **18.6** Courtesy of the Library of Congress **18.7** From the Collection of the Henry Ford, THF23871 **18.8** Courtesy of the Library of Congress **545** Joseph Lochner/National Geographic Image Collection **18.9L** Kansas State Historical Society **18.9R** Corbis/Bettmann **18.11** Widener Library **550** Lewis Wickes Hines/Courtesy of the Library of Congress **551T** Lewis Wickes Hines/Courtesy of the Library of Congress **551B** Courtesy of the Library of Congress **18.12L** Baker Library Historical Collections, Harvard Business School **18.12R** Baker Library Historical Collections, Harvard Business School **556** © Bettmann/CORBIS All Rights Reserved **18.13** Francis Johnson/Courtesy of the Library of Congress

CHAPTER 19

566 ICHIi-08428; Destruction of the battleship Maine in Havana harbor; in the Spanish-American War; Havana (Cuba) 1898 Feb. 15; Creator-Kurtz & Allison/Chicago Historical Society **566T** Frederic Remington Museum **566B** Courtesy of the Library of Congress **19.3** The Granger Collection, New York **19.4** Courtesy of Andy Moursund **19.5** © CORBIS All Rights Reserved **19.6** Provided courtesy HarpWeek., LLC **19.7** Widener Library, Harvard College Library, Harvard Depository **19.8** CORBIS-NY **19.9** Do You Graphics for "The National Archives" **19.11** © Bettmann/CORBIS **583** Science Museum/SSPL/The Image Works **19.12** Map of the Panama Canal from the Atlantic to the Pacific Ocean, 1913 (litho), American School, (20th century)/Private Collection/Peter Newark American Pictures/The Bridgeman Art Library International **19.13** Corbis/Bettmann **19.14** The Granger Collection, New York.

CHAPTER 20

593 Courtesy of the Library of Congress **20.4** Keene **20.5** Brown Brothers **20.6L** © CORBIS All Rights Reserved **20.6R** Cornell University, Carl A. Kroch Library, Division of Rare and Manuscript Collections **20.7** Courtesy of the Library of Congress **20.8** Jacob Lawrence born in Atlantic City, New Jersey, 1917, "The Migration of the Negro" 1940–41. Panel no. 1 "During the World War there was a great migration North by Southern Negroes." Tempera on masonite 12 × 18" (30.5 × 45.7 cm). Acquired through Downtown Gallery, 1942. In series of 60. [Odd numbers at Phillips]. E © 2010 The Jacob and Gwendolyn Lawrence Foundation, Seattle /Artists Rights Society (ARS), New York. **20.9** © Bettmann/CORBIS All Rights Reserved **607L** Poster Collection, Hoover Institution Archives **607R** Courtesy of the Library of Congress **20.10** From "World War I: A History in Documents" by Frans Coetzee and Marilyn Shevin-Coetzee, Oxford University Press. 2002 **610** © Bettmann/CORBIS All Rights Reserved **20.11L&R** Courtesy of the Library of Congress **20.14** © Bettmann/CORBIS All Rights Reserved **20.15** © CORBIS All Rights Reserved **619** © Bettmann/CORBIS All Rights Reserved **20.16** Property of the Westervelt Company and displayed in The Westervelt-Warner Museum of American Art in Tuscaloosa, AL.

CHAPTER 21

625 © Underwood & Underwood/CORBIS All Rights Reserved **21.1** The Center for American History, The University of Texas, No. 3_bb_4311 **21.2** © Terry Donnelly **21.4** Paramount/The Kobal Collection/The Picture-Desk **21.5** © Underwood & Underwood/CORBIS All Rights Reserved **21.6** Courtesy of the Library of Congress **21.8** © Bettmann/CORBIS All Rights Reserved **21.9** © Bettmann/CORBIS All Rights Reserved **21.10** © Bettmann/CORBIS All Rights Reserved **21.11** © Bettmann/CORBIS All Rights Reserved **641** © David J. & Janice L. Frent Collection/CORBIS All Rights Reserved **642T** Corbis/Bettmann **642B** Corbis/Bettmann **643** Janet Sommer/Getty Images Inc.—Hulton Archive Photos **21.12** Used with Permission of Documenting the American South, The University of North Carolina at Chapel Hill Libraries. **645** Courtesy of the Library of Congress **21.13** © Bettmann/CORBIS All Rights Reserved **21.14** Courtesy of the Library of Congress **649** Courtesy of the Library of Congress

CHAPTER 22

655 Courtesy of the Library of Congress **22.1L** James N. Rosenberg, American, (b. 1874). Oct 29 Dies Irae, 1929, Lithograph. Philadelphia Museum of Art, Lola Downin Peck Fund. **22.1R** © Bettmann/CORBIS All Rights Reserved **661** Picture History **22.4** Franklin D. Roosevelt Library **22.5** Franklin D. Roosevelt Library **22.6** © Bettmann/CORBIS All Rights Reserved **22.7** Reproduced with permission of The Kansas City Star © Copyright 2007 The Kansas City Star. All rights reserved. Format differs from original publication. Not an endorsement. **22.8** NARA/Getty Images **22.10** Marci Penner/Kansas Sampler Foundation **22.11** Hulton Images/Getty Images **22.12** Courtesy of the Library of Congress (LC-USF34-018191-E). Dorothea Lange **673T&B** Courtesy of the Library of Congress **675** Prentice Hall School **22.13** Courtesy of the Library of Congress **22.14** Courtesy of the Library of Congress **22.15** © UPI/CORBIS All Rights Reserved **22.16** Time & Life Pictures/Getty Images

CHAPTER 23

685 National Archives and Records Administration **23.3** National Archives and Records Administration **23.4** Mandeville Special Collections Library **23.5** U.S. Naval Historical Center, Collection of Fleet Admiral Chester W. Nimitz **23.6** Courtesy of the Library of Congress **23.7** TIME Life Magazine/Courtesy of the Library of Congress **23.8T** Courtesy of CSUN Oviatt Library, Special Collections & Archives **23.8B** Courtesy of the Library of Congress **23.9** Franklin D. Roosevelt Library **23.10** National Archives and Records Administration **696** Courtesy of the Library of Congress **23.11** Adel Precision Instruments **23.12L** Franklin D. Roosevelt Library **23.12R** The National Archives, Records of the Office of War Information. Do You Graphics **23.13** Horace Pippin (1888–1946), "Mr. Prejudice," 1943. Oil on canvas, 18 × 14 inches. Philadelphia Museum of Art, Gift of Dr. and Mrs. Matthew T. Moore. Photo by Graydon Wood. 1984-108-1 **23.16** National Archives and Records Administration **23.17** Ralph Crane/Time & Life Pictures /Getty Images/Time Life Pictures **706T** George Strock/Time & Life Pictures/Getty Images/Time Life Pictures **706B** National Archives and Records Administration **23.18** Robert Capa/Cornell Capa Photos/Magnum Photos, Inc. **23.19** National Archives and Records Administration **713** National Archives and Records Administration **23.21** Alfred Eisenstaedt/Stringer/Getty Images, Inc.

CHAPTER 24

719 © Bettmann/CORBIS All Rights Reserved **24.1** © Yevgeny Khaldel/CORBIS All Rights Reserved **24.3** The Granger Collection, New York **24.4** University College London **24.6** © Bettmann/CORBIS All Rights Reserved **24.7** W. Eugene Smith/Getty Images **24.9** © Sfc. Al Change/CORBIS All Rights Reserved **24.10** © Bettmann/CORBIS All Rights Reserved **24.11** Photofest **735T** © CORBIS All Rights Reserved **735Ba-b, d-e** © CORBIS All Rights Reserved **735Bc** Getty Images **24.12** MPI/Stringer/Hulton Archives/Getty Images **24.13** Elliot Erwitt/Magnum Photos, Inc. **740** © Bettmann/CORBIS All Rights Reserved **24.14** © Dorling Kindersley **24.16** John Waterman/Stringer/Hulton Archive/Getty Images **24.17** Keystone/Stringer/Hulton Archives/Getty Images **746** © CORBIS All Rights Reserved

CHAPTER 25

751 © Bettmann/CORBIS All Rights Reserved **25.1** © Bettmann/CORBIS All Rights Reserved **25.2** Courtesy of the Library of Congress **25.3&25.4** Dean Loomis/Time Life Magazine/Getty Images **759** © Bettmann/CORBIS All Rights Reserved **25.5** © Bettmann/CORBIS All Rights Reserved **25.6** Cecil Stoughton, White House/John Fitzgerald Kennedy Library, Boston **25.7** Hulton Archives/Getty Images **25.8** Mark Rothco(1903–1970), "Number 10". 1950. Oil on canvas. 7' 6⅜" × 57⅛". Gift of Philip Johnson. (38.1952) Location:The Museum of Modern Art, New York, NY, U.S.A. Digital Image © The Museum of Modern Art/Licensed by SCALA/Art Resource, NY. Estate of Mark Rothco © 2010 Artists Rights Society (ARS), NY **25.9** Bruce Davidson/Magnum Photos, Inc **25.10** Courtesy of the Library of Congress **767T** The Chicago Defender **767B** © Bettmann/CORBIS All Rights Reserved **769** AP Wide World Photos **25.11** Ernest C. Withers/Panopticon Gallery **25.12** © Jack Moebes/CORBIS All Rights Reserved **25.13** Fred Blackwell Photography/Wisconsin Historical Society

CHAPTER 26

779 Washington Post Writers Group **26.1** © Bettmann/CORBIS All Rights Reserved **26.2** Courtesy of the Library of Congress **26.3** Malcolm Browne/AP Wide World Photos **26.4** Lyndon Baines Johnson Library Collection **26.5** Kathy Hayes Associates **788** © Yoichi Okamoto/CORBIS All Rights Reserved **26.6** Trong Thanh/Doug Niven **26.7** Larry Burrows/ Time Life Pictures/Getty Images **26.9** Universal Press Syndicate **794** Eddie Adams/AP Wide World Photos **795** Larry Burrows/Getty Images **26.11** Courtesy of the Library of Congress **26.13** Ronald S. Haeberle/Time & Life Pictures/Getty Images **800** Time & Life Pictures/Getty Images **26.14** Howard Ruffner/Time & Life Pictures/Getty Images **26.15** © Hubert Van Es/CORBIS All Rights Reserved

CHAPTER 27

811 Santi Visalli, Inc/Contributor/Hulton Archives/Getty Images **27.1** Hank Walker/Getty Images **815** © Bettmann/CORBIS All Rights Reserved **27.3** Democratic National Committee **27.6** UPI/Corbis/Bettmann **822** Charles Moore/Black Star **823** Charles Moore/Black Star **27.7** © Bettmann/CORBIS All Rights Reserved **27.8** MPI/Hulton Archive/Getty Images **27.9** Tamio Wakayama **27.10** Courtesy of James Karales **27.11** Robert Altman Photography **27.12** Bob Gomel/Getty Images **27.13** Courtesy of the Library of Congress **833** © David J. & Janice L. Frent Collection/CORBIS **27.14** AP Wide World Photos **27.15** Steve Schapiro/Steve Schapiro **27.16** A 1967 Herblock Cartoon, copyright by "The Herb Block Foundation **27.17** NASA/Phototake NYC **27.18** Walter P. Reuther Library/ Wayne State University

CHAPTER 28

843 © H. Armstrong Roberts/ClassicStock/CORBIS All Rights Reserved **28.3** Stanley J. Forman/Stanley Forman **850T** A 1974 Herblock Cartoon, copyright by "The Herb Block Foundation" **850B** Paul Conrad/© Tribune Media Services, Inc. **28.4** Tribune Media Services, Inc. All Rights Reserved. Reprinted with permission. **28.5** Keene **28.6** Keene **857** From The New York Times 1981 © 2010 The New York Times. All Rights Reserved **28.8** Edward Kienholz, "The Illegal Operation". 1962. Sculptural installation of shopping cart, wooden stool, concrete, pots, blanket, hooked rug, medical equipment, polyester resin, pigment, etc. Dimensions: 59 × 48 × 54 in. Los Angeles County Museum of Art. Photograph © 2009 Museum associates/LACMA **860L** Corbis/Bettmann **860R** AP Wide World Photos **29.9** © Bettmann/CORBIS All Rights Reserved **28.10** Value RF/© Hirsham Ibrahim/Corbis Royalty Free **28.11** John Sotomayor/Redux/The New York Times **28.12** © W. Cody/CORBIS All Rights Reserved **28.13** Cindy Elgrably/Cindy Elgrably **28.14** AP Wide World Photos **28.16** The Herb Block Foundation/Courtesy of the Library of Congress

CHAPTER 29

875 Robert Clark/Aurora Photos, Inc. **29.1** Michael Samojeden/AP Wide World Photos **878T** © Reuters/CORBIS **878B** OLIPHANT © Universal Press Syndicate **29.2** Jeff Widener/AP Wide World Photos **29.3** CNN via Getty Images **29.5** Used by permission of Pelican Publishing Company, Inc. **29.6** © Najlah Feanny/CORBIS All Rights Reserved **29.7** Robert King/Getty Images, Inc. **29.10** © 2003 Brian Fairrington and PoliticalCartoons.com **29.12** © Andrew Holbrooke/CORBIS All Rights Reserved **29.13** Paul Watson/Toronto Star **29.14** Susan Meiselas/Magnum Photos, Inc. **29.15** Clay Bennett/© 2001 The Christian Scienc Monitor (www. CSMonitor. com) **899** The Permissions Group, Inc./ Ohman/TMS Reprints **29.16** USA Today **29.17** Courtesy of Anne Savage **29.18** From The New York Times Nov. 5, 2008 © 2010 The New York Times. All Rights Reserved. The New York Times/PARS International

Index

A

Abernathy, Ralph, 770
Abortion, 646
  controversy, 861
  demand for access to, 834
  Reagan and issue of, 859, 861
Abstract Expressionism, 764
Abu Ghraib prison, 900–901
Acheson, Dean, 724, 730, 732, 782
Ackerman, Amos T., 422
Acquired Immune Deficiency Syndrome (AIDS), 863
Adams, Henry, 444
Addams, Jane, 510, 534, 549, 554, 555
The Adventures of Huckleberry Finn (Twain), 462
The Adventures of Tom Sawyer (Twain), 462
Advertising, 480–481
  development of, 478
  images, *480*, *481*
  targeting female consumers, 644, *645*
Affirmative action programs, 834
Afghanistan
  al-Qaeda training bases in, 895
  attacked by United States, 896
  Soviet invasion of, 855, 856, 857
  withdrawal of Soviet forces from, 871
African American(s)
  civil rights of, and federal government, 699, 750
  colleges for, 411
  elected first U.S. president, 902
  freedom of movement for, 409
  invited to White House, 663
  leaders during Progressive Era, 554–555
  New Deal for, 679–680
  northward migration of, 500, *603*, 603–604, 621
  and Philippine-American War, 577–578
  serving during World War I, 609, 611
  in Vietnam War, 797
  women in paid workforce, 488
  workers, fears connected to, 486
  in World War II, 700
Agent Orange, 790
Agnew, Spiro, resignation of, 806, 851
Agricultural Adjustment Act (AAA) of 1933, 670
Agriculture. *See also* Farmers
  Dust Bowl's effect on, 670–671
  looming crisis in, 657
  spread of railroads and, 447
Aguinaldo, Emilio, 568, 577, 578
AIDS Coalition to Unleash Power (ACT-UP), 863
Alaska, 574
Alcatraz Proclamation, 839, 841
Alcohol, 632
Alger, Horatio, 490, 508
Ali, Muhammad, 830, *831*
Allende, Salvador, 851
Allies (World War I), 594, 717
  conflicting views among, on war's purpose, 601
  disproportionate U.S. aid to, 597
  money loaned to, 648, 650
  need for cash of, 596
  territorial ambitions of, 601
  U-boat attacks on ships of, 598
Allies (World War II), 688
  incendiary attacks of, 704
  Nuremberg War Crimes Trials held by, 710
  U.S. materiel sent to, 690
  war crimes trials for Japan held by, 714
al-Qaeda, 855, 874, 896
  fatwa of, 895
Altgeld, Richard, 524
Altman, Robert, 829
Amador, Manuel Guerrero, 584
Amazon.com, 889
America
  changes in family structure in, *889*, 889–890
  creation of empire for, 573–578
  and Holocaust, *709*
  impulse for expansion of, 562–563
  middle-class, 756–759
  response to Holocaust of, 708, 710
American Civil Liberties Union (ACLU), 635, 636
American Expeditionary Forces, *612*, 612
American Federation of Labor (AFL), 543, 603, 678, 683, 753
  goals of, 495
American Progress (Gast), *438–439*
American Protective Association (APA), 506
American Psychiatric Association, 862
American Railway Union (ARU), 524
Americans with Disabilities Act, 880
American Union Against Militarism, 598
Ames, Adelbert, 426
Amnesty Act., 423
Among the Sierra Nevada Mountains (Bierstadt), 452
Anarchists, 522–523, 634–635
Anderson, Archer, 429
Anderson, Sherwood, 632
Angel Island, 581–582
Anson, Adrian "Cap," 515
Anthony, Susan B., 421
Anti-Ballistic Missile (ABM) Treaty, 852
Anti-imperialists, 573, 574–575, 579, 589
Anti-Saloon League, 547, 632
Anti-Semitism, 686, 708, 709
Antitrust laws, 536, 539. *See also* Trusts
  suspension of, 667
Antiwar movement, 778, 796–798
  poster, 797
Appeasement, 687
Apple Computers, 847, 888
Arabic (British passenger ship), 598
Arabic Pledge, 598
Arango, Clemencia, 566
Arctic National Wildlife Refuge, 893
Arlington National Cemetery, 647
Armistice Day, 614, 615
Armour, Philip, 476
Armstrong, Louis, 642
Armstrong, Neil, 836
Army-McCarthy hearings, 741
Arnaz, Desi, 760
Asia
  banning of immigration from, 582
  Cold War spreads to, 781
  communism in, 781
Assembly lines, 541
"Atlanta Exposition" (Washington), 556
Atomic bomb(s)
  controversies continuing over, 713
  propaganda and, 734
  Soviet Union testing of, 729, 730
  U.S. stockpiling of, 729
  U.S. use of, 711–712, 713
Audubon Society, 864
Auschwitz, 708
Auto industry, 846
Axis, 688, 717

B

Babcock, Orville E., 423
Baby boom generation, 758
  comes of age, 828
Baker, Ella, 775
Baker, Howard, 849
Baker, James, 882
Baker, Ray Stannard, 536
Bakker, Jim, 866
Bakker, Tammy, 866
Baldwin, Roger, 635
Balkans, control of, 594
Ball, Lucille, 760
Banking
  deregulation, 887, 901
  institutions, revamping, 666
  system, reform of U.S., 539
Baseball, 515
Bataan Death March, 693
Bates, Daisy, 771, 772
Batista, Fulgencio, 745
Bay of Pigs operation, 745
Beals, Melba Pattillo, 772
The Beatles, 829
Beatniks, 763–764
Beats, 763–764, 777
  televised depiction of, 764
Begin, Menachem, 856
Belknap, William W., 423
Bell, Alexander Graham, 471
Bellamy, Edward, 491–492
Bennett, Clay, 897
Berkman, Alexander, 522–523
Berle, Adolf, 662
Berlin airlift, 726–727, *727*
Berlin, Irving, 516
Berlin Wall, 743–745, *744*, 784
  fall of, 878
Bernstein, Carl, 849
Berry, Chuck, 762
Bessemer-Kelly process, 475
Bevel, Jim, 773, 821
Bierstadt, Albert, 452
Big business
  domination of economy, 532
  emergence of, 470–477
  liberty suffocated by, *519*
  political influence of, 477
  power of, 476
  radio and, 630
  railroads as, 472
  resurgent power of, 602
  Rockefeller's contribution to rise of, 476
  tariffs and, 519
  Truman's campaign assault on, 754
  unchecked power of, 522
Bill Haley and the Comets, 762
bin Laden, Osama, 855, 895
  Afghanistan refuses to turn over, 896
Birmingham campaign, 821, *822*, *823*
  press and success of, 822
Birth control, 646
"The Bitter Cry of the Poor in New York" (Lowell), 505
Black Codes, 413, 414, 415
  in action, *415*
Black Friday, 423
Black, Hugo, 696, 815
Blacklists, 485, 541, 628
  Hollywood, 739

Blackouts, 694
Black Panthers, 832
Black Power, 832, 841
defining, 833
Black Star Line, 640
Black Thursday, 658
Black Tuesday, 658
Blitzkrieg (lightning war), 688
Blockade
around Central Powers, 597
Berlin, 726. *See also* Berlin airlift
during Cuban Missile Crisis, 745–747
Germany combats, 598
Block, Herb, 850, 870
Bloody Sunday, 827
Bolsheviks, 634
Bond, Julian, 767
Bonus March, 660, 683
Hoover's reaction to, 661
Boone, Daniel, 453
Bootlegging, 633
Borah, William, 615
Borjas, George J., 891
Born-again Christians, 866
Boston, Bernie, 778
Bourke-White, Margaret, 680
Boxer Rebellion, 580
Boycotts, 493, 546, 555, 768
sympathy, 753
Bradford, Susan, 404, 409
Bradley Martin Ball, 517
revulsion expressed over, 518
Brady, James, 867
Brain Trust, 662
Brandeis, Louis, 546
Brandenburg Gate, 744, *744*
Brand loyalty, 478
Brando, Marlon, 739, 762
Braun, Carol Mosley, 880
Brest-Litovsk, Treaty of, 601
Briand, Aristide, 649
Bribery, 519
Brinkmanship, 747
Britain
withdraws aid to Greece and Turkey, 724
in World War I, 596
in World War II, 688
Britain, Battle of, 688, 704
Brooklyn Bridge, 498
opening of, *499*
Brotherhood of Sleeping Car Porters, 824
Brown Berets, 838
Brown, Linda, 766
Brown, Minnijean, 772
Brown v. Board of Education of Topeka, 434, 766, 813, 847
Browne, Malcolm, 784
Bruce, Edward, 669
Brussels Pact, 728
Bryan, Hazel, 750, *751*
Bryan, William Jennings, *526*, 537, 572
anti-imperialism of, 573
"cross of gold" speech of, 526–527
and election of 1896, 526–527
resignation of, 598
Scopes trial and, 636–637
as Secretary of State, 596
Bryant, Anita, 862–863
Bryant, Roy, 766, 767, 768
Brzezinski, Zbigniew, 856, 857
Buchanan, Patrick, 885, 886, 892
Buchenwald, 709
Buckley, William F., 830
Buddhists, 784–785
Buffalo, 444, 454–455
wanton killing of, *454*
"Buffalo Bill's Wild West," 462
Buffalo Hunt Chase (Catlin), *444*
Bulge, Battle of the, 707
Bunau-Varilla, Philippe, 584–585
Bundy, McGeorge, 786
Bureau of Indian Affairs, 459, 838, 839
Bureau of Refugees, Freedmen, and Abandoned Lands. *See* Freedmen's Bureau
Burger, Warren, 847
Burnham, Daniel, 510–511
Burroughs, Floyd, 654
Burroughs, William S., 471
Burrows, Larry, 790, 795
Bush Doctrine, 898
Bush, George H. W., 868, 876–877
domestic policy in administration of, 880–881
and Gorbachev, 877
new world order of, 883, 903
Panama and Persian Gulf War, 881–883
sends troops to help UN peacekeepers, 894
Bush, George W.
after 9/11, 874
Bush Doctrine of, 898
compassionate conservatism of, 887
and disputed election of 2000, 886–887
Hussein and, 898, 899
Iraq War and, 898–901
issues ultimatum to Taliban, 896
and Kyoto Protocol, 892
low approval rates of, 901
neoconservative appointments of, 898
"No Child Left Behind" law and, 887
response to 9/11 attack by, 896–897
unpopularity of, 903
Business practices, modern, 472–473
Carnegie learns, 475
standardization, 472, *473*
Byrant, Carol, 766

C

Cabrini, Mother, 501
Cagney, James, 516
Cain, Richard H., 411
California
during Depression, 671–672
tax rebellion in, 865
Callaway, Howard "Bo," 799
Calley, William, 799, 800
Cambodia, 780
invasion and outrage, 803–805
Khmer Rouge in, 803
war extended to, 801
Camp David Accords, 856
Cane (Toomer), 642
Cannon, Lou, 871
Capa, Robert, 707
Capitalism
celebration of industrial, 489
championed, 489–491
communism and, 722
and community, *524*
criticism of, 491–492
desire for expansion of, 601
laissez-faire, 659. *See also* Laissez-faire
renewed public faith in, 666
spreading, 720
visions of industrial harmony under, 541–543
Capone, Al, 633
Caputo, Phil, 790, 791, 803
Carlisle Indian School, 459
Carmichael, Stokely, 832
Carnegie, Andrew, 451
"Gospel of Wealth" and, 489
and Homestead strike, 522–523
making steel and transforming the corporation, 474
philanthropy of, 489–490
reputation of, takes a hit, *522*
Carpetbaggers, 418
Carranza, Venustiano, 600
Cars, 626
changes brought by, 627–628
Carson, Rachel, 818
Carter Doctrine, 855, 881
Carter, Jimmy, 842, 852–853
establishes diplomatic relations with China, 855
fiscal policies of, 853
Iranian hostage crisis and, 856
"malaise speech" of, 854
and new paths in foreign affairs, 855–856
pardoning of draft resisters by, 853
Cash and carry policy, 687, 717
revision of, 688
Castro, Fidel, 745, 855
Catholics
parochial schools of, 507, 813
in Vietnam, 784
Catlin, George, 444, 462
Catt, Carrie Chapman, 605
Cattle, 449–450
Central business districts, 512
Central Intelligence Agency (CIA), 745, 782, 849, 876–877, 896
assistance to contras, 869
plots exposed, 851
use of water-boarding by agents of, 897
Central Park, 507
Central Powers, 594, 596
blockade around, 597
A Century of Dishonor (Jackson), 457
Chambers, Whittaker, 737–738
Chaney, James, 825, 826
Chaplin, Charlie, 630
Charity Organization Society, 505
Chávez, César, 838
Cheney, Dick, 883, 898
Chiang Kai-shek. *See* Jiang Jieshi
Chicanos, 838
Child labor, 548–549
exposing evils of, 550–551
family income provided by, 549
price of, *484*
sharp rise in, 484
Chile, 851
China, 579
Carter establishes diplomatic relations with, 855
communism in, 729, 730, 781
détente with, 806
economic relationship between United States and, 879
foreign activity in (1901), *580*
helps Ho Chi Minh, 782
Nixon visits, 805
Open Door Policy and, 579–580
pressures Hanoi to seek peace, 803
Rape of Nanking, 691
split between Soviet Union and, 786
Tiananmen Square, 879
Chinese
racism directed at, *486*
railroad workers, 441
violence against, 446
Chinese Civil War, end of, 729
Chinese Exclusion Act, 446, 486, 506, 581
Chivington, John M., 454
Chrisman sisters, 448, *448*
Churchill, Winston, 692
on Berlin airlift, 727
FDR and, 689
iron curtain speech of, 722
Stalin and, 703, 704, 721, 722
at Yalta Conference, 707

Church of the Transfiguration, 501
Cisneros, Evangelina, 566
Cities
diversity in, 501
emergence of ethnic enclaves in, 501–502
growth of, 500–501
improving services in, 552
new urban landscape of, 512–513
political machines in, 503–504
problems in Western, 448
reforms in, 507
troubles in, 502–503
City Beautiful Movement, 510–511
The City in History (Mumford), 759
City Lights Bookstore, 763–764
City, Sunshine and Shadow (Smith), *491*
Civil defense
drills, 735
fallout shelters and, 736
Civil disobedience, 772, 777
Civilian Conservation Corps (CCC), 668
Civil liberties
attack on, 737–738
and national security clash, 696
during World War I, 606, 608
Civil rights
activists, black, 829
advancing cause of, 679–680
of African Americans protected by federal government, 699, 750, 772
Johnson and, 827, 831, 832
Kennedy and, 819, 820, 821, 824
leaders, challenging traditional, 651
leaders during World War II, 699
mass media use for support for, 839
milestones, 1960–1965, *819*
protests, new direction in, 768
racial violence and, in 1920s, 638–643
Supreme Court's support for, 813
Truman and, 733, 753–754
Civil Rights Act of 1875, 426, 437
Civil Rights Act of 1964, 826
Civil Rights Bill (1866), 416
Civil Rights Cases, 433
Civil Rights Movement, 557, 822
double-victory campaign lays groundwork for, 700
faltering of, 835
fractures within, 830–831, 832, 834
in full bloom, 772–775
images, *822*, *823*
Kennedy and, 820, 821, 824
march from Selma to Montgomery, 826–827, *827*
new energy surges into, 750
new strategy of direct action for, 770
1960–1965, 819–827
nonviolent protest in, 768, 769, 770. *See also* King, Martin Luther, Jr.
pivotal phase of, 765
students as powerful force within, 775
training future leaders of, 773
turning point in, 825–826
wake-up call for, 767
Civil service law, passage of, 520
Civil War, end of, 404
Civil Works Administration (CWA), 668
Clark, Dick, 762
Clark, Jim, 827
Clark, Kenneth, 766
Clay, Cassius. *See* Ali, Muhammad
Clayton Anti-Trust Act, 539, 559
Clemenceau, Georges, 615
Clemens, Samuel Langhorne. *See* Twain, Mark
Cleveland, Grover, 493, 521
effect on Democrats of administration of, 526–527
and immigrant literacy test bill, 506
Pullman strike and, 524, 525
Clifford, Clark, 793
Climate change, 892–893
Clinton, Bill
authorizes Operation Desert Fox, 898
"Don't Ask, Don't Tell" policy of, 884
foreign policy dilemmas of, 894–896
formulates response to "ethnic cleansing," 895
issues embraced by, 903
NAFTA and, 885
new Democrats and, 884–885
retaliation against al-Qaeda by, 895
scandals surrounding, 885
Clinton, Hillary Rodham, 884, 901
Clinton, William "Bill" Jefferson. *See* Clinton, Bill
Closed shop, 541
Coca-Cola, 699
Cody, William "Buffalo Bill," 462
Cohan, George M., 516
Cold War
anti-Communist crusade during, 737–741
becomes global conflict, 734
damaging exposés about U.S. conduct in, 851
defined, 749
in Europe, *723*
focus from Europe to Asia, 780
at home, 718
hotspot, 745
key showdowns during, *726*
new moment of crisis in, 742
nuclear weaponry, *743*
opening phases of, 721–722
origins of, 720–721
post–, new threats in world, 894–901
Reagan changes rules of, 868–869
reshaping of, 803
second front in, 729
spreads to Asia, 781
thaw in, 870–871
United States declares victory in, 879
Collective bargaining, 541, 603
Collier, John, 671
Colonization. *See also* Imperialism
America and, 578
imperialist view of, 578
Colored Farmers' Alliance, 520
Commissioner for Indian Affairs, 671
Committee on Public Information (CPI), 605
Communism, 601
accusations regarding spreading of, 628
attempts to stop spread of, 724
capitalism and, 722
in China, 729, 730, 781
containing, 781
fear of domestic, 738
popular revolts against, 877, 879
rising: 1949, 729–730
struggle between democracy and, 780
threat probed by HUAC, 737
Communist Party, 665, 666, 737
dissolution of Soviet, 877
FBI infiltration of, 739
Communists, 665
deportation of, 634
Russian, 601
Company town, 524
Compromise of 1877, 427
Computer age, 847, 888–889
Comstock Act, 646
Comstock Lode, 450, 462
Concentration camps, 708, 709
German civilians viewing corpses in, *710*
Congress
approves Gulf of Tonkin Resolution, 787
bans all immigration from Asia, 582
declaration of war by, 600
promotes Western settlement, 440–441
Congress of Industrial Organizations (CIO), 679, 683, 753, 772
Congress of Racial Equality (CORE), 819, 825
Connor, Bull, 821, 822
Conrad, Paul, 850
Conscientious objectors, 610, 611
Consciousness-raising, 834
Conscription, 592, 611, 697, 790–791. *See also* Draft
Conservationists, 540
Conservatives, 668
ascendancy of, 842
attack New Deal, *663*
compassionate, 887
religious, 865–866. *See also* Fundamentalism
and Republican Party, 830. *See also* New Right
resistance from, 811
response to gay rights of, 862–863
view of Warren Court held by, 813
Conspicuous consumption, 517, 757
Consumerism, rise of, 629
Consumer Product Safety Commission, 864
Consumer protection movement, 864
Consumers
culture of, 482
during World War II, 697
Consumer spending, 657, 757–758
Containment, 781
philosophical foundation for, 722
refining of policy of, 728
strategy, broadening scope of, 729
Conti, Dennis, 800
Contraception, 646
demand for access to, 834
"The Contract with America," 885
Contras, 869
Convention of the Colored People of Virginia, 414
Coolidge, Calvin
efforts to maintain world peace by, 648
and Kellogg-Briand Pact, 649
Nobel Peace Prize awarded to, 650
Coral Sea, Battle of, 702
Corporation(s), 472, 497
criticism and support of, 758
international, 482, *482*
management, new forms of, 476
mergers of, 477, 519
railroad, 472
transforming, 474–476
Corruption, 520
Cotton Club, 642
Coughlin, Father Charles, 666–667
Council of Federated Organizations (COFO), 825
Freedom Schools founded by, 826, *826*
Counterculture, 750
assault on sexual taboos, 862
demise of, 837
drug use in, 829
environmentalists, 864
marriage between rock music and, 829
New Left and, 828–830
rejection of traditional values, 839
rise of hippie, 810
rise of youth-based, 796
Cowboys, 450, *450*, *464*
Cowper, Ernest, 592
Cox, Archibald, 849
Coxey, Jacob, 523
Coxey's Army, *523*, 523–524
Cox, James, 627
The Crack in the Picture Window (Keats), 758
Crazy Horse (Sioux chief), 456
Credit, 757
buying on, *756*, *757*

Credit Mobilier scandal, 423
Creel, George, 605
Cronkite, Walter, 793
Crosby, Ernest, 576
The Crucible (Miller), 739
Cuba, 564
  Soviet Union and, 745
  Spain and, 567–568
  U.S. decision to intervene in, 567–568
  U.S. ties with, 565
Cuban Missile Crisis, 745–747, 784
  choices and consequences regarding, 746
  hotline connection after, 747
Cullen, Countee, 642, *642*
Culture
  car, 626–628
  celebration of black, 642
  consumer, 482
  gradual rebirth of Native American, 671
  popular. *See* Popular culture
  reaffirming and strengthening Native American, 462
  spreading Western, 564
  teen, and rock-and-roll, 761–763
Curry, John Steuart, 620–621
Curtis, Edward, 540
Custer Battlefield National Cemetery, 465
Custer, George Armstrong, 455–456, 464, 465
Czechoslovakia, demise of democracy in, 725, 728
Czolgosz, Leon, 535

D

Dachau, 709
Darrow, Clarence, 636–637
Darwin, Charles, 490, 563, 611
  evolution theory of, 636
Daughters of the Confederacy, 428
Davis, Benjamin O., 700
Davis, Henry W., 408
Davis, Jefferson, 407
Davis, Joseph, 407
Davis, Richard Harding, 566, 570
Dawes Act, 671
Dawes, Charles G., 650
Dawes, Henry L., 458
Dawes Plan (1924), 650
Dawes Severalty Act, 458, 460, 467
  problems caused by, 459
Day of Wrath (Rosenberg), *658*
Dayton Peace Accords, 895
D-Day invasion, 705, 707, *707*
Dean, James, 763, 764
Dean, Loomis, 757
Debs, Eugene V., 524, 538, 636
  imprisonment and pardoning of, 608
DeCrow, Karen, 859
Deep Throat, 849
Defense of Marriage Act, 890
Defoliants, 790
Deforestation, 451
Democracy
  arsenal of, 688–690
  and communism, struggle between, 780
  desire to spread, to Middle East, 900
  spreading, 720
  Wilson's desire to export, 599, 601
Democratic Party
  black voters join, 680
  civil rights and, 753–754
  divided, 727
  and election of 1896, 526–527
  nominating convention of 1964, 814, 816, 841
  political machines associated with, 503
Democrats
  conservative Southern, 727, 752
  liberal, 853, 867, 889. *See also* Liberalism
  opposition to Persian Gulf War by, 882
Dempsey, Jack, 630
Denison House, 510
Department of Education, 853
Department of Homeland Security, 897
Department stores, 478–479
Department of Transportation, 817
Depression. *See also* Great Depression
  defined, 483
  economic trends in, *660*
  -era suffering, icon of, *673*
  industrial conflict and, 522–524
  repatriating Mexican immigrants during, 672
Deserving poor, 676
Détente, 803, 805
  success of, 806
  U.S. disaffection with, 855
Dewey, Thomas, 707, 727, 728, 754
DeWitt, John L., 694
The Diary of Anne Frank, 710
Diem, Ngo Dinh, 782
  opposition to, 783
  shortcomings of, 783
  treatment of Buddhists by, 784–785
  U.S. support for, 784
Dien Bien Phu, French defeat at, 782
Dime novels, 462
Diplomacy
  in 1920s, 647–651
  and East Asia, 589
  exerting U.S. influence through, 624
  Kissinger's use of, 803
  Nixon and, 805
  Theodore Roosevelt's use of, 579
  use of, by McKinley, 567
Disarmament, 647
Discretionary income, 756–757
Discrimination
  demands for end to Anglo-American, 838
  directed at Asians, 446, 486, 506, 581, 693
  FDR's executive order forbidding, 701
  gender, 834, 858, 859
  Jews and, 628. *See also* Anti-Semitism
  Native American, 461–462
  protesting racial, 701, 821
Diseases
  flu epidemic of 1918, 614
  Native Americans and epidemics of, 454
  during Spanish-American War, 571
  in tenement districts, 502
  transmission of, 586
Disenfranchisement movement, 433–434, *435*
Diversity
  in cities, 501, 503
  of ethnic Chicago, *502*
  of Native Americans in West, 442–443
  of workforce, 486
Dole, Bob, 884
Dollar Diplomacy, 587–588
Domino theory, 781
Donnelly, Ignatius, 520
"Don't Ask, Don't Tell" policy, 884
Dos Passos, John, 632, 665
Double-victory campaign, 699, 700
Douglas, Aaron, 642–643
Douglass, Frederick, 404, 421
Doves, 798
Draft. *See also* Conscription
  -card burnings, 797
  deferments, 791, 797
  reform, 801
  resisters pardoned by Carter, 853
Drive-in theaters, 760
Dr. Seuss, 689
Drugs, 829
Drys, 633
Du Bois, W. E. B., 434, 555, 556, 640
  criticism mounted by, 643
  view of Garvey held by, 641
Duc, Thich Quang, 784, *785*
Dukakis, Michael, 876–877
Duke, James B., 476
Dulles, John Foster, 742, 783
Duncan, David Douglas, 732
Dust Bowl, 670, 683
  dust storms of, *670*, 670–671
  refugees, 671–672, *672*
Dylan, Bob, 829

E

Eastern Europe
  communism in, 721
  end of Soviet domination in, 877
  Marshall Plan and, 724
  Soviets in, 722, 743
Easter Offensive, 805
East Germany, 728, 744
  fall of communism in, 877
Eastman, George, 471, 476
Eckford, Elizabeth, 750, *751*, 772
Economy
  ailing, 844, 846–847
  big business domination of, 532
  character of industrial, 483
  following Civil War, 424
  free market, 492
  globalization of American, 482, 884–885
  New South, 429–431
  precedent set for governmental management of, 660
  problems with, 901
  role of federal government in, in 1920s, 659
  during World War II, 698–699
Edison, Thomas, 471
Education
  for freedmen, 410–411
  laws, compulsory, 507
  for Native Americans, 458
  rise in, 513
  throughout Progressive Era, 549
Edwin, Marcus, 782
Eighteenth Amendment, 633
  repeal of, 634
Einstein, Izzy, 633
Eisenhower, Dwight D., 738
  demeanor of, 733
  domino theory embraced by, 781
  fiscal views of, 755
  increase in nuclear weaponry under, 742
  landslide elections of, 754
  McCarthy and, 741
  "military-industrial complex" speech, 755
  presidency of, 754–755
  sends federal troops to Little Rock, 772
  television and, 760
  urges private shelters to be built, 736
  and Vietnam, 782–783
  in World War II, 705
Eisenstaedt, Alfred, 714
Elections
  1868, 420–421, *421*
  1872, *424*, 424
  1876, 426–427, *427*
  1896, 526–527
  1912, 538, *538*
  1932, 654, 660
  1948, 727–728, 754
  1964, 814, 816–817
  1968, *798*, 836

1984, 867–868
1988, 876–877
2000, 886–887, *887*
2008, 901–902
Ellis Island, 506
Ellsberg, Daniel, 804–805
El Salvador, 869
Emancipation
African Americans' response to, 411
test cases, 406–408
Embargo, 691
oil, 842, 844, 883
Emergency Immigration Act (1921), 634
Emergency Relief Act (1932), 660
The Emigrant's Guide to Oregon and California (Hastings), 452
Empire(s). *See also* Imperialism
American, 573–578
calls for American, 562, 563, 572
European colonial, 563, *564*
Emporiums, 478–479
Energy
costs, 844
crisis, 853, *854*
U.S. usage of, 844
Enforcement Acts, 422
Engle v. Vitale, 814, 815
Enola Gay, 712
Entertainment industry, 515–516
Environment. *See also* Environmentalism
concerns about, 818, 893
preservation versus conservation of, 539–540
scandals pertaining to, 864
of West, 451
Environmentalism, 864. *See also* Environment
Environmental Protection Agency (EPA), 864
Equal Rights Amendment, 653
argument against, 644
Equal Rights Amendment (ERA, 1972), 859
Erie Canal, 584
Espionage, 738. *See also* Spies
Espionage Act (1917), 606, 608, 623, 635
Ethnic cleansing, 895
Ethnic enclaves, 501–502
New Right concerns about, 892
Eugenicists, 646
Europe
after World War I, 616, *617*
American loans to (1914–1925), *650*
Cold War in, *723*
far-flung empires of, *564*
imperialism of, 563–564
preventing war in, 649
reaction to Roosevelt Corollary of, 587
World War I in, 594, *595*, 596
European theater, World War II, *703*, 703–704, 705, 707–708
Evans, Walker, 654
Evers, Medgar, 824
Evolution, 490
challenges to teaching, 637
Darwin's views on, 636
Executive Order 9066, 694
Exodusters, 444–445, *445*
Exports, 482

F

Factory system, 532
foremen and managers in, 484
Fagan, David, 578
Fahey, James, 705
Fair Deal, 754
attack on, 754
curbing of, 755
Fair Employment Practices Committee, 699
Fair Housing Act, 832
Fair, Jim, 451
Fair Labor Standards Act, 677
Fairrington, Brian, 890
Fall, Albert B., 627
Fallout shelter(s), 736
sign for, *736*
Falwell, Jerry, 866
Families, changing face of, *889*, 889–890
Fannie Mae, 901
Farley, James, 790
Farmer, James, 819
Farmers. *See also* Agriculture
alleviating plight of, 520
benefits of new technology to, 626
demonstrations by, 665
during Depression, 657
environmental damage done by, 451
hard times for, 448–449
New Deal for, 670–671
tenant, 431, 432
Farmer's alliances, 520
Farm Security Administration, 654, 671
Fascism, 686
Fascist state, 686
Faubus, Orval, 771–772
FDR. *See* Roosevelt, Franklin Delano
Federal Bureau of Investigation (FBI), 737, 849
arrests after 9/11 made by, 897
infiltration of Communist Party by, 739
poster of slain civil rights workers, *825*
Federal deficit, 844
skyrocketing, 846
Federal Deposit Insurance Corporation (FDIC), 666
Federal Election Commission (FEC), 851
Federal Emergency Relief Administration (FERA), 668
Federal government. *See also* Government
demands made of, 654
Johnson and, 816
loss of confidence in, 842
prohibition and, 632
protecting civil rights of African Americans, 699, 750, 772
role in economy of, in 1920s, 659
support for industrialization, 471
during World War I, 602, 621
Federal Housing Authority (FHA), 666
Federal income taxes, 538–539
Federal Republic of Germany. *See* West Germany
Federal Reserve, 539
Federal Reserve Act (1913), 539, 559
Federal Trade Commission, 539, 559
Fellowship of Reconciliation, 700
Felt, William Mark, 849
Feminine Mystique (Friedan), 834
Feminists, 810
picket Miss America Pageant, *834*
successes of, 859
Ferguson, John H., 434
Ferraro, Geraldine, 867–868
Field, James G., 521
Fifteenth Amendment, 421, 437
circumventing, 433
Final Solution, 708
First Fort Laramie Treaty, 453
First Ladies, 663
First Red Scare (1919–1920), 634–635
anti-immigration given credence by, 635
Fisk, Jim, 423
Fitzgerald, F. Scott, 632
Fitzgerald, Zelda, 632
Fitzpatrick, Daniel R., 725
Five Power Treaty, 648
Flappers, 624, *625*
Flood, James, 451
"Flower Power" (Boston), 778, *779*
Foch, Ferdinand, 616
Fonda, Jane, 801
Food Administration, 602, 604
Ford, Gerald, 842, 849
assumes presidency, 806
pardoning of Nixon by, 851, 853
weakened presidency of, 851
Ford, Henry, 541–543, 678
Ford Motor Company, 541–543
worker housing, *542*
Foreclosures, 666
Foreign policy
under George H. W. Bush, 881–883
Carter's new paths in, 855–856
congressional reassertion of control over, 807
containment as new, 722
dilemma in Middle East, 844
focus of, 596
forays, 903
Kennan's view of needed, 722
key goal of, 718
mainstay of twentieth-century, 588
NSC-68 sets tone for, 781
priority of FDR, 691
triumphs of Reagan, 868–869
Truman orders review of, 729–730
Foremen, 484
Forman, Stanley, 847–848
Forrest, Nathan Bedford, 428
Fossil fuel consumption, 892–893
442nd Regimental Combat Team, 695
Four-Minute Men, 605
Fourteen Points, 601, 623
Fourteenth Amendment, 416–417, 437
limiting of, 434
violation of, 766
Fragging, 805
France
U.S. aid to, 781
and Vietnam, 780, 782–783
in World War I, 596
in World War II, 688
Frank, Anne, 708, 710
Franz Ferdinand (archduke of Austria), 594
assassination of, 687
Freddie Mac, 901
Free blacks. *See also* Freedmen
Freedmen, 406–408. *See also* Free blacks
cultivating sweet potatoes, *406–407*
education for, *410*, 410–411
forty acres and a mule for, 409–410
journeys of, 409
violence against, 416
Freedmen's Bureau, 408, 409
schools built by, 410
Freedom Rides, 819–820
attack on, *820*
Freedom Schools, *826*, 826
Freedom Summer, 774, 825–826
Free fire zones, 790
Freeman, Daniel, 440
Free silver, support of, 526–527
Free Speech Movement, 828
French, Daniel Chester, 479
Freud, Sigmund, 632
Frick, Henry Clay, 522
Friedan, Betty, 834
Friedenberg, Edgar, 762
Frontier, bringing market to, 479, 482
Frontier Thesis, 464, 467
Fundamentalism, 636–637
anti-gay rights stance of, 863
issues connected to, 865–866
Modernists' view of, 637
Funston, Frederick, 578
Fussell, Paul, 712

G

Galbraith, Kenneth, 756–757
Gallup polls, 663, 679, 798
Gandhi, Mahatma, 770, 772
Gans, Herbert J., 759
Garfield, James A., assassination of, 520
Garvey, Marcus, 640, *640*, 830
  accusations against, 641
  argument of, 641
Gas shortages, 842, *843*
Gast, John, 438
Gates, Bill, 847
Gatto, Victor, 530
Gay Liberation Front, 862
Gay Pride parades, 862
Gay rights, 862–863
Geisel, Theodore, 689
General Federation of Women's Clubs, 513
Geneva Accords, 782
Genocide, 710
Gentleman's Agreement, 581
George, Henry, 491, 495
German Democratic Republic. *See* East Germany
Germany. *See also* Nazi Germany
  defeat of, *720*, 721
  disarmament and reparations, 615, 616, 648, 650–651
  dominance of, 594
  four zones of occupation in, 726
  issues *Arabic* Pledge, 598
  negative images of, *607*
  reunification of, 877
  Schlieffen Plan and, 596
  sentiment against, 597
  sinks *Lusitania*, 598
  territory gained by, from Brest-Litovsk Treaty, 601
  unrestricted submarine warfare of, 592, 599, 621
Geronimo (Apache warrior), 457, 461
Ghost Dance movement, 461
GI Bill of Rights (1944), 757
Gibson, Charles Dana, 514
Gibson Girl, 514
Gilded Age, 532
  attitudes in American society during, 513
  concept of leisure time developed during, 515–516
  deadlocked presidential politics in, *518*
  lifestyles of rich and famous during, 517, 518
  nativism in, 506, *507*
  notion of, 498
Gingrich, Newt, 885
Ginsberg, Allen, 763–764
Gittings, Barbara, 862
Glass-Steagall Act of 1933, 666
Gleason, Jackie, 760
Globalization, of American economy, 482, 884–885
Global warming, 892–893
  carbon dioxide emissions, *893*
Godzilla, 734, *734*
Goethals, George W., 586
Goldman, Emma, 634
Gold standard, 526–527
Goldwater, Barry, 816–817, 830, 852
Goldwyn, Sam, 739
Gompers, Samuel, 495, 543
Goodman, Andrew, 825, 826
Goodnight, Charles, 449, 450
Gorbachev, Mikhail, 870
  and George H. W. Bush, 877
  resignation of, 877
Gore, Al
  and disputed election of 2000, 886–887
  global warming concerns of, 893
Gorgas, William C., 586–587
Gould, Jay, 423, 473, 489, 493
Government. *See also* Federal government
  anarchists' view of, 634
  bailout, 901–902
  contested visions of, 884–887
  corruption, ending, 552–553
  policies promoting industrialization, 471
  propaganda regarding atomic bombs, 734, *735*
  reforming, 552–553
  spending on work-relief, 668–669
Graduated income tax, 521
Grady, Henry, 429–430
Grange, 449, 467
Granger movement, 449, 520
Grant, Ulysses S., 420–421
  corruption scandals under, 423
Grayson, Cary, 620
Great Depression, 654. *See also* Depression
  early days of, 656–660
  economic weaknesses before, 656–657
  families on the move because of, 671–672
  helping industry and people during, 667–668
  Hoover's response to, 659–660
  length of, 659
  recovering from, 666–669
  revamping banking and financial institutions, 666
  stock market crash of 1929, 657–659
  temper of poor: passivity and anger, 664–665
Greater East Asia Co-Prosperity Sphere, 690
"Great Marianas Turkey Shoot," 704
Great Migration, 500
Great Plains, 443
  environmental damage done to, 451
  homesteading on, *448*
  Native American tribes of, 443–444
  wars on, 455–456
Great Society, 816, 817–818
  key legislative achievements, *818*
  unraveling of, 835–837
Greeley, Horace, 424, 445
Greenbacks, 519
Green Berets, 784, 786, 790
Greenough, Horatio, 453
Green Party, 886, 887
Greenpeace, 818
Greer (U.S. destroyer), 690
Grenada, 870
Grimké, Francis J., 609
Guam, 589
Guantánamo Bay, naval base at, 572
  prisoners held at, 897
Guevara, Ernesto "Che," 828
Gulf of Tonkin, 786–787
Gulf of Tonkin Resolution, 787
  Senate symbolically terminates, 803

H

Haber, Al, 828
Haeberle, Ron, 799
Haight-Ashbury, 837
Halberstam, David, 772, 789
Hall v. DeCuir, 433
Hamer, Fannie Lou, 816
Hamilton, Charles, 833
Hampton Institute, *554*, 555
Hanna, Mark, 541
Harding, Warren
  pardoning of Debs by, 608
  Teapot Dome scandal, 627
  Washington Conference and, 647
Hard money, advocates of, 519
Harlan, John Marshall, 434
Harlem Renaissance, 638, 640, 642–643
Harper, Frances, 421
Harper's Weekly, 416, 425
Harrigan, Edward, 516
Harriman, E. H., 536
Harrison, Benjamin, 521
Hart, Tony, 516
Hastings, Lansford W., 452
Haves and have-nots, 491
  growing gap between, *491*
Hawaii, 574
  annexation of, 568–569
  U.S. Pacific Fleet sent to, 684
Hawaiian Patriotic League, 569
Hawks, 798
Hay, John, 579–580, 584
Hay–Bunau-Varilla Treaty (1903), 585
Hayden, Tom, 828, 836
Hayes, Rutherford B., 426–427, 525
Haymarket Incident, 493, *493*, 495
Haywood, William D. "Big Bill," 543
Hearst, William Randolph, 565, 567
Helsinki Accords (1975), 852
Hemingway, Ernest, 632
Henderson, Fletcher, 642
Henry Street Settlement, 510
Hepburn Act, 537
Herblock, 836, 850, *870*
The Herd Quitters (Russell), *464*
Hickok, Lorena, 665
Hill, Anita, 880
Hill, Elsie, 644
Hill, James J., 536
Hinckley, John, 867
Hine, Lewis, 544, 549
  photographs of, *550–551*
Hippies, 829, *829*, 837
Hirohito (emperor of Japan), 712, 714
Hiroshima, atomic bomb dropped on, 712, 713, 729, 734
Hiss, Alger, 737–738
"The History of the Standard Oil Company" (Tarbell), 535
Hitler, Adolf, 616
  appeasement of, 687
  Final Solution of, 708
  invasions of, 687, 688, 690, 703
  in Paris, *688*
  signs non-aggression pact with Stalin, 688
  suicide of, 708
  treatment of Jews by, 709
  turns Germany into fascist state, 686
Hobart, Garrett, 567
Ho Chi Minh, *781*, 807
  accepts help from China, 782
  Americans' view of, 780
  background of, 780
Ho Chi Minh Trail, 789, 804
  hardships along, *789*
Hoffman, Abbie, 836
Holding companies, 477
Holland Tunnel, opening of, 626
Hollywood
  blacklist, 739
  catering to teenage tastes by, 762
  HUAC against, 739
  World War I propaganda effort by, 605
Hollywood Ten, 739
Holocaust, 709
  America and, *709*
  America's response to, 708, 710
  defined, 708
  Jews in, *709*
Homer, Winslow, 404
Homestead Act, 440–441
  flaw in original, 448
Homestead strike, 522–523
Home to Harlem (McKay), 643
Homosexuality, 862

Hoover, Herbert
background of, 656
Bonus March and, 660, 661
call for moratorium on international debts by, 651
differences between Roosevelt and, 654
as director of Food Administration, 602
response to Great Depression of, 659–660
Hoover, J. Edgar, 832
"Hoovervilles," 660, 661
Hopkins, Harry, 668
Horizontal integration, 475, 476
versus vertical integration, *475*
House, Edward, 599
House Un-American Activities Committee (HUAC), 737, 738
competing visions of, 740
against Hollywood, 739
Howard, O. O., 410
"Howl" (Ginsberg), 763–764
How the Other Half Lives (Riis), 508, 509, 812
Hughes, Charles Evan, 599, 647, 648, 650
Hughes, Langston, 642, *643*, 643
Hughes, Sarah, 786
Hull House, 510, 534, 549
Human rights
as guiding principle, 855
violations, 852
Humphrey, Hubert, 798, 836
Huntington, Collis B., 473
Hurricane Katrina, 901
Hussein, Saddam, 856
George W. Bush and, 898, 899
Clinton and, 898
fall of, 900
invasion of Kuwait by, 881–882
Huston, Zora Neale, 642
Hydrogen bomb, 735

I

Ickes, Harold, 668
"If We Must Die" (McKay), 642
Ikard, Bose, 450
The Illegal Operation (Kleinholz), 859
Immigrants. *See also* Immigration
discriminatory laws targeting, 693
German American, during World War I, 607, 608
hardships for Japanese, 581–582
illegal, 636
repatriating Mexican, 672
to trans-Mississippi West, 446
during World War I, 606
Immigration. *See also* Immigrants
banned from Asia, 582
barring of Chinese, 446, 486, 506
economic costs of, 891
illegal, 892
oversight of, 506
reduction in Japanese, 581
restrictions, 634–635
revamping of, 818
U.S. (1880–1920), *500*
wave of, 890, 892
Immigration Act of 1924, 634
quota system under, *635*
Immigration Act of 1965, 818
Immigration Restriction League, 506
Impeachment, 806
articles of, issued against Nixon, 849
Clinton survives, 885
trial of Andrew Johnson, 417
Imperialism, 591. *See also* Colonization
American, 573–574, 576, 578, 589
cloaked in self-determination rhetoric, 616–617
defined, 563
European, 563–564
Japanese, 690–691
"Incident" (Cullen), 642
Incredible Hulk, 734
Indian Appropriations Act, 453
Indian Reorganization Act (1934), 671
Indians of All Tribes, 839
Individualism, 532
Indochina, 780
Industrialists, 532, 534
antiunion, 541
child labor and, 548–549
innovative, 628
wartime rhetoric of, 699
during World War I, 603, 621
Industrialization
consequences of, 468
government policies promoting, 471
importance of steel to, 474
Industrial Revolution, 468
by the numbers, *470*
source of, 470–472
Industrial Workers of the World (IWW), 543, 559, 608
Inflation, 844
fear of, 519
high, 842
and unemployment, *846*
The Influence of Sea Power on History (Mahan), 562
Initiatives, 553
Integration
anger over court-ordered, 865
of buses in Montgomery, Alabama, 770
of lunch counters, 772–774
of public schools, struggle for, 770–772. *See also Brown v. Board of Education of Topeka*
supported by Du Bois, 640
Intelligence tests, 611, 628
for soldiers, *611*
Intercontinental ballistic missiles (ICBMs), 743
Interest rates, 846
Intermediate-Range Nuclear Forces Treaty, 870–871
Internal Revenue Service (IRS), 849
International Atomic Energy Agency, 898
International Business Machines (IBM), 847
International Longshoreman's Union, 543
Internet, 888–889
Internment camps, 694–695
Interstate Commerce Commission (ICC), 477, 536, 820
Interventionists, 684, 686
argument of, 688, 689
defined, 717
Inventors, 471
Investment, 482
Iran
hostages taken in, 856, 857
Shah of, 856, 857
war between Iraq and, 854, 856, 870, 881
Iran-Contra scandal, 870
Iranian hostage crisis, 856
ending, 857
Iraq
U.S. wars with. *See* Iraq War; Persian Gulf War
war between Iran and, 854, 856, 870, 881
Iraq War, 898, 900–901
controversy over, 900–901
pattern followed in, 900
weapons of mass destruction and, 898, 899
Iron curtain, 722, 749
Isolationism, 615, 621
Israel, 844
"I, Too, Sing America" (Hughes), 643
Iwo Jima, conquest of, 711
"Iwo Jima" (Rosenthal), *706*, 706

J

Jackson, Andrew, 525
Jackson, Helen Hunt, 457, 458, 459
Jacoby, Tamar, 891
James, William, 853
Japan
as American ally, 781
atomic bombs dropped on, 711–712
attacks planned by, 702
caves and bunkers of, 705, 711
edging closer to, 711
invasions of, 690–691
outrage against, 693
"picture brides" from, 581, *582*
relations between America and, 580–581
suicide tactics introduced by, 705
surrender of, 712, 714
U.S. purchases from, 846
war crimes trials for, 714
and Washington Conference, 647–648
Japanese Americans
civil liberties of, 696
protesting internment, *695*
relocation and internment of, 696
during World War II, 694–695
Jazz, 642–643
J. B. Williams C., 481
Jews
extermination of, 710. *See also* Holocaust
in Holocaust, *709*
in Nazi Germany, 686
in New York's East Side, 501
prejudice against, 628. *See also* Anti-Semitism
Jiang Jieshi, 729
Jihad, 895
Jim Crow, 432–433, 435
confronting harsh realities of, 765
dismantling, 813
law, overturning, 555
piecemeal dismantling of, 771
practices, acceptance of, 575
showing injustice of, 750
Jobs Corps, 814
Jobs, Steven, 846–847
Johnson, Andrew, 412–413
conflict between congressional Republicans and, 417
impeachment trial of, 417
leniency of, angers North, *413*
opposition to rights of freedmen and, 416
Johnson, James Weldon, 638, 642–643
Johnson, Lady Bird, 816
Johnson, Lyndon Baines, *787*, 810
and affirmative action programs, 834
assumes presidency, 786, *786*
background of, 786
civil rights and, 827, 831, 832
dilemma of, *836*, 836
Great Society, 816, 817–818
legislative successes of, 814
Pentagon Papers portrayal of, 805
and Vietnam, 786–787, 788, 798
War on Poverty, 814
withdraws from presidential race, 793, 796
Jolson, Al, 516
Jones, Cleve, 863

Jones, Joe, 669
Jones, Mother Mary, 543
Jones, Thomas, 450
Joseph, Chief (Nez Perce), 457
The Jungle (Sinclair), 552

K

Kamikaze pilots, 705, 711
Kaplan, Charles, 634
Karales, James, 827
Kazan, Elia, 739
  HUAC cooperation of, 740
Keats, John, 758
Kelley, Florence, 510, 534
Kelley, Oliver H., 449
Kellogg-Briand Pact (1928), 648, 649
Kellogg, Frank, 648, 649
Kelly, Mike "King," 515
Kemerer, Duncan, 612
Kennan, George F., 722
Kennedy, Jackie, 785, *786*
Kennedy, John F., 743, 810
  assassination of, 785–786
  and Bay of Pigs, 745
  civil defense measure ordered by, 736
  civil rights and, 819, 820, 821, 824
  and Cuban Missile Crisis, 745–747
  debate with Nixon, 761
  family portrait, *761*
  and Freedom Riders, 819–820
  Khrushchev and, 743, 745, 747
  and New Frontier, 812–813
  Pentagon Papers portrayal of, 805
  speaking with coal miners, *812*
  Vietnam and, 784–785
  visits Berlin Wall, 744–745
Kennedy, Robert, 820
  assassination of, 797
Kent State, shootings at, 803, *804*
  protests after, 804
Kerouac, Jack, 764
Kerry, John, 901
Khmer Rouge, 803
Khomeini, Ayatollah Ruhollah, 856
Khrushchev, Nikita, 742, 743
  Kennedy and, 743, 745, 747
Killing fields, 803
Kilpatrick, James Jackson, 771
Kim Il-sung, 730
King, Coretta Scott, 810
King, Martin Luther, Jr., 768, 769, 770, 831
  assassination of, 797, 810, 835
  Birmingham campaign, 821, *822*, *823*
  definition of Black Power by, 833
  on integrated Montgomery bus, *771*
  "Letter from a Birmingham Jail," 821
  March on Washington, 824
  Poor People's Campaign, 835
  A. Philip Randolph inspires, 699
  speaks out against war in Vietnam, 796–797
  weakening leadership of, 835
  wins Nobel Peace Prize, 826
King, Rodney, *880*, 880–881
King, Yolanda, 810, *811*
Kipling, Rudyard, 575, 576
Kissinger, Henry, 801, 852
  multipolarity vision of, 801
  use of diplomacy by, 803
"Kiss in Times Square" (Eisenstaedt), 714, *715*
Kleinholz, Edward, 859
Knights of Labor (KOL), 492–493
  achievements of, 493
  dissatisfaction within, 495
  inclusionary aspects of, 493
  strikes and, 494
Knights of the White Camelia, 422
Koehler, Robert, 468
Korea, division of, 730
Korean War, 729, 730–734, *731*
  geopolitical consequences of, 734
  MacArthur and, 731–733
  permanent cease-fire ends, 733
  Stalin and, 781–782, *782*
Korematsu v. United States, 696
Kramer, Larry, 863
Kristallnacht, 709
Kristol, Irving, 865
Ku Klux Klan, 422, 426, 437, 820, 825
  in the 1920s, 639
Kuwait, invasion of, 881–882
Kyoto Protocol, 892

L

Labor. *See also* Labor unions
  activism of working-class, 486, 494, 543
  alignment of Roosevelt with, 676–677
  anti-, legislation enacted, 753
  child. *See* Child labor
  dispute, federal troops sent to quell, 525
  expansion of clout of, 699
  movement, curtailing, 752–753
  movement upheaval of 1886, 493, 495
  organizers attacked, *678*
  power in numbers: organized, 492–493
  resurgence of, 678–679
  during World War I, 603
Labor Day, 492–493
Labor unions, 535, 541, 667. *See also* Labor
  difficulty of organizing, 484
  legitimacy of, 487
  opposition to NAFTA of, 885
  renewed efforts to organize, 492
  supporting, 676–677
  during World War I, 603
Ladies Memorial Association, 428
La Flesche, Susette, 457
Lafollette, Robert, 553
Laissez-faire, 428, 497, 518, 659
  challenges to notion of, 532
  consequences of, 522
  critics of, 491–492
  defined, 471
  efforts to curb, 474
  ethos of industrialists, 534
  Nast cartoon defending, *471*
Land
  conflict over Western, 456–457
  under Homestead Act, 440–441
  loss of Native American, *460*
Land grants, 471
Landon, Alf, 677
Landsmark, Ted, 847–848
Lange, Dorothea, 672, 673, 695
  photographs of, *665*, *672*, *673*
Lansing, Robert, 601
Laos, 780
  war extended to, 801, 804
La Raza (The Race), 838
Las Gorras Blancas (The White Caps), 457
Latin America
  American intervention in (1980–200), *869*
  American involvement in, *588*
  Roosevelt Corollary and, 587–589
Lawrence, Jacob, 603
Lawson, James, 770, 772–774, 775
League of Nations
  domestic opponents of, 615, 620
  Wilson and, 615–616, 617–620
League of Women Voters, 644
Lee, Robert E., 428–429
The Legacy of Conquest (Limerick), 464
Lehman Brothers, 901
Leisure, 515–516
Lend-Lease, 689–690, 717
  Truman and, 721
Leningrad, siege of, 704
Lenin, Vladimir, 601
Lesbianism, 862
Lesseps, Ferdinand de, 584
"Letter from a Birmingham Jail" (King), 821
Lever Food and Fuel Act (1917), 602
Levine, David, 787
Levitt, Abraham, 758
The Levittowners (Gans), 759
Levittowns, 758
Levitt, William, 758
Lewinsky, Monica, 885
Lewis and Clark expedition, 462
Lewis, John, 773, 819, 820, 831
Lewis, John L., 678–679
Leyte Gulf, Battle of, 705
Liberalism, 853
  critics of, 836
  momentum gained by, 814
  negative connotations of, 810
  rejection of, 842
Liberal Republicans, 424
Life Among the Paiutes (Winnemucca), 458
Life magazine, 693, 706, 707, 795, 799, 804
  photos, *822*, *823*
Liliuokalani, Queen, 569
Limerick, Patricia Nelson, 464
Limited Test Ban Treaty, 747
Lincoln, Abraham, Ten Percent Plan of, 408
Lindbergh, Anne Morrow, 631
Lindbergh, Charles A., 630–631
  nonstop solo transatlantic flight of, 630
  tragedy of, 631
Little Bighorn Battlefield National Monument, 465
Little Bighorn, Battle of, 456
  change to site of, 465
Little, Malcolm. *See* Malcolm X
Little Rock Nine, 770–772
Lloyd George, David, 615, 620
Loan, Nguyen Ngoc, *795*, 795
Lochner, Joseph, 545
Lochner v. New York, 544, 545
Locke, Alain, 642
Lockout, 522
Lodge, Henry Cabot, 575, 579
  Wilson and, 615–616, 618, 619, 620
Lomasney, Martin, 503
Long Drives, 449, 450
Long, Huey, 674, 675
Long telegram, 722, 749
Looking Backward (Bellamy), 492
Look magazine, 827
Lorch, Grace, 772
Lost Cause, 428–429
Lost Generation, 632
  writers, 633
Love Canal, 864
Loving, Oliver, 449, 450
Lowell, Josephine Shaw, 505
Ludendorff, Erich, 614
Ludlow Massacre, 544, 559
Lusitania (British passenger ship), 592
  sinking of, *593*, 598
Lynchings, 435, 555, 638, *638*, 651, 825
Lysergic acid diethylamide (LSD), 829

M

MacArthur, Douglas
  Korean War and, 731–733
  returns to Philippines, *704*, 704–705

Truman's firing of, 732
during World War II, 697
Mackay, John, 451
Mahan, Alfred T., 562
Mail order catalogs, 482
Maine (U.S. battleship), 560, 565, 567, 571
Malcolm X, 830–831
has change of heart, 831
rhetoric of, 833
Managers, 484
Man and Nature (Marsh), 452
Mandate system, 616
Manhattan Project, 711–712, 738
Soviet spies in, 712, 713
Manifest Destiny, 451, 452, 562
Mann-Elkins Act, 537
Manufacturers, 482
Many Marriages (Anderson), 632
Mao Tse-tung, 782, 786, 805. *See also* Mao Zedong
Mao Zedong, 729, 730. *See also* Mao Tse-tung
March on Washington, 824, *824*
Marijuana, 829
Marsh, George Perkins, 452
Marshall, George C., 724, 741
Marshall Plan, 724
aid approved by, *723*
differing views of, *725*
Marshall, Thurgood, 766, 880
Martin, Joseph, 732
Marx Brothers, 630
Mass market
bringing, to frontier, 479, 482
creating, 478–482
emergence of, 482
Mass production, 541, 624
Matzeliger, Jan, 471
lasting machine of, *471*
Mauthausen, 709
McAdoo, William G., 606
McCain, John, 901
campaign of, 902
McCarran Act, 737
McCarthy, Eugene, 836
McCarthy, Joseph, 739, 754
end of career of, 741
Murrow's exposure of, 741
McCarthyism, 739, 741
McCormick, Cyrus, 476
McCorvey, Norma, 861
McCoy, Joseph, 449
McFarlane, Robert, 855
McGovern, George, 805, 848
McKay, Claude, 642, *642*, 643
McKinley, William, 526–527
assassination of, 535, 634
authorizes annexation of Hawaii, 569
campaign poster (1900), *572*
ends Boxer Rebellion, 580
imperialism and, 573
Philippines and, 574, 575
sends *Maine* to Havana, 560
use of diplomacy by, 567
McKinstry, Carolyn, 821, 824
McNamara, Robert, 787
shift in views of, 792
McVeigh, Timothy, 895
Meadlo, Paul, 800
Meat Inspection Act (1906), 552
Medicaid, 818, 846
Medicare, 818
Mencken, H. L., 636
Mercie, Antonin, 429
Mexican Americans
activism of, 837–838
violence against, 700–701
Mexico
NAFTA and, 885
Pershing sent to, 600
Microsoft, 847, 888
Middle East, 594
after World War I, *617*
Carter and, 855–856
foreign policy dilemma in, 844
oil, reliance on, 844
and Persian Gulf (1947–1986), *845*
redrawing map of, 616–617
spreading democracy to, 900
Midway, Battle of, 702–703
Migrant Mother, *673*
Migrants
black, during World War II, 700
during Depression, 671–672
Migration
black, 603–604
great westward, 444–446
new perspective of westward, 464–465
rural-to-urban internal, 500
touched off by Homestead Act, 440
Mikilski, Barbara, 834
Milam, J. W., 766, 768
Military-industrial complex, 755
Miller, Arthur, 739
Mills, C. Wright, 758
Minimum wage, 754
raising, 813
Mining
booms, 450–451
environmental damage done by, 451
grievances related to, 544
labor policies and coal, 485
Missionaries, 443
in China, 579
Mississippi Freedom Democratic Party (MFDP), 814, 816
Mississippi Plan, 426
Missouri (U.S. battleship), 712
Modernism, 636, 637
Moley, Raymond, 662
Molly Maguires, 485
Molotov, Vyacheslav, 721
Moltke, Helmuth von, 596
Mondale, Walter, 867–868
Monkey trial. *See* Scopes trial
Monopolies
defined, 474
demonizing, *474*
weakening of, 538
Monroe Doctrine, 616
Montgomery Bus Boycott (1955–1956), 768, 770
Montgomery Improvement Association (MIA), 768, 769, 770
Montgomery Women's Political Council, 768, 769
Moody, Anne, 774–775, 824
Moonshine, 633
Moore, Charles, 822–823
Moral Majority, 866
Morgan, J. P., 489, 536, 539, 608
Morgan, Robin, 834
Morgenthau, Henry, 689, 708
Mormons, 445
Morrill Land Grant College Act (1862), 440
Morris, John Milt, 854
Morton, Ferdinand "Jelly Roll," 642
Moses, Bob, 773–774
Mother Earth, 634
Mr. Prejudice (Pippin), 700, *701*
Muckrakers, 553, 605
Muenter, Eric, 608
Muhammad, Elijah, 830
Muir, John, 539–540
Muller, Curt, 546
Muller v. Oregon, 546
Mumford, Lewis, 759
Munich Conference, 687
Munn v. Illinois, 449
Murphy, Edgar Gardner, 554
Murphy, Frank, 696
Murrow, Edward R., 741
Mussolini, Benito, 616, 703–704
Mustard gas, 612
Mutually assured destruction (MAD), 852
abandoning doctrine of, 868–869
"My Day" (E. Roosevelt), 740
My Lai, 798–799
massacre, disagreement over responsibility for, 800
villagers before execution, *799*

N

Nader, Ralph, 864, 886, 887
Nagasaki, atomic bomb dropped on, 712, 713, 729, 734
Nagumo, Chuichji, 684, 692
Napalm, 790, 796
Nash, Diane, 773, 774
Nast, Thomas, 424, 425, 471
cartoons, *425*, *471*, *519*
National Aeronautics and Space Administration (NASA), 742
National Alliance, 520
National American Woman Suffrage Association (NAWSA), 513, 605, 644
National Association for the Advancement of Colored People (NAACP), 434, 555, 638–639, 765, 766
assassination of leader of, 824
National Association of Colored Women, 513
National Child Labor Committee, 549, 550
National Civic Federation, 541
National Consumers' League (NCL), 546
National Industrial Recovery Act (1933), 667, 677
National Labor Relations Board (NLRB), 677
National Labor Union (NLU), 484–485
National Liberation Front (NLF), 783
National Organization for Women (NOW), 834, 859
National Park Service, 864
National Recovery Administration (NRA), 667
National Road, 584
National Security Council Memorandum 68 (NSC-68), 730, 781
National Security League, 598
National War Labor Board, 603, 698–699
National Woman's Party, 604
National Woman Suffrage Association (NWSA), 534
National Women's Party, 644
Nation, Carry A., *546*, 547
Nation of Islam, 830–831
Native Americans
activism of, 838–839
aided by New Deal, 671
diversity of, in West, 442–443
environmentalists' admiration for practices of, 540
forced assimilation versus cultural preservation and, 459
of Great Plains, 443–444
loss of lands by, *460*
mounting problems for, 453–455
persecution and persistence of, 461–462
under siege, 453–458
wars involving, 455–457
in World War II, 701
Nativism, 634
defined, 506

Nativism (*continued*)
denounced by political machines, 504
revival of, 506, *507*
Natural selection, 490
Navajo code talkers, 701
Nazi Germany
atrocities of, 708, 709, 710
Blitzkrieg of, 688
extermination camps in, 708
Jews in, 686
submarines of, 690
Nazi Party, 689
Neoconservatives, 865
advice to Clinton of, 898
view of Hussein held by, 883
Neutrality
banks accused of violating, 597
debate over, 621
favored by isolationists, 615
of FDR, 688
perils of, 596–600
U.S., spies and saboteurs during, 606
of Wilson, 600
Neutrality Act (1935), 687
Neutrality Act (1937), 687
Neutrality Act (1939), 688
Neutrality Acts, 687
New Deal, 557, 654, 683
accomplishments of, 681
for African Americans, 679–680
brings electricity to rural areas, 671
coalition, 680, 683, 727
conservatives attack, *663*
for farmers, 670–671
federal child labor law, 549
legislation, key, *662*
political end of, 681
programs and Eisenhower, 755
public works programs of, 668–669
reforms, 674–681
safety net of, 757
securing legacy of, 752–755
"The New Economics of Immigration" (Borjas), 891
New Frontier, 812–813
New Left, 796, 828–829
environmentalists, 864
splinter group, 836
The *New Negro* (Locke), 642
New Panama Canal Company, 584
New Right, 885
alliances created by, 865
changing family structure and, 889
fears of, 890, 892
rise of, 866
New South, 437
defined, 428
economy, 429–431
Newton, Huey, *832*, 832
New Western Historians, 464–465
New Woman, 514, *514*
and traditional woman, *514*
New York
extremes of income found in, 491
paid professional police department in, 507
Tammany Hall, 403, 420, 504
New York Stock Exchange, 658–659
The *New York Times*, 804–805
Nhu, Ngo Dinh, 783, 784
Nicaragua, 855, 869, 870
Nichols, Terry, 895
Nicolas II (tsar of Russia), 596
9/11 attack, 874, *875*, 905
Justice Department powers increased after, 887
U.S. reaction to, 896
1984 (Orwell), 730
Nineteenth Amendment, 605
Nixon Doctrine, 801
Nixon, Richard M., 855
announces "war on drugs," 837
articles of impeachment against, 849
and Cambodia, 803–805
as candidate of law and order, 836
debate with Kennedy, 761
disarmament agreement secured by, 805
family portrait, *761*
fiscal policies of, 847
Ford pardons, 851, 853
Israeli aid given by, 844
and Laos, 804
McCarthy and, 741
as member of HUAC, 738
multipolarity vision of, 801
and Native Americans, 839
peace with honor plan of, 798, 801, 803
resignation of, 849
trip to China of, 805
use of diplomacy by, 805
use of television by, 760–761
and Vietnam, 801, 803, 805–807
Vietnamization policy of, 801
Watergate scandal, 806, 848–849, 850
"No Child Left Behind" law, 887
No-Man's Land, 612, *613*
Non-interventionists, 684, 688
after Pearl Harbor, 692
defined, 717
desires of, 686
rise of fascism and, 686–687
slogan of "America First," 689, *689*
vision of, 687
Nonviolent protest, 768, 769, 770, 772–775
attacks during, 821
Malcolm X: an alternative to, 830–831
Noriega, Manuel, 881
Norris, George W., 600
North American Free Trade Agreement (NAFTA), 885
North Atlantic Treaty Organization (NATO), 722, 855, 895
Berlin airlift and, 725–727
purpose of, 728
North Carolina Mutual and Provident Insurance Company, 432, 433
Northern Farmers' Alliance, 520
Northern Securities Trust, 535, 536
North Korea, 730, 781
North, Oliver, 855, 870
North Vietnam, 783
Nixon resumes massive bombing of, 801, 803
NSC-68. *See* National Security Council Memorandum 68 (NSC-68)
Nuclear arms race, *743*
background of, 713
massive retaliation policy for, 742, 743
Nuclear fallout, 734
Nuclear reactors, 864
Nuclear war
averting, 742–747
fears of, 742
Nuclear weapons, 735, *743*
American monopoly on, 722
defensive war against, 734
government preparations for attack by, 736
increase of, under Eisenhower, 742
MacArthur and, 732
stockpiling of, 729
surviving attack from, 735, 736
testing of, 729
Nuremberg War Crimes Trials, 710
Nye, Gerald P., 687

O

Oakley, Annie, 462, *463*, 463
Obama, Barack, 901
makes history, *903*
message of, 902
"Out of Many, We Are One," *902*
O'Brien, William, 451
O'Connor, Sandra Day, 871
Office of Economic Opportunity, 814
Office of Indian Water Rights, 839
Office of War Information, 695
Oil
embargo, 842, 844, 883
reliance on Middle Eastern, 844
shortages, 854
U.S. dependence on foreign, 893
Oil wells, 626
Okinawa, capture of, 711
Olmsted, Frederick Law, 510–511
On the Road (Kerouac), 764
On the Waterfront, 739
Open Door Notes, 579, 580
Open Door Policy, 579–580
reaffirming, 647
Open shop, 541
Operation Desert Shield, 882
Operation Desert Storm, 883
Operation Just Cause, 881
Oregon Trail, 444, 453
Organization of the Petroleum Exporting Countries (OPEC), 844, 854
Orlando, Vittorio, 615
Orwell, George, 730
Oswald, Lee Harvey, 785
Ottoman Empire
joins Central Powers, 596
Our Country (Strong), 563

P

Pachucos, 701
Pacific Railway Act, 441
Pacific theater, World War II, *702*, 702–703, 704–705
ending, 711–714
Pacifists, 598, 600, 608, 610, 611
Packard, Vance, 757
Palestine, 617, 844
Palin, Sarah, 901
Palmer, A. Mitchell, 634
Panama. *See also* Panama Canal
Operation Just Cause in, 881
Panama Canal returned to, 855
revolt against Colombia by, 584
Panama Canal, 584–587, 881
building, *585*, 585–586
opening of, 589
reasons for, 584
returned to Panama, 855
Pan-American Exposition, 535
Panic of 1873, 424, 426, 449
Panic of 1893, 520, 522, 523
Panic of 1907, 539
Paris Peace Conference, 615–617
Paris, Treaty of (1898), 571–572, 573, 591
Parker, Alton B., 536
Parker, Dorothy, 628
Parks, Rosa, 768
makes history, 769
Parochial schools, 507, 813
Parr, Jerry, 867
Patriot Act, 897
Patrons of Husbandry. *See* Grange
Paul, Alice, 644
Paulson, Henry, 901, 902

Peace Corps, 813
Peace movement, 809
backlash against, 801
critics of, 778
discrediting, 797
energizing of, 790
Nixon's portrayal of, 801
Pearl Harbor, 569, 631
under attack, *692*
attack on, 684, *685*, 690
damage done at, 692
Japanese discrimination after, 693
Peck, James, 820
Peers, William, 799
Peik v. Chicago and North Western Railroad, 449
Pendleton Act (1883), 520
Pentagon Papers, 804–805
People's Party, 495, 520–522. *See also* Populists
and election of 1896, 526–527
People's Republic of China. *See* China
Perkins, Frances, 663
Perle, Richard, 898
Perot, Ross, 884
Pershing, John J., 600, 612
Persian Gulf War, *881*, 882–883
Operation Desert Storm, 883, 905
pattern followed in, 900
phases of, 883
Phelan, James D., 582
Philippine-American War, 577–578, 589
Philippine Insurrection, 577–578
Philippines
debate over colonizing, 573–574
Dewey sails to, 568
MacArthur returns to, 704–705
in World War II, 693
Philippine Sea, Battle of, 704
Phillips, David Graham, 553
Phillips, Sam, 762
Picasso, Pablo, 764
Pickets, 485, 628, 768
Pickford, Mary, 630
Pinchot, Gifford, 540
Pinkerton Detective Agency, 522
Pinkham, Lydia E., 552
Pinochet, Augusto, 851, 852
Pippin, Horace, 700
Plantations, freedmen forcibly returned to, *407*
Platt Amendment (1901), 572, 591
Pledge of Allegiance, 507, 814
Japanese girl saying, *696*
promoting loyalty and patriotism, *508*
Plessy, Homer A., 434
Plessy v. Ferguson, 433, 434, 555
overturning of, 765
"separate but equal" ruling in, 554
Plunkitt, George Washington, 505
Plunkitt of Tammany Hall (Plunkitt), 505
Poindexter, John, 870
Political action committees (PACs), 851
Political machines, 503–504, *504*
Politics
Gilded Age, *518*
out of touch, 519–520
Pollock, Jackson, 764
Poll tax, 433, 435
disenfranchisement through, *435*
Polygamy, 445
Pools, 476
Poor People's Campaign, 835
Popular culture
beginning of national, 516
in the fifties, 760–764
new forms of leisure and, 515–516
Population
density, 502
growth of U.S. urban, 500–501
Populists, 520, 667. *See also* People's Party
campaign to discredit, 520–521, *521*
Porter, Sylvia, 758
Postwar world
American supremacy in, 713
differing goals in, 720–721
Potlach, 443
Potsdam Conference, 712
Poverty. *See also* Urban poor
Powderly, Terence, 492
dissatisfaction with, 495
Powell, Colin, 882, 898
Powell Doctrine, 882, 883
Prager, Robert, 608
Preemptive war, 898, 905
launching, 899
Preservationists, 539–540
Presley, Elvis, 762, *763*, 764
parents of, 756
Price, Cecile, 825, 826
Price controls, lifting of, 853–854
"Price of Victory," *732*, 733
Princip, Gavrilo, 594
Printing press, steam-powered, 489
Prisoners of war (POWs), 789
Pro-choice movement, 861
Proclamation of Amnesty and Reconstruction. *See* Ten Percent Plan
Proctor, Redfield, 567
Prodigal Son (Douglas), *643*
"The Prodigal Son" (Johnson), 642–643
Profit, 484
margins, during World War II, 699
Progress and Poverty (George), 491
Progressive (Bull Moose) Party, 533, 538
Progressive Era. *See also* Progressives
African American leaders during, 554–555
angst of the middle class during, 532–533
competing views on transforming workplace in, 541–545
court decisions, 543
innovations, popularity of, 628
restoring childhood in, 548–549
stamping out vice during, 546–547
Progressive Party, 727
Progressives, 656, 668. *See also* Progressive Era
imperialism and, 564
limited progress of, 543–544
protecting women and children, 546
vision of, 533–534
Prohibition, 632–634, 651
1904 and 1917, *547*
crime associated with, 633
critics of, 633
repeal of, 633–634
Pro-life movement, 861
Propaganda, wartime, 571
directed at women, *697*
dissemination of, 605
effort by Hollywood, 605
focusing on Hitler and Nazism as enemy, 694
food campaign, 602–603
patriotism and, 606
posters, *593*, *602*, 604, *607*
skepticism toward, 597
Vietnamese, 789
Proposition 13, 865
Prostitution, 503
Public Broadcasting System (PBS), 817
Public Works Administration (PWA), 668
Puerto Rico, 564, 571, 589
Pulitzer, Joseph, 565
Pullman, George, 524
Pullman Palace Car Company, 524
Pullman strike, 524, 525, 538
Pure Food and Drug Act (1906), 552
Pyle, Ernie, 693–694

Q

Quayle, Dan, 889

R

Racial riots, 416, 604, 639, 700, 701, 810, 881
after King's assassination, 835
summers of, 831
Racism
anti-Chinese, 446, *486*
cartoon depicting, *571*
directed at Indians, 453
during Gilded Age, 513
and hiring policies, 488
Andrew Johnson plays on white, 417
Radical Republicans, 408, 415
control of Reconstruction taken by, 417
Radical Right, 835–836
Radioactive material, 734
Radios, 629–630
pocketsize transistor, 762
Ragged Dick (Alger), 490
Railroad Administration, 602
Railroads, 446, 449, *486*. *See also* Transcontinental railroad
effect of Pullman strike on, 524
federal management of, 602
fuel Western development, 447–448
growth of, 472
mixed feelings regarding, 473–474
promote westward settlement, *446*
regulatory problems with, 476
spread of, *447*
Rakes, Joseph, 847–848
Ranching, 449–450
Randolph, A. Philip, 699, 824
Range wars, 450
Rankin, Jeannette, 600
Rape of Nanking, 691
Rationing, 697
Ray, James Earl, 835
Readjusters, 428
Reagan, Ronald, 837
abortion issue and, 859, 861
anti-Communist activities of, 739
background of, 852
contribution of, 871
fiscal policies of, 868
foreign policy triumphs and scandals, 868–871
at home: setting a new course, 866–868
popularity of, 842
pro-business leaning of, 868
shooting of, *867*, 867
supply-side economics of, 867
and Western votes, 864
"The Real 'White Man's Burden'" (Crosby), 576
Recalls, 553
Recession, 483, 844, 846
Reconstruction
abandoned, 423–426
abuses under, 420
black churches during, 411
congressional, 415–417
end of, 426–427
eroding support for, 424
governments in South, creating, 419–420

Reconstruction (*continued*)
policy, divided opinions regarding, 408
preparing for, 406
presidential, 412–413, 415
retreat from, 423–424
Reconstruction Acts, 417
Reconstruction Finance Corporation (RFC), 667
Act of 1932, 660
Redeemers, 426, 437
rule of, 428
Red River War, 455
"The Red Summer of 1919," 639
Referendums, 553
Reform Party, 886
Reform(s)
currency, 519–520
draft, 801
to ensure social justice, 674–681
in home mortgage lending practices, 666
Kennedy's proposed, 813
Progressive, 538, 557. *See also* Progressive Era; Progressives
under Franklin Delano Roosevelt, 666
sought by Granger movement, *449*
urban, 507
Religion
among Plains tribes, 443
fundamentalism, 636–637. *See also* Fundamentalism
Religious Right, 865–866
Remington, Frederic, 462, 464, 566, 567
Republican Party
black voters abandon, 680
and election of 1896, 526–527
foundation for conservative resurgence within, 829–830
reshaping of, 865
in South, 418–419
three factions of, 419
Republicans
conflict between Johnson and congressional, 417
critical of Wilson, 616, 617–618
shifting electoral map in favor of, 846
The Rescue (Greenough), *453*
Reservations. *See also* Dawes Severalty Act
forcing of tribes onto, 456, 457
increased self-rule on, 839
Indian refusal to confinement to, 455
land set aside for, 453
The Return of Private Davis from the Argonne (Curry), *620*, 620–621
Rhee, Syngman, 730
Rhodes, James Allen, 803
Richardson, Elliot, 849
Ridenhour, Ron, 799
Ridgway, Matthew, 733
Righteous and Harmonious Fists, 580
Right to privacy, 813, 861
Riis, Jacob, 508, 509, 510, 535, 812
Robber barons, 476, 497
Robertson, Pat, 866
Roberts, Oral, 866
Robinson, Jo Anne, 768
Rock-and-roll, 762
Rockefeller, John D., 451, 532, 535–536, 544
mail bomb sent to, 634
and rise of trusts, 467–477
Rock music, 829
Roebling, Emily Warren, 498
Roebling, John, 498
Roebling, Washington, 498
Roebuck, Alvah C., 482
Roe v. Wade, 861
Rogers, Will, 671
Roosevelt Corollary, 587–589
Roosevelt, Eleanor
concerns about HUAC expressed by, 740
interest in civil rights of, 680
protest letter to, 675
role of, 663
stand on Equal Rights Amendment of, 644
Roosevelt, Franklin Delano
background of, 663
Churchill and, 689
death of, 711
differences between Hoover and, 654
election of, 660
Executive Order 9066, 694
"fireside chats" of, 663, 690
foreign policy priority of, 691
Lend-Lease and, 689–690
managing public appearances of, 664
neutrality of, 688
New Deal of, 662. *See also* New Deal
as politician, 662–663
Quarantine Speech of, 687
Randolph and, 699
repeal of prohibition by, 633
runs for third term, 688–689
sends U.S. Pacific Fleet to Hawaii, 684
Stalin and, 703
support for labor unions of, 676–677
Supreme Court and, 680–681
UN and, 721
at Yalta Conference, 707, 708
Roosevelt, James, 664
Roosevelt, Theodore, 495, 533, 538, 575
big stick of, *587*
conservationist vision of, 540
on "hyphenated Americans," 608
Muir and, 539–540
negotiates peace for Russo-Japanese War, 581
Panama Canal and, 584–587, *586*
Philippine Insurrection and, 578
at San Juan Heights, 570
Spanish-American War and, 567
trust-busting of, 535–537
Root, Elihu, 574
Rosenberg, Ethel, 737–738
Rosenberg, Harold, 764
Rosenberg, James, 658
Rosenberg, Julius, 737–738
Rosenthal, Joe, 706
Rothko, Mark, 764
Number 10, *764*
Rough Riders, 570
Rubin, Jerry, 836
Ruffner, Lena, 636–637, *637*
Rumsfeld, Donald, 852, 898
Rusk, Dean, 787
Russell, Charles, 464
Russell, Richard, 786–787
Russian Revolution, 628
fear caused by, 634
Russo-Japanese War (1904–1905), 579, 580–581, 647
Rust Belt, 846, 865
Rustin, Bayard, 774
Ruth, Babe, 629

S

Sacco, Nicola, 635
Sacco-Vanzetti Defense Committee, 635
Sadat, Anwar El, 856
Sagebrush Rebellion, 864
Saigon, fall of, 807
SALT I, 852
SALT II, 855
Sand Creek Massacre, 454
Sandinistas, 855, 869
Sanger, Margaret, 646, *646*
San Juan Heights, 570
Santa Clara County v. Southern Pacific Railroad, 476
Satellites, 742
Saturday Night Massacre, 849
Saudi Arabia, 882
Savage, Anne, 902
Savings and loan industry
bailout, 868
deregulation, 868
Savio, Mario, 828
Savoy, 642
Scalawags, 418
Schapiro, Steve, 835
Schlafly, Phyllis, 859, 860
Schlieffen, Alfred von, 596
Schlieffen Plan, 596
School busing, 847–848
anger over court-ordered, 865
protest, *848*
School prayer, 814, 815
Schwarzkopf, Norman, 883
Schwerner, Michael, 825, 826
Schwerner, Rita, 825
Scientific management, 543
Scopes, John, 636
Scopes Trial, 636–637, 651
Scott, Thomas A., 473, 475
Scowcroft, Brent, 877
Screen Actors Guild, 739
Scribner's Monthly, 487
Sculler, Robert, 866
Seale, Bobby, 832
Search-and-destroy missions, 791, 796, 798–799
Sears, Richard W., 482
Second Fort Laramie Treaty, 455, 466
Second Red Scare, 737
anti-Communist crusade during. *See* McCarthyism
Reagan during, 852
Security and Exchange Commission (SEC), 666
Sedition Act (1918), 606, 608, 623, 635
Segregation, 428, 435, 554
bus, ruled unconstitutional, 769, 770
challenges to constitutionality of, 765
demonstrating irreversible effects of, 766
sanctioning, 434
spread of, 433
Selective Service Act, 611
Self-determination, 601, 616
rhetoric cloaking imperialism, 616–617
Selma, Alabama, 826–827
Settlement houses, 510
Seuss, Dr., 689
Seventeenth Amendment, 553
Seymour, Horatio, 420–421
Shafter, William, 570, 571
Shamans, 443, 461
Shantytowns, 660
Sharecropping, *431*, 431–432
Share our wealth, 674
Shell shock, 612
Sheppard-Towner Act (1921), 644
Sheridan, Philip, 455
Sherman Anti-Trust Act, 477, 497, 519, 539. *See also* Trusts
trusts accused of violating, 536
Sherman Silver Purchase Act (1890), 519–520
Sherman, William Tecumseh, 409
Shipp, Thomas, 638
Shuttlesworth, Fred, 821
Sierra Club, 539, 818, 864
"The Significance of the Frontier in American History" (Turner), 464
Silent majority, 801, 847
Silent Spring (Carson), 818
Sinclair, Upton, 552

Sino-Soviet Treaty, 729
Sirhan, Sirhan, 797
Sit-down strikes, 679
Sit-ins, 772–775, *773*
awakening provoked by photos of, 774
resistance to, 774–775
during World War II, 700
Sitting Bull (Sioux chief), 444, 456, 462
Sixteenth Amendment, 538–539
Sixteenth Street Baptist Church, 824
Skyscrapers, 474, 512
Slaughterhouse cases (1874), 544
Slavery
abolishing, 408
to freedom, moving from, *432*
Slums, 502
Smiley, Glenn, 770
Smith, Abram, 638
Smith Act (1940), 737, 741
Smith, Joseph, 445
Smith, Mathew Hale, 491
Social Darwinism, 490–491, 497, 563, 611, 628
ideas about race and ethnicity, *629*
Social Gospel, 534
Socialism, 538
containing, 552
defined, 486
Socialist Party, 538, 608
Social Security, 674, 676, 754, 755, 846, 847
benefits, raising, 813
Society columns, 517
Soft money, proponents of, 519
Solidarity, 877
Somalia, 894–895
competing views of turmoil in, *894*
Somoza, Anastasio, 855
The Souls of Black Folk (Du Bois), 556
South
Lost Cause and, 428–429
Republican Party in, 418–419
violence in, 422
Southeast Asia
fear of Soviet control in, 781
stemming tide of communism in, 782–783
threat to, 788
U.S. ground forces sent to, 778
Southeast Asian Treaty Organization (SEATO), 783
Southern Christian Leadership Conference (SCLC), 770, 821
Chicago campaign, 831
workshops, 772, 773
Southern Democrats, 727, 752
Southern Farmers' Alliance, 520
South Korea, 730, 781
Truman sends military aid to, 731
South Vietnam, 782
American military "advisors" in, 784
campaign to create independent, 783
collapse of, 806–807
guerilla war in, 778
Southwest, 457
Soviet Union
atom bomb tests of, 729, 730
Cuba and, 745
détente with, 806
disarmament agreement signed by, 805
formation of, 601, 621
Hitler's invasion of, 688
hotline connecting United States and, 747
independence demanded by states of, 877
invasion of Manchuria by, 712
Middle East and, 844
pressures Hanoi to seek peace, 803
sends first astronaut into space, 813
split between China and, 786
United States and, 713, 718, 721, 725, 745–747, 852, 855
U.S. spies and, 737–739
Space race, 813
U.S. moon landing, 836–837, *837*
Spain
Cuba and, 567–568
declining might of, 564
U.S. conflict with, 565, 567
"Spaniards Search Women on American Steamers" (Remington), *566*
Spanish-American War, 535, 565–572, *568*
aftermath of, 571–572
Caribbean theater, *569*
end of, 571
fighting during, 568–571
start of, 568
stories and public opinion regarding, 566
Spanish Civil War, 686
Spanish Influenza pandemic, 614
Speakeasies, 633
Spear, Fred, 592
Special Field Order No. 15, 409
Spectator sports, 515
Speculators
homesteader, 440–441
land, 457, 458, 460
stock market, problems caused by, 657–658
Spencer, Herbert, 490–491
Sphere of influence, 579, 580
Spies
accusations about Communist, 737–741
German, 606, 608
Soviet, in Manhattan Project, 712, 713
Spirit of St. Louis, 630, *631*
Sputnik, 742, *742*, 813
Stagflation, 846
Stalingrad, Soviet victory at, 704
Stalin, Josef, 616
blockade of Berlin by, 726
brutality of, 721
Churchill and, 721, 722
death of, 742
fears of, 720–721
Korean War and, 781–782, *782*
Mao and, 729
revocation of blockade by, 728
signs non-aggression pact with Hitler, 688
Truman and, 722, 724, 726
U.S. concerns about, 722
U.S. fears regarding, 725–726
during World War II, 703, 704
at Yalta Conference, 707, 708
Standardization, 472
benefits of, *473*
Standard Oil Trust, 476, 532, 535, 536, *537*
Standing Bear (Ponca chief), 457
Stanford, Leland, 441
Stanton, Elizabeth Cady, 421
Starr, Ellen Gates, 510
Starr, Kenneth, 885
States' rights
advocates and prohibition, 633
Faubus sends troops to protect, 772
States' Rights Party, 727, 754
The Status Seekers (Packard), 757
Steel
Bessemer-Kelly process, 475
importance of, 474
industry, 476, 846
Steinem, Gloria, 860
Stein, Gertrude, 632
Stephens, Alexander, 413
Stevens, John Paul, 886
Stevenson, Adlai E., 754
Stewart, Alexander Turney, 478, 491
Stimson, Henry, 689, 690, 712
Stirling, Mary, 494
St. Louis (German passenger ship), 709
St. Louis World's Fair, 578
Stock, 472
Stockdale, James, 787, 789
Stockholders, 472
Stock market crash of 1929, 657–659, 683
overseas loans and, 651
Stokowski, Leopold, 642
Stone, I. F., 798
Stone, Lucy, 421
Stonewall riot, 862
Stoughton, Cecil, 786
Strategic Arms Limitation Treaty (SALT I), 805
Strategic Defense Initiative (SDI), 869
The Strike (Koehler), 468, *469*
Strikes, 494, 541, *752*, 753
in 1934, 678
air traffic controllers, 867
railroad, 468, 486
sit-down, 679, 752, 772
violence during, 485, 486, 518, 522, 533, *533*, 544
Strong, Josiah, 506, 534, 563
Student Nonviolent Coordinating Committee (SNCC), 775, 820, 825, 832
Students for a Democratic Society (SDS), 796, 828
St. Valentine's Day Massacre, 633
Suburbs
American dream or nightmare?, 759
defined, 512
lure of, *512*, 512–513
move to, 758
Suicide bombers, 900
Sullivan, Ed, 762
Sullivan, Louis, 511
Summer of Love, 837
Sun Belt, 846, 865
Sunday, Billy, 632
Supply-side economics, 867
Supreme Court
AAA declared unconstitutional by, 670
and disputed election of 2000, 886–887
employment rulings of, 544, 545, 546
first African American appointed to, 766
first female justice on, 871
Insular Cases (1900–1904), 574
interstate commerce rulings by, 449
and legal construction of "whiteness," 583
NRA declared unconstitutional by, 667–668, 677
overturns "separate but equal" ruling, 765
Plessy v. Ferguson, 433, 434, 554, 555
during Progressive Era, 543
Roe v. Wade decision, 861
Roosevelt and, 680–681
rules bus segregation unconstitutional, 769, 770
and school prayer, 814, 815
under Warren, 813–814
Swaggart, Jimmy, 866
Swastikas, 689
Swift, Gustavus, 476
Swinton, John, 487
Sylvis, William, 484–485

T

Taft, Robert, 754
Taft, William Howard, 537–538
expansion of U.S. influence over Latin America by, 587–588
and immigrant literacy test bill, 506
in Philippines, 578
Theodore Roosevelt and, 540
Takao Ozawa, 583
Takao Ozawa v. United States, 582

Taliban, 896
Tammany Hall, 420, 503, 505
power of, 504
Tarbell, Ida, 535–536
Tariffs, 471, 538, 628, 648, 657
high, 519, 520, 526
raising of, 659
Tax cuts, 846, 887
Tax revolt, California, 865
Taylor, Bob, 854
Taylor, Frederick Winslow, 543
Teach-ins, 797, 828
Teapot Dome scandal, 627
architectural spoof of, *627*
Technology
advertising and developments in print, 478
benefits to farmers of new, 626
impact on workforce of new, 483
industrial, 489
innovations in, 562
investment in new, 507
new furnace, 846
scramble to develop satellite, 742
steel, 475
Teenagers
in fifties, 761–762
TV programming exclusively for, 762
Telegraph, 455
cables, transatlantic, 562
Television, 733
age, arrival of, 760–761
and Birmingham campaign, 821
Civil Rights Movement and, 775
first political ads on, 754
Kennedy and Nixon debate, 761
programming for teenagers, 762
shows, early, 760
Vietnam War viewed on, 793
Teller Amendment (1898), 568, 572
Teller, Henry M., 568
Temperance, 546–547, 632
Tenant farmers, 431, 432
Tenements, 502
Tennessee Valley Authority (TVA), 671
Ten Percent Plan, 408, 437
Tenure of Office Act, 417
Terrorism. *See also* al-Qaeda; Lynchings
anarchist, 634
Internet and, 889
Islamic, 855, 870, 874, 887
post–Civil War, 421–422
return of, 426
Tet Offensive, 792–793
"Thank God for the Atom Bomb" (Fussell), 712
Their Eyes Were Watching God (Huston), 642
"The Jazz Age," 642
Thermonuclear hydrogen bomb, 729
Thind, Bhagat Singh, 583
Thirteenth Amendment, 408
38th parallel, 730, 732
This Side of Paradise (Fitzgerald), 632
Thomas, Clarence, 880
Thompson, Florence, 673
Thompson, Hugh, 799
Thoreau, Henry David, 772
Three Mile Island, 864
Thurmond, Strom, 727, 728, 754
Tiananmen Square, 879
Tilden, Samuel J., 426–427
Till-Bradley, Mamie, 766, 767, 768
Till, Emmett, murder of, 766–768
Tillman, Ben, 575
Time magazine, 693
Title IX (1972 Education Act), 859
Tito, Josip Broz, 796
Tojo, Hideki, 693
Tomb of the Unknown Soldier, 647
"Too Many Immigrants" (Jacoby), 891
Toomer, Jean, 642
Townsend, Francis, 674, 676
Trade
and Panama Canal, 584
U.S., with nations at war, *597*
Trail of Tears, 839
Transcontinental railroad, 438, 441, 584. *See also* Railroads
completion of, *441*
Trans-Mississippi West, 440
economic development in, 451
immigrants to, 446
major tribes of, *442*
migrant settlers flow into, 444–446
Transportation, 489
Treason, 738
Treaties, broken, 453, 454, 455
Triangle Fire (Gatto), *531*
Triangle Shirtwaist Factory fire, 530, 534
Tripartite Pact, 691
Trudeau, Gary, 792
Truman Doctrine, 724
Truman, Harry, 707, 752
assumes presidency, 711–712
authorizes "superbomb" development, 729
Berlin airlift and, 727
celebrates reelection, *728*
civil rights and, 733, 753–754
desegregation of military by, 728, 753
Fair Deal of, 754
federal employee loyalty program created by, 737
firing of MacArthur by, 732
hardliners in administration of, 781
and Ho Chi Minh, 780
Korean War and, 730–733
Lend-Lease and, 690, 721
loss of China and, 781, 784
orders review of foreign policy, 729–730
public disappointment with, 733
railroad strike and, 753
Stalin and, 722, 724, 726
UN and, 731
use of atomic bomb by, 713
Trust-busting, 536
Trusts, 536. *See also* Sherman Anti-Trust Act
defined, 476
political power of, *477*
Rockefeller and rise of, 476–477
Tugwell, Rexford, 662
Turner, Frederick Jackson, 464
Turner, Henry McNeal, 555, 577
Turner Thesis. *See* Frontier Thesis
Turning a Corner (Jones), *669*
Tuskegee Airmen, 700
Tuskegee Institute, 555, 700
Twain, Mark, 462
Tweed, William "Boss," 420, 504
Twenties, 624
age of flight: Charles A. Lindbergh, 630–631
car culture of, 626–628
cultural unrest during, 632–637
diplomacy during, 647–651
life for women in, 644–646
welfare capitalism and consumer culture, 628–630
Twenty-Fifth Amendment, 851
Twenty-First Amendment, 633–634

U

U-2, 743
U-boats, 598
Unemployment
benefits, raising, 813
in early thirties, 660
high, 842
inflation and, *846*
soaring, *667*
Union Pacific Railroad, 423
Unions. *See* Labor unions
United Auto Workers (UAW), 678, 679
United Farm Workers, 838
United Labor Party, 491, 495
United Mine Workers, 535, 543, 544, 678–679
United Nations (UN)
founding of, 708
peace agreement, Iraq and, 883
police force sent to Korea by, 731
pressuring of Stalin by, 724
resolution regarding Iraq, 882
and Franklin D. Roosevelt, 721
United States
attacks Afghanistan, 896
Chinese Open Door Policy and, 579–580
colonial expansion, possibilities for, 564
debate over colonies, 573–575
decision to intervene in Cuba, 567–568
economic relationship between China and, 879
emergence as world power of, 589
exports to Europe, 1914–1917, *597*
focus of foreign policy of, 596
foreign policy, mainstay of twentieth-century, 588
frustration in, 847–848
growing conflict between Spain and, 565, 567
hotline connecting Soviet Union and, 747
navy in 1890, 562–563
neutrality of, 596
protectorates, 588, 589
relations with Japan, 580–581
Soviet Union and, 713, 718, 721, 725, 745–747, 852, 855
stockpiling of atom bombs, 729
Universal Negro Improvement Association (UNIA), 640
Urbanization
brought by railroads, 448
dark side of, 506
Urban League, 604
Urban poor, *508*. *See also* Poverty
crime and, 503
living conditions for, 502
political machines and, 504
settlement houses for, 510
waning support for programs for, 835
U.S. Patent Office, 471
USS *Cole* (naval vessel), 896
USS *Maddox* (destroyer), 787
U.S. Steel, 536, 538
USS *Turner Joy* (destroyer), 787

V

Valentino, Rudolph, 630
Vance, Cyrus, 856, 857
Vandenberg, Arthur, 724
Vanderbilt, Alva, 517
Vanderbilt, William K., 489, 517
"The Vanishing Race" (Curtis), *540*
Van Vechten, Carl, 642
Vanzetti, Bartolomeo, 635
Vaudeville, 516
Veblen, Thorstein, 517

Versailles Peace Treaty, 615
fight at home over, 617–618, 620–621
global flow of reparation payments, *651*
harsh demands of, 616
punitive aspect of, 648, 650
ratification process, *618*
U.S. refusal to ratify, 620
Vertical integration, 475, 476
versus horizontal integration, *475*
Vietcong, 783
hideout, drawing of, *791*
infiltration of civilian population by, 791
Vietminh, 780
Communist advisors to, 782
Vietnam. *See also* Vietnam War
antiwar movement during, 796–798
civil war in, 783
Eisenhower and, 782–783
escalating importance of, 780–782
guerilla warfare in, 789
Johnson and, 786–787, 788, 798
Kennedy and, 784–785
map of, *793*
military dilemma in, 789
Nixon and, 801, 803, 805–807
partitioning of, 782
power of the press in, 794–795
taking over from French in, 782–783
withdrawal from, 805–807
Vietnamization, 801, 804
Vietnam Veterans Memorial, 807
Vietnam War. *See also* Vietnam
body counts in, 792, *792*
bombing campaign in, 789–790
controversy on home front during, 796–799
divisions caused by, 807
on the ground, 790–792
length of, 778
long road to, 780–787
My Lai, 798–799
by the numbers, *802*
origins of, 778
photographs from, *794*, *795*
and road to peace, 801–807
Tet Offensive, 792–793
Villa, Francisco "Pancho," 600
A Visit from the Old Mistress (Homer), *404–405*
Volstead Act (1919), 633
Volunteers in Service to America (VISTA), 814
Voting
female suffrage achieved, 604–605
for first time, *419*
women and, 534
Voting Rights Act of 1965, 827

W

Wabash, St. Louis & Pacific Railway Co. v. Illinois, 476
Wade, Benjamin, 408, 417
Wade-Davis Bill, 408
Wadsworth, James, 632
Wagner Act (1935), 677
Wallace, George, 798, 814
Wallace, Henry A., 689, 707, 727, 728, 754
Wall Street, 658–659
Wanamaker, John, 479
War bonds, 606
War Department, 699
Ward, Montgomery, 479, 482
War Industries Board (WIB), 602
War Manpower Commission, 697
Warner, Jack, 739
War on Poverty, 814
War Powers Resolution, 806
War Production Board (WPB), 697
War Refugee Board (WRB), 708
War Relocation Authority, 694
Warren Commission, 785
Warren Court, 813–814, 847
major decisions of, *814*
Warren, Earl, 847
Warsaw Pact, 728
Washington, Booker T., 434, 554–555, 556, 640
Washington Conference (1921–1922), 647, 653
treaties negotiated at, 648
Washington Post, 849
Watergate scandal, 806, 848–849
convictions related to, 851
through political cartoons, *850*
Watson, Paul, 895
Watson, Tom, 520, 527
Watts riot, 831
Wealth, distribution of, 868
Long's proposal for, 674, 675
unequal, 468, 491, 657
Weaver, James B., 521
Welfare capitalism, 541
and consumer culture, 628–630
Wellman, David, 737
Wells-Barnett, Ida B., 514, 555, 604
West
in art and literature, 462, 464
as cattle kingdom, 449–450
creating mythical heroes and images of, 462, 463
diversity of Native American, 442–443
economic transformation of, 447–451
historians reinterpret, 464–465
natives and newcomers to, 440–446
preservation versus exploitation views of, 452
Sagebrush Rebellion in, 864
war and conflict in, 456–457
West, Ben (mayor of Atlanta), 774
Western Europe, Truman Doctrine and, 724
Western Front, 611–612
German preparations to strike along, 601
No-Man's Land of, 612
size of, 623
trench warfare, 596, 597, 612, *613*
West Germany, 728, 744
West, Mae, 516
Westmoreland, William, 787, 788, 792
Wets, 632, 633
Weyler, Valeriano, 565, 567
Wheatley, Phillis, 410
Wheeler, Earle, 787
"Whiskey Ring" scandal, 423
White Brotherhood, 422
The White City, 510–511, *511*, 524
White House
African Americans invited to, 663
rules for press under Roosevelt, 664
suffragists picketing, *605*
"The White Man's Burden" (Kipling), 575, 576
White supremacy, 426, 638
Klan's call for, *639*
Redeemer politics and, 428
Whitman, Bert, 850
Whitman, Walt, 473
Who Said 'Creeping Socialism', 754, *755*
Widener, Jeff, 879
Wilhelm II (kaiser of Germany), 594, 596
Wilkie, Wendell, 689
Wilson, Charles E., 783
Wilson, Edith, 620
Wilson, Woodrow, 538
and attitude toward Western Hemisphere, 588
campaign slogans of, 599, *599*
child labor law signed by, 549
conscription implemented by, 611
endorsement of female suffrage by, 605
Fourteen Points of, 601, 623
illness and death of, 620
and immigrant literacy test bill, 506
League of Nations and, 615–616, 617–620
Lodge and, 615–616, 618, 619, 620
neutrality stance of, 596, 600
protests British blockade, 597–598
reelection of, 599
segregated offices under, 554
sends federal troops to mine strike, 544
wins Nobel Peace Prize, 620
Winnemucca, Sarah, 457–458, *458*
Wobblies. *See* Industrial Workers of the World (IWW)
Wolfowitz, Paul, 883
Woman's Christian Temperance Union (WCTU), 546–547
Women
in the 1920s, 644–646
expectations and new roles for, 513–514
firsts for, in thirties, 663
new roles and opportunities for, 488
role in Progressive causes of, 533–534
and work (1950–1990), *858*
during World War I, 604–605
during World War II, 697–698
Women's Army Corps (WAC), 697
Women's Christian Temperance Union (WCTU), 513
Women's liberation movement, 832, 834
divisions within, 859
Wood, Natalie, 763
Woodstock, 829
Woodward, Bob, 849
Woolworth, Frank W., 479
Workforce
diversity of, 486
exploitation, intimidation, and conflict regarding, 484–486
exploiting females in, *485*
hard times for industrial workers, 483–484
impact of new technology on, 483
luring women into, during World War II, *697*
rising number of women in paid, *488*
union members in industrial, 752
Workingmen's Benevolent Association (WBA), 485
Workplace safety, 544, 545
children and, 484
women and, 546
Works Progress Administration (WPA), 668–669
World Christian Fundamentals Association, 636
World's Columbian Exposition (1893), 510–511, 524
World Trade Center, attacks on
1993, 895
2001, 874, *875*, *896*
World War I
beginning of, 589, 594
conflicting views among Allies on purpose of, 601
countries involved in, 594
in Europe, 594, *595*, 596
Europe and Middle East after, *617*
final campaigns of, 614
gearing up for, 602–603
German spies and civil liberties during, 606, 608
and home front, 602–608
Hoover during, 656
memorial plaque, *501*
racial riots during, 604
raising an army for, 609, 611
rallying the public during, 605–606
sinking of *Lusitania* and, 592
twentieth century shaped by, 621
veterans, Bonus March of, 660, 661
wartime debts from, 648, 650–651
Western Front, 596, 597, 601, 611–612, *613*
World War II
approach of, 686–688
casualties from, 720
children and, *698*

World War II (*continued*)
combat photography, *706*
defeat, then victory, 702–705
ending Pacific war, 711–714
European theater, *703*, 703–704
final push in Europe, 705, 707–708
on the front lines, 702–708
on the home front, 693–701
human cost of global war, *714*
internment camps, 694–695
official beginning of, 688
origins of, *687*
Pacific theater, *702*, 702–703, 704–705
production of consumer goods during, 757
prosperity after, 756–758
prosperity, scarcity and opportunities for women, 695, 697–699
racial discord during, 699–701
war with Japan, 690–692
World War I as foundation for, 621
World Wide Web, 888
Wounded Knee Massacre, 461
Wovoka, 461
Wozniak, Stephen, 846–847
Wright, Moses, 768
Wrigley's Gum, 699

Y

Yalta Conference, 707, 708
Yellow press, 565, 567, 570–571
Yippies, 836
Yom Kippur War, 844
York, Alvin C., 610, 611
Young Americans for Freedom (YAF), 830
Young, James R., 560
Young Men's Christian Association, 604
Young, Neil, 804
Young, Owen D., 650
Young Plan, 650

Z

Zapruder, Abraham, 785
Zimmermann, Arthur, 600
Zimmermann Telegram, 600
Zoot-suiters, 700–701

PRESENT DAY UNITED STATES
CANADA
MEXICO
PACIFIC OCEAN
ATLANTIC OCEAN
Gulf of Mexico
WASHINGTON
OREGON
CALIFORNIA
NEVADA
IDAHO
MONTANA
WYOMING
UTAH
ARIZONA
COLORADO
NEW MEXICO
NORTH DAKOTA
SOUTH DAKOTA
NEBRASKA
KANSAS
OKLAHOMA
TEXAS
MINNESOTA
IOWA
MISSOURI
ARKANSAS
LOUISIANA
WISCONSIN
ILLINOIS
MICHIGAN
INDIANA
OHIO
KENTUCKY
TENNESSEE
MISSISSIPPI
ALABAMA
GEORGIA
FLORIDA
SOUTH CAROLINA
NORTH CAROLINA
VIRGINIA
WEST VIRGINIA
PENNSYLVANIA
NEW YORK
VERMONT
NEW HAMPSHIRE
MAINE
MASSACHUSETTS
RHODE ISLAND
CONNECTICUT
NEW JERSEY
DELAWARE
MARYLAND
RUSSIA
ARCTIC OCEAN
ALASKA
CANADA
HAWAII
PUERTO RICO (U.S.)
CUBA
BAHAMAS
Seattle
Olympia
Tacoma
Spokane
Portland
Salem
Helena
Billings
Boise
Bismarck
Fargo
Minneapolis
St. Paul
Pierre
Sioux Falls
Madison
Milwaukee
Grand Rapids
Lansing
Detroit
Toledo
Cleveland
Chicago
Gary
Davenport
Des Moines
Omaha
Lincoln
Cheyenne
Salt Lake City
Carson City
Sacramento
San Francisco
Stockton
Fresno
Bakersfield
Los Angeles
San Diego
Las Vegas
Denver
Colorado Springs
Pueblo
Topeka
Kansas City
Jefferson City
Wichita
Tulsa
Oklahoma City
Amarillo
Lubbock
Albuquerque
Santa Fe
Phoenix
Mesa
Tucson
El Paso
Fort Worth
Dallas
Austin
Houston
San Antonio
Corpus Christi
Shreveport
Jackson
Baton Rouge
New Orleans
Little Rock
Memphis
Nashville
Knoxville
Chattanooga
Huntsville
Birmingham
Montgomery
Atlanta
Columbus
Savannah
Mobile
Tallahassee
Jacksonville
Orlando
Tampa
St. Petersburg
Fort Lauderdale
Miami
Key West
Florida Keys
Straits of Florida
Lexington
Frankfort
Louisville
Indianapolis
Cincinnati
Springfield
St. Louis
Peoria
Columbus
Pittsburgh
Harrisburg
Philadelphia
Baltimore
Washington, D.C.
Annapolis
Dover
Trenton
New York City
Newark
Hartford
Providence
Boston
Concord
Portland
Augusta
Montpelier
Albany
Syracuse
Buffalo
Charleston
Columbia
Raleigh
Charlotte
Richmond
Newport News
Norfolk
Anchorage
Juneau
Kodiak Island
Aleutian Islands
Bering Sea
Gulf of Alaska
Kauai
Oahu
Honolulu
Molokai
Lanai
Maui
Hawaii
San Juan
Bayamón
Carolina
Ponce
Isla de Culebra
Isla de Vieques
Caribbean Sea
National boundary
State boundary
National capital
State capital
Other city

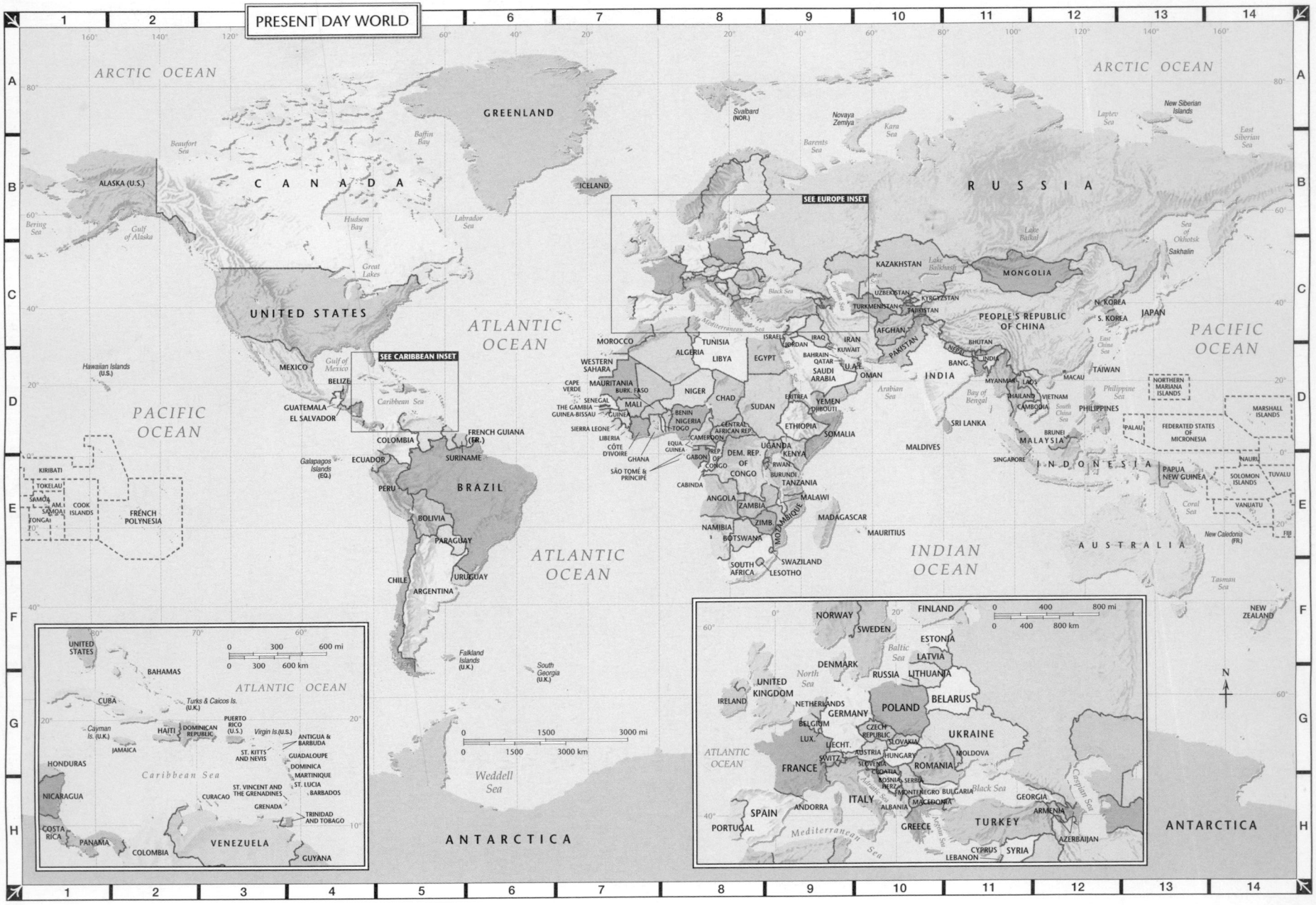
PRESENT DAY WORLD
ARCTIC OCEAN
GREENLAND
Svalbard (NOR.)
Novaya Zemlya
Barents Sea
Kara Sea
Laptev Sea
New Siberian Islands
East Siberian Sea
Beaufort Sea
Baffin Bay
ALASKA (U.S.)
C A N A D A
ICELAND
R U S S I A
Bering Sea
Gulf of Alaska
Hudson Bay
Labrador Sea
Great Lakes
Lake Baikal
Sea of Okhotsk
Sakhalin
SEE EUROPE INSET
KAZAKHSTAN
Lake Balkhash
MONGOLIA
UNITED STATES
ATLANTIC OCEAN
Black Sea
Caspian Sea
UZBEKISTAN
KYRGYZSTAN
TURKMENISTAN
TAJIKISTAN
N. KOREA
S. KOREA
JAPAN
PEOPLE'S REPUBLIC OF CHINA
PACIFIC OCEAN
Mediterranean Sea
AFGHAN.
PAKISTAN
MOROCCO
TUNISIA
ALGERIA
LIBYA
EGYPT
ISRAEL
JORDAN
IRAQ
IRAN
KUWAIT
BAHRAIN
QATAR
SAUDI ARABIA
U.A.E.
OMAN
NEPAL
BHUTAN
INDIA
BANG.
East China Sea
TAIWAN
MACAU
Hawaiian Islands (U.S.)
MEXICO
Gulf of Mexico
SEE CARIBBEAN INSET
BELIZE
GUATEMALA
EL SALVADOR
Caribbean Sea
WESTERN SAHARA
CAPE VERDE
MAURITANIA
BURK. FASO
NIGER
CHAD
SUDAN
ERITREA
YEMEN
DJIBOUTI
Arabian Sea
Bay of Bengal
MYANMAR
LAOS
THAILAND
VIETNAM
CAMBODIA
South China Sea
PHILIPPINES
Philippine Sea
NORTHERN MARIANA ISLANDS
MARSHALL ISLANDS
THE GAMBIA
GUINEA-BISSAU
SENEGAL
MALI
GUINEA
SIERRA LEONE
LIBERIA
CÔTE D'IVOIRE
GHANA
BENIN
NIGERIA
TOGO
CENTRAL AFRICAN REP.
CAMEROON
ETHIOPIA
SOMALIA
SRI LANKA
MALDIVES
PALAU
FEDERATED STATES OF MICRONESIA
BRUNEI
MALAYSIA
SINGAPORE
I N D O N E S I A
PAPUA NEW GUINEA
NAURU
SOLOMON ISLANDS
TUVALU
VANUATU
COLOMBIA
FRENCH GUIANA (FR.)
SURINAME
Galapagos Islands (EQ.)
ECUADOR
PERU
BRAZIL
BOLIVIA
PARAGUAY
CHILE
URUGUAY
ARGENTINA
KIRIBATI
TOKELAU
SAMOA
AM. SAMOA
TONGA
COOK ISLANDS
FRENCH POLYNESIA
EQUA. GUINEA
GABON
REP. OF CONGO
DEM. REP. OF CONGO
UGANDA
KENYA
RWAN.
BURUNDI
TANZANIA
CABINDA
SÃO TOMÉ & PRINCIPE
ANGOLA
ZAMBIA
MALAWI
MOZAMBIQUE
MADAGASCAR
NAMIBIA
BOTSWANA
ZIMB.
MAURITIUS
SOUTH AFRICA
LESOTHO
SWAZILAND
INDIAN OCEAN
A U S T R A L I A
Coral Sea
New Caledonia (FR.)
Tasman Sea
NEW ZEALAND
Falkland Islands (U.K.)
South Georgia (U.K.)
Weddell Sea
ANTARCTICA
0 1500 3000 mi
0 1500 3000 km
UNITED STATES
BAHAMAS
ATLANTIC OCEAN
CUBA
Turks & Caicos Is. (U.K.)
Cayman Is. (U.K.)
JAMAICA
HAITI
DOMINICAN REPUBLIC
PUERTO RICO (U.S.)
Virgin Is.(U.S.)
ANTIGUA & BARBUDA
ST. KITTS AND NEVIS
GUADALOUPE
DOMINICA
MARTINIQUE
ST. LUCIA
BARBADOS
HONDURAS
Caribbean Sea
NICARAGUA
CURACAO
ST. VINCENT AND THE GRENADINES
GRENADA
TRINIDAD AND TOBAGO
COSTA RICA
PANAMA
COLOMBIA
VENEZUELA
GUYANA
0 300 600 mi
0 300 600 km
NORWAY
FINLAND
SWEDEN
ESTONIA
Baltic Sea
LATVIA
DENMARK
North Sea
RUSSIA
LITHUANIA
UNITED KINGDOM
IRELAND
NETHERLANDS
BELARUS
POLAND
GERMANY
BELGIUM
LUX.
CZECH REPUBLIC
UKRAINE
LIECHT.
SLOVAKIA
AUSTRIA
HUNGARY
MOLDOVA
SWITZ.
SLOVENIA
ROMANIA
FRANCE
CROATIA
BOSNIA HERZ.
SERBIA
MONTENEGRO
BULGARIA
Black Sea
Adriatic Sea
ITALY
MACEDONIA
ALBANIA
GEORGIA
ARMENIA
SPAIN
ANDORRA
GREECE
TURKEY
PORTUGAL
Aegean Sea
Mediterranean Sea
CYPRUS
SYRIA
LEBANON
AZERBAIJAN
0 400 800 mi
0 400 800 km
N